37TH CONGRESS, Special Session. SENATE. Ex. Doc.

REPORT

ON THE

BATTLE OF MURFREESBORO', TENN.,

BY

MAJOR GEN. W. S. ROSECRANS, U. S. A.

WASHINGTON:
GOVERNMENT PRINTING OFFICE.
1863.

REPORT

OF

THE SECRETARY OF WAR,

COMMUNICATING,

In answer to a resolution of the Senate of the 10*th instant, a copy of Major General Rosecrans's report of the battle of Murfreesboro', or Stone river, Tennessee.*

MARCH 13, 1863.—Read and ordered to be printed. Motion to print 2,000 extra copies referred to the Committee on Printing. Report of committee in favor of printing 2,000 extra copies considered and agreed to.

WAR DEPARTMENT,
Washington City, March 13, 1863.

SIR: In compliance with the Senate resolution dated March 10, 1863, I have the honor to transmit herewith a copy of Major General Rosecrans' report of the battle of Murfreesboro', or Stone river, Tennessee. As soon as the sub-reports, which are voluminous, can be copied, they will be forwarded—in the event that the Senate has, in the mean time, adjourned—to the Secretary of the Senate.

I have the honor to be, sir, very respectfully, your obedient servant,

EDWIN M. STANTON,
Secretary of War.

The Hon. the PRESIDENT *of the Senate.*

HEADQUARTERS DEPARTMENT OF THE CUMBERLAND,
Murfreesboro', Tennessee, February 12, 1863.

GENERAL: I have the honor to submit herewith my report of the battle of Stone river, accompanying staff reports, maps, tabular statements, army corps and sub-reports, as follows:

1. Report of Colonel James Barnett, chief of artillery, including a tabular statement of artillery, &c., lost and captured during the battle of Stone river.
2. Report of Lieutenant Colonel Taylor, chief quartermaster, containing lists of wagons, animals, &c., lost and gained.
3. Report of Lieutenant Colonel Simmons, chief commissary of subsistence, containing losses of subsistence stores.

4. Report of Dr. Eben Swift, medical director, with complete lists of casualties.

5. Report of Captain Wiles, provost marshal general, containing a statement of prisoners lost and captured.

6. Report of Lieutenant Colonel Burke, tenth Ohio volunteers, commanding headquarters guard.

7. Lists of "special mentions," containing the names of officers and enlistsd men who distinguished themselves at Stone river, compiled from the official reports.

8. List of brigadier generals and colonels especially recommended for promotion.

9. Map of the battle-field.

10. Map of the country adjacent to Murfreesboro'.

11. Report of Major General Thomas, with reports of Generals Rousseau and Negley, and the sub-reports of the fourteenth army corps.

12. Report of Major General McCook, with the reports of Generals Johnson, Davis, and Sheridan, and the sub-reports of the twentieth army corps.

13. Report of Major General Crittenden, with reports of Generals Wood, Palmer, Van Cleve, and Hascall, and the sub-reports of the twenty-first army corps.

14. Report of Brigadier General Stanley, with the reports of the subordinate commanders of cavalry.

15. Report of Captain James St. Clair Morton, commanding pioneer brigade.

16. Report of Colonel Innes, commanding regiment Michigan mechanics and engineers.

17. Flags captured at battle of Stone river, also one captured at battle of Iuka.

18. Percentage of losses in brigades, divisions, and corps.

W. S. ROSECRANS, *Major General.*

Brigadier General L. THOMAS,
Adjutant General U. S. Army.

HEADQUARTERS DEPARTMENT OF THE CUMBERLAND,
Murfreesboro', Tennessee, February 12, 1863.

GENERAL: As the sub-reports are now nearly all in, I have the honor to submit, for the information of the general-in-chief, the subjoined report, with accompanying sub-reports, maps, and statistical tables of the battle of Stone river. To a proper understanding of this battle it will be necessary to state the preliminary movements and preparations.

Assuming command of the army at Louisville on the 27th day of October, it was found concentrated at Bowling Green and Glasgow, distant about 113 miles from Louisville; from whence, after replenishing with ammunition, supplies, and clothing, they moved on to Nashville, the advance corps reaching that place on the morning of the 7th of November, a distance of 183 miles from Louisville.

At this distance from my base of supplies, the first thing to be done was to provide for the subsistence of the troops and open the Louisville and Nashville railroad. The cars commenced running through on the 26th of November, previous to which time our supplies had been brought by rail to Mitchellville, 35 miles north of Nashville, and from thence, by constant labor, we had been able to haul enough to replenish the exhausted stores for the garrison at Nashville and subsist the troops of the moving army.

From the 26th of November to the 26th of December every effort was bent

On the 28th General McCook advanced on Triune, but his movement was retarded by a dense fog.
to complete the clothing of the army, to provide it with ammunition, and replenish the depot at Nashville with needful supplies, to insure us against want from the largest possible detention likely to occur by the breaking of the Louisville and Nashville railroad; and, to insure this work, the road was guarded by a heavy force posted at Gallatin.

The enormous superiority in numbers of the rebel cavalry kept our little cavalry force almost within the infantry lines, and gave the enemy control of the entire country around us. It was obvious from the beginning that we should be confronted by Bragg's army, recruited by an inexorable conscription, and aided by clouds of mounted men, formed into a guerilla-like cavalry, to avoid the hardship of conscription and infantry service. The evident difficulties and labors of an advance into this country, and against such a force, and at such distance from our base of operations, with which we were connected but by a single precarious thread, made it manifest that our policy was to induce the enemy to travel over as much as possible of the space that separated us, thus avoiding for us the wear and tear and diminution of our forces, and subjecting the enemy to all this inconvenience, besides increasing for him and diminishing for us the dangerous consequences of a defeat.

The means taken to obtain this end were eminently successful. The enemy, expecting us to go into winter quarters at Nashville, had prepared his own winter quarters at Murfreesboro', with the hope of possibly making them at Nashville, and had sent a large cavalry force into West Tennessee to annoy Grant, and another large force into Kentucky to break up the railroad. In the absence of these forces, and with adequate supplies in Nashville, the moment was judged opportune for an advance on the rebels. Polk's and Kirby Smith's forces were at Murfreesboro', and Hardee's corps on the Shelbyville and Nolensville pike, between Triune and Eaglesville, with an advance guard at Nolensville, while our troops lay in front of Nashville, on the Franklin, Nolensville, and Murfreesboro' turnpike.

The plan of the movement was as follows:

McCook, with three divisions, to advance by Nolensville pike to Triune.

Thomas, with two divisions, (Negley's and Rousseau's,) to advance on his right by the Franklin and Wilson pikes, threatening Hardee's right, and then to fall in by the crossroads to Nolensville.

Crittenden, with Wood's, Palmer's, and Van Cleve's divisions, to advance by the Murfreesboro' pike to Lavergne.

With Thomas's two divisions at Nolensville, McCook was to attack Hardee at Triune, and if the enemy re-enforced Hardee, Thomas was to support McCook. If McCook beat Hardee, or Hardee retreated, and the enemy met us at Stewart's creek, five miles south of Lavergne, Crittenden was to attack him, Thomas was to come in on his left flank, and McCook, after detaching a division to pursue or observe Hardee, if retreating south, was to move with the remainder of his force on their rear.

The movement began on the morning of the 26th of December.

McCook advanced on Nolensville pike, skirmishing his way all day, meeting with stiff resistance from cavalry and artillery, and closing the day by a brisk fight, which gave him possession of Nolensville and the hills one and a half mile in front, capturing one gun by the 101st Ohio and 15th Wisconsin regiments; his loss this day being about seventy-five killed and wounded.

Thomas followed on the right, and closed Negley's division on Nolensville, leaving the other (Rousseau's) division on the right flank.

Crittenden advanced to Lavergne, skirmishing heavily on his front, over a rough country, intersected by forests and cedar brakes, with but slight loss.

Crittenden had orders to delay his movements until McCook had reached Triune and developed the intentions of the enemy at that point, so that it could be determined which Thomas was to support.

McCook arrived at Triune and reported that Hardee had retreated, and that he had sent a division in pursuit.

Crittenden began his advance about 11 o'clock a.m., driving before him a brigade of cavalry, supported by Many's brigade of rebel infantry, and reached Stewart's creek, the 3d Kentucky gallantly charging the rear guard of the enemy and saving the bridge, on which had been placed a pile of rails that had been set on fire. This was Saturday night.

McCook having settled the fact of Hardee's retreat, Thomas moved Negley's division on to join Crittenden at Stewart's creek, and moved Rousseau to Nolensville.

On Sunday the troops rested, except Rousseau's division, which was ordered to move on to Stewantsbon; and Willich's brigade, which had pursued Hardee as far as Riggs's Cross Roads, and had determined the fact that Hardee had gone to Murfreesboro', when they returned to Triune.

On Monday morning McCook was ordered to move from Triune to Wilkinson's Cross Roads, six miles from Murfreesboro', leaving a brigade at Triune.

Crittenden crossed Stewart's creek by the Smyrna bridge and the main Murfreesboro' pike, and Negley by the ford two miles above; their whole force to advance on Murfreesboro', distant about eleven miles.

Rousseau was to remain at Stewart's creek until his train came up, and prepare himself to follow. McCook reached Wilkinson's Cross Roads by evening, with an advance brigade at Overall's creek, saving and holding the bridge, meeting with but little resistance.

Crittenden's corps advanced, Palmer leading, on the Murfreesboro' pike, followed by Negley, of Thomas's corps, to within three miles of Murfreesboro', having had several brisk skirmishes, driving the enemy rapidly, saving two bridges on the route, and forcing the enemy back to his intrenchments.

About 3 p. m. a signal message coming from the front from General Palmer that he was in sight of Murfreesboro', and that the enemy were running, an order was sent to General Crittenden to send a division to occupy Murfreesboro'.

This led General Crittenden, on reaching the enemy's front, to order Harker's brigade to cross the river at a ford on his left, where he surprised a regiment of Breckinridge's division, and drove it back on its main lines, not more than five hundred yards distant, in considerable confusion; and he held this position until General Crittenden was advised by prisoners captured by Harker's brigade that Breckinridge was in force on his front, when, it being dark, he ordered the brigade back across the river, and reported the circumstances to the commanding general on his arrival, to whom he apologized for not having carried out the order to occupy Murfreesboro'. The general approved of his action, of course, the order to occupy Murfreesboro' having been based on the information received from General Crittenden's advance division that the enemy were retreating from Murfreesboro'.

Crittenden's corps, with Negley's division, bivouacked in order of battle, distant 700 yards from the enemy's intrenchments, our left extending down the river some 500 yards.

The pioneer brigade, bivouacking still lower down, prepared three fords, and covered one of them, while Wood's divisions covered the other two, Van Cleve's division being in reserve.

On the morning of the 30th, Rousseau, with two brigades, was ordered down early from Stewart's creek, leaving one brigade there, and sending another to Smyrna to cover our left and rear, and took his place in reserve in rear of

Palmer's right, while General Negley moved on through the cedar breaks until his right rested on the Wilkinson pike, as shown by the accompanying plan. The pioneer corps cut roads through the cedars for his ambulances and ammunition wagons.

The commanding general remained with the left and centre, examining the ground, while General McCook moved forward from Wilkinson's Cross Roads slowly and steadily, meeting with heavy resistance, fighting his way from Overall's creek until he got into position, with a loss of some 135 killed and wounded.

Our small division of cavalry—say 3,000 men—had been divided into three parts, of which General Stanley took two, and accompanied General McCook, fighting his way across from the Wilkinson to the Franklin pike, and below it; Colonel Zahn's brigade, leading gallantly, and meeting with such heavy resistance that McCook sent two brigades from Johnson's division, who succeeded in fighting their way into the position shown on the accompanying plan, marked A, while the third brigade, which had been left at Triune, moved forward from that place, and arrived at nightfall near General McCook's headquarters. Thus, on the close of the 30th, the troops had all got into the position substantially as shown in the accompanying drawing, the rebels occupying the position marked A.

At 4 o'clock in the afternoon General McCook had reported his arrival on the Wilkinson pike, joining Thomas; the result of the combat in the afternoon near Greison's house, and the fact that Sheridan was in position there; that his right was advancing to support the cavalry; also that Hardee's corps, with two divisions of Polk's, was on his front, extending down towards the Salem pike, without any map of the ground, which was to us *terra incognita*. When General McCook informed the general commanding that his corps was facing strongly towards the east, the general commanding told him that such a direction to his line did not appear to him a proper one, but that it ought, with the exception of his left, to face much more nearly south, with Johnson's division in reserve, but that this matter must be confined to him who knew the ground over which he had fought. At 9 p. m. the corps commanders met at the headquarters of the general commanding, who explained to them the following

PLAN OF THE BATTLE.

McCook was to occupy the most advantageous position, refusing his right as much as practicable and necessary to secure it, to receive the attack of the enemy, or, if that did not come, to attack, himself, sufficient to hold all the force on his front; Thomas and Palmer to open with skirmishing, and engage the enemy's centre and left as far as the river; Crittenden to cross Van Cleve's division at the lower ford, covered and supported by the sappers and miners, and to advance on Breckinridge; Wood's division to follow by brigades, crossing at the upper ford, and moving on Van Cleve's right, to carry everything before them into Murfreesboro'. This would have given us two divisions against one, and, as soon as Breckinridge had been dislodged from his position, the batteries of Wood's division, taking position on the heights east of Stone river in advance, would see the enemy's works in reverse, would dislodge them, and enable Palmer's division to press them back, and drive them westward across the river, or through the woods, while Thomas, sustaining the movement on the centre, would advance on the right of Palmer, crushing their right; and Crittenden's corps, advancing, would take Murfreesboro' and then, moving westward on the Franklin road, get in their flank and rear and drive them into the country towards Salem, with the prospect of cutting off their retreat and probably destroying their army.

It was explained to them that this combination, insuring us a vast superiority on our left, required, for its success, that General McCook should be able to hold his position for three hours; that if necessary to recede at all, he should recede as he had advanced on the preceding day, slowly and steadily refusing his right, thereby rendering our success certain.

Having thus explained the plan, the general commanding addressed General McCook as follows: "You know the ground; you have fought over it; you know its difficulties. Can you hold your present position for three hours?" To which General McCook responded, "Yes, I think I can." The general commanding then said, "I don't like the facing so much to the east, but must confide that to you who know the ground. If you don't think your present the best position, change it. It is only necessary for you to make things sure." And the officers then returned to their commands.

At daylight on the morning of the 31st the troops breakfasted and stood to their arms, and by 7 o'clock were preparing for the

BATTLE.

The movement began on the left by Van Cleve, who crossed at the lower fords. Wood prepared to sustain and follow him. The enemy, meanwhile, had prepared to attack General McCook, and by 6½ o'clock advanced in heavy columns—regimental front, his left attacking. Willich's and Kirk's brigades, of Johnson's division, which being disposed, as shown in the map, thin and light, without support, were, after a sharp but fruitless contest, crumbled to pieces and driven back, leaving Edgarton's and part of Goodspeed's battery in the hands of the enemy.

The enemy following up, attacked Davis's division, and speedily dislodged Posts's brigade; Carlin's brigade was compelled to follow, as Woodruff's brigade, from the weight of testimony, had previously left its position on his left. Johnson's brigade, in retiring, inclined too far to the west, and were too much scattered to make a combined resistance, though they fought bravely at one or two points before reaching Wilkinson's pike. The reserve brigade of Johnson's division, advancing from its bivouac near the Wilkinson pike towards the right, took a good position, and made a gallant but ineffectual stand, as the whole rebel left was moving up on the ground abandoned by our troops.

Within an hour from the time of the opening of the battle a staff officer from General McCook arrived, announcing to me that the right wing was heavily pressed and needed assistance. But I was not advised of the route of Willich's and Kirk's brigades, nor of the rapid withdrawal of Davis's division, necessitated thereby—moreover, having supposed his wing posted more compactly, and his right more refused than it really was, the direction of the noise of battle did not indicate to me the true state of affairs. I consequently directed him to return, and direct General McCook to dispose his troops to the best advantage, and to hold his ground obstinately. Soon after, a second officer from General McCook arrived, and stated that the right wing was being driven—a fact that was but too manifest by the rapid movement of the noise of battle towards the north.

General Thomas was immediately despatched to order Rousseau—there in reserve—into the cedar brakes to the right and rear of Sheridan; General Crittenden was ordered to suspend Van Cleve's movement across the river, on the left, and to cover the crossing with one brigade, and move the other two brigades westward across the fields towards the railroad for a reserve. Wood was also directed to suspend his preparations for crossing, and to hold Hascall in reserve. At this moment fugitives and stragglers from McCook's corps began to make their appearance through the cedar brakes in such numbers that I became satisfied that McCook's corps was routed. I therefore directed General Crittenden to send Van Cleve in to the right of Rousseau; Wood to send Colonel Harker's brigade further down the Murfreesboro' pike; to go in and attack the enemy on the right of Van Cleve's; the pioneer brigade meanwhile occupying the knoll of ground west of Murfreesboro' pike, and about four hundred or five hundred yards in rear of Palmer's centre, supporting Stokes's battery, (see accompanying drawing.) Sheridan, after sustaining four successive attacks, gradually swung his right from a southeasterly to a northwesterly direction, repulsing the enemy four times, losing the gallant General Sill, of his right, and Colonel Roberts, of his left brigade, when, having exhausted his ammunition, Negley's division being in the same predicament and heavily pressed, after desperate fighting, they fell back from the position held at the commencement, through the cedar woods in which Rousseau's division, with a portion of Negley's and Sheridan's, met the advancing enemy and checked his movements.

The ammunition train of the right wing, endangered by its sudden discomfitures, was taken charge of by Captain Thruston, of the 1st Ohio regiment, ordnance officer, who, by his energy and gallantry, aided by a charge of cavalry and such troops as he could pick up, carried it through the woods to the Murfreesboro' pike, around to the rear of the left wing, thus enabling the troops of Sheridan's division to replenish their empty cartridge-boxes. During all this time Palmer's front had likewise been in action, the enemy having made several attempts to advance upon it. At this stage it became necessary to readjust the line of battle to the new state of affairs. Rousseau and Van Cleve's advance having relieved Sheridan's division from the pressure, Negley's division and Cruft's brigade, from Palmer's division, withdrew from their original position in front of the cedars, and crossed the open field to the east of the Murfreesboro' pike, about four hundred yards in rear of our front line, where Negley was ordered to replenish his ammunition and form in close column in reserve.

The right and centre of our line now extended from Hazen, on the Murfreesboro' pike, in a northwesterly direction; Hascall supporting Hazen; Rousseau filling the interval to the pioneer brigade; Negley in reserve; Van Cleve west of the pioneer brigade; McCook's corps refused on his right, and slightly to the rear on Murfreesboro' pike; the cavalry being still further to the rear on Murfreesboro' pike, at and beyond Overall's creek.

The enemy's infantry and cavalry attack on our extreme right was repulsed by Van Cleve's division, with Harker's brigade and the cavalry. After several attempts of the enemy to advance on this new line, which were thoroughly repulsed, as were also their attempts on the left, the day closed, leaving us masters of the original ground on our left, and our new line advantageously posted, with open ground in front swept at all points by our artillery.

We had lost heavily in killed and wounded, and a considerable number in stragglers and prisoners; also twenty-eight pieces of artillery, the horses having been slain, and our troops being unable to withdraw them by hand over the rough ground; but the enemy had been thoroughly handled, and badly damaged at all points, having had no success where we had open ground and our troops were properly posted; none which did not depend on the original crushing in of our right, and the superior masses which were in consequence brought to bear upon the narrow front of Sheridan's and Negley's divisions, and a part of Palmer's, coupled with the scarcity of ammunition, caused by the circuitous road which the train had taken, and the inconvenience of getting it from a remote distance through the cedars. Orders were given for the issue of all the spare ammunition, and we found that we had enough for another battle, the only question being where that battle was to be fought.

It was decided, in order to complete our present lines, that the left should be retired some two hundred and fifty yards to a more advantageous ground, the extreme left resting on Stone river, above the lower ford, and extending to Stokes's battery. Starkweather's and Walker's brigades arriving near the close of the evening, the former bivouacked in close column, in reserve, in rear of McCook's left, and the latter was posted on the left of Sheridan, near the Murfreesboro' pike, and next morning relieved Van Cleve, who returned to his position in the left wing.

DISPOSITION FOR JANUARY 1st, 1863.

After careful examination and free consultation with corps commanders, followed by a personal examination of the ground in rear as far as Overall's creek, it was determined to await the enemy's attack in that position, to send for the provision train, and order up fresh supplies of ammunition; on the arrival of which, should the enemy not attack, offensive operations were to be resumed.

No demonstration on the morning of the 1st of January; Crittenden was ordered to occupy the point opposite the ford, on his left, with a brigade.

About 2 o'clock in the afternoon the enemy, who had shown signs of movement, and massing on our right, appeared at the extremity of a field a mile and a half from the Murfreesboro' pike, but the presence of Gibson's brigade, with a battery, occupying the woods near Overall's creek, and Negley's division, and a portion of Rousseau's on the Murfreesboro' pike, opposite the field, put an end to this demonstration, and the day closed with another demonstration by the enemy on Walker's brigade, which ended in the same manner.

On Friday morning the enemy opened four heavy batteries on our centre, and made a strong demonstration of attack a little further to the right, but a well-directed fire of artillery soon silenced his batteries, while the guns of Walker and Sheridan put an end to his efforts there.

About 3 o'clock p. m., while the commanding general was examining the position of Crittenden's left, across the river, which was now held by Van Cleve's division, supported by a brigade from Palmer's, a double line of skirmishers was seen to emerge from the woods in a southeasterly direction, advancing across the fields, and they were soon followed by heavy columns of infantry—battalion front—with three batteries of artillery.

Our only battery on that side of the river had been withdrawn from an eligible point, but the most available spot was pointed out, and it soon opened fire upon the enemy. The line, however, advanced steadily to within one hundred yards of the front of Van Cleve's division, when a short and fierce contest ensued. Van Cleve's division giving way, retired in considerable confusion across the river, followed closely by the enemy.

General Crittenden immediately directed his chief of artillery to dispose the batteries on the hill on the west side of the river, so as to open on them, while two brigades of Negley's division, from the reserve, and the pioneer brigade, were ordered up to meet the onset.

The firing was terrific and the havoc terrible. The enemy retreated more rapidly than they had advanced. In forty minutes they lost two thousand men.

General Davis, seeing some stragglers from Van Cleve's division, took one of his brigades and crossed at a ford below to attack the enemy on his left flank, and, by General McCook's order, the rest of his division was permitted to follow; but when he arrived, two brigades of Negley's division and Hazen's brigade of Palmer's division had pursued the flying enemy well across the fields, capturing four pieces of artillery and a stand of colors.

It was now after dark, and raining, or we should have pursued the enemy into Murfreesboro'. As it was, Crittenden's corps passed over and, with Davis's, occupied the crests, which were intrenched in a few hours.

Deeming it possible that the enemy might again attack our right and centre, thus weakened, I thought it advisable to make a demonstration on our right by a heavy division of camp fires, and by laying out a line of battle with torches, which assisted the purpose.

Saturday, 3d day of January, it rained heavily from 3 o'clock in the morning. The ploughed ground over which our left would be obliged to advance was impassable for artillery. The ammunition trains did not arrive until 10 o'clock; it was therefore deemed unadvisable to advance, but batteries were put in position on the left, by which the ground could be swept, and even Murfreesboro' reached by Parrott shells.

A heavy and constant picket firing had been kept up on our right and centre, and extending to our left, which at last became so annoying that in the afternoon I directed the corps commanders to clear their fronts.

Occupying the woods to the left of Murfreesboro' pike with sharpshooters, the enemy had annoyed Rousseau all day, and General Thomas and himself requested permission to dislodge them and their supports, which covered a ford. This was granted, and a sharp fire from batteries was opened for ten or fifteen minutes, when Rousseau sent two of his regiments, which, with Spear's Tennesseeans and the 85th Illinois volunteers that had come out with the wagon train, charged upon the enemy, and, after a sharp contest, cleared the woods and drove the enemy from his trenches, capturing from seventy to eighty prisoners.

Sunday morning, the 4th of January, it was not deemed advisable to commence offensive movements, and news soon reached us that the enemy had fled from Murfreesboro'. Burial parties were sent out to bury the dead, and the cavalry was sent to reconnoitre.

Early Monday morning General Thomas advanced, driving the rear guard of rebel cavalry before him six or seven miles towards Manchester. McCook and Crittenden's corps following, took position in front of the town, occupying Murfreesboro'.

We learned that the enemy's infantry had reached Shelbyville by 12 m. on Sunday, but owing to the impracticability of bringing up supplies, and the loss of five hundred and fifty-seven (557) artillery horses, further pursuit was deemed unadvisable.

It may be of use to give the following general summary of the operation and results of the series of skirmishes closing with the battle of Stone river and occupation of Murfreesboro'.

We moved on the enemy with the following forces: Infantry, 41,421; artillery, 2,223; cavalry, 3,296; total, 46,940.

We fought the battle with the following forces: Infantry, 37,977; artillery, 2,223; cavalry, 3,200; total, 43,400.

We lost in killed: Officers, 92; enlisted men, 1,441; total, 1,533.

We lost in wounded: Officers, 384; enlisted men, 6,861; total, 7,245.

Total killed and wounded, 8,778; being 20.03 per cent. of the entire force in action.

Our loss in prisoners is not fully made out, but the provost marshal general says, from present information, they will fall short of 2,800.

If there are many more bloody battles on record, considering the newness and inexperience of the troops, both officers and men, or if there has been more true fighting qualities displayed by any people, I should be pleased to know it.

As to the condition of the fight, we may say that we operated over an unknown country, against a position which was 15 per cent. better than our own, every foot of ground and approaches being well known to the enemy, and that these disadvantages were fatally enhanced by the faulty position of our right wing.

The force we fought is estimated as follows:

We have prisoners from 132 regiments of infantry, (consolidations counted as one,) averaging from those in General Bushrod Johnson's division, 411 each—say, for certain, 350 men each—which will give—

132	regiments of infantry, say 350 men each	46,200 men.
12	battalions of sharpshooters, say 100 men each	1,200 men.
23	batteries of artillery, say 80 men each	1,840 men.
29	regiments of cavalry, say 400 men each, and }	13,250 men.
24	organizations of cavalry, say 70 men each, }	
220		62,490 men.

Their average loss, taken from the statistics of Claburne's, Breckinridge's, and Withers's divisions, was about 2,080 each. This for six divisions of infantry and one of cavalry will amount to 14,560 men; or to ours nearly as 165 to 100.

Of 14,560 rebels struck by our missiles, it is estimated that 20,000 rounds of artillery hit 728 men; 2,000,000 rounds of musketry hit 13,832 men; averaging 27.4 cannon shots to hit one man; 145 musket shots to hit one man.

Our relative loss was as follows: Right wing, 15,933 musketry and artillery; loss, 20.72 per cent. Centre, 10,866 musketry and artillery; loss, 18.4 per cent. Left wing, 13,288 musketry and artillery; loss, 24.6 per cent.

On the whole, it is evident that we fought superior numbers on unknown ground, inflicted much more injury than we suffered, were always superior on equal ground with equal numbers, and failed of a most crushing victory on Wednesday by the extension and direction of our right wing.

This closes the narrative of the movements and seven days' fighting, which terminated with the occupation of Murfreesboro'. For a detailed history of the parts taken in the battles by the different commands, their obstinate bravery and patient endurance, in which the new regiments vied with those of more experience, I must refer to the accompanying sub-reports of the corps, division, brigade, regimental, and artillery commanders.

Besides the mention which has been already made of the service of our artillery by the brigade, division, and corps commanders, I deem it a duty to say that such a marked evidence of skill in handling the batteries, and in firing low and with such good effect, appears, in this battle, to deserve special commendation.

Among the lesser commands which deserve special mention for distinguished service in the battle is the pioneer corps, a body of 1,700 men, composed of details from the companies of each infantry regiment, organized and instructed by Captain James St. Clair Morton, corps of engineers, chief engineer of this army, which marched, as an infantry brigade, with the left wing, making bridges at Stewart's creek; prepared and guarded the ford at Stone river on the nights of the 29th and 30th; supported Stokes's battery, and fought with valor and determination on the 31st, holding its position till relieved on the morning of the 2d; advancing with the greatest promptitude and gallantry to support Van Cleve's division against the attack on our left on the evening of the same day, constructing a bridge and batteries between that time and Saturday evening.

The efficiency and *esprit du corps* suddenly developed in this command, its gallant behaviour in action, and the eminent services it is continually rendering the army, entitle both officers and men to special public notice and thanks, while they reflect the highest credit on the distinguished ability and capacity of Captain Morton, who will do honor to his promotion to a brigadier general, which the President has promised him.

The ability, order, and method exhibited in the management of the wounded elicited the warmest commendations from all our general officers, in which I most cordially join. Notwithstanding the number to be cared for, through the energy of Dr. Swift, medical director, ably assisted by Dr. Weeds and the senior surgeons of the various commands, there was less suffering from delay than I have ever before witnessed.

The 10th regiment of Ohio volunteers, at Stewart's creek, Lieutenant Colonel S. W. Burke commanding, deserves especial praise for the ability and spirit with which they held that post, defended our trains, succored their guards, chased away Wheeler's rebel cavalry, saving a large wagon train, and arrested and retained for service stragglers from the battle-field.

The 1st regiment of Michigan engineers and mechanics, at Lavergne, under the command of Colonel James, fighting behind a slight protection of wagons and brush, gallantly repulsed a charge from more than ten times his number of Wheeler's cavalry.

For distinguished acts of individual zeal, heroism, gallantry, and good conduct, I refer to the accompanying lists of special mentions and recommendations for promotion, wherein are named some of the many noble men who have distinguished themselves and done honor to their country and the starry symbol of its unity. But those named there are by no means all whose names will be inscribed on the rolls of honor we are preparing, and hope to have held in grateful remembrance by our countrymen.

To say that such men as Major General George H. Thomas, true and prudent, distinguished in council, and on many a battle-field for his courage; or Major General McCook, a tried, faithful, and loyal soldier, who bravely breasted the battle at Shiloh and at Perryville, and as bravely on the bloody field of Stone river; and Major General Thomas L. Crittenden, whose heart is that of a true soldier and patriot, and whose gallantry often attested by his companions in arms on other fields, witnessed many times by this army long before I had the honor to command it, and never more conspicuously than in this combat, maintained their high character throughout this action, but feebly expresses my feeling of obligation to them for counsel and support from the time of my arrival to the present hour. I doubly thank them, as well as the gallant and ever-ready Major General Rousseau, for their support in this battle.

Brigadier General D. S. Stanley, already distinguished in four successful battles—Island No. 10, May 27; before Corinth; Iuka and the battle of Corinth—at this time in command of our ten regiments of cavalry, fought the enemy's forty regiments of cavalry, and held them at bay, or beat them whereever he could meet them. He ought to be made a major general for his service, and also for the good of the service.

As for such brigadiers as Negley, Jefferson C. Davis, Johnson, Palmer, Hascall, Van Cleve, Wood, Mitchell, Cruft, and Sheridan, they ought to be major generals in our service. In such brigade commanders as Colonels Carlin, Miller, Hazen, Samuel Beatty, of the 19th Ohio; Gibson, Gross, Wagner, John Beatty, of the 3rd Ohio; Harker, Starkweather, Stanley, and others whose names are mentioned in the accompanying report, the government may well confide. They are the men from whom our troops should be at once supplied with brigadier generals; and justice to the brave men and officers of the regiments equally demand their promotion to give them and their regiments their proper leaders. Many captains and subalterns also showed great gallantry and capacity for superior commands.

But, above all, the steady rank and file showed invincible fighting, courage, and stamina, worthy of a great and free nation, requiring only good officers, discipline, and instructions, to make them equal, if not superior, to any troops in ancient or modern times. To them I offer my most heartfelt thanks and good wishes.

Words of mine cannot add to the renown of our brave and patriotic officers and soldiers who fell on the field of honor, nor increase respect for their memory in the hearts of our countrymen.

The names of such men as Lieutenant Colonel J. P. Garesché, the pure and noble christian gentleman and chivalric officer, who gave his life an early offering on the altar of his country's freedom; the gentle, true, and accomplished General Sill; the brave, ingenious, and able Colonels Roberts, Millikin, Shaffer, McKee, Reed, Foreman, Fred. Jones, Hawkins, Knell, and the gallant and faithful Major Carpenter, of the 19th regulars, and many other field officers, will live in our country's history, as will those of many others of inferior rank, whose soldierly deeds on this memorable battle-field won for them the admiration of their companions, and will dwell in our memories in long future years, after God, in his mercy, shall have given us peace, and restored us to the bosom of our homes and families.

Simple justice to the gallant officers of my staff, the noble and lamented Lieutenant Colonel Garesché, chief of staff; Lieutenant Colonel Taylor, chief quartermaster; Lieutenant Colonel Symonds, chief commissary; Major C. Goddard, senior aide-de-camp; Major Ralston Skinner, judge advocate general; Lieutenant Frank S. Bowl, aide-de-camp of General Tyler; Captain Chas. R. Thompson, my aide-de-camp; Lieutenant Byron Kirby, 6th U. S. infantry, aide-de-camp, who was wounded on the 31st; R. S. Thoms, esq., a member of the Cincinnati bar, who acted as volunteer aide-de-camp, behaved with distinguished gallantry; Colonel Barnett, chief of artillery and ordnance; Captain S. H. Gilman, 19th U. S. infantry, inspector of artillery; Captain Jas. Curtis, 15th U. S. infantry, assistant inspector general; Captain Wiles, 22d Indiana, provost marshal general; Captain Michler, chief of topographical engineers; Captain Jesse Merrill, signal corps, whose corps behaved well; Captain Elmer Otis, 4th regular cavalry, who commanded the courier line connecting the various headquarters most successfully, and who made a most opportune and brilliant charge on Wheeler's cavalry, routing a brigade and recapturing 300 of our prisoners; Lieutenant Edson, U. S. ordnance officer, who, during the battle of Wednesday, distributed ammunition under the fire of the enemy's batteries and behaved bravely; Captain Hubbard and Lieutenant Newberry, who joined my staff on the field and acted as aids, rendered valuable service in carrying orders on the the field; Lieutenant Royse, 4th U. S. cavalry, who commanded the escort of the headquarters train and distinguished himself for gallantry and efficiency; all not only performed their appropriate duties to my entire satisfaction, but accompanying me everywhere, carrying orders through the thickest of the fight, watching while others slept, and never weary when duty called, deserves my public thanks, and the respect and gratitude of the army.

With all the facts of the battle fully before me, the relative numbers and positions of our troops and those of the rebels, the gallantry and obstinacy of the contest and the finale result, I say from conviction, and as public acknowledgement due to Almighty God, in closing this report, "*Non nobis Domine! non nobis sed nomine tuo da gloriam.*"

W. S. ROSECRANS,
Major General Commanding.

Brigadier General L. THOMAS,
Adjutant General U. S. A.

1.—REPORT OF COLONEL JAMES BARNETT, CHIEF OF ARTILLERY.

HEADQUARTERS DEPARTMENT OF CUMBERLAND,
Murfreesboro', Tenn., February 8, 1863.

SIR: I have the honor to submit, for the information of the general commanding, a summary from the reports of the batteries of this department, of their position, &c., at the late battle of Stone river.

RIGHT WING.

Second division, composed of the following batteries: Battery A, 1st Ohio artillery, Lieutenant Belding commanding, attached to General Willich's brigade; battery E, 1st Ohio artillery, Captain Edgarton, attached to Colonel Kirk's brigade; 5th Indiana, Captain Simonson, attached to Colonel Buckley's brigade, having the following guns: nine James's rifles, three 6-pounder smooth-bore, two 12-pounder howitzers, two 10-pounder Parrotts, two 12-pounder light field guns.

On the evening of the 30th of December battery A was placed in position in the rear of the brigade, on the extreme right of the right wing, with one section, the other two sections fronting the rear, horses unhitched but not unharnessed. At daybreak the horses were sent to water, with the precaution to return at the least alarm; firing commenced, teams returned quickly and hitched. The brigade falling back very fast, the battery retired to a slight eminence in the rear, but the enemy having got so far to the right that the guns were under a cross fire. Near this point three guns were taken by the enemy; two other pieces were taken rapidly to the rear, one gun having horses remaining was served with effect as opportunity was offered, firing about four rounds at each unlimbering. Upon reaching the Murfreesboro' pike this one gun was put in position with Captain Simonson's battery, where about ten rounds were fired. Upon being ordered to return, one wheel-driver and two horses being killed while limbering up, the piece was temporarily abandoned, but was brought off by the Louisville Legion with prolonge attached. This battery the next day was held in position with two guns near the Murfreesboro' pike in reserve, where it remained until ordered forward across the river. Company E, 1st Ohio artillery, Captain Edgarton, was posted, on the night of the 30th December, on the extreme right and in front of battery A, in position to guard a country road, horses harnessed all night. At daylight of 31st horses were sent to water; at the firing of the pickets horses were hitched in, or at least one-half, and others immediately returned. Two shells were thrown in the direction of the enemy, still invisible, and as they appeared six rounds of canister were thrown with great effect. The vigorous attack of the enemy in front and flank, and the loss of many horses, rendered it necessary to abandon the battery, after, however, a determined resistance, two cannoneers being bayoneted at the guns.

Captain Edgarton and Lieutenant Berwick were captured. 5th Indiana battery, Captain Simonson, was first put in position on the morning of the 31st, about one-half mile to the right of the six-mile pike, upon which the right wing advanced upon an open field, with the battery fronting to the west. Here the right section was temporarily detailed, by order of Colonel Baldwin, and ordered to the left and front. About four hundred yards from this position the battery fell back with the division, and were ordered, by Brigadier General Johnson, to take another position on the crest, about two hundred yards to the right of the Murfreesboro' pike, and near to the right of Major General Rousseau's division, which position it retained until ordered to retire.

The next ground taken was in the open space to the left, and about twenty-five yards from the railroad, where it remained until about sunset, when General Johnson ordered the battery to the left of his division, about one hundred and eighty-five yards to the right of the Murfreesboro' pike, opposite the headquarters of Major General Rousseau, where they remained until ordered to cross Stone river, January 5. The battery lost two guns.

First division.—The artillery in this division is composed of the following batteries, and had the following guns: 5th Wisconsin, Captain Piney, attached to Colonel Post's brigade; 2d Minnesota, Captain Hotchkiss, attached to Colonel Carlin's brigade; 8th Wisconsin, Captain Carpenter, attached to Colonel Woodruff's brigade. Four 10-pounder Parrotts, eight 6-pounder smooth-bore, four 12-pounder howitzers. Captain Piney's battery, which, with his brigade, was on the extreme right of the army, on the 30th, after driving the enemy to enable the skirmishers to advance to the open fields, or front, took position, with horses in harness, for the night. After dark two brigades of the 2d division took position on the right. On the morning of the 31st, upon the falling back of these two brigades, the battery changed front to the right, to meet the enemy rapidly approaching by the right and rear, supported by the 59th Illinois and posted in a cornfield, where they opened fire with canister, checking temporarily the advance of the enemy. However, being unopposed on the right, the position became untenable, and the battery was withdrawn, leaving Captain Piney dangerously wounded, with the loss of some eighteen horses and one gun. The balance of the battery was dragged to the rear by the assistance of the 59th Illinois. Near the Nashville pike it was charged upon by cavalry, who were driven off by the 4th regiment cavalry, and took position behind Overall's creek, on a hill to the right of the pike, where they remained all night.

The next morning their position was on the left of the pike, where breastworks were thrown up in a position to enfilade the enemy's lines. At this point a rebel battery opening was soon silenced by a few Parrott shot. In the afternoon of the next day the battery, with its brigade, were ordered to cross the Stone river, where they were put into position, throwing up breastworks, and where they remained until two o'clock on the morning of January 4, when they recrossed the river, taking their position on the right, where they remained until January 6, 1863.

2d Minnesota battery, Captain Hotchkiss.—This battery moved on the 30th with its brigade to the right of the Wilkinson pike, until the withdrawal of skirmishers, when the battery opened with canister and spherical case with effect. When the first line of the brigade had arrived at the point about one hundred and eighty yards from the house of Mrs. William Smith, two batteries, one about one hundred yards west of the house, and another on the east of the house, two hundred and fifty yards distant, opened fire on the 21st Illinois and 15th Wisconsin volunteers. These batteries were soon silenced by another to the right, about five hundred yards, enfilading. The brigade was driven off by a well-directed fire from this battery. Before daylight, on the morning of the 31st, the battery was retired two hundred yards; soon after which the brigade was vigorously attacked and obliged to fall back across the open fields and entered a wood about two hundred yards east of Gresion's house, when several rounds were fired with destructive effect.

The command was again retired about one mile, and went into position in the edge of a cedar grove, from whence they again retired to the railroad. The next position was near the Nashville pike, four miles from Murfreesboro'.

On January 2, under order of Major General Rosecrans, the brigade and battery were sent to the left, crossing Stone river at the ford, relieving Colonel Hazen, where they remained until January 4.

The 8th Wisconsin battery, Captain Carpenter, at about 11 o'clock, 30th December, were posted on the edge of a cotton-field, in front of a wood running parallel with the pike, facing southeast, placed in the interval between General Sill's right and the left of its (Colonel Woodruff's) brigade.

At about 3 o'clock the command was moved forward, with heavy skirmishing. The right of the brigade being well advanced, were halted, and remained until support should come up. The battery was placed at the angle of the fence, to protect the right and front, when it received a heavy fire, occasionally replying with shell, until towards night, when the enemy opened a heavy artillery fire on the right of Carlin's brigade, which was silenced in handsome style in a few minutes. Colonel Carlin's brigade being attacked at about the same time, this battery again opened with such effect as to effectually check the attack.

The enemy, on the morning of the 31st, made this attack in five lines, the battery opening a full fire of canister with terrific effect. After a determined resistance, being ordered back, several ineffectual attempts were made to get into position, but owing to the general stampede no stand could be made until they reached the Murfreesboro' pike, where they remained until Tuesday; being then ordered to the left, crossed the ford, and went into position on the extreme left, about two miles from the ford. On Saturday, January 3, the battery changed position again to the right, where they remained until ordered to Murfreesboro'.

3d division.—The batteries of this division are as follows: Battery G, 1st Missouri, Captain Hescock, attached to Colonel Schafer's 2d brigade; battery C, 1st Illinois, Captain Houtaling, attached to Colonel Roberts's 3d brigade; 4th Indiana battery, Captain Bush, attached to General Sill's 1st brigade, with the following guns: two 10-pounder Parrotts, four 12-pounder light field guns, two James's rifles, six 6-pounder smooth-bore, and four 12-pounder howitzers.

Battery G, 1st Missouri, Captain Hescock, moved on the morning of the 30th, at 7 a. m., with their brigade on the right and rear of the division, to the right of the Wilkinson pike, having Bush's battery on the left. Towards evening, Bush moving to the front, Captain Hescock took his place. The three batteries of the division concentrated their fire upon the enemy's batteries, silencing their fire. In the morning this battery and Captain Houtaling opened a heavy fire upon the enemy, who were engaging Generals Sill's and Davis's commands, until the enemy, who were pursuing General Johnson's command, gained their rear, when they moved to the front, to the position first held by the enemy, and then took position on the north side of the road, sending one section to re-enforce Captain Bush, engaging the enemy hotly until their ammunition was expended, when they retired through the cedars with the division. After gaining the open field, their guns were brought into action and fired until all the ammunition was expended. About 3 o'clock, January 1, they took a position south of the Murfreesboro' pike, and were not further engaged.

Battery P, 1st Illinois, Captain Houtaling, on the 30th, moved on the left of Captain Bush, and next to the Wilkinson pike, south side, opened fire, in concert with the other batteries of the division, at the enemy in front. On the 31st, at the falling back of General Johnson, this battery took position on the right of the pike, just in the edge of the timber, supported by Colonel Roberts's brigade, where he remained until all of his horses were killed and ammunition expended, when he was forced to abandon his guns, falling back and assisting at the guns of the other batteries of the division.

4th Indiana battery, Captain Bush, on the afternoon of the 30th, being on the right of Captain Houtaling, moved his battery to the front, and opened fire on the enemy at short range, with the other batteries, driving back the enemy. During the night the captain moved to a more commanding position. On the 31st the battle opened with this division by an attempt to capture this battery, which was gallantly defended by General Sill, when this brave officer fell between the guns. The battery fell back with the other batteries of the division, and took position on the north of the pike, sending one section, with Lieutenant Flansburg, to re-enforce Captain Houtaling; one Parrott section, with Lieutenant Tallifero, was at this time sent to Captain Houtaling, assisted by Captain Hescock, when, after a very warm resistance, and ammunition failing, the battery was compelled to retire, with the loss of two of his guns left in the cedars. The next position taken was on the south of the Murfreesboro' pike, with the division.

CENTRE.

First division.—The artillery of this division consists of the following batteries: Captain Stone, 1st Kentucky battery; Lieutenant Van Pelt, 1st Michigan battery; Company H, 4th United States artillery, Lieutenant Guenther, with the following guns: ten 10-pounder Parrotts, two James's rifles, two 6-pounder smooth-bore; 12-pounder light field guns.

Captain Stone, 1st Kentucky battery, was not ordered into position until January 1, when it was posted on the right of the Murfreesboro' pike, directly in front of the log-house, one section being stationed in the woods about 100 yards distant. The battery afterwards moved to the front edge of the woods, in rear of the brigade to which it was attached. At night it relieved Lieutenant Parsons's battery, which was stationed outside and in front of the woods commanding the cornfields and woods to the right and front, in which position it remained until January 3; at 4 p. m. relieved Captain Cox's half battery, which was about 50 yards to the left, posting a half battery in its place at night, shelled the fields and woods from both points; were not further engaged.

1st Michigan battery, Lieutenant Van Pelt, took position, in the morning of the 31st, on the left of the pike, three miles from Murfreesboro', where they remained during the day, serving their guns with effect; were relieved on the 1st of January, and took position about half a mile in rear of front line of battle. On the 2d of January moved a few hundred yards to the front, and took position on the right of the pike, remaining at this point through the day. On Saturday morning the battery moved to the front, behind earthworks, immediately beyond the pike, fronting the position occupied on Wednesday, remaining there all day and night, shelling the woods at sundown.

Company H, 4th artillery, Lieutenant Guenther. On the morning of the 31st, this battery moved through the cedars to the left of the pike with its brigade, but was returned, owing to the impracticability of operating in the woods, and took position in the open ground in time to check a rebel advance. From the cedars it then moved to a position on the rise of ground on the opposite side of the pike. On the appearance of the enemy at close range a heavy fire with canister shot was opened on them with such effect that they were driven back to the woods in disorder. The battery held this position until the morning of the 1st of January, when it was moved some distance to the rear, and after several changes of front, was ordered with the brigade to a point on the Murfreesboro' pike, beyond Stewart's creek: this order being countermanded, the battery camped near its old point. On the morning of January 3 fire was opened on a battery of the enemy which was annoying our troops, resulting in driving it from its position. During the forenoon the brigade and battery moved forward and occupied rifle-pits and epaulments which had been constructed for them. At dusk the battery opened fire with shell and spherical case shot on the enemy concealed in the woods and buildings and behind breastworks, &c., which, being followed by infantry, drove them from their position. The battery remained in position during the following day, and on the morning of the 5th removed to Murfreesboro'.

Second division, Brigadier General Negley.—The batteries of this division are as follows: Company M, 1st Ohio, Captain Schultz; company G, 1st Ohio artillery, Lieutenant Marshall; company M, 1st Kentucky, Lieutenant Ellsworth, with the following guns: two 12-pounder Wiard steel guns, two 6-pounder Wiard, four 12-pounder howitzers, two James's rifle, one 6-pounder smooth-bore, two 16-pounder Parrotts. The three batteries of this division were posted with the division on a slope of the west bank of Stone river, in advance, but joining the right of General Crittenden's line with General Sheridan on their right; Captain Schultz on the right of battery G, 1st Ohio; battery M, 1st Kentucky, on the left. The batteries opened fire on the enemy and drove them, holding the position during the day and night. On the 31st, these batteries, after holding their position under a murderous fire for some hours, having a large proportion of their horses killed, and being out of ammunition, were compelled to retire with the loss of six guns in getting through the cedars. Company M, on January 1, was posted on the left side of the railroad; changed position about one o'clock to the right of Murfreesboro' pike, where it remained until night. On January 2 these batteries were posted on the hill at the ford of Stone river to resist the attack on the left, which proved successful.

LEFT WING.

The batteries of the left wing are the following: Company M, 4th United States artillery, Lieutenant Parsons; company H, 4th artillery, Lieutenant Throckmorton; company B, 1st Ohio artillery, Captain Standart, attached to the second division; 10th Indiana, Captain Cox; 8th Indiana, Lieutenant Estep; 6th Ohio, Captain Bradley, attached to 1st division; 7th Indiana battery, Captain Swallow; 3d Wisconsin, Lieutenant Livingston; 26th Pennsylvania, Lieutenant Stevens, attached to the 3d division, with the following guns: four 3-inch rifles, ten 12-pounder howitzers, six James's rifles, twelve 6-pounder smooth-bores, sixteen 10-pounder Parrotts.

The first position taken by batteries H and M, under command of Lieutenant Parsons, was just to the right of Murfreesboro' pike, two and a half miles from Murfreesboro'. During the morning they retired for ammunition, and took a second position between the railroad and pike, and after firing away all their ammunition, they again retired. On the 2d of January they were moved to the front, and soon after took position at the hill near the ford, and participated in repulsing the enemy from our left.

Company B, 1st Ohio artillery, Captain Standart, on the 31st, was posted on the right of Lieutenant Parsons. After firing away his ammunition he retired for the day. On the 2d he was put in position on the hill, on the right of the pike commanding the cornfield occupied by Stokes's battery the day before. Being under a very heavy cannonading, three pieces were retired to a position under cover in reserve to the left of the pike. These three guns were in the afternoon moved to the left to resist the attack of the enemy.

Company F, 1st Ohio, Captain Cockerill, on the 31st, was placed in position on the left of Parsons's battery, and on the right of the pike; but during the morning retired and took position on the left of the railroad, and about four hundred yards from it, which position they held until the attack on the left, to which point Lieutenant Osborne moved four pieces, (the captain having been wounded.)

Captain Bradley, on the morning of the 31st, moved with Colonel Hacker's brigade on its advance to check the enemy on the right, and held with it its position through the day. On the 2d he held a position on commanding ground near to the right of the railroad. When the attack was made on the left, he changed front to fire to the left. 7th Indiana battery, Captain Swallow, on the 31st went into battery a short distance to the right of the pike, two and a half miles from Murfreesboro', and in the afternoon moved to the left of the railroad, going into battery on the right of Cockerill's battery. On the 2d this battery also was placed on the high ground to resist the enemy's attack at the ford.

8th Indiana battery, Lieutenant Estep.—This battery was placed on the opposite side of the pike, (left,) and rear of Captain Swallow's battery. On the 2d, having suffered severely from the enemy's artillery in the morning, he retired to repair damages, and when the attack was made on the left massed with the other batteries on the hill at the ford.

10th Indiana battery, Captain Cox, was placed in position in front, and on the left of the railroad, which he maintained on the 31st and afterwards. 26th Pennsylvania battery, Lieutenant Stevens, was posted on the left, and facing the pike, three miles from Murfreesboro', when the enemy appeared. As they fell back he moved forward, crossing the pike, taking position on the ridge, changing several times. On the 2d he changed front to fire to the left, and opened fire when the attack was made in that direction, 3d Wisconsin battery, Lieutenant Livingston, was commanding the ford on the 31st; they afterward moved across the river at the ford. When the attack was made on the 2d they recrossed and took position on the hill in line with the other batteries of the corps. Board of Trade battery, Captain Stokes, attached to Pioneer brigade, consisting of four six-pounders, smooth bore, two James's rifles, moved on the 31st promptly to the front and right of the pike, serving canister with effect. They afterwards moved still further to the front, holding a good position, commanding a cornfield and the woods beyond. After having held the position thirty-six hours the battery was ordered to the rear. On the 2d this battery was again put in position with the batteries to resist the attack from the left, and opened with the artillery force massed at that point a destructive fire, causing the enemy to retire. The losses in materiel and *personnel* I had the honor to report immediately after the battle.

The many gallant actions of battery officers and men are named by their immediate commanders in their reports, to which I respectfully refer for the details of their action. The practice of the batteries was good, and the precaution of the general commanding to fire low and be sparing of ammunition was heeded. Owing to the nature of the country, the loss of the guns was unavoidable, as in falling back on the right the horses could not be under cover, and the thick cedar thickets prevented the guns being brought off by hand.

Six guns, three caissons, three damaged forges, and two battery wagons were captured from the enemy, or recaptured; also five thousand four hundred and fifty-one muskets, with bayonets, scabbards, &c.

The whole number of men engaged in serving the batteries was eighty-six commissioned officers, twenty-seven hundred and sixty non-commissioned officers and privates.

I remain, colonel, your obedient servant,

JAMES BARNETT,
Colonel and Chief of Artillery.

Lieutenant Colonel C. GODDARD,
Assistant Adjutant General and Chief of Staff.

Report of loss sustained by the batteries of the fourteenth army corps.

Designation of battery.	Name of commanding officer.	OFFICERS.			ENLISTED MEN.			GUNS.		HORSES.			HARNESS LOST.		BATTERY WAGONS.		FORGES.		AMMUNITION.	Remarks.
		Killed.	Wounded.	Captured.	Killed.	Wounded.	Captured and missing.	Captured.	Disabled.	Killed.	Wounded.	Captured and missing.	Sets of lead.	Sets of wheel.	Lost.	Disabled.	Lost.	Disabled.	Number of rounds expended.	
Battery E, 1st Ohio artillery	Capt. Edgarton		2	2	10	5	20	6		75			28	14	1		1		7	
Battery A, 1st Ohio artillery	Lieut. Belding				1	5	23	3	1	73			22	11	1		1		25	
5th Indiana battery	Capt. Simonson				3	19	2	2		9	14		6						213	
Battery G, 1st Illinois artillery	Capt. Hescock	1			4	12	5			20		17					1		1,112	
Battery C, 1st Illinois artillery	Capt. Houghtaling		1	1	6	20	24	6		80		15			1		1		1,154	
4th Indiana battery	Capt. Bush				6	17	3	2		17		10					1		1,160	
5th Wisconsin battery	Lieut. Hill		1		1	5		1		21			6	3					726	
8th Wisconsin battery	Lieut. Stiles	1				4	1	2		18			4	2					375	
2d Minnesota battery	Capt. Hotchkiss		1		3	5	2			13			1	1					500	
1st Michigan battery	Lieut. Van Pelt				1	11				5	5		2						697	
1st Kentucky battery	Captain Stone					1	2					4							110	
Battery H, 5th U. S. artillery	Lieut. Guenther					5				3	4							1	558	
Battery Michigan artillery	Capt. Church																		170	
Battery M, 1st Ohio artillery	Capt. Shultz		1		1		1	1		9									750	
Battery G, 1st Ohio artillery	Lieut. Marshall				4	8	3	4		34		12							553	
Hewitt's Kentucky battery	Lieut. Nell				2	1		1		28			14	5					531	
Battery B, 1st Ohio artillery	Capt. Standart				3	13	3			21						1			1,610	
Batteries H, M, 4th U. S. artillery	Lieut. Parsons				2	14	6			20									2,299	
7th Indiana battery	Lieut. Swallow		1		4	7				1	4								406	
Battery F, 1st Ohio artillery	Capt. Cockerill		1		2	12					24								1,080	
3d Wisconsin battery	Lieut. Livingston					4				9									358	
26th Pennsylvania battery	Lieut. Stevens				2	7				7									1,650	
10th Indiana battery	Capt. Cox				1	4				72									1,442	
8th Indiana battery	Lieut. Estep					6	6			15	4								871	
6th Ohio battery	Capt. Bradley				2	2	1			16	5								500	
Board of Trade battery	Capt. Stokes		1		3	8	1			3		1							1,450	
Total		2	9	3	61	195	103	28	1	533	36	59	83	36	3	1	5	1	20,307	

Respectfully submitted.

JAMES BARNETT, *Colonel and Chief of Artillery.*

2.—REPORT OF LIEUTENANT COLONEL TAYLOR, CHIEF QUARTERMASTER.

HEADQUARTERS DEPARTMENT OF THE CUMBERLAND,
Office of Chief Quartermaster, Murfreesboro', February 1, 1863.

GENERAL: I have the honor to report herewith a statement of the losses of animals and means of transportation during the battle of Stone river; also a list of the animals, means of transportation, and other property, captured from the enemy and picked up on the field and at Murfreesboro', as reported by the quartermasters of the several divisions named. A large number of the wagons that were partially burned by the enemy have been recovered and turned into the repair shops. Some wagons, and a large number of animals reported as lost, have been picked up by the several regiments, and will be taken up and accounted for by the quartermasters in their monthly returns, so that the actual loss is much less than appears by the annexed statement.

Very respectfully,

JOHN W. TAYLOR,
Lieutenant Colonel and Quartermaster.

Major General W. S. ROSECRANS,
Commanding Department of the Cumberland.

Statement of public animals and means of transportation captured by the enemy, killed in battle, lost, and destroyed, from December 26, 1862, *until January* 16, 1863.

Command.	Wagons.	Ambulances.	Harness—sets.	HORSES.				Mules.	Animals.
				Draft.	Artillery.	Cavalry.	Total.		
RIGHT WING.									
Headquarters	10	1	60	----	----	----	----	60	60
1ST DIVISION.									
Headquarters	----	----	3	7	----	1	8	5	13
Ammunition and supply train	35	----	204	4	----	3	7	204	211
1st Brigade.									
Headquarters	----	----	4	3	----	1	4	----	4
22d Indiana volunteers	1	----	6	----	----	2	2	5	7
59th Illinois volunteers	2	1	12	----	----	2	2	11	13
74th Illinois volunteers	2	----	12	----	----	----	----	12	12
75th Illinois volunteers	1	----	6	----	----	----	----	12	12
5th Wisconsin battery	2	----	30	----	21	----	21	12	33
2d Brigade.									
Headquarters	----	----	24	----	----	1	1	24	25
21st Illinois volunteers	4	----	13	----	----	----	----	13	13
38th Illinois volunteers	2	----	14	1	----	----	1	15	16
15th Wisconsin volunteers	2	1	28	3	----	----	3	25	28

Statement of public animals, &c.—Continued.

Command.	Wagons.	Ambulances.	Harness—sets.	HORSES.				Mules.	Animals.
				Draft.	Artillery.	Cavalry.	Total.		
101st Ohio volunteers	4		2						
2d Minnesota battery					13		13		13
3d Brigade.									
Headquarters						4	4	1	5
25th Illinois volunteers	1		6			1	1	6	7
35th Illinois volunteers	1		6			4	4	6	10
81st Indiana volunteers	2		10	4		1	5	6	11
8th Wisconsin battery			8		18		18		18
36th Illinois cavalry, B comp						3	3		3
2d Kentucky cavalry, G comp.						7	7		7
2D DIVISION.									
Headquarters									
3d Indiana cavalry		1				30	30		30
Supply train	3		18					18	18
Ammunition train	2		12					12	12
1st Brigade.									
Headquarters									
15th Ohio volunteers		1	5	4			4	1	5
49th Ohio volunteers		2	4						
32d Indiana volunteers		1		1			1	1	2
39th Indiana volunteers	1	1	4	4			4		4
89th Illinois volunteers		2	2	2			2		2
1st Ohio art'ry, vol. battery A.		1	30		62		62		62
2d Brigade.									
Headquarters						7	7	7	14
34th Illinois volunteers				1			1		1
79th Illinois volunteers	1			2			2	1	3
29th Indiana volunteers	1	1	2	2			2	4	6
30th Indiana volunteers			1					2	2
77th Pennsylvania volunteers				2			2		2
1st Ohio artil'ry, vol. battery E.			82	7	75		82	6	88
3d Brigade.									
Headquarters	1		6					6	6
1st Ohio volunteers									
93d Ohio volunteers		1	4	5			5		5
5th Kentucky volunteers, (S.S.)	1		6	1			1	6	7
6th Indiana volunteers		1	6	1			1	6	7
5th Indiana battery			13		24		24		24
3d Indiana cavalry, 3 battal's									
3D DIVISION.									
Headquarters									
Ammunition and supply train	58		348					348	348

Statement of public animals, &c.—Continued.

Command.	Wagons.	Ambulances.	Harness—sets.	HORSES.				Mules.	Animals.
				Draft.	Artillery.	Cavalry.	Total.		
1st Brigade.									
Headquarters									
36th Illinois volunteers	1		6					6	6
88th Illinois volunteers	2	1	14	2			2	12	14
24th Wisconsin volunteers	1		6					1	1
21st Michigan volunteers									
4th Indiana battery	1	1	8	2	43		45	6	51
2d Brigade.									
Headquarters	1		6					6	6
2d Missouri volunteers	1		4					4	4
15th Missouri volunteers									
44th Illinois volunteers									
73d Illinois volunteers	1		6					6	6
1st Missouri, battery G	1		6		37		37	6	43
3d Brigade.									
Headquarters	1		6					6	6
27th Illinois volunteers	2	2	16					16	16
42d Illinois volunteers	1	2	8					8	8
51st Illinois volunteers	2	1	14	18			18	18	36
22d Illinois volunteers	1		6					6	6
1st Illinois battery	1		8		85		85	8	93
CENTRE.									
1ST DIVISION.									
2d Brigade.									
3d Ohio volunteers	1							4	4
88th Indiana volunteers	1		4	1			1		1
1st Michigan battery				10			10		10
4th Brigade.									
Headquarters				1			1		1
1st batt. 18th infantry, U. S.			2					10	10
2d batt. 18th infantry, U. S.		1	2					2	2
5th United States artillery					15		15		15
2D DIVISION.									
Headquarters and division train	5		90					90	90
2d Brigade.									
Headquarters				1			1		1
18th Ohio volunteers				6			6	4	10

Statement of public animals, &c.—Continued.

Command.	Wagons.	Ambulances.	Harness—sets.	HORSES. Draft.	HORSES. Artillery.	HORSES. Cavalry.	HORSES. Total.	Mules.	Animals.
3d Brigade.									
Headquarters	2	----	12	1	----	1	2	8	10
74th Ohio volunteers	1	1	6	2	----	----	2	4	6
37th Indiana volunteers	4	1	16	1	----	----	1	12	13
21st Ohio volunteers	4	1	1	6	----	----	6	----	6
78th Pennsylvania volunteers	1	----	14	1	----	9	10	----	10
1st Ohio artillery, battery E	----	----	28	----	46	----	46	----	46
Hewitt's Kentucky battery	1	----	19	----	18	----	18	----	18
1st Ohio artillery, battery M	----	----	1	----	9	----	9	1	10
5TH DIVISION.									
2d Brigade.									
Headquarters	15	----	88	5	----	----	5	84	89
105th Ohio volunteers	4	----	8	----	----	----	----	16	16
80th Illinois volunteers	5	----	10	1	----	----	1	20	21
123d Illinois volunteers	4	----	12	----	----	----	----	24	24
101st Indiana volunteers	4	----	10	----	----	----	----	20	20
19th Indiana battery	2	----	4	----	10	----	10	----	10
LEFT WING.									
1ST DIVISION.									
Supply train	----	----	----	----	----	----	----	2	2
6th Ohio battery	----	----	2	----	16	----	16	----	16
10th Indiana battery	----	----	----	----	22	----	22	1	23
8th Indiana battery	2	----	12	----	18	3	21	12	33
26th Ohio volunteers	1	1	8	4	----	----	4	6	10
58th Indiana volunteers	2	----	12	----	----	----	----	12	12
3d Kentucky volunteers	1	----	6	----	----	----	----	6	6
13th Michigan volunteers	----	----	6	----	----	----	----	6	6
2D DIVISION.									
Supply train	2	----	6	----	----	----	----	12	12
90th Ohio volunteers	1	----	----	----	----	----	----	----	----
110th Illinois volunteers	----	----	----	----	----	----	----	1	1
9th Indiana volunteers	----	1	1	2	----	----	2	----	2
3D DIVISION.									
Supply train	2	----	8	----	----	----	----	7	7
3d Wisconsin battery	----	----	----	----	11	----	11	----	11
26th Pennsylvania battery	----	----	----	----	7	----	7	----	7
7th Indiana battery	----	----	----	----	5	----	5	----	5
Detached.									
Michigan engineers and mechanics	3	----	41	21	----	----	21	20	41
3d Ohio cavalry	1	----	6	----	----	----	----	6	6
Captain Warren's supply train	6	----	----	----	----	----	----	----	----
Total loss	229	28	1,540	139	555	80	774	1,334	2,108

List of animals, means of transportation, and other property captured from the enemy and picked up on the battle-field, from January 1 *to January* 16, 1863, *as per reports of division quartermasters.*

Command.	Wagons.	Ambulances.	Mules.	Horses.	Total number of animals.	Harness, single—sets.	Hides.	Cotton.	Bran.
							No.	*P'nds.*	*Bush's.*
RIGHT WING.									
2d division	----	----	20	50	70	----	------	------	------
3d division	----	----	------	4	4	----	------	------	------
CENTRE.									
8th division	9	----	18	15	33	12	------	------	------
LEFT WING.									
1st division	1	1	17	7	24	----	------	------	------
3d division	----	1	2	6	8	----	------	------	------
DETACHED.									
10th Ohio	3	----	14	1	15	19	------	------	------
Captain Boyd, a. qm	----	----	------	6	6	----	------	------	------
1st brigade pioneers	4	----	4	------	4	21	------	------	------
Chief army police	1	----	143	103	246	2	------	------	------
Captain C. F. King, a. qm	----	----	------	------	------	----	------	8,680	3,500
Lieut. Col. J. W. Taylor, qm	----	----	5	4	9	----	1,069	------	------
Total	18	2	223	196	419	54	1,069	8,680	3,550

3.—REPORT OF LIEUTENANT COLONEL SIMMONS, CHIEF COMMISSARY OF SUBSISTENCE.

HEADQUARTERS ARMY OF THE CUMBERLAND,
Office Ch. C. S., Murfreesboro', February 14, 1863.

COLONEL: I have the honor to submit herewith a statement of stores lost and picked up by the several commands of the centre and left wing, commanded by Major Generals Thomas and Crittenden, on the battle-field and between Stone river and Nashville, during the late action on Stone river.

No report of stores lost on the right wing has been furnished me.

Very respectfully, your obedient servant,

SAMUEL SIMMONS,
Lieutenant Colonel and Chief

Lieutenant Colonel C. GODDARD,
Assistant Adjutant General and Chief of Staff.

Statement of subsistence stores lost and taken up on and near the battle-field, during the battle of Stone river, about January 1, 1863.

FOURTEENTH ARMY CORPS.

First division, Captain G. R. Paul, commissary of subsistence.

Lost.—8,700 pounds of fresh beef, 3,874 pounds of fresh bacon, 39 barrels of flour, 10,123 pounds of hard bread, $61\frac{22}{32}$ bushels of beans, 225 pounds of rice, 891 pounds of roasted coffee, 187 pounds of tea, 1,388 pounds of sugar, 320 pounds of adamantine candles, 120 pounds of tallow candles, 1,380 pounds of soap, 42 gallons molasses, 220 pounds of mixed vegetables.

Taken up.—4,500 pounds of fresh beef, 29,873 pounds of bacon, $5\frac{64}{196}$ barrels of flour, 38,382 pounds of hard bread, $32\frac{18}{32}$ bushels of beans, $2{,}537\frac{5}{16}$ pounds of rice, 4,681 pounds of roasted coffee, 91 pounds of tea, 6,835 pounds of sugar, 80 gallons vinegar, 360 pounds of adamantine candles, 1,532 pounds of soap.

Second division, Captain W. J. Kane, commissary of subsistence

Lost.—4 barrels of pork, 6,432 pounds of fresh beef, 500 pounds of bacon, 5 barrels of flour, 150 pounds of coffee, 1,400 pounds of sugar, 40 gallons of molasses.

TWENTY-FIRST ARMY CORPS.

First division, Captain S. D. Henderson, commissary of subsistence.

Lost.—38 head of cattle, estimated to weigh 600 pounds each, net.

Second division, Lieutenant C. C. Peck, assistant commissary of subsistence.

Lost.—4,500 pounds of bacon, 5,000 pounds of hard bread.

Third division, Captain J. O. Stanage, assistant commissary of subsistence.

Lost.—1,295 pounds of bacon, 3,922 pounds of roasted coffee, 46 pounds of tea, 893 pounds of soap.

4.—REPORT OF DR. EBEN SWIFT, MEDICAL DIRECTOR.

HEADQUARTERS DEPARTMENT OF THE CUMBERLAND,
Murfreesboro', January 25, 1863.

COLONEL: Herewith I have the honor to transmit a brief report of the transactions of the medical department of the army of the Cumberland, together with the reports of the medical directors of the right, left, and centre.

On the morning of the 26th of December last, pursuant to orders from the commanding general, the army moved forward from camp near Nashville towards Murfreesboro', the right on the Nolinsville and the centre on the Franklin pikes, while the left advanced direct on the Murfreesboro' road.

Soon after Major General McCook, in command of the right wing, left his camp on Mill creek, he encountered the cavalry of the enemy, and skirmished with them till he reached Nolinsville. About a mile in advance of this place the enemy made a determined stand with a battery in position, but was soon routed, with the loss of one of his guns and several prisoners. We had three men killed and seven wounded in Davis's division. The heavy rain of the morning had subsided, and now the country was enveloped in fog or mist.

The same day Major General Thomas, in command of the centre, moved across the country from the Franklin to the Nolinsville pike; sent aid to General Davis, who he learned was engaged, and on the following day marched to Stewartsville, on the Murfreesboro' pike. He remained here till the morning of the 29th, when he advanced to the support of the left wing, which had preceded him, and was now near Murfreesboro'.

On the 30th General Negley's division of this portion of the army joined with Sheridan, who occupied the left of General McCook's command, which had moved up from Nolinsville on the Wilkinson pike, and now occupied a position nearly parallel with the enemy, the left resting on the Wilkinson pike, and the right extending southwesterly in a line in a direction with the river. In this movement of the right from near Nolinsville, General Stanley, in command of a division of cavalry in advance, encountered the enemy in considerable force and drove him beyond Triune. The cavalry lost one killed and five wounded, and in another affair the much lamented Major Rosingartin was killed, and Major Ward mortally wounded; ofthe Anderson cavalry six privates were also wounded. These were taken with the command in ambulances, and placed in hospital at the crossroads.

Major General Crittenden, in command of the left wing, while advancing along the Murfreesboro' pike, met the enemy, on the 27th, at Lavergne, and put him to flight. In this engagement we lost two killed and thirty-two wounded. These latter were left in hospital at Lavergne in charge of medical officers, and were subsequently removed to Nashville. On the 29th this grand division of the army moved into position on the extreme left, with General Palmer on the right, resting on the Murfreesboro' pike and joining Negley, of the centre, and General Wood occupying the ground from Palmer to the river, General Van Cleve in reserve of this, and General Rousseau in rear of the centre.

General Rosecrans, with his entire staff, advanced from Nashville on the Murfreesboro' pike, and, having reached the head of the column, turned off to the right over a heavy mud road, visited General McCook's command, and returned to his camp in the rear of Lavergne about 4 o'clock the following morning. Here he remained contemplating the movements of the enemy, till the following day, when he moved on to Stewartsville. The next day, (the 29th,) late in the evening, he visited General Crittenden's headquarters, and remained in consultation all night with the chief officers of his command.

On the following morning one of our batteries, in position a little to the left, and in advance of the general, opened fire upon a battery of the enemy still more to the left, and on elevated ground, which, replying, killed one of the escort, Private Dolan, of the 4th United States cavalry, and wounded the adjutant of the 7th Indiana volunteers in the shoulder; at the same time a private of an infantry regiment not engaged, was killed. The general and his staff now fell back three or four hundred yards to the sloping ground on the left of the road, where he remained all day.

About 11 o'clock the heavy picket firing on our left ceased, and opened generally along our right, where General McCook was being engaged. The enemy was strongly intrenched behind earthworks extending from the river, on our extreme left, across our front in almost a direct line; then far along our right, but receding from the Wilkinson to the Franklin pike, through heavy timber.

The left wing lost to-day three killed and eighteen wounded; the centre, fourteen killed and fifty-three wounded; and the right, twenty-four killed and one hundred and five wounded.

Field hospitals were established for the left and centre, in houses and tents along the Nashville pike; and for the right wing, in the same manner, on the Wilkinson pike and neighborhood.

Before leaving Nashville I had approved of full and complete requisitions, at the suggestion of Surgeon Murray, United States army, my predecessor, for the three grand divisions of the army. I had also in reserve tents, bedding, etc., for a field hospital for more than 2,500 men, which I ordered up from the rear on the 29th, as soon as I learned the enemy had made a stand near Murfreesboro'. At the same time I ordered forward twenty ambulances—all that we had on hand at Nashville. Surgeons were detailed to perform operations when decided on after consultation, for dressing, and such other duties as the reception and disposition of the wounded and circumstances required.

Early on the morning of the 31st, the enemy, during the night having massed a heavy force on our right, fiercely attacked Johnson's and Davis's divisions, which he forced back; and Sheridan's, being heavily pressed, was obliged to recede. The hospitals, wounded, and nearly all the medical supplies of this wing of the army thus fell into the hands of the enemy. We were also called on to lament in sadness the loss of General Sill, and many noble and brave officers and men.

About 9 o'clock the commanding general, with his staff, dashed boldly forward to the front of the left wing, and in person directed the movements of troops and placed batteries in position. His daring presence so near the enemy's line brought down upon him an angry and spiteful fire of musketry, round shot and shell, almost at point-blank range. But utterly disregarding this metallic storm, our brave commander moved calmly on from left to right, cheering and inspiring our faltering troops. And throughout the day wherever the tide of battle most fiercely raged, General Rosecrans bore his charmed life and ubiquitous presence. The noble Garesché was killed by his side, and his aids, Lieutenant Kirby severely, and Lieutenant Porter slightly, wounded. Sergeant Richmond and four privates of his escort were also killed or wounded, the former mortally.

Much the heaviest loss sustained to-day fell upon our regular battalions, brigaded under command of Lieutenant Colonel O. S. Shepherd, in holding the cedar brake, on the right of the centre, against the columns of the enemy sweeping down upon them after having forced back our entire right wing. This loss amounted to 561 killed and wounded, more than one-third of their numbers; in fact, I might probably better say, nearly one-half.

Our casualties in killed and wounded did not fall short of 4,000 men, including about 1,500 of the right wing, 1,200 of whom, wounded, fell into the hands of the enemy.

The ambulance corps, though temporarily organized, worked admirably. As soon as the fire of the enemy slacked at any point along our lines, and became only desultory, the ambulances dashed in at a brisk trot, and snatched our wounded from their picket lines. In justice, I should add, the enemy did not fire on these brave men when they knew their humane mission—friend and foe, no longer combatants, being equally the objects of their care.

In the early part of the day Dr. Weeds, assistant medical director, went to the rear to take charge of the property pertaining to the field hospitals, and placed it in proper position. About 10 o'clock Surgeon McDermot, medical director of the right wing, reported to me that his hospitals and wounded, hospital supplies and medical officers had fallen into the hands of the enemy, and asked for instructions. I directed him to a cedar brake on the left of the road, half a mile to the rear, where I instructed him to make a temporary field hospital, constructing the shed, roof, and beds for the wounded from cedar boughs, to make his requisition on Dr. Weeds for supplies, and report to me when he could receive the wounded. Visiting this place an hour later I found it untenable, or, at least, unsafe, on account of round shot and shell from the enemy occasionally falling upon it. I then directed Surgeon McDermot to find suitable buildings on the pike to the rear.

It became necessary, in order to accommodate so many wounded, to make use of tents, and my field hospital having arrived, I was enabled to afford comfortable shelter for all. In the mean time my attention was drawn to a large number of wagons, ambulances, caissons, &c., moving from different points to the river, more to the left. I soon learned they had come in disorder from the right, and were looking for safety over an uneven, rocky ford on the opposite river bank. This Babel-like confusion was somewhat augmented by the approach of the enemy, who now charged upon this flank. They were, however, driven back before much property had been destroyed. I had succeeded in drawing out many of the ambulances before crossing the ford. Three were reported to me as having been taken by the enemy and burned; the remainder subsequently did good service.

During the day the enemy's cavalry made a descent upon our hospitals at the Nashville pike; but, beyond some confusion and embarrassment, they did little harm. Our own cavalry, commanded by Captain Otis, speedily drove them away, and recaptured all we had lost.

During the night I visited the hospitals within our lines along the pike and off of it, to the rear, and was gratified to find the wounded well provided and attended. At daylight surgeons, nurses, and attendants were busily engaged in the labor they had begun the morning before.

As the fighting on the 1st of January was confined to brisk skirmishing, and but few casualties resulting therefrom, we were able to complete our organization, and finish the heavy work so suddenly thrown upon our hands the day before. Many of the slightly wounded, and those who were able to ride in empty wagons, and walk, I ordered to Nashville, 25 miles to the rear.

After a brisk engagement the following morning, without any marked results, the day passed much as the preceding, till 5 o'clock, when the enemy came down with an overwhelming force upon our left flank, driving, for a while, everything before him. But emerging from the heavy timber upon the open ground, he was met by terrific volleys of grape, round shot, and shell from 52 pieces of artillery, placed in position by Captain Mendenhall, on the opposite river bank. The enemy faltered, they fell back, and soon this living mass was in full retreat. Our loss, not exceeding 500 men, was comparatively small, his being estimated at nearly three times that number.

Then, as on other occasions, the ambulance corps behaved well. It was dark when the battle ceased, but while occasionally only shot fell from the baffled foe, our wounded were on the road, and less than an hour later they were all comfortably provided for in the rear. Lieutenant ———, who had charge of this branch of the medical service, deserves favorable mention for his zeal and industry; for though he could not share, from indisposition, the more bold and daring occupation of his brave comrades, he contributed much to the comfort of the wounded.

Saturday morning found our army bivouacked in mud, drenched with rain, without shelter, and almost without food, but still hopeful and cheerful. None were sick—few complaining. Our heavy lines of pickets on all sides were all day engaged, and at night General Rosecrans's division stormed their rifle-pits in front, carried them, and held them. Our loss in this affair and throughout the day was not large. This proved to be our last encounter with the enemy.

On the following day we were engaged in the mournful task of burying our lamented dead. I visited the hospitals on the Wilkinson pike and neighborhood, now again within our lines, and found the wounded generally well cared for. Surgeon Marks and other medical officers, as also the attendants, left in these hospitals by direction of Surgeon McDermot, medical director of the left wing, I am happy to state, with but few exceptions, did their duty faithfully and well.

Their labors were great and harassing, and not unattended with danger. On the 31st, when the ground was fiercely contested, and only yielded to an overwhelming force, some buildings were pierced by round shot and musketry, wounding attendants in the earnest discharge of their duty.

During the battle of Wednesday, a portion of Negley's division of the centre fell into the hands of the enemy. These have been reported to me as having received the same care and attention as their own wounded by the medical officers of their army. In fact, they have said to me they had been "well treated," and "had no reason to complain."

Surgeons Bogue, Johnson, Bretsford, and Wright are highly commended for their gallantry in maintaining their position with their wounded comrades when the hospitals of this portion of the army came within the enemy's lines. In strong contrast with these and many other devoted and self-sacrificing men, it becomes my painful duty to say that V. D. Miller, assistant surgeon 78th Pennsylvania volunteers, is reported to me by the medical director of his corps as having "basely deserted his post."

Surgeon Phelps, medical director of the left wing, is entitled to the highest praise for his zeal and untiring industry in the establishment of the largest field hospital in the rear, for professional skill, and devoted attention to the wants of the wounded. Surgeon Blair also deserves credit for the comfortable provision made for those intrusted to his care, in tents, and shelters made of tent flags. The wounded here, as elsewhere, under canvas did well, and most clearly established, in the opinion of all, the advantages derived from free ventilation thus afforded over hospitals in ordinary dwellings of wood or brick, notwithstanding a liberal provision of windows and doors.

I am gratified to say my conservative views were generally adopted, and that amputations were seldom performed without consultation. Many excisions were made, which are doing well, and some cases were treated as compound fractures with marked success.

Surgeon Muscroft, medical director of General Rousseau's division, established a hospital in the rear, and accommodated comfortably a large number of wounded. Many of the serious cases are in an advanced stage of recovery. His zeal, skill, and industry are commendable. Also Surgeon James, medical director of the cavalry division, and Cumfort, of the Anderson Troop, did faithful service. Assistant Surgeon Taylor has been assiduous in his attentions to sick and wounded.

Lieutenant Colonel Northcote, unable longer to bear the fatigue and exposure incident to duty in the lines, on account of ill health, aided me greatly in organizing parties of stragglers, with whom he policed camps and procured wood, water, and straw.

Captain Monger, with his company, was detailed to guard property and enforce discipline in and about the field hospitals; and Captain Stackpole, to provide and issue subsistence stores as required. These gentlemen did their duties well, and gave universal satisfaction. The duties of these officers, like those of the medical department, though not of the brilliant nature of their more fortunate comrades in front, were essential to the comfort of the brave wounded, and deserve well of their commanding general and country.

I must crave your indulgence for again mentioning the ambulance corps.

The service performed was highly creditable. The drivers and assistants, among the former of whom I desire to mention F. M. Figett, private, company M, 21st Kentucky volunteers, were kind, prompt, and zealous in the discharge of their duty. This service was often necessarily continued into the night, and near the enemy's lines. Yet these brave men, unarmed, untiring, and unflinching, in the face of danger, gathered their bleeding comrades from under the guns of the enemy, and bore them to the rear.

My orderly, Private Bassett, 4th United States cavalry, deserves creditable mention for his unceasing devotion to duty, and the prompt manner in which he conveyed my directions on the field. My clerk, William Dorner, private in the Anderson Troop, who, I am gratified to know, has been highly recommended for a commission, also served faithfully and assiduously at the hospitals in the rear.

The commissary and quartermaster's departments are entitled to our thanks for timely and efficient aid in furnishing supplies and transportation, and in the preparation of hospitals for the reception of sick and wounded here and at Nashville. My thanks are also due to my assistants, Doctor Weeds and Surgeon Phelps, whom I have previously mentioned, for their prompt and efficient co-operation, and for valuable suggestions conducive to the comfort and best treatment of the wounded; to Surgeon Thurston, assistant medical director at Nashville, also, for his zeal, energy, and rare professional abilities displayed in providing for the wounded sent him from the battle-field. Surgeons McDermot and Bebe were untiring in their labors, and afforded me valuable aid. Their observations on treatment of wounded, etc., as shown in their report herewith appended, should receive attention.

From the difficulty of individualizing, where so many are distinguished, I have mentioned but few officers as deserving of commendation for faithful and conscientious attention to duty. I am sorry to say, however, that there are those whose conduct has been bad, whose names at an early day will be forwarded to the commanding general for his action. Among these are two officers, who left the field to look for hospitals beyond Stewart's creek, and did not soon return. Reported to me by Colonel Burke, 10th Ohio volunteers.

Under the present standard of professional ability among subordinate medical officers, too much stress cannot, in my opinion, be laid upon the importance of securing supervisory talent of the highest order. The rank now common to corps, (medical directors,) is most inadequate to the responsibility, extent of authority, and respect attaching to such a position; while the pay and emoluments pertaining thereto are a poor inducement to skilful practitioners to abandon a lucrative practice at home for the drudgery, exposure, and, at best, brief honors of service with troops in the field. While the medical officers now acting in this capacity are comparatively the best fitted therefor among those open to selection, I am of opinion that the standard of professional administrative capacity of such officers should be elevated, and that increase of rank, (it may be local,) of pay and emoluments to medical directors, will insure the availability to the department of a much higher order of talent than is at present accessible.

It appears to me that the liberality of the government and the people, which grants such liberal donations of money and supplies for sanitary purposes, might be most advantageously applied to securing more valuable personal attentions to the objects of these laudable efforts.

I append hereto a complete return of the killed and wounded of the various subdivisions of the army, with a tabular statement of the location and nature of the wounds.

Very respectfully,

EBEN SWIFT,

Surgeon, U. S. A., Medical Director, Department of the Cumberland.

Tabular statement showing the location of 3,102 *wounds received in the army of the Cumberland during the late battle of Stone river.*

Head and face	282	Hand	245	Thigh	432
Breast	134	Neck	59	Leg	626
Shoulder	259	Back	57	Knee	94
Arm	347	Abdomen	52	Ankle	45
Forearm	21	Groin	11	Foot	141
Elbow	16	Hip	159		
Waist	22	Side	100		

The remaining wounds are unknown or too slight in their nature to be mentioned.

EBEN SWIFT,
Surgeon U. S. Army, Medical Director.

General summary of casualties during the battle of Stone river.

Corps and detachments.	Killed.		Wounded.		Total.
	Officers.	Enlisted men.	Officers.	Enlisted men.	
Right wing	30	573	100	2, 481	3, 184
Centre	16	308	94	1, 619	2, 037
Left wing	42	527	180	2, 663	3, 412
Staff and escort of general commanding	1	3	2	3	9
Fourth U. S. cavalry	....	3	1	8	12
Chicago Board of Trade battery	....	3	1	5	9
Pioneer brigade	....	7	3	21	31
Cavalry division	3	17	3	61	84
Total	92	1, 441	384	6, 861	8, 778

List of casualties during the battle of Stone river.—Detachments.

Lieutenant Colonel Julius P. Garesché, assistant adjutant general and chief of staff—killed December 31, 1862.

Killed.—Sergeant James B. Richmond, company K, 4th United States cavalry, on escort duty; Private Daniel McDonald, company D, 4th United States cavalry, on escort duty; Private E. W. Grubb, Anderson Troop, on escort duty, December 31; Private C. P. Cole, company L, 4th United States cavalry; Private John Stagg, Board of Trade battery; Private —— Wiley, Board of Trade battery; Private —— Finney, Board of Trade battery.

Wounded.—Captain Eli Long, company K, 4th United States cavalry, arm; Second Lieutenant Byron Kirby, 6th United States infantry, aide-de-camp on staff of general commanding, severely; Lieutenant Porter, aide-de-camp on staff of general commanding, slightly; Lieutenant T. D. Griffin and Sergeant —— Adams, Board of Trade battery; Private Patrick Kern, company B, 4th United States cavalry; Private Charles Smith, company B, 4th United States cavalry; Private William Dalton, company C, 4th United States cavalry; Private George Deiter, company D, 4th United States cavalry; —— Stuckler, farrier, 4th United States cavalry; Private Joseph Kohler, company G, 4th United States cavalry; Private Samuel Tate, company I, 4th United States cavalry; Private William Ellis, company K, 4th United States cavalry; Private A. Jennett, company L, 4th United States cavalry; Private Jackson Howard, Board of Trade battery; Private James Bloom, Board of Trade battery; Private —— Canberry, Board of Trade battery; Private —— Carver, Board of Trade battery.

Summary.

Killed	7
Wounded	18
Total	25

First brigade, first division of cavalry.

Colonel Minor Milkins, 1st Ohio cavalry, killed; Major A. B. More, 1st Ohio cavalry, killed; Adjutant W. H. Scott, 1st Ohio cavalry, severely wounded.

Killed.—Lieutenant T. L. Condid, company L, 1st Ohio cavalry; Corporal N. Poland, company D, 1st Ohio cavalry; Corporal C. E. Aldrive, company N, 4th Ohio cavalry; Corporal M. R. Tiffin, 3d Ohio cavalry; Corporal Jacob Henry, 3d Ohio cavalry; Privates John Wessel, company E, 3d Kentucky cavalry; James Galispie, company A, 7th Pennsylvania cavalry; Henry Fry, company I, 7th Pennsylvania cavalry; Orlando Hawly, company I, 4th Michigan cavalry; F. Senteim, company L, 1st Ohio cavalry; George McConnell, company A, 4th Ohio cavalry; Marias Ecke, company B, 4th Ohio cavalry; Allen McComp, company I, 4th Ohio cavalry; John Hersh, company N, 4th Ohio cavalry; James Walker, 3d Ohio cavalry; Byron Staunton, 3d Ohio cavalry; Henry Winslow, 3d Ohio cavalry; S. C. Chapin, 3d Ohio cavalry.

Wounded.—Captain —— Wertham, company C, 1st Tennessee cavalry, slightly; Lieutenant T. V. Mitchell, company H, 4th Michigan cavalry, severely; Sergeant John Castillo, company H, 3d Kentucky cavalry, severely; Sergeant Charles T. Trago, company B, 7th Pennsylvania cavalry, severely; Sergeant A. J. Kingsley, company C, 7th Pennsylvania cavalry; Sergeant —— Sutton, company B, 4th Michigan cavalry, severely; Sergeant —— Lowland, company K, 4th Michigan cavalry, severely; Sergeant —— Palmer, company K, 4th Michigan cavalry, severely; Sergeant John Queal, company G, 1st Ohio cavalry, severely; Sergeant Henry Long, company G, 1st Ohio cavalry, slightly; Sergeant John C. Cooper, company B, 1st Ohio cavalry, slightly; Sergeant J. W. Ward, 3d Ohio cavalry; Sergeant Thomas Hanfimer, 3d Ohio cavalry; Corporal —— Voght, company B, 4th Michigan cavalry, severely; Corporal —— Moore, company K, 4th Michigan cavalry, severely; Corporal Charles Lentherby, company B, 4th Ohio cavalry, severely; Corporal I. Krona, company L, 4th Ohio cavalry, severely; Corporal Em. Cooper, company L, 4th Ohio cavalry, severely; Corporal Alver Moris, company L, 4th Ohio cavalry, severely; Corporal W. E. Rextor, company E, 1st Ohio cavalry, slightly; Bugler John Decker, company M, 3d Kentucky cavalry, severely; Privates Philip Peters, company H, 3d Kentucky cavalry, severely; Charles Spitunagle, company C, 3d Kentucky cavalry, severely; Robert More, company M, 3d Kentucky cavalry, severely; Edwin Cranmer, company B, 7th Pennsylvania cavalry, severely; M. Gilded, company F, 7th Pennsylvania cavalry, slightly; John Patridge, company I, 7th Pennsylvania cavalry, slightly; Samuel Kraver, company I, 7th Pennsylvania cavalry, slightly; Henry Baker, company K, 7th Pennsylvania cavalry, slightly; William Maddan, company K, 7th Pennsylvania cavalry, slightly; —— Narns, company D, 4th Michigan cavalry, slightly; —— Pendergrast, company B, 1st Tennessee cavalry, severely; A. Mutlerborough, 3d Ohio cavalry; Perry Duval, 3d Ohio cavalry; Daniel Ryretz, 3d Ohio cavalry; Jos. Bundaugh, 3d Ohio cavalry; William Bacon, 3d Ohio cavalry; Chas. Lentherly, company B, 4th Ohio cavalry, severely; George Tealdecamp, company C, 4th Ohio cavalry, severely; Charles Dubur, company D, 4th Ohio cavalry, severely; E. J. Harn, company G, 4th Ohio cavalry, severely; W. A. B. Young, company H, 4th Ohio cavalry, severely; Henry Hess, company H, 4th Ohio cavalry, severely; John Hamilton, company I, 4th Ohio cavalry, severely; Edward Duncan, company I, 4th Ohio cavalry, severely; M. Heis, company K, 4th Ohio cavalry, severely; Rorenzo E. Wilber, company L, 4th Ohio cavalry, severely; Benjamin Brown, company L, 4th Ohio cavalry, severely; Calvin Floyd, company L, 4th Ohio cavalry, severely; Frederick C. LeCount, company L, 4th Ohio cavalry, severely; Hugh Duffy, company M, 4th Ohio cavalry, severely; J. Hardy, company G, 1st Ohio cavalry, severely; J. Harris, company H, 1st Ohio cavalry, severely; Thomas Dunann, company F, 1st Ohio cavalry, severely; James Parker, company F, 1st Ohio cavalry, severely; William Lewis, company G, 1st Ohio cavalry, slightly; Lewis Holland, company B, 1st Ohio cavalry, slightly; John Lambert, company H, 1st Ohio cavalry, slightly; A. W. Little, 3d Ohio cavalry; D. Hawley, 3d Ohio cavalry; John Britton, 3d Ohio cavalry; Albert Parry, 3d Ohio cavalry; W. Englebreadt, 3d Ohio cavalry; James R. Conley, company A, 4th Ohio cavalry.

Summary.

Killed	20
Wounded	64
Total	84

A list of the casualties of the Pioneer Brigade, department of the Cumberland, from December 29, 1862, *to the 5th of January*, 1863, *inclusive.*

Acting Colonel Lyman Bridges, 1st battalion, wounded in the leg; Lieutenant Colonel E. B. Dodd, 1st battalion, wounded in the leg and foot.

Killed.—Corporal James Brown, company B, 1st battalion; Privates Horace C. Cooper, 1st battalion; George Bowmaster, company E, 2d battalion; Amos Hake, company I, 3d battalion; William Trimble, company C, 3d battalion; Peter Wagoner, company C; J. A. Head, company F, 3d battalion.

Wounded.—Lieutenant John Richel, 1st battalion; Sergeant Amos Wilson, company K, 2d battalion; Sergeant W. E. Mason, company F, 3d battalion; Privates Thomas Lane, 1st battalion; Adam Ritzel, company F, 1st battalion; Levi Beam, company C, 1st battalion; John Van Acre, company C, 1st battalion; Henry Borham, company R, 1st battalion; B. Greenleaf, company G, 1st battalion; J. A. Reed, company D, 2d battalion; William Ferguson, company H, 2d battalion; David Smith, company H, 2d battalion; C. Calier, company C, 2d battalion; T. A. Scott, company F, 3d battalion; John Dirk, company A, 3d battalion; C. Pelson, company A, 3d battalion; Benjamin Wagoner, company C, 3d battalion; Charles Dregg, company C, 3d battalion; B. N. Blankenship, company H, 3d battalion; Timothy Gorfert, company F, 3d battalion.

Missing.—Private Amos Reed, company C, 3d battalion.

Summary.

Killed	7
Wounded	22
Missing	1
Total	30

Statement of the killed and wounded of the 20th corps, army of the Cumberland, in the battle before Murfreesboro'.

Commands.	Officers.		Non-commissioned officers.		Privates.		Total.		Aggregate.
	Killed.	Wounded.	Killed.	Wounded.	Killed.	Wounded.	Killed.	Wounded.	
FIRST DIVISION.									
First brigade.									
22d Indiana	......	5	......	8	7	26	7	39	46
59th Illinois	......	......	3	5	4	38	7	43	50
74th Illinois	......	......	4	8	4	25	8	33	41
75th Illinois	......	2	......	4	2	16	2	22	24
Second brigade.									
21st Illinois	2	4	5	25	40	169	47	198	245
38th Illinois	2	5	10	17	22	88	34	110	144
101st Ohio	1	4	2	14	15	107	18	125	143
15th Wisconsin	2	3	2	13	11	56	15	72	87
Third brigade.									
25th Illinois	1	3	4	13	11	63	16	79	95
35th Illinois	1	1	1	11	9	41	11	53	64
81st Indiana	2	1	3	12	1	35	6	48	54
5th Wisconsin battery	......	......	3	......	1	4	1	7	8
8th Wisconsin battery	1	......	......	......	......	4	1	4	5
SECOND DIVISION.									
First brigade.									
49th Ohio	2	7	4	9	10	80	16	96	112
39th Indiana	......	2	1	14	29	93	30	109	139
32d Indiana	......	......	......	10	12	31	12	41	53
15th Ohio	......	4	1	3	16	89	17	96	113
89th Illinois	1	......	1	3	8	4	10	45	55
Second brigade.									
77th Pennsylvania	......	2	......	5	4	22	4	29	33
29th Indiana	1	1	......	......	3	21	4	22	26
30th Indiana	1	2	5	23	23	75	29	100	129
79th Illinois	1	3	2	12	16	65	19	80	99
34th Illinois	1	2	5	35	12	63	18	100	118
Third brigade									
6th Indiana	......	1	3	5	12	46	15	52	67
1st Ohio	......	1	1	7	7	30	8	38	46
93d Ohio	......	4	4	6	8	31	12	41	53
5th Kentucky	1	5	7	14	10	61	18	80	98
1st Ohio vol. artillery	......	......	1	......	1	4	1	5	6
5th Indiana battery	......	1	1	4	2	13	3	18	21

Statement of killed and wounded, 20th army corps, &c.—Continued.

Commands.	Officers.		Non-commissioned officers.		Privates.		Total.		Aggregate.
	Killed.	Wounded.	Killed.	Wounded.	Killed.	Wounded.	Killed.	Wounded.	
THIRD DIVISION.									
First brigade									
88th Illinois	1	3	5	7	10	44	16	54	70
36th Illinois	1	19	3	23	44	140	48	182	230
24th Wisconsin	1	......	1	8	17	50	19	58	77
21st Michigan	......	4	5	14	13	66	18	84	102
Second brigade.									
2d Missouri	1	......	......	7	1	15	2	22	24
15th Missouri	3	4	1	3	10	37	14	44	58
44th Illinois	1	4	1	11	4	29	6	34	40
73d Illinois	1	5	2	4	19	43	22	52	74
Third brigade.									
22d Illinois	......	3	5	11	24	83	29	97	126
27th Illinois	......	2	1	10	8	43	9	55	64
42d Illinois	4	......	5	20	16	98	25	118	143
51st Illinois	1	4	4	4	2	46	7	54	61
4th Indiana battery	......	......	1	2	4	17	5	19	24
1st Illinois artillery	......	1	1	4	4	15	5	20	25

Statement of the killed and wounded of the 14th army corps, army of the Cumberland, during the battle of Stone river.

Commands.	Officers.		Non-commissioned officers.		Privates.		Total.		Aggregate.
	Killed.	Wounded.	Killed.	Wounded.	Killed.	Wounded.	Killed.	Wounded.	
FIRST DIVISION.									
First brigade.									
33d Ohio				4	2	17	2	21	23
94th Ohio		2		7	2	15	2	24	26
2d Ohio	1	4	2	7	5	22	8	33	41
10th Wisconsin					3	15	3	15	18
38th Indiana	1	2	3	19	10	65	14	86	100
Second brigade.									
15th Kentucky	2	1	1	4	5	24	8	29	37
88th Indiana		3	2	11	6	34	8	48	56
3d Ohio		1	4	13	13	53	17	67	84
42d Indiana		6	3	13	14	68	17	87	104
Third brigade.									
1st Wisconsin		1		4		3		8	8
21st Wisconsin		1				1		2	2
2d Kentucky cavalry				2		2		4	4
79th Pennsylvania				3	2	5	2	8	10
24th Illinois						4		4	4
Fourth brigade.									
15th U. S. infantry	1	4	1	13	9	54	11	71	82
16th U. S. infantry		7	1	22	15	104	16	133	149
18th U. S. infantry	2	11	10	32	43	173	55	216	271
19th U. S. infantry	1	1		11	6	35	7	47	54
Battery H, 5th U. S. art.				1		4		5	5
SECOND DIVISION.									
Second brigade.									
18th Ohio	1	8	8	21	17	86	26	115	141
19th Illinois	1	7	4	21	9	55	14	83	97
11th Michigan	2	6	5	12	23	66	30	84	114
69th Ohio	1	6	3	15	1	32	5	53	58
Third brigade.									
21st Ohio	1	4	7	14	16	85	24	103	127
74th Ohio		5	4	21	5	66	9	92	101
37th Indiana	2	5	4	27	19	74	25	106	131
78th Pennsylvania		5	3	19	13	103	16	125	141
First brigade.									
1st East Tennessee				2		9		11	11
2d East Tennessee		1		1		3		5	5
Bat. G, 1st Ohio vol. art.			1	2	2	7	3	9	12
Bat. M, 1st Ohio vol. art.		1	1				1	1	2
Bat. M, 1st Kentucky		1			1	2	1	3	4

Statement of killed and wounded, 21st army corps, (left wing,) battle of Stone river.

Commands.	Officers.		Non-commissioned officers.		Privates.		Total.		Aggregate.
	Killed.	Wounded.	Killed.	Wounded.	Killed.	Wounded.	Killed.	Wounded.	
FIRST DIVISION.									
First brigade.									
26th Ohio	1	2	4	15	4	68	9	85	94
58th Indiana	1	5	2	27	12	63	15	95	110
3d Kentucky	1	11	8	22	4	57	13	94	107
100th Illinois	2	5	......	3	6	14	8	22	30
10th Indiana battery	......	......	......	1	1	4	1	5	6
Second brigade.									
57th Indiana	......	6	......	12	10	43	10	61	71
40th Indiana	......	5	......	6	4	41	4	52	56
15th Indiana	1	6	6	21	32	108	39	135	174
97th Ohio	......	......	......	3	2	15	2	18	20
8th Indiana battery	......	......	......	2	......	6	......	8	8
Third brigade.									
51st Indiana	......	2	2	3	3	31	5	36	41
64th Ohio	1	3	5	6	18	46	24	55	79
13th Michigan	......	1	6	13	16	53	22	67	89
65th Ohio	2	9	6	8	24	114	32	131	163
73d Indiana	2	2	......	......	18	50	20	52	82
6th Ohio battery	......	1	......	3	......	6	......	10	10
SECOND DIVISION.									
First brigade.									
1st Kentucky	......	1	3	8	11	44	14	53	67
2d Kentucky	......	......	3	5	15	23	8	28	36
31st Indiana	......	2	4	16	1	28	5	46	51
90th Ohio	......	5	3	4	13	61	16	70	86
Bat. F, 1st Ohio vol. art.	......	1	......	......	2	12	2	13	15
Second brigade.									
41st Ohio volunteers	2	6	3	15	12	78	17	99	116
6th Kentucky	2	4	......	9	9	58	11	71	82
9th Indiana	1	4	5	17	5	72	11	93	104
110th Illinois	1	3	......	3	6	21	7	27	34
Third brigade.									
36th Indiana	2	6	6	24	9	53	17	82	99
24th Ohio volunteers	4	4	5	7	3	50	12	61	73
6th Ohio volunteers	2	4	5	20	8	80	15	104	119
23d Kentucky	......	2	4	13	3	35	7	50	57
84th Illinois	1	6	10	23	20	96	31	125	156
Bat. B, 1st Ohio vol. art	......	......	2	......	3	6	5	6	11

Statement of killed and wounded, 21st army corps, &c.—Continued.

Commands.	Officers.		Non-commissioned officers.		Privates.		Total.		Aggregate.
	Killed.	Wounded.	Killed	Wounded	Killed.	Wounded.	Killed.	Wounded.	
THIRD DIVISION.									
First brigade.									
9th Kentucky	4	12	3	6	12	65	19	83	102
11th Kentucky	......	4	1	20	6	61	7	85	92
19th Ohio	4	2	6	28	12	99	22	129	151
79th Indiana	1	6	......	2	5	43	6	51	57
26th Pennsylvania bat	......	.	......	1	2	6	2	7	9
Second brigade.									
44th Indiana	1	3	......	4	7	45	8	52	60
13th Ohio	2	4	4	13	16	51	22	65	87
86th Indiana	1	4	4	6	19	57	24	67	91
59th Ohio	......	3	1	6	3	29	4	38	42
3d Wisconsin battery	......	......	......	1	......	3	1	3	4
Third brigade.									
51st Ohio	......	5	5	24	19	100	24	129	153
35th Indiana	......	7	9	10	17	43	26	60	86
8th Kentucky	1	9	1	14	7	42	9	65	74
21st Kentucky	1	4	1	5	4	3	6	12	18
7th Indiana battery	......	1	......	1	4	5	4	7	11
	15	64	35	141	133	652	184	853	1,037

5—. REPORT OF CAPTAIN WILES, PROVOST MARSHAL GENERAL.

HEADQUARTERS DEPARTMENT OF THE CUMBERLAND,
Office Provost Marshal General,
Murfreesboro', Tennessee, February 9, 1863.

GENERAL: I have the honor herewith to forward a complete report of confederate prisoners captured by the army under your command at the late battle of Stone river, showing the number of regiments and other organizations represented, the number of the same from each State, the number of officers and enlisted men captured from each regiment or organization, the entire number of officers and enlisted men captured, and to what arm of the service they belong. The total number of prisoners captured is shown to be three thousand six hundred and ninety-four.

Taking into account the number and character of the organization, and using the lowest possible estimate of the strength of each, it can be shown, beyond controversy, that the enemy's force exceeded our own by at least one-third.

Complete reports of the number captured by the enemy from our own forces have not yet been received. From the best information received up to the present time the number will not exceed twenty-eight hundred, and in all probability the estimate is too large.

I am, general, very respectfully, your obedient servant,

WILLIAM M. WILES,
Captain and Provost Marshal General.

Major General W. S. ROSECRANS,
Commanding Department of the Cumberland.

OFFICE PROVOST MARSHAL GENERAL,
DEPARTMENT OF THE CUMBERLAND,
Murfreesboro', Tennessee, February 9, 1863.

The following is a complete report of confederate prisoners captured by the army under command of Major General W. S. Rosecrans, at the battle of Stone river, January 3, 1863, showing the number of regiments and other organizations represented, the number from each State, the number of officers and enlisted men captured from each regiment or organization, the entire number of officers and enlisted men captured, and to what arm of the service they belong :

Confederate officers and enlisted men captured.

Regiment.	No. of regiment.	Officers captured.	Enlisted men captured.	Total officers and enlisted men captured.
Alabama regiments, (infantry)	1		22	
	2		1	
	3		5	
	4	1	1	
	9		1	
	14		1	
	16	2	36	
	19	1	22	
	22	1	10	
	23		2	
	24		34	
	25	1	16	
	26		14	
	28	1	30	
	32	2	79	
	33		22	
	34	1	10	
	37	1		
	39	2	14	
	41	1	93	
	44		1	
	45		18	
	51		10	
Total	23	14	442	456

Confederate officers and enlisted men captured—Continued.

Regiments.	No. of regiment	Officers captured.	Enlisted men captured.	Total officers and enlisted men capturde.
Arkansas regiments, (infantry)	1	5	50	
	2	3	63	
	3	1	3	
	4	1	30	
	5	2	33	
	6	3	30	
	7		6	
	8	4	29	
	13		3	
	15	1	8	
	19		1	
	30	2	22	
Total	12	22	278	300
Confederate States, (infantry)	1		3	
	3		56	
	4		1	
	5	2	18	
	8	8	75	
Total	5	10	153	163
South Carolina, (infantry)	10	1	19	
	19		13	
Total	2	1	32	33
Florida regiments, (infantry)	1 & 3	4	69	
	4	3	99	
	6		1	
	9		1	
Total	4	7	170	177
Georgia regiments, (infantry)	1		4	
	2	1	2	
	5		10	
	43		1	
Total	4	1	17	18
North Carolina regiments, (infantry)	16		11	
	25		10	
	29		15	
	39	1	13	
	60	2	45	
Total	5	3	94	97

Confederate officers and enlisted men captured—Continued.

Regiments.	No. of regiment.	Officers captured.	Enlisted men captured.	Total officers and enlisted men captured.
Kentucky regiments, (infantry)	2	1	54	....
	4	4	42	....
	6	2	32	....
	8	....	2	....
	9	2	23	....
	13	....	1	....
Total	6	9	154	163
Texas regiments, (infantry)	4	1	....	....
	9	....	28	....
	10	....	19	....
	11	....	18	....
	14	....	18	....
	15	....	11	....
	19	....	1	....
	26	....	1	....
Total	8	1	96	97
Tennessee regiments, (infantry)	1	1	34	....
	2	....	19	....
	3	....	26	....
	4	1	34	....
	5	....	22	....
	6	1	27	....
	8	7	47	....
	9	....	16	....
	11	4	53	....
	12	3	38	....
	13	....	38	....
	15	....	16	....
	16	3	44	....
	17	5	44	....
	18	1	32	....
	19	....	27	....
	20	....	24	....
	23	....	45	....
	24	....	16	....
	25	1	38	....
	26	2	35	....
	27	....	4	....
	28	3	24	....
	29	1	27	....
	30	....	40	....
	31	....	9	....
	32	1	4	....
	33	1	17	....
	37	1	12	....
	38	....	22	....
	39	....	4	....

Confederate officers and enlisted men captured—Continued.

Regiments.	No of Regiment.	Officers captured.	Enlisted men captured	Total officers and enlisted men captured.
Tennessee regiments, (infantry)--Continued.	41	--------	4	--------
	44	3	54	--------
	45	4	49	--------
	47	1	27	--------
	50	1	4	--------
	51	--------	16	--------
	80	1	2	--------
	134	2	16	--------
Total	39	48	984	1,032
Louisiana regiments, (infantry)	1	1	46	--------
	11	--------	3	--------
	13 & 20	9	239	--------
	16 & 25	2	119	--------
	40	--------	1	--------
Total	5	12	408	420
Mississippi regiments, (infantry)	3	--------	1	--------
	5	--------	9	--------
	7	1	15	--------
	8	1	28	--------
	9	3	28	--------
	10	--------	27	--------
	12	--------	1	--------
	13	--------	1	--------
	17	--------	1	--------
	21	--------	1	--------
	24	1	33	--------
	20	--------	1	--------
	27	2	12	--------
	29	2	23	--------
	30	4	62	--------
	32	--------	1	--------
	37	--------	2	--------
	41	--------	30	--------
	45	5	89	--------
Total	19	19	365	384

Various infantry organizations.

Name.	State.	Officers captured.	Enlisted men captured
Tennessee Sharpshooters	Tennesee		2
Bluff City Sharpshooters	do		2
Blythe's Mississippi Sharpshooters	Mississippi	1	25
Mississippi Sharpshooters	do		4
Captain Cox's signal corps			1
Cox's Sharpshooters			3
Georgia Sharpshooters	Georgia		3
Chalmer's Sharpshooters			2
Austin's Sharpshooters		1	1
Hyde's company; Ross's regiment			1
Holleman's Regiment			1
Dake's regiment			1
12 organizations.		2	46

RECAPITULATION OF INFANTRY.

State.	No. of regiments represented.	No. of officers captured.	Enlisted men captured.
Alabama	23	14	442
Arkansas	12	22	278
Confederate States	5	10	153
South Carolina	2	1	32
Florida	4	7	170
Georgia	4	1	17
North Carolina	5	3	94
Kentucky	6	9	154
Texas	8	1	96
Tennessee	39	48	984
Louisiana	5	12	408
Mississippi	19	19	365
	132	147	3,193
Various organizations	12	2	46
Total infantry	144	149	3,239

State regiments.

No.	State.	Officers captured.	Enlisted men captured.	No.	State.	Officers captured.	Enlisted men captured.
1	Georgia		1	1	Tennessee		43
2	do		12	2	....do		2
3	....do		5	3	....do		4
3	Georgia battalion		4	4	....do		14
1	Confederate		7	1	Alabama		23
3	....do		19	2	....do		5
8	....do		4	3	....do		3
1	Arkansas		4	8	....do		1
2	... do	1	1	14	....do		2
4	....do		1	51	....do	1	5
4	Texas	1		1	Kentucky		5
8	....do	1	19	4	....do		2
10	....do		10	6	....do		4
11	....do		5				
14	....do		5	29	Total	4	211
15	....do		1				

Cavalry—various organizations.

Name.	Officers captured.	Enlisted men captured.	Name.	Officers captured.	Enlisted men captured.
Gilbert's Tennessee	....	2	Morris's battalion	....	1
Wheeler's command	....	1	Aid to General Morgan	1	....
Burnett's Tennessee cavalry	....	2	Willard's legion	....	1
McCann's Tennessee cavalry	....	1	Second mounted infantry	....	1
Tennessee battalion	....	1	Buford's body guard	....	1
Douglas's Tennessee battalion	....	9	Tyffis's battalion	....	4
Durke's Kentucky cavalry	......	1	Rody's cavalry	....	1
Cox's Kentucky cavalry	....	1	Buckin's cavalry	....	1
Morgan's Kentucky cavalry	....	1	Woodward's cavalry	....	2
Howard's cavalry	....	1	Hollman's cavalry	....	1
Breckinridge escort	....	1	Terry's Texas Rangers	....	1
Wharton's escort	....	5			
Ashley's cavalry	....	1	Total	1	41

Artillery.

Name of battery.	Officers captured.	Enlisted men captured.	Name of battery.	Officers captured.	Enlisted men captured.
Cobb's Kentucky	....	4	Moser's	....	4
First Kentucky	....	1	Robinson's	....	1
Mark's Alabama	....	1	Redman's	....	1
Semple's Alabama	1	2	Phipps's	....	1
Calvert's Arkansas	....	1	Scott's	....	1
First Texas	....	1	Sunden's	....	1
Fourteenth Georgia	....	5	Walton's	....	2
Jackson's Florida	....	4	Darden's	....	1
Napier's	....	1	Stuben artillery	....	1
Burns's	1	....	Washington (La.) artillery	....	3
Wright's	....	4			
McTyres'	....	1	Total	2	47
Ketchum's	....	6			

RECAPITULATION.

	No. of regiments represented.	No. of various organizations represented.	No. of batteries.	Entire No. of organizations represented.	Officers captured.	Enlisted men captured.	Total officers and enlisted men captured.
Artillery	....	....	23	23	2	47	49
Cavalry	29	24	....	53	5	252	257
Infantry	132	12	....	144	149	3,239	3,388
Grand total	161	36	23	220	156	3,538	3,694

WM. M. WILES,
Captain and Provost Marshal General.

6.—REPORT OF LIEUTENANT COLONEL BURKE, TENTH OHIO VOLUNTEERS, COMMANDING HEADQUARTERS GUARD.

HEADQUARTERS 10TH OHIO VOLUNTEERS,
Murfreesboro', Tennessee, January 28, 1863.

COLONEL: I beg leave to submit the following report of my command, while posted at Stewart's creek bridge, from the 31st December 1862, to the 22d of January 1863.

I remained at Stewart's creek with eight companies of the regiment, in charge of headquarters train, after detaching two companies of my command, under Captain John E. Hudson, to accompany headquarters in the field.

On the 31st December information reached me that the trains of the 28th brigade had been attacked and captured near Smyrna, at nine o'clock in the morning of that day; and at a later hour learning that the rebel cavalry were destroying it. I despatched a party to the scene, succeeded in saving eight wagons loaded with supplies.

I had sufficient force to have saved this train entirely, but owing to the extreme negligence of the quartermaster in charge of the train, in not reporting the fact of capture to me at an early hour, the enemy were enabled to carry away and destroy a large portion of it.

The force that attacked that train was very small, and I understand there was a guard with it, all of whom were paroled.

We were threatened with attack at the bridge during the whole day. I had the large train corralled in close order, and by extreme vigilance prepared to resist any attack during the night.

A large number of stragglers came back from the front, from an early hour of the day. I deployed a line of skirmishers across the country, from the pike to the railroad, with instructions to shoot down every straggler who attempted to force the line and marched into camp at night over 1,100 of these men.

Regiments of stragglers were organized, officered by my own commissioned and non-commissioned officers, and put on duty.

On January 1, 1863, I was re-enforced by four companies of the 4th Michigan cavalry, under Lieutenant Colonel Dickinson, and a section of company D, 1st Ohio battery, under Lieutenant Newell.

Rebel cavalry threatened the post during the day, and their advanced guard was twice repulsed by my pickets and reserve. Concluding not to attack, at Stewart's creek, this force consisting of Wheeler's, Wharton's, Buford's, John H. Morgan's and McCann's rebel cavalry, with too pieces of artillery, passed on toward Lavergne, where they attacked Colonel Innis, 1st Michigan engineers, at one o'clock. I apprised Colonel Innis of the movements of this force at an early hour.

About one o'clock a squadron of affrighted negroes came charging at full gallop from Murfreesboro' towards Stewart's creek, and with such impetuosity and recklessness that over one hundred passed the bridge before I could check the progress of the main cavalcade. They were dismounted and some of them ducked by my men. This was the advance of what seemed to me to be the whole army, cavalry men with jaded horses, artillery and infantry soldiers, breathless and holding on to wagons, relating the most incredible defeats and annihilation of the army, and their respective regiments came streaming down the road and pouring through the woods on their way towards the bridge. In vain did my small guard stationed on the road try to check this panic. Officers drew their revolvers, but the fugitives heeded them not.

My regiment was in line on the hill-side, and I promptly fixed bayonet, marched at double quick to the bridge and drew up a line before it, sending out, at the same time, two companies deployed as skirmishers, on the right and left, to prevent the passing of the creek by fording. The fugitives crowded in thousands and at one time pressed closely up to the bayonets of my men. I ordered the battalion to load, and determined to fire if the crowd did not move back; seeing which, many took flight back toward the front. At this critical moment I was rendered most valuable assistance by Lieutenant Runderhook, 4th United States cavalry, and his men, who were stationed at the bridge with their camp and train.

To him I assigned the duty of getting the stragglers into line, and nobly did his men execute his orders.

Riding through the panic-stricken crowds, the cavalry men drove them into a *field*, where a good line was formed and every straggler taken and made "dress up." When I had a regiment formed in this manner, I assigned it officers and marched it across the bridge, stacked arms and rested it. In this manner I secured over four thousand men. I must mention here the fact that the prominent movers in the panic, were the quartermasters in charge of trains. There was only one who behaved with anything like courage and coolness, the quartermaster of the Pioneer brigade.

Later in the day I was notified by Colonel Innis that he was attacked fiercely by rebel cavalry; that a demand for surrender had been made twice, and asking to be re-enforced, I promptly despatched four companies of the 4th Michigan cavalry, and the section of artillery (Rodman guns) to his assistance, and ordered them to move up at a trot, holding my own forces ready to support them.

After the lapse of two hours, during which the cannonading of Colonel Innis's stockade was kept up by the rebels, (hearing the report of each gun,) Mr. Reily, a citizen, made his escape through the rebel lines, bearing a despatch from Colonel Innis, requesting me to re-enforce him, and the astonishing information, that the troops I sent up under Lieutenant Colonel Dickinson were on their way back to me without having fired a shot, and that the rebels were burning the trains.

I quickly decided to save the trains and leave the bridge to the protection of the regiments of stragglers, set out at a rapid pace for Lavergne with my own command. I met the section of artillery returning, as well as part of the cavalry, ordered them to fall in behind me, and sent a strong support of infantry to the guns.

The scene on the road was indescribable. Teamsters had abandoned their wagons and came back mounted on their mules and horses; wagons were packed across the road and many capsized on the side of the pike; horses ran wild through the woods, and although men were allowed by me to pass as wagon guards, there were none at their posts. They had left the road and were bivouacing in small parties in the woods, evidently careless of the fate of the trains.

The woods towards Lavergne were filled with small bodies of rebel cavalry, which were quickly dislodged by my skirmishers and driven off. I reached Colonel Innis, at Laverge, at seven o'clock, and assisted him in arranging the trains and forwarding them to Nashville.

I detached four companies of my regiment, and Lieutenant Colonel Dickinson's command, and sent them back to Stewart's creek at daylight next morning, remaining myself at Lavergne, collecting supplies from the trains; gathering in cattle abandoned by our men, and sending them to the front,

With the remaining portion of my command I joined the garrison at Stewart's creek, on the 7th of January, and immediately set to work putting it in a defensible condition, by erecting a stockade and throwing up a small redoubt to cover the bridge.

I was relieved in command there by Lieutenant Colonel Carroll, commanding 10th Indiana volunteers, on the 22nd of January, and reported for duty at headquarters.

In connexion with the disgraceful panic of the first of January, I would mention the names of the following officers: Lieutenant Gilbert, 2nd Tennessee cavalry, who had his horse hitched up to a wagon on the road, and who abandoned it with the teamsters, joining in the stampede.

Lieutenant Newell, 21st Michigan, and the regimental quartermaster, 79th Pennsylvania, who abandoned the train of the 28th brigade, and although within my lines, never communicated the fact of capture, until it was too late to pursue the enemy.

Out of a crowd of runaway teamsters, I took the names of four men who cut loose their mules from the wagons and left them to their fate: Henry W. Davis, 25th Illinois; Scott Cunningham, 25th Illinois; Henry Denney, 59th Ohio; Jacob Rohrer, 101st Ohio. A number of commissioned officers came back with the men, but on seeing the obstacles interposed to their passage, they returned voluntarily to the front.

My officers and men performed their duty faithfully and strictly. I was rendered signal assistance by Lieutenant Runderbrock, 4th United States cavalry, and the non-commissioned officers and men of his command, as also Lieutenant Maple, Anderson troop, who with their commands were constantly on duty, reporting the movements of the enemy, and assisting in effectually checking the disgraceful and causeless panic.

I would respectfully mention the name of Captain Perkins, assistant quartermaster, headquarters quartermaster, who evinced the utmost zeal and vigilance, and assisted most materially in the defence of the post and in restoring order amongst the trains.

I have the honor to be, colonel, with great respect, your obedient servant,

J. W. BURKE,

Lieutenant Colonel, commanding 10th Ohio Volunteer Infantry

Colonel C. GODDARD,

Acting Adjutant General and Chief of Staff.

7.—NAMES SPECIALLY MENTIONED FOR IMPORTANT SERVICES AND PARTICULAR ACTS, &c., IN OFFICIAL REPORTS.

Brigadier Generals R. W. Johnson, P. H. Sheridan, and Jefferson C. Davis, commanding divisions in the right wing, for gallant conduct during the battle, and for prompt support and conscientious attention to duty during their service with the right wing.

Brigadier General D. S. Stanley, chief of cavalry, commanded advance of right wing during its advance from Nolansville, is specially mentioned for energy and skill.

Brigadier General Hascall, commanding 1st brigade, deserves commendation and gratitude of his country.

Brigadier General Cruft, 1st brigade, for holding an important position, and for extricating his command from the mass of confusion around him.

Brigadier Generals I. J. Wood, H. P. Van Cleve, and John M. Palmer, specially mentioned for distinguished gallantry and the skill with which they handled their command. Generals Van Cleve and Wood were wounded, but remained with their commands until after the battle was over.

Brigadier General J. S. Negley, specially mentioned for the courage and skill displayed in handling his command.

Surgeon McDermott, medical director, staff of Major General McCook, for gallant conduct in the field and great care and consideration for the wounded.

Surgeon G. D. Beebe, medical director, staff of Major General Thomas, for great zeal, energy, and efficiency.

Surgeon A. T. Phelps, medical director, on staff of Major General Crittenden, for prompt attention to the wounded, great energy and efficiency in discharge of his duties.

Colonel Minty, commanding 4th Michigan cavalry, 1st brigade, deserves credit for the management of his command on the march and in the several engagements.

Colonel Muny, 3d Kentucky cavalry, rendered important and distinguished service, gallantly charging and dispersing the enemy's cavalry in their attack on our train on Wednesday, 31st.

Colonel Zahm, 3d Ohio cavalry, contributed greatly by his personal example to the restoration of order and confidence in that portion of the 2nd brigade stampeded by the enemy's attack on Wednesday.

Colonel W. H. Gibson, 49th Ohio volunteers, commanded Willich's brigade, has been several times before recommended for promotion, and is again recommended by General Johnson for meritorious conduct ; is also specially mentioned by Major General McCook and Major General Crittenden.

Colonel Charles Anderson, 93d Ohio volunteers, honorable mention for gallant conduct by Major General Rosseau.

Colonel Wallace, (15th Ohio volunteers,) Colonel Dodge, (30th Indiana volunteers,) Colonel Baldwin, (6th Indiana volunteers,) remembered for promotion for coolness and courage on the field of battle.

Colonel G. D. Wagner, 15th Indiana volunteers, commanding brigade, has commanded a brigade for a year, is recommended for promotion for brave and skilful conduct during the late battle.

Colonel C. G. Harker, 65th Ohio volunteers, has commanded a brigade for a year, is recommended for promotion for brave and skilful conduct. He is also specially mentioned by Major General McCook for valuable services with the right wing.

Colonel Jno. W. Blake, 40th Indiana volunteers, recommended to be dishonorably discharged for being so drunk as to be unfit for duty before going into action, on the 31st ; was ordered in arrest by his immediate commander, Colonel Wagner, and was next heard from in Nashville, claiming to be wounded and a paroled prisoner.

Colonel Hazen, 41st Ohio volunteers, commanded a brigade, is specially mentioned for courage and skill in handling his troops and for maintaining an important position.

Colonel W. Grose, 36th Indiana volunteers, commanded a brigade, is specially recommended for coolness and bravery in fighting his troops against a superior force.

Colonels Sedgwick, (2d Kentucky volunteer infantry,) Engart, (1st Kentucky volunteer infantry,) Rose, (90th Ohio volunteer infantry,) and Osborne, (31st Indiana volunteers,) displayed marked gallantry on the field, and handled their respective commands with skill and judgment.

Colonel Samuel Beatty, 19th Ohio volunteer infantry, commanding brigade, for coolness, interpidity, and skill.

Colonel Tyffy, 59th Ohio volunteer infantry, is recommended for coolness, intrepidity, and skill ; is also specially mentioned by Major General McCook for valuable service with the right wing.

Colonel Grider, 9th Kentucky volunteer infantry, commanded brigade, and is specially mentioned for gallantry and coolness under trying circumstances.

Colonel O. S. Loomis, 1st Michigan artillery, rendered most important service throughout the battle.

Colonel John Starkweather, 1st Wisconsin volunteer infantry, commanding brigade, especially mentioned for coolness, skill, and courage.

Colonels William Sirnell, (78th Pennsylvania volunteer infantry,) Granville Moody, (74th Ohio volunteers,) and Hull, (37th Indiana volunteers,) for the skill and ability with which they handled their respective commands.

Colonels Grensel, (36th Illinois volunteers,) and Bradley, (51st Illinois volunteers,) are especially commended for skill and courage.

Colonel Sherman, 88th Illinois volunteers, honorably mentioned for distinguished service.

Lieutenant Colonels Hotchkiss, (89th Illinois volunteer infantry,) and Jones, (39th Indiana volunteers,) recommended for promotion for meritorious conduct.

Lieutenant Colonel W. W. Berry, commanding Louisville legion, specially mentioned for gallant and meritorious conduct; is also specially mentioned by Major General Rosseau for retreating in good order before an overwhelming force, and drawing off, by hand, a section of artillery he had been ordered to support.

Lieutenant Colonel Shephard, 18th United States infantry, commanding brigade, specially mentioned by Major General L. H. Rosseau.

Lieutenant Colonel Neibling, commanding 21st Ohio volunteer infantry, for skill and ability during the battles.

Lieutenant Colonel Laibold, 2d Missouri volunteer infantry, specially commended for skill and courage.

Lieutenant Colonel McCreary, 21st Michigan volunteers, honorably mentioned for distinguished services.

Major Voline, 3d Indiana cavalry, on the 27th, engaged the enemy on the Nolansville pike and put them to flight.

Captain Otis, commanding 4th United States cavalry, with his regiment, rendered important and distinguished service, gallantly charging and dispersing the enemy's cavalry, in their attack upon our train on Wednesday the 31st.

Major Lyne Sterling, assistant adjutant general, specially mentioned by Major General Crittenden for gallantry in the battle, general efficiency, and eighteen months faithful service.

Majors John H. King, (15th United States infantry,) Carpenter, (19th United States infantry,) Slemmer, (16th United States infantry,) and Townsend, (18th United States infantry,) commanding their respective regiments, are specially mentioned for distinguished gallantry and ability. Major Carpenter was killed and Majors King and Slemmer wounded.

Majors Miller, (36th Illinois volunteers,) Chandler, (88th Illinois volunteers,) and Hibbard, (24th Wisconsin volunteers,) honorably mentioned.

Captain John Mendenhall, 4th United States artillery, chief of artillery and topographical engineer, Staff Major General Crittenden recommended for promotion for general efficiency, and personal bravery, and good conduct in battle.

Captains Chambers, (51st Indiana volunteer infantry,) and Gladwin, (73d Ohio volunteer infantry.) These brave officers with one hundred and twenty men drove a large force of the enemy from a covered position, and unmasked his battery.

Captain Standant, company F, 1st Ohio artillery, for the gallant manner in which he handled his guns and brought them off the field.

Captain Edgarton, company E, 1st Ohio artillery, was guilty of a grave error in taking over a part of his battery horses to water at an unseasonable hour, and thereby losing his guns.

Captain G. R. Thruston, 1st Ohio volunteer infantry, is especially mentioned by Major General McCook and others for particular acts of gallantry, skill and good conduct. Mentioned by Generals Sheridan, Johnson, Davis, and by Colonel Carlen, commanding brigade.

Captains Hale, (75th Illinois volunteers,) and Litson, (22d Indiana volunteers,) specially mentioned for gallant conduct in skirmishing.

Captains Crofton, (16th United States infantry,) Fulmer, (15th United States infantry,) and Mulligan, (19th United States infantry.) These three infantry captains commanded their respective battalions after their majors had been disabled, and behaved with great gallantry and skill, although opposed by an overwhelming number.

Captain Gunther, company H, 5th artillery, deserves great credit and special mention.

Captain Hescock, 1st Missouri battery, specially mentioned for bravery and skill in the battles, and for general efficiency.

Captain Bridges, 19th Illinois volunteers, continued in command of his regiment after receiving a painful wound.

Lieutenant Belding, commanding company A, 1st Ohio artillery, recommended for promotion for saving three guns of his battery, (Goodspeed's.)

Lieutenant Richard Jervis, 8th Indiana battery, behaved in a cowardly manner, by retiring his section at a critical moment, without notifying his company commander. He is recommended for dismissal.

Lieutenants Lambressord, (19th Illinois volunteers,) and Wyman Murphy, (21st Missouri volunteers,) inspectors of pioneer brigade, are specially mentioned in two reports for gallant conduct and energy.

Assistant Surgeon N. S. Fish, 3d Indiana cavalry, fled during the battle to Nashville, and is recommended by Major General McCook for dismissal. This man passed himself off as an assistant surgeon and proved to be a private. Case being attended to.

Enlisted men recommended for gallant conduct during the battle of Stone river, Tennessee.

Quartermaster Sergeant Colburn, (33d Ohio volunteers,) 1st Sergeant German, (8th Missouri battery,) Sergeants Fergusson, (company G, 59th Illinois volunteer infantry,) Holen, (company G, 64th Ohio volunteer infantry,) McKay, (company E, 41st Ohio volunteer infantry,) McMahon, (company H, 41st Ohio volunteer infantry,) R. B. Rhodes, (1st Ohio volunteer cavalry,) Jason Hurd, (19th Ohio volunteer infantry,) H. A. Mills, (78th Pennsylvania volunteer infantry,) A. R. Weaver, (78th Pennsylvania volunteer infantry,) F. Meeklin, (78th Pennsylvania volunteer infantry,) P. A. Weaver, (74th Ohio volunteer infantry,) Corporals James F. Slater, (2d Indiana cavalry volunteers,) J. P. Patterson, (company G, 41st Ohio volunteer infantry,) M. Hughes, (78th Pennsylvania volunteer infantry,) and Private R. G. Pindle, (company L, wagoner,) are especially recommended by Colonel Murray, colonel of 3d Kentucky cavalry.

Privates A. F. Freeman and Abijah Lee, (orderlies with Brigadier General Davis,) James Gray, (company E, 39th Indiana volunteer infantry,) William Hayman, (2d Indiana volunteer cavalry,) William Brown, (57th Ohio volunteer infantry,(Nelson Shields, (13th Ohio volunteer infantry,) J. T. Mitchel, (company B, 35th Ohio volunteer infantry.)

Special mention of gallantry, &c. Lieutenant Colonel Houszam, (77th Pennsylvania volunteer infantry,) Captains Brigham, (69th Ohio volunteer infantry,) Cop, (10th Indiana battery,) James L. Meade, (38th Illinois volunteer infantry,) Lieutenants John L. Dillon, (38th Illinois volunteer infantry,) Jones, (Post's brigade.)

1st. 78th Pennsylvania regiment captured a rebel flag from 26th regiment, Tennessee, assisted by other regiments of General Negley's division.

2d. Lieutenant Gunther's battery and the 2d Ohio volunteers captured the flag of the 36th Arkansas volunteers.

3d. 15th Indiana volunteers, Lieutenant Colonel Wood commanding, charged and captured 173 prisoners from 20th Louisiana regiment.

4th. 13th Michigan volunteers gallantly recaptured two guns belonging to Captain Bradley's battery.

5th. Carlin's brigade lost half its field officers in killed and wounded.

6th. 5th Kentucky volunteers dragged from the field by hand a section of artillery, through deep mud and under heavy fire.

7th. Four color bearers of the 21st Illinois were shot down, yet the colors were borne safely through the fight.

HEADQUARTERS DEPARTMENT OF THE CUMBERLAND,
Murfreesboro', Tennessee, March 10, 1863.

GENERAL: Enclosed I transmit a "special mention" of Colonel John Kenneth, 4th Ohio cavalry, whose gallant and meritorious services were by accident not mentioned in my report.

Please cause this to be filed with others.

W. S. ROSECRANS, *Major General.*

Brigadier General L. THOMAS,
Adjutant General, United States Army, Washington, D. C.

HEADQUARTERS DEPARTMENT OF THE CUMBERLAND.
Murfreesboro', March 8, 1863.

Special mention of Colonel John Kenneth, 4th Ohio cavalry, who commanded the second brigade of the cavalry division accompanying Crittenden's corps, behaved with great gallantry and efficiency throughout the entire engagement, commencing on the 26th December and terminating on the 2d of January last.

His cavalry drove the rebel cavalry from near Lavergne and followed them during our advance.

On the 31st during all the day the cavalry of his brigade was scattered, but with those parts he could command, from time to time, during the battle, he behaved with distinguished gallantry, charging the rebel cavalry in person. He rallied some of our cavalry, and stopped stragglers to the rear, and captured a number of rebel prisoners.

His unwearied labors and conspicuous courage on former occasions, as well as during the battle of Stone river, have endeared him to this army, and it is a matter of deep regret that a functional disease compelled him to quit the service.

He well deserves to be a brigadier general in the cavalry service.

W. S. ROSECRANS, *Major General.*

11.—REPORT OF MAJOR GENERAL THOMAS.

HEADQUARTERS (CENTRE) 14TH ARMY CORPS,
DEPARTMENT OF THE CUMBERLAND,
Murfreesboro', January 15, 1863.

MAJOR: I have the honor to submit to the major general commanding the department of the Cumberland the following report of the operations of that part of my command which was engaged in the battle of Stone river, in front of Murfreesboro'. It is proper to state here that two brigades of Fry's division, and Reynold's entire division, were detained near Gallatin and along the Louisville and Nashville railroad, to watch the movements of the rebel leader, Morgan, who had been, for a long time, on the watch for an opportunity to destroy the railroad. Rousseau's, Negley's, and Mitchell's divisions, and Walker's brigade of Fry's division, were concentrated at Nashville, but Mitchell's division being required to garrison Nashville, my only available force was Rousseau's and

Negley's divisions, and Walker's brigade of Fry's division, about thirteen thousand three hundred and ninety-five (13,395) effective men.

December 26.—Negley's division, followed by Rousseau's division, and Walker's brigade, marched by the Franklin pike to Brentwood, at that point taking the Wilson pike. Negley and Rousseau were to have encamped for the night at Owen's store. On reaching the latter place, Negley hearing heavy firing in the direction of Nolansville, left his train, with a guard to follow, and pushed forward with his troops to the support of Brigadier General J. C. Davis, commanding the advanced division of McCook's corps, Davis having become hotly engaged with the enemy posted in Nolansville, and in the pass through the hills south of that village Rousseau encamped with his division at Owen's store, Walker, with his brigade, at Brentwood. During the night a very heavy rain fell, making the cross-road almost impassable, and it was not until night of the 27th that Rousseau reached Nolansville with his troops and train. Negley remained at Nolansville until 10 a. m. on the 27th, when, having brought his train across from Wilson's pike, he moved to the east over an exceedingly rough by-road, to the right of Crittenden, at Stewartsboro', on the Murfreesboro' pike. Walker, by my orders, retraced his steps from Brentwood, and crossed over to the Nolansville pike.

December 28.—Negley remained in camp at Stewartsboro', bringing his train from the rear. Rousseau reached Stewartsboro' on the night of the 28th. His train arrived early next day.

December 29.—Negley's division crossed Stewart's creek, two miles southwest and above the turnpike bridge, and marched in support of the head and right flank of Crittenden's corps, which moved by the Murfreesboro' pike to a point within two miles of Murfreesboro'. The enemy fell back before our advance, contesting the ground obstinately with their cavalry rear guard. Rousseau remained in camp at Stewartsboro', detaching Starkweather's brigade, with a section of artillery, to the Jefferson pike crossing of Stone river, to observe the movements of the enemy in that direction. Walker reached Stewartsboro' from the Nolansville pike about dark.

December 30.—A cavalry force of the enemy, something over four hundred strong, with two pieces of artillery, attacked Starkweather about 9 a. m., but were soon driven off. The enemy opened a brisk fire on Crittenden's advance, doing but little execution, however, about 7 a. m. During the morning Negley's division was obliqued to the right, and took up a position on the right of Palmer's division of Crittenden's corps, and was then advanced through a dense cedar thicket, several hundred yards in width, to the Wilkinson crossroad, driving the enemy's skirmishers steadily, and with considerable loss. Our loss comparatively small. About noon, Sheridan's division of McCook's corps approached by the Wilkinson crossroad, joined Negley's right, McCook's two other divisions coming up on Sheridan's right, thus forming a continuous line, the left resting on Stone river, the right stretching in a westerly direction, and resting on high wooded ground, a short distance to the south of the Wilkinson crossroads, and, as has since been ascertained, nearly parallel with the enemy's entrenchments thrown up on the sloping land bordering the northwest bank of Stone river. Rousseau's division, (with the exception of Starkweather's brigade,) being ordered up from Stewartsboro', reached the position occupied by the army about 4 p. m., and bivouacked on the Murfreesboro' pike in rear of the centre. During the night of the 30th I sent orders to Walker to take up a strong position near the turnpike bridge over Stewart's creek, and defend the position against any attempts of the enemy's cavalry to destroy it. Rousseau was ordered to move by 6 a. m. on the 31st to a position in rear of Negley. This position placed his division with its left on the Murfreesboro' pike, and its right extending into the cedar thicket through which Negley had marched on the 30th. In front of Negley's position, bordering a large open field, reaching to the Murfreesboro' pike, a heavy growth of timber extended in a southerly direction towards the river. Across the field, running in an easterly direction, the enemy had thrown up rifle pits, at intervals, from the timber to the river bank, to the east side of the turnpike. Along this line of entrenchments, on an eminence about eight hundred yards from Negley's position, and nearly in front of his left, some cannon had been placed, affording the enemy great advantage in covering an attack on our centre. However, Palmer, Negley, and Sheridan, held the position their troops had so manfully won the morning of the 30th against every attempt to drive them back, and remained in line of battle during the night.

December 31.—Between 6 and 7 a. m., the enemy having massed a heavy force on McCook's right, during the night of the 30th, attacked and drove it back, pushing his divisions in pursuit in echelon, and in supporting distance, until he had gained sufficient ground to our rear to wheel his masses to the right and throw them upon the right flank of the centre, at the same moment attacking Negley and Palmer in front with a greatly superior force. To counteract the movements, I had ordered Rousseau to place two brigades, with a battery to the right and rear of Sheridan's division, facing towards the west, so as to support Sheridan, should he be able to hold his ground, or to cover him should he be compelled to fall back. About 11 o'clock General Sheridan reported to me that his ammunition was entirely out and he would be compelled to fall back to get more. As it became necessary for General S. to fall back, the enemy pressed on still further to our rear, and soon took up a position which gave them a concentrated cross-fire of musketry and cannon on Negley's and Rousseau's troops at short range. This compelled me to fall back out of the cedar woods and take up a line along a depression in the open ground, within good musket range of the edge of the woods, whilst the artillery was retired to the high ground to the right of the turnpike. From this last position we were enabled to drive back the enemy, cover the formation of our troops, and secure the centre on the high ground. In the execution of this last movement the regular brigade, under Lieutenant Colonel Shepherd, 18th United States infantry, came under a most murderous fire, losing twenty-two officers and five hundred and eight men in killed and wounded, but, with the co-operation of Scribner's and Beatty's brigades and Guenther's and Loomis's batteries, gallantly held its ground against overwhelming odds. The centre having succeeded in driving back the enemy from its front, and our artillery concentrating its fire on the cedar thicket on our right, drove him back far under cover, from which, though repeatedly attempting it, he could not make any advance.

January 1, 1863.—Repeated attempts were made by the enemy to advance on my position during the morning, but they were driven back before emerging from the woods. Colonel Starkweather's brigade of Rousseau's division, and Walker's brigade of Fry's division, having reinforced us during the night, took post on the right of Rousseau and left of Sheridan, and bore their share in repelling the attempts of the enemy on the morning of the 1st inst. For the details of the most valuable service rendered by these two brigades on the 30th and 31st of December, 1862, and the 1st, 2d, and 3d of January, 1863, I refer you to their reports. In this connexion I also refer you to the report of Lieutenant Colonel Parkhurst, commanding 9th Michigan infantry, (on provost duty at my headquarters,) for the details of most valuable services rendered by his command on the 31st December and 1st and 2d of January. Negley's division was ordered early in the day to the support of McCook's right, and in which position it remained during the night.

January 2.—About 7 a. m. the enemy opened a direct and cross fire from his batteries in our front, and from a position on the east bank of Stone river to our left and front, at the same time making a strong demonstration with infantry, resulting, however, in no serious attack. Our artillery—Loomis's,

Guenther's, Stokes's, and another battery, the commander's name I cannot now recall—soon drove back their infantry. Negley was withdrawn from the extreme right and placed in reserve behind Crittenden's right.

About 4 p. m. a division of Crittenden's corps, which had crossed Stone river to reconnoitre, was attacked by an overwhelming force of the enemy, and, after a gallant resistance, compelled to fall back. The movements of the enemy having been observed and reported by some of my troops in the centre, I sent orders to Negley to advance to the support of Crittenden's troops, should they want help. This order was obeyed in most gallant style, and resulted in the complete annihilation of the 26th Tennessee (rebel) regiment and the capture of their flag; also, in the capture of a battery, which the enemy had been forced to abandon at the point of the bayonet.—(See Negley's report.)

January 3.—Soon after daylight the 42d Indiana, on picket in a clump of woods about eight hundred yards in front of our lines, was attacked by a brigade of the enemy, evidently by superior numbers, and driven in with considerable loss. Lieutenant Colonel Shanklin, commanding the regiment, was surrounded and taken prisoner whilst gallantly endeavoring to draw off his men from under the fire of such superior numbers. From this woods the enemy's sharpshooters continued to fire occasionally during the day on our pickets. About 6 p. m. two regiments from Colonel John Beatty's brigade, Rousseau's division, co-operating with two regiments of Spear's brigade of Negley's division, covered by the skillful and well-directed fire of Guenther's 5th United States artillery and Loomis's 1st Michigan batteries, advanced on the woods, and drove the enemy not only from its cover but from their intrenchments a short distance beyond.

For the details of this gallant night attack, I refer you to the reports of Brigadier General Spears, commanding third brigade of Negley's division, and Colonel John Beatty, commanding second brigade Rousseau's division. The enemy having retreated during the night of the 3d, our troops were occupied during the morning of the 4th in burying the dead left on the field. In the afternoon one brigade of Negley's division was advanced to the crossing of Stone river, with a brigade of Rousseau's division in supporting distance in reserve.

January 5.—My entire command, preceded by Stanley's cavalry, marched into Murfreesboro', and took up the position which we now hold. The enemy's rear guard of cavalry was overtaken on the Shelbyville and Manchester roads, about five miles from Murfreesboro', and after sharp skirmishing for two or three hours was driven from our immediate front.

The conduct of my command, from the time the army left Nashville to its entry into Murfreesboro', is deserving of the highest praise, both for their patient endurance of the fatigues and discomforts of a five days' battle and for the manly spirit exhibited by them in the various phases in this memorable contest. I refer you to the detailed reports of the division and brigade commanders, forwarded herewith, for special mention of those officers and men of their commands whose conduct they thought worthy of particular notice.

All the members of my staff, Major G. E. Flynt, assistant adjutant general, Lieutenant Colonel A. Von Schrader, 74th Ohio, acting inspector general, Captain O. A. Mack, 13th United States infantry, acting chief commissary, and Captain A. J. Mackay, chief quartermaster, were actively employed in carrying my orders to various parts of my command, and in the execution of the appropriate duties of their office. Captain O. A. Mack was dangerously wounded in the right hip and abdomen whilst conveying orders from me to Major General Rousseau. The officers of the signal corps, attached to my headquarters, did excellent service in their appropriate sphere, when possible, and as aides-de-camp, carrying orders. My escort, composed of a select detail from the 1st Ohio cavalry, commanded by First Lieutenant J. D. Barker, of the same regiment, who have been on duty with me for nearly a year, deserve commendation for the faithful performance of their appropriate duties. Private Guiteau was killed by a cannon shot on the morning of January 2. Surgeon G. D. Beebe, medical director, deserves special mention for his efficient arrangements for moving the wounded from the field and giving them immediate attention.

Annexed hereto is a consolidated return of the casualties of my command. The details will be seen in the accompanying reports of division and brigade commanders.

Very respectfully, your obedient servant,

GEORGE H. THOMAS,
Major General U. S. Volunteers Commanding.

Major C. GODDARD,
Assistant Adjutant General and Chief of Staff.

Consolidated report of casualties of the centre, 14*th army corps, in the five days' battle before Murfreesboro', Tenn., commencing December* 31, 1862, *and ending January* 4, 1863.

	IN ACTION.				LOST IN ACTION.												
					Killed.		Wounded.		Missing		Horses.			Guns.	
	Commissioned officers.	Enlisted men.	Horses.	Guns, (artillery.)	Commissioned.	Enlisted.	Commissioned.	Enlisted.	Commissioned.	Enli-ted.	Killed.	Wounded.	Missing.	Lost.	Disabled.
1st division, Maj. Gen. Rousseau.	303	5,883	..	18	8	171	43	903	3	324	8	5	..	....	....
2d divison, Brig. Gen. Negley ...	237	4,632	257	13	11	167	47	704	1	308	62	24	9	6	1
1st brigade, 3d division, Col. M. B. Walker...............	97	2,243	..	6	....	...	4	19	...	1	...	....	....	....	....
	637	12,759	257	37	19	338	94	1,626	4	633	70	29	9	6	1

HEADQUARTERS 14TH ARMY CORPS,
Murfreesboro', Tenn., May 16, 1863.

COLONEL: My attention having been called by Major General Rousseau to the fact that Colonel B. F. Scribner's brigade had not been mentioned by the major general commanding the department for the part it took in the battle of Stone river, I cheerfully submit the following statement, premising that in my official report of the battle of Stone river it was my earnest endeavor to do equal justice to the commands of Colonels Beatty, Scribner, and Lieutenant Colonel Shepperd, as well as to all other troops under my command, and thought that the best way of so doing, without extending my report to too great length, was to give a succinct narrative of the events of the battle, and then refer to the reports of the subordinate commanders for more detailed information. This I did, with the more confidence in the justice of that course, from the fact that after a careful reading of the different reports I perceived no discrepancy in the accounts given in those reports of the events of the battle in which different portions of my command acted together. In my official report is the following: "As it became necessary for General Sheridan to fall back, the enemy pressed on still further to our rear, and soon took up a position which gave them a concentrated cross-fire of musketry and cannon on Generals Negley and Rousseau's troops at short range. This compelled me to fall back through the cedar woods and take up a line along a depression in the open ground, within good musket range of the edge of the woods, whilst the artillery was retired to the high ground on the right of the turnpike. From this last position we were enabled to drive back the enemy, cover the formation of our troops, and secure the centre on the high ground.

"In the execution of this last movement the regular brigade, under Lieutenant Colonel Shepperd, 18th United States infantry, came under a most murderous fire, losing 22 officers and 508 men in killed and wounded; but, with the co-operation of Scribner and Beatty's brigades and Guenther and Loomis's batteries, gallantly held its ground against overwhelming odds"—thus connecting these three gallant brigades together in the honorable and distinguished work of covering the formation of the troops on the elevated ground in their rear, when the enemy was straining every nerve to gain possession of the same point. I now quote Colonel Scribner's report of the part taken by his brigade at this period of the battle:

"From near the Wilkinson pike I was ordered to move back in great haste to near our position on the Nashville pike, which order was faithfully obeyed. My right had just emerged from the woods when the enemy, which had just been repulsed in their efforts to take the batteries before mentioned, were seen retreating in disorder in a northwesterly direction, through a narrow neck of woods, and were opened upon by the 94th Ohio and the two right companies of the 38th Indiana.

"I then threw my skirmishers forward and advanced about 600 yards into the woods, when my line became masked by General Negley's division, who were falling under heavy fire from the enemy, who appeared to be advancing from a point south of the direction taken by the retreating column. I opened my line to permit that portion of General Negley's command, who had expended their ammunition, to pass, which was done in good order, a portion of them forming in my rear. Here the ninety-fourth Ohio was ordered to the pike, leaving me but two regiments, the thirty-eighth Indiana and tenth Wisconsin, the latter now on the left. General Negley having halted his right some twenty-five paces obliquely in front of my line, I wheeled my right, under heavy fire, to connect with him. Here I appeared to be nearly surrounded—a heavy column turning my left—to prevent which I ordered the tenth Wisconsin to change front to the rear on their first company, thereby forming a right angle with the thirty-eighth Indiana. This position was scarcely taken when the enemy came down upon us in great fury; they appeared to be massed in several lines, and their heads seemed to be in terraces, not twenty-five yards before us. For twenty minutes these two regiments maintained their ground, completely checking the advance of the enemy's column. Here the thirty-eighth Indiana lost their brave Captain Fouts, besides nearly one-third their number in killed and wounded. Lieutenant Colonel Griffin and Major Glover both had their horses shot under them and their clothing perforated by balls. The tenth Wisconsin nobly vied with their comrades on the right, and I am convinced that both regiments would have suffered extermination rather than have yielded their ground without orders. But the order came, and we fell back and formed on the pike fronting the woods, but the enemy did not venture to follow further than the skirts of the timber. Having reformed my brigade, I soon after advanced my right to the woods from which we had just emerged, deploying skirmishers from the ninety-fourth Ohio through the neck of timber, with my left resting on the pike. Here we remained the rest of the day, under the fire of the enemy's sharpshooters, and ever and anon the shot and shell from their battery on the left of us. A ball from the former struck Colonel Frizell on the shoulder, so wounding him that he was borne from the field on which he had nobly performed his duty."

Colonel Scribner's brigade was at this time to the right of the regular brigade, and advanced into the cedars.

It gives me much pleasure to be able to testify further that the efficiency of this brigade, so long commanded by Colonel Scribner, is second to none in this army.

Very respectfully, your obedient servant,

GEORGE H. THOMAS,
Major General U. S. V. Commanding.

Lieutenant Colonel C. GODDARD,
A. A. G., Headquarters
Department of the Cumberland.

HEADQUARTERS DEPARTMENT OF THE CUMBERLAND,
May 18, 1863.

I forward with pleasure General Thomas's special notice of the part taken by Colonel Scribner in the battle of Stone river. It supplies an omission in the report of General Rousseau, which was the reason why a notice of it did not appear in my report.

W. S. ROSECRANS,
Major General.

HEADQUARTERS 9TH REG'T MICHIGAN INFANTRY VOLS.,
(Centre) 14*th Army Corps, Dep't of the Cumberland, January* 4, 1863.

MAJOR: I have the honor to make the following report of the part taken by the 9th regiment Michigan infantry in the recent advance of the army, and in the five days' battle before Murfreesboro'.

On the morning of the 26th day of December this regiment, as the provost guards to the corps d'armée of Major General George H. Thomas, marched two miles out from Nashville on the Franklin pike, and crossed over to the Nolinsville pike, and proceeded upon that road as far as the Edmonson pike, a distance of seven miles, and marched out one mile on the Edmonson pike and encamped for the night.

On Saturday morning the regiment, with headquarters train, returned to the Nashville pike, and marched to a point one mile south of Nolinsville and seventeen miles from Nashville.

On Sunday morning the regiment marched across from the Nolinsville pike to the Murfreesboro' pike, and encamped with headquarters, about five miles south of Lavergne, and remained there until Tuesday morning, when the regiment moved out on the Murfreesboro' pike to Overall's creek, about two miles in rear of our front, and established headquarters for the general.

During the several days' marches the regiment picked up many stragglers from the army in front, and sent them forward to their commands.

On Wednesday morning, about two hours after the commencement of Wednesday's battle, I noticed many stragglers crossing the fields from the direction of the right wing of our army, and sent out forces and brought them in, until I had from one to two hundred collected, when I discovered several cavalry men approaching with great speed from the direction of our front, and very soon discovered that a large cavalry force, together with infantry and a long transportation train, were in the most rapid retreat, throwing away their arms and accoutrements, and many of them without hats or caps, and apparently in the most frightful state of mind, crying, "We're all lost."

I at once concluded it was a stampede of frightened soldiers, and before many had passed me I drew my regiment up in line of battle across the road, extending on either side, and ordered my men to fix bayonets, and to take the position of guard against cavalry. This was done with celerity, and with much difficulty, without firing upon the frightened troops. I succeeded in checking their course, and ordered every man to face about. Within half an hour I had collected about one thousand cavalrymen, seven pieces of artillery, and nearly two regiments of infantry. Among them was a brigadier general. The cavalry, or most of it, belonged to the 2d brigade, and, if I am not mistaken, was commanded by Colonel Zahm. The infantry was from different regiments belonging to General Johnson's division. One colonel succeeded in escaping my lines, and passed on toward Nashville.

From the reports made by these troops I did not know but the enemy were in pursuit in force, and consequently I organized the forces I had collected and formed them in line of battle on the crest of the hill the other side of Overall's creek, planting the artillery on the left and centre.

In a short time Colonel Walker came up from the rear with a brigade of troops, and took position on the left. After we had occupied this position a short time a small force of the enemy's cavalry appeared on the opposite side of the creek and attacked our transportation train, which I had directed to proceed moderately toward Nashville. I directed a pursuit by a cavalry force, and about the same time Captain Church, of the 4th Michigan battery, and of Colonel Walker's brigade, opened a fire upon them, and they were soon dispersed, losing some few of their men. During the remainder of the day there were several attacks by the enemy's cavalry, and they were as frequently repulsed, and with considerable loss, by the cavalry force which I had stopped, but the cavalry of the 2d brigade did not seem very determined in their pursuit.

In the afternoon I was ordered by General Thomas to take position with my regiment on the south side of the creek, which I did, and then collected a large force of straggling infantry, and which, during the evening, were, most of them, returned to their regiments.

Late in the evening I was ordered to advance with my regiment to General Thomas's headquarters, near General Rosecrans's headquarters, which I did. About three o'clock on Thursday morning I received orders to proceed to Nashville with my regiment in charge of headquarters train, and about four o'clock I moved with the regiment in charge of the train.

No casualties occurred on the march until about one o'clock, when about nine miles this side of Nashville I discovered a general stampede in the train in my rear, which was not directly under my charge. I immediately formed my regiment across the road and stopped the train and fugitives. Very soon there were several cavalry men came up and reported that the train was attacked at Lavergne, about six miles in our rear. I succeeded in checking the stampede and stopping the alarmed cavalry men, teamsters, and negroes, who had gotten up the stampede. Among the cavalry men stopped was a Captain Skinner, of the 3rd Ohio cavalry. I reached Nashville about half past five o'clock with my train, and the long train in my rear, and pitched my camp on the site occupied previous to leaving Nashville. After I had my camp pitched, I received orders from General Morgan's aid to remove my regiment inside the fortifications early the next day, which I did, and about five o'clock in the evening received orders from General Thomas to return to the front with eight days' rations, and between three and four o'clock on Saturday morning I marched from Nashville with my regiment, with a small train. When about nine miles this side of Nashville I rescued a lady with a carriage, horse, and servant, which a party of rebel cavalry had captured. The cavalry fled on our approach, and I had no means of pursuit.

When I reached Lavergne I was informed by Colonel Innis, of the 1st

Michigan fusileers, that a large body of cavalry were about to attack his regiment, stationed there. I halted my regiment and prepared to assist Colonel Innis in his defence; but after waiting two hours for their attack, I proceeded on my march to this place without any other incident, and reached here last evening about seven o'clock with the regiment and train.

In stopping the rout which seemed to be prevailing among our troops on Wednesday morning, my officers and men, without one exception, behaved with great coolness, and are entitled to much credit for the determined and successful effort in preventing a disgraceful rout of a large portion of the right wing of the army.

I remain, major, very respectfully, your obedient servant,

T. G. PARKHURST,

Lieutenant Colonel commanding 9th Michigan Infantry Volunteers,

Major GEORGE E. FLYNT, *A. A. G. and Chief of Staff.*

HEADQUARTERS FIRST BRIGADE, THIRD DIVISION,
FOURTEENTH ARMY CORPS, DEPARTMENT OF THE CUMBERLAND,
Camp before Murfreesboro', Tenn., January 11, 1863.

MAJOR: On the night of the 30th ult. the first brigade made a night march from Nolinsville to Stewartsboro'. The road was very heavy, rough, and intricate, and most of the night was occupied in the march. The fourth Michigan battery, belonging to the brigade, got through without accident, but in a manner unknown to the "oldest inhabitant."

On the 31st the brigade was ordered to join the forces near Murfreesboro'. This order would have been promptly obeyed, but at the moment it was received a messenger came into camp with the news that a body of rebel cavalry, numbering from one to two thousand men, had attacked and were burning the supply train belonging to General McCook's corps, at Lavergne. I immediately ordered the seventeenth, thirty-first, and thirty-eighth Ohio regiments, and one section of the fourth Michigan battery, to move with all possible haste to the relief of the train; lest an attack might be made upon our camp, in the absence of the troops, I left the eighty-second Indiana volunteers drawn up in line of battle, with four pieces of the fourth Michigan battery for its defence. The distance from my camp to Lavergne was a little more than two and a half miles, and though the infantry moved with great rapidity, we were unable to reach Lavergne before nearly all the wagons and their contents had been destroyed. By pushing forward the artillery with all haste, I was able to get the two guns which I had taken into position, on the hill about one third of a mile on this side of the town, before the rebels had succeeded in paroling near all the men connected with the train. Many of the rebel cavalry were engaged in trying to drive away the mules belonging to the train, but the timely administration of shells, by Lieutenant Wheat, put an effectual stop to driving away the mules, but drove the rebels pell-mell into the woods on the right and left of the road. Captain Patton, of the first Ohio cavalry, who had joined me on the march with twenty of his men, supported, as well as could be done, by the thirty-first Ohio volunteers, now made pursuit, and succeeded in capturing five prisoners. The other two regiments having come up, a sufficient detail was made, under the direction of Major Ward and Captain Stinchcum, to secure all the mules and harness, with two wagons, which were not burnt, and a considerable amount of camp and garrison equipage, all of which was for the time being secured, and has since been sent back to Nashville. The rebels had broken and rifled the trunks and valises of the officers, taking everything in the way of clothing and other property of value from them. Having done the best that I could, under the circumstances, in the way of saving property, and, as I have since learned, having killed several and wounded others, I marched my command back to camp, on reaching which I immediately ordered Colonel Hunter, of the eighty-second Indiana volunteers, to move with his regiment on the road leading to Nashville, to collect together and bring forward all the trains which he might meet coming this way. This was accordingly done, the regiment making a forced march to Nashville the same night, and returning the next day to rejoin the brigade at this place, at about eight o'clock at night. This regiment rendered important service, checking and forcing back fugitives. About eleven o'clock p. m. of the 30th I was ordered to move forward as soon as relieved by General Stanley. At half-past seven of the 31st General Stanley relieved me, and again ordered me to move to the front. Whilst on the march, and near the crossing of Stewart's creek, I received an order from Major General Rosecrans to take up a strong position and defend the trains at the creek. I hastened forward, and at the creek was met by a large number of fugitives, flying to the rear, and spreading most exaggerated reports of disaster to the right wing of our army. I immediately brought the fourth Michigan battery into position on the high hill east of the road, and formed my infantry in line of battle, to support it. The tenth Ohio volunteers, commanded by Colonel Burke, was drawn up in line of battle on the west side of the road. Our position was such as to completely command the road, as well as a wide area stretching off to the front. I here stopped the first stampede, compelling men who had thrown away their guns to pick them up again and return to the field. We had remained here but a few moments until I received an order from Major General Thomas, again directing me to move to the front, and join my brigade to General Rousseau's division. I was also at this point notified by General Stanley that he would move forward on my right flank with a force of cavalry. It was about nine o'clock a. m. when I again moved forward, throwing a line of skirmishers to the front, for the twofold purpose of driving back fugitives and giving me timely warning if an enemy should approach. About ten o'clock a. m. I reached the headquarters of Major General Thomas, and here, learning from you that but a short time previous a large body of rebel cavalry had menaced that part of the field, I again took up a position in the cornfield fronting the headquarters, throwing my battalion into squares, and masking a section of guns in the centre of each square. I remained in this position but a few moments, until another stampede of mules, negroes, fugitives, and cowards of every grade were seen swarming to the rear. At this moment Captain McKay, of General Thomas's staff, rode up and requested me, if possible, to check the stampede. I at once reduced my squares, forming a line of battle, with my right resting upon the road. The appearance of this force appeared to reassure and give confidence to the runaways—men and mules all stopped. Again receiving your instructions to move to the front, I advanced on this side of the creek, but was here again met by an order directing me to watch my right flank with great vigilance, as the rebel cavalry was again in strong force menacing that part of the field. I again formed a line of battle, taking advantage of a piece of woodland lying to the right of the road, from a piece of high land, immediately in front of which I had a good view of the field to our right. I remained here a short time, and no enemy approaching I moved forward to the front. At one o'clock I reached the point on the turnpike in front of General Rosecrans's headquarters on the field. Here, in accordance with your instructions, I reported to General McCook, who ordered me to take up a position on his left, which I did, and remained here comparatively inactive, until about sundown, when I was ordered by General Johnson to move to the front, which I did, forming a double line of battle, and throwing out a strong body of skirmishers. We remained in this position all night, without fires.

My skirmishers were busy all night, almost constantly exchanging shots with those of the enemy. At three o'clock a. m., January 1, I was sent for to report at General Thomas's headquarters in person, which I did, and was there instructed to watch my front with great vigilance, and keep a strong body of skirmishers in advance to prevent any surprise. This I did, and daylight had no sooner broken upon us than I saw the wisdom of the warning that I had received, as the enemy showed himself in strong force upon the margin of the woodland immediately on my front. General Johnson had in the meantime ordered me to move to the left, about the distance of a brigade front, formed in two lines. The ground I then occupied was covered with a somewhat dense cedar forest. I directed my men to throw up a breastwork upon our front, which they very soon did, constructing it of loose rocks and logs gathered together for that purpose. So well was this work constructed, and with such rapidity, that by ten o'clock we had a strong line of defences, which were continued by other troops on our right, who evinced equal energy, skill, and industry.

The 4th Michigan battery, under command of Captain Church, assisted by Lieutenants Wheat, Corbin, and Sawyer, acted an important part in this morning's operations. Twice during the early hours of the morning the enemy showed himself upon our front. Captain Church had placed his guns in the most commanding positions, and whenever the opportunity offered the most destructive fire I ever witnessed from artillery was poured upon the rebel masses as they thickened upon the margin of the opposite woods. Other batteries, however, to our right and left, opened their fire, with perhaps equal effect.

It is not my business to speak of what they did, further than to admit the noble part that they took in the work. I watched the progress, and observed the effect of my own shot, and saw the rebel masses torn down and scattered before it, like leaves before a storm.

One rebel battery on our extreme right, and one or two guns in front of our centre, replied with shell and round shot, many of which struck in the timber, and fell crashing and bursting in dangerous proximity, but not a man of the brigade was injured by them. The day was spent in skirmishing upon the front, and in these artillery duels, in one of which a rebel gun on our right front was dismounted in a very handsome manner by a shot from Lieutenant Wheat's section of the 4th Michigan battery, which was sent with the accuracy of a rifle ball. About eight o'clock of the night of the 1st, I was ordered by General Sheridan to send a strong reconnoitering party to the front, which I did. The enemy were found in force but a short distance in front of our line, and apparently engaged in the same business. In this reconnoissance I had three men from the 17th Ohio volunteers wounded. John Zeigler, of company A, Corporal Edward Lacy, and W. R. Sain, of company B. The first two were severely, the third but slightly wounded.

On the morning of the second the enemy could again be seen threatening our front, but so vigorous and well directed was the fire from Church's battery and others upon the right and left of our position that no body of soldiers could have attacked our front successfully, covered as it was by the batteries. Heavy skirmishing continued upon our front all through the fore part of the day, until the action on our left appeared to command silence upon every other part of the field, there being no firing on our front. I reported in person to Major General Thomas that the enemy appeared to have withdrawn, upon which he ordered me to advance to the front with my brigade and test the fact. I immediately obeyed his order. My men leaped over their breastworks, formed their lines, and moved to the front with a veteran steadiness and determination. The enemy had again shown himself upon our front, and that at closer proximity than at any time during this or the preceding day. Stone's battery had opened fire upon such a line as to compel me to move my left directly under it; and finding that the elevation of his guns was not such as to enable me to do so in safety, I sent an officer to him with the request that he would change the direction of his pieces. The officer in command of the battery seems not to have understood my message, and for a few moments the fire from this battery threatened to do us greater injury than anything coming from the front, knocking the branches of trees to pieces and scattering them around us. Several shells from this battery also bursted in our very midst, but fortunately did us no injury. We had not advanced more than three hundred yards beyond our breastworks when the rebel infantry opened a rapid fire on our right from the cornfield adjacent, and from the pickets in front of our centre. My lines advanced under this fire, with the utmost steadiness and good order, a distance of seventy-five or eighty yards before a shot was returned. I then gave the order to commence firing. The front line, composed of the 17th and 31st regiments, delivered a steady and well directed fire. Then, as previously instructed, falling upon the ground to load, the 38th Ohio and 82d Indiana immediately advanced and delivered their fire, lying down to load. I then gave the order to fix bayonets, intending to finish the job with that weapon. The enemy, however, had fled precipitately before our volleys behind their breastworks in the woods. There being no corresponding movement on my right, and the battery on our left keeping up a most pertinacious fire, which put my lines in great peril should I advance, I withdrew the brigade again behind the breastworks. In this advance upon the enemy I had one man severely wounded from the 17th Ohio volunteers—Thomas Outcalt, private of company K; four men from the 82d Indiana volunteers—Robert H. Rigg, private, company C, shot in the hip—badly hurt; Henry C. McCoy, private, company C, dangerously wounded in the abdomen; William Manott, private, company F, badly wounded in the thigh; James A. May, company I, wounded in the hand; and six men from the 31st Ohio volunteers—John Kisic, company G; John Sheldon, company G; M. P. Murry, company K; Corporal David Kiser and John Shoe, of company K; and David Condon, of company A. About half-past seven in the evening I was again ordered, by General Sheridan, to make a reconnoissance in front. For this purpose I detailed two companies from each of the Ohio regiments under my command, and placed them under command of Lieutenant Colonel Choate, of the 38th Ohio regiment, assisted by Lieutenant Colonel Davis, of the 82d Indiana volunteers, and Captain Stinchcum, of the 17th Ohio volunteers. This force had not advanced above a quarter of a mile to the front before they were fired on by the enemy. A brisk skirmish ensued, which was kept up for about half an hour. In this affair I had six men wounded, five from the 38th Ohio volunteers—Lieutenant Hanna, company A, slightly; Sergeant John J. Wilsey, severely; Private Levi Lovejoy, severely; Private John Simmons, severely; Private James Rogers, severely—all of company A; Sergeant Brice H. Jay, company K, severely; Captain Stinchcum, of the 17th Ohio volunteers. On the morning of the 3d, being ordered to maintain great vigilance in watching the movements of the enemy to our front, I placed the brigade under arms, advancing my rear line and massing it upon the front under the breastworks. Here we remained pretty much all day, exposed to the inclemency of the weather and suffering a good deal, but without complaint. The officers and men uniformly behaved well while under my command, and I find no lack of zeal, patience, or courage. With the night of the third closed the active struggles of this great conflict. The first brigade has sustained few casualties compared with others. We have tried to perform our duty; we have done the work assigned us in the best manner we knew how. We are in good condition to perform any service which may be required of us, and will do it cheerfully, whatever it may be, as we have ever heretofore done.

Respectfully submitted.

M. B. WALKER,
Colonel Commanding First Brigade.

Major GEORGE E. FLYNT.

HEADQUARTERS FIRST BRIGADE, THIRD DIVISION,
(CENTRE) 14TH ARMY CORPS, DEPARTMENT OF THE CUMBERLAND,
Camp near Murfreesboro', Tennessee, January 10, 1863.

MAJOR: I have the honor to report the casualties of the first brigade during the engagement before Murfreesboro'; they are as follows:

Seventeenth Ohio volunteers.

Wounded.—Captain Stinchcum, acting topographical engineer on Colonel Walker's staff, slightly in the side by a spent ball; Corporal Ed. Lacy and Zeigh John, company A, severely; William R. Sain, company B, slightly; Private Thomas Outcalt, company K, severely. Total 5.

Thirty-eighth regiment Ohio volunteers, Colonel E. H. Phelps.

Wounded.—Lieutenant T. B. Hanna, in the hand, slightly; Sergeant John J. Wilsey, in both thighs; Privates John J. Simmons, in the wrist, seriously; James Rogers, thigh, seriously; Simeon Lovejoy, in the back, seriously; Brice H. Jay, commissary sergeant, in the leg, flesh wound. Total, 6.

Eighty-second Indiana volunteers, Colonel M. C. Hunter.

Wounded.—Sergeant Albert Galtry, company B, missing; Sergeant Henry C. McCoy, company C, in the side; Private Robert H. Rigg, company C, in the hip; Private William Minett, company F, in the thigh; Private James A. May, company I, in the hand. Total, 5.

Thirty-first regiment Ohio volunteer infantry, Lieutenant Colonel Lister.

Wounded.—Corporal David Kiser, slightly; Privates John Kissic and John Sheldon, company G, slightly; M. P Murry, company K, slightly; John Shoe, company C, slightly; David Condon, company A, slightly. Total, 6.

Very respectfully,

R. McQUILKIN,
Captain and Acting Assistant Adjutant General.

Major GEO. E. FLYNT,
Assistant Adjutant General Fourteenth Army Corps.

LIST OF CASUALTIES AT THE BATTLE OF MURFREESBORO'—FIRST DIVISION, (CENTRE,) FOURTEENTH ARMY CORPS.

Thirty-third Ohio volunteers.

Killed.—Privates John Vandenaw, and Charles Felter, company B.

Wounded.—Corporals Samuel Rolby, John Derush, and N. C. Tompkins, company A, and Sam Vurelee, company G; Privates Cornelius Canter, Cyrus Dixon, John Hogan, A. J. Orin, John Porter, Jos. L. Rogers, and Sam White, company A; Samuel Pullen, W. Howell, Jos. Sences, company B; W. A. Sing, George Barleen, company C; M. Tidd, company E; George Therenin, Thomas Casetolt, company F; Samuel Dutton and James Browing, company G.

Ninety-fourth Ohio volunteers.

Killed.—Privates Harry Hughs, Jacob Ain, company I; and Jas. Lockhart, company K.

Wounded.—Colonel Commanding J. W. Frizell; Captain —— Stel, company E; First Sergeant B. C. Mitchell, company C, and Sergeant J. R. Martin, company K; Corporals A. Close, company A; George Detro, Josiah Reed, company I; S. D. Taylor, company K; and George Dolinger, company B; Privates John Sedenstich, W. H. Hayne, D. Jenkins, company A; H. McLuse, John Reese, company F; Eli Fenlers, company D; Jacob Elter, Jas. Phaley, company I; John Roberts, E. Chambers, company C; L. C. Cartel, company E; T. B. White, M. Hardin, company K; and John Ginn, company B.

Second Ohio volunteers.

Killed.—Colonel Commanding Y. Kell; Corporals C. M. Wingett, company A, and A. J. Ward, company B; Privates Jas. Flord, W. C. Goodpaster, George W. Hughs, L M. Hill, company C, and J. Walker, company I.

Wounded.—Acting Major O. C. Maewell; 1st Lieutenants R. C. Chanebers, company I, (died in hospital,) and L. Van Horn, company I; Sergeants —— Henry, company D; —— Dougherty, company H; Jas. Phillips, company K; Corporals W. P. Long, company A; A. J. Ward, company B; N. Huffman, company C; J. C. Haslett, company E; —— Bahill, company F; and J. H. Morison, company K; Privates C. C. Cranston, M. W. Anderson, company A, (died in hospital;) W. Jackson, company B; W. E. Henry, G. W. Myers, W. Gaskill, company C; James Doyle, M. Galliram, J. Clifford, A. Smith, J. Simpson, company D; T. Ross, R. Duncan, J. M. Gray, company F; Elijah Mattock, John M. Lense, W. Dunn, W. Michals, company G; N. Frints, H. Dunham, George Seigel, company I; and George Lowry, company K.

Tenth Wisconsin volunteers.

No names furnished.
Killed, three; wounded, fifteen.

Thirty-eighth Indiana volunteers.

Killed.—William Ellis, William B. Smith, and Henry J. Affle, company A; Captain James E. Fouts, company C; Privates Henry Bessic and Lyman B. Goulds, company D; Corporal William T. Carpenter and Private James Taylor, company E; Privates Elijah Kemple and Thomas J. Smith, company F; Private Jehu Measel and Corporal Benjamin Treeal, company G; Private James Webb, company H; Corporal William Ballard, company K.

Wounded.—Samuel W. Hobson, John W. Affle, A. Buchanon, Jeff. McCahea, John T. Peyton, Leander Free, William J. Hannee, William J. Aberman, Moses W. Affle, J. W. Leatherman, Samuel Granger, William Furguson, and E. M. Lenard, company A; George Hessey, Charles Bonames, Samuel Roby, H. Roby, and Bugler John N. Foote, company B; Corporals John A. Sipes and Leander Jackson, Privates John Raison, William Johnson, Robert L. Campbell, Albert Newbolt, and Henry Stonehouse, and Second Lieutenant Milton Davis, company C; Sergeant Peter Dobbins, Corporals James Hanley and James C. McLain, Privates A. Williams, Peter Wolf, and John Fitzgerald, company D; Corporal Benjamin Goodman, Privates William F. Boldt and George W. White, company E; Sergeant William Tucker, Corporal Thomas Mitchell, Privates George Apperson, James Bathoff, John F. Baugh, Henry Briggs, David Cole, Henry Frank, Jacob Hartman, M. B. Jenkins, Francis

James, Thomas Kelly, John Overman, John Rouff, Christian Staffinger, and Alford Young, company F; Corporal John Carlton, Privates Jonathan Brinson, Hosea Carlton, W. J. Jackson, Samuel McCormic, Jacob Hosier, J. S. Kumple, J. A. Smith, and Robert Smith, company G; Corporals Samuel F. Smith and A. T. Buchanan, Privates Thomas Gray, Robert Duncan, John J. Tundy, and James Rodgers, company H; Second Lieutenant Thomas Hawkins, Sergeants Abel Jacknear and Benjamin Webb, Privates Joseph Harkins, William G. Ellis, Joseph Moore, Lewis Collins, and H. Hammon, company J; Corporals Abraham Kempt, Hiram Brewer, David Jones, and William Reggle, Privates Enoch Seaton, P. Cunningham, David Allen, John Snell, C. Wanosian, and James McGuin, Sergeants Walter Seacot and James Seaton, company K.

Missing.—Private Henry Henson.

First Wisconsin volunteers.

Wounded.—Sergeant George Tibbets, company D; Corporal F. H. Farr' company K; Private L. W. Peterson, company F; Private Harvey Arnold company I; Captain D. C. McNean, company E; Corporal Andrew Bunteen company A; Private Baptist De Marra, company B; Color Corporal Azra D Bundy, company C.

Twenty-first Wisconsin volunteers.

Wounded.—Private Benjamin Turney, (since died,) company D; Lieutenant A. B. Smith, company I.

Second Kentucky cavalry.

Wounded.—Private Benjamin Tarley, company D.

Seventy-ninth Pennsylvania volunteers.

Killed.—Private Mark Erb, company G.

Wounded.—Privates John Shovy, Samuel Pickel, and Isaac Quigly, company G; Private William Patton, company H; Private Michael Brant, company E; Private Henry Hock, (accidentally,) company F; Corporal Benjamin Bones, company E; Corporal Elias Hollins, company G; Sergeant J. H. Friday, company G.

Twenty-fourth Illinois volunteers.

Wounded.—Privates Christ Lages, (since died,) and George Kreeman, company D; Private Charles Shuttla, company G; Private Jacob Hartman, company B.

Fifteenth Kentucky volunteers.

Killed.—Colonel James Foreman; Captain A. S. Bane, company F; Corporal Robert Robb, company A; Private M. Leary, company A; Private William Crady, company C; Private John Hoback, company F; Private Edward Boyle, company G; Private Weber, company I.

Wounded.—Privates William Sanders, G. W. Fields, Harry Hall, and J. B. Carrica, company A; Privates J. Whortenburry, W. S. Stevens, W. A. Richardson, Joshua Morrow, and John Cogwell, company B; Lieutenant Frank Foadel, company C; Sergeant J. T. Chambers, company C; Private George Ford, company C; Private Joseph Rosteller, company D; Privates William Malott, John Lawsman, John Patterson, Philemon Olds, Frederick Plump, and Hiram Potts, company E; Privates W. S. Thompson and J. C. Skinner, company F; Sergeant William Hepford, company H; Corporal John Randall, company H; Sergeant Constantine Schultz, company I; Privates Hahnemenn, Michael Grunt, Philip Hoffman, and Frank Glosson, company I; Private Charles Harrington, company K.

Eighty-eighth Indianna volunteers.

Killed.—Private Henry Collins, company B; Sergeant William S. Jones, company C; Private Charles M. Scott, company F; Private Ira Pryor, company H; Corporal John Hull, company H; Private Mark Fraks, company I; Privates Jacob Boyer and Ruben Barnes, company H.

Wounded.—Colonel George Humphrey; First-Lieutenant Philander Smith, company H; Second-Lieutenant John G. Gohcen, company E; Corporal J. Baughman, company A; Privates John Zimmerman and William Krouty, company A; Sergeants Andrew Linn and H. P. Smith, company B; Corporal Moses Kiser, company B; Privates John Renahan and James Douglass, company B; Corporal Dorsey Scudder, company C; Private H. Diffindaffer and John Leepeer, company C; Color Sergeant Hiram Thomas, company C; Privates John Bishop, Eldridge Burke, and Marion Griswold, company C; Corporal Edward Wilson, company C; Privates Joshua Sweet, Josephus Marsh, Michael Broward, Chris. Parker, Washington Perkins, Albert Snyder, and Edward Johnson, company D; Privates Mahl Sipes, Robert K. Brown, Samuel H. Smith, Enos Reed, William M. Natt, John H. Furguson, and Martin Baggs, company E; Private James Patterson, company G; Corporal Franklin Thomas, company H; Sergeant William A. Ree, company H; Privates Michael Johnson and Samuel R. Stopher, company H; Privates John Middleton, Aseph S. Prescott, Henry L. Schcraeder, and Jonathan Kellett, company I; Corporal Charles Evans, company I; Corporal James Walker, company H; Privates William Boyd, Moses Ward, Israel Thompson, and David J. Browman, company H.

Third Ohio volunteers.

Killed.—Sergeant George McAlvain, Corporal John Conway, and Private H. K. Bennett, company A; Private J. D. Figley, company B; Private Chas. Winnegand, company C; Privates Mahleen Neer and John Baker, company D; Sergeant William McCarty and Private Frank Burley, company F; Privates John B. Nailer and H. Tuckerneyers, company G; Corporal Richard Hughs, company H; Privates John Mottram, Levi H. Courtright, and James W. Wright, company I; Privates C. A. McDonald and T. J. McCollough, company K.

Wounded.—Corporals Samuel A. Frazer and James B. Duelen, and Privates George Cobb, F. W. Mechum, Charles T. Palmer, Benj. F. Palmer, William Worly, and John Kerceller, company A; Sergeant Samuel L. French, Corporal Robert J. Dennis, and Privates William H. Barnes, Charles B. Case, Owen E. Moore, John Neill, and Michael Wolf, company B; Sergeants Henry Sanderson and D. Walker, Corporal J. J. Shinn and Aaron Herr, and Privates W. H. Cook, W. C. Light, John Mann, H. Morison, J. Woodyard, A. Wharff, A. Scott, G. A. Richie, B. O. Cussins, Rufus H. Smith, and Alonzo Riddle, company C; Corporal W. O. Munson and Privates R. F. Singleton, George P. Fuller, Noah Spring, and John W. Signer, company E; Corporal John W. Loring and Privates Jerome Galbrieth, James Tarbet, Henry Smith, John Reed, and Jacob Bowers, company F; Sergeant H. Bender and Privates Henry Barry, William Chase, and E. English, company G; Captain Leroy S. Bell, George A. Ball, William S. Wywick, and Privates Albert Asher, Thomas Deryer, William

Boodle, and Nathaniel Levett, company H; Sergeant Elias C. Nicholas and Privates Robert Glenn, Charles W. Wood, W. R. Willits, John Benedict, Jasper Mann, and John B. Cazy, company I; Sergeants G. B. Cooper and W. J. Hurst, Corporal M. Givergin, and Privates S. O. Harra, J. W. Patterson, J. Jeffries, and J. Barcus, company K.

Forty-second Indiana volunteers.

Killed.—Sergeant C. Goldsmith and Private Henry P. Stone, company A; Private William C. Seikman, company B; Sergeant W. H. Shuyler and Private James E. Hammond, company C; Private James Hamilton, company D; Corporal John Nixon, company E; Privates Joseph Guest, Deidrick Knise, James H. McGregor, and A. H. Still, company F; Privates Hubbard Pride and Terry Taylor, company G; Private Austin Bolin, company H; Private Duquesne Elder, company I; Privates W. H. Clifford and Rinaldo Edward, company K.

Wounded.—Sergeant Nat. Matheny, and Privates John Trimble, William Carter, Nathaniel Black, and William Schroeder, company A; Sergeant Joseph Cox, Privates John Kelly and John Bossee, company B; Sergeant E. C. Grigsby, Corporal A. Baum, and Privates John Lindsey, James Saucer, Roger Barber, and D. C. Gillum, company C; Captain John Eigenman, Corporal William Garrison, and Privates D. T. Tennison, Michael Foley, and Thomas Galley, company D; Lieutenant J. R. Ashmead, Corporal John W. Smith, and Privates Elijah Smith, Joseph Malone, Thomas W. Ward, Ephraim Rutledge, Pickney Williams, and S. L. Hutchinson, company E; Captain William M. Cockrum, Lieutenants John Q. A. Stell and J. C. White, Sergeant James M. Harper, Corporal Charles Oring, and Privates R. M. Martin, William Mason, John P. Simpson, William A. Reavis, Beach Compton, Henry Gillum, H. J. Kestner, John C. Martin, James W. McCleary, Asa Mason, Elias Skelton, and James H. Simpson, company F; Corporal Richard McGeehee and Privates William D. Burras, John W. Ellis, Chas M. Crocker, Willis Wallace, James Wallace, Andrew Potts, Michael Austin, N. T. Carroll, William Johnson, W. D. Risley, N. F. Wallace, and Joseph Swan, company G; Privates George R. Goodman, William Cook, Peter Doering, Ezekial Beard, Henry Jones, James Tumbleton, James B. Payne, and Samuel Crow, company H; Sergeant Nathan Price, Corporal A. N. Thomas, and Privates James Cartwright, John Lichlyter, Samuel Garland, Graves Mead, P. W. Chappel, Calvin Coe, James Penner, Levi Hale, and M. Christson, company I; Lieutenant E. M. Knowles, Sergeant L. M. Neeves, Corporals J. M. Martin and A. Ashley, and Privates Pleasant Shepard, John Coleman, M. Matthews, Frank Ross, and George Thompson, company K.

Second Kentucky cavalry.

Wounded.—Sergeant Thomas Hall and Private James Sanders, company A; Corporal James Turley, company D.

Fifteenth United States infantry.

Killed.—Captain J. Bowman Bell; Sergeants Irwin, Kane, Movicth, Somison, Brown, Hugck, Skanable, and Lovejoy; Corporals McFadden, Underwood, Harp, Mantle, Gibson, and Blaw; Privates McCall, and Van Suttle, company A; Private Wangle, company B; Private Skapple, company C; Private Detweiler, company D; Privates Quinn, Genick, company E; Privates Hemer, Brown, company H.

Wounded.—Major King, Captain Wise, Lieutenant Occleston, Privates Lemon, Flynn, Brice, Hasler, McGuin, Ogden, Ayers, Moran, Masters, Kelley, and Acker, company A; Privates Adams, Finley, Loore, McGuire, Daily, and Wray, company B; Privates Spencer, Findley, Mauk, Strauss, and Schweikert, company C; Privates Benton, Rowey, Rouly, Stolter, Sponeilee, Williams, and Umbaugh, company D; Privates Scholers, Barker, Gillooly, Osterlee, Suhoff, Vackum, Sifers, and Farr, company E; Privates Davis, Fletcher, and Schisck, company F; Privates Gilbert, Sozo, Saneber, and Slusser, company G; Privates Chappman, Gissneyer, Mowell, Sutten, Snyder, Ramsey, Geph, and Henwick, company H.

Sixteenth United States infantry.

Killed.—Corporal Robinson; Privates Hendelong, Lewis, Snelivan, Frost, Ginsback, Clark, Féyso, Williams, Pooler, Patterson, Cheadle, Stockdale, White, Palmer, and Simmons.

Wounded.—Major Slemmer; Captains Barry, King, and Dykeman; Lieutenants Bartholomew, Bowen, and Howland; Sergeants Howe, Whalen, Hamilton, Perkins, Judson, Thomas, Wagner, Edson, Martin, Scott, Potter, McNeil, and Brickner; Corporals Dewin, Vigor, Kinkaid, Oteel, Donohoe, Reese, Hastings, Greenbalgh, and Kastner; Privates Gillock, Dolan, Hilton, Hogan, Dudley, Adams, Spice, Velson, Kane, Dorsey, Kelly, Devine, Larcomb, Hutchinson, Fjitterstrom, Donohue, McQuade, Kenmp, McCaughy, Fahy, Lade, Lester, Love, Griffin, Gollon, Gilhoed, Kollinger, Orteril, Stone, Wagner, Owens, Batten, Black, Healey, Brody, Conway, Hawley, Mewer, Mead, Roach, Russell, Mix, Wrightman, Mesmer, Burton, Growney, Kavanaugh, Kinston, Jones, McMahon, Shannon, Straw, Winters, Willic, Wescott, Banyan, Boyle, Crotine, Garveny, Halihan, Kunltson, Livingston, Lathrope, McCarthy, Mannahan, McLane, Sykes, Tuneblood, Taylor, Gillespie, Henry, Donnelly, Wale, Wild, Boyce, Dubie, Gray, Keith, Smith, Thompson, Galliger, Waidham, Caldwell, Barnard, Kelly, Sawyer, Padden, Kahaley, Kirkpatrick, Miller, Harper, Daney, Dorey, Crabben, Anderson, Olson, Olson, Rawson, Smith, Stratee, Findle, Page, Williams, and Hilton.

Eighteenth United States infantry.

Killed.—Captain Charles Kneass; Lieutenant John F. Hitchcock; Sergeants White, Dobbins, Maderia, and Headley; Corporals Phillips, Wilcox, Harcourt, Long, Conwall, and Linbaugh; and Privates Harrison, Holsbach, Kay, Tussleman, Patterson, Ayers, Masterton, Scolan, Ennis, Kelly, Harper, Pike, Wasmer, Edkert, Jones, Armstrong, Oikeil, Shwarp, Scheck, Blessing, Robins, Fenenkouf, Adair, Plumley, Savage, White, Elsbach, Cowles, Smith, McGinnis, Carmain, Hancock, Murphy, Anderson, Fisher, Sherman, Redman, Gallivan, Boglin, Dashil, Ralfstock, Sherler, and Palmer.

Wounded.—Captains Charles Denison, A. B. Thompson, Henry Haymond, Douglass, Hull, and Wood; Lieutenants M. F. Ogden, Carpenter, McConnell, Simons, and O'Dail; Sergeants Owens, Schwartz, Looker, Wilder, Wiles, Smith, Horton, Duncan, Mathew, Leibole, Flezal, Williams, Davis, Wallace, Barr, Todd, Ell, and Peters; Corporals Gaisuch, Davis, Hannahs, Brooks, Bell, Allen, Bartlette, Tooker, Johns, Barnes, Miller, Hines, Seibole, and Falter; Privates Lanowe, Myers, Moore, Medick, Peckham, Stupelt, Smith, Seigle, Barker, Dailey, Frizzell, Fitzgerald, Hardwick, Kuntz, Pepper, Shaffer, Welsh, Dixon, Riddle, Schreckingaust, Mossey, Washburn, Welch, Welch, Quiner, Habstile, Broggar, Gaddis, Eberly, Rumsey, Johnson, White, Plum, Steihoff, Williams, Boulten, Clark, Fetters, Harkley, Moriarty, Schultz, Helpman, Brown, Constwright, Dodds, Maxwell, Connell, Price, Rose, Rhodes, Shepherd, Swank, Hawley, Maley, Wallace, Mangar, Young, Coen, Myer, Thomas, Weisoth, Barrett, Edwards, Hickman, Hill, Converse, Homer, Nasey, Frank, Davy, Sheet, Tesley,

Harris, McClintock, Seibt, Marshall, Livament, Beemerdafer, Browncan, Morgardidge, Medow, Place, Trewan, Argo, Brooks, Cantile, Goble, Hogan, Howald, Saken, O'Connor, Strassel, Wilson, Shafersberger, Robinhood, Hamilton, Gulerwood, Hilgert, Bolan, Dixon, Wety, Kelley, Thorp, Baugham, Brink, Higgins, Jones, Owen, Stone, McBride, Beardsley, Grey, Hartman, McInsery, Rhodes, Senett, Villiers, Weaver, Baker, Bowen, Divine, Handley, Jones, Jones, Waterfield, Price, Clark, Headington, Howard, Kerchner, King, McCauley, Rither, Luther, Howard, Scharck, Brown, Douglas, Endrass, Haas, Jacobee, Rose, McConnel, Beard, Baker, James, Jackson, McKenzie, Connor, Riddle, Oaith, McCarty, Harvice, Hofler, Swezer, Sigman, Deal, Kerstelle, McCormick, Daniels, Fernel, Kelleen, Coleman, Cunningham, McQuary, Parsons, Seaton, Schaffrex, Stoufer, Taylor, Wilson, Young, and Caty.

Nineteenth United States infantry.

Killed.—Major S. D. Carpenter and Lieutenant J. J. Wagoner; Privates John Quinn, Haggerty, Aaron Luther, Gorman, Higgins, and Boyer.

Wounded.—Sergeants Harrison, Steaffer, Sloan, Howe, Williams, and Little; Corporals Jepalery, John Stewart, Davis, Nester, and Smith; Privates Breese, Brunnon, Faller, Fizy, Lynch, Martin, Cask, Cain, Cope, Lanthan, Slawson, Earnigle, Bennett, Crosby, Griffiths, Hunt, Rayer, Sways, Hall, Gause, Hook, Kroman, Smith, Springer, Adams, Brown, Doran, Delaney, Gilford, Haney, Tulbits, Tatew, Hipps, Powers, and Fitzpatrick.

Fifth United States artillery.

Wounded.—Corporal Charles Allbyon; Privates Thomas Brown, F. N. James, Michael McGrath, and James Bryen, company H.

List of casualties at the battle of Murfreesboro'.—First brigade, 3d division, centre.

Seventeenth Ohio—Private Thomas Outcult, company K, compound fracture, elbow joint; Private John Zigler, company K, comminuted tibia; Private Edward Lacy, company K, flesh wound, leg.

Thirty-eighth Ohio—Sergeant John Welsey, company A, flesh wound, both hips; Private John Simmons, company A, compound fracture, right fore-arm; Private James Rodgers, company A, flesh wound, left thigh; Private Simon Lovejoy, company A, flesh wound, lumber reg.; Second Lieutenant Thomas B. Nanne, flesh wound, finger; Private Brice Jay, company K, flesh wound, thigh.

Eighty-second Indiana.—Private William Minnett, company F, compound fracture, femur; Private Robert Bigg, company C, flesh wound, groin; Sergeant Henry McCoy, company C, flesh wound, right side; Private James May, company G, finger shot off; Private Joseph Cooper, company G, all fingers, right hand; Private Oscar Vengre, company A, half hand shot away.

List of killed and wounded in the tenth regiment volunteers, battle of Stone river.

Tenth Wisconsin volunteers.—Private John Long, company A, killed; Private Michael Coulon, company D, killed; Private Irwin Clark, company D, killed; Private Dewitt Griffin, company A, wounded arm and thigh, severe; Private Thomas H. Morison, company A, wounded scalp; Private Rufus R. Cowles, company B, wounded abdomen, since died; Private Nelson Corrison, company B, wounded thigh, slightly; Sergeant Martin Jenkins, company C, wounded face, severe; Private Bela G. Bishop, company C, wounded shoulder, severe; Private George Dewey, company E, fore-arm, slightly; Private Ruben T.

Crosby, company F, wounded elbow, not severe; Private Kasper Wachter, company G, wounded shoulder, severe; Private George Lane, company G, wounded, contusion of arm; Private Edward O. Flaherty, company G, wounded head, said to be severe; Sergeant Augustus M. Kennison, company H, wounded, contusion, back, slightly; Private Joseph M. Ginnis, company H, wounded through calf of leg; Private Andrew Scow, company K, wounded leg, severe; Private Washburn Blatchly, company K, wounded arm, slight; Private W. S. Holdridge, company K, wounded slight, did not see him; Captain J. W. Roley, company B, contusion fore-arm, one bone fractured.

Killed, 3; wounded, 17; missing, 4.

NASHVILLE, TENNESSEE,
January 11, 1863.

SIR: I have the honor to report the part taken by my command, the 3d division of the army, in the battle of Murfreesboro', begun on the 31st ultimo, and ended on the 3d instant.

Early on the morning of the 30th ultimo, in obedience to the order of General Thomas, my division moved forward towards Murfreesboro', from Stewartsboro', on the Nashville and Murfreesboro' turnpike, about nine miles from the latter place. On the march forward several despatches from General Rosecrans reached me, asking exactly where my command was, and the hour and minute of the day. In consequence we moved rapidly forward, halting but once, and that for only five minutes. About 10½ o'clock a. m. we reached a point three miles from Murfreesboro', where Generals Rosecrans and Thomas were, on the Nashville and Murfreesboro' turnpike, and remained during the day, and bivouacked at night.

At about 9 o'clock a. m. on the 31st the report of artillery and heavy firing of small arms on our right announced that the battle had begun by an attack on the right wing, commanded by Major General McCook. It was not long before the direction from which the firing came indicated that General McCook's command had given way and was yielding ground to the enemy. His forces seemed to swing around toward our right and rear. At this time General Thomas ordered me to advance my division quickly to the front, to the assistance of General McCook.

On reaching the right of General Negley's line of battle, General Thomas there directed me to let my left rest on his right, and to deploy my division off towards the right as far as I could, so as to resist the pressure on General McCook. We consulted and agreed as to where the line should be formed. This was in a dense cedar brake, through which my troops marched in double-quick time, to get into position before the enemy reached us. He was then but a few hundred yards to the front, sweeping up in immense numbers, driving everything before him. This ground was new and unknown to us all. The woods were almost impassable to infantry, and artillery was perfectly useless, but the line was promptly formed; the 17th brigade, Colonel John Beaty commanding, on the left; the brigade of regulars, Lieutenant Colonel O. L. Shephard commanding, on the right; the 9th brigade, Colonel B. F. Scribner commanding, was placed perhaps a hundred yards in rear and opposite the centre of the front line, so as to support either or both of the brigades in front as occasion might require. My recollection is that perhaps the 2d Ohio and 33d Ohio regiments filled a gap between General Negley's right and the 17th brigade, occasioned by the effort to extend our lines far enough to the right to afford the desired aid to General McCook.

The 28th brigade, Colonel John C. Starkweather commanding, and Stone's battery of 1st Kentucky artillery, were at Jefferson Crossing, on Stone river, about eight miles below.

Our lines were hardly formed before a dropping fire from the enemy announced his approach. General McCook's troops, in a good deal of confusion, retired through our lines and around our right under a most terrific fire. The enemy in pursuit furiously assailed our front, and greatly outflanking us passed around to our right and rear. By General Thomas's direction I had already ordered the artillery—Loomis's and Guenther's batteries—to the open field in the rear. Seeing that my command was ouflanked on the right, I sent orders to the brigade commanders to retire at once also to this field, and riding back myself I posted the batteries on a ridge with open ground, parallel with our line of battle, and as my men emerged from the woods they were ordered to take position on the right and in support of these batteries, which was promptly done. We had perhaps four or five hundred yards of open ground in our front. While the batteries were unlimbering, seeing General Van Cleve close by, I rode up and asked him if he would move his command to the right, and aid in checking up the enemy by forming on my right, and thus giving us a more extended line in that direction in the new position taken. In the promptest manner possible his command was put in motion and in double-quick time reached the desired point in good season. As the enemy emerged from the woods in great force, shouting and cheering, the batteries of Guenther and Loomis, double shotted with cannister, opened upon them; they moved straight ahead for a while, but were finally driven back with immense loss. In a little while they rallied again, and as it seemed with fresh troops, and assailed our position, and were again, after a fierce struggle, driven back. Four deliberate and fiercely sustained assaults were made upon our position, and repulsed. During the last assault I was informed that our troops were advancing on the right, and saw troops not of my division, led by General Rosecrans, moving in that direction.

I informed General Thomas of the fact, and asked leave to advance my lines; he directed me to do so; we made a charge upon the enemy and drove him into the woods, my staff and orderlies capturing some seventeen prisoners, including a captain and lieutenant, who were within a hundred and thirty yards of the batteries. This ended the fighting of that day, the enemy in immense force hovering in the woods during the night, while we slept upon our arms on the field of battle. We occupied this position during the three following days and nights of the fight. Under General Thomas's direction I had it entrenched by rifle pits and believe the enemy could not have taken it at all.

During the day the 28th brigade, Colonel Starkweather, was attacked by General Wheeler's cavalry in force, and some of the wagons of his train were burned before they reached him, having started that morning from Stewartsboro' to join him. The enemy were finally repulsed and driven off with loss. Starkweather's loss was small, as will be seen by his report of the action. In this affair the whole brigade behaved handsomely. The burden of the fight fell upon the 21st Wisconsin, Lieutenant Colonel Hobart commanding. This regiment, led by its efficient commander, behaved like veterans.

From the evening of the 31st until the ensuing Saturday night no general battle occurred in front of my division, though firing of artillery and small arms was kept up during the day and much of the time of small arms during the night. The rain on the night of the 31st, which continued, at intervals, until the Saturday night following, rendered the ground occupied by my command exceedingly sloppy and muddy, and during much of the time my men had neither shelter, food, nor fire; I procured corn, which they parched and ate, and some of them ate horse steaks, cut and broiled from horses upon the battle-field. Day and night in the cold, wet, and mud, my men suffered severely, but during the whole time I did not hear one single man murmur at the hardships, but all were cheerful and ever ready to stand by their arms and fight. Such endurance

I never saw before. In this severe trial of their patience and their strength they were much encouraged by the constant presence and solicitous anxiety of General Thomas for their welfare.

On the evening of Saturday, 3d instant, I asked permission of General Thomas to drive the enemy from a wood on our left front, to which he gave his consent. Just before night I directed the batteries of Guenther and Loomis to shell the woods with six rounds per gun, fired as rapidly as possible; this was very handsomely done, and ended just at dusk, when the 3d Ohio regiment, Lieutenant Colonel O. H. Lawson, and the 88th Indiana, Colonel George Humphreys, both under command of the brigade commander, Colonel John Beatty, moved promptly up to the woods. When near the woods they received a heavy fire from the enemy, but returned it vigorously and gallantly and pressed forward. On reaching the woods a fresh body of the enemy, attracted by the fire, moved up on their left to support them; on that body of the enemy Loomis's battery opened with shell. The fusilade was very rapid and continued for perhaps three quarters of an hour, when Beatty's command drove the enemy at the point of the bayonet, and held the woods. It turned out that the enemy was posted behind a stone breast-work in the woods, and when ousted about thirty men were taken prisoners behind the works.

This ended the battle of Murfreesboro'. On the morning of the 31st six companies of the 2d Kentucky cavalry, Major Thomas I. Nicholas commanding, were ordered down to watch and defend the fords on Stone river, to our left and rear. The cavalry of the enemy several times, in force, attempted to cross these fords, but Nicholas very gallantly repulsed them with loss, and they did not cross the river. I should have mentioned that on Friday evening, late, I was directed by General Thomas to place a regiment in the woods on our left front as an outpost, and with the view to hold these woods, as they were near our lines and the enemy could greatly annoy us if allowed to hold them. Our skirmishers were then just leaving the woods. I ordered the 42d Indiana, Lieutenant Colonel Shanklin commanding, to take that position, which he did. But early the next morning the enemy in large force attacked Colonel Shanklin, first furiously shelling the woods, and drove the regiment back to our lines, taking Shanklin prisoner.

It was this woods that was retaken on Saturday night, as before described

The troops of my division behaved admirable. I could not wish them to behave more gallantly. The 9th and 17th brigades, under the lead of their gallant commanders, Scribner and Beatty, were, as well as the 28th brigade, Colonel Starkweather, veterans; they were with me at Chaplin Hills, and could not act badly.

The 28th brigade held a position in our front after the first day's fighting and did it bravely, doing all that was required of them, like true soldiers.

The brigade of United States infantry, Lieutenant Colonel O. L. Shephard commanding, was on the extreme right. On that body of brave men the shock of battle fell heaviest, and its loss was most severe. Over one-third of the command fell killed or wounded. But it stood up to the work, and bravely breasted the storm, and, though Major King, commanding the 15th, and Major Slemmer, ("old Pickens,") the 16th, fell severely wounded, and Major Carpenter, commanding the 19th, fell dead in the last charge, together with many officers and men, the brigade did not falter for a moment.

These three battalions were a part of my old 4th brigade at the battle of Shiloh.

The 18th infantry, Majors Townsend and Caldwell commanding, were new troops to me, but I am proud now to say we know each other.

If I could, I would promote every officer, and several non-commissioned officers and privates of this brigade of regulars, for gallantry and good service in this terrific battle. I make no distinction between these troops and my brave volunteer regiments, for in my judgment there never were better troops than those regiments in the world.

But the troops of the line are soldiers by profession, and with a view to the future, I feel it my duty to say what I have of them. The brigade was admirably and gallantly handled by Lieutenant Colonel Shephard.

I lost some of the best and bravest officers I had; Lieutenant Colonel Kell, commanding the 2d Ohio, was killed. After he fell his regiment was efficiently handled by Major Anson McCook, who ought to be made colonel of that regiment for gallantry on the field.

Colonel Forman, my brave boy colonel, of the 15th Kentucky, also fell; Major Carpenter, of the 19th infantry, fell in the last charge. His loss is irreparable. Many other gallant officers were lost, whose names will appear in the list of casualties.

Of the batteries of Guenther and Loomis I cannot say too much; Loomis was chief of artillery for the 3rd division, and I am much indebted to him. His battery was commanded by Lieutenant Van Pelt; Guenther is but a lieutenant. Both of these men deserve to be promoted, and ought to be *at once.* Without them we could not have held our position in the centre.

I fell in with many gallant regiments and officers on the field of my command; I wish I could name all of them here. Whilst falling back to the line in the open field, I saw Colonel Charles Anderson gallantly and coolly rallying his men. Colonel Grider, of Kentucky, and his regiment efficiently aided in repulsing the enemy. The 18th Ohio, I think it was, though I do not know any of its officers, faced about and charged the enemy in my presence, and I went along with it. The 11th Michigan and its gallant little colonel (I do not know his name certainly, but believe it is Stodart) behaved well. And the 6th Ohio infantry, Colonel Nick Anderson, joined my command on the right of the regular brigade, and stood manfully up to the work. I fell in with the Louisville Legion in retreat, Lieutenant Colonel Berry commanding. This regiment, though retreating before an overwhelming force, was dragging by hand a section of artillery, which it had been ordered to support. A part of General McCook's wing of the army, it had fallen back with the rest, but through the woods and fields, with great difficulty, bravely brought off the cannon it could no longer defend on the field. When I met it, it faced about and formed line of battle with cheers and shouts.

To Lieutenant McDowell, my assistant adjutant general; Lieutenant Armstrong, 2d Kentucky cavalry; Lieutenant Millard, 19th United States infantry; inspector general, Captain Taylor, 15th Kentucky infantry; and Lieutenant Alf. Pirtle, ordnance officer, my regular aids, and to Captain John D. Wickliffe, and Lieutenant W. G. Jenkins, both of the 2d Kentucky cavalry, aides for that battle, I am much indebted for services on the field.

The wounded were kindly and tenderly cared for, by the 3d division medical director, Surgeon Muscroft, and the other surgeons of the command. Captain Paul, my division commissary, rendered valuable services during the whole time of the battle. The musicians of the division carried the wounded from the field faithfully and fearlessly.

Lieutenant McDowell was wounded; my orderlies, Damas, Emery, and the rest, went through the whole fight, behaving well; Emery was wounded; Lieutenant Carpenter, of the 1st Ohio infantry, one of my aides, was so badly injured by the fall of his horse that I would not permit him to go on the field; Lieutenant Hartman, of the 79th Pennsylvania infantry, a member of my staff, was ill with fever, and unable to leave his bed.

It should be mentioned that the 88th Indiana, Colonel Humphreys commanding, being placed at one of the fords on Stone river where our forces were temporarily driven back, very opportunely rallied the stragglers, and promptly crossed the river and drove the enemy back. In this he was aided by the stragglers, who rallied and fought well. The colonel was wounded by a bayonet thrust in the hand, in the attack of Saturday night on the enemy in the woods in our front.

I enclose, herewith, the report of brigade commanders, which will show the list of casualties.

I have the honor to be, &c.,

LOVELL H. ROSSEAU,
Major General.

Major GEO. E. FLYNT,
Chief of Staff (Centre) 14th Army Corps,
Department of the Cumberland.

HEADQUARTERS FIRST BRIGADE,
Murfreesboro', Tennessee, January 10, 1861.

SIR: I have the honor to report the following killed and missing of this command:

COMMISSIONED OFFICERS KILLED.

Captain James E. Fouts, thirty-eighth Indiana; Lieutenant Colonel John Kell, second Ohio; First Lieutenant R. C. Chambers, second Ohio.

COMMISSIONED OFFICERS WOUNDED.

Colonel James W. Frizell and Captain Steele, ninety-fourth Ohio; Captain Maxwell, Captain J. C. Hazlett, and First Lieutenant Van Horn, second Ohio; Second Lieutenant Milton F. Davis, Second Lieutenant Thomas S. W. Hawkins, and First Lieutenant Alexander Martin, thirty-eight Indiana; Captain J. W. Robey, tenth Wisconsin.

ENLISTED MEN KILLED.

Thirty-eighth Indiana.—William R. Smith, Henry A. Apple, and William Ellis, (corporal,) company A; Henry F. Bressie and Lyman B. Gould, company D; William Carpenter, (corporal,) company E; James Hawkins and Green W. Ellis, company I; William Bullard, (corporal,) company K; Benjamin Truax, (corporal,) company G; James H. Wells, company H.

Thirty-third Ohio.—John Vanduman and Charles Fetters, company B.

Ninety-fourth Ohio.—Jas. Lockhart and James Taylor, company G; Elijah Kemple and Thomas I. Smith, company F.

Second Ohio.—Morrill W. Anderson, Christopher Hamilton, and Calvin Winget, (corporal,) company A; Andrew J. Ward, company B; James W. Flora, George W. Hughes, Lefayette N. Hill, and William C. Goodpastine, company C; Jacob Arm and James Walker, company I.

Tenth Wisconsin.—John H. Long, company A; Irwin Clark and Michael Conolon, company D.

ENLISTED MEN WOUNDED.

Thirty-eighth Indiana.—Elijah Leonard, James Leatherman, Moses Apple, Samuel M. Granger, William G. Overman, John W. Apple, William Furguson, Alexander Buchanan, William T. Hawhee, William Lewis, Jefferson McCabe, John F. Peyton, and Samuel Holdson, (first sergeant,) company A; Charles

Banames, George Hessick, Samuel Robey, and John H. Foote, (bugler,) company B; Leander Jackson, (corporal,) John Lipe ,(corporal,) John Robinson, Albert A. Newbald, Robert Campbell, William Johnson, and Henry Stoneman, company C; Peter S. Dobbins, (sergeant,) James F. Manley, (corporal,) James B. McLane, (corporal,) Peter Wolfe, Absolem Williams, and John Fitzgerald, company D; Benjamin F. Goodman, (corporal,) George W. White, and William F. Boldt, company E; George Apperson, John Butorf, Francis M. James, Marcelus B. Jenkins, Christopher Staffinger, Alfred H. Young, John T. Baugh, Henry Briggs, David M. Cole, Henry Frank, James Hartman, Thomas Kelly, John Overman, and John Rouf, company F; William I. Jackson, James Masier, James T. Rumple, John Carlton, Hosea A. Carlton, Robert Smith, James A. Smith, Jonathan Mesle, and Samuel McCormick, company G; Samuel F. Smith, (corporal,) Alexander Buchanan, Thomas J. Gray, James W. Rogers, John J. Tandy, and Robert Duncan, company H; Henry T. Henson, Lewis Cullins, Henry Hammond, Jos. Moore, George Hazlewood, Abel A. Jackman, (sergeant,) Benjamin Webb, (sergeant,) and Ernest Sleischer, (corporal,) company I; James H. Seyton, (sergeant,) Walter L. Lacat, (sergeant,) Abraham Kemp, (corporal,) Hiram Brewer, (corporal,) David Jones, Wm. Rigglee, David Allen, Chris. Kanarian, John Suell, and Pat. Cunningham, company K.

Second Ohio.—William P. Long, (corporal,) company A; William Jackson, company B; Amos Huffman, W. S. Henry, G. W. Myers, and W. Gaskill, company C; A. W. Henry, (sergeant,) A. Smith, J. Simpson, J. Clifford, J. Doyle, and M. Galiver, company D; J. L. Bahill, (corporal,) Theodore Ross, Richard Duncan, and John M. Guy, company F; William Dunn, Walter Nichols, Elijah Matlock, and John M. Lees, company G; William Dougherty, (sergeant,) company H; Newton Frintz, Henry Dunham, and W. Congrave, company I; James Phillips, (sergeant,) Isaac Morrison, (corporal,) and George Lourie, company K.

Thirty-third Ohio.—Samuel Baxby, (corporal,) John Derush, (corporal,) Cornelius Canter, Cyrus Dixon, John Hogan, A. J. Orin, John Porter, Jos. L. Rogers, and Samuel White, company A; James Severs, Samuel Pullin, and William Howell, company B; William A. Long and George Barteon, company C; Moses Tidd, company E; John Thurman, company F; Samuel Purdam, (corporal,) Samuel Dolten, and Jas. Browning, company G.

Ninety-fourth Ohio.—A. Clase, (corporal,) J. H. Seidenstick, A. H. Haines, and Daniel Jenkins, company A; George S. Dallinger, (corporal,) John Grim, and John Bronton, company B; B. C. Mitchell, (first sergeant,) John Roberts, and Emery Chambers, company C; Eli H. Fenton and Henry Hughes, company D; Hiram McClure and I. F. Reese, company F; S. D. Taylor, (corporal,) Thomas Homer, and Fluvius Tovender, company G; Jacob Arm, George Detro, (corporal,) Josiah Reed, (corporal,) James Etter, and James Faley, company I; J. R. Martin, (sergeant,) and T. B. White, company K; Lewis Cottrell, company E.

Tenth Wisconsin.—Thomas H. Morrison, company A; Rufus Cowles and Tilson Covison, company B; Martin D. Jenkins, (sergeant,) and Bela S. Bishop, company C; George Dewey, company D; Rueben T. Crosby, company F; Edward O'Flaherty, Casper Watcher, and George Lane, company G; Augustus H. McKimpson, (sergeant,) and James McGinnis, company H; Washburn Blatchley, Andrew Show, and William S. Holdridge, company K.

ENLISTED MEN MISSING.

Thirty-third Ohio.—James Lewis, company B; Thomas Hale and Jacob Bettis, company F; Jos. Jett, company G.

Second Ohio.—Jos. Ashmore, company B; John Wiggins and Samuel T.

Cross, company E; John V. Brown, company G; Jos. Wellington, company H; John Barinford and John Call, company K.

Ninety-fourth Ohio.—G. G. Guy, Abraham Kauffman, J. A. Shuman, and Malcolm Young, company A; W. H. Johnston and Albert Harner, company C; D. A. Swaggart, (sergeant,) Jas. Miller, (corporal,) T. A. Kemph, (corporal,) Isaac Corer, C. C. Guy, John Eckert, John H. Yoe, W. H. Martin, Martin Sesler, J. H. Townsed, J. R. P. Weaver, Lovenius Wilson, I. H. Wikel, T. C. Dunn, and Mike Clohessey, company E; Jas. Harinsh, company G; N. M. Browder, Titus Dove, A. G. Marshal, William Carter, S. D. Heck, J. B. Heck, and Buelis Binkley, company K.

Tenth Wisconsin.—Cornelius Barbee and De Witt Griffin, company A; Byron P. Tafft, company F; Benjamin Hulett, (corporal,) company G; Henry Banks, (corporal,) and Jos. Collimer, (corporal,) company H.

Thirty-eighth Indiana.—Enoch Seyton, company K.

SUMMARY.

Commissioned officers killed	9
Commissioned officers wounded	9
Enlisted men killed	30
Enlisted men wounded	167
Enlisted men missing	51
Wounded and missing	1
Total loss	261

B. F. SCRIBNER,
Colonel 38th Indiana Volunteers,
Commanding 1st Brigade, 1st Division, (Centre) 14th Army Corps.

Captain M. C. TAYLOR, *A. A. A. G.*

Report of killed, wounded, and missing in second brigade, first division, (centre) fourteenth army corps, department of the Cumberland, during the three days, engagement before Murfreesboro', Tennessee.

OFFICERS, NON-COMMISSIONED OFFICERS, AND MEN KILLED.

Third Ohio volunteer infantry.—George M. McIlvane, (sergeant,) and Henry K. Bennett, company A; James E. Suttles, company B; J. D. Figley, company C; Mahlon Neer, John W. Baker, and Charles Winegand, company D; William McEater, (sergeant,) and Frank Burley, company F; John B. Nailor and Henry Peckmeyerr, company G; Richard Hughes, (corporal,) company H; John Motram, Levi H. Courtwright, and James W. Wright, company I; Chas. A. McDonald, company K.

Fifteenth Kentucky volunteer infantry.—J. B. Freeman, (colonel;) A. S. Bayne, (captain;) R. M. Robb, (sergeant,) John B. Carico, Michael O'Leary, and William P. Sanders, company A; W. M. Stevens, company B; J. W. Holack, company F; Edward Boyle, company G; Bernhard Wiber, company I.

Forty-second Indiana volunteers.—Chancy Goldsmith, (sergeant,) and Henry P. Stone, company A; William C. Sukman, company B; W. H. Shuller, (sergeant,) and James E. Hammond, company C; James Hamilton, company D; John Nixon, (corporal,) company E; Jos. Guest, Jas. H. McGregory, D. Kruse, and A. H. Steel, company F; Herbert Pride and Terry Trayler, company G; Austin Bolin, company I; Warrick H. Clifford and Rinaldo Edward, company K.

Eighty-eighth Indiana volunteers.—Henry Collins, company B; William S. Jones, (sergeant,) company C; Elias M. Scott, company F; John Hull, (corporal,) and Ira Pryor, company H; Reuben Barnes and Jacob Boyer, company K; Mark Frakes, company I.

First Michigan artillery.—Jared Nichols, company A.

WOUNDED.

Third Ohio volunteer infantry.—John Conway, (corporal,) William Wortz, John Percella, Samuel A. Frazier, (corporal,) James B. Duden, (corporal,) Geo. Cobb, Francis Meechum, Charles T. Palmer, and Benjamin F. Strahl, company A; Samuel L. French, (sergeant,) R. J. Dennis, (corporal,) William H. Barnes, Charles B. Case, Owen E. Moore, and M. Wolf, company B; Henry Saunderson, (sergeant,) D. Walker, (sergeant,) W. H. Cook, W. C. Light, John Mann, J. J. Shinn, H. Morrison, J. Woodyard, A. Wharff, A. Scott, G. A. Richie, and B. O. Coussins, company C; Aaron Herr, (corporal,) Rufus H. Smith, and Alonzo S. Ruddle, company D; William O. Murison, (corporal,) R. F. Singleton, George P. Filcher, Noah Spring, and John W. Tignor, company E; John W. Loring, (corporal,) Jerome Gilbraith, James Torbet, Henry Smith, John Reed, and Jacob Bowers, company F; Henry Bender, (sergeant,) H. Baney, William Chase, and E. English, company G; Captain L. S. Bell, Geo. A. Ball, (corporal,) William S. Wirrick, Albert Asher, Thomas Dewar, William Boodle, and Nathan Jewett, company H; Ellis C. Nichols, (sergeant,) Robert Glenn, Chas. Wood, Wendell Willetts, Jonathan S. Benedict, Jasper Munn, and John B. Casey, company I; George B. Cooper, (sergeant,) W. J. Hurst, (sergeant,) —— McGivigen, (corporal,) S. O. Harra, J. M. Patterson, J. Jeffries, and J. Barcus, company K.

Fifteenth Kentucky.—W. H. Hall, (corporal,) George W. Fields, James Douglas, company A; William McCook, (sergeant,) William A. Richardson, (corporal,) John M. Whortenbery, John Cogwell, Joshua F. Morrow, company B; L. F. Todd, (first lieutenant,) Isaac F. Chamber, (sergeant) George Ford, James Dever, Thomas Dever, company C; James Rostetter, company D; John Lausman, Fred. Plump, John Patterson, Hiram Potts, P. Olds, William Malott, company E; Milton Davis, John C. Skinner, W. Y. Thompson, John Daley, company F; William Hefford, (sergeant,) John Randall, company H; Constantine Shultz, (sergeant,) Frank Closen, (corporal,) Michael Grand, Philip Hoffman, Bernard Hineman, company I; Charles Harrington, company K.

Forty-second Indiana.—Nathaniel Mathany, (sergeant,) Nathaniel Black, John Findle, William Schroder, William Carter, company A; John Bossee, Jos. Cox, (sergeant,) John Kelley, company B; B. C. Grigsby, (sergeant,) W. B. Whitney, (sergeant,) A. Baum, (corporal,) John Linsey, James Lancer, Roger Barber, D. C. Gillum, company C; John Eigenman, (captain,) William H. Garrison, (corporal,) D. T. Tennyson, M. Foley, Thomas Galley, company D; J. R. Ashmeade, (second lieutenant,) John W. Smith, (corporal,) J. S. Stubblefield, (sergeant major) Elijah Smith, Jos. Malone, Thomas J. Ward, Solana Hutchison, Eph. Rutledge, company E; H. C. Gillum, H. J. Kistner, James W. McCleary, John H. Martin, R. M. Martin, Asa Mason, Wm. Mason, Elias Skelton, John P. Simpson, James H. Simpson, William A. Reeves, Wm. M. Cockrum, (captain,) J, Q. A. Steele, (first lieutenant,) J. C. White, (second lieutenant,) James W. Harper, (sergeant,) Charles Ohning, (corporal,) Beach Compton, company F; M. Austin, William D. Burras, N. F. Carroll, John W. Ellis, Charles McCracken, M. D. Hisely, Willis E. Wallace, N. F. Wallace, James P. Wallace, Richard McGahee, (corporal,) company G; George R. Goodwin, James Tumbleton, Peter Doering, Ezekiel Beard, company H; Nathaniel Pierce, (sergeant,) A. N. Thomas, (corporal,) P. W. Chepel, Calvin Coe, James Cutright, G. Meade, Mideon Chrisistison, Samuel Garland, Levi Hale, John

Sichlyter, James Penner, Jasper M. Martin, (corporal,) Alvis Ashley, (corporal,) John Coleman, Miles Mathews, Frank Ross, George Thompson, Pleasant Shephard, S. F. Tyner, company I; E. M. Knoles, (lieutenant,) F. M. Nuves, (sergeant,) company K.

Eighty-eighth Indiana.—George Humphreys, (colonel;) Isaiah Binghan, (corporal,) George J. Link, John N. Zimmerman, William Krontz, company A; Andrew J. Linn, (sergeant,) Henry P. Smith, (sergeant,) Moses Kiser, (corporal,) John Kruhan, (corporal,) James Douglass, company B; Dorsey Scudder, (corporal,) John S. Lepper, Henry Deffenderfer, Edward Wilson, Marion E. Griswold, Hiram W. Thomas, (color sergeant,) Joshua Sweet, John Bishop, E. Birk, company C; Josephus Marsh, C. Parker, Albert Snyder, Isaac Nesbit, Edward Johnson, Washington Perkins, M. Browand, Jos. D. Stoper, (lieutenant,) company D; Mahlon Sipe, Joseph G. Gohen, Robert K. Brown, Samuel H. Smith, Enos Reed, company E; W. N. Nutt, John H. Fergisun, Martin Boggs, company F; James Patterson, company G; Philander Smith, (lieutenant,) William A. Rix, (sergeant,) F. B. Thomas, (corporal,) M. Johnson, Samuel R. Stanfer, company H; John Middleton, Asoph S. Prescott, Henry S. Schraeder, Jonathan Kellett, Charles W. Evans, (corporal,) William Boyd, David J. Bowman, James Walker, Israel Thompson, Moses F. Ward, company I.

First Michigan Artillery.—Henry M. Woorrington, (quartermaster sergeant,) Marcus A. Gague, (corporal,) Lineas H. Stephens, Charles E. Hastings, Asa B. Cornell, Martin Kelly, John E. Ellsworth, John H. Dillon, Henry C. Heartwell, Fred. Upton, company A.

OFFICERS, NON-COMMISSIONED OFFICERS, AND ENLISTED MEN MISSING.

Third Ohio volunteers.—Silas Welsh, Erasmus Welsh, and Walter Vandine, company A; William H. McCartney and Henry Ramer, company B; I. C. Coleman and D. Light, company C; William Runyan and William H. Vananda, company D; Jacob Young, William Piers, William Mussleman, Levi W. Ewing, and R. S. Ewing, company E; H. E. Miller, company G; John Smith, company H; Geo. Early, (sergeant,) Frederick A. Miller, Melville Maxwell, Jno. Miller, Smith Oliver, and Frank Doty, company I; Edward McGafee, company K.

Fifteenth Kentucky volunteers.—C. S. Duvall and John A. Tucker, company A; James W. Gray, (1st lieutenant,) company B; George Clark, Seth Duncan, John Lafollet, and William Crady, company C; James Collier, John Hornback, and Frederick Walter, company D; W. A. Phelps, (sergeant,) F. A. Dougherty, James Hite, and E. J. Jackson, (corporal,) company F; George Mueler, (corporal,) Frederick Andre, and D. Merkee, company I.

Indiana volunteers.—Daniel Watson, Richard Nash, John Allbacker, Thomas Dennison, and Granville Witherspoon, (corporal,) company A; Elijah Kinkaid, company B; J. L. Phelleps, F. M. Brady, (corporal,) J. W. Carpenter, and William Bentle, (musician,) company C; John Scammerhorn, (lieutenant,) John Ireton, and Joseph Hust, company D; James C. Kain, (sergeant,) W. H. McCleary, (corporal,) and D. Mason, company F; Smith Newson, (sergeant,) John Daley, (musician,) and Ephraim Smith, company E; William Pride, and William A. Myers, (corporal,) company G; Joseph Pheffer, W. Niblack, (musician,) and James W. Bolin, company H; W. C. Stevenson, (musician,) John W. Hines, Joseph H. Denton, Thomas H. English, James H. Hughes, and James F. Jones, company I; Willis Brown, Amos Parker, William A. Keith, and James M. Shanklin, (lieutenant colonel,) company K.

Eighty-eighth Indiana volunteers.—Henry Albert and William Pearson, Aaron Woolestern, (sergeant,) Joseph M. Henderson, and John Webb, company D; Charles Wiebke, Robert Lanoning, and Jabez Bonze, company F; William A. Goorich, Cyrus Forken, Jonathan Cummings, and Ira M. Woodyard (corporal,) company G; Edwin Smurr, (musician,) company H; Smith Barclay, George Fowler, James W. Hasell, and Jno. B. Celford, company I; Daniel Doney, company K.

1*st Michigan Artillery.*—Sylvester T. Dwight, and Jerona C. Mathers, company A.

	Killed.			Wounded.			Missing.			Total.
	Commissioned officers.	Enlisted men.	Total.	Commissioned officers.	Enlisted men.	Total.	Commissioned officers.	Enlisted men.	Total.	Killed, wounded and missing.
Third Ohio volunteer infantry............	...	17	17	1	65	66	...	23	23	106
Fifteenth Kentucky volunteer infantry....	2	8	10	1	31	32	1	17	18	60
Forty-second Indiana volunteer infantry....	...	17	17	6	75	81	2	32	34	132
Eighty-eighth Indiana volunteer infantry ...	...	8	8	4	47	51	...	19	19	78
First Michigan battery,	...	1	...	...	10	10	...	2	2	13
Total............	2	51	53	12	228	240	3	93	96	389

JOHN BEATTY,
Colonel 3d Ohio, commanding Second Brigade, First Division.

James S. Wilson,
First Lieutenant Third Ohio, and A. A. A. G.

List of casualties of 28th brigade in the engagement before Murfresboro', Tennessee, January 1st, 2d, and 3d, 1863.

OFFICERS, NON-COMMISSIONED OFFICERS, AND MEN KILLED.

79*th Pennsylvania regiment.*—Abram Strong, company A; Mark Ert, company G.

24*th Illinois regiment.*—C. Lage, company D.

OFFICERS, NON-COMMISSIONED OFFICERS, AND ENLISTED MEN WOUNDED.

79*th Pennsylvania regiment.*—Sergeant J. H. Friddy, company E; Henry Koch, company F; Elias Hollinger, Isaac A. Genkley, and Samuel Picke, company G; W. K. Palton, company H.

24*th Illinois regiment.*—Jacob Hartman, company B; George Krumm, company D; Charles Scuttler, company G.

1*st Wisconsin regiment.*—Corporal Andrew Bunteen, company A; Bartese Demond, company B; Captain D. C. McVean, company E; Azaira Bundy, company G.

1*st Kentucky battery.*—Patrick Carran.

MISSING IN THE 28TH BRIGADE.

79th Pennsylvania regiment.—None.

24th Illinois regiment.—Principle Musician Theo. Louner.

1st Wisconsin regiment.—Hospital Steward J. R. McCullough; Thomas Morgan and William Huyck, company H.

RECAPITULATION.

79th Pennsylvania regiment.—Killed, 2; wounded, 8. Total, 10.

24th Illinois regiment.—Killed, 1; wounded, 3; missing, 1. Total, 5.

1st Wisconsin regiment.—Killed, 0; wounded, 4; missing, 3. Total, 7.

1st Kentucky battery.—Wounded, 1. Total, 1.

Total killed, wounded, and missing, 23.

H. A. HAMBRIGHT,
Colonel 79th Pennsylvania Commanding.

C. A. SEARLES, *Lieutenant and A. A. A. G.*

Report of killed, wounded and missing in 4th brigade, 1st division, (centre) 4th Army Corps, department of the Cumberland, during the three days' engagement before Murfreesboro', Tennessee.

OFFICERS, NON-COMMISSIONED OFFICERS, AND MEN KILLED.

15th United States infantry.—Edward Quinn, (sergeant,) William B. McCall, and M. Van Suttle, company A; William W. Wise, (captain,) and William Kapple, company C; J. B. Bell, (captain,) and Isaac Detweler, company D; Sutton B. Quinn, and Gustavus Garie, company E; Chester Brown, Jacob Hexamer, John Gessinger, and Benjamin Giph, company H.

16th United States infantry—N. Hindelong, James Lewis, and Dennis Sullivan, company A; Nathan Frost, Nicholas Ginsbach, Zach. White, Lemuel K. Palmer, Aaron Simmons, Hastner, (corporal,) Duddy, and Bowers, company B; Frank Clark, company C; Ferd. Ferguson, company D; Robert Robinson, (corporal,) and J. Williams, company F; George L. Povler, and George H. Patterson, company G; Charles Alletzon, (corporal,) Thomas Burns, Erastus Chedle, and Harrison Stockdale, company H.

18th United States infantry.—James Harrison, Nicholas Holabach, B. W. Wilcox, (corporal,) James Adair, James A. Anderson, James S. Fisher, David Dedmon, Amos Sherman, John F. Pierce, and Gordon Beard, company A; Nathan Ray, John Fusselman, William Patterson, Charles Argus, Francis Masterton, J. L. Hitchcock, (lieutenant,) J. Limbaugh, (corporal,) J. R. Leibole, (corporal,) M. Gallivan, George Shuler, and Abram Coombs, company B; Charles L. Kneass, (captain,) F. M. Phillipi, (corporal,) Thomas J. Long, (corporal,) J. H. Tuman, William Cornwall, George Eckhert, Isaac B. Jones, Frank Kelly, and George B. Smith, company C; Hugh Scolan, Samuel Palmer, Elisha Harper, V. Ferrenkoaf, Peter Murphy, Joseph Wasmer, Arthur D. Cantrill, and Jere Howard, company D; William Baglin, Samuel Daihl, Jos. Elsbech, William Ernis, M. Khapsbock, Alfred M. Ginnis, Amos Robins, and T. F. Armstrong, company E; Henry Headley, (sergeant,) Jacob Bike, George F. White, (first sergeant,) Samuel Dobbins, (first sergeant,) William D. Madeira, (first sergeant,) John J. Carman, Mahlon Hancock, William H. Himes, (corporal), company F; S. D. Carpenter, (major;) J. L. Harcourt, (corporal,) James O'Neill, Martin Swang, and Charles Schreck, company G; James F.

Mohr, M. McGrath, Jacob Blessing, Henry B. Plumley, Patrick Sarage, and Elias White, company H.

Nineteenth United States infantry.—John Quinn and Aaron Lather, company A; S. C. Higgins, company D; John Bayer, company E; B. Haggerty and Edward Gorman, company F.

WOUNDED.

Fifteenth United States infantry.—Pat. Kane, (sergeant,) A. K. McFaden, (corporal,) David S. Flynn, Fidel Keisler, Jesse Gwynn, Frank Maguire, Eugene A. Ogden, George Sagers, Michael Moran, Alfred H. Masters, and Thomas Kelly, company A; James Acker, Robert Adams, Patrick Daily, Samuel Finley, Henry Holtkoff, Joseph Loose, James McGuire, David R. Spenser, and George A. N. Wray, company B; O'Rourke, (sergeant,) Morrett, (sergeant,) Underwood, (corporal,) Findley, Mauck, Strauss, Schieickert, and Astomyer, company C; J. Loomison, (sergeant,) William Thorp, (corporal,) Daniel Henderson, (corporal,) Alfred Benton, James M. Williams, Charles M. Umbaugh, Noah Statler, John C. Roney, H. W. C. Roney, Jesse Spoucilor, Abram M. Mills, and Hiram Conner, company D; James P. Brown, (1st sergeant,) David E. Scholas, George Parker, Peter Cillouly, John A. Osterle, John Imkof, Robert Raisin, Gottleib Nukom, Nathan Rix, John Sifers, G. Washington Foor, and Orson W. Beebe, company E; Huyck, (sergeant,) Moll, (sergeant,) Kanable, (sergeant,) Mantle, (corporal,) Gibson, (corporal,) Davis, Ketcher, and Schrock, company F; Joseph S. York, (captain,) H. S. Lovejoy, (sergeant,) Ezra Gilbert, David Lose, Sam'l J. Landis, and Alfred Slusser, company G; W. B. Occleston, (1st lieutenant,) W. W. Blair, (sergeant,) Henry Chapman, Robert Howell, Charles Sutter, George Snyder, Alexander Ramsay, Thomas Prestley, and John H. King, (major,) company H.

MISSING.

J. H. Lemon, Francis Bruce, Kernan, company A; Myron Parks, Corporal McRussell, Bruce, and O'Flaherty, company B; Lewis, Hardy, Dorr, McKinney, Carrigan, and Loth, company C; Benjamin Closson, company D; D. Pontrois, company E; Kennedy and Miller, company F; T. S. Dunning, H. R. Moore, M. Fressel, and C. P. Van Duyn, company G; A. Frandensteine, company H.

WOUNDED.

Sixteenth United States infantry.—Major A. J. Slemmer, Robert P. Barry, (captain,) John C. King, (captain,) N. L Dykeman, (captain,) W. H. Bartholomew, (first lieutenant,) John Power, (first lieutenant and adjutant,) James C. Howland, (first lieutenant,) James H. Howe, (commissary sergeant,) F. J. Pattee, (sergeant,) G. McNeil, (sergeant,) W. G. Scott, (sergeant,) Privates Gillick, Dolan, Hilton, Hogan, Dundon, Adams, Spice, Nelson, Kane, Dorsey, Kelly, Devine, Larcombe, Hutchinson, Fretterstrom, Donohue, McQuaid, Kinney, Nolan, McCaughey, and Fahy, company A; J. Buckner, (sergeant,) M. Whalen, (sergeant,) Hamilton, (sergeant,) Greenhalgh, (corporal,) Privates Lade, Leslie, Love, Griffin, Golton, Gilhoed, Kottinger, O'Neill, Stone, Wagner, Rahaley, Kirkpatrick, Miller, Harper, Daney, Dorcey, Crabbee, Anderson, B. Olson, J. Olson, Ranson, Smith, Strater, Frindle, Page, McWilliams, and Hilton, company B; M. Thomas, (sergeant,) Privates Owens, Batten, Black, and Healy, company C; W. Wagner, (sergeant,) Privates Brotz, Conway, Harley, Meiner, Mead, Roach, Russell, Nix, Wrightman, Wrightman, and Mesmer, company D; Privates F. O'Neil, Burton, Growney, Kavanaugh, Kinston, Jones, McMahon, Shannon, Straw, Venters, Wielie, and Wescott, company E;

Judson, (sergeant,) Derwin, (corporal,) Kinkaid, (corporal,) Vigor, (corporal,) Privates Bengan, Boyle, Crotine, Garvey, Halihan, Knutson, Livingston, Lathrope, McCarthy, Minnihan, McLane, Sykes, Trueblood, and Taylor, company F; Charles Perkins, (sergeant,) Privates Gillepsie, Heney, Donelly, Wirt, and Weld, company G; H. H. Edson, (sergeant,) Seth Martin, (sergeant,) Thomas Donohue, (corporal,) N. W. Reese, (corporal.) H. B. Hastings, (corporal,) Privates Boyce, Dubi, Grey, Keith, Smith, Thompson, Gallagher, Nordham, Caldwell, and Brainard, company H.

MISSING.

Canfield, company B; Carroll, O'Neill, Sympson, and Scott, company E; Finnigan, company G; Kelly, Sawyer, and Padden, company H.

WOUNDED.

Eighteenth United States infantry.—Henry Douglass, (captain,) J. M. McConnell, (first lieutenant,) G. S. Carpenter, (second lieutenant,) Samuel Gorsuch, (corporal,) Privates William Larrowe, Ebenezer Myers, George Moore, George A. Medick, William H. Peckham, Henry Strufelt, Henry D. Smith, Frederick Seigle, J. J. Brown, S. A. Rose, W. H. Maxwell, P. McDonald, A. Courtwright, P. Brown, J. A. Shepard, O. Rhoads, T. L. Swank, H. F. Helpman, William Marshall, J. W. McBride, A. D. Tagg, J. Micklejohn, Z. Durham, (sergeant,) J. Matthew, (sergeant,) George F. Fass, (corporal,) P. Birk, and J. H. Dodds, company A; Jos. Owens, (sergeant,) F. M. Davis, (corporal,) Privates William Barker, William Frizzell, Patrick Daily, M. Schwartz, (sergeant,) Richard Fitzgerald, R. C. Hardwick, M. Kuntz, Edward Pepper, J. B. Shaffer, M. Welsh, C. L. Denison, (captain,) William P. Seibole, (sergeant,) T. P. Hanly, M. Maly, R. S. Carrady, P. Mangan, J. Linamant, E. Coen, M. H. V. Young, William R. Wallace, E. S. Johns, J. C. Baker, J. Jackson, Isaac James, and J. McKenzie, company B; Amos Flegal, S. S. Bartlett, H. Bemesdafer, S. A. Bowman, William M. Morgaridge, J. Wedrow, James Place, William M. Wallace, (sergeant,) J. Burns, (corporal,) William H. Diehl, A. J. Conner, J. T. Haurice, J. McD. Haurice, J. Hoffler, F. Kersteller, G. McCarty, F. M. Orth, H. M. Riddle, T. Sigman, J. Campbell, and J. Sweagan, company C; D. L. Wood, (captain,) D. M. Hannahs, (corporal,) Privates George Meyers, William H. Thomas, O. M. Wescott, Patrick Barrett, J. P. Ell, (sergeant,) M. Peters, (sergeant,) J. Falter, (corporal,) William Plum, G. W. Stierhoff, M. E. Williamson, H. Boulter, J. Clark, S. Fetters, J. Converse, J. Horner, M. L. Ogden, (first lieutenant,) S. C. Williamson, (sergeant,) John Argo, George Brooks, L. Goble, T. Hogan, D. Laken, J. O'Connor, and M. Strassel, company D; M. E. Looker, (first sergeant,) Jesse Brooks, (corporal,) F. Edwards, T. H. Hickman, Samuel Hill, Isaac Wilson, George Shaferberger, Hi. Rolinhood, John Hamilton, Levi Greenwood, Jacob Hilgert, A. B. Thompson, (captain,) J. Dares, (sergeant,) J. H. Foakes, (corporal,) C. Beardsley, William Grey, J. A. Hartman, L. McInverney, M. B. Shirk, G. H. Smith, William Viller, D. C. Weaver, M. B. Rhoads, T. Barr, (sergeant,) J. McCormick, P. Fennel, P. Killeen, T. B. Daniels, and George W. Caty, company E; D. S. Wilder, (sergeant,) C. W. Bell, (corporal,) M. Bolan, T. H. Clark, J. S. Headington, I. N. Howard, F. Kerchner, D. Kring, William E. McCauley, J. S. Risher, Alexander White, J. Simons, (first lieutenant,) Daniel Baker, Andrews Bowers, D. Devine, J. Handelley, (died in hospital,) R. J. Jones, (died in hospital,) John C. Jones, D. M. Price, G. Waterfield, D. S. Kissen, D. S. Todd, (sergeant,) William H. Hines, (corporal,) since dead; C. Miller, (corporal.) A. F. Young, (corporal,) J. Coleman, E. Cunningham, M. McCuaig, J. W. Parsons, J. M. Saxton, J. S. Shaffner, F. Stonefer, G. H. Taylor, and J. Wilson, company F; R. B. Hall, (captain,) J. J. Adair, (quartermaster's sergeant,) J. F. Weiler, (sergeant,) J. C. Smith, (sergeant,) Privates T. Nasey, M. Frank, H. Davy, J. Shutt, J. Lesley, J. Dixon, A. Welty, A. Kelley, N. Thorp, J. Baughman, W. T. Grimer, and M. Cackler, company G; R. Horton, (first sergeant,) Privates B. Brink, A. Higgins, T. Luther, Patrick Hoare, C. Schrauck, George Brown, J. Endrass, H. Douglass, N. Haos, D. Hackney, D. W. Jones, John Harris, J. Jackbolle, J. Moriarty, J. S. McClintock, G. H. Owen, G. Rose, T. Schultz, F. Seibt, and George W. Stone, company H.

MISSING.

E. C. Beach, (sergeant,) Private Riefenberg, company A; A. R. Brownig, company C; M. Kacer and Benjamin Lawhead, company E; I. C. Colby and John Priest, company F.

WOUNDED.

Nineteenth United States infantry.—Privates William Beam, Eli Wells, and William Schultz, company A; W. H. Harrison, (first sergeant,) John H. Topky, (corporal,) Privates T. Brennon, Patrick Cain, J. C. Cope, William H. Fallen, William Figg, E. Herrington, F. Lamsham, G. W. Lawson, and Patrick Lynch, company B; H. B. Shaffer, (sergeant,) J. Shrot, (corporal,) B. Davis, (corporal,) Privates E. Bennett, J. Crosby, George Emigh, I. Griffith, I. L. B. Harnden, C. Hunt, S. Imay, and A. Snyder, company C; Charles Stears, (sergeant,) Privates W. D. Dewey, S. Gause, H. Hook, C. Kronman, F. T. Shore, A. Smith, and T. E. Fall, company D; W. H. Hoover, (sergeant,) T. J. Smith, (corporal,) J. Hester, (corporal,) Privates C. Adams, J. E. Brown, J. M. Doran, J. Dunlewy, D. Gilford, J. A. Harvey, H. T. Tibbitt, and P. Tatem, company E; W. H. Williams, (sergeant,) J. A. Little, (sergeant,) Privates J. Powers, L. Hipp, and J. B. Cockefair, company G.

Fifth United States battery.—B. F. Burgess, company H.

MISSING.

James Kelley, company A; John Neckl, company B; John Reese, company C; H. Robinson, company D; W. D. Bennett, Edward Haggey, J. Sallet, J. B. Smith, and E. T. Swamk, company E; William O. Randall, D. W. Pollock, and I. A. McClain, company F.

The report of each battalion being signed properly by the commandants.

HEADQUARTERS 2D KENTUCKY CAVALRY,
Murfreesboro', January 10, 1863.

SIR: The following is a correct list of the killed, wounded, and missing from our regiment during the three days' engagement before Murfreesboro.

Thomas Hall, (sergeant,) and Private James Saunders, company A; Benjamin F. Surley, (corporal,) company D; Samuel McGowan, (corporal,) company H.

Very respectfully, your obedient servant,

JOHN E. STILWELL, *Adjutant.*

Captain M. C. TAYLOR.

CAMP OF THIRD DIVISION, FOURTEENTH CORPS,
Near Murfreesboro', Tenn., January 9, 1863.

SIR: I have the honor to make the following report of the part taken by the batteries of artillery of this division in the battle of "Stone river," and the events during the march from Mill Creek, December 26, 1862, and after the battle up to January 6, 1863.

The batteries marched with the several brigades on the morning of December 26 in the following order: Houghtaling's battery, with Colonel Roberts's brigade on the Nolensville pike; Hescock's battery, with General Sill's brigade, on the road to the left of the pike *via* Patterson's Mill; Bush's battery, with Schæffer's brigade, on the Nolensville pike, in reserve. Nothing was done this day by the artillery. Encamped about one mile from Nolensville. On the 27th marched at dawn of day towards Triune, formed line of battle with expectation of an engagement, the men and horses suffering very much on account of the heavy rains for the last few days and deep mud. Did not move on the 28th. Spent the day preparing the batteries for battle.

Marched on the 29th on the Bully Jack road towards Murfreesboro'. Saw but little of the enemy—no fighting. Encamped near Wilkinson's Crossroads, about seven miles from Murfreesboro'. Marched on the morning of the 30th, at seven o'clock a. m. Found the enemy strongly posted in our front, about three miles from Murfreesboro'.

The batteries having been assigned to brigades as follows: Hescock's battery to Schæffer's brigade; Houghtaling's battery to Colonel Roberts's brigade; and Bush's battery to General Sill's brigade, took post with their brigades—Houghtaling's on the right of the Wilkinson pike; Bush's on the right of Houghtaling's; Hescock's on the right and rear; all supported by their respective brigades. But little firing was done during the forenoon. In the afternoon Bush moved with his battery to the front and opened on the enemy at short range. Hescock took the position left by Bush, all three batteries concentrating their fire on the points of timber in front, shelling the enemy's battery and driving back his skirmishers. The casualties were confined to Bush's battery, he having lost four enlisted men and several horses. His battery was placed in an exposed position and nobly did their duty.

During the night Bush moved his battery to a more commanding position; the other batteries remained on the hill facing the enemy.

The events of the 31st relative to the batteries of this division are difficult to detail, but may be made intelligible to any one conversant with the ground or taking any part in the action. The battle opened in the division by an attempt to capture Bush's battery. It was gallantly defended by General Sill until his brigade was completely turned. The brave general fell dead between the guns. The battery then fell back to the position occupied by the other batteries of the division. In the mean time Houghtaling's and the Missouri batteries were firing into the enemy's ranks and batteries that were engaging. General Sill and General Davis continued to do fearful execution among them until the enemy who were pursuing General Johnson's surprised and defeated division gained the rear of the division, when all the batteries moved to the front to the position just held by the enemy, and from which the division had driven him.

Houghtaling advanced first and took position on the right of the pike, (south side,) just in the edge of the timber, supported by Colonel Roberts's brigade, where he remained until his last horse was killed or wounded, and his last round of ammunition expended, and the enemy demanding of his men to surrender. He was forced to abandon his battery, after a gallant fight for a most important position. His loss will be found in his statements already submitted to you.

Bush took position on the north side of the pike, doing his duty bravely; the Missouri battery also on the north side of the pike. These two batteries were exposed to a fire of artillery from their front and rear, and of sharpshooters on their flank.

Captain Bush re-enforced Captain Houghtaling with one section of his battery, under First Lieutenant D. Flansbourg. Captain Hescock also sent his Parrott section, under First Lieutenant R. C. W. Taliaferro. Lieutenant Taliaferro fell dead fighting bravely his guns, being shot through the head. The two batteries on the north side of the pike engaged the enemy in front and rear until their ammunition was expended, when they retired through the cedar woods with the division. Captain Bush was compelled to abandon two of his guns in the dense cedar trees for the lack of horses, the enemy charging his cannoneers. After gaining the open ground three guns of the Missouri battery were brought into action and fired on the enemy what little ammunition remained, until ordered to retire and replenish. Thus ended the operations of the 31st.

The batteries took a position, by order of General Sheridan, with the division on the south of the Nashville and Murfreesboro' pike, about three o'clock a. m., January 1, 1863, where they remained until January 6, 1863. Nothing of note occurring, except on the first, when a brigade of the enemy appeared in our front and was handsomely repulsed in five minutes, leaving forty of his dead.

The loss of guns, &c., in the division I believe to have been unavoidable, and necessary to the successful resistance of the enemy's attack, which was made in heavy masses, and I do not think the officers can be blamed, as they could not do otherwise without most disastrous results to the army.

The loss of the batteries was severe, but they are in good discipline and ready for service.

I have the honor to be, very respectfully,

H. HESCOCK, *Captain 1st Missouri State Artillery, Chief of Artillery, 3d Division.*

Lieutenant GEORGE LEE,
Acting Assistant Adjutant General, 3d Division.

HEADQUARTERS 5TH INDIANA BATTERY,
Camp in field, January 5, 1863.

SIR: I have the honor to report that on the morning of the 27th of December this command marched with the brigade from its bivouac on the Nolensville pike, half mile south of Nolensville, Tennessee. After marching about two miles the battery was ordered forward with the brigade, which was advancing in line of battle on the right of the pike, cannonading being heard directly in our front. Colonel Baldwin, brigade commander, ordered one piece forward, which fired three shots at the enemy's cavalry, who were in sight, retreating on the opposite hill; we then advanced a short distance, and two Parrott guns were ordered in the woods to the right of the pike, where six rounds were fired at the enemy who were apparently cavalry, drawn up in line of battle, supported by a bat, tery planted on the left of the pike; their artillery ceased firing, and their cavalry retreated when we advanced, but too late to properly support the brigade, who had charged through the village of Triune. The cause of delay was a bridge being destroyed, and very heavy ground bordering on each side of the creek when we passed beyond. With a light twelve-pounder we fired two shots at the enemy retreating through a wood. The command then encamped half a mile south of Triune, where it remained, and was employed in inspecting ammu nition until the morning of the 29th of December, when four pieces of the battery was ordered to report to General Willich, under whom they marched, without any event worthy of notice, to within four miles of Murfreesboro', Tennessee. At this place, at about 1 o'clock, the four pieces rejoined the brigade, when the whole command went with the brigade upon a reconnoissance two miles to the right of the main body of the division, from which the command returned at about 8 o'clock p. m., and went into bivouac in the woods near brigade and division headquarters. We received permission to unhitch the horses, but not to unharness, and early on the morning of the 31st an order was sent to us by the brigade commander to hitch, which we did without watering the horses. At about half past 7 a. m. two light twelve-pounder guns were ordered out to a position about 800 yards southeast from the camp, facing a large cornfield, the enemy appearing in very heavy force. I was then ordered to return and get the other four guns in position as quickly as possible, which was done, placing them to the right and rear of the first pieces posted. The light twelve-pounder guns in the advance position was under command of 1st Lieutenant H. Rankin; the brigade commander is better informed as to their actions than I am, as they were under his immediate eye. I simply noticed that they fired very rapidly, and were the last troops which passed to the rear upon my left; they fired in that position 17 rounds from one piece, and 23 from the other—nearly all canister; some of the rounds were double charges. The four guns under my immediate command commenced firing shell; we had fired about 15 rounds when a very large body of our own troops appeared to our right oblique, retreating rapidly—it was the remains of Kirk's brigade. Colonel Dodge, of this brigade, had hardly time to inform me that a very large body of the enemy were in close pursuit, when they appeared. Three of the four guns opened upon them with canister and checked them in front and to the right oblique, but more appearing almost directly on our right flank—our infantry were out of sight to the rear—when the order was given to leave the field. The command succeeded in getting away with but two of the four pieces. At these two positions there were three men killed and twenty-one wounded; also twenty-three horses disabled. We retreated through a dense woods, and had great difficulty in getting our carriages through. I endeavored to go as much to the left as possible, as I noticed that our troops were less disorganized in that direction. With two pieces we made an ineffectual stand in the woods about midway between the two pikes at a point five or six hundred yards to the right of the Murfreesboro' pike; under the direction of the brigade and division commanders, with three of our own pieces and one of battery "E," 1st Ohio light artillery, we succeeded for a time in checking the enemy, but the infantry fell back, and we were ordered to retire the battery. At this point about 42 rounds of ammunition were fired. It was a splendid position, and I regretted leaving it; one man was wounded and several horses disabled. We then fell back across the pike and the railroad, and became again separated from the brigade. I then reported to general Johnson, who ordered me in position on a point to the left of the railroad, where we remained until about 3 o'clock p. m., and were then ordered to our present position, on the right of the Murfreesboro' pike. Upon the following morning we had a short artillery duel with a four-gun battery in front of us. In the afternoon the enemy appeared advancing with about a brigade, and we opened fire, firing about twenty-five rounds. We have been lying in our present position since.

Very respectfully, yours, &c.,

PETER SIMONSON,
Captain 5th Indiana Battery.

Lieutenant GEORGE H. BURNS,
Acting Assist. Adj't General, 3d Brigade, 2d Division.

HEADQUARTERS BATTERY M, 1ST O. V. A.,
Camp near Murfreesboro', January 16, 1863.

Report of the casualties of Battery M, 1st O. V. A.

Killed.—Corporal William Bettberg.
Wounded.—Captain Frederick Schultz, leg and arm, (slightly.)

F. SCHULTZ,
Captain Commanding Battery M, 1st O. V. A.

Endorsed: Received, headquarters 3d brigade, 2d division, centre, Murfreesboro', January 12, 1863, Lieutenant A. A. Ellsworth, commanding 1st Kentucky battery. Official report of part taken by his battery at the "battles of Stone river," from December 30, 1862, to January 4, 1863. Headquarters 3d brigade, 2d division, centre, Murfreesboro', January 27, 1863. William Sirwell, colonel 78th Pennsylvania volunteer infantry, commanding 3d brigade, &c.

HEADQUARTERS 2D DIVISION, 14TH ARMY CORPS.
Murfreesboro', February 5, 1863.

Respectfully forwarded.

JAS. S. NEGLEY,
Brigadier General Commanding.

HEADQUARTERS HEWETT'S BATTERY, KEN. VOL. ART'Y,
Murfreesboro', Tennessee, January 12, 1863.

SIR: In obedience to orders received from headquarters 7th brigade, 8th division, 14th army corps, I have the honor to make the following report of the part taken by Hewett's battery, Kentucky volunteer artillery, in the recent engagement before Murfreesboro', Tennessee.

On the evening of December 29, 1862, in obedience to orders from General Negley, I placed the battery in position near the old toll-gate, and on the right of battery G, 1st Ohio volunteer artillery, commanded by Lieutenant Marshall. Early on the morning of the 30th I received orders from Colonel Miller to move about three-fourths of a mile to the right and front, through a dense cedar thicket, and over a rough and newly-made road. Here I remained partly under cover of the cedars until about 10 o'clock a. m., when I received orders from General Negley to move a short distance to the left and front, taking a position fronting an open field, where the enemy had a battery of four guns bearing on us. During the day fired about fifty rounds of shell and solid shot at his battery and intrenchments without receiving any reply. As night approached, withdrew the battery and placed it under cover of the wood, where we remained during the night.

Early in the morning of the 31st received orders from Colonel Miller to bring my command in position on the left, and near an old log-house, supported on my right and front by the 21st Ohio volunteer infantry, where I remained without further orders for about fifteen minutes, when observing the enemy, in large column, marching on a battery and some infantry stationed about three hundred yards to my left, I opened an oblique fire on him, and soon discovered him retiring to his intrenchments, where I kept up a brisk and well-directed fire, receiving, at the same time, a heavy fire from his artillery for about fifteen or twenty minutes, when a cessation appeared. I soon after noticed a heavy mass of his infantry moving on our support, to my right and front, accompanied by a section of artillery which was brought into position about five hundred yards to my right and front; also a section placed to my left and front at about the same distance. Here we were subject to a heavy cross-fire of canister. I immediately ordered a return fire of canister double shot, firing as rapidly as possible for about twenty minutes, doing good execution. The enemy was soon seen retiring, and I ordered the use of shell to follow his retreat, briskly kept up for about fifteen minutes, when the enemy commenced a well-directed fire from his artillery direct upon my command. After shelling him rapidly for about three-fourths of an hour, one of my guns (a small rifled gun) was disabled. I continued shelling as rapidly as possible for some time after, and finding my horses were fast being crippled by the shells continually exploding in our midst, I ordered a change of position of the battery to the left that I might break the range of his artillery bearing heavily upon us. While my order was being executed, I noticed that our infantry and artillery were retiring at the same time that a heavy fire was being poured into our right, and almost into our rear. Receiving no orders to retire, made the change of position of the battery to the left, and opened fire on the enemy now fast approaching; but I soon found it impossible to do more without losing the whole battery, and ordered it limbered to the rear, and to retire into the cedar thicket, now being cut off from the road we came in the day previous. Being principally in the rear of our retiring forces, was subject to a heavy fire from the enemy following our retreat, and having all, except one horse that moved my 6-pounder smooth-bore gun, shot, was compelled to leave it, also one caisson belonging to the 10-pounder Parrott gun, containing about fifty rounds of amunition. The remainder of the battery we succeeded in saving; some of the carriages moved out with two horses, having had over half my horses killed and crippled. Fired during the day four hundred and ninety-three rounds of ammunition, losing two men killed and one wounded.

Early on the morning of January 1, 1863, reported to General Negley the Parrott gun, and sent on the field in charge of Lieutenant Spence. I then took the remainder of the battery, now unserviceable, to the rear; at the same time procuring 22 rounds of Parrott ammunition, and was subsequently ordered to move the unserviceable portion of the battery to Nashville, which I did, and immediately returned; but while on the road was attacked, and lost the rear chests of one caisson. Lieutenant Spence was placed on the left centre for a short time; then receiving orders to move to the right, and take position with Marshall's battery, where he remained until about 12 o'clock m., January 2, when ordered to move to the left centre, and take position as on the day previous. About 4 p. m., a heavy force of the enemy was discovered moving on our left and front, driving in our skirmishers. He immediately ordered shell to be fired into him as rapidly as possible, and at the same time receiving a heavy cross-fire from the enemy's artillery. Not long after, the batteries on his right and left retired, and retired about forty yards to the rear; found that the limber contained about 10 rounds of shell and few canister; immediately ordered the gun to its former position, using all the shell, and reporting the same to Captain Loure; was ordered to remain and use the canister in case a second attack was made; but the enemy being repulsed and driven beyond their intrenchments, he retired, moving the gun about one-fourth of a mile to the rear. Forty-two rounds of ammunition was expended, receiving little damage except a few horses wounded. On the morning of the 3d I failed to procure ammunition, and remained as on the night previous.

Early on the morning of the 4th procured seventy-five rounds of ammunition, and reported to Colonel Miller, who ordered me to move to the left centre, and placed my gun in position with Marshall's battery. About 3 o'clock p. m. was ordered to advance on Murfreesboro', and moved about one mile, and remained during the night. Early on the morning of the 5th forded the river, and passed through Murfreesboro'.

I take great pleasure in referring to the valuable assistance rendered by Lieutenant Spence, whose heroic bravery inspired the men with courage, and his conduct is deserving of public commendation.

My non-commissioned officers and privates deported themselves like veterans who fight for the cause of their country.

Our loss in killed was two—Godfrey Hautt, 9th Ohio volunteer infantry, on detached duty with the battery; Lewis Sagers, 78th Pennsylvania, on detached duty with the battery. Wounded, one—Milton Crawhorn.

A. A. ELLSWORTH,
Lieutenant Commanding Hewitt's Battery,
Kentucky Volunteer Artillery.

W. H. CIST,
Acting Assistant Adjutant General,
7th Brigade, 8th Division, 14th Army Corps.

HEADQUARTERS 1ST BRIGADE, 1ST DIVISION, CENTRE,
Near Murfreesboro', Tennessee, January 9, 1863.

I have the honor to submit the following report of the part borne by my command in the engagements before Murfreesboro' on the 31st December and three succeeding days.

At daylight we left our bivouac and moved about a mile to the front, and formed the second line of your division, two regiments extending into the cedar thicket on the right, and the left extending to the Murfreesboro' and Nashville pike. My line was disposed from right to left in the following order: 10th Wisconsin volunteers, Colonel A. R. Chapin; 94th Ohio, Colonel J. W. Frizell; 38th Indiana, Lieutenant Colonel D. F. Griffin; 33d Ohio, Captain E. J. Ellis; 2d Ohio, Lieutenant Colonel John Kell. Having just finished loading arms, I received your orders to proceed, in double-quick time, to the assistance of the right wing, and to follow the 17th brigade. on the Pioneer road, into the woods. When the 17th brigade halted in the woods, I was ordered by General Thomas to move to the right, and soon after formed my line of battle near the Wilkinson pike, when we were opened upon by the enemy's battery.

When near this position, the 33d and 2d Ohio were, by your order, detached and moved back near to the position we first occupied, to support our batteries stationed there, and nobly did they defend them; for soon after the enemy fiercely charged them and were handsomely repulsed, the 2d Ohio capturing the colors of the 30th Arkansas—a victory dearly bought, by the loss of the gallant Lieutenant Colonel Kell, commanding. From near the Wilkinson pike I was ordered to move back, in great haste, to near our position on the Nashville pike, which order was faithfully obeyed. My right had just emerged from the woods, when the enemy, which had just been repulsed in their efforts to take the batteries before mentioned, were seen retreating in disorder in a northwesterly direction through a narrow neck of woods, and were opened upon by the 94th Ohio and the two right companies of the 38th Indiana. I then threw my skirmishers forward, and advanced about six hundred yards into the woods, where my lines became masked by General Negley's division, who were falling back under a heavy fire from the enemy, who appeared to be advancing from a point south of the direction taken by their retreating column. I opened my line to permit that portion of General Negley's command who had expended their ammunition to pass through which was done in good order, a portion of them forming in my rear. Here the 94th Ohio was ordered to the pike, leaving me but two regiments, 38th Indiana and 10th Wisconsin, the former now on the right. General Negley having halted his regiments some twenty-five paces obliquely in front of my line, I wheeled my right under heavy fire to connect with him. Here I appeared to be nearly surrounded, a heavy column turning my left, to prevent which I ordered the 10th Wisconsin to change front to the rear on their first company, thereby forming a right angle with the 38th Indiana volunteers. This position was scarcely taken when the enemy came down on us in great fury; they appeared to be massed in several lines, and their heads seemed to be in terraces not twenty-five yards before us. For twenty minutes these two regiments maintained their ground, completely checking the advance of the enemy's column. Here the 38th Indiana lost their brave Captain J. E. Fouts, besides nearly one-third their number in killed and wounded.

Lieutenant Colonel D. Griffin and Major Glover both had their horses shot under them and their clothing perforated by balls. The 10th Wisconsin nobly vied with their comrades on the right, and I am convinced that both regiments would have suffered extermination rather than have yielded their ground without orders. But the order came, and we fell back and formed on the pike fronting the woods, but the enemy did not venture to follow us further than the skirts of the timber. Having reformed my brigade, I soon after advanced my right to the woods from which we had just emerged, deploying skirmishers from the 94th Ohio, through the neck of the timber, with my left resting on the pike. Here we remained the rest of the day under the fire of the enemy's sharpshooters, and ever and anon the shot and shell from their batteries on our left fell among us. A ball from the former struck Colonel Frizell on the shoulder, so wounding him that he was borne from the field on which he had nobly performed his duty.

At 4 o'clock on the morning of the first of January you ordered me to take my command back to a point on the pike, near the place we occupied before the battle, in order that they might build fires and warm themselves and get something to eat.

Upon receiving your caution to protect myself from an attack on the left, and from your allusion to a ford in that direction, I ordered Lieutenant Alex. Martin, assistant inspector general on my staff, and Lieutenant M. Allen, topographical engineers, to reconnoitre the position. Upon their reporting the feasibility of the crossing, I ordered Lieutenant Martin to conduct the 2d Ohio, Major McCook, to the position. Soon after, firing was heard in this direction, and a stampede occurred among the wagons and hospitals. I ordered the 10th Wisconsin to support the 2d Ohio, and placed them behind the embankment of the railroad. These dispositions had scarcely been made when your order came for me to hurry to the front again with my command. Having obeyed this order, and after some manœuvring, we were placed in position, the 33d Ohio extending across the neck of woods into which my right threw out skirmishers the evening before, with a battery on the right and left, commanding the fields on either side of the woods. On the right of the 33d Ohio came the 94th Ohio and 38th Indiana in the edge of the undergrowth on the crest of the slope from the field west of the Nashville pike. On the right of the 38th Indiana was another battery. The 10th Wisconsin and 2d Ohio were held in reserve, in order to re-enforce any part of the line that was menaced. This position was maintained without material change during the subsequent days of the fight. Our skirmishers were kept out during the time, and employed in discovering and dislodging the sharpshooters, who, during the hours of daylight, almost continuously annoyed us. I cannot too highly praise Captain Ellis, commanding 33d Ohio, for the vigilance of himself and men in their exposed position in the woods. At times the enemy from the woods below would essay to advance, when every man would be at his post, and often the batteries would open upon them. While here Captain Ellis had his horse shot under him. Breastworks of logs and rocks had been constructed to protect the line; also a few rifle-pits dug.

On the evening of the 2d, when the enemy so vigorously attacked our left, the moving of their forces in that direction could be seen from my position, which fact was promptly reported. I caused my skirmishers to advance and take precaution against demonstration upon my position; the attempt was made just before dark, the enemy forming in the edge of the woods in our front, where Captain Cox's 10th Indiana battery, on the right of the 33d Ohio, opened his fire upon them, driving them back.

I deem it improper to close this report without commending in high terms the manner in which my command bore the hardships of this terrible conflict. They suffered from cold, rain, fatigue, and hunger, without a murmur. These attributes, when added to their bravery, make soldiers of which the country may be proud. I also feel it my duty to praise the courage and efficiency of my staff—Lieutenant Fitzwilliam, acting assistant adjutant general and aide-de-camp; Lieutenant Martin, inspector, who was wounded above the knee by a shell; Lieutenant George H. Hollister, acting assistant commissary of subsistence, missing, after displaying great gallantry in his transmission of your orders to me; Lieutenant Mundy Allen, topographical engineers—all of whom have endeared themselves to me by their prompt and intelligent performances of their appropriate duties. I would, in an especial manner, mention the name of one of my orderlies, Josiah F. Mitchell, company B, 33d Ohio volunteers, who displayed marked courage and intelligence.

I went into the fight with 1,646 officers and men, minus two companies, 33d Ohio, under Major Ely, 10th Wisconsin, who were detached to guard the train. My losses are:

Regiments.	KILLED.		WOUNDED		Missing men.
	Officers.	Men	Officers	Men.	
38th Indiana volunteers.	Capt. J. E. Fouts.	14	Lt. S. W. Hawkins. Lt. M. T. Davis.	84	*3
33d Ohio volunteers		2		19	4
2d Ohio volunteers	Lt. Col. John Kell.	9	Capt. Hazlett Capt. Maxwell Lt. Van Horn Capt. Steel	29	3
94th Ohio volunteers		2	Col. Frizell	25	29
10th Wisconsin volunt'rs		3	Capt. J. W. Roby	15	6
Total	2	30	8	172	45

* Wounded.

For list of names of killed and wounded see accompanying paper.

Your obedient servant,

R. F. SCRIBNER,

Colonel 38th Indiana Volunteers, Commanding 1st Brigade, 1st Division, Department of Cumberland.

Captain M. C. TAYLOR,

Acting Assistant Adjutant General.

NINTH BRIGADE, THIRD DIVISION,
Camp at Murfreesboro', January 7, 1863.

COLONEL: I have the honor to report, briefly, the part taken by the 2d regiment Ohio volunteers, in the action of the 31st of December, 1862, and the following days On the morning of the 31st, after being ordered into the woods on our right centre, with the balance of the brigade, and before being engaged, Lieutenant Colonel Kell, then in command of the regiment, was ordered by Captain McDurel, assistant adjutant general on Major General Rousseau's staff, in person, to leave the position assigned us in the woods, and move to the support of Captain Guenther's battery H, United States artillery, then stationed on the left of the main Murfreesboro' turnpike.

He did so without, I believe, reportng to you, as the exigency of the case would not admit of it. The regiment was formed on the flank of the battery, and, in conjunction with it, successfully repulsed the efforts of a brigade to cap ture it, killing and wounding many of the enemy, and capturing about thirty prisoners and a stand of colors belonging to the 30th regiment Arkansas volunteer infantry.

At this time you made your appearance from the woods with the balance of the brigade, and from that time, until we occupied this place, we were under your eye. Our loss was eleven officers and men killed and thirty-four officers and men wounded; among the former, Lieutenant Colonel John Kell, commanding the regiment, and First Lieutenant Richard Chambers, company F; among the latter First Lieutenant Lafayette Van Horn, company I, mortally, and Captains Maxwell and Hazlett severely. I cannot refrain from expressing my regret at the loss of Lieutenant Colonel Kell and Lieutenant Chambers, particularly the former. Brave, competent, and energetic, he had proven himself on several occasions well qualified for the position he held. His death is greatly to be deplored, and his loss will be severely felt by the regiment.

With a very few exceptions the regiment behaved well, and at some future time I will particularly recommend deserving men for promotion.

I have the honor to be,

A. G. McCOOK,
Major 2d Ohio Volunteers, Commanding.

Colonel B. F. SCRIBNER,
Commanding 9th Brigade.

HEADQUARTERS 38TH INDIANA VOLUNTEERS,
On the field, in front of Murfreesboro', January 4, 1863.

SIR: I have the honor to report the following as the part taken by my command in the action of December 31 in front of Murfreesboro', and subsequent operations in the field since that date. At daylight on the morning of December 31, the command occupying the centre of your brigade moved to the front on the Nashville turnpike, and about eight o'clock a. m. moved, through a dense cedar forest, towards the right wing of the army, which was then hotly engaged by the enemy. After manœuvring for about an hour we were ordered to retire, left in front through the same forest, to near the position first occupied on the right of the pike in the timber. Here the enemy was discovered in strong force on our right and rear, charging towards the turnpike. The command was, by your order, immediately faced by the rear rank, and moved down on the flank of the enemy, who was now retiring before a column of our troops, moving from the pike. In this movement the 94th Ohio was on our right, and the 10th Wisconsin was on our left. Company H, Captain Poindexter, commanding, and company B, First Lieutenant Lenace commanding, were deployed forward as skirmishers, moving steadily on the skirmishers of the enemy, capturing six of them, who were sent to the rear. Continuing our movements about 600 yards, we met the left of General Negley's command, who were now retiring before a heavy column of the enemy, and moved into position to their support. The left of this command having passed to the rear through our ranks, their centre came into postion on our right, and some sixty yards to the front. By your command the battalion was wheeled to the left, and moved forward with our left, *now our right*, joining their line. Before we were fairly in position, the enemy opened a heavy fire, and the troops on our right fell back, leaving the left of the battalion, now the right, exposed. I then moved the line by the flank, striving to continue the connexion. The enemy now opening on our line, we at once faced to the front, and kept up a continuous fire for the space of twenty minutes, checking the enemy's advance, and holding him in check until your orders to retire to the pike were received. This was done in order, forming there on the right of the 2d Ohio volunteers. The enemy now appearing in force on the front, by your order we changed front forward on left company and advanced into the cornfield in front of the Chicago Board of Trade Battery. Lying down, in this position we remained from two o'clock p. m. until dark, exposed to the fire of the enemy from the woods in front, awaiting their expected advance, night closing the engagement; we lay in this position, with pickets advanced, until daylight, when we were relieved and retired to the woods in our rear. At half past seven o'clock the engagement again opened on the front, when, by your orders, we moved forward on the double quick and were assigned to position on the right to support Guenther's battery. In this position we have remained to present date, exposed to the fire of the enemy's sharpshooters and from their batteries on the front. In the engagement of December 31 the command lost, in killed, Captain James E. Fouts and thirteen men. Wounded and missing, supposed to be in the enemy's hospital, three men wounded, and in our hospital, Second Lieutenant M. T. Davis, company C, Second Lieutenant Thomas S. W. Hawkins, company I, and eighty-one men: total killed 14, wounded 86. For list of names of killed and wounded I respectfully refer you to accompanying report. I cannot close without commending, for their coolness and bravery on the field, each officer and soldier of my command engaged during the five days. Though suffering at times severely from cold, hunger, rain, and fatigue, yet not a murmur was heard nor a duty flinched from. To Major J. B. Glover I am indebted for every support in command of the skirmishers, and during the hottest of the fight he was ever at his post; his horse received two wounds, himself barely escaping. My adjutant, George H. Devol, was ever on the alert, and renderd much valuable assistance. Of our chaplain, Rev. L. E. Caison, too much cannot be said. In his attention and devotion to the wounded he was untiring, making this his especial duty. We have the satisfaction of knowing that all were cared for properly and efficiently. In the death of Captain Fouts we lament the loss of a brave officer, a true patriot, and a warm friend.

Very respectfully,

D. F. GRIFFIN,

Lieutenant Colonel, Commanding 38th Regiment Indiana Volunteers.

GEORGE H. DEVOL,

A. A. A. G. 1st Brigade, 1st Division, "Centre."

HEADQUARTERS 94TH REGIMENT OHIO VOLUNTEERS,
Army of the Cumberland, in the field.

In obedience to orders from headquarters, I have the honor to forward the following report of the part taken in the battle of Wednesday, December 31, 1862, and the following days, by the 94th regiment.

My command, forming part of the 9th brigade, was ordered to move forward towards Murfreesboro', on the Nashville and Murfreesboro' pike. After marching about one and a half (1½) mile, we turned to the right and went a quarter of a mile, and halted in the woods. After waiting a short period we were again moved forward to the right and front in double quick, halted, formed in line of battle, and for the first time came under fire of the enemy. Shells bursting over and around us, soon we were ordered to move to the right. After marching a short distance we were halted. Remaining in that position about twenty minutes, we were again ordered to move by the right. We then marched towards the Murfreesboro' pike, and halted at the edge of the woods. At the time the enemy left the woods and charged one of our batteries. The foe broke and fled precipitately. We commenced firing on our right, and threw company B out as skirmishers on our left.

We were then ordered into the open field in line, halted, and delivered several rounds at the retreating foe. Received orders to fix bayonets, which done, we moved in double quick across the field, following the enemy. We halted at the edge of the woods, remaining but a short time; threw out company G as skirmishers, advanced into the woods about seventy-five yards, and halted. After remaining here for some time we received orders to move out to the right and up to the top of the hill, which we did, passing one of our batteries there; from this point we crossed the pike, forming in line along the east side. From this point I was ordered back to bring up ammunition. The regiment remained here about thirty minutes. We had several wounded at this point by the enemy's artillery.

The regiment was then ordered forward, over the crest of the hill and into the woods, by order of General Rousseau. Companies B and G were advanced from this point as skirmishers; they were soon brought in, and the whole command marched by the left flank to join on the right of the 38th Indiana, then in the open field. In this position we were ordered to lie down. Many of our men were wounded by the enemy's sharpshooters. We did not remain long in this position, but returned to the woods, and after a very brief stay we were ordered out again, but not quite so far advanced, and less exposed to the sharpshooters. Shortly after this our gallant colonel, whose cheerful courage and constantly encouraging presence had contributed effectively to the calmness and prompt obedience of the entire command, was severely wounded, and instantly carried from the field.

At this juncture the command fell for a short time upon Major King. Our left here joined on the right of the 38th Indiana; this position we held during the night, throwing out pickets to the front. No disturbance occurred of any importance.

On Thursday, January 1, 1863, 5 a. m., we were ordered to report ourselves on the Murfreesboro' pike, which being done, we were marched back to about the position we started from the morning before; but we did not have long to remain at this point. We had hardly stacked arms and broken ranks till we heard that familiar sound, "Fall in." We were marched back again towards Murfreesboro' in double quick. After going about one mile we were ordered off to the right of the pike, and formed into line. Soon General McCook ordered us over to the left of the pike; we were, however, soon ordered back to the point at which we left the pike; at which place we were formed into column of companies, then marched forward to the right and front, to the crest of a hill, and halted facing south, formed a line in a few moments. We were ordered to change front forward on first company, which being done, we marched forward, and were halted in the edge of a thicket. Here we remained till 3 p. m., when we were pushed to the further edge of the thicket, facing southwest.

During the night and day following we threw up breastworks of such material as was at hand. On the evening following (January 2) we threw out heavy pickets, and this position we occupied, with nothing to disturb us, excepting the annoyance of the enemy's sharpshooters, until January 5, when ordered to March.

During the five days we were on the field, among those wounded was Captain Steele, bold and brave, who, though suffering from severe sickness, commanded his company with praiseworthy success until removed from the field. The officers, without exception, acted well their parts, and in perfect concert. The men, obedient and prompt, were easy to command, and are worthy of high commendation.

Of our chaplain, Rev. William Allington, I do not think too much can be said. I wish there were more such in our army. He followed the regiment wherever it went, picking up the wounded, and carrying them off the field; and after we were through with a day's fight, he would spend his nights at the hospitals administering to the wounded.

The above report is as near correct as I am able to make it.

Yours, most respectfully,

S. A. BASSFORD,

Lieut. Col., Commanding 94th Regiment Ohio Volunteer Infantry.

Colonel B. F. SCRIBNER,

Commanding 9th Brigade, 3d Division.

HEADQUARTERS TENTH WISCONSIN VOLUNTEER INFANTRY,

Camp at Murfreesboro', Tennessee, January 9, 1863.

SIR: I would most respectfully report that at 12 o'clock m., December 30, 1862, the 18th regiment Wisconsin volunteer infantry, with the other regiments of the brigade, had arrived at a point on the Nashville and Murfreesboro' pike, three and one-half miles from Murfreesboro'. Heavy skirmishing was going on at the time in the cedar wood to the right of the pike. We did not get engaged that day. At 7 o'clock a. m., December 31, we got under arms, and shortly after moved on the pike towards Murfreesboro' about one-half mile. We then moved towards the wood on the right, and soon engaged the enemy. After some hot work they gradually retired, followed up by our brigade.

About this time the 2d Ohio and 33d Ohio were detached, and my regiment, with the 38th Indiana and 94th Ohio, continued to advance under a pretty hot skirmish fire. After having advanced some distance we were attacked by a strong force, which we held for some time until we began to receive a flank fire from the right. Orders were received to retire behind the line of the 17th brigade, which we did; and as I was about to get my regiment into line, I saw that the 17th brigade was also retiring. I moved to the rear with them and formed my line on their right and the left of Loomis's battery. There I remained until retired by your order about daylight the next morning.

At about 7 o'clock on the morning of the 1st January we were again moved rapidly forward on the pike to near our old position, where we remained all through the battle, but did not have any general engagement with the enemy after the 31st December.

I went into the battle with eleven officers and two hundred and fifty men.

My loss is three killed, one officer slightly wounded, fifteen enlisted men wounded, and six missing.

My loss would probably have been much larger, but the nature of the ground where we were engaged in the woods was such that the men had some protection.

Very respectfully, your obedient servant,

A. R. CHAPIN,
Colonel 10th Regiment Wisconsin Volunteer Infantry.

ACTING ASSISTANT ADJUTANT GENERAL, *9th Brigade.*

HEADQUARTERS SECOND BRIGADE,
First Division, Murfreesboro', Tennessee, January 9, 1863.

SIR: In the recent engagement before Murfreesboro' the casualties in my brigade were as follows:

Third Ohio infantry, Lieutenant Colonel Lauson commanding.—Enlisted men killed, 17; wounded, 65; missing, 23; commissioned officers wounded, 1. Total, 106.

Fifteenth Kentucky volunteer infantry, Colonel J. B. Foreman commanding.—Commanding officers killed, 2; wounded, 1; missing, 1. Enlisted men killed, 8; wounded, 31; missing, 17. Total, 60.

Forty-second Indiana volunteer infantry, Lieutenant Colonel Shanklin commanding.—Commanding officers wounded, 6; missing, 2. Enlisted men killed, 17; wounded, 75; missing, 32. Total, 132.

Eighty-eighth Indiana volunteer infantry, Colonel George Humphrey commanding.—Commanding officers wounded, 4. Enlisted men killed, 8; wounded, 47; missing, 19. Total, 78.

First Michigan battery, Lieutenant Van Pelt commanding.—Enlisted men killed, 1; wounded, 10; missing, 2. Total, 13.

Colonel Forēman, 15th Kentucky, was killed in the cedar woods on the morning of the 31st ultimo. He was a brave man and an excellent officer. Captain Bayne, of the same regiment, fell at the same time while urging his men forward. Lieutenant Colonel Shanklin, 42d Indiana volunteer infantry, was surrounded by a superior force on the morning of January 3, and taken by the enemy. Colonel George Humphrey, 88th Indiana, was wounded, on the night of January 3, in expelling the enemy from the woods in our front. He behaved gallantly throughout the fight. Captain L. S. Bell, 3d Ohio infantry, wounded at the same time, conducted himself with great courage.

Lieutenant Colonel Lauson, 3d Ohio; Lieutenant Colonel Briant, 88th Indiana; Captain I. H. Bryant, 42d Indiana; Lieutenants Du Barry and Wildman, 88th Indiana; Lieutenant I. B. McRoberts, 3d Ohio; Lieutenants Harroll and Orr, 42d Indiana; Mr. James K. Patterson, Evansville, Indian, and Acting Assistant Adjutant General James S. Wilson, deserve especial praise. Colonel O. A. Loomis, Lieutenants Van Pelt and Hale, of the 1st Michigan battery, rendered most important service throughout the entire battle. No men could have conducted themselves with more courage and ability. There are other officers and men who should be mentioned favorably, but the reports of regimental commanders have failed to reach me, and it is impossible therefore to give them the credit they deserve.

My brigade had three separate encounters with the enemy on the first day. On the second and third day it was in front a portion of the time. Skirmishing, on the night of the 3d of January, two regiments led by myself drove the enemy from their breastworks in the edge of the woods in our front. I trust the conduct of the brigade throughout may be satisfactory.

I am, captain, very respectfully,

JNO. BEATTY,
Colonel, Commanding 2d Brigade.

Captain M. C. TAYLOR,
Acting Assistant Adjutant General, 1st Division.

HEADQUARTERS TWENTY-EIGHTH BRIGADE,
Camp at Jefferson, near Stone river, December 31, 1862.

SIR: I have the honor to report that on the 30th instant the train of the 28th brigade, consisting of sixty-four wagons, loaded with camp equipage, stores, officers' baggage, knapsacks, &c., which was sent from Stewartsboro' at 8½ a. m. for this point, unprotected save by the convalescents and a small guard left to the rear for protection, ten wagons loaded with rations, the head of the train had just arrived in camp, and while in process of being parked the rear and centre of the same was attacked by a portion of General Wheeler's cavalry brigade; while the remainder of his brigade, he being in command, as also a part of a brigade under command of Colonel Allen, advanced on both sides of the highway for the purpose of attacking the brigade force and destroying the whole train. The outposts and pickets, however, being on the alert, met the enemy at the front and held them in check until the brigade was formed and ready for battle. I immediately ordered the train at double quick to be parked, sent the 21st Wisconsin, under Colonel Hobard, to the front and to rear of train; ordered the 1st Wisconsin, Colonel Bingham, to deploy right and left from the centre as skirmishers, and to press forward; moved one regiment, the 24th Illinois, under Colonel Mihalotzy, to the bridge crossing the river together with one section of artillery, and then advanced to the front with the 79th Pennsylvania, Colonel Hambright, and two sections of artillery, 1st Kentucky, Captain Stone. My advance, the 21st Wisconsin, was soon hotly engaged, and being pressed severely by the enemy in front and on the left they passed to the right of the highway and occupied a hill, upon which was a log-house, giving them a good fighting position. The 2d Kentucky cavalry, Captain Craddock, about fifty strong, was then sent to the left and front to feel the enemy, and at once become engaged; the right wing of the 1st Wisconsin was rallied on the right, and placed in rear of the 1st section of artillery, which was then upon the hill occupied by the 21st Wisconsin, opening with shell. The 79th Pennsylvania was placed in rear of the left wing of the 1st Wisconsin, which was skirmishing to the front. One section of artillery opened upon the enemy in front as between my infantry on the right and left. The engagement at this time became general as between the enemy's 1st and 21st Wisconsin volunteer infantry and two sections of the 1st Kentucky battery, the enemy acting principally on foot, supported by two field howitzers. The enemy was, however, finally repulsed, and left the field after severe fighting, the engagement lasting two hours and ten minutes, the brigade following one and a half miles, when, deeming my rear unsafe, I ordered the command to retire, and went into camp on the north side of Stone river, near Jefferson.

The enemy's force, as near as could be ascertained, was some thirty-five hundred strong; strength of my force was about one thousand seven hundred. The enemy's loss in killed, as learned from prisoners taken since the fight, was 83. Their loss in wounded must have been very severe; but as the wounded and dead were carried away mostly by the cavalry upon their horses, it is impossible to give their loss with certainty. Eight prisoners were taken and paroled, two of whom were mortally wounded. A lieutenant colonel of Wheeler's brigade was also mortally wounded.

Casualties upon our side were as per recapitulation, the chief part of the loss being convalescents who were with the train when attacked. Twenty wagons from the rear of the train were taken and destroyed by fire, with the contents thereof, consisting of camp and garrison equipage, officers' and men's clothing, &c. The troops under my command acted with great coolness and bravery—no flinching, no running, but the utmost coolness shown by all, adding another creditable mark to the old 28th brigade. Staff officers and orderlies carried orders fearlessly to different parts of the field, entitling them to great credit and to my thanks.

Yours, respectfully,

JOHN C. STARKWEATHER,
Colonel 1st Wisconsin Volunteers, Commanding 28th Brigade.

Captain M. C. TAYLOR,
Acting Assistant Adjutant General, 3d Division.

	CASUALTIES.				
	Killed.	Wounded.	Missing.	Prisoners.	Total.
79th Pennsylvania	......	1	1	5	7
21st Wisconsin	1	3	37	......	41
1st Wisconsin	......	4	13	3	20
1st Kentucky battery	......	......	1	1	2
24th Illinois volunteers	......	......	52	......	52
	1	8	104	9	122

NOTE.—The missing are prisoners taken with train, most of them being convalescents, and will undoubtedly be paroled.

HEADQUARTERS TWENTY-EIGHTH BRIGADE,
Camp near Murfreesboro', Tennessee, January 6, 1863.

SIR: I have the honor to report that on the 31st ultimo the 28th brigade left Jefferson, in accordance with orders, and reported at 5 p. m. for duty, bringing in one field howitzer, belonging to 5th Wisconsin battery, and some two hundred and fifty cavalry, of different regiments, as also many stragglers from infantry regiments, that were found on the Jefferson and Lavergne pike and roads adjacent thereto, who had participated in the fight in front cf Murfreesboro' that day or the day previous. On the 1st instant the brigade was manœuvred, changing positions, fronts, &c., &c., going into camp, formed in line, with battalions doubled on the centre, left resting on the Nashville and Murfreesboro' pike, right on the left of General Johnson's troops. The following morning the brigade was ordered by General Rousseau to deploy into line and advance to the front to the support of our batteries then in action. The change of position was made, and the gallant 28th brigade moved to the front to give such support with unflinching courage, amid a most tremendous rebel fire of solid shot and shell, and remained in such supporting position until another change was made, when it was sent to the extreme front and ordered to hold the same, which post it occupied, the 2d, 3d, and 4th changing position from time to time, as the nature of circumstances seemed to require, supporting batteries, pioneer corps, &c., in digging trenches; and although not brought into place where its own fire could be made to tell effectively, yet from the duties performed by it, under the continued and severe fire of shot and shell of he enemy, it is entitled to all praise. Casualties as per recapitulation.

Yours, respectfully,

JOHN C. STARKWEATHER,
Colonel 1st Wisconsin, Commanding 28th Brigade.

Captain M. C. TAYLOR,
Acting Assistant Adjutant General, 3d Division.

Recapitulation of casualties.

	Killed.	Wounded.	Missing.	Total.
24th Illinois volunteers	1	3	0	4
79th Pennsylvania volunteers	2	8	0	10
1st Wisconsin volunteers	0	4	3	7
1st Kentucky battery	0	1	0	1
Total	3	16	3	22

HEADQUARTERS THIRD BRIGADE,
Murfreesboro', Tenn., January 11, 1863.

List of casualties in 28th brigade, December 30, 1862.

79*th Pennsylvania.*—Samuel Gruel, company A, prisoner; John Bowker, company B, Jacob Gongary, company H, Solomon Shupp, company I, and C. Kreider, company K, paroled prisoners; Thomas Leonard, company I, wounded; George Bolinger, company D, prisoner.

1*st Wisconsin.*—Privates E. Tweedy, Bernard Hook, company A, prisoners; Privates George Downing, Nicholas Pifer, company B, prisoners; Privates E. C. Wallace, Michael Flynn, company C, missing; Privates Gabriel Cornish, W. B. Baker, company D, missing; Private Henry Bloomer, company D, paroled prisoner; Private John Ames, company E, missing; Private Henry Holderness, company E, paroled prisoner; Private S. W. Peterson, company F, wounded; Privates Lucius E. Knowles, Amos Greengo, company G, prisoners; Private Frank Davis, paroled prisoner; Sergeant Waldo Tibbetts, Private Harvey Arnold, company I, wounded; Corporal Freeman H. Farr, company K, wounded and paroled; Privates Francis M. Ruth, company K, and Alexander McDonald, company I, missing.

21*st Wisconsin.*—Private B. S. Turney, company D, killed; Private Charles Goutermont, company F, wounded; Lieutenant A. B. Smith, company I, wounded; Corporal P. A. Maloney, company A, wounded; Corporal A. Peck, Privates James A Washburn, J. B. Corey, company A; Corporal F. E. Wickwire, Privates A. Grignon, John Brockway, company B; Private Thomas Hewitt, com pany C; Corporal Sylvester Greely, Privates Miles H. Fenno, J. W. Recksford, James Walcot, company D; Privates Christopher Johnston, Hiram Taylor, company E; Corporals C. C. Currier, B. F. Phelps, Privates William R. Bills, L. Holland, Frank Lewis, Sterling S. Ross, Charles Sabin, J. J. Smith, John Smith, William J. Smith, Llewellyn Shurtleff, D. S. Thayer, company F; Privates Thomas Tohill, William Bolman, Musician William Hilse, company H; Captain S. B. Nelson, First Sergeant James H. Hodges, Sergeant James M. Tendell, Privates J. C. Prouty, Rudolph Staunton, Silas Lovely, A. F. Ham, Henry Cain, and Benjamin Miles, company I, missing.

1*st Kentucky battery.*—Privates L. W. Joice and C. McCarty, prisoners.

24*th Illinois.*—Lieutenant Henry Wendt, quartermaster; Corporals Jacob Metzler, G. Reitsch, Privates Jacob Kinn, Henry Elend, Frederick Brink, company A; Corporal Simon Hang, Privates John Kensing, A. Berchtold, Frank Miller, A. Goerhtz, company B; Corporal C. Ahlheim, Privates Adam Kaemnerer, Joseph Degouecey, Charles Gans, Henry Diesback, company C; Sergeant Louis Rosenstrel, Corporal Max Schoele, Privates Nicholas Schneider,

Mathial Kill, John Rahler, company D; Privates George Buergle, Frederick Buehrer, Ernest Mieth, August Alp, company E; Corporal Mathias Kunst, Privates Hachenberg, Christopher Klas, George Zuellig, John Goosen, company F; Privates Edward Ewers, Philip Enders, Eberhard Weinrich, Henry A. Mueller, Christopher Pfetzing, company G; Privates Jacob Stoetzler, Ferdinand Ochs, Frederick Paulson, C. Schmidt, Peter Roth, H. Beste, August Gsoell, company H; Privates Adam Simon, C. Bergmann, Joseph Schmidt, John Ring, C. Lanz, company I; Corporal M. Eisenback, Privates Louis Buechen, Philip Pollack, Joseph Dollinger, and Rudolph Willmer, paroled prisoners.

Recapitulation.

	Killed.	Wounded.	Missing.	Total.
79th Pennsylvania	..	1	6	7
1st Wisconsin	..	4	16	20
24th Illinois	..	..	53	53
21st Wisconsin	1	3	37	41
1st Kentucky battery	..	..	2	2
	1	8	114	123

H. A. HAMBRIGHT,
Colonet 79th Pennsylvania Commanding.

C. A. SEARLES, *Lieutenant and A. A. A. G.*

Respectfully,
JOHN C. STARKWEATHER,
Colonel 1st Wisconsin Volunteers, Commanding 28th Brigade.

Captain M. C. TAYLOR,
Acting Assistant Adjutant General, 1st Division.

HEADQUARTERS BRIGADE UNITED STATES REGULAR TROOPS,
THIRD DIVISION, (ROUSSEAU'S,) CENTRE FOURTH ARMY CORPS,
Camp at Murfreesboro', Tennessee, January 10, 1863.

SIR: I have the honor, respectfully, to report the operations of this brigade, under my orders during the recent five days' battle before this place.

The brigade on going into action consisted of first battalion, 15th infantry, United States army, comprising 16 officers and 304 enlisted men for duty, Major King commanding.

First battalion, 16th infantry, United States army, and company B, second battalion, same regiment attached, comprising 15 officers and 293 enlisted men, Major Slemmer commanding; company H, battery, 5th artillery, United States army, comprising 3 officers and 120 enlisted men for duty, Captain Guenther commanding.

First battalion, 18th infantry, United States army, and companies A and D, third battalion, same regiment attached, comprising 16 officers and 272 enlisted men, Major Caldwell commanding.

Second battalion, 18th infantry, United States army, and companies B, C, E, and F, third battalion, same regiment attached, comprising 16 officers and 298 enlisted men, Major Townsend commanding.

Six companies, A, B, C, D, E, and F, first battalion, 19th, United States army, comprising 10 officers and 198 enlisted men, Major Carpenter commanding.

Making a total of 77 officers and 1,485 enlisted men, not including the staff officers and commanding officer of the brigade, four in number, and one acting sergeant major, (Commissary Sergeant Gill, third battalion.)

The balance of the brigade, including the sick, were left behind to guard the brigade and battalion trains, where they did good service, under the respective battalion quartermasters, in repelling the attacks of the enemy's cavalry, saving thereby the entire trains of the brigade.

The musicians were under the orders of the various surgeons.

The brigade, thus constituted and in the order enumerated, went first into action under your eye and general supervision at about half-past 9 o'clock a. m., on the 31st December, 1862, forming line in the dense cedar forest to the right of the turnpike and railroad, with design of succoring the right wing of the army under Major General McCook. After being placed partially in quick time in position and *line* the rebel enemy attacked briskly the two battalions, 15th and 16th, on the right of the battery. On observing that the battery and the three battalions to the left were separated from and not in view of these two battalions, I sent my acting adjutant general, Lieutenant Sutherland, with orders to Major King to take the command on the right, while I proceeded towards the centre and left of the brigade to bring them into this contest, which was shortly terminated by the 15th and 16th being forced to retire with considerable loss, not, however, without having checked the advance of the enemy, who soon succeeded in possessing the flank by their long extended line, and having at first been deceived by the enemy, who advanced dressed in American uniform, and without firing till within a short distance, supported by a heavy line behind.—(See official report of Captain J. Fulmer, commanding first battery, 15th infantry.)

A regiment, believed to be the 6th Ohio volunteers, withstood the fire of the enemy along with these two battalions.

On arriving on the left of the brigade, I found that the battery had fortunately received your orders to retire by the same narrow cut in the cedar forest by which the brigade first entered. The three battalions of the 18th and 19th were directed to accompany this movement just in time to save the battery from capture and under fire of the advancing enemy.

In this first conflict in the cedar forest Captain Bell, of the 15th, was killed, and Captain Yorke and Lieutenant Occleston, 15th, severely wounded, and also about 8 enlisted men were killed and 42 wounded.

After emerging from the cedar forest the battalions of the brigade drew up in their proper positions to the right and left of the battery, which had taken position, from which, by its effective fire, the advancing lines of the enemy were driven back and dispersed from view in the forest.

While waiting in this position, the enemy's batteries to the front, along the turnpike and railroad, were throwing shot and shell upon our ground, by which Captain Dennison, second battalion, 18th, lost his leg, and the heroic first sergeant, George F. White, of company F, third battalion, his life; other men of the brigade were also killed and wounded.

At about 12 m. the brigade, including the battery, were again directed to advance to the front along the railroad and turnpike, and after reaching the further side of the open ground was suddenly directed to the right, to enter again the cedar forest to sustain troops which were receding, exhausted of ammunition. This movement was made in pursuance of orders directly from yourself and Major General Thomas.

The brigade being halted just along the edge of the forest, the battery was ordered to retake the former slightly elevated site near the railroad.

The brigade having the battalion of the 19th shifted at the request of its commanding officer, Major Carpenter, from extreme left to position in line, between the battalions of the 15th and 16th, was projected about fifty yards into the dense cedar forest towards the enemy, and after allowing our retiring regiments to pass through the line to the rear, the fire was opened in return to that of the pursuing enemy. The excellence of the firing by file by all the battalions of the brigade could not be excelled, and was terrifying and destructive to the enemy, who were brought to a stand for about twenty minutes.

During this stubborn combat most of our losses in killed and wounded took place; Major Slemmer, commanding 16th, wounded at its commencement. The enemy's lines extending, however, beyond both flanks of the brigade, enabled them to pour an incessant fire from three directions, the front and left and right flanks; and the brigade being supported by any other forces on either flank and having secured the required time for the receding regiments to reform, I thought it proper to order a retreat, which was probably quite long enough deferred.

Just after the order to retreat was given a regiment came up in line in the open field on the extreme right of the brigade, but its fire, though brisk, came too late, and was unavailing against so large a force as filled the forest, three lines being discernible.

It is proper here to remark that notwithstanding the loss in the brigade had been nearly half its strength, the battalions evidently gave ground with reluctance, probably not having looked to such result and being too much engaged to know the full extent of their losses. The retreat of the brigade across the open field was done handsomely and with as much order as was desirable, having view to prevent further loss of life. On this retreat Major King, commanding the 15th, and Captain Douglass, acting field officer of the first battalion, 18th infantry, were wounded, causing them both to retire to the hospital.

The brigade was at this time re-formed in line near the railroad, in proper place to the right and left of the battery, as directed in previous orders for the formation in line of battle, and in this position remained the balance of the day and during the following day, within reach of the enemy's cannon.

In this last terrific combat in the cedar forest many brave men and officers perished.

Four officers killed and eighteen wounded, and seventy-eight enlisted men killed, and four hundred and thirty enlisted men wounded, exclusive of the missing.

At the moment of retreating a few steps, the brave and gallant Major Carpenter, commanding the 19th infantry, fell from his horse with six mortal wounds, regretted by all who knew him. The left wing of the brigade, 1st and 2d battalions, 18th infantry, was during the remainder of the battle committed mostly to Major Townsend, the right wing deprived of its field officers, requiring, as I thought, more of my attention.

About the middle of the afternoon an extended line of men was discovered far to our front, advancing with our national colors, and having passed over a slight rise descended into a corresponding depression, partially concealing them, when a white flag with a dark ball in its centre was substituted, after which they unfurled the rebel flag. Whereupon Captain Guenther directed the fire of his battery, causing the line to break in double quick time to their left flank and disappear into the cedar forest.

Though occasionally visited by the enemy's shot but little heed was given to it, and thus closed the action of the brigade the first day, being the last of the year, the 31st of December, 1862. During the night our wounded were gathered together as far as the enemy's pickets would permit.

A short time before daybreak of new year's day the brigade retired, according to orders, to a point in the rear of the commanding general's headquarters, to meet an attack on our right. Some shiftings of position took place till about 2 o'clock p. m., when it marched towards Stewart's creek, and on arriving near there it was ordered back in double-quick time, which being executed, and night coming on, the brigade bivouacked on the left of the road way and near the commanding general's headquarters.

On the third day, the 2d instant, the brigade marched before breakfasting to the front to meet the enemy's attack, and we retained this position during the day and following night, the battery assisting to silence the enemy's batteries, and effect the repulse of the enemy in their attack on the left wing of the army under General Crittenden in the afternoon.

On the 3d inst., the fourth day, the brigade and battery moved forward to the stand-point of the first day, the 31st of December, 1862, where slight embankments were thrown up, principally by the men of the brigade, and encamped within them, though rendered almost untenable by heavy rains, which filled them partially with water and made the adjoining ground miry. As this day closed, and at dark, a severe attack was made by some portion of the division upon the enemy in front, which resulted in gaining possession of the enemy's first line of breastworks for a time, and subsequently abandoned them, owing to exhausted ammunition.

On the 4th instant I reported at half past 7 a. m. that the enemy had evacuated our front. The brigade held the same position, employing the day and following night in the sad duty of collecting our dead, who were interred with military honors just in front of our intrenchments and on the stand-point of the brigade and battery, maintained from the first till the last day's conflict.

The heavy rains on the 2d and 3d instants covered this position and the trenches with mud and water, in which the whole brigade had to stand or recline while seeking to obtain a little rest. Not a murmur escaped the lip in all this trying and painful as well as arduous and dangerous service. On the contrary, cheerfulness and alacrity were evident on the countenances, and this while subsistence was so scarce as to force a consumption of horses killed in the battle. It is hoped that the bearing and whole career of this brigade of regular troops during the five days' conflict were of a character to meet the approbation of the major general commanding the division.

The brigade was not without the ambition of deserving also the commendation of Major General Thomas, commanding the centre, whose experience has been so successful and so long, and likewise of the commander-in-chief, whose uniform success inspired confidence. In fine, the brigade having combatted so well we need hardly search for examples, but should rest satisfied that there are none to excel it in courageous action and mournful losses. Of 77 officers with the battalions 5 were killed and 21 wounded, some mortally; and of 1,366 enlisted men 90 men killed and 469 wounded, many mortally, besides 47 missing, supposed to be prisoners.

The casualties of the battery were not so great, on account of its position and of its fire dispersing every line of the enemy approaching sufficiently near; at one time completely routing the 2d Arkansas rebel regiment, causing it to abandon its colors, which were picked up by skirmishers of the 2d regiment of Ohio volunteers before the officer sent for it reached the ground where the regiment was broken, and 22 rebel prisoners were taken during the day.

Captain Gunther's battery attached could scarcely have been excelled for the skill and effectiveness of its fire, and the cool, brave conduct of its officers and men. For six days and nights the harness was never taken from the horses either for food or water, the horses being kept patiently on the alert at the pieces.

Appended is a list of the officers killed and wounded, and a consolidated report of the total killed and wounded. Also the reports of the chiefs of battalions and of the battery. They are admirably drawn and exhibit more minutely the operations of the particular commands, and are of great interest.

The honor of this brave conduct of the brigade belongs properly to the chiefs of battalions and of the battery, respectively, Majors King, Carpenter, Plummer,

Townsend and Caldwell; and after Majors King and Plummer were wounded, and Major Carpenter was killed, to their successors, Captains Crofton, 16th, Fulmer, 15th, Mulligan, 19th infantry, and also to Captain Gunther, commanding company H, battery, 5th artillery. Great credit is reflected by the good condition of their respective commands.

The brigade staff, Captain Kinney, quartermaster, 1st Lieutenant Mills, commissary, and 1st Lieutenant Sutherland, 18th infantry, acting adjutant general of the brigade, accompanied me into action with the brigade, and performed the duties of carrying orders and all the other duties required of them with courage, zeal and ability. Assistant Surgeon Lindsly, acting brigade surgeon, and Acting Surgeons Patton and Henderson were actively and zealously occupied at the various hospitals during the whole time. Dr. Lindsly visited at different times the field.

Resting in the hope that this brigade, but recently organized, has displayed in this great battle of five days' duration a career worthy the approbation of the government and the cause in which engaged,

I have the honor, respectfully, to subscribe myself, very truly, your humble servant, &c.,

O. L. SHEPHERD,
Lieutenant Colonel 18th Infantry, U. S. A., Commanding Brigade.

Major General LOVELL H. ROSSEAU,
Commanding 3d Division, Centre 14th Army Corps.

List of commissioned officers killed and wounded.

HEADQUARTERS BRIGADE UNITED STATES REGULAR TROOPS,
Third Division, Centre 14th Army Corps, January 10, 1863.

Killed.—Major S. D. Carpenter, 19th infantry; Captain William W. Wise, 15th infantry; Captain J. B. Bell, 15th infantry; Captain Charles L. Kneass, 1st battalion, 18th infantry; Second Lieutenant J. L. Hitchcock, 2d battalion, 18th infantry.

Wounded.—Major John H. King, 15th infantry; Major A. J. Slemmer, 16th infantry, severely; Captain Joseph S. Yorke, 15th infantry, slightly; Captain Robert P. Barry, 16th infantry, severely; Captain John C. King, 16th infantry, severely; Captain Newton L. Dykeman, 16th infantry, slightly; Captain Henry Douglass, 1st battalion, 18th infantry, slightly; Captain D. L. Wood, 1st battalion, 18th infantry, slightly; Captain R. B. Hull, 1st battalion, 18th infantry, severely; Captain Charles E. Dennison, 2d battalion, 18th infantry, severely; Captain A. B. Thompson, 2d battalion, 18th infantry, severely; Captain Henry Haymond, 3d battalion, 18th infantry, slightly; First Lieutenant W. B. Occleston, 15th infantry; First Lieutenant W. H. Bartholomew, 16th infantry, severely; First Lieutenant John Power, adjutant 16th infantry, severely; First Lieutenant James C. Howland, 16th infantry, slightly; First Lieutenant Joseph McConnell, 1st battalion 18th infantry, severely; First Lieutenant Morgan L. Ogden, 2d battalion 18th infantry, severely; First Lieutenant James Simons, 2d battalion 18th infantry, severely; Second Lieutenant G. L. Carpenter, 1st battalion 18th infantry, severely; Second Lieutenant John J. Adan, 1st battalion 18th infantry, slightly.

O. L. SHEPHERD,
Lieutenant Colonel 18th Infantry, United States Army,
Commanding Brigade.

Consolidated report of casualties in brigade U. S. regular troops, 3d division, "Centre" 14th Army Corps, in the five days' battles before Murfreesboro', Tennessee, commencing December 31, 1862, *and ending January* 4, 1863.

Regiment.	Commanded by—	Officers.			Enlisted men.						Horses.	
		In action.	Killed.	Wounded.	In action.	Killed.	Wounded.	Prisoners.	Missing.	Total enlisted.	Killed	Wounded.
Brigade headquarters.	Lt. Col. O. L. Shepherd	4	..	..	1	..	....	..	..	....	....	....
Co. H, bat. 5th art ..	1st Lt. F. L. Guenther	3	..	..	120	..	5	..	..	5	8	5
1st bat. 15th infantry	Capt. Jesse Fulmer...	16	2	3	304	10	74	2	15	101	....	....
1st bat. 16th infantry	Capt. R. E. A. Crofton	15	..	7	293	16	147	..	16	159	....	....
1st bat. 18th infantry	Major J. N. Caldwell .	16	1	6	272	28	115	2	..	145	....	....
2d bat. 18th infantry	Maj. Fred'k Townsend	16	1	5	298	30	98	3	2	133	....	....
1st bat. 19th infantry	Capt. J. B. Mulligan ..	10	1	..	198	6	55	..	7	68	....	....
		80	5	21	1,486	90	494	7	40	611	8	5

HEADQUARTERS BRIGADE U. S. REGULAR TROOPS,
3d Division, "Centre," 14th Army Corps,
Camp at Murfreesboro', Tennessee, January 10, 1863.

O. L. SHEPHERD,
Lieut. Colonel 18th Infantry, Commanding Brigade.

HEADQUARTERS FOURTH BRIGADE,
FIRST DIVISION, FOURTEENTH ARMY CORPS,
Camp at Murfreesboro', Tennessee, February 18, 1863.

SIR: I desire respectfully to state that, owing in part to Captain H. Douglass, 1st battalion 18th infantry, not being a commander during the recent battle, I have forgotten him in my reports, therefore I desire respectfully to give an outline of his service.

He was commander of the 1st battalion from its organization, in the fall of 1861, and continued so through all the trying campaign of Mill Springs, and up to the 26th of May, 1862, just before entering Corinth, and has ever since been acting field officer.

In the performance of said duty he was distinguished in the battle of Perryville, and wounded in the great battle of Stone river, during the heavy conflict in the cedars, on the 31st December, 1862.

Having his wound dressed, and with his arm in a sling, he reported for duty as the brigade moved to the front, on the 2d of January, but was directed shortly after to go again to the hospital.

He has always been brave and zealous, and is again in command of his battalion, which owes much of its instruction to him. I hope it may not be too late to have justice done him.

I am, colonel, very respectfully, your obedient servant,

O. L. SHEPHERD,
Colonel United States Army, Commanding Brigade.

Colonel GODDARD,
Assistant Adjutant General and Chief of Staff,
Department of the Cumberland.

HEADQUARTERS FIRST BATTALION
FIFTEENTH UNITED STATES INFANTRY,
Camp at Murfreesboro', Tennessee, January 10, 1863.

SIR: I have the honor to report that on the morning of December 31, 1862, the 1st battalion 15th United States infantry, comprising eight companies, entered into action before Murfreesboro', Tennessee, under the command of Major John H. King.

The number of enlisted men present and entering into action was 304; Lieutenant Ogilby, battalion adjutant, and the following company officers, to wit: Captains Fulmer, Wise, Bell, Ketettas, and Yorke, and Lieutenants Jewett, Wikoff, Woodward, Occleston, King, Semple, Galloway, and Grey were present and participated in the engagement. The average strength of the battalion on entering into action was 319, officers and men.

This battalion, with the others of the brigade of regulars, commanded by Lieutenant Colonel Shepherd, 18th United States infantry, advanced several hundred yards into a dense forest of cedars, about 9 o'clock on the morning of the 31st instant, to engage the enemy. The 15th, with the 1st battalion of the 16th infantry on the left, were moved a short distance from the other battalions of the brigade and formed in line of battle. Captain Ketettas's company was immediately ordered forward as skirmishers, and, as such, he advanced them some 400 yards beyond our line. He had been enticed thus to advance by the action of scattering rebels in our front, who, wearing our style of uniform, feigned to be of us. This piece of deception, however, was timely detected, and a heavy firing between the skirmishers was immediately commenced. Ours were driven back, and the enemy, in two or three lines of battle, hurriedly advanced with a strong line of skirmishers in front. Our line of battle suffered somewhat by mistaking a body of rebels dressed in our uniform for our troops. When commanded to open upon the enemy, the battalion poured in a heavy fire upon them, but were soon compelled to give way to the vastly superior numbers of the enemy. We fired retreating until we reached the rear of the position just that moment taken by the 6th regiment Ohio volunteers. Here we halted to re-form our line, but, while so doing, the overwhelming numbers of the rebels and the fierce onslaught they made on the 6th Ohio forced these gallant volunteers to fall back also, whereupon we moved out of the woods, returning the enemy's fire, and, under cover of Guenther's battery, succeeded in taking favorable position and re-forming our line. It was in this engagement that Captain Bell was killed, Captain Yorke wounded, and, I fear, mortally, and Lieutenant Occleston severely wounded.

The battalion re-formed, advanced, and again took position in the woods, as also the others of the brigade. This was done promptly and with a zeal highly creditable to men who had only a few moments before been under a most galling and terrible fire. Very soon we were again engaged with the enemy, and, after a spirited engagement for a while, were ordered to fall back. Then it was that Major King was wounded and the command of the battalion devolved upon me. I continued the movement, firing upon the enemy, and moved to the support of Guenther's battery. In this affair Captain Wise fell mortally wounded, and has since died.

For the remainder of that day we acted in support of Guenther's battery, and remained on the front of our lines that night until nearly daybreak, when we moved to the rear. Later in the morning we moved forward again, first supporting the centre, then the right.

Friday morning we again moved to the front, supporting Guenther's battery, and remained there until the battle of that day ended.

Advancing a short distance on Saturday morning, we threw up entrenchments in face of the fire of the enemy's skirmishers and sharpshooters. These we occupied Saturday night, supporting Guenther's battery during the brilliant and successful attack made upon the enemy's lines that night.

In addition to the casualties already named, the battalion had eighty-four enlisted men killed and wounded, ten of whom are positively known to have been killed outright, two captured, and fifteen missing, who have doubtless either been killed, wounded, or captured. The aggregate casualties to officers and men number 106.

The conduct of the officers and of the men engaged merits commendation, and the battalion, in all of the advanced movements into the cedars, and in the several actions engaged, did well in aiding to check and drive back the largely superior numbers of the enemy confronted by the brigade of regulars.

I am, sir, very respectfully, your obedient servant,

JESSE FULMER,
Captain 15th United States Infantry, Commanding 1st Battalion.

First Lieutenant ROBERT SUTHERLAND,
18th Infantry, Acting Assistant Adjutant General,
Brigade of Regulars.

List of casualties in the 1st battalion U. S. infantry, in the action before Murfreesboro', Tennessee, December 31, 1862.

CONSOLIDATION OF COMPANY REPORTS.

	Officers.		Enlisted men.				
	Killed.	Wounded.	Killed.	Wounded.	Captured.	Missing.	Aggregate.
Field and staff	......	1	......	......	......	......	1
Company A	......	......	3	11	......	2	16
Company B	......	......	1	9	......	1	11
Company C	1	......	1	8	2	3	15
Company D	1	......	1	12	......	1	15
Company E	......	......	2	12	......	1	15
Company F	......	......	......	8	......	2	10
Company G	......	1	......	5	......	4	10
Company H	......	1	2	9	......	1	13
Total	2	3	10	74	2	15	106

I certify that the above is correct.

J. FULMER, *Capt. 15th U. S. Infantry,*
Commanding 1st Battalion.

JANUARY 10, 1863.

Report of killed, wounded, and missing of the field and staff of 1st battalion Fifteenth United States infantry, in the action before Murfreesboro', Tennessee, the 31st day of December, 1862.

Wounded.—Major John H. King, commanding 1st battalion.

Respectfully,

F. D. OGILBY,
First Lieutenant 15th Infantry, Adjutant,
Per FULMER.

Captain J. FULMER,
15th United States Infantry,
Commanding 1st Battalion.

Report of killed, wounded, and missing of company A, 1st battalion Fifteenth infantry, December 31, 1862.

Number of men engaged, 47.

Killed.—Sergeant Edward Quinn; Privates William B. McCall and Martin Van Suttle.

Wounded.—Sergeant Patrick Kane; Corporal Andrew H. McFaden; Privates David S. Flynn, Fidel Heisler, Jesse Guyun, Frank Maguire, Eugene A. Ogden, George Sagers, Michael Moran, Alfred H. Masters, and Thomas Kelley.

Missing.—Private James H. Lemon and Francis Bruce.

Killed, 3; wounded, 11; missing, 2.

HORACE JEWETT,
First Lieutenant 15th Infantry, Commanding Company A.

CAMP AT MURFREESBORO', *January* 10, 1863.

List of casualties in company B, 1st battalion 15th United States infantry, in the battle before Murfreesboro', Tennessee, on the 31st day of December, 1862.

Killed.—Private John Waugh.

Wounded.—Private James Acker, Robert Adams, Patrick Daily, Samuel Finley, Henry Kolthoff, Joseph Loose, James McGuire, David R. Spencer, and George A. N. Wray.

Missing in action.—Private Myron Parks.

Killed, 1; wounded, 9; missing, 1.—Total, 11.

Very respectfully,

R. P. KING,
First Lieutenant 15th Infantry, Commanding company B.

Captain JESSE FULMER,
Commanding 1st Batalion, 15th U. S. Infantry.

Report of killed, wounded, and missing of company C, 1st battalion 15th infantry, December 31, 1862.

Number of men engaged, 32,

Killed.—Captain William W. Wise, (mortally wounded, died January 3, 1862;) Private William Kapple.

Wounded.—Sergeants O'Rourke, (captured,) and Morrett; Corporal Underwood; Privates Findley, Mank, Strauss, Schiveikert, Astermyer.
Captured.—Corporals Betzer and Titsworth.
Missing.—Privates Levis, Hardy, and Dorr, (supposed captured.)

JAS. Y. SEMPLE,
First Lieutenant 15th Infantry, Commanding Company C.

List of casualties in company D, first battalion fifteenth United States infantry, in the battle before Murfreesboro', Tennessee, on the 31st day of December, 1862.

STATION CAMP AT MURFREESBORO', *January* 10, 1863.

Killed.—Captain J. Bowman Bell, and Private Isaac Petweler.
Wounded.—Sergeant Isaiah Lomison, Corporals William Sharp and Daniel Henderson, Privates Alfred Benton, James M. Williams, Charles H. Umbaugh, Noah Stotler, John C. Roney, H. W. C. Roney, Jesse Spouciller, Abram M. Mills, and Hiram Conner.
Missing in action.—Private Benjamin Closson.
Killed, 2; wounded, 12; missing, 1. Total, 15.

ROMAN H. GRAY,
Second Lieutenant Fifteenth U. S. Infantry.

Captain JESSE FULMER,
Commanding First Battalion Fifteenth U. S. Infantry.

List of the killed, wounded, and missing of company E, first battalion fifteenth United States infantry, in the action near Murfreesboro', Tennessee, December 31, 1862.

Killed.—Privates Sutton B. Quinn and Gustavus Garrick. Total, 2.
Wounded.—First Sergeant James P. Brown, Privates David A. Scholes, George Barker, Peter Gillonly, John A. Osterle, John Imhof, Robert Raisin, and Gottleib Nukom, Nathan Rix, John Sifers, G. Washington Foor, Orsin H. Beebe. Total, 12.
Missing.—Private David Pontus.

HENRY KETELTAS,
Captain Fifteenth Infantry, Commanding Company.

Report of killed, wounded and missing of company F, first battalion, fifteenth infantry, in the action before Murfreesboro', Tennessee, December 31, 1862.

Wounded.—Sergeants Huyck, Moll and Kanable; Corporals Mantle and Gibson; Privates Davis, Fletcher and Shrock.
Missing.—Privates Kennedy and Miller.
Wounded, 8; missing, 2. Total, 10.

CHAS. WIKOFF,
First Lieutenant, Fifteenth Infantry, Com'g Co. F.
Per FULMER.

List of casualties in company G, fifteenth United States infantry, in the late battle before Murfreesboro', on the 31st day of December, 1862.

Wounded.—Captain Joseph S. Yorke, severely; Sergeant Harry S. Lovejoy, slightly; Privates Ezra Gilbert, Daniel Lose, Samuel J. Landis, and Alfred Slusser. Total, 5.

Missing in action.—Privates Theodore S. Dunning, Henry R. Moore, Michael Tressel, and Charles P. Van Duyn. Total, 4.

Respectfully submitted,

S. E. WOODWARD,
First Lieutenant Fifteenth Infantry, Com'g Co. G.

Captain JESSE FULMER, *Commanding Battalion.*

List of killed, wounded and missing, of company H, first battalion, fifteenth United States infantry, in action at the battle of Stone river.

Killed.—Privates Chester Brown and Jacob Hexamex.—2.

Wounded.—First Lieutenant W. B. Occlestone, Corporal W. D. Blair, Privates John Gissinger, (since died in hospital,) Henry Chapman, Robert Howell, Charles Sutter, George Snyder, Alexander Ramsey, Benjamin Geph, (since died in hospital,) Thomas Prestly.

Missing.—Adam Frandensteine. Total, 13.

The company went into action with 34 men and one commissioned officer.

Loss in killed, wounded and missing.......35
13
—
22
=

Total now with the company.......12

N. S. GALLOWAY,
Second Lieutenant, Commanding Company H.

HEADQUARTERS 1ST AND 2D BATTALION 16TH INFANTRY,
Camp at Murfreesboro', Tennessee, January 10, 1863.

COLONEL: I have the honor to submit the following as a report of the part taken by the 1st battalion and company B 2d battalion 16th infantry, under my command, in the late actions before Murfreesboro', during the 31st December, 1862, and the 1st, 2d, 3d, and 4th January, 1863.

At 7 o'clock a. m. on the morning of December 31, 1862, this command (then under Major A. J. Slemmer, 16th infantry,) was ordered to move to the front from the bivouac where we had rested the night previous. We marched about a mile in the direction of Murfreesboro', and were then marched into line of battle on the right of the turnpike, the 1st battalion 15th infantry being on our right, and 1st battalion 18th infantry on our left. Here we stacked arms and rested for some time. About a quarter past 9 o'clock we were ordered into a thicket of cedars; when we had arrived about three-quarters of a mile from the edge of the thicket we moved into line of battle, changing our front to the right to oppose the advancing columns of the enemy. Company "B" 1st battalion, under command of First Lieutenant Bartholomew, was thrown to the front in skirmishing order to cover the front of our line. In about five minutes these skirmishers were driven in and formed on the right of the battalion. The enemy was now seen advancing in line and at the same moment opened a deadly fire on our ranks. The command, however, succeeded in checking their advance, the men behaving with the greatest possible coolness and aiming with accuracy. The battalion on our right having moved to the rear, it became necessary to fall back, which we did, by the right of companies to the rear. The men performed this movement with the same order and regularity they would in an ordinary drill. Having fallen back about one hundred paces, we came into line, faced to the front, and returned the enemy's fire. Again, for want of support we were obliged to retire, and did so as before for about another hundred yards. Maintaining this position for some minutes, we found it necessary to make a retreat to where we could be supported, as the enemy was moving his line on our right and left and threatening to surround us. We then moved by the right of companies to the rear, out of the woods and across a cotton field, where the enemy poured musketry and round shot upon us, but without doing much injury. We continued our retreat across the turnpike to the railroad, where we joined the remainder of the brigade and were ordered to support battery "H" 5th artillery. We remained in this position till about half past eleven o'clock a. m., when we were again ordered into the cedars. We advanced this time about thirty yards from the edge of the woods, when we became engaged, and a most terrific conflict issued. Almost at the commencement of this action Major A. J. Slemmer was so seriously wounded as to be obliged to fall to the rear; about the same time Adjutant John Power was dangerously wounded. After remaining in this position for about twenty-five minutes, and seeing the right of the brigade retire in order, we were compelled reluctantly to fall back, as the enemy outflanked us on our right and left. The men moved out of the woods by the right of companies with great regularity, notwithstanding the fearful fire to which they were exposed. As we crossed the open field between the woods and railroad the fire was terrible, and the men fell before it in great numbers until the enemy were driven back by the fire from battery "H" 5th artillery, attached to brigade. Arrived at the railroad, we again formed and remained with the rest of the brigade in support of the above battery. We continued in this position all the afternoon, continually exposed to artillery fire from the enemy's batteries. About four o'clock next morning we were ordered to the rear about a mile, where we obtained some rest. About eight o'clock a. m. we were again put in position on the right centre. From this position we were ordered to the right. In the afternoon we were ordered to proceed to Stewart's creek, and on arriving within a mile of the creek were ordered back at a double-quick, when we immediately faced about and retraced our steps in double-quick time. About sundown we arrived near our original position, the men being very much exhausted by hardships they had undergone and the rapidity of the march. We were moved into bivouac in a belt of woods near the centre of the general position. Next morning formed us again near the front and centre supporting battery "H" 5th artillery. Here we remained in reserve until about two o'clock p. m., when we moved back to our bivouac of the night before. Here we remained about half an hour, when we were again ordered to the position occupied by us during the morning, owing to an impetuous attack on the left, under General Crittenden, by the enemy. In this position we remained all the afternoon and that night. Next morning a battery opened on us from the enemy, but was soon silenced by battery "H" 5th artillery. We then moved still further to the front, where we threw up a line of earthworks, and the men slept on their arms in the trenches. That night so completely were the men exhausted from want of rest and food, that they slept in about six inches of water. Next morning it was discovered that the enemy had abandoned their position and were in full retreat. The command remained guarding these trenches till the morning of the 5th January when we marched to Murfreesboro'.

During these five days the men suffered very much for want of food, and were so much reduced that some of them ate roasted horse flesh. Fifteen officers and two hundred and ninety-three enlisted men went into action.

The following is a list of the officers of the command who were engaged. Major A. J. Slemmer, Captains R. E. A. Crofton, R. P. Barry, James Biddle, N. L. Dykeman, and J. C. King; First Lieutenants A. W. Alleyn, E. McConnell, W. H. Bartholomew, John Power, (battalion adjutant,) W. W. Arnold, J. C. Howland, and R. E. Kelleg; Second Lieutenants S. E. St. Onge and W. J. Wedemeyer.

All the officers and men behaved with great coolness and courage, and notwithstanding the great sufferings it was necessary for them to endure, they performed their duties without a murmur.

Subjoined you will find a list of killed, wounded, and missing; of the latter number I am convinced that few, if any, are stragglers, as some who were at first reported missing, it has since been discovered are wounded and were unable to avoid being taken by the enemy.

I have the honor to remain, very respectfully, your obedient servant,

R. E. A. CROFTON,
Captain 16th Infantry, Commanding.

Lieutenant Colonel O. L. SHEPHERD,
Commanding Brigade Regular Troops.

List of officers and enlisted men killed, wounded, and missing, of the sixteenth United States infantry, at the battle of Murfreesboro', December 31, 1862.

OFFICERS.

Wounded.—Major A. J. Slemmer, commanding regiment, severely; Captain Robert P. Barry, company A, severely; Captain John C. King, company D, severely; Captain Newton L. Dykeman, company H, slightly; First Lieutenant W. H. Bartholomew, company B, first battalion, severely; First Lieutenant John Power, adjutant, first battalion, severely; First Lieutenant James C. Howland, company D, slightly.

ENLISTED MEN.

Killed.—First battalion: Privates Nicholas Hindelong, James Lewis, and Dennis Sullivan, company A; Nathan Frost and Nicholas Ginsbach, company B; Frank Clark, company C; Fernando Fergusson, company D; Corporal Robert Robertson and Private J. Williams, company F; George L. Pooler and George H. Patterson, company G; Erastus Cheadle and Harrison Stockdale, company H.

Second battalion: Zachariah White, Lemuel K. Palmer, and Aaron Simmons, company B.

Wounded.—First battalion: Commissary Sergeant James H. Howe, mortally; Sergeants Flavius J. Pattee, G. McNeil, and W. G. Scott, company A; J. Buckner, company B; Morris Thomas, company C; W. Wagner, company D; Judson, company F; Seth Marten and H. H. Edson, company H; Charles Perkins, company G; Corporals Greenhalgh and Kastner, company B; T. O'Neil, company E; Dervin, Kinkaid, and Vigor, company F; Thomas Donohoe, N. W. Reese, and H. B. Hastings, company H; Privates Gillick, Dolan, Duddy, (from missing,) Hilton, Hogan, Dundon, Adams, Spice, Nelson, Kane, Dorsey, Kelley, Devine, Larcomb, Hutchinson, Fjetterstrom, Donohoe, McQuaid, Kinney, Nolan, McCaughy, and Fahy, company A; Lade,

Leslie, Love, Griffin, Golton, Gilhoed, Kottinger, Bowers, (from missing,) O'Neil, Stone, and Wagner, company B; Owens, Batten, Black, and Healy, company C; Brotz, Conway, Harley, Meiner, Mead, Roach, Russel, Nix, Wrightman, and Mesmer, company D; Burton, Grawney, Kawanaugh, Kinston, Jones, McMahon, Shannon, Straw, Venters, Wielie, and Wescott, company E; Bengan, Boyle, Crotine, Garvey, Hulihan, Knutson, Livingston, Lathrope, McCarthy, Minnihan, McLane, Sykes, Trueblood, and Taylor, company F; Gillespee, Heney, Donelly, Wirt, and Wild, company G; Boyce, Dubi, Grey, Kieth, Smith, Thompson, Gallagher, Nordham, Caldwell, and Brainard, company H.

Second battalion: Sergeants M. Whalen and Hamilton, privates Rahaley, Kirkpatrick, Miller, Harper, Daney, Dorcey, Crabree, Anderson, B. Olson, J. Olson, Rawson, Smith, Strater, Frindle, Page, McWilliams, and Hilton, company B.

Missing.—First battalion: Privates *Duddy* and Kernan, company A; *Bowers*, Bruce, and O'Flaherty, company B; McKinney, Carrigan, and Loth, company C; Finnigan, company G; Kelley, Sawyer, and Padden, company H; Carroll, O'Neil, Sympson, and Scott, company E.

Second battalion: Corporal McRussell and private Canfield, company B.

RECAPITULATION.

Officers wounded		7		7
Enlisted men killed		16		16
Enlisted men wounded	2 +	125	=	127
Enlisted men missing	2 –	18	=	16
Total		166		166

NOTE.—Duddy, company A, and Bowers, company B, first battalion, found wounded.

HEADQUARTERS FIRST BATTALION EIGHTEENTH INFANTRY,
Camp near Murfreesboro', Tenn., January 6, 1863.

SIR: Herewith I have the honor to transmit a list of the killed and wounded in my battalion in the battle of the "Cedars," near Murfreesboro', December 31, 1862. I went into the battle with 1 adjutant, 1 sergeant major, 6 captains, 8 lieutenants, and 272 enlisted men; aggregate, 288. Captain Kneass was killed, Captains Douglass, Wood, and Hull, wounded, Lieutenants McConnell, Carpenter, and Adair, wounded, 1 sergeant and 3 corporals killed, 6 sergeants and 4 corporals wounded, 23 privates killed, and 99 wounded; total and aggregate loss, 145. All did their duty well, were cool, deliberate, and firm under the terrific fire that thinned our ranks, and not one gave way, until the order to rejoin the battery attached to our brigade was given. We were under fire on the 1st, 2d, and 3d of January, 1863, and in the trenches on the day and night of the 3d instant, but sustained no loss. During the four days and nights on the battle-fields near Murfreesboro', notwithstanding the cold, mud, and rain, and want of rations, part of the time, not a murmur was heard; all exhibited the same coolness and unflinching devotion to their country and flag that they had shown on the battle-field at Perrysville, Ky., when composing a part of General Steadman's brigade, which was exposed to a terrific fire on that field. Captain Douglass acted as field officer on the 31st December, 1862, and rendered valuable service, and, notwithstanding his painful wound, joined the battalion on the 2d of January, and remained on duty with it during that day. My battalion adjutant, Lieutenant R. L. Morris, rendered valuable service on the field; his horse was wounded. My horse was wounded and disabled. My battalion quartermaster, Lieutenant Benham, Quartermaster Sergeant Price, and Commissary Sergeant Livsey, with a small escort and the teamsters, all did their duty well, in defending and conducting the battalion train in safety to Nashville. In conclusion I beg leave respectfully to recommend the following named non-commissioned officers for promotion, for their bravery and meritorious conduct in the battle of December 31, 1862, near Murfreesboro', Tenn.: Sergeant Major Reuben F. Little, Sergeant Allen C. Barrows, company F, First Sergeant Ralph Horton, company H, and First Sergeant Isaac D'Isay, company A; and also Sergeant E. C. Beach, company A, Sergeant Carpenter, company F, Quartermaster Sergeant Price, and Commissary Sergeant Livsey, for certificates of merit.

Very respectfully, your obedient servant,

J. N. CALDWELL, *Major Eighteenth Infantry,*
Commanding First Battalion Eighteenth Infantry.

The ACTING ASSISTANT ADJUTANT GENERAL, *Brigade of Regulars.*

HEADQUARTERS EIGHTEENTH U. S. INFANTRY,
Camp near Murfreesboro', Tennessee, January 6, 1863.

SIR: In compliance with instructions from brigade headquarters, I have the honor to submit the following list of killed and wounded in the battle of the Cedars, near Murfreesboro', Tennessee, December 31, 1862.

Company A, first battalion, eighteenth United States infantry.

Killed.—Privates James Harrison and Nicholas Holsback. Total, 2.

Wounded.—Captain Henry Douglass, (slightly,) Second Lieutenant G. S. Carpenter, (severely,) Corporal Samuel Gorsuch, Privates William Larrowe, Ebenezer Myers, George Moore, George W. Medick, William H. Peckham, Henry Strupelt, Henry D. Smith, and Frederick Siegle. Total, 9.

Captured while bringing the wounded from the field.—Sergeant Edward C. Beach, and Private Charles Riefenberg. Total, 2.

Company B, first battalion, eighteenth United States infantry.

Killed.—Nathan Ray, John Fusselman, William Patterson, (doubtful,) Charles Argus, and Francis Masterton. Total 5.

Wounded.—First Sergeant Joseph Owens, Sergeant Maurice Schwartz, Corporal Francis M. Davis, Privates William Barker, William Frizzell, Patrick Dailey, Richard Fitzgerald, Robert C. Hardwick, Michael Kuntz, Edward Pepper, John B. Shaffer, Michael Welsh, Henry P. Dixon, John Riddell, and Jacob Schrechingaust. Total, 15.

Company C, first battalion, eighteenth infantry.

Killed.—Captain Charles L. Kneass, and Corporal Francis M. Phillipi. Total, 2.

Wounded.—Privates James B. Massey, Vendreith Washburn, Wellington D. Welch, John Welch, John Quinn, John Herbstritt, John Brugger, Frank P. Gaddis, George Eberly, Richard Rumsey, Peter Johnson, and Sergeant Daniel C. Fletcher. Total, 12.

Company D, first battalion, eighteenth United States infantry.

Killed.—Private Hugh Scolann.
Wounded.—Captain D. L. Wood, (slightly,) Corporal David M. Hannahs, Privates George Meyer, William H. Thomas, Owen M. Wescott, and Patrick Barrett. Total, 5.

Company E, first battalion, eighteenth infantry.

Wounded.—First Sergeant Martin E. Looker, Corporal Jesse Brooks, Privates Frederick Edwards, Thomas H. Hickman, Samuel Hill, Isaac Wilson, George Shafersberger, Hiram Robinhood, John Hamilton, Levi Greenwood, and Jacob Hilgert. Total, 11.

Company F, first battalion eighteenth United States infantry.

Killed.—Sergeant Henry Headley, and Private Jacob Bike. Total, 2.
Wounded.—Sergeant Daniel S. Willder, Corporal Charles W. Bell, Privates Michael Bolan, Henry H. Clark, Jaret Headington, Isaac N. Howard, Frederick Kerchner, Daniel Kring, William E. McCauley, James S. Risher, and Alexander White. Total, 11.

Company G, first battalion, eighteenth infantry.

Killed.—Corporal Joseph L. Harcourt, Privates James O'Neill, Martin Schwank, and Charles Schreck. Total, 4.
Wounded.—Captain Robert B. Hull, (severely,) Second Lieutenant John J. Adiar, (slightly,) Sergeant Joseph F. Weller, John C. Smith, Privates Thomas Nasey, Martin Frank, Henry Davy, Isaac Shutt, John Lesley, James Dixon, Aaron Weltz, Andrew Kelly, Newton Thorp, Josiah Baughman, W. T. Grimer, and Marvin Cacklen. Total, 14.

Company H, first battalion, eighteenth infantry.

Killed.—Private Jacob Blessing, Henry B. Plumley, Patrick Savage, and Elias White.—Total, 4.
Wounded.—First Sergeant Ralph Horton, Privates Barnard Brink, Ambrose Higgins, Frederick Luther, Patrick Hoare, Christian Schranck, George Brown, John Endrass, Henry Douglass, Nicholas Haas, David Hackney, David W. Jones, John Harris, John Jackoble, John Moriarty, John S. McClintock, Gabriel H. Owen, Gideon Rose, Thomas Schultz, Frederick Seibt, and George W. Stone. Total, 21.

Company A, third battalion, eighteenth infantry.

Killed.—Corporal B. W. Willcox, Privates James Adair, James A. Anderson, and James S. Fisher. Total, 4.
Wounded.—First Lieutenant Joseph McConnell, (severely,) Privates Henry F. Helpman, William Marshall, John McBride, A. D. Tagg, and James Michlejohn. Total, 6.

Company D, third battalion, eighteenth infantry.

Killed.—Privates Samuel Palmer, Elisha Harper, Valentine Ferrenkoaf, and Peter Murphy. Total, 4.
Wounded.—Sergeants John P. Ell and Mahlon Peters, Corporal John

Falter, Privates William Plum, George W. Steirhoff, Michael E. Williamson, Henry Boulter, John Clark, Samuel Fetters, Jasper Converse, and James Horner. Total, 11.

RECAPITULATION.

	Killed.	Wounded.	Missing.
Captains	1	3	0
Lieutenants	0	3	0
Sergeants	1	6	1
Corporals	3	4	0
Privates	23	99	1
Total	28	115	2

Aggregate: 145 in the battle of December 31, 1862.

The battalion was under fire on the 1st, 2d and 3d of January, 1863, and in the trenches on the day and night of the 3d, but met with no loss.

Very respectfully, your obedient servant,

J. N. CALDWELL,
Major Eighteenth U. S. Infantry, Com'g First Battalion.

The ACTING ASSISTANT ADJUTANT GENERAL,
Regular Brigades.

HEADQUARTERS SECOND BATTALION EIGHTEENTH U. S. INFANTRY,
Camp at Murfreesboro', Tennessee, January 10, 1863.

SIR: I have the honor to report that, pursuant to the orders of the lieutenant colonel commanding the brigade, about 7 o'clock on the morning of the 31st December, 1862, my battalion, comprising sixteen officers and 298 enlisted men, being one of the battalions of the brigade of regulars, accompanied that brigade into action. My orders were to support and defend Lieutenant Guenther's battery, company H, 5th artillery. While thus employed, Captain Charles E. Dennison, commanding company B, and the right general guide, Sergeant Joseph Matthew, were severely wounded, and First Sergeant George F. White, of company F, 3d battalion, was killed. Subsequently the brigade and battalion took position in a dense forestof cedars for the purpose, as was understood, of holding in check the advancing enemy while a rearrangement of our own line of battle might be effected. We maintained this position for over twenty minutes, when we received the orders of the brigade commander to retire, having, however, achieved the result expected and required, but not without great loss—nearly one half of the command—as will be observed in the annexed list of casualties. During the subsequent days of the battle we were continuously under arms and under the fire of the enemy's cannon, and were moved from place to place wherever our presence seemed to be required. The last thirty-six hours of the battle we assisted in throwing up and holding intrenchments commanding the central portion of the field, the occupancy of which, owing to the heavy rains, became one of hardship and trial.

It affords me pleasure to state that there was not a single instance of cowardice in the battalion, and that both officers and men did completely and effectively their whole duty.

The names of the officers of the battalion in the engagement of the 31st are as follows: Major Frederick Townsend, commanding battalion; First Lieutenant Frederick Phisterer, adjutant of the battalion; Captain Henry R. Mizner; Captain Charles E. Denison, wounded severely; Captain Henry Belknap; A.

B. Thompson, wounded severely; Captain William J. Fetterman; Captain Henry Haymond, wounded slightly; Captain A. B. Denton; First Lieutenant M. L. Ogden, wounded severely; First Lieutenant H. G. Radcliff; First Lieutenant James Simons, wounded severely; First Lieutenant Henry B. Freeman; Second Lieutenant William H. Bisbee; Second Lieutenant John F. Hitchcock, killed, and Second Lieutanant Wilbur F. Arnold. Total, 16.

First Lieutenant William P. McClery, quartermaster of the battalion, was with the train, where he displayed conspicuous gallantry in defending it from capture with its guard and the sick.

I beg to call the attention of the brigade commander to the following enlisted men of my battalin, who were conspicuous for their gallantry in the engagement on the 31st: Sergeant Major John S. Lind; Sergeant Samuel C. Williamson, company D, 2d battalion; Sergeant Charles B. Meredith, company D, 2d battalion; Corporal Sylvester S. Bartlett, company C, 2d battalion; Lance Coporal Paul Fisher, company D, 2d battalion; Private William H. Maxwell, company A, 2d battalion; Private Jacob Kline, company D, 2d battalion; Private James McKenzie, company B, 3d battalion; James Hofler, company C, 3d battalion.

I have the honor to remain, very respectfully, your obedient servant,

FREDERICK TOWNSEND,
Major 18th United States Infantry, Commanding.

First Lieutenant R. SUTHERLAND,
Assistant Adjutant General, Brigade of Regulars.

WASHINGTON, D. C., *February* 23, 1863.

GENERAL: I neglected, in my report of the doings of the 2d battalion of the 18th United States infantry in the recent battles in front of Murfreesboro', Tennessee, to mention among the names of certain enlisted men conspicuous for good conduct on the field, and at all times, the name of my mounted orderly, Private Jacob Troutman, of company D. He was of very great assistance to me in carrying and bringing orders, and displayed a degree of intelligence and bravery worthy of strong commendation. In justice to this excellent soldier I trust, general, that you will permit this notice of him to be appended as supplemental to my official report.

I have the honor to be, general, your obedient servant,

FREDERICK TOWNSEND,
Major 18th Infantry, Commanding 2d Battalion.

Brigadier General LORENZO THOMAS,
Adjutant General United States Army,

Consolidated list of casualties in the 2d battalion of the 18th United States infantry during the battle near Murfreesboro', Tennessee, December 31, 1862.

Company.	Killed.		Wounded.		Prisoners.	Missing.
	Commissioned officers	Enlisted men.	Commissioned officers.	Enlisted men.	Enlisted men.	Enlisted men.
A, 2d battalion	....	4	....	14	....	....
B, 2d battalion	1	3	1	9	....	....
C, 2d battalion	....	2	....	7	....	1
D, 2d battalion	....	1	1	10	....	....
E, 2d battalion	....	5	1	11	1	....
F, 2d battalion	....	....	1	9	....	....
B, 3d battalion	....	2	....	5	....	....
C, 3d battalion	....	5	....	14	....	....
E, 3d battalion	....	3	1	6	....	1
F, 3d battalion	....	5	....	13	2	....
Total	1	30	5	98	3	2

Commissioned officers and enlisted men killed, 31; wounded, 103. Prisoners and missing, enlisted men, 5.—Total, 139.

FREDERICK TOWNSEND,
Major 18th United States Infantry, Commanding 2d Battalion.

FREDERICK PHISTERER,
First Lieutenant 18th U. S. Infantry, Adjutant 2d Battalion.

List of casualties in company A, 2d battalion United States infantry during the battle of the 31st of December, 1862, near Murfreesboro', Tennessee.

Killed.—Privates David Redmon, Amos Sherman, John M. Pierce, and Gideon Beard. Total, 4.

Wounded.—First Sergeant Zenas Dunham, in foot, since amputated; Sergeant Joseph Matthieu, severely, abdomen; Corporal George T. Fass, slightly, leg. Privates Pharaoh Brink, slightly, leg; Joseph H. Dodds, severely, in foot; Ira J. Brown, severely, hip; Salathiel A. Rose, dangerously, side and back; William H. Maxwell, severely, arm shattered; Patrick McDonald, dangerously, leg; Amya Courtright, slightly, hand; Preston Brown, dangerously, groin; John A. Shepard, dangerously, breast; Orville Rhodes, slightly, side of head; Thomas L. Swank, severely, arm shattered. Total, 14.

WILLIAM J. FETTERMAN,
Captain 18th United States Infantry, Commanding Company.

List of casualties in company B, 2d battalion 18th infantry, during the engagement before Murfreesboro', from December 31, 1862, to January 3, 1863.

Killed.—Lieutenant J. L. Hitchcock, Corporals John Limbaugh and Jacob R. Leibole, and Private Michael Gallivan. Total, 4.

Wounded.—Captain Charles E. Denison, solid shot in knee, leg since amputated; Sergeant William P. Leiboler, in leg, rifle ball. Privates Thomas P. Hunley, through arm and breast; Michael Maly, through both thighs; Roseline S. Conady, through right thigh; Patrick Mangan, through right arm; John Linament, flesh wound in leg; Edmund Coen, slight flesh wound; Martin H. V. Young, left breast and wrist, and William R. Wallace, slight wound, left hand. Total, 10.

H. G. RADCLIFF,
First Lieutenant 18th Infantry, Commanding Company B, 2d Battalion.

List of casualties in company C, 2d battalion 18th infantry, January 1, 1863.

Killed.—Corporal Thos. J. Long and Private John Henry Teiman. Total, 2.

Wounded.—Sergeant Amos Flegal, ball entered near upper left and came out near lower right breast; Corporal Sylvester S. Bartlett, flesh wound in right shoulder; Privates Isaac Bemesdarfer, ball entered near right shoulder and came out near lower right breast; Samuel A. Bowman, in lower jaw; William Morgaridge, slightly in the back with a spent ball; Joseph Tredrow, in the hand slightly; James Place, ball passed through the flesh of the thigh. Total, 7.

Missing.—Musician Albert R. Browning. Total, 1.

A. B. DENTON,
Captain 18th Infantry, Commanding Company.

List of casualties in company D, 2d battalion 18th infantry, in the battle before Murfreesboro', Tennessee.

Killed.—Private Joseph Wasmer. Total, 1.

Wounded.—First Lieutenant Morgan L. Ogden, flesh wound in the shoulder; Sergeant S. C. Williamson, flesh wound in the leg; Privates John Argo, slightly; George Brooks, severe wound in the leg; Arthur D. Cantrill, severe wound in the leg, since died; Jeremiah Howald, severely, since died; Lenhard Goble, severely in the shoulder; Thomas Hogan, severely in the lungs; David Laken, arm broken; Jarral O'Connor, severely in arm, breast, and foot; Michael Strassel, slightly in the ear. Total, 10.

W. F. ARNOLD,
Second Lieut. 18th U. S. Infantry, Com'g Company D, 2d Battalion.

List of killed, wounded, and missing in company E, 2d battalion 18th United States infantry, during the action before Murfreesboro', Tennessee, from December 31, 1862, to January 3, 1863.

Killed.—Privates William Baglin, Samuel Daihl, Joseph Elsbeck, William Ennis, and Martin Rhapsbock. Total, 5.

Wounded.—Captain A. B. Thompson, seriously; Sergeant Joseph Davis, slightly; Corporal James H. Fowkes, slightly; Privates Charles Beardsly, slightly; William Grey, seriously; John A. Hartman, seriously; Lott McInerny, slightly; Martin B. Shirk, slightly; George H. Smith, slightly; William Viller, seriously; Dewitt C. Weaver, seriously; Milford B. Rhoads, slightly. Total, 12.

Taken prisoner.—Mannassah Kaln. Total, 1.

W. H. BISBEE,
Lieutenant 18th Infantry, Commanding Company.

List of killed, wounded, and missing in company F, 2d battalion 18th infantry, at the battle of Murfreesboro', Tennessee, December 31, 1862.

First Lieutenant James Simons, severely in hip and shoulder; Privates Daniel Baker, severely in shoulder; Andrew Bowers, severely in thigh; Daniel Devine, slightly in back; James Handley, severely, (died since in hospital;) Richard I. Jones, severely, (died since in hospital;) John C. Jones, slightly in hip; David M. Price, slightly in hand; George Waterfield, severely in shoulder; David S. Kissen, wounded and missing. Total, 10.

HENRY HAYMOND,
Captain 18th Infantry, temporarily commanding Company.

List of casualties in company B, 3d battalion 18th United States infantry, battle of Murfreesboro', December 31, 1862.

Killed.—Privates George Shuler and Abraham Coombs. Total, 2.

Wounded.—Corporal Elias H. Johns, left side, severely; Privates John C. Baker, severely; John Jackson, severely; Isaac James, abdomen and thigh, severely; James McKenzie, both legs, severely. Total, 5.

HENRY BELKNAP,
Captain 18th Infantry, Commanding Company.

List of killed and wounded of company C, 3d battalion 18th United States infantry, during the engagement before Murfreesboro', Tennessee, December 31, 1862.

Killed.—Privates William Cornwall, George Eckert, Isaac B. Jones, Frank Kelly, and George B. Smith. Total, 5.

Wounded.—Sergeant William Wallace, side, slightly; Corporal James Burns, neck, slightly; Privates William H. Diehl, knee, slightly; Andrew J. Conner, left arm, (since amputated;) John T. Hawice, both shoulders, severely; John McD. Hawice, right knee, severely; John Hoffler, ankle and arm, severely; Felix Kerstetter, leg, severely; George McCarty, right arm, severely; Fred. W. Orth, both arms, severely; Hugh W. Riddle, arm, severely; Theo. Sigman, hand, slightly, taken prisoner; James Campbell, supposed wounded, in hospital; James Sweagar, both legs, severely. Total, 14.

H. G. RADCLIFF,
First Lieutenant 18th Infantry, Com'g Company C 3d Battalion.

CAMP NEAR MURFREESBORO', TENNESSEE,
January 8, 1863.

List of killed, wounded, and missing in company E, 3d battalion 18th infantry, in the action of December 31, 1862, near Murfreesboro', Tennessee.

Killed.—Privates A. M. McGinnis, Amos Robins, and Sidney F. Armstrong. Total 3.

Wounded.—Captain Henry Haymond, wounded slightly in right knee; Sergeant Thomas Barr, right arm broken; Privates James McCormick, slightly in leg; Philip Fennel, slightly in thigh; Peter Killeam, slightly in face; Thomas B. Daniels, slightly in thigh, and George W. Caty, in thigh, nature of wound not known.

Missing.—Private Benjamin Lawhead, supposed to have been wounded and taken prisoner.

HENRY HAYMOND,
Captain 18th Infantry, Commanding Company.

List of casualties in company F, 3d battalion 18th United States infantry, in action near Murfreesboro', Tennessee, December 31, 1862.

Killed.—First Sergeants George F. White, solid shot through body; Samuel Dobbins, color bearer, rifle shot, head; William D. Madeira, rifle shot, head; and Privates John J. Carmean and Mahhon Hancock.

Wounded.—Sergeant David S. Todd, ankle, slightly; Corporals William H. Himes, leg—since dead, January 5th; Charles Miller, hip, missing; Albert F. Young, rifle shot; Privates Jacob Coleman, shoulder; Edward Cunningham, body; Malcolm McCraig, back and foot; John W. Parsons, left side; James M. Saxton, and Isaac S. Shaffner, missing; Francis Stoufer, arm; George H. Taylor, and John Wilson, rifle shot.

Prisoners.—Privates Isaac C. Coldby and John Priest.

HENRY R. MIZNER,
Captain 18th U. S. infantry, Commanding Company F, 3d Battalion.

HEADQUARTERS FIRST BATTALION NINETEENTH U. S. INFANTRY,
Camp near Murfreesboro', January 8, 1863.

SIR: I have the honor to report that six companies of the first battalion of the 19th regiment United States infantry, under command of Major S. D. Carpenter, with the regular brigade, under command of Lieutenant Colonel O. L. Shepherd, 18th infantry, were ordered to the front, and entered into action on the morning of the 31st of December, 1862, before Murfreesboro', at 9½ o'clock a. m.

The battalion was ordered by the brigade commander to take its position in the brigade on the left of the 18th infantry, supporting the left of Guenther's battery H, 5th artillery. About 10 o'clock a. m. the brigade, with the battery, was ordered into the cedars to the assistance of Negley's division; but after finding there was no possibility of securing a position, the battalion, in company with the battery, retired from the cedars in excellent order, under a most destructive fire. After taking our position on the hill near the railroad, we were again, about 12 m., ordered, with the remainder of the brigade, to advance in line of battle into the cedars. We there engaged an overwhelming force of the enemy for full twenty minutes. It was as we received the order to retire that

Major Carpenter fell, receiving six mortal wounds, dying instantly. The fire from the enemy at this time was terrific. Our men were falling on all sides. At this point the command of the battalion devolved upon myself, being the senior officer present. We fell back, in pursuance of orders, to the support of Guenther's battery, which had taken its position on the hill near the railroad, which position we maintained throughout the day.

The next day, January 1, 1863, at daybreak, we were ordered, with the brigade and battery, to the right to assist McCook's corps, where we remained in position until after midday, when we were ordered to proceed up the Murfreesboro' pike in the direction of Nashville, to Stewart's creek, to protect a provision train which was threatened by the enemy. After proceeding about four miles up the road we were ordered to the right about and double-quicked to the centre of the line of battle.

On the second of January, at daybreak, we took our position on the hill by the railroad in front of the cedars, which we held during the day and throughout the night. The next day, the 3d, we commenced intrenching the front and centre, under cover of our skirmishers, and that night, our breastworks being completed, were occupied and held by us until after the enemy had left our front, which fact was reported by me to the colonel commanding the brigade shortly after sunrise the 4th instant.

The battalion lost one commissioned officer killed, (the major commanding;) enlisted men, six killed, fifty-five wounded, and missing, seven, the greater part of the latter known to be in the hands of the enemy.

Twenty-two of the enemy fell on the 21st into our hands and were turned over to an escort of cavalry by order of Lieutenant H. Millard, of General Rousseau's staff, by Lieutenant Stansbury.

The following officers participated: 1st Lieutenants Andrews, Stansbury, and Jones; 2d Lieutenants Wagoner, Lowe, Curtis, Miller, Johnson, and Carpenter. The conduct of the officers and men throughout the five days' battle was excellent, the battalion taking part and sharing with the brigade in all its hardships, deprivations, and arduous duties, in its movements over the entire field, at one time supporting the right of General McCook's corps, at another assisting General Crittenden's, and on the last day and night intrenching and holding the centre of our own division.

I take pleasure in mentioning the energy and efficiency displayed by Drs. Henderson, of this battalion, and Lindsey, of the 18th infantry, acting brigade surgeon, in the care and treatment of our wounded, all of whom, I am credibly informed, are well cared for in comfortable hospitals.

I enclose herewith a consolidated list of the killed, wounded and missing of the battalion during the five days' battle, also copies of the reports from the commandants of companies of casualties, &c.

Very respectfully, your obedient servant,

JAS. B. MULLIGAN,

Captain 19th Infantry, U. S. A., Commanding 1st Battalion.

Lieutenant ROBERT SUTHERLAND,

18th Infantry, Assistant Adjutant General, Regular Brigade.

Consolidated list of casualties, killed, wounded, and missing, of the 1st battalion of the 19th regiment United States infantry, during the five days' battle before Murfreesboro', Tennessee, ending January 4, 1863.

Officers killed.—Major S. D. Carpenter, commanding battalion.

Enlisted men.

Company.	Killed.	Wounded.	Missing.
Company A	2	3	1
B	....	11	1
C	....	10	1
D	1	9	1
E	1	17	......
F	2	5	3
Total	6	55	7

Most of the missing known to be in the hands of the enemy.

JAS. B. MULLIGAN,
Captain 19th Infantry, U. S. A., Commanding 1st Battalion.

List of the killed, wounded, and missing of company A, 1st battalion 19th regiment of infantry, United States army, in the action of December 31, 1862, near Murfreesboro', Tennessee.

Killed.—Privates John Quinn and Aaron Luther.

Wounded.—Privates William Beam, in the back; Eli Wells, in the leg; William Shultz, in the head.

Missing.—Private James Kelley.

W. R. LOWE,
Second Lieutenant, Commanding Company.

List of the killed, wounded, and missing in company B, 1st battalion 19th regiment of infantry, United States army, in the action of December 31, 1862, near Murfreesboro', Tennessee.

Wounded.—First Sergeant William H. Harrison; Corporal Joseph H. Topky; Privates Thomas Brennon, Patrick Cain, Joseph C. Coke, William H. Fallen, William Figg, Edward Herrington, Frank Lansham, George W. Lawson, and Patrick Lynch.

Missing.—Private John Neckl.

JOSEPH J. WAGGONER,
Second Lieutenant, Commanding Company.

List of killed, wounded and missing of company C, first battalion nineteenth regiment of infantry, United States army, in the action of December 31, 1862, *near Murfreesboro', Tennessee.*

Wounded.—Sergeant H. B. Shaffer, through the body; Corporal John Shrot, in the spine; Corporal Benjamin Davis, in the arm; Privates Elisha Bennett, in the foot, badly; Jacob Crossby, in the shoulder; George Emigh, in the groin, dangerously; Joseph Griffith, in the side; J. L. B. Harnden, in the leg; Cornelius Hunt, in the hand; Samuel Smay, left leg broken; Aaron Snyder, in the hand.

Missing.—Private John Reese, deserted his flag.

CHAS. H. MILLER,
Second Lieutenant, Commanding Company.

List of the killed, wounded, and missing of Company D, first battalion nineteenth regiment of infantry, United States army, in the action of December 31, 1862, *near Murfreesboro', Tennessee.*

Killed.—Private S. C. Higgins.

Wounded.—Sergeant Charles Stears, in the foot; Privates Williston D. Dewey, ditto; Stephen Gause, thigh; Henry Hook, right side; Christ'n Kronman, nose; Franklin T. Shore, thigh and back; August Smith, nature of wound not known; Daniel Springer, foot; Townsend E. Fall, left leg broken.

Missing.—Private Henry Robinson, supposed to have been wounded and taken prisoner.

A. H. ANDREWS,
First Lieutenant, Commanding Company.

List of the killed, wounded, and missing of Company E, first battalion nineteenth regiment of infantry, United States army, in the action of December 31, 1862, *near Murfreesboro', Tennessee.*

Killed.—Privates John Bayer.

Wounded.—Sergeant W. H. Hover, in the head; Corporal Thomas J. Smith, ditto; Corporal Jacob Hester, right arm broken; Privates Charles Adams, in the face; James C. Brown, hand; John M. Doran, thigh; James Dunlevey, left hand; David Gilford, wrist; James A. Harvey, right foot; Henry F. Tibbitts, hip; Paul Tatem, abdomen.

Missing.—Privates Woodford D. Bennett, Edward Huzzey, Jacob Sallet, John B. Smith, Phillip Shram, and E. T. Swank.

JACOB D. JONES,
First Lieutenant, Commanding Company.

List of the killed, wounded, and missing of Company E, first battalion nineteenth regiment of infantry, United States army, in the action of December 31, 1862, *near Murfreesboro', Tennessee.*

Killed.—Privates Barnard Haggerty, Edward Gorman.

Wounded.—Sergeants William H. Williams, James A. Little; Privates John Powers, Leander Hipp, Joseph R. Cockefair.

Missing.—Privates William A. Randall, David W. Pollock, John J. McLain.

ALFRED CURTIS,
Second Lieutenant, Commanding Company.

HEADQUARTERS EIGHTH DIVISION,
Camp near Murfreesboro', Tennessee, January 8, 1863.

SIR: I have the honor to submit the following report of the operations of the troops of my command in the engagements with the enemy on Stone river:

On Tuesday morning, December 30, 1862, the 8th division, composed of the 7th and 29th brigades, Schultz's, Marshall's, and Nell's batteries, was posted on a rolling slope of the west bank of Stone river, in advance, but joining the extreme right of General Crittenden's line, and the left of General McCook's.

In the rear and on the right was a dense cedar woods with a broken, rocky surface. From our position several roads were cut through the woods in our rear, by which to bring up the artillery and ammunition trains.

In front a heavy growth of oak timber extended towards the river, which was about a mile distant. A narrow thicket crossed our left diagonally and skirted the base of a cultivated slope which expanded to the width of a mile as it approached the Nashville pike. This slope afforded the enemy his most commanding position, (in the centre,) on the crest of which his rifle pits extended, with intervals, from the oak timber immediately in my front, to the Nashville pike, with a battery of four Napoleon and two iron guns, placed in position near the woods, and about eight hundred yards from my position. Behind this timber on the river bank the enemy massed his columns for the movements of the next day. Their skirmishers were driven from our immediate front after a sharp contest, in which the 19th Illinois and 78th Pennsylvania volunteers displayed admirable efficiency. The position of my command was held under a heavy fire, until darkness terminated the skirmishing in our front, by which time we had inflicted considerable loss upon the enemy.

In the mean time General Sheridan's division came up and formed line of battle his left resting on my right, and began to advance, driving the enemy until he had passed the centre of my right brigade. While General Sheridan was in this position I changed my front slightly, bearing it more to the left to avoid masking a portion of Sheridan's command. The troops remained in this position and in order of battle all night, cheerfully enduring the rain and cold, awaiting the morrow's sun to renew the contest. Early the next morning, and before the heavy fog had drifted away from our front, the enemy in strong force attacked and surprised General McCook's right, commencing a general action, which increased in intensity towards his left. Sheridan's division stood its ground manfully, supported by the 8th division, repulsing and driving the enemy at every advance. The enemy still gained ground on General McCook's right, and succeeded in placing several batteries in position which covered my right. From these, and the battery on my left, which now opened, the troops were exposed to a converging fire, which was most destructive. Haughtaling's, Schultz's, Marshall's, Bush's, and Nell's batteries were all ordered into action in my front, pouring destructive volleys of grape and shells into the advancing columns of the enemy, mowing him down like swarths of grain.

For four hours the 8th division, with a portion of Sheridan's and Palmer's divisions, maintained their position amid a murderous storm of lead and iron, strewing the ground with their heroic dead. The enemy, maddened to desperation by the determined resistance, still pressed forward fresh troops, concentrating and forming them in a concentric line on either flank. By 11 o'clock Sheridan's men, with their ammunition exhausted, were falling back. General Rousseau's reserve and General Palmer's division had retired in rear of the cedars to form a new line. The artillery ammunition was expended; that of the infantry reduced to a few rounds; the artillery horses were nearly all killed or wounded; my ammunition train had been sent back to avoid capture; a heavy column of the enemy was marching directly to our rear through the cedars; communication with Generals Rosecrans or Thomas was entirely cut off, and it was manifestly impossible for my command to hold the position without eventually making a hopeless, fruitless sacrifice of the whole division. To retire was but to cut our way through the ranks of the enemy. The order was given and manfully executed, driving back the enemy in front, and checking his approaching columns in our rear.

All the regiments in my command distinguished themselves for their coolness and daring, frequently halting and charging the enemy under a withering fire of musketry. On approaching General Rousseau's line the battalion of regulars, under command of Major King, at my request, gallantly charged forward to our assistance, sustaining a severe loss, in officers and men, in the effort.

Colonels Stanley and Miller now promptly re-formed their brigades with the remaining portions of the batteries, and took position on the new line, as designated by Major General Thomas. Shortly afterwards the 29th brigade was ordered to the left to repel an attack from the enemy's cavalry on the trains. The troops remained in line all night and the next day in order of battle until noon, when the division was ordered to the right of General McCook's line, in expectation of an attack upon his front.

The next day, January 2, at one o'clock p. m., my command was ordered to the support of General Crittenden's, on the left, and took position in the rear of the batteries on the west bank of Stone river. About 3 p. m. a strong force of the enemy, with artillery, advanced rapidly upon General Van Cleve's division, which, after sustaining a severe fire for twenty or thirty minutes, fell back in considerable disorder, the enemy pressing vigorously forward to the river bank. At this important moment the 8th division was ordered to advance, which it did promptly, the men crossing the river and charging up the steep bank with unflinching bravery. The 21st, 18th, 69th, and 74th Ohio, 19th Illinois, 11th Michigan, 37th Indiana, and 78th Pennsylvania volunteers displaying their usual promptness and gallantry. Four pieces of artillery and a stand of colors belonging to the 26th (rebel) Tennessee were captured at the point of the bayonet, and a large number of prisoners, the enemy retreating in disorder.

It is proper to mention here that the artillery practice of Shultz's, Mendenhall's, Standart's, Nell's, Marshall's, and Stokes's batteries, which were acting temporarily under my orders in this engagement, was highly satisfactory, giving the enemy great tribulation.

The promptness displayed by Captain Stokes in bringing his battery into action by my orders, and the efficient manner with which it was served, affords additional evidence of his marked ability and bravery as an officer and patriot. In the same connexion I feel permitted to speak in complimentary terms of the gallant Morton, and his pioneer brigade, which marched forward under a scathing fire to the support of my division.

The enemy having fallen back to their intrenchments, my division recrossed the river and resumed its former position.

On the evening of the 4th the 29th brigade was moved forward to the north bank of Stone river, near the railroad, as an advance force. On the same day General Spear's 1st Tennessee brigade was assigned to the 8th division. This brigade distinguished itself on the evening of the 3d in a desperate charge on the enemy, a report of which is included in General Spear's report, annexed.

On the morning of the 5th I was ordered to take command of the advance and pursue the enemy towards Murfreesboro'.

By 9 a. m. the 8th division, Colonel Walker's brigade, pioneer brigade, and General Stanley's cavalry force, had crossed the river and taken possession of Murfreesboro' without having met any resistance, the rear guard of the enemy retreating on the Manchester and Shelbyville roads, our cavalry pursuing, supported by the 29th brigade on the Shelbyville pike, and by Colonel Byrd's 1st East Tennessee regiment on the Manchester pike.

The rear guard of the enemy, (three regiments of cavalry and one battery,) was overtaken on the Manchester pike, five miles from Murfreesboro'. Colonel Byrd fearlessly charged this unequal force of the enemy, driving him from his position with a loss of four killed and twelve wounded; enemy's loss not ascertained.

Our army marched quietly into Murfreesboro', the chosen position of the enemy, which he was forced to abandon after a series of desperate engagements.

The joyful hopes of traitors have been crushed—treason receiving another fatal blow.

My command enthusiastically join me in expression of admiration of the official conduct of Generals Rosecrans and Thomas. During the most eventful periods of the engagements their presence was at the point of danger, aiding with their counsels and animating the troops by their personal bravery and cool determination.

I refer to my command with feelings of national pride for the living, and personal sorrow for the dead. Without a murmer they made forced marches over almost impassable roads, through drenching winter rains, without a change of clothing or blankets, deprived of sleep or repose, constantly on duty for eleven days, living three days on a pint of flour and parched corn. Ever vigilant, always ready, sacrificing their lives with a contempt of peril, displaying the coolness, determination, and high discipline of veterans, they are entitled to our country's gratitude. Pennsylvania, Ohio, Kentucky, Indiana, Michigan, and Tennessee, may proudly inscribe upon their scrolls of fame the names of the 78th Pennsylvania volunteers; 18th, 21st, 69th, and 74th Ohio; Schultz's and Marshall's batteries, (Ohio;) the 11th Michigan; 19th Illinois; 37th Indiana; Nell's section, Kentucky battery, and Spear's Tennessee brigade.

I respectfully refer to the reports of General Spear, Colonels Miller and Stanley, which I approve and append hereto, for a detailed account of the part taken by each portion of the command, and for special reference to the meritorious conduct of individuals in their respective commands.

In addition to which I make honorable mention of the bravery and efficient services rendered by the following named officers and men, for whom I earnestly request promotion:

East Tennessee brigade.—Brigadier General Spears, commanding; Colonel T. R. Stanley, commanding 18th Ohio volunteer infantry; Colonel John F. Miller, commanding 29th Indiana volunteer infantry; Captain James J. C. C. Morton, commanding pioneer regiment.

Chicago battery.—Captain James H. Stokes, commanding.

15th United States infantry.—Major John A. King, commanding.

4th Indiana battery.—Captain Rush, commanding.

4th Ohio battery.—Captain W. A. Standart, commanding.

8th division.—Captain James A. Lowrie, A. A. G.; Lieutenant Frederick H. Kennedy, A. D. C.; Captain Charles F. Wing, A. Q. M.; Major F. H. Gross, medical director; Captain James R. Haden, orderly officer; Lieutenant W. W. Barker, A. D. C; Lieutenant Robert H. Cochran, provost marshal; Lieutenant Thomas Riddle, A. A. C. S.; Lieutenant Charles C. Cook, A. A. D. C.; Lieutenant W. D. Ingraham, topographical engineer; Captain Frederic Schultz, Lieutenant Joseph Hem, battery M, 1st Ohio artillery; Lieutenants Alexander Marshall, John Crable, Robert D. Whittlessy, battery G, 1st Ohio artillery; Lieutenants A. A. Ellsworth, W. H. Spence, Nell's section Kentucky artillery; Lieutenant H. Terry, 3d Ohio cavalry; Sergeant H. B. Fletcher, company K, 19th Illinois volunteers; Corporal K. G. Rice, company K, 1st Wisconsin volunteers; Private James A. Sangston, company C, 79th Pennsylvania volunteers; Sergeant Charles Kamboun, company K, 74th Ohio volunteers; Private William Longwell, orderly, 7th Pennsylvania cavalry.

Escort.—Sergeant George C. Lee; Corporal E. H. Daugherty; Privates Henry Zimmerman, Henry Schwenk, John Higgins, Leon Starr, Daniel Walker, John D. McCorkle, Abraham Kepperly, George Gillen, John Cunningham.

The following is an approximate report of the casualties of my command during the battles before Murfreesboro', Tennessee, December 30 *and* 31, 1862, *and January* 2 *and* 3, 1863.

Second division, centre, 14th army corps.	Went into action.				Lost in action.										
					Killed.		Wounded		Missing.		Horses			Guns.	
	Commissioned officers.	Enlisted men.	Horses.	Guns	Commissioned.	Enlisted.	Commissioned.	Enlisted.	Commissioned.	Enlisted.	Killed.	Wounded	Missing.	Lost.	Disabled.
1st E. Tenn. brigade..	66	734	8	..	....	3	1	22	....	....	..	1	..	....	..
29th brigade..........	93	1,719	37	..	8	77	25	259	....	94	5	3	5	....	..
7th brigade..........	71	1,948	....	..	3	79	20	415	1	193	..	..	..	....	..
Infantry	230	4,401	45	..	11	160	46	696	1	178	5	4	5	....	..
Schultz's battery......	2	75	56	4	....	1	1	....	....	1	5	4	..	1	..
Marshall's battery....	3	110	116	6	....	5	....	5	....	14	34	12	..	4	..
Nell's battery........	2	47	40	3	....	1	....	3	....	6	18	6	4	1	1
Artillery	7	232	212	13	....	5	1	8	....	21	57	20	4	6	1
Total...........	237	4,632	257	13	11	167	47	704	1	38	62	24	9	6	1

My command captured from the enemy upwards of 400 prisoners, four brass pieces of field artillery, and one stand of regimental colors.

I have the honor to remain, very respectfully, your obedient servant,

JAMES S. NEGLEY, *Brigadier General.*

Major GEORGE E. FLYNT, *Chief of Staff.*

HEADQUARTERS FIRST TENNESSEE BRIGADE,
Hawthorn's, near Murfreesboro', Tenn., January 9, 1863.

GENERAL: I herewith beg leave to submit the following report, which is intended to embrace the action of the troops under my command, from the 2d inst. up to the present date.

At 12 o'clock m. on January 2, 1863, when at Nashville, Tenn., I was ordered by Brigadier General Johnson, military governor of the State, to immediately take command of the 1st and 2d East Tennessee volunteer infantry, and such other troops as would be assigned me by Brigadier General Mitchell, commanding post, which were the 11th Michigan volunteer infantry, about 300 men strong, commanded by Captain ———; the 85th Illinois volunteer infantry, Colonel Moore commanding, 350 to 400 men strong, together with two ections of the 10th Wisconsin battery, commanded by Captain Barber; as company of cavalry under Lieutenant ———; also Colonel Pickins, commanding 300 mounted volunteers of the 3d Tennessee cavalry, which forces were placed under my command for the purpose of conducting and protecting a train of 303 wagons loaded with commissary stores for the army then before Murfreesboro'.

I assumed command of the said forces at the junction of Market street and Murfreesboro' pike at 5 o'clock p. m., at which place I took up the line of march, throwing out skirmishers and otherwise disposing the forces under my command in such manner as I believed would best protect the train.

After marching all night I reported myself and command to Major General Rosecrans's headquarters at 5 o'clock on the morning of the 3d instant, and by his order turned over the train to his commissary.

Major General Rosecrans then ordered me to report to General McCook, which I complied with, and after receiving orders and instructions from General McCook I placed the artillery under my command in position, drew up the infantry in line of battle, and the enemy failing to make any demonstrations in front on the right wing we stacked arms and took refreshments. At this time I was ordered by General Rosecrans to turn the cavalry in my command over to General Stanley, which was done. The skirmishing in front of General Thomas's division becoming heavy, I was ordered by General Rosecrans to change my position and report to General Thomas, which I did, and by his order took a position in front of his division, relieving troops that had held said position during the night. I received further orders from General Thomas to place my artillery in reserve and to throw up an intrenchment of my force, in doing which, two of my men, privates in the 1st and 2d East Tennessee regiments, were wounded.

I was also authorized by General Thomas, if I thought proper, to throw out skirmishers, consisting of three or four companies, and retake and drive the enemy from a piece of woods in our front. After my force had finished the intrenchments, I was informed by an aid of General Rousseau that he would co-operate with me in throwing out skirmishers and in retaking the woods and driving the enemy from the same as soon as the artillery had began shelling the woods, which was to be the signal for advance. In accordance to this I threw out two companies (company A, Captain Duncan, and company B, Captain Sawyer) from the 1st East Tennessee regiment, also company A, Captain Masney, of the 2d East Tennessee regiment, and one company of the 85th Illinois, and one company of the 14th Michigan as skirmishers, at the same time that skirmishers were thrown out from General Rousseau's division.

Shortly after sundown the signal was given by shelling the woods, and the skirmishers advanced. The skirmishing becoming heavy, my force advancing in front, and General Rousseau's upon the right, it was soon discovered as they approached the woods the enemy was there in strong force and intended to maintain his position with the greatest obstinacy, so much so that I thought fit to order up Lieutenant Colonel Milton, commanding 2d East Tennessee regiment, to support the skirmishers in front.

By this time the skirmishers had driven the enemy back and gained the edge of the woods. Colonel Milton was ordered to advance as near as possible to the woods, and then to order his men to lie flat on the ground. By that time darkness had set in. I ordered Colonel Byrd, with the 1st East Tennessee regiment, to take his position behind the intrenchments, while I ordered Lieutenant Colonel Philips, of the same regiment, to take command of the 14th Michigan regiment, and to flank the enemy upon the left and rear, and I ordered the skirmishers to withdraw in good order and retreat behind the 2d Tennessee regiment, which at this time was pouring a galling fire into the enemy, while a hot fire was kept up by General Rousseau's skirmishers on the right and from the Michigan regiment on the left, which was kept up until the enemy abandoned his position, being completely routed. The engagement lasted from 6 to near 8 o'clock, during most of which time Major General Thomas was a spectator on the field.

I then ordered my forces to retire behind the intrenchments, throwing an advance picket forward to hold the position we had taken.

The force under my command in this engagement was composed of regiments and parts of regiments: of the 1st regiment East Tennessee volunteer infantry, 400 men; of the 2d regiment East Tennessee volunteer infantry, 400 men; of the 14th regiment Michigan volunteer infantry, 300 men; of the 85th regiment Illinois volunteer infantry.

The loss in my command of Tennessee troops was four wounded from the 1st regiment, and seven wounded from the 2d regiment East Tennessee volunteers. None killed or missing. The 14th regiment Michigan volunteers, commanded by Lieutenant Colonel Philips, of the 1st East Tennessee, reported two killed and three wounded. The regiment left for Nashville, as soon as the engagement was over, with the 8th Illinois regiment, which during the engagement was held as a reserve and had no casualties.

Nineteen prisoners were taken and sent to corps headquarters. The loss of the enemy is not known, but said to be considerable, his strength being variously estimated at from one to two brigades.

On the morning of the 4th instant I received an order from Major General Rosecrans informing me that I, together with my command, had been permanently attached to the eighth division, commanded by Brigadier General Negley. On the evening of the same day I was ordered by General Negley to hold myself in readiness to march at a moment's warning. At 10 o'clock at night I received an order from General Negley to order one of my regiments to report to Colonel Miller, commanding seventh brigade, for picket duty, which order was complied with by sending forward Lieutenant Colonel Milton in command of the 2d East Tennessee regiment at 1 o'clock a. m. on the 5th. On the morning of the 5th I received a verbal order from General Negley to immediately move forward with the remaining force under my command, consisting of the 1st East Tennessee infantry, Colonel R. K. Byrd, and 6th East Tennessee infantry, Colonel Jos. A. Cooper, also two sections of a battery (10th Wisconsin) commanded by Captain Beebee, and support Colonel Miller, who was in advance engaged in building a bridge over Stone river for the purpose of crossing infantry, the railroad bridge having been burned and injured by the enemy to such an extent as to render it unsafe. Being detained, Colonel Byrd and Colonel Cooper set their men to repairing the railroad bridge and crossed about the same time that Colonel Miller's rear crossed the other bridge, marching through the town of Murfreesboro', with my force in the rear of Colonel Miller's brigade. I was there ordered by General Negley to take and occupy a position near the crest of the ridge on the Manchester pike, which position I now occupy.

In the mean time, the cavalry having advanced upon the rear of the enemy then in our front, and the skirmishing becoming heavy, I was ordered by General Negley to support the cavalry with one regiment of infantry and one section of artillery, which I did by immediately ordering Colonel Byrd's regiment of East Tennessee, 400 men strong, and Captain Beebee with one section of artillery, to go forward and report to Brigadier General Stanley, commanding the cavalry in front.

The enemy had retreated to a point in the woods, near the Manchester pike, five miles from Murfreesboro', where they had stopped and formed "line of battle."

On the arrival of Colonel Byrd's and Captain Beebee's commands a sharp fight took place, both sides using artillery and small arms, which resulted in a complete rout of the enemy—not, however, without some loss to us; Colonel Byrd losing three men killed, and twelve wounded, mostly slight.

About the time the fight was going on between our infantry and cavalry force and the enemy, I received a verbal order from General Negley to advance to the front with the remaining force under my command, which I did as rapidly as possible; but before I could arrive on the battle-field General Stanley, with his brigade of cavalry, and Colonel Byrd, with his gallant Tennesseeans, aided by Captain Beebee's shells, had succeeded in driving the enemy so that not one could be seen.

All the troops under my command behaved well, and Colonel R. K. Byrd, of the 1st East Tennessee, and Lieutenant Colonel Philips, of the same regiment, are both said to have distinguished themselves ; Colonel Byrd having his horse shot and wounded, and several balls passing through his clothes. Several prisoners were taken.

The loss of the enemy has since proved to be some thirty in killed, besides wounded, which he took off.

The 2d sections of the 10th Michigan battery were not permanently attached to my command, and have since been ordered back to Nashville.

Herewith I enclose the reports of Colonel Cooper, 6th East Tennessee regiment volunteer infantry, describing the march from Nashville to this point, and his encounter with the enemy on his way.

All of which is respectfully submitted.

I am, general, your obedient servant,

JAMES G. SPEARS,

Brigadier General, Commanding 1*st Tennessee Brigade.*

Brigadier General JAMES S. NEGLEY,

Commanding 8*th Division,* 14*th Army Corps.*

Command.	Went into action.			Lost in action.			
				Killed.	Wounded.		Horse.
	Commissioned officers.	Enlisted men.	Horses.	Enlisted.	Commissioned.	Enlisted.	Wounded.
1st East Tennessee, 400	33	367	4	3	......	16	1
2d East Tennessee, 400	33	367	4	......	1	6	......
14th Michigan, 300*	......	......	......	......	......	......	......
85th Illinois, 350*	......	......	......	......	......	......	......
Total	66	734	8	3	1	22	1

* Ordered out of my command immediately after the action. I have no report from these regiments.

HEADQUARTERS 6th EAST TENNESSEE VOLUNTEERS,

Camp near Murfreesboro', Tennessee, January 9, 1863.

SIR : Permit me to submit this my official report of the march of my regiment from Nashville to Murfreesboro', in obedience to Special Order No. 8, as follows :

["Special Order No. 8.]

"HEADQUARTERS 1ST BRIGADE, TENNESSEE VOLUNTEERS,
"*Nashville, Tennessee, January* 3, 1862.

"Colonel Cooper, with his entire command for duty, will at once take up the line of march upon the Murfreesboro' pike. They will take two days' rations. They will report on said road to Colonel Daniel McCook.

"By command of General Spears.

"D. C. TREWHITT,
"*Assistant Adjutant General.*"

Complying with the above order, we took up the line of march at 8 o'clock. We marched out to the junction of the pike, where we lay in the rain about three hours waiting for the commanding officer, Colonel Daniel McCook. He arrived about 12 o'clock, and gave the following order:

"The two regiments in advance of you will march in front with the regiment of regular cavalry, all except fifty, the remaining fifty will act as rear guards for the whole. Your regiment, the 6th Tennessee, will march immediately in rear of the train."

We then took up the line of march to Murfreesboro.' We marched, without halting, about six miles, arriving this side the Lunatic Asylum. There we, together with a part of the 2d East Tennessee cavalry which had come up with us, met a body of the enemy. The cavalry, filing to the right, engaged the enemy, who consisted of two or three regiments of cavalry, supported by a small piece of artillery. The cavalry fired one or two rounds and fled in confusion, running through the trains. Just previous to this occurrence I received orders from Colonel McCook to move my regiment forward, on the left, to the loss of the rise. I marched forward in double quick, gained the point designated just in time to arrest the charge of the enemy. I engaged the enemy in a smart skirmish for some ten or fifteen minutes, killing some six or eight, and wounding several, and capturing ten prisoners. I met the enemy and repulsed them without assistance from the front. Immediately after skirmish a battalion of infantry came up on the left and assisted us in holding the position. We met the enemy and whipped them without the loss of a man either in killed, wounded, or missing. My men acted with great coolness and bravery.

The train was soon reorganized, and we were again on the march. We arrived at Lavergne without interruption. At that point the two regiments in advance and the battalion which came up during the skirmish were mounted on the train, leaving my command on foot in rear of the train. I rode forward and asked Colonel McCook what I should do. He first said I had better encamp there with my command. I then told him it was "most too far from shore for me to cast anchor." He then ordered me to march on as fast as I could on foot, so that if they were attacked we could come up to their assistance, and said "he was ordered to go through that night." I obeyed said order, keeping in my rear the one hundred cavalry first mentioned, and a portion of the 2d Tennessee cavalry, until we arrived inside the lines. I then halted, let the cavalry pass, aud went into camp for the night. Next morning at daylight I took the line of march, and marched to headquarters of Major General Rosecrans, where I reported to Brigadier General James G. Spears. All of the above I respectfully submit. I had in all when I went to the skirmish, and also when it ended—present, 12 commissioned officers and 213 enlisted men.

I am, very respectfully, your obedient servant,

JOSEPH A. COOPER,
Colonel 6th East Tennessee Infantry.

Captain D. C. TREWHITT,
Ass't Adj. General, 1st Brigade, East Tennessee Volunteers.

HEADQUARTERS TWENTY-NINTH BRIGADE,
Battle-field near Murfreesboro', Tenn., January 4, 1863.

SIR: Before the smoke of battle is over, and while the dead lie uninterred, I desire to make the following important report:

On the 30th December the 8th division occupied the extreme right of the advance of the army at this point, my brigade occupying the right. The enemy were in our immediate front and extending to our right. It was expected that General McCook would occupy our right and first engage the enemy there. I directed Colonel Scott, with his regiment, (the 19th Illinois,) as skirmishers, to protect our right flank, but not to bring on an engagement, as you had orders not to do so at that time. It, however, became necessary to occupy some buildings in a field from which we were annoyed by the enemy, and Colonel Scott drove them from the place and afterwards held it. We were then annoyed from a barn and brickkiln in our advance and right, and Colonel Scott charged and drove them away. Quite a number of the enemy were killed in these skirmishes and some two or three of our men.

During the day General McCook came up on our right and sharply engaged the enemy. At night we lay on our arms, and early on the morning of the 31st December our skirmishers advanced and drove the enemy's skirmishers partly through the woods in our front, and General McCook engaged them on our right, but eventually fell back; and then a very heavy force was precipitated on our front and right, and on the 7th brigade, to my left. This infantry force was supported by a battery on our front and one in intrenchments on our left, and the fire was very severe; but the brigade (as also did the 7th brigade, on my left) sustained the fire without falling back, and poured such a well-directed fire upon the enemy that they faltered, and their ranks were thinned and stayed; but the troops on our right and left had fallen back so far as to bring the enemy on three sides of us and fast closing on our rear. At this time General Negley directed the division to cut its way through, to join our other troops in the rear This we did in good order, halting at two points and checking the enemy by a well-directed fire, which, by this time, they had learned to fear.

After we had formed in line behind the crest of a hill, an officer from another division rode to the front of the 8th Ohio and ordered them forward, himself leading the way, and made the charge upon the enemy in the woods; but the enemy was so strong there the regiment was compelled to fall back with heavy loss. As soon, however, as I saw the move, I called upon the 11th Michigan to follow me to their support, which they did most gallantly; but I soon called them off, as they had no support and the fire was murderous. I exceedingly regretted this order from an officer not having command over me, and without consulting yourself or me, and many of my men were left on the field. Early in the action of this day I discovered that Colonel Casselly, of the 69th Ohio volunteers, was so drunk as to be unfitted to command, and I ordered him to the rear in arrest, and placed Major Hickox in command, who soon after was injured by the concussion of a shell so as to be unfit for duty, and thus the regiment was left without a commander. I, however, knew nothing of this for some time after; but members of my staff found them scattering, rallied them, and directed the senior officer present, Captain Putnam, to take command. Captain Brigham, the senior captain of the regiment, had been out with skirmishers, and was not at this time with the regiment. The regiment did but little service in the action, but the company officers did what they could, and in that way helped us some.

I recommend the dismissal of Colonel Casselly from the service. I cannot for a moment tolerate or pass over such flagrant conduct. I saw nothing of him after the action, but have learned that he was wounded and has gone to Nashville. A man who will come to the field of battle, having the lives of so many in his keeping, in such a situation, no matter what his social position, is totally unfit for any command.

On the 2d of January the enemy attacked the left flank of our army in strong force of infantry and artillery, and soon drove our scattered forces to the rear. General Rosecrans and General Negley were both on the ground occupied by the 8th division, and ordered my brigade forward across Stone river to stay the advancing forces. This was done with a will, the 19th Illinois leading, accompanied by the 7th brigade. They met the enemy with cheers, and with such determination that very soon the enemy gave way, followed closely by us, and were driven from every position of the hill, through the woods, and through an open field to woods beyond. In this gallant charge my brigade charged a battery and took three brass pieces. We occupied the field, and soon re-enforcements came to our relief, but it was nearly dark, and did not deem it prudent to advance further without orders, as there was a battery in the woods beyond which took effect upon us at short range. I here rallied my men and formed a little in rear of the crest of the hill. It was now about dark, and upon your order I withdrew my command to our former position. In this engagement, as also in the one of the 31st December, the 7th brigade acted in concert with my own, and sometimes the two, to some extent, were intermingled, but fought together without confusion; and thus the troops from Pennsylvania, Ohio, Indiana, Illinois, and Michigan stood side by side, each vieing with the other in the conflict.

With the exception of Colonel Cassilly, I know of no conduct worthy of censure, but much to commend. They acted with that bravery expected of well-disciplined troops fighting in a just cause. They stood manfully and bravely the appalling fire of a much larger force, and in the last engagement met and repulsed the enemy in superior force, elated with a supposed victory. The officers and men, almost without exception, behaved with the most determined bravery. Colonel Stoughton, of the 11th Michigan, was in the thickest of the fight, encouraging his men, and throughout both engagements acted with the most distinguished gallantry. Good judgment was also displayed by him in rallying his own men and others of my brigade at the crest of the hill in the last engagement during my temporary absence on another part of the field.

Colonel Scott, of the 19th Illinois, was also where danger was most imminent, and by his coolness and bravery aided his regiment in their gallant defence the first day, and charge the second. He was seriously wounded in the second engagement and carried off the field cheering and encouraging his men.

Lieutenant Colonel Given, of the 18th Ohio, was also at his post, and the thinned ranks of that regiment show how well they exposed themselves to the missiles of the enemy. He was cool, brave, and judicious.

Those officers, by their coolness and bravery, as well as good judgment and promptness of action, aided me in all my orders, and thus, by combined action and cool bravery, the brigade sustained the most determined shocks and repulsed the enemy at all points.

It would be invidious in me more particularly to specify individual cases of bravery. When all do well it is hard to particularize.

It is but just, however, to speak in commendation of Captain Brigham, of the 69th Ohio; under his leadership a part of the regiment was in front of the battle in the last engagement and behaved most gallantly. The regiment is a good one, and only needed a leader the first day to have taken a more active part in that engagement.

The members of my staff—Lieutenants Bishops, Temple, Platt, Sweeny, Rarick, and Cunningham—all were prompt and efficient in carrying my orders and aiding me, no matter what the danger. The same may also be said of my orderlies and clerks, Coffin, Mercer, and Adams, and Agnew and Riley, who were prompt and efficient.

I deem it but an act of simple justice to say of our division commander that in all he was cool, prudent, and determined. In the first engagement, when we were surrounded on all sides by the enemy, (the right and left having retired far to our rear) he said to me, "We must cut our way through," and gallantly led the division for that purpose, but the enemy wisely opened a way for us, and only closed upon us at a respectful distance. If we have acquitted ourselves with honor, much of it is due to his careful training, his cool self-possession, and the confidence we all feel in him.

Surgeons Bogue, Johnson, and Elliott, and their assistants, rendered all the aid in their power in alleviating the sufferings of the wounded. It is also claimed by some of my men that the 19th Illinois also took the enemy's colors on the second day. The same is also claimed by the 7th brigade. Suffice it to say that the colors were taken, the two brigades acting in concert. And while I desire for my brigade all credit for gallantry, I would not in the least detract from the other which was side by side with us.

In this engagement many of my valuable officers and men were killed and wounded.

Our thinned ranks show how well they faced the enemy. The last engagement was against the enemy's best troops in superior force. They had never before been beaten, but now they were driven in confusion, leaving hundreds of the dead and dying on the field.

Captain Schultz, with his battery, rendered me efficient service, and was ready and enthusiastic in executing my orders. He did his duty well. On the first day one of his pieces became entangled in the woods and was abandoned. We more than compensated this loss the second day.

I append a list of the casualties, and propose hereafter to make a more detailed report.

Very respectfully, your obedient servant,

T. R. STANLEY,
Colonel Commanding.

Captain JAMES A. LOWRIE,
A. A. G. and Chief of Staff, 8th Division.

Report of casualties.

HEADQUARTERS 29th BRIGADE,
Camp near Murfreesboro', Tenn., January 10, 1863.

Command.	Went into action.				Lost in action.								
					Killed.		Wounded.		Miss'g	Horses.			Guns.
	Commissioned officers.	Enlisted men.	Horses.	Guns, artillery.	Commissioned.	Enlisted.	Commissioned.	Enlisted.	Enlisted.	Killed.	Wounded.	Missing.	Lost.
Brigade staff	7		7							1	1	1	
18th Ohio volunteers	23	423	4		3	26	6	112	23	1			
19th Illinois	23	350	5		2	18	7	75	8		2		
11th Michigan	17	423	14		2	28	6	72	25	2		4	
69th Ohio	23	523	7		1	6	6	45	38	1			
Battery M	2	75	56	4		1	1		1	5	4		1
Total	95	1,794	93	4	8	79	26	304	95	10	7	5	1

Respectfully submitted.

——— ———,
Colonel Commanding.

M. D. TEMPLE,
Lieutenant and Acting Assistant Adjutant General.

HEADQUARTERS 7TH BRIGADE, 8TH DIVISION,
Murfreesboro', Tennessee, January 6, 1863.

SIR: In compliance with your request, the following report of the operations of my command before Murfreesboro' is respectfully submitted.

On the evening of December 29 my command took a position in a field on the right of the Nashville pike, in the rear of General Palmer's line, and bivouacked for the night. At daylight on the 30th, by order of General Negley, I took a position on the right of General Palmer's division, on the edge of a dense cedar woods fronting to the south, and deployed skirmishers from the 78th Pennsylvania and 37th Indiana in front, across and to the left of the six-mile pike, to act in conjunction with the skirmishers of Colonel Stanley's brigade on my right. A brisk fire was kept up between the skirmishers and the enemy's sharpshooters, in the open field to the left and in the woods in front, until the arrival of General Sheridan's division on the right, when our skirmishers were withdrawn for Colonel Roberts's command.

During the day General McCook's forces advanced on the right, so that his left rested on our right flank, when a change of front to the left was made by General Negley's division.

The enemy had remained quiet on the open field (now almost directly in my front) in his intrenchments, which were plainly visible, and had kept a battery of four pieces in position at his works all day without firing.

Marshall's and Ellsworth's batteries attached to my brigade, and posted in a small open field, fired an occasional shot into the works without eliciting reply. My command lost about twenty men killed and wounded during the day.

Skirmishers were kept out well to the front during the night, and two regiments of my command, with the batteries, were posted in the open field.

On the morning of the 31st skirmishing was resumed along our line, and heavy firing was heard in the night along General McCook's line. The firing on our right gradually increased and neared our position, until a continuous roar of artillery and musketry was heard directly in our rear, and the advancing columns of the enemy were on our right and front.

Here I received orders from General Negley to hold my position to the last extremity.

For this purpose I executed a partial change of my front, and placed my troops in the convex order, as follows: the 78th Pennsylvania, Colonel Sinvell, on the right at the brow of a small hill, the right resting near Schultz's battery of Colonel Stanley's brigade; the 37th Indiana, Colonel Hull, on the right centre; the 74th Ohio, Colonel Moody, on the left centre, behind a rail fence; Marshall's battery on a small hill in the open field to the left of the 74th Ohio; the 21st Ohio, Lieutenant Colonel Neibling, on the left in a thicket, fronting the enemy's works; and Ellsworth's battery near the log-house between Palmer's right and the 21st Ohio. Simultaneously with the advance of the enemy from the right, a heavy force advanced from the enemy's works on my left wing.

The batteries at the enemy's works were manned and opened over the heads of the enemy's infantry. Before my regiments were properly in position a most terrific fire was opened upon every part of the line by infantry and artillery, but there was no wavering, and as the advancing columns of the enemy approached they were met by a well-directed and terribly destructive fire from our line.

The batteries were worked with admirable skill, and the firing along our whole line was executed with credible precision. The enemy halted, but did not abate his fire. The roar of musketry and artillery now became almost deafening, and as the unequal contest progressed it became more terrible; once the strong force in the open field in front of my left wing attempted a bayonet charge on the 21st Ohio, but were gallantly met and repulsed with great slaughter. On one of the flags was inscribed "Rock City Guards." The battle continued with unabating fierceness on both sides until the sixty rounds of ammunition, with which my men were supplied, was nearly exhausted.

The 37th Indiana was the first to report a want of ammunition, and withdrew a short distance to the rear for a supply; the 74th Ohio and 78th Pennsylvania filling up the interval. The teamsters of the ammunition wagons had moved to the rear, and when ammunition was being brought forward they turned and fled. Colonel Hull again led his regiment forward, and fired the few remaining cartridges on the persons of the men, taking also such as could be had from the dead and wounded.

At this juncture the troops on our right retired, and some unauthorized person ordered Colonel Sinvell to retire his regiment. This regiment was fighting gallantly, and holding the position on the crest of the hill; but, on receiving the order, retired to the cedars in the rear. Seeing this, I immediately ordered Colonel Sinvell forward to the same position. This order was obeyed promptly, and the men again took position in admirable order. Soon after this a heavy force was observed to advance on General Palmer's left, and a hard contest ensued.

General Palmer's right brigade held their ground for a short time, and then began to retire; just at this time I received orders from General Negley to retire, slowly, with my command into the woods. My troops were nearly out of ammunition; the enemy was advancing on my right flank and on my left; the fire in front was no less destructive than it had been during the engagement.

The movement was executed in good order by the infantry, but it was impossible for the artillery to obey; nearly all the horses had been killed, the ground was soft and muddy, and the men had not the strength to haul away the pieces. Five guns were lost; four were saved by the men of the batteries, assisted by the infantry.

On reaching the woods I halted the command and formed a "line of battle," faced by the rear rank, and delivered several well-directed volleys into the enemy's ranks now crossing the open field over which I had retreated. This checked the advance of the enemy for a short time, strewing the ground with his dead. Being closely pressed on both flanks, and receiving fire from three directions, I again retired my command, the men loading while marching, and firing to the rear as rapidly as possible. In this way my command retreated for the Nashville pike, in a northeast direction.

While in the forest, being closely pressed in the rear, the enemy in strong force was encountered on the line of retreat, when a destructive fire was opened upon my column which caused them to break to the right. My men did not run, but marched to the pike, carrying many of our wounded. When near the pike, and when rallying his men, Colonel Hull, of the 37th Indiana, was severely wounded and disabled. He had fought bravely and gallantly during the whole engagement.

The 21st Ohio, Lieutenant Colonel Neibling, rallied near the pike, and, at the request of General Rousseau, took a position for the support of a battery then at work near the road. Ammunition was furnished, and the regiment fought with the battery over an hour, and then rejoined my command on the left of the road where I had organized and obtained ammunition.

During this entire engagement, and under all these terribly appalling circumstances, both officers and men of my command behaved with admirable coolness and bravery. Examples of heroic daring and gallantry were everywhere to be seen, but where all acted so well it is difficult to make special mention without doing injustice to many.

The cool courage and distinguished gallantry of Colonel William Sinvell, 78th Pennsylvania volunteers; Colonel Granville Moody, 74th Ohio, (who was wounded early in the engagement and refused to leave the field;) Colonel J. S. Hull, 37th Indiana, and Lieutenant Colonel James M. Neibling, 21st Ohio, regimental commander, deserve the highest praise, and the skill and ability with which these brave officers performed their responsible duties cannot be too highly applauded. The other field officers and company officers and also Lieutenants Marshall and Ellsworth, of the artillery, displayed that high courage and determined bravery which marks the veteran soldier.

Too much cannot be said in praise of both officers and men. The losses in my brigade, killed and wounded in the action, amounted to over five hundred men.

In the evening of the 31st I was ordered by General Negley to take a position on the centre front across the Nashville road for support to the batteries in position at that place. My command remained in this position until the next morning, when I was ordered to take position as reserve for General Hascall's division to the left of the railroad. In the afternoon of the 1st of January I received orders to march my command to the support of the right of General McCook's corps. I took position as directed, and remained there all night in the open field, and until about one o'clock p. m. on the 2d, when I was ordered to the support of General Crittenden's corps on the left. I took position, as ordered by General Negley, in an open field, in rear of the battery on the left of the railroad and near the bank of Stone river.

About 4 o'clock p. m. a furious attack was made by the enemy upon General Beatty's (or Vancleve's) division, then across the river. The fire of the enemy was returned with spirit for a time, when that division retired across the river and retreated through my lines, which were then formed near the bank of the river, my men lying down partly concealed behind the crest of a small hill in the open field.

As soon as the men of Beatty's division had retired entirely from our front I ordered my command forward—the 78th Pennsylvania on the right; the 21st Ohio on the left, to advance under cover of the hill along the river bank; the 37th Indiana and 74th Ohio in centre. The 29th brigade moved forward in the same direction, the 18th Ohio on the right, and formed partly in the intervals between the regiments of my right wing. The enemy advanced rapidly, following Vancleve's (Beatty's) division, and gained the river bank, all the time firing rapidly across at my line. My troops opened fire from the crest of the hill; the enemy halted and began to waver. I then ordered the men forward to a rail fence on the bank of the river. Here a heavy fire was directed upon the enemy with fine effect, and although in strong force, and supported by the fire of two batteries in the rear, he began to retreat. Believing this an opportune moment for crossing the river, I ordered the troops to cross rapidly, which they did with great gallantry under fire from front and right flank.

Here the 18th Ohio, part of the 37th Indiana, and part of the 78th Pennsylvania were ordered by some one to proceed up the river on the right bank to repel an attack from a force there firing on my right flank. The colors of the 78th Pennsylvania, and, I think, 19th Illinois, were the first to cross the river—the men followed in as good order as possible. While my troops were crossing a staff officer informed me that it was General Palmer's order that the troops should not cross. The enemy was then retiring, and many of my men across the stream.

I crossed in person and saw the enemy retiring. Taking cover behind a fence on the left bank, the men poured a heavy fire into the ranks of the retreating force.

The 21st Ohio had crossed the river on the left and was ascending the bank and fast going into the woods. When in this position I received another order, purporting to come from General Palmer, to recross the river and support the line on the hill. The force on the right of the river was then advancing in the cornfield and driving the enemy, thus protecting my right flank, and having no inclination to turn back I ordered the troops forward. Colonel Stoughton, of the 11th Michigan, formed his regiment and moved along the bank of the river, while the other troops moved forward to his left. The 21st Ohio came in on the extreme left and advanced in splendid style.

In crossing the river, the men of the different regiments had to some extent become mixed together, yet a tolerable line was kept under the colors of the 78th Pennsylvania, 19th Illinois, and 74th Ohio, and the men moved forward with spirit and determination.

The enemy's batteries were posted on an eminence in the woods near a cornfield in our front, and all this time kept up a brisk fire, but without much effect. His infantry retreated in great disorder, leaving the ground covered with his dead and wounded.

When within about one hundred and fifty yards of the first battery, I ordered the 78th Pennsylvania volunteers to charge the battery, which was immediately done by the men of that regiment, and the 19th Illinois, 69th Ohio, and perhaps others. The 21st Ohio coming opportunely on the left, the battery, consisting of 4 guns, was taken and hauled off by the men.

The colors of the 26th Tennessee (rebel) at the time of the charge were near the battery, and were taken by men of the 78th Pennsylvania, and brought to the rear.

Another battery, further to the front, all this time kept up a heavy fire of grape and canister upon our forces, but without much effect.

Seeing my troops in the disorder which follows such success, and being nearly out of ammunition, I sent a staff officer back to General Negley for re-enforcements with which to pursue the enemy.

I ordered the troops to halt and reform, so as to hold the ground until relieved by other troops. This being done, a large body of troops were soon brought to our lines, when I withdrew my command to reform and procure ammunition. At this time Colonel Stanley crossed the river and took command of the regiments of his brigade on that side of the river. I brought my troops across to the right bank of the river by order of General Negley, reformed them, supplied them with ammunition, and took position as support for the batteries on the hill in front.

The troops in this action behaved most gallantly, and deserve the highest credit for their bravery. Of the officers who participated in this engagement, honorable mentioned should be made of Colonel William Sinvell, 78th Pennsylvania; Colonel Jas. R. Scott, 19th Illinois, who was severely wounded while leading his regiment; Colonel William L. Stoughton, 11th Michigan; Colonel Granville Moody, 7th Ohio; Lieutenant Colonel Neibling, 21st Ohio; Lieutenant Colonel Elliott, commanding 69th Ohio; Major J. C. Bell, 74th Ohio; Lieutenant Colonel Ward and Major Kimball, 37th Indiana; Captain William Inness, 19th Illinois; Captain Fisher and Lieutenant McElroy, 74th Ohio. The gallantry of these officers, and of many others, cannot be excelled.

To my staff officers I am greatly indebted for their efficient and valuable services in both these engagements, as well as for their general efficiency and faithfulness.

Major A. B. Bonnaffon, 78th Pennsylvania volunteers, topographical engineer; First Lieutenant Henry M. Cist, acting assistant adjutant general; Lieutenant Alf. Ayars, 78th Pennsylvania volunteers, aide-de-camp; First Lieutenant S. F. Chenny, 21st Ohio, aide-de-camp; First Lieutenant F. I. Tedford, 74th Ohio, brigade inspector, all deserve the highest credit for the ability displayed in the discharge of their duties, and for distinguished gallantry and cool courage on the field.

I am also under many obligations to Lieutenant Robert Manque, brigade quartermaster, and Lieutenant Frank Riddle, brigade commissary, for the able manner in which they discharged their duties.

Chaplain Lozier, of the 37th Indiana, rendered valuable service by his labor for the comfort of the men, and in taking care of the wounded. His bravery and kindness were conspicuous throughout.

I am informed that Surgeon Anderson, 37th Indiana, brigade surgeon, performed his duties in a highly satisfactory manner.

Privates Nicholas J. Vail, 19th Illinois, and W. J. Vance, 21st Ohio, acted as orderlies, and deserve honorable mention for their efficiency and bravery; they are both worthy of promotion to the rank of lieutenant. I also recommend for promotion Sergeants H. A. Miller, A. R. Weaver, F. Mechling, Corporal W. Hughes, 78th Pennsylvania volunteers, and Sergeant P. A. Weaver, 74th Ohio, for deeds of valor on the field.

There are many others whose names have not been furnished.

You will please find appended a list of killed and wounded, amounting in the aggregate to ——.

I am, captain, very respectfully, your obedient servant,

JOHN F. MILLER,
Colonel 29th Indiana Volunteers, Commanding Brigade.

Captain J. A. LOWRIE,
Assistant Adjutant General.

Report of Casualties.

Command.	Went into action.				Lost in action.										
					Killed.		Wounded.		Missing.		Horses.			Guns.	
	Commissioned officers.	Enlisted men.	Horses.	Guns, artillery.	Commissioned.	Enlisted.	Commissioned.	Enlisted.	Commissioned.	Enlisted.	Killed.	Wounded.	Missing.	Lost.	Disabled.
78th Pennsylvania....	15	540	....	..	1	17	4	123	....	45	..	..	..	....	..
74th Ohio........	18	381	....	..	....	12	5	66	1	84	..	..	..	....	..
37th Indiana..........	17	437	....	..	2	28	6	105	....	9	..	..	..	....	..
21st Ohio.............	21	590	....	..	....	22	5	121	....	55	..	..	..	....	..
Battery G, 1st Ohio V. A.	3	110	116	6	....	5	....	5	....	14	34	12	..	4	..
1st Kentucky battery..	2	47	40	3	....	1	....	3	....	6	18	6	4	1	1
Total..........	76	2,105	156	9	3	85	20	423	1	213	52	18	4	5	1

JNO. F. MILLER,
Colonel 29th Indiana Volunteers, Commanding 7th Brigade.

HENRY M. CIST,
Acting Assistant Adjutant General.

List of casualties of the 7th brigade, commanded by Colonel John F. Miller, in the engagements of December 31, 1862, and January 2, 1863, before Murfreesboro', Tennessee.

Wounded.—Colonel John F. Miller, 29th regiment Indiana volunteers, in neck; N. J. Vale, 19th regiment Illinois volunteers, in left arm; Sergeant W. L. Lowrie, of escort, 78th Pennsylvania volunteers, in hand; James Carroll, of escort, 78th Pennsylvania volunteers, in leg.

Report of the 78th regiment Pennsylvania volunteers, commanded by Colonel William Sinvell.

Wounded.—Sergeant Major F. Muhling, in head, slightly.

Company A.—Wounded: Lieutenants John M. Marlin, in shoulder, slightly; William R. Maize, in leg; Corporal Samuel L. Serene, in leg; Privates William Cochran, in ankle; Thompson Kelly, in shoulder; James Little, in neck; David McElroy, in leg; Sergeant James M. Miller, in shoulder; Privates James Carroll, in leg; James Guthrie, in shoulder; Adam Keep, in leg, slightly; Robert Ewenswell, in shoulder. Missing: Privates James Buchannan, George F. Curry, John C. Lewis, James D. Lane, Jefferson Palmer, James H. Robinson, and David K. Rankin. Prisoners: George McGoughy.

Company B.—Wounded: Sergeants D. K. Thompson, in arm, slightly; W. C. Patkink, in head, slightly; Privates A. J. Cowan, sub-luxatio; Robert Lewis, in thigh; William Youn, in both thighs; Amos Dinger, in abdomen; Elias Diebler, in leg; G. W. Donerspiher, in head, slightly; Solomon Hinnes, in thumb, (amputated;) John J. Spencer, in hip, slightly; Corporals William Mathews, in leg, severely; Mark Sullivan, in leg, slightly; Privates Eli Hendrichs, in arm, severely; John B. Nevill, in leg, severely.

Company C.—Wounded: Sergeants Andrew Brown and William H. Thomas, in leg, (flesh;) Corporal William H. H. Miller, knee, (flesh;) Privates Thomas Kepler, leg, (flesh;) Reuben Hilliard, both thighs; Samuel Mohney, leg, (flesh;) William McMillen, hip; David R. Myers, breast; Albert C. Slocum, hand; Samuel Lowry, hip, slight; Lewis Sagers, left lung; Solomon Burkhouse, knee. Missing: Michael Riley, Abraham Forney, Alfred Maitland, William H. Frazier, Sergeant William Lattimer.

Company D.—Killed: Private Nathan Kern. Wounded: Privates Jacob Neff, in knee; A. B. Wike, foot; Isaac Kern, slightly; Jeremiah Cook, tibia.

Company E.—Killed: Reuben Latshaw. Wounded: Lieutenant James H. Anchors, and a prisoner; Sergeants James G. Briggs, in leg; Thomas M. Graham, and a prisoner; Corporal Jerry Hummel, leg; Privates John Brady, hand; Samuel Burford, arm; David Daniels, right leg; George W. Hogan, side; William Hays, right knee; Charles Myers, wrist; James A. McElwaine, head; George P. Marsh, knee; William S. Mortimer, side; Gibson J. Moore, leg; George W. Nichols, head; Christian Snyder, head; James H. Seip, shoulder; James R. Tutsworth, head; H. H. Whiteshell, back; Chambers Yurgling, thigh; Eli M. Call, do.; J. W. Williams, do.; E. W. Slator, do.; Christian Over, do.; James McNutt, side; A. J. Readon, thigh; Joseph W. Dislor, head. Missing: Private Alen Anchors.

Company F.—Killed: Privates H. S. Weaver, Philip Griffith, Dennis Conway, James Henry. Wounded: James Penman, head, (mor.;) Michael Sullivan, leg and testicles; Sergeant Absalom R. Weaver, side; Privates Lewis Lossa, leg; David Alter, shoulder and face; Samuel Slusser, thigh; George W. Taylor, hip; Jonathan Needam, leg; Peter Saplee, back. Missing: Private William Street. Prisoners: Corporals John S. Davidson and Robert Mitchell; Privates A. J. Kistler, James Adams, John F. Barr, Benjamin F. Haws.

Company G.—Killed: Corporals Arthur Myrtle and Morrison Hall; Private James M. Erwin. Wounded: Sergeant John C. White, arm; Corporal George G. Boreland, heel; Privates Henry F. Soxman, hip and thigh; James McCrachen, upper arm; James N. McLeod, foot; James M. Cousins, hand; John Hall, knee; William A. Haggerty, leg; Daniel Murphy, thigh; James Shannon, leg, and a prisoner; John G. Bowser, hand; Hugh Hooks, mouth; Charles Henry, foot; John H. Thompson, knee. Prisoners: John Croyle and Daniel McMullen. Missing: Simon Cousins.

Company H.—Killed: Privates James Myers and James Runyan. Wounded: Captain William S. Jack, leg; Sergeant C. F. Smith, head; Corporals John Moore, foot; U. J. Miller, not known; Privates Thomas Sykes, head; George Rose, leg; John C. Black and William Christly, left shoulder; E. Frank, right arm; A. Shindler, head; Dallas Thompson, left hip; E. Wilson, head. Missing: Henry Forct and J. A. Black.

Company I.—Killed: Privates John Chapman, James Cochlin, George Ressinger, and James Curran. Wounded: Sergeant William C. Murphy, foot; Sergeant John D. Hall, knee; Privates Samuel A. Gray, thigh; Aaron Eakman, leg; James McMeans, arm; James Updegraff, head; William H. Grey, leg; Harrison Daugherty, head; Jesse A. Clement, leg; and James A. Champin, thigh. Missing: Corporals H. V. Ashbough and William Young. Prisoners: Corporal Lewis S. Hill; Privates Thomas Dunlop and Johnston McElroy.

Company K.—Killed: Lieutenant Mathew J. Halstead. Wounded: Sergeant W. W. Smith, thigh; Corporals Enoch Gillem, thigh; William Martin, arm; and S. P. Henry, foot; Privates Peter A. Painter, hand; Adam Aikens, (supposed to be killed,) head; George H. Altman, thigh; David Prunhard, slightly; William Maxwell, slightly; A. Lloyd, slightly; Enoch Hastings, slightly; H. C. Bengough, slightly; Levi Step, slightly; John S. Hartman, head, (severely;) M. C. Bowser, thigh; W. W. Ronney, foot; Levi H. Smith, slightly; and S. A. McClellan, slightly. Missing: Henry Claypole, Samuel

Painter, John Yormkins, and J. C. Smith. Not known: A. Copely and Solomon Sipes. Prisoners: John G. Stroyic, M. Davis, and R. A. Malone.

Recapitulation.—Killed, 16; wounded, 133; missing, 23; prisoners, 16; total, 188.

Report of killed, wounded, and missing, 74th Ohio volunteer infantry, commanded by Colonel Granville Moody.

Colonel Granville Moody, slightly wounded.

Company A.—Killed: Corporal Isaac J. Smith; Privates Wyatt C. Jones and Jacob Burhert. Wounded: Sergeant A. C. Mahern; Corporals Samuel Schooley and James R. Hayslett; Privates David S. Wilson, Barney Warters, Michael McNamara, Jesse Curry, and Jacob Shirk. Missing: Alexander Walthal and Charles Hunter.

Company B.—Killed: Private James A. Blessing; Wounded: Sergeant James McCarr; Privates John A. Seuss, William H. Pratt, Ephraim Dickerson, Jacob Widemott, Jesse Levers, H. C. Edwards, and James A. Boone. Missing: Patrick McNary, Edward Pressinger, George B. McClellan, and Charles Lucas.

Company C.—Wounded: Sergeant A. B. Castler; Privates Henry G. Forbes, Alfred Harrold, Samuel J. Miller, William McDaniel, Ira S. Owens, James H. Seldomidge, Philip Tracy, Charles M. Wolfe, and Chancy White.

Company D.—Wounded: Privates Philip Mineheart, John D. Collins, John Andrew, R. Galloway, John Coppsock, Pat'k Castello, J. McCune, William McAfee, Thomas Hunter, and A. Ames. Missing: Corporals J. H. McClung and Samuel Galloway; Privates James Hamilton, J. G. Stewart, Henry Frock, Uill Drummond, and William Heirman.

Company E.—Wounded: Corporal John Fax; Privates Ed. Snider, Wesley Snider, Garrett Luscott, Samuel Putterbough, Peter Shmead, Jacob Callenbough, Clayton Haims, Eli Trustee, William Duffy, John Furgerson, Henry Snyder, and Jacob M. Krist.

Company F.—Killed: Sergeant William H. Smith and Private B. G. Hughes. Wounded: Captain Walter Crook; Lieutenant M. H. Peters; Sergeants Enos S. Walters, Cyrus Philips, and Orderly Sergeant Charles C. Dobson; Corporals David Brosman and Edw. Shumer; Privates R. N. Elder, George W. Beck, Pat. McCann, Charles Braily, (mortally,) Jonathan Townsens, John A. Brian, and Jacob Caudle.

Company G.—Wounded: Orderly Sergeant M. K. McFadden and Sergeant Theodore Leggett; Corporal L. Baker; Privates Hiram Cox, John Handy, William Chambers, James C. Mansfield, and Abraham Dennis. Missing: Charles Weaver.

Company H.—Wounded: Captain James H. Ballard; First Lieutenant David Snodgrass; Sergeants Ruper A. Sparr (mortally wounded, since died,) and John W. Dewn; Corporals Philip Stumm, Albert F. Johnston, and Daniel Heim; Privates Calvin Carl, Dudley Day, Joseph Wyburn, John A. Durnard, Augusta Houmard, John Clover, Joseph Early, and George Wise. Missing: Corporal Fred. Shull; Privates Christopher Cline, Morris Halley, and Urs. Tagge.

Company I.—Killed: Private John Hawkins. Wounded: Lieutenant Robert Cullem; Sergeant John Trohie; Privates Michael Cormell, Terrence McLaughlin, James McCarthy, and Michael Brannon.

Company K.—Killed: Corporal John D. Holson. Wounded: Corporal

William Carter; Privates David Sleeth, Philip Umrich, Robert C. Stewart, and Joseph C. Underwood. Missing: Corporal John M. Carson.

RECAPITULATION.

Killed in both days' fight	8
Wounded in both days' fight	93
Missing in both days' fight	24
Total	125

Report of killed, wounded, and missing of the thirty-seventh regiment Indiana volunteers, commanded by Colonel James Hall.

Company A.—Killed: Privates James Bebe, Lemuel Jackson, and William L. Ross. Wounded: Sergeants James H. Brown and John Grossman; Corporals James M. Powell, William H. H. Davis, Ira Castleton, and A. W. Smither; Privates Oliver Bruner, William Cole, John Hannah, James Harper, John Laswell, Theodore Hess, John B. Montcurf, George A. Myers, J. C. Myers, Ludlow McKestrick, Jesse Moreland, and Josephus Main. Missing: Privates John Hasty, Reuben Sutton, George Buchannan, and Lafayette Keely.

Company B.—Killed: Privates George W. Rodgers, Oliver W. Barnard, Isaac Snyder, and Josiah Eglarts. Wounded: Sergeants Jacob W. Stone and James Colten; Corporals Elis W. Fister, Brice B. Moore, and John McCrady; Privates James D. George, John P. Trueman, Alen C. Rose, William Fisk, John S. Price, Samuel Thompson, Julius M. Anderson, and Andrew M. Bell.

Company C.—Killed: Private James R. Pate. Wounded: Captain Thomas M. Pate; Sergeant Mitchell H. Day; Corporal Josiah M. Green; Privates John Lawler, George McKay, and James A. C. Herm. Missing: Sergeant Chapman A. Blanchard and Private Joseph Powell.

Company D.—Killed: First Lieutenant Jesse B. Holman; Privates Nicholas Aliger and Silas Hall. Wounded: Lieutenant Pye; Sergeants Andrew Von Sickle and Robert Wilson; Corporals Jonas Wise, Mehton Day, and John Hallett; Privates Levi Cochran, John Buchannan, Arthur McCane, Thomas Lawrence, Warren Mergan, Obediah Francisco, Isaac Stearns, John McCane, Edward Hollinsbee, James Robets, Benjamin Stevens, Christian Snedaker, Lysander Webster, John Coils, Moody Lockulger, and Granville Newbury.

Company E.—Wounded: Sergeant Charles W. Sherman and Private Thomas Stevens.

Company F.—Killed: Captain Charles Stewart; Privates John F. Godert, Samuel C. Smith, James S. Brennoughs, John W. Sanks, and Henry Cravens. Wounded: Sergeants Eliager Cole and John F. Spencer; Privates William F. Roland, William H. Green, Samuel Herndon, Heartly Yanksoger, and William J. Shull.

Company G.—Killed: Sergeant Peter Kerr; Privates William Sutton and Robert Craig. Wounded: Captain H. E. Lord; Sergeant H. C. Baughman; Corporals Charles E. Woodapple and Samuel Bayless; Privates Robert Allen, H. C. Anthony, D. W. Cinnery, C. E. Louse, John Hamlin, John Miller, James McCann, Charles Young, Perry Lynche, James Hetrick, Elisha H. Glisson, W. Goshorn, Ira M. Kulir, A. Taylor, Edward M. Small, and J. J. Hinas.

Company H.—Killed: Corporals Samuel Williams and Harrison Robbins; Private William R. Murray. Wounded: Sergeants John L. Hice and John Reat; Privates William G. Shafer, James Brick, William H. Thompson, Anderson Owens, John S. Dunglass, and Alfred Watson.

Company I.—Killed: Corporal Beardon Jones and Private Reuben Jones. Wounded: Captain William H. Dougherty; Sergeant Robert Huff; Corporal

Theodore Aug; Privates Levi Morris, John Stoll, Andrew Massey, Nicholas Burlbaugh, Ezekial Childors, and Joshua Shaw. Missing: Corporal Robert Blashin and Private John Taylor.

Company K.—Killed: First Lieutenant Isaac Aburmatha and Private Andrew B. Kirkham. Wounded: Captain John W. McKell; Sergeants John Patton and James H. Rankin; Privates John E. Brown, Thomas M. Gainess, James W. Mitchell, David L. Mitchell, John P. Moreloch, Harrison Stewart, and James H. Ruddell.

Report of killed, wounded, and missing of 21st regiment Ohio volunteer infantry, commanded by Lieutenant Colonel James M. Nerbling.

Company A.—Killed: First Sergeant Louis Diebley; Privates Abraham Kleckner, William Bradford, and Daniel Swartz. Wounded: Sergeant Erastus Biggs and Corporal Albert Hasner; Privates Jacob Wyne, Godfrey Newser, Jacob Hazen, John Boley, Sylvan Koons, William Kise, James Morrison, Jacob Morning, Levi Bonsher, and Jonathan Fellers; Corporal Joseph Wilson; Privates James Blake, Russell Kennion, Sylvester Hawkins, and Joseph Morning.

Company B.—Killed: Private Franck C. Arnold. Wounded: Privates Jacob F. Oman, George Montgomery, Clay C. Martin, John Cram, Jacob Bashop, Martin Keibler, and Joseph Oring. Missing: Privates Adam Walters, David Swan, John Engle, and Abraham Cortright.

Company C.—Killed: Second Lieutenant E. B. Wiley; Corporal Seneca Hodge. Wounded: First Lieutenant J. W. Knaggs; Sergeant Asa C. Spafford; Privates Daniel Braner, David Defiance, James McLargin, Newton Barkshamer, Benjamin Everly, Joseph Cox, Samuel Coly, and Fred. Newnberger. Missing: Privates Almond Farnson, E. B. Clough, and H. H. Huston.

Company D.—Killed: Corporal William L. Trusk. Wounded: Lieutenant W. C. Allen; Sergeant Alexander C. Anderson; Corporal Valentine Coyn; Privates William Burn, Abraham Boughman, William McKinis, Henry D. Hashberger, Isaac S. Stouk, Aaron Gargery, John H. Askam, Hiram McDowell, and Nathaniel Trusk. Missing: Sergeant Celestin Cochard; Privates George M. Payne and James M. Stout.

Company E.—Killed: Privates Wilson S. Musser and Westley Johnston. Wounded: Corporals William Rawles and Nat. Smith; Privates Samuel Gru, Emanuel Schamp, Charles Palmer, Levi M. Brunson, Horace Genter, and Solomon Hoy. Missing: Daniel Richard, John Rittich, and Loyal B. Wirt.

Company F.—Killed: Privates John Wilkinson, Edson G. Reed, Solomon Scowden, and Cyrus S. Stoker. Wounded: Sergeant S. M. Biggs; Corporal D. P. Stoher; Privates John G. Slater, Shannon Shoemaker, George W. Carr, Ralph C. Watson, Philip Deitz, Joshus Snoyer, John Sheely, Dannis R. Sloker, and James H. Mays.

Company G.—Killed: Joseph Heminger, Wallace Lewis, and William R. Thomas. Wounded: William Boyer, Thomas Collins, Lenias Jenkins, John M. Edgcomb, Henry Copus, Philip Haynes, Daniel Miller, John Copus, Robert Shoemaker, Franklin Archer, Levi H. Clabough, and Samuel S. Burman. Missing: Adam Helfrich and Charles A. Taylor.

Company H.—Killed: Privates John H. Craner, Nicholas Voget, Silas McDonald, and William Taylor. Wounded: Privates Tilman Peters, Christopher Gundy, Liberty Warner, Samuel Batyfisher, George Smith, Edwin Courtner, James Y. Dean, John Hamilton, Harvey Hensted, Levi Brisbin, Henry Hoobler, and Silver Daish. Missing: Westley Seeling and John Foreman.

Company I.—Killed: Corporal A. J. Vern; Private Elias Jackson. Wounded: Lieutenant James J. Bumpus; Sergeant Robert H. Caldwell; Corporals Maxwell C. Reynolds and James M. Parker; Privates James Reynolds, Alexander Ingraham, W. H. Cheeny, Eli Laines, Lyman Wright, John Anderson, Wilson Hutchinson, and John Fitsgiven. Missing: Privates Everson Wainwright and Garrett Kertting.

Company K.—Killed: Sergeant David N. Loomis; Private Samuel Burke. Wounded: Lieutenant William B. Wirker; Corporal Sidney R. Patterson; Privates Guy Morgan, William Krose, Jesse Walker, William Shanks, James Banks, James A. Forrest, Sherman Bushnell, James Pember, Charles Myers, and William Forrest. Missing: John Myers and John Coner.

Report of the 1st Kentucky battery commanded by Lieutenant H. H. Spence.

Killed.—Privates Lewis Sagers and Godfrey Hautt. Wounded: Milton Crawhorn.

Report of the 1st Ohio Volunteer battery, commanded by Lieutenant Alexander Marshall.

Killed.—Corporal Thomas Strong, Privates Spencer Yuman, Samuel Burford and John Woodworth. Wounded: Sergeant George W. Bills, Corporal Henry Clayne, Privates James W. Fife, badly, shoulder; Charles A. Whitting, thigh; Edward Beverstock, foot; William Jones, head; James H. Clinton, hand; Henry Yetter, badly, arm; Henry Wilds, slightly, hand. Missing: Privates Jachson Hochet, George B. Cox, William Voltz, Henry Yetten, and Artificer Samuel Brigam.

RECAPITULATION.

78th regiment Pennsylvania volunteers	188
74th regiment Ohio volunteers	125
37th Indiana volunteers	152
21st Ohio volunteers	159
1st Kentucky battery	3
Battery G, 1st Ohio volunteers	18
	645

List of killed and wounded of the 2d division (centre) 14th army corps during the battle near Murfreesboro', December 30th and 31st, 1862, and January 1st, 2d, and 3d, 1863, (29th brigade, Colonel Stanley.)

EIGHTEENTH OHIO VOLUNTEERS.

Killed.—Company A: Corporals Josiah Simmons and Augustus S. Royal, and Privates Marshall Blucker, John F. Mowbray and James Hodsden. Company B: Private Robert Wakefield. Company C: Sergeant James Light, and Privates Joseph Cathiel and Henry Folley. Company D: Corporal William Rainer, and Privates Harrison Dart and Oscar F. Clark. Company E: 2d Lieutenant W. W. Blacker; Sergeants John Pearce and John Davis; Privates Dallas Farley, Thomas E. Wroton and James F. Morton. Company F: Private Harrison Sheets. Company G: Privates J. C. Springer and John Pratchard. Company K: Privates W. H. Thompson, Silas D. Wolf, Thomas Long and William Moore,

Wounded.—Company A: Lieutenant Colonel Josiah Given; 2d Lieutenant Edmund C. McLarren, leg; Sergeant Henry C. Roby, arm, amputated; Corporal David A. Woodland, flesh wound of thigh; Privates Eben. Fennimore, mortal wound of pelvis; Henry W. Purcell, left lung, mortal; Allen Riddell, neck, slight; George Cader, middle finger, amputated; Henry Hays, contusion; Jackson Mackerly, arm, flesh wound; Robert Goff, arm, flesh wound; William Christian, shoulder, slightly; Thomas Goodwin, shoulder, slightly; Enoch Smith, toe, slightly, and Edward E. Traite, leg, flesh wound. Company B: Captain Asbell Fenton, ankle, seriously; Corporals E. W. Ellis, thigh, flesh wound; Archibald Fitzgerald, arm, slightly; George Caylor, leg, slightly; Privates James Buzzard, arm, slightly; Miles Bowen, abdomen, mortally; A. U. Ball, leg, flesh wound; L. S. Bancroft, shoulder, resection; J. H. Chapman, leg; R. Campbell, breast; S. Clawson, contusion by shell; John Hamilton, wrist; A. H. Reames, arm; L. H. Runnand, leg; Asa Scott, fracture of arm; C. L. Williams, arm; E. Wyant, shoulder. Company C: Captain John M. Welsh, leg; 1st Lieutenant A. W. S. Minear, left lung, seriously; Sergeant John W. Root, wrist and arm; Corporals Samuel Hamrick, arm, flesh wound; Jasper Witham, thigh, flesh wound; Privates Ervin Cannor, arm, flesh wound; Hiram Hinhead, head, flesh wound; Isaac McDonald, leg, flesh wound; Daniel North, leg, flesh wound; William Stiles, leg, flesh wound; George Stout, arm, flesh wound; Jonathan Snow, head. Company D: Sergeants A. S. Camp, wrist; Nelson Gaskell, side; Privates Morton Bailey, both legs; John P. Carsey, leg; E. Jones, leg; A. A. Lasler, leg; Felix Riley, arm; William A. Young, head; William Blazer, arm; William Scott, leg. Company E: Captain Philip E. Taylor, abdomen, mortally; Corporals A. R. Hart, foot; James Quinn, resection, elbow joint and wound; Privates Charles Davis, shoulder; Sherman Freese, hip, flesh wound; John L. Grey, hand, seriously; W. H. McDonald, left arm, amputated; G. W. Day, hip, flesh wound; Edward Proctor, arm; John D. Sampson, hand; Oliver B. Tootle, leg. Company F: Sergeants David J. Seawright, wound of knee; William J. Byers, hand; Corporals Thomas H. Wade, head; Thomas P. Byar, head; Privates Harrison Sheets, Holland C. Beard, shoulder; James S. Connor, arm; John Hall, hand; William B. Irvin, finger; John Kendall, hand; James A. Nixon, leg, amputated; Austin W. Pickins, fracture, scapular; Isaac Washington, thigh, flesh wound; Company G: Sergeant William Quigley, thigh, flesh wound; Corporal B. Griffith, knee, amputated; Privates Wm. C. Bowers, abdomen, mortal; John Sanders, arm, flesh wound; S. S. McDivitt, hand, finger amputated; John Charlton, shoulder; H. C. Smith, leg; George Beet, arm. Company H: C. S. Simmons, chest, mortal; A. C. Hamilton, leg; P. M. Phillips, head; Samuel McElroy, foot; Patrick Foard, arm, amputated; Wilson Seft, neck, slightly; Wesley Bader, head; William Malone, head; George Call, leg; Adam Gregory, leg. Company I: Captain C. C. Ross, contusion of side; Sergeants L. D. Carter, contusion of back; William Wright, leg, flesh wound; Privates James B. James, thigh, flesh wound; Thomas A. Towers, hip, shell wound; Henry Crowley, thigh, fracture; James M. Lyons, finger; A. W. Boggs, shoulder. Company K: Captain George Stevens, chest, mortally; Corporal Joseph Haggins, side; Privates Joseph Fullerton, face and arm; Abraham Baringer, face; P. J. Hartly, head; Milton Bosworth, back; George W. Angel, leg, amputated; L. A. Pullin, abdomen; George Hallman, left hand; John Willis, neck; George J. Rice, leg.

NINETEENTH ILLINOIS VOLUNTEERS.

Killed.—Company A: Corporal Ira A. Pease, and Privates D. L. Holmes and Thomas A. Moore. Company B: Corporal George Ryerson, and Privates Isaac L. Knigan, Charles W. Leason, and James O. Jones. Company C: Corporal Henry Sevezy. Company F: Captain Chandler and Private Samuel Griffin. Company H: Private Jesse Maxwell. Company I: Private John

Britton. Company K: Sergeant Daniel W. Griffin and Private James C. Fullerton.

Wounded.—Company A: Sergeant William H. Wildey, contusion of arm; Sergeant Rosco G. Sylvester, head, slightly; Corporal Charles Kerr, leg, slightly; Privates Joseph L. Seagle, left side, slightly; M. Kennedy, arm, flesh wound; Samuel Worden, arm, flesh wound; Charles H. Tuthill, wrist; J. H. Edgell, leg, flesh wound; R. P. Blanchard, side, flesh wound; George Utts, abdomen, mortal. Company B: Captain Alexander Marchison, shoulder, contused; 2d Lieutenant John H. Hunter, thigh, serious; Sergeant Thomas Robinson, arm and shoulder; Corporal H B. North, hand, slightly; Privates Columbus Morgan, abdomen, mortal; George Dugan, hand, slightly; Thomas Turnbull, hand, severe; Thomas Oziah, face, slightly; George T. Shaver, arm and thigh; William Douglas, foot; Joseph M. Seacox, arm, flesh wound; Walter Clark, knee, slightly. Company C: 1st Lieutenant Washington L. Wood, hand, severe; Corporal Delevan Craft, leg; Corporal Charles Idair, neck; Privates John Iris, hand; Webster Daniels, wrist; Frank Seguin, side and arm; Wilkins M. Baltis, knee; Edward McKelly, knee; Peter Bouckwort, arm. Company D: Corporal Henry C. Daggy, side and leg, mortal; Corporal William B. Taylor, leg, severe; Sergeant Jonas Goldsmith, back, mortal; Corporal Robert McCrackin, side, mortal; Privates John Tansy, back, slightly; Thomas Willard, leg, flesh wound; Joseph Smith, head, flesh wound; Henry C. Carter, left leg; Samuel Madden, shoulder, flesh wound; Jacob Bolls, left side, severe. Company E: Sergeant Joseph Huntington, finger, amputated; Corporal Peter Guthrie, back; Corporal Alex. M. L. Frazer, back, slightly; Privates David McArthur, face, flesh wound; Thomas King, thigh, flesh wound; John G. P. Noble, back, mortal; George Joell, abdomen; John Stephens, both thighs, arm and shoulder; John Hays, thigh, flesh wound; Thomas Welsh, thigh. Company F: Privates Christopher Moore, left shoulder; Abraham Hess, right side; John Coleman, right hand; William Afland, right leg. Company H: Captain P. A. Garriott, leg, flesh wound; Sergeant V. C. Johnson, leg, contusion; 2d Lieutenant W. L. Wood, abdomen, mortal; Corporals Lloyd B. Thomas, right knee; John H. Snyder, thigh, flesh wound; Sumner Harrington, side, contusion; William Hagerty, left arm, contusion; Privates George B. Sickles, left shoulder, severe; George F. Fleming, arm, flesh wound; Henry E. F. Wells, left arm, amputation elbow joint; James W. Carson, right wrist; John Benham, leg, fracture; James F. Coleman, head; Josiah Suter, wound and fracture of leg; Metellus Stoughton, thigh, flesh wound; Charles G. Bates, wrist, contusion. Company I: Privates Joseph Malt, thigh; Richard Doring, right arm; Henry Harmes, back; Warren F. Hogan, left shoulder. Company K: 2d Lieutenant V. B. Bell, head; Sergeant L. H. Scadin, leg; Corporal F. Russell, head; Privates R. Periolet, thigh; Peter Smith, face; Edgar Bullen, side; Charles Kent, ear; Col. Joseph K. Scott, thigh and groin.

ELEVENTH MICHIGAN VOLUNTEERS.

Major Sylvester Smith, seriously wounded in the face.

Killed.—Company A: Private Edward Timmer. Company B: Corporal Orim Nichols and Privates Oliver Busby, Daniel Haynes, and William Johnson. Company C: Privates David C. Leonard, James Fisher, and Bennet Smilts. Company E: Lieutenant Thomas Flynn; Sergeant Ezra Spencer and Privates Hiram Everett, Thomas Manning, and Robert McIlvain. Company F: First Lieutenant Joseph Nelson and Sergeant Jeremiah C. Peck. Company G: Privates Oscar Angel, Perry DeForest, Cyrus W. Gilbert, Silas Kelly, Joseph Kettinger, and Sylvester Nichols. Company H: Corporal James W. Gayer and Privates Chauncey Green and William Chamberlain. Company I: Sergeant

Ariel Palmer and Privates James W. Wait and George E. Jewett. Company K: Privates Thomas Rughity, Simon Hamelton, and Joseph Miller.

Wounded.—Company A: Captain David A. Smith, neck, slightly; Corporal E. D. White, leg, slightly; Privates Robert Carpenter, breast, slightly; David Rockwell, shoulder, slightly; Henry Clark, side, slightly; Anson Spencer, left arm, severely; William Wood, leg, severely; William H. H. Platt, hip, severely; C. L. Carpenter, shoulder, severely; Henry Damon, scalp; Daniel Rose, contu sion of thigh; William Lemongen, contusion of side; Byron Barker, contusion of head; Julius Tompkins, head, slightly; Stephen Haxley, head, slightly. Company B: Privates Hennan Adams, left hand; Joseph Bowen, shoulder; Bradley Mosher, head; Levi McGinnis, left foot: Frederick Watman, thigh; Deny Nichols, arm; Oliver Swart, back, slightly; Andrew Silverwood, left foot; Halsey Miller, neck. Company C: Lieutenant L. H. Howard, leg, slightly; Privates William Patten, hand, slightly; Jacob Hackenberg, right side, slightly; Charles Leonard, scalp, slightly. Company D: Corporal D. L. Byrnes, amputation left arm; Privates John George, shoulder, severely; John Quail, shoulder, slightly; William Robson, hand, slightly; B. F. Bordner, arm, slightly. Company E: Privates George Quay, slightly; Andrew Knapp, slightly; Bradley Lane, slightly; William Sherman, severely; Benjamin Clubine, back, severely; Peter V. Dobbs, back, severely; Frank Bouter. Company F: Second Lieutenant Ephraim Hall, neck; Corporal Meron M. Comstock, thigh, slightly; Private William Sprafford, shoulder, slightly. Company G: Lieutenant F. H. Briggs, leg, slightly; Sergeant James Bouter, head, slightly; Corporal Charles Myers, shoulder, slightly; Privates James R. Hass, right arm, slightly; Andrew Kershmar, face, slightly; Charles M. Nichols, head, slightly; James Ross, left arm, slightly; John Austin, amputation right ankle; Stephen Andrews, forearm, severely; David F. Barret, leg, severely; Augustus E. Dickenson, hand, severely; Jesse M. Nash, right lung, mortally; Martin Farmer, right arm; Martin V. B. Williams, right side, slightly. Company H: Privates Harvey Vanderhoof, left arm and right shoulder; E. A. Green, back; Dennis Ussuick, face. Company I: Corporal Marcus I. Baker, face; Privates Walter F. Halleck, face; L. Barnes, thigh, slightly; Eli Lamkin, foot, slightly; George Francisco, head, slightly. Company K: Lieutenant P. H. Hugan, face, slightly; Sergeants Elmer Bradley, right leg, slightly; John H. Johnson, head and leg, severely; Coleman Darkin, right hand, severely; John D. Hugin, thigh, severely; Corporals James Boulton, left shoulder, severely; Frank Papin, thigh, severely; Privates Myron Bragg, back, severely; Alphonso Cherrey, right arm, severely; Anson Farmer, left hand, severely; Homer Goodale, hip, severely; Harry William, head, severely; Adam Sehr, right hand, severely; Jacob M. Pommell, shoulder, severely; Daniel Rapp, back, severely; Peter Seely, hand, severely; Edward Finch, head and arm, slightly; Daniel Patterson, hip, slightly.

SIXTY-NINTH OHIO VOLUNTEERS.

Colonel Cassidy wounded in the arm; Adjutant Boynton wounded in the knee.

Killed.—Company B: Sergeant McGillan. Company E: Corporal P. B. Albright and Private J. J. Stoker. Company G: Corporal Brown. Company H: Captain Counsellor.

Wounded.—Company A: Lieutenant L. E. Hicks, shoulder; Sergeant S. Scott, shoulder; Corporal T. Tetuch, thigh; Privates R. Merchant, leg; J. Bragg, leg; H. F. Colferm, leg; J. Simpson, arm; L. Halse, leg; B. Stewart, leg, mortally. Company B: Lieutenant Tucker, shoulder, slightly; Privates D. Stebbins, ankle, slightly; W. Porter, face, slightly; J. Bulger, left hand, slightly; J. Halse, left hand, slightly. Company C: Privates Longfellow, back, severely, and P. Burch, cheek, slightly. Company D: Sergeant King, hand; Corporal Desor, neck, slightly; Privates H. Stolle, back, slightly; R. Wilson, leg, slightly; H. Zumi, hand, slightly; A. Hawkins, shoulder, slightly; D. Shadetaker, thigh, slightly; H. Haskins, shoulder, mortally. Company E: Sergeant Perry, hand; Privates M. Jones, neck; J. Yenatles, thigh; G. A. Davis, arm; James Red, side. Company F: Sergeant G. Shedd, shoulder; Privates J. J. Simmons, foot; J. M. Havens, leg. Company G: Captain Patten, leg and side; Corporals F. Buck, arm; Pritts, knee; Privates J. Holter, neck; Joel Wagoner, shoulder; Howell, hand. Company H: Sergeant Eckridge, leg; Corporal J. Brobeck, abdomen, slightly; Privates J. Peterson, thigh, slightly; G. Wiederlich, back, slightly. Company I: Corporals Williams, amputation of leg; McKelvey, amputation of leg; Kildon, leg; McAllister, leg, flesh wound; Private R. R. Wells, flesh wound. Company K: Corporals Jones, side, flesh wound; Graham, thigh, flesh wound; Privates Garvan, hip; N. Johnson, side.

SUMMARY.

18th Ohio volunteers.		
Killed	26	
Wounded	115	
Missing, (not included above)	26	
	—	167
19th Illinois volunteers.		
Killed	14	
Wounded	83	
Missing, (not included above)	11	
	—	108
11th Michigan volunteers.		
Killed	30	
Wounded	84	
Missing, (not included above)	25	
	—	139
69th Ohio volunteers.		
Killed	5	
Wounded	53	
	—	58
Total		472

List of killed and wounded, second division, (centre,) fourteenth army corps, seventh brigade, Colonel Miller commanding.

TWENTY-FIRST OHIO VOLUNTEERS.

Killed.—Company A: Sergeants Levi Dibley and Erastus Biggs, Privates David Swartz and William Bradford. Company B: Private F. C. Arnold. Company C: Lieutenant Enoch B. Ariby, and Corporal Seneca Hadjee. Company D: Private William Brask. Company E: Privates W. S. Musser and Wesley Johnson. Company F: Privates Edson J. Reed, Solomon Sconton and Cyrus Stoker. Company G: Privates Joseph Heninger, William Thomas and Wallace Lewis. Company H: Privates John H. Bromer and Nicholas Vogle, Sergeant Silas McDonald, and Corporal William Taylor. Company I: Corporal Alonzo J. Vean and Private Elias S. Jackson. Company K: Sergeant David Loomis and Private Samuel Berk.

Wounded.—Company A: Corporals Albert Hasner, thigh; Joseph Wilson, arm; Privates James B. Coke, thigh; Henson Russell, thigh; John Roley, leg; John Fuller, thigh; Levi F. Boucher, head and leg; William Wise, head and leg; Godfrey Musser, chest; James Morrison, head; Lyman Hoons, head; Jacob Hoison, arm; Jacob Wise, face; Asa Babcock, shoulder; Joseph Swining, wrist. Company B: Privates Clay C. Morton, arm; John Crone, face; George Montgomery, face; Jacob Oman, face; Jacob Bishops, leg and feet; Martin Hibler, arm; Joseph Craig, arm. Company C: Lieutenant James W. Nagge, shoulder and side; Sergeant Asa C. Spafford, neck and wrist; Privates David David Bromer, leg; Newton Backham, arm; Joseph Cox, leg; Benjamin Eberly, arm; Fred'k Nurembarger, feet. Company D: First Lieutenant Charles W. Allen, thigh; Sergeant Alexander Anderson, head; Corporal Valentine Corn, leg and hand; Privates William Bumna, head; Abraham Bauhusen, shoulder; William McKinnous, neck; Hiram McDowell, hip; John Askham, neck; H. D. Harsbruger, leg; Nathaniel Praste, arm. Company E: Corporals William Ralls, side; Nathaniel Smith, shoulder; Samuel Grica, leg; Privates Emanual Shamp, hand; Charles Palmer, leg; Levi M. Bronson, wrist; Horace Ginter, feet; James H. Maise, hand; Solomon Hay, breast. Company F: Sergeant S. M. Biggs, leg; Corporal David Stoker, chest; Privates John G. Slater, arm; R. C. Watson, leg; E. S. Shoemaker, leg; George Harr, leg; Philip Deet, head; Joshua Swire, leg. Company G: Privates Thomas Collins, foot; P. M. Edgecome, face; Henry Capin, arm; William Boyer, hand; Jenkins Lewis, hip; David Miller, leg; P. H. Haines, leg; John Copus, leg; Frank Archer, thigh; Levi Clabaugh, arm; Robert W Shoemaker, arm; S. S. Bummern, hand. Company H: Privates Gilman Peters, leg; Christopher Grundy, Liberty Warner, head; Samuel Pennyfeather, shoulder; Irvin Cantreas, mouth; James Y. Dean, shoulder; John Hamilton, leg; Harvey Husteet, chest; Levi Brisbin, chest; Henry Harbler, face; Silas Daisk, arm; George Smith, arm. Company I: Second Lieutenant James H. Bumbar, leg; Sergeant Robert H. Caldwell, shoulder; Corporals M. C. Reynolds, thigh; James M. Parker, feet; Privates James Reynolds, arm; Alexander E. Ingraham, shoulder; William H. Cheny, hand and chest; Eli Larnes, leg; Lyman Wight, leg; John Anderson, leg; Filson Huchison, leg; John Fitzgibbon, hand. Company K: First Lieutenant William Wicker, hand; Corporal Cyrus J. Patterson, abdomen; Privates Guy Morgan, head; James Pembe, feet; Charles Myers, side; J. Walson, arm; James A. Forrest, side; Ira Forrest, leg; James Banks, head; Sherman Bushnell, feet.

SEVENTY-FOURTH OHIO VOLUNTEERS.

Killed.—Company A: Corporal Isaac J. Smith and Privates Wyatt K. Jones and Jacob Bushest. Company B: Private James A. Blessing. Company F: Sergeant William H. Smith and Private B. J. Huger. Company H: Sergeant R. A. Sparks. Company I: Private John Hawkins. Company K: Corporal John D. Halson.

Wounded.—Colonel Granville Moody, horse shot under him. Company A: Sergeant O. C. Mehan, Corporals Samuel Schooly and James A. Haslit and Privates David Wilson, Barney Waters, Michael McMonoh, Jesse Curry, and Jacob Scirk. Company B: Privates James McCare, John A. Sceiss, William H. Pratt, Ephraim Dickerson, Jacob Wildersmith, Jesse Scevest, Henry C. Edwards, and James A. Bone. Company C: Privates Femy Forbs, Alfred Hanold, Samuel F. Miller, William L. McDaniel, Ira S. Owens, James H. Seldonmidge, Philip Tracy, Charles M. Wolf, Chauncey White, and Sergeant A. B. Coster. Company D: Privates P. Minchard, (mortally,) James I. Collins, John Andrew, R. Galloway, I. Coppick, B. Costello, I. McCune, William McAfee, F. Hunter, and A. Ames. Company E: Corporal John Cox and Privates Edward C. Snyder, Wesley Snyder, Garrett Ginscott, Jacob Butterfaugh, Peter Smead, Jacob Cullenbrugh, Clayton Havens, Ell. Trubee, William Duffee, and John Ferguson. Company F: Captain Walter Crook, Lieutenant M. H. Peters, Sergeants Enos H. Walters, Cyrus Philips, and Charles C. Dodson, and Corporals Eden Sherman and David Bossman, and Privates M. W. Elders, George W. Peck, Patrick McCarin, and Charles Brakey, mortally. Company G: Sergeants M. K. McFadden and Theodore Seggick, Corporal Leander Baker and Privates Hiram Cox, John Haudy, William Chambers, Joseph Mansfield, and Abraham Dennis. Company H: Lieutenant David Snodgrass, Sergeant John M. Deroe, Corporals Joseph H. Ballard, Philip W. Stumin, Albert F. Johnson, and Daniel Herin, and Privates Calvin Curl, Dudley Day, Joseph Hybern, John A. Donnard, Augusta Humard, John Glover, Joseph Harley, and George Wise. Company I: Lieutenant Robert Cullen, Sergeant John Toohie, and Privates Michael Connell, Terrence McLaughlin, James McCarthy, and Michael Brannon. Company K: Corporal William Carter and Privates David Sleth, Philip Mininck, Robert Stewart, and Joseph Underwood.

THIRTY-SEVENTH INDIANA VOLUNTEERS.

Killed.—Company A: Privates Jasper Beebe, W. Ross, and Lemuel Jackson. Company B: Privates Isaac M. Snyder, Josiah Egberts, and G. W. Roberts. Company C: Private James R. Pate. Company D: First Lieutenant Jesse B. Holman, Privates Nicholas Olizes and Silas Hall. Company F: Corporal Charles Stewart, and Privates James L. Burrows, Henry Craven, John F. Goddart, Samuel C. Smith, and David Banks. Company G: Sergeant Peter Krin, and Privates Robert Craig and William Sutton. Company H: Corporal Samuel Williams and Privates Harrison Robins and Robert Murray. Company I: Reuben Jones. Company K: First Lieutenant Isaac Abnethy and Private Andrew B. Kirk.

Wounded.—Company A: Corporals John H. Brown, John Groseman, James M. Pavell, V. H. Lavis, Ira Casteller, and Privates William Cole, John Hannah, James Harper, John Haswell, John Moncrief, James Myers, Ludlow McKittrick, Jesse Moreland, Joseph Main, A. W. Smith, Theodore Hess. Company B: Sergeants James Coulten, J. W. Stone; Corporals B. B. Moore, E. H. Foster, L. L. Andrews, M. Bell and Privates James D. George, Oliver W. Barnard, John S. Price, John P. Freeman, Allen C. Rose, William Fish, Samuel Thompson, Myer Bowers, John McCrady. Company C: Captain Thomas W. Pate, Sergeant M Day, Corporal J. S. Green, and Privates John Fowler, George McKay, James Ferren, John Garbet. Company D: Second Lieutenant William Rye, Sergeants A. Vanside, Robert P. Wilson; Corporals Machlin Day, James Wise, and Privates John Buchanan, Levi Cochran, John Coles, Obadiah Francisco, Ed. Hollenbee, Thomas Lawrence, Moody Lothridge, Arthur McGiven, Warren Morgan, John McKnew, James Roberts, Benjamin Stevens, Christian Sindaker, Lysander Webster, and Granville Newbury. Company E: Sergeant W. Sherman, and Private Thomas Stevens. Company F: Sergeants John F. Spinceo, Eleazer Cole, and Privates William Boland, William Green, Hartey Gorkager, and W. I. S. Hull. Company G: Captain E. Woodapple, and Privates Samuel P. Baylons, Robert Allen, Dennis Conway, James Hettrick, I. M. Keeler, John P. Luvick, Cyrus Lown, James S. McCann, John Miller, Henry Stone, and Charles A. Ming. Company H: Sergeants D. Wise, John Ross, and Privates I. W. Shaffer, James N. Breck, William A. Shapson, I. S. Douglas, Andrew Owens, and Alfred Watson. Company I: Captains William N. Doughty, and Theodore Any; Corporal I. B. Jones, and Privates Levi Morris, John Stote, —— Childers, Nicholas Bullon, D. E. Masey, John Shaw, and Robert Huffday. Company K: Captain John McKee, Sergeants John Patten, James W. Rankin, and Privates Daniel Lichtbell, J. H. Ruddell, John P. McCullough, John McGinnis, and Harrison Stewart.

SEVENTY-EIGHTH PENNSYLVANIA VOLUNTEERS.

Killed.—Sergeant J. D. Hull, company I; Corporals Authur L. Myrtle, Mespen Hull, company F; Privates Mathan Reain, company C; Henry S. Wean, Philip Griffiths, Dennis Conway, James Hervey, J. S. Thompson, J. M. Eram, company F; James Myart, James Bergan, company H; John Johnson, James Conklin, George Beniser, James Cunan, company I.

Wounded—Captains Enoch Williams, company K; George B. Borlam, company F; W. S. Jack, James Moore, company H; First Lieutenant John F. Moreland, Second Lieutenant William R. Maize, company A; Sergeants James M. Miller, company A; W. C. Patrick, D. H. Thompson, A. J. Cowan, company B; Andrew Brown, James G. Briggs, William H. Thomas, company C; Reuben Lotsham, company E; A. B. Sreiner, John C. White, company F; W. C. Murphy, company I; C. F. Smith, company H; W. H. Smith, M. Melling, company K; Corporals Samuel S. Seram, company A; William H. Miller, company C; William Mathews, company B; Privates William Carlan, Thomas Kelley, James Little, David K. McElroy, James J. Carroll, James Guthrie, Adam Keep, Robert Ewonsable, company A; Robert Lewis, William Yount, Amos Dinger, Elias Diller, J. W. Dospike, Solomon Hines, John J. Spencer, Mark Sullivan, Eli Hendrick, John P. Neville, company B; Thomas Kepler, Solomon Buckouse, Reuben Hellcterd, Samuel Mohoning, William McMillen, David R. Miges, Albert C. Slaum, Samuel Lovesy, Lewis Sayers, Jacob Neff, A. B. Wrike, Isaac Rein, Jeremiah Cook, Thomas M. Grecken, Jeremiah Humerld, John Brade, Samuel Boffand, David Daniels, George W. Hagen, William Hays, Charles Myers, J. A. McElodine, George P. Marsh, William J. Mortimer, company C; Gibson Meese, George Nichols, James H. Seep, J. R. Teetsworth, D. H. Whitehill, Charles Kingley, Charles McNutt, A. J. Runder, Joseph M. Disler, company E; James Penman, M. Sullivan, Lewis Lord, David Alten, Samuel Slireer, George J. Taylor, James Neadam, Peter Sepper, J. S. Davidson, Henry F. Sexman, James M. Crakem, James N. McLeod, James M. Cousins, John Hall, Wm. A. Hegarty, David Murphy, James Shassan, J. J. Bower, Hugh Stotes, Charles Hany, company F; D. Thompson, Thomas Sytus, George Rose, John Black, John Chisty, E. French, A. Shender, E. Nelson, company H; Samuel Gray, Aaron Eatman, James McMeans, James Utograph, W. H. Gray, Harrison Dephertz, Jasper Clements, Jos. A. Chempson, company I; William Martin, S. R. Henry, Adam Akins, J. H. Altman, David Pritchard, James L. Hatman, I. I. Strout, M. Danes, R. A. Malon, I. C. Smith, M. C. Bower, W. W. Boovey, I. Sirth, S. A. McClellan, M. I. Halstead, company K.

SUMMARY.

21st regiment Ohio volunteers.

Killed	24	
Wounded	103	
	——	127

74th regiment Ohio volunteers.

Killed	9	
Wounded	92	
	——	101

37th regiment Indiana volunteers

Killed	25	
Wounded	106	
	——	131

78th regiment Pennsylvania volunteers.

Killed	16	
Wounded	125	
		141
Total		500

East Tennessee brigade.

FIRST REGIMENT EAST TENNESSEE VOLUNTEERS.

Wounded.—Company B: Private Samuel Bew, thigh and elbow joint. Company C: Jesse McCrury, flesh. Company G: Jesse Devers, toe. Company H: George Hanold, face. Company I: James Bowman, leg; William Lone, knee; H. C. Heart, malleolus. Company K: Sergeant P. K. Diggs, flesh; Corporal William Reed, hip; Privates I. M. McGill, fore-arm; G. W. Diggs, slight.

SECOND REGIMENT EAST TENNESSEE VOLUNTEERS.

Wounded.—Company D: Private Markus Renfrore, foot. Company F: Captain Sneed, arm. Company G: Privates Alfred Baurdergrift, thigh; Joseph Thomas, thigh. Company I: Sergeant Robbins, foot.

SUMMARY.

First regiment East Tennessee volunteers, killed	0	
First regiment East Tennessee volunteers, wounded	11	11
Second regiment East Tennessee volunteers, killed	0	
Second regiment East Tennessee volunteers, wounded	5	5
Total		16

Batteries.

FIRST REGIMENT OHIO VOLUNTEER ARTILLERY.

Killed.—Battery G: Corporal Thomas Strong, and Privates Spencer Tuman and John Wordsworth. Battery M: Corporal William Redback.

Wounded.—Battery G: Captain Shultz, arm and leg; Sergeant George W. Bills, neck; Corporal Henry Claque, side; Privates Samuel Benford, arm; James W. Fife, shoulder; Charles A. Whiting, thigh; Edmund Beverstock, foot; William Jones, head; James H. Clinton, hand; Henry Wields, hand.

FIRST REGIMENT KENTUCKY ARTILLERY.

Killed.—Battery M: Private Hart Godfrey.

Wounded.—Battery M: Lieutenant A. A. Ellsworth, slight; Privates Lewis Jagers, arm, shoulder, and back; Milton Crawhome, slight.

SUMMARY.

First regiment Ohio artillery, battery G, killed	3
First regiment Ohio artillery, battery G, wounded	9
First regiment Ohio artillery, battery M, killed	1

First regiment Ohio artillery, battery M, wounded	1
First regiment Kentucky artillery, battery M, killed	1
First regiment Kentucky artillery, battery M, wounded	3
Total	18

GENERAL SUMMARY.

Twenty-ninth brigade	75 killed,	335 wounded.
Seventh brigade	74 killed,	426 wounded.
First East Tennessee brigade	0 killed,	16 wounded.
Artillery	5 killed,	13 wounded.
Total	154	790

List of killed and wounded during a skirmish on Rolling Fork, Hardin county, Ky., December 29, 1862, second brigade, third division, (centre) fourteenth army corps.

Killed.—Private Thomas P. Burton, company F, fourth Kentucky regiment.

Wounded.—Lieutenant Henry W. Pollis, company C, first regiment Ohio artillery, fatally, died December 30; Privates Louis W. Finney, company D, tenth regiment Indiana volunteers, fatally, died December 30; John C. Osborne, company A, tenth Indiana volunteers, very slightly.

SUMMARY.

Killed	3
Wounded	1
Total	4

HEADQUARTERS FIRST TENNESSEE BRIGADE,
Cacottson's, near Murfreesboro', January 11, 1863.

SIR: In obedience to your circular, under date of 10th inst., just received, I have the honor to submit the following report of killed and wounded in the two Tennessee regiments under my command, during the three days' engagement before Murfreesboro'.

The fourteenth Michigan infantry and the eighty-fifth Illinois infantry, attached to my command on the 3d instant, were ordered to Nashville immediately after the engagement of that night. I am therefore unable to furnish the information regarding their loss.

FIRST EAST TENNESSEE VOLUNTEER INFANTRY.

Killed.—Corporal Leander P. Peters, and Private John R. Davis, company K; Private Oliver H. P. Phibbs, company H.

Wounded.—Privates Samuel Pugh, company B; Jesse McCranny, company C; Corporal George I. G. Crandell, and Privates David G. Farmer and Jesse Deavers, company G; Privates George Werreld and W. H. Hatmaker, company H; James Boman, William Lane, Henry C. Heart, John Brashears, and

Hugh W. Bicket, company I; Sergeant Priestley K. Diggs, Corporal William M. Reed, and Privates James McGill and George W. Diggs, company K.

SECOND EAST TENNESSEE VOLUNTEER INFANTRY.

Wounded.—Captain John L. Snead and Private Joseph Johnson, company F; Sergeant Alfred A. C. Robbins and Private Alfred Vandergrift, company I; Sergeant Mark C. Benfro, company D; Privates Isaac Thomas and William Sarsett, company K.

None missing.

Respectfully,

P. G. SPEARS,
Brigadier General Com'g First Brigade.

Captain JAMES A. LOWRY,
Assistant Adjutant General.

HEADQUARTERS FIRST BRIDADE,
January 17, 1863.

CAPTAIN: The foregoing is a copy of the report sent to your headquarters on the 11th instant. Whether it ever reached you we do not know.

Respectfully, by command of General Spears,
P. W. CANDIS, *Aide-de-Camp.*

Captain JAMES A. LOWRY,
Assistant Adjutant General.

[Indorsed.]

Received, headquarters third brigade, second division, centre, Murfreesboro', January 10, 1863. Colonel J. M. Neibling, commanding twenty-first Ohio volunteer infantry, United States army.

Official report of the part taken by the twenty-first Ohio volunteer infantry at the battles of Stone river, from December 30, 1862, to January 4, 1863.

HEADQQARTERS THIRD BRIGADE, 2D DIVISION, (CENTRE,)
Murfreesboro', January 27, 1863.

Respectfully forwarded.

WILLIAM SIVWELL,
Commanding Third Brigade.

HEADQUARTERS SECOND DIVISION, 14TH ARMY CORPS,
Murfreesboro', February 5, 1863.

Respectfully forwarded.

JAMES S. NEGLEY,
Brigadier General Commanding.

CAMP TWENTY-FIRST OHIO VOLUNTEER INFANTRY,
Near Murfreesboro', Tennessee, January 10, 1863.

SIR: I respectfully submit to you the following report of the action of my regiment in the battle of Stone river.

After a march occupying three days, during which skirmishing with the enemy was fierce and continuous, by your order I bivouacked my regiment upon the field on the evening of the 29th December ultimo, in its brigade position. On the morning of the 30th December, ultimo, my regiment was thrown into position with reserve corps on the right centre. Sharp picket fighting occupied the day, and on the morning of the 31st December ultimo the enemy made his appearance on the centre and right wing; the battle raged with uninterrupted fury, and we lay upon the field during the night. I cannot picture to you the gallant conduct of my men during the fight of the 31st ultimo. Officers and men universally fought with desperation and bravery. January 1st the enemy refused to show himself in force on the centre, and at night we again slept on the field. January 2d indicated fight. At 3 o'clock p. m., by your orders, my regiment took position to support General Van Cleve's division on the left. At about 4 o'clock p. m. the enemy in force showed his front in pursuit of our retreating troops. Lying down in line we watched the approach of the enemy exulting over his fancied success. A charge was ordered, and although my regiment was much impeded by the disorganized flight of infantry, artillery, and riderless horses, my regiment reached the opposite bank of Stone river and engaged the enemy. The struggle which ensued was desperate and bloody. We succeeded in driving him beyond his line of artillery, which he left on the field as trophies. The enemy was completely routed, and night closed pursuit, leaving us in possession of a battle-field two miles in extent. I could mention many instances of individual heroism. Captain Caton, company H, gallantly bore the colors across the river in the charge. Captains McMahon, Canfield, and Allan were conspicuous in the struggle. Lieutenant Wiley, of company C, commanding company A, fell mortally wounded. Lieutenants Knaggs, Allen, and Bumpus fell severely wounded while cheering their men to the charge. Lieutenant Colonel Stoughton and Major Walker deserve all praise for their efficient and prompt action during the fight; indeed, all vied with each other in the performance of their several duties. I herewith append a list of the killed, wounded, and missing, for whom, amidst our cheers of victory, let us not forget to drop a soldier's tear.

Very respectfully, &c.,

JAMES M. NEIBLING,
Colonel Commanding 21st Regiment Ohio Volunteer Infantry.

Colonel JOHN F. MILLER,
Commanding 7th Brigade, 8th Division, 14th Army Corps.

[Indorsed.]

Received at headquarters 3d brigade, 2d division, centre, Murfreesboro,' January 5, 1863.

Colonel Granville Moody, commanding 74th Ohio volunteer infantry.

Official report of the part taken by the 74th Ohio volunteer infantry at the battles of Stone river, from December 30, 1862, to January 4, 1863.

HEADQUARTERS THIRD BRIGADE, SECOND DIVISION, CENTRE,
Murfreesboro', January 27, 1863.

Respectfully forwarded.

WILLIAM SIVWELL,
Colonel 78th Pennsylvania Volunteers, Commanding 3d Brigade.

HEADQUARTERS SECOND DIVISION, FOURTEENTH ARMY CORPS,
Murfreesboro', February 4, 1863.

Respectfully forwarded.

JAMES S. NEGLEY,
Brigadier General Commanding.

HEADQUARTERS 74TH REGIMENT OHIO VOLUNTEER INFANTRY,
Camp near Murfreesboro', Tennessee, January 5, 1863.

SIR: I have the honor to report the results of the engagements of the 31st of December, 1862, and the 2d of January, 1863, as affecting the 74th regiment Ohio volunteer infantry, under my command.

Colonel Miller, commanding the 7th brigade, 8th division of the 14th army corps, was pleased to assign to my command the position of the left centre of the brigade. In the action of the 31st December we were posted on the slope of an eminence facing and commanding the position held by the Rock City guards, and other regiments, composing one of the most efficient brigades of the rebel forces, under General Withers. I am justly proud, sir, of my regiment. The brave and persistent men of my command promptly obeyed every order on that field of blood and deadly strife, and contributed largely to the glorious victory which has driven the entire rebel force from their chosen field, and has placed us in undisputed possession of Murfreesboro', Tennessee.

Allow me, in this connexion, to note the gallant action of the 21st Ohio volunteer infantry, Colonel Neibling, on our left, the 37th Indiana on our right, under command of Colonel Hall, and the 78th Pennsylvania, Colonel Sivwell. These regiments displayed the utmost bravery, inspiring all around with the high resolve to emulate their devotion to the cause in which we have mutually invested our all.

I take the greatest pleasure in reporting the gallant conduct of all the officers of the 74th regiment.

Major Thomas C. Bell, the only field officer with me, did his whole duty in the several engagements in the nine days' battle. Cool, fearless, prompt, he proved himself to be the right man in the right place.

I desire to record the superior qualities evinced by the adjutant of the regiment, Lieutenant William F. Armstrong, of company C. In addition to his marked business habits, to which the regiment is greatly indebted, his bravery and efficiency on the battle field entitle him to distinguished consideration. Our line officers, too, without exception, have won the highest regards by their eminently good conduct before the enemy and in the fiery ordeal through which they passed. Lieutenants William McGinnis, commanding company H; Richard King, commanding company B; Robert Stevenson, commanding company C; Robert Hunter, commanding company D; Captain Joseph Fisher and Lieutenant H. H. Fleming, of company E; Captain Walter Crook, and Lieutenants M. Peters and Joseph Hamill, of company F; Lieutenant T. C. McElravy, commanding company G, with Lieutenant George Brecker, of same company; Captain Joseph Ballard and First Lieutenant Snodgrass, of company H; Lieutenant Robert Cullen, of company I, and William H. Reed, second lieutenant of company K; these officers, sir, all did their duty bravely; there was no flinching in any one of them; each faced the iron hail unmoved; each was in his place superintending the movements and cheering their men in the terrible work they were called on to perform.

Lieutenant Peters was severely wounded in the wrist and was compelled to retire about the middle of the action on the 31st. Lieutenant Snodgrass was last seen just before the closing struggle, cheering his men, clapping his hands, saying, "Work away, my lads; we are gaining ground!" Noble fellow! He was wounded shortly afterward, and is reported amongst the missing. We fear he was mortally wounded. Captain Crook and Lieutenant Cullen were also wounded in the action of the 31st, the latter dangerously. Captain Ballard was wounded in the shoulder slightly.

In the action of the 2d January the 74th regiment occupied its position in the brigade and aided in the decisive repulse of the rebel forces under General Cheatham and Hanson, in which they were driven over Stone river, and over the hill and through the fields beyond, where our soldiers made the successful charge on the rebel batteries as they belched their fiery fury on the federal forces. At the close of that eventful onward movement the flag of the 74th was waving on the outer lines amidst the rejoicings of its stern supporters, and there remained till recalled by the order of General Negley to reform his division in the rear of the artillery in the centre.

The review which I have made of the battle fields over which we have together made our way during this nine days' struggle shows the awful effectiveness of our arms, the desperate obstinacy which characterizes our troops, and warrants the belief that though our pathway may be over bloody fields and thickly-planted graveyards, yet, the flag of Washington, Jefferson, Jackson, and the heroes of our glorious Union, endeared by a thousand precious memories, and the symbol of a greater, grander destiny, shall be upheld and be borne along and aloft till it shall again float in unquestioned supremacy over all its ancient domain,

The following reports I have just received from our company commanders, and forward by Sergeant James Worden to headquarters.

Allow me to say in behalf of the 74th regiment officers and men that, with such commanders as Major General Rosecrans, General Negley, and Colonel John F. Miller, we are prepared to go forward and follow the fortunes of the flag with increasing confidence in the cause of our country against its rebel foes.

I have the honor to be your obedient servant,

GRANVILLE MOODY,
Colonel Commanding 74th Regiment Ohio Volunteer Infantry.

HENRY M. CIST, *Acting Assistant Adjutant General.*

[Indorsed.]

Received, headquarters 3d brigade, second division, (centre,) Murfreesboro', Tennessee, January 14, 1863.

LIEUT. ALEX. MARSHALL,
Commanding Battery G, 1st Ohio Volunteer Artillery.

Official report of the part taken by his battery at the battles of Stone river from December 30, 1862, to January 4, 1863.

HEADQUARTERS 3D BRIGADE, SECOND DIVISION, (CENTRE,)
Murfreesboro', January 27, 1863.

Respectfully forwarded.

WILLIAM SIVWELL,
Colonel 78th Pennsylvania Volunteers, Commanding 3d Brigade, &c.

HEADQUARTERS SECOND DIVISION, 14TH ARMY CORPS,
Murfreesboro', February 5, 1863.

Respectfully forwarded.

JAS. S. NEGLEY,
Brigadier General Commanding.

HEADQUARTERS BATTERY G 1st OHIO VOLUNTEER ARTILLERY,
Murfreesboro', Tennessee, January 11, 1863.

SIR : In obedience to orders from headquarters 7th brigade, eighth division, 14th army corps, I have the honor to report part taken by battery G 1st Ohio volunteer artillery, in the late engagement before Murfreesboro', Tennessee.

On the morning of December 29, 1862, the battery was ordered out on a reconnoissance. Leaving the Murfreesboro' pike at Stewartsboro', followed up Stewart creek one mile, discovered the enemy's cavalry in the woods on the opposite side of the creek, fired twelve rounds from rifled 12-pounder, causing them to disperse. We then moved forward and to the right, taking position as indicated, until 2 p. m., when we crossed the creek with the brigade, advanced on a by road running nearly parallel with the Murfreesboro' pike. Entering the pike at Wilson's creek, about five miles from Murfreesboro', advanced on the pike two and a half miles, took position on a slight elevation, on the right of the pike, where we remained during the night, with horses harnessed and hitched in. At daylight on 30th, per order, Colonel Miller moved about three-fourths of a mile to the right and front over a new and rocky road through a cedar thicket; remained in this vicinity during the day, occupying several positions in a narrow cornfield and in the thicket, within range of the enemy's battery and rifle-pit, located in an open field in front. At four p. m. fired about fifty rounds, shelling the woods on our right occupied by the enemy's skirmishers, whose fire was severe, also the battery and rifle-pit in front. Some of our shells falling into the rifle-pit caused considerable scattering. We remained in this position in the cornfield during the night; we elicited no reply from the enemy's battery during the whole day. At six p. m. removed the right section out on the right of the section in the cornfield, and remained in this position hitched in during the night. At daylight of the 31st opened with the four guns stationed in the cornfield, shelling the woods to the right, and the battery and rifle-pit in front, as the night before. About eight a. m. moved the centre section down to the left about forty rods, taking position near two log-houses in rear of the cornfield, a dense thicket across the cornfield directly in front, open country to the left and front, where the enemy was in position. Remained in this position about thirty minutes without firing. Then moved this section up and took position in centre of the battery; worked the battery to about eleven a. m. The enemy up to this time fired but few rounds from their batteries in our front, firing being mostly from their skirmishers in the woods, when, in obedience to Colonel Miller's order, moved to the right, partially changed front. The batteries of the enemy opened over the advancing infantry a heavy fire before we had fairly got into position; ordered the caissons under shelter a short distance in the rear and opened upon the rapidly advancing enemy with canister; as our support advanced we moved our pieces forward by hand and worked them as rapidly as possible. One of our 12-pounder howitzers being disabled, the trail having been cut nearly off by a shot, ordered it to the rear; went to work with canister, the enemy advancing in the woods close upon us; as our infantry support advanced we advanced our pieces by hand to the fence close to the woods, that we might hold an interval in their lines, and continued firing canister as fast as possible; during this time our horses were suffering severely from fire from the enemy—had them replaced by the teams from battery and forge wagon, which I had ordered up the day before, leaving the battery and forge wagon a mile and a half in the rear in charge of artificers; all of my spare horses were soon used up and several taken from the caissons; had three men killed and several wounded. Saw the enemy moving down the open field in masses on our left flank, and the firing extending far to our rear on our right flank; and one of our 12-pounder rifles having a shot wedged and but three horses remaining, I ordered Lieutenant Crabb to take the two disabled pieces and caissons to the rear through the cedar swamp, and ordered the remaining four pieces to fix prolonge, to fire retiring; the enemy had already been twice repulsed, when they moved upon both our flanks and front with renewed ranks and vigor, which caused our support to give way. I ordered the battery to retire to the woods in our rear, two pieces having but three horses and two four horses each. My own, Lieutenant Whittlesey's, and one sergeant's horse were killed; three of the guns moved off as ordered, prolonge of the left piece, 12-pounder Wiard, broke, at the same the lead rider was shot, the gunner mounted his team when the off-wheel horse was killed and the off-lead horse was wounded, which prevented us from using the limber. I then ordered a limber of one of the pieces already in the woods out, to draw the remaining 12-pounder off the field into the woods. We had no sooner started back when I found the right and centre of the brigade had fallen back, and the left (21st Ohio) was coming in, leaving the pieces about forty yards outside of our lines, between us and the enemy, which was fast closing in on us with a heavy fire. Saw that it was impossible to reach the gun. I ordered the limber back and gun limbered up; moved back through the cedar swamp in rear of brigade. There being no road, I was considerably bothered to work my way through. As the brigade was moving rapidly and the enemy pressing close upon us, two more of my wheel horses were shot and one rider, when I was obliged to leave two more guns, having but one wheel and middle horse on each piece. Sergeant Farwell, together with Sergeant Bills, took the remaining piece, passed the pieces left, and worked their way through and took position on the right of Captain Stokes's battery, where I found them and went to work, using up the balance of our ammunition—about forty rounds. As soon as joining this piece I sent to inform Lieutenant Crabb where I was, and to get that portion of the battery which had succeeded in getting out, together with the battery and forge wagon, which was a short distance in the rear. After expending the ammunition of the piece I was with, moved it to the rear, and left it in charge of Lieutenant Whittlesey, with the battery and forge wagon. I then proceeded to find Colonel Barnett or Lieutenant Edson in relation to ammunition, when I met Lieutenant Crabb, who informed me that our piece and four caissons had moved up the pike. I ordered him to have the carriages all halted, and to send back the 6-pounder ammunition. After waiting some time, sent my orderly back to hurry up the 6-pounder ammunition. At dark moved over to the left of the railroad, and remained during the night with the 1st Kentucky battery, Lieutenant Ellsworth commanding, having previously reported to General Negley and Colonel Miller the condition of the battery and where I was; was ordered to remain in that vicinity. Early on the morning of January 1, 1863, I proceeded out the pike; met sergeant with the 6-pounder caisson, who had been unable the night previous to find the gun. Sent sergeant forward with the caisson, when the piece in command of Lieutenant Whittlesey moved up and took position on the left of Captain Shultz's battery, in an open field on the left centre, joining General Crittenden's corps. I soon met Lieutenant Crabb with the 12-pounder howitzer, who informed me that when he came up with the 12-pounder howitzer, the afternoon of the 31st, the enemy was about making a charge upon our transportation, when he placed the piece in position, fired fifteen rounds of shell, doing good execution, where he remained during the night with a brigade of cavalry. I found that our loss for December 31, 1862, summed up forty-three horses, four guns, three limbers, two caissons and limbers, three men killed and wounded, and twelve missing. I then moved the 12-pounder howitzer to the front, and took position with the other piece. Procuring fifty rounds for howitzer and eighty rounds for 6-pounder, Wiard immediately reported to Colonel Miller, commanding brigade, and General Negley, commanding division. About half-past ten shifted our position about 200 yards to our front and left; remained in this position about an hour, when we received orders to move immediately to the right, across the pike, into a cedar thicket, and took position in centre of Missouri battery. About 3 p. m. was ordered to move with division to the rear and right; finally took position in corn-field on the extreme right, in company with Captains Standart's, Shultz's, and Ellsworth's batteries, fixed prolonge, where we remained until dark, when we moved back close to the pike under cover of an elevation, where we remained during the night. At daylight on the morning of January 2, again moved up on the elevation. At about 12 m., received orders to move over and take position on left centre, same as day previous. The skirmishers kept up a lively fire along our front until 4 p. m., when I observed the enemy moving in masses through the open country on the opposite side of the river on our left and front, driving back our forces on the opposite side of the river, when we commenced shelling them as fast as possible, receiving a cross fire from the enemy's artillery. Soon Captain Shultz, on our left, and Captain Swallow's, battery on our right, fell back. I then ordered prolonge fixed, and retired about forty yards; commenced firing, when I had one man and three horses killed on the piece. At the same time the enemy was repulsed and the ground retaken.

January 3, held the same position as the day previous; fired several rounds on the enemy, shelling the woods to the right and front as our men advanced. Late on January 4, advanced with division on Murfreesboro' pike about one mile; camped on the right of pike. Early on the morning of the 5th forded the river and passed through Murfreesboro'.

Our losses are, killed: Corporal Thomas Strong and Privates Spencer Inman, Samuel Burford, and John Woodworth. Wounded: Sergeant G. W. Bills, Corporal Henry Clagen, and Privates James W. Fife, Charles A. Whiting, Edward Beverstock, William Jones, James H. Clinton, and Henry Wilds. Missing: Jackson Hockett, George B. Cox, and William Volts, all privates. Total killed, wounded, and missing, 16. Horses killed, 34; horses captured by the enemy, 12. Total horses killed and captured, 46.

I take pleasure in referring to the valuable assistance rendered me by Lieutenants Crabb and Whittlesey. Their gallant and heroic bearing not only inspired the men with courage, but is deserving of public commendation.

Orderly Sergeant Slimy and Sergeants Bills, Farwell, and Mitchell, by their promptness in the execution of orders, and by their unflinching courage in scenes of danger, merit particular mention. Others in the command evinced soldierly qualities of no common order. To mention their names might seem invidious.

I wish to make special mention of Quartermaster Treat, whose energy and perseverance in keeping the men supplied with rations during the severe weather of seven days that we were separated by miles from our transportation, and his promptness in looking after, collecting together, and reporting to me property and men which, in the confusion of falling back, had separated from the command.

Respectfully submitted.

ALEXANDER MARSHALL,
Lieutenant Commanding Battery G, 1st Ohio Volunteer Artillery.

HENRY M. CIST,
Lieutenant and Acting Assistant Adjutant General.

Official report of casualties of the 29th brigade, 8th division.

18TH REGIMENT OHIO VOLUNTEERS.

Lieutenant Colonel Josiah Given, (commanding regiment,) wounded in arm; Adjutant A. W. S. Minear, wounded in breast; Sergeant Major Dow L. Carter, wounded in hip.

Company A.—Killed: Corporals Isaiah Timmons and R. S. Augustis, Privates John F. Mowbray, M. M. Blacher, and James Hodsdew. Wounded: Second Lieutenant E. McLaren, left leg; Sergeant Henry C. Roby, right arm, (amputated;) Corporals D. A. Woodland, thigh; Albert Toops, slightly; Privates Ebenezer Finemore, left thigh, (since died of wound;) H. W. Purcell, breast, (since died of wound;) Allen Reddin, mouth; Enoch H. Smith, foot; Edward Trewitt, leg; Jackson Mackerly, arm; W. A. Christian, shoulder; George Goder, finger; Robert Goff, slightly; Henry Hays, (on duty;) Thomas Goodwin, left leg. Missing: Private Franklin Maddox, (supposed a prisoner.)

Company B.—Wounded: Captain Ashbel Fenton, ankle; Corporals R. F.

Wakefield, breast; E. W. Ellis, hip; A. Fitzgerald, arm; George Kailor, leg; Musician H. S. Honnold, shoulder, (supposed a prisoner;) Privates Niles Bowin, abdomen, (since died of wound;) James Bussan, arm; A. M. Ball, thigh; A. H. Buck, thigh; L. S. Barcroft, breast; A. C. Chapman, leg; S. Clanson, back; Robert Campbell, breast; Harvy B. Gill, hand, (prisoner;) J. S. Hamilton, hand, (prisoner;) P. Scharlotterbock, arm; Asa S. Scott, shoulder, (prisoner and paroled;) Dennis Wilson, knee; Charles T. Williams, hand; E. Weant, breast; A. H. Kames, hand, (prisoner;) L. H. Kennard, ankle. Missing: Private Perley Waldron and Musician F. W. Dollison, (supposed a prisoner.) Prisoners: J. B. Clark and J. N. Hutchinson.

Company C.—Killed: Privates Joseph Cheehill and Henry J. Folly. Wounded: Captain Johnson M. Welch, calf of leg; Sergeant J. W. Root, hand; Corporals Jasper Witham, leg; Samuel Hamerick, arm; Privates George Stout, arm; Imni Coman, arm; Hiram Kincade, head; Isaac McDonnald, leg; Jacob McDonald, hip; William Stitts, leg; Jonathan Snow, head. Missing: Sergeant James Light and Private Henry Taylor. Prisoners: Private Wesley Taylor and Musician E. W. Jemle.

Company D.—Killed: Corporals James S. Vanpelt and William Ranier and Private Oscar Clark. Wounded: Sergeants A. S. Camp, wrist; Nelson Gaskill, side; Privates William Crosby, leg; Eli C. Meek, leg; John P. Caisey, leg; A. A. Ladley, leg broken; William Scott, leg; Enis Jones, leg; Hamsone Dart, thigh; Martin Baley, leg; William A. Young, hand; Felix Baley, arm; William Blayce, arm.

Company E.—Killed: Second Lieutenant W. W. Blacker, Sergeants John Pierce and John T. Davis, Privates D. Fesley and T. E. Morter. Wounded: Captain Philip E. Taylor, leg and side, (since died of wounds;) Corporals A. Hurst, foot; James Quim, arm; Privates Charles Davis, shoulder; S. Freese, leg; J. L. Guy, hand; W. E. McDonald, arm; G. W. O'Day, leg; E. B. Proctor, arm; J. D. Sampson, head. Missing: Privates William Gill, James Morter, Charles Stough, O. B. Foote, and William Whitten. Prisoners: Musician John Tatman, Corporal J. N. Fustin, and Private Joseph Garrett.

Company F.—Killed: Privates Charles B. McDonald and Harrison Sheets. Wounded: Sergeants David J. Searight, slightly; William J. Byeer, slightly; Corporal Thomas P. Byns, head; Privates James Maxon, leg; Austin W. Perkins, shoulder; James S. Comer, arm; Isaac Washington, leg; John C. Brand, John Hill, John Kendle, and William Irnill, slightly. Prisoner: Corporal Thomas H. Wade.

Company G.—Killed: Privates John C. Spinger and John Pratchard. Wounded: Sergeant William F. Quigley, leg; Corporal Belford Griffith, leg; Privates Lawrence Young, hip, (since died of wound;) William C. Bowers, side, (since died of wound;) S. S. McDisilt, hand; John D. Sanders, arm; George W. Bute, arm; John Charlton, shoulder, (prisoner;) Hiram C. Smith, leg. Prisoner: Musician William E. Barron.

Company H.—Wounded: Privates Charles S. Simmons, side, (since died of wound;) Patrick Ford, arm; A. C. Hamilton, leg; Wilson Liff, neck; William Franklin, shoulder; P. W. Phillips, slightly; George Gale, leg; Samuel McElroy, foot; Wesley Rader, face; Adam Gregory, leg; William Maline, hand. Missing: Privates Samuel Weeks, G. P. Winman, (supposed a prisoner,) and Thomas Bourn, (supposed a prisoner.)

Company I.—Wounded: Captain Charles C. Ross, breast; Sergeant W. W. Right, leg; Privates Thomas A. Tomas, thigh; H. W. Cawley, thigh; James D. James, thigh; William G. Jewell, thigh. Missing: Corporal H. McClafflim, (supposed a prisoner.)

Company K.—Killed: Privates W. H. Thompson, Silas D. Wolf, Thomas Long, and William Moor. Wounded: Captain George Stivers, shoulder, (since died of wound;) Corporal Joseph Huggins, left arm; Privates P. J. Hartley, neck; Milton Bosworth, shoulder; G. W. Angell, foot; Joseph Fullerton, nose;

George J. Rice, leg; Lewis A. Pullen, side; George Hallman, right hand; G. Barringer, left cheek; E. W. Tucker, left side; George Willis, left shoulder.

19TH REGIMENT ILLINOIS VOLUNTEERS.

Company A.—Killed: Corporal Ira A. Plase, Privates Deville L. Holmes and Thomas A. Moore. Wounded: Sergeants William H. Wildey, arm; R. G. Sylvester, head; Corporal Charles Kerr, leg; Privates R. P. Blanchard, side; E. H. Edgele, leg; M. C. Kennedy, leg; Joseph L. Slagle, side; Charles H. Rishill, head; George Ultz, abdomen, (since died of wound;) Samuel Worden, shoulder, slightly. Missing: C. A. Muloy.

Company B.—Killed: Corporal George Ryerson, Privates J. O. Imes, Charles W. Leason, and Isaac L. Kenyon. Wounded: Captain Alexander Murchison, back; Second Lieutenant John H. Hunter, thigh; Sergeant Thomas Robison, shoulder; Corporal H. B. Worth, finger; Privates Walter Black, knee; J. M. Leacox, arm; William Douglass, foot; Columbus Morgan, bowels; T. W. Oziah, lip; George T. Sham, arm and thigh; Thomas Turnbull, thumb; George Dugan, thumb. Missing: Corporal J. L. Kennedy.

Company C.—Wounded: First Lieutenant W. L. Wood, hand; Corporals Henry Sneezy, (since died of wound;) Delevan Craft, leg; Privates John Ives, hand; Webster Daniels, hand; Peter Barhwort, arm; Charles Adair, neck; Wilkins M. Battis, leg; Frank Seguin, arm and side; Edward McKulee, leg.

Company D.—Killed: Corporal Robert McCracken. Wounded: Sergeant Jonas Goldsmith, side; Corporal H. Clay Doggry, hip; William B. Taylor, leg; Privates John Tansey, back, and prisoner; Thomas Willard, leg; Henry E. Carter, leg; Jacob Balls, breast; Joseph Smith, head; Samuel Wadden, shoulder. Missing: Privates James H. Haynie and M. W. Smith.

Company E.—Wounded: Corporal Joseph E. Huntington, hand; Privates John E. A. Stevens; David McArthur, face; John Hays, hip; John G. P. Noble, (since died of wound;) Thomas C. Welsh, hip; Thomas King, thigh; George Joel. Missing: Corporal Peter Guthrie, Privates Daniel McVery and William Patterson.

Company F.—Killed: Captain Knowlton H. Chandler and Private Samuel Griffin. Wounded: Privates Abraham Hess, side; Christopher Moore, shoulder; William Alfred, leg; John Coleman, hand.

Company H.—Killed: Private Jesse Maxwell. Wounded: Captain Peachy A. Garrett, leg; Second Lieutenant Washington Wood, bowels, (since died of wound;) Corporals Lloyd D. Thomas, knee; John H. Snyder, thigh; Privates Henry E. Wells, arm; James F. Coleman, eye; Josiah Suter, leg; Mettelous Stoughton, thigh; Charles G. Bates, wrist. Wounded and prisoners: First Sergeant Voleny C. Johnson, leg; Corporals Summer Harrington, side; William Hagerty, arm; Privates George F. Fleming, arm; George B. Sickles, shoulder; James W. Carson, wrist; John Benham, ankle. Prisoner: U. P. Benson. Missing: George Kearnes.

Company I.—Killed: Private John Fritham. Wounded: Privates Henry Harmer, Frank Hogan, shoulder, and missing; Richard Doning, arm; Joseph Mate, leg. Missing: L. M. Jones.

Company K.—Killed: Sergeant Daniel W. Griffen. Wounded: Second Lieutenant V. Bradford Bell, head; Sergeant L. H. Scadden, leg; Corporal F. Russell, head; Privates I. Fullerton, (since died of wound;) E. Rullen, side; P. Smith, mouth; R. Priolet, thigh; Charles Kent, ear. Missing: Privates Joseph Dayer and Thomas Johnson.

69TH REGIMENT OHIO VOLUNTEERS.

Colonel William B. Cassilly, arm; Adjutant J. W. Baynton, leg.

Company A.—Wounded: Acting Lieutenant L. E. Hicks, shoulder; 1st Sergeant J. S. Scott, shoulder; Corporal D. Tetrick, thigh, (supposed prisoner;) Privates B. Stewart, leg, (died January 6;) L. Hulsey, leg; B. Marchant, calf of leg, (supposed prisoner;) J. Bragg, leg; A. T. Cloffern, leg, (by cavalry horse;) and E. Sempson, arm.

Company B.—Killed: Sergeant J. McGillan. Wounded: Acting Second Lieutenant Joseph Tucker, shoulder; Sergeants D. Stibbens, ankle; W. Porter, hand, (prisoner;) and J. Hulsey, hand.

Company C.—Wounded: Sergeants W. Longfellow, loin; P. Burch, cheek. Missing: Sergeant I. Schellenboch, Privates A. J. Garner, J. Dinkfellow, and A. Grosserman.

Company D.—Wounded: Captain J. Devor, neck; Privates R. Willson, leg; H. Zumi, hand; A. Hawkins, shoulder; and D. Strudebaker, thigh. Missing: Privates A. Dynes, S. Deforest, and D. West.

Company E.—Killed: Corporal D. P. Allbright and Private J. J. Stoker. Wounded: Sergeant Perry, hand; Privates V. Jones, neck; J. Vanatles, thigh; George A. Davis, arm; and James Pea, side. Missing: Privates J. Hunsbarger and J. Landon, (prisoner.)

Company F.—Wounded: Sergeant George Shedd, shoulder; Privates J. J. Simmons, foot; and Jesse M. Hamens, leg. Missing: Privates S. C. Miller, A. Drexalins, S. Waters, and T. H. Seagrist.

Company G.—Killed: Corporal J. Brown. Wounded: Captain W. Patton, leg and side; Corporals F. Buck, arm; and F. Pretz, knee; Privates J. Holler, throat; Joel Wagoner, shoulder; and Joe Howell, hand. Missing: First Sergeant W. Tilton, Sergeant David Russell, Privates L. B. Kerfoot, F. Hill, E. J. Manche, (prisoner,) W. Barnhard, (prisoner,) L. Otis, (prisoner, paroled,) R. Pleger, (prisoner, paroled,) G. Kleim, (prisoner, paroled.)

Company H.—Killed: Captain L. C. Counsellor. Wounded: Sergeant G. W. Eskridge, leg; Corporal J. Brobeck, stomach; Privates C. Patterson, thigh; and G. Weederlick, back. Missing: Privates James Justes, W. P. Mayer, and W. Case.

Company I.—Wounded: Corporals McKilvey, leg, (died January 10;) J. W. Williams, leg, (amputated;) and J. McAlister, hand, (supposed prisoner;) R. R. Wells, hand; Private Kiedow, leg. Missing: Privates James Penn, T. C. Brumell, and Hend. Vance.

Company K.—Wounded: Corporal W. Jones, side; Privates Charles Graham, D. Gowan, hip; and N. Johnson, side. Missing: Corporal J. Mahon, Privates S. B. Romick, B. Graham, J. Nulan, J. McCurdy, and J. C. McGaw.

11TH MICHIGAN VOLUNTEERS.

Major Sylvester B. Smith, wounded in face.

Company A.—Killed: Private Edward Timna. Wounded: Captain David Oakes, neck; Corporal Edward D. White, leg; Privates Anson Spencer, left arm; William Wood, leg; Loomis Carpenter, shoulder; Robert Carpenter, breast; David Rockwell, shoulder; Henry Clark, side; Daniel Rose, thigh bruised; William Lemunjon, side; Byron Baker, head; Julius Tompkins, head; Stephen Huly, head; Drummer William Platt, hip. Missing: Corporal A. B. White, Privates Byron Thomas and Rollin O. Eaton.

Company B.—Killed: Corporal Orrin Nichols, Privates Oliver Busby, Daniel Haynes and William Johnson. Wounded: Privates Andrew Silverwood, hip; Frederick Waltman, right thigh; Levi McGinness, left foot; Harman Adams, left hand; Joseph Bowen, left shoulder; Dorry Nichols, left arm. Missing: Dexter

Avery, Bradley Mother, Oliver Swart, Robert Thomas, G. W. Vanvantenbury, and Halsey Miller.

Company C.—Killed: Privates James Fisher, Daniel C. Leonard, and Bennet Smelts. Wounded: Second Lieutenant L. H. Howard, leg; Privates William Palten, hand; Jacob Hockenburgh, right side; Charles Leonard, over left eye. Missing: Sergeant Cyrus Sherman.

Company D.—Wounded: Sergeant William Robson, hand; Corporal D. Le Burnes, left arm; Corporal B. Y. Bordner, arm; Privates John George, shoulder; John O. Nayler, shoulder. Missing: Privates James Eberhard, Thos. A. White, Jesse J. Christy, Simpson D. Long, William H. Lucus, and Henry Burkson.

Company E.—Killed: First Lieutenant Thomas Flynn, Sergeant Ezra Spencer, Privates Hiram Everett, Thomas Manning, Robert McIlvain, and Joseph Le Roy. Wounded: Corporal Daniel Chase; Privates William Sherman, back; Benjamin F. Clubine, left side; Peter V. Dolber, right side; Frank M. Buter, arm; George Quay, back; Andrew Knapp, back; Bradley L. Lane, finger. Missing: Privates Samuel Quaco, James W. Beck, and Washington Antony.

Company F.—Killed: First Lieutenant Joseph Wilson and Sergeant C. Peck. Wounded: Corporal Myron M. Comstock, thigh; Privates William Spafford, shoulder. Missing: Second Lieutenant Ephraim G. Hall, and Private Edward B. Hopkins.

Company G.—Killed: Privates Oscar Angle, Perry Deforrist, Cyrus W. Gilbert, Silas Kelly, Joseph Killinger, and Sylvester Nichols. Wounded: First Lieutenant Thomas H. Briggs, leg; Sergeant James Boughton, head; Corporal Charles Myers, shoulder; Privates Jesse Nash, lung, (since dead;) John Austin, ankle; Stephen Andrews, arm; David F. Barrett, leg; Augustus E. Dickinson, hand; Martin Tanner, right arm; Andrew Kershner, face; James R. Hass, right arm; Charles N. Nichols, head; James Rose, right arm; Martin V. B. Williams, side. Missing: Privates Chancy W. Granger and Almerin C. Currier.

Company H.—Killed: Corporal George W. Guyer, Privates William Chamberlain and Chancy B. Green. Wounded: Privates Henry Vanderhoff, left arm; Ed. A. Green, back; Dennis N. Sewick, face. Missing: Musicians Abel Coon and Stillman Hedge.

Company I.—Killed: Sergeant Ansel Palmer, Privates James W. Wright and George E. Jewett. Wounded: Privates Marcus D. Baker; Lynn Barnes, thigh; Elijah Lampkins, foot; George Francisco, head. Missing: Privates Napoleon B. Sprague and Walter F. Halleck.

Company K.—Killed: Privates Thomas Brightly, Simon Hamiltons, and Joseph Miller. Wounded: First Lieutenant Patrick Keeyan, right cheek; First Sergeant John H. Johnson, head and left leg; Sergeants Coleman Dokin, right hand; John D. Keegan, thigh; Elmer Bradley, right cheek; Corporals James Bolton, left shoulder; Frank Papane, right thigh; Privates Myror Bragg, back; Homer Goodall, left hip; Alpheus Cheney, right arm; Anson Farmer, hand; William Horris, head; Adam Lehr, right hand; Jacob M. Pound, right shoulder; Daniel Rapps, back; Peter Leeley, head; Edward Finch, hand and arm; David Patterson, hip. Missing: Richard Privates Evans, Daniel Griswold, and Barthomer Rhodes.

Respectfully submitted.

T. R. STANLEY, *Colonel Commanding.*

WILLIAM D. TEMPLE,
Lieutenant and Acting Assistant Adjutant General.

HEADQUARTERS 69TH OHIO VOLUNTEER INFANTRY,
Camp near Murfreesboro', Tennessee, January 10, 1863.

Agreeably to orders, I submit the following report of the part the 69th regiment Ohio volunteers took in the battles of "Stone river," omitting all the incidents up to the morning of December 31, 1862.

The 69th regiment occupied the left of the 29th brigade, Negley's division, and was ordered to advance about 6 a. m. across the Nolensville pike; did so, and sent out three companies to the front. Remained in that position one and a half hour. Received an order to fall back to the right of Shultz's battery, which was executed in good order, the regiment sustaining a heavy fire from front and flank during that time Remained in that position, fighting, until the division was ordered to retire back as far as the pike; there the regiment was reformed. During all these moves and fighting we had many killed and wounded. During this time Colonel Cassilly was wounded through the arm severely. Major Hickcox had his horse shot under him, falling on him, and so severely bruising him as to compel him to leave the field. The command was then turned over to Captain Putnam, he being the senior officer present. Was ordered up to the front and sustained a heavy fire; was then ordered to retire by General Negley in person. During this day's fighting I was back at Stewart's creek—left there with a detachment of two hundred men. Arrived on the battle-field at 5 p. m. and took command.

Thursday was occupied in skirmishing with the enemy on our right. Nothing of special interest occurred during the day. Friday, January 2, was ordered to the left, where we took up a position and kept it until 3 p. m. At this time the division on the left of Stone river was attacked by the enemy, and after a short fight fell back. At this time we were ordered out into a corn-field, and lay down until the enemy came within three hundred yards. We then arose, fired, and charged up to the bank of Stone river, and halted a few minutes and fired across the river. Then crossed the river, and reformed, and charged them for half a mile and assisted to take a battery. The enemy having fallen back, we slowly retired to the woods, and took care of our wounded and dead, which I am sorry to say was heavy. (A full list has already been forwarded to brigade headquarters.) It was now dark, and we were ordered out on picket in front.

Saturday, January 3, nothing of interest occurred. January 4, was on picket; relieved in the evening. January 5, came on through Murfreesboro', since which time we have been encamped in our present camp.

I am, colonel, your obedient servant,

J. F. ELLIOTT,
Lieutenant Colonel, Commanding 69th Ohio Volunteer Infantry.

Colonel T. R. STANLEY,
Commanding 2d Brigade, 2d Division, Centre.

HEADQUARTERS 19TH REGIMENT, ILLINOIS INFANTRY,
Camp near Murfreesboro', Tennessee, January 10, 1863.

SIR: I would respectfully submit to you my report of the part taken by the 19th regiment Illinois infantry in the late engagements before Murfreesboro'.

On Tuesday morning, December 30, the regiment, under command of its colonel, Joseph R. Scott, was by your orders deployed as skirmishers to take possession of and hold certain buildings on the Nolensville pike. On the north side of said pike, on our front, and right opposite the above buildings, was a brickyard, in which we found the enemy in strong numbers. We succeeded, after a short struggle, in driving in their line of skirmishers, which had been thrown out, taking possession of the designated places. We held the position thus gained until relieved, about 12 m., by the 42d Illinois on our right and the 18th Ohio on our left.

We then retired, and were held as a reserve, remaining in that position until next morning, the 31st. At about 9 a. m. of the 31st we became engaged with a large force of the enemy. By your orders we changed our position for the purpose of protecting and preventing, if possible, our right wing from being turned, which, after some two hours' hard fighting, the enemy succeeded in doing. We retired, falling back in line of battle to the cedar forest, where we halted, but were ordered to fall back still further. We again made a stand some fifty yards from the edge of the forest, engaging the enemy alone. We held our position perhaps half an hour, but our colonel, seeing that we were in danger of being outflanked, ordered a retreat, which was done in good order, falling back to the railroad.

By your orders we changed our position several times during the day, but we were not engaged in action. On Thursday, January 1, 1863, we changed our position several times, but did not become engaged with the enemy. On the 2d, about 3½ p. m., the enemy suddenly attacked our left with great fury, and after some severe fighting, the left gave way. We were then ordered forward to their support. Charging upon the enemy, we drove them back. Crossing Stone river, we forced them beyond their batteries, capturing four of their guns, remaining masters of the field.

Early in the engagement our colonel, whilst gallantly leading his men, fell severely, but not dangerously, wounded, the command then devolving upon me; and I here take great pleasure in testifying to the bravery and good conduct of both officers and men in my command. But where all did their duty so nobly, it would be unjust to discriminate.

Enclosed please find list of casualties in my command. Trusting the above may prove satisfactory,

I am, very respectfully, your obedient servant,

ALEX. W. RAFFEN,
Lieutenant Colonel, Commanding 19th Illinois Infantry.

T. R. STANLEY,
Colonel, Commanding 29th Brigade.

Indorsed: Headquarters nineteenth regiment Illinois volunteers, Murfreesboro', January 10, 1863, A. W. Raffen, lieutenant colonel, commanding. Report part taken by the nineteenth regiment Illinois volunteers in the engagements of December 30 and 31, 1862, and January 2, 1863, on Stone river, Tennessee.

HEADQUARTERS 2D DIVISION, 14TH ARMY CORPS,
Murfreesboro', February 9, 1863.

Respectfully referred to department headquarters.

JAS. S. NEGLEY, *Brigadier General.*

List of killed, wounded, and missing of the nineteenth regiment Illinois infantry, at the battle of Stone river, Tennessee, December 30 and 31, 1862, and January 2, 1863.

Colonel Joseph R. Scott, wounded in thigh; Major James V. Guthrie, wounded in face.

Company A.—Killed: Corporal Ira A. Pease, and Privates Devillo L. Holmes, and Thos. A. Moore. Wounded: Sergeants William H. Wildey, arm, and R. G. Sylvester, head; Corporal Charles Kerr, leg; Privates R. P. Blanchard, side; J. H. Edgell, leg; M. C. Kennedy, leg; Jos. H. Slagle, side;

Chas. H. Tuthill, hand; George Uttz, abdomen, (died January 2, 1863;) Samuel Warden, shoulder. Missing: Chris. A. Mulvey.

Company B.—Killed: Corporal George Ryerson, and Privates Isaac L. Kenyon, Charles M. Leason, and J. C. Jones. Wounded: Captain Alex. Murchison, back; Second Lieutenant John H. Hunter, thigh; Sergeant Thomas Robson, shoulder; Corporal H. B. Worth, finger; Privates George Dugan, thumb; Thomas Turnbull, thumb; George T. Sharrer, thigh; T. W. Oziah, lip; Columbus Morgan, bowels, (died January 7, 1863;) William Douglass, foot; J. M. Leacox, arm; Walter Clark, knee. Missing: Corporal J. L. Kennedy.

Company C.—Wounded: First Lieutenant Washington L. Wood, hand; Corporals Henry Sweezy, body, (died January 3, 1863,) and Delevan Craft, leg; Privates John Ivis, hand; Webster Daniels, hand; Peter Bourkwort, arm; Charles Adair, neck; Wilkins M. Battis, leg; Frank Sequin, arm; Edward McKeebe, leg.

Company D.—Killed: Corporal Robert McCracken. Wounded: Sergeant Jonas Goldsmith, side, (died January 1, 1863;) Corporal William B Taylor, leg; Privates John Tansey, back, (paroled January 4, 1863;) Thomas Williard, legs; Henry E. Carter, leg; Jacob Bolls, breast; Joseph Smith, head; Samuel Madden, shoulder. Missing: Privates Henry Clay Daggy, James H. Haynie, and Murray W. Smith.

Company E.—Wounded: Corporals Peter F. Guthrie, back, (prisoner;) Joseph C. Huntington, hand; Alex. McL. Frazier, back; Privates David McArthur, face; John Hays, hip; John G. P. Noble, abdomen, (died of wounds;) Thomas C. Welsh, hip; Thomas King, thigh. Missing: Privates John E. A. Stephens, George Joel, Daniel McVeoy, and William Patterson.

Company F.—Killed: Captain Knowlton H. Chandler and Private Samuel Griffin. Wounded: Abraham Hess, side; Christopher Moore, shoulder; Wm. Afland, leg; John Coleman, hand.

Company G.—Detached as an artillery company by order of Major General Rosecrans.

Company H.—Killed: Private Jesse Maxwell. Wounded: Captain Peachy A. Garriott, leg; Second Lieutenant Wellington Wood, bowels, (died January 5, 1863;) Sergeant Volney C. Johnson, leg, (prisoner;) Corporals Sumner Harrington, side; William Hagerty, arm, (prisoner;) Lloyd B. Thomas, knee; John H. Snyder, thigh; Private Henri E. Wells, arm; George F. Fleming, arm, (prisoner;) George B. Sickles, shoulder; James W. Carson, wrist, (prisoner;) John Benham, ankle, (prisoner paroled;) James F. Coleman, eye; Josiah Suter, leg; Mettellus Stoughten, thigh; Charles G. Bates, wrist. Missing: George Kerns.

Company I.—Killed: Private John Triteau. Wounded: Privates Henry Harms, back; Richard Doring, arm; Joseph Matt, leg. Missing: Privates Frank Hogan and Lyman M. Jones.

Company K.—Killed: Corporal Daniel W. Griffin. Wounded: Second Lieutenant V. Bradford Bell, head; Sergeant Sutherland H. Scadin, leg; Corporal J. Frank Russel, head; James C. Fullerton, mortally; Edgar M. Bullen, side; P. Smith, mouth; Robert Periolet, thigh; Chas. Kent, head. Missing: Privates James A. Dwyer and Thomas Johnson.

HEADQUARTERS 37TH INDIANA VOLUNTEERS,
Camp near Murfreesboro', Tennessee, January 10, 1863.

SIR: I have the honor to submit the following report of the part taken by the 37th Indiana volunteers in the engagement at Stone river, near Murfreesboro', Tennessee, commencing December 30, 1862, and ending January 3, 1863.

On the morning of the 30th, the regiment, Colonel Hull commanding, moved through the cedar thicket to the right of bivouac, and there rested, only two companies, D and E, taking part in skirmishing.

On the morning of the 31st the regiment was moved to the open field to support Marshall's battery, where it remained until about 9 a. m., when we changed front, still supporting same battery. While there, one piece was disabled by the horses all being killed and cannoneers leaving.

The regiment then advanced to the woods on the front, which position was held until 12 m. The troops on the right giving way, Colonel Hull called up three pieces of artillery while in that position, which did great execution in the centre. He also ordered two pieces on the right, which were of great support to the maintaining of the position. We were assisted at one time by the 74th Ohio volunteers, also by the 78th Pennsylvania volunteers, which passed over us.

During the entire time we were in this position the cross fire of the enemy from each flank, in addition to that we were meeting in front, was exceedingly galling.

About 12 o'clock m. we were ordered to retire in support of Neel's battery As we approached the thicket, the fire from the enemy's batteries became extremely harassing, so much so that the battery which we supported was compelled to retire. We then moved by left flanks to engage the enemy, who was approaching by brigade, at which time we were broken up by a regiment passing through our lines. We again collected our men, when the 11th Michigan volunteers also passed through our lines, causing some confusion.

The regiment again formed near the centre of the woods, and moved in column of battle to the outer edge, where Colonel Hull was wounded by a musket ball, passing through his left hip, entirely disabling him for duty, at which time the command was turned over to me.

I moved the regiment to the pike, where I received ammunition, which we were entirely out of.

The brigade then being again formed, we rested, not being placed in action again that day.

On the morning of the 1st January, 1863, we were moved to the right, where the enemy was expected to press.

There we remained during the day and night following, resting on arms, but unengaged.

On the afternoon of the second we were moved to the left centre, where we were placed to support a battery or batteries. While there, the forces across the river gave way. The 7th brigade then being ordered to charge, I crossed the brow of the hill and engaged the enemy that had approached the river, drove them back, and held the position under extremely heavy fire from cannon and musketry. I remained in that position until dark, when I was ordered back about two hundred yards, where I remained in that position until after noon of the 4th, when the forces moved for Murfreesboro'.

Colonel Hull's actions during the engagement of the 31st were such as merit the highest praise. He at all times was at his post coolly, bravely, nobly doing his entire duty, causing his willing men to be more energetic. I cannot mention any individual case of bravery among the officers or men without doing injustice to every unmentioned one. Officers and men labored with that energy and presence of mind which distinguishes the *soldier* from the coward.

I return my heartfelt thanks to each and every officer and enlisted man for their noble co-operation during the entire engagement.

I trust their country will be mindful of them.

Very respectfully, your obedient servant,

WILLIAM D. WARD,
Lieutenant Colonel, Commanding.

Lieutenant HENRY M. CIST,
Acting Assistant Adjutant General, 7th Brigade.

Indorsed: Received headquarters 3d brigade, 2d division, centre, Murfreesboro', January 10, 1863. Lieutenant Colonel William D. Ward, commanding 37th Indiana volunteer infantry. Official report of the part taken by the 37th Indiana volunteers at the "battles of Stone river," from December 30, 1862, to January 4, 1863.

HEADQUARTERS 3D BRIGADE, 2D DIVISION, CENTRE,
Murfreesboro', January 27, 1863.

Respectfully forwarded.

WILLIAM SIRWELL,
Colonel 78th Pa. Voluuteer Infantry, Commanding 3d Brigade, &c.

HEADQUARTERS 2D DIVISION, 14TH ARMY CORPS,
Murfreesboro', February 5, 1863.

Respectfully forwarded.

JAMES S. NEGLEY,
Brigadier General Commanding.

HEADQUARTERS 11TH MICHIGAN VOLUNTEER INFANTRY,
In the field near Murfreesboro', Tennessee, January 4, 1863.

SIR: Agreeably to orders, I submit the following report of the part taken by the 11th regiment Michigan infantry in the recent engagement: On the morning of the 31st December heavy firing was heard to our right and front, and apparently rapidly approaching the position occupied by the 29th brigade. My regiment was im-immediately formed and marched to the brow of the hill near brigade headquarters. The skirmishing soon after indicated the approach of the enemy to the right of this position, and under orders from Colonel Stanley, and at the request of General Rousseau, the regiment was formed in line of battle under cover of a ledge of rocks about one hundred yards in this direction. The skirmishing continued with much spirit for about half an hour, when a heavy roar of musketry and artillery indicated that the principal attack of the enemy was being made immediately to our left and rear. I immediately gave orders to change front to the rear on the first company, which was promptly executed under a heavy fire, and the regiment advanced to the brow of the hill, from which Shoull's battery had first been drawn, under a galling fire, and poured a well-directed fire into the advancing columns of the enemy, and continued to load and fire with great coolness and bravery until the orders came to fall back. The fire of the enemy was apparently concentrated upon this point, and was terrific. The slaughter was great, and men and officers fell on every side. The regiment fell back about one hundred yards, and was again formed, and poured a fire into the enemy as he raised the brow of the hill, and then retired to the corner of the cedars in our rear. Here some confusion was at first manifested; a large number of regiments had fallen back here for protection, and the enemy's artillery and infantry opened upon us from all sides except to our left towards the Murfreesboro' pike. Order was, however, promptly restored by our division and brigade commanders, and then my regiment, with the others, moved back in good order, keeping up a steady fire on the enemy. When near the cleared field, to the right of the Murfreesboro' pike, the regiment was rallied and held the ground for twenty or thirty minutes, checking the advance of the enemy. It was then marched about half-way across the open field to the pike, when orders came to charge back into the cedars. My regiment promptly obeyed my orders, rallied on their colors and charged back into the woods with great gallantry, checking the enemy by their sudden and impetuous charge. After delivering our fire, orders came from the brigade commander to retire, and the regiment fell back in good order to the left of the Murfreesboro' pike. Here closed the active operations of the day.

On the 2d of January instant the regiment was again called into action. In the afternoon of that day we were posted in an open field in the rear of —— battery, on the left wing of the army, and about one hundred yards to the right of Wilson's creek. Between three and four o'clock the enemy made a heavy attack, with artillery and infantry, on our front. My command was kept lying upon the ground, protected by a slight hill, for about thirty minutes. At the expiration of this time the enemy had driven back our forces on the opposite side of the creek, and one regiment crossed in great disorder, many without arms, and rushed through our ranks. As soon as the enemy came within range across the creek, my regiment, with the others of this brigade, rose up and gave him a destructive fire, and immediately charged over the creek, the enemy falling back under cover of the woods. In crossing the creek my line of battle was necessarily broken, and I led them forward to a fence on a rise of ground, and formed them in line, when they immediately opened an effective fire on the enemy, who in a short time retreated through the woods. The regiment promptly advanced to the edge of the woods, and delivered a rapid fire on him as he retreated across the open field. The 11th was among the first who crossed the creek and assisted in capturing four pieces of artillery abandoned by the enemy in their flight. At this time my ammunition was nearly exhausted, and I, with the other regiments in the advance, formed a line of battle and held our position until recalled across the creek. I cannot speak too highly of the bravery of the troops under my command. They fought with the coolness of veterans, and obeyed commands under the hottest fire with the precision of the parade ground. Lieutenants Wilson and Flynn were killed while gallantly discharging their duties as company commanders. Major Smith and Lieutenants Hall, Briggs, and Howard were wounded, the two former severely, and are prisoners of war. The officers of my command, without exception, behaved with great gallantry, coolness, and fortitude. When all nobly discharged their duty, it would perhaps be unjust to discriminate.

The following are the casualties as far as known at this time:

Killed	25
Wounded	70
Missing	23
Aggregate loss	118

I am, very respectfully, your obedient servant,

WILLIAM L. STOUGHTON,
Colonel 11th Regiment Michigan Infantry.

M. D. TEMPLE,
Acting Assistant Adjutant General.

Indorsed: Headquarters 11th regiment Michigan volunteers, Murfreesboro', January 4, 1863, William L. Stoughton, colonel commanding. Report part taken by the 11th Michigan infantry in the battle of Stone river, December 30 and 31, 1862, and January 2, 1863.

HEADQUARTERS 2D DIVISION, 14TH ARMY CORPS,
Murfreesboro', February 9, 1863.

Respectfully forwarded to department headquarters.

JAS. S. NEGLEY,
Brigadier General.

HEADQUARTERS 18TH REGIMENT OHIO VOLUNTEER INFANTRY,
Before Murfreesboro', January 4, 1863.

I have the honor to report that on the 30th of December the 18th Ohio volunteers, under my command, with Captain A. Fenton, acting major, and Lieutenant A. W. S. Minear, adjutant, took position with the reserve on the left of the centre wing. At 1 o'clock p. m., under your orders, I took position in the woods to the west of the Winston pike, joining with the left of the right wing.

At the instance of the commander of the left flank regiment of the right wing, I relieved three of his companies then deployed as skirmishers and engaging the enemy. My skirmishers soon started the enemy, and would have cleared the woods but for an order received from the right not to advance our part of the line, whereupon I fell back to the first position, preserving an alignment with my right. At 5 o'clock p. m. I was relieved by the 11th Michigan, and I moved to the rear, where I remained all night. On the morning of the 31st I again took position with the reserve, but was soon ordered forward to support the battery. At — a. m. I was ordered to take position in rear of the position and fronting to the rear, it having been discovered that the enemy had turned our right. No enemy appearing at that point, I was ordered to take position again on the hill and support the battery. I found the battery men much endangered by the enemy's skirmishers to the right. I deployed a company and soon removed them. I was then ordered to take position in the woods on the left, the enemy having made his appearance in that direction. When moving to that position a very considerable consternation was observed among our forces, many of the regiments moving to the rear. Observing that a regiment still held the position, I moved rapidly to its rear; that regiment was lying down so that my men were enabled to remain in their rear and engage in the firing. This position was rendered necessary, other regiments having moved into the only available position on the right and left. By the combined efforts of the forces there the enemy was driven from the woods, but very soon a piece of artillery was brought into position against us. I hastened to where our battery was to ask that it might be brought to bear against the enemy's piece that was then doing fearful havoc among our ranks. I learned that for want of ammunition none of our pieces were available. In the midst of this terrible fire I received your order to fall back, which I did, my men preserving perfect order. During this engagement Captain A. Fenton, who was acting major, and whose services proved of inestimable value, fell wounded, and was placed on a horse and started to the rear; since that nothing has been heard of him, and I have reason to fear that he has fallen into the enemy's hands. After falling back as ordered to the point near the Nashville pike, I received your order to take a position in line with the 19th Illinois, and in rear of a line formed, as I understood, by a part of General Rousseau's command. We had scarcely taken our position when the enemy engaged the first line, which, after some minutes, retired under a terrible fire from the enemy. Anticipating the movement, I caused my men to lie down, and cautioned them to hold their fire until the enemy closed on them. The first line passed over my men closely followed by the enemy. My men, observing well the caution I had given, poured a well-directed fire into the enemy, which checked them, but soon their second line pressed upon me, when I, with the rest of the line, fell back. Immediately on the appearance of the enemy the 19th Illinois was moved to another position on his flank, so that no other regiment remained on the line with me. I moved to the rear gradually, returning the enemy's fire, until I found myself on open ground, when I ordered my men to move double-quick to a point covered from the enemy's fire, where I rallied my men and reformed my ranks, which had become somewhat broken in the retreat. Just as I had accomplished this, General Rousseau ordered me to charge the woods again, encouraging the men to charge by taking the lead in person. The men, already breathless from fatigue, approached the close woods but slowly, yet in perfect order, notwithstanding the enemy from the cover of the woods met us with a withering fire. My men bravely charged upon the hidden enemy and drove them back into the woods, where they held them at bay for some twenty minutes. Seeing that I was unsupported and standing against a much stronger force, and that some fifty of my command had already fallen, I ordered a retreat, returning to the same place from which I had started under General Rousseau's order. In this engagement Captain P. E. Taylor fell mortally wounded, also Lieutenant Minear, adjutant, fell severely wounded. I was then, with the balance of the brigade, withdrawn from the field for that day.

My command was not actively engaged again until the afternoon of the 2d instant. I took position in rear of the battery in our centre about four o'clock, when the enemy appeared to our left. I was ordered by General Negley to move to the support of the battery on the left, and to take covering behind the buildings near the position. When I arrived there I saw the enemy's columns advancing under cover of the woods to our left, the head of his column almost to the creek. I immediately deployed my column and moved my line forward to a fence, from which my men sent a well-directed fire against the enemy. At this point Captain J. M. Welch, who was acting major, was carried from the field severely wounded, also Sergeant L. D. Carter, aiding me as adjutant. Seeing that our fire brought the enemy to a halt, and that our forces were advancing, I ordered my men forward across the stream, which was promptly under execution, when I discovered the enemy moving on our right in the woods in heavy force, evidently intending to attack us on our flank. I immediately ordered a halt and rallied my men who had not already crossed the stream, leaving those who had crossed, as I supposed to the command of Captain Welch, of whose wounds I was not informed. I rallied my men, getting many men from other regiments, and moved towards the woods on the right. Finding my ranks very imperfectly formed, I called a halt to allow the men a moment's rest and to prepare my ranks for a charge bayonet. Just as I halted a regiment arrived in my rear and passed on. Just then I received an order from General Palmer to move forward, which I did, taking position on the right of the other regiment. The line soon pressed the enemy back, discovering which I moved my line forward; but, finding that the other regiment did not advance, I caused my bugler to sound a retreat, so as to join my forces with the other regiment. Just as the line was moving to the rear a man on the right called out "they are flanking us from the woods on the right." This caused some of the men to retreat hastily. I hastened to the open ground, from which I saw that the report was false. When I rallied those that had fled, and returned to the woods again, we continued to reply to the enemy's fire until darkness set in, when I withdrew, other forces having arrived to hold the ground. In this charge Captain George Stivers, a most valuable officer, fell mortally wounded. The behavior of all my officers in these various engagements was such as that I may only say every one did all that he could or that any one in his position could have done, and, as to my men, I can praise no one above another. All did well alike, except three or four cowards, who deserted their posts and went back to Nashville.

I hereto append a list of our loss.

Your obedient servant,

JOSIAH GIVEN,

Lieutenant Colonel, Commanding 18th Ohio Volunteer Infantry.

Colonel T. R. STANLEY,

Commanding 29th Brigade.

HEADQUARTERS EIGHTEENTH REGIMENT OHIO VOLUNTEERS,
Murfreesboro', January 22, 1863.

SIR: The enclosed list of names are members of the eighteenth regiment Ohio volunteers, who were wounded and taken prisoners by the enemy in the late battle of Stone river and paroled; they are now in Murfreesboro'. I would respectfully ask what disposition shall be made of them.

I am, very truly, yours,

CHARLES C. ROSS,
Captain Commanding.

Major C. GODDARD,
Acting Assistant Adjutant General.

List of paroled wounded prisoners of the eighteenth regiment Ohio volunteers, taken in the late battle of Stone river, now in Murfreesboro'.

Captain Ashbel Fenton, company B; Sergeant John W. Root, company C; Corporals James Quinn, company A, and Buford Griffeth, company G; Privates Enoch Smith, company A; Asa S. Scott, L. S. Bancroft, and L. H. Kenard, company B; Irwin Connon and I. McDonald, company C; Sherman Freese, John L. Guy, W. H. McDonald, and George W. O'Day, company E; Samuel S. McDivitt, company G; James D. James, company I; George W. Angell, company K.

12.—REPORT OF MAJOR GENERAL McCOOK.

HEADQUARTERS RIGHT WING 14TH ARMY CORPS,
In Camp 2½ miles south of Murfreesboro', Tenn., January 8, 1863.

MAJOR: In compliance with telegraphic orders from the general commanding, received at my camp on Mill creek, five miles south of Nashville, at 4½ o'clock a. m., on the morning of the 26th of December, 1862, I put the right wing of the 14th corps in motion towards Nolensville, Tennessee. The 1st division, Brigadier General Jefferson C. Davis commanding, marched, at 6 a. m., upon the Edmondson pike, with orders to move upon that road to Prim's blacksmith shop, from whence it was to march direct, by a country road, to Nolensville.

The 3d division, Brigadier General Philip H. Sheridan commanding, also marched at 6 a. m., and upon the direct road to Nolensville. The 3d division, Brigadier General R. W. Johnson commanding, (the reserve of the right wing,) followed the 3d division upon the direct road.

The advance guards of Generals Davis's and Sheridan's columns encountered the enemy's cavalry about two miles beyond our picket line. There was continuous skirmishing with the enemy until the heads of these columns reached Nolensville.

About one mile beyond the town the enemy made a determined stand in a defile and upon a range of hills that cross the turnpike at this point, lining the slopes with skirmishers, and placing a six-gun battery on a commanding position, endeavoring to repel our advance.

They were attacked in front and their position handsomely turned by General Carlin's brigade, of Davis's division, capturing one piece of their artillery and several prisoners.

After taking possession of the defile and hills the command was encamped.

On the night of this day I was visited by the general commanding, who gave me verbal orders to move forward, in the morning, to Triune, seven miles distant, and attack Hardee's corps, supposed to be quartered at that place.

At this camp I was joined by Brigadier General D. S. Stanley, chief of cavalry, with the 1st and 2d Tennessee regiments and the 15th Pennsylvania cavalry.

Preparations were made to move forward at daylight—the cavalry under

General Stanley in the advance, followed by the 2d division, under General Johnson.

It having rained all the day previous, and the entire night, there was a dense fog which prevented us from seeing one hundred and fifty yards in any direction.

The column having moved about two miles to the front, they again encountered the enemy, consisting of cavalry, infantry, and artillery.

The fog at this time being so thick that friend could not be distinguished from foe, and our cavalry having been fired upon by our infantry skirmishers, on the flanks, the enemy being conversant with the ground, my troops strangers to it, and from prisoners captured having learned that Hardee's corps had been in line of battle since the night before, I did not deem it prudent to advance until the fog lifted, and I ordered the command to halt until the work could be done understandingly.

The fog having lifted at 7 o'clock p. m., an advance was immediately ordered, driving the enemy's cavalry before us.

On nearing Triune we found that the main portion of their forces had retired, leaving a battery of six pieces, supported by cavalry, to contest the crossing of Nelson's creek, which has steep and bluff banks. The enemy having destroyed the bridge, it was with difficulty that artillery could be crossed. On the approach of our skirmishers the battery, with the cavalry, took flight down the Eaglesville road. It now being nearly dark, and a severe and driving rain-storm blowing, they were pursued no further.

Johnson's division crossed and camped beyond Nelson's creek, repairing the destroyed bridge.

On the morning of the 28th instant, I ordered out a strong reconnoissance under Brigadier General Willich, to learn whether the enemy had retired to Shelbyville or Murfreesboro'. Pursuing seven miles down the Shelbyville road, it was found that the enemy had turned to the left, having taken a dirt road which led into the Salem pike, thence to Murfreesboro'.

Leaving the 3d brigade of Johnson's division at Triune, I marched on the 29th, with my command, on the Bullejacks road towards Murfreesboro'. The road being a very bad one, the command did not reach Wilkinson's Crossroads (five miles from Murfreesboro') until late in the evening.

My command was encamped in line of battle: Sheridan's division on the left of Wilkinson's pike; Davis's division on right of same road; Woodruff's brigade guarding the bridge over Overall's creek; the two brigades of Johnson's division watching the right.

On that evening, believing that the enemy intended giving our army battle at or near Murfreesboro', I ordered the brigade left at Triune to join the command without delay, which it did on the 30th.

At one o'clock on the morning of the 30th I received an order from General Rosecrans to report in person at his headquarters, on the Murfreesboro' pike, and arrived there at 3.30 a. m. I received my instructions, which were that the left of my line should rest on the right of General Negley's division, and my right was to be thrown forward until it became parallel, or nearly so, with Stone river, the extreme right to rest on or near the Franklin road.

My entire command advanced at 9½ o'clock a. m., Sheridan's division moving down the Wilkinson turnpike until its advance encountered the enemy's pickets. The line of battle was then formed, the left of Sheridan's division resting upon the Wilkinson pike, and immediately upon General Negley's right; the remainder of Sheridan's division was deployed to the right, the line running in a southeasterly direction.

Davis's division, which had already been deployed, moved up, his left resting upon Sheridan's right, Johnson's division being held in reserve.

Our front was covered with a strong line of skirmishers, who soon became sharply engaged with the enemy's sharpshooters and skirmishers.

The line moved forward, but slowly, as the enemy contested stubbornly every inch of ground gained by us. The ground was very favorable to them; they were under cover of a heavy woods and cedar thicket. At 12 m. on the 30th the house of a Mr. Harding came within our lines. From that point I ascertained where the enemy's line of battle was, our skirmishers being then about 500 yards from it.

The right, under General Davis, moved handsomely, but slowly, into position, as the ground over which he had to march was hotly contested by the enemy's skirmishers.

At 1 p. m. word was sent to General D. S. Stanley, chief of cavalry, that Colonel Zahm, commanding three regiments of cavalry on my right flank, was hard pressed by a superior force. I ordered one brigade of my reserve division to report to General Stanley, who conducted it to the Franklin road. On his approach the enemy pressing Colonel Zahm retired, and the brigade was ordered back to its former position. At 2 p. m. a citizen living on the Franklin road, and about one-half mile in front of the enemy's line of battle, was sent me under guard by General Stanley. He reported as follows: "I was up to the enemy's line of battle twice yesterday, and once this morning, to get some stock taken from me. The enemy's troops are posted in the following manner: the right of Cheatam's division rests on the Wilkinson pike; Withers is on Cheatam's left, with his left resting on the Franklin road; Hardee's corps is entirely beyond that road, and his left extending towards the Salem pike."

This man was sent immediately to the general commanding, and subsequently returned to me, with the report that his information had been received. I also sent a report to the general commanding by my aide-de-camp, Captain Horace N. Fisher, that the right of my line rested directly in front of the enemy's centre. This made me anxious for my right. All my division commanders were immediately informed of this fact, and two brigades of the reserve division, commanded, respectively, by Generals Willich and Kirk, two of the best and most experienced brigadiers in the army, were ordered to the right of the line, to protect the right flank and guard against surprise there.

At 6 o'clock p. m. I received an order from the general commanding to have large and extended camp fires made on my right to deceive the enemy, making them believe that we were massing troops there. This order was communicated to General Stanley, commanding cavalry, and carried into execution by Major R. H. Nodine, 25th Illinois, engineer officer on my staff.

On the evening of the 30th the order of battle was nearly parallel with that of the enemy, my right slightly refused, and my line of battle in two lines. Two brigades of the reserve re-enforced the right of the line, and the 3d brigade of the reserve was posted in column about 800 yards in rear of the right. On the evening of the 30th Sheridan's left rested on the Wilkinson road, and on the right of Negley's division, and the line then ran in a southeasterly direction through an open wood, thence in front of and partly through a cedar thicket, until General Davis's right rested near the Franklin road. Kirk's brigade was on Davis's right, Willich's brigade placed on a line nearly perpendicular to the main line, forming a crotchet to the rear, to avoid the possibility of my right being turned by anything like an equal force.

My line was a strong one—open ground in front for a short distance.

My instructions for the following day were received at about 6½ p. m. on the 30th, which were as follows:

"Take a strong position; if the enemy attacks you, fall back slowly, refusing your right, contesting the ground inch by inch. If the enemy does not attack you, you will attack him, not vigorously, but warmly; the time of attack by you (General McCook) to be designated by the general commanding."

I was also informed that Crittenden's corps would move simultaneously with my attack into Murfreesboro'; written instructions were sent by me to each division commander on the night of the 30th, explaining to each what would be required of them on the 31st.

At about 6.30 a. m. on the 31st a determined and heavy attack was made upon Kirk's and Willich's brigades on the extreme right. They were attacked by such an overwhelming force that they were compelled to fall back. General Kirk being seriously wounded at the first fire upon his main line, General Willich having his horse killed early in the action, and he falling into the hands of the enemy, the two brigades were deprived of their immediate commanders and gave way in confusion. Colonel Post's brigade, on the right of Davis's division, and, in fact, my entire line to Sheridan's left, was almost simultaneously attacked by a heavy force of the enemy. The attack in front of Davis and Sheridan was repulsed several times, and had not the heavy turning columns of the enemy on my right succeeded so well, my line could have been maintained, and the enemy driven back to his barricades, which extended from the Wilkinson pike, with but a short interval, three-fourths of a mile, beyond the Franklin road. General Sheridan's division was ably manœuvred by him under my own eye. As soon as it became evident that my lines would be compelled to give way, orders were given to reform my line in the first skirt of timber in rear of my first position. The enemy advancing so rapidly upon my right, I found this impossible, and changed the point of reforming my line to the high ground in rear of the Wilkinson pike. Moving to the left of my line, and in rear of Sheridan's division, I here met General Rousseau in a cedar wood posting his division to repel the attack. I then ordered my line to fall still further back and form on the right of Rousseau. I gave General Johnson orders in person to form his division in rear of Rousseau. Rousseau's division having been withdrawn to the open ground in rear of the cedar woods, the last position became untenable, and my troops were retired to the Nashville pike, where my wing, except Schaffer's brigade of Sheridan's division, was reassembled and replenished with ammunition. On arrival at the pike I found Colonel Harker's brigade, of Wood's division, retiring before a heavy force of the enemy. I immediately ordered Roberts's brigade, of Sheridan's division, to advance into a cedar wood and charge the enemy and drive him back. Although this brigade was much reduced in numbers, and having but two rounds of cartridges, it advanced to the charge under the gallant Colonel Bradley, driving the enemy back with the bayonet, capturing two guns and forty prisoners, and securing our communication on the Murfreesboro' pike at this point.

This brigade is composed of the 22d, 27th, 42d, and 51st Illinois volunteers; the 27th particularly distinguished itself. About eleven a. m. Colonel Moses B. Walker's brigade arrived upon the field, and reported to me for duty; they were assigned to General Sheridan's command, to whose report I refer for the good conduct of this brigade. On the afternoon of the 31st the right wing assumed a strong position; its left, composed of Walker's brigade, resting near a commanding knoll, its line running nearly northwest along the slope of a ridge, covered with cedar growth, the right resting upon the Murfreesboro' pike. On the slope strong barricades were erected, which could well have been defended by single lines. The second line and Gibson's brigade (late Willich's) was used as a reserve. The right wing, excepting Davis's division and Gibson's brigade, did not participate in any general engagement after the 31st.

There was constant skirmishing in my front until the night of the 3d. On the 4th the enemy left his position in front of the right, and evacuated Murfreesboro' on the night of the same day. On the 6th the right wing marched to its present camp, two and a half miles south of Murfreesboro', on the Shelbyville pike.

The reports of Generals Johnson, Davis, and Sheridan, division commanders, are herewith enclosed.

Accompanying General Johnson's report you will find the reports of the brigade, regimental, and battery commanders carefully prepared.

I have been thus particular, on account of the commanding general's despatch to the general-in-chief, and also from erroneous reports sent to the public by newspaper correspondents.

The attention of the general commanding is particularly called to Colonels Gibson and Dodge; also to Lieutenant Colonel Jones's report, who commanded the pickets in front of Willich's brigade.

Captain Edgarton, commanding battery of Kirk's brigade, certainly was guilty of a grave error in taking even a part of his horses to water at such an hour; he is in the hands of the enemy, therefore no report can be had from him at present.

In strict compliance with my orders, and the knowledge I possessed of the position of the enemy, which was communicated to my superior, also to the generals under my command, I could not have made a better disposition of my troops.

On subsequent examination of the field, I found the statements of the citizen, referred to in my report correct, as the barricades extended fully three-fourths of a mile beyond the Franklin road.

I am well satisfied that Hardee's corps, supported by McCowan's division, (late of Kirby Smith's corps,) attacked Kirk's and Willich's brigades.

About the same time Withers's division attacked Davis, and Cheatam's division attacked Sheridan; Cheatam's and Withers's divisions compose General Polk's corps. I was in the rear of the centre of my line when this attack commenced; therefore I did not see all the column that attacked and turned my right; but it can be safely estimated that the rebel force outnumbered ours three to one. After leaving my line of battle, the ground in rear was, first, open fields; second, woods; then a dense cedar thicket; and over such ground it was almost impossible for troops to retire in good order, particularly when assailed by superior numbers.

My ammunition train, under the charge of my efficient ordnance officer, Captain Gates P. Thruston, 1st Ohio volunteers, was at an early hour ordered to take a position in rear of the centre of my line. It was there attacked by the enemy's cavalry, which was handsomely repulsed by a detachment of cavalry under the direction of Captain H. Pease, of General Davis's staff, and Captain G. P. Thruston, ordnance officer.

The train was conducted safely to the Nashville pike, Captain Thruston cutting a road through the cedar wood for the passage of the train.

To Brigadiers R. W. Johnson, Philip H. Sheridan, and Jeff. C. Davis I return my thanks for their gallant conduct upon the days of the battles, and for their prompt support and conscientious attention to duty during their service in the right wing. I commend them to my superiors and my country.

To Brigadier General D. S. Stanley, chief of cavalry, my thanks are particularly due. He commanded my advance from Nolensville, and directed the cavalry on my right flank. A report of the valuable services of our cavalry will be furnished by General Stanley. I commend him to my superiors and my country.

For the particular instances of good conduct of individuals I refer you to the reports of division commanders.

I cannot refrain from again calling the attention of my superiors to the conspicuous gallantry and untiring zeal of Colonel W. H. Gibson, of the 49th Ohio volunteers. He succeeded to the command of Willich's brigade, and was ever prompt to dash upon the enemy with his gallant brigade when opportunity permitted. I have repeatedly recommended him for promotion; he has again won additional claims to his reward.

Colonel Harker, commanding a brigade of Wood's division, performed gallant service under my supervision, as also did Colonel Fyffe, of the 59th Ohio. They are commended to my superiors.

To my staff—Lieutenant Colonel E. Bassett Langdon, inspector general; Major R. H. Nodine, engineer officer; Major J. A. Campbell, assistant adjutant general; Captain Gates P. Thruston, ordnance officer; Captain B. D. Williams, aide-de-camp; Captain J. F. Boyd, assistant quartermaster; Captain O. F. Blake, provost marshal; Major Caleb Bates, volunteer aide-de-camp; Captain Horace A. Fisher, volunteer aide-de-camp and topographical engineer—my thanks are due for their conspicuous gallantry and intelligence on the field. My escort, under command of Lieutenant Theckston, 2d Kentucky cavalry, and my orderlies, behaved gallantly. When my horse was shot, Orderly Cook, of the 2d Indiana, promptly replaced him with his own. The officers of the signal corps were ever ready to perform any service in their line or as aids.

The report of Surgeon C. McDermont, the medical director of the right wing, is also submitted.

Surgeon McDermont's gallantry on the field and his great care for the wounded is worthy of great praise.

My entire medical corps behaved nobly, except Assistant Surgeon W. S. Fish, of the 3d Indiana cavalry, who fled to Nashville. He is recommended for dismissal.

The casualties of my wing are five hundred and forty-two killed, and two thousand three hundred and thirty-four wounded.

The nation is again called to mourn the loss of gallant spirits who fell upon this sanguinary field. First of these, Brigadier General J. W. Sill, commanding first brigade, third division. He was noble, conscientious in the discharge of every duty, brave to a fault; he had no ambition save to serve his country. He died a Christian soldier in the act of repulsing the enemy.

Such names as Roberts, Shaffer, Harrington, Stern, Williams, Read, Housem, Drake, Wooster and McKee, all field officers, and many other commissioned officers of the right wing, who fell vindicating their flag, will never be forgotten by a grateful country.

Complete lists of the killed and wounded will be furnished from each regiment. All of which is respectfully submitted.

There will be a map of the field sent forward to-morrow.

A. McD. McCOOK,
Major General Volunteers, Commanding Right Wing.

Major C. GODDARD, *Chief of Staff, Tenth Army Corps.*

HEADQUARTERS RIGHT WING FOURTEENTH ARMY CORPS,
In Camp near Murfreesboro', Tennessee, January 11, 1863.

MAJOR: I have the honor to submit the following report of the casualties in my command during the late engagements before Murfreesboro':

Commands.	Killed.		Wounded.		Missing.		Aggregate.	
	Officers.	Men.	Officers.	Men.	Officers.	Men.	Officers.	Men.
1st Brigade 1st Division.								
22d Indiana volunteers	......	7	5	34	......	18	5	59
59th Illinois volunteers	......	7	......	43	......	30	......	80
74th Illinois volunteers	......	8	1	34	......	42	1	84
75th Illinois volunteers	......	2	2	19	......	59	2	80
5th Wisconsin battery	......	1	1	5	......	6	1	12
Total	......	25	9	135	......	155	9	315
2d Brigade 1st Division.								
21st Illinois volunteers	2	55	7	180	......	59	9	294
15th Wisconsin volunteers	2	13	5	65	1	33	8	111
101st Ohio volunteers	4	19	2	121	......	66	6	206
38th Illinois volunteers	2	32	5	104	......	34	7	170
2d Minnesota battery	......	3	1	5	......	1	1	9
Total	10	122	20	475	1	193	31	790
3d Brigade 1st Division.								
25th Illinois volunteers	1	15	3	72	......	5	4	92
35th Illinois volunteers	1	10	1	49	......	25	2	84
81st Indiana volunteers	2	4	1	46	1	15	4	65
8th Wisconsin battery	1	......	......	4	......	1	1	5
C. B. cavalry	......	......	......	2	......	......	......	2
2d Kentucky cavalry, G	1	......	......	2	......	6	1	8
Total	6	29	5	175	1	52	12	256
Total 1st division	16	176	34	785	2	400	52	1,361
1st Brigade 2d Division.								
General officers	......	......	......	......	1	......	1	......
15th Ohio volunteers	......	17	2	68	1	127	3	212
49th Ohio volunteers	2	18	6	88	......	108	8	214
32d Indiana volunteers	......	12	......	40	......	115	......	167
39th Indiana volunteers	1	30	2	116	2	229	5	375
89th Illinois volunteers	1	9	1	45	......	94	2	148
Battery A	......	1	......	4	......	24	......	29
Total	4	87	11	361	4	697	19	1,145
2d Brigade 2d Division.								
General officers	......	......	1	......	......	......	1	......
34th Illinois volunteers	2	19	2	98	2	72	6	189
79th Illinois volunteers	1	23	3	68	3	121	7	212
29th Indiana volunteers	1	14	2	66	1	51	4	131
30th Indiana volunteers	1	30	2	108	2	70	5	208
77th Pennsylvania volunteers	1	4	1	28	2	28	4	60
Battery E	......	10	......	5	2	......	2	15
Total	6	100	11	373	12	342	29	815

Report of casualties.—Continued.

Commands.	Killed.		Wounded.		Missing.		Aggregate.	
	Officers.	Men.	Officers.	Men.	Officers.	Men.	Officers.	Men.
3d Brigade 2d Division.								
1st Ohio volunteers	......	8	1	46	......	81	1	135
93d Ohio volunteers	......	12	1	45	......	64	1	121
6th Indiana volunteers	......	17	......	50	1	36	1	103
5th Kentucky volunteers	1	18	7	73	......	26	8	117
5th Indiana battery	......	3	1	18	......	1	1	22
3d Indiana cavalry	......	4	......	6	......	15	......	25
Total	1	62	10	238	2	223	12	523
Total 2d division	11	249	32	972	17	1,262	60	2,483
1st Brigade 3d Division.								
General officers	1	......	1	......	......	......	2	......
36th Illinois volunteers	1	45	3	144	6	13	10	202
88th Illinois volunteers	1	13	2	48	......	48	3	109
24th Wisconsin volunteers	1	19	1	55	......	98	2	172
21st Michigan volunteers	......	18	7	82	......	36	7	136
4th Indiana battery	......	6	......	17	......	3	......	26
Total	4	101	14	346	6	198	24	645
2d Brigade 3d Division.								
General officers	1	......	......	......	......	......	1	......
2d Missouri volunteers	......	7	......	40	1	14	1	61
16th Missouri volunteers	3	9	4	51	......	5	7	65
44th Illinois volunteers	1	28	4	104	......	17	5	149
73d Illinois volunteers	1	15	3	61	1	7	5	83
1st Missouri battery	1	5	......	13	......	1	1	19
Total	7	64	11	269	2	44	20	377
3d Brigade 3d Division.								
General officers	1	......	......	......	......	......	1	......
22d Illinois volunteers	......	21	5	109	2	54	7	184
27th Illinois volunteers	1	8	2	67	......	25	3	100
42d Illinois volunteers	1	18	......	96	1	45	2	159
51st Illinois volunteers	1	6	4	37	......	9	5	52
1st Illinois battery	......	5	2	19	......	25	2	49
Total	4	58	13	328	3	158	20	544
Total 3d division	15	223	38	943	11	400	64	1,566
Grand total	42	648	104	2,700	30	2,062	176	5,410

The names of each, by regiment and company, will be forwarded as soon as can be obtained.

Respectfully submitted.

A. McD. McCOOK, *Major General Commanding.*

General summary of casualties of right wing.

Regiments.	No. of killed	No. of wounded.	Total.
FIRST DIVISION.			
22d regiment Indiana volunteers	7	39	46
5th Wisconsin battery	1	7	8
15th Wisconsin volunteers	15	72	87
74th Illinois volunteers	8	33	41
59th Illinois volunteers	7	43	50
35th Illinois volunteers	11	53	64
25th Illinois volunteers	16	79	95
75th Illinois volunteers	2	22	24
21st Illinois volunteers	47	198	245
2d Minnesota battery	2	5	7
81st Indiana volunteers	6	48	54
101st Ohio volunteers	18	125	143
8th Wisconsin battery	1	4	5
38th Illinois volunteers	34	110	144
Total	175	813	1,013
SECOND DIVISION.			
49th Ohio volunteers	16	96	112
15th Ohio volunteers	17	96	113
93d Ohio volunteers	12	41	53
1st Ohio volunteers	8	38	46
39th Indiana volunteers	30	109	139
32d Indiana volunteers	12	41	53
6th Indiana volunteers	15	52	67
30th Indiana volunteers	29	100	129
29th Indiana volunteers	4	22	26
89th Illinois volunteers	10	45	55
79th Illinois volunteers	19	80	99
34th Illinois volunteers	18	100	118
5th Kentucky volunteers	18	80	98
Battery A, 1st Ohio artillery	1	5	6
5th Indiana battery	3	18	21
77th Tennessee volunteers	4	29	33
Total	216	952	1,168
THIRD DIVISION.			
36th Illinois volunteers	45	159	204
88th Illinois volunteers	15	55	70
24th Wisconsin volunteers	19	58	77
21st Michigan volunteers	18	84	102
42d Illinois volunteers	21	109	130
22d Illinois volunteers	25	88	113
51st Illinois volunteers	6	48	54
27th Illinois volunteers	8	55	63
73d Illinois volunteers	22	52	74
44th Illinois volunteers	6	34	40
15th Missouri volunteers	14	44	58
2d Missouri volunteers	2	22	24

General summary of casualties of right wing—Continued.

Regiments.	No. of killed.	No. of wounded.	Total.
4th Indiana battery	5	16	21
1st Missouri artillery, company G	6	13	19
1st Illinois artillery, company C	5	20	25
Total	217	857	1,074
Aggregate	608	2,647	3,255

Respectfully forwarded.

C. McDERMONT,
Surgeon U. S. Volunteers, Medical Director of Right Wing.

A. McD. McCook,
Major General Commanding.

Medical Director's Office, Right Wing,
Murfreesboro', January 14, 1863.

Sir: I transmit, for the information of the commanding general, the accompanying report of the casualties that occurred in the right wing during the late battle of Murfréesboro'.

While the loss of so many brave men must be a source of profound sorrow to the general, it will afford him some satisfaction to know that the wounded were not neglected. Throughout the severe and protracted struggle our surgeons exerted their utmost energies in alleviating the sufferings and promoting the comfort of their unfortunate brethren, and succeeded as far as it was possible to do so with the means at their disposal.

When, on the second day of the battle, it became evident that the territory occupied by our hospitals would fall in possession of the enemy, I directed a sufficient number of surgeons and attendants to remain in charge, and not to desert the wounded in any event. These gentlemen were exposed to much danger, as the contending armies swept past; but they remained faithfully at their posts, and were unceasing in their attentions to the wounded during the three days that elapsed before the recovery of this territory by our troops.

The enemy took from them a large portion of their medical and hospital stores and instruments, and our men were compelled to seek for dressing materials, bedding, &c., among the families in the rear of the lines. Much kind assistance was received from citizens in the vicinity, and no violence was experienced at the hands of the confederate soldiers.

It affords me much pleasure to bear testimony to the efficiency and self-denial of the medical officers of the right wing. During that long week of hardship and exposure they labored day and night, regardless of their own safety and comfort, and only anxious for the well-being of the wounded intrusted to their care.

I have the honor to remain, your most obedient servant,

C. McDERMONT,
Surgeon United States Volunteers, Medical Director Right Wing, 14th Army Corps.

Major Campbell,
Assistant Adjutant General, Right Wing, 14th Army Corps.

General summary of killed and wounded at the battle of Stone river, near Murfreesboro', Tennessee, from December 30, 1862, to January 3, 1863, of right wing, 14th army corps, department of the Cumberland.

FIRST DIVISION, (John L. Teed, medical director.)

Regiments.	Killed.	Wounded.	Total.
38th Illinois volunteers	34	110	144
22d Indiana volunteers	7	39	46
5th Wisconsin battery	1	7	8
15th Wisconsin volunteers	15	72	87
74th Illinois volunteers	8	33	41
59th Illinois volunteers	7	43	50
35th Illinois volunteers	11	53	64
25th Illinois volunteers	16	79	95
2d Minnesota battery	2	5	7
75th Illinois volunteers	2	22	24
81st Indiana volunteers	6	48	54
101st Ohio volunteers	18	125	143
21st Illinois volunteers, (not reported.)			
8th Wisconsin battery	1	4	5
Total	128	640	768

SECOND DIVISION, (S. Marks, medical director.)

Regiments.	Killed.	Wounded.	Total.
34th Illinois volunteers	18	100	118
77th Pennsylvania volunteers	4	28	32
79th Illinois volunteers	19	80	99
30th Indiana volunteers	29	100	129
6th Indiana volunteers	15	52	67
1st Ohio volunteers	8	38	46
93d Ohio volunteers	12	41	53
5th Kentucky volunteers	18	80	98
32d Indiana volunteers	12	8	20
39th Indiana volunteers	30	109	139
15th Ohio volunteers	17	96	123
1st Ohio artillery, battery A	1	5	6
89th Illinois volunteers	10	45	55
49th Ohio volunteers	16	96	112
5th Indiana battery	3	18	21
Total	212	906	1,118

THIRD DIVISION, (D. J. Griffiths, medical director.)

Regiments.	Killed.	Wounded.	Total.
88th Illinois volunteers	15	55	70
21st Michigan volunteers	18	84	102
36th Illinois volunteers	45	159	204
27th Illinois volunteers	9	35	44
24th Wisconsin volunteers	19	58	77
51st Illinois volunteers	6	48	54
22d Illinois volunteers	25	88	113
42d Illinois volunteers	21	109	130
44th Illinois volunteers	6	34	40
73d Illinois volunteers	22	52	74
2d Missouri volunteers	2	22	24
15th Missouri volunteers	14	44	58
Total	202	788	990

NOTE.—This division reports no batteries.

General summary of right wing, 14th army corps, department of the Cumberland, (C. McDermont, medical director.)

Divisions.	Killed.	Wounded.	Total.
First division	128	640	768
Second division	212	906	1,118
Third division	202	788	990
Total	542	2,334	2,876

HEADQUARTERS 1ST DIVISION, RIGHT WING, 14th ARMY CORPS,
January, 1863.

MAJOR: I have the honor to submit the following report of the part taken by the division under my command in the recent operations against the enemy's forces in the vicinity of Triune and Murfreesboro'.

On the morning of the 26th ultimo, in compliance with instructions received from the general commanding the right wing, I broke up camp at St. James's chapel, on Mill creek, and advanced upon Nolensville, *via* the Edmondston pike, as far as Prim's blacksmith shop; from thence my advance was over a rugged country road, rendered almost impassable by the incessant rain which had been falling in torrents during the entire morning.

The enemy's pickets were discovered by my cavalry escort, composed of company B, 36th Illinois volunteers, under command of Captain Shirer, within a few miles of our camp. This small force of cavalry being the only mounted force under my command, I ordered them to the front with instructions to drive in the enemy's pickets, and to attack him on his flanks at every opportunity. So effectually was this done that the infantry and artillery were enabled to move with little interruption to within a mile of Nolensville. By this time I had learned from reliable information, through citizens as well as cavalry scouts, that the enemy occupied the town in some force, both of cavalry and artillery.

The first brigade, consisting of the 22d Indiana, 74th Illinois, 75th Illinois, and 59th Illinois regiments, and the 5th Wisconsin battery, commanded by Colonel P. Sidney Post, was immediately deployed for an advance upon the town. Pinney's 5th Wisconsin battery was posted so as to command the town and all approaches from the southwest. The enemy's cavalry was seen by this time taking position on a range of hills southwest of town, and was evidently attempting to flank our position. A few shells from Pinney's battery soon caused them to fall back. A battery, which by this time they had succeeded in getting into position, opened fire, but was, after a few rounds, silenced by Pinney's guns.

The second brigade, consisting of the 21st Illinois, 38th Illinois, 15th Wisconsin, and 101st Ohio regiments, and the 2d Minnesota battery, commanded by Colonel Carlin, had by this time formed a line of battle on Post's right, and moving rapidly forward, soon engaged the enemy's dismounted cavalry in a sharp skirmish.

The third brigade, consisting of the 25th Illinois, 35th Illinois, 81st Indiana regiments, and the 8th Wisconsin battery, commanded by Colonel Woodruff, was deployed on the right so as to check any effort which might be made to attack my flank from this direction. Carlin advanced in excellent order, driving everything before him until ordered to halt, having dislodged the enemy from his position entirely.

By this time I ascertained that the enemy would probably make another effort to resist our advance about two miles further on; and notwithstanding it was late in the afternoon, and the men were much fatigued from a hard day's march through rain and mud, I could not forego the opportunity thus offered in giving them another chance to signalize their courage and endurance. Ascertaining the enemy's exact position as well as I could, I ordered the advance.

Their lines were soon discovered, occupying a range of high, rocky hills through which the Nolensville and Triune pike passes, known as "Knob's Gap." This was a favorable position to the enemy, and well guarded by artillery, which opened fire at long range upon Carlin's lines. Hotchkiss's and Pinney's batteries were rapidly brought into action and opened fire, while Carlin's brigade charged the battery, carried the heights in his front, and captured two (2) guns. Post's brigade carried the heights on the left of the road with but little resistance, while Woodruff's brigade drove in the enemy's skirmishers on the extreme right.

The day had now closed, and I ordered the troops to bivouac, in accordance with instructions from the general commanding, who arrived at this time upon the ground, followed by Generals Sheridan and Johnson's divisions.

The steady courage and soldierly zeal displayed on this occasion by both officers and men gave ample assurances of what could be expected of them in the coming struggle at Murfreesboro'.

On the 27th, in accordance with the general's instructions, the division took position at the junction of the Bole Jack road with the Nolensville pike, one mile from Triune, where it remained in bivouac until the morning of the 29th, at which time the advance was resumed. In compliance with instructions, I moved forward on the Bole Jack road as far as Stewart's creek, a few miles beyond which it was reported by our cavalry the enemy had shown himself in considerable force. The general commanding arriving at this time in person at the head of the column, ordered a halt until the divisions in rear could be brought up.

Brigadier General Stanley, commanding the cavalry in advance, soon reported the road clear, and the march was resumed without obstruction until the entire command reached the Wilkinson pike, six miles from Murfreesboro'. The division bivouacked during the night at Overall's creek, three and a half miles from Murfreesboro', the left brigade resting on the Wilkinson pike.

On the morning of the 30th the division moved forward and took position on General Sheridan's right, about three hundred yards south of and parallel to the Wilkinson pike, in which position it remained until two o'clock p. m. A few companies of skirmishers thrown to the front in a skirt of timbered land soon found those of the enemy, and for several hours a brisk skirmish was kept up with varying results. About two o'clock p. m. the general commanding ordered a general advance of the whole line. This the enemy seemed at first disposed to resist only with his skirmishers; gradually, however, as both parties strengthened their lines of skirmishers, the contest became more animated. Our main lines steadily advanced, occupying and holding the ground gained by the skirmishers until about half an hour before sunset, when the enemy's position was plainly discerned, running diagonally across the old Murfreesboro' and Franklin road.

The enemy's batteries now announced our close proximity to their lines. Carpenter's and Hotchkiss's batteries were soon brought into position and opened fire. Woodruff's and Carlin's brigades by this time felt the fire of the enemy's main lines, and responded in the most gallant manner. Post's brigade, moving steadily forward on the right, after a most obstinate resistance on the part of the enemy, succeeded in driving his skirmishers from a strong position in our front, forcing them to retire upon his main lines. Night soon brought a close to the contest.

Receiving directions at this time from General McCook to desist from any further offensive demonstration further than what might be necessary to hold my position, I ordered the troops to rest for the night on their arms. Two brigades of General Johnson's division, heretofore held in reserve, arrived and took position on my right about sunset, thus extending our line of battle beyond the old Franklin and Murfreesboro' road. These brigades were commanded by Generals Willich and Kirk.

The night passed off quietly until about daylight, when the enemy's forces were observed by our pickets to be in motion. Their object could not, however, with certainty, be determined until near sunrise, when a vigorous attack was made upon Willich's and Kirk's brigades. These troops seemed not to have been fully prepared for the assault, and with little or no resistance retreated from their position, leaving their artillery in the hands of the enemy. This left my right brigade exposed to a flank movement, which the enemy was now rapidly executing, and compelled me to order Post's brigade to fall back and partially change its front. Simultaneous with this movement the enemy commenced a heavy and very determined attack on both Carlin's and Woodruff's brigades. These brigades were fully prepared for the attack, and received it with veteran courage. The conflict was fierce in the extreme on both sides. Our loss was heavy, and that of the enemy no less. It was, according to my observations, the best contested point of the day, and would have been held but for the overwhelming force moving so persistently against my right. Carlin, finding his right flank being so severely pressed and threatened with being turned, ordered his troops to retire.

Woodruff's brigade succeeded in repulsing the enemy and holding its position until the withdrawal of the troops on both its flanks compelled it to retire. Pinney's battery, which I had posted in an open field upon my extreme right, and ordered to be supported by a part of Post's brigade, now opened a destructive fire upon the enemy's advancing lines. This gallant and distinguished battery, supported by the 22d Indiana and 59th Illinois regiments, together with a brigade of General Johnson's division commanded by Colonel Baldwin, 6th Indiana volunteers, for a short time brought the enemy to a check on our right. Hotchkiss's battery had also by this time taken an excellent position near the Wilkinson pike, so as to command the enemy's approach across a large cotton-field in his front, over which he was now advancing. The infantry, however, contrary to expectations, failed to support this battery, and after firing a few rounds was forced to retire.

In accordance with instructions received during the night, announcing the plan of operations for the day, I desisted from any further attempts to engage the enemy, except by skirmishers thrown to the rear for that purpose, until my lines had reached within a few hundred yards of the Nashville and Murfreesboro' pike, when I again determined to form my lines and resist his further advance. To this order but few of the regiments responded, their ranks being much thinned by killed and wounded; and not a few had availed themselves of the favorable opportunity offered by the dense woods through which we were compelled to pass to skulk like cowards from the ranks. The reserve forces here moved to the front and relieved my command from any further participation in the engagement until late in the afternoon, when, in compliance with instructions, I took position on the right. My skirmishers were immediately thrown out, and soon engaged the enemy's, until night brought a close to hostilities for the day.

During the 1st and 2d of January the division occupied this position in skirmishing with the enemy's pickets until late in the afternoon of the 2d, when I received orders from General Rosecrans to hasten to the support of a part of General Crittenden's command, who had been for some time hotly engaged with the enemy across the river, on our extreme left.

Moving as rapidly as possible across the river to the field of battle, I found our gallant troops forcing the enemy back on his reserves. The brigade of Colonel Woodruff being in the advance, only arrived in time to participate in the general engagement.

After relieving the troops of General Palmer and Colonel Beatty, and particularly the brigade of Colonel Hazen, which had so nobly vindicated their courage in the then closing conflict, I ordered a heavy line of skirmishers to be thrown out. The enemy's lines were soon encountered, and a renewal of the engagement seemed imminent. A few rounds of grape and canister from one of our batteries, however, caused them to withdraw, and night again brought a cessation of hostilities.

During the night I disposed of my troops in such manner as would best enable me to repel an attack, and, in compliance with instructions, I directed rifle-pits and breastworks to be thrown up. This was done, and morning found us well prepared for any emergency, either offensive or defensive.

The following day (3d of January) considerable skirmishing was kept up, without abatement, from early in the morning until dark.

During the night I received orders from General Crittenden to withdraw my command from the east bank of the river, and to report with it to General McCook. This movement was executed between the hours of one and four o'clock in the morning, during which time the rain fell incessantly.

The pickets about this time reported the enemy as having been very active in their movements during the latter part of the night, and their convictions that he was evacuating his position. Further observations, made after daylight, found this to be the case.

The following list of casualties shows a loss in the division during the several engagements above described, as follows:

Commissioned officers.—Killed	16
" " Wounded	34
" " Missing	2
Enlisted men.—Killed	176
" " Wounded	784
" " Missing	399
Total killed, wounded, and missing	1,411

The division lost three pieces of artillery and captured two. In the list of officers killed are the names of Colonel Stern, 101st Ohio; Colonel Williams, 25th Illinois; Lieutenant Colonel Wooster, 101st Ohio; Lieutenant Colonel McKee, 15th Wisconsin; Captain Carpenter, 8th Wisconsin battery, and Captain McCulloch, 2d Kentucky cavalry, of my staff, whose noble deeds of valor on the field had already placed their names on the list of brave men. The history of the war will record no brighter names, and the country will mourn the loss of no more devoted patriots than these.

Among the wounded are Colonel Alexander, 21st Illinois; Lieutenant Colonel Tanner, 22d Indiana; Captain Pinney, 5th Wisconsin battery, and Captain Austin, acting assistant adjutant general, on the staff of Colonel Woodruff, whose names it affords me special gratification to mention.

From the 26th of December until the close of the engagement on the 4th of January at Murfreesboro', no entire day elapsed that the division, or some part of it, did not engage the enemy. During a great part of the time the weather was excessively inclement, and the troops suffered much from exposure.

A heavy list of casualties and much suffering were unavoidable under the circumstances.

It affords me pleasure, however, to be able to report the cheerful and soldier-like manner in which these hardships and privations were endured by the troops throughout. History will record and the country reward their deeds.

My staff, consisting of Lieutenant T. W. Morrison, acting assistant adjutant general; Captain H. Pease, inspector general; Captain McCulloch, aide-de-camp, (killed;) Lieutenant Frank E. Reynolds, aide-de-camp; Lieutenant Thomas H. Dailey, aide-de-camp; Surgeon J. L. Teed, medical director; Captain Shriver, ordnance officer; Lieutenant R. Plunket, provost marshal, and Private Frank Clark, clerk to assistant adjutant general and acting aide-de-camp, deported themselves throughout the entire campaign as well as on the battle-field with distinguished zeal and conspicuous gallantry.

While expressing my high regard and appreciation of the general commanding, I desire also to tender my thanks to yourself, major, and to Colonel Langdon, Major Bates, Captains Thruston, Williams, and Fisher, of his staff, for the prompt and efficient manner in which the field duties were performed by them.

During the several engagements in which the division participated, the conduct of many subaltern officers attracted my admiration by their conspicuous gallantry, and whose names I regret cannot be mentioned in this report; they will be remembered in future recommendations for promotion.

I am, major, very respectfully, your obedient servant,

JEFFERSON C. DAVIS,
Brigadier General, Commanding Division.

Major J. A. CAMPBELL,
Assistant Adjutant General, Right Wing, 14th Army Corps.

Report of killed and wounded at the battle of Stone river, near Murfreesboro', Tennessee, fought December 30, 1862, *to January* 3, 1863.—*Right wing, fourteenth army corps, first division, Dr. Jno. L. Teed, medical director.*

TWENTY-SECOND REGIMENT INDIANA VOLUNTEERS.

Killed.—Company E: Sergeant Patrick Madden and Private S. W. Seap. Company G: Private Bernard Kelly. Company H: Privates John Summerville, Levi Baldwin, and John Clark. Company K: Private Conrad Corn.

Wounded.—Lieutenant Colonel Thomas B. Tanner, prisoner. Company A: Corporal Thomas Blitton, thigh; Privates John Brooke, back; Thomas Myrick, arm; William Putts, slightly. Company B: Second Lieutenant W. H. Ireland, leg; Privates G. W. Boas, leg; Thomas Thompson, side and arm. Company C: Corporal William Seal, side; Privates Josephus Smith, leg and face; D. A. Whiteman, leg and face. Company D: Privates George Morris, ankle; Alfred Cofman, ankle and hand. Company E: Privates Thomas Wilson, thigh broken; Wm. H. Davis, thumb; Levi Kelso, hand; W. H. Brott, hand; W. W. Thompson, foot and leg; Josiah W. Snider, shoulder. Company F: Second Lieutenant W. F. Riggs, thigh; Private R. W. Fugate, hand. Company G: Corporal George Ball, arm; Privates George Thomger, abdomen, mortally; Robert Pedegren, leg. Company H: Captain Wm. Powers, leg and ankle; Sergeant William Emood, ankle; Corporals Jasper Ross, foot; Albert Blose, elbow; Privates Levi W. Brant, breast; Wesley Ruthinford, heel; John Patrick, leg: W. Chappell, leg; Allen Falles, wrist. Company I: Corporal James Bell, ankle; Privates John Miller, arm; James F. Martin, shoulder. Company K: Captain R. M. Sitson, knee.

FIFTH WISCONSIN BATTERY.

Killed.—Private Cephas Adair.

Wounded.—Sergeant Elijah Broth, thigh; Corporal Oscar F. Pinney, finger; Privates David S. Welty, thigh; I. C. Forbs, arm and head; Martin Campbell, arm and side; George Thomas, knee and leg; Michael Ward, side.

FIFTEENTH REGIMENT WISCONSIN VOLUNTEERS.

Killed.—Lieutenant Colonel David McKee. Company B: Corporals Peter O. Sarsin and Torgrin M. Kelson. Company C: Privates Gunder Hawson, Maltiro Malpison, and Kund Finkleson. Company D: Privates Nils Nilson and Ole Sec. Company E: Captain John Ingimmosen. Company F: Privates Ole A. Kunsen, Kund Snisers, and John Flack. Company H: Corporal Andrew F. Fosse and Private Hans Gildhausen. Company K: Private John Martinsen.

Wounded.—Company A: Privates Henry Elligsen and Ole Larsen. Company B: Sam. I. Olsen, arm, thigh, and leg; Albert A. Nelson, arm; A. Lyser ture; S. Anderson, left foot; Lewis Nelson, leg; Enoch A. Basnis, shoulder. Company C: Corporal Samuel Johnson, thigh; Privates Larentz Olsen, thigh; Burt Osmudkin, leg; Tobjom Hanshid; Ole Begisen, foot; Peter Jorgensen, knee; Jacob Jordhe, side; Rund Hansen, thigh. Company D: First Sergeant Iver Brant, shoulder; Privates Halse Absen and John Wartz, hand. Company E: Second Lieutenant J. A. Brown, leg; Sergeant Guirden Gundusen, finger; Corporal A. Johnson, neck and jaw; Privates Christopher Lee, leg; Asbjorm Sacariasen; Ole Mileshen; Jacob I. Lee; Iren Anderson, arm; Ole Syndboe, arm; Aaron Kulsoig, arm. Company F: Captain Charles Gashaneson, foot; First Lieutenant Thomas Simonson, thigh; Sergeants Johan Oberg, leg; Niles J. Gilbert, hip; Corporals Gilbert Paulson and Andw. Thomson; Privates Too Tackinson; Charles A. Unbeck, ankle; Elling Ellinksen; Albert Allen, hip; Forger Forgessen; Frend Bjngepen, hip; Ole T. Olsen, foot; Ole Chlinshasen, arm; Ole Wilson, leg. Company H: Captain George Wilson, thigh; Sergeants Ole Back, abdomen; Ormond Topepen, thigh; Corporals Hans Inglitriglsen, shoulder; Thomas Thomson, foot and thigh; Miles I. Gide, foot; Privates Lars O. Dokhen; Peter Petersen, thigh and shoulder; Thomas O. Laudwig, leg; Elling P. Simer, shoulder; Halsen Jorgensen, eye; Lorentz Nilsen, thigh; Kund Petersen; Nils Emerson; Kund Larsen; Charles E. Balstad; Gaber Hawser, shoulder; Martin Gorginser; Gabriel E. Lenmond, arm; Jonas Thompson, arm. Company K: Sergeant Kund R. Alsen, leg; Corporals Kund Annudsen, forearm; Moses Gimager, leg; Privates Andrew Gilbert, thigh; Ira Jacobsen, thigh; Ole W. Wingar, leg; J. K. Hundbye.

SEVENTY-FOURTH ILLINOIS REGIMENT.

Killed.—Company A: Corporal William Ankhart. Company G: Corporal W. Barren, Private F. F. Fickmier. Company H: Sergeant H. S. Post and Private A. J. Butterfield. Company K: Sergeant R. R. Gaylord, Corporal M. C. Felenly, Private M. W. Bamler, and Captain's Servant Butler Ward.

Wounded.—Company A: Sergeants James S. Cowan, W. F. Liffingnal, Corporal W. H. Hitchcock, Privates E. Parkhust, S. Riddle, and M. Mepler. Company B: Privates C. Flinn, C. M. Stevens, L. M. Kelly, and E. W. Parane. Company C: Sergeant B. A. Chaplain, Private W. A. Miller. Company D: Private D. C. Shermerhorn. Company F: Sergeant H. Hengle, Privates W. O. Prebles and R. Lagrange. Company G: Privates E. Mutmiller, A. Westcrook, and G. Straker. Company H: Sergeant —— Hurlbut, and Privates O. W. Brown, Z. Rice, M. Sturleen, S. Thayer, C. Hind. Company I: Corporal C. Hunt and Private S. Jerame. Company K: Corporals F. W. Shennett, I. B. Corkers, and Privates F. Caswell, John R. Vail, and A. Anderson.

FIFTY-NINTH ILLINOIS REGIMENT.

Killed.—Company C: Privates James H. Shuts and Henry Banmen. Company D: Sergeant John J. Rathen and Private Andrew J. Watts. Company F: Private Jacob A. Hanser.

Wounded.—Company A: Privates Gaham Martin, George Glendon, Joseph Byron, and Thomas J. Hooper. Company B: Corporal Joseph K. Dennis and Private Wesley B. Adams. Company C: Privates Joel Hyatt, James Elidge, Jasper Huelchison, Manhac Pendam, George Kerr, John Cluley, Henry Dabbs, and Samuel J. Jacobs. Company D: Corporal John Eagan, and Privates Charles B. Hannason, Joseph Walter, Henry Deidtrick, Thomas Fabin, and Hutcheson McCauly. Company E: Corporal Chesley Allen, and Privates Nemiah C. Brann, William Bostwick, Frederic Oldendorth, Heman Smith, George Semen, and John Shutt. Company F: Corporal Thomas J. Sluper and Privates Jacob Flint, John A. P. Kelley, James Slusser, and Levi A. Sharke. Company G: Sergeant Alfred C. Barber, and Corporal Reuben A. Cumings. Company H: Corporls George M. Sharke, Alexander C. Pepper, and Privates Jesse Adams, Patrick Reynolds, Ford White, and Albert B. Salta. Company I: Private Richard Ferden. Company K: Corporal Addis Downing, Privates Robert Drake, William Hyse, and Marcus S. Brue.

THIRTY-FIFTH ILLINOIS REGIMENT.

Killed.—Company B: Sergeant George Morrison, Privates William Mason, Moses Buchanan, L. D. Taylor, Peter Green, and Richard Fitzgerald. Company C: Privates David Maze and H. M. Scranton. Company E: Private J. B. Chambers. Company H: 1st Lieutenant H. McConnell and Corporal William McVicar. Company I: Private Isaac M. Nelson. Company K: Private Seward Powell.

Wounded.—Sergeant Major Samuel W. Burch. Company A: Privates John Samby, William R. King, Ebenezer Westfall, and Patrick Roan. Company B: 1st Sergeant B. F. Smith, and Corporals J. D. Burrows and A. J. Davis. Company C: Corporals S. R. Whiteside and Charles Sharke, and Privates Jeremiah Payne, Perry A. Crocker, John Shules, James J. Filrick, and Zibidas Smith. Company D: Sergeant Sandusky Wright, Corporal Thomas O. Wiskins, and Privates Thomas C. Gorman, Ezra C. Price, Candy O'Donel, Charles E. Torrence. Clark Butler, Samuel Snider and Thadeus S. Coffin. Company F: Corporals William Delay and S. H. Green, and Privates G. W. Songer, Patrick McKinney, Thomas Young, and Charles Miller. Company G: Sergeant Samuel Morrison, Corporal Herman Swartz, and Privates Jacob Fanshire, William Wright, and William Forest. Company H: Sergeant James Cox, Corporal William Brown, and Privates William Goben, James McCallister, W. H. Nichols, Wesley Oglesby, John Simons, W. Brockman, Jesse Hosk, and James Rogers. Company I: Privates Charles Wynn and Charles W. Draper. Company K: 2d Lieutenant D. K. Kagaz, and Privates Jacob Musser, Isaac McCasson, M. F. Trapp, and Richard Holleman.

TWENTY-FIFTH ILLINOIS REGIMENT.

Killed.—Colonel Thomas D. Williams; Sergeant Major John C. McCray. Company B: Corporal Daniel D. Dale and Private John Burley. Company D: Privates James E. Bowen and David D. Baird. Company E: Private James M. Simple. Company F: Corporal William Johns. Company G: Sergeant Merrill P. Rich and Private Jno. Gillen. Company I: Sergeant Jno. W. Moppin; Privates William Hank and J. H. Groover. Company K: Privates Lewis Bates and George Hindman.

Wounded.—Company A: Sergeant Aaron Newlon, leg; Privates George Brady, knee; Michael Bickel, arm; Anderville Wall, forearm; Henry Barth, scalp; Cyrus Bellus, scalp; Amin Wrightwine, face; Thomas Agnew, arm; Jacob Garrard, chest. Company B: Captain Samuel D. Wall, forearm; Corporal S. M. Fairchilds, hip; Privates Heisler H. Ludington, shoulder; W. H. Ward, hand. Company C: Sergeants Archibald Logan, ankle; Isaiah Humrickhamer, leg; Albert Dolby, arm; Corporal Fidilia Hull, skull; Privates Joseph R. Morris, hip; James F. Ramey; David B. Smith, leg; Henry C. Millicam, hand; James Thompson, chest; Coleman Lyons, knee; Sylvester Niblock, leg; Joseph R. Walters, hand. Company D: Sergeant Arnold F. Addams, chest; Corporal Milvin L. Porter, thigh; Privates Joseph A. Duoss, leg; Jos. C. Collisen, leg; John C. Wilson; Wm. Mills, arm; John Galbreth, arm; J. E. P. Eberhart, thigh. Company E: Privates Martin Shaffer, thigh; William P. Walker. Company F: Sergeant John Campbell, abdomen;

Corporals Philip Jones, face; David Patterson, thigh; Privates M. V. B. Allen, chest; William C. Ayers, abdomen; Edward W. Bishop, thigh; Daniel Harrington, scalp; Elam Page, arm; Jos. Guhl, leg; James Pibles, arm; Alfred Lyman, shoulder. Company G: Second Lieutenant Samuel Dickson, thigh; Privates —— McIlheny, leg; R. W. Bryan, scalp; Eugene Ballard, hand; John D. Davis, scalp; John T. Fox, forearm; Thomas B. Hixon, forearm; James Hayworth, arm; Robert Robinson, chest; Onlin Oberger, shoulder. Company H: First Lieutenant J. H. Hastings, chest; Sergeant Reuben L. Robinson, arm; Corporals James Walker, thigh; Charles Allison, thigh; Privates Samuel Bonfield, forearm and hand; G. P. McOnaid, forearm; W. H. Newcomb, leg; William F. Prose, abdomen; W. B. Lackville, leg; Joseph Vincent, leg. Company I: Sergeant Josiah Statcher, shoulder; Corporal G. W. Hawk, hip; Privates John Schlunaker, chest; Thomas Houston, shoulder; John Campbell, leg; Adam Killgore, shoulder. Company K: Sergeants James M. Tracy, abdomen; Harrison Goodspeed, hand; Privates John Clashill, leg; Christian Harter, leg; Thomas Johnson, thigh; Henry Mack, forearm; John Morgan, hip; Nicholas Coney, ankle.

SECOND WICONSIN BATTERY.

Killed.—Privates John O'Brien and John Flynn.

Wounded.—Second Lieutenant W. H. Hardin, thigh; Privates E. A. Whitefield, hip; Charles Ford, forearm; E. G. Bloomfield, side; Charles Nozzle, shin.

SEVENTY-FIFTH ILLINOIS REGIMENT.

Killed.—Company K: Private Sidney Merriman. Company C: Private Washington Wood.

Wounded.—Company A: Private Adniram I. Collins, hip. Company B: Sergeant Chancy B. Hubbard, neck. Company C: Privates George Fuller, arm; Hiram Brown, arm. Company E: Second Lieutenant James H. Blodgett, hip. Company F: Corporal Elisha T. Towrlittal, leg; Private Samuel Shore, chest. Company G: Corporal Edwin J. Lany, leg; Privates Addison Hickert, hand; John C. Kaiser, back. Company H: Private Jos. Hanprick, back. Company I: Captain Robert Hale, leg; Privates William Hampton, arm; James Kollins, leg; Augustus Quade, neck; Osland Orcutt, slightly. Company K: First Sergeant Burkley Barrett, hand; Sergeant Jonathan Hyde, leg; Corporal Walter Simons, leg; Privates James Morehead, hip; John Ninger, hand; Fletcher Vickey, leg.

THIRTY-EIGHTH ILLINOIS REGIMENT.

Killed.—Company A: Privates Jacob S. Killinger, Reuben H. Lightfoot, T. O. McCasland, John McPherson, F. Galmer, Thomas Stofford, and Algernon Hood. Company B: Privates Frederick A. Hollis and Henry Smith. Company C: Privates Theodore Williams and Philip Donns. Company D: Privates Alfred A. King, Nicholas Malone, Jos. S. Allen, Abr. Plunket, John B. Chapman, Albert Bradbury, and C. C. Warran. Company E: First Lieutenant John S. Dillon, Corporals Casswell Haddock and David Sawyer, and Private Cooper C. Mayhew. Company F: Captain James P. Mead, and Corporals Booth B. Patton, Nathan E. Baker, David I. Davidson, Thomas Dal-. ton, Thomas Stout, James Wilkins, and Joel D. Wells. Company G: Corporal James Franks and Private J. H. Davis. Company I: Private Moses F Adamson and Henry Gorman.

Wounded.—Company A: Captain Henry L. Alden, shoulder; First Sergeant C. H. Egleston, hand; Corporals John Mott, side; Newton C. Jones; Privates

Patrick Tobin, hand; William Henny; Nicholas Kohls, shoulder; Thomas C. Caney, shoulder; Edward Carrigan, leg; Patrick Chance, arm; David Plair, arm; Joseph Cary, arm; James Looch, arm; Joseph Ray, knee; Thomas Sheban; W. C. Paffinbuger; John Kentgler; William Rashnor; Michael Kail; Jos. Smith; William Wilch, left arm. Company B: Privates H. G. Henry, right hand; David J. Hughes, chest; Jos. Thompson, chest; Jefferson H. Turner, back; David Martin; John A. Johnson, left leg. Company C: Sergeant Samuel Campbell, left leg; Corporals James Carpenter, knee; Ben. F. Carpenter, hand; Privates Christopher Carrol, knee joint; Dan. Clair, chest; Thomas Glening; Patrick Jackson; Michael Kennedy. Company D: Privates John Maran, thigh; William Plunket; Robert B. Moss; Simeon Bridnell; William Boyd; Ezra Hickox; Jesse Pearson; Jos. H. Mullen; Benjamin F. Bromfield; James P. Moore. Company E: Privates Peter Ander, right arm; P. Argath, left knee; James Dicken, both knees; Timothy Hipen, thigh; F. A. Bishop; Isaac McGoren; Ansel Pearce; John Detuck; Joseph Floyd; Z. Strait; R. S. Starkweather. Company F: Second Lieutenant Samuel K. Wistcott, face and neck; First Sergeant Francis U. Jeffries, thigh; Sergeant Robert McFarland; Corporals Thomas Conebaugh, mouth; Reuben Lawrence; Isaac Fleming, knee and arm; Privates William Shutts, hip; John Lamb, thigh; Alexander Stevens, hand; Henry Taylor; John W. Chambers; John W. Lowrine; James B. Stenner; Johan Ham; John A. Hayne; Geo. H. Seylmer; Frank Richmond; James Stund; Albert S. Wilcox. Company G: First Lieutenant W. F. Chapman, right arm; Sergeants A. McIntire and E. Hines; Corporals B. M. Hayden and J. D. Hazzard; Privates Jacob Wideman; Samuel Knols; J. Whiteman, leg; J. Conrad, leg; J. Ebersault; Conrad Hinehaisdt, leg; G. W. Norman;. W. H. Reynolds; J. Wal. Company H: First Lieutenant A. E. Goble, knee; Privates G. W. Dimbar, hand; T. H. White; J. W. Trabes; H. Kilburn; John Ashen; Daniel Roberts. Company I: Sergeant J. A. Petteguin; Corporals Wright Bunton; J. S. Stone; Privates John A. Kelsey, shoulder; Charles Pickford, knee joint; Alfred McKibben, leg; William Batson; George Harper; I. I. Lambert; Dudley McKibben. Company K: Peter A. Scoot, right leg, since died; Andrew Burnside, hand; John McDonnell; John W. Lee; Abey Hawkins.

EIGHTY-FIRST INDIANA REGIMENT.

Killed.—Company A: Corporal Hiram Spencer. Company B: First Sergeant William D. Morgan, and Corporal Albin Prather. Company C: Private Christian McNaman. Company H: Sergeant A. G. Mansfield. Company K: Second Lieutenant Samuel Wild.

Wounded.—Company A: Corporal Wilfred Shirley, shoulder; Private Adam M. Edleman, chest. Company B: Sergeant Peter H. Bohart, hand; Privates Henry Kemple, face; James Seeler, face; Francis M. Dailey, arm; James N. Norris, hand; George McCarty, forearm. Company C: Sergeant W. E. Abbott, leg; Corporal James R. Fox, arm; Privates Thomas J. Stephens, chest; Walter Walter, face. Company D: Sergeant Felix J. Monroe, leg; Privates Geo. N. Johnson, thigh; P. Monroe, ankle; William Hughes, chest; Parker M. Truelock, chest; Riley S. Adams, wrist. Company E: Sergeant Ellison Howell, shoulder; Corporal John Newton, forearm; Privates Thomas McCarty, leg; William Blake, hip; Ruther Miller, leg. Company F: Sergeant Wesley Johnson, thigh; Musician Elza Denny, hand; Privates Samuel Weaver, leg; Osborn T. Landon, arm; Henry R. Green, hand; Aaron Hockman, ankle; Thomas Talbot. Company G: Privates John Patrick, thigh; Daniel Hadney, foot: W. Lanman, knee; Alvin H. Gregg, leg. Company H: Sergeant Jos. Cole, abdomen; Corporals William Wood, thigh; Henry Guerdon, leg; Private John Francis, leg. Company I: Captain W. D. Everett, scalp; Privates John Carmcy, os calcis; Charles Green, thigh; Henry B. Abbott, thigh; Andrew

Nichols, hip; Martin Buttorf, leg. Company K: Sergeants Oliver P. Anderson, foot; Levi Riddle, thigh; Corporal J. J. Mulsselder, foot; Private James A. Butt, skull.

ONE HUNDRED AND FIRST OHIO REGIMENT.

Colonel Leander Stern, wounded in the spine.

Lieutenant Colonel M. F. Wooster, wounded in both legs.

Killed.—Company A: Private Edward Kennyan. Company C: Second Lieutenant J. B. Biddle, Privates John J. Morn and Henry Kile. Company E: Sergeant Peter Snyder, Privates Isaac Farnsworth and Adam Shearer. Company F: Privates John Keer, David Miller, John Scott, Aaron C. Shively, and Garret Taylor. Company G: Privates Curtiss B. Mulnix and Andrew Mickle. Company K: Corporals G. W. Hewlitt and D. R. Newhouse, Privates Moses Parkhurst and Sylvester Bealby.

Wounded.—Company A: First Lieutenant A. R. Hillyer, both legs; Sergeant Andrew J. Tackson, thigh; Privates G. W. Gettinger, both legs; Chester Carr, thigh; Miles Cartwright, hand; Thomas Enoe, side; Sidney Hoff, leg; Cyrus B Prosser, side; John Smith, jr., hand; John Stimpson, forearm; S. O. K. Perry, forearm; Enoch Wilbur, arm; John Williams, right hand; and George P. Rady, left arm. Company B: Sergeant Simon Huntingdon, leg; Privates Charles B. Dennis, hip; Albert Thineman, ankle; Jacob Jury, thigh; H. J. Bly, shoulder; O. A. Rice, thigh; and J. T. Marshall, thigh. Company C: Sergeants John P. Beach, thigh; and John A. Roberts, leg; Corporal Martin Yummell, arm; Privates Gilbert Newell, thigh; Samuel Shoup, thigh; John Wolf, leg; William George, side; Henry Reperberger, breast; William Keller thigh; Jacob Omevey, head; David Fortney, face; Newlen Taylor, leg; James Holsaple, leg; Fred. Wingert, leg; William Kinney, leg. Company D: Captain E. T. Marsh, shoulder; Sergeants L. O. Rowland, both legs; E. M. Hume, left leg; Charles Penfield, breast; and George N. Mead, arm; Privates H. W. Townsend, nose; J. E. Terry, cheek; Charles Beedster, forehead; W. C. Wicks, hand; Charles B. Rose, leg; Job Peterson, leg; George Lower, leg; Charles Scott, head; George Lawrence, breast, mortal; Charles Pickery, leg; and L. L. Lerry, leg. Company E: Second Lieutenant R. D. Lord, thigh; Corporal W. P. Wordin, thigh; Privates William Currie, thigh; William Doly, both legs; James Harvey, groin; John Hawley, left thigh; J. K. Kirkland, hand; S. Lewis Lowrie, groin; Henry W. Smith, hand; William Reynolds, arm; Wallace Stately, hand and thigh; and Isaac Williams, head. Company G: Lieutenant J. P. Fleming, arm; Sergeants John S. Millman, leg and hand; and A. B. C. Denman, foot; Corporal John White, groin; Privates Andrew Bradley, leg; C. D. Morehouse, shoulder; E. Andrews, side; Malichi Humphrey, head; John Howey, arm; Horace Romsdall, hip; George Hewitt, leg; Elisha Smith, head; Peter Griner, hip and privates; and Lyman Russell, leg. Company H: Sergeant D. W. Hade, leg; Corporal S. Grivesheat, left foot; Privates John Thompson, shoulder; Edward Carrigan, thigh; D. B. Andrews, arm; Jacob L. Yeager, thigh; Charles W. Bell, left shoulder; B. F. Bell, left shoulder; Jacob T. Nomman, leg; Peter Schellung, leg and right arm; Jacob Bessey, right leg; Henry Koller, hip; James B. Fox, leg; James S. Ames, hip; and James H. Stewart, hip. Company I: Corporals S. F. Arnt, testicles; Jack Sheats, left leg; and Joseph Vanest, hip; Privates Jacob Beardley, ankle, died since; J. A. Killinger, thigh; R. McMeen, shoulder and hand; A. Decit, leg; Mathias Heng, forearm; John Fravor, leg fractured; Fred. Myers, thigh and hip; Thomas Kaup, contused leg; Philip Jordan, leg; William More, shoulder; John Doughley, knee; and G. W. Gittinser, hip. Company K: Sergeant L. Shayer, wrist; Corporals G. W. Winked, left arm; and Joseph Powell, wrist; Privates Mark Howlton, leg; John Shinser, arm; Geo. Kemper, thigh; Jerry Nicklas, hand; Solomon Saum, thigh; John Mohler, foot; John Dickens, breast; John Hoover, knee; Hiram Bealby, hip; Cyrus G. Norton, shoulder; and Clark Dayt, hip.

EIGHTH WISCONSIN BATTERY.

Killed.—Captain Stephen J. Carpenter.

Wounded.—Privates Joseph H. Worby, left thigh; William A. Bowers, back; Peter Murkley, right shoulder; Thomas Gannt, arm fractured.

TWENTY-FIRST ILLINOIS REGIMENT.

Killed.—Company A: Second Lieutenant Joseph C. Avoid, First Sergeant Robert Dimes, Corporal Alexander Bucher, Privates Jacob Canniff, W. H. Higgins, Elijah Smith, Hugh Bacon, Oliver Woolman, Charles Peters, John Ruby, and John F. Wise. Company B: Privates Thomas J. Ashmore, William Russell, John H. Bedford, John H. Ashman, and William Ferguson. Company C: Second Lieutenant Emanuel Weigle, Privates Isaac Grooms, Alumbia Phillips, and James Rathburn. Company D: Privates Ira W. Noel and James Byers. Company E: First Sergeant Joel B. Wright and Private Gotliff Heller. Company F: Privates Leroy Blace, J. A. Conghanower, Elliot A. Goodnough, William Lewis, James F. Carter, Richard Hamilton, Aaron Laus, and H. M. Smith. Company G: Corporal William Nash and Private —— McInary. Company H: Private S. C. Comstock. Company I: Corporal Alfred Harrison, Privates H. B. Longnecker, Hiram Philips, John W. Martin, Henry Hardy, Allen M. Patton, James G. Gillmore, Joseph W. Maxwell, and William H. Dean. Company K: Corporal E. A. Richardson, Privates R. F. Richardson, and Martin Mitchell.

Wounded.—Colonel J. W. S. Alexander, right foot; Adjutant C. B. Steele, right side bruised. Company A: Corporals Joseph Wagoner, side, severely; and Rudolph Zorger, shoulder, severely; Privates David Crawford, left thigh; Jonathan Bell, left thigh; S. D. Morgan, right hand; Z. B. Wills, right hand; John Leigh, left ankle, amputated, died January 7; William A. Steward, foot, slightly; Alexander Hogan, hand, slightly. Company B: Sergeants S. P. Payne, cheek; and S. F. Williams, thigh, severely; Corporal James Sell, thigh, severely; Privates Aaron Elliot; William W. Buchanan, foot; Allen Gorden, thigh; Wesley Hoge, hip, severely; Marion Landaon, arm, amputated, died since; John Maynard, thigh, severely; Thomas T. Robinson, arm, severely; Columbus Halbrook, shoulder, severely; Henry Horton, wrist, slightly; and John Amkler, shoulder. Company C: Sergeant B. F. Stark, neck, severely; Corporals L. W. B. Lowry, mortally, died; William F. Dawson, finger, slightly; Privates D. Argo, leg, severely; Patrick Britt, left lung; Isaac Graham, leg, severely; John McLaughlin, leg, severely; Joseph Phillips, leg, severely; Andrew Eden, chest, severely; Reuben Learamary, chest, severely; Aaron More, ankle, severely; Allen J. Newport, breast; Wiley M. Leslie, mortally, died; John Garver, leg, severely; William Hamline, hand, slightly; Michael Moynabon, hip, slightly; Abraham Marshall, hand, slightly; and Henry Rogers, back, slightly. Company D: Lieutenant J. S. Taylor, left ankle; First Sergeant C. A. Lingkendale, head, slightly; Privates John C. Achemon, thigh, fractured; Edward Coffin, hip, severely; N. B. Modesett, right lung; J. S. Cross, slightly; George W. Earle, hip, slightly; C. Montgomery, abdomen, mortally; James Osborne, right lung; J. W. Riley, shoulder, slightly; Lewis P. Bunting, abdomen, mortally; James A. Aden, lung, severely; James Gillogly, thigh, fractured; Jacob Goode, wounded and missing; W. S. Bromelton, neck, severely; James Badgley, leg, severely; William Hazlett, leg, severely; John Daniels, leg, severely; Samuel H. Ford, leg, severely; William Grace, leg slightly; A. Hagerman, thigh, severely; James Humback, breast, severely; John Maddox; James Neal; Henry R. Potts, hip, severely; James G. Russell, arm, slightly; Levi Romin, shoulder, severely; Henry Stroop, thigh, severely; William Smallwood, hip and legs; H. Warner, left arm; and D. Haws, jaw. Company E: Sergeant William Bunkson, neck, slightly; Corporals G. F. Greene, thigh, severely; Samuel Boggs, finger, slightly; Privates J. J. Adams, neck, slightly; John A. Abbot; Israel J. Aiken; Andrew M. Brown, thigh, severely; G. W. Bone, thigh, severely; G. W. Baker, foot, severely; Alexander Freeland, foot, severely; Simeon Greeg, arm, slightly; George R. Jenkins, jaw, slightly; W. B. Kennedy, arm, slightly; Louis Kennedy, jaw, slightly; Joel M. Lansdon, leg; Joseph A. Lansdon, head; John B. Ruse, head, slightly; John Buck, abdomen, slightly; Andrew Lynn, thigh, slightly; James H. Black, thigh; Robert Bean, thigh; Robert S. Crowder, severely; Samuel Kennedy, severely; Thomas A. Lanaden, leg, severely; Thomas A. Strayhoun, thigh, amputated; and Andrew Wilson, hand, slightly. Company F: First Sergeant John M. Bell, hip, slightly; Sergeants John Hunter, arm, fractured; Corporals J. F. Everett, hip severely; J. M. Shuts, chest; and Alexander Campbell, hip, slightly; Privates Daniel Carlel, hip, severely; John M. King, face, slightly; James Ingle, leg, severely; Elias Pittijohn, head, severely; Joseph Robertson, arm; Stephen D. Jones, leg, slightly; and James Willis, finger, slightly. Company G: Sergeant C. S. Burrows, knee, severely; Corporal J. D. Whitaker, leg, severely; Privates C. Leatherman, hand, slightly; M. Fanning, leg, slightly; J. A. Flemming, shoulder, severely; S. A. King, thigh, severely; R. R. Buntney, thigh; Joseph Read, neck, severely; Samuel Shultz, neck, severely; G. W. Hamilton, chest, severely; and D. S. Shultz, hand, slightly. Company H: Corporals William Harlan, shoulder and back; and Joseph H. Pitman; Privates George Parke, chest, mortal, dead; Stephen D. Framan, abdomen, mortal, dead; James H. Baker, thigh, slightly; Henry Donaldson, thigh, severely; Noah Homaday, foot, severely; John N. Harduck, thigh, severely; James H. King, leg, severely; Samuel Poorman, arm, severely; William F. Sandy, leg; Martin Wilson, leg, slightly; David B. Miller, leg, slightly; James H. Baker, thigh, slightly; Thomas P. Bennett, thigh, slightly; Henry Haller, leg, slightly; Samuel J. Jones, thigh, severely; Thomas Kendall, arm, slightly; John Phillips, thigh, amputated, died; Joshua Ross, chest, severely; Henry Schofer, chest, severely; William Price, arm, slightly; and Abraham Whitehead, leg, slightly. Company I: Captain Christian K. Knight, thigh, severely; Lieutenant Charles Howe, side, severely; Corporals Archibald Maxwell, thigh, severely; G. W. Bean, head, severely; and Samuel W. Cammons, arm, severely; Privates John G. Brown, groin, severely; James F. Carges, head, severely; Joseph Burr, leg, severely; G. W. Bean, head, slightly; William Carver, thigh; Solomon Jones, back, mortal, died; E. P. Fitch, arm, slightly; Isaac Foster, leg, slightly; Harvey R. King, arm, slightly; Jacob Sangston, face, severely; Alonzo W. Passons, leg, severely; Leander Padgett, ankle, severely; James M. Shaw, arm and chest; William Spilkey, leg, severely; Hiram Wood, knee, severely; Philip Dorsett, foot; John F. Dean, hand, slightly; Thomas Burr, thigh, slightly; John Hipple, leg, slightly; and John Muskunmut, leg, slightly. Company K: First Sergeant W. M. Abrahams, thigh, fractured; Sergeants Isaac M. Shup, leg, slightly; and William F. Payne, leg, bruised; Corporals James Nokes, head, slightly; and Thomas Alexander, thigh, severely; Privates John C. Bridges, arm and side, severely; T. Dodd, head, severely; John Davis, arm, slightly; Arch. Ford, thigh, severely; William Garnett, thigh, severely; D. Gardner, arm, slightly; M. Haley, abdomen and arm; William R. Hant, back, slightly; John W. Lee, leg, severely; Oliver P. Payne, hand and thigh; George H. Payne, arm and side; Thomas J. Rush, leg, slightly; Thomas Rich, hand, slightly; Charles F. Stair, leg, slightly; Thomas Forhey, thigh, severely; Jacob Weaver, hip, severely; Thomas Wills, thigh, severely; Lomas E. Vining, thigh, slightly; John Sites, shoulder, severely; John H. Hays, foot, severely; Harvay Shook, hand, severely; G. W. Short, foot, severely; and Albert A. Worthey, leg, slightly.

FORTY-NINTH OHIO REGIMENT.

Killed.—Lieutenant Colonel L. Drake. Captain Amos Keller. Company C: Sergeant William Myers, Corporal Joseph Slough, and Privates Joseph Porter, E. P. Holten and Daniel Meysner. Company E: Private J. W. Ferris. Company F: Corporal Isaac Ferry and Private J. N. Anderson. Company G: Sergeant Joseph Busrom and Private R. Kummel. Company I: Private William Lyle and Austin Hammel. Company K: Privates Charles Brhetten and Henry Megsel, neck.

Wounded.—Major ——— Porter; Captain G. H. Calves, shoulder; Lieutenants Milton Conzill, thigh; A. H. Celler, shoulder; ——— Ray, leg; and ——— Lottas, ankle; Adjutant J. C. Norton, leg; Sergeants S. C. Miller; S. B. Stewart, elbow; and F. Warner, thigh; Corporals J. C. Ley, thigh; W. C. Blackmead, thigh; Nathan Roberts; C. B. Morgan; William Hindman, shoulder; and J. Ferry, shoulder; and Privates S. A. Darborough, hand; G. W. Mulholland, hand; Dana Craims; Adam Brets; George Benham, right lung; Martin Butler, hand; Samuel Solsby, head; David Grisles, head; J. Wannotler, ankle; Samuel Clerc, thigh; C. H. Buder, leg; John C. Kample, knee; George M. Weelholle, leg; Eli Warner, hip; J. G. Shuts, leg; William Burlee, thigh; Albert Dodge, thigh; L. S. Bertes, heel; William Harberger, hip-joint; Levi Henry; William Lisle, thigh; Peter Liffer, right lung; H. L. Bud, hip; A. C. Pagler, leg; William Inregoom, arm, severely; John Lawrence, hip; D. W. Smith; J. Sileso; M. J. Lutz, right side; John D. Meyer, knee; John Caldwell; W. S. Varner, thigh; W. Himrman, hand; Thomas Berit, lungs; J. Lorslin; thigh; Albert Doze, thigh; Amon Sohle; Eli Warner; A. Bicker, leg; Austin Eller; Oliver Jacobs, foot; Lorenzo Emminger, foot; Robert Colwell; Henry Burnell, arm; R. J. Smith, shoulder; R. King, hand; William H. Muznon; F. S. Roberts, elbow and hand; John Lawrence, foot; A. C. Pazilion; J. N. McConnell, thigh; C. W. Everett, thigh; Elis Hole, thigh, severely; J. R. Bossler, leg; J. C. Clarlsett, thigh; R. Camey, ankle-joint; C. Benin, leg; Cylus Bland, thigh; Samuel Cove; J. P. Kedger; C. H. Barder, leg; C. J. Keller; B. C. Shins, hand; Simon Miller, hand, severely; G. H. Coast; J. A. Kinpple; J. M. Cartwright, leg, severely; H. S. Reed, hand; William Hapenberger, shoulder; Peter Lefler, elbow; Thomas Barker, arm, slightly; W. A. Barshing; J. E. Harston, hand; J. S. Carber, foot; John Foley; F. W. Bendier, shoulder; Warren White, back; David Frank, and Thomas Barshong.

EIGHTY-NINTH ILLINOIS REGIMENT.

Killed.—Company E: Private James Nichols. Company F: Privates Moses Beaver and E. Tonlin. Company G: Dewitt C. Landon, George W. Murray, and David H. Bestor. Company H: Captain Henry L. Willet, Corporal W. H. Litsey, and Private Henry Huggins. Company I: Private W. Holdeen.

Wounded.—Adjutant Edward F. Bishop, face. Company A: Sergeant John H. More; Musician Justus D. Payne, thigh, severely; and Privates James J. Eagan; Franklin H. Miller, foot; Louis Saunders. Company C: Corporal H. H. Warner, thigh, severely. Company D: Privates Mader Olenin; Frank Gangin, shoulder; Ralph Pardy, leg; Eli Morris, hip; Alonzo Anderson. Company E: Privates Patrick McGrath; James Wilderick; Hiram H. Prain;

James T. Copp; J. S. Priscote; Ira Bridgeport, thigh; Henry Felsh, thigh; Joseph Goyer, shoulder. Company G: Musician William Ferman; and Privates John Herlick; David Kerr, face; Herman Rosenlief, thigh; Wilfred Whitney; Robert Wilson, slightly; D. E. Shrouse; and C. V. Bainbridge. Company H: Orton H. Barnes; James Snowball; Ole H. Johnson; F. W. Goddard; Thomas N. Modly, leg, severely; and William J. Cooper, leg, slightly. Company I: Musician A. W. Parker; and Privates A. Bigley; Joseph Gutherie, ankle; J. J. Lloyd; Charles Nelson; and Henry Shicter, hip, severely. Company K: M. Schebinger; Frank Driesel, leg; John P. Adams; Frederick L. Phillips; leg, slightly; John Reed, leg, slightly.

FIFTEENTH OHIO REGIMENT.

Killed.—Company B: Privates Absolem Sime and Levi Frost. Company C: Private John Massman. Company E: Private George Hutchinson. Company F: Corporal William Caffay; Privates John Craig, John Hescht, W. Bell, J. R. Bark, E. Brown, A. Ralston, and W. Nelson. Company H: Private Elias Evans. Company I: Privates Lucus Brown, John M. Charly, William Whitney, and Samuel Cotes.

Wounded.—Lieutenant Colonel Asken, thigh and side; Major McClenahan, shoulder. Company A: Privates W. T. Kenney, left leg; J. S. Brown, neck; J. Hammond, thigh, severely; James W. White, forearm, slightly; J. Krissinger, left shoulder; and J. D. Patterson, back, slightly. Company B: Corporals M. Cune, thigh, severely; J. Blachr, thigh, severely; and —— Niles, leg, severely; Privates A. Milner, right leg, severely; J. Adams, knee, slightly; Thomas Evans, leg, severely; J. A. Penrose, leg, severely; A. Ross, right leg; A. Williams, leg, severely; A. Allison, leg, severely; W. Silders, left leg; W. Calvert, shoulder; B. Chance, forearm, slightly; John Frazer, right hand; and J. Adamson, leg. Company C: Privates Theo. Jolly, left arm and chest; A. Harding, thigh, mortally; M. S. Byrd, left thigh; D. Buggs, hip; Albert Noe, right hip; and D. Cartwright, head, slightly. Company B: Privates G. M. Chambers, hip and leg; E. Shambriege, left hand; W. A. Ward, face, slightly; C. Factor, knee, slightly; D. Somford, thigh, slightly; and J. P. Moulton, right ear. Company D: Privates John Hehn, left shoulder, slightly; John Hesser, left leg; A. E. Miller, forearm, and H. Shriver, thigh. Company E: Privates J. E. Diesert, thigh; Calvin Etzel, shoulder; P. Shackelford, arm and leg, severely; J. E Stewart, forearm; George Billop, thigh, slightly; John Dantford, abdomen; W. G. Malin, thigh; J. Gardner, shoulder and neck; H. Brooks, leg, slightly; J. Fenton, foot, slightly; J. Picheing, foot, slightly; J. Dillon, shoulder, slightly; C. Henderson, hand, slightly, and L. Hillies, thigh. Company F: Privates L. Fowler, both legs; M. Madden, shoulder, severely; J. Bowles, nose; C. Brandon, thigh; A. Gurlock, hip, slightly, and J. M. Hays, hand. Company C: Privates William H. Patterson, foot; J. Taylor, mouth, severely; Jacob Egerly, thorax; George Maycook, hand, slightly; P. C. Hayflick, arm; and C. V. Cracraft, face. Company G: Privates S. A. Walker, head; J. C. McCowley, neck, slightly; and W. Whip, thigh. Company H: Captain —— Douglass, side, severely; Privates William Angervim, head, slightly; Willlam Crales, thigh, severely; James Updegrove, shoulder, slightly; C. Miller, leg; W. H. Pier, shoulder, severely; David Cappin, forearm, slightly; P. Beamer, leg; William Crone, forearm; Elias Temboz, forearm; and H. H. Nice, leg. Company I: Privates William M. Connel, ankle, severely; James Iniasger, shoulder; Lewis Goshome, leg, slightly; George Stull, shoulder; W. M. Connell, ankle; W. J. White, forearm; W. Morton, neck; Joseph Sheely, side and A. J. Simons, cheek. Company K: Privates J. J. Renard, leg, severely; P. Russle, leg; F. Sanders, thigh, severely; F. Fawcett, hand, slightly; L. B Grimes, shoulder, slightly; and J. Thompson, hand.

BATTERY A.—FIRST REGIMENT OHIO ARTILLERY.

Killed.—Private Conrad Least.

Wounded.—Sergeant Richard H. Rodgers, knee; Privates S. B. Cuthbert, leg; D. A. Bishop, leg; John C. Whitney, head, slightly; and V. B. Stanford, forearm.

THIRTY-NINTH INDIANA REGIMENT.

Killed.—Company A: Sergeant Alex. Jamison; Corporal Abraham Hie; Privates H. C. Barker, A. Crane, Leander Free, Lafayette Ferguson, William W. Jones, Charles Kelly, William Banner, Benj. Contions, G. W. Plotner, and Peter Wright. Company D: Private Jeremiah Houthy. Company E: Privates Henry Hering and John Donahey. Company F: Sergeant S. F. Fobes; Privates S. F. Cox, A. J. McClintock, B. F. Davis, J. W. Overman, and Allen Walton. Company G: Privates Henry Somers and H. J. Pierce. Company I: Sergeant J. Benham; Privates J. Amkenbough, J. H. Cozart, O. P. Lewis, A. Murphy, M. S. Householder, and J. J. Householder.

Wounded.—Company A: Sergeants Robert Schelling and Samuel C. Jones; Corporal D. W. Rowe; Privates H. W. Jones, A. Harold, Arnold Davis, J. F. Beriss, J. S. Hawkins, W. F. Galriel, Ralph Jones, D. W. Jones, J. W. Larkins, John Marlin, W. V. Powell, O. P. Swain, and George Taylor, thigh. Company C: Privates H. McClennan, shoulder; G. H. Bassett; James Hilton, chest, and Eugene Plump, leg. Company D: 1st Sergeant J. A. Boering; Sergeant George Ogden; Privates G. W. Shilling, and Andy Julian, thigh. Company E: Privates J. A. Andholson, James McDaniel, Milton Johnson, Beaty Boughton, Newton Barker, Isaac Bowen, John Ball, Levi Ball, Austin Serman; Thomas Kurely, leg and ankle; E. Shillds, hip and thigh; David Vance, and Isaac Ray. Company F: 1st Sergeant H. C. Snyder; Sergeant R. W. Stringer; Corporal A. O. Cady, arm; Privates G. W. Barnett, hip; James Basset, W. Clayborn, William Edmonds, John Griffy, D. Gartlemen, Johnson Haydon, G. W. Hoffman, H. W. Kelty, H. M. Clintock, W. Pettell; William Peel, arm; A. Rodgers, shoulder; John Shiks, chest; J. Sullivan, and B. J. Winslow, leg. Company G: Lieutenant John Levil: Sergeant F. C. Stevenson; Privates John Barker, knee; J. G. Symons, leg and thigh; Levi Bichart, chest; Samuel Kesslor, chest; ——— Jackson, and W. H. Harrold. Company H: Sergeant William Todd; Corporals James Grove, hip and leg; James McCesby, head; D. Caise, arm; Privates J. M. Kreller, hip; G. S. Kreller, chest; Fred. Weidmeiso; John Fisher, head; and William Templer, arm. Company I: Corporal B. F. Dill; Privates Howard Huffman, hip; B. Lenord Burkard, thigh; A. Echalmon; Jacob Echalmon; J. M. Fitzgerald, hip; Thomas Griffin; M. W. Linsey, arm; A. J. Bennington, Martin Shive, George Schmidt, Davis Lee, F. W. Brown, J. L. Masters, and G. Burchman. Company H: Privates G. Gadker, thigh; Charles Love; A. Robins, shoulder; M. Fisk, Charles Mitchell, Daniel Both, M. Stenly, ——— Stochman, Milton Jones, and C. Morris. Company D: Privates L. Julian, James Berder, and John Wilson. Company G: Privates M. Godard, Newton Deer, and Hugh Tucker. Company F: Private Henry Millenbrock. Company K: Privates Milton Stocheld and John L. Jones.

THIRTY-SECOND INDIANA REGIMENT.

Killed.—Company A: Privates John Boedle, Jacob Osterly, and Bemhartt Mardorf. Company C: Private Frederick Pepper. Company D: Sergeant Lewis Irving; Private August Steinmler. Company F: Private Frederick Myer. Company G: Sergeant Bauctanstins Hurst. Company F: Sergeant Henry Kaiser. Company G: Private John Weidhurst. Company K: Privates Joseph Proctker and Jacob Gessner.

Wounded.—Company A: Privates John Wyp, head; John Stengel, arm; Louis Scherimyer, back; Frank Marks, head. Company B: Sergeant Frederick Know, breast; Privates Frederick Urlow, leg; Jacob Forthofer, thigh. Company C: Privates Louis Beith, leg; David Fisher, head and leg; Christian Lepper, breast; Peter Bittner, leg. Company D: Corporal George Duchle, hand; Privates Abraham Weinackle; John Benner; John Tabert, leg; Balthers Binar, leg. Company E: Privates Wilhelm Schœfield, thigh; W. H. Helwing, breast. Company F: Privates Christian Bussim, left shoulder; Herman Derrenger, leg; George Schenk, breast; Gotlieb Wittman, arm; Anton Weigle, leg. Company G: Sergeant Nathial Schrockdelsker, knee; Privates William Becker, arm and leg; Louis Schilling; John Osterman. Company H: Privates Philip Eckard; August Koble; Joseph Baerle; Conrad Miller; Ludwig Wagoner. Company I: Private Christian Gross, hand. Company K: Sergeant Fritz Netzer, knee; Corporals Christian John, hand; Fritz Weber, hand; John Lewsins, hand; Privates Frederick Bretthaner, leg; Henry Brepner, left arm; Robert Kamp; Frederick Richerick, hand.

FIFTH INDIANA BATTERY.

Killed.—Corporal Jas. M. Waters; Privates Daniel Rickards and Phillips Geddis.

Wounded.—Lieutenant Henry Rankin, shoulder; Sergeant Joseph Henghey, knee; Corporals John English, hip; Wm. Henry, side and neck; and Robert Bolton; Privates Wesley Amos, thigh; David Bricker, leg; Stephen McKeizer, wrist; John Mendenhall, left foot; David Myers, left leg; Wm. Plummer, foot; and Jacob Shoemaker, knee.

FIRST OHIO VOLUNTEERS.

Wounded.—Company E: Private T. B. Cure, hip. Company I: Private W. S. Brown, right thigh.

NINETY-THIRD OHIO VOLUNTEERS.

Wounded.—Company A: Private Samuel Rowlands, right leg. Company F, Privates Miles McNaf, right arm, and John Magner, right thigh.

NINETY-FOURTH OHIO VOLUNTEERS.

Wounded.—Company I: Private Christian Wise, left knee.

FIFTH KENTUCKY.

Killed.—Company A: Private John Sutten. Company C: Privates Henry Miller, and Mike Conly. Company D: Sergeant Ely Tamill, Corporals Benj. Dren and Pat. Burk, and Privates Arthur Graham, G. Pliffer, and Conrad Bround. Company E: Corporals Adam Menkirk and John Gottchalk, and Private George Beanmister. Company G: Corporal John Lacy and Private Michael Fallon. Company H: Corporals Wm. Summers and Jas. McDaniels. Company I: Captain Alexander Ferguson and Corporal John Moore.

Wounded.—Lieutenant Colonel Wm. W. Berry, wrist; Major Jas. L. Treanor, slightly. Company A: Sergeants James Cullen, knee, and Daniel Clinton, thigh; Corporals Benj. D. Edsill, arm, and Robert Cosgrave; Privates W. W. Cassidy, leg; Robert Johnson, hand; Thomas Lofters, arm; Pat. Vale, hip; and J. McCormick, hip. Company B: Privates Jos. Connor, arm; Jas. Wooman, arm; Alex. Mullen, leg; William Steward, hip; Thos. Murry, hand; and John Malz, hip. Company C: Captain Asa Speed, abdomen; Sergeant Wm. Shaw, abdomen; Corporal John Brown, thigh; Privates Thos. Ely, arm; Jacob Barber, hand; John Crown, neck; Lewis Sergant, head. Company D: Corporal David Hard, abdomen; Privates Austin Sweeny, both thighs; Pat. Gilligan, leg; John Marion, knee; Michael Keenan, leg; Ben. Patrick, both legs; John McCormick, leg; Francis M. Tucker, face and leg; Sebastin Mill; leg, and James Donnelly, shoulder. Company E: Lieutenant Frank Dissel, abdomen; Sergeant Fred Knoiner, foot; Corporal Bumhurdt Leimon, shoulder; Privates Jacob Arent, foot; Bumhardt Kiel, ankle; and Phil. Schnieder, side. Company F: Privates O. H. Johnsen, leg; Albert H. Laycock, neck; Andrew J. Smith, leg; John Stratton, leg; Wm. Snapp, leg, amputated. Company G: Corporals Walter Lacy, thigh; Wm. Shomaker, thigh; and Charles Anderson, thigh; Privates Martin Brophes, hand; Francis Schaffer, back; Benj. Conklin, leg; August Depoir, neck; Daniel Dunn, thigh; Thomas Farren, shoulder; and Thomas White, leg. Company H: Privates John Hoffman, hand; Squire Cable, hand; Antoines Berringer, arm; Chas. Fleckhammer, shoulder; Wm. Factor, hip; Geo. Halabaum, thigh; Fred. Jones; Frank Klespie, arm; Wm. Sherrer, thigh, fractured; Andrew H. Ward, wrist; and James R. Williams, arm. Company I: Privates Wm. Carter, hip; Henry Hailman, hip; T. H. Johnson, arm; and Herman Shroeder, legs. Company K: Lieutenant John D. Sheppard, left lung; Corporals Theo. Mennypeny, leg; and Elisha Chandler, leg; Privates Thos. Eagan, hip; James R. Carter, both legs; Michael Conner, arm; John J. Galely, leg; W. H. Roes, back; and Mike Higgins, thigh.

NINETY-THIRD OHIO REGIMENT.

Killed.—Company A: Corporal Jasper Fry. Company C: Private Wayne Thompson. Company F: Sergeant William Lane, Corporal Swain Corson, Privates William Ogg, George Kimbal, and James Kennedy. Company G: Private George B. Saylor. Company H: Sergeant Joseph Wiley, Privates Henry Siler and Alfred Shiler. Company K: Corporal William McKee.

Wounded.—Company A: Captain William H. Martin, shoulder; Corporal Ira B. Hearn; Privates William Hillrigle, arm; Daniel Lehman, William Sicklider, and Francis Kapp. Company B: Sergeant ——— Tingler, breast; Corporals Jesse Fister, knee, and ——— Wolf, shoulder; Privates ——— Shortz, leg; ——— Irvin, face. Company C: Lieutenant J. T. Patton, both thighs; Sergeants S. S. Lodler, shoulder; J. Falconer, arm and groin; J. Merill, arm; Privates W. C. Stewart, forearm, and Z. Dody, knee. Company D: Private John A. Logan, arm. Company E: Sergeants A. H. Mason, leg, and Jacob Vogle, thigh; Privates O. W. Weichmar, ankle; H. B. Ulm, ankle; H. Hippait, ankle. Company F: Privates Richard Straw, ——— Flichtimger, Enny Carle, John Wagner, and ——— McNiff. Company G: Privates J. W. Johnson, J. H. Ramsay, and Martin C. Bemmel. Company H: Lieutenant Daniel Sherman, elbow; Sergeants F. W. Austin, elbow, and ——— Logan, arm; Private Albert Brown, both thighs. Company I: Privates J. Hammond, breast; J. Easser, leg; J. Cline. Company K: Lieutenant George Shultz, Corporal Martin Etter, and Private Benjamin Strails.

FIRST OHIO REGIMENT.

Killed.—Company B: Private Frederick Burbam. Company C: Private Mathew Webster. Company D: Privates Samuel Berby, Charles Scobie, and Eugene Roberts. Company H: Corporal Curtis McKinney, Privates Henry Sharp and J. M. Donner.

Wounded.—Company A: Privates J. W. Reed, right side; Freeman Wolf, leg; Newal A. Webb, leg. Company B: Sergeant Jacob Ryner; Private William Fabier, wrist. Company C: Privates James Galloway, thigh; Joseph Platt, scalp; Thomas Dickenstal, leg, (amputated;) Franklin Luray, leg; Charles A. Stone, arm. Company D: Lieutenant Alex. Vairan, foot; Corporal George Jamison, thigh; Privates Horace Cowan, neck; Hugh Gray, leg and side; Robert Waterson, thigh. Company E: Privates Reuben Parker, arm; George H. Patton, thigh; J. L. Houser, thigh. Company H: Privates Danair Milhauzen, left hand; Danair McChist, left hand; Ed. Murey, leg; Joseph Slack, thigh. Company I: Sergeants William May, chest; J. W. Faucett, thigh; Corporals James Robinson, left thigh; Peter Trapp, forearm; Privates Samuel Lockheart, head; Michael Sullivan, shoulder; James Waller, thigh; Henry C. Neff, forearm; M. W. Fulk, shoulder; Ed. Dubler, thigh; John Marquis, shoulder; Frank Prouse, shoulder; Thomas Fox, shoulder. Company K: Sergeant C. W. Bowelle, head; Privates A. Keefer, side; Lewis A. Spemyk, arm.

SIXTH INDIANA REGIMENT.

Killed.—Company A: Corporal George A. Benepil and Private William Ellis. Company B: Corporal Seely Jayne; Privates B. F. Simpson, William Jolly, and James Shoemaker. Company C: Privates Ira Roberts, Samuel Stall, and Enqs Clark. Company G: Privates James Reay and John W. Sharp. Company H: Private James H. Earl. Company K: Corporal John F. Harrell; Privates John H. Hyatt and Ed. McVay.

Wounded.—Company A: Lieutenant J. C. Whaley, hip; Corporal Samuel Storms, shoulder; Privates George Smith, foot; James Stephenson, left hip; George Messmore, knee; John W. Anderson, hand; Ebenezer Marcus, knee. Company B: Sergeant John E Tillman, both legs; Privates James Kitts. thigh; Stephen Jayne, both legs; John Dixon, shoulder; B. F. Hargrave, left side; T. R. Munroe, shoulder; E. M. Adkins, leg; William Fungrater, leg. Company C: Privates D. B. Simonton, chest, since died; G. Cummins, right arm; Robert C. Gray, left arm; William Dunlap, shoulder; Virgil Brown, head; Newton Young, right arm. Company D: Privates Jonathan Easts, leg; Casper Land, right leg; William Conway, left wrist; John Long, ankle; William Wallace, shoulder. Company E: Corporal W. S. Meads, hand; Privates Joseph Underwood, hand; Theodore Johnson, hand. Company F: Privates Elijah Baily, head; Cornelius Underunk, breast. Company G: Privates A. G. Cotton, left hip; Gideon Powell, leg; Alexander Bradford, hip. Company H: Corporal George H. Sheets, head; Privates J. P. Fanon, right leg; William P. Gosswell, right arm; James H. Voris, left arm; Robert Chillis, left knee; William H. Johnson, right shoulder; J. D. Griffith, right ankle. Company I: Privates Virgil Baker, left knee; Nathan H. Floyd, both legs; Henry Dixon, scrotum; William Underwood, right side; Mathew Doyle, hand. Company K: Privates S. W. Jackson, neck; J. F. Jordan, arm; W. P. Ensminger, over right eye; John Breese, finger; Thomas W. Lewis, thigh and finger.

THIRTIETH INDIANA REGIMENT.

Killed.—Company A: Lieutenant E. B. Stribly, Privates Christian Mickler, Lawrence White, and W. D. Allen. Company B: Corporals William Rosesaugh, William Roberts, and Daniel Walker; Privates N. M. Reynolds, and E.

Middleton. Company C: Corporal J. W. Hathaway, Privates William Archy and James Morrow. Company D: Privates William Vlealfield and J. W. Newbit. Company E: Corporal Alfred Harris, Privates George Johnson and William Topono. Company F: Private Curtis Bronse. Company G: Corporal T. J. Rambo, Privates Eli Wheeler, Myron Ames, and Namon Pence. Company H: Corporal N. Osborn, Privates W. Meller, George Long, William Fick, and George Coal. Company K: Corporal David Zigler and Private David Swank.

Wounded.—Company A: Sergeant J. W. Stribly; Privates Joseph Vanyier, C. Stribly, P. Schrona, A. Wilson, F. Hutchins, and M. Storms. Company B: Privates Robert Smidley, G. W. Johnson, F. Menhide, S. Frank, D. Koons, G. Bartly, J. Bentford, William Felters, W. H. Sloan, and F. Fisher. Company C: Sergeant Anderson Cooly; Corporals Isaac Pancake and Joseph S. Olcott; Privates Charles Allen, George Garber, William P. Johnson, H. M. Marker, Talman Morris, Joseph Miller, William Parker, and R. Vanderford. Company D: Sergeant Thomas Meads; Corporal Robert Bell; Privates Henry Richards and George Penbrook. Company E: Sergeant George R. Murphy; Corporals Charles S. Muny, John H. Rhodes, and Edward Struck; Privates John Whitera, William Mann, Samuel Shann, Henry Bush, Charles V. Fair, Thomas Hogarth, and Simeon Malone. Company F: Corporal John C. Bloomfield; Privates Samuel Wygart, David Skinner, William Snooks, Henry Hayner, and James Vanferson. Company G: Sergeant R. P. McFarland; Corporal Harrison Merrick; Privates C. B. Ellsworth, W. H. Yoder, J. W. Walbum, Silas Latta, Elias Butt, and W. W. Wilson. Company H: Sergeants J. Likens, —— Hogei and —— Connor; Corporals —— Whisong, William Freeman, and —— Burnhart; Privates —— Bean, A. Coller, N. Kedricorn, J. George, A. Long, William Sutes, John Marcum, R. McCush, G. Muny, A. Reeder, N. M. Showers, S. Ulm, A. Skinner, J. Lockmier, and S. Dilno. Company I: Captain J. M. S. Britcher; Lieutenant John Moore; Corporal Peter Hemmer; Privates George Armstrong, Daniel Bowman, T. Carlier, Alfred Clark, Oliver P. Evey, William Ford, William Harris, William Hight, Henry Kist, Silas McCook, Jeremiah Now, John Meritney, Andrew Pern, A. H. Beck, and W. Hapner. Company K: Corporal D. D. Copies; Privates W. Nelson and G. A. Potter.

SEVENTY-NINTH ILLINOIS REGIMENT.

Killed.—Colonel Sheridan P. Reed. Company A: Sergeant Joseph Thomas. Privates Thomas Berry, Henry Loop, and George Lifter. Company C: Privates Wesley Strickland and George Green. Company D: Private George Yeakee. Company E: Privates William Dillin and Phenias Coffin. Company F: Privates Jay Guinniss, Wiley Jones, Joseph Walkin, and John J. Miller. Company G: Corporal Boeman Jacobs and Private David Ball. Company H: Joseph H. Smith and B. F. G. Fuller. Company K: Private Henry Wansly.

Wounded.—Company A: Privates John Cook, side; Francis Cuady, left thigh; Benjamin Lane, head; George Hiddle, left shoulder; and A. M. Robineru, right shoulder. Company B: Privates Michael Lames, face; Albert Carter, right hand; Henry Bentz, shoulder; Eleazer Smith, lung; Jacob Franna, left thigh; Chinton Davis, left foot; William Vincent, right hand; Benjamin Watts, left forearm; Peter Gregors, head; and Jeremiah Viatch, left thigh. Company C: Lieutenant John H. Patton, ankle; Sergeant Abednego Sanders, right knee; Corporals John M. Shank, left hand; Hamilton Elliott, right knee; Privates George W. Rigg, mortally; Jacob Luimon, back; John Jones, side of head; and Isaac M. Ewing, left hand. Company D: Captain Thomas A. Young, back; Corporal William Greenleaf, right hand; Privates Francis J. Pastor, right thigh; John Shance, right leg; Josiah Wallett, right side; Emsley J. Troyden, mortally; Thomas Patterson, left side; and Jno. Hotston, both thighs. Company E: Lieutenant Henry S. Albin, thigh; Sergeant Harvey

Peters, mortally; Privates James H. Lyon, right thigh; G. Crise, left shoulder; Jno. L. Stevens, right side; Edwin Drake, right side; Asa Craft, right leg; William Bracket, mortally; Owen Brown, hand; George Pittill, right arm; and Andrew Wiley, left hand. Company F: Sergeant Milton F. Craig, mortally; Corporals Henry B. Kieler, left side of head, and George Reddick, left leg and shoulder; Privates John Taylor, right side of head; John W. Cunningham, left leg; J. M. Farr, left side; Cornelius Ramsey; Charles Cleelfiter, finger, left hand. Company G: Sergeant James Madden, left side; Privates Theodore Elliott, knee; Thomas Brandon, left shoulder; Orlando Genil, right leg; Richard Clark, right foot; and Stephen Grimes, left arm. Company H: Corporal Asa Williams, right knee; Privates Samuel Heicky, mortally; Harvey Zink, mortally; T. R. Ogden, left thigh; William Hollin, left leg; Charles Cass, right foot; S. Stanly, right leg; John Kidden, left knee; Jacob H. Titus, left side; and W. H. Roberts, left leg, Company J; Alexander Chambers, left hand; Enoch Harris, left thigh; Benedict Martin, head; Alonzo McKee, left leg; and Marion Rolster, left shoulder. Company K: Sergeant Josephus Daman, left leg; Corporals Hewitt McKinny, right thigh, and Cyrus Brannock, right foot; Privates George Moxen, left thigh; Larkin Lane, right hip; John Jenkins, right ear; and Stacy Darning, mouth.

SEVENTY-SEVENTH PENNSYLVANIA REGIMENT.

Killed.—Company D: Private Augustus Mace. Company E: Privates John Haker and John Buler. Company K: Private Alexander Brown.

Wounded.—Lieutenant Colonel Peter B. Hensum, left hip, since died. Company A: Lieutenant John E. Walker, knee; Private Henry Tennary. Company B: Privates William Tomes, leg, and Edwin Bratt, hip. Company C: Sergeant Scott R. Crawford, leg; Corporals William Kinth, both legs, and Samuel A. Gethy, left thigh; Privates William Ganster, right leg; David Sutter, ankle; William Dixon, breast and wrist; Andrew Hindland, right eye; John Higgins, face; Henry Grecknawall, left finger. Company D: Private William Robinson, breast. Company E: Privates Thomas Harely; E. J. Murphy; J. E. Clark, back; Alfred Ray, breast; Enoch Eckler, head. Company F: Privates Michael Short, shoulder; William Brian, hand; George Heamer, knee. Company G: Corporal James Foster, breast; Private Patrick Galliger, face. Company K: Corporal Robert McMillan, right thigh; Privates William J. Prentiss, breast; John Gamble, shoulder; Lewis H. Buler, hip.

THIRTY-FOURTH ILLINOIS REGIMENT.

Killed.—Company A: Private G. S. Woodworth. Company C: Corporal Charles Santee. Company D: Corporal John Dole and Privates Henry Pecks and William Hendle. Company E: Sergeant Marcus D. Bennett, Corporal George J. Dougherty, and Privates Henry D. Krouch and A. M. Pratt. Company G: Captain W. C. Greenwood and Private S. R. Cully. Company H: Corporal S. R. Kurtz and Privates A. S. Tyler, A. A. Willoby, and Charles Easter. Company I: Private James Masters. Company K: Sergeant James M. Peaden and Private Riley Marcoti.

Wounded.—Company A: Corporals John Gibner, leg; J. P. Durstin, left thigh; John Gorgan, hip, chin, and neck; J. M. Maiden, wrist; Hershell H. Smith, left foot. Company B: Corporal W. F. Nichols, right leg; Private Philip Besor, right leg. Company C: Lieutenant Daniel Riley, left knee; Corporals W. A. Leity, ankle; John Lalsoman, left thigh and arm; G. W. Bissler, both hands; David Wingard, knee and arm; Privates J. H. Bowers, left leg; Henry Brown, right leg; Thomas Brown, face; Robert Caldwell, ankle; Patrick Fayher, right thigh; Herman Groith, shoulder and face; Henry

Hoffmaster, left side; J. B. Hoff, right leg; Jacob F. Hirsel, left shoulder; William H. Hopper, left thigh; Philip Keysier, right thigh; Erl. O. Neal, left leg; John Bonch, left ear; Ben. Boyce, right side; J. H. Stephens, head; R. E. Young, left leg. Company D: Sergeant D. C. Young; Corporals L. J. Tussey; John Chambers, arm; Privates E. Brewer, leg; O. P. Barber, arm; H. C. Carr, forearm; Wellington Ealor; Henry Law; George Pierce, left hip; Jos. Shellmier, elbow; James Lyman, leg. Company E: Captain Oscar Van Tasset, forearm; Sergeants John F. Gunty, thigh; Patrick McCarty; Robert Dean; Corporals George F. Cheeshire, hip and arm; Austin S. Fox, hand; J. C. Groover; Privates Fred. Tyers; William Jovine; Charles Miner; Lawrence Coffried; John Zenk; Michael Kenham; A. H. Blakely; Triar Richardson; Charles Butterfield, head; F. C. Brown, right leg; J. H. Gull, chest; A. F. Herington, knee; E. F. Merritt, arm. Company F: Corporals William Steel, hip and thigh, and J. B. Taylor, left shoulder; Privates Ed. Pankherd, knee, and Christian D. Taylor, hip and thigh. Company G: Sergeant Edwin Olls, leg; Corporal Elias Bacherman, back, severely; Privates Samuel Hindman, forefinger and jaw; S. C. Barber, leg; H. J. Sultith, lung, (head.) Company H: Sergeant Peter Householder, side; Corporals Levi J. Holinsinger, neck; E. G. Lawrence, leg; Privates A. Billing, right hip; H. H. Bennett, head; John Goddington, wrist; George Detwiller, shoulder and wrist; John Cosut, thigh; Jacob S. Grove, right thigh; Levi E. Hays, right hip; W. W. Johnson, left shoulder; Davis W. Morteith, leg; Lewis Miller, right elbow; E. Rife, right side; Otho Sice, shoulder. Company I: Sergeants Joseph Feller, left groin; Philip Gelwicks, right leg; Levi Lower, left heel; John C. Gelwicks, thigh; Corporals George Robbins, leg; Hiram H. Mayward, groin; Privates K. Ransom, right leg; Joseph Saver, right wrist; Philip Quicktremer, back; Peter Farrel, leg; Christian Bachman, leg; Jesse H. Berlin. Company K: Privates Nathan Conner; Daniel Madder, wrist; Nelson O'Hara, both thighs and knee; W. J. Rodgers, left side; Thomas Gaddis, right hip.

TWENTY-NINTH INDIANA REGIMENT.

Killed.—Company C: Privates Robert Donnely and Adam Sigrider. Company E: Private Joseph Chresnel. Company G: Captain —— Stebbins. Company I: Private Wm. Crawford.

Wounded.—Company A: Privates Hugh Guthrie, foot; Anson Brown, right leg. Company B: Private John Stonebreaker, right leg. Company C: Privates James Houghton, left thigh; John Bach, left foot; Henry Holmes, thigh; John Schofer, arm; B. H. Brown, arm; and James Chine, left thigh. Company D: Privates J. H. Dunlap, hand; Albert H. Har, shoulder; and Silas E. Bascom, right thigh. Company E: Lieutenant P. Dunn, right foot; Privates Wm. Cline, left foot; John Tuttle, right lung; Austin Sargant, left thigh; Wm. H. Steavson; and Daniel White, right leg. Company G: Private O. Bushnell, face and knee. Company I: Privates Geo. Mopholder, lung, (dead;) Sylvester Crawford; and F. M. Smith, right leg.

FORTY-SECOND ILLINOIS REGIMENT.

Killed.—Colonel Roberts. Company A: Privates Eli Carson and John Minnich. Company B: Lieutenant Julian Letterman and Private Fred. Litsney. Company C: Privates Franklin Bush and Warren Reynolds. Company E: Privates D. C. Arnold and A. J. Northrop. Company H: Lieutenant Cyrus B. Chipman, Sergeant William H. Perry, Corporals P. Paddock and C. M. Harrison, and Private A. Jeffers. Company I: Corporal Alexander Smith and Privates Gorden J. Carpenter and John Therson. Company K: Sergeant Perry C. Bowen and Ordandott Benson.

Wounded.—Company A: Corporals Anthony Daly, severely, and Dwight A. Linedler, severely; Privates Duncan Hamilton, severely; Frederick Dreghorm, severely; George Stole, severely; Charles A. Jacques, severely; and Henry J. Schott, severely. Company B: Privates Patrick Shirts, severely; Hermann Peters, severely; George Godfrey, severely; William Bincint, severely; Swartz Andrews, severely; Peter Shoemaker, severely; and Henry Dougherst, severely. Company C: Sergeants John Abarebeen, shoulder and wrist: Orill Powell, right arm; and Barnard Powell, right leg, slightly; Corporal Martin L. Holt, right leg, slightly; Privates William Cornish, arm; Benjamin J. Gardner, head; Orlin L. Higgins, leg; Rolin H. Egerton, arm; Wilbert Writing, arm; John Wallace, arm; and Charles Johnson, thigh, severely. Company D: Sergeants M. J. Sheridan, leg, severely, and John W. Hill, left hand; Corporal Henry Wells, shoulder; Privates William O. Kelsey, foot; Thaddeus Mott, foot; Nicholas Machin, thigh; Nathaniel Redford, arm; Adam Stuoyer, thigh; Richard Hill, leg; David B. Whitmore, arm; William B. Watson, arm; and Julius J. Worcester, arm. Company E: Sergeant Leonard B. Norton, shoulder; Corporals Henry Lucas, shoulder; O. F. Mowery, shoulder; Byron J. Dart, shoulder; Charles Schrode, shoulder; and C. Herman, shoulder; Privates Hiram Caston, thigh; G. Henderson; Kon. M. Donald; John Peters, thigh; and John Fillitson, hip. Company F: Sergeant Charles Ledyard, hip; Corporal C. R. Perkins, both legs; Privates Charles Ashling, knee; George Round; R. B. Welch, slightly; J. G. Oldritch, slightly; J. D. Somes, severely; William Buykdall, slightly. Company G: Sergeant George W. Bagnall, elbow; Privates Edward A. Kely, thigh; James W. Barber, head; Daniel Beamer, leg; Charles E. Dix, slightly; John D. Dorkey, head; Burnett Herle, head; Charles M. Verdy, arms; William Slatterly, hand; and Benjamin Singer, leg. Company H: Sergeant Stephen H. Reynolds, hand; Corporal James Pusard, arm; Privates James L. Perdy, shoulder; William Billings; J. Colomb; Linly J. Ford; J. P. Fry; J. A. Gibson; J. Stenhauser; P. Sash; J. H. Jarmer, and F. E. O. Vogland. Company I: Corporal Charles Limstrom; Privates George W. Boardman; Edward Fauaix; Christian Johnson; Henry Hale; Benjamin Morse; John Petty; Aaron C. Smith, severely; William Smith; Henry W. Shoemaker, severely; and Joseph Faller, slightly. Company K: Sergeant James M. McDelan, thigh; Corporal J. G. Beard, leg; Privates P. F. Arst, hip; Peter Semly, leg; C. Nichols, leg; E. B. Edmonds, thigh; and Thomas Condon, leg.

FIFTY-FIRST ILLINOIS REGIMENT.

Killed.—Company A: Lieutenant John S. Weith. Company B: Corporal Mathew Mansfield and Private Hill Stason. Company C: Sergeant Thomas Barnes. Company E: Corporal John D. Jones. Company H: Private George Monderaut.

Wounded.—Major Chas. W. Davis. Company A: Privates John Kelly, John Connel, and Thomas Hays. Company B: Captain James S. Boyd, Privates Samuel Wilson, Silas Cunmings, James Miller, James Brannon, William Gavin, Eli Shreeve, Patrick Clark, David Beak, William Gardner, William Dinsmore, and Jerome Morgan. Company C: Privates Frederick W. Camps, Ethan Hoover, Robert Crawford, Rufus Dunnan, and J. R. Loback. Company E: Sergeant Benton Runnel, Corporal John S. Dougherty, Privates Anderson Bailor, James Nelson, William Pilkington, and George E. Chapman. Company F: Privates Thomas W. Marcus, David A. Shaffer, and Thomas H. Mason. Company G: Corporal John Nelson, Privates H. Gibson, Patrick Lyons, and Lewis Bonnshear. Company H: Captains Stephen M. Alliston and C. B. Whiston, Privates Henry Gibson, and Jeremiah Miller. Company K: Sergeant Henry A. Bush and Private Elon Clark.

TWENTY-SECOND ILLINOIS REGIMENT.

Killed.—Company A: Corporal Thomas Kirkham. Company B: Sergeant William Davis, Privates Pat. McHessing and John C. Perrine. Company C: Corporal G. Vote and Private William Arthur. Company D: Sergeant T. C. P. White, Privates A. D. Albert and A. Pettyoyher. Company E: Privates E. R. Wheeler, Samuel Davenport, and John Fisher. Company F: Privates Charles Bochman and Charles Gilbert. Company I: Sergeant John A. Beck, Privates John Macks, John Rose, and Thomas Malone. Company K: Corporal Fred. Lewis, and Privates Jerome Donnovan and John McGow.

Wounded.—Company A: Sergeant Obed Turk, Corporals Albert Mace, J. Pickering, Fred. Carter, Privates Jacob Engler, F. Mellink, A. Rider, Robert MacDonald, William Mace, John Sesmir, and William Umberge. Company B: Sergeant Henry D. Rossiter, Corporal E. Olden, Privates Ed. Hilton, Thomas Lincoln, S. S. Alford, Loomis Robb. Company C: Captain William A. Gregory, Sergeant A. H. Quinn, Privates N. Ames, John Kamp, and C. M. Galloway. Company D: Sergeant Joel Basely, Corporal Robert Beams, Privates E. Heal, John Alexander, N. Coleman, H. O. Tile, M. Handly, and O. Stevans. Company E: Captains Jas. Murry and Jas. Collins, Privates Peter McVay, John Luggs, M. V. Cornelius, and P. P. S. Dewy. Company F: Captain H. Bornemann, Corporal Charles Seigfried, Privates C. B. Murdoff, J. Larsen, Loomis Vessels, and George Schmidt. Company G: Sergeants A. Lamb, J. F. Gregory, Clinton B. Hall, and Mirlin Ireland; Corporals A. F. Williams and —— Hoffman; Privates G. W. Blankinship, L. W. Cunningham, G. W. Cunningham, William Gilmore, M. Hogan, Jacob Van Patten, Nathaniel Scott, Harvey Simpson, Charles Gates, and William Hammond. Company I: Captain N. A. French, Sergeant D. H. Cowle; Corporals William Gray and John R. Allen; Privates A. Gibson, M. Kavanaugh, Calvin Hodges, Wisley Lafferty, and A. S. Carlton. Company K: Sergeant Fred. Welty, Corporal —— Besslar; Privates M. Hennyberry, E. Jones, L. L. Jenkins, M. Keting, Pat. McVary, Pat. McAvery, J. Aver, J. Pendergrass, William Thomas, George Thomas, and James Fusil.

FIRST ILLINOIS ARTILLERY REGIMENT.

Killed.—Company C: Sergeant G. W. Cooper; Privates Ashbury Smith, John Wilder, John Bennett, and Charles Zeisig.

Wounded.—Company C: Captain Charles Hauteling; Sergeant Charles P. Whiteman; Corporals M. P. B. Channel, O. D. Gries, and J. A. Fitzimmons; Privates Lafayette Bruneville, Martin Zohner, A. Dallas, John Doherty, Adam Eley, Jacob Goddard, Henry Miller, John B. Nettles, Michael Leary, Samuel Peterson; W. S. Robinson, Jesse Richardson, William Stephens, W. E. Dobson, and Jacob Shenk.

TWENTY-FOURTH WISCONSIN REGIMENT.

Killed.—Company A: Private Charles Cooksen. Company B: Privates G. Rockwell, R. Joyce, and J. Cockrane. Company C: Privates E. Eckhart and R. Panca. Company D: Lieutenant Nix, Privates G. Gregg and S. Hennessy. Company E: Privates D. Springshead, A. Quenand, and J. R. Colman. Company G: Corporal Frank Hall. Company H: Private John Eder. Company I: Private W. Regan. Company K: Privates J. Gibbert, Aug. Gage, and N. B. Brooks.

Wounded.—Company A: Privates George Trecker, hand; F. Fowler, right leg; Peter Comeilie, ankle. Company B: Privates Jas. Smythe, unknown; G. Merrick, abdomen; S. Williams, right leg; D. Newcomb, breast; A.

Weber, neck; Ph. Ward, face. Company C: Sergeant W. Mash, shoulder; Corporals Thomas Wyck, face; G. Nockerneame, face; Privates G. Beck, right leg; M. Bergner, hip; Fr. Zettela, shoulder; H. Giger, right arm. Company D: Private Pat. Ryan, leg. Company E: Privates John Banett, leg; W. Queesnan, unknown; James Harvey, left arm; G. Krause, left thigh. Company F: Privates John Dunn, foot and leg; John McKey, hand; John James, leg; George Creighton, right hand; Frank Kittridge, left thigh; M. Parkinson, wrist. Company G: Sergeant H. W. Carter, leg; Privates John James, thigh; M. Smith, thigh; Harry Weldon, leg. Company H: Privates M. Reily, unknown; F. Parker, morea; D. Murphy, unknown; J. Weiskoff, unknown; Charles Bish, hand. Company I: Corporal J. Berth, arm; Privates J. Cameron, knee; B. F. Marshall, arm; —— Galdrielson, finger; M. Fanencamp, hand; J. French, head; C. Andacher, left thigh. Company I: H. Ulrich, left arm; Ed. Curly, head and hand; N. Hurm, leg; M. Hulman, leg. Company K: D. Saulsbury, left leg; John Guller, shoulder; M. Steffins, unknown; Aug. Wrase, arm; Stephen Smith, foot; Jacob Bender, head; Harvey Baker, penis.

TWENTY-SEVENTH ILLINOIS REGIMENT.

Killed.—Company A: Privates Fred'k Geiger, George Genner, Chas. Pitran, Fred'k Wiseman. Company G: Corporal Wm. D. Mallory; Company H: Private Jas. A. Martin.

Wounded.—Company A: Private Casper Pillman, leg. Company B: Sergeant G. W. Edwards, right arm; Corporal Wm. Hiatt, finger; Privates Pat. Beny, hip; Thos. Hoffman, hip. Company C: First Sergeant Geo. W. Clark, hand shot off; Sergeant F. F. Clark, side; Corporal Wm. A. Osborn, thigh; Privates Wm. Bean, thigh; Thos. Connor, wrist; Wm. Huston, thigh; John Litzman, cheek; Donly Toland, hand; James Macksell. Company D: Sergeants Nathan F. Page, shoulder; John Kennedy, leg; Privates Frank Mott, shoulder; George W. Mallory, shoulder; Andrew W. Johnson. Company E: Sergeant A. M. Boggs; Corporal M. S. Rankin, wrist; Privates Thos. J. McConnell, leg; J. M. Hoyt, arm; John Lowrey, thigh; S. R. Davis, thigh; John O'Riley, foot; A. J. Shiffer; Wm. Moore, leg; L. M. Cook, leg. Company F: Privates Job Fritz, chin; Jas. Brown, ear and shoulder. Company G: Sergeant S. B. Atwater, leg; Privates Joel N. Woodward, face; M. Chamberlin, shoulder; J. F. Eiley, chest. Company H: Corporal Pitia W. Bowen, shoulder; Privates Wm. F. Bewcher, hand; R. Clark, back; Disney Crane, arm;; Jesse Dougherty, legs; Jas. Gray, shoulder; Fred. B. King, hip; Joshua Tyler, arm; Orlando F. Whipky, hip; Elias Worther, arm; Philip Wolf, back and side. Company I: Lieutenant W. S. Bryan, leg; Privates Wm. W. Williams, eyes; J. G. Heaps, arm; John Hall, leg; J. N. Holcomb, arm; C. M. Owen, lung; Lewis Dennis, leg; James Wilburn; F. M. Hartly; A. J. Graham, shoulder; D. B. Frank, neck; Wm Stilwell, leg. Company K: Colonel Harrington, face and thigh; Privates Charles Creamer, breast; Thomas Davidson, leg; John Surgent.

THIRTY-SIXTH ILLINOIS REGIMENT.

Killed.—Company A: Corporals Thomas Fenner and Orlando Nash; Privates Moses F. Gibbs and Thomas Stimler. Company B: Sergeant Daniel McCheny; Private F. Thompson. Company C: Privates Joseph Baxter, W. T. Artimus, D. H. Buchanan, and James Elder. Company D: Sergeant Alexander Stickels; Privates Samuel Yonnes and James Thorp. Company E: Corporals William Benedict and W. Burgess; Privates Nicholas Mahan, Benjamin Sayer, David Vandeuser, Augustus Castor, and James Baird. Company F: Sergeant Michael Boomer; Privates W. H. Jones, K. Spradling, James

Foster, Charles Wangler, A. P. Vanorden, and Cornelius Seward. Company G: Privates Henry Morton and Salmon Heulse. Company H: First Lieutenant L. L. Onson; Corporals Alfred Riggs and Alvin S. Banker; Privates Alonzo Ray, W. M. Floyd, W. M. Hutchings, and Robert Archibald. Company I: Corporal T. Ellis. Company K: Privates George Linhart, George Hall, George R. Pollock, Asoph Adams, and George W. Johnson.

Wounded.—Major Silas Miller, left thigh. Company A: First Lieutenant S. H. Wakeman, arm; Sergeants Alexander Robertson, lung; Alec Sand, hand; Leroy Saulsbury, leg; Corporals B. D. C. Rowland, abdomen; Cyrus Dean, right leg; John W. Aldrich, left hand; Privates J. N. Minor, hand; C. A. Brown, right arm; Freeman Derklee, left leg; John Flood, elbow; Alexander Henderson, right lung; John H. Hewitt, hips; David Munro, neck; M. H. Sabine, left leg; Daniel W. Brown, left leg; Charles Plummer, right ankle; John A. White, left leg. Company B: Captain B. F. Campbell, thigh; Second Lieutenant George S. Douglass, right ankle and thigh; Corporals Henry B. Latham, leg; D. Hazleton, leg; Privates Henry Alcott, leg; William Race, left hand; John Otter, right foot; Adams Reits, left leg; William Vanolin, both thighs; James Campbell, right hand; Thomas McConnel, right leg; James H. Woodward, right breast. Company C: Privates R. J. Colwell, right foot; James L. Dryden, right arm; A. A. Ecklerser, right hand; John B. Edger, right side; Thomas B. Gormly, left arm; William Hartzell, right hand; Fred. Kercher, head; Warren Kingsly, right arm; Ether Kech, head; Francis McClanahan, left hand; James McPherson, face; Walter Reeder, right thigh; John Shock, right side; James H. Smith, shoulder; Abraham Stewart, left arm. Company D: Corporals John C. Taylor, right hand; C. H. Thompson, left cheek; James A. Smith, right side; Harry Kemble, right temple; Privates Henry T. Birch, left thigh; L. Barmsmile, right hip; Allen Averel, left hip; Thomas Welsh, right leg; Samuel Tucker, right shoulder; N. Erickson, left leg; C. H. Johnson, right hand; C. N. Olson, left shoulder; D. R. Seymour, slightly; F. Henning, severely. Company E: Captain A. M. Hobbs, breast; First Sergeant C. Smith, slight; Sergeant Lucius Heminsny, right shoulder; Corporals Daniel Darnill, slight; D. Burnside, slight; Privates Henry Haight, left leg; Fred. Bier, left arm; Alfred Bullard, right leg; James N. Donn, left elbow; James Brown, left side; Clines Butterman, left thigh; Charles W. Doty, right cheek; Aaron Darnell, both hips; Oscar Howe, right arm; James F. Hanell, left hand; William Himler, left shoulder; James S. Hatch, left arm; Gilbert Ketchum, right hand; Elisha E. Lloyd, right hand; James E. Moss, left leg; George Merrill, left side; Lyon Perry, right shoulder; Walter Ralston, left hand; Charles H. Schofield, left shoulder; Joel Wagner, face; Joseph Howard, right side. Company F: Lieutenant George W. Mossman, forehead; Sergeant William J. Bond, both legs; Corporal W. H. Mossman, head; Privates S. S. Smith, right arm; William H. Carter, head; Stephen Cummins, head; Ed. Dopp, right leg; W. Huggert, left side; John Jordan, left leg; Anteni Myers, left leg; Lewis Allen, both hips; Alfred Tomblin, left arm; Albert H. Wolf, back of neck; William Thompson, neck. Company G: Corporals Robert B. Herrie, hand; Daniel Kennedy, right arm; Privates George W. Moody, leg; Jesse H. Brown, neck; J. H. Chamberlain, left arm; Joseph Herbert, left shoulder; Robert Jordan, right shoulder; W. F. Boseman, right thigh; William Seversis, right leg; P. Buchanan, left leg broken. Company H: Second Lieutenant Myron A. Smith, leg; First Sergeant H. M. Crittenden, left arm; Sergeant N. B. Sherwood, right temple; Sergeant John C. Wolf, left arm; Corporal Daniel Hartman, left arm; Privates Charles Crawford, left leg; Jackson Carrol, forehead; Jerome C. Ford, left thigh; John H. Sackett, right hip; David D. Warrick, right shoulder; Myron Harris, right leg; Monroe Troop, left hand; Calvin T. Jones, right lung; Ed. H. Robinson, left leg. Company I: Captain C. K. Merrill, leg; Sergeant D. S. Smith, leg; Privates D. McClung, arm;

Frederick Wetzke, hand; William Varnier, right thigh; John Rosh, thigh; A. Miller, left arm. Company K: First Lieutenant John F. Elliott, left leg; Sergeants John Gordon, right leg; Eldridge Adams, left leg; H. Folson, slightly; Corporals Frank Micks, right thigh; Fred. Hazelhurst, chest; Privates Sidney Wagner, thigh; Brinton Holz, right hip; Samuel W. Gandy, head; Allen Buess, left shoulder; P. Vamrickleton, right leg; Ed. Reeder, right hand; Eugene Alchun, left hand.

Missing.—Company H: Private Robert Kee.

SECOND MISSOURI REGIMENT.

Killed.—Colonel Schæffer, commanding 2d brigade. Company G: Private Tim. O'Brien.

Wounded.—Company A: Corporals William Heitz, right thigh; L. Reinken, left leg. Company B: Bugler J. Mueller, right lower hip; Privates Henry Fenmere, right hand; ——— Eleaser, left arm; Henry Stieman, right arm. Company D: Sergeants H. Kreeler, left hand; J. Wenf, thigh; Privates ——— Bloomer, left leg; C. Huffman, right arm; John Eckard, small of back. Company F: Sergeants Charles Newbert, left shoulder; ——— Vatts, left knee; Privates ——— Erb, leg; L. Katslasser, shoulder; M. Krill, right leg. Company G: Privates George Rendenback, right thigh; Fred. Tissing, leg. Company H: Corporal A. Brandenberg, leg. Company K: Privates George Hellniger, right foot; ——— Saetz, left hip.

FORTY-FOURTH ILLINOIS REGIMENT.

Killed.—Company K: Captain ——— Hosmer; Corporal ——— Johnson.

Wounded.—Captain W. W. Barret, back of head. Company A: Sergeant ——— Dagget, right calf; Privates Patrick O'Brien, head; J. Resbonkonig, head; R. Michlick, upper lip; Lewis Sponknash, right elbow. Company B: Second Lieutenant ——— Parker; Sergeant J. E. Conklin, forehead; Corporal L. D. Wilbur, left ankle; Privates Byron Daren, left calf; George Joles, contusion right arm. Company C: Sergeant D. F. Spring, right calf; Privates H. Coller, left hip; John Allen, contused hip; J. J. Mills, right shoulder. Company E: Captain Ernest Moldenhawer, breast; Adjutant ——— Ranson; Sergeant Ashmud Ruhberg; Privates ——— Manhies; George Apponzeller; ——— Tilman; Charles Halber, right hand. Company F: Sergeant ——— Isom, right shoulder; Privates J. Office, head; B. F. North, left foot; ——— Howe, left leg. Company G: Sergeant C. Wells, right leg; Corporal H. A. Dobson, left arm; Privates J. Murphy, right elbow; J. J. Chaplin, right breast. Company H: Sergeant ——— Evans, left shoulder; Private A. Hamilton, right shoulder. Company I: Private ——— Lacy, left leg. Company K: Corporals Julius Hager, left calf; ——— Norton, left leg; Privates Henry Schmidt, right arm; Udo. Dicks, elbow; George Benson, right finger.

FOURTH INDIANA BATTERY.

Killed.—Corporal W. A. Stoddard; Privates James E. Dale, James Hill, Ed. Nergert, and William Mundell.

Wounded.—Corporal Edgar J. Abbot; Privates C. O. Law, James Small, Robert Harris, William Berdoit, Andrew T. Mitchell, William Abbott, Edwin Smith, Elias Brice, Jesse Baily, John Disard, Simeon Ashton, James Hanold, Charles Lockard, Edwin Logan, and Edwin D. Arnold.

TWENTY-FIRST MICHIGAN REGIMENT.

Killed.—Company A: Private Nelson G. Merril. Company B: Corporal Milton M. Mansfield; Privates Charles D. Hilton and Augustus Hean Ausky. Company C: Private Lester M. Jones. Company D: Private Lyman A. Frost. Company E: Corporal Edwin Rathburn; Privates Theo. Bloomis and Irwin McClain. Company F: Private Christianson Johnson. Company G: Private Jona. Stoddard. Company H: First Sergeant A. A. Sawyer; Privates Septimus Carlton and Charles B. Chillman. Company I: Sergeant William F. Sceer; Privates Robert Morse and Amerson Kachvond. Company K: Corporal Julius F. Barrett.

Wounded.—Adjutant Morris B. Wells, right arm. Company A: Sergeant Carlos D. Loring, shoulder; Privates James Swaggard, left arm; Valentine Bretts, nose; James Bartlett, right leg; George W. Tyler, finger; John W. Westbrook, both legs. Company B: Lieutenant B. D. Fox, right foot; Sergeants William A. Thompson, shoulder; Ezra D. Johnson, left foot; Corporal Edward Barry, hand; Privates DeWitt Aldrich, hand; Edward L. Parker, left thigh; George W. Davis, left thigh; John M. Knapp, right arm; Joseph Largo, left leg; Swet Timothy, back; Daniel W. Wood, hand. Company C: Captain Leonard O. Fitzgerald, face, thigh, and right hand; Sergeant A. C. Leonard, left leg; Corporals Ansel P. Hosier, right leg and arm; William Crabb, right arm three times; Privates John Smith, leg; John O. Kelly, leg; Nelson Killman, right leg; Alvin R. Palmer, finger; Allen Roush, neck. Company D: Privates Harry B. Tripp, foot; Edward Sanderson, foot; D. W. West, ankle; William Whipple, left hip and leg; Joseph H. Canfield, ankle; Elvin Gurnsy, face; James B. Ewit, left foot. Company E: Corporal John Fredricks, side; Privates Charles C. Anderson, arm; William McCoy, leg; Christopher Stone, right side; John S. Alden, right arm; Alexander Cole, right thigh; Joseph Brown, left leg; James Gollesphy, left arm. Company F: Lieutenant John F. Loase, neck and leg; Privates Joseph E. Giles, left leg; William S. Campbell, ankle. Company G: Captain Henry C. Albee, arm and side; Privates J. Sullivan, side; M. Camhoul, arm; J. D. Wilt, right leg; E. Wilbott, right hand; C. Klehan, right leg; Oscar Blood, left arm; H. Cooly, right arm; A. Gottschilling, right hand. Company H: Sergeant Charles E. Beckaup, left leg; Corporal Theodore N. Chapin, ankle; Privates John Moffit, both legs; William R. Foot, both thighs; Charles S. Middler, left side and leg; John G. Dumason, hip; Michael Jaherthofer, left leg; Webster B. Ewing, right leg; William James, side; Milo Willard, right hand. Company I: Sergeants A. A. Olcott, right hand and thigh; Samuel Wooldridge, left thigh; Corporal Sanford White, leg; Privates A. Lowery, knee; James G. Putnam, side; William Gearman, right arm; A. E. Wheelock, side and head; H. Marker, right leg; George D. King, left leg. Company K: Lieutenants A. G. Russell, right arm; Eli E. Barrett, thigh; Sergeant E. B. Potter, arm; Privates Albert Stuck, face; Chas. Lock, leg; Chas. Philips, arm; P. C. Goldsmith, arm; William Bowser, face; Henry Shimer, leg.

EIGHTY-EIGHTH ILLINOIS REGIMENT.

Killed.—Company B: First Lieutenant Thomas F. W. Gillick, Privates Abram Weaver, Henry Millering. Company C: Corporals William T. Owens, Samuel H. Mick, Charles Walker. Company D: Privates Hugh T. Logan, William H. Davis. Company H: Private John Dan. Company I: First Sergeant Eugene Aleyford, Corporal Frederick M. Hollow. Company K: Privates John Roman, George Helm, John Peters.

Wounded.—Company A: Captain George W. Smith, leg; Privates James

B. Sutherland, thumb; Daniel G. Walty, hip; S. R. Gordon, foot. Company B: Privates Andrew Mory, right thigh; Theodore F. Kent, left foot. Company C: First Sergeant Henry C. Griffin, right wrist; Privates Clark O. Mickvise, back; Louis Claremont, back; John Kelly, right shoulder; John Sheriden, shoulder; Thomas Hughes, face; J. S. Cunningham; Henry Mapes, left heel. Company D: Privates Chis. Brinkmar, right forefinger; William J. Campbell, arm; G. H. Myers, right leg; John Patterson, right side; M. McCasson, arm. Company E: Corporal Daniel Palmer, head and right thigh; Privates J. B. Fritz; Thomas Kehoe, left thigh; Archie Vanhauter, palm of hand. Company F: Sergeant Edwin C. Miller, shoulder; Corporal C. F. Hearig, hand; Privates Thomas Morris, hand; John F. Harper, back; David Shreeves, leg; Willard Elyea, arm; Julius Fessedie, thigh; Howard Gittings, thigh; William Woodruff, arm. Company G: Corporal Naden Cox; Privates Thomas Berdan, arm; William H. Cummings, head; C. F. Gerring, right thigh; Jacob Hanmick, arm; Abram Keldar, right hand; John McDonald, left elbow; William Melvin. Company H: First Sergeant Henry C. Bingham, neck; Privates W. H. Bullon, finger and leg; Andrew Allen, Alonzo A. Hyde. Company I: Privates Loder Fumer, head; James B. Hall, hand; Samuel Semblick, right thigh; Jacob Sigwall, Richard Vaucher. Company K: First Lieutenant H. C. McDonald, Corporal Andrew Cox.

SEVENTY-THIRD ILLINOIS REGIMENT.

Killed.—First Sergeant C. B. Mantle and Privates Ed. M. Shrake and James O'Neal, company A; Privates Norris Johns and Richard Robinson, company B; Privates John Dye and James H. Yoho, company C; Captain Edward Allsop, and Private W. B. Tipton, company F; James S. Price, company G; Privates David Lancaster and George Martin, company H; Corporal G. W. Dilman, company K.

Wounded.—Major William A. Presson, side; Sergeant Major Henry Carter, left hand. Company A: First Lieutenant Ed. W. Bennett, leg; Corporal James A. Armstrong, right leg; Privates David C. Fletcher, right leg; S. C. Robins, left arm; W. H. Maxwell, shoulder; W. R. Constant, right hand; A. J. Perry, left shoulder; William Meredith, right shoulder; A. B. Hiath, left hip; D. H. Bechtel, right hip; R. Montgomery, right breast; Jacob Ruppler, right arm; J. C. Chambers, right finger; C. B. McDonald, left arm. Company B: Privates Jacob Heildebrand, left shoulder; Calvin F. Randolph, hips; Martin Freeman, left arm; A. J. Reid, head; William B. McNicholas, hip. Company C: Private John J. Harstead, head. Company D: Privates Sam'l Richards, leg; Ed. Williamson, both hands; Samuel D. Gava, left shoulder; D. Clover, left hip; J. Conze, both legs. Company E: Lieutenant B. Presser, leg; Private George Pirce, right foot. Company F: Lieutenant William Barrick, right arm; Sergeant Harvey Long, foot; Privates William R. Martin, right breast; A. Montgomery, breast; Benjamin Pounds, leg; Ransom Kelsey, left leg; Isaac C. Coil, right hip; William Toberman, left hand; Benj. Hobbs, right leg; Charles Kelly, head; William Weaver, ankle. Company H: Corporal Thomas Wade, head; Privates Thomas Bradburn, left breast; Henry Bennett, hand; John J. Genler, hand and face; Richard Bickendyke, foot. Company I: Sergeant Elisha T. McComas, left knee; Privates George Landgive, left foot; J. W. Fisher, left hip; L. W. Emmons, left thigh; A. M. Cassedy, left leg; J. M. Dewy, breast; H. M. Caughman, mouth; Hugh McLaughlin, back; Samuel D. Foster, foot. Company K: First Sergeant D. M. Davis, shoulder; Privates Henry Hinchcliff, both legs; Joseph Jarvis, left arm; Harrison Tamer, right thigh.

FIFTEENTH MISSOURI REGIMENT.

Killed.—Company C: Captain M. Zimmerman; Private Philip Hostetter. Company B: Second Lieutenant ——— Tunceus. Company D: ——— Diel. Company E: Second Lieutenant ——— Bellner; First Sergeant ——— Grandjean. Company F: Privates Freid Holloway, Henry Schnob, and Henry Feihrer. Company G: Mich. Hausler. Company K: Privates John Bowming, ——— Schnaesser, and Christ. Gerber.

Wounded.—Company A: Private Herman George, back. Company B: Captain ——— Ernst, shoulder; Corporal John Baily, arm; Musician Theoph. Suter, thigh; Privates Gabriel First, back; and ——— Reber, head. Company C: Bugler George Addelmott, thigh; Privates John Operus, ——— Speilman, shoulder; ——— Sedden, thigh; and ——— Blanders. Company D: First Lieutenant ——— Shroeder, breast. Company E: Privates Anton Lung, foot and arm; Nick. Decker, leg; M. Heicht, breast; John Roeth, leg; ——— Speilberger, head. Company F: Second Lieutenant ——— Molarhard, leg; First Sergeant Geischten, arm; Sergeant James Ratch, head; Privates Bemaner, head; Fred. Halslop, wounded and prisoner; ——— Reiterman, and ——— Miller, leg. Company G: Privates J. Battinghoffer, arm; ——— Byer, thigh; Chris. Jung, Gottleib Debler, George Domberg, Henry Urich, George Hen, head; and Andrew Oth, hip. Company H: ——— Winzing, leg; and ——— Barmdel, leg. Company I: Privates Julius Riel, calf; Victor Senn, eye; Simeon Brendle, foot. Company K: Second Lieutenant Jacob Lieb, head; Privates Andrew Myers, thigh; John Kneckenback, M. Kneckenback, John Kurtz, Philip Barker, and ——— Steiner.

TWENTY-SECOND ILLINOIS REGIMENT.

Killed.—Company A: Privates James Essington. Company E: Private Samuel McAdams. Company H: Private James Frazer. Company K: Private Nicholas Solesby.

Wounded.—Company A: Sergeant Hobart Fink, ankle; Corporal S. Smith, arm; Privates John Ford, thigh; John Grob, knee; and Andrew Reeder, knee. Company E: Privates Jackson Green, arm; and James Alderman, side. Company H: Private Audolph Jacobi, legs. Company K: Private Barney Cull, hand.

THIRTY-SIXTH ILLINOIS REGIMENT.

Killed.—Company A: Privates Henry Clasen and F. A. Burmaster. Company K: Private George Munsol.

Wounded.—Company A: Private M. G. Townsend, thigh. Company B: Captain W. A. Blakesler, leg. Company C: Private J. F. Young, wrist. Company G: Privates Robert Brandt, leg; and William Gould, neck. Company K: Privates N. Sanders, thigh; James H. Hogan, hip; Joseph Leveran, hand; Lucien Bulton, ankle and knee; John Peterson, hip; John McCreeny, thigh.

FORTY-SECOND ILLINOIS REGIMENT.

Killed.—Company C: Private William E. Emery and ——— Franklin.

Wounded.—Company C: Captain James Lighton, face; Sergeant Jehud Hull, thigh; Privates George W. Hand, pelvis; C. Carcenus, thigh; F. C. Hook, foot; Alfred Ericcson, hip; Peter McConnel, face; and J. Bowen, leg. Company D: Private H. Shroyer, thigh. Company H: Private M. Sash, foot.

FIFTY-FIRST ILLINOIS REGIMENT.

Wounded.—Company B: David Beall, finger. Company D: Reuben Jefferson, leg; and Milton Kingston, leg. Company G: Samuel McFadden, hip.

Company K: Sergeant Charles Hill, scalp; Privates A. W. Duffey, shoulder; and Charles Peterson, arm.

EIGHTY-EIGHTH ILLINOIS REGIMENT.

Killed.—Company B: Private Abram Wern.

Wounded.—Company F: Privates E. A. Day, ankle; M. H. Watts, knee; and Levi D. Drake, foot. Company H: Captain George W. Smith, left leg.

TWENTY-FOURTH WISCONSIN REGIMENT.

Killed.—Company K: Private Henry Pluff.

Wounded.—Company A: Lieutenant George Bleyer, leg. Company D: Private J. M. Jeffries, body and both hands. Company K: Private J. W. Powell, shoulder.

FOURTH INDIANA BATTERY.

Wounded.—Sergeant John Young, head; Privates Charles Howe, arm; and W. C. Kirk, thigh.

HEADQUARTERS 1ST BRIGADE, 1ST DIVISION,
RIGHT WING 14TH ARMY CORPS,
In camp south of Murfreesboro', January 9, 1862.

LIEUTENANT: I have the honor to submit the following report of the part taken by the 1st brigade in the late engagements resulting in the taking of Murfreesboro'.

In compliance with the order of Brigadier General Davis, commanding division, we left camp, at St. James Chapel, at daylight on the 26th day of December, 1862, and marched in the direction of Nolensville, this brigade being in advance. We soon came upon the enemy's cavalry. Company B, 36th Illinois cavalry, under the direction of Captain Pease, of Brigadier General Davis's staff, occupied the road, and the 59th Illinois infantry was thrown out as skirmishers on each side of it. A lively skirmish was kept up until we reached Nolensville, when the enemy appeared in force and opened upon the brigade with artillery.

The left of our line of battle rested upon the pike, the right occupying a hill commanding the town. Captain Pinney's 5th Wisconsin battery opened upon the enemy and drove them from the town.

A large force of cavalry was seen moving to the right and dismounting with the evident intention of attacking our right and rear and dislodging us from the hill. The 22d regiment Indiana infantry was moved to the right to repel this attack, and Colonel Carlin's and Woodruff's brigades, deployed, by order of Brigadier General Davis, upon our right, soon came up, and the enemy were driven from their position and forced to withdraw their artillery.

This brigade, on the left of the line of battle, moved forward up the pike leading to Triune—Pinney's battery being, on the pike, the 22d Indiana and the 74th Illinois on its right, and the 75th and 59th Illinois on its left. The enemy were posted in a position of great natural strength about two miles from Nolensville, on the right and left of the pike, with one section of artillery on and the remainder near the road. Pinney's battery, from a knoll to the left of the pike, opened at short range with all his guns, and this brigade, on the left of Colonel Carlin's, marched steadily forward, driving the enemy from the hill, where they were compelled to abandon one piece of artillery. This march had been made in a drenching rain, and the men, exhausted by their exertions upon the muddy road and the excitements of the day, bivouacked on the field, for the possession of which they had fought. The following day this brigade marched in rear of Colonel Carlin's nearly to Triune, it raining constantly and being very cold.

December 29 we marched in rear of Colonel Woodruff's brigade, on the "Bole Jack," road, towards Murfreesboro'. About two miles from Overall's creek, by order of Brigadier General Davis, I deployed the brigade on the right of the road, and moved forward nearly to the creek, where we bivouacked in the rain without fires.

In the morning of December 30 we marched across the fields on the right of the Wilkinson pike, the 74th and 75th regiments Illinois infantry deployed on the right of Colonel Carlin's brigade, and being the right of the entire army, the 59th regiments Illinois infantry in reserve to support the battery, and the 22d regiment Indiana infantry in a position to protect the right flank from the enemy's cavalry, which were continually hovering about and engaging the skirmishers. I directed Captain Sher, who, by order of Brigadier General Davis, reported to me with company B, 36th Illinois cavalry, to throw out skirmishers and march upon our right flank, where he repeatedly engaged and drove back the cavalry threatening our line. The skirmishing in front grew more brisk, and late in the afternoon the enemy were found in force, strongly posted, and opened upon us with artillery from our front and right, killing one and wounding several men. Captain Hale, acting as major of the 75th Illinois, and Lieutenant Hall, of my staff, each had a horse killed under them.

General Kirk's brigade at this time moved into position upon our right.

Captain Pinney's battery drove back the enemy from our front, and under cover of his fire our skirmishers were advanced to the open field, when night closed the contest. The men lay down without fires or shelter, and in the morning were awakened and standing in order of battle one hour before the first dawn of light. The battery horses stood at their pieces during the night ready for any emergency.

As soon as it become light the enemy were discovered moving in great numbers towards our right and nearly parallel with our line, with the evident design of turning the right wing of the army. I immediately despatched Lieutenant Jones, of my staff, to inform Brigadier General Davis.

The right of the brigade extended into a dense and almost impenetrable thicket of cedars, connecting there with the left of General Kirk's brigade, and in that direction nothing could be seen on account of the thicket. For more than half an hour the enemy's dark columns flowed towards our right where the volleys of musketry and their advancing cheers from that direction assured me that they had driven the brigades on our right from their position, and were already in our rear, and I accordingly changed front nearly perpendicularly to the rear to meet them.

The 74th Illinois, Colonel Jason Marsh, and the 75th Illinois, commanded by Lieutenant Colonel J. E. Bennett, were stationed behind a fence in the edge of the timber. By order of Brigadier General Davis several companies were added to our force of skirmishers, and under his direction Pinney's battery took position in a cornfield with the 59th Illinois infantry, commanded by Captain H. E. Payne, supporting it on the left. Perceiving that the enemy were still far beyond our right, I deployed my reserve regiment, the 22d Indiana, Colonel Gooding commanding, on the right of the battery. The 6th regiment Indiana infanty, having been separated from its brigade, was placed about four hundred paces in rear as a reserve.

Captain Pinney opened upon the advancing line with all his guns, and when they came within range of his canister and the fire of the supporting regiment the execution was so great that the entire line recoiled before it, but after temporary confusion they were rallied and lay down. The enemy opened a battery upon the hill and advanced a second line.

Captain Pinney's guns were splendidly handled, and great credit is due to

Lieutenants Humphreys, Gardner, and Mr. Knight, and to the men of the company for their promptness and skill. No shots were wasted over the heads of the enemy. For about thirty minutes this fierce contest continued, while the enemy on our right had advanced so as to again endanger our rear.

As those in front rallied and charged upon the battery on the double quick, the 59th Illinois regiment fixed bayonets to receive them, but with the large force unopposed upon our right the position was already untenable, even though that in front were repulsed, and I ordered the battery withdrawn.

Captain Pinney was dangerously, if not mortally, wounded. He fell and was left on the spot where he executed his most gallant deeds. Lieutenant Colonel Tanner, of the 22d Indiana, and many others seriously wounded, were left upon the field.

Eighteen of the battery horses were disabled, and one gun in consequence could not be brought off. One Parrott gun had but two wounded horses before it. I ordered the 59th regiment to drag the guns to the rear. As the battery reached the Nashville pike it was charged upon by cavalry and partially captured, but they were quickly driven away by the 4th regiment regular cavalry, and crossing Overall's creek it took a position, under the direction of Lieutenant Hall, on a hill to the right of the Nashville pike, from which it repeatedly shelled, and drove back the enemy's cavalry endeavoring to take possession of the road.

The 74th and 75th Illinois regiments fell back across the cotton-field, and under the direction of Lieutenant Jones, who also rallied a number of detachments from other regiments, made a determined resistance, again checking the foe. The fresh troops from the reserves here relieved the brigade, and I proceeded to the pike, reformed my shattered battalions, and supplied them with ammunition.

I was soon ordered by Brigadier General Davis to move up the pike and take position on the right of the line, and here, exhausted, the men lay down for the night. The next morning I was ordered to occupy the open field to the left of the pike, where I caused a breastwork to be thrown up, the battery being in position to enfilade an enemy's lines attempting an attack. A strong force of skirmishers was thrown out, covering our front and right. The enemy opened a battery upon us, but after a few well-directed shells from Pinney's Parrott gun they ceased firing. During the following day the constant skirmishing was kept up on our front, and a number of prisoners were taken. Late in the afternoon we were ordered to cross Stone river. The stream was swollen from the heavy rains, but the entire brigade, hearing the volleys of musketry on the other side, plunged into it with cheers and debouched upon the field which was still being contended for, and, rapidly forming, hurried to the front. All that stormy night the men who had been previously soaked in fording the river stood by their arms without fires, the 22d Indiana and 75th Illinois busily engaged in constructing a breastwork. During the night our pickets, under charge of Major Dutcher, of the 74th Illinois, contested for the possession of the fields and woods in our front, and advanced a considerable distance. Substantial breastworks were completed during January 3 under a constant fire of sharpshooters, and at night, in a pouring rain, the men again lay upon their arms. At 2 o'clock the next morning the battery was ordered to recross the river, and at 4 o'clock, in a torrent of rain, the brigade forded the swollen stream and took its former position on the right, where it remained until January 6, when, passing through Murfreesboro', we encamped at this place.

During the long contest, and notwithstanding the extreme inclemency of the weather and the scarcity of provisions, no word of complaint was heard. Officers and men seemed alike anxious to do their full duty as patriot soldiers. In our advance they pushed forward boldly, and when greatly superior numbers were hurled against them they awaited the onset with the utmost coolness and determination. The temporary confusion which occurred when they fell back was caused, to a considerable extent, by the large force of skirmishers thrown out to check the enemy, having been driven towards the left instead of directly upon their own regiments. The deliberation and order with which the 74th Illinois retired is especially commended.

During the series of engagements the several regimental commanders displayed great persistence and resolution, and everywhere encouraged their men.

Too much praise cannot be awarded to the dauntless and skilful Captain Pinney, whose characteristic conduct elicited compliment even from his foes.

I herewith transmit the reports of the regimental and battery commanders, together with a full list of casualties.

The gallant bearing of Captain Hale, of the 75th Illinois, who had chief command of the skirmishers; of Captain Litson, of the 22d Indiana, and of Sergeant P. S. Furguson, of company G, 59th Illinois, one of the skirmishers, is deserving of mention. Assistant Surgeon Corbus, of the 75th Illinois, and Assistant Surgeon Bunce, of the 59th Illinois, remained with and took care of our wounded while the fight was raging around them.

The zeal and decision shown by Lieutenants Jones, Hall, Hatch, and Baker, members of my staff, and the intrepidity of my faithful orderly, George Fogle, demands my highest commendation.

The names of the self-constituted messengers who carried to Nashville with such unparalleled celerity the tidings of the battle of December 31 have already been forwarded. In the hour of trial showing themselves false as the news they manufactured and disseminated, their infamy only makes more bright by contrast the imperishable record of those who nobly struggled or bravely fell in that unequal contest.

I have the honor to be, very respectfully, your obedient servant,

P. SIDNEY POST,
Colonel Commanding 1st Brigade.

Lieutenant T. W. MORRISON,
Acting Assistant Adjutant General, 1st Division.

List of casualties in the first brigade, first division, right wing, fourteenth army corps, in the engagements before Murfreesboro'.

Twenty-second regiment Indiana infantry, (Colonel Gooding.)

Lieutenant Colonel Thomas B. Tanner, severely wounded and a prisoner.

Company A, (Second Lieutenant John Gooding.)—Wounded: Corporal Thomas Bliten, severely in thigh; Privates John Brooks, severely in back; Thomas Myrar, slightly in left arm; William Putz, slightly in left arm.

Company B, (First Lieutenant A. D. Sawyer.)—Wounded: Second Lieutenant W. H. Inland, slightly in left leg; Privates G. W. Boas, slightly in left leg; Thomas Thompson, severely in left leg and arm.

Company C, (Captain W. H. Taggard.)—Wounded: Corporal William Seal, severely in left thigh; Privates Josephus Smith, slightly in left leg and face; David A. Whitehorn, slightly in right leg. Prisoner: William Hobbs.

Company D, (Second Lieutenant Patrick Carney.)—Wounded: Privates George W. Morris, slightly in left ankle; Alfred Coffman, slightly in left hand. Missing: Corporal George Bard; Privates Elerius Barwill, Walter Harrison, and Calvin Ogle.

Company E, (Captain W. H. Snodgrass.)—Killed: Sergeant Patrick Madden and Private Samuel W. Leap. Wounded: Privates Thomas A. Wilson, severely in right thigh; William H. Davis, slightly in thumb; Levi Kelso, severely in right hand; Henry W. Bard, slightly in left hand; William Thompson, severely in right foot; Josiah W. Snyder, severely in left shoulder. Missing: Frederick Holt, James Cain, and Henry Jordan.

Company F, (Captain E. H. Stepleton.)—Wounded: Second Lieutenant William T. Briggs, slightly in left thigh; Private Ruel W. Fugit, severely in left hand. Missing: Abraham Holcraft, Delaney W. Fague, and William Vandusen.

Company G, (Sergeant A. J. Moss.)—Killed: Private Bernard Kelly. Wounded: Corporal George Ball, slightly in arm; Privates George Thoymer, dangerously; Robert Belligrew, slightly in leg.

Company H, (Captain William Powers.)—Killed: Privates John Summerville, Levi Balwin, and John Clark. Wounded: Captain William Powers, slightly in leg and ankle; Sergeant William Ewood, slightly in ankle; Corporals Jasper Ross, severely in foot; Albert Close, slightly in elbow; Privates Levi W. Brandt, slightly in left breast; Wesley Rutherford, slightly in hand; John Patrick, severely in thigh; William Chappel, slightly in leg; Allen Fuller, severely in wrist. Missing: Sergeant John Moore, Privates William Rude and Washington Hogg.

Company I, (Second Lieutenant R. V. Marshall.)—Wounded: Corporal James A. Bell, severely in left ankle; Privates John Miller, severely in arm; James F. Martin, slightly in shoulder. Missing: Corporal Wilson S. Dean.

Company K, (Captain R. H. Litson.)—Killed: Private Conrad Coon. Wounded: Captain R. H. Litson, severely in knee. Missing: Privates Thomas Horsman, John Horton, James O'Neal, and John Prentice.

Recapitulation.

Commissioned officers wounded	5
Enlisted men wounded	39
Enlisted men killed	7
Enlisted men missing	18
Total killed, wounded, and misssing	64

Fifty-ninth regiment Illinois infantry, (Captain H. E. Paine.)

Acting Adjutant Second Lieutenant Heslip Phillips, missing; Quartermaster Frederick Brashear, (supposed prisoner;) Commissary Sergeant Thomas Melvin, (supposed prisoner;) Sergeant Major John Ford Smith, (supposed prisoner.)

Company A, (Second Lieutenant D. M. Baily.)—Captain Clayton Hale, (supposed prisoner.) Wounded: Privates Graham Martin, severely in left side; John Glendon, slightly in shoulder; Joseph N. Byron, slightly in thigh; Thomas J. Hooper, severely and missing. Missing: Corporal Richard Allen; Privates Nathan B. Westbrook, Andrew Ryan. Prisoner: Private Joel B. Godfrey.

Company B, (Lieutenant James Johnson.)—Wounded: Corporal Joseph R. Dennis, severely and missing; Private Wesley B. Adams, slightly.

Company C, (Lieutenant D. M. Henderson.)—Killed: Privates James H. Sheets, Henry Barnum. Wounded: Joel Hyatt, James Elidge, Jasper Hutchison, Marshal R. Purdam, George Herr, John Cheeley, (slightly,) Henry Dabbs, (slightly,) Samuel J. Jacobs, (slightly.)

Company D, (Captain O. W. Frazier.)—Killed: Sergeant John J. Kathan; Private Andrew J. Watts. Wounded: Privates Charles B. Hinnason, slightly, in hand; Joseph Walter, slightly in head; Henry Diedrich, slightly in abdomen; Corporals John Egan, slightly, missing; Andrew Sacket, slightly missing; Private Huchison Macauley, severely, missing; Corporal John Goos, missing. Prisoners: Privates George A. Brewer, Samuel W. Beard, Charles N. Brown, Jesse Hedrick, James Peterkin, Peter Spohn.

Company E, (Lieutenant J. H. Knight.)—Wounded: Corporal Chesley Allen, slightly in breast; Privates William Bostwick, slightly in hand; Frederick

Oderdorph, slightly in head; Herman Smink, slightly in hand; George Semer, slightly in hand; John Shult, slightly in hip; Nehemiah C. Braun, severely, missing; Charles A. McNabb, missing.

Company F, (Lieutenant Reuben Maddox.)—Killed: Private Jacob A. Houser. Wounded: Privates Jacob Flint, slightly; John A. P. Kelly, slightly; Corporal Thomas J. Slusser, severely, missing; Privates James Slusser, severely, missing; Levi H. Sharp, slightly, missing. Prisoners: Corporals Wesley Kitchen, Tilghman H. Jones.

Company G, (Captain G. S. Hackney.)—Killed: Sergeant Alfred C. Barber; Corporal Reuben A. Cumings. Missing: Privates Felix Morris, Davidson May. Prisoners: Sergeant William W. Oakes; Private Henry F. McLining; Musician George R. Strickland.

Company H, (Lieutenant H. Wiley.)—Wounded: Corporals George M. Sparks, Alexander C. Pepper; Privates Jesse Adams, Patrick Reynolds, Ford White, Albert B. Latta. Missing: Obediah McNanny.

Company I, (Lieutenant James Johnson.)—Wounded: Private Richard Ferden. Missing: Private Samuel Fisherman. Prisoner: Henry Newwus.

Company K, (First Lieutenant John M. Van Osder.)—Wounded: Corporal Addis Downing; Privates Robert Drake, William Kyse, Marcus S. Rue, missing. Prisoners: Corporal Lewis Roloson, Private Patrick Powers.

Recapitulation.

Enlisted men wounded	43
Enlisted men killed	7
Missing	10
Prisoners	20
Total killed, wounded, and missing	80

Seventy-fourth regiment Illinois infantry, (Colonel Jason Marsh.)

Company A, (First Lieutenant Josiah W. Leffingwell.)—Killed: Corporal William Urkhart. Wounded: Sergeants J. S. Cowen, slightly in thigh; William Leffingwell, severely in leg; Corporal W. H. Hitchcock, severely in shoulder and side; Privates E. Parkhurst, severely in shoulder and face; S. Riddle, slightly in leg; H. Heesler, slightly in arm. Missing: Privates W. W. Wattles, J. D. Cherry, D. Dobsen, D. Benjamin, S. Smith, C. Raffee, C. A. Streeter, and J. Vance.

Company B, (Captain D. O. Buttolph.)—Wounded: Privates F. Flinn, C. M. Stevens, S. M. Kelley, and C. W. Corwin.

Company C, (Second Lieutenant John F. Squire.)—Wounded: Sergeant B. A. Champlain, slightly; Private W. A. Millen, slightly. Missing: Privates H. L. Wooley and S. R. Stevenson.

Company D, (Captain Jonathan H. Douglass.)—Wounded: Private George C. Shermorhorn, slightly in knee. Missing: Privates David Pryse and George W. Bliss.

Company E, (First Lieutenant Alpheus Blakesley.)—Wounded: Private W. Weaver, slightly in hand. Missing: Sergeant W. E. Lippet, Corporal H. F. Covey, and Privates W. Rodgers, R. Banks, N. Clothier, J. Shaw, M. Jarvis, M. Brown, and William Craig.

Company F, (Captain Henry C. Parker.)—Wounded: Sergeant H. Heagle, seriously in leg; Privates W. O. Jackless, seriously in right shoulder; R. Lagrange, slightly in arm. Missing: Privates W. Garber, L. Lowe, H. Olrain, L. Sanders, B. Buffington, F. Jones, and M. Fitzgerald.

Company G, (Captain Browman W. Baun.)—Killed: Corporal W. Baieren,

Private F. Pichmyer. Wounded: Corporal J. Wartmiller, Privates A. Westbrook and G. Spraker. Missing: Sergeant J. F. Hawthorn, Privates J. J. Campbell, E. McMobbin, J. D. Moor, G. Petrie, H. Wade, and J. Edmond.

Company H, (Captain Thomas J. Bryan.)—Killed: Sergeant H. S. Post and Private A. J. Butterfield. Wounded: Sergeant —— Hurlburt, in leg; Privates A. W. Brown, seriously in right side; Z. Rice, slightly in foot; M. Sarver, seriously in hip; S. Thayer, slightly in leg; C. Hins, in hand; J. H. Canos, in leg, missing. Missing: Privates T. H. Chambers and M. Rawley.

Company I, (Captain William Irvine.)—Wounded: Corporal C. Hunt and Private S. Jenoine. Missing: Privates J. Andrew and G. Inglet.

Company K, (Captain Butler Ward.)—Killed: Sergeant R. R. Garlick, Corporal M. C. Hulmly, and Private W. Parmler. Wounded: Captain B. Ward, in head and breast; Corporals T. W. Sheratt, in head; J. B. Caspers, in side; Privates F. Caswell, in leg and arm; J. P. Vale, in arm; A. Anderson, seriously. Missing: A. M. Ondner and J. Thorson.

Recapitulation.

Commissioned officers wounded	1
Enlisted men wounded	34
Enlisted men killed	8
Missing	42
Total killed, wounded, and missing	85

Seventy-fifth regiment Illinois infantry, (Lieutenant Colonel J. E. Burnett.)

Company A, (Second Lieutenant William Parker.)—Wounded: Private Adoneram J. Collins, slightly in hip. Missing: Privates Frederick A. Clark, Michael McDonald, William S. Peacock, James Yarrow, and Enoch Pinkerton.

Company B, (Sergeant Elisha Bull.)—Wounded: Sergeant Chauncey B. Hubbard, seriously in leg. Missing: Privates Gaylord Jennigs and Levi Dunner.

Company C, (First Lieutenant George R. Shaw.)—Killed: Private Washington Wood. Wounded: Privates George W. Fuller, slightly in right arm; Hiram Brown, slightly. Prisoner: Joseph Wagley.

Company D, (Captain A. McMoore.)—Missing: Captain A. McMoore, Corporals Benjamin Congonour, Julius A. Ballow, Privates Aurand Aurns, Harvey Mahan, Shelton S. Osborn, Silas Richardson, and John Goodel.

Company E, (Captain William S. Frost.)—Wounded: Second Lieutenant James H. Blodget, in hip, prisoner. Missing: Sergeants Henry Hill and Agnella S. Christopher, and Private Dennis Carroll Prisoner. John Morrill.

Company F, (Captain Addison Storey.)—Wounded: Corporal Elisha F. Furtillot, severely in left leg; Private Samuel Shore, slightly in side. Missing: Corporal Washington Niver, Privates Joseph Carr, John C. Herman, Arthur McGinnis, Ira Corbey, Aaron O'Neil, and Musician James B. Ayres.

Company G, (First Lieutenant David Sandford.)—Wounded: Corporal Edwin J. Larry, seriously in leg; Privates Addison A. Heckhart, slightly in hand; John C. Kaiser, in back. Missing: Cornelius Comans, Lyman Webster, and Michael Mungan.

Company H, (First Sergeant Frank Bingham.)—Wounded: Privates Jos. Haubrick, slightly; James Moorehead, slightly, prisoner. Missing: Second Lieutenant Abner R. Hurless, Sergeant Seth Hawkins, Corporals Oliver Osborn, Frederick Mitchell, James Haley, John Wood, Privates Jacob Funt, Patrick Maley, Simon Regner, Charles Thorp, Ulrich Folstead, John Yeager. Prisoner: Edward Bates.

Company I, (Second Sergeant Augustus Johnson.)—Wounded: Privates Orland Orcutt, slightly; Augustus Quade, in neck; James Collins, seriously in leg;

William Hampton, slightly in hip. Missing: Privates Harrison Butcher, James McBride, Gilbert W. Jennings, Edmond Rainlow. Prisoners: Privates James M. Wyth and William Quade.

Company K, (First Lieutenant William H. Thompson.)—Killed: Private Sidney Merriman. Wounded: Sergeant Barkley Barrett, slightly in hand; Corporal Walter Simon, slightly in hand; Privates John Unger, slightly in hand; Fletcher Vickey, slightly in hand. Missing: Corporals Ebon Backus, George Danner, Privates Frederick Donner, Thomas Steele, John Woodburn, Frederick Mason, William Miller, Edward Prentice, and Jonathan Hide.

Recapitulation.

Commissioned officers wounded	2
Enlisted men wounded	19
Enlisted men killed	2
Missing	53
Prisoners	6
Total killed, wounded, and missing	82

Fifth Wisconsin battery, (Captain O. F. Pinney.)

Killed.—Private Charles Adair.

Wounded.—Captain O. F. Pinney, severely in thigh; Sergeant Elijah Booth, slightly in thigh; Privates David Wilty, severely in back; Josiah C. Forbes, in head and arm; Michael Ward, slightly in side; Martin Campbell, severely in side.

Missing.—Privates John G. Thomas, William Wilty, Charles A. South, and James Stewart.

Prisoners.—Privates William Dunn and John C. Smith.

Recapitulation.

Commissioned officers wounded	1
Enlisted men wounded	5
Missing	4
Killed	1
Prisoners	2
Total killed, wounded, and missing	13

Recapitulation.

Regiments.	Commissioned officers wounded.	Enlisted men.				Aggregate.
		Killed.	Wounded.	Missing.	Prisoners.	
22d regiment Indiana infantry	5	7	34	18	......	64
59th regiment Illinois infantry	......	7	43	10	20	80
74th regiment Illinois infantry	1	8	34	42	......	85
75th regiment Illinois infantry	2	2	19	53	6	82
5th Wisconsin battery	1	1	5	4	2	13
Total	9	25	135	127	28	324

HEADQUARTERS 2D BRIGADE, 1ST DIVISION,
RIGHT WING, 14TH ARMY CORPS,
January 6, 1863.

SIR: I have the honor to submit the following report of the operations of this brigade since leaving Knob Gap, near Nolensville, December 27, 1862.

The brigade took up the line of march on the morning of the 27th, in a heavy rain, in the direction of Triune, bivouacking within one mile of that place, where it remained during the 28th, moving on the morning of the 29th in the direction of Murfreesboro.' That night we bivouacked on Blackman's farm, 4½ miles west of that town. Early on the morning of the 30th we crossed Overall's creek, on the right of the Wilkinson pike, and took up our position in a heavy wood south of the Asa Grissom's house. At 2 o'clock p. m. I was ordered to advance, passed through a cornfield, entering another heavy wood, where my skirmishers first met those of the enemy. Before making this advance, Brigadier General Davis, commanding division, informed me that my brigade was to direct the movements of the division, and that Colonels Post and Woodruff, commanding, respectively, the 1st and 3d brigades, were ordered to keep on a line with me. My skirmishers, under Lieutenant Colonel McKee, 15th Wisconsin volunteers, continued to drive those of the enemy through the wood for about one-fourth of a mile, when I halted and sent a request to Colonels Post and Woodruff to keep pace with my advance.

At this point my skirmishers, having suffered severely, were withdrawn, and my battery (2d Minnesota, Captain W. A. Hotchkiss,) opened on the enemy with canister and spherical case, inflicting serious damage. I then threw forward another line of skirmishers, under Lieutenant Colonel McMakin, 21st Illinois volunteers, which advanced so slowly that my front line of battle soon closed upon it, driving in, however, the skirmishers of the enemy. My first line of battle was now within one hundred and eighty (180) yards of the enemy's line, at the house of Mrs. William Smith. At this point a battery about one hundred (100) yards west of the house opened with canister upon the 21st Illinois volunteers, and another on the east of the house, two hundred and fifty (250) yards distant, on the 15th Wisconsin volunteers, killing and wounding a number of my men. Here it was my intention to halt until the 1st and 3d brigades should come up on my right and left, respectively; but Colonel J. W. S. Alexander, commanding 21st Illinois volunteers, without instructions from me, ordered his regiment to charge on the battery in his front. His command was moving with a shout at the double-quick step, within eighty (80) yards of the battery, already abandoned by its cannoneers, when a very heavy fire was opened upon it by infantry, which lay concealed behind fences and outhouses, on the right and left of the battery. This fire killed and wounded a large number of the 21st Illinois volunteers, and threw the left companies into some disorder, when the regiment was halted and formed on the right of the 15th Wisconsin volunteers.

The fight was now fairly opened and continued vigorously until night by the front line of my infantry and the battery which had been placed between the two regiments. The batteries in our front were soon silenced, but another was then opened on my right flank, distant about five hundred (500) yards, which completely enfiladed my lines and considerably injured us, but this, too, was driven out of sight by Captain Hotchkiss, after a vigorous and well-directed fire.

Again I sent a request to Colonels Post and Woodruff to come up, but they continued to remain in rear of my lines. I maintained my position during the night, having at dark relieved my front line by the 38th Illinois volunteers and 101st Ohio volunteers.

My loss during this day, in killed, wounded, and missing, was about one hundred and seventy-five (175) officers and men. Before daylight on the morning of the 31st December, perceiving indications of an advance by the enemy, I retired my battery about (200) two hundred yards. At daylight the enemy advanced. Seeing that the troops on the right and left of my line would not come up, I fell back with my infantry, on a line with my battery, and made a stand, the 21st Illinois volunteers about (200) two hundred yards to the rear, and on the right of 101st Ohio volunteers; the 15th Wisconsin volunteers were posted in the rocks in front of my battery, and the 38th Illinois volunteers on the left of the 101st Ohio volunteers.

My men were falling rapidly on the front line, and wishing to increase the fire on the enemy, I sent an order to Colonel Alexander to advance and form on the right of the 101st Ohio volunteers, and to Colonel Heg, 15th Wisconsin volunteers, to form on the left of the 38th Illinois volunteers, and to my battery to retire. To my surprise I received in reply from Colonel Alexander, that he was already so hotly engaged that he could not come forward. The startling intelligence was also at this moment communicated to me, by one of my orderlies, that all our forces on our right had left the ground. Immediately afterwards a heavy fire of musketry and artillery from the enemy, from my right flank and rear, unmistakably announced that I was also attacked from that direction.

On my left Woodruff's brigade had left the ground. My command was thus exposed to fire from all points, excepting the left of my rear. When too late to retire in good order, I found that I was overpowered, and but a moment was wanting to place my brigade in the hands of the foe. I decided to retreat by the left flank, when my horse was shot under me and I myself struck, and all my staff and orderlies dismounted or otherwise engaged, which prevented me from communicating the order to the regimental commanders. The rear line, then consisting of the 21st Illinois volunteers, was the first to withdraw, by the order of Lieutenant Colonel McMahin, then commanding, Colonel Alexander having been wounded. Colonel Stern and Lieutenant Colonel Wooster, of the 101st Ohio volunteers, having been shot down, and the ranks of that regiment dreadfully thinned by the fire of the enemy, it gave way and retreated. The 38th Illinois volunteers held its position until the enemy was within a few steps, and then retired. This regiment would have suffered far more severely in its retreat had not a heavy fire from the 15th Wisconsin volunteers, judiciously posted by Colonel Heg, to its left and rear, kept the enemy in check until it had left the wood and partially reformed along the fence, on the right of the 15th Wisconsin volunteers, where an effective fire was kept up, holding the enemy at bay.

This only gave the foe on our right and left the more time to envelop us. All that now remained of my brigade crossed two open fields and entered a wood about (200) two hundred yards east of Grissom's house.

The regiments were painfully reduced in numbers, but I formed a line at this point and several volleys of musketry and artillery were fired with destructive effect upon the ranks of the enemy; but the foe was still on our right at Grissom's house, with none of our forces at that point to oppose them, and being informed that General Davis had ordered a still further withdrawal, I retired my command about a half mile to our rear and again endeavored to rally the men, but it was evident that they were so utterly discouraged that no substantial good could result, while no supports were in sight.

At another point about half a mile further to our rear I rallied all who could be found, and took a strong position in the edge of a cedar grove, holding it until the enemy came up, when my men fired one volley and broke without orders. I conducted them to the rear, passing through the lines of our reserve,s and halted at the railroad, where we remained during the afternoon collecting our scattered men. During the two days' fight the loss of officers was so great that some companies had not *one* to command them, and others not even a sergeant. Our regimental colors were all borne off the field flying, though four (4) color-bearers in succession, of the 21st Illinois volunteers, were shot down, and two (2) of the color guard 38th Illinois volunteers, three (3) of the color guard 15th Wisconsin volunteers, and four (4) of the color guard 101st Ohio volunteers, fell.

Our artillery was all brought off in safety.

I have to report the loss of many officers who were ornaments to our army, and who will be mourned by all who knew them. Colonel L. Stern, 101st Ohio volunteers, Lieutenant Colonel David McKee, 15th Wisconsin volunteers, and Lieutenant Colonel M. F. Wooster, 101st Ohio volunteers, were unsurpassed in all the qualities that make up the brave soldier, the true gentleman, and the pure patriot. Captain James P. Meade, 38th Illinois volunteers, fell, shot three times, while bravely fighting the enemy with his revolver after his regiment had retired. Lieutenant John L. Dillen, 38th Illinois volunteers, commanding company E, fought with a musket until he was shot once, when he drew his sword and cheered on his men till he fell dead. Other instances of equal gallantry were observed in the other regiments, but to recount all would give my report an undue length. The long, sad list of killed and wounded forms the truest eulogium on the conduct of the troops composing this brigade, and it is by that list I wish it to be judged.

Of the ten field officers in the regiments, three were killed and two wounded. Seven horses were shot under the regimental field and staff officers. Of my orderlies, Private Pease, company B, 36th Illinois volunteers, had his horse shot under him while carrying my orders. Private Knox, same company, also had his horse shot under him, and while endeavoring to procure another horse for me, was wounded by a grape shot, and again by a Minie ball; and Corporal Hart, 38th Illinois volunteers, was stunned and disabled by a cannon ball.

I deem it my duty to call the special attention of the general commanding the 14th army corps to Colonel John W. S. Alexander, 21st Illinois volunteers, and Colonel Hans C. Heg, 15th Wisconsin volunteers. While every field officer under my command did his duty faithfully, Colonels Alexander and Heg, in my opinion, proved themselves the bravest of the brave. Had such men as these been in command of some of our brigades, we should have been spared the shame of witnessing the rout of our troops and the disgraceful panic, encouraged, at least, by the example and advice of officers high in command.

Lieutenant Colonel D. H. Gilmer, commanding 38th Illinois volunteers, was always at his post, and attended to his duty. Major Isaac M. Kirby, 101st Ohio volunteers, took command of the regiment after the fall of the brave Colonels Stern and Wooster, and conducted it to the rear, reduced to about one hundred (100) men. Captain W. A. Hotchkiss, commanding 2d Minnesota battery, with all his officers and men, deserve credit for their gallantry in the fight, and energy in preventing the loss of the battery. Among the staff officers of this army who made themselves useful in rallying the scattered men, Dr. L. F. Russell, 2d Minnesota battery; Lieutenant S. M. Jones, 59th Illinois volunteers; Captain Thurston, aide-de-camp to Major General McCook; and Chaplain Wilkins, 21st Illinois volunteers, came especially under my observation.

On the night of the 31st December this brigade was ordered to take up its position near the Nashville pike, four miles from Murfreesboro'.

January 1, 1863, slight skirmishing with the enemy continued during the day, in which we killed several, capturing thirteen prisoners, and paroling eleven others wounded. At 3.30 o'clock p. m., January 2, while hard fighting was progressing on our left, I received orders from General Rosecrans to report to him in person. He directed me to "take my command to the left, form it in two lines, and, should I find our forces repulsed by the enemy, to allow our men to pass through my lines, and on the approach of the enemy, give a whoop and a yell and go at 'em." With a brigade which, in three days' hard fighting, had been reduced from two thousand to seven hundred, and greatly discouraged, I felt serious apprehension that I would not be able to fulfil the expectations of the general, and, to prepare him for such a result, I informed him of the condition of my brigade. He said: "Tell them they *must* do it for us and for the country." I told him I would do my best. My men fell into ranks with the utmost alacrity, and marched to the scene of the conflict, a great portion of the way on the double-quick, crossing Stone river at a ford. All apprehensions that I had previously entertained now vanished. I felt confident that they would not only charge the enemy, but would repulse them. Before reaching the ground designated, however, I learned that the enemy had already been driven back in confusion. I continued my march, and, under the direction of Brigadier General Davis, placed my command in the advance, relieving the command of Colonel Hazen. It was now dark. We maintained our ground till the morning of January 4, when we returned to our position on the right.

My loss in killed, wounded, and missing in the engagement at "Knob Gap," near Nolensville, December 26, and the battles of the 30th and 31st December, 1862, and in front of the enemy east of Stone river, January 2, and 3, 1863, is as follows, viz:

Regiment or corps.	KILLED.		WOUNDED.		MISSING.		
	Officers	Men.	Officers.	Men	Officers	Men.	Total.
21st Illinois volunteers...	2	55	7	180	......	59	303
15th Wisconsin volunteers,	2	13	5	65	1	33	119
101st Ohio volunteers....	4	19	2	121	......	66	212
38th Illinois volunteers...	2	32	5	104	......	34	177
2d Minnesota battery....	......	3	1	5	......	1	10
Total.............	10	122	20	475	1	193	821

I cannot close this report without expressing my obligations to the following named officers of my staff for their zeal, fidelity, and courage in all the severe engagements embraced in this report, viz: Captain S. P. Voris, 38th Illinois volunteers, acting assistant adjutant general; Captain W. C. Harris, 38th Illinois volunteers; Lieutenant Albert Woodbury, 2d Minnesota battery; and Lieutenant Walter E. Carlin, 38th Illinois volunteers; also to my faithful orderlies, Pease, Knox, Asrick, and Hael. Private Alex. C. Hosmer, 101st Ohio volunteers, my clerk, though not required to go into the battle, was constantly at my side to carry my orders.

Regimental reports and lists of casualties are herewith enclosed; also a report of the engagement at "Knob Gap," near Nolensville, December 26, 1862.

A topographical sketch, showing the ground passed over, and positions occupied by this brigade on the 30th and 31st December, 1862, is herewith enclosed.

Very respectfully, your obedient servant,

WM. P. CARLIN,

Colonel 38th Illinois Volunteers, Commanding.

Lieutenant P. W. MORRISON,

Acting Assistant Adjutant General.

HEADQUARTERS 3D BRIGADE, 1ST DIVISION,
Right Wing 14th Corps, January 5, 1863.

SIR: I have the honor to report the operations of the 3d brigade, 1st division of the right wing, in the five days' battle before Murfreesboro'.

This brigade having held the advanced position on Overall's creek in the afternoon and night of Monday, December 29, was the base of formation for the line of battle on Tuesday morning. At an early hour on the morning of the 30th I received instructions that we would move forward in line of battle.

I was directed to join my left with Brigadier General Sill's brigade, holding the right of the 2d division under Brigadier General Sheridan, and that Colonel Carlin, commanding the 2d brigade of the 1st division, would connect his line with my right.

This brigade was accordingly formed in two lines, the 35th Illinois regiment, Lieutenant Colonel Chandler, on the right; the 25th Illinois regiment, Colonel T. D. Williams commanding, on the left, in the first line of battle; and the 81st Indiana regiment, Lieutenant Colonel Timberlake, in the second line in reserve, the extreme left on the right of ——— turnpike; the 8th Wisconsin battery, of four guns, Captain Carpenter commanding, being placed in the interval between Brigadier General Sill's right and my left. my front was curtained with two companies of skirmishers detailed from the 25th and 35th Illinois regiments, under the command and immediate supervision of Major MacIlvain, of the 35th Illinois regiment. The commands to my right and left were formed in the same manner. We moved forward on the morning of Tuesday, the 30th, at about 10 o'clock, and halted on the edge of a large cotton-field immediately in front of a wood running parallel with the turnpike, our lines facing Murfreesboro', which was in a southeast direction. This was about 11 o'clock a. m.

No enemy being visible in our front, I caused a few shells to be thrown into the woods beyond, but met no response. The topography of the country in this line and in my front was a cotton-field, which we then occupied, at the further end of which was a belt or strip of timber, ending at a cornfield on my left and front, and immediately in front of Brigadier General Sill's right. This cornfield extended to a narrow, heavily timbered wood bordered by a rail fence. Beyond this timber was a cornfield receding towards a ravine terminated by a bluff wood bank, along the foot of which, in the ravine, was the enemy's line of battle, with its supports and artillery on the elevation.—(See plate.)

We remained in position until about 3 o'clock p. m., when my skirmishers were ordered forward to occupy the belt of timber, which they did. Major MacIlvain, who was in command, reported to me that the enemy's skirmishers were in the furthest wood to our front and left, and desired me to send him a further support of one company, which was sent him, with orders to press their skirmishers back. The skirmishing soon commenced briskly, and my brigade was ordered to advance, which it did in admirable order, and was halted in the first belt of timber. Desiring to know the position of the enemy's line and the situation of their skirmishers, I proceeded to the line of skirmishers to assist in directing their movements and urge them on, and having given them directions in person, returned to my command to be ready to move forward to their support. The wood was so thick and brushy on my right, that it was difficult to see further than the left of the 2d brigade; but as I discovered it advancing, we moved forward also, to protect its flank. Sheridan's division had halted some one hundred yards in rear of my brigade, his line of skirmishers joining my line of battle. At this juncture my skirmishers commenced falling back rapidly, and I endeavored to get the officer in command of those of Sheridan's division to advance to their support, as those of my brigade had not only driven the enemy from my front but General Sill's also; but as he had no orders to move forward, he refused. The emergency being imminent, Colonel Williams was ordered to detach the left company of his regiment, and deploy it forward as skirmishers, to relieve or strengthen those engaged as circumstances might require, while the brigade was advanced to support them.

The command passed forward in splendid order, and soon became hotly engaged, and drove the enemy back through the woods and cornfield in their own lines. As we were now far in advance of any support upon the left, I deemed it advisable to halt and wait for them to come up, and therefore took position in rear of the rail fence, my right nearly at right angles to my line of battle, thereby obtaining an oblique as well as direct fire; but the space to be occupied by this brigade was so great that the 81st Indiana regiment was ordered up to complete my line, thereby leaving me no reserves.

The battery was placed in the angle of the fence to protect my right and front. Shortly after taking this position, Brigadier General Sill joined me on the left. We remained in position, receiving a heavy fire and occasionally replying with shell, until towards night, when the enemy opened a heavy artillery fire apparently on the right of Colonel Carlin's brigade. This discovering their battery, and mine being in good range and position to enfilade theirs, Captain Carpenter was ordered to silence their battery, which he did in handsome style in about five minutes. An attack of infantry was then made from the same point on Colonel Carlin, and as their lines presented the same advantage, Captain Carpenter again opened fire with such terrific effect that their yells of pain, terror, and anguish, as our shells exploded in their dense ranks, could be distinctly heard where we stood. So well was the battery served that their attack ceased, and darkness closed the conflict.

We slept on our arms without fires, prepared for the battle which we well knew would open on the morrow. During the night we discovered what appeared to me to be a continued movement of troops, which led me to believe that the enemy were massing troops on our right, which information I had the honor to report to my immediate superior, Brigadier General Davis. As soon as day dawned I examined the line of battle, and, as I had no supports, placed three (3) pieces in battery on my left, and pointed out to Brigadier General Sill the weakness of the line at this point, and requested him to order up some regiments of his brigade, held in reserve, to strengthen his right and protect my left, feeling certain that the enemy meditated an attack, and that it would be made at that place. He agreed with me, and immediately ordered up two regiments, who remained there but a short time, and then resumed their former positions as reserves. Deeming the knowledge of this fact of paramount importance, I despatched a staff officer to Brigadier General Davis to give him the information. Afterwards the general informed me that I must hold the position as best I could, for he had no supports to send me. Almost simultaneously with the withdrawal of the reserves ordered up by Brigadier General Sill, the enemy made their attack in five (5) heavy lines, and we were immediately engaged. Captain Carpenter's battery opened with terrific effect with grape and canister, and they were mowed down as grass beneath the sickle, while the infantry poured in a well-directed and very destructive fire. Sheltered by the rail fence, they were partially protected, and fired with the coolness of veterans. As soon as the battle became general the 24th Wisconsin, which joined my left, gave way, leaving my battery and left flank exposed to an enfilading fire. I finally succeeded in rallying them as a reserve. At this moment the right of Brigadier General Sill's brigade commenced to swing to the rear, and Colonel Carlin's was discovered falling steadily back. I then received orders to take position to the rear some 300 yards, in the belt of timber. I informed the staff officer who brought the order that we could maintain our position if supported. He said the order was peremptory, and I hastened to execute it, but not until I was flanked both on the right and left. The brigade moved to the rear in good order, and halted on the new line; but the right and left continuing the march, and being severely pressed, we made a vigorous charge and drove the enemy back in our front, and, strange to say, not only carried our point, but swung the enemy's lines upon right and left with it. Had we been supported here, they would have been routed; as it was, we regained our position occupied when the battle opened, but could hold it but a moment, when we were forced to yield to superior numbers, and steadily fell back to the ground from which the charge was first made. From this point we charged a second time, compelling the enemy to yield ground, but our ammunition beginning to fail, and no wagons to be found from which to replenish the stock, the brigade was ordered to hold its position as best it could, and if pressed too hard to fall steadily back until the battery could be got into position to protect their movement across the cotton-field. I placed the battery in position, and gave the officer in command, Sergeant German, directions where to fire, pointing out to him the position of the brigade, and what he was required to do.

The ammunition of the regiments now entirely failing, and a perfect rout appearing to have taken place, the brigade fell back to the ground occupied by them on the morning of Tuesday. At this time the whole wing was in the utmost confusion, and I used every endeavor to rally and organize them, but without avail. There seemed to be no fear, no panic, but a stolid indifference unacountable. Officers and men passed to the rear, nor words nor exhortation could prevent them.

In three different positions I used every exertion to reform our lines, but it became impossible. Reaching the Murfreesboro' pike a stampede, or panic, commenced in the wagon train, but succeeding in getting a regiment across the road, it was stopped, and by a vigorous charge of cavalry saved from the enemy.

We were then placed in reserve to our division along the Murfreeboro' pike, and there waited in anxious expectation to make or repel attacks until the afternoon of Friday, when we were ordered to move in double-quick to the extreme left to support the division who were being driven in by the enemy, and although fatigued and worn out by exposure to the rain, without tents or blankets for seven days, and want of sleep, (two days of which time we had had nothing to eat but parched corn,) the command, with yells of joy, rushed forward, and, after fording the river three times, pushed the enemy back with the greatest rapidity, the ground being covered with rebel dead and wounded. We went into position about two miles from the ford, and on the extreme left. During the night we threw up an abatis of rails, and laid on our arms without fires in a drenching rain. The next morning, Saturday, January 3, we expected an attack, but none occurred during the day. That night we changed position to the right again, nothing but picket skirmishing having occurred during the day. When the morning of Saturday passed without an attack, I became satisfied, in my own mind, that the enemy were evacuating Murfreesboro', and so expressed it.

I cannot speak in too high terms of the gallant conduct of the officers and men under my command. If indomitable daring, cool courage, and invincible bravery in the midst of the turmoil of such a battle, when all space seemed occupied by some deadly missile, amid carnage and noise, be any proof of heroism, they certainly possess it. Many instances of personal daring and feats of individual prowess were visibly performed, but I must refer you to the reports of subordinate commanders for names and instances. To the officers and men of the 25th and 35th Iillinois regiments and 8th Wisconsin battery I owe especial thanks for the determined bravery and chivalric heroism they evinced throughout; and also to the officers and men of the 81st Indiana, a new regiment, the first time under fire, who, with but a few exceptions, manfully fronted the storm of battle, and gave earnest proof of what may hereafter be expected of them. I desire to call the attention of the commanding officer to the gallant conduct of Lieutenant Colonel Chandler, commanding 35th Illinois, whose cool, steady courage, admirable deportment, and skilful management evinced the soldier, true and tried, and who at all times proved himself worthy of the trust he holds. Major MacIlvain, of the same regiment, I cannot praise too much: his good management and skilful handling of the skirmishers, of which he was in charge, elicited encomiums of well-merited compliment—at all times cool, determined, and persevering. Lieutenant Colonel Timberlake and Major Woodbury, of the 81st Indiana, displayed manly courage, and held their regiment firm and steady under heavy fire; for officers young in the service their efforts are worthy of imitation. Captain W. Taggert, who succeeded to the command of the 25th Illinois regiment, behaved as a soldier should, everywhere efficient, and ever ready to execute orders. First Sergeant German, of 8th Wisconsin battery, merits much praise for the cool, skilful, and determined manner in which he served his battery after he succeeded to the command.

To my staff, Captain George Austin, acting assistant adjutant general, Captain A. C. Keys, Lieutenant C. P. Ford, Lieutenant John F. Isom, Lieutenant William R. McChesney, and Lieutenant H. S. Parks, I owe especial thanks for the manner they served upon the field, carrying my orders, wherever required, through a hail-storm of shot, shells, and bullets, regardless of all save the performance of their duty.

During the conflict it became necessary, in the absence of staff officers on duty, to make use of orderlies to supply their places. In connexion herewith I take great pleasure in testifying to the brave conduct of Orderlies A. T. Freeman and Abijah Lee, of my escort. Amid the glorious results of a battle won, it gives me pain to record the names of the gallant men who offered up their lives on the altar of their country; but we must drop the tear of sorrow over their resting-place, and offer our heartfelt sympathies to their relatives and friends, trusting that God will care for them, and soothe their afflictions. And while we remember the noble dead, let us pay a tribute of respect to the gallant Colonel T. D. Williams, 25th Illinois regiment, who died in the performance of his duty. He fell with his regimental colors in his hands, exclaiming "We will plant it here boys, and rally the old 25th around it, and here we will die." Such conduct is above all praise, and words can paint no eulogium worthy of the subject. And here let me call the attention to the conduct of Captain Carpenter, of 8th Wisconsin battery, who fell gallantly serving his guns until the enemy were within a few yards of their muzzles. He died as a soldier would wish to die, with his face to the foe, in the smoke and din of battle.

The casualties of the command are small, in comparison to the fire they received and the service did.

The 35th Illinois lost 2 commissioned officers wounded, 8 privates killed, 49 wounded, and 32 missing; the 25th Illinois, one (1) commissioned officer killed and 3 wounded, 14 privates killed, 69 wounded, and 35 missing; the 81st Indiana, 2 commissioned officers killed, 2 wounded, and 1 missing, 3 privates killed, 40 wounded, and 39 missing; the 8th Wisconsin battery, 1 commissioned officer killed, 4 privates wounded, and 19 missing. Total, 4 commissioned officers killed, seven (7) wounded, and 1 missing, twenty-five (25) privates killed, 162 wounded, and 125 missing. Aggregate killed, wounded, and missing, 324.

I hope a portion of those missing may yet return, as all cannot have been made prisoners

I have the honor to submit the above report to your consideration, and remain, dear sir, yours, most respectfully,

W. E. WOODRUFF,
Colonel, Commanding 3d Brigade.

Lieutenant P. W. MORRISON,
Acting Assistant Adjutant General, 1st Division.

HEADQUARTERS SECOND DIVISION, RIGHT WING,
January 8, 1863.

I have the honor to submit the following report of the operations of the second division, under my command, beginning December 26, 1862, the day upon which it left Nashville, and terminating on January 6, 1863:

The second division is composed of the following troops:

First brigade, Brigadier General A. Willich commanding.—49th Ohio Colonel Gibson; 15th Ohio, Colonel Wallace; 39th Indiana, Lieutenant Colonel Jones; 32d Indiana, Lieutenant Colonel Eskelmeyer; 89th Illinois, Lieutenant Colonel Hotchkiss; Goodspeed's battery, 1st Ohio artillery.

Second brigade, Brigadier General E. N. Kirk commanding.—29th Indiana, Lieutenant Colonel Dunn; 30th Indiana, Colonel Dodge; 77th Pennsylvania, Lieutenant Colonel Houssem; 34th Illinois, Lieutenant Colonel Bristol; 79th Illinois, Colonel Read; Edgarton's battery, Ohio artillery.

Third brigade, Colonel P. P. Baldwin commanding.—6th Indiana, Lieutenant Colonel Tripp; 5th Kentucky, (Louisville Legion,) Lieutenant Colonel Berry; 1st Ohio, Major Stafford; 93d Ohio, Colonel Anderson; Simonson's Indiana battery.

Major Kleim's battalion of 3d Indiana cavalry was assigned to duty with the second division.

Agreeably to orders, the three divisions constituting the right wing of the 14th army corps, marched from their camps near Nashville, taking the Nolensville pike, and arrived in that village same day, 4 o'clock p. m. On the following day the same divisions, with mine in advance, marched to Triune. The rebel rear guard contested the ground inch by inch, and the day was passed constantly skirmishing with them, with no loss on our side, but several casualties on their part. Triune was occupied by my division about 4 p. m. The following day (December 28) the command remained in Triune. A reconnoissance to ascertain the direction the enemy had retreated was made by a brigade of my command, commanded by Brigadier General A. Willich. It having been ascertained that the enemy had retreated towards Murfreesboro', I was ordered to leave a brigade at Triune, and on the 29th to march on Murfreesboro', on what is known as the Bolizack road. Colonel P. P. Baldwin's 3d brigade was left at Triune. The command arrived at Wilkinson's Crossroads about 8 p. m. on the 29th, and an order sent at once to Colonel Baldwin to move forward his brigade, which arrived early on the afternoon of the 30th. My division was in reserve on the 29th. On the following morning, December 30, General Sheridan's division was ordered to advance in line of battle, covering the Wilkinson pike, while General Davis's division marched in the same order on the right of General Sheridan. My division being held in reserve, was marched in column on the pike. There being no troops on General Davis's right, and General Sheridan's left being guarded by General Crittenden's left wing, I was ordered to oblique to the right, covering the right of General Davis's division. About 2 o'clock p. m. I received an order from Major General McCook to look well to my right, as General Hardee, (rebel,) with his corps, was on the right flank of our column. I ordered the 2d brigade, Brigadier General Kirk commanding, to take position with his brigade, his left resting against the right of General Davis, his right refused so as to cover our right flank. About dark I placed General Willich's brigade on the right of Kirk's refusing his right, and directing a heavy line of skirmishers to be thrown forward, connecting on the left with those of General Davis, and extending to the right and rear, near the Wilkinson pike. This line of skirmishers was thrown forward about six hundred yards and near those of the enemy. My 3d brigade, Colonel Baldwin commanding, was held in reserve. At dusk on the evening of the 30th the troops occupied the position as indicated by the accompanying map. In consultation with Major General McCook late in the afternoon of December 30, he informed me that he had reliable information to the effect that the centre of the rebel line of battle was opposite to our extreme right, and that we would probably be attacked by the entire rebel army early on the following morning. His prediction proved true. He also informed me that he had communicated this information to the commanding general. I expected a change in the programme for the following day, but none was made. My brigade commanders were called together and the operations of the following day fully explained to them. Every arrangement was made for an attack. Two gallant and experienced officers commanded my advanced brigades, and every precaution taken against surprise. At 6.22 on the morning of the 31st, the outpost in front of my division were driven in by an overwhelming force of infantry, outnumbering my forces greatly, and known to contain about 35,000 men. At the same time my extreme right was attacked by the enemy's cavalry.

The gallant Willich and Kirk soon opened a heavy fire of musketry and artillery upon the advancing columns, causing wavering in the ranks, but fresh columns would soon replace them, and it was apparent that to fall back was a "military necessity." Edgarton's battery, after firing three rounds, had so many of his horses killed as to render it unmanageable. He, however, remained with it, and continued to fire until he fell by a severe wound, and he and his battery fell into the hands of the enemy. Before falling back the horse of General Willich was killed, and he was wounded and taken prisoner. About the same time General Kirk received a severe wound, which disabled him. Seeing the pressure upon my lines, I ordered up my reserve brigade, under the gallant Baldwin. The troops of his brigade advanced promptly and delivered their fire, holding their ground for some time, but they too were compelled to fall back. The troops of this division were compelled for the first time to yield the field temporarily, but the heroes of Shiloh and Perryville did not abandon their ground until forced to do so by the immense masses of the enemy hurled against them, and then inch by inch. The ground over which the division passed, covered with the enemy's dead and those of our own men, shows that the field was warmly contested. Several times the lines were reformed and resistance offered, but the columns of the enemy were too heavy for a single line, and ours would have to yield. Finally the flank of my division reached the line of General Rousseau's, when it was reformed and fought until out of ammunition, but my efficient ordnance officer, Lieutenant Murdoch, had a supply in readiness, which was soon issued, and the division assisted in driving the enemy from the field in their last desperate struggle of the day. Soon the curtains of darkness fell upon the scene of blood, and all was quiet, awaiting the coming of morn to renew hostilities. Morning came, but the enemy had withdrawn. January 1 was a day of comparative quiet in camp, few shots being fired, but many preparations made for a heavy battle on the following day. General Crittenden's wing was attacked in force on the 2d, and one of my brigades (Colonel Gibson's) was sent to re-enforce him. For the gallant part taken by it reference is made to the report of Major General Crittenden. The enemy evacuated Murfreesboro' on the night of the 3d. On the 6th I was ordered to remove my camp to a point on the Shelbyville road four miles south of Murfreesboro'.

The conduct of officers and men under my command was good. (The Louisville legion, under the gallant Lieutenant Colonel Berry, brought off by hand one of the cannon, after the horses were killed.) They yielded the ground only where overpowered, offering an obstinate resistance at every point; some few in each regiment becoming panic-stricken, fled to Nashville for safety. Captain Simonson managed his battery with skill and courage, and with it did good execution. He lost two guns, but not until the horses had been killed and the guns disabled. Goodspeed's battery lost three guns and quite a number of horses. This battery was handled well and did good execution, under Lieutenant Belden. Reference is respectfully made to the reports of regimental and brigade commanders, for the list of those who by their bravery and good conduct rendered themselves conspicuous. After the capture of General Willich his brigade was commanded temporarily by Colonel Wallace, fifteenth Ohio, but was afterwards replaced by Colonel Gibson, forty-ninth Ohio. General Kirk becoming disabled, was replaced by Colonel Dodge, thirtieth Indiana, while the third brigade was commanded throughout by Colonel Baldwin. These four colonels have demonstrated their fitness for command on several bloody fields, and are recommended to my superiors for promotion. Their coolness and courage rendered them conspicuous throughout the bloody engagement. Major Kleim and his battalion, of the third Indiana cavalry deserve special mention. Under their gallant leader the battalion was always in front, and rendered efficient service.

To Captains Bartlett, Hooker, Thruston, and McLeland, and Lieutenants Taft, Hill, and Shultz, of my staff, my thanks are due for their efficiency and promptness in carrying orders to all parts of the field.

My medical director, Surgeon Marks, and the medical officers of the division, were untiring in their exertions to alleviate the sufferings of the wounded, and to them my thanks are due. My escort, composed of the following named men of the third Kentucky cavalry, who accompanied me throughout the engagement, deserve special mention for their good conduct: Sergeant William C. Miles; Privates George Long, Thomas Salyers, John Christian, John Whitten, James Bowen, B. Hammerslein, and R. A. Norah. Private Bowen's horse was killed by a cannon ball.

The loss of the division was as follows: killed, 260; wounded, 1,005; missing, 1,280, (supposed to have been captured.)

Very respectfully, your obedient servant,

R. W. JOHNSON,
Brigadier General of Volunteers, Commanding.

Major J. A. CAMPBELL,
Assistant Adjutant General.

HEADQUARTERS BATTERY H, 5TH ARTILLERY,
January 10, 1863.

SIR: I have the honor to make the following report of the operations of the battery under my command, in the recent engagements near Murfreesboro', Tennessee:

The battery arrived near the battle-field with the brigade of regulars of which it forms a part, on the morning of December 30, 1862. On the morning of December 31 it was moved forward with the brigade, and after a short halt, proceeded through a dense grove of cedars to take a position. Finding it impossible to operate with the battery in so dense a wood, I reported to General Rousseau, who, after seeing the impossibility of taking up a proper position, ordered the battery into action in the open field, which it had previously left. The battery was formed in time to check the advance of the enemy from the cedars, and was then moved to a position on a rise of ground on the opposite side of the pike.

A heavy column of the enemy advanced from the cedars, but was finally driven back in disorder by the fire of canister from the battery. On the afternoon of the 31st the enemy again moved forward in heavy force from a position to our left and front, but were unable to advance under the fire of the different batteries which was concentrated upon them. Though the battery changed positions several times in order to follow up the movements of the troops, its main position was on the rise of ground already spoken of, and on which it camped at night.

On the morning of January 1, 1863, the battery was moved some distance to the rear, and after several changes of position was ordered back with the brigade of regulars towards a point on the Murfreesboro' pike beyond Stewart's creek. After proceeding some miles, the order being countermanded, the brigade and battery returned, and about nightfall camped in the woods near the old position. On the morning of January 2 the battery moved forward and took position—remaining in position during the day, and camping on the same ground at night. On the 3d the brigade and battery were moved forward and occupied rifle-pits and epaulements which had been constructed for them. At dusk the battery opened fire with shell and spherical case shot on the enemy concealed in the woods, in buildings, and behind breastworks, etc., and the attack being followed up by the infantry the enemy were driven from the position and the grounds occupied by our troops, who were subsequently withdrawn. The battery remained in position during the following day, and on the morning of the 5th of January took up the line of march towards Murfreesboro', encamping some distance beyond the town in the evening.

To Lieutenant Colonel Shephard, 18th infantry, commanding brigade, and to Majors Carpenter, 19th infantry; King, 15th infantry; Caldwell and Townsend, 18th infantry, and Slemmer, 16th infantry, commanding battalions, and to their officers and men I am indebted for the gallant support afforded me during the series of engagements. My officers, Second Lieutenant Israel Ludlow and J. A. Fessenden, deserve honorable mention for their display of coolness, gallantry, and judgment.

Sergeants Egan, Reed, Metcalf, Brode, Bickel, Ervin, and Manbeck behaved with conspicuous courage, and to the other non-commissioned officers and privates of the battery, without exception, I am indebted for faithful services.

I have the honor to append the following list of causualties in my command:

Wounded.—Corporal Charles Allitzon, and Privates Thomas Burns, James F. Mohr, Michael McGrath, and Benjamin F. Burgess.

Total wounded, 5. Total of horses killed, 10. Total of horses wounded, 5. Rounds of ammunition expended, 558.

Very respectfully, your obedient servant,

F. L. GUENTHER,

First Lieutenant 5th Artillery, Commanding Battery H, 5th Artillery.

First Lieutenant ROBERT SOUTHERLAND,

18*th Infantry, Acting Assistant Adjutant General, Brigade of Regulars.*

Report of killed, wounded, and missing, 3d division, right wing, in the engagement from December 26, 1862, to January 6, 1863.

REGIMENTS.	GENERAL OFFICERS.			FIELD OFFICERS.			COMPANY OFFICERS.			ENLISTED MEN.			Total loss of commissioned officers.	Total loss of enlisted men.	Aggregate.
	Killed.	Wounded.	Missing.	Killed.	Wounded.	Missing.	Killed.	Wounded.	Missing.	Killed.	Wounded.	Missing.			
FIRST BRIGADE.															
1st brigade			1												
15th Ohio					1	1		1		17	68	127	3	212	215
49th Ohio				1	1		1	5		18	88	108	8	194	202
32d Indiana										12	40	115		167	167
39th Indiana							1	2	2	30	116	229	5	375	380
89th Illinois							1	1		9	45	94	2	148	150
Battery A										1	4	24		29	29
Total			1	1	2	1	3	9	2	87	561	697	18	1, 125	1, 143
SECOND BRIGADE.															
2d brigade		1													
34th Illinois							2	2	2	19	98	72	6	189	195
79th Illinois				1				3	3	23	68	121	7	212	219
29th Indiana						1	1	2		14	66	51	4	131	135
30th Indiana						1	1	2	1	30	108	70	5	208	213
77th Pennsylvania				1				1	2	4	28	28	4	60	64
Battery E									2	10	5		2	15	17
Total		1		2		2	4	10	10	100	373	342	28	815	843

THIRD BRIGADE.															
1st Ohio	......	......	......	......	......	......	......	1	......	8	46	81	1	135	136
93d Ohio	......	......	......	......	1	......	......	......	......	12	45	64	1	121	122
6th Indiana	......	......	......	......	......	......	......	......	1	17	50	36	1	103	104
5th Kentucky	......	......	......	......	2	......	1	5	......	18	73	26	8	117	125
5th Indiana battery	......	......	......	......	......	......	......	1	......	3	18	1	1	23	23
Total	......	......	......	......	3	......	1	7	1	58	232	208	12	498	510
3d Indiana cavalry	......	......	......	......	......	......	......	......	......	4	6	15	......	25	25
Grand total	......	1	1	3	5	......	8	26	13	249	972	1,262	58	2,463	2,521

R. W. JOHNSON,
Brigadier General of Volunteers, Commanding.

HEADQUARTERS 1ST BRIGADE, 2D DIVISION, RIGHT WING,
Murfreesboro', January 5, 1863.

CAPTAIN: The capture of Brigadier General Willich renders it my duty to report to Brigadier General Johnson, commanding division, the participation of this command in the events of the last ten days. In accomplishing this task, I shall address myself to a concise narrative of occurrences that "the truth of history may be vindicated," the memory of our heroic slain honored, and that justice may be done to the brave survivors, who, by their energy and stubborn courage, maintained a conflict for six days, and vanquished the *grand army* of our foe.

Leaving camp near Nashville, December 26, 1862, the first and second days' march was without incident, and took us through Nolensville to Triune, twenty miles. The following day we reconnoitred the country seven miles to our front in the direction of Shelbyville, and developed the fact that the rebel forces had retreated the day and night previous in the direction of this place. In that reconnoissance we made forty-one prisoners of war. On the 29th we moved upon this place, reaching the Salem road, four miles distant, after dark, and slept upon our arms in rear of General Davis's division. On the 30th we advanced upon this position, acting as a reserve to the ——— of the right wing, and were not brought under fire that day. In the evening we took up a position on the extreme right of our army on the Franklin road. General Kirk's brigade was in front, with pickets thrown out to the margin of open fields. To his rear and near his right, in open woods, was Edgerton's battery in position, with a narrow cleared field in front. To the right of this battery, and on a line perpendicular to the rear of General Kirk's right, were the reserves of the 29th and 32d Indiana of this command, portions of each being on picket duty. The direction of the Franklin road is due east and west at this point, and it was covered by General Kirk's right, his line of battle fronting east and in advance of a lane running north and south, eight yards wide, and intersecting the road at right angles. In this angle is a field of open woods, three hundred and thirty yards square. South of this is an unenclosed space covered by a few trees, and near a hundred yards wide, through which the Franklin road is located. At the fence, to the right of Edgerton's battery, five companies of the 39th Indiana were camped in line of battle, fronting south. To their right, the 32d Indiana occupied a like position. Inside of the wooded field, and within thirty yards of the fence, the 49th Ohio was formed in line of battle, fronting south, its left resting within one hundred yards of the lane and its right within a like distance of the west enclosure.

In its rear the 89th Illinois was in double column closed in mass fronting south. Perpendicular to the rear of the right of the 49th was the 15th Ohio, in line near the fence fronting west, its left wing resting within sixty yards of the 49th. In the southwest corner of this wooded field, Goodspeed's battery was parked in oblong square. North and west of this field, and south and east of the unenclosed space, were cleared fields. The picket line of General Kirk covered his front and flank, connecting with that of this brigade, at a fence six hundred yards south of the left of the reserve of the 39th Indiana. The pickets of the 39th were advanced seven hundred yards in front of the reserve, in an open cornfield. The pickets of the 32d joined those of the 39th, and covered our flank and rear. At 3 o'clock a. m. Colonel Jones was ordered to patrol the woods six hundred yards in front of his pickets. No indications of the presence or purposes of the enemy were discerned.

Here I beg leave to call attention to the very concise and satisfactory report of Lieutenant Colonel Jones, commanding 39th Indiana, and also to the report of Lieutenant Colonel Erdelmeyer, commanding 32d Indiana. These dispositions had been made, and these precautions adopted by General Willich. At dawn of day orders were received to build fires and make coffee. In a few moments after, I met General Willich, who remarked that he would be absent a few moments at the headquarters of General Johnson, and in case anything occurred in front of our pickets, he directed me to rally the 39th and 32d to their support. At twenty-five minutes past six, and soon after meeting the general, firing was heard on General Kirk's right. The brigade was instantly ordered to take arms, and Lieutenant Miles of the staff, was despatched for General Willich. He was found, and started for his command, but his horse was shot under him, and he was made a prisoner before giving an order. The enemy advanced upon our position with four heavy lines of battle, with a strong reserve held in mass. All these were in full view before the lines of General Kirk gave way. His left extended a great distance beyond our extreme right, and was thrown forward so that his lines were, to some extent, oblique to ours. To the right of our position, and near the Franklin road, he took position with an immense force of cavalry. In fact, the centre of Hardee's corps attacked our right. His lines were advanced with great rapidity, and his force could not have been less than thirty-five thousand, besides cavalry. Portions of Polk's and Smith's corps were engaged. The lines of General Kirk soon yielded to an assault which no troops in the world could have withstood. The 32d and 39th moved promptly, but were embarrassed by the retiring forces, and their safety endangered by an assault in overwhelming numbers upon front and flanks. Lieutenant Belding moved back with four guns, but was so hotly pressed that he could not put them in position with safety; he had done nothing in his original position, because the lines falling back in our front were between his guns and the enemy's lines. He and his men stood at their pieces until the enemy's lines were within fifty yards, when they fell back, leaving two guns on the field, owing to the killing of horses attached to one, and the breaking of the pole of the other. The 49th remained in its position until ordered to retire, and fought desperately at every rod. The 15th Ohio, Colonel Wallace, delivered six rounds before falling back, whilst the 32d and 39th Indiana bravely contested the ground on the right. The courage and activity of these regiments kept the enemy in check until our artillery horses could be hitched, and the dead of the foe showed the telling effect of their fire. With cavalry on their right, infantry assailing them on the left, and heavy masses rushing to the assault in front, these regiments were directed to retire, as the only escape from annihilation or capture. Edgerton's battery, after being uncovered by the lines of General Kirk, opened fire, but before three rounds were delivered the enemy reached the guns and captured the pieces. Unchecked, the foe rushed on, and as his advance reached Goodspeed's battery, his second line reached Edgerton's battery, and that gallant officer being wounded and made prisoner, his men continued to defend themselves with their gun swabs. The 15th Ohio, Colonel Wallace, had got into position, and under cover of its fire the 49th Ohio and 89th Illinois were directed to retire by the flank. The 32d and 39th were now retiring in good order. At this juncture, learning nothing of General Willich, I felt it my duty to exert myself as far as possible to save the command. Goodspeed's battery, under command of Lieutenant Belding, was ordered to retire to a position beyond an open field, and Lieutenant Colonel Drake was directed to place the 49th Ohio in position at the same point. Here I had hoped to rally the whole brigade, but Lieutenant Colonel Drake was killed, and Major Porter, of the 49th, was severely wounded; my horse was shot, and most of our field officers were disabled or dismounted by the enemy's fire. From my position, looking to our centre, I could see our whole line falling back rapidly in some disorder, though a constant fire was kept up to the right. Lieutenant Colonel Jones was bravely rallying his men, and large numbers separated from other regiments were moving directly west, instead of to our centre. Lieutenant Belding and Lieutenant Scovill with one gun moved to the centre, whilst Lieutenant Day, in charge of three guns, moved back towards the Wilkinson road, with our extreme right. After retiring for nearly a half mile, and rallying and fighting at every available point, my second horse was killed, placing it again out of my power to communicate with our centre. Soon after, a line was rallied and formed, extending west to a small creek, and Lieutenant Belding's gun was got in position; beyond the creek Lieutenant Colonel Jones and myself rallied under cover of a fence and cedar thicket. As the enemy's columns neared our irregular lines, they were met by a rapid and deadly fire, and Lieutenant Belding opened fire at the same time with terrible effect; the rebel columns were checked and fell back across the open ground; here they opened on us with artillery, and again advanced their infantry, our line falling back.

After thus rallying and meeting the enemy several times we arrived with our flank on the Wilkinson road, a short distance west of our ammunition train; here we were charged by the enemy's cavalry and lost one gun, all of us being in the enemy's power. My sword was demanded, but just at that instant a detachment of our cavalry made a dash for our rescue, and in the confusion of the moment most of us fought our way out and escaped.

The division train was got under motion, and we moved rapidly and in considerable disorder to the Nashville road, closely pursued by the enemy's cavalry. Here the colors of the 39th Indiana were captured. At this moment I learned that a considerable portion of this brigade had reached the centre; that General Willich had been killed or captured, and that Colonel Wallace was in command of the brigade. A complete panic prevailed: teams, ambulances, horsemen, footmen, and attaches of the army, black and white, mounted on horses and mules, were rushing to the rear in the wildest confusion. I exerted myself to arrest this panic, and hastened down the road until I met Colonel Walker with his brigade, who promptly formed in line of battle, and put his artillery in position. With this assurance the tide was quite checked, and placing a strong guard of cavalry across the road, Colonel Walker moved his command to the front, compelling every able-bodied soldier to fall in. I hurried them back to the front, and thus hundreds, if not thousands, were compelled to return to their commands.

In the evening this brigade was reorganized, and by order of General Johnson, took position on our extreme right, in rear of Colonel Carlin's brigade of the first division. Though repulsed and sustaining severe loss in officers and men the day previous, the first of January found us thirteen hundred strong, and eager to participate in the dangers and struggles of the field. I was directed to reconnoitre the woods to the right and rear of our position, which was accomplished under the observation of Major Generals Rosecrans and McCook. Though within range of the enemy's battery, we reached the woods unobserved and soon met his sharpshooters, and discovered that he was massing his infantry under cover of these woods, with the apparent design of attacking our extreme right. In withdrawing we were harassed by shot and shell from his batteries, but sustaining no loss, we were soon directed to reoccupy the woods, and promptly took up our position with the 15th Ohio and the 32d Indiana and 89th Illinois in line of battle—their front covered by skirmishers, and the 39th Indiana and 49th Ohio, under Lieutenant Colonel Jones, as a reserve. The enemy's cavalry made a dash upon our position, but were gallantly repulsed by our skirmishers. The movements of the enemy on the right having *averted* the serious attention of General Rosecrans, troops were promptly placed in position to our left, and our lines withdrawn to the margin of the woods—our flank covered by a strong force of cavalry. The prompt movements of our forces, and the splendid manœuvring of the commander-in-chief, defeated the designs of the enemy, and no further attack was made.

Leaving this position on the morning of the 2d, by order of General Johnson, we were placed in an important position, so as to sustain the right, centre, or left, in case of a reverse to either. In the evening a terrible assault was made upon our extreme left, and our forces were repulsed. We were ordered to make a charge with the bayonet. The brigade moved out and deployed in splendid style. It moved with alacrity and perfect order, clearing the field and reaching the river, where we were ordered to halt. Our right flank was exposed to the enemy's infantry concealed in the woods on our right, whilst he annoyed us with his battery across Stone river.

General Palmer attempted to drive the foe from the woods, but meeting with strong resistance his aid appealed to me for re-enforcements, and the 32d Indiana was detached for that service. They met and repulsed two regiments, driving them across the river at the point of the bayonet. Nothing could exceed the gallantry and enthusiasm that this heroic regiment exhibited in this emergency. Our brigade changed the fortunes of the hour, and, under cover of our lines, the enemy was driven back and three pieces of artillery captured. Though under arms night and day, and manœuvring, we were not again brought within range of the enemy's musketry.

I must mention the fortitude and good cheer with which the officers and men submitted to the hardships and exposure of four long days and nights, without adequate rations or shelter; they cheerfully subsisted partly on parched corn, and rested in drenching rains.

On visiting the field over which we retired on the 31st abundant evidence was presented of the desperate struggle. Our men rallied whenever summoned, and delivered their fire with deadly effect. Though the enemy's wounded and many of his dead had been removed, it is safe to affirm that his killed exceeded our's as three to two, and that vast numbers were wounded. It was before our fire that General Rains, of the rebel army, was killed, and a vast number of subordinate officers and men killed and wounded. Every rod of ground over which we retired was marked by the blood of the foe, and our men reached the centre with empty cartridge-boxes. Our loss was terrible, but unavoidable, and is, to a great extent, compensated by the result ultimately obtained. We went into action with 2,458 men and 113 commissioned officers. In killed we lost 96, including 4 officers; in wounded we lost 365, including 14 officers; and our missing reach 682, including 6 officers. Many of our missing escaped and are safe in the rear, but it is probable that 400 were made prisoners.

Lieutenant Colonel Drake, 49th Ohio, fell at the post of duty, bravely cheering his men. By his death the State has lost a valued citizen, his community an ornament, his family a noble husband and kind father, and the army a most gallant and faithful soldier.

Captain Keller, of the same regiment, fell as heroes love to fall. A true patriot and accomplished soldier, he carried with him into camp and field all the graces of Christianity.

Captain Willett, of the 89th Illinois, fell whilst bravely leading his command, and such were his accomplishments as a gentleman and soldier that it will be difficult to fill his place.

Throughout these trying days and nights officers and men did their duty nobly, with a few exceptions—a few officers failed to earn the confidence of their men, and some privates sought safety in flight.

The 15th Ohio evinced the greatest courage, and many of its officers deserve special mention. Colonel Wallace, always prudent, energetic, and brave, fully sustained his high reputation as a soldier, and was the admiration of all who witnessed his conduct. Lieutenant Colonel Askew fell early on the 31st, whilst heroically cheering his men.

Captain Dawson was especially distinguished for thrilling heroism and persistent courage. This officer, conspicuous in so many battles, and so well qualified, merits, and should receive, honorable promotion.

Adjutant Du Bois, of the same regiment, deserves special mention for gallantry and good conduct.

The 49th Ohio sustained its high reputation, and though it lost ten officers it faced the foe at every point. Captain Gray, as ranking officer, had charge of a portion of the regiment on the 31st, and proved himself brave, prudent, and competent for any command. Adjutant Worton was especially heroic, and excited general admiration by his inflexible courage and great activity. Both these officers merit, and I hope will receive, promotion. Captains McCormac and Tyler were ever active, brave, and self-possessed in the midst of dangers, and showed themselves worthy and competent to command.

The splendid conduct of the 32d Indiana fully sustained its claims to confidence. Every officer and man did his duty heroically. Lieutenant Colonel Erdelmeyer, commanding, and Major Glass and Captain Monk were especially conspicuous throughout the long struggle.

Lieutenant Colonel Hotchkiss, commanding 89th Illinois volunteers, deserves the highest praise for his coolness and skill in action. He drew off his men in good order, fighting as he withdrew, and showed himself worthy of any command. This gallant officer has given to the service one of its best regiments, and has justly earned promotion. Major Hall and Captain Whiting, brave and valuable officers, I regret to say, were made prisoners. All the officers and men of this regiment did their duty promptly and earned the confidence of their companions in arms. Captain Williams, commanding during the illness of Lieutenant Colonel Hotchkiss, is an efficient and competent officer.

The 39th Indiana, Lieutenant Colonel Jones commanding, fought with desperation and terrible effect. Its list of casualties shows that where it moved the battle raged most fierce. Men could not have evinced greater courage and heroism. Captains McCleland, Cody, McCoy, Graham, and Captain Herring, acting major, merit the highest praise for their activity and energy. Lieutenant Colonel Jones discharged his duties in the most gallant manner; ever active and brave, he rallied his men at every point, and yielded only before overwhelming numbers. He met the foe in hand-to-hand conflict, and owes his escape to the skilful use of his side-arms. I beg leave to urge the name of this most meritorious officer upon the executive of his State for promotion.

I cannot too highly commend the good conduct of Lieutenants Belding, Scoville, and Day, of battery A, 1st Ohio artillery, and the men under their command. The loss of three guns was from no fault of any one. Lieutenant Belding did splendid execution upon the enemy's column, and proved himself worthy of a command. I cannot too strongly urge his promotion upon the executive of Ohio.

Surgeons Kinckler, Parks, Suttle, Kelly, and Pitman, as well as Dr. Corey, hospital steward of the 49th Ohio, remained on the field and labored for days and nights, unaided, in caring for our wounded. For thus faithfully performing their duty, at the risk of maltreatment and possible captivity, they have secured the confidence and respect of this command.

On the evening of the 31st, Captain Smith, Lieutenants Green, Miles, and McGrath, of General Willich's staff, reported to me for duty, and in all the subsequent operations of the command these gallant officers were vigilant and prompt in every duty, and to them I am under especial obligations for suggestions on the field. Though not acting under my personal observation on the 31st, they were in the thickest of the fight, and officers of experience speak of their conduct as being most intelligent and heroic in rallying our forces. James Purdy, mounted orderly, merits especial praise for his activity and courage throughout the week of battles.

I must express the deep regret of officers and men at the capture of Brigadier General Willich; having the confidence of the brigade, and being a soldier of education and experience, his removal from the command at this juncture is a public misfortune.

To Brigadier General Johnson we are under obligations for constant vigilance, unremitting energy, and his many acts of kindness and expressions of confidence towards this command.

In the name of the brigade, I am allowed to thank Major General McCook and the general-in-chief for their flattering attentions on the field, and for their repeated exhibitions of confidence in our efficiency, prudence, and courage.

I am, most respectfully,

W. H. GIBSON,
Colonel, Commanding 1st Brigade.

Captain J. R. BARTLETT,
Acting Assistant Adjutant General.

HEADQUARTERS EIGHTY-NINTH ILLINOIS INFANTRY,
1ST BRIGADE, 2D DIVISION, RIGHT WING,
In camp near Murfreesboro', January 7, 1863.

I have the honor to submit the following report of the part taken by this regiment in the series of engagements between the federal and rebel forces near Murfreesboro', Tennessee, and upon the approaches thereto, commencing on December 26, 1862, and ending on January 4, 1863, when the latter, under General Bragg, were defeated by the army of General Rosecrans and forced to evacuate all their positions in and about Murfreesboro'.

This regiment left camp in front of Nashville, with the brigade, on the morning of December 26, taking the Nolensville pike and moving slowly with the column, (as the enemy had to be driven by the advance,) through Nolensville, Triune, and along the Murfreesboro' and Franklin road, arriving, on the night of the 30th, at a point about three and one-half miles due west from Murfreesboro', where, just after dark, the brigade was put in position on the extreme right of our right wing, about 200 yards in rear of and at right angles with Kirk's brigade. My regiment was formed in double column at half distance, in rear of the 49th Ohio, which was formed in line, (fronting south.) The 15th Ohio formed in line (fronting west) on my right flank, with battery A, 1st Ohio artillery, near the right flank of the 49th Ohio and the left flank of the 15th Ohio, the 32d and 39th Indiana regiments being on picket, covering the front of our position both south and west, thus protecting the rear of the extreme right (Kirk's brigade) of the right wing. In this position my men bivouacked without fires for the night. At half-past 5 o'clock on the morning of December 31, as my men were building fires for cooking, rapid firing was heard on Kirk's front, which was almost instantly followed by the men of his brigade rushing in confusion and indiscriminately through our ranks and over my men, closely followed by a heavy column of rebel infantry. The enemy's fire being very severe and heavy upon us, and the large number of fugitives passing through and covering my front, together with peremptory orders communicated to regimental commanders of his brigade by General Willich the night previous, made it impossible for me to make a deployment or otherwise advantageously change my position. To protect my men as much as possible from the enemy's fire I ordered them to lie down. In that position they remained without confusion until my left wing was uncovered of fugitives and the enemy within fifty yards of my position, when I ordered that wing to fire, which was done with good effect, the colors of the leading column of rebels falling. Having received no orders as yet, and seeing the other regiments of the brigade falling back, I gave the order to retire by the right flank on double-quick, which was done (but with some confusion) to a lane, about 400 yards in a northwesterly direction, where I placed Captains Willett, Whiting, and Comstock, and Lieutenant Wells's companies in a very good position. But few of our shots were wasted, the colors of the leading column of the enemy again falling under our fire; but, being closely pressed, I ordered the companies to retire on the same line of direction to a point on a small creek about 500 yards distant, where I placed Captains Rowell's and Blake's companies under the partial cover of a thicket, and their fire most materially checked the enemy's advancing skirmishers, allowing me time to cross the creek with and partially reorganize my command, (Captain Rowell gradually following.) Following the line of the creek I again crossed to a point some 500 yards southeast of the 2d division hospital, where, in an open field, I joined a portion of each of the 49th and 15th Ohio and 32d Indiana regiments. The enemy's cavalry appearing on our right, and their infantry approaching on our left flank, threatening to cut us off, I moved by the left flank, (the other regiments following,) in a northeasterly direction, to a position in the woods on the south side of the Wilkinson pike, and about equidistant from the hospitals of the 1st, (General Davis's,) and the 2d, (General Johnson's,) divisions, a position from which our fire, at short range over an open field, thinned the ranks and partially checked the advance of the rebels' closely pressing columns. At this point, being informed of the loss of General Willich and Colonel Gibson, the next senior officer, the command of the brigade was assumed by Colonel Wallace, of the 15th Ohio. The forces (to me unknown) which here formed upon the right and left flanks of our brigade having retired in obedience to orders, I retired my regiment in line and in good order, making several stands in the same woods with the balance of the brigade, to and near the right of General Rousseau's division, where I was ordered by General Johnson to take position in a cedar thicket, on the right with some troops (to me unknown) who were in front and joining on the right of said division. Soon afterwards, the troops on my right and left of the line which they and I commonly held having unexpectedly and rapidly retired, and my position just then receiving the brunt of the enemy's artillery and musketry fire, and my ammunition being exhausted, I retired my regiments by the flank to the rear, there replenishing my ammunition and resting my men, who had, up to this time, taken and delivered an unceasing fire for nearly five hours.

Later in the day, being informed of the position of the balance of the brigade, I at once rejoined them, when I was put in position on the right of the same, thus unitedly forming the second line of infantry (General Davis's division being in front) on the extreme right of the right of the right wing, where we bivouacked that night without fires. The operations of the regiment during the subsequent four days were in common with the brigade, and were not of a character to need from me particular mention, with the exception of the part taken by it on the night of Friday, January 2, when, under the command of Captain Williams, (myself being unable to take active command,) it had the responsible position of guarding the ford and supporting Captain Stokes's (Chicago Board of Trade) battery, while the forces under General Negley made the successful charge upon the enemy's right. The behavior of the officers and men during this period, particularly in the trying action of the 31st, was, in steadiness and bravery, all that could be required by any commander. This phrase fully expresses my estimate of their conduct: "Every man that day did his duty." Where bravery and obedience were so general it is difficult for me to make personal discrimination, but, among my non-commissioned officers, I particularly commend for their gallantry in rallying to my colors fugitives from other commands, Sergeant Major John M. Farquar and Sergeant Erastus O. Young, of company "A;" also Captain Button G. Cody, of the 39th Indiana, and Lieutenant Seifert, of the 32d Indiana, who tendered their services to me on the field and fought gallantly in my ranks.

The following is the list of casualties during the period specified.

Very respectfully, your obedient servant,

C. W. HOTCHKISS,
Lieutenant Colonel Commanding.

Captain CARL SCHMITZ,
Assistant Adjutant General.

List of the killed, wounded, and missing in the eighty-ninth regiment Illinois volunteer infantry in the series of engagements commencing December 31, 1862, *and ending January* 4, 1863.

Killed.—Captain Henry S. Willett and Corporal Wm. H. Litsey, company H; Privates Jas. Nichols, company E; Moses Beaver and Elijah Tonlin, company F; De Witt C. Scudder, Geo. W. Murray, and David H. Bestor, company G; Henry Huggins, company H; Wm. Holdren, company I. Total, 10.

Wounded.—Adjutant Ed. F. Bishop; Sergeants John H. Moore, company A; —— Olinier, company D; Jas. F. Copp and J. S. Prescott, company F; Corporal H. H. Warner, company C; Privates Jas. I. Egan, Franklin H. Mellen, and Louis Saunders, company A; Frank Granger, Ralph Purdy, Eli Morris, and Alonzo Henderson, company D; Patrick McGrath, James Wildrick, and Hiram H. Crain, company E; Ira Bridgeford, Henry Fitch, and Joseph Goyer, company F; John Herlick, David Kerr, Herman J. Rosenleaf, Wilfred H. Whitney, Robert Wilson, David E. Sprouse, and Charles V. Bainbridge, company G; Orton H. Barnes, James Snowball, Ole H. Johnson, F. W. Godard, Thomas N. Mosley, and Wm. J. Cooper, company H; A. Bigley, Joseph Guthrie, Joseth J. Loydd, Charles Nelson, and Henry Shecter, company I; Michael Schabinger, Frank Diesel, John P. Adams, Fred. L. Phillips, and John Reed, company K; Musicians Justus D. Payne, company A; Wm. Forman, company G; A. W. Parker, company I. Total, 45.

Missing.—Major Duncan J. Hall; Captain Thos. Whiting, company G; Sergeant Joseph Cushman, company F; Corporals Jay R. Lowrey, company A; Richard M. Vanegen, company B; Matthew W. Claxton, company C; George Shears, Andrew Golden, and George L. Richards, company E; Jason Wallace, company F; Thomas H. Berry and George H. Wagoner, company G; Sergeant Ed. Humphrey, company D; Corporals David Labouty, David S. Allen, and Oliver Bunker, company D; Privates Robert Armstrong, Charles Lord, Roger Duffy, Gardner Fuller, Jasper Luper, Philip Mulinix, Franklin Russell, Henry Sterling, and Enoch D. T. Sharp, company A; John C. Mercer, company B; Jacob Becker, Charles Davis, Peter Hussey, Daniel Nellis, Pat. H. NcNamee, Thomas Maroney, Robert Purcell, Wesley Wilson, George M. Jones, and Marvin J. Spoor, company C; Joseph Zach, L. W. Beardsley, W. H. Milcham, Charles Fisher, Marion King, Mada Rubidi, Henry Tinsley, Wm. Voorhes, John Miller, W. S. Rice, Jackson Arnold, Wm. D. Walker, and Leo Laurent, company D; H. G. Bramble, C. M. Bryant, Thomas Clark, S. G. Eggleston, F. W. Le Comte, R. B. Mack, John Pinegar, Daniel Porter, Wm. Saddler, Wm. H. Simmons, and Jubal Shaw, company E; Joseph Babbitt, James Perkins, Russell Huntley, Washington Cox, Curtis B. Knox, Wm. Chamberlain, Addison Weaver, Reuben L. Kelly, Wm. Golden, and Henry Couch, company F; Hiram Cole, James Livingston, W. H. Nesbitt, Andrew Topper, and George Wells, company G; W. H. Delancy, Nels Christianson, Jos. Haigh, John B. Smith, and John Whitehead, company H; J. R. Marmon, A. G. Rouse, Henry J. Lowe, Robert Smith, Wm. H. Bissell, John Cole, and Wm. R. Piventon, company I; George Nugent, Thomas Creighton, Wm. Reed, Thomas Rogers, and John Nelson, company K; Musicians Marcus H. Perry, company C; Walter Huff, company F. Total, 94.

CAMP NEAR MURFREESBORO', TENNESSEE,
January 7, 1863.

SIR: I have the honor to submit the following report of operations of the 39th regiment of Indiana volunteers since December 25, 1862.

Nothing of note occurred after breaking camp near Nashville, Tennessee, until the regiment arrived on the field of operations in the enemy's front, near Murfreesboro', Tennessee, where it arrived December 30, 1862. On the evening of the same day the 1st brigade, to which the regiment belongs, was moved to the extreme right of the right wing of the army, the line of battle of the brigade being nearly at right angles with that of the right wing.

I was ordered to detail five (5) companies from the 39th Indiana for pickets during the night. My orders were to join the left of my line with the right of General Kirk, and join my right on the left of the picket line of the 32d, and leave the five (5) reserve companies in line of battle facing towards my picket line. Companies A, B, C, D, and K, were detailed, and having deployed A, C, and D, as skirmishers, with B and K as supports, I joined picket lines with General Kirk and 32d Indiana, as ordered. The following diagram will aid in explaining the operations of the 31st:

DIAGRAM.

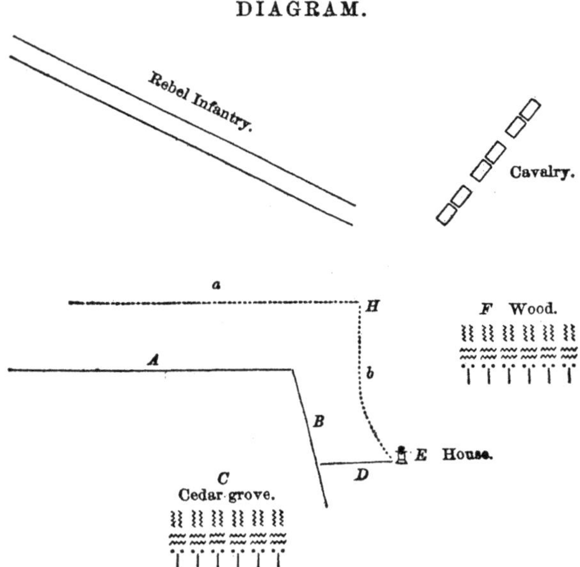

A, line of battle of right wing; B, position of reserve companies of 39th Indiana; dotted line *a*, General Kirk's pickets; dotted *b*, picket line of 39th Indiana, distant from the reserve one-half mile; line extends through open corn-field from point H to house E. About 3 o'clock a. m, December 31, 1862, I received orders from General Willich to throw forward one company to patrol the wood F in our front, and distant about 600 yards. Captain Herring, acting major, immediately sent company B forward for that purpose. At early daylight General Willich ordered me, in case there should be any indication that the rebels had placed a battery in our front, to move my picket line at once to the wood F, and hold it until the brigade could give me support. I went immediately to the picket line, and, learning from the patrol that no indication of the enemy had been seen, I was on the point of ordering company B from the front when several shots were fired from the pickets on our left, who gave way at the point H, leaving our flank exposed. I ordered Lieutenant Stanley to reconnect his line with General Kirk and hold his ground. At the same time I ordered all the company reserves on the picket line, forming a very strong skirmish line. Scarcely had this disposition been made when Kirk's pickets again gave way, and three regiments of rebel infantry, moving abreast in line of battle, were interposed between my picket line and the reserve companies.

Seeing that the rebel line of battle was oblique to that of our right wing, and supposing that our brigade would either charge obliquely on the 39th Indiana or place the batteries in position to enfilade the rebel lines, I, partly to support such a movement and partly to secure an opportunity to rally the pickets on the reserve, ordered Captain Herring to move the pickets in double-quick time by the right flank and take position behind the fence D, and open fire on the advancing foe, at the same time sending Lieutenant Neal to the house E to open the fence and show the companies where to commence filing to the right. We succeeded in rallying company A and parts of companies D and K behind the fence, when the enemy opened upon us a murderous fire. Lieutenant Neal fell mortally wounded, and of the few who took position there nearly one-half were either killed or wounded. Twice did our fire cause the enemy's lines to halt and waver, but he quickly rallied and moved forward. Had we been supported here either with infantry or artillery the enemy would have been repulsed with great slaughter. But no support came. Three rebel standards were within thirty feet of the fence when I ordered the men to double-quick to the cedar thicket C, where they again made a stand and covered the retreat of Goodspeed's battery. Here I first learned that my five reserve companies, under command of Captain Cady, senior captain, had charged front forward on seven companies and had bravely held their ground until the regiment on their left had given way and they were forced to abandon their position. They retired in good order for some distance when their ranks were thrown into confusion by the rush of stragglers through their lines. Seeing our colors at a distance, I ordered the skirmishers to fall back at once and join them. I met Colonel Gibson near this point, and we selected a ground on which to rally our two regiments; but ignorance of the topography of the country and the operations of our cavalry threw me so far over to the right as to separate me from Colonel Gibson and involve me in difficulty with the rebel cavalry, which was swarming on our flank. The division train being threatened by this cavalry, I rallied as many men as possible to its support and escorted it safely and in good order to the Nashville pike. Here both myself and the other officers did our utmost to file the regiment to the right and join the centre of our army, but at this time the panic on the pike was at the highest and our men were swept away as by a whirlwind, leaving me but a handful of men and officers. With these, after having been under a murderous fire for over eight hours, with our colors lost and men dispirited, I joined General Johnson near the rear of the centre of our army. Had I been better acquainted with the topography of the country I might have saved more men; but hour after hour elapsed and I received no orders, and I did not even know where to direct my line of retreat; yet every obstacle, thicket, fence or ravine, was taken advantage of, and at no time was our fire relaxed. Our loss was terrible. We had thirty-one killed, including one lieutenant; one hundred and eighteen wounded, including two lieutenants, and two hundred and thirty-one missing, including one captain and one lieutenant. Of those reported missing I have reason to believe that very many are wounded, though, perhaps, slightly. How well the regiment fought let the above fearful list proclaim. Over thirty fell behind the fence D, while opposed to ten times their number, yet no man left his post until ordered. Lieutenant Neal, acting adjutant, fell here; no truer gentleman, no better soldier or braver man, belongs to the great patriot army. He fell at his post doing his duty; he is no longer with us, but his name is in his country's history and his memory is enshrined in the hearts of all who knew him well. Lieutenant Leawel was also wounded while in the discharge of his duty. He is a brave man and good officer. Most of the company officers acted manfully. I am under obligations to Captains McCoy, McClelland, Cody and Graham, Lieutenants Foot, Stanly, Mitchel, Clark, Hamilton and Scott for efficient and timely aid. Of Captain Thomas Herring, acting major, I cannot say too much in his praise; always at the post of danger, brave and cool, aiding here in rallying the men and there in directing the fire so as to render it most effective. He deserves well of his regiment and his country. Private James Gray, of company E, behaved nobly. No commissioned officer did more that day to rally the men than he did; he deserves promotion. Sergeants Boyce, Jones, Crozier, Noah Davis, Daniel Wilkins and Mark Molike are also worthy of mention. Assistant Surgeon John Gray did everything mortal man could do in caring for the wounded, and richly merits the deepest gratitude of the regiment and friends of the wounded. On January 1, 1863, the 49th Ohio and 39th Indiana were consolidated at the request of Colonel Gibson, commanding brigade, and the request of the officers of the 49th. I assumed command of the two. My command took an important part in the manœuvring in the right wing January 1, and also in the bayonet charge of the brigade on the evening of January 2. In this charge the men were in excellent spirits, and never in the history of the two regiments would they have fought with greater desperation than on that night. Three men of the 49th Ohio were wounded by shells thrown from the enemy's batteries. My thanks are due to Captains Hays, Gray, and Tyler; also to Lieutenant Kesler and Adjutant C. McNorton. Their untiring energy and zeal roused the drooping spirits of their men, and excited enthusiasm out of despondency.

Very respectfully,

F. W. JONES,

Lieutenant Colonel, Commanding 39th Indiana.

Captain CARL SCHMIDT, *A. A. G.*

HEADQUARTERS 32D INDIANA VOLUNTEERS,

Camp near Murfreesboro', Tenn., January 7, 1863.

SIR: I respectfully submit to you the official report of the part taken by the 32d Indiana volunteers in the late battle at Murfreesboro' and in the events of the days preceding.

The regiment left the camp near Mill creek on the morning of the 26th of December, 1862, and marched to Nolensville. On the 27th the regiment advanced to Triune. On the 28th, having the advance guard of the brigade, participated in a reconnoissance towards Shelbyville. On the 29th we left Triune, crossing over to within four miles of Murfreesboro'. On the 30th, the battle having commenced, the regiment moved up to the road and performed picket duty on the right flank of the extreme right of the army corps. On the morning of the 31st, firing having been heard on our left, Lieutenant S. Green, of the staff of General A. Willich, ordered me to draw in the pickets and move up to the brigade. Before I was able to summon seven companies of my command and form them in line, facing towards the centre, I observed the enemy's columns advancing and firing. At the same time a great portion of our battery, guns, caissons, and battery teams, together with a dense mass of infantry, in disorder, came rushing towards us, and breaking through the regiment, forced our men to give way and fall back. The confusion and panic having then become general, I was unable to reassemble the regiment until we had retreated along the creek for nearly three-quarters of a mile, when we succeeded in rallying about 200 of our men. I would respectfully state that Lieutenant Belling, of Captain Goodspeed's battery, had retreated with me with one gun, and by firing several times on the enemy checked their flanking columns. We then moved towards the centre of the engagement, firing on the enemy's cavalry at different times, and met at a rise of the ground the rest of the division, where Colonel Wallace, of the 15th Ohio, directed me to fall in line with his regiment. The enemy advancing at that time, we fought there for more than an hour, and being relieved by fresh troops, fell back and joined the brigade. In the afternoon of the 1st of January we moved to a strip of woods on the right of the first hospital on the Nashville road, and remained there during the night, picketing.

On the 2d we moved with the brigade as reserve to the centre of the right wing. Towards 5 o'clock the brigade was ordered to charge on the enemy on the left of our centre. While the regiment advanced in line of battle towards Stone river, General Palmer rode up and ordered me to move the regiment by the right flank into a strip of woods on our right occupied by the enemy. On approaching said woods I received their fire and threw out my skirmishers to cover my advance. We then charged and drove them back to the edge of the hill, where the heavy firing commenced, the enemy contesting every inch of ground. My skirmishers, advancing on the right and left, unexpectedly found themselves within fifteen yards of the enemy, lying below the crest of the hill. At that time a regiment came up to our support on the right. They fired one volley and fell back in disorder. A second regiment (31st Indiana) came up in fine style, and at the right moment, assisted us in driving the enemy from his position, causing him to retreat precipitately and in great disorder across Stone river. It having grown night for nearly two hours it was impossible to gain more advantages or better results of the fight, keeping our position until relieved by General Palmer's pickets, after which we returned to camp.

The casualties of December 31 amount to 2 killed, 13 wounded, and 115 missing; of January 2, 10 killed, 27 wounded, none missing.

List of killed, wounded, and missing.

Killed.—Company A: Privates William Roedel, Jacob Ostertag, and Berhard Mardoff. Company C: Private Frederick Pepper. Company D: Sergeant Louis Young, and Private A. Stemler. Company E: Private Frederick Meier. Company F: Sergeant Henry Kaiser. Company G: Sergeant Bancratz Hurst and Private Henry Weidenhorst. Company K: Privates Jacob Gessner, and Joseph Roetken.

Wounded.—Company A: Privates John Wyss, Louis Schermeyer, John Stengel, and Frank Marx. Company B: Orderly Sergeant Frederick Knorr, Privates Frederick Urlan, and Jacob Forthoffer. Company C: Privates Louis Peitsch David Fischer, Christian Lipper, and Peter Rittner. Company D: Corporal G. Deuschle, Privates B. Binder, J. Faber, J. Remer, and A. Weihnacht. Company E: Privates Henry Hellwich, and William Schoepple. Company F: Privates Christian Bussian, George Schunck, Gottlieb Weidman, and Anton Weigle. Company G: Sergeants Math. Schwedelsicker, Frederick Becker, Louis Schilling, and Private Nic. Ostermann. Company H: Privates Philip Ecker, Aug. Kelbe, Joseph Bahole, Conrad Mueller, and Louis Wagner. Company I: Private Christian Gross. Company K: Sergeant Fritz Notzer, Corporals Christian Jahn, John Zensius, Fritz Weber, Privates Philip Rickerick, Frederick Britthaus, Robert Camp, and Henry Roesmer.

Missing.—Company A: Privates Jacob Schuler, Sib. Walff, Jacob Hunt, Jacob Keihr, John Frick, Frank Rolfus, John Brumley, and William Muerke. Company B: Sergeant Peter Kraemer, Corporals Louis Nagel, Louis Wolff, Privates John Ardner, Henry Binkhoff, John Betz, Eberh'd Brown, Otto Brehn, Peter Brisbow, John Fick, Conrad Flaerke, John Treund, Adolf Kerner, Jacob Pfaertner, Ernst Schlegel, Peter Schnabel, Philip Schwertzer, Peter Spely, Aug. Stroh, George Weber, Peter Wendel, and Charles Zucknegel. Company C: Privates John Adam, Charles Aehle, Aug. Defloh, Wilhelm Degg, Christian Kessner, Michael Mueller, D. Sultan, Christian Schercher, Frederick Zreimer, William Ackermann, John Anger, and Louis Ellerbrook. Company D: Corporal M. Frisch, Privates Peter Zwickel, C. Sander, M. Vogel, F. Gaebler, F. Young, T. Ingenthron, George App, J. A. Schmitt, and G. Sturn. Company E: Musician Julius Berndt, Privates Math. Brosatt, Nicholas Fillbeck, George Graff, Gustav Klein, Frederick Locher, Tac Meyer, John Rolfes, George Stegmeyer, and D. Sandmann. Company F: Corporal Adam Liebler, Privates Frederick Aehler, Michael Dehninger, William Berg, John Bohleber, Samuel Gfroerer, Adam Kauffman, Adrian Muttag, Frederick Ochs, Martin Ritter, Adolf Sommer, and Herman Tiemeyer. Company G: Corporal Albert Raupp, Privates Henry Haefner, Christian Arnold, John Besenfelder, John Hummel, Henry Mitz, William Ott, John Sauer, Michael Goeppner, John Waltz, and Anton Schmitt. Company H: Corporals Christ. Kray, Gallero Koenig, Privates Henry Blanke, George Mantz, John Lutz, John Ulrich, Aloes Busch, Julius Weber, John Faunicke, Caspar Huch, Thomas Taercher, James Humpher, and John Schoenstein. Company I: Privates Peter Schuessler, Joseph Hamm, Peter Eckenfels, Louis Hacke, Michael Capeller, Marcellus Ossamowsky, Conrad Rollfing, Vall. Steiger, Frederick Stemper, William Walter, Anton Palest, and Mc. Wendel. Company K: Privates Philip Decker, George Denzer, Berthold Kamp, George Stroebel, and Fritz Kunow.

I have the honor to be, very respectfully, your obedient servant,

FRANK ERDELMEYER,

Lieutenant Colonel, Commanding 32d Indiana Volunteers.

Colonel W. H. GIBSON, *Commanding 1st Brigade.*

HEADQUARTERS 15TH INFANTRY OHIO VOLUNTEERS,

January 7, 1863.

In accordance with orders from Colonel Gibson, commanding brigade, I have the honor to report to you the part taken by the 15th Ohio in the march from Nashville to Murfreesboro', and the engagements in which the 15th participated. We were first engaged with the enemy on the morning of December 31, 1862, about 7 o'clock, when I found the enemy approaching in our rear, and received the order from Colonel Gibson to move out and form line of battle; to do this I countermarched the regiment and took up a position about ten rods in front of my camp. By the time this was accomplished, the — brigade, in rear of the 1st brigade, had given way, and, with the balance of our brigade, were in full retreat. We held this position only long enough to cover the retreat of our forces, when I gave the order to fall back. It was at this point where the brave and gallant Lieutenant Colonel Askew fell, severely wounded in the thigh, and was taken prisoner, and the no less brave Captain Douglass and Lieutenant Hillis also fell; Captain Douglass wounded in the breast, and Lieutenant Hillis in the thigh; both fell into the enemy's hands; all of the above have been paroled, and are now within our lines. Major McClennahan was slightly wounded in the shoulder, but made his escape on foot with the regiment. Five men of the regiment were killed at this point. The retreat was through an open field, with a high fence to cross before we could get under cover of the woods. Most of my killed and wounded occurred at or near this fence. Having placed this fence between us and the enemy, we fell back in good order, keeping up a brisk and deadly fire on the advancing foe. I rallied the regiment about one half mile from my camp, being greatly assisted by Captain Dawson and Adjutant Du Bois, both of whom showed themselves to be brave and gallant officers. At this time I found myself in command of the brigade, and my report of the 15th for the balance of the day will be included in that of the brigade, which was rallied here, and with one piece of artillery, under Lieutenant Belding, we checked the advance of the rebel column. Lieutenant Belding is deserving of great praise for the admirable manner of handling his piece; from the effects of three shots not less than one hundred of the enemy fell. When in command of the brigade, Adjutant Norton, of the 49th Ohio, Captain Schmitt, Lieutenant Mills, Lieutenant Green, and Lieutenant McGrath, of General Willich's staff, rendered invaluable assistance in rallying the men, in charging the enemy, and conducting the retreat. Captain Dawson took command of the 15th Ohio, Major McClennahan not feeling able to do so, and once when there was danger of the men breaking in wild confusion, he seized the colors of the 15th, and by a united cheer the brigade was again formed and checked again the enemy's advance; the brigade fell back at last in rear of General Rousseau's lines and formed again, and held the rebels' advance in check, but were again compelled to fall back by the overwhelming numbers of the enemy in rear of General Van Cleve's division, who put a stop to the further advance of the enemy. · On the evening of this day I learned with pleasure of the safety of Colonel Gibson, who took command of the brigade. Under his direction the 15th took part in the manœuvring on the right the following day, and on the succeeding day was present in the charge made by the 1st brigade upon the right of the enemy, and in which but one man of the 15th was injured, Sergeant Malin, who was struck by a piece of shell in the thigh. Major McClennahan rejoined the regiment on the 3d, having been ordered to do so by the brigade commander. I am pleased to mention with pride the gallant bearing of all the company officers of the 15th who took part in the action of the 31st and the following days of the conflict. They did their whole duty under the trying circumstances under which they were placed.

Lieutenant Fowler was wounded slighly in the right leg, and taken prisoner on the 31st, but he is now within our lines.

From the 31st of December to the evening of the 4th of January, the loss of the 15th was: Killed, 17; wounded, 68; missing, 127.

Your obedient servant,

WM. WALLACE,
Colonel, Commanding 15th Infantry Ohio Volunteers.

Captain C. SCHMITT,
A. A. G. 1st Brigade, 2d Division,
Right Wing 14th Army Corps.

P. S.—I cannot close my report without speaking in terms of highest commendation of Dr. Kelly, of this regiment, who remained with our wounded, and by his untiring efforts succeeded in having our unlucky braves made as comfortable as the nature of the circumstances would permit.

Report of the casualties of the 49th Ohio volunteers, in the action of December 31, 1862.

Lieutenant Colonel Levi Drake, killed; Major B. S. Porter, wounded.

Company A.—(Captain S. F. Gray.)—Killed: Corporals William Clark, George W. Platt, Privates Charles Witherbee and John Roller. Wounded: Second Lieutenant T. F. Ray, slightly; Privates Ebenezer Henderson, S. M. Dixon, slightly; G. W. Brookes, slightly; James Linch, slightly; Martin Butler, slightly; Salamus Bowlby, slightly; James Gilpin, slightly; George Benham, slightly; and A. J. Ryan, slightly. Missing: Sergeant G. W. Vail, Corporals Edward Bearse, William Bowring, Henry H. Ludwig, Privates Henry C. Stevens, Ephriam Edwards, John W. Davis, David Bender, and Josiah Kimmell.

Company B.—(Captain J. E. McCormick.)—Wounded: Orderly Sergeant W. T. Lutz, slightly; Privates John Festler, slightly; David P. Grubb, severely; Daniel W. Smith, slightly: Theodore Gibson, severely; and James H. Vannater, severely. Missing: Sergeant David H. Dagwall, Corporals David Stewart, B. H. Fansey, Philip Miller, Privates John Clevidence, David A. Bennett, David M. Winn, Pleasant Tracy, M. L. Shade, Andrew Berkert, William Stevenson, Oliver Ragan, Samuel Myser, W. H. Black, H. Clay Myres, William Bayer, G. W. Pancoast, and A. P. Havens.

Company C.—(Captain Amos Keller, fatally wounded, since died.)—Killed: Corporal Joseph Stough; Privates Joseph Porter Moore, Edward Patrick Hatten, Daniel Messmore, and William Myres. Wounded: First Lieutenant Aaron H. Keller, severely; Privates Silas Bland, slightly; Samuel Core, slightly; James P. Rader, slightly; Ohen H. Rader, slightly; Oliver J. Keller, slightly; Bradford Charles Spicer, slightly; George T. Cost, slightly; and John C. Knipple. Missing: Second Lieutenant Andrew G. Brown, Privates Uriah Bower, Roswell Dame, Henry Shaffer, John Wood, John P. Cost, William Nagle, and Philip Blom.

Company D.—(Captain G. W. Culver.)—Wounded: Captain George W. Culver, slightly; Second Lieutenant Milton Cowgill, slightly; Corporals J. C. Loy, slightly; W. P. Blackburn, slightly; Privates Nathan Ravert, slightly; C. B. Morgan, slightly; G. W. Mulholland, slightly; S. A. Dorborough, slightly; David Cramer, slightly; and Amos Bretz, slightly. Missing: Privates Henry Campbell, William Michaels, James Zint, Marshall Eckelbery, William Dean, and Wilson Carr.

Company E.—(Lieutenant Jacob Miller.)—Killed: Private James W. Ferris. Wounded: Corporal Aaron Sohr, severely; Privates Eli Warner, severely; William Hinneman, severely; William A. Carlisle, severely; Almon Riker, severely; Justin Eller, slightly; Oliver G. Jacobs, slightly; Lorenzo Emmons, slightly; Robert Caldwell, slightly; Henry Pennell, slightly; Benjamin F. Smith, slightly; Pliny Trumbo, slightly; Ruben King, slightly. Missing: Corporals Franklin Crowell, Winfield G. Stevens, Privates Sidney J. Graham, Walter Young, James Caldwell, David A. Sprout, Franklin S. Richards, Gideon Sabins, Alexander Bowman, and David Williams.

Company F.—(First Lieutenant John Kessler.)—Killed: Corporal Isaiah Terry and Private I. N. Anderson. Wounded: Second Lieutenant I. O. Totten, slightly; Sergeant L. Laughlin, slightly and missing; Corporal Eli Lewman, slightly; Privates Albert Dodge, severely; I. G. Shutts, slightly; Thomas Burdell, slightly; L. S. Porter, slightly; and William Burdue, slightly. Missing: Sergeant C. W. England, Corporals W. H. H. Wadsworth, C. C. Laughlin, Privates M. Rogers, W. Addelspeher, George Davis, Gustavus Baesch, Jonathan Durfree, and Michael Baker.

Company G.—(Second Lieutenant I. H. White.)—Killed: Sergeant Joseph

J. Basom, Private Washington Rummell. Wounded: Corporals John W. Reynolds, slightly; John Caldwell, slightly; John D. Myers, severely; and Private William H. Vance, slightly. Missing: Second Lieutenant Isaac H. White, Corporal Richard L. Hudson, Privates John W. Currell, Charles W. Cooley, Benjamin F. Culver, Mathias Fowwather, James S. Gibson, George B. Good, John Henry, Amos E. Kitchen, William Robenall, Samuel Sower, William Storm, Walter Weber, and Jerome Williams.

Company H.—(First Lieutenant H. Chance.)—Wounded: Orderly Sergeant Clayton Everett, severely; Sergeants Francis R. Stewart, slightly; Frederic Werner, severely; Corporal Simpson P. Miller, slightly; Privates Elisha Hale, severely; John W. Bossler, slightly; John W. Chilcote, slightly; Reuben Casey, and Carolus Simon. Wounded and Missing: Corporal Isaac W. Lenard, severely; Privates John Johnson, slightly; Niloba H. Glick, slightly; Samuel Nesbitt, slightly; Julius Leitner, severely; and Jeremiah C. Hartz. Missing: Privates Allva Angel, George W. Fritcher, Daniel B. Musgrove, Henry Wickard, Theodore Whitman, Charles Werner, and Simeon G. Crawford.

Company I.—(Captain M. E. Tyler.)—Killed: Privates William I. Lisle, and Austin Himmell. Wounded: Sergeant John M. Cartwright, slightly; Privates Hiram L. Reed, slightly; William Hashberger, severely; Peter Leffler, severely; Thomas Barker, slightly; William A. Bushong, slightly; James E. Huston, slightly; James S. Carver, slightly; John Fahey, slightly; Thomas W. Prentiss, seriously; Warner White, prisoner, slightly; Samuel Terrell, slightly; and Thomas Van Buskirk, fatally. Missing: Sergeant Ezra Phelps, Corporals George D. Harris, Arthur Bell, Privates Uriah Johnson, Andrew Clark, David Jack, Samuel Faltner, Jonas Lenhart, William H. Craig, and Jacob Leffler.

Company K.—(Lieutenant S. M. Harper.)—Killed: Privates Charles Whittem and Henry Messel. Wounded: Corporal William H. Musgrave, severely; Privates John Lawrence, severely; Franklin S. Brobst, slightly; Alexander C. Parjelis, slightly; and J. M. McConnell, (nature of wound not known.) Missing: Privates Silas Debolt, William Emerson, Henry K. Funk, James R. Green, Samuel T. Kearns, Edward P. Marble, Wilson S. Orm, Nathan Zimmerman, and Jesse Dicken.

Recapitulation.

Company	A.—	Killed	4 ...... Wounded	10	...... Missing	9
"	B.	"	0	"	6	" 18
"	C.	"	5	"	9	" 8
"	D.	"	0	"	10	" 7
"	E.	"	1	"	13	" 10
"	F.	"	2	"	8	" 10
"	G.	"	2	"	4	" 15
"	H.	"	0	"	15	" 13
"	I.	"	2	"	13	" 11
"	K.	"	2	"	5	" 9
Total,		killed	18	wounded	93	missing 108

Aggregate, 219.

Respectfully submitted,

O. B. HAYS,
Captain, Commanding.

D. R. Cook,
Sergeant Major and Acting Adjutant.

HEADQUARTERS FIRST REGIMENT OHIO VOLUNTEERS,
In Camp, January 5, 1863.

CAPTAIN: I have the honor to report the part taken by my regiment in the recent battles and skirmishes about Murfreesboro'.

On the morning of the 27th of December, 1863, when about a mile below Nolensville, the enemy appeared in our front. I was ordered by you to form a line of battle on the right of the pike, my left resting on the right of the 6th Indiana, and deploy two companies as skirmishers, and to advance. I did so, deploying company B, Lieutenant Dumbusch commanding, and company D, Lieutenant Hayward commanding. We had severe skirmishing all day, but drove the enemy before us, and encamped near Triune. On the morning of the 30th of December we were ordered to join our division, which had preceded us the day before, within about four miles of Murfreesboro'. We arrived about four o'clock, and, after making a reconnoisance on our right, we fell back and bivouacked for the night in a piece of woods in the rear of our division. On the morning of the 31st, about half-past six o'clock, I heard what I thought to be heavy skirmishing on our right. I immediately ordered my command under arms, and marched to and halted on the edge of the woods just to the right of where we bivouacked the night previous. A few moments after, by your orders, I moved forward at a double-quick across a large open field and formed my line behind a rail fence, on a line with the 6th Indiana, (they occupying a piece of woods to my left,) with two pieces of Simonson's battery between us, the 79th Illinois and 30th Indiana occupying the right, the 79th in reserve. I ordered Lieutenant Hayward, company D, to deploy the first platoon of his company as skirmishers. This had hardly been done when the enemy appeared in our front in three distinct lines of battle, followed by columns closed in mass, several batteries of artillery, and a large amount of cavalry, the left of their lines extending not less than one-fourth of a mile to the right of the 30th Indiana. As soon as they arrived within about one hundred and fifty yards of my line, I opened fire, which checked their advance for about fifteen minutes. Their line then in front of me seemed to separate, and I saw them marching by the flank to the right and left of us. Immediately after this manœuvre the two regiments on my right gave way and left my flank entirely unprotected. The enemy's left then changed their front to the right and marched diagonally towards my right. At this moment the 6th Indiana was forced from their position, the enemy immediately taking possession of the fence they occupied. They then again appeared in my front and opened an enfilading fire on my regiment. Finding it was impossible to hold my position without being annihilated, I ordered my regiment to fall back, intending to take a position in the rear of the Louisville Legion, who were at that time supporting me. My regiment started back in good order, but coming in contact with the Louisville Legion, (Colonel Berry having just ordered a change of front forward on first company to protect our right,) we became entangled with them, as we did also with the 93d Ohio, whom you had ordered to our support. I then fell back in some confusion to the woods occupied by me some half hour previous. Here I tried to form my line, but again became entangled with a part of the first brigade. My regiment became scattered and it was impossible to get them into line until we had fallen back through the woods into a cotton field and into another piece of woods. Here, by your help and the united efforts of my officers, I succeeded in rallying part of my regiment and took position on the left of Colonel Berry, who had also succeeded in rallying part of his regiment. Here the enemy was checked and driven back a short distance, but they soon rallied and came down in a solid mass, and we were obliged again to retire. In a short time after I rallied a portion of my regiment, and meeting Captains Trapp and O'Connell, who had succeeded in doing the same, (in all amounting to about 100 men,) I halted and formed a line. Here I was joined by a portion of the 93d Ohio, under the command of Lieutenant Harmon. I took command of the whole. At this moment I received an order from General Johnson to proceed immediately to a certain point, but the guide missed the place, so I took a position on the left of a regiment, (I do not know what regiment,) who were hotly engaged with the enemy. Here I remained until I was ordered to fall back in the rear of General Rousseau's division. Soon after Colonel Anderson, of the 93d Ohio, came up and took command, and was ordered to proceed in the direction of the river; that we were needed there. Word soon came that our division was again forming on the left of the railroad running towards Nashville. I immediately proceeded to that point, where I found about 100 more men of my regiment, under command of their respective officers. By your order, I again moved forward with the balance of our brigade to the support of another brigade who were hotly contesting the ground we now occupy. After a short and severe fight the enemy were driven off, and with considerable fighting and skirmishing it has been held ever since.

The loss in my regiment is heavy, so far as heard from. 8 non-commissioned officers and privates killed; 1 officer and 46 non-commissioned officers and privates wounded, and 81 missing; a partial list of which you have already received. My officers and men behaved most gallantly, and I do not think there are any soldiers in the world that could have done better under the circumstances. I would most respectfully recommend for your favorable consideration Captain Kuhlman, company B, acting field officer; Captain Trapp, company G; Captain O'Connell, company F; Captain Pomeroy, company E; Captain Prentiss, company H; Captain Hooker, company A; Captain Snodgrass, company I; First Lieutenant Henry Dumbusch, company B, commanding; First Lieutenant George Hayward, company D, commanding; Adjutant Samuel W. Davies, and Second Lieutenant Kuhlman, company B, commanding company C; Second Lieutenant R. Chappel, commanding company K; Second Lieutenant Denny, company G, and Second Lieutenant Varian, not yet assigned to any company. They are all justly entitled to the thanks of their superiors for their gallant conduct in the past few days. All have been engaged in the service during the breaking out of the rebellion; have been in several engagements, and proved themselves worthy the confidence reposed in them. A more gallant and braver set of officers never entered a field. I would also mention our surgeons, Drs. Wilson and Barr. They performed their duties faithfully and unflinchingly.

I had forgotten to mention that some time during the day a portion of my regiment, under Lieutenant Dumbusch and Adjutant Davies, gallantly repulsed a charge of the enemy's cavalry, and drove them off altogether.

Very respectfully, your obedient servant,

J. A. STAFFORD,
Major 1st Regiment Ohio Volunteers, Commanding.

Captain BURNS,
Acting Assistant Adjutant General 4th Brigade.

HEADQUARTERS L. L., 5TH REGIMENT KENTUCKY VOLUNTEER INFANTRY,
In Camp, January 8, 1863.

SIR: Having been called upon to furnish a report of the operations of my command from the 26th day of December, 1862, to the 4th day of January, 1863, inclusive, I have the honor to submit the following:

On the morning of the 26th of December, 1862, being on picket duty with my regiment, I received orders to join the column marching southward on the Nolensville road; we reached Nolensville at three o'clock the next morning.

At daylight of the 27th I was ordered forward, and marching three miles we found the enemy, with some artillery, prepared to obstruct our march. We were thrown out on the right of the road, and immediately pushed at them, but they fell back to a new position; and this was repeated time and again throughout the day, till we reached a point one mile south of Triune. We traversed in line of battle this day some four or five miles of country, made up of corn and cotton fields, thickets, swamps, and woods. I sustained no loss in this skirmish. Sunday morning, December 28, I was ordered to support General Willich in a reconnoissance; no enemy was found, and we returned to camp. On Monday General McCook's command having moved off towards Murfreesboro', distant some fifteen miles, we were left near Triune to prevent the enemy interrupting the march of the main column; here we remained till the morning of the 30th, when we marched off towards Murfreesboro' and rejoined the division, which we found moving into position beyond Wilkinson's Crossroads. In a short time orders came for us to support a cavalry reconnoissance of the country lying to the right of our front. No enemy was found in this direction and we returned to the division; we were then placed in position as a reserve for the other two brigades of General Johnson's command, occupying the extreme right of the army. Early the next morning I received orders to form a line of battle 150 paces in rear of the 1st regiment Ohio volunteers; this done, the command forward was given. (In this advance Captain A. H. Speed, of company C, was struck in the abdomen by a spent ball and severely injured, but, like a true soldier, he retained the command of his company until late in the evening, when he was ordered to the hospital.) When the 1st Ohio reached a fence on the crest of a hill it became hotly engaged; at the same time there was rapid firing from the 6th Indiana on the left, and also from some regiment on the right of the 1st Ohio; a section of Simonson's battery had been moved to the front, to the left and abreast of the 1st Ohio; a battery of the enemy immediately opened upon it, and their shells killed and wounded many of my men; presently I observed the regiment to the right of the 1st Ohio in full retreat, and in a few minutes I saw the 1st Ohio moving to the rear. I could see no enemy on account of the intervening ridge, and supposing that the 1st Ohio had exhausted their ammunition, I instantly prepared to take its place, but just before it reached my lines, to my utter amazement, a mass of the enemy appeared, moving obliquely upon my right flank. A change of front was imperative; whilst executing this movement, refusing my right to the enemy, the 1st Ohio passed through the right of my regiment and threw into great confusion my four right companies; their officers promptly arrested this, and I here take occasion to thank Captain John Lucas, commanding company F; First Lieutenant Thomas Forman, commanding company A; First Lieutenant Joseph E. Miller, commanding company D; and Second Lieutenant A. Sydney Smith, commanding company I, for their steadiness at this trying moment. In the meantime my left getting into position poured its fire into the steadily advancing columns of the enemy. But the troops to my left were giving way, and the enemy getting a battery into position, almost enfiladed me; the right of the division was completely crushed in, and I had no connexion, consequently no protection, here. It was soon manifest that I must fall back or be isolated. A new position was taken some two hundred paces in rear of our first, and here I believe we could have successfully resisted the enemy, but some general, I don't know who, ordered the entire line to fall back still further; and those who like rapid movements would have been more than satisfied with the celerity with which some of the floating fragments of regiments obeyed him. Pending this movement, my attention was called, by Colonel Baldwin, to a piece of artillery abandoned by those whose business it was to look after it. A full battery of the enemy were playing on it at the time. I immediately yoked the Legion to it, and, with Huston and Thomasson as the wheel horses, it was dragged to the railroad, where the new line was forming. I was shortly ordered to move by the flank further up the railroad, where a position was taken that was not assailed on this day.

I had gone into the fight with 320 muskets, a portion of my command being on detached service; nineteen (19) men were killed, including Captain Ferguson, of company I, who was one of our best officers; eighty (80) were wounded, among the latter were seven (7) commissioned officers, viz: Lieutenant Colonel W. W. Berry, shot through the wrist; Major John L. Treanor, wounded by a shell in the thigh; Captain A. H. Speed, wounded in the abdomen; Captain L. P. Lovett, slightly in the thigh; First Lieutenant Frank Dissell, mortally; First Lieutenant John D. Sheppard, seriously through the left lung; and First Lieutenant William H. Powell, slightly in the shoulder, and twenty-six missing. Some of these, I am mortified to say, ran away at the first fire; their names shall be duly reported. During the engagement my color-bearer was shot, and down went the flag, but like lightning it gleamed aloft again in the hands of three men, struggling who should have it. Their names are John B. Scheible, company E; Charles Fleckhammer, jr., company H; and Sergeant John Baker, company D. The latter bore it throughout the remainder of the day. Private William Shumaker, of company G, was badly shot through the thigh, but persisted in fighting with the regiment till he was forced to the rear by order of his captain. I commend him for his devotion. Sergeant Major Willett deported himself most bravely, and deserves promotion. Adjutant Johnstone rendered me every assistance in his power, and I especially thank him.

On the morning of the 1st of January I received orders to move further to the front. There was no general advance of our lines, though constant skirmishing through the day. Captain Thomasson had command of the skirmish line, and by his adroitness was mainly instrumental in the capture of 95 prisoners. The enemy held a dense wood about three hundred yards in front of us, in the edge of which were some cabins occupied by sharpshooters. I proposed to push forward my skirmishers and dislodge them, provided those on my right and left were simultaneously advanced. This, though ordered, was not done, and I did not deem it safe to expose my flanks; but towards evening the fire of these riflemen became so annoying that I was determined, at any cost, to stop it. I ordered Captains Hurley and Lindenfelser to move with their companies directly upon the houses and burn them. Across the open fields they dashed, the enemy having every advantage in point of shelter. Captain Huston was then ordered to their support, and the place was literally carried by assault, the houses burned, and five of the enemy left dead upon the spot. This was the last we heard of the sharpshooters. The daring displayed by officers and men in this affair deserves especial consideration. But one man was hurt—Corporal Moneypenny, shot through the leg. The skirmishing in which my command took part on the days succeeding this was of an uneventful character, and I forego the details.

Respectfully, your obedient servant,

WM. W. BERRY,
Lieutenant Colonel, Commanding.

Captain WM. MANGAN,
Acting Assistant Adjutant General, 3d Brigade,

HEADQUARTERS 93D REGIMENT,
Camp near Murfreesboro', Tennessee, January 5, 1863.

SIR: In obedience to your order I beg leave to submit the following report:

At one o'clock on the morning of the 27th of December the regiment left Mill creek for Nolensville, at which place we arrived at 4 a. m. We went into camp one mile south on the Nolensville road; at 7 a. m. took up our line of march. The brigade commenced skirmishing with the enemy about four miles south of Nolensville. We were then ordered to file to a field on left of Nolensville road, and were supports to the 6th Indiana volunteers. We marched in the above order until we arrived at Triune; here quite a brisk skirmish ensued, but, as the enemy's cavalry retreated before us on the road to Eagleville, my regiment was not engaged. Went into camp on the farm of —— Perkins at 4 p. m. On the morning of the 28th was ordered on picket to relieve the 79th Illinois volunteers, Colonel Reed commanding; remained until 12 m., the 29th, when brigade was moved back a short distance beyond Triune. Here we camped until 7 a. m. the 30th, when we started to join our division, which was encamped three miles northwest of Murfreesboro'; arrived at 3 p. m. We were then immediately ordered to report to General Stanley, chief of cavalry. After reporting to General Stanley, company "A" of my regiment was deployed as skirmishers through a cotton-field, and drove in rebel cavalry. The regiment then advanced through cotton and corn fields and meadows some mile and a half, when we were drawn up in line of battle, and marched so nearly one-half mile, when a very large cavalry force was seen drawn up in line of battle. We advanced to a fence and commenced firing at them; but, the range being so great and our loads having been long wetted, our shots did no apparent execution. We were then ordered to fall back, Stanley's cavalry covering our retreat. The rebel cavalry advanced a short distance, but made no demonstration. We were then ordered to go into the division encampment at the intersection of the Murfreesboro' road and a county road, crossing it about two miles from Murfreesboro'. This we did; but, finding that our brigade had been in the meantime ordered to act as reserve of the 1st and 2d brigades, under advice of General Willich, I ordered up the regiment and marched it into the reserve camp about a mile back and near General Johnson's headquarters, and remained in this camp all night. Upon the attack by the enemy immediately in our front, a little before 7 a. m. on the 31st, the brigade was ordered out to re-enforce our front division lines. The other regiments having been placed in their several positions, the 93d was ordered by myself to form line of battle upon the left of the 5th Kentucky, in the rear of which it had marched. But this movement was arrested by an order from Colonel Baldwin, with an order for it to remain in its form of column, and to await further orders. This order was obeyed, and the regiment (with two slight changes in advance as the other regiments marched forward into the open field to their second positions) so remained awaiting orders. All this time the 93d was in the woods of our encampment, parallel to the field in which the 1st Ohio and 5th Kentucky were marching and forming their lines, whilst the 6th Indiana, in line of battle, occupied the fence at the head of this woods, and between it and the adjacent fields on the south. No further orders were given to the regiment, though twice asked for. In retreat the 1st Ohio fell back from the second position in line of battle. When that event took place, and whilst the two regiments in the field were retreating back to their first position, I ordered and began a deployment of my regiment as skirmishers across the woods, and extending from the left flank of these two regiments to the road on the east. Whilst in the actual process of this movement the colonel commanding the brigade intercepted it, and ordered the regiment to form in line of battle to the left flank of the two other regiments. I ordered the skirmishers to rally on the right wing, which had not yet begun its deployment, and the colonel commanding brigade then gave me orders, in person, to retreat. The regiment being still in line of battle I ordered it to about face, and to march in slow time. This order was executed for a little time in some regularity. The enemy poured into the woods and pressed on to our rear. The regiment, like the rest of the retreating troops, of course, much increased its speed, so that, by the time it passed out of the woods into the cotton-field to the northward, the march had degenerated into a run. At this point and in the cotton-field the men of my regiment suffered quite severely. Notwithstanding, however, the number of killed, wounded, and scattered, a small remnant of the 93d was rallied with those of the division, and it may be from some other divisions, and formed in line of battle in the large woods, containing in all several hundred men. This line was again faced to the front and marched a short distance against the enemy, which by this time passed the cotton-field, entered the woods, and were again flanking our right in very great force. Another retreat having been ordered, this whole body of troops retreated once again under the support of General Crittenden's wing. No other event of special interest occurred in the regimental history of this day, except that several of its officers and many of its men, after being separated from the regiment, united themselves to other regiments, and fought gallantly during the subsequent conflict. Several of these men were thereby killed and wounded. In a temporary absence from my regiment, in order to have two slight wounds looked at and dressed by a surgeon, the remnant of mine, with that of his regiment, was left with Major Stafford, of the 1st Ohio volunteer infantry. Upon rejoining my regiment I received orders from Lieutenant Colonel Michler, aide-de-camp of General Rosecrans, to form on the extreme right of the line of battle. This I did, and then rejoined the colonel commanding and what was left, at that time, of the brigade. These little and trivial details seem to make a sufficient record of my regiment's share in these great proceedings; for a fuller statement of the various casualties to my command I beg leave respectfully to refer to previous reports and this accompanying addendum.

Total number killed, as far as heard from, 12; total number wounded, as far as heard from, 45; total number missing up to date, 64.

Very respectfully, your obedient servant,

CHARLES ANDERSON,
Commanding 93d Ohio Volunteer Infantry.

Colonel BALDWIN,
Commanding 3d Brigade.

List of casualties in the Ninety-third Ohio volunteers.

Killed.—Corporal Joseph Fry, company A; Private Wayne Thompson, company C; Sergeant Willard P. Lane, Corporal Swain Corson, and Privates William Ogg and George B. Kumter, company F; Privates James Kennedy and George B. Sayler, company G; Sergeant Joseph Wiley and Privates Henry Siler and Alfred Shister, company H; Corporal William McKee, company K.

Wounded.—Captain William H. Martin, Corporal Ira B. Ham, and Privates William Hellrigle, Daniel Lehman, William Lichlider, and Francis Kappe, company A; Sergeant Tingle, Corporals Jesse Foster and Wolf, and Privates Sholtz and Lerin, company B; First Lieutenant J. T. Patton, Sergeants L. L. Sadler, J. Falconer, and J. Neville, and Privates W. C. Stewart, and Z. Dodge, company C; Private John N. Logan, company D; Sergeants A. H. Mason and Jacob Voegel, and Privates O. W. Weidman, H. B. Ulm, and H. Hipart, company E; Privates Richard Shaw, Flichinger, Emery Carle, John Wagner, and McNeff, company F; Privates J. W. Johnson, Joseph H. Ramsay, and Martin C. Benit, company G; Second Lieutenant Daniel Shewman, Sergeant F. W. Austin, and Private Albert Brower, company H; Sergeant Logan and Privates J. Hammond, J. Esser, and J. Cline, company I; First Lieutenant George Schultz, Corporal Martin Ellen, and Private Benjamin Sharts, company K.

List of casualties in the Fifth Kentucky volunteers.

Killed.—Private John W. Sutton, company B; Privates Henry Miller and Mike Connelly, company C; Sergeant Elijah Tansille, Corporals Benjamin Drew and Patrick Burke, and Privates Costhar Graham, G. Ptiffer, and Conrad Braund, company D; Corporal Adam Newkirk, and Privates John Gottschalk and George Beaumister, company E; Corporal John Lacy and Private Michael Fallon, company G; Corporals William Summan and James McDonald, company H; Captain Alexander Ferguson and Corporal John Moose, company I.

Wounded.—Lieutenant Colonel W. W. Berry and Major J. L. Treanor, First Sergeant James F. Cullen, Sergeant Paul Clinton, Corporals Benjamin D. Edsill and Robert Cosgrove, and Privates W. W. Cassiday, Robert Johnson, Thomas Loftus, Patrick Vale, and Jeremy McCormick, company A; Captain L. P. Lorett and Privates James Conan, James Wooman, Alexander Mullen, William Stewart, Thomas Murray, and John Metz, company B; Captain Asaph Speed, Color Sergeant William Shaw, Corporal John Brown, and Privates Thomas Sly, Jacob Barbee, John Cronin, and Lewis Sergeant, company C; Corporal David Hard and Privates Aust D. Sweeney, Patrick Gilligan, John Manion, Michael Keenan, Benjamin Patrick, John McCormick, Francis M. Tucker, Sebastian Mill, and James Donnelly, company D; First Sergeant Frank Dissell, Sergeant Frederick Knomer, Corporal Barnhardt Seiner, and Privates Jacob Asent Barnhardt Kiel, and Philip Schneider, company E; First Lieutenant W. H. Powell, and Privates C. H. Johnson, Albert H. Laycock, Andrew J. Smith, John Stratton, and William Schnapp, company F; Corporals Walter Lacy, William Shoemaker, and Charles Anderson, and Privates Martin Brophy, Francis Shaiffer, Benjamin Concklin, August Depoir, Daniel Dunn, Thomas Ferrar, and Thomas White, company G; Corporal John Hoffman and Privates Squire Cable, Antone Bessinger, Charles Flickhammed, William Factor, George Haltubaum, Frederick Jones, Frank Klespie, Thomas McNickle, William Shever, Andrew H. Ward, and James P. Williams, company H; Privates William Carter, Henry Hailman, Thomas H. Johnson, and Henry Schroder, company I; First Lieutenant John D. Sheppard, Corporals Thomas Manypenny and Elisha Chandler, and Privates Thomas Eagan, James R. Carter, Michael Conner, John J. Gately, William H. Ross, and Michael Higgins, company K.

Missing.—Private Patrick Carney, company A; Robert Beatly, Peter Sutton, William Rodricker, and Thomas Frothingham, company B; Corporal Henry Hoos, and Privates James Hagerman, James Carroll, Benjamin Davis, George Hughes, John McLaughlin, and Peter O'Connell, company C; Privates Paul D. Kauffer, Philip Kline, Joseph Stoltz, William Stranch, and Victor Gienlich, company E; Privates James H. Hughes, Jacob Munger, Matthew Mutchler, and John M. Wirley, company F; Private Thomas Burns, company G; Privates Harrison Summers and Frederick Brunner, company H; Privates John A. Donahoo and Thomas J. Craddock, company K.

List of casualties in the First Ohio volunteers.

Killed.—Company A: Private Matthew Webster. Company B: Private Fred. Bierbaum. Company D: Privates Samuel Bearsby, Charles Scoby, and Eugene Roberts. Company H: Private Henry Sharp. Company K: Private Jas. M. Doman, Corporal Austis L. McKinney.

Wounded.—Company A: Corporal Robert Shannon. Privates John W. Reed, Nimrod A. Webb, Freeman D. Wolf, and Wesley Bennet. Company B: Sergeant Jacob Reuner, and Private Wm. Trabien. Company C: Privates

Thomas Dickensheels, James Galloway, Frank Savoy, Charles A. Stone, and Joseph Platt. Company D: Lieutenant Alex. Varian, Corporal George Jeunsen, and Privates Hugh Gray, Robert Waterson, and Horace Conant. Company E: Corporal Reuben Parker, and Privates George H. Potter, and James L. Houser.. Company G: Sergeant W. F. S. May, Corporal Peter M. Trapp, and James Robinson; Privates Nicholas W. Fulk, Henry C. Neff, James W. Allen, Oliver L. Lockhart, and Michael Sullivan. Company H: David McLeisch, Dawin Melhizio, Edwin Murray, and Joseph Slack. Company I: Privates Frank Prouse, John Marquis, Emanuel Dubbs, Patrick Bonner, Geo. W. Faucett, and Thomas Fox, bugler. Company K: Sergeant Charles W. Bodle, Privates Alexander Kiefer, and Lewis L. Speigh.

Missing.—Company A: Sergeant Charles Young, Privates John Heberling, Jacob H. Hassan, Jessee Lewis, William Rockey, William Shetzley, Edward Stover, and Edward Thornbury. Company B: Privates Michael Koppnut, Daniel Heintz, Joseph Liebold, and Christ. Stolz. Company C: Privates Josiah A. Swain, Joseph Snell, Henry Carse, and J. M. Smith. Company D: Privates James Saley, and William Witherup. Company E: Private Richard Driver, William Key, James Miller, Allan A. Moore, William Moses, Theodore Parker, and Corporal James Shepherd. Company F: Sergeant Henry C. Coy, Privates Robert M. Dixon, Patrick Sexton, Michael Sherlock, and Ezekiel Burney. Company G: Privates John A. Cox, James M. Day, Thomas J. Hopkins, and Corporal John H. Willenham. Company H: Private Joseph Martin. Company I: Privates Joseph Fountain, Charles Blythe, John J. Craig. Company K: Corporal J. L. McKinney, Privates Dennis Howard and J. D. Lyon.

List of casualties in the Fifth Indiana battery.

Killed.—Corporal James M. Waters; Privates Daniel Richards and Philip Gaddis.

Wounded.—First Lieutenant Henry Rankin; Sergeant Joseph H. Hughey; Corporals John J. English, William Henry, and Robert Bolton; Privates Wesley Ames, David Bricker, Stephen McKinsie, John Menderhall, Jacob Shoemaker, Daniel Myers, William Plummer, W. S. Brown, (company I, 1st Ohio volunteer infantry attached;) Christian Wise, (company I, 94th Ohio volunteer infantry attached;) J. B. Kurl, (company E, 1st Ohio volutneer infantry attached;) Samuel Roland, company A, (93d Ohio volunteer infantry attached;) Miles McNeff, and John Wagner, (company F, 93d Ohio volunteer infantry attached.)

List of casualties in the Sixth Indiana volunteers.

Killed.—Corporal G. A. Benefield, Private W. T. Ellis, company A; Corporal Seby Jenfor, Privates B. F. Simpson, William Jolly, and James T. Shoemaker, company B; Privates Samuel Steele, Ira Roberts, and D. B. Simonton, company C; Private James Ray, company G; Privates James Earle, and John W. Sharpe, company H; Corporal John T. Harrol, Privates John H. Hipput and Edward McNery, company K.

Wounded.—Corporal Samuel M. Storms, Privates George Smith, George Stephenson, John W. Anderson, Jeff Cooprider, and Ebenezer Marquis, company A; Sergeant John E. Tillman, Privates James S. Kitts, Stephen Jaspre, John Dixon, B. F. Hargrove, F. R. Monroe, Edward Askins, and William Fingate, company B; Privates Enos Clarke, Gordon Cummings, Robert Gaye, Virgil A. Brown, Wallace Dunlop, and William Young, company C; Privates Jonathan Eads, Caspar Leind, William Conway, John Long, and William Wallace, company D; Corporals James S. Meads, and Thomas W. Lewis, Privates James Underwood, Thomas Johnson, and John Brees, company E; Privates Elijah Bailey, and Cornelius Underwood, company F; Privates Alexander Bradford, and Gideon Powell, company G; Privates A. J. Cotton, John F. Farrow, George A. Sheets, William P. Gossnel, James H. Vorhis, Robert Chillis, William H. Johnson, and J. D. Griffith, company H; Privates Virgil Baker, Nathan H. Glazel, Henry Dixon, William Underwood, and Matthew Doyle, company I; Privates Lem. W. Jackson, James T. Jordan, James R. Castner, and William P. Ensminger, company K.

Missing.—James Flynen, David S. Subyers, Dan. Conaway, Moses Lewis, and John McCarty, company A; Sergeant Caleb W. Whitmore, company B; Sergeant James Dilton, Privates William H. Dodd, Nathan T. Raper, William C. Gay, and Joseph M. Luckey, company C; Privates Charles Irish, August Sherlock, Patrick O'Brien, Norman B. Cook, James A. Duncan, Dominick Barrett, Carl A. Ramspot, and Alfred Vanote, company D; Sergeant J. Milholland, Privates W. J. Cosby, R. M. Truman, James Tewland, N. O. Ramsay, and Goe. Tolson, company E; Privates M. B. Cook, and Leonidas Bryant, company F; Privates Edward Martin, George W. Smith, Aaron Day, and Martin B. Cole, company H; Privates McMahon, and James Gorbit, company I; John W. Wilson.

Total.—Killed, 59; wounded, 235; missing, 102.

P. P. BALDWIN,
Colonel, Commanding 3d Brigade.

WILLIAM MANGAN,
Captain, Acting Assistant Adjutant General.

HEADQUARTERS 6TH INDIANA VOLUNTEERS,
In camp near Murfreesboro', Tennessee, January 4, 1863.

SIR: I have the honor to report the part taken by my regiment in the skirmish fight on the 27th, also in the battle of the 31st ultimo.

On the morning of the 27th, while on the march, some two and a half miles north of the village of Triune, on the Nolensville pike, we encountered the enemy near the intersection of the Bole Jack road and pike. I immediately deployed in line of battle on the right of the road, my left resting on the road, being supported on my right by the 1st Ohio, and the 93d Ohio in reserve. I at once advanced as skirmishers company A, Captain Kavanagh, and company B, Lieutenant McGannon commanding, when a running fight commenced; Captain Simonson, of the 5th Indiana artillery, shelling the enemy from the hill-tops, being energetically replied to by the enemy's guns. The fight continued until we arrived at Triune, where the rebels made a stand, when we charged double-quick their battery, and drove them from the field. We pursued them some two miles, they contesting each rod of ground, when they again made a stand. We again drove them from their position in precipitate retreat. Night coming on put an end to our day's labor. I cannot speak in too high terms of commendation of the gallantry of the officers and men of my command during the entire day; when we consider that for eight hours they fought under the hardest rain of the season, and in mud to the ankles, pressing forward to the mark of their high calling with the utmost cheerfulness, their endurance was worthy the highest commendation.

On the 30th we marched from Triune to the field which was to be the scene of the battle of Murfreesboro', a distance of sixteen miles, where we arrived at 5 p. m., when we were at once *sent* some two and a half miles to the right of the right wing of the army; being informed that the enemy were in too large force to enable us to maintain our position, we returned at 9 o'clock to position first taken. At 7 a. m., on the 31st, I was posted in line of battle behind a rail fence, my right resting on an open field; a stalk-field in front, extending far to my left, a wood in rear, and also extending to my left. On my right, some seventy-five yards to the front, was a section of Simonson's 5th Indiana battery; to the right of it lay the 1st Ohio, behind a fence; also on my right, some seventy-five yards to rear, lay the Louisville Legion, also securely posted behind a fence, the whole supported by the 93d Ohio, Colonel Anderson. I promptly deployed as skirmishers the 1st platoons of company A, Captain Kavanagh, and company B, Lieutenant McGannon commanding. Some half hour after my skirmishers returned, being driven in by the enemy, their skirmishers in close pursuit. A few shots from my line served to hold them in check, when their main line advanced, deployed column after column, making some four or five lines approaching our front. When within one hundred yards I ordered my men to fire, and they went at it with a right good will, it having been difficult to restrain them so long. Our fire caused the enemy to waver, and checked their advance; they were not idle, but threw upon us their leaden hail, which caused my men to hug closer their frail defence, delivering their fire with the steadiness of veterans. At this time the artillery ceased on my right, and in a few minutes the 1st Ohio gave way and fell back on the Louisville Legion, who in turn also fell back before an overwhelming force of the enemy, who were passing my right flank in line of battle, their right passing within fifty yards of the right of my regiment, which produced some unsteadiness in one or two companies of my right, they getting out of place for the purpose of firing into the enemy's flank as they passed. I promptly rallied them to the *fence*. In the mean time the line in front had advanced to within twenty-five yards of my line. A rebel regiment had crossed the fence on my left; those advancing on the 1st Ohio and Louisville Legion, on my right, were already some one hundred yards to my rear, and being closely pressed in front, I gave the order to "Fall back slowly and in good order," which was executed at a double-quick. At one time I had some wavering in ranks in consequence of some unauthorized person giving an order to fall back to the men instead of to me, but I rallied them without difficulty, and continued the fight. I fell back to a point some two hundred yards east of the Nolensville pike, when I formed the regiment in line, faced about, intending to renew the fight, but seeing General McCook, reported to him for orders. He ordered me to "march my regiment to the rear," which I did, hauling up on the Nashville pike, thence to the railroad, when I reported to you.

On the 1st, 2d, and 3d instant my command bore a full share of the skirmish fighting on our part of the line; the particulars need not be mentioned here. I would do violence to my own feelings did I close this report without mentioning the good conduct and soldierly bearing of the men of my command. To the company officers I am greatly indebted for the steadiness of their several companies. I would be glad to name some of them, but where all have so ably done their duty it would be invidious to do so. I must, however, acknowledge the able, prompt, and energetic assistance I received from Major C. D. Campbell throughout the engagement.

Herewith please find a list of our loss in killed, wounded, prisoners, and missing.

Company A.—(Captain Delany Kavanaugh, prisoner.)—Killed: Corporal George A. Bencefield and Private William T. Ellis. Wounded: Corporal Samuel M. Storms, arm; Privates George Smith, foot; James Stevenson, hip; J. W. Anderson, hand; Jeff. Cooperider, slightly; George Messmore, and Eben Marquis. Missing: James Flynn, David S. Salyers, Dom. Conaway, and Moses Lewis. Captured: John McCarty.

Company B.—(Lieutenant P. C. McGannon,)—Killed: Corporal Luly Jayne, Privates Benjamin F. Simpson, William Jolly, and James Shoemaker. Wounded: Sergeant John E. Tillman, Privates James S. Kitts, Stephen Jayne, John

Dixon, B. F. Hargrove, T. R. Monroe, E. M. Adkins, and William Fungate. Prisoners: Sergeant C. Whitmore and J. M. Wilson.

Company C.—(Lieutenant Cummings.)—Killed: Privates Samuel Stull, Ira Roberts, and David B. Simonton. Wounded: Privates Enos Clark, Gordon Cummings, Robert Guy, Virgil A. Brown, Wallace Dunlap, and William N. Young. Missing: Sergeant James Dillon, Privates William H. Doll, Nathan T. Rappee, William C. Guy, and Joseph M. Luckey.

Company D.—(Captain Samuel Russell.)—Wounded: Privates Jonathan Eades, ankle; Caspar Land, leg; William Conway, John Long, and William Wallace. Missing: Privates Charles Irish, Aug. Scherloch, Patrick O'Brien, Norman B. Cook, James A. Duncan, Dominick Barrett, Carl A. Ramspot, Alfred Van Note, and Charles Donahue.

Company E.—(Lieutenant O. F. Rodarmel.)—Wounded: Corporal T. S. Meeds, Privates James Underwood, and Thomas Johnson. Missing: Sergeant Millholland, Privates J. W. Cosby, R. M. Freeman, and James Fewland. Prisoners: Privates J. N. O. Ramsay and George Tolson.

Company F.—(Lieutenant A. J. Newland.)—Wounded: Privates Elijah C. Bailey and Cornelius Underwood. Prisoner: Private M. B. Cook. Missing: Private L. Briant.

Company G.—(Captain Samuel T. Finney.)—Killed: Private James Ray. Wounded: Privates Alexander Bradford and Gideon Powell.

Company H.—(Captain Frank P. Stroder.)—Killed: Privates James Earle and John W. Sharp. Wounded: Privates A. G. Cotton, John P. Farrow, George H. Sheets, William P. Gosnell, James H. Voorhis, Robert Chillis, W. H. Johnson, and J. D. Griffith. Missing: Privates Edward Martin and George W. Smith. Prisoners: Privates Aaron Day and Martin B. Cole.

Company I.—(Captain S. D. Huckleberry.)—Wounded: Privates Virgil Baker, knee; Nathan H. Gloyd, Henry Dixon, William Underwood, and Matthew Doyle. Missing: Privates John McMahon and James Gorbett.

Company K.—(Lieutenant George B. Green.)—Killed: Corporal J. F. Harrel, Privates J. H. Hyatt and Edward McVay. Wounded: Corporal T. W. Lewis, Privates Simon W. Jackson, James T. Jordan, James R. Casner, William P. Ensminger, and T. W. Lewis.

I am sir, very respectfully, your obedient servant,

H. TRIPP,

Lieutenant Colonel 6th Indiana Volunteers, Commanding.

Colonel P. P. BALDWIN,

Commanding 3d Brigade.

HEADQUARTERS SECOND BRIGADE, SECOND DIVISION,

In Camp near Murfreesboro', Tenn., January 8, 1863.

SIR: In compliance with your order of the 7th instant I have the honor to respectfully submit the following report of the operations of this command since the 26th of December last up to the evening of the 31st ultimo.

On the morning of the 26th of December last this brigade left camp near Nashville under command of Brigadier General E. N. Kirk and marched out on the Nolensville pike about twelve miles, where we camped during the night. Although there was heavy skirmishing in our front and on each flank, we were in nowise engaged with the enemy on that day, as there was a heavy force of federal troops in front of this brigade and between it and the enemy.

On the morning of the 27th we were ordered to resume the march, and on that day the brigade was in advance of our whole forces, with the exception of the cavalry, which was thrown out as skirmishers in advance. About one mile from where we had bivouacked for the night, the enemy made his appearance in considerable force, composed of cavalry and supported by artillery, all of which opened upon us, and he showed a disposition to contest the ground over which we wished to pass. The 34th regiment Illinois volunteers and the 29th Indiana were promptly deployed as skirmishers, each regiment retaining a good reserve, and thrown forward with instructions to push on as rapidly as possible, which order was obeyed with alacrity and skill, and the other regiments of the brigade moved forward in line of battle, the 30th Indiana supporting Edgarton's battery. Owing to a dense fog, which enveloped everything so that we could not distinguish the troops of the enemy from our own, it was deemed prudent to halt until the fog partially disappeared, when we again moved forward, with continued skirmishing on our front, until we gained an elevated position overlooking the village of Triune. Here the enemy were in plain view, drawn up in line of battle, the centre of their line being in the village. Edgarton's battery opened upon them immediately with splendid effect, soon throwing them into disorder and disabling at least one piece of their artilery, as I have good reason to believe. While in this position a very heavy rain commenced, accompanied with fog, rendering an advance immediately hazardous. The fog disappeared again in about an hour, when we again advanced; but owing to the ground being very much softened by the rain, the men's clothes so saturated with water, that it was impossible to do so at the rate of speed desired. The enemy had destroyed a bridge across a stream that runs through the edge of the town, thus compelling the artillery to make a detour of nearly a mile to a ford, and by this means gained time to collect his scattered forces and withdraw. On that night we bivouacked about one mile south of Triune.

During that day this brigade lost none in killed or wounded, but inflicted considerable loss upon the enemy. The officers and men engaged showed themselves to be cool, skilful and courageous, and behaved splendidly. We stayed at the above-mentioned place all of the 28th, and on the morning of the 29th took up our march for Murfreesboro'. During this day nothing of importance occurred. We bivouacked that night in an open field, without fires and in a drenching rain. On the morning of the 30th we were ordered out to take a position, preparatory to an expected attack upon the enemy. Heavy skirmishing and fighting was going on in front of us during the whole day, in which we took no active part until about 3 o'clock p. m., at about which time we arrived at the extreme right of the line of our army. At that time the enemy had a battery of artillery stationed directly in front of this brigade, which was pouring a destructive fire into some troops on our left, belonging to Brigadier General J. C. Davis's division. General Kirk immediately ordered Captain Edgarton's battery to open upon it, which order was complied with with great execution, dismounting one of the enemy's pieces and killing quite a number of men in a very few moments, and driving him from his position. There was no more firing either from artillery or infantry that evening or night. The brigade was formed in line of battle—the 34th Illinois, Major A. P. Dysart commanding, on the extreme right, the 29th Indiana, Lieutenant Colonel Dunn commanding, next on the left; the 30th Indiana, Colonel J. B. Dodge, next, and the 77th Pennsylvania, Lieutenant Colonel Housum commanding, on the left; Edgarton's battery (E. 1st Ohio artillery) in the rear and to the left of the 34th Illinois, in a cedar grove, with rather a dense thicket immediately in front of the three left regiments. A strong picket line was thrown out from 150 to 200 yards in front, with a cornfield in front of their (the picket) line. Every precaution that was possible was taken to prevent surprise and to give seasonable warning of the approach of the enemy. The brigade was up and under arms for nearly or quite an hour before daylight. Just after daylight a part of the horses of the battery were unhitched from the caissons and taken to water, which was close by.. Just at this moment the enemy made his appearance on our front and right in immense force and formed in close columns, with a front equal to the length of a battalion in line, and ten or twelve ranks in depth. General Kirk immediately ordered the 34th Illinois to advance to near where the picket was stationed, in order to check (at least) the advance of the enemy and save the battery, if possible, which movement was promptly executed under an awful fire, which almost annihilated the picket line, or line of skirmishers, which it really was, and killed or wounded a large number in the line some 150 or 200 yards in the rear. The battery under command of Captain Edgarton immediately opened with canister upon the enemy, and only had time to fire eight rounds before the battery was taken. Nearly or quite one-half of the horses were killed, or wounded so as to be unmanageable, by the first fire from the enemy, and it was impossible to remove it from the ground. Captain Edgarton and his officers and men fought nobly, as the number of killed and wounded will testify, and did everything possible to maintain their ground against an overpowering force. The captain was taken prisoner while assisting to work his guns, and Lieutenant Berwick was bayonetted and taken prisoner while assisting him. General Kirk was seriously wounded at almost the first fire, and I then succeeded to the command of the brigade. The fire the enemy received from us, although well directed and as effective as a fire from two ranks generally is, produced no visible effect upon him as he moved his heavy column forward upon a double-quick. General Rains, who commanded a part of their column fell dead or mortally wounded at this point. The enemy then moved to the left oblique, or nearly, by his left flank, until his centre was opposite our extreme right, when he moved forward again, changing direction to his right as he did so, so as to bring his whole force upon our most exposed point. We held our ground until our ranks were not more than twenty yards from the enemy; when I was forced to retire, having no support and seeing that it was a needless waste of life to contend in that position with at least twenty times the number of men I then had left, which was done in the best order possible, across a cornfield in the rear and to the left of our first position to a field, one side of which was on rising ground and overlooking the ground over which the enemy must advance to attack. I here formed the 30th Indiana, at that time under command of Lieutenant Colonel O. D. Hurd, of that regiment, and the 79th Illinois, Colonel J. P. Reed commanding, that had just reported to me, (it having been detailed to guard a train the day before, and had just arrived upon the field,) behind a fence on the rise of ground before spoken of. Before the 79th Illinois reached the fence, and while it was at least 200 yards distant from it, the enemy made his appearance and instantly poured a terrible fire into their ranks; although a new regiment, they advanced with a firmness that would have done credit to veterans, and, after reaching the fence, poured a terribly destructive fire into the enemy. Here, assisted by Captain Simonson's (5th Indiana) battery, this brigade was unsupported, except by the 3d brigade, that was on our left, and almost alone succeeded in checking the enemy, bringing his columns to a halt, and requiring the utmost exertions of his officers to keep his men from flying in disorder from the field, during all of which time a tremendous fire was kept up. The enemy finally succeeded in throwing his left wing forward across the fence, thus outflanking this brigade and dislodging us from that position; but the number of dead left by him on that ground for five days afterwards show conclusively that it was by far the dearest position to him that he gained that day. Colonel Reed, of the 79th Illinois, was killed instantly while bravely urging his men on. In his death the service has lost a fine officer, a brave soldier and a true man. Adjutant Stribley, of the 30th Indiana, was also killed here. The service contained no braver or cooler officer than he. The 77th Pennsylvania, Lieutenant Colonel Housum, commanding at the time of the occurrences above mentioned, was some 600 yards on the left of the troops under my immediate command, acting with a brigade in General Davis's division. While hotly engaged with the enemy Colonel Housum was wounded severely, of which he died shortly afterwards. He was a cool, clear-headed, courageous officer and gentleman.

After being driven from the fence I retired my command to a piece of woods in the rear of my former position, the enemy closely following up with infantry on our rear, and cavalry on his left flank. I halted my command twice, and formed a line and undertook to hold him in check, but it was impossible to do but little, owing to our weakened condition and the absence of all support. I finally fell back to near the Murfreesboro' and Nashville turnpike, and made up my mind that the enemy must be stopped there. I had at that time the seventy-seventh Pennsylvania, Captain Rose commanding, twenty-ninth Indiana, Major Collins commanding, and about 100 men belonging to the thirtieth Indiana, thirty-fourth Illinois, and seventy-ninth Illinois, in all about, at that time, 500 men. By command of Brigadier General Johnson I formed my little force on the right of Captain Simonson's battery, which was in action with one of the enemy's batteries, which was soon silenced, immediately after which it (Captain Simonson's battery, was placed in another position. I wish to be pardoned for testifying here to the skill, efficiency, and courage displayed by Captain Simonson and his officers and men during that day. I then moved my command some 150 yards to the right of where it had been while supporting the battery, into a piece of woods, and took a good position for defence. Some troops belonging to some other division moved in on my left just at that moment, and a moment after the remains of the column that made the first attack in the morning made its appearance, coming up on a double-quick. I immediately gave the command, forward, and my command met them, poured in a deadly volley and rushed forward. Their advance was stopped, their line wavered, and in a moment was in full retreat, and thus the brigade that received the first attack from this column in the morning had the satisfaction of giving it the first repulse it received during the day. I followed them but a short distance, when I got a regiment to relieve the command I had left, as they were entirely out of ammunition, and, by order of General Johnson, I took them back and formed along the railroad and got a supply. I was then ordered back to the bank of the river, where I awaited further orders. While there an officer rode up and informed me that the enemy's cavalry were attempting to cross the river some distance below, near an hospital, and that it was important that we should have a force there. There was no superior officer near, and I took the responsibility of at once moving to the point designated and forming in line. The enemy seeing us approach promptly fell back, but not until he had taken quite a number of prisoners, as I understand. I then returned to the turnpike, and at dark bivouacked in the woods near by, where we spent the night. On the morning of the 1st instant I placed my command in line, under your directions, and we immediately threw up a line of breastworks, behind which we bivouacked until the evening of the 3d instant, without any movement on our part, with the exception that on the 2d instant, at about 9 o'clock p. m., I was ordered to take four companies from my command, and a like number from the third brigade of this division, and advance to our front until I reached the Franklin turnpike or found the enemy in force. It was a very dark night, and I took my little command according to your orders, deployed the whole as skirmishers and started. I first crossed an open field or fields nearly to the woods in our front, where I could distinctly hear the enemy chopping and moving either artillery or heavy wagons. When we got about twenty yards from the edge of the woods, I distinctly heard officers giving commands to their men, and, fearful that I was going into a trap, I ordered my men to fire, which was promptly obeyed, and my suspicions confirmed, as the enemy returned a withering volley in reply; found at least ten times the number I had with me. Having ascertained that the enemy were in heavy force near our lines, thereby accomplishing the purpose for which I was sent out, I ordered my men to retire, which they did in good order, losing but four wounded; none killed. The officers and men under my command during this terrible battle behaved with great coolness and courage under the most trying circumstances. I cannot help but bring to the notice of the commanding general the gallant conduct of Captain T. E. Rose, of the 77th regiment Pennsylvania, who took command of his regiment after Lieutenant Colonel Housum was wounded, and who, by his skill, perseverance and energy, kept his regiment well together, and by his example urged on his men to attack the enemy when all around was disorder and confusion. Major Collins, of the 29th Indiana, took command of that regiment about 9 o'clock a. m. on the 31st, after Lieutenant Colonel Dunn had by some means become separated from his command, fought nobly. Major Buckner, of the 79th Illinois, took command of that regiment after the death of Colonel Reed, and gallantly rallied his men, and showed himself worthy of a higher position than he now holds. Major A. P. Dysart, commanding the 34th Illinois, distinguished himself in his efforts to arrest the enemy's progress, and his regiment stood by him until it was utterly impossible for the same number of men without support to do so longer. Lieutenant Colonel Hurd commanding, and Major Fitzsimmons, (who was taken by the enemy,) of the 30th Indiana, showed that they were worthy of the positions they occupy. Both needlessly, almost, exposed themselves, and were untiring in their efforts to stop the progress of what seemed a victorious enemy. I can but express my heartfelt thanks to my staff for their conduct on the field—firm, cool, energetic and fearless, their assistance was invaluable. Captain D. C. Wagner, acting assistant adjutant general; Captain E. P. Edsall, acting assistant inspector general; Lieutenant J. C. McElpatrick, topographical engineer, and Lieutenants Baldwin and Walker, aids, were untiring in their efforts to rally the troops, and to their exertions the whole right wing of the army is, in my opinion, indebted. Dr. George W. Hewitt, acting brigade surgeon, was untiring in his exertions in behalf of the wounded, and was captured while at his post by the enemy; as was also Dr. Hostetter, of the 34th Illinois, Dr. Keen, of the 29th Indiana, and Dr. McAllister, of the 79th Illinois, were all taken where a surgeon should be in time of action, attending to the duties of their profession. While in the enemy's lines they were engaged night and day in taking care of our wounded. They have all been released since, and their horses retained by the enemy, in pursuance, as they report, of orders of General Wharton. Surgeon Downy, of the 77th Pennsylvania, was fortunately spared and stayed with the brigade. He was of invaluable service to those who were so unfortunate as to require the attention of a surgeon. The medical department of this brigade was in splendid condition; thanks to Dr. Hewitt and division medical director, Dr. Mark, and notwithstanding our loss in surgeons the wounded were well cared for. Chaplain Bradshaw, 79th Illinois, and Chaplain Decker, of the 34th Illinois, exposed themselves in the most fearless manner in taking care of the wounded, taking them off the field, &c., and proved themselves to be well worthy, at least, of the positions they occupy.

This brigade met with a serious loss in the person of General Kirk, early in the engagement; he fell at the head of his brigade, trying manfully to resist and repel the overwhelming force thrown against it. Accompanying please find a summary of killed, wounded, and missing of this command. The missing are, a large majority of them, I fear, wounded and in the hands of the enemy; also, please find reports of regimental commanders of this brigade and complete list, by name, of casualties.

Respectfully submitted.

J. B. DODGE,
Colonel 30th Indiana, Commanding 2d Brigade.

Captian BARTLETT, *A. A. A. General.*

P. S.—Excuse me for calling the attention of the general commanding to a gallant charge made by the 77th Pennsylvania, while they were separated from this brigade and were acting in concert with a brigade in Brigadier General J. C. Davis's division. A battery in possession of the enemy made its appearance directly in their front, and opened upon them. Lieutenant Colonel Housum ordered a charge upon it, which was obeyed instantly by his command; the cannoneers were either killed or wounded, the horses disabled so they could not move back; the 77th had possession of Captain Edgarton's battery, which the enemy had brought along with them, for a few moments, but before they could do anything more than compel the enemy to spike the guns, a heavy force of infantry made its appearance in their front and flank, and they were compelled to retire, during which movement Lieutenant Colonel Housum was mortally wounded.

J. B. DODGE,
Colonel 30th Indiana, Commanding 2d Brigade, 2d Division.

General summary of killed, wounded and missing in the second brigade, second division, (right wing,) in the battle before Murfreesboro', Tennessee, on December 31, 1862.

Regiments.	No. taken into action.			Field officers.			Comp'y officers.			Enlisted men.			Total loss.		
	Field and staff officers	Company officers	Enlisted men.	Killed.	Wounded.	Missing.	Killed.	Wounded.	Missing.	Killed.	Wounded.	Missing.	Commissioned officers.	Enlisted men.	Aggregate.
34th regiment Illinois volunteers	5	19	330	--	--	--	2	2	2	19	98	72	6	189	195
79th regiment Illinois volunteers	5	16	416	1	--	--	--	3	3	23	68	121	7	212	219
29th regiment Illinois volunteers	6	18	313	--	--	1	1	2	--	14	66	51	4	131	135
30th regiment Illinois volunteers	4	21	463	--	--	1	1	2	1	30	108	79	5	208	213
77th regiment Pennsylvania vol	3	16	288	1	--	--	--	1	2	4	28	28	4	60	64
Edgarton's battery	--	--	----	--	--	--	--	--	--	--	----	----	--	----	----
Total	23	90	1,810	2	--	2	4	10	8	90	368	342	26	800	826

Very respectfully submitted,

J. B. DODGE,
Colonel 3d Regiment Indiana Volunteers, Commanding 2d Brigade.

Owing to the absence of the officers and men of battery E, 1st Ohio volunteer artillery, I am unable to procure a report of casualties, &c., as required by your order.

Very respectfully, your obedient servant,

D. C. WAGNER,
Captain and Acting Assistant Adjutant General.

HEADQUARTERS 79TH REGIMENT ILLINOIS VOLUNTEERS,
In the Field near Murfreesboro', January 7, 1863.

SIR: I have the honor to report to you that the 79th regiment Illinois volunteers left camp near Nashville on the 26th December, under command of Colonel S. P. Read, for Murfreesboro', *via* Nolensville, but was not in action until Wednesday, December 31. This regiment was detailed on the morning of the 30th as rear guard of the division train, and at night encamped on the right and to the rear of the brigade, as ordered, throwing out a strong line of skirmishers to the front and right. On the morning of the 31st the men were under arms at daylight, about which time the brigade was attacked in front by such a heavy force that it began to fall back. Colonel Read requested that I should go forward and learn of Colonel Dodge, who was then in command of the brigade, (General Kirk having been wounded,) what he should do. I did so, and told him that the 79th was ready and waiting to do anything it could. He directed me to tell Colonel Read to hurry the regiment forward as soon as possible; which was done, he bravely leading his men on to the field amid a destructive fire from the enemy. The regiment marched up on the "double-quick," until it arrived on the right of the 30th Indiana, becoming the right of the brigade, and commenced pouring a deadly fire into the ranks of the enemy. It was not long before I heard some one say that Colonel Read had fallen. I went immediately to where he was lying, and found that he had been shot directly in the forehead; thus falling at his post and facing the enemy. My attention was at once called (by one of the officers) to the fact that the enemy was flanking us on the right. I directed the men to fire right-oblique, but could not check them. They rushed forward, opening on us a deadly cross-fire. I saw that in a few moments we would be surrounded, and consequently ordered a retreat, which was made across an open field to the woods—a distance of some three hundred yards—exposed all the time to a destructive fire of artillery and musketry, killing and wounding a great many of our men. At the woods I tried to rally the men, but we were so closely pursued by overwhelming numbers that it was impossible. The regiment became very much scattered, although the officers did all they could to keep them together. Many of them joined other regiments and fought during the day. I was able to keep enough men together in the brigade to form a nucleus around which to rally. A few of our men acted cowardly; but the regiment, as such, fought as bravely as men could. As to the officers, I must say, to my personal knowledge, that Captains Van Deven, Young, Low, Martin, Lacy, and Pinnell, and also Lieutenants Mitchel, Williams, Fatton, Albin, Jacobs, Braddock, and Biglow, stood to the work, and have gained a name as brave officers. I must speak of Adjutant Lamb, as doing his duty as none but a faithful officer, likewise.

Assistant Surgeons McAllister and Wheeler, who stayed with the wounded and dying, although they were compelled thereby to fall into the hands of the enemy for a time, they have done their part to the utmost to both officers and men. Last, but not least, the chaplain, C. S. Bradshaw, was with us all day, assisting to carry off the wounded. He conducted himself in such a manner as to command the love and esteem of both officers and men. Sergeant Major Harding did his part with true courage. Sergeants Boyle, of company C, and Harding, of company D, also deserve a great deal of credit for the manner in which they rallied their men, their commanders having been wounded early in the action. For numbers and names of killed, wounded, and missing I refer you to report already made.

Respectfully submitted.

ALLEN BUCKNER,
Major, Commanding 79th Illinois Volunteers.

To Captain D. C. WAGNER,
Acting Assistant Adjutant General.

List of killed, wounded, and missing in the 79th regiment Illinois infantry volunteers.

Killed.—Colonel Sheridan P. Read. Company A: Sergeant J. H. Thomas, and Privates Henry Loop, George Lefler, and Thomas Berry. Company C: Privates George H. Green and Wesley Stricklen. Company D: Privates George Yeakle and A. Y. Trogden. Company E: Sergeant Harvey W. Peters, and Privates William Brackett, William Dillon, and Phineas Coffin. Company F: Sergeant Milton H. Craig, and Privates Joseph Walker, Wiley Jones, John J. Milliss, and J. Guinnip. Company G: Corporal Bosman Jacobs, and Private David Ball. Company H: Privates J. H. Smith and B. T. G. Fuller. Company K: Privates Henry Wamsley and Slacy Davenney.

Wounded.—Company A: B. F. Lane, J. Cook, F. Canady, G. Hiddle, and A. Robertson. Company B: W. B. Watts, Edgar Smith, William Vincent, Clinton Davis, Henry Bould, Peter Greggers, Albert Castor, Michael James, Jacob Fraghen, and Jerry Veatch. Company C: Second Lieutenant John H. Patten, Sergeant A. Saunders, Corporals H. Elliott and J. H. Shank, and Privates John T. Jones, Jacob Leinen, George H. Rigg, (since died,) and J. N. Ewing. Company D: Captain T. A. Young, and Privates F. J. Paster, T. M. Elliott, John Chance, D. Green, T. Patterson, John Holston, J. Wallet, and William Greene. Company E: Second Lieutenant H. S. Albin, and Privates Asa A. Craft, Edwin Drake, Jas. H. Lyons, George Crist, Aden Wylie, George Pettit, J. L. Stewart, Owen Brewer, and John H. Boyce. Company F: Corporals George H. Redick and Henry B. Kille, and Privates Irison T. Crail, Jacob N. Furr, J. W. Cunningham, John Taylor, and Charles Clatfeller. Company G: Sergeant James Maden, and Privates Thomas Branden, Steven Grimes, H. D. Clark, and Olando Gomel. Company H: Privates T. R. Ogden, S. Stanley, J. H. Tetes, J. F. Redden, P. H. Zink, S. Hickney, W. H. Roberts. Company I: Privates Joseph M. Rolston, Enoch Harris, Alexander Chambers, and Alonzo McKee. Company K: Sergeant Josephus Danner, Corporal Hugh McKenney, and Private Thomas Davenny.

Missing.—Company A: Privates C. P. Lake, L. Crumb, J. Conce, and S. Forhner. Company B: Sergeant John Abbott, Corporal Benjamin F. Shreves, and Privates John Dorjohn, Charles Howard, Cyrenius James, Samuel Randolph, Henry Randolph, Thomas Jester, Frederick Stoltz, Peter Schnack, and Hans Schnack. Company C: Corporals Alfred Lycan and J. S. Bradley, and Privates J. M. David, George Brundedge, Stephen Baylon, Frank Ray, G. W. Barnhardt, Jacob M. Jones, Charles H. Squire, Peter Stepp, and John Sullivan. Company D: First Lieutenant D. Elliott, and Privates George Elliott, H. Carpenter, Wm. Merriman, James Mehard, William Baxter, Dory Baxter, John Hart, G. R. Batty, M. Arbigast, James Price, D. Clouser, M. Sumner, P. Rader, John Cooper, John Adams, John Grover, John Pharis, L. Smith, John Hicks, Henry Pane, D. N. Price, and William Starr. Company E: Sergeant David N. Howard, Corporal John P. Ross, and Privates William R. Brown, Peter Cheesem, Harrison Entler, Spencer Gillogly, John Harris, Job Irish, William P. McWilliams, John Shee, and George Van Asdall. Company F: Privates C. W. Smith, Edmund Smith, James Ingle, Ruben Touts, George W. Reedy, Samuel Reedy, Lord B. Miller, W. W. Gilbert, and John Hazl. Company G: Captain O. O. Bagley, Sergeants John Counly and Harvey Ingram, Corporal J. S. Reaves, and Privates D. M. Callahan, Daniel DeHart, J. S. Reader, J. H. Ingram, George Ingram, J. R. Willis, John Thomason, William Sears, Isaac Coshet, James Ferman, Alexander Hooper, Nelson Steepelton, and Richard West. Company H: Sergeant C. T. Estes, Corporals W. L. Kester, Asa Williams, and J. W. Davis, and Privates A. J. Boggs, C. Cass, J. M. Goodman, R. Howell, M. P. Norton, A. Shutton, J. W. Tites, J. C. Cole, and J. S. Bell.

Company I: First Lieutenant Henry Week, Second Lieutenant William Williard, Sergeant James Dolson, Corporal Iradel Evans, and Privates Cyrus Patten, Thomas Rolston, James S. Briggs, William Partlow, Daniel Thompson, George F. Hampston, and Elijah Goodwin. Company K: Sergeant William H. Bassett, Privates William T. Aldridge, David Bowen, William Collins, S. H. Compton, Stephen Elless, Jesse Evans, Andrew Hays, John Jenkins, Ames Lackey, George Neer, Levi Rimmel, William B. Templeton, and Henry Wood, and Drummer Orlando B. Whorton.

Respectfully submitted.

ALLEN BUCKNER,
Major, Commanding Regiment.

JANUARY 7, 1863.

CAMP NEAR MURFREESBORO', TENN.,
January 7, 1863.

SIR: I have the honor to report the part taken by the 29th regiment Indiana volunteers in the advance on Murfreesboro' from Nashville, and the battles before that place. On the morning of the 26th December last we struck tents, sending the train back to Nashville, and left camp, following in the order of march the 30th Indiana and 34th Illinois. The divisions of Generals Davis and Sheridan *preceeded* the 2d, and in the skirmishing with the enemy on the road and near Nolensville we had not an opportunity to take a part.

On the 27th the 2d division and 2d brigade were the advance forces, and in regular order the 29th regiment Indiana volunteers followed the 34th Illinois. We had not marched over one mile when sharp skirmishing was heard ahead between our cavalry and that of the enemy. Pushing rapidly forward to the summit of a ridge, beyond which the skirmish was going on, we became exposed to the fire of a masked battery of the enemy, which opened on the head of the column with shot and shell. Advantage was taken by Generals Johnson and Kirk of a cedar thicket, covering this ridge, to move the 34th Illinois and 29th Indiana to the left of the road and towards the enemy. Orders were immediately given by General Kirk to Colonels Bristol and Dunn to throw out skirmishers to cover their regiments, the 34th Illinois and 29th Indiana, which were drawn up in line of battle in front of the thicket, but in an open field. The skirmishers, being ordered forward, moved over the ground just wrested from the enemy by our cavalry, until they reached the top of another ridge, divided by a narrow valley from the rebel battery. Here we were ordered to halt, to await the issue of an artillery duel between it and Captain Edgarton's battery, (E, 1st Ohio artillery,) attached to the 2d brigade, as well as the lifting of a dense fog, which rendered a hasty movement to the front extremely perilous. When objects at a distance could be distinctly seen and the rebel battery silenced, we were again ordered forward, without seeing the enemy until we had reached a hill overlooking the town of Triune. Large bodies of rebel cavalry were posted in the town and in our front on the left of the road, about three-quarters of a mile distant. Our artillery was again brought into action, leaving us the privilege of witnessing the hurried retreat of both bodies of the rebels. When we next advanced they moved their cannon towards us and *plied* the advancing regiments with shot, shell, and grape shot. Supporting their artillery we discovered a large force of dismounted cavalry, posted on a hill covered with timber, whose leaden compliments attracted our attention. The skirmishers were ordered forward on "double-quick," but the torrent of rain which poured down on us had made their clothing and the ploughed field so heavy, the efforts of the men at a "double-quick" were painful and almost futile. They pushed on, however, as rapidly as possible, and by a well-directed fire drove the rebels from the woods, and prevented them again forming within rifle range.

The rebel artillery retreated towards Triune, taking advantage of every rise of ground to check our advance, until the skirmishers of the 29th Indiana had almost secured a position in the woods to the rebel right, from which the capture of the rebel guns was perfectly feasible, when the bugle again sounded a halt, and the rebels moved off rapidly. "Forward" once more, and the line of skirmishers had reached the top of another ridge and halted, leaving the reserve at its base, when we were surprised by the sudden appearance of a regiment of cavalry on our left, within twenty yards, and moving leisurely to the front. I ordered the reserve to wheel to the left and fire, which was heard by the rebels, who instantly quickened their pace to a gallop, but were unable to pass in time to save their entire column. Several were seen to reel in their saddles and all changed direction by the left flank, making for the woods. Immediately afterwards a squad appeared, made a demonstration on the deployed line, (company A, 29th Indiana,) but failed to intimidate the men or force the line. With a shout the skirmishers rushed forward, poured in a galling fire, unhorsed four or five, took one prisoner, badly wounded; while company F, 29th, on reserve at the same time, forced another to surrender without a wound. This cavalry force was the 1st confederate regulars, and I only regret that the fear that this might be Colonel Stokes's cavalry, which had all day supported our left, but of whose personal appearance I was ignorant, rendered their loss so slight. We advanced half a mile further, when we bivouacked for the night. After we had reached our final halting place, the federal (Stokes's) cavalry emerged from the woods on our left, but at sufficient distance to leave a gap through which the rebels escaped. Until December 30, we were not again engaged in any movement or preparation for the attack on Murfreesboro'. On this day we moved in reserve to the column of General Davis until 3 p. m., when the 2d brigade, 2d division, was ordered to the right of General Davis's division, which was threatened by rebel cavalry. The 77th Pennsylvania and 38th Indiana were thrown forward as skirmishers, to the first of which the 29th acted as reserve. We moved forward until we reached the reserve of General Davis's right, where the rebel cavalry were distinctly visible in line of battle, but not within range. Captain Edgarton's battery, having taken position, soon put them to flight. While in line at this point we were exposed to the fire of the rebel battery supporting their skirmishers, but it was immediately silenced by ours. About dusk a line of battle was decided upon, and by order the 29th Indiana took position on the left of the 34th, which supported the battery on a line leading to Murfreesboro' and behind a dense thicket of cedars. Steps were at once taken to guard against surprise; a large company (B) of our regiment was sent out as pickets, with instructions to act as skirmishers, should the enemy appear, our line connecting that of the 34th Illinois on the right, and the 30th Indiana on our left, both of which lines were established sufficiently in advance to command a wide range of vision, and enable the regiments to form in time to meet any attack; the night passed without alarm on our line until about 3 a. m., when a shot fired on the picket line, to our right, brought every man to his place in ranks. About daylight we were alarmed by general firing on the picket line, and immediately afterwards by shouting in front, but to our right. The men instantly grasped their loaded guns, while I, by Lieutenant Colonel Dunn's order, rode to the front, along the lane, to ascertain the cause of the firing, and the force coming down on us emerging from behind the thicket, I saw a heavy column moving rapidly down on the 34th Illinois, firing as they advanced, and opposed bravely and vigorously by the pickets and skirmishers. Riding further down the lane to obtain a view of the open country beyond the thicket, I saw a column of like proportions moving down on the 29th Indiana.

I galloped back to the regiment with this information, and found that Lieutenant Colonel Dunn, anticipating, had thrown forward another large company (C) to support the pickets and skirmish amongst the cedars. This company, ably and gallantly led by Lieutenant S. O. Gregory, pushed forward through the entangled mass until within a few yards of the rebels, and only fell back when overpowered, leaving some of his men killed and wounded. Situated as our regiment was, we dared not fire lest we killed our own men, whom we could not see, from which circumstance we were obliged to receive the storm of bullets without a response; and the resistance of our skirmishers under Lieutenants Gregory, Hess, and McComber, was so obstinate that the rebel column had advanced within twenty yards of our line before they received a shot from us. Our first fire, delivered lying down, partially checked the advance, and enabled the men to load and fire four or five times; but while engaged in front, the column which pressed on the 34th Illinois and the battery had moved so far forward as to uncover our line, giving them the opportunity to deliver a raking fire upon us. The troops on our right had fallen back, and Lieutenant Colonel Dunn considered the peril of his situation demanded a retreat. We fell back about eighty rods and formed behind a cornfield fence, every man loading and firing in retreat; through which field the rebels were pushing vigorously, but as no other troops appeared ready to sustain the shock, the regiment was moved some rods further to a piece of woods, where we took our position in line of battle. The 30th Indiana now made its appearance from a cornfield in front and to our left, and moving still further to the left, took position behind a fence facing the advancing enemy, who had not yet emerged from the woods at that point. To gain a position beside the 30th Indiana, Lieutenant Colonel Dunn moved by the flank, under cover of the woods, until directly in its rear, but forty rods distant, when a section of Simonson's battery came up and unlimbered directly in our front. The rebel infantry now poured into and through the cornfield, meeting with obstinate resistance from the 30th Indiana and 79th Illinois, and the artillery, which the 29th now supported. Here we lost Captain Frank Stebbins, company G, who was struck by a 12-pound ball in the thigh, causing his death very soon. He had bravely led his men, and by his own conduct inspired them with courage and daring. Up to this time we had the discreet and tried leadership of Lieutenant Colonel Dunn, and the valuable assistance of Captain Jenkins acting field officer; but the former got separated and cut off from the regiment, and the latter going a short distance to the rear for ambulances to carry off our wounded, of whom we had a great number, was also cut off from us. We did not see Lieutenant Colonel Dunn again, nor Captain Jenkins until the afternoon, but both we heard were busy, rallying the runaways and stragglers at the pike and railroad, until the former was taken prisoner, and the latter had turned over his men to their respective regiments. The artillery limbered up, moved to the rear, passing General Davis's division hospital, which we followed until we reached the woods near the hospital, where we found the 77th Pennsylvania, under Captain Rose, in line of battle. I at once formed the 29th on its right to await the rebel onset. All seemed pushing to the rear, and finding our shattered forces unsupported, we again moved in perfect order still further towards the pike; and again formed our line, having the 93rd on the right, and I believe a Kentucky regiment on the left. The artillery did not halt here, and before any enemy appeared in front we found our small force flanked on the right by rebel infantry and cavalry, and on the left by an unknown force. Again we moved leisurely back to a point designated by General Johnson as one suitable to make a stand. This was on the elevated ground west of the pike, on the east side of which we saw a large force of federal troops congregated. Colonel Dodge, (30th Indiana,) now commanding our brigade, placed us in position in a thicket, our left resting on the section of artillery planted on the most elevated point, and supported on the right by the

77th Pennsylvania, its right resting on the woods. Sharp cannonading ensued, but a few minutes' hot work satisfied our artillerists that they could not contend with two batteries and hold their position. They retired to the pike. Colonel Dodge now directed us along the woods to the road, where we again formed our line. The yells of the rebels coming through the cedar woods became plainer and plainer; the balls rained amongst us. When within range, and in sight, the order to advance was given by Colonel Dodge. With a yell the line rushed forward, determined to stop the sweeping tide or die. This very unexpected attack on the victorious column entirely changed the aspect of affairs; for the first time that day it was checked; it tried to withstand the withering fire, but soon gave way, at first slowly, but as our line rushed on the retreat became a rout. We still pushed on rapidly, few in numbers, but determined, with orders not to waste ammunition, and followed the running horde until every cartridge was expended, when Colonel Dodge, after great exertions, got the troops to take our places. We fell back to the railroad for ammunition, when intelligence was brought that our rear, in the vicinity of the hospitals and train, was threatened by cavalry. To repel this attack we were marched to a point near the hospitals, when we stood in line half an hour, but no enemy appearing we again moved to the railroad. After this our force changed its position, as the heavy firing indicated a bloody contest, but we were not again under fire. At night we bivouacked on the pike.

Morning brought with it signs of a renewal of yesterday's fight, and we were placed in position on the edge of the cedar grove, nearest the enemy's line, where the men at once went to work, securing their position with breastworks and abattis. The 29th had no share in any of the ensuing contests, and were entirely occupied on picket duty, and standing to arms, on every alarm, to resist any attack on our line. Volunteers were called for to drive the enemy's skirmishers into the woods and burn some loghouses, in which their sharpshooters found shelter and excellent positions to annoy us; amongst the number were several of the 29th Indiana, one of whom was killed.

Nothing further of importance occurred, unless I mention the fatigue duty performed by details from this regiment, which succeeded in finding and burying our dead and all our wounded, except those who fell into the enemy's hands.

I cannot close without paying a tribute of praise, well merited and proudly given, to the officers and men of my command, who, Spartan like, rallied at every call around our glorious old flag, and who would not desert it when all around looked dark and hope had almost fled. Allow me to mention, with feelings of extreme gratification, the names of those who nobly did their duty.

First, Adjutant Coffin, who, exposed more than any other, carrying orders to different parts of the line, never once quailed before the storm. He is an excellent officer, fearless, prompt, and deserving the highest praise.

Captains Stebbins, Jenkins and McCaslin Moore. First Lieutenants Melandy, who, though wounded, would not leave until trampled by cavalry. N. P. Dunn, who stuck to the flag, severely wounded, until forced by his companions to retire to a hospital; A. Dunlap, J. Houghton, G. Malvon, ——— Henderson, and Hess; also Second Lieutenants S. O. Gregory, commanding company C, and Lieutenant Hess, commanding company B, directed the skirmishers; Junius McGowan, O. P. Butler, William McDonald, ——— Cutler, McComber, and P. Sabin.

While the storm raged without, Surgeon Kean and the Rev. Mr. Shaw, chaplain, were busy dressing wounds, and doing all they could to alleviate the sufferings of our wounded. Assistant Surgeon Griffith, hospital steward, and corps were elsewhere engaged, but all were busy with their duties. I would not pass over the names of the non-commissioned officers, who, with very few exceptions, were heroes in the fight, giving a noble example to the men, and assisting very materially in maintaining order and discipline, but this report is already too long, and I close.

Accompanying this is a list of casualties.

Respectfully, your obedient servant,

J. P. COLLINS,
Major, Commanding 29th Indiana Volunteers.

Captain D. C. WAGNER, *A. A. A. General,*
2d Brigade, 2d Division, Right Wing 14th Army Corps.

HEADQUARTERS 29TH REGIMENT INDIANA VOLUNTEERS,
In Camp near Murfreesboro', Tennessee, January 7, 1863.

SIR: I have the honor to submit the following list of casualties in the actions near Murfreesboro', Tennessee:

Company A.—Killed: Privates Christian Gibbons and Caleb Talbot. Wounded: First Lieutenant R. W. Melandy; Orderly Meletus McGowan; Corporals Henry Hanna, Andrew Somerlett, and Jos. J. Delabaugh; Privates John A. Berger, Anson Brown, George Brown, Frederick Klock, Hugh Guthrie, and J. M. Phenicie.

Company B.—Killed: Orderly George McKean. Wounded: Privates Albert B. Fox, John Lawrence, J. W. Stonebraker, and Webster Paxton.

Company C.—Killed: Corporal Robert Dwinwiddie; Privates John E. Cox, Adam Sigrider, and Richard McLane. Wounded: Corporals Oscar B. Rockwell and John Shafer; Privates Leroy Burback, James Cline, Henry Cline, Fletcher Garres, Henry H. Graves, W. J. Graves, Harvey Holmes, James M. Hoffman, J. H. Michael, Norvel Phillips, John Phillips, Berger H. Bown, and Tristram Pike.

Company D.—Wounded; Private William Stephenson; Sergeants J. H. Dunlop and Jos. Phillips; Privates C. P. Adams, A. H. Highway, Silas Bascom, William Bell, and Jeremiah Smith.

Company E.—Killed: Corporal Joseph Chestnut; Privates Theodore Thompson and John Tuttle. Wounded: First Lieutenant Palmer Dunn; Sergeant Austin Sergeant; Corporals George Myers and Robison B. Reed; Privates J. V. Pownell, Enoch Smith, H. Grable, Aaron Booth, William J. Cline, William Jones, Allen Brown, and Corporal Daniel M. White.

Company G.—Killed: Captain Frank Stebbins. Wounded: Sergeants C. Bushnell and A. W. Warnett, and Corporal E. Towelten.

Company H.—Killed: Private William Delancy. Wounded: Private David Reno.

Captain Shuler ran to Nashville at the commencement of the action, and is supposed to be running still.

Company I.—Killed: Privates William Crawford and George Moseholder. Wounded: Corporal A. Z. Norton; Color Sergeant L. Hunt; Privates Sylvester Crawford, Thomas O. Neil, and Jos. Gibbens.

Company K.—Wounded: Privates George Wiley, John A. Lamb, F. M. Smith, M. P. Kizer, and John Hildebrand.

Killed, 14; Wounded, 65.

Missing.—Company A: Corporal Woodward, Privates Thomas J. Baker, John Dennis, William Kerns, Lewis Phenicie, Elias F. Conrad, Elijah Waller, and Chester Coe. Company B: Corporal Jacob Miller, Privates Thomas Buchanan, James P. Boyd, Cornelius M. Boyd, Benjamin McCurmsah, Philip Row, William Chesay, and William Stover. Company C: Privates Harvey Holmes and Valentine Long. Company D: Privates Jeremiah Ormsby, Joseph Johnston, and Abram Shafer. Company E: Privates Allen Brown, John H.

Grable, John V. Reed, Oliver Philley, William H. Jones, and Michael Foley. Company F: Sergeants William Isey and Samuel Gillmore, Privates Amos Roberts, Michael Snyder, Stephen Rollins, David M. Love, John McCormick, and John Lehman. Company H: Privates David Rayone, Andrew Adams, and William Delaney. Company I: Sergeant Charles Tucker, Privates A. C. Norton, Alphonso Kidwell, John Bonton, and Thomas O'Neill. Company K: Orderly Sergeant Charles Purdy, Corporal Peter D. Shoeff, Privates Milton P. Keyser, Frederic Nagley, Charles Ream, George Ringie, John Hughes, J. Donohoe, George Wyle, William Cline, and John Hildebrand.

Killed, wounded, and missing, 135.

——— ———

Acting Assistant Adjutant General,
Second Brigade, Second Division.

HEADQUARTERS 34TH ILLINOIS VOLUNTEERS,
Camp near Murfreesboro', Tennessee, January 7, 1863.

SIR: In compliance with circular, dated January 7, 1863, from headquarters 2d division, requiring a minute statement of regimental commanders of the operation and casualties of their respective regiments from the time of leaving camp near Nashville, Tennessee, up to the expiration of the battle at Murfreesboro', I have the honor to submit the following report:

On Friday, December 26, 1862, this regiment, under command of Lieutenant Colonel H. W. Bristol, left camp near Nashville, Tennessee, and marched that day to one-half mile south of Nolensville, where we encamped for the night. Next morning, December 27, 1862, the 2d brigade being in advance, the 34th Illinois was in the advance of the brigade. After advancing nearly three-quarters of a mile General Kirk ordered Colonel Bristol to throw forward four companies of his regiment on the left of the pike as skirmishers. Companies A, F, G, and B were detailed for that purpose, and placed under command of myself and Captain Van Tassel. We moved forward, the remaining companies of the regiment marching immediately in the rear of the skirmish line as a support, the skirmish line advancing, driving the enemy through Triune, and halting about one mile south of that place near dark. The distance skirmished over that day was near five miles. Although exposed to the enemy's fire from their artillery and musketry nearly all the day, we had no one killed, wounded, or missing. We went into camp that night a short distance to the rear of where we had advanced with our skirmish line, and remained in camp at that place the next day (being Sunday) without performing any duties, only those required on that day. On the morning of December 29, 1862, we were ordered back towards Nashville two and a half miles, and turned off the pike on a dirt road, to the right, leading in the direction of Murfreesboro', and, after marching six miles, went into camp between 10 and 11 o'clock that night. The 34th Illinois was rear guard for the brigade teams that day.

On the morning of the 30th, 1862, about two o'clock a. m., we moved forward in the direction of Murfreesboro' three miles, when we were ordered to the right. The 34th Illinois was ordered to support Captain Edgarton's battery, which was moved to the extreme right of our lines, and opened fire on a rebel battery that was firing into the right flank of Davis's division. General Kirk ordered two companies of this regiment to be thrown out as skirmishers, A and B, under the command of Captain Van Tassel, extending the line across an open field to a piece of woods about one hundred rods further to the right than our troops occupied. Captain Edgarton's battery soon silenced the rebel battery; and it was now near dark. Colonel Bristol, being unwell, was compelled to leave the regiment, and the command then fell upon myself. I received orders that I was to picket immediately in my front, and that General Kirk would join his pickets on the right. This was done shortly after dark. I was then ordered to encamp the remainder of my regiment in the rear of the left of my picket line, and within thirty rods of the same. Everything was quiet through the night. Just before daylight I had my regiment under arms, and moved them forward some four rods in advance of where I was encamped, so that I could more conveniently deploy into line, as I had my regiment in double column. A few minutes after daylight one of my lookouts reported to me that the enemy was moving down on us with an overwhelming force. I immediately sent word to General Kirk, and rode immediately myself to find General Willich, who was encamped in my rear not more than thirty rods. I failed to find the general; they told me he had gone to see General Johnson. I informed some of the officers of his brigade that the enemy was advancing. I hurried back to my regiment, and I then received an order to advance my regiment, and try to hold the enemy in check, which was done. After advancing out in the open field about fifteen rods the enemy opened upon us, my men returning the fire. They were now exposed to the fire of more than five times their number, as I only had 354 men, including the officers. Ten or twelve of my men were killed and some sixty odd wounded before I received an order to fall back in support of the battery. I gave the oider for them to fall back; not one of my men or officers left their post before I gave them the order. When we returned to the battery everything was confusion; the first brigade was not in position, and was engaged, many of them, cooking their breakfast. I endeavored to hold the battery with what few men I had, but it was of no use; the enemy were fast surrounding us, and the only alternative was to retreat or be taken prisoners. I gave the order for them to retreat, and would, I think, have been able to keep them together, but they got mixed up with the first brigade, and were carried too far to the left, where many of them were taken prisoners. I rallied some fifty of my men, and made a stand behind a rail fence, about three-quarters of a mile from where I formed my first line, and opened a destructive fire on a regiment of cavalry that was bearing down upon us; but, finding it impossible to hold that position, I had to fall back to near the pike, when I was ordered to assist our train with what few men I had left.

January 1, 1863.—What was left of my regiment was put in with the 30th Indiana, and took part with that regiment, under the command of Captain Hostetter, company I, 34th Illinois volunteers, I being sick, and unfit for duty. They were engaged in skirmishing from behind breastworks that were erected. January 2d they were engaged the same as on the 1st, and on the 3d the same routine of duty. The 34th Illinois lost no one killed or wounded after the battle of December 31, 1862.

I need not particularize the services of any officers under my command, for both officers and men did their duty nobly; although being compelled to retreat, they stood firm till we were overwhelmed by superior numbers.

I attach a list of killed, wounded, and missing. Many of the missing I have no doubt are wounded and in the hands of the enemy.

All of which is respectfully submitted.

ALEXANDER P. DYSART,
Major, Commanding 34th Illinois Volunteers.

Captain D. C. WAGNER,
A. A. General, 2d Brigade, 2d Division.

List of killed, wounded, and missing, in the different companies of the 24th regiment Illinois volunteers, in action before Murfreesboro', Tennessee, December 31, 1862.

Killed.—Company A: Private George L. Woodworth. Company C: Corporal Charles Santee. Company D: Corporal John D. Dole; Privates William Windle and Henry Pecks. Company E: Sergeant Marcus M. Bennett; Corporal George J. Doughty; Private Henry D. Krouch. Company F: Corporal Jeremiah C. Grover; Private Archibald M. Pratt. Company G: Privates S. R. Cully and H. J. Sutliff. Company H: Corporal Secust R. Wertz; Privates Asa L. Tyler, H. A. Willaby, and Charles Easton. Company I: Private James Masters. Company K: Sergeant James M. Peadan, and Private William Riley Norcutt.

Wounded.—Company A: Corporal John Gibner; Privates John Durstin, John Gorgas, James M. Maiden, and Herschel H. Smith. Company B: Corporal Wilber F. Nichols; Private Phil. T. Resser. Company C: First Lieutenant D. Riley; Corporals W. A. Seitz, J. E. Laxman, G. W. Kessler, and David Wingard; Privates J. H. Bowers, Henry E. Brown, T. W. Brown, (prisoner,) R. M. Colwell, P. Fahey, John Gillott, H. Grothe, H. Hoffmaster, (prisoner,) J. Hoof, J. Hunt, W. H. Knepper, P. Kegauxe, E. O'Neil, John Rouch, B. Royce, (prisoner,) and J. H. Stephens, in head. Company D: Sergeant D. C. Young, (prisoner;) Corporals Samuel J. Tussey and John Chambers; Privates Eugene Brewer, Charles P. Barber, (prisoner,) Henry C. Case, Wellington Eaton, Henry Law, George Pierce, Joseph Shellhamer, James Sigman, and William Savage. Company E: Sergeants Patrick McCarty (prisoner,) and Robert Karr; Corporal George F. Cheshier, (prisoner;) Privates Frederic Fyers, William Devine, Charles E. Miner, Lawrence Coffield, John Zink, (missing,) Michael Renaham, A. S. Blakely, (prisoner,) and Freer Richardson. Company F: Captain Oscar Van Tassell; Sergeant John T. Gantz; Corporal Austin S. Fox; Privates Charles Butterfield, Thomas C. Brown, John H. Gull, Arnold S. Harrington, Edmund F. Merritt, Edward Bankhurst, Kenton D. Taylor, William Steel, and James B. Taylor. Company G: Captain M. G. Greenwood, (since died;) Sergeant Edward Cates; Corporal Elias Baughman; Privates Samuel Hindman, and Samuel C. Barber. Company H: Second Lieutenant J. M. Smith; Sergeant Peter Householder; Corporals Levi R. Holsinger, and Elmnar G. Lawrence; Privates H. H. Bennett, Ananicus Billig, John Coddington, John Cost, George Detwilder, Jacob L. Grove, Levi Hays, W. W. Johnson, David V. Meredith, U. S. A. Howison, Lewis Miller, Ernest C. Reif, and Otho Tice. Company I: First Sergeant Joseph Teeter; Sergeants Levi Sarver and John C. Gelwick; Corporals Hiram H. Maynard, and George Robbins; Privates Christian Bushman, (missing,) Jesse N. Berlin, Peter Farrell, Philip Quickbeuner, Caleb Ransom, Joseph Savver, (missing.) Company K: Privates Thomas Gaddes, Nathan Conner, William Rogers, Nelson O. Harra, Daniel Madden, and Nathan Isenhoner,

Missing.—Company A: Privates L. T. Babcock, George B. Brandt, John Crichton, Charles Crickton, Henry Cornell, Charles Slocumb, H. Clay Smith, and Charles D. Wilson. Company B: Sergeants David L. Eagle and Oscar Olmsted; Corporal Daniel White; Musicians Charles Wood and George A. Quackenbush; Privates Smith Ring, William Dow, Patrick O'Connell, Patrick McDonald, William Messmore, Jacob G. Ressor, Charles L. Parkhurst, Andrew J. Harp, John Lansing, Julius J. Brown, William L. Hubbard, and Daniel Richards. Company C: Privates Thomas Hays and R. E. Young. Company D: Captain William S. Wood; Sergeants Major Wood and Spencer Conn; Privates Edward Doyle, Orlando Redney, and Morris Johnson. Company E: First Lieutenant Edward H. Weld; Corporal De Wayre R. Calkins; Privates John W. Dunlava, Hiram H. Benner, Martin Cartle,

Patrick Hare, Patrick Hughes, Thomas E. Kellogg, Dennes Finley, and William Harrison. Company F: Musician Virgil E. Reed; Privates Lewis C. Bronson, Uriah Beechly, Eliot Taylor, Elbridge S. Weley, and Joseph Wolf. Company G: First Sergeant T. G. Carney; Sergeant H. C. Pratt; Corporal Tim Geidna; Privates H. H. Smith, George Apple, A. Shuman, and J. H. Ellis. Company H: Musicians J. L. Harrison and John Brown; Privates James T. Askey, August Hickmam, Nelson Kellogg, Chapman Mann, Christian Niel, and John Shaw. Company I: Privates Adam Lawver, Fred. J. Reman, and Alfred Nurd. Company K: Sergeants William S. Wright and Austin Umbarger; Corporals Rufus S. Cusick and Zedekiah Thomlinson; Privates Samuel J. Richards, Charles C. Lyons, and William Stapelton.

HEADQUARTERS 30TH INDIANA VOLUNTEERS,
Camp near Murfreesboro', Tennessee, January 7, 1863.

SIR: In accordance with circular dated January 7, 1863, issued from headquarters 2d division, requiring a minute statement from regimental commanders of the operations of their respective regiments, including casualties, I have the honor to report that on Friday, December 26, 1862, this regiment under command of Colonel J. B. Dodge, left camp, near Nashville, Tennessee, marched half a mile south of Nolensville, where we encamped for the night. Next morning, December 27, 1862, the 2d brigade being in advance, we left camp at sunrise, moved in the same direction on the turnpike as the day previous. After advancing one and a half miles were ordered into line of battle to support Captain Edgarton's battery, in which manner we moved three or four miles, and until dark, when we were ordered out on outpost picket. On the next day, December 28, 1862, after being relieved from picket, we remained in camp without any actual service. On December 29, 1862, we moved back towards Nashville two miles and took a cross road leading towards Murfreesboro', and after moving six miles camped for the night. On December 30, 1862, we moved towards Murfreesboro' three miles, when we were ordered off to the right, and after throwing forward two companies each from the right and left flanks as skirmishers, moved forward one mile in line of battle, and bivouacked for the night in a cedar thicket. On the morning of December 31, 1862, the enemy moved upon us in force about daylight, driving in our pickets, making it necessary for us to fall back, or move out by the flank to the right; the latter movement was made with the loss of one man slightly, and one mortally, wounded, except upon the picket line, which being doubled during the night by two additional companies, to insure vigilance and safety, suffered severely upon being driven in. The movement by the flank was a fortunate one for us, for had we remained any longer in that position we would have been cut to pieces or taken prisoners by the enemy who were in great force on our front. After moving to the right and rear about half a mile, we formed a line of battle in a meadow behind a fence, where we were joined by the remnants of the four companies who were on picket the night before. After sending out two companies as skirmishers across a field to a fence directly in our front, we moved up to the same place and the action commenced. General Kirk having been wounded early in the morning, and Colonel Dodge of this regiment having taken command of the 2d brigade, the command of this regiment fell upon the undersigned. After the regiment upon our left and we had sustained the enemy's fire for some time, the 79th Illinois volunteers advanced to our immediate right and supported us gallantly, but being outflanked by a superior force of the enemy, and exposed to a heavy cross-fire, they fell back, and we were obliged to do the same, having no support whatever, and having suffered heavy loss as hereinafter stated;

in retiring the men became very much scattered, but were mostly collected again, and then we were ordered to the front on the right of the Murfreesboro' turnpike, three miles from the town.

January 1, 1863.—After erecting breastworks we remained behind them, without any further active service except skirmishing on picket-line.

January 2.—The same routine of duty as the day previous, except in the evening, when the left wing was sent out with parts of other regiments of this brigade as skirmishers to feel the position of the enemy, but after receiving a severe fire and supposing the enemy to be in force, we returned their fire briskly for some time and then retired to the breastwork.

January 3.—Same routine of picket duty as the day previous. It is unnecessary for me to particularize the services of any officer or man, for both officers and men performed their duties well and gallantly.

I have also a statement of the killed, wounded, and missing to submit, as follows, to wit:

Major G. W. Fitzsimmons, taken prisoner.

Killed.—Company A: Assistant Adjutant E. B. Stribley; Privates Christian Winkler, Lawrence White, and W. D. Allen. Company B: Corporals William Rosebrugh, (color guard,) William Roberts, and Daniel Walker; Privates N. M. Reynolds, and E. Middleton. Company C: Corporal J. W. Hathaway; Privates William Archey, and James Morrow. Company D: Corporals William Hatfield, and J. W. Nesbit. Company E: Corporal Alfred Harris; Privates George Johnson, and William Popeno. Company F: Private Kirtis Browse. Company G: Corporal J. P. Rambo; Privates Myson Ames, Eli Wheeler, and Naaman Pence. Company H: Corporal Nathaniel Osburn; Privates George Cole, William Phyke, George Long, and William Miller. Company K: Corporal David Gigler, and Private Daniel Swank.

Wounded.—Company A: Sergeant J. W. Stribley; Privates R. Myers, C. Stribley, P. Schrom, J. W. Vogier, A. Wilson, F. Huchin, and M. Strous. Company B: Privates Robert Smidbey, G. W. Johnson, F. Musheide, S. Funk, D. Koons, G. Bartley, W. Benford, William Felters, W. H. Sloane, and F. Fisher. Company C: Sergeant Anderson Corle; Corporals Isaac Pancake, and Jos. S. Olcott; Privates Charles Allen, George Gorber, William P. Johnson, H. M. Marker, Tollmon Morris, Joseph Miller, William Parker, Francis Vedder, and Richard Vanderford. Company D: Sergeant Thomas Mead; Corporal Robert Bell; Privates Henry Richards and George Pembrook. Company E: Sergeant George E. Murphey; Corporals C. L. Murray, J. H. Rhodes, and Edward Strack; Privates John Whiton, William Morrow, Samuel Shane, Henry Bush, Charles Fair, Thomas Hogarth, and Lennan Maloney. Company F: Corporal J. C. Bloomfield; Privates Samuel Wygant, David Skinner, William Shool, Henry Hanes, and J. D. Vanfersan. Company G: Sergeant Robert McFerson; Corporal Harrison Merrills, and C. G. Cookinghan; Privates C. B. Elsworth, W. H. Yoder, J. W. Walburn, Silas Latta, Oris Butt, and W. W. Wilson. Company H: Sergeants J. D. Likens, Perry Hodges, and L. D. Conner; Corporals J. C. Whyson, Peter Barnhardt, and William Freeman; Privates W. H. H. Beard, Alvin Coller, Leslie Delano, Nathan Frederickson, James George, Leslie Fisher, John High, John Hammon, Joseph Lockenmire, Asbury F. Long, William Lutz, Perry Mullen, John Marcum, Reason McCush, George Murray, Albert Reed, Levi Rutan, B. F. Sponhower, N. M. Showers, Alexander Skinner, and Samuel Ulane. Company I: Captain J. M. Butcher; Second Lieutenant John Moore, (missing;) Corporal Peter Hemmer; Privates George Armstrong, Daniel Bowman, Timothy Carsher, Alfred Clark, Oliver P. Every, William Fordjum, Wade Harris, William Hight, Henry Rist, Silas McCush, Jeremiah Noll, John Puntney, and Andrew Tom. Company K: Corporal Daniel D. Coppes; Privates Wallis Nelson, George Potter, Adam Beck, and Nelson Hoppner.

Missing.—Company A: Privates W. Allen, J. Slemler, William Frederickson, J. Harvey, M. Sucker, W, Gunslerberger, J. Johnson, and J. Lockwood. Company B: Second Lieutenant W. R. Williams; Privates G. Fogle, A. Harper, E. Hall, W. Hall, R. McCutcheon, H. Yager, Isaac Scott, D. Vandemark, and J. Pennland. Company C: Corporals Hirah Goodspeed, John Airgood, Henry Gunder, Henry Serried, and Thomas Cullison. Company D: Corporal Henry Kelby; Privates Henry Wyant, William Schlawtroff, William Strong, and Thomas Devese. Company E: Privates Frank Sten, William Sten, Joshua Kelby, and Joseph Bryant. Company F: Sergeants Philo Elinwood and William G. Gibbon; Corporal Hugh A. Young; Privates Lewis Wright, Weir D. Carver, Francis Coon, J. Lease, Sterling Monroe, William Monroe, and Jeremiah Noel. Company G: Sergeant Samuel Shepardson; Corporal Charles N. Buck; Privates C. N. Wheeler, Charles Moon, G. D. Rhinehart, John McNeel, Charles Isley, Lewis Airgood, Ruben Mosier, and M. V. B. Leidign. Company H: Sergeant J. W. McKay; Privates William Franks, Harman Meed, Wesley Miller, John A. Provines, and Calvin Marshall; Private Lorenzo Piatt, (missing and prisoner.) Company I: Musician Levi Peddycord; Privates Orlan Tremaires, and John Andrews. Company K: Privates David Lampa, (prisoner,) Dewatt Shuster, George Epart, Jacob W. Leavely, John Lehman, David Cristner, and Peter Baker.

RECAPITULATION.

	Killed.	Wounded.	Missing and prisoners.	Command'g officers	Enlisted men
Field officers	......	......	1	3	......
Staff officers	1	......	......	1	......
Company A	4	8	8	2	51
Company B	5	10	10	2	48
Company C	3	12	5	1	52
Company D	2	4	5	1	41
Company E	3	11	4	2	38
Company F	1	6	10	2	39
Company G	4	9	10	3	59
Company H	5	27	7	2	64
Company I	......	16	3	3	32
Company K	2	5	7	2	39
Total	30	108	70	24	463

All of which is respectfully submitted.

O. D. HURD,
Lieutenant Colonel Commanding Regiment.

Captain D. C. WAGNER.

HEADQUARTERS 77TH REGIMENT PENNSYLVANIA VOLUNTEERS,
In Camp near Murfreesboro', January 8, 1863.

SIR: I have the honor to make the following report of the 77th regiment Pennsylvania volunteers, from the time of leaving camp near Mill creek, December 26, 1862, to January 3, 1863, viz:

We broke up our camp near Mill creek December 26, sent our wagon train to Nashville, and took up our march in the direction of Shelbyville, on the Nolensville turnpike, and encamped in the evening a short distance beyond Nolensville.

December 27.—We continued our march in the same direction and on the same road. At 8 a. m. we encountered the enemy within two miles of Triune. We were immediately placed in position with the balance of our brigade on the left of the road. Our front line was composed of the 29th regiment Indiana volunteers on the left, the 34th Illinois volunteers on the right, and the 30th Indiana volunteers in the centre. Our regiment and the 79th regiment Illinois volunteers were held in reserve, but advanced with the brigade, our regiment covering the 29th Indiana volunteers. Skirmishers were thrown forward by each of the three first-named regiments, as also were two companies of the 77th regiment Pennsylvania volunteers, who occupied the extreme left of the line. In this manner we advanced towards Triune, driving the enemy from his position, and took possession of the town, the enemy retreating towards Shelbyville. We encamped about a mile beyond Triune, near the turnpike.

December 28.—We remained in camp where we stopped the evening before.

December 29.—We retraced our march on the same road for two miles and turned off on a dirt road running an easterly course into the Salem turnpike, at the junction of which two roads we silently and without fires encamped for the night.

December 30.—We marched towards Murfreesboro' on the Salem turnpike for about three miles, when we were thrown into column, by division, into the woods on the right of the road with the balance of our brigade and division. At this time heavy skirmishing was going on on our left and in front. We advanced for a short distance, when our regiment and the 30th regiment Indiana volunteers were ordered to change front to the right, deploy column, and throw out skirmishers. We then advanced, moving towards the right of the general line of battle for about a quarter of a mile. We then changed front to the left and occupied a dense cedar grove. The position of our regiment was now on the right of the 22d regiment Indiana volunteers, of General Davis's division. It was here that we received a heavy fire from a rebel battery that was stationed to the right and in front of us in an open field by the edge of a woods at a distance of 500 yards. After a sharp skirmish it was silenced, when we threw out our pickets and remained for the night. Our position was now on the left of our brigade and on the right of Davis's division.

December 31.—We were under arms at 4 a. m., and at daylight we discovered the enemy in large force within sixty yards of our pickets, who immediately commenced firing when the enemy advanced to a furious attack. As the pickets retired our regiment advanced to meet the enemy and resisted their attack with desperate valor, repulsing the forces immediately in front with great slaughter, and compelling them to retire across the brook where we first found them posted and into a cornfield beyond. This was the first attack that was made on our lines; but almost at the same time the enemy's column's on our left, which were directed on those regiments on our right, pressed furiously onward bearing down everything before them. Those on our right fell back after a short but desperate resistance, as was shown by the great mortality on both sides. Soon after this the regiment on our left changed position to our rear, leaving our regiment completely isolated and battling against great odds, with the danger of being surrounded. We were ordered to retire for about 150 yards and then march to the right, in order, if possible, to reattach ourselves to the balance of our brigade which had been driven from its first position. While doing this we fell in with a portion of General Davis's division and were advised that we had better co-operate with that division for the present, as our brigade had by this time retired so far that it would consume much valuable time in finding it that could be used at this particular juncture to great advantage by re-inforcing one of his, Davis's divisions. We posted ourselves on the right of Davis's division in front of which was a rebel battery, at a distance of about 400 yards. A little to the right and in front of this was Edgarton's battery which had been previously captured by the rebels in the onset, and was still in their possession. It was here that our regiment charged alone, recapturing Edgarton's battery, and up to the guns of the rebel battery through a hurricane of grape and canister, until we were confronted by several thousands of the rebel infantry, when, as we were unsupported, we were obliged to retire to the line from which we started on the charge, leaving our much loved battery in the hands of the rebels, as we had no means of moving it off. Yet we were repaid for this desperate charge as much as for any we made during the day, in damaging the enemy and holding him in check. We retired in good order and halted and reformed in our previous position on the right of Davis's division. Here Colonel Housem fell. The battle was here hotly contested for some time, when our forces began to give way, fiercely pursued by the enemy who came near taking a battery of ours at this place. As soon as the battery was safely off we retired to the fence on the opposite side of the field, where we stood alone for some time contending with the rebels, until they commenced scaling the fence on our right and left, when we retired to the woods and again made a stand. We thus continued for some time taking advantage of everything that came in our way, moving slowly, and our line never broke once throughout the day; but we fought every time we could find a line to rest on, or wherever we could gain a position in whtch we could for a minute successfully make a stand. When we came near the Nashville and Murfreesboro' turnpike we fell in with a portion of the 29th Indiana volunteers, under the gallant Major Collins, also a portion of the 30th Indiana volunteers. These, with our regiment, were now joined together as the remnant of the old 5th brigade under Colonel Dodge as brigade commander. We were posted in the edge of the woods by General Johnson, on the right of General Van Cleve's division which had just come up. The rebels were now coming on with tenfold more impetuosity, and our men were ordered to lie down quietly behind a fence which partly protected us. We waited here until the rebels were within a short distance, when we up and delivered our fire with such great effect that the rebels began to give way. We now pitched into them with whoop and yell, all the time delivering a most destructive fire, and soon the whole rebel column was in full retreat; we drove them half a mile, when our ammunition gave out and we were relieved, when we retired to the railroad to obtain a fresh supply. This was the first check of importance that the rebels received, as it saved our ammunition train and secured for our forces an important position. From the break of day until 12 m. our regiment was under constant fire, and terribly our ranks were thinned. At night our regiment went on picket.

January 1, 1863.—We remained under arms on the crest of the hill where we ended our final charge on the 31st ultimo. At 4 p. m. we received a heavy fire from a rebel battery which was soon silenced.

Janaary 2.—Remained in the same position as on the 1st. A heavy battle was fought on our left in which we took no part. In the evening we went on picket. A heavy skirmish took place immediately in front of our line.

January 3.—Still remained under arms in our old position. At night, in the midst of the rain, the last final struggle was made, in which we took no part.

During this great battle our little regiment did no discredit to the old Keystone State. Officers and men stood up and did their duty nobly. Among those noted for conspicuous valor I must mention Adjutant S. F. Davis, who rendered me invaluable assistance throughout the battle. Also Captain T. Phyfer, company K; Captain William W. Robinson, company E; Captain A. Philips, company G, and Captain J. J. Lawson, company C, all of whom cheered and encouraged their men throughout the battle with a coolness which belongs to none but vetern officers. That our line never broke shows that our men fought like veterans.

We went into the action with 288 men. We lost in killed, 5, including Lieutenant Colonel Housem; in wounded, 29, including one commissioned officer; missing, 29, including two commissioned officers. Total, 63. Of those missing the greater part are either killed or taken prisioners.

I must not forget to mention the valuable services and noble conduct of Dr. Downie, the assistant surgeon of our regiment. He remained with us throughout the battle, and disylayed the most indomitable energy and courage in attending to our wounded, and in superintending the whole medidal department which came within his sphere.

I regret to say that, notwithstanding the great valor displayed by our regiment as a body, there were some miserable cowards who skulked away during the excitement of the battle, and left their comrades to perform their duty. I have carefully obtained their names and rank, however, and shall forward them without delay.

I have the honor to be, most respectfully, your obedient servant,

TOM ELLWOOD ROSE,

Captain, Commanding 77th Regiment Pennsylvania Volunteers.

D. C. WAGNER,

Acting Assistant Adjutant General, 2d Brigade.

HEADQUARTERS 77TH REGIMENT PENNSYLVANIA VOLUNTEERS,

In Camp, January 8, 1863.

SIR: The following is a correct list of the casualties of the 77th regiment Pennsylvania volunteers, in killed, wounded and missing, in the battles before Murfreesboro,' Tennessee, December 31, 1862:

Lieutenant Colonel Peter B. Housem commanding, mortally wounded in hip, since died.

Wounded.—Company A: First Lieutenant John E. Walker commanding, wounded in knee; Privates Henry Tennary, and Jackson Smith, in leg. Fifty-five men taken into action.

Missing.—Corporal James Cannon; Private Frederick Rensinger.

Company B: First Lieutenant John W. Krepps, commanding. Thirty men taken into action.

Wounded.—Privates Jones, in hip, and Edwin Bratt, in leg.

Missing.—Privates Wm. Acker, and David Darby.

Company C: Captain Joseph J. Lawson commanding. Thirty-seven men taken into action.

Wounded.—Sergeant Scott R. Crawford, in both legs, (left leg amputated;) Corporals William Keith, in left thigh, (leg amputated,) and Samuel A. Gettys, in right leg; Privates William Gansta, in ankle, (prisoner;) David Stiller, in breast and left wrist, (prisoner;) William Dixon, in right eye; Andrew Hindlind, face; John Higgins, left index finger off; Henry Greenawatt, right arm.

Missing.—Privates Charles McFarland, and Richard Mitchel.

Company D: First Lieutenant Henry B. Thompson commanding. Twenty-four men taken into action.

Killed.—Private Augustus Mace.

Wounded.—Private Wm. Robinson, in breast.

Missing.—Second Lieutenant Thomas G. Cochran; Privates, John C. Shirley, Jacob Blinsinger, and Joshua Keenar.

Company E: Captain William A. Robinson commanding. Twenty-six men taken into action.

Killed.—Privates John A. Hake, and John A. Buler.

Wounded.—Privates Thomas Hardey, not known where, (prisoner;) Edward

J. Murphy, not known where, (prisoner;) Johnston E. Clark, not know where, (prisoner;) Alfred Ray, slightly in breast; Enoch Eckel, slightly in hand.

Missing.—Privates James Rodgers, and Jacob S. Bartholomew.

Company F: First Lieutenant John S. McDonal commanding. Forty-two men taken into action.

Wounded.—Privates Michael Short, in shoulder; William Bivin, in hand; and George Heavner, in knee.

Missing—.Captain Henry Wishart; Corporals George M. Cooper, and Milton M. Horton; Privates Randal Childers, and James Lippincott.

Company K: Captain Frederick T. Pyfer commanding. Thirty-five men taken into action.

Killed.—Private Alexander Brown.

Wounded.—Corporal Robert McMullen, right thigh, (prisoner;) Privates William J. Prentis, in breast and arm, (prisoner;) John Gambe, in shoulder, (prisoner;) and Dennis H. Buler, hip.

Missing.—Privates Charles Mackinson, Alexander Stewart, and William Clark.

Company G: Captain Alexander Philips commanding. Thirty-nine men taken into action.

Wounded.—Corporal James Foster, in breast; Private Patrick Gallagher, in face.

Missing.—Sergeants George Buchanon, and Edwin Morgan; Corpoal James Brown; Privates William Davis, Owen Williams, Edward Jones, James Forester, Thomas Jordon, and Wadsworth Wetherbee.

Respectfully submitted,

CAPTAIN COMMANDING REGIMENT.

Captain D. C. WAGNER,
Acting Assistant Adjutant General.

HEADQUARTERS 3D BRIGADE, 2D DIVISION, RIGHT WING,
In camp near Murfreesboro', January 8, 1863.

I have the honor to submit a report of the operations of this brigade from the time of its leaving camp, December 26, until Saturday, January 3.

This brigade moved with the division, and on the 27th engaged in the skirmishing about Triune. I deployed the first Ohio and the sixth Indiana on the right of the road, these regiments being supported by the ninety-third Ohio and Louisville legion, the battery taking post on the road, and later in the day being posted near the right of my line. We drove the enemy and bivouacked beyond Triune.

This brigade remained at Triune to cover the extreme right, in obedience to your order, and rejoined the division on the 30th in the woods to the right of Wilkinson pike, about three miles from Murfreesboro'.

At 2 o'clock this brigade moved off two miles to the right, to support a cavalry reconnoissance, Colonel Anderson's regiment being sent forward to support the cavalry while the remainder of the brigade was held in reserve at a point on the Salem pike.

The brigade returned to the woods, near the headquarters of the division, after dark, and bivouacked there.

At daybreak next morning I was informed by stragglers, who were running across the field in my front, of the attack on Generals Willich's and Kirke's brigades.

I immediately ordered the brigade under arms and proceeded to form line of battle in the edge of timber facing the large open fields over which I knew the enemy must come to attack me.

I deployed the Louisville legion on the right, and was proceeding to post the first Ohio in the centre, and the sixth Indiana on the left, holding the ninety-third Ohio in reserve, to protect either flank, when you ordered me to move the first Ohio across the open field and post it at the fence. The sixth Indiana was moved forward and posted in the edge of a skirt of timber to the left of the first Ohio, the thirtieth Indiana and seventy-ninth Illinois being posted on the right; a section of the fifth Indiana battery was posted between the first Ohio and sixth Indiana. The Louisville legion moved to within supporting distance of the first Ohio, and the ninety-third Ohio held in reserve in the woods near the edge of the field. These dispositions were scarcely made when the enemy, in immense masses, appeared in my front at short range, their left extending far beyond the extreme right of my line. My infantry and artillery poured a destructive fire into their dense masses, checking them in front; but their left continued to advance against my right. Here four pieces that Captain Simonson had posted near the woods, in rear of my first line, poured in a terrible fire; but the enemy came in such overwhelming numbers that, after half an hour's stubborn resistance, my line was compelled to retire, not, however, until the enemy had flanked my right and were pouring in an enfilading fire. Had my line stood a moment longer it would have been entirely surrounded and captured. Falling back to the edge of the woods, I endeavored to make a stand. I moved the ninety-third Ohio up to the left of the Louisville legion; but my line was again forced back, almost before I had got the ninety-third in position. Ordering Colonel Anderson to retire in good order, I succeeded, after making several short stands in the woods, in forming the brigade near the railroad. Under your orders I took position on the right of the Nashville pike, together with the rest of the division, and held it during the succeeding skirmishes, throwing up a breastwork of logs, rails, &c.

Nothing occurred here but unimportant skirmishing, sometimes quite warm, but always resulting in our driving the enemy. A house about 300 yards from our line was held by the enemy's skirmishers, who annoyed us exceedingly by their fire. It was captured and burned by two companies of the Louisville legion, after a severe fight. Too great praise cannot be awarded to the regiments of this brigade and Simonson's battery for the coolness and steadiness with which they resisted the attacks of an overwhelming force, and the readiness with which they rallied and formed again when the enemy had broken their lines. The Louisville legion gallantly drew off, by hand, a disabled gun belonging to Cotter's battery.

It may be proper for me to state here, with reference to the line formed in the woods after leaving the open field, that I am informed by reliable officers that the line could have been held had not the right been ordered to fall back by some general not known to the writer.

I beg leave to refer you to the accompanying reports of regimental and battery commanders for details:

Colonel Charles Anderson, commanding ninety-third Ohio; Lieutenant Colonel W. W. Berry, commanding Louisville legion; Lieutenant Colonel H. Tripp, commanding sixth Indiana; Major J. A. Stafford, commanding first Ohio; and Captain P. Simonson, commanding fifth Indiana battery, displayed the greatest coolness, courage, and skill in the management of their respective commands.

Colonel Anderson and Lieutenant Colonel Berry were wounded early in the engagement of Wednesday, but refused to leave the field.

Captain Simonson's battery did good service, and was handled bravely and skilfully. Two pieces, under command of Lieutenant Rankin, did effective service in my first line, he continuing to work his guns after being severely wounded. I regret to report the loss of two pieces of the battery, owing to the horses all being killed and the gunners disabled.

I am indebted to Lieutenant G. H. Burns, assistant acting adjutant general, rof his valuable assistance, and also to Lieutenant Patterson, first Ohio, and Adjutant J. J. Siddell, for their coolness and readiness in transmitting orders to the hottest parts of the field.

Dr. E. S. Swain, brigade surgeon, remained with the wounded, after the enemy drove us back, and rendered them every assistance in his power.

I append a list of killed, wounded, and missing, amounting to 56 killed, 242 wounded, and 137 missing.

I have the honor to be, very respectfully, your obedient servant,

P. P. BALDWIN,
Colonel Commanding 3d Brigade.

Brigadier General R. W. JOHNSON,
Commanding 2d Division.

HEADQUARTERS 3D DIVISION, RIGHT WING, 14TH ARMY CORPS,
Camp on Stone river, Tennessce, January 9, 1863.

MAJOR: In obedience to instructions from the headquarters right wing, I have the honor to report the following as the operations of my division from the 26th day of December, 1862, to the 6th day of January, 1863.

On the 26th day of December I moved from camp, near Nashville, on the Nolensville pike, in the direction of Nolensville. At the crossing of Mill creek the enemy's cavalry made some resistance, but were soon routed, one lieutenant and one private of the enemy being captured.

On approaching Nolensville, I received a message from General Davis, who had arrived at Nolensville, *via* the Edmonson pike, that the enemy were in considerable force in his front, and requesting me to support him. On the arrival of the head of my division at Nolensville, General Davis advanced upon the enemy's position, about two miles south of that place, supported by my division. The enemy had here made a stand in a gap of the mountains, but after a sharp conflict with General Davis's command were routed and one piece of artillery captured.

On the next day (27th) I supported General Johnson's division in its advance on Triune, where the enemy were supposed to be in considerable force.

The town was taken possession of after a slight resistance, the main portion of their forces having evacuated the place.

On the 28th of December I encamped at Triune. On the 29th I supported General Davis's division, which had the advance from Triune on Murfreesboro', encamping that night at Wilkinson's Crossroads, from which point there is a good turnpike to Murfreesboro'.

On the next day (the 30th) I took the advance of the right wing on this turnpike towards Murfreesboro', General Stanley, with a regiment of cavalry, having been thrown in advance.

After arriving at a point about three miles from Murfreesboro', the enemy's infantry pickets were encountered and driven back, their numbers constantly increasing until I had arrived within about two miles and a quarter of Murfreesboro'. At this point the resistance was so strong as to require two regiments to drive them. I was here directed by Major General McCook to form my line of battle, and place my artillery in position.

My line was formed on the right of the pike and obliquely to it; four regiments to the front, with a second line of four regiments within short supporting distance in the rear, with a reserve of one brigade in column of regiments, to the rear and opposite the centre. General Davis was then ordered to close in and form on my right.

The enemy all this time keeping up a heavy artillery and musketry fire upon my skirmishers.

The enemy continued to occupy with their skirmishers a heavy belt of timber to the right and front of my line, and across some open fields and near where the left of General Davis's division was intended to rest. General Davis was then directed by Major General McCook to swing his division, and I was directed to swing my right brigade with it until our continuous line would front nearly due east. This would give us possession of the timber above alluded to, and which was occupied by the enemy's skirmishers in considerable force. This movement was successfully executed after a stubborn resistance on the part of the enemy, in which they used one battery of artillery. This battery was silenced in a very short time by Bush's and Hescock's batteries of my division, and two of the enemy's pieces disabled.

At sundown I had taken up my position, my right resting in the timber, my left on the Wilkinson's pike, my reserve brigade of four regiments to the rear and opposite the centre.

The killed and wounded during the day was seventy-five men. General Davis's left was closed in on my right, and his line thrown to the rear, so that it formed nearly a right angle with me. General Negley's division of Thomas's corps was immediately on my left, his right resting on the left-hand side of the Wilkinson pike.

The enemy appeared to be in strong force, in a heavy cedar woods, across an open valley varying from 300 to 400 yards.

At two o'clock on the morning of the 31st General Sill, who had command of my right brigade, reported great activity on the part of the enemy immediately in his front. This being the narrowest point in the valley, I was fearful that an attack might occur at that point. I therefore directed two regiments from the reserves to report to General Sill, who placed them in position in very short supporting distance of his lines. At four o'clock in the morning, the division was assembled under arms, and the cannoneers at their pieces. About fifteen minutes after seven o'clock in the morning, the enemy advanced to the attack, across an open cotton-field, on Sill's front. This column was opened upon by Bush's battery, of Sill's brigade, which had a direct fire on its front; also by Hescock's and Houghtaling's batteries, which had an oblique fire on its front, from a commanding position near the centre of my line. The effect of this fire upon the enemy's columns was terrible. The enemy, however, continued to advance until they had reached nearly the edge of the timber, when they were opened upon by Sill's infantry at a range of not over fifty yards. The destruction to the enemy's columns which was closed in mass, being several regiments in depth, was terrible. For a short time they withstood the fire, manœuvred, then broke and ran—Sill directing his troops to charge, which was gallantly responded to, and the enemy driven back across the valley and behind their intrenchments. In this charge I had the misfortune to lose General Sill, who was killed. The brigade then fell back in good order, and resumed its original lines. The enemy soon rallied and advanced to the attack on my extreme right and in front of Colonel Woodruff, of Davis's division. Here unfortunately the brigade of Colonel Woodruff gave way, also one regiment of Sill's brigade, which was in the second line. This regiment fell back some distance into the open field and there rallied, its place being occupied by a third regiment of my reserve. At this time the enemy, who had attacked on the extreme right of our wing against Johnson, and also on Davis's front, had been successful, and the two divisions on my right were retiring in great confusion, closely followed by the enemy, completely turning my position and exposing my line to a fire from the rear. I hastily withdrew the whole of Sill's brigade, and the three regiments sent to support it, at the same time directing Colonel Roberts, of the left brigade, who had charged front and formed in column of regiments, to charge the enemy in the timber from which I had withdrawn those regiments. This was very gallantly done by Colonel Roberts, who captured one piece of the enemy's artillery, which had to be abandoned.

In the mean time I had formed Sill's and Schaefer's brigades on a line at right angles to my first line, and behind the three batteries of artillery, which were placed in a fine position, directing Colonel Roberts to return and form on this new line.

I then made an unavailing attempt to form the troops on my right on this line, in front of which there were open fields, through which the enemy was approaching under a heavy fire from Hescock's, Houghtaling's, and Bush's batteries.

After the attempt had proved to be entirely unsuccessful, and my right was again turned, General McCook directed me to advance to the front and form on the right of Negley. This movement was successfully accomplished under a heavy fire of musketry and artillery, every regiment of mine remaining unbroken.

I took position on Negley's right, Roberts's brigade having been placed in position at right angles to Negley's line, facing to the south, the other two brigades being placed to the rear and at right angles with Roberts's, and facing the west, covering the rear of Negley's lines. I then directed Houghtaling's battery to take position at the angle of these two lines, Captain Hescock sending one section of his battery under Lieutenant Taliaferro and one section of Bush's battery to the same point, the remaining pieces of Hescock's and Bush's batteries were placed on the right of Negley's line facing towards Murfreesboro'. In this position I was immediately attacked, when one of the bitterest and most sanguinary contests of the day occurred.

General Cheatam's division advanced on Roberts's brigade, and heavy masses of the enemy, with three batteries of artillery, advanced over the open ground which I had occupied in the previous part of the engagement, at the same time the enemy opening from their intrenchments in the direction of Murfreesboro'.

The contest then became terrible; the enemy made three attacks and were three times repulsed, the artillery range of the respective batteries being not over 200 yards. In these attacks Roberts's brigade lost its gallant commander, who was killed.

There was no sign of faltering with the men, the only cry being for more ammunition, which unfortunately could not be supplied, on account of the discomfiture of the troops on the right of our wing, which allowed the enemy to come in and capture our ammunition train.

Schaefer's brigade being entirely out of ammunition, I directed them to fix bayonets and await the enemy. Roberts's brigade, which was nearly out of ammunition, I directed to fall back, resisting the enemy. Captain Houghtaling, having exhausted all his ammunition, and nearly all the horses of his battery having been killed, attempted, with the assistance of the men, to withdraw his pieces by hand. Lieutenant Taliaferro, commanding the section of Hescock's battery, having been killed, and several of his horses shot, his two pieces were brought off by his sergeant, with the assistance of the men. The difficulty of withdrawing the artillery here became very great, the ground being rocky and covered with a dense growth of cedar. Houghtaling's battery had to be abandoned; also two pieces of Bush's battery.

The remaining pieces of artillery in the division were brought through the cedars, with great difficulty, under a terrible fire from the enemy, on to the open space on the Murfreesboro' pike, near the right of General Palmer's division.

In coming through the cedars two regiments of Schaefer's brigade succeeded in obtaining ammunition, and were immediately put in front to resist the enemy, who appeared to be driving in our entire lines.

On arriving at the open space I was directed by Major General Rosecrans to take those two regiments and put them into action on the right of Palmer's division, where the enemy were pressing heavily.

The two regiments went in very gallantly, driving the enemy from the cedar timber and some distance to the front. At the same time I put four pieces of Hescock's battery into action near by and on the same front. The other two regiments of Schaefer's brigade, and the thirty-sixth Illinois, of Sill's brigade, were directed to cross the railroad where they could obtain ammunition. I then, by direction of Major General McCook, withdrew the two regiments that had been placed on the right of Palmer's division, also Captain Hescock's pieces, that point having been given up to the enemy in the rearrangement of our lines.

These regiments of Schaefer's brigade, having supplied themselves with ammunition, I put into action, by direction of Major General Rosecrans, directly to the front and right of General Wood's division on the left-hand side of the railroad.

The brigade advanced through a clump of timber and took position on the edge of a cotton-field, close upon the enemy's lines, relieving the division of General Wood, which was falling back under heavy pressure from the enemy.

At this point I lost my third and last brigade commander, Col. Fred. Schaefer, who was killed. The brigade, after remaining in this position until after it had expended its amunition, was withdrawn to the rear of this timber, where it was again supplied and joined by the 36th Illinois. I was here directed by General Rosecrans to form a close column of attack and charge the enemy should they again come down on the open ground.

The remaining portion of the evening this gallant brigade remained in close column of regiments, and under the fire of the enemy's batteries, which killed about twenty of the men by round shot. In the mean time Colonel Roberts's brigade, which had come out of the cedars unbroken, was put into action by General McCook at a point a short distance to the rear, where the enemy threatened our communication on the Murfreesboro' pike. The brigade having but three or four rounds of ammunition, cheerfully went into action, gallantly charged the enemy, routing them, recapturing two pieces of artillery and taking forty prisoners. The rout of the enemy at this point deserves special consideration, as they had here nearly reached the Murfreesboro' pike.

On the night of the 31st I was placed in position on the Murfreesboro' pike, facing south, and on the ground where Roberts's brigade had charged the enemy, General Davis being on my right.

On the 1st of January heavy skirmish fighting, with occasional artillery shots on both sides, was kept up till about three o'clock p. m., when a charge was made by a brigade of the enemy on my position. This was handsomely repulsed and one officer and eighty-five men of the enemy captured.

Colonel Walker's brigade, of Thomas's corps, was also placed under my command temporarily, having a position on my left, where the same character of fighting was kept up. On the 2d January Colonel Walker sustained two heavy attacks, which he gallantly repulsed. On the 3d skirmishing took place throughout the day. On the 4th all was quiet in front, the enemy having disappeared.

On the 5th nothing of importance occurred, and on the 6th January I moved my command to its present camp on Stone river, three miles south of Murfreesboro', on the Shelbyville pike.

I trust that the general commanding is satisfied with my division. It fought bravely and well. The loss of Houghtaling's battery and one section of Bush's battery was unavoidable. All the horses were shot down or disabled, Captain Houghtaling wounded, and Lieutenant Taliaferro killed.

My division alone and unbroken made a gallant stand to protect the right flank of our army, being all that remained of the right wing. Had my ammunition held out I would not have fallen back, although such were my orders if hard pressed. As it was, this determined stand of my troops gave time for a rearrangement of our lines.

The division mourns the loss of Sill, Schaefer, and Roberts; they were all instantly killed, and at the moment when their gallant brigades were charging the enemy. They were true soldiers, prompt and brave. On the death of these officers, respectively, Colonel Grensel, 36th Illinois, took command of Sill's brigade; Lieutenant Colonel Laiboldt, 2d Missouri, of Schaefer's, and Colonel Bradley, 51st Illinois, of Roberts's brigade. These officers behaved gallantly throughout the day.

It is also my sad duty to record the death of Colonel F. A. Harrington, of the 27th Illinois, who fell heroically leading his regiment to the charge.

I refer with pride to the splendid conduct, bravery, and efficiency of the following regimental commanders, and the officers and men of their respective commands:

Colonel F. S. Sherman, 88th Illinois; Major F. Ehrler, 2d Missouri; Lieutenant Colonel John Weber, 15th Missouri; Captain W. W. Barrett, 44th Illinois, wounded; Major W. A. Presson, 73d Illinois, wounded; Major Silas Miller, 36th Illinois, wounded and a prisoner; Captain P. C. Oleson, 36th Illinois; Major E. C. Hibbard, 24th Wisconsin; Lieutenant Colonel N. H. Walworth, 42d Illinois; Lieutenant Colonel F. Swamvick, 22d Illinois, wounded and a prisoner; Captain Samuel Johnson, 22d Illinois; Major W. A. Schatill, 27th Illinois; Captain Wescott, 51st Illinois.

I respectfully bring to the notice of the general commanding the good conduct of Captain Wescock, chief of artillery, whose services were almost invaluable; also Captains Houghtaling and Bush, and the officers and men of their batteries. Surgeon D. J. Griffiths, medical director of my division, and Dr. McArthur, of the board of medical examiners of Illinois, were most assiduous in their care of the wounded.

Major N. F. Deitz, provost marshal, Captain Morhardt, topographical engineer, Lieutenant George Lee, acting assistant adjutant general, Lieutenants R. M. Denning, Frank H. Allen, E. M. De Bruin, J. S. Forman, and —— Somard, aides-de-camp, officers of my staff, were of the greatest service to me, delivering my orders faithfully, and promptly discharging the duties of their respective positions.

The ammunition train, above alluded to as captured, was retaken from the enemy through the good conduct of Captain Thruston, ordnance officer of the corps, and Lieutenant Douglass, ordnance officer of my division, who, with Sergeant Cooper, of my escort, rallied the stragglers and drove off the enemy's cavalry.

The following is the total of casualties in the division: Officers killed, 15; wounded, 38; missing, 11. Total of officers, 64. Enlisted men killed, 223; wounded, 943; missing, 400. Total of enlisted men, 1,566. Aggregate, 1,630. Of the 11 officers and 400 enlisted men missing many are known to be wounded and in the hands of the enemy.

Prisoners were captured from the enemy by my division as follows: 1 major, 1 captain, 3 lieutenants, and 216 enlisted men; total, 227.

I am, sir, very respectfully, your obedient servant,

P. H. SHERIDAN,
Brigadier General Commanding.

Major J. A. CAMPBELL,
Assistant Adjutant General, Right Wing, Fourteenth Army Corps.

Officers killed.

Brigadier General J. W. Sill, commanding first brigade; Colonel F. Schaefer, 2d Missouri infantry, commanding second brigade; Colonel George W. Roberts, 42d Illinois infantry, commanding third brigade.

FIRST BRIGADE.

Thirty-sixth Illinois regiment.—Second Lieutenant Soren P. Olson, company F.
Eighty-eighth Illinois regiment.—First Lieutenant Thomas F. W. Gulich, company C.
Twenty-fourth Wisconsin regiment.—Second Lieutenant Christian Nix, company D.

SECOND BRIGADE.

Fifteenth Missouri regiment.—Captain Medchier Zimmerman, company C; Second Lieutenant Christian Quincius, company, B; Second Lieutenant Charles Kelner, company E.
Forty-fourth Illinois regiment.—Captain A. J. Hosmer, company F.
Seventy-third Illinois regiment.—Captain Edwin Alsop, company F.
First Missouri Light Artillery.—First Lieutenant R. C. M. Taliaferro, company G.

THIRD BRIGADE.

Twenty-seventh Illinois regiment.—Colonel F. A. Harrington.
Fifty-first Illinois regiment.—Second Lieutenant John S. Keith, company A.
Forty-second Illinois regiment.—Second Lieutenant F. Lettman, company B.

Officers wounded.

FIRST BRIGADE.

Thirty-sixth Illinois regiment.—Major Silas Miller*; First Lieutenant S. H. Wakeman,* company A; Captain B. F. Campbell,* company B; Captain Albert Hobbs,* company E; Lieutenant G. W. Moseman, company F; Captain O. B. Merrill,* company I; First Lieutenant John F. Elliott,* company K.
Eighty-eighth Illinois regiment.—Major G. W. Chandler; Captain G. W. Smith, company A; First Lieutenant H. C. McDonald, company K.
Twenty-fourth Wisconsin regiment.—Second Lieutenant George Blyer, company A.
Twenty-first Michigan regiment.—First Lieutenant B. D. Fox, company B; Captain S. O. Fitzgerals, company C; Captain A. C. Alber, company G; Lieutenant M. B. Wells, regimental adjutant; Lieutenant Albert G. Russell, company K.

SECOND BRIGADE.

Fifteenth Missouri regiment.—Captain George Ernst, company B; Lieutenant Martin Schroeder, company D; Second Lieutenant George Mohrhardt, company F; First Lieutenant Jacob Lupp, company K.
Forty-fourth Illinois regiment.—Captain Wallace W. Barrett, company B, commanding regiment; Second Lieutenant S. W. Parker, company B; Captain Ernst Moldenhower, company E; Lieutenant James R. Ransom, adjutant.
Seventy-third Illinois regiment.—Major W. A. Preston; Doctor March, assistant surgeon; Lieutenant E. W. Bennett, company A; Lieutenant B. Presson, company C; Lieutenant William Barrick, company F.

THIRD BRIGADE.

Twenty-seventh Illinois regiment.—Second Lieutenant W. S. Bryan, company I.

* Known to be in the hands of the enemy.

Forty-second Illinois regiment.—Captain J. Leighton, company C.

Fifty-first Illinois regiment.—Major Charles W. Davis; Captain James S. Boyd, company B; Lieutenant Henry A. Buck, company K.

Twenty-second Illinois regiment.—Lieutenant Harry Clifth, adjutant; Lieutenant William S. Ford, company A; Captain Wm. A. Gregory, company C; Lieutenant S. M. Galloway, company D.

First Illinois artillery.—Captain Charles Houghtaling, company C.

Officers missing.

FIRST BRIGADE.

Thirty-sixth Illinois regiment.—Second Lieutenant Myron Smith, company H.

Twenty-first Michigan regiment.—Second Lieutenant Eli E. Barnett, company K.

SECOND BRIGADE.

Second Missouri regiment.—Second Lieutenant Leo Kenith, company A.

THIRD BRIGADE.

Fifty-first Illinois regiment.—Lieutenant Archibald L. McCormas, company E.

Twenty-second Illinois regiment.—Lieutenant Colonel F. Sivanwick; Lieutenant Andrew Young, company K; Captain H. Bourman, company F; Second Lieutenant William Lishman, company K.

First Illinois artillery.—Second Lieutenant Joseph R. Channel, company C.

List of non-commissioned officers killed.

FIRST BRIGADE.

Twenty-first Michigan regiment.—Sergeant A. A. Sawyer, company H; Sergeant Wm. T. Scarr, company I; Corporal Merrifield, company B; Corporal Edwin Rathline, company E; Corporal Julius F. Barrett, company K.

Twenty-fourth Wisconsin regiment.—Sergeant Geo. S. Rickwell, company B; Corporal Frank S. Hale, company G.

Eighty-eighth Illinois regiment.—Corporal Wm. T. Owen, company C; First Sergeant Eugene A. Lyford and Corporal Fred. W. Holton, company I.

Thirty-sixth Illinois regiment.—Corporal Thomas Fenner, company A; Sergeant David McClorg, company B; Sergeant Alexander Stickler and Corporal William C. Benedict, company D; Sergeant Romier Michael and Corporal Alfred Riggs, company F; Corporals Wm. Hutchings, Orlando W. Nash, and Alon Riniker, company H; Corporal Aseph Adams, company K.

Fourth Indiana battery.—Sergeant John Young and Corporal William A. Stoddard.

SECOND BRIGADE.

Second Missouri regiment.—Sergeant Fred. Grandliner, company B; Corporal Peter Hagely, company G; Sergeant John Schmidt, company H.

Fifteenth Missouri regiment.—Sergeant George Grandehemp, company E; Corporal Henry Schwab, company F.

Forty-fourth Illinois regiment.—Sergeant Chester Kreft, company B; Sergeant Asmus Ruhberg, company E; Sergeant Cyrus R. Wells, company G; Sergeant S. McCormick and Corporals Teophil Lacey and Isaac Price, company I; Corporal John Johnson, company K.

Seventy-third Illinois regiment.—Sergeant C. B. Mantle, company A; Sergeant Elisha T. McCormas, company I; Corporal George W. Oulman, company K.

THIRD BRIGADE.

Twenty-seventh Illinois regiment.—Corporal Wm. D. Malaby, company G; Corporal James A. Martin, company H.

Forty second Illinois regiment.—Sergeant J. Hall, company E; Sergeant C. B. Chipman, and Corporals M. Mattocks and E. M. Harrison, company H; Corporal A. Smith, company I; Sergeant O. E. Rowan and Corporal O. N. Benson, company K.

Fifty-first Illinois regiment.—Sergeant J. M. Mansfield, company B; Sergeant Thomas Barnes, company C; Corporal John D. Jones, company E.

Twenty-second Illinois regiment.—Corporal Gotlieb Vogel, company C; Corporal C. Gibert, company F; Corporal Wm. L. Lewis, company K.

First Illinois artillery.—Sergeant George Cooper, company C.

List of non-commissioned officers wounded.

FIRST BRIGADE.

Twenty-first Michigan regiment.—Sergeant Charles D. Loring, company A; Sergeant W. E. Thornton, company B; Sergeant A. C. Leonard, company C; Corporal John Frederick, company E; Sergeant Charles E. Belknap, company H; Corporal F. W. Chapin, company H; Sergeants A. A. Alcote and Samuel Walbridge, company I; Corporal Sanford White, company I; Sergeant E. B. Potter, company K.

Twenty-fourth Wisconsin Regiment.—Corporal George H. Tucker, company A; Sergeants George Cole and Charles Swan, company B; Corporals Henry B. Furness and Albert Weber, company B; Corporals Charles C. Mayer and Gustave Weckerman, company C; Corporal George Creighton, company F; Sergeant H. W. Carter, company G; Corporals B. F. Marshall and C. Galvidson, company I.

Eighty-eighth Illinois regiment.—First Sergeant Henry C. Griffin, company C; Sergeant Edwin C. Miller and Corporal Clinton L. Haring, company F; First Sergeant H. L. Brigham and Corporal Charles Walker, company H; Corporal Andrew Cox, company K.

Thirty-sixth Illinois regiment.—Sergeant Alexander Robinson and Corporal Benjamin D. Rowland, company A; Corporals Henry B. Letham and Wm. H. Blakslee, company B; Corporal John C. Taylor, company D; First Sergeant O. Smith, Sergeant L. F. Hemenway, and Corporals D. Dammell and D. Burnside, company E; Sergeants S. F. Smith and William Eybond, and Corporal William Mossman, company F; First Sergeant H. N. Crittenden, and Sergeants Nelson B. Sherwood, J. C. Wolfe, and D. Hartman, company H; Sergeant T. Folson and Corporal Frank Week, company K.

Fourth Indiana battery.—Corporal Edgar S. Abbott.

SECOND BRIGADE.

Second Missouri regiment.—Corporal Louis Rinken, company A; Corporal Henry Ulrich, company C; Sergeants Joseph Weizt, Any Kreuter, Gustave Kessler, and Corporals Conrad Hoffman and H. Eggemann, company D; Sergeant F. Wenckel, company E; Sergeants J. Vatter, Charles Naebert, and L. Kattwasser, company F; Corporal A. Brandenberry, company H.

Fifteenth Missouri regiment.—Sergeant William Milke, and Corporals Fred. Blum, John Beeli, and John Sallenback, company B; Sergeant Louis Arendt and Corporal Ulrich Frei, company E; Sergeants James Levichten, Joseph Ratsch, and John Geill, and Corporal Henry Miller, company F; Sergeant

John Horr, company G; Sergeant Victor Senn and Corporals Simon Brandley and Julius Rieth, company I.

Forty-fourth Illinois regiment.—Sergeant Jacob Daget, and Corporals John Rieth and John Fuchs, company A; Sergeants Martin Derfin and Jacob E. Conchlin, and Corporals Byron Goodrich and Jesse O'Carry, company B; Sergeant Jackson Ebner, and Corporals William F. Spring and Wesley Oickle, company C; Sergeants James U. Asom, George P. Coons, and George W. Allen, company F; Sergeant Albert Dobson and Corporal Charles Coon, company G; Sergeants William F. Licking, Alonzo Evans, and Henry T. Smith, and Corporals Cornelius Quick and Orson D. Ramsdell, company H; Sergeants John A. Hall and Morris H. Taylor, and Corporal Edwin R. Bliss, company I; Sergeant John Neppart, and Corporals Leopold Norton and Charles Egan, company K.

Seventy-third Illinois regiment.—Sergeant Major Henry Castle; Corporal J. T. Armstrong, company A; Sergeant William Commire, company H; Sergeant D. M. Davis, company K.

First Missouri artillery.—Sergeant Hiram Jennings and Corporal John E. Stoltze, company G.

THIRD BRIGADE.

Twenty-seventh Illinois regiment.—Sergeant G. W. Edwards, company B; Sergeants G. W. Clark and Franklin T. Clark, and Corporal W. A. Osborne, company C; Sergeants Nathan Y. Page and John Kennedy, company D; Sergeant A. M. Boggs and Corporal M. L. Rankin, company E; Sergeant S. A. Atwater, company G; Corporal Peter W. Bower, company H.

Forty-second Illinois regiment.—Corporal A. Daily, company A; Sergeant P. Short, company B; Sergeants J. Aberdeen and B. J. Powell, and Corporal M. S. Holt, companyC; Sergeants M. J. Sheridan and J. N. Hill, and Corporal H. Wells, company D; Sergeant L. R. Norton and Corporal H. Lucas, company E; Sergeant —— Ledyard, company F; Sergeant G. W. Bagnall, company G; Sergeant S. H. Reynolds and W. H. Perry, and Corporal J. Pusard, company H; Corporals C. A. Linstrann and J. Voller, company I; Sergeant J. N. McClellan and Corporal J. G. Beard, company K.

Fifty-first Illinois regiment.—Sergeant Barton Bumell, company E; Corporal John S. Dougherty, company C; Corporal David A. Schaefer, company F; John Nelson, company G.

Twenty-second Illinois regiment.—Sergeant Major Henry Garague; Sergeant Henry D. Roseter, company B; Sergeants T. C. P. White and Joel Pailsey, and Corporal Robert Reams, company D; Sergeant William H. Kershner, company E; Sergeant William Lamb, company G; Sergeant Martin Ireland and Corporals A. D. A. Henson, John Hoffman, and Ehlmer Wilson, company H; Sergeant William Livingston and Corporals Arick Gibson and William Gray, company I; Corporal James Gale, company K.

First Illinois artillery.—Sergeant C. P. Whitman and Corporals Martin Chamel, Oscar D. Grey, and Thomas A. Fitzsimons, company C.

List of the missing.

FIRST BIGADE.

Twenty-first Michigan regiment.—Sergeants Ezra D. Johnson and John Cleveland, company B; Sergeant George N. Westlake and Corporal Henry Widdecomb, company E; Corporal Charles Dickinson, company G.

Twenty-fourth Wisconsin regiment.—Sergeant C. C. Lowell and Corporal Darwin C. Merrill, company A; Corporal N. L. Burdrick, company B; Corporal Louis A. Stave, company I; Sergeant J. M. Arnold and Corporal F. Fowler, company K.

Eighty-eighth Illinois regiment.—Sergeant George S. Collins, company A; Corporal William R. Batten, company C; Corporal J. O. Marks, company D; Sergeant James B. Felson and Corporals F. Uhlrick, G. W. Champlin, and Jacob Springer, company F; Corporal H. W. Alexander, company G; Drum Major G. W. Foster.

Thirty-six Illinois regiment.—Sergeant D. Smith, company I.

THIRD BRIGADE.

Twenty-seventh Illinois regiment.—Corporal Thomas Sauter, company A; Corporals William H. Mays and Robert McDonald, company C; Corporal W. W. Williams, company I.

Forty-second Illinois regiment.—Corporals D. McGrath and T. Fay, company B; Corporal J. Howland, company C.

Fifty-first Illinois regiment.—Sergeant John W. Terry, company B; Corporal William Carr, company C; Corporal Charles Peterson, company K.

Twenty-second Illinois regiment.—Sergeant Obed Fink and Corporal Thomas Kirkham, company A; Sergeants William H. Davis and A. P. Wilson, company B; Sergeant H. H. Doane, company C; Corporals James Collier and James Murry, company E; Sergeant Charles Baader and Corporal Augustus Hoffman, company F; Sergeant John Gregory and Corporal Robert Malory, company G; Sergeant D. H. Coles and Corporals John A. Beck, John Allen, and D. A. McClinton, company I; Sergeant Fritz Walby, company K.

First artillery.—Corporal Josiah Bagley, company C.

List of privates killed.

Thirty-sixth Illinois regiment.—Henry Clayton, Thomas Staunton, Frederick H. Burmaster, Moses F. Gibbs, and George M. Johnson, company A; Frank. Thompson, company B; Joseph Baxter, James Elder, Daniel H. Buchanan, and William F. Arthurs, company C; James Thorp, and Samuel Young, company D; Benjamin Sayers, Nicholas Meehan, Augustus Haskin, William Burgess, and James Baird, company E; James Foster, Cornelius Seward, Richard H. Spaulding, Charles Womgler, and Augustus Vanorden, company F; Zalman F. Heelse, Harvey D. Norton, and David Vanderstand, company G; Robert Archibald, Washington M. Floyd, William H. Jones, and Lorenzo D. Keys, company H; Leander Ellis, company I; George Lenhard, George Monroe, George Pollock, and George Hall, company K.

Eighty-eighth Illinois regiment.—Abraham Weaver, and Henry Millering, company B; Samuel Meek, company C; Hugh L. Logan, and William H. Davis, company D; John Darr, company H; John Roman, George Helen, and John Peters, company K.

Twenty-fisrt Michigan regiment.—Nelson G. Merrill, company A; Charles C. Hilton, and Augustus Manausky, company B; Lester M. Jones, company C; Lyman A. Frost, company D; Theodore Bloomis and Ira McClain, company E; Christinson Johnson, company F; Joseph Stoddart, company G; Septimus Carlton and Charles B. Gilman, company H; Robert Morse, and Almersen D. Rathburn, company I.

Twenty-fourth Wisconsin regiment.—C. J. Cochran, company A; Leonard Cochran, Richard Joyce, company B; Charles Parkenson, and Rheinholdt Eckhardt, company C; Richard M. Jeffers, George Gregg, and Sylvester Hennisey, company D; Abraham Quinman and David H. Springstead, company E; John Coleman, company F; John Eder, company H; William Regan, company I; N. B. Brooks, J. Gilbert, A. Gage, and H. Pfuff, company K.

Fourth Indiana battery.—James E. Date, William Mundell, James Hill, and Edmund Nugent, company K.

Second Missouri regiment.—Herman Kramer, Herman Ernst, Henry Stehr, and Timothy O'Brien, company F.

Fifteenth Missouri regiment.—Philip Hofsteker, company C; Henry Dill, (bugler,) company D; Henry Frihner and Frederick Holloway, company F; Michael Henster, company G; Christian Gerber, company K.

Forty-fourth Illinois regiment.—Michael Weihing, Joseph Leinning, Herman Miller, Henry Junker, and Mathew Sitian, company A; Lucius Clark, Edwin Benton, and Joseph Newman, company B; George Heinz, Emanuel Theelman, and George Appenzeeler, company E; George Bellows and Levi W. Faulkner, company F; Charles Beeler and Lewis Christian, company G; Albert Corey and George Thompson, company H; John E. Hall and Joshua Hall, company I; Christian Bushing and Henry Frank, company K.

Seventy-third Illinois regiment.—James O'Neal and E. M. Snake, company A; Morris R. T. Solnis and Richard Robinson, company B; John Dye and James Tole, company C; Wm. B. C. Lipton, company F; J. L. Price, George Martin, Thomas Bradbury, and David Lancaster, company G.

First Missouri artillery.—Maxwell Brewer, David Forrest, George M. Johnson, George Martin, and Henry Detman, company G.

Twenty-seventh Illinois regiment.—Frederick Gugar, Charles Petrau, Frederick Wiseman, and George Gerner, company A; Andrew W. Johnson, company D; Andrew S. Phifer, company F.

Forty-second Illinois regiment.—Eli Carson, John Mennich, F. Fitsky, company A; F. Burt, W. E. Emery, and W. E. Reynolds, company C; D. C. Arnold and A. J. Northrop, company E; A. Jeffrey, company H; G. J. Carpenter and John Thirson, company I.

Fifty-first Illinois regiment.—G. D. Martin, J. H. Slayton, company B; George Sturdivant, company H.

Twenty-second Illinois regiment.—J. H. Perrin and P. M. Hermsey, company B; William Arthur, company C; Anson Dabbott, Abner Pettijohn, company D; Samuel McAdams, Samuel Davenport, E. R. Wheeler, and John R. Fisher, (drummer,) company E; E. Bachman, company F; John Mark, Wm. J. Ross, and Thomas Melone, company I; William Defoe, Evan Jones, John Megann, Nicholas Solesby, and J. Donnivan, company K.

First Illinois artillery.—Asbury Smith, John Wiley, John Bennett, and Charles Ziscry, company C.

List of privates wounded.

Thirty-sixth Illinois regiment.—Alexander C. Lind, Leroy Salsbury, Cyrus F. Dean, John W. Aldrich, Charles A. Brown, Freeman S. Dunkley, John Flood, Alexander F. Henderson, John A. Hewitt, Darius Mussie, Merrill H. Sabin, Charles L. Themur, Milton S. Townsend, and John A. White, company A; Emra D. Haselton, Henry Alcot, Vanwyck Race, John Olt, Adam Reitz, William Vanohlen, James Campbell, and Thomas McConnell, company B; Robert J. Colwell, James L. Dryden, Albert O. Eckleston, John R. Edgar, Thomas B. Gromley, William Hartsell, Ferdinand Hercher, Warren Kintsee, Ethan Kerch, Francis McClauhan, Walter Reeder, John Stook, James S. Smith, Abraham Steward, and Joseph Young, company C; O. H. Thomson, Joseph A. Smith, Harvey Kimball, Henry T. Burch, Lynder K. Barrister, Thomas Welch, Samuel Tucker, Nelson Eckerson, O. N. Johnson, O. W. Oleson, and Lewis R. Seymor, company D; Frederick Beir, Alfred Ballard, James Brown, Charles C. Drane, Charles W. Doty, Aaron Darnell, Uriah Foster, Oscar Howe, Henry Haigh, James Harral, William Hanker, James S. Hatch, Gilbert Ketcham, Elias Lloyd, George W. Laniger, Henry Mullen, James E. Moss, George E. Merrill, Cyrus Perry, Walker S. Ralston, Charles H. Sufield, and Joel Wagrin, company E; William Curtis, Stephen Cummings, Edwin Dopp, William A. Haggett, John Jordan, Anton Myre, Lewis Oleson, Alfred Tomlin, Albert H. Wullft, and William Thompson, company F; William Goold, Robert B. Harrie, Daniel Kennedy, Peter Bradler, William Chamberlin, Joseph Hebert, Robert Jordan, George W. Moody, Wilbar Roseman, William F. Severans, Peter Buchanan, Frank Small, and Milton G. Yarnell, company G; Charles Crawford, Jackson Conner, Jerome Ford, John Sackett, David D. Warwick, Myron Harris, and Munroe Thorp, company H; Frederick Wilsk, William Varnee, John Roth, and Anton Miller, company I; John Jordan, Eldrich Adams, Frederick Hazelhurst, Sydney Wauzen, Henry Buten, Charles Miner, Owen Wood, Henry Hogan, Lemuel Grundy, John Peterson, Paul Van Winklin, Eugene Albso, Harlem Sanders, and Lucian Butten, company K.

Eighty-eighth Illinois regiment.—James B. Sutherland, Daniel G. Watts, and Griffen R. Borden, company A; Andrew Murry and Thomas F. Kent, company B; Clark O. Wickwire, Louis Claremont, John Kelly, John Sheridan, Thomas Hughes, Isaac S. Cunningham, and Henry Mapes, company C; Charles Brinkman, Martin M. Casson, William J. Campbell, G. H. Meyer, and John Patterson, company D; J. R. Frietz, Thomas Hehoe, Archie Vanhorn, and A. Heishbalz, company E; Levi L. Drake, Eben A. Day, Martin Watts, Thomas Norris, John T. Harper, David Shreeves, Willard Elyea, Julius Lisseda, Howard Gettings, and William Woodruff, company F; Thomas Berdan, William H. Cumings, C. T. Gurding, Jacob Karmisky, Abram Kelder, and John McDonald, company G; W. H. Billen, Andrew Allen, and Alonzo A. Hyde, company H; Landon Tanner, James B. Hall, Samuel Limbler, and Jacob Sigwalt, company I.

Twenty-first Michigan regiment.—James Bartlett, George W. Tyler, and John W. Westbrook, company A; Edward Barry, Edward W. Barker, John M. Knapp, Francis Lapreze, Joseph Loze, Timothy Sweet, and Daniel W. Wood, company B; John Smith, John O. Kelley, William Crabb, Ansil P. Hosier, Nelson Kelmer, Eli Gleason, Calvin H. Palmer, Allen Rouch, John Irvin, Leslie P. Mosely, and Byron W. Tomlison, company C; Henry B. Tripp, Edmond Sanderson, D. W. West, William Whipple, Joseph H. Canfield, and Alvin Gurney, company D; Charles C. Anderson, William McCoy, Christopher Storr, John S. Alden, Alexander Cole, Joseph Brown, and James Gallisphy, company E; John F. Lease, Jasper E. Giles, and William L. Campbell, company F; J. Sullivan, M. Camhout, J. Dewitt, E. Walcott, C. Klon, O. Blood, and A. Gouschling, company G; John Moffat, William R. Foot, Charles S. Medler, John G. Dunnavan, Michael Johnston, Webster B. Ewing, William Jones, William McKinney, Charles Watkins, and Miles Willard, company H; A. Lowrey, H. Johnson, Edwin Mead, James Bateman, William Gearman, A. E. Wheelock, H. Manker, and George D. King, company I; Albert Stuck, Charles Rock, Charles Phillips, P. C. Goothsite, and William Bowen, company K.

Twenty-fourth Wisconsin regiment.—Peter C. Cornelius and Franklin D. Fowler, company A; Charles Ellmaker, George B. Merrick, David Newcomb, Joe Smythe, Phillip Ward, and L. J. Williams, company B; Gotlieb Beck, Frederick Zettibee, Henrick Geiger, and Mervtz Berngen, company C; Patrick Ryan and Michael Hickey, company D; John D. Barrett, James Harvey, George Krause, and William Quinman, company E; John Dunn, Frank Kittridge, and William Parkinson, company F; Henry Welden and Martin Smith, company G; Thomas C. Parker, Charles Bish; James Viskouf, Morris Bielty, and Daniel Murphy, company H; C. Aubacher, George Cameron, Edward Carley, H. Ulrich, John French, and Augustus Hunn, company I; H. Beker, H. Baldwin, J. H. Bender, F. G. Chapman, J. Gelter, D. Salsbury, L. R. Smith, William Small, A. W. Wranser, and J. Powell, company K.

Fourth Indiana battery.—Charles O. Lau, William C. Kirk, James Small, Robert Hainer, William Perdoil, Andrew T. Mitchell, William Abbott,

Edmond Smith, Elias Price, Jesse Bailey, John Discard, Simon Ashton, James Harold, Charles Lockwood, Edmond J. Logan, and Edwin V. Arnold.

Second Missouri regiment.—Matthew Stiels and Wolf Lanasberger, company A; Henry Lerrence, Salmon Ellison, and John Miller, (bugler,) company B; Henry Steinmann and Nicholas Steinmudy, company C; Henry Kreniter, Herman Blunmee, Theodore Geilo, Kaner Maer, Minolph Brodefield, and Joseph Fritz, company D; Hern Trappil and John Erhardt, company E; John Ahrens and Martin Krill, company F; John Ringenbach, Patrick Murrin, Fritz Diesing, Moses Roach, and Thomas Schmidt, company G; Fritz Strieber and Charles Oestermann, company H; George Faher and Antoys Menger, company I; Justin Goltz and Hern Hellinger, company K.

Fifteenth Missouri regiment.—William Schaefer and Herman Gocke, company A; Theophilus Sutter, (drummer,) Gabriel Fuerst, Michael Fruder, Christian Reber, and Conrad Schurtz, company B; George Andermass, (bugler,) Jacob Loder, John Krusger, Edward Spelman, and John Operer, company C; Philip Gaertner, company D; Nicholas Decker, John Roth, Martin Hecht, Samuel Speigelburg, and Anton Lang, company E; Cajetan Bermauer, Frederick Hasleck, and Joseph Reiterman, company F; Joseph Berper, Joseph Buettokoffer, Gotlieb Doeberli, Christian Jenny, Andrew Oth, George Dreer, George Darnberny, and Henry Ulrich, company G; Loui Baumettler and Thomas Vincent, company H; Frederick Kissling, company I; Philip Becker, Augustus Kuntz, John Richenbach, Andrew Meyer, George Boming, Valentine Schardt, and Bathasas Grunnicpelder, company K.

Forty-fourth Illinois regiment.—John Borlenbach, Jacob Ehrhardt, Robert Miehlick, Patrick O'Brien, John Reuben Koning, John Schroeder, Louis Schuggnagg, and Benedict Waldroya, company A; Ven Dunham, Daniel E. Declute, Byron Derrin, Hamilton Johnson, Edward Cobb, Edward Pues, A. Sherman, John Miser, John Weaver, John Shear, George Pearce, Ira W. Brooks, Julius Hubbard, Luther A. Russell, George G. Patterson, and Lewis W. Wilber, company B; Jacob C. Rosenberger, John W. Argabright, John Allen, Henry Benedict, William T. Boyd, Alexander J. Cutter, Benjamin F. Freeman, George O. Grist, Donald McDonald, John J. Miles, Alfred Piles, Samuel Showers, William Weiber, and Henry Murphy, company C; George Benson, Charles Halleen, and Henry Matip, company E; James M. Atherson, Benedict L. Creek, Thomas Evans, Michael Epelving, William G. Howe, John Kettles, Francis M. Lindsay, James Offile, and Frederick G. Smith, company F; A. C. Delancy, John Murphy, Theodore Collins, Daniel Hubbard, John Van Altine, Joseph R. Champlin, Franklin Luck, Charles Baker, Michael Fulman, Herman Calson, and George Knapp, company G; Abraham M. Beebe, Benjamin F. Morris, and Arthur Hamilton, company H; James Lacey, William C. Rhina, John W. McGill, Andrew J. Young, and Franklin S. Parker, company I; John Eckerman, Charles Bayer, Julius Haager, John O. Neil, Henry Decker, Udi Dirks, Henry Schmidt, and Matthias Lernis, company K.

Seventy-third Illinois regiment.—C. B. McDaniels, A. J. Perry, Jacob Rufle, William A. Mindette, A. B. Hoyte, William R. Constandt, S. C. Robbins, P. M. Chambers, W. Maxwell, and D. C. Fletcher, company A; Jacob Hilderbrand, Calvin Randolph, Martin L. Freeman, William B. McNicholls, Andrew J. Reid, Joshua Bailey, and Alexander H. Wright, company B; John T. Halstear and Samuel Sigler, company C; Samuel Garner, David Glover, Edward Williamson, Samuel Richards, and William Cromis, company D; George Pierce, company E; William Martienia, Benjamin Powers, Berry Hobbs, Rousen D. Kelsey, Isaac C. Cail, Charles W. Kelley, William Sabermann, and Harvey Long, company F; Joseph Yates, George Johnston, Isaac Lytle, Jas. Anthony, Charles McVane, Henry Bennett, Richard Bickenrike, Thomas Battle, Thomas Ware, James Lancaster, Elijah Basin, and Edward Preston, company H; John W. Fisher, Leonidas Emery, George F. Londgribe, Alex. M.

Cassiley, Jas. W. Denny, Hiram T. Coffman, Samuel S. Foster, and Hugh McLaughlin, company I; H. Hinchchiff, J. Jarvis, and H. Franer, company K.

First Missouri artillery.—Bernard Hays, Robert Beaumer, Louis Dumont, John Morrison, Henry Rieling, Moses Rosenthal, Nicholas Stimtz, Cornelius Vanderburgh, Wilson Dawson, Edward P. Gerad, and Jacob Meng, company G.

Twenty-seventh Illinois regiment.—Casper Bellman, company A; Patrick Berry and John T. Huffman, company B; William C. Bean, Thomas Conner, William Huston, John Sitsman, and Dowy Faland, company C; Frank Molt and George W. Mallony, company D; John Lowry, John O. Reiley, S. R. Davis, J. M. Hoyt, and T. J. McConnell, company E; L. N. Cook, William Moore, Joseph Brown, and Joseph Fritz, company F; Joel N. Woodward, Manville Chamberlain, and John F. Esslie, company G; O. F. Whipley, Elias Worthen, W. F. Boucher, Roberta Clara, Disney Crani, Jesse Dougherty, Jas. Gray, Fred. B. King, Joshua Taylor, and Philip Wolfe, company H; Louis Dennis, Jas. A. Fronk, J. G. Heaps, John Hall, Richard Judkins, J. N. Holcomb, Charles M. Owen, Alex. J. Graham, William Stillwell, and H. C. Ladd, company I; Charles Cramer and Thomas Davidson, company K.

Forty-second Illinois regiment.—D. A. Lincoln, D. Hamilton, F. Dreghorn, George Stoll, Charles A. Jaynes, and H. I. Schott, company A; H. Peters, G. Copely, William Vincent, S. Anderson, Peter Shoemake, H. Longharst, and L. Helsey, company B; J. Bowen, C. C. Alkins, L. R. Carver, William Cornish, A. Emickson, G. Hand, F. S. Hooks, O. L. Higgins, P. McConnell, J. C. Purdy, W. Whiting, John Wallace, and Charles Johnson, company C; W. O. Kelsey, T. L. Mott, N. Mashin, N. Redford, A. Schroyer, R. Hill, William Watson, and J. J. Worcester, company D; O. F. Momany, B. J. Dart, S. Schrode, C. Herman, H. Caston, G. Henderson, A. McDonald, J. Peters, and J. Tillotson, company E; C. R. Perkins, C. Ashling, G. Round, R. B. Welch, J. D. Aldrich, J. D. Jones, and William Kuykindall, company F; C. Aikley, D. W. Beaman, B. Herle, Charles M. Kelley, W. Slattens, and B. Siminger, company G; William Bellings, J. Calomb, J. A. Gibson, I. Stzenhaas, M. Losh, J. H. Tanner, and F. E. O. Vogland, company H; G. W. Boardman, N. Hover, C. Johnson, H. Kate, and J. Petty, company I; F. A. Ernst, P. Lemley, C. Nichols, E. B. Edmonds, and T. Condom, company K.

Fifty-first Illinois regiment.—John Kelly, company A; James Brannan, Silas A. Cumming, Patrick Clark, James Gilchrist, William Gavin, Fletcher Sheve, and Samuel Wilson, company B; Fred. A. Camp, Rufus A. Dunkin, Ethan Hover, and Joseph R. Labach, company C; D. F. Beal, William Dismore, William Gardner, Reuben Jefferson, Milton Kingston, and Jerome Mangan, company D; Andrew Barlie, George Chapman, James Nelson, and Wilie Pilkerton, company E; Thomas J. Mason, company F; Thomas Hays, Patrick Lyon, Timothy McFadden, and Lewis Barnshane, company G; Henry T. Gibson and Jerry Miller, company H; and Anthony W. Duffie, company K.

Twenty-second Illinois regiment.—A. Pickering, Jacob Essington, Jacob Engle, Robert McDonald, and Andrew Reader, company A; John Camp and M. Whaler, company C; M. Hanley, H. O. File, Alva Stephen, and J. W. Coleman, company D; Peter Dewey, M. V. Cornelius, John Suggs, Frank Shinn, and John Koonce, company E; J. Larsen, George Smith, A. Schuthris, and William Zimmerman, company F; G. W. Blankship, S. W. Cunningham, C. B. Hall, John Hewsley, G. N. Cunningham, W. W. Elliott, M. Hogan, Thomas Huggins, Dennis Ryan, and Jacob Vanpattent, company G; W. P. Allen, W. H. H. Ireland, B. A. McGuire, A. F. Williams, James Frazier, —— Richards, and William Hewman, company H; John Ford, M. Cavenaugh, Wesley Lafferty, M. McGary, William McGashen, T. D. Lewis, Calvin Hodge, and James Ralney, company I; George Thomas, L. Jenkins, A. McMinneman, Joseph Owen, John Arbs, Thomas Williams, James Pendgost, M. Hendeberg, William Thomas, and Barney Call, company K.

First Illinois artillery.—Lafayette Bonarville, Martin Zahner, Archibald M. Dallas, John Dougherty, Adam Ellis, Jacob Godert, Michael Leary, Henry Milder, John B. Nettle, Samuel Patterson, William P. Robinson, Jesse Richardson, William M. Stevens, William M. Dobson, and Jacob Sheuk, company C.

List of privates missing.

FIRST BRIGADE.

Twenty-first Michigan regiment.—James Swaggart, Valentine Brutz, John Rouleader, Hoziel D. Bartlett, George W. Housman, Thomas J. Hall, William A. Amba, Hiram Minier, company A; Dennis Aldrich, Daniel C. Alcumbrand, Daniel W. Mills, Walter M. Nixon, Henry J. Russell, William J. Wooley, Sherman C. Bennett, Henry L. Trucus, James H. Finney, Benjamin C. Hardy, company B; James B. Emnett, company D; Thomas Fox, John L. Bailey, Addison Clark, Daniel Tompkins, James Kent, D. B. Blakeley, company E; Loren Bink, Martin Feng, company H; N. C. Cooley, John Eskhoft, Peter Duchain, company I; Henry Schene, Hiram Barrett, company K.

Twenty-fourth Wisconsin regiment.—Alexander Yessen, Amandus Selby, company A; W. E. Daggett, Berkly Farrell, W. F. Webber, Thomas Duke, J. H. Alexander, E. A. Douglass, Guy Derry, Wm. Davis, N. O. Hamilton, I. Q. Walker, company B; Jarry Bollman, William Denitz, John Zwiebel, William Rahlman, Merritz Ischope, Adam Bulles, Henry Millec, John Ruddan, Conrad Riehel, company C; John Kuntzky, William Clark, Jacob Gnitz, Henry O. Lee, Walter Lindman, Michael Mackendon, Gardner H. Buzzell, Henry Brustom, R. I. Phelan, company D; Albert Blanchard, Ansel Strong, George Brewan, company E; John James, Al. Brandage, William Dolan, Pat. Feniter, Thomas Gaynor, John Ghortz, Warren D. Weehar, George W. Shan, Charles Sullivan, John P. Thomas, John H. Lorley, company F; John Anderson, H. Dennis Gilmore, Philip Gallagher, Samuel Morrison, William Hall, Christian Kreimer, Michael McLaughlin, Philip Pfluger, Thomas Ronake, Edward Thomson, John Wright, William I. Bemorit, William Ham, company G; John Cook, Patrick Flood, John Washing, Oliver Subish, John A. Nelson, Henry Bichler, Eugene Kelley, James Geary, Thomas Leston, John Kiefe, Arnold Boyd, Thomas H. McElroy, Edgar W. Rose, company H; H. Assman, William Curley, M. Huberman, R. Jones, H. Kuffenkraum, James Lawrence, I. P. Gleason, John Saner, company I; E. T. B. Day, T. Duffy, A. Harver, P. Honer, D. Sinson, H. Stevenson, H. Wescott, company K.

Eighty-eighth Illinois regiment.—George L. Maxon, Lofty C. Hayden, company A; George W. Rodney, Robert Dodson, C. Rogers, Charles E. Francis, company B; Edwin B. Beckwith, Samuel Harper, Chas. L. Fuller, Edwin T. Ralph, Andrew A. German, company C; Peter Brown, company D; F. G. Tanner, John E. Martindale, Ebenezer Hardee, John Barns, Patrick Sheridan, company E; George Burgu, James K. Burgu, Hardin Hancock, William Comstock, William N. Smith, William Hill, Joseph Ryan, Howard Hogan, Robert Sparks, James O'Neil, company F; William Granfield, Charles Ross, William Fisk, John M. Staub, William Melvin, company G; Charles H. Graham, Morris McGrath, Samuel Troat, C. Pangborn, (musician,) C. Walworth, company H; Richard Vaughn, company I; Peter Golden, Thomas Taut, F. Schall, company K.

Thirty-sixth Illinois regiment.—Isaac N. Minner, Edwin H. Robinson, Albert Shan, John F. Scott, company A; Elnathan Weeden, Adam Campbell, Jacob Winn, Carl Ecklart, Joel Wilder, company B; Frank Hemming, Oliver Edmond, company D; William Woolenreiber, company E; Canute Phillips, company F; Jesse Brown, company G; Robert Ker, company H; D. M. Carry, company I; Allen Bursse, Edward Reader, Joseph Leurman, George Gates, company K.

SECOND BRIGADE.

Second Missouri regiment.—Louis Benny, company A; Jacob Salmirt, Philip Kissler, and John Pennelton, company B; Peter Schroeder, company C; August Gunter, company F.

Fifteenth Missouri regiment.—Blandus Henster, company C; Henry Kurtz, company D; August Roth, company H; Leonhardt Stinns, company K.

Forty-fourth Illinois regiment.—Bulip Renter, (drummer,) Franz Rentz, and Lewis Tobems, company A; Spencer Mitchell, company B; Thomas Quay, company C; Jacob Adoff, company E; Thomas Barnett, James A. Mansker, and Thomas Taylor, company F; Floyd Babcock and James Jany, company G; John R. Cunningham, Joseph M. Stockton, Alfred C. Musgrove, and Martin Scott, company I; Philip Mans and Lewis Vogel, company K.

Seventy-third Illinois regiment.—F. A. Fortune, Jesse Umphues, John Langley, and John Huckleberry, company A; William F. Ballard, company B.

First Missouri battery.—James Reegan, company G.

THIRD BRIGADE.

Twenty-seventh Illinois regiment.—Henry Schauz, company A; Thaddeus Combs and L. D. Brown, company B; Albert Hamonds, Frederick Hammond, and Julias Vandewater, company C; J. T. Folley, W. H. Ross, Samuel Rochester, and John F. Wedford, company E; D. W. Cox and Bruce Tenny, company F; Benjamin F. Swafford, company G; Ivens W. Eaton, (musician,) M. F. Hartly, James G. Wilber, James H. Shear, Patrick Lynch, Charles G. Stillwell, and George W. Carroll, company I; George Bately, Philip Holmes, Hugh Hays, Frederick Newman, James Sergeant, and Sylvester Thompson, company K.

Forty-second Illinois regiment.—W. H. H. Miller and William Town, company A; S. Simonton and W. Swader, company B; J. F. Davis, C. Seriquest, W. H. Reice, M. B. Sweet, D. Stewart, J. B. Godair, G. D. Sims, and M. Voris, company C; S. Robbins, company D; William Suggett, G. W. Clark, J. Neville, J. Ryan, G. Spicer, R. H. Thimfell, and N. Wall, company E; G. M. Lane, and J. C. Holmes, (bugler,) company F; J. W. Barbour, J. D. Dockery, C. E. Dix, and E. Johnson, company G; J. Borroughs, William Wood, L. J. Ford, and E. M. Fry, company H; R. Evans, E. Fanen, P. La Plant, B. Morse, R. C. Smith, W. Smith, H. W. Shoemaker, A. J. Wilkinson, and E. N. Blakeslee, company I; and J. D. Edwards, company K.

Fifty-first Illinois regiment.—Samuel Smith, Fritz Harter, Albert Maace, John Seum, William Hurburget, Frink Millonk, Adam Arend, M. Burchard, M. Branger, and Jacob Scharlie, company A; Lawrence Alford, J. Homberget, Aleek Loughton, J. D. Ochiltree, Ellis F. Olden, Louis Robb, Samuel E. Armley, and Samuel E. Jones, company B; Robert T. Crawford, William Duscal, and M. O. Shanisan, company C; Samuel Martin, Jacob Miller, and James Winters, (wagoner,) company D; and Stephen McAllister, company G.

Twenty-second Illinois regiment.—S. M. Kinleff, company C; W. A. Elam, J. H. Armstrong, J. N. McCollum, and William K. Jackson, company D; James Aldeman, James McCullum, Jackson Green, Peter Derry, Josiah Suggs, Calvin Case, Peter McVey, and J. D. Stewart, company E; Anson Aufluimer, Conrad Bettendoff, Henry Beek, J. Hochiel, Christian Jeune, Jno. Kennick, R. Keller, M. Mongett, C. Leefried, and S. Wessell, company F; John Bealy, William R. Cunningham, William Gilmore, L. L. Jones, and C. F. Lackey, company G; Charles Gates, Nathaniel Scott, James H. Simpson, John H. Sullivan, John H. Schaffer, Calvin P. White, and James McHenry, company H; D. A. H. Clinton, Frederick Ahloens, Frederick Brunner, G. K. Caison, R. S. Coulter, J. Mathews, Jno. Malone, and Clias Repert, company

I; C. Hazard, M. Keating, Patrick McVorey, Patrick M'Avoy, Robert Bailey, Patrick D. Maley, John Edwards, and G. T. Stout, (musician,) company K.

First Illinois artillery.—Huston Bushby, William A. Carl, John L. Clark, Irwin Cole, Josiah Robinson, John Russell, George Thuler, Harly Sherwood, and Charles Seales, company C.

Fourth Indiana battery.—Edward Gilbert, company G.

Twenty-fourth Wisconsin regiment.—Fred. Burnson, company G; Daniel Buckley, Gernt Kerkestine, John W. Montgomery, Dalas Worth, and Adolph Walters, company E.

Prisoners paroled.

Twenty-first Michigan regiment.—Privates Edwin B. Ellenwood, Henry C. Nichols, and Samuel J. Clease, company F.

Fifty-first Illinois regiment.—Private William Cromwell, company A; Privates Charles Hill, company K.

Twenty-second Illinois regiment.—Private A. Perry, company C; Corporal Jas. Collier, company E; Private M. A. French, company I.

Second Missouri regiment.—Corporal Henry Drees and Privates Louis Ellenbroch, Augustus Mark, Alois Steindard, and Henry Statts, company D; Privates Henry Meyer and August Jammhausen, company K.

Forty-fourth Illinois regiment.—Sergeant Major Edgar J. Davis; Private Martin Orthus, company E.

Recapitulation.

Commissioned officers killed	15	
Commissioned officers wounded	39	
Commissioned officers missing	9	
		63
Non-commissioned officers killed	53	
Non-commissioned officers wounded	156	
Non-commissioned officers missing	48	
		257
Privates killed	166	
Privates wounded	719	
Privates missing	369	
		1,254
Paroled		17
Total		1,591

P. H. SHERIDAN,
Brigadier General, Commanding 3d Division, Right Wing.

Official.

R. W. DENNING,
Lieutenant and Aide-de-Camp.

HEADQUARTERS 1ST BRIGADE, 3D DIVISION, RIGHT WING,
Camp on Stone River, Tennessee, January 10, 1863.

SIR: Not being in command of the brigade until General Sill's death, Wednesday morning, December 31, 1862, I am unable to give a very correct report of its operations previous to that time, but have succeeded from what I observed myself, and by reports of other regimental commanders, in getting very near, if not quite, a correct report of the movements of the brigade.

In obedience to orders from General Sill, the brigade was under arms from 4 o'clock a. m. Tuesday, December 30, till 8 o'clock, on the Wilkinson pike, about five miles from Murfreesboro', and at 9 o'clock we moved forward; this brigade being the centre of the division. Skirmishers were deployed and soon were engaged with the enemy's skirmishers. When within about two miles from Murfreesboro' the brigade was ordered by General Sill to the right of the pike, and formed the first line of battle on the edge of the timber in the following order: 36th Illinois on the right, 88th Illinois on the left, Bush's 4th Indiana battery in the centre; the 21st Michigan supporting the 88th Illinois, and the 24th Wisconsin supporting the 36th Illinois. Sharp skirmishing was kept up until 3 o'clock p. m., when General Sill ordered an advance, and the brigade moved forward, (changing front to the left;) the regiments keeping their relative positions across a cornfield, and the battery was advanced into the woods beyond, supported by the 36th Illinois and five companies of the 24th Wisconsin. Soon after the advance into the woods, a battery of the enemy opened on us from the low ground across a cotton-field, and in the edge of a strip of timber, scarce 500 yards distant, and then ensued a terrific artillery duel between our battery and the enemy's, which finally resulted in their battery being silenced and withdrawn. It now being near dark, our battery was moved to the rear, just out of the woods, and the brigade formed in nearly the same relative positions as at first, and lay upon their arms all night, with strong lines of skirmishers out as pickets.

Soon after daylight, on the morning of the 31st, the enemy advanced out of the woods on the opposite side of the cotton-field (referred to before) in great force immediately on our front, but were met by such a fire from our artillery and infantry that they were finally repulsed and driven back with great loss across the cotton-field. About this time, 7 o'clock a. m., while directing the movements of the brigade, our brave General Sill was struck in the face by a musket ball and instantly killed. I then received your order to take command of the brigade. The enemy having turned our right, and again advancing in force I moved to the rear with the 24th Wisconsin and 88th Illinois, and across the road, where I formed on the left of the 88th Indiana, Woodruff's brigade, leaving the 21st Michigan to support Hescock's battery, where they were assailed by great numbers of the enemy, but held their ground until the battery was moved, when they retired in good order, losing heavily in killed and wounded.—(See report of Lieutenant Colonel McCreary.) Having expended all the ammunition of the two regiments with me, I retired to and got a supply from the train of General Rousseau, ours having been cut off.

I then reformed my line on the east of the railroad and moved forward to the Murfreesboro' pike. Here I received orders from General McCook to move to the extreme right of our line to support the cavalry, who were threatened by the rebel cavalry, and in some danger of being flanked. I formed and supported the 5th Wisconsin battery, and remained in this position until dark, after which I retired the 88th Illinois to the rear of the battery, and detailed the 24th Wisconsin for picket duty, Colonel Kenneth supporting my pickets with his cavalry. At 2 o'clock a. m. January 1 I received your order to move the brigade to the vicinity of your headquarters; when, in accordance with your orders, I formed line of battle in the rear of Colonel Liebold's brigade in the following order: 36th Illinois on the right, 4th Indiana battery, 88th Illinois, and 24th Wisconsin on the left, the 21st Michigan being for the time joined to the 3d brigade, Colonel Bradley commanding; where we lay during the 1st, 2d, and part of the 3d of January, 1863, inactive with the exception of being ordered to form double column on Friday, January 2, to support the left wing (then heavily engaged with the enemy) if necessary, but were not needed. Saturday, January 3, we moved, by your order, the whole brigade (the 21st Michigan having joined) to the position before held by General Davis's division, to the right and front of our former position, where we remained inactive until Tuesday, January 6, when we moved to our present camp, south of Murfreesboro'.

I am unable to give sufficient praise to the officers commanding the different regiments in the brigade—all have done their duty; but I must say that in regard to Major Miller, Captain Olson, and Adjutant Biddulph, of the 36th Illinois; Colonel Sherman and Major Chandler, of the 88th Illinois; Lieutenant Colonel McCreary and Adjutant M. B. Wells, of the 21st Michigan; Major Hibbard and Adjutant McArthur, of the 24th Wisconsin, they behaved with great coolness and presence of mind—ever ready to obey my command. Of my staff I would especially notice Lieutenant J. B. Watkins, acting assistant adjutant general; Lieutenant J. L. Mitchell, aide-de-camp; Lieutenant N. G. Bouton, brigade quartermaster, who was very active in procuring ammunition, and Quartermaster Sergeant Fred. Colburn, 33d Ohio, acting as volunteer aid to General Sill, and after his death, in the same capacity to me, and who showed great coolness and activity in carrying orders during the thickest of the fight. Brigade Surgeon D. W. Young deserves especial notice for his untiring efforts to care for the wounded.

In General Sill we all feel that we have lost an able commander and a kind friend; though but a short time with us, he had endeared himself to the whole command by his quiet, unassuming disposition, combining gentleness with strict discipline, courageous in action almost to a fault, we all feel that the brigade and the service have lost an officer hard to be replaced.

I enclose with this the reports of the commanders of the different regiments; also a complete list of casualties, the aggregate of which is as follows: Killed, 102; wounded, 369; missing, 200; total, 671.

I am, sir, yours, very respectfully,

N. GRENSEL,
Colonel, Commanding 1st Brigade, 3d Division.

Lieutenant GEORGE LEE,
Acting Assistant Adjutant General, 3d Division.

HEADQUARTERS 24TH WISCONSIN INFANTRY VOLUNTEERS,
Camp on Stone River, Tennessee, January 8, 1863.

LIEUTENANT: I have the honor to submit the following report of the part taken by the 24th regiment Wisconsin volunteers in the late engagements resulting in the taking of Murfreesboro', viz:

On the morning of Tuesday, December 30, 1862, I marched the regiment from camp right in front, following in rear of Bush's battery, with two companies deployed as flankers, according to orders from General Sill. About an hour's march from camp, and while firing was going on in front, I received an order to add one company to the flankers, and move them out further from the column, which order was carried out. Soon after, I received an order from General Sill to move my regiment forward, and form line two hundred paces in rear of the 36th Illinois. These dispositions being made, an order was received to have the men lie down. I remained in this position, just in the edge of the woods on the left of a white house, (afterwards used as a hospital,) and on the right of Bush's battery.

I remained there until ordered to advance by General Sill, keeping directly in rear and two hundred paces distant from the 36th Illinois. Advancing to the open field beyond an old log-house, I halted and ordered the men to lie down, the enemy having opened on the advance with artillery very effectually served.

Soon after, I was directed by an aid to send five companies to the woods in our front to support Bush's battery, which was then hotly engaged with the enemy's artillery. The five companies were sent under the command of the acting field officer. I remained in the field with the balance of the regiment, which was in a very exposed position, and had lost several men from the enemy's artillery, until ordered by General Sill to bring down the balance of my command to the support of the battery, as the enemy were about to make an effort to capture it. The artillery firing then ceased, night having put an end to the action. I was ordered by General Sill to have a picket posted, the balance to lie down on their arms, and allow half of each company to go to the rear and do some cooking. I posted one company as pickets, and allowed the men to boil some coffee; then placed them in line. The night was intensely cold, and the men were nearly frozen.

At 3 a. m., 31st, General Sill came down to the regiment and said we would be supported from the reserve brigade. The men were then awake and ready for action. At early dawn two regiments came into the woods, and formed line at right angles with my left. They remained a few moments, and were marched away.

Soon after, firing began, and the pickets were driven in by the enemy's skirmishers directly in my front. Their column of attack came close on the rear of their skirmishers, and I ordered the men to fire. At the same time my attention was directed to a column coming out of the wood on my right flank. They were in line and advancing very rapidly. (I counted five battle flags.) I immediately sent word to General Sill that the enemy were in force on my flank. About the same time the regiment on my right, formed at right angles, fell back; a battery which had fired four rounds very effectively, followed them, leaving my flank entirely unprotected. I maintained my position waiting for orders, until the enemy were in the woods in my rear, and had come up on my flank and delivered a cross fire, doing me considerable damage. No orders having been received, and thinking it improper to remain longer in this position, I ordered the regiment to break to the rear by companies. Some of the officers not hearing the order, the left wing did not move with the right, and the regiment came off in some disorder, but was quickly reformed in the open field to the right of the log-house used for a hospital. No regiment could have formed line more rapidly than they did, after retreating, surrounded on all sides by confused masses of fugitives—the veterans of some of the hardest battles of the war. Where such troops flee, new recruits assuredly deserve praise for standing their ground. I then received the first orders during the day from Colonel Grensel, to move my regiment up to a fence and have them lie down. My left then formed on the right of the 15th Missouri. An order given by Colonel Shaefer for that regiment to move, left me entirely alone unless I advanced with them, which was done. Moving up to the second fence in my front, I again ordered the men to lie down.

Soon after, an aid from General Sheridan directed me to move my regiment up to the woods. The order was obeyed, when I joined the 88th Illinois, and was thereafter under the immediate command of Colonel Grensel. By his direction we marched through the cedar swamp, a terrific fire of artillery and infantry roaring all around us. I crossed the railroad and marched up the Murfreesboro' pike, placed my men, as per orders from him, in a thicket, with directions to deploy skirmishers and watch for the enemy's cavalry, which was annoying our train. Remained in this position some time. Was ordered up still further to the right and placed behind a rail fence, which position I occupied for about one hour. Again moving up the pike by Colonel Grensel's direction, I supported one gun of the 1st Ohio battery. Night coming on, I was directed to post three companies as pickets, keeping the remainder in reserve.

On the morning of January 1, 1863, under direction of Colonel Grensel, I brought the regiment back to the pike, and, following the 88th Illinois, marched down to the cedar swamp, a mile beyond Stone river, with orders to erect temporary breastworks. In this position I remained until the evening of the 2d, when, by directions of the colonel commanding, I moved my regiment on to the grounds occupied by a regiment on my right, which had marched. On the morning of the 3d I marched again, by directions of the brigade commander, to the left of Bush's battery, my right resting on the 36th Illinois, in which position we remained until we marched to this our present camp.

I cannot too highly speak of the men who passed through all the trials of the two days' fighting and the following four days of suspense, worse than the battle itself. Exhausted and cold, they stood their ground like veterans, and fought as good soldiers.

I desire to make special mention of the conduct of Captains Root, Austin, and Philbrook, and Lieutenants Balding, Chase, Nix, Chivas, Hasting, Goldsmith, Horning, Elmore, Parsons, Batth, Kennedy, Holton, and Green. The surgeons (Major Hasse and Captain Wheeler) were not under my immediate observation, but I am informed they performed their duties nobly. To the chaplain of the regiment I return thanks for his kind attention to the wounded.

To the adjutant of the regiment (Arthur McArthur, jr.) I am more than indebted for his aid and efficient service rendered during the engagements. Young and gallant, I bespeak for him an honorable career. Of the sergeant major (Frank W. Biddle) and Sergeants Drake and Kersson, I would make favorable mention. Sergeant Cobourn, of company A, deserves special notice for bringing off the body of Lieutenant Nix, mortally wounded.

Enclosing you a list of the casualties, and desiring, on behalf of the officers of the regiment, to acknowledge our indebtedness to the colonel commanding the brigade for his care and attention after assuming command, I have the honor to be your obedient servant,

E. C. HIBBARD,
Major, Commanding 24th Wisconsin.

Lieutenant WATKINS.
Acting Assistant Adjutant General, 1st Brigade, 3d Division.

HEADQUARTERS 21ST REGIMENT MICHIGAN INFANTRY,
Camp on Stone River, January 7, 1863.

LIEUTENANT: I have to report to you the following as the action taken by this regiment in the recent engagement in front of Murfreesboro':

On the morning of the 30th ultimo we took position on the hill, between Captains Hescock's and Houghtaling's batteries, to act as a support to the 88th Illinois, Colonel Sherman, who had previously taken position a few rods in front. About 3 o'clock p. m. we were moved forward into the cotton-field, still retaining the same relative position to the 88th. We remained here until after dark, when we were ordered to move to a grass plot a few rods to our right, where we remained during the night. Before daylight we were ordered to occupy the same ground we had occupied the evening previous. Soon after daybreak an attack was made in force by the enemy upon our front and to our right. After a fierce contest the forces on our front and right retired. At this time the enemy were delivering a murderous fire upon our front and right flank. After delivering our fire, and observing him closing in in heavy force upon us, I ordered the regiment to fall back. Owing to a barn and outbuildings which we were compelled to pass, the regiment was for the time being thrown into some confusion; but it was with much difficulty that I could compel the men to leave the cover they had taken behind the fences and buildings, where they were delivering a well-directed fire.

We immediately formed upon the right of the 88th Illinois, and were ordered to move a few rods to the rear and left, and were then ordered to support Hescock's battery until further orders, it having taken position a little to our left

The battery soon changed position to a point of woods, where we followed in support. It was immediately engaged, and a heavy force of the enemy's infantry made their appearance on our front and left. As soon as they had advanced to within short musket range I opened a telling fire upon them, which was continued until the battery had retired, when we fought our way back to the woods in good order. We again took position in the woods, but receiving a heavy fire on our front and flank, we were obliged to fall back. We made another stand further back in the woods, and fought our way back to the clearing; after which I fell back beyond the railroad, where we remained until along towards evening, when we joined the brigade near Overall's creek. The next morning we were ordered to recross the creek, and took position on the right of the pike, and to the left of the 24th Wisconsin, in support of Colonel Bradley's brigade, where we remained without action until the next morning, when we moved to the right, occupying the ground previously held by the 36th Illinois, in which place we remained until we took up our line of march for this place. Both officers and men, with few exceptions, behaved with coolness and bravery. I am indebted to Major Hunting and Adjutant M. B. Wells for valuable assistance, especially the latter, whom I recommend to your favorable notice.

The list of casualties are as follows:

Officers wounded	7
Enlisted men wounded	82
Enlisted men killed	18
Elisted men missing	36
Total	143

Very respectfully,

WILLIAM B. McCREARY,

Lieutenant Colonel, Commanding 21st Michigan Infantry.

Lieutenant J. B. WATKINS,

Acting Assistant Adjutant General, 1st Brigade, 3d Division.

HEADQUARTERS 88TH REGIMENT ILLINOIS INFANTRY,
Camp on Stone River, Tennessee, January 7, 1863.

COLONEL: I have the honor to make report to you of my regiment during the recent battle of Stone river, near Murfreesboro', Tennessee.

On the morning of the 30th day of December, at 7 o'clock, by order of Brigadier General Sill, then commanding your brigade, I marched my regiment on the pike towards the town of Murfreesboro'. At 9 o'clock a. m. we were ordered to the right of the pike, where skirmishing with the enemy was being had. We formed in line of battle in front of Houghtaling's and Hescock's batteries, and threw out the two flank companies as skirmishers, with companies F and G as reserves.

We skirmished moderately with the enemy until about 3 o'clock p. m., when an advance was made, and I took position with the regiment in a cotton-field on a ridge, just in rear of a strip of bottom land, with my skirmishers a short distance in advance. During the remainder of the day skirmishing was brisk, and Captain G. W. Smith, of company A, while bravely directing his company as skirmishers, was wounded in the leg and obliged to leave the field. Night having set in, we were ordered to remain on the field all night and keep our skirmishers out as pickets.

On the morning of the 31st the men were in line of battle at daybreak, and skirmishing with the enemy began soon after. About 7 o'clock they made an advance across the "bottom," one brigade charging directly upon my regiment. I ordered the men to hold their fire until the enemy were within short musket range, when the skirmishers having nearly all rallied on the battalion, I ordered them to rise up and fire, which they did with a coolness and daring worthy of veteran soldiers, and which checked the enemy in his advance and drove him back into the timber. We held our position until forced to retire by the enemy advancing in overwhelming numbers from the timber to our right.

Our retirement was made in good order, but with great loss of men. We re-formed our line, when I was informed that General Sill was killed, and that you were in command of the brigade.

The enemy having broken our right, I retreated, under your direction, across the Wilkinson pike into the cedars, where we again made a stand, and held our position, checking the enemy's advance, until ordered to retire.

About noon we went out on the Nashville and Murfreesboro' pike, to support the cavalry in resisting the attacks of the enemy on our trains. We camped at night on a hill just beyond Overall's creek.

At 4 o'clock the next morning (January 1, 1863) we marched back to the battle-field, and took position on the right, where we lay in line of battle all this and the two following days, anticipating an attack from the enemy, but which was not made.

During the engagement I was ably assisted by all my officers present, Lieutenant Colonel Chadbourn and Lieutenant Ballard, adjutant, being absent, sick. Major Chandler was the only field assistance I had; and I take special pleasure in mentioning Major Chandler, whose conduct throughout the conflict was characterized by calmness and the most determined bravery. His services were invaluable to the regiment, as his gallant example infused itself into the spirits of the men, making them cool and steady when obliged to retire in the face of the enemy. Although wounded, and having his horse shot under him, he remained steadily at his post until the close of the battle.

It gratifies me to be able to make honorable mention of the officers commanding companies, viz: First Lieutenant George Chandler, company A; Captain W. A. Whiting, company B; Captain George A. Sheridan, company C; Captain John A. Bross, company D; Captain Levi P. Holder, company E; First Lieutenant James A. S. Hanford, company F; Second Lieutenant Dean R. Chester, company G; First Lieutenant Charles F. Boal, company H; Captain J. J. Spaulding, company I; Captain D. E. Barnard, company K; all of whom remained steady under fire, always at their posts urging their men on in repelling the enemy. The lieutenants assisting were cool and brave, and worthy of the offices they filled. The conduct of my sergeant major, N. P. Jackson, was worthy of a soldier, being cool and brave, ever ready to carry out my orders, though bullets were flying thick around him.

During the engagement on the 31st, while at his post, Lieutenant Thomas F. W. Gullich, of company C, fell, shot through the head. In his death his company and country have lost a faithful officer and a gallant soldier.

Herewith you will find a list of the killed, wounded, and missing of my regiment.

Very respectfully, yours,

F. T. SHERMAN,
Colonel, Commanding 88th Regiment Illinois Volunteers.

Colonel N. GRENSEL,
Commanding 1st Brigade, 3d Division, 14th Army Corps.

HEADQUARTERS 36TH ILLINOIS VOLUNTEERS,
January 9, 1863.

The 36th Illinois regiment, Colonel N. Grensel commanding, was called into line at 4 o'clock on Tuesday morning, 30th December, 1862, and stood under arms until daylight, to the left of the Wilkinson pike, our right resting upon it, and five miles from Murfreesboro'. At 9 o'clock a. m. we moved forward to Murfreesboro'; two companies were deployed as skirmishers to the right of the road, and were soon engaged with the enemy's skirmishers. When two miles from Murfreesboro' the regiment was deployed in the cornfield to the right of the pike, and two companies were deployed forward as skirmishers, as ordered by General Sill. The regiment lay in line in this field until 2 o'clock p. m., at which time the whole line was ordered to advance. The skirmishers kept up a sharp fight, the enemy's line retreating, and ours advancing. We drove the enemy through the timber and across the cotton-field, a low, narrow strip stretching to the right, into the timber. A rebel battery, directly in front of the 36th, directed a heavy fire on us. Our skirmishers advanced to the foot of the hill near the cotton-field, and here kept up a well-directed fire. We were ordered to support Captain Bush's battery which was brought into position in the point of timber where our right rested, and opened fire with terrible effect upon the enemy. We remained as a support until nearly dark, when Captain Bush went to the rear, the enemy's battery, or rather its disabled fragments, having been dragged from the field. In this day's engagement the regiment lost 3 killed and 15 wounded. Total, 18. We occupied the hill during the night, and our skirmishers were in line at the edge of the cotton field.

On the morning of the 31st of December, soon after daylight, the enemy advanced in strong force from the timber from beyond the cotton-field opposite our right. They came diagonally across the field. Upon reaching the foot of the hill they made a left half wheel, and came up directly in front of us. When the enemy had advanced up the hill sufficiently to be in sight, Colonel Grensel ordered the regiment to fire, which was promptly obeyed. We engaged the enemy at short range, the lines being not over ten rods apart. After a few rounds the regiment supporting us on our right gave way. In this manner we fought for nearly half an hour, when Colonel Grensel ordered the regiment to charge. The enemy fled in great confusion across the cotton-field into the woods opposite our left, leaving many of their dead and wounded upon the field. We poured a destructive fire upon them as they retreated, until they were beyond range.

The 36th again took position upon the hill, and the support for our right came forward. At this time General Sill was killed, and Colonel Grensel took command of the brigade. A fresh brigade of the enemy advanced from the direction that the first had come, and in splendid order. We opened fire on them with terrific effect. Again the regiment on our right gave way, and we were again left without support. In this condition we fought until our ammunition was exhausted, and until the enemy had entirely flanked us on our right. At this juncture Major Miller ordered the regiment to fall back. While retreating Major Miller was wounded, and the command devolved upon me. We moved back of the cornfield to the edge of the timber, a hundred rods to the right of the Wilkinson pike, and two miles from Murfreesboro', at 8 o'clock a. m. Here I met General Sheridan, and reported to him that the regiment was out of ammunition, and that I would be ready for action as soon as I could obtain it. We had suffered severely in resisting the attack of superior numbers. I had now only one hundred and forty men; the regiment fought with great obstinacy, and much is due Colonel N. Grensel for his bravery in conducting the regiment before being called away. Adjutant Biddulph went to find the ammunition wagon, but did not succeed. I then informed Quartermaster Bonton that I needed cartridges, but he failed to find any except size fifty-eight, the calibre of most of the arms being sixty-nine. I was now ordered by Major General McCook to fall back to the rear of General Crittenden's corps. I arrived there about 10 o'clock a. m. I here obtained ammunition, and despatched the adjutant to report to Colonel Grensel the condition and whereabouts of the regiment. He returned without seeing the colonel. Lieutenant Watkins soon rode up, and volunteered to take a message to Colonel Grensel or General Sheridan. He, also, returned without finding either officer. I now went in search of General Sheridan myself; found him at 12 o'clock; reported to him the regiment (what there was left of it) ready to move to the front. He ordered that I should hold the regiment in readiness, and await his orders. At 2 o'clock p. m. I received orders from General Sheridan to advance to the front on the left of the railroad, and connect my command temporarily with Colonel Lubold's brigade. We were here subject to a very severe artillery fire. A twelve-pound shell struck in the right of the regiment, and killed Lieutenant Loren L. Olsen (a brave and faithful officer, commanding company F) and Corporal Riggs, and wounding three others. At dark we were moved by Lieutenant Denning one-quarter of a mile to the rear, where we remained for the night. At 3 o'clock of the morning of the 1st of January, 1863, by order of General Sheridan, we marched back to his headquarters on the Nashville pike, a distance of half a mile, where, at daylight, I reported to Colonel Grensel. As ordered by him, we took position to the right of Captain Bush's battery, and fronting west. We built a barricade of logs and stone, and remained through the day ready to receive the enemy, but no attack was made. On the morning of the 2d the regiment was in line at 4 o'clock; stood under arms until daylight. We remained ready for action through the day until 4 o'clock p. m., when, by order of Colonel Grensel, we moved to the right on the line formerly occupied by General Davis. During the night considerable skirmishing occurred on our front. On the morning of the 3d instant the regiment stood under arms from 4 o'clock until daylight. At 8 o'clock a. m., by order of Colonel Grensel, we changed position to the right and somewhat to the rear, letting our right rest upon the Nashville pike. On the morning of the 4th we were under arms at 4 o'clock; no fighting occurred on our part of the line during the day. In the action throughout, the regiment behaved in the most gallant manner. The officers, with only a single exception, distinguished themselves for bravery and coolness; the men with unflinching courage were always ready, and met the enemy with a determination to conquer. I tender my thanks to Adjutant Biddulph for the gallant and efficient manner in which he assisted me, and also to the other officers for their gallant action throughout the stormy conflict, which resulted in victory. I append to this report a list of casualties.

PORTER C. OLSON,
Captain, Commanding 36th Illinois Volunteers.

Lieutenant J. B. WATKINS,
Assistant Adjutant General.

HEADQUARTERS 2D BRIGADE, 3D DIVISION,
Right Wing, January 7, 1863.

I have the honor to submit to you a report of the part taken by the brigade I have now the honor to command in the battle in front of Murfreesboro'.

The brigade, then in command of the lamented Colonel Fred. Schaefer, was assigned a position as reserve of the 3d division on the 30th of December, and took no part in the engagement on our left on that day. Shortly after daybreak next morning, the 31st of December, Colonel Schaefer received orders to re-enforce General Sill's brigade with two regiments; and the 15th Missouri volunteers and 44th Illinois volunteers, under command of Lieutenant Colonel Weber, of the 15th Missouri volunteers, were accordingly sent to General Sill, with orders to report to him for duty. The 2d battalion of the 73d Illinois volunteers, under command of Major Presson, was detached to protect Captain Hescock's battery, while the other battalion of the 73d Illinois volunteers and the 2d regiment Missouri volunteers were held in reserve. The 15th Missouri volunteers and 44th Illinois volunteers had a position assigned to them, about thirty yards in rear of General Sill's brigade, when, after a short interval, Lieutenant Colonel Weber received orders to advance in double-quick. The order was promptly executed, and Lieutenant Colonel Weber found himself in front of the enemy, the artillery previously stationed there having retreated, leaving one Parrott gun, supposed to belong to Carpenter's battery, Davis's division, behind. The two mentioned regiments kept up a strong firing, and even when one regiment on their left broke and ran, they held their position until attacked from the flank and front at once. Lieutenant Colonel Weber then retreated in good order, keeping up a constant firing until he, being heavily pressed by the enemy, reached a cornfield, where he halted.

Soon afterwards our troops on the left advanced again on the enemy, when Lieutenant Colonel Weber also rapidly advanced to a place about fifty yards in advance of his previous position, and formed in line of battle. He had the gun, above referred to, dragged by his men to the rear of his column, from where it afterwards was removed to a safer place. Lieutenant Colonel Weber contested his ground admirably until the enemy advanced six columns deep, and the ammunition of the 15th Missouri volunteers gave out, the 44th Illinois volunteers having previously withdrawn. Then the order to retreat was given and carried out without improper haste until the edge of the timber was reached, when the pressure by the enemy was so hard that it became necessary to resort to the double-quick. By the time the 15th Missouri volunteers and 44th Illinois volunteers rejoined the brigade, orders were given to retreat across the pike towards a piece of cedar woods, and two companies of the 2d Missouri volunteers were deployed as skirmishers to retard the rapid advance of the enemy. The whole brigade, with the exception of the 1st battalion of the 73d Illinois volunteers, under temporary command of Captain Bergan, and being a short distance from the main body, arrived safely at the woods above mentioned, at the edge of which the 2d Missouri volunteers behind natural and very favorable fortifications of huge and deeply cut rocks opened a brisk fire on the enemy, which kept him at bay for a considerable length of time. The 1st battalion of the 73d Illinois volunteers was at the same time attacked by the enemy, but repulsed them. When in the attempt to join the brigade, the battalion was, by the advance of General Rousseau, separated, but keeping up a constant firing crossed the pike, and took a position in the cedar grove. Here Captain Bergan, commanding the battalion, withstood three different charges of a whole rebel cavalry brigade, and was shortly afterwards enabled to join his brigade. By this time the ammunition of the 2d Missouri volunteers had given out, as well as that of the rest of this brigade, and they were ordered into the thicket of the cedar grove.

After the lapse of one hour the brigade was enabled to receive ammunition, and had a new position assigned to them on the Chattanooga railroad. Colonel Schaefer ordered the 15th Missouri volunteers to deploy in a cornfield, whilst the balance of the brigade held the railroad and kept up such a galling and well aimed fire that the enemy, though of a strength to which our force was hardly comparable, and fighting with the utmost desperation, was again and again repulsed. The 15th Missouri volunteers being in danger of being outflanked, retreated towards the position of the brigade, and it was at that moment, when about giving orders to said regiment, that the true soldier and brave man, my lamented predecessor, Colonel Fred. Schaefer fell. By order of General

Sheridan, I assumed forthwith the command of the brigade, the 36th Illinois volunteers, commanded by Captain Olson, having been detached to it; and after taking up another favorable position on the line of the railroad, I was enabled to hold the enemy in check, in spite of his desperate endeavors, until night broke in and the bloody drama of that day was ended.

On the 1st day of January, at 2 o'clock a. m., my brigade was ordered to take a position in front of an open field edged by heavy timber, and I had, as soon as daylight permitted, heavy breastworks erected along the whole front I was to protect; and keeping a vigilant lookout, I held that position until the 6th of January, when I was ordered to advance to the present camp.

The officers and men of the brigade all behaved as would naturally be expected of veteran soldiers who have heretofore earned the highest praise for their bravery and gallantry, and to enumerate single ones would hardly be in justice to the balance.

Among those who laid down their lives for our holy cause I particularly lament Captain Zimmerman and Lieutenants Kellner and Quintzins, of the 15th Missouri volunteers; Captain Alsop, of the 73d Illinois volunteers; Captain Hosmer, of the 44th Illinois volunteers; Lieutenant Taliaferro, of the 1st Missouri artillery. May their relatives find a consolation, as their comrades do, in the thought that the death on the battle-field for the righteous cause, wins immortal laurels for the slain!

I cannot omit to mention Captain Hescock's battery, which on the 31st of December, as oftentimes before, did splendid execution. The skill and bravery of its officers is almost proverbial, and need not be further commented on by me than to express my heartiest gratification, that they stood by me, as formerly, with a right good will and telling courage.

Enclosed I have the honor to transmit a list of the casualties in my brigade.

I am, sir, your very obedient servant,

B. LAIBOLDT,

Lieutenant Colonel 2d Infantry, Missouri volunteers,
Commanding 2d Brigade, 3d Division, Right Wing.

First Lieutenant GEORGE LEE,
Acting Assistant Adjutant General, 3d Division.

HEADQUARTERS 3D BRIGADE, 3D DIVISION,
Right Wing 14th Army Corps, January 8, 1863.

SIR: I have the honor to report, for the information of the general commanding, the part taken by the 3d brigade in the operations before Murfreesboro' ending January 4.

On the morning of December 30, 1862, the brigade, under command of Colonel G. W. Roberts, advanced on the Winchester pike, having the right of the column. About 9 o'clock we came on the enemy's skirmishers, engaged with a regiment of General Negley's division. The 22d Illinois was thrown out on the left, and the 42d on the right of the pike, as skirmishers, and soon forced the enemy back.

Houghtaling's battery was sent to the high ground, just in the edge of heavy timber on the right, and the 27th and 51st Illinois formed in line of battle to the rear of the reserves of the 22d and 42d, and on the left of the battery. We had active work with the enemy's skirmishers all day, the battery occasionally shelling them, but they were generally out of range. At noon the 51st Illinois relieved the 42d Illinois, and occupied the right of the brigade line of skirmishers for the balance of the day. About dark the skirmishers were withdrawn, and the brigade bivouacked on the field. The losses for the day were seven killed and thirty-five wounded.

On the morning of the 31st the brigade was under arms at daylight, and soon after formed line of battle. The enemy's columns opened out from the opposite woods, and Colonel Roberts ordered a skirmishing force to advance and feel the timber on our left. Companies A and B, 27th Illinois, were thrown out under Major Smith, the balance of the regiment being held in reserve—its left resting on the pike. About 8½ a. m. Colonel Roberts ordered the 22d, 42d, and 51st to charge the enemy's columns, and gallantly led them in person. The 42d and 51st charged in line with the 22d, in rear of the 42d, at battalion distance. These regiments went forward at the double-quick, and cleared the wood in front of our lines, the enemy giving way before we reached him. The line was halted, and opened fire in the timber. After some ten minutes, the line on our right giving way, we were ordered to retire to the lane leading at nearly right angles with the pike, and take a new position. Very soon the whole brigade was moved to the left and rear, and formed in the cedar woods on the pike, east of the hospital. Houghtaling's battery was posted so as to sweep the open ground and timber the brigade had lately occupied. The 42d and 22d were thrown to the left and rear of the battery, and the 27th and 51st formed on the pike fronting south. The whole command was soon hotly engaged with the enemy advancing on the east and south. The 27th changed front to rear on first company, and the 51st moved by the right flank so as to form an angle with the 27th Illinois. Company K, 51st Illinois, under Lieutenant Moody, was thrown out in advance of the battery to the east, to skirmish the woods, and remained there until driven in. Houghtaling's battery was worked with great spirit and vigor during the whole action; it, as well as the regiments of the brigade, was exposed to a cross fire from rebel batteries situated at the brick-kiln, and at the point occupied by Houghtaling on the 30th, as well as a heavy fire of small arms.

There the brigade met its chief loss; 400 were killed or wounded in two hours. Colonels Roberts and Harrington fell about quarter before 11 o'clock. At this time the ammunition of the battery and of the infantry was nearly exhausted. Being hard pressed by a superior force, and nearly surrounded, it was thought necessary to retire. At about 11 o'clock I withdrew the 51st in concert with the 27th, under Major Smith; both regiments moving by the right flank in good order. Houghtaling's battery was left upon the field, after firing the last round of ammunition and losing more than half the horses; being outflanked on both sides, it was impossible to bring it off in its crippled condition. I was not informed of the fall of Colonels Roberts and Harrington until after the 22d and 42d had moved. Those regiments, after suffering a loss of half their numbers, retired towards the Nashville pike, striking it near the grounds held by General Palmer's division, and, being separated from the brigade, reported to him.

The 27th and 51st were the last regiments to leave the ground, the regiments of General Negley's command having already retired. As soon as I was informed that the command of the brigade devolved on me, I sent Captain Rose, of Colonel Roberts's staff, to report to General Sheridan for orders, and fell back through the timber towards the pike.

Not being able to find General Sheridan, I reported to General Davis, who ordered me to reinforce Colonel Harker's brigade, then engaged with the enemy, who was endeavoring to turn our extreme right, and get possession of the road. I took in the 27th and 51st in line of battle, just as our troops were falling back in some disorder, and after delivering a volley or two charged a rebel brigade of five regiments, routing them completely and taking some 200 prisoners. This was the final effort on the right. About 1 p. m. we stacked arms and supplied the men with ammunition, the 22d and 42d joining soon after.

On the morning of January 1 we stood to arms at 3 o'clock, expecting an attack, and after daylight built a breastwork in front of the brigade line. In the afternoon a brigade of the enemy issued from the timber opposite our position and advanced on our line. As soon as they were in range I opened with small arms and shell, driving them back in disorder.

Observing that a part of them had skulked in the rocks, I sent out a strong line of skirmishers under Lieutenant Hanbeck, of the 27th Illinois, and captured 2 lieutenants and 117 men, mostly of the 3d confederate. The brigade occupied the same position on the 2d and 3d and 4th of January, skirmishing more or less with the enemy every day.

The entire loss of the brigade is 3 commissioned officers killed; 12 wounded; 58 enlisted men killed; 328 wounded; 161 missing; making a total of 562: This loss occurred on the 30th and 31st. I think there is a considerable number of wounded men in the hands of the enemy, who are now reckoned among the missing, but having no positive knowledge of their condition we account for them in that way.

I cannot forbear to express the sorrow felt by the whole command at the loss of its senior officers, Colonels Roberts and Harrington. They had served with the brigade since last April, and had each been in command of it for a considerable time. Long service had made the command familiar with them, and inspired them with confidence in their judgment and skill.

They fell in exactly the line of their duty, and each met a soldier's death bravely.

L. P. BRADLEY,
Colonel Commanding Brigade.

Lieutenant GEORGE LEE,
Acting Assistant Adjutant General, Third Division.

13.—REPORT OF GENERAL CRITTENDEN.

HEADQUARTERS LEFT WING, *January* 15, 1863.

COLONEL: In obedience to orders, I left camp near Nashville on the 26th December, and reached the point where the battle of Stone river was fought, just before dusk on the evening of the 29th. The march from Nashville was accompanied by the skirmishing usual when an army moves towards any enemy posted near by and in force; the gallant and handsome things done by several different portions of my command during this march have been mentioned in detail by the immediate commanders conducting the advance and leading the skirmishers. The seizure of two bridges, one by General Hascall and the other by Colonel Hazen, the gallant charge of the troops of Hascall's brigade at Lavergne, and the counter charge and capture of 25 of the enemy by a company of the new regiment, 100th Illinois, when charged by the enemy's cavalry, are worthy of notice.

It was about dusk, and just at the moment when Generals Wood and Palmer had halted to gather up their troops, that I reached the head of my command. These two generals had their divisions in line of battle, General Wood on the left and General Palmer on the right, the enemy in sight and evidently in heavier force than we had yet encountered them; it was evident they intended to dispute the passage of the river and to fight a battle at or near Murfreesboro'.

At this moment I received an order to ocupy Murfreesboro' with one division, camping the other two outside; I immediately gave the order to advance, and the movement was commenced; Wood was ordered to occupy the place, General Palmer being ordered, at General Wood's suggestion, to keep in line with Wood's division, and advance with him until we had forced the passage of the river. At this time it was dark. General Wood had declared when he received the order that it was hazarding a great deal for very little, to move over unknown ground in the night, instead of waiting for daylight, and that I ought to take the responsibility of disobeying the order. I thought the movement hazardous, but, as the success of the whole army might depend on the prompt execution of orders by every officer, it was my duty to advance. After General Wood had issued the order to advance, and General Palmer had received his, also, they both came to see me, and insisted that the order should not be carried out. I refused to rescind the order, but consented to suspend it for one hour, as General Rosecrans could be heard from in that time. During the interval the general himself came to the front and approved of what I had done. In the mean time Colonel Harker had, after a sharp skirmish, gallantly crossed the river with his brigade and Bradley's battery, and Hascall was already in the river advancing when the order to suspend the movement was received. As soon as possible I recalled Harker, and to my great satisfaction this able officer, with consummate address, withdrew from the actual presence of a vastly superior force his artillery and troops, and recrossed the river without any serious loss. During the night General McCook came over to see the commanding general, and reported that he was on the Wilkinson pike, about three miles in rear of our line, and that he should advance in the morning. The next morning (the 30th) early my line of battle was formed, Palmer's division occupied the ground to the right of the turnpike, his right resting on General Negley's left—General Negley having advanced into the wood and taken a position on the centre to connect with General McCook when he should come into line. General Wood was to occupy that part of our front to the left of the turnpike, extending down the river. General Van Cleve was held in reserve, to the rear and left. This position of our forces was, without material change, maintained all day, though the skirmishing during part of the day was very heavy, particularly on our extreme right, where McCook was coming up. Then, when it assumed almost the proportions of a battle, I proposed to cross the river with my corps and attack Murfreesboro' from the left, by way of the Lebanon pike, but the general, though approving the plan of attack, would not consent that I should move until McCook was more seriously engaged. On the morning of the 31st, when the battle begun, I occupied the front near the turnpike, General Palmer's division on the right, General Wood's on the left, General Van Cleve in reserve to the rear and left. About 8 o'clock, when my troops under Van Cleve were crossing the river as ordered, and when all was ready for an advance movement, it became evident that our right was being driven back; orders were received and immediately issued, recalling Van Cleve and stopping the advance. Van Cleve was ordered to leave a brigade to guard the ford; Matthews's brigade, Colonel Price commanding in Colonel Matthews's absence, was left; and to hurry with all possible despatch to try and check the enemy to the right and rear. One brigade of his division, Colonel Tyffe's, had already been ordered to protect the train then threatened near the hospital; and General Van Cleve moved at once and quickly to the right with Beatty's brigade. He arrived most opportunely, as his own and Colonel Beatty's reports show, and checked the enemy. The confusion of our own troops, who were being driven from the woods at this point, hindered him for some little time from forming his men in line of battle; this difficulty, however, was soon overcome, his line rapidly formed, and one small brigade, commanded by the gallant Colonel Beatty, of the 19th Ohio, under the direction of General Van Cleve, boldly attacked vastly superior forces of the enemy, then advancing in full career, checked their advance and drove them back. Being soon re-enforced by Tyffe's brigade and Harker's brigade of Wood's division, the enemy were pressed vigorously too far, they came upon the enemy massed to receive them, who, outnumbering them and outflanking them, compelled them to fall back in turn; this they did in good order, and fighting with such effect that the enemy drew off and left them, and they were able to hold their position during the remainder of the day; from this time the great object of the enemy seemed to be to break our left and front, where, under great disadvantages, my two divisions, under Generals Wood and Palmer, maintained their ground. When the troops composing the centre and right wing of our army had been driven by the enemy from our original line of battle to a line almost perpendicular to it, the first and second divisions of the left wing still nobly maintained their position, though several times assaulted by the enemy in great force. It was evident that it was vital to us that this position should be held, at least until our troops which had been driven back could establish themselves on their new line. The country is deeply indebted to Generals Wood and Palmer for the sound judgment, skill, and courage with which they managed their commands at this important crisis in the battle. The reports of my division commanders show how nobly and how ably they were supported by their officers; and the most melancholy and convincing proof of the bravery of all who fought in this part of the field is their terrible list of the killed and wounded, for with them there was no rout and no confusion; the men who fell, fell fighting in the ranks. Generals Wood and Van Cleve being wounded on the 31st, their commands devolved of course on other officers, General Hascall taking command of Wood's division, and Colonel Beatty of Van Cleve's, on the first of January. It was a fortunate thing that competent and gallant officers took command of these noble divisions on the night of the 31st. With the consent of the general commanding, I reunited my command, bringing them all together on the left of the turnpike; and before daylight, by orders from the general commanding, we took up a new line of battle about 500 yards to the rear of our former line; Hascall's division was ordered to rest their right on the position occupied by Stokes's battery, and his left on General Palmer's right; General Palmer was to rest his left on the ford, the right extending towards the railroad and perpendicular to it, thus bringing the line at right angles to the railroad and turnpike, and extending from Stokes's battery to the ford.

On the morning of 1st January Van Cleve's division again crossed the river, and took position on ground the general considered it important we should hold, extending from the ford about half a mile from the river, the right resting on the high ground near the river, and the left thrown forward so that the direction of the line should be nearly perpendicular to it. These changes in position having been accomplished, the day passed quietly, except continued skirmishing and occasional artillery firing. The next day, January 2, large forces of the enemy's infantry and artillery were seen to pass to their right, apparently contemplating an attack. Lieutenant Livingston, with Drury's battery, was ordered over the river, and Colonel Grose's brigade, of Palmer's division, was also crossed over, taking post on the hill near the hospital, so as to protect the left and rear of Beatty's position.

About 4 o'clock p. m. on the evening of the 2d a sudden and concentrated attack was made on the 3d division, now commanded by Colonel Beatty; several batteries opened at the same time on this division. The overwhelming numbers of the enemy, directed upon two brigades, forced them, after a bloody, but short conflict, back to the river. The object of the enemy (it is since ascertained) was to take the battery which we had on that side of the river; in this attempt it is most likely they would have succeeded, but for the sound judgment and wise precaution of Colonel Beatty, in changing the position of his battery. It was so late when the attack was made that the enemy, failing in their enterprise to capture our battery, were sure of not suffering any great disaster in case of a repulse, because night would protect them. They not only failed to capture our battery, but lost four of their guns in their repulse and flight. As soon as it became evident that the enemy were driving Colonel Beatty, I turned to my chief of artillery, Captain John Mendenhall, and said, "Now, Mendenhall, you must cover my men with your cannon, without any show of excitement or haste." Almost as soon as the order was given the batteries began to open, so perfectly had he placed them; in twenty minutes from the time the order was received 52 guns were firing upon the enemy. They cannot be said to have been checked in their advance—from a rapid advance they broke at once into a rapid retreat. Re-enforcements soon began to arrive, and our troops crossed the river and pursued the flying enemy until dark.

It is a pleasant thing to report that officers and men from the centre and right wing hurried to the support of the left, when it was known to be hard pressed. General J. C. Davis sent a brigade at once without orders, then applied for and obtained orders to follow immediately with his division; General Negley, from the centre, crossed with a part of his division; General McCook, to whom I applied for a brigade, not knowing of Davis's movement, ordered immediately Colonel Gibson to go with his brigade, and the colonel and the brigade passed at double-quick in less than five minutes after the request was made. Honor is due to such men. On the night of the 2d General Hascall, with his division, and General Davis, with his, camped a little in advance of the position which Beatty had occupied; General Palmer, commanding 2d division, camped with two brigades in reserve to Hascall's and Davis's divisions, and the remaining brigade on this side of the river. In this position these troops remained until Saturday night, when the river beginning to rise, and the rain continuing to fall, it was feared we might be separated from the rest of the army, and all recrossed the river, except Palmer's two brigades, which remained, and did not come back until it was ascertained the next day, Sunday, that the enemy had evacuated Murfreesboro'.

I feel that this report of the part taken by my command in the battle of Stone river is very imperfect. I have only endeavored to give a general outline of the most important features of the battle. The reports, however, of the division, brigade, and regimental commanders, together with the report of the chief of artillery, accompanying this report, give a detailed and good account of the memorable incidents which occurred in this protracted fight.

Reports of the division commanders show how nobly they were sustained by their subordinate officers, and all reports show how nobly the troops behaved. Generals Wood and Van Cleve, though wounded early in the battle of the 31st, remained in the saddle and on the field throughout the day, and at night were ordered to the rear. General Palmer, exposing himself everywhere and freely, escaped unhurt, and commanded the 2d division throughout the battle.

To these three division commanders I return my most earnest and heartfelt thanks for the brave, prompt, and able manner in which they executed every order, and I very urgently present their names to the commanding general and to the government as having fairly earned promotion

After the 31st General Hascall commanded Wood's division, the 1st, and Colonel Beatty the 3d, Van Cleve's. To these officers I am indebted for the same cheerful and prompt obedience to orders, and the same brave support which I received from their predecessors in command, and I also respectfully present their names to the commanding general and the government as having earned promotion on the field of battle. There are numerous cases of distinguished conduct in brigade as well as regimental commanders, mentioned by my division commanders as meriting promotion. I respectfully refer the general commanding to division, brigade, and regimental reports, and solicit for the gallant officers and men who have distinguished themselves for conduct and bravery in battle the honors they have won. We have officers who have commanded brigades for almost a year, though they have but the rank of colonel; in such cases, and in all like cases, as where a lieutenant commands a company, it seems if the officers have capacity for their commands on the field, that they should have the rank the command is entitled to.

The report of Captain Mendenhall, chief of artillery to the left wing, shows the efficiency, skill and daring with which our artillery officers handled their batteries. Division and brigade commanders vie with each other in commendations of our different batteries; some of these batteries fighting, as they did, in all parts of the field, won praises from all. To these officers also attention is called, with a sincere hope that they may be rewarded as their valor and bearing deserve.

Major Lyne Starling, assistant adjutant general to the left wing, has been for nearly eighteen months the most indefatigable officer I ever knew in his department. His services to me are invaluable. On the field here, as well as at Shiloh, he was distinguished even amidst so many brave men for his daring and efficiency.

Captain R. Loder, inspector general for the left wing, has entitled himself to my lasting gratitude by his constant and able management of his department. It is sufficient to say that the gallant and lamented Colonel Garesché told him in my presence, but a short time before the battle, that he had proven himself to be the best inspector general in the army. On the field of battle bravery was added to the same efficiency and activity which marked his conduct in the camp.

Captain John Mendenhall, who has been mentioned already as chief of artillery to my command, but of whom too much good cannot be said, is also topographical engineer on my staff. In this capacity, as in all where he works, the work is well and faithfully done. His services at Shiloh, of which I was an eye-witness, his splendid conduct as chief of artillery, his uniform soldierly bearing, point him out as eminently entitled to promotion.

To the medical director of the left wing, Dr. A. J. Phelps, the thanks of the army and the country are due, not only for his prompt attention to the wounded, but for his arrangements for their accommodation. He took good care not only of the wounded of my command, but of more than two thousand wounded from orher corps and from the enemy. Since the battle I have visited his hospitals, and can bear testimony to the efficiency of the medical department of this wing.

Captain Louis M. Buford and Lieutenant George Knox, my aides-de-camp, were brave, active, and efficient helps to me all through the battle. Captain Buford was struck just over the heart, fortunately by a ball too far spent to penetrate, and which only bruised. The captain and Lieutenant Knox were frequently exposed to the heaviest firing as they fearlessly carried my orders to all parts of the field.

Captain Case, of the signal corps, tendered his services as a volunteer aid, and proved himself a bold soldier and an efficient aid.

Two other officers of the same corps, Lieutenants Jones and ———, tendered their services as aids, and were placed on my staff during the battle, and I thank them sincerely for their services.

Lieutenant Brunner, of the 3d Kentucky cavalry, who commanded my escort, was quietly brave on the battle-field as he is mild and gentlemanly in the camp. I thank him and the brave men he commands for their fearless discharge of their duties amidst so many hardships and perils.

Before concluding this report it will be proper to add that when I speak of a quiet day I mean to speak comparatively. We had no quiet days, no rest from the time we reached the battle-field until the enemy fled; skirmishing constantly, and sometimes terrible cannonading. On the 2d, which we call a quiet day until about 4 o'clock p. m., the first division, under Hascall, laid for a half hour in the early part of the day under the heaviest cannonading we endured. Many men were killed, but he and his brave soldiers would not flinch.

The appended summary of the killed and wounded furnished by my medical director demonstrates with what fearful energy and earnestness the battle was contested in my command.

Report of the killed, wounded and missing, left wing.

First division.—Killed: Officers, 11; enlisted men, 200; total 211. Wounded: Officers, 56; enlisted men, 859; total 915. Missing: Enlisted men, 167; total, 167.

Second division.—Killed: Officers, 15; enlisted men, 191; total, 206. Wounded: Officers, 49; enlisted men, 1,031; total 1,080. Missing: Officers, 6; enlisted men, 257; total, 263.

Third division.—Killed: Officers, 17; enlisted men, 216; total, 233. Wounded: Officers, 52; enlisted men, 854; total, 906. Missing: Officers, 4; enlisted men, 387; total, 391. Grand total, 4,372.

Most respectfully, your obedient servant,

T. L. CRITTENDEN,
Major General Commanding.

Colonel C. GODDARD, *Chief of Staff.*

HEADQUARTERS LEFT WING, 14TH ARMY CORPS,
January 10, 1863.

MAJOR: I have the honor to submit the following report of the operations of the artillery in the left wing from December 26, 1862, to January 2, 1863.

This army marched from camp, near Nashville, 26th December; the left wing marching on the Murfreesboro' pike.

26th.—About 3 p. m. our advance was brought to a stand still, near Lavergne, by a rebel battery; it was opposed by a section of artillery, serving with the cavalry, which, being unable to dislodge the enemy, our advance battery (Captain Standart's battery B, 1st Ohio) was, after a little delay, put in position and opened fire, soon silencing the enemy's battery.

27th.—General Hascall took the advance with his brigade and Lieutenant Estep's 8th Indiana battery; they marched steadily forward till the enemy was driven across Stewart's creek—the battery halting only when it was necessary to fire; two pieces were posted near, covering the bridge.

28th.—Some artillery was so disposed as to check the enemy should he attempt to destroy or retake the bridge.

29th.—Lieutenant Parsons, commanding batteries H and M, 4th artillery, being in a commanding position, threw a few shells about 9 a. m., driving the enemy's pickets from the opposite woods. Our column advanced across the bridge at 10 a. m., meeting with little resistance till within about three miles of Murfreesboro'. Our troops were placed in line of battle as they came up, the artillery remaining with their divisions.

30th.—About 9 a. m. the enemy opened upon Captain Cox's 10th Indiana battery, (which was between the pike and the railroad, and in front partially covered by woods.) Captain Bradley's 6th Ohio battery at once took a position to the left of the woods and in a cornfield. The two batteries soon silenced that of the enemy. One shot killed a man near where a number of general and staff officers were standing, and another passing through battery H, 4th artillery, killed one man and wounded another, besides disabling a horse.

31st.—The left wing started to cross Stone river about 8 a. m., but before a division had crossed intelligence was received that the right was falling back. Colonel Fiffe's brigade, which was about crossing, was ordered to countermarch and move at double-quick to the right. Captain Swallow's 7th Indiana battery operated for a time with this brigade, shelling the rebel cavalry from the brick hospital, &c. Colonel Beatty's brigade, having recrossed the river, advanced to the support of the right wing, but the 26th Pennsylvania battery, Lieutenant Stevens commanding, being unable to follow the brigade through the woods, took a position near the pike, and received the enemy with shot and shell as he advanced after our retreating columns, and, I think, did his part in checking him. He advanced as they retreated, and took a position in a cornfield on the right of the pike, near the three-mile post, and again opened upon the enemy. The position of this battery underwent several changes during the rest of the day, but remained in the same immediate vicinity. Lieutenant Livingston, having recrossed the river with brigade, took a position commanding the ford, and about 12 m. opened upon the enemy's cavalry, while attempting to drive off some of our wagons which had crossed the river and were near a hospital we had established on the other side. They were driven away with little booty.

The batteries of General Wood's division (Cox's 10th Indiana, Estep's 8th Indiana, and Bradley's 6th Ohio—all under command of Major Race, of the 1st Ohio artillery) fought with the brigades with which they were serving. I had no occasion to give special orders to either of them during the day. The batteries of General Palmer's division served with it during the morning, rendering good service. Captain Standart's battery B, 1st Ohio, fell back with General Cruft's brigade, and was not again engaged during the day.

Captain Cockerill, during the afternoon, was ordered to the front, and he took a position in the cornfield on the left of the woods, where the enemy was making such desperate attempts to force back the left. At this place Captain Cockerill was severely wounded in the foot, and the command of the battery devolved upon Lieutenant Osburn. Two guns of this battery were disabled from their own firing, the axles being too weak. One of the limbers of this battery was blown up during the day. Lieutenant Parsons, commanding batteries H and M, 4th artillery, was ordered up to support the left about 4 p. m., and took a position in rear of the woods near the railroad, and after he had expended all his ammunition I sent Captain Swallow's 7th Indiana battery to replace him. These batteries did much to repell the enemy, as he advanced with the evident determination to drive us back at all hazards, if possible.

During the night the batteries were resupplied with ammunition, and I directed them to take positions as follows, before daylight, viz:

Lieutenant Livingston, (3d Wisconsin,) commanding ford on the extreme left; Captain Swallow, (7th Indiana,) on his right near the railroad; Lieutenant Stevens, (26th Pennsylvania,) also near railroad, but on the left of Captain Swallow. The batteries of the first division between the railroad and the pike. Captain Bradley, (6th Ohio,) on the left; Captain Cox, (10th Indiana,) on the right; and Lieutenant Estep, (8th Indiana,) in the centre. The 2d division batteries near the pike, in reserve.

During the morning Lieutenant Livingston was directed to cross the river; he was assigned a position by Colonel Beatty, and Captain Swallow took his place commanding the ford. Lieutenant Parsons was ordered to a position on General Rousseau's front by General Rosecrans, and Captain Cox was moved across the pike, near the Board of Trade battery, to support the right of his division, which had moved its right to that point. After dark Captain Standart was ordered to relieve the Board of Trade battery. No firing, except now and then a shell at the enemy's pickets was fired, during the day.

2d January.—Early in the forenoon the enemy opened his batteries, first upon our left, which was not responded to—their shot and shell doing no harm. They then opened more furiously upon the troops and batteries near the railroad and pike. Several of our batteries replied and soon silenced them. When the enemy had nearly ceased firing the Board of Trade battery (Captain Stokes) opened with canister upon Captain Bradley's battery and Colonel Harker's brigade, wounding several men and horses.

Captain Standart, with 3 pieces, Captain Bradley, 6th Ohio, and Lieutenant Estep, 8th Indiana, retired a short distance to fit up, they having received more or less injury from the enemy. Captain Bradley fell back on account of being fired into by Captain Stokes. He returned to his former position, after a little while, but Captain Standart and Lieutenant Estep remained in reserve. I then ordered Lieutenant Parsons, with batteries H and M, 4th artillery, to a position on the ridge to the right of Captain Swallow, (who was on the highest point of the ridge covering the ford,) and Lieutenant Osburn, battery F, 1st Ohio, to a position perhaps a hundred yards to the right of Lieutenant Parsons. During the afternoon Colonel Beatty changed the position of Lieutenant Livingston's 3d Wisconsin battery to near the hospital, (across the river.)

About 4 p. m., whilst riding along the pike with General Crittenden, we heard heavy firing of artillery and musketry on the left. We at once rode briskly over, and arriving upon the hill near the ford saw our infantry retiring before the enemy. The general asked me if I could not do something to relieve Colonel Beatty with my guns; Captain Swallow had already opened with his battery. I ordered Lieutenant Parsons to move a little forward and open with his guns; then rode back to bring up Lieutenant Estep, with his 8th Indiana battery. Meeting Captain Morton with his brigade of pioneers, he asked for advice, and I told him to move briskly forward with his brigade, and send his battery to the crest of the hill, near the batteries already engaged. The 8th Indiana battery took position to the right of Lieutenant Parsons. Seeing that Lieutenant Osburn was in position, (between Lieutenants Parsons and Estep,) I rode to Lieutenant Stevens, (26th Pennsylvania battery,) and directed him to change front, to file to the left and open fire; and then to Captain Standart, and directed him to move to the left with his pieces; he took position covering the ford. I found that Captain Bradley had anticipated my wishes, and had changed front to fire to the left and opened upon the enemy; this battery was near the railroad. Lieutenant Livingston's 3d Wisconsin battery, (which was across the river,) opened upon the advancing enemy, and continued to fire till he thought he could no longer maintain his position, when he crossed over, one section at a time, and opened fire again. The firing ceased about dark.

During this terrible encounter of little more than an hour in duration forty-three pieces of artillery, belonging to the left wing, the Board of Trade battery of six guns, and the batteries of General Negley's division, about nine guns, making a total of about fifty-eight pieces, opened fire upon the enemy. The enemy soon retired, our troops following; three batteries of the left wing, besides those of General Davis, crossed the river in pursuit.

During this engagement Lieutenant Parsons had one of his howitzers dismounted by a shot from the enemy, but it was almost immediately replaced by one captured from the enemy and brought over by the 19th Illinois regiment.

The following are the casualities, &c., in the several batteries.

Designation of battery.	Commanding officer.	Commis'd officers wounded.	Enlist'd men.			Horses.			Guns.		Rounds of ammunition expended.
			Killed.	Wounded.	Missing.	Killed.	Disabled.	Missing.	Disabled by enemy.	Disabled by firing.	
Batteries H and M, 4th artillery	Lt. C. C. Parsons	.....	2	14	6	20	....	....	1	......	2,299
Battery B, 1st Ohio	Capt. Standart	......	3	13	3	21	....	....	......	......	1,610
Battery F, 1st Ohio	Capt. Cockerill	1	2	12	....	24	..	....	.....	2	*1,080
Battery 7th Indiana	Capt. Swallow	1	4	7	....	1	4	4	......	......	406
Battery 3d Wisconsin	Lt. Livingston	......	...	4	...	9	....	....	......	......	358
Battery 26th Pennsylvania	Lt. Stevens	......	2	7	...	7	...	....	.....	......	1,650
Battery 8th Indiana	Lt. Estep	......	....	6	6	15	4	....	.....	.....	871
Battery 10th Indiana	Capt. Cox	......	1	4	...	12	...	....	......	2	1,442
Battery 6th Ohio	Capt. Bradley	......	2	2	1	16	5	....	......	....	500
	Total	2	16	69	16	125	13	4	1	4	10,516

* This battery had a limber blown up on the 31st.

Captain Cockerill and Lieutenant Buckmar were both wounded on the 31st The former commanded battery F, 1st Ohio, and the latter belongs to the 7th Indiana battery.

Major Race, 1st Ohio artillery, chief of artillery in the 1st division, and the several battery commanders, with their officers and men, all, with *one exception*, deserve most grateful mention for their coolness and bravery throughout the battle.

Lieutenant Parsons, commanding batteries H and M, 4th artillery, and his officers, Lieutenants Cushing and Huntington, deserve great credit for their courage under the hottest of the enemy's fire; they were probably under closer fire and more of it than any other battery in the left wing, and perhaps in the army. I am more than pleased with the way they behaved, as well as the brave men that were under them. Captain Bradley, 6th Ohio battery, deserves particular notice for the manner in which he handled his battery.

The *one exception* above referred to is Lieutenant Richard Jervis, of the 8th Indiana, who is represented to have acted in a very cowardly manner, by retiring a section of the battery at a critical moment, without orders, or notifying his battery commander.

I am, major, very respectfully, your most obedient servant,

JOHN MENDENHALL.
Captain 4th Artillery, Chief of Artillery.

Major LYNE STARLING,
Assistant Adjutant General.

NASHVILLE, *Tennessee, January* 6, 1862.

SIR: On the morning of the 26th ultimo the left wing of the 14th army corps broke up its encampment in the vicinity of Nashville, and moved toward the enemy. Reliable information assured us that he was encamped in force at and in the vicinity of Murfreesboro'; but as his cavalry, supported occasionally by infantry, had extended its operations up to our outposts, and as we had been compelled, for some days previous to the movement on the 26th ultimo, to fight for the greater part of the forage consumed by our animals, it was supposed we should meet with resistance as soon as our troops passed beyond the line of our outposts. Nor was this expectation disappointed. The order of march on the first day of the movement placed the 2d division, General Palmer, in advance, followed by my own. Several miles northward of Lavergne, a small hamlet nearly equidistant between Nashville and Murfreesboro', parties of the enemy were encountered by our advance guard, a cavalry force, and a running fight at once commenced. The country occupied by these bodies of hostile troops affords ground peculiarly favorable for a small force to retard the advance of a larger force. Large cultivated fields occur at intervals on either side of the turnpike road, but the country between the cultivated tracts is densely wooded, and much of the woodland interspersed with thick groves of cedar. The face of the country is undulating, presenting a succession of swells and subsidences. This brief description is applicable to the whole country between Nashville and Murfreesboro', and it will show to the most casual observer how favorable it was for covering the movements and designs of the enemy in resisting our progress. The resistance of the enemy prevented our troops from gaining possession of the commanding heights immediately south of Lavergne during the first day's operations, and delayed the arrival of my division at the site intended for its encampment until some time after nightfall. The darkness of the evening and the lateness of the hour prevented such a reconnoissance of the ground as is so necessary in close proximity to the enemy;

but to guard effectually against surprise a regiment from each brigade was thrown over forward as a grand guard, and the front and flanks of the division covered with a continuous line of skirmishers. The troops were ordered to be roused an hour and a half before dawn of the following morning, to get their breakfasts as speedily as possible, and to be formed under arms and in order of battle before daylight.

An occasional shell from the opposing heights, with which the enemy commenced to greet us shortly after the morning broke, showed these precautions were not lost.

As it was understood from the commanding general of the corps that the right wing was not so far advanced as the left, the latter did not move forward until 11 o'clock a. m. on the 27th. At this hour the advance was ordered, and my division was directed to take the lead. The entire cavalry on duty with the left wing was ordered to report to me; being satisfied, however, from the nature of the country that its position in advance would be injudicious, and retard rather than aid the progress of the infantry, I directed it to take position in rear of the flanks of the leading brigade. I ordered Hascall's brigade to take the advance and move in two lines, with the front and flanks well covered with skirmishers. The other brigade, Wagner's and Harker's, were ordered to advance on either side of the turnpike road, prepared to sustain the leading brigade, and especially to protect its flanks. These two brigades were also ordered to protect their outward flank by flankers. In this order the movement commenced. Possession of the hamlet of Lavergne was the first object to be attained. The enemy was strongly posted in the houses and on the wooded heights in rear, whence he was enabled to oppose our advance by a direct and cross fire of musketry. Hascall's brigade advanced gallantly across an open field to the attack, and quickly routed the enemy from his stronghold. This was the work of only a few minutes, but more than twenty casualties in the two leading regiments proved how sharp was the fire of the enemy. The forward movement of Hascall's brigade was continued, supported by Estep's 8th Indiana battery. The enemy availed himself of the numberless positions that occur along the entire road to dispute our further progress, but he could not materially retard the advance of troops so determined and enthusiastic. They continued to press forward through the densely wooded country, in a drenching rain-storm, until they reached Stewart's creek, distant some five miles from Lavergne, Stewart's creek is a narrow and deep stream, flowing between high and precipitous banks. It is spanned by a wooden bridge with a single arch. It was a matter of cardinal importance to secure possession of this bridge, as its destruction would entail much difficulty and delay in crossing the stream, and perhaps involve the necessity of constructing a new bridge. The advance troops found on their arrival that the enemy had lighted a fire upon it, but he had been pressed so warmly there had not been time for the flames to be communicated to the bridge. The line of skirmishers and the 3d Kentucky volunteers, Colonel McKee's regiment, dashed bravely forward, though exposed to a fire from the opposite side, threw the combustible materials into the stream and saved the bridge. While this gallant feat was being performed the left flank of the leading brigade was attacked by cavalry. The menaced regiments immediately changed front to the left, and a company of the 100th Illinois, Colonel Bartleson's regiment, succeeded in cutting off and capturing seventy-five prisoners with their arms, and twelve horses with their accoutrements. The result of the day's operations was some twenty-odd casualties, wounded in Hascall's brigade, and some thirty-five prisoners taken from the enemy. The enemy fell back in great disorder from Stewart's creek. He left tents standing on the southern bank of the creek, and on this encampment the ground strewn with arms. Sunday, the

28th ultimo, we remained in camp, waiting for the troops of the right wing and centre to get into position.

Monday, the 29th, the advance was resumed. Wagner's brigade, of my division, was deployed on the left or eastern, and a brigade of General Palmer's division on the right or western side of the road. Cox's 10th Indiana battery supported Wagner's brigade. Moving, *pari passu*, the two brigades advanced, clearing all opposition till we arrived within two miles and a half of Murfreesboro'. Harker's brigade was disposed on the left of Wagner's in the advance, and Hascall's held in reserve.

On arriving within two miles and a half of Murfreesboro', the evidences were perfectly unmistakable that the enemy was in force immediately in our front, prepared to resist seriously and determinously our further advance. His troops, displayed in battle array, were plainly to be seen in our front. Negley's division, which was to take position in the centre and complete the connextion between the right and left wings, was not up, but seven miles in the rear. Van Cleve's division, which was to support the left, was in rear of Negley's; nor had the right wing, McCook's command, got into position. Consequently I halted the troops in advance, reported the fact to General Crittenden, commanding the left wing, and desired further orders. Up to this moment the information received had indicated, with considerable probability, that the enemy would evacuate Murfreesboro', offering no serious opposition. But observations assured me, very soon after arriving so near to the town, that we should meet with a determined resistance, and I did not deem it proper to precipitate the force in advance, two divisions, my own and General Palmer's, on the entire force of the enemy, with the remainder of our troops so far in the rear as to make it entirely possible, perhaps probable, that a serious reverse would occur before they could support us. Furthermore, the afternoon was well nigh spent, and an attempt to advance would have involved us in the obscurity of the night, on unexamined ground, in the presence of an unseen foe, to whom our movements would have rendered us fearfully vulnerable.

The halt being approved, my division was disposed in order of battle, and the front securely guarded by a continuous line of skirmishers, thrown out well in advance of their reserves. The right of the division, Wagner's brigade, rested on the right of the turnpike, and occupied a piece of wooded ground, with an open field in front of it. The centre, Harker's brigade, occupied a part of the wood in which Wagner's brigade was posted, and extended leftward into an open field, covered in front by a low swell, which it was to occupy in case of an attack, and General Hascall's brigade was posted on the left of the division, with its left flank resting nearly on Stone river. The entire division was drawn up in two lines. Stone river runs obliquely in front of the position occupied by the divisions, leaving a triangular piece of ground of some hundreds of yards in breadth in front of the right, and narrowing to almost a point opposite the left.

Such was the position occupied by my division Monday night. It remained in this position Tuesday, the 30th, the skirmishers keeping up an active firing with the enemy. In this encounter of skirmishers, Lieutenant Elliott, Adjutant of the 57th Indiana, was very severely wounded. In the afternoon I had three days' subsistence issued to the men, and near nightfall, by order, twenty additional rounds of cartridges were distributed to them. Commanders were directed to instruct their men to be exceedingly vigilant, and report promptly any indication of a movement in the front by the enemy. The artillery horses were kept attached to the pieces. Between midnight and daylight Wednesday morning I received a message from Colonel Wagner to the effect that the enemy seemed to be moving large bodies of troops from his right to his left. I immediately despatched the information to the headquarters of the left wing, and I doubt not it was sent thence to the commanding general, and by him distributed to the rest of the corps. The division was roused at 5 o'clock Wednesday morning; the men took their breakfasts, and before daylight were ready for action. Shortly after dawn I repaired to the headquarters of the left wing for orders. I met the commanding general there, and received orders from him to commence passing Stone river, immediately in front of the division, by brigades. I rode at once to my division, and directed Colonel Harker to commence the movement with his brigade; despatching an order to General Hascall to follow Colonel Harker, and an order to Colonel Wagner to follow General Hascall. While Colonel Harker was preparing to move I rode to the front to examine the ground. A long wooded ridge within a few hundred yards from the stream extends along the southern and eastern side of Stone river. On the crest of this ridge the enemy appeared to be posted in force. During the morning some firing had been heard on the right, but not to a sufficient extent, however, to indicate that the troops were seriously engaged. But the sudden and fierce roar and rattle of musketry which burst on us at this moment indicated that the enemy had attacked the right wing in heavy force, and soon the arrival of messengers, riding in hot haste, confirmed the indications. I was ordered to stop the movement of crossing the river, and to withdraw two brigades to the rear for the purpose of re-enforcing the centre and right. General Hascall's and Colonel Harker's brigades were withdrawn, and the latter, under an order from the commanding general, moved to the right and rear. I ordered Colonel Wagner to hold his position in the wood at all hazards, as it was an important point, and so long as it was held, not only were our left, front, and flanks secured, but the command of the road leading to the rear preserved. The vigorous attack on our right and centre extended to the left, and our whole line became seriously engaged. Not only was the extreme left exposed to the attack in front, but was much harassed by the enemy's artillery posted on the heights on the southern side of Stone river. But the troops nobly maintained their position, and gallantly repulsed the enemy. Cox's battery was most splendidly served and did most excellent service in repulsing this attack. A slackening of the enemy's fire at this moment in the attack on our centre and left, and other indications that his forces were breaking in the centre, rendered the juncture apparently favorable for bringing additional and fresh troops into action.

Hascall's brigade was now brought forward and put in position on the right of Wagner's brigade. But the abatement of the enemy's fire was but the lulling of the storm, soon to burst with greater fury. The attack was renewed on our centre and left with redoubled violence. Hascall's brigade had got into position in good season, and aided, in gallant style, in driving back the enemy. Estep's battery, generally associated with Hascall's brigade, had been detached early in the morning and sent to the right and rearward to aid in driving back the enemy from our centre and right.

The falling back of the right wing had brought our lines into a crotchet. This rendered the position of the troops on the extreme left particularly hazardous, for, had the enemy succeeded in gaining the turnpike in his attack on the right, the left would have been exposed to an attack in reverse. This danger imposed on me the necessity of keeping a rigid watch to the right to be prepared to change front in that direction should it become necessary. Again the enemy was seen concentrating large masses of troops in the fields to the front and right, and soon these masses moved forward to the attack. Estep's battery was now moved to the front to join Hascall's brigade. The artillery in the front line, as well as those placed in the rear of the centre and left, poured a destructive fire on the advancing foe, but on he came until within small arm range, when he was repulsed and driven back. But our thinned ranks and dead and wounded officers told, in unmistakable language, how largely we were suffering in those repeated attacks. Colonel McKee, of the 3d Kentucky volunteers, had been killed, and Colonel Hines and Lieutenant Colonel Lennard, of the 57th Indiana, and Colonel Blake and Lieutenant Colonel Neff, of the 40th Indiana, with others, wounded. During this attack the 15th Indiana volunteers, commanded by Lieutenant Colonel Wood, countercharged one of the enemy's regiments and captured one hundred and seventy-three prisoners. The capture was made from the 20th Louisiana. While this attack was in progress I received a message from General Palmer, commanding the 2d division of the left wing, that he was sorely pressed and desired I would send him a regiment, if I could possibly spare one. I sent an order to General Hascall to send a regiment to General Palmer's assistance, if his own situation would warrant it. He despatched the 58th Indiana volunteers, Colonel G. P. Buell's regiment, to report to General Palmer. The regiment got into position, reserved its fire until the enemy was in close range, and then poured in a withering discharge, from which the foe recoiled in disorder. Our extreme left next became the object of the enemy's attention. His skirmishers were seen ascending the slope on the opposite side of the river, and also working their way down the stream, apparantly with the design of gaining our left flank and rear. A few well-directed shots of grape and canister from Cox's battery drove them back. This battery did most useful service in counter-battering the enemy's artillery posted on the heights on the southern side of the river. The afternoon was now well advanced, but the enemy did not seem disposed to relinquish the design of forcing us from our position. Heavy masses were afresh assembled in front of the centre with a view, evidently, of renewing the onset, but the well-directed fire of the artillery held them in check, and only a small force came within range of our small arms, which was readily repulsed. The enemy concluded his operations against the left, as night approached, by opening on it with his artillery. Cox's and Estep's batteries gallantly and effectually replied, but darkness soon put a conclusion to this artillery duel; and when the night descended and brought a period to the long and bloody contest of this ever-memorable day, it found the 1st and 2d brigades, Hascall's and Wagner's, occupying, with some slight interchange in the position of particular regiments, the ground on which they had gone into the fight in the morning; every effort of the enemy to dislodge them had failed; every attack had been gallantly repulsed.

I cannot speak in too high terms of the soldierly bearing and steadfast courage with which the officers and men of these two brigades maintained the battle throughout the day. Their good conduct deserves and will receive the highest commendation of their commanders and countrymen. The commanding general of the enemy has born testimony, in his despatch, to the gallantry and success of their resistance. Cox's and Estep's batteries were splendidly served throughout the day and did the most effective service. They lost heavily in men and horses, and it was necessary for Estep to call on the 100th Illinois volunteers for a detail to aid in working his guns. I have previously remarked that the 3d brigade, Colonel Harker, was detached early in the day and sent to re-enforce the right; it remained on that part of the field during the entire day; I am unable, consequently, to speak of its services from personal observation, but its extremely heavy list of casualties show how hotly it was engaged, and what valuable service it rendered. I am sure it fully met the expectations I had ever confidently entertained of what would be its bearing in the presence of the foe. Bradley's 6th Ohio battery was associated with this brigade during the day, was skilfully handled, and did most effective service. It lost two of its guns, but they were spiked before they were abandoned. They were subsequently recaptured by the 13th Michigan volunteers, attached to the brigade. From all I have learned of the service of the 3d brigade and Bradley's battery, I am sure they deserve equal commendation with the two brigades and batteries which so stoutly held the left. An official report of events so thrilling as those of the battle of the 31st ultimo, made from personal observation amid the din and roar of the conflict, and unaided by the reports of the subordinate commanders, must necessarily present but a brief and meagre outline of the part enacted by the troops whose services it professes to portray. A report so prepared may, entirely unintentionally on the part of the writer, do injustice to particular troops and officers. From inability of reference to the reports of subordinate commanders I cannot give any detail of the heavy casualties of the battle of the 31st. I must leave them to be reported, with the subsequent casualties, by my successor in command. The absence of such reports prevents me from signalizing by name such regimental and company officers as particularly distinguished themselves. But where all did so well, it would be difficult, perhaps invidious, to discriminate among them. To my brigade commanders, Brigadier General Hascall, commanding 1st brigade, Colonel Wagner, 15th Indiana volunteers, commanding 2d brigade, and Colonel Harker, 65th Ohio volunteers, commanding 3d brigade, my warmest thanks are due for their valuable assistance, their hearty co-operation, and intelligent performance of duty throughout the whole of the trying day. For these services, and for their gallant and manly bearing under the heaviest fire, they richly deserve the highest commendation and the gratitude of their countrymen. Colonels Wagner and Harker have long and ably commanded brigades, and I respectfully submit it would be simply an act of justice to confer on them the actual and legal rank of the command they have so long exercised. To Surgeon W. W. Blair, 58th Indiana volunteers, Captain M. P. Bestow, assistant adjutant general, First Lieutenant J. L. Yargan, 58th Indiana volunteers, aide-de-camp, Captain F. R. Palmer, 13th Michigan volunteers, inspector general, and Major Walker, 2d Indiana cavalry, volunteer aide-de-camp, my thanks are due and cordially given. Captain L. D. Myers, division quartermaster, Captain J. D. Henderson, commissary of subsistence to the division, and First Lieutenant Martin, 21st Ohio, signal officer, but for some time engaged in performing the duties of acting assistant quartermaster, great credit is due for the intelligent and efficient performance of duty in their respective departments. Captain Bruce, 58th Indiana volunteers, ordnance officer of the 1st brigade, deserves credit for valuable services rendered in the ordnance department, for the entire division, during the absence of the division ordnance officer.

My division is composed of regiments from the States of Illinois, Indiana, Ohio, Michigan, and Kentucky. To the relatives and personal friends of those who have fallen in defence of their country I would respectfully offer my sympathy and condolence. About 10 o'clock Wednesday morning, during one of the heaviest attacks, I was struck by a Minie ball on the inside of the left heel. Fortunately, the ball struck obliquely, or the injury would have been much severer. My boot was torn open, the foot lacerated, and a severe contusion inflicted. I did not dismount from my horse until 7 o'clock in the evening. The coldness of the night, combined with the injury, made my foot so painful and stiff as to render it evident I would not be effective for immediate service. I was ordered by the commanding general of the corps to repair that night by ambulance, with an escort, to this city. It was with extreme regret I found myself in a condition to make it necessary, on account of my injury, to leave the division I had formed and so long commanded; but the regret was alleviated by the reflection that I had left the division under the command of an able and experienced officer, one who had long served with it, knew it well, and in whom it had confidence.

I am still confined to my room, but trust ere long to be able to resume my duties.

I am, very respectfully, your obedient servant,

TH. J. WOOD,
Brigadier General of Volunteers.

Major LYNE STARLING,
Assistant Adjutant General, Left Wing, 14*th Army Corps.*

DAYTON, *Ohio, January* 28, 1863.

SIR: In my official report of the operations of my division, from the time it moved from Nashville, on the 26th ultimo, to the date of my relinquishing command of it, I omitted to mention the passage of Stone river the evening of the 29th ultimo, by the 3d (Harker's) brigade.

After the division had arrived within two and a half miles of Murfreesboro', in obvious view of the enemy's battle array, halted, as explained in my former report, and precautionary dispositions commenced for the night, an order was received to contiue the advance on Murfreesboro'. The order was received just at night-fall, when darkness was beginning to shroud the ground to be passed over with obscurity. The movement was at once commenced, but was subsequently suspended by General Crittenden, until further communication could be had with the commanding general of the army. Before, however, the order was suspended, Harker's brigade had crossed Stone river under a galling fire, driven in the enemy's outposts, and seized a strong position, which it held until nearly 10 o'clock that evening.

The commanding general having approved the suspension of the order, and it not being prudent to leave the brigade in so exposed a position, it was ordered to recross the river. It performed the retrogade movement handsomely, in good order, and with perfect success, though confronted by an entire division (Breckinridge's) of the enemy. This fact was learned from a prisoner, captured when the brigade first crossed the river. Bradley's 6th Ohio battery accompanied the brigade in the entire movement.

I desire to repair the omission in my previous report, and request that this communication be made part of it. It will readily be perceived how the omission occurred, when it is remembered that my original report was prepared without the aid of the reports of subordinate commanders, and written under the compound embarrassment of inconvenience from my wound, and suffering from a quotidian intermittent fever, with which I had been afflicted for ten days previous to the battle of the 31st ultimo.

I am, sir, very respectfully, your obedient servant.

TH. J. WOOD,
Brigadier General of Volunteers.

Major LYNE STARLING,
Assistant Adjutant General, Chief of Staff, Crittenden's Corps.

HEADQUARTERS 1ST DIVISION, LEFT WING,
Murfreesboro', Tennessee, January 10, 1863.

I have the honor to submit the following report of the operations of this division during the recent battles after the command devolved upon me, on the evening of December 31, 1862. At that time the division was considerably scattered, as Colonel Harker's brigade had been in action during the 31st on the extreme right and had not returned. Colonel Wagner's was in position to the left of the railroad, where it had been in action during the day, and my brigade was to the right of the railroad. About 11 p. m. of that day Colonel Harker returned with his brigade, and the division was once more together. At this time I received an order to send all the wagons of the division to the rear, and, shortly after this was executed, I received an order from General Crittenden to fall back so that my right should rest on the position occupied by Stokes's battery and my left on the right of General Palmer's division. This brought the new line of the division about 500 yards to the rear of the one of the day before. The line of the division was now nearly at right angles with the railroad, with the centre of the line resting on it; the 1st brigade, Colonel Buell, on the right; the 3d, Colonel Harker, in the centre; and the 2d, Colonel Wagner, on the left.

In this position we lay all the next day, January 1, 1863, with nothing more to break the silence than picket firing and an occasional artillery duel. The division lost, however, several killed and wounded during the day. Each of my brigades were in line of battle, and I was occupying so much front that it kept the men constantly on the alert. Most of the other divisions had one or two brigades in reserve, and could therefore relieve their men some. We maintained this position during the night of the 1st and till about 8 a. m. in the morning of the 2d, the batteries occupying the intervals between brigades. At this time the enemy opened upon us the most terrific fire of shot and shell that we sustained during the entire engagement. It appears that during the night before they had massed and masked several batteries in our front, so they opened on us from a line of batteries one quarter of a mile long all at once. They had our range perfectly, so that their fire was terribly effective from the first. Estep's battery, on the right of my line, being in a very exposed position and receiving a very heavy fire, had to retire at once, not, however, till so many horses had been killed as to render it necessary for two of the pieces to be hauled to the rear by the infantry. Bradley's battery, with Colonel Harker in the centre, having a better position and longer range guns, opened a brisk fire on the enemy in return, and had every probability of maintaining their position until Stokes's battery, in their rear, undertook to open on the enemy with grape, which took effect on Bradley's men, instead of the enemy, and compelled Bradley to retire. The infantry, however, along my entire line, though suffering severly from the enemy's fire, all maintained their position. After about half an hour this firing ceased, and nothing further worthy of note happened till about 4 o'clock in the afternoon of that day. At this time General Van Cleve's division, which was stationed across Stone river to our left, were suddenly attacked by a heavy force of the enemy under Breckinridge, and so fierce was the onslaught that the division was compelled to give way almost immediately. General Jefferson C. Davis and General Negley were immediately ordered to their relief with their divisions, and, as soon as they had time to get over, the attack was checked and the enemy began to retire. At this time I received an order from General Crittenden to cross with my division, and immediately put the different brigades in motion. While crossing at the ford one or two pieces of the enemy's artillery were playing upon us, but, as it was then dusk, their firing was not accurate and I think we sustained no loss in crossing. By the time we were over it was quite dark and the firing had nearly ceased. Negley's division was returning, and Davis's had taken up a position a little in advance of where Van Cleve's division was attacked, his right wing resting on the bank of the river. I moved up and went into position on the left of Davis, my left inclining somewhat to the rear to prevent it from being turned. General Davis and myself then fortified our fronts as well as we could with the logs, stones, and rails at hand, and remained in this position that night, the next day, (January 3,) and till about 12 o'clock that night, without anything more than picket firing transpiring. I should remark that it rained very hard all day January 3 and during the night, so that our men and officers suffered severely. By this time the rains had so swollen the river that General Crittenden became apprehensive that it would not be fordable by morning, and we might be cut off from communication with the main body of our army. He therefore ordered us back, and my division took up a position in reserve near General Rosecrans's headquarters, arriving there about 2 o'clock at night, completely drenched with mud and rain. They had now been on duty four days and nights, some of the time with nothing to eat, and all the time in the front, where they had to be constantly on the alert. The next morning we heard that the enemy had retreated and the battle was over. The conduct of the division throughout was admirable, and it can be truthfully said concerning it that it held its original position and every other position assigned it during the whole four days, and this is more than can be said of any other division in the entire 14th army corps. I am under great obligations to my brigade commanders, Colonels Wagner, Harker, and Buell. Colonel Wagner had his horse shot under him, on the 31st, and his clothes completely riddled with bullets. He nevertheless stood by throughout, and ably and gallantly performed his duty. The conduct of Colonel Harker was equally brave and efficient. They have each commanded brigades for nearly a year now, and it seems to me that common justice demands that they now receive the promotion they have so gallantly earned. Colonel Buell came in command of the 1st brigade in consequence of my taking command of the division, and, although comparatively inexperienced, he performed every duty gallantly and well. All the officers of the division, with a single exception, behaved gallantly and did well, therefore I need not discriminate. The exception was Colonel John W. Blake, of the 40th Indiana, and I consider it my duty to draw the line of distinction broad and deep between those who do well and those who prove recreant. He became so drunk as to be unfit for duty before going into action on the 31st, and was sent to the rear in arrest by his immediate commander, Colonel Wagner. The next that was heard of him he was in Nashville, claiming to be wounded and a paroled prisoner. For this bad conduct I recommend that he be dishonorably discharged the service. For more minute particulars, and for a complete report of the part performed by the different brigades, I refer you to the reports of brigade commanders, herewith enclosed. My staff officers, including Captains Palmer and Bestow of General Wood's staff, not heretofore mentioned by me, all performed their duty gallantly and ably assisted me in every way possible.

I would also refer to my report as brigade commander, as that gives more in detail and more truthfully than any other report the operations of Colonel Wagner's and my brigade on the 31st, they being both under my personal observation and control after the heavy fighting commenced that day.

The casualties in the division were as follows:

The 1st brigade went into action with seventy-one officers and one thousand four hundred and fifty-four enlisted men, and lost—Officers: killed, 4; wounded, 21. Enlisted men: killed, 42; wounded, 278; missing, 34.

The 2d brigade went into action with eighty-six officers and one thousand three hundred and eighty-nine enlisted men, and lost—Officers: killed, 2; wounded, 18. Enlisted men: killed, 54; wounded, 269; missing, 32.

The 3d brigade went into action with ninety-seven officers and one thousand seven hundred and ninety enlisted men, including the 6th Ohio battery, and lost—Officers: killed, 5; wounded, 17. Enlisted men: killed, 104; wounded, 312; missing, 101.

Recapitulation.

The division went into action with two hundred and fifty-four commissioned officers and four thousand six hundred and thirty-three enlisted men, and lost—Officers: killed, 11; wounded, 56. Enlisted men: killed, 200; wounded, 859; missing, 167. Total killed, 211; wounded, 915; missing, 167. Total killed, wounded, and missing in the division, 1,293.

All which is respectfully submitted.

MILO T. HASCALL,
Brigadier General Volunteers, Commanding 1st Division, Left Wing.

Official: E. R. KERSTETTER,
Captain and Assistant Adjutant General.

Major LYNE STARLING,
Assistant Adjutant General, Left Wing.

HEADQUARTERS 1ST DIVISION, LEFT WING,
Murfreesboro', January 17, 1863.

In the hurry of making out my official report as division commander I neglected to allude to the very valuable services rendered by Surgeon W. W. Blair, medical director of this division, during and since the recent battles. His services were such as merit special commendation, and I desire that this may be forwarded as a part of my report in justice to Dr. Blair. He reports to me that all the regimental surgeons were efficient and rendered valuable service.

I am, sir, respectfully,

MILO T. HASCALL,
Brigadier General Volunteers, Commanding 1st Division, Left Wing.

Major STARLING,
Assistant Adjutant General, Left Wing.

HEADQUARTERS 1ST DIVISION, LEFT WING,
Murfreesboro', January 10, 1863.

Having just received the report of the batteries attached to my division, I hasten to forward them to the general, in order that he may allude to them in his report as their merits deserve. It will be seen by their reports that they all did their duty nobly, with perhaps a single exception on the part of one of the officers attached to Estep's battery. I allude to Richard H. Jervis, 2d lieutenant of that battery, who behaved badly throughout the entire four days' action. I recommend that he be dishonorably discharged the service on account of this bad conduct. I have already alluded to the distinguished services of these batteries both in my brigade and division reports, and only desire further to add that, with the exception above alluded to, the conduct of both officers and men was admirable. Particular credit is due to Major Race, in command of the batteries, for the gallantry and good judgment displayed by him throughout the entire four days. The conduct of Stokes's battery, in firing upon Bradley's battery on the 2d of January, was such as, in my judgment, demands immediate investigation, in order that the parties guilty of such gross carelessness may be properly punished.

I am, sir, most respectfully,

MILO T. HASCALL,
Brigadier General Volunteers, Commanding 1st Division, Left Wing.

Major STARLING,
Assistant Adjutant General, Left Wing.

ARTILLERY HEADQUARTERS 1ST DIVISION, LEFT WING,
January 7, 1863.

DEAR SIR: I have the honor to submit to you the official report of the commanding officers of the batteries of this division. About 9 o'clock a. m. of the 31st December, 1862, Captain Cullen Bradley, 6th Ohio light battery, by orders moved his battery, with Harker's brigade, to the extreme right of our lines, where they engaged the enemy's artillery (two four-gun batteries supposed) and infantry in a most severely contested battle. Before superior numbers of the enemy, the brigade and battery (after repulsing the first attack of the enemy) were oblige to retire, but not without disputing every inch of ground, Captain

Bradley being obliged to leave two of his guns on the field. They were soon after retaken by the 13th Michigan, Colonel Shoemaker, whose timely support forced the enemy to retire. Captain Bradley's battery was under my immediate observation, and the conduct of Captain Bradley, his subordinate officers, and men was such as to entitle them to great credit. The conduct of this battery on the 2d January, under the fire of three batteries of the enemy, was gallant in the extreme. The enemy's batteries were nearly silenced, when Captain Stokes's battery opened, 300 yards in rear of Bradley, with canister, at a distance of at least twenty-two hundred yards from the enemy's guns. Captain Bradley had five men and five horses wounded by their fire, and was obliged to retire. I respectfully ask an investigation into the conduct of Stokes's battery on this occasion. Captain J. B. Cox, 10th Indiana battery, and Lieutenant George Estep, commanding 8th Indiana battery, were closely engaged during the battle of the 31st December, on the left of our lines, supported by General Hascall's and Colonel Wagner's brigades. Captain Cox was under the fire of three batteries of the enemy for seven hours during the day, but succeeded in administering to them all in a manner perfectly satisfactory to me, and to the great discomfiture of the enemy. On the 2d January, when in position on the right, he repulsed with canister a desperate charge of a brigade of the enemy's infantry. Captain Cox, his officers, and men behaved with great gallantry and bravery. Lieutenant Estep's battery, by a free use of case shot and canister, on the 31st December, succeeded in repulsing three successive charges of the enemy's infantry, and otherwise during the three day's battle did most excellent service. Lieutenant Estep, Lieutenant Voris and Winsor, and the non-commissioned officers and men of this battery, with few exceptions, behaved with commendable coolness and bravery. Lieutenant Richard Jervis acted in a most cowardly manner. I will devote a special communication to his case.

For full particulars of the engagements and losses I respectfully refer you to the accompanying reports of battery commanders.

Respectfully submitted,

S. RACE,
Major, Chief of Artillery 1st Division, Left Wing.

Captain E. R. KERSTETTER,
Assistant Adjutant General.

On the morning of the 31st December I was ordered to move my battery across the railroad (my left was then resting on the railroad) and prepare for battle. I immediately obeyed by crossing and placing the right section immediately on the left of the railroad, and the left and centre sections about two hundred yards further north. The entire battery then engaged a battery of the enemy immediately in front, which we compelled to cease firing. Simultaneously with this two other batteries opened upon us, and shortly afterwards were joined by the one that had been silenced. They completely showered the shot and shell, but with little damage. This unequal contest was kept up for about four hours, and was only deviated from on the appearance of heavy columns of their troops, upon which we would open the entire battery and disperse them in great disorder. We would then resume the work on their artillery. About 1 o'clock p. m. I relieved one section of the battery at a time for a short time, to retire for ammunition. They came up again to the work supplied with ammunition, when the engagement was renewed somewhat similar to the fight in the forenoon, except that more frequently we had to drive back their infantry. About 3 o'clock my ammunition was exhausted, with the exception of canister, which I ordered they should hold to disperse a large force then bearing down on us in front. We held our fire until they were within four hundred yards, when we could completely see the devices on their colors. We completely broke up their lines and scattered them in great disorder over the field in front. Being then only under fire of their batteries, and having no projectiles to reach them, I withdrew from the field. When near the hospital, about one-fourth of a mile in the rear of my former position, I discovered the enemy's skirmishers deployed out and advancing. I at once drove them back with canister. During the day I silenced each one of the batteries in my front and on my flank several times. They had a cross fire on us during the entire day. We were at one time fighting four batteries, but my men, not the least disheartened, were determined to hold their position at all hazards, which one, I believe, was the only one held by any battery on the field. On this day I had one man killed and six slightly wounded.

On the 1st of January I was removed to the right wing, and about 10 o'clock drove back a brigade of infantry who were advancing. On the 2d day of January, in the evening, our skirmishers were thrown forward and drew the fire of a brigade in ambush. This we expected, and had prepared by cutting the fuzes the proper length and getting the proper elevation and range, and showered their ranks with shrapnell, every one bursting precisely at the spot needed. They became badly disorganized and fled in great disorder.

To Lieutenants Naylor, Cox, Cosner, and Clifford, I return my warmest thanks for their coolness, gallantry, and promptness in obeying commands. Their actions deserve the highest commendation.

To my sergeants and corporals, and to the members of my battery, too much could not be said. They fought gallantry for seven hours, and until they were completely exhausted from their excessive labor; but it is enough to say that the whole battery, men and officers, did their whole duty as soldiers, and maintained their original position on the 31st against three, and part of the time four batteries, and the determined charges of the enemy's troops. The battle-field in front is the witness of their execution.

All of which is respectfully submitted.

CAPTAIN J. B. COX,
10th Indiana Battery.

Major RACE,
Chief of Art'y, 1st Div'n of Left Wing of the Army of the Cumberland.

[Annexed is a list of casualties.]

Killed.—William Wooley.

Wounded.—Sergeant Cox, in leg; Private Bryden, in toe; Private Arnold, in shoulder, very slight; Private Shable, in hip, very slight.

HEADQUARTERS 6TH OHIO BATTERY, ON BATTLE-FIELD,
Near Murfreesboro', Tennessee, January 5, 1863.

SIR: have the honor to submit the following official report of the engagement of December 30 and 31, 1862, and January 1 and 2, 1863, viz: At 8 o'clock a. m., December 30, 1862, the battery was put in position on the left bank of Stone river, and near camp, and engaged a four-gun battery of the enemy at a range of fifteen hundred yards, who held a high, strong, and commanding position on the opposite bank of the river, and silenced the enemy's battery after an engagement of fifteen minutes, expending seventy-two rounds of shell and solid shot, sustaining no damage except the loss of one sponge bucket, struck by an enemy's shot. At 8 p. m., December 31, the battery, in accordance to rders, proceeded to the right of our lines. At 10.30 a. m. engaged two four-gun batteries of the enemy, supported by two brigades of infantry, at a range of two hundred and fifty yards. We received a galling fire from the infantry as well as the batteries. We held our position twenty minutes, pouring a heavy and destructive fire upon the infantry, at the same time engaging the batteries with good effect, expending one hundred and fifty rounds of case shot and canister, and sustained a loss of one man wounded, and two horses killed. Our left flank having been turned, I retired my battery and took a position five hundred yards in the rear; again opened upon the enemy, (with case and canister,) who were advancing in force; after an engagement of five minutes, and expending twelve rounds of ammunition, I was again compelled to retire my battery and abandon two pieces of the battery, one of which I had spiked, (since removed,) and sustaining a loss of one man killed, two men wounded, and one man missing; also eight horses killed and three wounded. About this time Colonel Shoemaker charged the enemy with the 13th Michigan regiment, driving them off the field and recovering the guns, and for which Colonel Shoemaker should receive full credit.

About 8 a. m., January 1, 1863, I again changed position to the front lines, and, in conjuuction with several batteries, opened upon the enemy with case-shot and shell, at a range of two thousand yards, driving them back, expending fifty-four rounds of ammunition and sustaining no damage. January 2, while occupying a position on the front line, the enemy advanced eighteen guns, (supposed,) and opened fire upon my battery with solid shot and shell. About 8 a. m. I was supported upon the right by two six-gun batteries, which gave way early in the action and retired. I silenced the enemy's guns and held the position, expending one hundred and seventy-seven rounds of ammunition, and sustaining a loss of five men wounded, five horses killed, and three horses wounded. About this time Captain Stokes's Chicago battery opened upon my battery several rounds of canister, from a position two hundred and fifty yards in rear, and from which I sustained much damage. At 2 p. m. the enemy advanced a heavy column upon our left lines, and supported by two four-gun batteries. My battery took a strong position, and opened upon the enemy at a range of three thousand yards, with good effect, expending thirty-five rounds of shell, and sustaining no damage. I take pleasure in noticing the promptness and coolness displayed by First Lieutenant O. H. P. Ayres, Second Lieutenant A. P. Baldwin, and First Sergeant G. W. Smetts for the manner in which they managed their respective sections; Lieutenant Ayres having been slightly wounded, also his horse being wounded, and Lieutenant Baldwin having his horse shot.

The following non-commissioned officers and privates greatly distinguished themselves, viz: Sergeants G. W. Howard, H. Hartman, T. O. Casey, S. Miller, and J. Hersh; Corporals N. Poole, H. A. Collier, and Acting Corporal S. O. Kimbrick. Corporal E. H. Neal is entitled to much credit for the promptness and carefulness he displayed in keeping the caissons well screened and for keeping the battery well supplied with ammunition. Privates W. C. Stough, J. Robinett, D. H. Evans, J. G. Banger, and Frank Leslie greatly distinguished themselves. The whole company, with but few exceptions, displayed great coolness and are entitled to much credit.

Enclosed find statement of losses in the battery.

Respectfully,

CULLEN BRADLEY,

Captain, Commanding 6th Ohio Light Battery.

Major T. RACE, *Commanding Artillery,*

1st Division, 14th Army Corps, Department of the Cumberland.

Expended 500 rounds of ammunition during the several engagements.

December 31, 1862.—Private S. M. Scott, killed; Sergeant G. W. Howard, mortally wounded, since died; Privates Willard Cory, lost right arm; J. Cackler, slightly wounded in right hand; and William Barr, missing.

January 2, 1863.—Lieutenant O. H. P. Ayres, wounded in left arm, slightly; Sergeant S. Miller, arm, severely; Corporals J. Hersh, left arm, severely; H. A. Collier, head, slightly; and Private R. Caldwell, right arm, severely, attached from the 21st brigade. Private J. Baird, right leg, severely.

Horses killed during the several engagements, 16; wounded, 5.

The above statement I believe to be correct.

CULLEN BRADLEY,
Captain, Commanding 6th Ohio Light Battery.

P. S.—The following men were wounded by the fire of Captain Stokes's battery, viz: Sergeants Hersh and Miller, and Corporal Collier; Privates Caldwell and Baird, and five horses. I desire an investigation, that the blame may rest upon the right person that caused the battery opened.

HEADQUARTERS EIGHTH INDIANA BATTERY,
In the field, near Murfreesboro', Tennessee, January 4, 1863.

I have the honor respectfully to submit the following official report of the 8th Indiana light battery on the 31st day of December, 1862, and the 1st and 2d days of January, 1863.

I put my battery in position on Wednesday morning about 9 o'clock, by order of General Rosecrans, on the west side of the railroad, supported on the right by two batteries, and on the left by the 19th infantry, (regulars;) fired 114 rounds (at a range of 800 yards) at the enemy, who were driving back our infantry advance. I then advanced the battery seventy-five or eighty yards, supported, as in the first position, by the two batteries on my right and the 19th infantry on my left. At this position the enemy in three lines made three desperate charges, and were as often repulsed by my battery. I expended 70 rounds of canister, and was compelled four or five times to double charge the pieces in order to drive the enemy; this beginning at a range of 90 yards, and increasing as the enemy became confused and retired. I also fired from this position 106 rounds of shrapnell and solid shot, at a range of about 800 yards, at the lines of the enemy advancing on our right. I then received an order from General Hascall, commanding the brigade of the division, to take a position on the left of the pike in the direction of Murfreesboro', which I did, supported by his entire brigade, *as good soldiers as ever went to battle.* I commenced firing at a range of 400 yards, the enemy bringing up his forces in three lines, and making desperate charges on the centre, but was repulsed by my battery and the gallant men of General Hascall's brigade. I was twice in this position, and fired 226 rounds, my men all the time exposed to a galling fire of musketry. Late in the afternoon I was ordered to a position on the east side of the railroad, supported by three regiments of the 26th Ohio, 57th Indiana, and an Illinois regiment. Here I expended 66 rounds, shelling the enemy from the woods, near the creek, from which he had driven a portion of our troops during the afternoon. I remained in this position until after dark, and then retired to the camp of the previous night. Loss during the day eight horses killed and disabled, and four men wounded.

On the morning of the 1st of January I was put in position before daylight, in line of battle, by Major Race. An hour or two after daylight the enemy commenced an advance on our front; I opened fire, in connexion with other batteries, and drove him back; no loss during the day; expended forty-six rounds. Remained in position all night, and on the morning of the 2d expended thirty-four rounds, shelling the woods at different points, where the enemy could occasionally be seen from my position. About 9 o'clock my battery was fired upon by two rebel batteries, (12 guns supposed,) at a range of 2,000 yards; it being beyond my range I was forced to retire my battery, leaving for the time being two pieces on the field. Some of the horses of one of the limbers were severely wounded, and became so badly frightened by the bursting of the enemy's shell that the drivers were unable to control them; they ran to the rear in spite of every effort made to bring them to the pieces. I was not long, however, in recovering both pieces, after repairing the loss of horses in the battery from the battery and forge wagons. I remained quiet in line until about 4 o'clock. I was then ordered to take a position on the left, which I did. I was well supported by infantry, but do not know what troops they were. I commenced firing, at a range of about 700 yards, at what I supposed to be a brigade of the enemy's infantry holding a point of woods; I am positive that my battery from this position did the enemy great injury; expended 123 rounds. I retired the battery for ammunition, and again took a position to the left of my first and near the creek; here I engaged a rebel battery at a range of 900 yards, and succeeded in silencing it, expending 86 rounds. We soon after crossed the creek and remained during the night.

I am sorry to say that Second Lieutenant Richard Jervis, on Wednesday, at a trying and critical moment, retired a section of my battery without my order or knowledge, and that he otherwise behaved badly during the day. He claimed, on the morning of the second day's fight, to be unwell, but said (this was before daylight) if he should feel better in the course of an hour or two he would come out to the field and report for duty; this was the last I saw of him till the fight was over; I am informed that he went back to the rear to one of the hospitals.

First Lieutenant Jeremiah Voris and Second Lieutenant Samuel Winsor have my thanks for their efficient service at all times during the engagement; they were brave and unflinching in the discharge of duty. I am also indebted to Orderly Sergeant William Stokes for the promptness with which he supplied the battery with ammunition. My sergeants, corporals, and men, with three exceptions, behaved with commendable coolness and bravery.

I am, very respectfully, your obedient servant,

GEORGE ESTEP,
First Lieutenant, Commanding 8th Indiana Battery.

Major S. RACE,
Commanding Artillery of First Division, Left Wing.

I neglected to state that my loss on the third day was four men wounded, eleven horses killed and disabled.

ESTEP.

List of wounded.

Sergeant Henry F. Smith, severely. Corporals William Hamilton, severely; Joseph Mauriscen, slightly. Privates Adam Hershner, severely, (attached from 13th Michigan regiment;) Robert Otto, slightly; Middleton H. Hargrave, slightly; Henry Shuler, slightly, (attached from 26th Ohio regiment;) Cornelius Daisey, slightly, (attached from 56th Ohio regiment.)

List of killed and wounded, 1*st division, left wing,* 14*th army corps, in the battle before Murfreesboro', as reported by A. J. Phelps, medical director, left wing.*

TWENTY-SIXTH REGIMENT OHIO VOLUNTEERS.

Wounded. —Brigadier General T. J. Woods.

Killed.—First Lieutenant G. D. McClelland, company G. First Sergeant B. Putnam, company K. Corporals F. Singer, company H, and William D. Chandley, company B. Privates O. Mullen, company A; John Allen, company I; J. Goodhue, company C; J. Kanns, J. Fag, and Sergeant J. Jennings, company G.

Wounded.—2d Lieutenant L. B. Foster, company A, left leg below knee, severely; 2d Lieutenant F. M. Williams, company K. Sergeant F. B. Hart, company A, contusion right knee, slightly; Corporal J. W. Cooley, middle finger, right hand, slightly; Privates P. Hatchfield, right leg, both bones fractured, severely; P. Mea, side and shoulder contused; J. Bower, left arm contused, slightly; M. Boyer, left arm contused, slightly; C. W. Carson, right arm contused, severely; C. Thoughro, right leg fractured, fibula, died, tetanus, January 7; Jesse Stutesman, left index finger, slightly; H. Shuler, right leg, both bones fractured; G. Kinch, thumb and cheek, slightly, company A. First Sergeant William L. Heiser, company B, shoulder contused by shell, severely; Sergeants J. W. Ruley, left hand severely lacerated; A. Rodgers, left hand, severely; Corporal J. B. Doyle, left hip, severely; Privates William H. Cook, left leg, severely; S. Connor, right thigh and hand, severely; J. Castell, right leg, severely; C. Carmean, slightly; T. Donahue, slightly; J. Finley, both thighs, severely; A. James, scalp, severely; J. Warshlaff, leg; R. P. Pinkerton, right leg; H. Renick, left shoulder, slightly; J. Simmes, right foot; N. Teems, mortal, died January 7, 1863; J. Van Gundy, company B, chin, slightly. J. Sherwood, mortally; C. Martin, left knee, severely; A. T. Brown, left chest, severely; J. Ashburn, right thigh and leg; and A. Taylor, right hand, company C. Sergeant D. McKensie, right leg, severely; Privates H. McGrath; A. G. Beer, right leg amputated, upper third; J. Gregg, left arm, severely; J. Brown, J. Roberts, right chest, company D. Corporal L. Reed, right leg, slightly; Privates J. Mishey, left hip lacerated by shell, severely; and H. Stounom, left hand and right side, severely, company E. Sergeants A. Turner, left leg; and A. Gonner, right forearm, company F. Corporals A. C. Tillett, left foot; F. Scarborough, left forearm and fractured near elbow; Privates M. Brill, E. Thompson, right hand, severely; R. Thomas, company F, left shoulder contused; Corporal W. Cusbaum, mortally; Privates J. F. Evans, left cheek, severely; J. M. Morgan, right hand, slightly; F. McCormick, left forearm contused; J. Mosher, right leg, severely; J. Moore; J. Ritter, J. S. Williams, elbow joint implicated; C. Daisey, left arm fractured, humeris; and J. Rees, right side above hip, severely, company G. C. Bartholomew, mortally; J. Castle, right leg severely; H. Martin, left arm, slightly; J. Thatcher, and C. Chapman, left hand, two fingers amputated, company H. Privates G. Best, face, slightly; J. Graham, right thigh and leg, severely; J. Oliver, head, slightly; and H. D. Posts, right arm, slightly, company I. Corporals J. Moore, left thigh, severely; and J. Morris, left thumb shot off, company K. Privates W. Singer, right thigh and left leg; W. Steele, left elbow joint; Z. Powell, forefinger, slightly; D. Crisman and D. Laughlin, left hand, slightly, company K. Privates Samuel Chestnut, slightly, and Abram Knapp, slightly, company B. Charles Davis, finger; and W. Worlem, left ankle contused, company C. Private Arthur Glenn, left leg fractured, severely, company G. Privates Lyman A. Cook, right side, slightly; and Adam Gasage, hand, slightly, company C.

SIXTY-FOURTH OHIO VOLUNTEERS.

Killed.—Captain J. B. Sweet, company K; Sergeant John McIlvain; Corporal William B. Robinson; Privates Daniel Slater, John Kelso, James Eckless, and Charles M. Hetherington, company A. Corporal John Bensy; Privates Jacob Walter, John Ward, and George Snyder, company B. Corporals Levi Dare, and William Bober; Private William Phillips, company C. Privates S. Hem and Reuben Ramsay, company F. Privates Abraham Bretz, B. H. Ross, David Geese, and D. Cunen, company H. Privates James Kaliker and Nicholas Baker, company I. Sergeant And. Bumgarden and Private Patrick McMay, company K.

Wounded.—Privates Andrew Laird, left foot, severely; Reuben Hulit, leg, slightly; and Jason Thorp, hand, slightly, company A. Sergeants Henry Partridge, leg, slightly; and A. C. Crammer, foot, slightly, company B; Corporal Charles Partridge, hand, slightly; Privates Almond Partridge, hand, severely; William Brown, both legs, mortally; Jacob Helbert, mortally; John Smith, legs, slightly; and William Freese, head, slightly, company B. Privates William Ebly, leg, severely; Ephraim Simpson; Thomas Gatton, ankle, amputated; George Stewart, lumbar region, slightly; and Martin Bonser, company C. Private James Irwin, shoulder, company D. Privates Hinton M. Barns, finger, slightly; Peter Hass, leg, resection; Henry Applegate, leg, severely; John Kersh, knee, slightly; Noah W. Coyle, shoulder, severely; Thomas Barkinson, leg, slightly; and Alonzo Akins, company E. Privates Eli Wilson, both hands, severely; Andrew Peters, breast. Corporal Daniel Majors, thigh. Privates Asa Farnum, thigh; John Lockhart, wrist, slightly; John Broshans, left breast, severely; Albert Gun, John Long, and Marion Trimble, abdomen, slightly, company F. Private Joseph Erborn, foot, severely; and Corporal Osborne, foot, slightly, company G. Sergeant William Ritchie, arm. Privates Daniel Ruhle, left cheek; Daniel Manar, thigh, severely; George Marvin; Peter Weston, ankle, severely; George H. Cummings, hand, slightly; and Henry Shatzer, left breast, company H. Private George Marshall, thigh, severely; Corporal Jefferson Houser, leg, severely; Privates Patrick Powers, hand, slightly; John Stukey, breast, slightly; Henry Dittenhafer, leg, severely; Thomas Duford, abdomen, mortal; and Timothy Dugan, company I. Privates Lewis Sily, leg, severely; Samuel Hantzten, neck, mortal; and John Ashcraff, company K. Lieutenant and Adjutant Chauncey Woodruff, leg, severely. Lieutenant Warner Young, ankle, severely, company E. Lieutenant Joseph Ferguson, company I, thigh, severely.

Summary.—Killed, 24; wounded, 55—total, 79.

THIRD REGIMENT KENTUCKY INFANTRY.

Killed.—Colonel Samuel M'Kee, and Private George Jokes, company A; Sergeant S. Collier and Corporal Henry Lynch, company B; Corporal Daniel Cox, company C; Corporal Hugh Carter and William Dye, company D; Sergeant M. Buster, Corporal A. J. Hughes, B. F. Coffey, and Private A. Booker, company H; Privates Green Williams and Martin A. Vankuk, company K.

Wounded.—Captain Daniel R. Collier, leg, slight, company B; Captain L. H. Ralston, leg, severe, company C; Lieutenant B. F. Powell, ankle, slight, company A; Lieutenant W. J. Hogan, ankle, slight, company B; Lieutenant Mathew Cullin, knee, severe, company D; Lieutenant C. F. Gumstead, hip, severe, company E; Lieutenant Daniel Severance, leg amputated, mortal, company F; 1st Lieutenant James M. Bristow, right leg, severe, and 2d Lieutenant H. B. Carter, right leg, sever, company H; 1st Lieutenant Joseph Carson, right arm, slight; and 2d Lieutenant William D. Murray, knee, slight, company I. Corporal John Jones, left ankle, severe, company A; Corporal Thomas C. Griffith, hand, slight; Privates James Gibson, head, severe; Joseph Adams, hip, severe;

Corpora l William Childers, shoulder, slight; Corporal Thomas Price, hand, severe; Corporal Samuel Cowe, shoulder, slight; Private Thomas Smith, face, slight; Private Lorrey Jackson, foot, slight; Sergeant John Brough, foot, slight; Privates William Connelly, shoulder, and William Forbes, shoulder, severe, company B; Sergeant R. D. Compton, left thigh, severe; Corporal Wesley Tarten, side, slight; Private W. Baston, right wrist, slight; Private Thomas Dick, hand, severe, company C. Company D: Corporals William Chumely, leg, severely; Joseph Rainwater, hand, slight; John Harlton, hand, slight; Silas Rainwater, hip; Joseph Hopper, shoulder. Company E: Sergeants George W. Cleck, arm; Olin C. Yates, leg; Privates Henry Rybee, breast; William M. Baston, arm; William Long, thigh; A. E. Hurt, forearm; P. H. Baston, left side; Fayette Hunt, hand; James M. Estes, shoulder, and M. H. Watson, leg. Company F: Privates Samuel Powell, arm; John E. Dougherty, hand fractured; James R. Head, shoulder; Corporal John L. Ball, shoulder; Privates Reuben Delaney, left arm; John C. Dollins, right leg; John Mason, left arm; George Severance, hip and groin; James Hendrickson, right shoulder; William Wardlow, left arm; John W. Leach, left arm; William Playforth, right knee; John C. Cogle, thigh; James L. Payne, head; Lewis Rose, thigh; J. P. Ballard, thigh; James Dishon, thigh. Company G: Corporals A. Hereford, foot fractured; J. P. Ropplewell, left arm; Adrian River, left arm; Reuben Weston, knee fractured; Privates J. A. Hann, both legs; John A. Sutherland, left groin; Stuben Rexorat, head; Thomas Hadley, left leg; Sim. Cox, side. Company I: Sergeants L. Ellis, chin and shoulder; David Stevens, right side; Corporal Barnett Hayes, forefinger; Privates R. Risley, shoulder; Edward McPherson, arm; James Cummings, face. Company H: Privates L. G. Lampler, left shoulder; Joseph Griffin, right arm; M. P. Pitman, right arm; Thomas Ballard, right arm; J. C. Sutherland, right arm; Andrew Carter, neck and shoulder; Edward Pryor, hip; Thomas Stockton, right elbow; Simpson Pilty, arm; William Pilty, breast; John Pryor, arm. Company K: Sergeant Henry J. Nickols, right shoulder; Corporal Eli Wells, hand; Privates J. P. A. Tickleter, right thigh; Samuel P. Watson, arm, and Charles Lawson, arm.

Killed, 13; wounded, 90—total, 103.

FIFTY-FIRST INDIANA REGIMENT.

Killed.—Corporal William Duckworth; Privates Joseph Servis and David Budd, company A; George W. Holbrook, company F, and Sergeant S. J. Beard, company H.

Wounded.—Privates John Stout, side, ribs fractured, and Joseph Fleece, leg, slightly, company A; Robert Gore, shoulder, severely, company B; Reuben Templeton, hand, and Joseph A. Mundy, mortally, company C; Martin J. Phillips, leg; John Byers, arm; Hennan Buchsthall, groin, slightly; J. M. Peck, hip, slightly, and A. L. Hewitt, knee joint, severely, company E; Corporal Lewis Leywell, shoulder contused, and Privates Henry Nepper, hip, slightly; G. J. Smith, hand, slightly, and Thomas Ferris, hand, slightly, company F; Captain T. M. Constant, hand, and Private Harvey Ward, mortally, company G; Lieutenant Alfred Gude, leg; Sergeant Thomas A. Kieth, thigh, slightly; Corporal William Roberts, hand, slightly; Privates M. Hollingsworth, hand, slightly; Franklin Jerrold, arm, slightly; Aaron Wolverton, hand, slightly; W. W. Bruce, hand, slightly; George W. McKinley, side, slightly; J. R. Edmunds, hand, slightly; James H. Cable, hand, slightly, and Daniel A. McKee, arm, slightly, company H; Privates J. J. Jater, leg; John Trimble, leg; Nathan Riley, arm, slightly; Andrew Roach, shoulder, mortally; M. D. Losey, hand, slightly, and James Aldrich, company I; Privates Jerome Dyas, arm, slightly, and Samuel Measton, mortally, company K.

Summary.—Killed, 5; wounded, 36—total 41.

SEVENTY-THIRD INDIANA REGIMENT.

Killed.—Privates Edmund Welch and John Early, company A; Privates W. H. Moore, Hiram Babcock, J. Brittenham, and George Pall, company C; Captain Miles Tibbits, Private H. Tibbets, and Gilbert Warren, company F; Captain Peter Doyle, and Privates Henry Thornton and John Fidler, company H; W. H. Hardee, G. McCurdy, and John Brown, company I; Privates C. Agustral, James McNally, J. F. Stephens, Cary Weston, and Wiley W. Peck, company K.

Wounded.—Major William Kimball; Lieutenant E. Williamson, thigh, severely, company I; Privates George Clark, side, slightly; E. S. Evans, and Martin Nicholas, company A; Privates Samuel Moon, shoulder severely, and Henry Shultz, company B; Privates Frederick Stone, ankle, fractured tibia; Jacob Lay, hip, slightly; Egbert Truman, thigh, severely; Moses Alonzo, thumb, severely; Ezra Martin, Samuel D. Martyr, W. W. Fulmer, and John A. Ronig, foot, company C; Privates S. Primly, head, severely, and S. M. Reeler, ear, slightly, company D; Privates H. W. Smith, breast and shoulder, and S. A. Samuelson, shoulder, severely, company E; Privates W. M. Genard, thigh; Daniel G. Long, arm; Peter Jacobs, thigh and hip; Andrew Jacobs, elbow; S. B. Fife, leg; William Vooris, leg, and Joseph Wirgale, company F; Privates John Kills, elbow, severely, and William Elmer, thigh, severely, company G; Privates C. H. Wight, hip and abdomen; Christian Kelmer, arm and shoulder; Oscar McIlvain, wrist and arm, severely; Thornton Tyson, head, slightly; Abner Healy, leg, severely, and Samuel Burns, company H; Privates James H. Reed, hip; John J. Asher, hip; William F. Iseminger, thigh, slightly; Stephen Thorton, finger, slightly; John C. Sone, finger, and H. W. Adams, company I; Privates James Brown, side, slightly; Henry Kilburn, shoulder and back, severely; C. S. Goodwin, arm slightly; Charles Warren, head, severely, and William Reynolds, fracture of skull, company K; Privates Ephraim F. Lane, company C; John H. Sapp, company D; Jacob Kudig, back, company E; James Stickling, back, severely, company F; William McDougle, knee, severely, company G; Adam E. Sanderson, arm, severely, and John F. Hood, thigh, severely, company H; H. W. Adams, thigh, severely, company I.

FIFTY-SEVENTH INDIANA REGIMENT.

Killed.—Private S. D. Fort, company A; Private John Barket, company B; Privates Thornton Freeman and Calim Warhold, company D; Privates Wesley W. Seward and Edmund Gregory, company F; Privates Andrew Rhodes and J. Anderson, company G; Privates Thomas Orr and John Penland, company K.

Wounded.—Colonel C. C. Hines, right thigh, severely; Lieutenant Colonel G. W. Leonard, leg, severely; Adjutant Henry C. Elliott, breast, severely; Lieutenant S. F. Smith, ankle, severely, company F; Captain C. W. Burket, head, slightly, company I; Lieutenant S. J. Teel, hip, slightly, company K; Corporal Joseph Brooks, arm, and Privates G. Tist, right thigh, and Martin B. Thom, both knees, company A; Privates George Minor, right thigh; Amos Draker, left leg, flesh-wound; Frank M. Hunt, head, flesh-wound, and Henry C. Hunt, arm, flesh-wound, company B; Privates Merritt Lamb, left hip; John Osborn, left hip, flesh-wound; Albert Jeffries, arm; M. K. Martin, right hip, company C; Privates B. F. Chewworth, right hand; Elias Manning, leg, severely; Pole Ritchie, arm, severely, and John Emman, company D; Privates John Fitz, mortally; Solomon Raymond, right hand, severely; Abraham McConnell, face, and Thomas Bules, right foot, severely, company E; Corporal Dewitt Mackell, right leg, severely; Sergeant A. G. Hardin, hand, slight; Privates Alonzo McLaughlin, left arm, severely; William Graves, shoulder, and Henry

Cloud, hand, company F; Sergeant B. F. Rhodes, hand, and Privates C. S. Edmunds, left knee, and J. M. Cooper, hand, severely, company G; Sergeant William Smith, right arm, and Privates Elias D. Green, head, O. S. Preble, leg, severely, and P. S. McKenny, hand, slight, company H; Sergeant C. A. Thomburgh, thigh, slight; Corporal Parker Terrill, head, slight, and Privates George Barney, left thigh, John W. White, arm, and M. Galloway, right hand, company I; Sergeants M. J. Cram and S. A. Brown, left side of neck; Corporal J. Stealy, hip; Privates George Method, hip; M. Baulk, right arm; William Buderhistle, right arm; John Staley, hip, severely; Hiram Meed, foot, severely; Hiram Leman, arm; L. B. Baker, arm; John Rink, shoulder, severely; John Goodnight, leg, slight; O. L. Bear, right arm; George Holdman, shoulder; Z. Hendrickson, thigh; M. R. Phillips, thumb; George W. Creame, shoulder, and George W. Butcher, shoulder, company K; First Sergeant W. H. McLaughlin, left cheek, company A.

Summary.—Killed, 10; wounded, 61—total, 71.

FIFTEENTH INDIANA VOLUNTEERS.

Killed.—Sergeant Richard Kesler, Corporal Ed. Palmer, and Privates John Curran, James Williams, and Henry Hoaglin, company A; Sergeant —— Lanberger, Corporal Jonas Hoover, and Privates Henry Cooper, Michael Hennesy, and Frank Markle, company B; Privates John Frazer, John A. Morgan, William Livergood, Henry McDougal, Fred'k Myers, and R. Barney, company C; Captain R. J. Templeton, Corporal J. A. Williams, Privates C. M. Brishong and C. P. Huff, company D; Privates John A. Small, Emery Williams, Abram Littinger, and Henry Staffin, company E; Private William R. Conrad, company F; Privates George W. Moore, P. H. Madden, John Junglius, and Jesse Venters, company H; Privates William Mayer, William Cockfair, John Davis, and Jeff. Wolf, company I; Sergeant Mathias M. Dickey, and Privates Isaac A. Chambers, Isaac Lebo, William Kneefick, Esau Fisher, and Robert B. Simpson, company K.

Wounded.—Company A: Lieutenant Alonzo Pearce, deafened by explosion of shell; Sergeant Clayton Podd, hand; Privates D. Phipps, hand; Henry Allen, ankle; Hirden Barksdale, hand; Christopher Boan, chest; W. R. Brown, thigh; Lewis Crane, thigh; E. Erwin, thigh; Simon Downey, thigh; C. D. Crane, hip; Peter Edrubum, back; Michael Griffin, chest; William Hayler, thigh; George Leath, hand; Ira Treadwell, hand. Company B: Captain J. E. George, spine; First Sergeant William A. Pegg, hand; Corporal Jacob Telford, side; Privates W. H. Hogle, chest; James Parks, side; P. T. Clark, side; Peter Clogham, hip; John Garesty, hip; William Hill, hip; Ed. Huntinger, face; Robert Logan, hip; Chreffield Lucia, thigh; William Melvin, arm; Henry Shearer, hand; Jas. Sweeny, leg. Company C: Lieutenant J. P. Monroe, abdomen; Sergeants William Dougal, scrotum, and L. A. Foster, shoulder; Corporals J. E. Threadgall, arm, and J. M. Brewer, arm; Privates David Boyle, head; William A. Daffron, leg; Bruce Dolson, leg; Jos. Fluallen, leg; J. C. Foster, Timothy Murphy, James N. Rich, and John Mooney, slightly; John D. Long, George Miller, Lewis Straton, John B. Underwood, and Obadiah Vaughn, severely; Milton P. Wilson, chest; John M. Wilson, hand, slightly. Company D: Lieutenant Mark Walker, head; First Sergeant M. A. Maxin, arm; Sergeant William Snyder, leg; Corporals G. W. Snodgrass, leg; Fred. Ghering, leg, and Abram Gaskill, hand; Privates Fred. Adams, leg; — Benedict, foot; John Barnes, head; Abram Davenport, leg; William Hanley, leg; W. E. Edwards, shoulder; Benjamin Hawk, leg; John Kennedy, leg; Benjamin Booth, head; John H. Barnes, leg. Company E: Privates H. B. Beal, leg; Joseph F. Bilto, foot; Charles P. Crews, chest; William Hartman, head and back; Jeff. Castle, leg; Samuel Dent, leg; William R. Smith, hand; John W. Luna, head; William

P. Moore, thigh; William R. Hess, arm; H. H. Mercer, hand; Robert A. Jailors, leg and chest. Company F: Corporal John Harges, neck; Privates James Greer, hip; Theodore Olds, thigh; J. Stineberger, hand. Company G: Lieutenant J. W. Smith, thumb; Corporal Henry Wederbrust, arm; Privates John D. Stockton, leg and chest; James Rippets, leg and chest; H. Shanster, hand; L. Richards, left lung; Lemuel Shelden, leg; N. F. Maxwell, arm fractured; J. Burns, side; A. Jamison, face; Lewis Page, hand; John Rose, hand; B. Thumber, thigh; A. Wilson, face; M. D. Foster, leg. Company H: Privates George W. Lewis, leg and chest; William Kennedy, leg and chest; Charles D. Hyatt, leg and chest; M. D. C. Foster, leg and chest; Russell Wing, leg and chest; George Plumb, head; P. Lally, foot; B. F. Muselman, thigh; John Osborn, leg. Company I: Privates Henry C. Putnam, arm; Daniel Shaffer, hand; M. Macy, arm; Jeff. Wolf, arm. Company K: Sergeants J. W. McGure, thigh; W. G. Welch, leg; Jacob Custer, head; Corporals J. F. Henning, thigh, and Henry Buckhart, head and back; Privates Frank McCourtney, arm; John Shook, head; Adolph Lidon, shoulder; Frank Bower, hand; Andrew Jackson, face; Edward Edwards, hand; Frank Hekok, thigh; John Webb, back; John Smith, neck; Henry Hazleton, thigh; John Devore, shoulder; A. Titus, leg; R. B. Bright, face; George A. Griffith; thigh, Andrew Heaton, temple; Charles Fruit, face; Isaac Wyant, thigh.

Summary.—Killed, 41; wounded, 133—total, 174.

ONE HUNDREDTH REGIMENT ILLINOIS VOLUNTEERS.

Major C. M. Hammond, wounded slightly in right leg; Sergeant Major W. P. Harbottle, contusion of spine.

Killed.—Company A: Second Lieutenant Charles F. Mitchell. Company C: Privates John Hopkins and Fred. Kahar. Company D: Private George W. Hess. Company K: Second Lieutenant Morris Worthington, Privates Giles S. Greenmanner, George Askins, and Andrew Thiel.

Wounded.—Company A: Privates Michael Worthy, hand, and John Haynes, contusion of head, (since died.) Company B: First Lieutenant A. A. Osgood, head; Privates Stephen James, right leg; William Cludes, face; Philip Shear, knee; Stephen Hook, knee. Company C: First Lieutenant ——— Bez, spine; Second Lieutenant M. Macdonald, head; Corporal John H. Gent, left shoulder; Private Michael Sullivan, left leg. Company D: Sergeant John Fellows, head; Privates Edward Mellan, left leg; Ephea Englennyer, left thigh. Company H: Private John Shoemaker. Company I: Privates George Irish, body contused, and James Titball, right leg. Company K: First Lieutenant ——— Kelly, shoulder; Privates William Mundy, thigh; Alf. Carter, head.

Summary.—Killed, 8; wounded, 22—total, 30.

NINETY-SEVENTH REGIMENT OHIO VOLUNTEERS.

Killed.—Company B: August Reamish. Company G: John Rodecker.

Wounded.—Company A: Private Jacob B. Brice, right foot. Company B: Private Isaac M. Donald, face. Company C: Color Sergeant Murray Hussen, face and shoulder; Privates James Huffman, elbow; Israel Garnett, arm. Company D: Privates Benjamin Linsey, hand; James Livery, chest and back; Stephen Cogle, chest; Osten Harvey, left shoulder; E. Faulk, shoulder. Company E: Corporals William Edgill, severely, and Llewelleyn Eckelbagh, face. Company G: Private George Robertson, head. Company H: John Moore, hand. Company I: Privates Samuel Browning, both legs, and Mathias Tapyer, head. Company K: Privates Moses Dozer, head, and Charles Clappill, foot.

Summary.—Killed, 2; wounded 18—total 20.

THIRTEENTH REGIMENT MICHIGAN VOLUNTEERS.

Killed.—Company A: William Z. Hurin. Company B: Private William Withey. Company C: Corporal Oscar A. Budsell, Privates Lafayette Randall, Alden S. Hurd, and K. S. Wolcott. Company D: Corporals R. H. Paxton and John R. Scott. Company F: Sergeant Walter Delony, Corporal George Gould, Privates John S. Young and Samuel Hamlin. Company G: Privates S. Caslin, George A. Hillan, Charles Reed, and Martin Crespo. Company I: Corporal Walter Wever, Privates Elin Pratt, Jacob Southwick, W. D. Loomis, and W. H. Edmonds. Company K: Private John Walker.

Wounded.—Company A: Privates A. Swartout and Lee C. Glasby, hand. Company B: Sergeant Joseph Miller, foot; Corporals F. Grey, thigh; Orris Slater, thigh; Elias Arming, scalp; Cyril LaDoux, thigh; Lewis Carles, foot; Richard Carmedy, right leg, (amputated.) Company C: Corporals R. E. McArthur, ear; Henry Fox, shoulder; H. C. Burnes, penis; Privates George Tower, arm; Oliver P. Storey, arm; Josiah F. Clark, forearm; Walter Putnam, shoulder; William Moyer, toe; D. A. Bush, head; Harvey Johnson, head; John Wynn, thigh; M. Newton, neck. Company D: Sergeant A. Tibbets, thigh and leg; Corporal John Lyttleness, shoulder joint; Privates William Yetter, shoulder joint; Robert E. Furgerson, side; I. K. Judd, hand; Seth Crosby, elbow. Company E: Lieutenant John E. McIver, scalp; Sergeant Julius Lillie, side; Corporals C. C. Webb, arm; Joseph DeWaters, thigh; Privates S. Barney, thigh; John Moorehouse, thigh; Chester Shwarts, thumb; John Trick, hand. Company F: Sergeants A. O. Taylor, armpit; D. R. Corrie, forearm; Privates John T. Burkill, arm; Eli Martin, thigh; Hugh McGillick, left shoulder and lung; Hiram Geoffrey, thigh; Henry Rodgers, hip; Thomas Jackson, leg. Company G: Corporal C. B. Rumels, arm; Privates W. E. Allen, eye and ear; W. G. Ray, hand; H. K. Waterman, foot; Lucius Cleveland, arm. Company H: Corporal George P. Coon, face and neck; Privates John A. Rich, thigh; Jesse McBain, wrist; T. White, scalp. Company I: Corporals Henry Holt, elbow; David Harmon, thumb; Privates John Hackhouse, side; B. Vanderhoop, side; John W. Purdy, face; H. Brundage, arm; Ward V. Smith, face; Charles O. Edwards, arm; Milo Hawkes, arm; Stephen Brown, thumb; Wilson Henry, neck. Company K: Corporal W. H. McConnell, hip; Privates Samuel Holten, arm; W. C. Hamlin, back; William Anderson, groin.

Summary.—Killed, 23; wounded, 66—total 89.

FIFTY-EIGHTH REGIMENT INDIANA VOLUNTEERS.

Killed.—Company A: Sergeant William M. Kany; Privates Elias Skelton, E. B. Endicoff, and Joseph Reins. Company B: Private John Van Wagoner. Company C: Privates J. H. Hall and Henry Frusty. Company D: Private Henry Coale. Company E: Lieutenant Francis Blackford. Company G: Private Noah Miller. Company H: Private Andrew Cunningham. Company I: Corporal A. McDonald and Private Frank Ferethy. Company K: Private Albert Goodman.

Wounded.—Lieutenant and Adjutant C. C. Whiting, posterior part of thorax. Company A: Corporals A. M. Bryant, head, and M. Reaves, slight; Privates Alfred Trafer, wounded mortally; Willy Knowles, arm; Jesse Knowles, arm; John Crow, leg; George Benchfield, leg; Joseph Davisi, thigh; James Drysdale, thigh fractured; H. V. Hayes, head; Silvester Miner, arm; Henry Beck, arm; George Willis, shoulder; —— Huckenson, shoulder contused; S. D. Bennet, arm; Moses Witherspoon, head; S. W. Curray, slight; J. M. Stonant, arm, slight; James Chorn, arm, slight; R. Smith, E. Love, slight; Henry Corner, slight; John Baldwin, slight, and E. Lincoln, slight. Company B: Private Green B. Yager, arm, slight. Company C: Captain William Downing, neck, serious; Sergeant P. W. Spain, back, severely; Corporals C. C. Haddock, hand, severely; John Johnson, leg, slightly, and J. Dye, leg, slightly; Privates L. Roberts, leg, slightly; David Hoke, abdomen, severely; A. R. Wood, arm, fractured; H. I. Wright, foot, slight; John J. Phillips, leg, slight; John G. Grossen, leg, slight; Robert Chew, head, mortal, and George W. Aloes. Company D: Lieutenant George W. Witmore; Sergeants D. C. Barret, leg, severe; William M. Mumford, arm, severe; D. T. Davis, and M. M. Coleman, arm, slight; Corporal D. Van Niggle; Privates A. Jones, mortally; James Anderson, arm, slight; L. Christmas, face, severe; Johnson Wheeler, leg fractured; Thomas Duncan, leg fractured; A. C. Myers, John Morick, leg; James Cunningham, and A. H. Cochran. Company E: Captain A. H. Alexander; Sergeant John D. Norman, foot, severely; Privates Z. Pierce, slight; H. Hughes, arm, slight, and Elijah Black, arm, slight. Company F: Sergeants L. C. Mason, slight, and H. Barrett, slight; Corporal John Emerson, slight; Privates Henry McCoy, mortally; L. Cleveland, leg, slight; John Browne, arm; R. E. Embree, Calvin Burch, and William Sanders. Company G: Sergeant R. J. Brown, side, severely; Privates Henry Brinton, thigh, severely; Milton Holden, head, severely; Hany Amos, arm, severely, and John A. Berdin, arm, severely. Company H; Lieutenant William Adams, foot, severely; Corporals John H. Gower, elbow joint, amputated, and James Wood, leg, amputated; Privates James S. Newman, femur, mortally, and W. M. Kindall, arm. Company I: Sergeant W. L. Shaw, thigh, severely; Corporals V. Mead, head, severely; George W. Ernest, spine, mortally; George W. Martin, abdomen, severely; George Varm, head and face, severely, and Jacob Mead, arm, fractured; Privates W. H. Doads, arm, slight; George Williamson, arm, slight; T. J. Smith, hand, slight; Lewis Staliens, hand, slight; Edward Blair, foot, slight; and James Meley, arm, slight. Company K: Sergeants Jesse B. Miller, face, severe; George W. Wilden, leg, severe, and John W. Pace, severe; Privates W. Young, James Bahanan, and Alfred Poe.

Summary.—Killed, 19; wounded, 91—total, 110.

SIXTY-FIFTH REGIMENT OHIO VOLUNTEERS.

Killed.—Company A: Sergeants Wm. Hibbits and Wm. Buchanan; Private Milon Hammil. Company B: Sergeant Thomas Hale; Privates E. W. Day, Almon Alleston, J. M. Johnston, James Morfit, James Kintz, Bontin Speakman, John Champion, Joseph Bull, and Harvey Allen. Company C: Sergeant H. L. Welden; Corporal Martin Burnham. Company G: Second Lieutenant D. Vankirk; Privates George B. McClellan, Samuel Cormick, and Wm. Donaldson. Company H: Privates John McCloy, John Kimble, V. Duncan, Henry Lyon, Wm. Gillespie, and Wm. Herrick. Company I: Captain Jacob Chistofel; Corporal Peter Clark; Private Peter Smith. Company K: Privates Cyrus Myers, Christopher Schmidd, John Workman, and James Packer.

Wounded.—Lieutenant Colonel A. Cassil, severely contused; Major H. A. Whitbeck, neck, slight; Captain R. M. Vorrhees, abdomen, slight, company F; Adjutant W. H. Massy, knee, serious; First Lieutenant A. A. Gardner, back, serious; Second Lieutenant Frank Reader, thigh fractured, company A; Second Lieutenant J. P. Brown, shoulder, severe, company H; Second Lieutenant Peter Markell, left thigh, severe, company K; Second Lieutenant R. S. Rook, both hips, severe, company B; Sergeants A. Kimber, left leg, severe, and John Boyd, left leg, severe; Privates Clark Jordan, right knee, slight; H. C. Jennings, arm and shoulder, severe; John Nicoli, shoulder and side, severe; Adam Markham, thigh, severe; J. Aterholt, shoulder; J. Murphy, throat, and M. Clark, right arm, company G; Sergeant H. Leasenby, right hand; Privates H. B. Roder, wrist, severe; J. G. Davis, wrist, severe; J. M. Funk, head, severe W. Page, ankle, severe, and J. E. Boleander, hand, company K; J. L. McKibbin, right side; C. Brishart, right thigh, severe; Jacob Miller, right side; E. Gregory, finger, slight; L. Alman, hip, serious; R. W. Corey, left forearm; Jas. Perkins, face fract. R. sap. max.; Henry J. Young, hip and abdomen, mortal; R. B. Black, wrist, severe; D. Carpenter, wrist and head; W. Jeffrey, hand, slight; Martin Smith, hip, serious, and M. L. Smith, ankle, serious, company C; Frederick Mosier, face, serious; Amos Pingard, right hand, serious; John Long, thigh and ankle, slight; Daniel Griffith, breast and arm; Z. Wood, breast and arm; W. Thompson, breast and arm; I. M. Clark, leg; W. Jackson, back, and J. Wright, shoulder, slight, company D; John Myers, right leg, seriously; John A. Legree, right leg, seriously; Edward Kingsby, right leg, slight; John Desmond, mortally; Peter Cashen, right leg factured, severe; M. Amich, right leg, slight; Henry Sentill, shoulder; J. M. Scott, breast and shoulder; A. Shecker, face, and J. Mayler, face, company I; B. M. Stockdale, right hand, slight; W. George, arm; E. Stires, right leg, and W. H. Ramson, hip, severe, company H; Corporal G. G. Clement, right side, mortal; Privates Daniel Elliott, ankle; David Harris, lung, mortal; D. D. Shaub, ankle, slight; Lloyd Fording, ankle, severely; Edward Crocker, shoulder, and Peter Gustmer, face and hand, company E; Corporal M. S. Terrill, face, serious; Privates Peter Green, left side; J. J. Shellenberger, right foot; J. H. Wyman, side; James Morris, side; A. A. Layman, left shoulder; J. Lybonger, arm fractured; Amos Hembert, arm; Hollis Marsh, mortally; Daniel Caldwell, breast, severe; L. Johnson, left hand, and J. Young, left breast, company A; James Shaeffer, right ankle; Samuel Moore, hand; William Day, shoulder; Michael McBride, leg; William Moore, hand; George Linkerson, head; J. C. Knid, thigh; J. Hile, thigh, and G. W. Crow, hip, company F; A. R. Bretz, mortally; M. A. Rodgers, left hip; Wm. Farmyhill, face, fractured lower jaw; John Ganglaw, left hip; George F. Ball, right arm and thigh, severe; George Beel, right arm and thigh, severe; J. C. May, right shoulder; J. Shoe, left hand; S. Moore, back, severe; J. C. Sneeder, back, severe; H. Keer, breast; W. Hale, abdomen, mortal, and J. Humes, right hand, company B; Cyrus Marvin, shoulder, and James Mirick, hand, company A; John Goshon, left side; Lloyd Fording, left shoulder, and John Humes, hand, company B; J. C. Byron, hand, and John Coleman, company C; Corporals Elias Aldrich, right arm and hip, and Ira C. Herrick, face; Privates James L. Denton, right leg and hand, and John Bailey, shoulder, company D; Henry A. Dagget, arm; Abram Hany, leg, severe; G. L. Pope, face, and Perry Roof, hand, company E; Sergeant John Sullivan, knee; Corporal Horace Curtis, left leg; Privates James Nolan, right leg; M. M. Parks, shoulder, and Hugh Taylor, prisoner, company G; James Paisle, arm; W. Taylor, back, severely, and Adam Glascon, privates, company H; Charles Rauschaulb, shoulder; Jacob Weisen, back; Lewis Bretz, thigh; Ira B. Horner, thigh, and Edward Hougsby, hip, company I; William Hall and John Reece, prisoners, company C.

Summary.—Killed, 35; wounded, 125; missing, 3—total, 163.

FORTIETH REGIMENT INDIANA VOLUNTEERS.

Killed.—Company A: Privates John Montgomery. Company B: Robert Atchison and Jacob Huling. Company D: G. W. Harney.

Wounded.—Company A: Corporal William Shellington, hip; Privates S. Fremm, left thigh; William Heulton, right arm; James Patten, right hand; William Morris, right leg; N. Morris, foot; Samuel Combe, forearm; William Marcey, A. Shaw, R. Wilson, right leg, and J. Sheets, ear, slight. Company B: Captain —— Harney, right arm, slightly; Lieutenant W. Griswold, thigh; Sergeant B. Murphy, leg, slight; Privates William McCarmah, arm, slight; M., Miller, leg, amputated; C. Massett, hip; H. Philaburn, left arm; Daniel Ramsay, left thigh; Sanford Stahl, William Naustenight and Thomas Helsey, right arm. Company C: Captain H. D. Wallace, right arm, slightly. Company D:

Lieutenant W. L. Coleman, head; Privates G. D. Davis, parietal bone; John L. Lewis, neck, and James Meek, foot. Company E: Sergeant A. Kobb, right arm, severe; Corporal T. D. Henderson, thigh, severe; Privates P. Hartman left hip; S. R. Wise, right foot; S. M. Jackson, left leg, and A. M. Hilt, left arm.. Company F: T. T. Dunmore, right forearm, and W. H. Duly, left hip. Company G: J. N. Patterson, left arm; William Sonborges, left hip; E. C. Moore, right forearm, and H. H. Seely, right forearm. Company I: Sergeant A. Ruth, foot; Privates D. Richardson, foot; David Benson, right thigh; James Hicks, left leg; A. Whitmore, P. S. Bailley, J. C. Morfoot, John Groves, A. Beld, and Joseph Davis. Company K: Lieutenant H. L. Hazlerigg, right leg; Sergeant W. N. Chambers, left arm; and Private H. Veach, right hand.

Summary.—Killed, 4; wounded, 52—total 56.

EIGHTH AND TENTH INDIANA AND SIXTH OHIO BATTERIES.

Killed.—Tenth Indiana: Private William Wooley.

Wounded.—Tenth Indiana: Sergeant Joseph Cox, hip and breast, severe; Privates John Kench, spine contused; Robert Shable, thigh; Frank Arnold, right breast; and Edw. Bordin, foot. Sixth Ohio: Lieutenant O. H. P. Oyers, left arm, slight; Sergeants George W. Howard, lung, mortal; Stewart Miller, right arm, severe; Corporal H. A. Collier, head, slight; Privates Samuel W. Scott, lung, mortal; William Coney, right arm, amputated; John Cackler, hand; Joel Hersch, left arm, severe; R. Caldwell, right arm, severe; and E. H. Beard, right leg, severe. Eighth Indiana: Sergeant Henry S. Smith, left leg; Corporal Joseph Morrison, left cheek; Privates Wm. Hamilton, right shoulder; William H. Hargrave, elbow; Robert Otter, foot; Adam Hershmer, right leg; Coon Dacey, left arm; and Henry Shulk, mid-finger.

General summary.—Killed, 202; wounded, 921—total, 1,123.

HEADQUARTERS 1ST BRIGADE, 1ST DIVISION, LEFT WING,
Near Murfreesboro', Tennessee, January 6, 1863.

SIR: I have the honor to submit the following report of the operations of my brigade, (formerly the 15th brigade, 6th division, but under the new nomenclature the 1st brigade, 1st division, left wing,) on the eventful 31st of December, 1862. During the night of the 30th I had received notice through General Wood, our division commander, that the left wing (Crittenden's corps) would cross Stone river, and attack the enemy on his right. My brigade was posted on the extreme left of our entire line of battle, and was guarding and overlooking the ford, over which we were to cross. On the morning of the 31st heavy firing was heard on the extreme right of our line, (McCook's corps,) but as they had been fighting their way all the distance from Nolensville, as we had from Lavergne, no particular importance was attached to this, and I was getting my brigade into position, ready to cross, as soon as General Van Cleve's division, which was then crossing, was over. All this time the firing on the right became heavier and apparently nearer to us, and our fears began to be aroused that the right wing was being driven rapidly back upon us. At this juncture Van Cleve halted his division, and the most terrible state of suspense pervaded the entire left, as it became more and more evident that the right was being driven rapidly back upon us. On and on they came, till the heaviest fire was getting nearly around to the pike leading to Nashville, when General Rosecrans appeared in person, and ordered me to go with my brigade at once to the support of the right, pointing towards our rear, where the heaviest fire was raging. General Van Cleve's division, and Colonel Harker's brigade, of our division, received the same order. I at once changed the front of my brigade to the rear, preparatory to starting in the new direction, but had not proceeded more than 200 yards in the new direction before the crowd of fugitives from the right wing became so numerous, and the fleeing mule-teams and horsemen so thick, that it was impossible for me to go forward with my command without its becoming a confused mass. I therefore halted, and awaited developments. General Van Cleve's and Colonel Harker's, not meeting with so much opposition, pressed forward and got into position beyond the railroad, ready to open on the enemy as soon as our fugitives were out of the way. They soon opened fire, joined by some batteries and troops belonging to the centre, (General Thomas's corps,) and Estep's battery, of my brigade; and after about one hour's firing along this new line, during which time I was moving my command from point to point, ready to support any troops that most needed it, the onslaught of the enemy seemed to be in a great measure checked, and we had reasonable probability of maintaining this line. During all this time my men were exposed to a severe fire of shot and shell from a battery on the other side of the river, and several were killed. About this time an aid of General Palmer came galloping up to me, and said, that unless he could be supported his division would have to give way. Palmer's division formed the right of General Crittenden's line of battle on the morning of the 31st. After consulting with General Wood, he ordered me to send a regiment to support General Palmer; accordingly I sent the 3d Kentucky regiment, commanded by Lieutenant Colonel Samuel McKee. Before the regiment had been ten minutes in its new position, Captain Kerstetter, my adjutant general, reported to me that Colonel McKee had been killed and the regiment badly cut up. I therefore moved at once, with the other three regiments of my command, to their relief. The line they were trying to hold was that part of our original line of battle lying immediately to the right of the railroad. This portion of our original line, about two regimental fronts, together with two fronts to the left, held by Colonel Wagner's brigade, was all of our original line of battle, but what our troops had been driven from; and if they succeeded in carrying this, they would have turned our left, and a total rout of our forces could not then have been avoided. Seeing the importance of the position, I told my men it must be held, even if it cost the last man we had. I immediately sent in the 26th Ohio, commanded by the gallant Major William H. Squires, to take position on the right of the 3d Kentucky, and support them, and despatched an aid for Estep's 8th Indiana battery to come to this point, and open on the enemy. No sooner had the 26th got into position, than they became hotly engaged, and the numerous dead and wounded that were immediately brought to the rear told how desperate was the contest.

The gallant Lieutenant McClellan, of that regiment, was brought to the rear mortally wounded, and expired by my side in less than five minutes from the time the regiment took position. And still the fight went on, and still brave men went down. The 3d Kentucky, now reduced to less than one-half its original numbers, with ten out of its fourteen remaining officers badly wounded, were still bravely at work. In less than ten minutes after the fall of Lieutenant Colonel McKee, the gallant Major Daniel R. Collier, of that regiment, received two severe wounds—one in the leg, and the other in the breast; Adjutant Bullitt had his horse shot from under him; but nothing could induce either of them to leave the field. Equally conspicuous and meritorious was the conduct of Major Squires and Adjutant Franklin, of the 26th Ohio. Major Squires's horse was shot three times through the neck; nevertheless, he and all his officers stood by throughout, and most gallantly sustained and encouraged their men. Estep's battery came up in due time, and taking position on a little rise of ground in rear of the 26th and 3d Kentucky, opened a terrible fire of shot and shell over the heads of our infantry. In about one hour after the 26th Ohio got into position this terrible attack of the enemy was repulsed, and they drew back into the woods, and, under cover of an intervening hill, to reform their shattered columns and renew the attack.

I now took a survey of the situation, and found that along the entire line to the right and left of the railroad, which had not yet been carried by the enemy, I was the only general officer present, and was, therefore, in command, and responsible for the conduct of affairs. Colonel Hazen, commanding a brigade in General Palmer's division, was present with his brigade, to the left of the railroad, and Colonel Gross, commanding another brigade in the same division, was also present with what there was left of his brigade, and most nobly did he co-operate with me with the 6th and 24th Ohio, to the right of the railroad, while Colonel Wagner, commanding the 2d brigade in the 1st division, left wing, nobly sustained his front, assisted by Colonel Hazen, to the left of the railroad. I now relieved the 3d Kentucky regiment, who were nearly annihilated and out of ammunition, with the 58th Indiana regiment, of my brigade, commanded by Colonel George P. Buell, and this being a much larger regiment than the 3d Kentucky, filled up the entire space from where the right of the 3d Kentucky rested to the railroad. I then threw forward the right of the 6th Ohio regiment, of Colonel Gross's brigade, which was on the right of the 26th Ohio, so that its line of battle was more nearly perpendicular to the railroad, and so its fire would sweep the front of the 26th Ohio and 58th Indiana, and supported the 6th Ohio with Estep's battery, on a little eminence to its right, and brought up the 97th Ohio, Colonel Lane, from Wagner's brigade, to still further strengthen the right. This disposition being made, I galloped a little to the rear and found General Rosecrans, and called his attention to the importance of the position I was holding, and the necessity of keeping it well supported. He rode to the front with me, approved the disposition I had made, spoke a few words of encouragement to the men, cautioning them to hold their fire till the enemy got well up, and had no sooner retired than the enemy emerged from the woods and over the hill, and were moving upon us again in splendid style and in immense force. As soon as they came in sight the 6th and 26th Ohio and Estep's battery opened on them, and did splendid execution. But on they came, till within one hundred yards of our line, when Colonel Buell, of the 58th Indiana, who lost three men, but had not fired a shot, ordered his men to fire. The effect was indescribable; the enemy fell in winrows, and went staggering back from the effect of this unexpected volley. Soon, however, they came up again and assaulted us furiously for about one and a half hour, but the men all stood their ground nobly, and at the end of that time compelled the enemy to retire as before. During the heat of this attack a heavy cross fire was brought to bear on the position I occupied, and Corporal Frank Moyer, 3d Ohio volunteer cavalry, in command of my escort, was shot through the leg, and my adjutant general, Captain E. R. Kerstetter, was shot through his coat, grazing his back. The regiments all behaved splendidly again, and the 58th Indiana won immortal honors. Lieutenant Blackford, of that regiment, was shot dead, and several of the officers, including Captains Downey and Alexander, badly wounded. Estep's battery was compelled to retire from the position assigned it, after firing half a dozen rounds, but it did terrible execution while there. The 6th and 24th Ohio did noble service, as did the 97th; but their immediate commanders will, no doubt, allude to them more particularly. Thus ended the third assault upon the position. I should have remarked that the 100th Illinois regiment, the other regiment composing my brigade, which was in reserve during the first engagement described above, had, under instructions of Colonel Hazen, moved to the front, on the left of the railroad, where they fought splendidly in all the actions that took place on the left of the road. There was no formidable attack made on them, though they were almost constantly under fire of greater or less severity, particularly from shot and shell, and suffered quite seriously in killed and wounded. Lieutenant Morrison Worthingham, of that regiment, was killed while gallantly sustaining his men, and six other commissioned officers, including Major Hammond, were wounded. Their operations being to the left of the railroad, and in a wood, did not come so immediately under my personal observation, but their conduct, from Colonel Bartleson down, was such as leaves nothing to be desired. The 58th Indiana having now been over three hours in action, and the 26th Ohio about four hours, were exhausted and very near out of ammunition; I therefore relieved the 58th Indiana with the 40th Indiana, from Colonel Wagner's brigade, and the 26th Ohio was relieved by the 23d Kentucky. There was now not more than an hour of day left, and though the enemy was continually manœuvring in our front, no formidable attack was made upon us except with artillery. The enemy having been three several times repulsed from their attack on that position, seemed satisfied to keep at a respectful distance, and the sun set upon us masters of the situation. We had sustained ourselves and held the only position of the original line of battle that was held throughout by any portion of our army. To have lost this position would have been to lose everything, as our left would then have been turned, and either rout or capture inevitable. To the "fearless spirits who hazarded and lost their lives on this consecrated spot" the country owes a deep debt of gratitude. No purer patriot, more upright man, and devoted Christian than Colonel McKee, of the 3d Kentucky, ever offered up his life in defence of his country. To the members of my staff present with me in the field, Captain Edmund R. Kerstetter, assistant adjutant general; Lieutenant James R. Hume, aide-de-camp; and Lieutenant James R. Warner, inspector general, I am under the greatest obligations. They were constantly with me in the thickest of the fight, ably and gallantly assisting me in every way possible. My escort was also faithful and efficient. With the exceptions already alluded to, all of us were so fortunate as to get through unscathed.

The casualties in the brigade were as follows: the 3d Kentucky regiment went into action with thirteen officers and three hundred men, and lost—

Officers—Killed, 1; wounded, 9. Enlisted men—Killed, 12; wounded, 77; missing, 34.

The 58th Indiana regiment went into action with nineteen officers and three hundred and eighty-six enlisted men, and lost—

Officers—Killed, 1; wounded, 4. Enlisted men—Killed, 16; wounded, 91.

The 100th Illinois went into action with twenty-seven officers and three hundred and ninety-four enlisted men, and lost—

Officers—Killed, 1; wounded, 6. Enlisted men—Killed, 5; wounded, 33.

The 26th Ohio went into action with twelve officers and three hundred and seventy-four men, and lost—

Officers—Killed, 1; wounded, 2. Enlisted men—Killed, 9; wounded, 77.

Recapitulation.

The brigade went into action with seventy-one officers and one thousand four hundred and fifty-four enlisted men, and lost—

Officers—Killed, 4; wounded, 21. Enlisted men—Killed, 42; wounded, 278; missing, 34.

Total killed, wounded, and missing in brigade, 379.

For more minute reports of the parts performed by the different regiments I transmit herewith their respective reports. During the evening of the 31st I was notified that, in consequence of the indisposition of General Wood and a wound received during the day, he was relieved of the command of the division, and that the same would devolve upon myself; I therefore turned over the command of the brigade to Colonel George P. Buell, of the 58th Indiana, and assumed the command of the division.

All of which is respectfully submitted.

MILO S. HASCALL,
Brigadier General Volunteers, Commanding Brigade.

Captain M. P. BESTOW,
Acting Assistant Adjutant General, 1st Division, Left Wing.

Official: ED. R. KERSTETTER,
Captain and Assistant Adjutant General.

HEADQUARTERS 1ST BRIGADE, 1ST DIVISION,
LEFT WING, ARMY OF THE CUMBERLAND,
Near Murfreesboro', Tenn., January 5, 1863.

SIR: Brigadier General Hascall having assumed command of the division on the night of the 31st of December, A. D. 1862, the command of this brigade devolved upon me, by orders issued to that effect. At the time of assuming this command the position of the brigade was on the right of the division, in front, which point we held until the morning of the 1st instant, when we fell back, before daylight, to the rear, as reserve for the division. This position we retained until 8 o'clock p. m. of the same day, when we again moved forward to the front, occupying the ground then held by the pioneer brigade, on the right of the division. Pickets were then thrown forward, so that the enemy's advance was within easy range of their guns, and the brigade lay on their arms during the night. Early on the morning of the 2d instant sharp skirmishing began between our advance posts and the enemy, followed shortly afterwards by a most terrific shower of shell and shot in our midst from guns having been massed and masked against us during the night, killing three and wounding ten men of the brigade. During the day there was considerable skirmishing, and occasional shells fell among us. Half an hour before dark we formed line of battle by order, and moved forward some six hundred yards, but, finding no enemy, were ordered to cross Stone river, where we lay during the night in reserve, under arms, in a drenching rain-storm. On the morning of the 3d instant we moved into the works thrown up during the night, taking position on the right of the division, relieving the 20th brigade, where we remained quietly during the day and night, laing on our arms. But nothing worthy of note transpiring, and being ordered, we recrossed Stone river at half past two o'clock on the morning of the 4th instant, taking up the position in the rear, which our brigade now occupied, as reserve.

The list of casualties from the night of the 31st of December, 1862, in this brigade, to this date, is—

	Enlisted men killed.	Enlisted men wounded.
26th Ohio volunteer infantry	2	8
58th Indiana volunteer infantry	0	2
100th Illinois volunteer infantry	1	0
3d Kentucky volunteer infantry	0	0
Total loss	3	10

No commissioned officer killed or wounded.

It gives me great pleasure to state that all the officers of the brigade conducted themselves with true spirit and becoming bravery, and were keenly alive to the great dangers of their respective commands, each endeavoring to guard them from the fire of the enemy. Where all do nobly, no individual cases of bravery need be cited. For more minute details I would respectfully refer you to the individual reports of the regimental commanders on file.

Very respectfully,

GEO. P. BUELL,
Colonel Commanding.

Captain KERSTETTER,
Assistant Adjutant General 1st Division.

HEADQUARTERS 100TH ILLINOIS VOLUNTEER INFANTRY,
On the Battle-field, near Murfreesboro', Tennessee, January 5, 1863.

SIR: I have the honor to submit the following report of the part taken by the 100th regiment Illinois volunteer infantry during the 31st December, 1862.

On the morning of the 31st December, 1862, while a portion of General Van Cleve's command were returning from the ford of the creek, (which up to that time had been guarded by the 100th Illinois and 58th Indiana,) not carrying out their original intention of crossing, my regiment was ordered to follow, in column of companies, the 26th Ohio, which we did, and moving with them towards the right, we at last took our position in line of battle on the right of the 58th Indiana and in the rear of the 26th Ohio, amid a scene of almost indescribable confusion, other regiments moving amongst us, ambulances and wagons hurrying to the rear, and scattered cavalrymen and negroes urging their horses to their utmost speed, seeking a place of safety. We moved with the brigade further on, until we came within range of the enemy's cannon, and were exposed for a time to a heavy cross-fire of artillery. After remaining thus for a short time, the fire on the right becoming momentarily heavier, I moved, in pursuance of orders, across the railroad, the regiment resting at right angles with the road, the right wing on the right of the railroad, and the left wing on the left of it. I noticed at this time, and shortly before, that our troops on the right were falling back, belonging, I presume, to General McCook's corps, and I was ordered to throw my men parallel to the railroad, which I did. The bank of the excavation being too high for a part of the regiment to fire in that position, I ordered them to get out of it and lie down on the left side of the railroad. The firing in this direction was pretty heavy, but my men were not called on to reply. I observed some troops falling back in considerable confusion. Some of them were rallied and formed in the excavation we had left, towards my right, but not in any considerable number. I am unable to say who they were. At this point a shell, which killed five men of an adjoining regiment, so affected my sergeant major that he is bent to the ground with an injury which will probably affect him for life.

I had noticed about this time that the firing was drawing near on the left of the position I then occupied, parallel with the railroad, and was apprehensive that our troops on the left side of the road might be taken on the flank. About this time Colonel Hazen, of the brigade, directed me to file to the left. Asking him his name, and being myself convinced of the necessity of the movement, I complied, and moved forward in a line at right angles with that just left until I came up with the 110th Illinois, Colonel Casey. We halted here, and for a short time participated in a sharp fire of musketry, which finally ceased, leaving us to bear nothing except a cannonade, which gradually lulled. There was another regiment at this time behind us, but what one I know not. After a short time this was withdrawn, and I was left alone with the 110th Illinois.

There was at this point an open space—a cotton-field—in our front, and in a short time I discovered a large body of the enemy on the other side, across the field, apparently moving to attack us. The 110th at this time had formed on my left. I regarded the situation as extremely perilous, and informed General Hascall, who was not far distant, of the same. He replied that he saw it likewise, but we must hold it. Shortly after a force of our own was thrown across the field in our front, but was soon withdrawn. Informing my men that this was a good time to show what they were and make a reputation, and announcing my determination to them that they should stay there, I ordered them forward, and halted them at the edge of the wood. The 110th said they would stay with us, and moved likewise. I commanded the men to lie down, but the enemy, having necessarily discovered us, opened upon us with a perfect storm of shot, and shell, and grape. A battery of our own in a short time replied behind us, and for the space of three or four hours the scene was fearful. Although so much exposed, I cannot but be thankful that we suffered so little, commensurate with our danger. The most of our loss, however, was incurred here. Second Lieutenant Worthingham was instantly killed by a shell. Second Lieutenant Mitchell, company A, was mortally wounded in the hip by a musket or rifle ball, of which he afterwards died. They were both deserving officers, and did their duty nobly. Major Hammond had a narrow escape, having the skirts of his coat torn and a slight wound in the calf of his leg. First Lieutenant George Bez and Second Lieutenant McDonald, both of company C, were somewhat wounded, but I think not severely. First Lieutenant Kelly, company K, was wounded severely in the right shoulder. Second Lieutenant McConnell, company I, was somewhat bruised by the limb of a tree striking him on the head, but has since returned to duty. The list accompanying this report will show the number of enlisted men and others killed and wounded.

Night at last closed in and ended this unequal combat—unequal, because our men were compelled, to a great extent, to be spectators and sufferers without being allowed to be actors in the scene. I threw out skirmishers to the front of the regiment, and the men were ordered to lie down on their arms and forbidden to make fires. Our skirmishers soon came upon the enemy seeking his wounded, and through misapprehension some of my men took the horse of a rebel surgeon and four prisoners. I sent the horse back, and directed the messenger to say, without mentioning from whom the messenger came, that it was regretted that the men were taken, but, under the circumstances, they could not be released at present, but would be at the first fitting opportunity. The men themselves were quite pleased at the idea. Two more were brought in to me, being reported to have given themselves up and to be anxious to leave the confederate service. I questioned them, and finding that it was entirely voluntary on their part I sent them to General Hascall, who took charge of them. I also sent out an ambulance under charge of Dr. Woodruff, who brought in a number of our own wounded from the field. The others, the next day, I sent to the rear. I had no paper on which to express the facts, but if they can be identified hereafter, (as they can be by some of my regiment,) they ought to be returned.

The following is a list of the killed and wounded:

Killed.—Commissioned officer: Second Lieutenant Morrison Worthington, company K. Enlisted men: Privates John Hopkins and Frederick Rahm, company C; Andrew Thiel, company B; Giles L. Greeman, company K; Musician George Hess, company D.

Wounded.—Commissioned officers: Major C. M. Hammond, slightly; Second Lieutenant Charles F. Mitchell, company A, mortally, (since dead); Second Lieutenant John S. McDonald, company C, slightly in the head; First Lieutenant George Bez, company C, slightly; Second Lieutenant John McConnell, company I, slightly; First Lieutenant John E. Kelly, company K, severely in right shoulder. Non-commissioned staff: Sergeant Major William P. Harbottle, severely in spine. Enlisted men: Privates Benedict Wenger, Alonzo M. Jones, Michael Worthy, Henry Kellog, Constant Bruchet, James Dowling, James Dore, all slightly; John Haines, severely, company A. Privates William Cludas, severely in the face; Stephen I. Roka, severely in the head; Philip Shears, slightly in the neck, company B. Sergeant Wade McFadden, severely; Private Michael Sullivan, slightly in the arm, company C. Sergeant John Fellows, slightly in the thigh; Privates Edward Hyland, severely in the breast; Ephraim Anglemeir, slightly in the knee; Patrick Martin, slightly in the head; Tiberius Taylor, slightly in the eye; Conrad Lyring, slightly in the head, company D. Privates John McDonald, slightly in the face; Henry Stalder, slightly in the arm, company E. Privates Augustus Wadsworth, slightly in the head; Selah Spaulding, slightly in the leg, company F. Corporal John C. Ghent, severely in the shoulder; Private William R. Moore, slightly in the arm, company H. Privates Jas. Tidball, severely in the leg; Dennis Smith, slightly, company I. Privates Erastus Rudd, slightly in the head; Samuel Heredon, slightly in the head; Eli Heredon, severely in the thigh; William Monday, severely; David C. Elderkin, slightly, company K.

Recapitulation.

Killed—Commissioned officer	1
Enlisted men	5
Wounded—Commissioned officers	6
Enlisted men	32
Non-commissioned staff	1
Total	45

Of the above, one commissioned officer died shortly after.

I have not included in the above some of those who have been killed and wounded from among men detailed from the regiment in other parts of the service.

Troops, I think, could not have behaved better than did the 100th. Considering that it was a new regiment; that since being mustered into the United States service its time has been almost entirely consumed in marching, precluding proper opportunities of drilling, and that its officers generally were new, it must be confessed, I trust and think, it did well. Where all did well, then, it is unnecessary to specify individual cases.

Respectfully,

F. A. BARTLESON,
Colonel 100th Illinois Infantry.

Captain ED. R. KERSTETTER,
Assistant Adjutant General, — Brigade.

HEADQUARTERS 100TH ILLINOIS INFANTRY,
January 5, 1863.

The following is a continuation of my report, after the 31st December, 1862, commencing with the operations of the 1st January, 1863, being supplementary to a report just made to General Hascall, through his adjutant general.

Very early the next morning (1st January, 1863) we were ordered to change our position, which we did, but nothing was done that day. About 9 or 10 o'clock p. m. an order came to proceed to the front, which we did in conjunction with the rest of the brigade, and relieved the pioneer corps, which was on duty there. Everything passed off quietly at night; but in the morning, while my regiment, which had been in the front line all night, was being relieved by the 26th Ohio, the enemy opened on us with artillery. We took up our position, notwithstanding, and were subjected, for a considerable space of time, to one of the most severe fires that troops can experience. The men lay in that position all day, without rations that day or the night before, and sunk deep in the mud. This made the second night without sleep, and, one might say, almost without food. Private George H. Atkins, company K, was killed by a solid shot, which penetrated him and severed his arm from his body.

We were here the spectators, to a considerable extent, of the fight on the left, which took place on the afternoon of the 2d. Near dark our regiment, with the remainder of the brigade, after being formed in line, and our skirmishers skirmishing with the enemy, proceeded to ford the creek on the left, which we did, and at last bivouacked in a terrible rain for the night.

On the morning of January 3, with the rest of our brigade, we took our position behind the rail barricades or breastworks, relieving the 20th brigade. Nothing transpired, except one of the most constant rains, lasting day and night. Early the next morning we recrossed to our present position.

Troops could not have behaved better than did the 100th. Considering that it is a new regiment; that its time has been mostly occupied heretofore in marching, furnishing but small opportunity for drilling; that most of its officers were new, it must be acknowledged that it did good service. Where all do well, it is unnecessary to specify individual cases.

The following is a list of the killed: Private George H. Atkins, company K.

The above brings down the report to the time of occupying this present camp.

Respectfully,

F. A. BARTLESON,
Colonel 100th Illinois Infantry.

Captain I. G. ELWOOD,
Acting Assistant Adjutant General 15th Brigade.

HEADQUARTERS TWENTY-SIXTH OHIO VOLUNTEER INFANTRY,
In Field, January 5, 1863.

SIR: I have the honor to report the following part taken by the 26th Ohio volunteer infantry in the action of the 31st December, 1862. On the morning of the 31st, after being placed in position near the railroad, the regiment was ordered to the front, near the turnpike, where the enemy were making a fierce attack on our forces. The regiment was thrown forward as a support to the 24th Ohio volunteer infantry, which, being too hotly pressed, fell back, thus throwing the 26th Ohio volunteer infantry on the front. While in this position the enemy made three distinct attacks on this portion of our lines, and were gallantly repulsed by the men. At the close of the third attack I was ordered to withdraw my regiment to the railroad for the purpose of refilling the cartridge-boxes of the men. The regiment was then ordered forward to the support of the battery on the left of the 100th Illinois volunteers, and shortly afterwards was ordered to report to Colonel Waggoner, commanding 21st brigade, and was by him placed as a support to portions of two regiments engaged in preventing the enemy from crossing the creek. The regiment held this position until the close of the day, and was then thrown forward some distance, and a heavy picket thrown forward. The casualties of this day amount to one commissioned officer killed, two commissioned officers wounded; seven enlisted men killed, and sixty-four wounded.

The conduct of the men and officers of the regiment was excellent, and, notwithstanding the example set by troops of other divisions, they held their ground and remained cool and firm, retiring only when ordered, and then in perfect order.

I have the honor to be, very respectfully, yours,

W. H. SQUIRES,
Captain Commanding 26th Ohio Volunteer Infantry.

Captain ELWOOD,
Acting Assistant Adjutant General 15th Brigade,
Left Wing, 14th Army Corps.

HEADQUARTERS 26TH OHIO VOLUNTEER INFANTRY,
In Field, January 5, 1862.

SIR: I have the honor to report the following movements on the part of the 26th Ohio volunteer infantry on the 1st of January, 1863: At an early hour in the morning I was ordered to fall back with my regiment from the position in which I had been placed by Colonel Waggoner and join the 15th brigade. We were then drawn back, and formed a reserve near and at right angles to the railroad. At night the regiment was thrown across the railroad and into a hollow for the purpose of allowing the men to build fires. At nine o'clock p. m. we were ordered forward to relieve the pioneer brigade, and the regiment was formed in rear of the 58th Indiana as a support. This position was held all night. There were no casualties in the regiment on this day.

January 2.—On the morning of the 2d of January the regiment was ordered forward to relieve the 100th Illinois and support the 8th Indiana battery on our left flank, and the Board of Trade battery, on the centre and right. Immediately after taking this position the batteries of the enemy opened on our artillery, and severe firing ensued. During the day the enemy's skirmishers advancing under cover annoyed our line, and were twice driven back by our own skirmishers. Immediately after sundown the regiment, with the brigade, was thrown across the creek, and, being held in reserve, were thrown back into the woods and allowed fires, The casualties of this day were two men killed and eight wounded, most of which were caused by the artillery of the enemy.

January 3.—On the morning of the 3d of January the regiment was ordered to relieve the 64th Ohio volunteer infantry and occupy the breastworks built during the previous night. In this position the regiment remained during the day and night, nothing of interest occurring, and no casualties taking place.

January 4.—On the morning of the 4th of January the regiment recrossed the creek and was placed in camp in the present position.

In conclusion, I will add, that the 26th Ohio volunteer infantry entered into the engagement of December 31 with 374 guns, and has lost during the interval a total of one commissioned officer killed and two wounded, and nine enlisted men killed and seventy-two wounded. Many others were struck, and so slightly wounded as not to unfit them for duty, and are, therefore, not mentioned in this report. I cannot mention, in particular, any of my officers, as each one seemed to vie with each other in deeds and examples of good conduct. The men, with a very few exceptions, behaved nobly, though a few, I regret to say, skulked to the rear.

I have the honor to be yours, very respectfully,

W. H. SQUIRES,
Captain Commanding 26th Ohio Volunteer Infantry.

Captain ELLWOOD,
Acting Assistant Adjutant General 15th Brigade.

HEADQUARTERS 58TH REGIMENT INDIANA VOLUNTEERS,
Near Murfreesboro', Tennessee, January 5, 1863.

SIR: I have the honor to report that the 58th regiment of Indiana volunteers, under my command, entered the late action near Murfreesboro', Tennessee, at thirty minutes past 11 o'clock a. m. on the 31st day of December, 1862, with 386 men, exclusive of commissioned officers. This regiment in the battle was posted on the right of the railroad, fronting towards town, forming a part of the left wing of the army engaged. Each man was, prior to the action, furnished with from sixty to eighty rounds of cartridges; and after engaging the enemy under very severe fire for three hours and twenty minutes the regiment was relieved by the 40th Indiana volunteers.

It gives me great pleasure to state that during the action both officers and enlisted men showed no desire nor symptom to retire from the contest, but all stood firmly at their posts and fought nobly and bravely. I would also state that John J. Hight, chaplain of the regiment, deserves commendation for his efficient services rendered on the field and in the hospitals, caring for the wounded.

I have to report the following loss in this day's engagement, to wit:

Second Lieutenant Francis B. Blackford, of company E, was killed while bravely encouraging his men to fight for their cause. Captain William A. Downey, Captain Ashbury Alexander, Second Lieutenant William Adams, and Lieutenant Charles C. Whiting, were all wounded while performing their duty with great zeal and efficiency at their respective posts.

Of enlisted men killed in action there were sixteen, and seventy-three wounded in such a manner as to disable them for present service. There were also twenty-four men slightly wounded.

I have also to report three men captured by the enemy with the regimental wagons at some distance from the field of battle, and also three men missing; making a total loss to the regiment as follows:

Killed.	
Commissioned officer	1
Enlisted men	16
Wounded.	
Commissioned officers	4
Enlisted men disabled	73
Enlisted men missing	3
Total loss in this day's action	97
Captured.	
Enlisted men (not in action)	3
Total	100

At the close of the action this day, Brigadier General Hascall being called to the command of the division, I took command of the brigade, and left the command of the regiment to Lieutenant Colonel James S. Embree, who has since commanded it.

Respectfully,

GEORGE P. BUELL,
Colonel Commanding.

Captain KERSTETTER,
Assistant Adjutant General.

HEADQUARTERS 58TH REGIMENT INDIANA VOLUNTEERS.

SIR: I have the honor to report that the 58th regiment of Indiana volunteers came under my command on the evening of the 31st day of December, 1862, after the close of that day's action, George P. Buell, colonel of the regiment, having been called to the command of the brigade.

About daybreak of the first day of January, 1863, this regiment received orders and took position as part of the reserve on the left wing of the army, and retained that position during the entire day, and consequently was not in action.

At 10 o'clock p. m. of the same day the regiment was posted on the front line in the left wing of the army, and retained this position until 9 o'clock p. m. of the 2d of January, 1863. During this time the regiment was not engaged in action, but was, at about 10 o'clock a. m. of the 2d of January, subjected to a severe fire from the enemy's artillery, discharging into their ranks a large number of solid shot and shells, by which two enlisted men were severely wounded.

About 5 o'clock p. m. of this day an attack was made by the enemy on the right flank of the regiment while the regiment was being moved to a new position which it had been ordered to occupy. The front of the regiment was immediately changed, and skirmishers thrown forward to meet the skirmishers of the enemy, and soon succeeded in driving the enemy from the field without loss to the regiment. At 9 o'clock a. m. of the second day of January the regiment, in pursuance of orders received, crossed the river on the left, and took position on the front line of the left wing of our army, which position it held until the morning of the fourth day of January, 1863, when it was moved to its present position in the field, in the rear of the army.

During the time the regiment held position south of Stone river, to wit, the night of the second and the day and night of the third of January, the regiment was not engaged in action.

The loss of the regiment during the time covered by this report was but two, to wit, two enlisted men wounded.

Respectfully,

JAMES T. EMBREE,
Lieutenant Colonel Commanding
58th Regiment Indiana Volunteers.

HEADQUARTERS THIRD KENTUCKY VOLUNTEERS,
Near Murfreesboro', January 5, 1863.

SIR: By order of Colonel George P. Buell, I herewith submit a report of the part taken by the 3d regiment Kentucky volunteers in the action on Thursday, January 1, 1863.

By order of Colonel Buell I moved my regiment at 2 o'clock a. m. west of the railroad, and formed on the right of the 100th Illinois, the 58th Indiana and 26th Ohio in our rear. We remained here all day, ready at any time to meet an attack, but nothing of note took place, an occasional shell passing over the regiment, which we shielded ourselves from by lying flat on the ground. At 8 o'clock p. m. we moved to a skirt of woods about five hundred yards to the front, and relieved the 3d battalion of pioneers, where we remained during the night.

Friday, January 2, 1863.—We remained in the position occupied the night previous, and during part of the time were under a heavy fire from the enemy's batteries. About five o'clock p. m. we marched with the balance of the brigade across the river, where we formed in line in an open field. After standing under arms for some time in a drenching rain we withdrew to a skirt of woods on the right of our position, where we bivouacked for the night.

Saturday, January 3, 1863.—About 7 o'clock a. m. we marched to the front and took position in the second line in rear of the fortifications, where we remained until about 1 o'clock p. m., when we moved forward and occupied the position previously held by the 58th Indiana, where we remained until about 2 o'clock a. m.

Sunday, January 4, 1863.—We recrossed the river about 2 o'clock a. m., and went into camp on the west of the railroad. The day was mostly spent in gathering up and burying the dead.

Respectfully, yours,

D. R. COLLIER,
Major Commanding.

Captain J. B. ELWOOD,
Acting Assistant Adjutant General, 15th Brigade.

HEADQUARTERS THIRD REGIMENT KENTUCKY VOLUNTEERS,
Camp near Murfreesboro', January 5, 1863.

SIR: By order of Brigadier General Milo T. Hascall, commanding brigade, I herewith submit a report of the part taken by the third regiment of Kentucky volunteers in the action at this place on Wednesday, December 31, 1862.

At 10 o'clock a. m. the regiment was ordered to form, and was marched to its first position on the east of the railroad, fronting towards the right of our army, where the battle was raging fiercest, and our forces, overwhelmed by superior numbers, were falling back, contesting stubbornly inch by inch the ground which they were forced to give up. Our regiment, with the 26th regiment Ohio volunteer infantry on our right, formed the front line, while the 58th regiment Indiana volunteers, with the 100th Illinois volunteers on its right, formed the second line. We lay in that position until about 10 o'clock, when we were ordered to the front to the support of Colonel Hazen's brigade, which was being attacked by greatly superior numbers. We crossed the railroad, and marching by the right flank at double-quick, filed to the right across the turnpike, and formed in an open field on the right of the 9th Indiana, of Colonel Hazen's brigade, our left resting on the turnpike. The men were ordered to lie down, and immediately the firing commenced, the enemy having advanced in two lines to within two hundred yards of our position. We held our position under a galling cross fire until 1 o'clock p. m., when a regiment which had formed on our right giving way, we were ordered to fall back about twenty-five yards across the turnpike to guard against a flank movement which the enemy threatened from the woods on our right. We occupied our new position about an hour, when our ammunition having been entirely expended, and the guns becoming so foul that it was impossible to load them, we were ordered to fall behind the railroad, about fifty yards in rear of our old position, to fix bayonets and receive the enemy, should they approach nearer, with the cold steel. We lay in this position until 4 o'clock p. m., when we were ordered to the rear to replenish onr stock of ammunition and clean the guns.

We marched half a mile to the rear, and had scarcely filled our cartridge-boxes and wiped out the guns when we were called upon by the commanding officer of —— battery to support him against a strong force of the enemy, who were approaching our left from the east side of the river. A few rounds from the battery caused the enemy to retire. We were in line on the left of the battery when General Rosecrans came up, and in person ordered us to advance and take position in a cornfield within about two hundred yards of the river. This position we held until about 2 o'clock a. m. of Thursday, the men lying on their arms.

The regiment went into the fight with Samuel McKee, colonel commanding,

Major Daniel R. Collier, acting lieutenant colonel, Adjutant W. A. Bullitt, acting major. There were in the regiment thirteen officers of the line, and three hundred (300) men, rank and file.

Colonel McKee fell at 11 o'clock, after we had been engaged half an hour, and when the contest was at its height. A Minie ball striking him over the right eye, he fell from his horse and expired almost immediately. A truer patriot, a braver man, or a better Christian never fell fighting in defence of truth and liberty—worshipped by his men, respected and loved by the officers, our colonel would have desired no fitter mausoleum than that in the midst of dead and dying comrades. I was wounded twice during the engagement, but did not leave the field. The horse of Adjutant Bullitt was shot under him. Our hospital was captured by the enemy about 12 o'clock m., and our surgeon, Hector Owens, was taken prisoner, but released after having been kept four days. Our men and officers, without exception, acted bravely, and to give you a list of those who distinguished themselves would be but to give you our muster-roll. Out of thirteen officers of the line, nine were disabled; of the enlisted men there were—

Killed	12
Wounded	77
Missing	34
Total	123

Many of the wounded have died since the report was compiled. The number of killed and wounded is here stated as it was the day of the fight.

Respectfully,

DANIEL R. COLLIER,
Major Commanding Third Kentucky Infantry, Volunteers.

Captain EDW. R. KERSTETTER,
Assistant Adjutant General, 15th Brigade.

HEADQUARTERS 2D BRIGADE, 1ST DIVISION, LEFT WING,
ARMY OF THE CUMBERLAND,
On the field near Murfreesboro', Tennessee, January 6, 1863.

SIR: I have the honor to report the following as to the position and part taken by my brigade in the great battle of the last few days. On the morning of the 31st ultimo my command was formed in order of battle, the right resting on the Murfreesboro' road, about two miles from the town, and the left resting to the left of the railroad; one section of Cox's battery commanding the pike, the remainder of the battery posted so as to command either side of the railroad. While in this position I received an order to move forward; my skirmishers immediately became engaged with the enemy, and the enemy's artillery shelling my lines. There was a fearful battle going on at this time on our extreme right. I received orders to proceed no further, but if attacked to hold my position. General Hascall's and Colonel Harker's brigades were posted on my left, but were soon after withdrawn; this made it necessary to extend my line to the left, so as to prevent the enemy crossing Stone river, at a ford which had been held by Colonel Harker, and that I was now ordered to hold at all hazards by General Wood. I accordingly moved all my brigade to the left of the railroad, with one section of Cox's battery at the railroad; the other sections were posted directly in front of the ford, on the crest of a hill, supported by the 57th Indiana volunteers, and in such position as to rake the front both to the right and left. Directly in front of this position, on the opposite side of the river, on an elevation defended by earthworks were posted two of the enemy's batteries and a large force of infantry, under command of General Breckinridge. This was mainly the position of my command when the enemy made the first vigorous assault in front, which, after a long and continued struggle, was repulsed with great slaughter of the enemy, but to return in still greater force. Learning that General Hascall, on the right of the road, was hard pressed, I sent the 97th Ohio to re-enforce him, which did good service as they took position on the flank, and were sheltered by the nature of the ground from the fire of the enemy, and which prevented the enemy from raking our lines from the woods on the right; Colonel Lane maintained this position throughout the day. The enemy at this time had gained the woods on this side of the river, and I ordered the 15th Indiana, supported by the 57th Indiana, to advance to meet them. Captain Cox's battery, supported by the 40th Indiana, opened on them with canister, and soon drove them back; at the same time they were repulsed in front by General Hascall, but only to return, as before, in greater force, this time evidently determined to carry my position, as a brigade was thrown on this side of the river, under cover of the woods in my front, at only about 300 yards distant. Cox's battery had exhausted nearly all of their ammunition, and had tried in vain to procure more, which made it necessary for me to rely mainly on the infantry to dislodge the enemy from this position. I preferred making the attack myself rather than waiting an assault from them: I ordered forward the 15th Indiana, supported by the 57th Indiana, being all the troops I had in hand, the 40th Indiana being hotly engaged on the right of the railroad, with the left resting upon the river, so as to completely enfilade the enemy's line. At this time Colonel Hines and Lieutenant Colonel Leonard, of the 57th Indiana, were severely wounded, and had to leave the field. From this position I directed Lieutenant Colonel Wood, commanding 15th Indiana volunteers, to charge the enemy at a double-quick, and nobly did he and his men execute the order, killing, wounding, and capturing nearly one entire regiment, and driving two others in utter rout from the field; and nobly was the movement seconded by the 57th Indiana volunteers, although they had lost all their field officers, they poured volley after volley into the enemy, thereby aiding greatly to the success of the movements. Captain Cox's battery gave them the last shot they had in the locker, thereby making the route complete. The 15th Indiana lost in this charge about thirty killed and near one hundred wounded; but the rebels were not yet whipped, as they returned again in force, my infantry slowly retiring, and fighting their way back; by this time we were prepared for their reception, as Captain Cox had procured some ammunition, and I had ordered Lieutenant Estep's 8th Indiana battery into position with four guns; when the enemy came within canister range they were literally swept away and driven back in utter confusion. The artillery was supported at this time by the 26th Ohio, under command of the gallant Major Squires. Night coming on put an end to the conflict. And allow me to say I found my command as far to the front as they were in the morning, and the noble dead of this brigade lay nearer the enemy's position than that of any other. It must be remembered that during the entire day the enemy's guns directly in my front, at a thousand yards distant and defended by earthworks, from the effect of our artillery kept up a continual fire of shot and shell, and every movement of my troops had to be made under this fearful fire. And I desire thus publicly to state of the men of my command, that in this trying ordeal they proved themselves soldiers of the highest order; they remained in this position during the night without fire, shivering with cold as they lay upon the bloody field, yet not a murmur escaped them. To Captain Cox's battery, officers and men, I am greatly indebted for the result of this day; they were under a continual fire, and much of it a cross fire from the enemy's artillery, which was securely protected while Captain Cox was in an open field without even a tree to screen him from view; yet when their ammunition was exhausted the only cry of the captain and his men was for more ammunition.

The morning of the first, in accordance with orders from General Hascall, I formed my command on the right of Colonel Beatty's division, whose left rested upon the river, some half a mile to the rear of the position of the day before, with Colonel Harker upon my right. Soon after daylight the enemy attacked us warmly, but were soon driven off by the artillery. My advance still held the ground on the left of my position of the 31st ultimo, which the enemy seemed determined to drive me from. I re-enforced this point and held it during the day, although repeatedly attacked by the enemy. Things remained in this position until the morning of the 2d. The enemy having, during the night, thrown across the river in our front a large force, they opened upon our lines with a fearful storm of artillery, which, however, did but little execution on my lines, but was directed to Colonel Harker's command, on my right; they were soon silenced and driven off by our artillery. The enemy again attempted to drive my men from the woods on the left. I obtained re-enforcements for that position from General Cruft, which enabled us to hold that position until the attack in the evening, made upon Colonel Beatty, when I was ordered by General Hascall to cross the river to his support. When we arrived on the opposite side the enemy were already repulsed. Night coming on we lay upon the field. The troops under my command were not engaged on the 4th. Allow me, in closing this report, to say that, with one single exception, the commanders of regiments and field officers showed themselves worthy of the positions they hold. Lieutenant Colonel Wood, 15th Indiana, had his horse shot under him; Colonel Lane, 97th Ohio, behaved with the coolness of a veteran; Lieutenant Colonel Neff, commanding 40th Indiana volunteers, unfortunately was wounded early in the action, devolving the command on Major Leaming, to whom I am under obligations for the manner in which he handled his regiment; Colonel Hines, 57th Indiana, was wounded about the middle of the afternoon while at the head of his regiment gallantly leading them to the attack of the enemy. Lieutenant Colonel Leonard was wounded about the same time, devolving the command of that regiment on Captain McGraw, who deserves special commendation for the manner in which he performed his trust. It is impossible for me to name the officers who did well, as they nearly all did so, but will leave with the regimental commanders the duty of doing them justice; but must be allowed to pay one last tribute to the noble dead, Captains Foster and Templeton, of the 15th Indiana, who fell while leading the men in their charge upon the foe. May their country not forget them. The exception above alluded to in my commendation of officers was Colonel J. W. Blake, 40th Indiana volunteers, who, upon the field, became so intoxicated as to be entirely unfit for duty. I ordered him to report to General Wood under arrest, since which time I have not seen him, but report says he is in Nashville a paroled prisoner. This was about noon of the day of the 31st, before his regiment had become engaged.

The casualties are as follows:

Fifteenth Indiana volunteers—Officers: 2 killed and 7 wounded. Enlisted men: 36 killed, 136 wounded, and 7 missing. Total killed, wounded, and missing, 188.

Fifty-seventh Indiana volunteers.—Officers: 6 wounded. Enlisted men: 11 killed, 55 wounded, and 6 missing. Total killed, wounded, and missing, 78.

Fortieth Indiana volunteers.—Officers: 5 wounded. Enlisted men: 4 killed, 63 wounded, and 13 missing. Total killed, wounded, and missing, 85.

Ninety-seventh Ohio volunteers.—Enlisted men: 3 killed, 15 wounded, and 6 missing. Total killed, wounded, and missing, 24.

Total number of men of the brigade killed, wounded, and missing, 375; total number of men engaged, 1,475; number of men for duty on the morning of the 2d, 1,100.

The 15th Indiana volunteers captured 171 prisoners belonging, most of them, to the 13th Louisiana.

The members of my personal staff present on the field, Captain Henry C. Tinney, acting assistant adjutant general, Captain Warren, and Lieutenant W. M. Casterline, aides-de-camp, and of my escort, who rendered me efficient service during the engagement, frequently carrying orders through such a storm of bullets that it was extremely doubtful whether they would live to deliver them.

Which is respectfully submitted.

Your obedient servant,

G. D. WAGNER,
Colonel Commanding.

HEADQUARTERS 40TH INDIANA VOLUNTEERS,
Near Murfreesboro', Tennessee, January 9, 1863.

SIR: On the 26th ultimo the 40th Indiana volunteers, commanded by Colonel John W. Blake, marched from Nashville in the direction of Murfreesboro' and camped near the village of Lavergne. The pickets from this regiment covering the right of the brigade, and one-half of the regiment having been thrown forward for this purpose, the entire picket line of the brigade being made the charge of Lieutenant Colonel Neff, of this regiment. The night passed quietly, but early on the morning of the 27th firing commenced between our outposts and those of the enemy who occupied the village, which was kept up briskly for some time, and terminated with a few rounds of artillery firing on either side. The regiment had one man wounded in this skirmish. At about midday we again took the road, and without further casualty marched to Stewart's creek and encamped, remaining till the morning of the 29th, when we crossed the creek and moved forward amid occasional skirmishing till arriving about two and half miles from Murfreesboro', where we halted, our right resting on the turnpike at the toll-gate, and the left resting on the railroad. We remained at this point till the morning of the 31st without casualty, having picketed the front on the nights of the 29th and 30th.

On the 31st firing was heard off to our right from both artillery and small arms, indicating an important movement in that direction. but the regiment made no change of position, keeping the men ready for instant action. About 9 a. m. the troops to our right were discovered to be falling back, and we were ordered to retire and move to a position from which we could advance to their support. The enemy were soon repulsed, however, and we were then ordered to take position in rear of Cox's battery, and on a line with that the regiment occupied on the morning, our right resting on the railroad, the left extending nearly at right angles from it. In this position we were exposed to the fire from the enemy's guns, and lost some men wounded. We remained here but a short time, when we were ordered to retire the regiment slowly, which order was about being executed when General Palmer, mistaking the 40th for the 9th Indiana, ordered it to remain. Some time was consumed in explaining the mistake, which kept the regiment to the rear of the line of the retiring brigade. The movement on the part of the 40th Indiana was being executed with much confusion and greatly to the dissatisfaction of the company officers, as well as to Lieutenant Colonel Neff and myself. The confusion arising from the intoxication of Colonel Blake, who was discovered to be utterly unfit to command. These facts were reported to Colonel Wagner, who promptly put Colonel Blake in arrest, and ordered Lieutenant Colonel Neff to assume command. Shortly thereafter an order came from Colonel Wagner directing that the regiment advance at once and engage the enemy, but this order was found to be impracticable, as there were at that moment two lines immediately in front of us; Lieutenant Colonel Neff, however, directed the adjutant to say to the officer commanding the front line that the 40th was ready to relieve him, but it was ascertained that the enemy's guns engaging this line were silenced, and that our assistance was not required. In a few minutes another order came from Colonel Wagner directing the regiment to the support of General Hascall's brigade, which was now engaging the enemy and occupying the ground which we had been resting on in the morning. The regiment was reported to General Hascall and was by him ordered to take a position with the right resting at the old house near the toll-gate, and the left extending across the railroad, which struck the line about the colors, and lie down. This ground being elevated several feet above that occupied by the front line, placed the regiment in a position much exposed to the fire of the enemy, which was at this time very heavy, both artillery and musketry. Many of our men were wounded here, one mortally, and three more killed outright. It was while lying here that I was advised that Lieutenant Colonel Neff was severely wounded in the arm and had quit the field in consequence thereof. After having laid about three-fourths of an hour on this spot we were ordered to relieve the 58th Indiana, which occupied the advance line in our front. I called up the regiment and advanced at once, notifying the officer commanding the 58th of my purpose. The 58th was withdrawn and the 40th took their place. For some minutes after getting into position we were only annoyed by artillery fire, but soon we observed a brigade of the enemy moving toward us in order, with the evident intention of attacking us. On nearing the ruins of the burnt brick building in our front, one regiment was detached from the brigade and bore down upon us; I allowed them to gain a point within easy range of musketry fire, and directed the regiment to open upon them, which they did with great briskness, and with such effect as to repulse the enemy handsomely. When I found the enemy had been effectually driven back I ordered my command to cease firing, and immediately set about replenishing the cartridge-boxes with ammunition, and quietly awaited any further advance on the part of the enemy, which, however, was not made. Nightfall found the regiment occupying the same ground upon which we had bivouacked since arriving on the 29th. The regiment remained in position with a picket thrown forward till 4 o'clock a. m. of the 1st instant, when we were ordered to retire, which we did quietly, and took a position a few rods to the left of the railroad and about half a mile to the rear of the one abandoned. Nothing of any moment occurred to the regiment on the 1st; we kept the front well covered with skirmishers and kept in readiness for any attack.

On the 2d, early in the day, we were subjected to a vigorous artillery fire from the enemy, which, however, had no serious result. On the evening of the 2d, at nearly sundown, the enemy attacked the troops on the left of our position, and the regiment threw forward an additional skirmishing company to support our line, which, being in the open field, was much exposed, and had been subjected, throughout the day, to a vicious fire from the outposts of the enemy, who were concealed by the timber in front, which resulted in wounding Captain Wallace and two of his men. The enemy were repulsed on the left, and the regiment was directed to move to that part of the field. Crossing the river, we moved forward to the advanced line, and taking position, remained till the evening of the 3d, when we were relieved and retired to the skirt of woods on the bank of the river, where we bivouacked till 4 a. m. of the 4th, when we were withdrawn to the rear, recrossing the river and taking position on the turnpike one mile in advance of the general hospital. Shortly after arriving here we learned that the enemy had evacuated.

Our loss during the engagement was 4 killed and 68 wounded; among the latter were Lieutenant Colonel Neff, Captains Wallace and Harvey, First Lieutenant Griswold, and Second Lieutenants Coleman and Hazelrigg.

In conclusion, I must state that the conduct of the regiment under the most trying circumstances was worthy of all praise. The coolness and quiet determination of officers and men were admirable, and not less so the cheerfulness of spirit with which the hardships and exposure to cold and rain were born. The regiment did its duty faithfully; I know no higher praise that can be given it.

HENRY LEAMING,
Major, Commanding Regiment.

Captain N. C. TINNEY,
Acting Assistant Adjutant General, 21st Brigade.

List of killed and wounded in the battle of Murfeeesboro' in the 40th Indiana volunteers.

Colonel John W. Blake, said to have been wounded in the left arm; Lieutenant Colonel Elias Neff, wounded in left arm severely.

Killed.—Company A: Private John Montgomery. Company B: Privates Robert Atchison and Jacob Walling. Company D: Private George W. Hawey.

Wounded.—Company A: First Sergeant John A. Baer, shoulder, slightly. Corporals S. Leaming, leg, severely; W. Shellington, leg, slightly; and W. Hutton, side, slightly; Privates S. Cambee, elbow, severely; W. Manary, leg, slightly; W. Morris, foot; William Morris, foot and leg, severely; Joseph Patton, leg, severely; R. Wilson, leg; N. Howard, arm, slightly; J. Sheetz, head and shoulder, slightly; S. Elliott, shoulder, slightly; P. Illianfritz, belly, slightly; and J. P. Julien, side, slightly. Company B: Captain O. C. Harvey, head, slightly; First Lieutenant W. Griswold, thigh, severely; Sergeant G. S. Murphy, arm, slightly; Sergeant J. Brower, back, slightly; Corporal H. S. Phillaburm, shoulder, slightly; Privates Thos. Helvey, arm; W. McConaha, hand and breast; C. Merrett, head and shoulder; D. Ramsey, breast, slightly; S. Staley, hip, severely; W. Vanschouick, back, slightly; C. M. Cook, leg, slightly; and M. Miller, foot shot off. Company C: Captain W. D. Wallace, arm, severely; Corporal Josiah Leavis, hand, slightly; Privates P. G. Beaty, thigh, slightly; J. Monfort, side, slightly; J. Linnet, neck, slightly; J. Groves, arm; A. Bell, shoulder; and A. Whitmore, face. Company D: Lieutenant William Coleman, head, severely; Privates G. B. Davis, head, severely; J. L. Lewis, head, slightly; and J. Meek, arm, slightly. Company E: First Sergeant R. Kolb, hand; Corporal T. D. Henderson, leg; Privates P. Wiltsman, back; S. K. Wise, foot; S. N. Jackson, head, severely; and A. McNutt, head and foot. Company F: Privates F. N. Linsmore, head, slightly; W. H. Dooley, hip, slightly; J. Muldoon, thigh, slightly; and M. A. Brockway, arm, slightly. company G: Sergeant W. W. Cuonutt, arm, slightly; Privates Joseph Patterson, thigh, severely; H. C. Seeley, arm, severely; E. C. Moore, arm, severely; W. Longberger, hip, slightly; Luke Conner, hip, slightly; O. Jones, leg, slightly; and W. Silvers, hip, slightly. Company H: Private John Briley, foot. Company I: First Sergeant E. A. Routh, hip; Privates L. R. Richardson, hip; L. Benson, thigh; and J. Hicks, knee. Company K: Second Lieutenant H. L. Hazelrigg, leg, severely; Corporal H. W. Chambers, head, slightly; and Private Horatio Veatch, head, severely.

HEADQUARTERS 40TH INDIANA VOLUNTEERS,
Near Murfreesboro', Tennessee, February 22, 1863.

SIR: I send you below a complete list of the killed and wounded of the 40th Indiana volunteers at the battle of Stone river, near Murfreesboro', Tennessee:

Killed.—Company A: Private John Montgomery. Company B: Privates Robert Atchison and Jacob Walling. Company D: Private George W. Hawey.

Wounded.—Colonel John Blake and Lieutenant Colonel Elias Neff. Company A: First Sergeant John A. Baer; and Corporals Sylvester Leaming, William Shellington, and William Hutton; Privates Samuel Camber, William Manary, Walter Morris, William Morris, Joseph Patton, Reuben B. Wilson, Nelson Howard, Jacob Sheetz, Scott Elliott, Peter Illianfritz, and James P. Julian. Company B: Captain Orpheus C. Harvey; First Lieutenant Willard Griswold; Sergeants Grimes L. Murphy and Jeremiah Brower; Corporal Henry S. Phillabaum; Privates Thomas Helvey, William McConaha, Charles Morrett, David Ramsey, Sanford Staley, William Van Schoyck, Cassius M. Cook, and Milton Miller. Company C: Captain DeWitt Wallace; Corporal Josiah Davis; Privates Peter T. Batey, John Monfort, James Sennett, George Grover, Ambrose Bell, and Adam Whitmore. Company D: Second Lieutenant William S. Coleman; Privates George B. Davis, John L. Lewis, and James Meek. Company E: First Sergeant Richard Kolb; Corporal Thomas D. Henderson; Privates Peter Writsman, Salatiel K. Wise, Silas N. Jackson, and Andrew McNutt. Company F: Privates Francis N. Dinsmore, William H. Dooley, James Muldoon, and Marcus A. Brockway. Company G: Sergeant William W. Curnutt; Privates Joseph Patterson, Horace C. Seeley, Elijah C. Moore, William Lonberger, Luke Conner, Oliver Jones, and William Silvers. Company H: Private John Briley. Company I: First Sergeant Eugene A. Routh; Privates Daniel H. Richardson, David Benson, and James Hicks. Company K: Second Lieutenant Henry L. Hazelrigg; Corporal Henry W. Chambers; and Private Horatio Veach.

Very respectfully, your most obedient servant,

W. LEAMING,
Major 40th Indiana Volunteers, Commanding Regiment.

ADJUTANT GENERAL U. S. A.

SIR: I have the honor to report to you the part taken by the 97th regiment Ohio volunteers, infantry, in the late engagement in front of Murfreesboro', commencing the 31st day of December, 1862, and ending the 3d day of January, 1863.

On the night of the 30th of December we were, by your order, placed in the front, our advance pickets being deployed on the left bank of Stone river. On the morning of the 31st, at the commencement of the engagement, our position was on the north side of the Nashville and Chattanooga railroads, one-fourth of a mile from the river. At 9 o'clock a. m. the enemy commenced feeling for our position with shot and shell, and by your order I moved my regiment by the left flank to a position in an open field, one-fourth of a mile from the railroad, and deployed one company to the river as skirmishers. We remained in this position, under a fire from the enemy's artillery and infantry, until 11 o'clock a. m. Our casualties up to this time were: wounded, Jacob G. Brill, private, company A; Mathias Tapier, private, company I, and Samuel Browning, private, company I, the latter having since died from the effects of his wounds.

By your order I now moved to the south side of the railroad to re-enforce General Hascall. We found the enemy vigorously assaulting his lines with artillery and infantry. Our place was assigned us by General Rosecrans in person, who ordered us to take the position and hold it. We advanced to the place designated, which was on the south side of the Nashville and Murfreesboro' turnpike, returning the fire of the enemy until near sundown, when he withdrew to the cover of the woods, leaving us in posession of the ground. At nightfall I threw out one company as pickets a hundred paces to the front, instructing the officer in command to avail himself of the opportunity to carefully note any movement of the enemy. Near midnight he informed me that he could distinctly hear the tramp of horses and rumbling of artillery moving from our right to our left. Upon investigation I was satisfied that the enemy was massing his forces on our left, and forthwith informed you of the fact. At 2 o'clock on the morning of the 1st of January I informed General Rosecrans of this movement of the enemy, when he immediately arranged to relieve us from this position, which we had held since noon of the preceding day. Our casualties during our absence from your brigade were: wounded, Isaac McDonald, private, company B; Israel Garrett and J. C. Huffman, privates, company C; Austin Harvey and Evan Foulke, privates, company D; Lewellyn Echelberry, sergeant, company E; George Robinson, private, company G, and John Moore, private, company H; A. M. Hasom, color sergeant, killed; August Reinsch, private, company B, and John Rodecker, private, company G.

At 3 o'clock on the morning of the 1st I reported my regiment to you, and was assigned a place in the front line about a half mile to the rear of the position occupied by me at the beginning of the engagement. We remained here during the day with no other annoyance than an occasional shot or shell from the enemy's guns. At night we bivouacked on the spot. On the morning of the 2d our skirmishers were advanced a half mile to the front, where they remained undisturbed until quarter before 3 o'clock p. m., when the enemy attacked our forces across the river and our skirmishers were driven back. We were here subjected to a cross fire from the enemy's guns for more than an hour, wounding Charles H. Claspbell, corporal, company K; Purley Dickson, sergeant, and Benjamin Kinsey, private, company D.

At 5 o'clock p. m. we crossed Stone river and remained on its right bank until the morning of the 4th without further event.

Our loss during the whole engagement was three killed, fifteen wounded, and six missing. The officers and men in my command everywhere acquitted themselves nobly, and we never lost a position after once taking it.

I have the honor, colonel, to be your obedient servant,

JOHN A. LANE,
Colonel 97th Regiment Ohio Volunteer Infantry.

Colonel G. D. WAGNER.

HEADQUARTERS 57TH INDIANA FOOT VOLUNTEERS,
In field near Murfreesboro', January 8, 1863.

SIR: I have the honor to submit the following report of the killed, wounded, and missing of the 57th Indiana foot volunteers in the late action before Murfreesboro', Tennessee:

Engaged in action: Two field officers, one staff officer, one non-commissioned staff, sixteen line officers, and 311 enlisted men. Aggregate, 331.

KILLED AND WOUNDED.

Adjutant Henry C. Elliott, severely wounded in right shoulder by musket ball on morning of the 30th ultimo.

Colonel C. C. Hines, severely wounded by cannon ball in right thigh on the 31st ultimo.

Lieutenant Colonel George W. Leonard, severely wounded by buckshot in calf of leg.

Company A.—First Sergeant W. H. McLaughlin, slightly wounded; Corporal Joseph Brooks, severely wounded in right arm; Private Granvill Fisk, slightly wounded; Private Lorenzo D. Fort, severely wounded on 31st, died on 2d in hospital.

Company B.—Killed: Private John Burket. Wounded: Privates Amos Draher, mortally; Henry C. Hunt, in left breast, slightly; Frank M. Hunt, in head, slightly; George Minor, in thigh, slightly; Martin V. B. Thorn, in knee, slightly.

Company C.—Wounded: Privates John Osborn, Milter R. Maston, Merritt Lamb, William Lamb, Albert C. Jeffries.

Company D.—Killed: Privates Thornton Freeman and Calvin W. Arnold. Wounded: Musician V. H. Richter, seriously in arm; Corporals E. E. Manning, seriously, and John Ensman; Private B. Tickenoucth, slightly in hand.

Company E.—Killed: Private John F. Fitz. Wounded: Privates Abram McConnell, nose and left cheek; Thomas Bayles, right ankle; Solomon Rinard, accidentally, right hand.

Company F.—Killed: Sergeant Wesley W. Seward and Private Edwin A. Gregory. Wounded: Lieutenant S. J. Smith, leg; Sergeant Albert S. Hardin, right arm, slightly; Corporal Dewitt G. Markle, leg, seriously; Privates William H. Graves, right shoulder, seriously; Alonzo McLaughlin, left arm shot away; Henry C. Cloud, hand, slightly.

Company G.—Killed: Privates John Adamson and Andrew Rhoades. Wounded: Sergeant B. F. Rhoades, and Privates Charles Edwards and Jasper Cooper.

Company H.—Wounded: Sergeant William Smith, arm, severely; Privates Henry C. S. Poole, leg, severely; Pleas. L. McKinney, hand, slightly; and Elias D. Green, head, severely.

Company I.—Wounded: Captain Calvin W. Burket, head, slightly; Sergeant Charles H. Thornbury, leg, severely; Corporal Parker Smith, head, slightly; Corporal More Galway, hand, slightly; Privates George W. Barry, leg, severely; and James White, arm, slightly.

Company K.—Killed: Privates Thomas Orr and John Freeland. Wounded: Second Lieutenant Stanton J. Peeble, hip, slightly; Sergeants Martin J. Crum, hand, and George R. Brown, foot; Corporals Joel Stickly, hip, and George Methore, rump; Privates Noah Rarisch, arm, seriously; S. W. Crummar, shoulder, seriously; William Britwhistle, shoulder, seriously; John Staley, hip, seriously; Hiram Lanner, arm, seriously; Hiram Meck, foot, seriously; Daniel P. Baker, arm, seriously; John Rink, shoulder, seriously; John Goranight, leg, slightly; Orlandor L. Baer, arm, slightly; George Holdenan, shoulder, seriously; Zacharias Hendrickson, thigh, slightly; Melvin R. Phillips, thumb, slightly.

Killed, 11; wounded, 61. Total, 72.

Near 2 p. m. on December 31, 1862, in consequence of Colonel Hines and Colonel Lennard being wounded, the command devolved upon me.

Very respectfully, your obedient servant,

Captain JOHN G. McGRAW,
Commanding 57th Indiana Volunteers.

FIFTEENTH REGIMENT INDIANA VOLUNTEERS,
Camp near Murfreesboro', Tennessee, January 9, 1863.

SIR: I have the honor to present you, herewith, a report of the operations of the regiment during the late engagements before Murfreesboro'. During the advance on the enemy's position the regiment was not actually engaged prior to the 31st ultimo. On the 29th, companies B and F were in advance as skirmishers, and company F had one man wounded. On the morning of the 31st, while supporting Cox's battery, we were ordered to *take* and hold a point of woods on the (then) extreme left of the lines; companies G and F were thrown forward as skirmishers. Finding the enemy so strong that the skirmishers could not dislodge him, I ordered the regiment to fix bayonets and charge, which was executed in a most brilliant style, driving the enemy out in confusion, killing and wounding a large number, and taking over two hundred prisoners from a Louisiana brigade, having in it the 13th, 16th, and 20th Louisiana, (among others.) Being unable, from insufficient force, to send a proper guard, a portion of the prisoners escaped while on the way to the rear. We, however, delivered over to the provost one hundred and seventy. The enemy having been completely driven out, skirmishers were left to hold the position, and the regiment was withdrawn in order to escape the heavy raking fire which the enemy's batteries were pouring on us. On the last grand advance of the enemy, when their right was in fair range of the woods, the regiment again took the position and held it under a most terrific fire, until the enemy was finally routed for the day, when it was withdrawn for the same reason as before. By your order it was soon after placed in a grove to the left of our last position, where we bivouacked for the night. In the subsequent engagements the regiment was not actually engaged, but at different periods was exposed to a very heavy fire from the enemy's batteries, during which several men were killed and wounded. All behaved nobly. It cannot be expected that I should mention names where all did so well. Captains Foster and Templeton died gallantly performing their duty, as did their dead comrades. The more fortunate living were fit compeers for the noble dead. Major Camparet was very active wherever duty called him; Adjutant Nicar fearlessly faced the fire to which the command was exposed, and, in addition, volunteered to bear messages to the battery and other exposed places in rear, (I having no mounted man for the purpose.) Captain White, company F, having skirmishers in charge, performed his duty well during the day, and at night cheerfully volunteered to do the picket duty for the command. It may be proper for me to say that during the entire time of privation and fatigue—being ten days' continuous duty in a very inclement season—the cheerfulness and fortitude of the men were only equalled by their courage on the field of battle. The regiment went into action with 24 commissioned officers and 416 enlisted men; aggregate, 440. The list of killed, wounded, and missing is appended.

Respectfully submitted.

G. S. WOOD,
Lieutenant Colonel, Commanding 15th Indiana volunteers.

Colonel G. D. WAGNER,
Commanding 21st Brigade.

Killed, wounded, and missing of the 15th Indiana volunteers.

Killed.—Company A: Sergeant Richard Kester, Corporal William E. Parmer, Privates John Curran, Henry Hogeland, and James Williams. Company B: Corporal Jonas Hoover, Privates Michael Hennessy and Benjamin F. Markel. Company C: Corporals John Morgan, Royal E. Barney, Privates John Trager and Frederick Ulque. Company D: Captain Robert

J. Templeton, Corporal Isaac N. Williams, Privates Columbus M. Bushong and Commodore P. Huff. Company E: Corporal John A. Schmall, Privates Adam Sittinger, Henry Staffen, and Emory Williams. Company F: Private William Coward. Company G: Captain Joel W. Foster, Corporal Calvin R. Zener, Privates Robert J. Douglas and W. D. Kelley. Company H: Privates John E. Jungling, Patrick Madden, George W. Moore, and Jesse Vincer. Company I: Privates William A. Cockafair, William H. Muir, and John Davis. Company K: Sergeant Mathias M. Dickey, Privates Israel Lebo, Isaac N. Chalmers, William Kenifeck, Esau Fisher, and Robert B. Simpson.

Total killed.—	Captains	2
	Sergeants	2
	Corporals	6
	Privates	28
Aggregate killed		38

Wounded.—Company A: Second Lieutenant Alonzo Pearce, severe concussion; Sergeants Clayton H. Todd, slightly; David Phipps, slightly; Corporals Wesley Day, slightly; John Cassell, slightly; Henry Allen, severely; Privates Hiram Barkdale, severely; Christian Bond, dangerously; Carlton D. Crane, severely; Lewis Crane, severely; Simon Downey, slightly; Peter Edenbern, slightly; Elza Irwin, severely; Jonathan Gibbs, slightly; Michael Griffin, dangerously; William T. Hagler, severely; George H. Seath, slightly; Jacob Paulding, slightly; Isaiah Treadwell, severely; and James Downey, slightly. Company B: Captain John E. George, severely; First Sergeant William A. Pegg, dangerously; Sergeant Michael Sandenberger, mortally, since died; Corporals Jacob Tilford, severely; William H. H. Hogle, severely, since died; John Parks, severely; Privates Pierce T. Clark, severely; Peter A. Cloyher, slightly; John Gaseytty, slightly; William Hill, severely; Edwin Hunterugan, severely; Robert Logan, severely; Chefield Lucien, severely; William Melvin, severely; Henry Shearer, severely; and James Sweeney, severely. Company C: Second Lieutenant John F. Monroe, severely; Sergeants Louis A. Foster, slightly; William Dougall, severely; Corporal John M. Brewer, severely; Privates David Boyle, severely; John Cojel, slightly; William M. Daffern, severely; Bruce Dalson, severely, since died; Joseph Fluallen, slightly; James C. Foster, slightly; William Livergood, severely, since died; John D. Long, leg shot off; Henry McDowell, dangerously, since died; George Miller, severely; John Mooney, slightly; Timothy Murphy, slightly; James S. Rich, severely; John B. Underwood, slightly; Milton Wilson, dangerously; Holbert Fullem, severely; and John M. Wilson, slightly. Company D: Second Lieutenant Mark Walker, severely; Sergeants William Snyder, slightly; M. A. Maxson, dangerously; Corporals Frederick Gherring, severely; George W. Snodgrass, severely; Privates Frederick M. Adams, severely; John Baws, severely; Benjamin Booth, slightly; John H. Burns, slightly; Abraham Davenport, severely; Wallace E. Edwards, severely; Benjamin Hawks, slightly; William Hawley, severely; John Kennedy, dangerously; Benedict Clemings, severely; and David Ream, slightly. Company E: Corporals William S. Hess, slightly; Jefferson Cassell, severely; Privates Henry B. Beal, severely; Joseph J. Bettour, severely; Samuel F. Dent, severely; William Hartman, severely; Charles P. Curr, slightly; John W. Lynn, severely; Henry Mercer, severely; William P. Moore, severely; James Ripeto, slightly; Robert F. Sayler, dangerously; William R. Smith, slightly; and John D. Stockton, severely. Company F: Corporal John Harjis, severely; Privates Thomas Olds, severely; Joseph Steinberger, slightly; and Joseph A. Green. Company G: First Lieutenant John H. Smith, slightly; Corporals Herman Shauster, severely; Henry Weidabush, severely; Privates J. F. Burns, slightly; Simeon Jamison, slightly; Louis Page, slightly; Samuel Richards, dangerously; John Rose, slightly; Lemuel Shelden, severely; Burton Shurber, slightly; Alexander Wilson, slightly; and A. F. Maxwell, severely. Company H: Marcus D. L. Foster, severely; Charles D. Heait, severely; William Kennedy, slightly; Patrick H. Lalley, slightly; Benjamin F. Musselman, slightly; John Osborne, slightly; George Plum, severely; Russell Wing, severely; Moses S. Jones, slightly; James M. Carr, slightly; George Lewis, severely; and Harrison Moore, slightly. Company I: Corporals Samuel Hazi, severely; Andrew J. Colkins, slightly; Privates William H. Macy, slightly; Henry C. Putnam, slightly; Daniel P. Shafer, slightly; and Moses W. Corey, slightly. Company K: Second Lieutenant John M. Jones, severely; First Sergeant Tipp W. McClure, severely; Sergeants Jacob Custer, slightly; William G. Welch, slightly; Corporals Jacob F. Henning, severely; Henry Buckherst, slightly; Privates Reuben R. Bright, slightly; Francis M. Bowen, slightly; Edward Edwards, severely; George A. Griffith, severely; Henry Hazelton, severely; Andrew J. Heaton, slightly; Franklin Hickox, severely; Andrew Jackson, slightly; Francis McCourtney, severely; John Shook, severely; Adolph Sidon, slightly; John W. Smith, slightly; John Webb, slightly; Isaac F. Wyant, slightly; and John Devose, dangerously.

Total wounded.—Commissioned	6
Enlisted	136
Aggregate	143

Missing.—Company B: Private Henry Cooper, supposed to be killed. Company F: Privates Isaac Ross, prisoner, and Francis Hudson, prisoner. Company G: Privates Samuel Carr, no information in regard to him, and Charles Taylor, no information in regard to him. Company I: Private Thomas J. Wolfe, no information in regard to him. Company K: Sergeant Matthew Sharp went to rear, supposed to have deserted.

Total missing.—Enlisted	7

Summing up.—Killed	38
Wounded	143
Missing	7
Grand total	188

HEADQUARTERS 3D BRIGADE, 1ST DIVISION, LEFT WING,
14th ARMY CORPS, DEP'T OF THE CUMBERLAND,
Murfreesboro', Tennessee, January.

SIR: I have the honor to submit the following report of the operations of the troops under my command from the 29th ultimo to the 4th instant, inclusive.

The 3d brigade, 1st division, left wing, 14th army corps, department of the Cumberland, formerly the 20th brigade, 6th division, consisting of the 51st regiment Indiana volunteers, Colonel A. D. Streight commanding; the 13th regiment Michigan volunteers, Colonel M. Shoemaker commanding; 73d regiment Indiana volunteers, Colonel G. Hatheway commanding; 64th regiment Ohio volunteers, Lieutenant Colonel A. McIlvaine commanding; 65th regiment Ohio volunteers, Lieutenant Colonel Cassil commanding; and the 6th Ohio

Independent battery, commanded by Captain Cullen Bradley, left Stewart's creek about 10 a. m. on Monday, the 29th ultimo, marching most of the time in line of battle, with the right of the line a little in the rear of the left of the 2d brigade, Colonel Wagner commanding. Our skirmishers soon came upon the enemy's cavalry, engaging them briskly, and driving them slowly before them. We proceeded in this manner, cautiously feeling our way until our left arrived at the left bank of Stone river, which was reached about 4 p. m. Up to this time we had suffered no casualties from the enemy's skirmishers. We took up a position near Stone river, about 400 yards to the left of the Nashville and Murfreesboro' pike, 2d brigade, Colonel Wagner commanding, being on the right, and the 1st brigade, General Hascall commanding, being on the left, and somewhat to the rear, owing to the conformation of the ground. We remained in this position until about dark, when we received orders to proceed to Murfreesboro'. Stone river being fordable in our front, we at once commenced crossing the stream. Throwing a strong line of skirmishers over the stream, orders were given to the 51st Indiana volunteers, 13th Michigan, and 73d Indiana to cross simultaneously, form on the opposite bank, press forward and seize the commanding heights beyond, while the 64th and 65th Ohio, with Bradley's battery, were directed to follow as rapidly as possible. The skirmishers had barely left the bank of the river before they were vigorously attacked by those of the enemy, concealed in a thicket and behind a fence in our front. Our skirmishers, in no way daunted by this fierce assault of the enemy, pressed gallantly forward, driving the foe until they came upon the enemy in force. The skirmishers were soon supported by the front line of the brigade. The enemy seemed to have been entirely disconcerted by this bold movement of our troops, and fell back in confusion. In this movement our loss was two men killed and three wounded. This slight loss must be attributed to the able manner in which the officers of the brigade conducted their commands. A prisoner taken reported an entire division of the enemy on my front—movements along my entire front and flanks indicated that a strong force was near me. I reported this to the general commanding the division, at the same time stating that I could hold the position until re-enforced. I soon received orders to recross the stream, which I did, occupying nearly the same ground as before crossing. This movement was so quickly executed as not to excite the suspicion of the enemy. Too much praise cannot be accorded to the brave officers and men of this brigade for their bravery and skill in driving a concealed enemy from a strong position after nightfall, and holding their ground in the face of an enemy three times their numbers. Though little was accomplished by this feat, it nevertheless made manifest the indomitable courage of the men under the most trying circumstances, and augured well for the more severe work which awaited them. On December 30 the 64th Ohio, being on picket and outpost duty, was somewhat annoyed by the enemy in the slight skirmishing in the front, losing one man killed. About 8 a. m. the enemy's battery, stationed on an eminence near the right bank of Stone river, opened a severe fire of shot and shell upon my camp. Bradley's battery was ordered in position to engage that of the enemy. After a severe engagement of fifteen minutes Captain Bradley succeeded in silencing the enemy's battery. My command sustained no loss in this engagement. Aside from this, it was generally quiet on my front during the day.

About 8 a. m., December 31, I received orders from General Wood, commanding division, to cross the river with my command. The movement was commenced, in obedience to General Wood's orders, but was suspended for a few moments by an order emanating from Major General Crittenden, commanding the left wing. While awaiting further orders Major General Rosecrans passed my command, and gave me direct instructions to proceed immediately to the support of the right wing of our army, which was yielding to the overwhelming force of the enemy at that point. We had hardly commenced moving towards the right when a confederate battery, located on the south bank of the river, opened upon us, killing one man and wounding two. Not stopping to reply to this battery we pressed steadily forward. On approaching the right much confusion was visible; troops marching in every direction; stragglers to be seen in great numbers, and teamsters in great consternation endeavoring to drive their teams, they knew not whither. My progress was impeded by the confusion, while the enemy was pouring shot and shell upon us from, at least, three different directions, wounding several men in my command. The brigade was, however, extricated from this perilous position as soon as possible, and pressed on to a position on the extreme right of our line, Colonel Fyffe's brigade, of General Van Cleve's division, being immediately upon our left. After reaching this last position my brigade marched in two lines, the 51st Indiana on the right, the 65th Ohio on the left, the battery a little retired and opposite the interval between the 65th and 51st, the 64th Ohio on the right of the second line, the 73d Indiana on the left, with the 13th Michigan in rear of the caissons. We marched in this order about half a mile, when our skirmishers came up with those of the enemy, and the fire became brisk in front. About this time a battery from the enemy, situated in a cornfield, and nearly opposite my right flank, opened upon my command with canister. In order to get a commanding position for my artillery, and at the same time guard well my right flank, which I was fearful the enemy would attempt to turn, I moved the command a little to the right. While this movement was being executed a staff officer from the command upon my left reported a strong force of the enemy in his front. I replied that my right was in danger, and that a strong force and battery was in front. No sooner had I taken a position on the crest of the hill than a most vigorous engagement commenced. The position selected for my brigade proved a most fortunate one. The enemy was completely baffled in his design to turn my right; not only were the batteries in my front silenced and the enemy there repulsed, but a most destructive fire from Bradley's battery played upon the heavy columns of the enemy then pressing the troops upon my left. This engagement had continued about twenty minutes when it was reported to me that the troops on my left had given way, and that the enemy was already in rear of my left flank, and about two hundred yards from it, pouring a destructive cross fire upon my troops. At this time my command was in a most precarious situation, with a strong foe in front, which, though repulsed, could not be followed up for want of support, my right threatened, and my left already turned. It therefore became necessary to change the disposition of my command and fall back. The commander of the 65th Ohio anticipated my order, when he found his left turned, and fell back in good order. I directed this regiment to make a stand behind a rail fence running obliquely to the first line of battle. During this movement this regiment was subject to a most galling fire from the enemy, but they stood up under it nobly, and fought desperately. While this movement was being executed, the 73d Indiana was left in position on the second line, and the battery retired to a position about four hundred yards to the rear, when it again opened. The 64th Ohio was now ordered to change its front to the left and charge the enemy. The direction was indicated to the commanding officer, but unfortunately he moved too far to the right. Though this regiment handsomely repulsed the enemy in its front, it did the work of the other regiments already in position, and leaving the left of the 73d Indiana exposed, and permitting the enemy to advance much further than could have been done had my design been carried out. I do not, however, desire to censure the commanding officer of this regiment, who acted most gallantly through the engagement, but attribute it to a misunderstanding of the order. Bradley's battery, having taken its second position, opened again with great effect upon the advancing enemy, but, being in an exposed position, it was again ordered to withdraw, being badly crippled by loss of horses; two pieces were abandoned, one of which was spiked. The command was now ordered to fall back, and form on a rocky eminence covered with cedars, being a very strong position. The 13th Michigan, from their position, opened upon the enemy with telling effect, and, having caused his ranks to waver, followed up the advantage with a charge, supported by the 51st Illinois volunteers, which had now come to our relief. They completely routed the enemy. The 13th Michigan retook the two pieces of artillery abandoned by our battery, and captured fifty-eight prisoners. For this act of gallantry Colonel Shoemaker and his gallant regiment are deserving of much praise.

The enemy thus driven from our right did not again attempt to annoy us in that quarter. How far the brave troops of this brigade contributed towards repulsing the strong columns of the enemy designed to turn the right flank of our army, and thus preventing most disastrous consequences to our army, must be inferred by the position occupied by this command, and the part it took in the engagement. Too much praise cannot be bestowed upon Colonel Shoemaker, commanding 13th Michigan volunteers; Colonel Hathaway, commanding the 73d Indiana volunteers; Lieutenant Colonel McIlvain, commanding the 64th Ohio volunteers; Lieutenant Colonel Cassil, who commanded the 65th Ohio volunteers until injured by the falling of his horse, and Major Whitbeck, though wounded in action, remained in command of the 65th Ohio volunteers, after Lieutenant Colonel Cassil was injured, and Captain Bradley, commanding 6th Ohio battery, for their bravery and good conduct during this engagement. My thanks are also due to Colonel A. D. Streight, commanding 51st Indiana volunteers, for valuable information of the movements of the enemy during this engagement. From the less exposed position of his regiment, it suffered less than any other regiment of my command. On the evening of the 31st I received orders from the major general commanding to rejoin the 1st division, which was done about 11 p. m. On January 1 this division was moved a little to the right and rear. My brigade occupied a central position of the division, on the front line of battle, and a short distance to the left of the Murfreesboro' pike. We were hardly in position before the enemy drove in our skirmishers. Bradley's battery, in conjunction with several others on our front, opened a most destructive fire of case shot and shell, driving the enemy from our front and sustaining no loss. On January 2, Bradley's battery being in position on a small eminence on our front, supported on the right by the 64th and 65th Ohio, behind a small clump of trees, and on the left by the 51st Indiana volunteers, lying in a skirt of timber, while the 13th Michigan and 73d Indian were in reserve, three batteries of the enemy opened upon us. They were promptly responded to by Captain Bradley and other batteries on my right, when the most fearful artillery engagement ensued which I had yet had the experience to witness. The enemy, having our range quite perfectly, poured upon us a most destructive fire, causing the battery on our right to be abandoned, but Captain Bradley continued his well-directed firing until the enemy's batteries were silenced. While this engagement was going on Captain Stokes's battery, posted in our rear, opened upon us, mistaking us for the enemy. It is due to Captain Stokes, however, to say that I believe this firing was commenced without his orders, and was stopped by him as soon as it was possible to do so, but not until we had sustained some injury. During the engagement we had one man killed and eleven wounded. On the evening of the same day, when the enemy attacked the left flank of our army with great vigor, Bradley's battery was again placed in position, and did good service in silencing those of the enemy. About dark on the evening of the 2d instant we were ordered to cross Stone river. My brigade was placed in the front line, my right resting on the left of General Davis's division. We were hardly in position before the enemy opened upon us, killing one man of the 64th Ohio. During the night we constructed a musket breastwork of rails, and remained on the front until about 9 a. m., January 3, when we were relieved, and ordered to the rear in reserve, where we remained until about 3 p.m., when we were again ordered to the front to relieve Colonel Wagner's brigade, and occupied a position on the left of the 1st division. We remained in this position until about one a.m., January 4, when we received orders to recross Stone river. We crossed the stream, and took a position in rear of the main body of our force, and about five hundred yards to the left of the railroad, where we remained until our troops had occupied Murfreesboro'. The loss in killed, wounded, and missing, during these six days' engagements, was as follows:

Fifty-first Indiana.—Killed: enlisted men, 7. Wounded: officers, 2; enlisted men, 32. Missing: enlisted men, 9. Total, 50.

Sixty-fourth Ohio.—Killed: officers, 1; enlisted men, 23. Wounded: officers, 3; enlisted men, 61. Missing: enlisted men, 17. Total, 105.

Thirteenth Michigan.—Killed: enlisted men, 17; Wounded: officers, 2; enlisted men, 70. Total, 89.

Seventy-third Indiana volunteers.—Killed: officers, 2; enlisted men, 22. Wounded: officers, 3; enlisted men, 48. Missing: enlisted men, 36. Total, 111.

Sixty-fifth Ohio volunteers.—Killed: officers, 2; enlisted men, 33. Wounded: officers, 8; enlisted men, 92. Missing: enlisted men, 38. Total, 173.

Sixth Ohio battery.—Killed: enlisted men, 2. Wounded: officers, 1; enlisted men, 7. Missing: enlisted men, 1. Total, 11.

Total loss in killed, wounded, and missing, 539.

The following is a correct list of the killed and wounded officers of my command:

Of the 51st Indiana, Captain Francis M. Constant, company G, and Second Lieutenant Alfred Gude, wounded.

Of the 64th Ohio, Captain Joseph B. Sweet, killed; First Lieutenant Warner Young, wounded; First Lieutenant Joseph B. Ferguson, wounded; First Lieutenant and Regimental Adjutant Chancey Woodruff, wounded.

Of the 13th Michigan, Captain Clement C. Webb, company E, wounded; Second Lieutenant John E. McIvor, company E, wounded.

Of the 73d Indiana, Captain Miles N. Tibbets, company I, killed; Captain Peter Doyl, company K, killed; Major William Krimbill, wounded.

Second Lieutenant Emanuel Williamson, company I, wounded; Second Lieutenant John Butterfield, company K, wounded.

Of the 65th Ohio, Captain J. Christofel, killed; Second Lieutenant Dolsen Van Kirk, killed; Lieutenant Colonel A. Cassil, wounded; Major H. N. Whitbeck, wounded; Captain R. M. Voorhies, company F, wounded; First Lieutenant A. A. Gardner, wounded; Second Lieutenant and Regimental Adjutant William H. Massey, wounded; Second Lieutenant Peter Markel, wounded; Second Lieutenant Joel P. Brown, wounded; Second Lieutenant Frank Pealor, wounded; and Acting Lieutenant R. S. Rook, wounded.

Of the 6th Ohio battery, First Lieutenant O. H. P. Ayres, wounded.

From the 29th to the 2d, inclusive, my brigade occupied some portion of the front, and during each day some portion of the forces under my command were engaged with the enemy, and sustained greater or less losses. For the cheerful manner in which they stood up under these fatigues and exposures they are entitled to commendation. I cannot close this report without paying a tribute of respect to the memory of the soldierly Sweet, the conscientious Christofel, and the intelligent and noble-hearted Van Kirk, who fell while manfully encouraging their men in the trying hour of battle. The country will do justice to the memory of the brave soldiers who so gloriously fell on the morning of the 31st of December. Great praise is due to Dr. J. M. Todd, 65th Ohio, acting brigade surgeon, for the care and professional skill extended to our wounded after the battle.

Where all behaved so gallantly it would be unjust to particularize, but I cannot refrain from mentioning in terms of special praise the name of Captain

Cullen Bradley, of the 6th Ohio battery, attached to my brigade. This gallant officer, ever at his post, was always ready to engage the enemy whenever he opened upon our troops, and managed his battery with so much judgment and skill as to silence those of the enemy in every instance. Such valuable services and such meritorious conduct, I believe, will not be overlooked.

I therefore take great pleasure in recommending Captain Bradley for some position commensurate with his merit and ability in the artillery branch of the regular service. Of both officers and men under my command I can speak in tones of unqualified praise for their bravery and good conduct throughout the engagement in front of Murfreesboro'. I must also mention a circumstance worthy of notice which occurred on Friday, the 2d instant.

The enemy's sharpshooters, taking advantage of the woods in our front, and to our right and left, had crept up sufficiently near our camp with the evident intention of picking off our general and field officers. They annoyed us exceedingly, firing at every mounted officer or man who appeared near the front. Desirous of dislodging this concealed foe, I directed the skirmishers to advance and clear the woods if possible. Captain Chambers, of the 51st Indiana, had command of the skirmishers, consisting of forty men from his own company; company B, 73d Indiana volunteers, Captain Gladwyn, commanding; company D, 73d, Lieutenant Grimes commanding; company W, 65th Ohio, Lieutenant Joel Brown commanding; company E, 65th Ohio volunteers, Lieutenant Kinman commanding; Lieutenant Mathias, commanding company K, 65th Ohio volunteers, and company G, 64th Ohio volunteers, Sergeant Holen commanding. This little detachment numbering only one hundred and twenty men. The enemy's force was much larger. Our skirmishers drove them until they were checked by the enemy's batteries.

Thus these brave men not only drove a concealed enemy from a strong hiding place, but elicited valuable information concerning the position of his masked batteries. This act of gallantry elicited the praise and admiration of all who witnessed it. To my personal staff, Captain S. L. Coulter, acting assistant adjutant general; Lieutenant A. B. Case, acting assistant inspector general, and D. L. Wright, aide-de-camp, I am indebted for valuable assistance throughout this memorable battle. For details I would most respectfully refer you to the reports of regimental commanders.

I have the honor to be, sir, very respectfully, your obedient servant,

C. G. HARKER,

Colonel 65th R. O. V., Commanding Brigade.

Brigadier General HASCALL,

Commanding 1st Division, Left Wing, 14th Army Corps.

CAMP NEAR MURFREESBORO',

January 4, 1863.

SIR: In compliance with your request, I have the honor to report that the 73d regiment Indiana volunteers, under my command, left Nashville on the morning of the 26th, taking the Murfreesboro' road, camping that night near Lavergne. The next day we marched in line of battle through the fields and cedar thickets amidst a drenching rain, encamping at night on the camping ground of the enemy, which bore abundant evidence of having been hastily evacuated. In the course of the day we passed several of his camp grounds strewed with many signs of very recent occupation. Some skirmishing was had to-day by one of my flanking companies. The next day being Sunday, we remained quiet in camp. The enemy had been here in considerable force, and, in this connexion, I may be permitted to mention that a company from my command and one from that of

Colonel Streight's crossed the river to a camp still in possession of the enemy's pickets, where were found more than 100 cavalry sabres, several rifles and other arms, which were taken possession of without much resistance, and brought to our camp. On Monday morning the line of march was resumed; passing through the same kind of country as on yesterday, (very rough and broken,) we came to Stone river, not far from where the railroad crosses the stream, and about two miles from Murfreesboro', the enemy being strongly posted on a rise of ground on the opposite bank. After nightfall my command waded the river amidst a shower of balls with which our reception was greeted. My command was quickly formed and marched in line of battle up the hill, during which time my skirmishers kept up a vigorous fire with those of the enemy, who retired at our approach. Halting under the brow of the hill, we waited the attack which we had reason to expect, and doubtless would have experienced had it not been that the very boldness of our advance intimidated him. We were near enough to distinctly hear his officers urge their men forward, appealing in the name of their "country and their rights" to make the attack; but they came not. We then recrossed the stream and bivouacked for the night near its bank. The next day skirmishing was indulged in with successful issues. Heavy firing was kept up on our right and left most of the day. On the morning of the 31st ultimo, the enemy apparently making a more vigorous attack on the right wing of the army than at any time before, we were sent in that direction, and were soon engaged with him. The 65th Ohio had taken position in a piece of woodland. In obedience to orders I took my command to their support. They soon became engaged with a heavy column which was pressing against it with great force. Well did they sustain themselves till by great superiority of numbers they were compelled to give way. Passing over my command, which at the time was lying down, we, in turn, were instantly engaged. Twelve rounds were fired with great spirit and effect, when it was seen that the enemy was retreating in disorder, taking an oblique direction to the left. I ordered an advance, and well, indeed, was it obeyed—passing forward on the double-quick, the ground recently occupied by the 65th Ohio was attained, the enemy still flying before us. There being no support for us on our left, and the battery on our right (which in the beginning of the engagement had rendered good service) having been withdrawn, the enemy bringing up his reserve, crossed an open field on our left, and subjected us to an enfilading fire for several moments of a most destructive character. Being thus left entirely alone, and finding it impossible to withstand such fearful odds, I withdrew in a somewhat disordered state, but soon rallied and again took position in front. My horse having been shot in the early part of the engagement, I was compelled to remain on foot the remainder of the day, when, by your kindness, I was furnished with another. That night we bivouacked on the same ground as the night before. From that time to the evening of the 3d we were in the front, being more or less exposed to the shells of the enemy, sustaining some loss thereby. We took no active part in any of the actions that ensued, with the exception of having 20 men engaged, with others of the brigade, in gallantly driving about 300 sharpshooters from a piece of woodland, where they had annoyed us for a day or two. It affords me great pleasure to say to you that all of my command behaved most nobly through all the trying scenes they were called to pass; and where all behaved so well, it would be invidious to make especial mention of any.

In conclusion, I would remark that my command numbered, on the morning of the 31st ultimo, 309 enlisted men, 19 line officers, 3 field and staff. The casualties of that day were as follows: enlisted men killed, 22; enlisted men wounded, 49; Captains Miles H. Tibbets and Peter Loyle, company H, killed; Second Lieutenants Emanuel Williamson, company I, and John Butterfield, company K, wounded; also Major William Krimbrill, slightly wounded in the knee, and 36 missing. My judgment is that fully one-half of those missing are killed or wounded, and part of the others taken prisoners.

Respectfully submitted.

G. HATHAWAY,
Colonel 73d Indiana.

Colonel C. G. HARKER,
Commanding 3d Brigade, 1st Division.

IN CAMP NEAR MURFREESBORO', TENNESSEE,
January 6, 1863.

SIR: The 65th Ohio volunteers, under command of Lieutenant Colonel Cassil, left its bivouac, near Duck creek, on Monday morning, December 29, 1862. In the advance its position was on the left wing of the front line of the brigade. Two companies were deployed as skirmishers, who very soon encountered a strong cavalry picket of the enemy. This force contested our advance at times sharply, but disappeared near Stone river. When within a couple of miles of the same river several shells were thrown at us from cannon, which soon retired. In this skirmishing we sustained no loss, but several of the enemy's saddles were seen to have been emptied and the horses straggling. We reached the heights on the north side of the river about three o'clock p. m., where we lay in line till after sundown. Orders were received to advance upon Murfreesboro' that night. I was in command of the companies of skirmishers and immediately threw them across the river, and commenced the ascent of the opposite heights. Passing the skirt of woods we encountered the enemy's skirmishers strongly posted to the front on the crest of the hill, and on my left behind a rail fence. A galling fire brought our line to a halt, but we soon cleared the hill, and, advancing over the crest, we found ourselves within thirty paces of a regiment of rebels, who, in their confusion, were rallying with great difficulty. I at once retired the line to the woods, where we remained till the whole brigade had recrossed, when we were quietly withdrawn. Sergeant Snider, acting orderly, was wounded in the face, which was the only injury our regiment suffered. The regiment itself crossed the stream in good order under fire of the rebel skirmishers, and remained in line behind the skirt of woods till it recrossed with the brigade. Tuesday we lay in bivouac near the river, and went on picket at night. In accordance with Colonel Harker's order, we were ready to move at daybreak, with sixty rounds of cartridges to a man. We received marching orders about eight o'clock a. m., and moved at once forward. The enemy's sharpshooters and a battery on the opposite hill began a fierce fire of ball and shell upon us as we returned up the heights. When on the summit a shell exploded in the ranks of company B, killing one and wounding two. We double-quicked under a storm of shell after the brigade, which was some distance ahead, moving to the support of the right wing. When the brigade was formed to advance through the open field to the right of General Van Cleve's division, our regiment was placed on the left of the front line, with the 51st regiment Indiana volunteers on our right, and the 73d regiment Indiana volunteers to our rear. Company I, Captain Christofel, was deployed to the front as skirmishers, but having suffered severely, was, in a short time, relieved by company K, Lieutenant Brown. When near the skirt of timber protruding from the main forest, we marched by the right flank to support the 6th Ohio battery. We were again moved towards the enemy and placed behind a rise of ground. We suddenly found them in line at a short distance, and immediately commenced firing. The enemy, though in brigade front, three columns deep, staggered, concealed himself as far as possible, and did not venture to advance under our fire. Meanwhile, General Van Cleve's division giving way, the line of the enemy on our left advancing, completely outflanked us, and we were suffering under a raking cross fire. We held the position for about thirty minutes, and fell back, in accordance with orders, formed behind the 73d regiment Indiana volunteers, and moved by the flank to oppose the advancing right of the enemy. We took our position behind a rail fence, and again held the enemy in check for about twenty minutes. At length, being nearly cut off by the enemy on the right, we retired behind the line of battle, resting in the wood near the pike. We had suffered severely; out of sixteen officers with the regiment two had been killed and eight wounded. Second Lieutenant Van Kirk, commanding company A, fell in the advance; Captain Christofel, of company I, some time in the retreat. Both were doing their duty unflinchingly and manfully. Lieutenant Colonel Cassil having been disabled by the fall of his horse at the second stand of the regiment, I then took command. We rejoined our division at night near the position we left in the morning.

On Thursday, January 1, 1863, we lay in front in support and to the right of the 6th Ohio battery during the furious cannonading, and were annoyed by sharpshooters during the whole day. We picketed at night. Our skirmishers covered the front on Friday. The regiment lay in a little clump of wood, in support of the battery, and exposed to the most terrific shelling during the morning. In the p. m. our skirmishers, in conjunction with those of the brigade, cleared the wood in front of rebel skirmishers and sharpshooters, were in turn shelled out, and again took possession and held it. Near night, and the close of the engagement on the left, we moved over the river, threw up a defence of rails to the front, and remained there through the rain till morning. We were retired till Saturday night, when we again picketed the left front. About two o'clock Sunday a. m. we were marched back to our present bivouac.

The following is the list of the casualties of the regiment:

Lieutenant Colonel Cassil, severe sprain by the fall of his horse; Major Whitbeck, slightly wounded in the neck; Adjutant Massey, severely in leg, slightly in face and hip; Captain Jacob Christofel, killed; Captain Vorhees, through the side; First Lieutenant Gardner, through side; Second Lieutenant Van Kirk, killed; Second Lieutenant Markel, through hip; Second Lieutenant Brown, in the shoulder; Second Lieutenant Pealer, through thigh; and Acting Second Lieutenant Rook, in thigh. Of 382 enlisted men in the engagements during the week, 34 were killed, 100 wounded, 38 missing—total 172. Of the missing, some are known to be prisoners, others are serving in hospitals, and a few stragglers are still coming up.

I will not particularize, when all, officers and men, conducted themselves so coolly and fought so determinedly against such desperate odds; nor need I mention their patience under such privations and exposures in midwinter.

HORATIO WHITBECK,
Major, Commanding 65th Regiment Ohio Volunteers.

Captain COULTER,
Acting Assistant Adjutant General 3d Brigade.

HEADQUARTERS SIXTH OHIO BATTERY,
On Battle-field, near Murfreesboro', Tenn., January 5, 1863.

SIR: I have the honor to submit the following official report of the engagements of December 30 and 31, 1862, and January 1 and 2, 1863, viz:

At 8 a. m, December 30, 1862, the battery was put in position on the left bank of the Stone river, and near camp, and engaged a four-gun battery of the enemy's at a range of fifteen hundred yards, who held a high, strong, and commanding position on the opposite bank of the river, and silenced the enemy's battery after an engagement of fifteen minutes, expending seventy-two rounds of shell and solid shot, sustaining no damage excepting the loss of one sponge bucket, struck by an enemy's shot. And at 8 a. m., December 31, 1862, the battery, in accordance to your order, proceeded to the right of our lines. At 10.30 a. m. engaged two four-gun batteries of the enemy, and supported by two brigades of infantry, at a range of two hundred and fifty yards; we received a galling fire from the infantry, as well as the battery. I held the position twenty minutes, pouring a heavy and destructive enfilading fire upon the infantry, at the same time engaging the battery with good effect, expending one hundred and fifty rounds of case shot and canister, and sustaining a loss of one man wounded and two horses killed. Our left flank having been turned, I retired my battery and took up a position five hundred yards in rear, and again opened upon the enemy with case and canister, who were advancing in force. After an engagement of five minutes, and expending twelve rounds of ammunition, I was again compelled to retire my battery, and to abandon two pieces of the battery, one of which I had spiked, (since removed,) and sustaining a loss of one man killed, two men wounded, and one man missing; also, eight horses killed and three wounded. About this time Colonel Shoemaker charged the enemy with the 13th Michigan regiment, driving them off the field and recovering the guns, and for which Colonel Shoemaker should receive full credit.

About 8 a m., January 1, 1863, I again changed position to the front lines, and, in conjunction with several batteries, I opened upon the enemy with case shot and shell, at a range of two thousand yards, driving them back, expending fifty-four rounds of ammunition, and sustaining no damage.

January 2, while occupying a position on the front lines, the enemy advanced eighteen guns, (supposed,) and opened upon my battery with solid shot and shells about 8 a. m. I was supported upon the right by two six-gun batteries, which gave way early in the action and retired. I silenced the enemy's guns and held the position, expending one hundred and seventy-seven rounds of ammunition, and sustaining a loss of five men wounded, five horses killed, and three horses wounded. About this time Captain Stokes's Chicago battery opened upon my battery, firing several rounds of canister, from a position two hundred and fifty yards in my rear, and from which I sustained much damage. At 2 p. m. the enemy advanced a heavy column upon our left lines, and, supported by two four-gun batteries, my battery took up a strong position, and opened upon the enemy, at a range of three thousand yards, with good effect, expending thirty-five rounds of shell, and sustaining no damage.

I take great pleasure in noticing the promptness and coolness displayed by First Lieutenant O. H. B. Ayres, Second Lieutenant A. P. Baldwin, and First Sergeant G. W. Smetts, for the manner in which they managed their respective sections; Lieutenant Ayres having been slightly wounded, also his horse being wounded, and Lieutenant Baldwin having his horse shot. The following non-commissioned officers and privates greatly distinguished themselves, viz: Sergeants G. W. Howard, H. Hartman, T. O. Cassey, S. Miller, and J. Hersh; Corporals N. Poole, H. A. Collier, and Acting Corporal W. Kinsbreck. Corporal C. H. Neal is entitled to much credit for the promptness and carefulness he displayed in keeping the caissons well screened, and for keeping the battery suppled with ammunition. Privates W. Stough, J Robbinet, D. H. Evans, J. G. Barger, and F. Leslie greatly distinguished themselves, and the whole company, with but few exceptions, displayed great coolness, and are entitled to much credit. Enclosed please find statement of losses in the battery.

Respectfully,

CULLEN BRADLEY,

Captain, Commanding 6th Ohio Light Battery.

Colonel C. G. HARKER,

Commanding 3d Brigade, 1st Division, Left Wing,

14th Army Crops, Department of the Cumberland.

HEADQUARTERS 13TH REGIMENT MICHIGAN VOLUNTEERS,
In Camp near Murfreesboro', Tenn., January 8, 1863.

SIR: My report of the 5th, having been made in great haste, was necessarily very brief. I would, therefore, for the better understanding of the movements of this regiment during the several days of battle commencing on the 29th ultimo and ending on the 3d instant, submit the following: On the evening of the 29th, when ordered to cross the river, we were on the left, the 51st Indiana in the centre, and the 73d Indiana on the right. My regiment commenced crossing as soon as our skirmishers were fairly on the other side. The skirmishers were company A, commanded by Lieutenant Van Arsdale, and company F, commanded by Lieutenant James R. Slayton. They drove the enemy rapidly, the regiment following quite closely upon them. When in line in the cornfield, after receiving the third volley from the enemy, we were ordered to fix bayonets and prepare to receive a charge of cavalry. As my regiment was somewhat in advance of the 51st Indiana, and my right covering their left, I moved my regiment to the le t and rear, so as to connect with the 51st Indiana, but still leaving my left somewhat in advance, and in such a position as would have enabled us to enfilade any force which might charge the centre. Our position was now a very strong one, being in the edge of the woods. Here we remained until ordered to recross the river.

On the 31st, being in reserve when our brigade was placed in position on the extreme right of the army, we occupied an open field just in rear of where the 64th and 65th regiments Ohio volunteers and 73d regiment Indiana volunteers were engaged with the enemy. When the battery retired we were ordered to fall back to the position we held when the enemy advanced upon us. When they opened fire upon us the other regiments of the brigade had passed by our right to the rear, and we did not see them again until the close of the engagement. My regiment was in line during the battle, and delivered their fire with such precision and rapidity that the whole force of the enemy were brought to a stand at the fence in our front, and held there for at least twenty minutes, when their left, which extended considerably beyond my right, having advanced so as to make it apparent that they would soon turn my right flank, I gave the order to retire, but again formed the regiment within twelve or fifteen rods of the first line. The enemy advanced so as to occupy our first line, but broke and retreated precipitately when charged by us. The 51st Illinois advanced only to within about three rods of our first line, and then threw forward skirmishers. My regiment charged past the first line, and to the right down to near the fence and full thirty rods in advance of our first position, overtaking and capturing the enemy, from the place where the guns were recaptured, which was to the right and in front of our first line of battle, to the houses in our front, and into the cornfield, on a line with the houses. The artillery ceased firing a short time before we opened upon the enemy, and fell back out of sight, with all but the guns which had had their horses killed, and were captured. The enemy broke up the guns of our dead on the first line of battle while they occupied it. A lieutenant whom we captured informed me that our fire was very destructive, and that their loss in wounded must largely exceed ours.

On the 1st instant my regiment was exposed to a scattering fire all day, but was not actually engaged. At night we were ordered to the extreme front, to protect the 6th Ohio battery, and lay all night on our arms.

On the 2d instant, while supporting our battery, my regiment was exposed to a terrible fire from the artillery of the enemy, the number of guns playing upon us at one time being, as stated by Captain Bradley, eighteen. Though necessarily inactive, my regiment steadily maintained their position for over an hour, when one of our batteries commenced playing upon us from the rear. I then withdrew my regiment a few rods to the left, to a less exposed situation. In the afternoon we crossed Stone river with our division, and remained there doing duty both Friday and Saturday nights. On Sunday morning we recrossed the river, and bivouacked near the hospitals.

I am, sir, very respectfully, your obedient servant,

M. SHOEMAKER,
Colonel Commanding.

Captain S. S. COULTER,
Acting Assistant Adjutant General, 3d Brigade, 1st Division, Left Wing, General Rosecrans's Army.

HEADQUARTERS 64TH REGIMENT OHIO VOLUNTEERS,
In the field, January 5, 1863.

SIR: I have the honor herewith to report the number killed, wounded, and missing in this command, from the 27th of December, 1862, to the 3d day of January, 1863, inclusive:

Commanded by Lieutenant Colonel Alexander McIlvaine.

Company A, commanded by 1st Lieutenant Samuel Wolff:

Killed.—Sergeant John W. McIlvaine; Corporal William A. Robinson; Privates Charles H. Hetheringter, Daniel W. States, John Kelso, and James E. Ehlens.

Wounded.—Corporals Andrew Laird, severely, in the foot, and John Russell, severely, in the side. Privates Reuben Hulet, slightly, in leg; Jason Sharp, slightly, in hand; and Homer Culbertson, seriously, in left foot.

Missing.—Private Jacob Reining.

Company B, commanded by 2d Lieutenant Thomas E. Tillotson:

Killed.—Corporal John W. Berry; Privates Jacob Halbert, George Snyder, John T. Ward, and Jacob Walker.

Wounded.—2d Lieutenant Thomas E. Tillotser; Sergeants Henry Partridge, slightly, in the leg, and Asa Crammer, slightly, in the foot; Corporals Charles Partridge, seriously, in hand, and William Fils, slightly, in head; Privates William Brown, severely, in both legs; Alma Partridge, severely, in leg; John Smith, slightly, in leg, and Henry Hildebrand, slightly, in shoulder.

Missing.—Corporal Walter Stafford.

Company C, commanded by Captain R. C. Brown:

Killed.—Private William H. H. Phillips.

Wounded.—Corporal Samuel H. Morrison, in ankle; Privates William H. Eby, severely, below knee; Thomas Getten, in leg, since amputated; George H. Stewart, slightly, in back, and Samuel G. Williams, slightly, in hand.

Missing.—Corporal Levi Darron; Privates William Cohen and Ephraim Simpson.

Company D, commanded by 1st Lieutenant Henry H. Kling:

Wounded.—Color Sergeant James Irvin, slightly, in shoulder.

Missing.—Privates William P. Wilkins, John Matlin, and James Taurybill.

Company E, commanded by 1st Lieutenant Warner Young:

Wounded.—1st Lieutenant Warner Young, severely, in ankle; Privates Henry Applegate, severely, in leg; Alonzo G. Akers, severely, in leg; Norton M. Burns, slightly, in hand; Noah L. Coil, seriously, in shoulder; Peter Haas, severely, in leg; John Hersh, slightly, in knee; and Thomas Parkison, slightly, in leg.

Company F, commanded by 2d Lieutenant Norman K. Brown:

Killed.—Corporal John C. Coun; Privates Simon Herring and Reuben Ramsey.

Wounded.—Sergeants John Bleaker, severely, in left arm, and Lewis High, slightly, in cheek; Corporals Asa D. Farnam, severely, in hip, and Henry David

Major, severely, in hip; Privates John Brouches, severely, left breast; Alfred Guier, slightly, in right arm; John Linkhart, severely, right wrist; Andrew Peters, severely, breast; Joseph Sproul, severely, arm; Jackson M. Trimble, slightly, in abdomen, and Eli C. Wilson, severely, in left arm and right hand.

Missing.—Private Joseph J. Bravo.

Company G, commanded by Sergeant James L. Hall:

Killed.—Private Samuel Maurer.

Wounded.—Captain Samuel Neeper, slightly, in knee, by explosion of shell while on picket, near Lavergne, December 27, 1862; Corporal Andrew Ozman, slightly, in right foot; Private Joseph Urban, slightly, right foot.

Company H, commanded by 1st Sergeant David Cummins:

Killed.—Corporal James Curran; Privates David Gies and Abraham Bretz.

Wounded.—Sergeant William Ritchey, slightly, in arm; Privates G. W. Cummins, slightly, in hand; Daniel Marvin, severely, thigh; George Marvin, slightly, right leg; J. W. Packer, slightly, right arm; H. A. Schatzer, severely, in left breast; W. P. Weston, severely, in left ankle; Daniel Ruhl, slightly, left cheek; and B. H. Ross, slightly, in left arm.

Company I, commanded by 1st Lieutenant Joseph B. Ferguson:

Killed.—Private Nicholas Baker.

Wounded.—1st Lieutenant Joseph B. Ferguson, severely, in thigh; Sergeant George O. Marshall, severely, in thigh; Corporal Jefferson A. Houser, in leg; Privates Thomas Dunford, mortally, in both legs; Henry R. Dettenhafer, in leg; Timothy Dugan, in leg; James Kalahen, severely, in thigh; John Stuckey, slightly, in breast; Patrick Powers, slightly, in hand; and Robert White, slightly, in arm.

Missing.—Privates Samuel Dubewees, John Tarman, and Joseph Sallow.

Company K, commanded by Captain Joseph B. Sweet:

Killed.—Captain Joseph B. Sweet; Privates James Armitage, Patrick McNary, and John Reagan.

Wounded.—Privates Joseph Barnes, slightly, in left shoulder; Peter Gant, severely, in face; Lewis Lilley, severely, in leg; and Samuel Kautzhert, severely, in head.

Missing.—Sergeant John Ashcroft; Privates Charles Berdwell, Wilson Morrow, David Morrow, and John Swangin.

Field and staff.—Adjutant Chauncey Woodruff, wounded severely in leg.

The above is a correct report of the casualties in this regiment, so far as can be ascertained from company commanders now present.

The command arrived on the south bank of Stone river on the evening of December 29, 1862, and crossed to the opposite or Murfreesboro' side after nightfall on same evening, and formed as reserve to the remainder of the 20th brigade. Recrossed the river during the same night, and next morning, while on duty on the front, had one man killed by the enemy. On the morning of the 31st was ordered from the left to the right of the line, and occupied the second line on the right. It was discovered that the enemy was approaching on the left flank; ordered the command forward on 10th company, and by order fixed bayonets and successfully drove them for some distance, when the command became isolated and was ordered to fall back.

Among the casualties of officers of my command I seriously regret the loss of Captain James B. Sweet, who fell while bravely leading his company into the thickest of the engagement. As an officer, and true and devoted soldier, Captain Sweet bore the well-merited love and respect of all those who knew him. Having adopted military life as a profession, and for a long time served in the regular army, he was proficient in all the high qualifications that pertained to his calling. In him this country and cause have lost a brave and patriotic officer. Of those wounded, honorable mention is justly due to First Lieutenant Warner Young' First Lieutenant Joseph B. Ferguson, and First Lieutenant and Regimental Adjutant Chauncey Woodruff, each of whom exerted themselves to their utmost to press forward their respective commands to the charge, and only ceased their labors when overcome by the exhaustion occasioned by their wounds. I learn with pleasure that although seriously, none were mortally wounded. The officers who survived the battle did honor to the State they hail from and the cause they nobly fought for. Of those who commanded companies, the names of each can be honorably mentioned in justice to them. Captain R. C. Brown, of company C; First Lieutenant Samuel Wolff, of company A; First Lieutenant Henry H. Kling, of company D; Second Lieutenant Norman K. Brown, company F; Second Lieutenant T. Eugene Tillotson, company B; and First Sergeant James L. Hall, of company G; and First Sergeant David Cummins, of company H; also Second Lieutenant George R. Hall, of company K, and Sergeants Cuneman and Holden, of companies I and E, respectively, who commanded the companies to which they were attached, after their immediate commanders had been either killed or wounded; also, Second Lieutenant Thomas E. Ehlers, who assisted in the command of company A. The above-named officers did their duty regardless of the danger to which they were exposed at every step while gallantly leading their men forward to meet and charge the enemy. The file-closers, without exception, manfully stood up to their work, and I cannot, in justice to them all, single out any one for special subject of remark, and too much praise cannot be attached to their patriotism and heroic military bearing. The men in the ranks all did their duty, and did it well, and they are heroes, all. While we deeply regret, and truly sympathize with the friends of those who were either killed or wounded, we are, as they can be, consoled with the thought that they all fell while bravely battling for their country's right and the overthrow of rebellion.

ALEXANDER McILVAINE,
Lieutenant Colonel Commanding.

Colonel CHARLES G. HARKER,
Commanding 20th Brigade.

BATTLE FIELD,
Near Murfreesboro', Tennessee, January 4, 1863.

SIR: I have the honor to submit the following report of the part taken by my regiment in the battle near Murfreesboro', from the 29th ultimo to the 2d instant, inclusive.

At about 4 o'clock p. m. I arrived on the west bank of Stone river, about one-half mile north of the Murfreesboro' and Nashville pike, and two miles from Murfreesboro', where I was ordered to halt until further orders. Here I remained until about dark, when I received orders to cross the river, preparatory to moving upon Murfreesboro'. Being fully aware that the enemy occupied the opposite bank, and as none of our troops had at that time crossed the river, it became necessary to proceed somewhat cautiously, in order to avoid the danger of running into an ambuscade; consequently I deployed companies A and F to act as skirmishers, and ordered them to cross in advance and engage the enemy briskly, and, if possible, to seize the heights on the east side of the river. No sooner had my skirmishers crossed than the enemy opened a brisk fire from under cover of a strong fence but a few yards distant. My skirmishers were ordered forward at a double-quick, and charged upon the enemy, who instantaneously fled from their hiding-places. At this moment it became evident, from the brisk firing of the enemy, that large numbers of them were concealed in the standing corn on the hill-side; and fearing that my skirmishers would be overwhelmed, I ordered the whole regiment forward at a double-quick, but before the regiment had entirely crossed the river Captain Russell informed me that the enemy was advancing in line of battle just beyond the crest of a ridge, about four hundred yards to our front. I at once determined to seize the crest before the enemy could get there, if possible; consequently the whole line was ordered forward on the run, and although the whole ridge seemed to issue forth a continuous flame of fire, not a man faltered, but each seemed to strive to reach the desired point in advance of his comrades. The boldness of the movement, and the alacrity with which it was executed, together with the brisk and well-directed fire of my men, struck terror to the enemy, who fell back in great confusion at our approach. I was at this moment ordered to advance no further, but hold my position. I then ordered my men to lie down so as to conceal them as much as possible, and in a few moments the enemy were plainly seen advancing upon our position. They were allowed to advance to within thirty paces, when fire was opened upon them with such effect that they hardly waited to reply, but broke and fled again. Re-enforcements soon arrived on my right and left. We remained in our position without further molestation until about 10 o'clock at night, when I was notified that orders had been given to retire to the opposite bank of the river. After waiting until the balance of the troops had recrossed, my regiment was marched by the rear rank to the river, when it recrossed also. In the mean time my skirmishers were gradually withdrawn. The regiment was marched about five hundred yards from the ford where it bivouacked for the night. Slight skirmishing was all that occurred of interest until the morning of the 31st, when it became evident from the terrific roar of artillery and musketry that the enemy was turning the extreme right of our army. We were at once ordered to the right and rear double-quick. We had moved but a short distance, when we came within range of the enemy's artillery; and, although several were wounded when we had no chance of striking a blow at the enemy, yet my men moved a distance of over a mile as regularly as they could have moved had we been on drill; and even when we came in contact with excited teams and teamsters, every command I gave was promptly obeyed, without confusion. After marching about two and one-half miles we reached the extreme right of the army. We had hardly reached our position, when we were ordered forward in line of battle, across open cotton and corn fields. Companies A, B, and F were deployed as skirmishers to cover my extreme right and front. We had proceeded in this order but about one-half mile, when my skirmishers approaching the crest of a ridge in front, running at an angle of about fifteen degrees to the right, were fired upon by a large force of the enemy concealed in the standing corn to my front and right. I at once ordered the whole line forward at a double-quick. My skirmishers came in sight of the enemy in a moment, when our well-directed fire soon put them to flight. I was here again, by rapid movements, particularly fortunate in getting the advantage of the enemy in my position. We had a fair chance at them while they were retreating some four hundred yards, and large numbers of them were killed and wounded. Although the troops to my left were attacked desperately, the enemy did not attempt to bring infantry against me after his repulse. Shortly after I had obtained full possession of the ridge, I was informed by Lieutenant Colonel Colescott, then in command of the skirmishers, that large masses of troops were seen moving towards a piece of woods to my left and front. I at once notified Colonel Harker, and requested that the 6th Ohio battery, Captain Bradley, be sent to the ridge occupied by my regiment. The battery was promptly on the ground, but not too soon, for by the time it was in position the enemy had engaged the troops to my left. Captain Bradley opened a most terrific fire, thus enfilading their ranks who were in column four regiments deep, at a distance of not to exceed five hundred yards. Their dead were literally piled in heaps by the terrific fire from the battery. Nothing else could have saved our troops to my left from total destruction. The battle had been raging for about three-quarters of an hour when I was notified that the division on our left was falling back; consequently my position would have to be abandoned. At this moment Colonel Harker ordered me to fall back, which was done in good order, bringing off all my wounded. Having received no orders as to what point I should fall back to, I formed in line of battle on the first advantageous ground, expecting to give the enemy battle, but was again ordered to fall back to the position first occupied on the extreme right, and at once deployed companies H and C as skirmishers. The enemy again approached our lines on the left, which formed an angle of about fifteen degrees to the front of our position. My skirmishers and the troops to my left were but handsomely engaged when the enemy broke and fled from the field in great confusion. It was now nearly night, and the contest was ended for the day. Other troops were brought up, and we were again ordered to the position occupied on the previous day and bivouacked for the night. Early the next morning we were ordered into position about one-half mile to our right and rear, where we remained through the day. Companies H and G, and one company from the 73d Indiana, were sent forward as skirmishers to drive the enemy from a piece of woods about one-half mile to our front, which was occupied in short order. This was all the engagement my men were in on that day.

January 2, I took company H, together with several volunteers from my regiment, and drove the enemy from the woods formerly occupied by the 21st brigade. The contest was severe in the extreme for a short time, but the boys soon got the advantage, and the woods were ours. Ten of the enemy were left dead on the ground. This was the last engagement in which my men participated. Our entire loss in killed is seven, wounded thirty-four, and missing nine. Members of my regiment took nineteen rebel prisoners, one a major, and one a captain. From careful observation on the various grounds fought over by my men, I am convinced that we have killed not less than sixty of the enemy, and by adding five times that number, the usual proportion of the wounded to the killed, and we have a grand total of three hundred and sixty. These figures, though seemingly large for the amount of loss sustained by us, I feel confident could be fully verified by the facts. Most of the ground fought over by my regiment has not been covered by other troops, and in nearly every case we have been placed where it was easy to decide which were our killed. The success attending us in most cases, and our small loss, I think, is attributable in a great measure to the advantage taken of the ground.

Feeling grateful beyond expression for the brave soldierly bearing and prompt manner in which both officers and men performed every duty assigned them, I feel a great delicacy in mentioning names, being fully convinced that it is more owing to the difference in circumstances than to the difference in men. Nevertheless, Captain Russell, company A, Captain Chambers, company H, Captain Flinn, company F, and the officers and men under them, are justly entitled to honors for distinguished services at different times during their various engagements with the enemy, though I do not wish to detract one star from the imperishable glory won by other worthy members of my regiment.

I have the honor to be your obedient servant,

A. D. STREIGHT,
Colonel 51st Indiana Volunteers.

Colonel CHARLES G. HARKER,
65th Ohio Volunteers, Commanding 20th Brigade.

HEADQUARTERS 2D DIVISION, LEFT WING,
14TH ARMY CORPS, DEPARTMENT OF CUMBERLAND,
Camp near Murfreesboro', January 9, 1863.

MAJOR: I have the honor to submit, for the information of the general commanding, the following report of the operations of this division, from and including the 27th December up to and including the 4th of January, instant.

At 11.20 a. m. on the 27th December, while in camp near Lavergne, I received orders to move forward, following the division of General Wood, and to detach a brigade to proceed by the Jefferson pike, and seize the bridge across Stewart's creek. The duty of conducting this operation was assigned to Colonel Hazen. How well and skilfully it was done will be seen by his report, which is herewith forwarded.

The brigades of Cruft and Grose reached the west bank of Stewart's creek late in the afternoon of the 27th, and bivouacked there until the morning of the 29th.

During all the day, Sunday, 28th, the enemy's pickets were in sight across the creek, firing upon us occasionally at long range, but did us no harm. On Monday morning, 29th December, at 9 o'clock, I was ordered to deploy one regiment as skirmishers; to dispose of my other troops so as to support it, and move forward at 10 o'clock precisely, and continue to advance until the enemy were found in position. This disposition was made. A few minutes before 10 o'clock Parsons was ordered to shell the woods to our front, and at 10 o'clock Grose's brigade moved forward, skirmishing with the enemy, supported by the 1st brigade, Hazen not having yet joined me.

The command advanced steadily, driving the light force of rebel skirmishers before it to the top of the hill, some mile and a half on this side of Stewart's creek, and being under the impression that the divisions of Wood and Negley were to advance with me, to my right and left, I halted for them to come up.

In a few minutes Wood's advance came up on the left of the pike, and the two divisions moved forward, constantly skirmishing (though much heavier on Wood's front than my own) to the ground occupied that night, afterwards the theatre of the battle of the 31st.

During this day the casualties were 10 wounded in Grose's brigade—none severely.

On the morning of the 30th my division was formed as follows: 3d brigade (Grose's) in two lines, the left resting on the pike; 1st brigade (Cruft's) to the right, extending across the point of woods, his extreme right retired to connect with General Negley's left, and Hazen's brigade in reserve. There was considerable skirmishing during the day, the greater portion of which fell upon Cruft's brigade, which was in rather unpleasant proximity to a point of woods to his front and right, held by the enemy in strong force.

About 4 o'clock I was ordered to advance and open the enemy with all my artillery.

This was not done, probably, as soon as the order contemplated. The ground occupied by the batteries at the time the order was received was low and confined; upon pushing forward the skirmishers of the 1st brigade to clear the way to a good artillery position, in the open field to the front, the rebels were found numerous and stubborn. Learning very soon that a mere demonstration was intended, all my batteries opened, and I am satisfied damaged the enemy considerably. The skirmish attending this movement was quite brisk, the troops engaged doing themselves great credit. This closed the operations of the day.

On the morning of the 31st Cruft's brigade retained its position of the day before. Hazen's brigade had relieved Grose, who had fallen back to a point some two hundred yards to the rear, and was formed in two lines nearly opposite the intervals between the 1st and 2d brigades; Standart's battery on the extreme right; Parson's near the centre.

Early in the morning I rode to the right of my own command, and then the battle had commenced on the extreme right of the line. Soon afterwards, near 8 o'clock, General Negley, through one of his staff, informed me he was about to advance, and requested me to advance to cover his left. I gave notice of this to the general commanding, and a few minutes later received orders to move forward. I at once ordered General Cruft to advance, keeping closed up well towards Negley; Colonel Hazen to go forward, observing the movements of Wood's right; and Grose to steadily advance, supporting the advance brigades, and all to use their artillery freely.

My line had advanced hardly a hundred yards, when, upon reaching my own right, I found that General Negley had, instead of advancing, thrown back his right, so that his line was almost perpendicular to that of Cruft, and to his rear; and it was also apparent that the enemy was driving General McCook back, and were rapidly approaching our rear.

Cruft's line was halted by my order. I rode to the left to make some disposition to meet the coming storm, and by the time I reached the open ground to the south of the pike the heads of the enemy's column had forced their way into the open ground to my rear.

To order Grose to change front to the rear was the work of a moment, and he obeyed the order almost as soon as given, retiring his new left so as to bring the enemy under the direct fire of his line; he opened upon them in fine style and with great effect, and held his ground until the enemy was driven back.

In the mean time General Negley's command had, to some extent, become compromised by the confusion on the right, and my 1st brigade was exposed in front and flank to a severe attack, which also now extended along my whole front. Orders were sent to Colonel Hazen to fall back from the open cotton-field into which he had moved. He fell back a short distance, and a regiment from Wood's division, which had occupied the crest of a low wooded hill between the pike and the railroad, having been removed, he took possession of that, and there resisted the enemy. At that time, near 11 o'clock, as I think, my command was all engaged with the enemy; Hazen on the railroad; one or two regiments to the right; some troops in the point of woods south of the cotton-field, and a short distance in advance of the general line, amongst whom I was only able to distinguish the gallant Colonel Whitaker and his 6th Kentucky; still further to the right Cruft was fighting, aided by Standart's guns; and to the rear Grose was fighting with apparently great odds against him.

All were acquitting themselves nobly, and all were hard pressed. I could see that Grose was losing a great many men, but the importance of Hazen's position determined me, if necessary to do so, to expend the last man in holding it. I gave my attention from that time chiefly to that point.

The 100th Illinois came up on the left of the railroad and fought steadily. As soon as Colonel Grose was relieved of the enemy in his rear, he again changed front, moved to the left and co-operated with Colonel Hazen. One regiment was sent to my support from General Wood's command, which behaved splendidly. I regret my inability either to name the regiment or its officers. Again and again the attack was renewed by the enemy, and each time repulsed; and the gallant men who had so bravely struggled to hold the position occupied it during the night.

For further details of the day's operations I respectfully refer to the reports of the brigade and regimental commanders, which are herewith forwarded, and confess my obligations to them all for their assistance during the day. Brigadier General Cruft deserves great praise for so long holding the important position occupied by him on our right, and for skilfully extricating his command from the mass of confusion around it.

Standart fought his guns until the enemy was upon him, and then brought them off safely, while the 2d Kentucky brought off by hand three guns abandoned by General Negley's division.

Colonel Hazen proved himself a brave and able soldier by the courage and skill exhibited in forming and sheltering his troops, and in organizing and fighting all the materials around him for the maintenance of his important position.

Colonel Grose exhibited great coolness and bravery, and fought against great odds. He was under my eye during the whole day, and I could see nothing to improve in his management of his command.

I shrink from the task of specially mentioning regiments or regimental officers. All did their duty, and from my imperfect acquaintance with regiments, I am apprehensive of injurious mistakes.

I recognized during the battle the 41st Ohio, which fought until it expended its last cartridge, and was then relieved by the noble 9th Indiana, which came into line under a heavy fire with a shout which inspired all with confidence. The 84th, 110th, and 100th Illinois I knew; all new regiments, and all so fought that even the veterans of "Shiloh" and other bloody fields had no occasion to boast over them. The 84th stood its ground until more than one-third its numbers were killed or wounded. The 6th Ohio, the 24th Ohio, the 23d Kentucky, and the 36th Indiana were pointed out to me, and I recognized the brave Colonel Whitaker and his fighting men doing soldiers' duty. I only saw the regiments of Cruft's brigade fighting early in the day; I had no fears for them where valor could win. Indeed, the whole division fought like soldiers trained under the rigid discipline of the lamented Nelson, and by their courage proved that they had caught a large portion of his heroic and unconquerable spirit.

During the whole day I regarded the battery under the command of Lieutenant Parsons,. assisted by his lieutenants, Cushing and Huntington, as my right arm, and well did the brilliant conduct of these courageous and skilful young officers justify my confidence. My orders to Parsons were simple: "Fight where you can do the most good." Never were orders better obeyed!

The reported conduct of the other batteries attached to the division is equally favorable. They were in other parts of the field.

My personal staff—Captain Norton, acting assistant adjutant general; Lieutenants Simmons and Child; Lieutenant Croxton, ordnance officer; Lieutenant Hays, division topographical engineers; Lieutenant Shaw, 7th Illinois cavalry—were with me all day on the field, and carried my orders everywhere with the greatest courage. Lieutenant Simmons was severely injured by a fragment of a shell.

On the 1st day of January this division was relieved and placed in reserve. On Friday, the 2d, Grose's brigade was ordered over the river to the left to support the division of Colonel Beatty, and during the action the brigade of Colonel Hazen was also ordered over to co-operate with Grose; whilst the 1st brigade, Cruft's, was posted to support a battery on the hill near the ford. For an account of the part the 2d and 3d brigades took in the affair of Friday afternoon reference is had to the reports of the officers in command.

During the heavy cannonade the 1st brigade maintained its positions with perfect coolness. While the engagement was going on across the river a rebel force of what seemed to be three small regiments entered the clump of woods in front of the position of our batteries on the hill near the ford. These troops were in musket range of our right across the creek, and I determined at once to dislodge them.

Seeing two regiments, one of which was commanded by Colonel Garric, and the other by Colonel Altemire, I ordered them to advance to the edge of the woods and deploy some companies as skirmishers. They obeyed me cheerfully and pushed in. Not being willing to leave the repulse of the enemy a matter of doubt, or to expose these brave fellows to the danger of heavy loss, I ordered up two of Cruft's regiments, and upon approaching the edge of the woods halted them, told them it was my purpose to clear the woods at the point of the bayonet. To inspire them with coolness and confidence, the preparations for the charge were made with great deliberation. To get the proper direction for the line, guides were thrown out and the proper changes were made, bayonets fixed, and these two regiments, 31st Indiana and 90th Ohio, ordered to clear the woods. They went in splendidly. It was done so quickly that the rebels had hardly time to discharge their pieces. They fled with the utmost speed.

All these regiments behaved handsomely. With this report will be forwarded a list of the casualties of my command, and from its fearful proportions demonstrates its hard service.

Commands.	Killed.			Wounded.			Missing.			Aggregate.
	Officers.	Enlisted men.	Total.	Officers.	Enlisted men.	Total.	Officers.	Enlisted men.	Total.	
1st brigade	....	44	44	9	218	227	6	120	126	397
2d brigade	5	41	46	17	318	335	....	52	52	433
3d brigade	10	97	107	22	456	478	....	74	74	659
Standart's battery	....	5	5	....	12	12	....	3	3	20
Parsons's battery	....	2	2	....	14	14	....	6	6	22
Cockerill's battery	....	2	2	1	13	14	....	2	2	18
Total	15	191	206	49	1,031	1,080	6	257	263	1,549

I have the honor to be, very respectfully,

J. M. PALMER,
Brigadier General Commanding Division.

Major L. STARLING,
Adjutant General and Chief of Staff, &c.

HOSPITAL OF THE SECOND DIVISION, LEFT WING,
Army of the Cumberland.

SIR: As acting medical director of your division, I have the honor to respectfully submit the following report of casualties in the several days' battle before Murfreesboro'.

The number of killed in the 1st brigade	43
Wounded	185
The number of killed in the 2d brigade	50
Wounded severely, 77; slightly, 215	292
Number of killed of the 3d brigade	89
Wounded severely	484
Total killed and wounded	1,143

From the fact that our hospital was nearer the battle-field than any other, we were during the fight necessarily crowded with hundreds of the wounded from other divisions, making our duties very responsible and laborious. And I cannot in justice submit this report without making honorable mention of all the medical officers in your division. They have shown themselves equal to their responsible duties, and have been untiring in their efforts both day and night to alleviate the sufferings of the wounded who have come under their notice; and more especially would I make honorable mention of Dr. J. B. Armstrong, acting brigade surgeon of the 1st brigade, and Dr. S. H. Kersey, acting brigade surgeon of the 3d brigade, who were selected as operating surgeons, and they have proved themselves abundantly competent to the task, and have not allowed themselves one moment's rest while the suffering needed their attention.

Their devotion to their suffering fellow-soldiers should win for them the esteem and unbounded confidence of all who know them.

Very respectfully,

M. G. SHERMAN, *Acting Medical Director,*
Second Division, Left Wing, of the Department of the Cumberland.

Brigadier General J. M. PALMER,
Commanding.

Report of battery B, First Ohio Light Artillery, second brigade, General Palmer's division, (left wing of the army.)

On December 26 was ordered to march; took up line of march towards Murfreesboro'; in the afternoon moved to the front, and fired on the enemy at and in the vicinity of Lavergne. One man wounded by premature discharge. 27th, 28th, and 29th, no casualties; on the 30th was ordered to the right of the 22d brigade, and in the afternoon fired at long range for one hour; one horse killed. On the 31st, in the morning, took same position; was soon ordered to advance and move in connexion with Brigadier General Negley's division, which was on my right, the battery being on the right of the 22d brigade. General Cruft's brigade, General Negley's division, not moving to the front, and the artillery that was on my left being moved off, changed our section from the right to the left of the 22d brigade. The fight at this time was general along our front and right and left of our position near the fence; the enemy showing himself in great numbers on the left, brought all the guns to bear on the cotton-field. The division of General Negley at this time gave way; we received a heavy fire from our right, held our position for a short time, and the ammunition being expended, were forced to retire, the enemy following us close.

The caisson was ordered out and pieces followed, and 86 rounds in the boxes were sent to the supply trains. Filled up the limbers of the pieces and sent the caisson to the rear, it being all the ammunition that I could get. Loss: One killed, nine wounded, three since died, two missing, 15 horses killed.

In the afternoon of January I was ordered up the pike by General Rosecrans. Not having anything to do, was ordered to relieve Captain Stokes, Chicago Board of Trade battery. Lieutenant Baldwin took the same position with three pieces, and Lieutenant Sturgis with three pieces, as was occupied by Captain Stokes's battery.

In the morning the enemy opened a heavy fire on the three pieces of Lieutenant Baldwin, who was soon forced to retire. Lost one man killed and five horses. Lieutenant Sturgis, not replying to the enemy's fire, retained his position. In the afternoon was ordered to the left with three pieces, and opened fire as the enemy was being successfully repulsed. Remained on the field for the night.

On the 3d of January, in the evening, Lieutenant Sturgis opened fire on the woods in his front, and the enemy's pickets being driven back, was relieved from picket duty. 1,610 rounds of ammunition expended. The battery wagon, being among the wagon trains, was broken down; the axles have been used to repair carriages, and contents have been taken by different batteries. Lieutenants Baldwin and Sturgis, as well as every one in the battery, did their whole duty.

Very respectfully, your obedient servant,

W. E. STANDART,
Captain Company B, First Ohio L. Artillery.

Brigadier General PALMER,
Com'g Second Division, Left Wing of the Army.

IN CAMP NEAR MURFREESBORO', TENNESSEE,
January 7, 1863.

SIR: I have the honor to report the part taken by battery E, 1st regiment Ohio artillery, in the movement of the federal army on Murfreesboro' and the battles before that town.

Leaving camp near Nashville December 26, 1862, but marching in rear of two other divisions, the 2d was not that day engaged. We bivouacked south of Nolensville, and early on the morning of the 27th instant started on the road to Triune. Before we had proceeded more than one mile, heavy skirmishing was heard in front, and one section of our battery was ordered forward by General Kirk. Our place in the march being in rear of the 2d regiment, when the head of the column had reached the top of a ridge, beyond which cavalry skirmishing was still going on, a masked battery of the enemy on the left and commanding the road opened on it. Our pieces were at once unlimbered, and, after firing twelve rounds, got no response from the enemy's guns. The infantry skirmishers had filed off the road to the left, and our entire battery now moved rapidly after them. Leaving the pike, the skirmishers moved to the top of another ridge, and, our battery following, was at once placed in position there, from which point it opened fire from every gun, driving the rebels out of range. Here we were ordered to await the uplifting of a very heavy fog, and, when the infantry moved forward, again sought the pike, which we followed until the skirmishers reported the enemy again in sight and in line of battle. A fine position, on a hill overlooking Triune, and within the range of the rebel cavalry, in line of battle facing our left, was found here, and four pieces opened from this eminence, throwing shot and shell into and beyond the town, and into the rebels on the right and left. When we first came in sight of Triune the road was filled with rebel cavalry, and one section, unlimbering in the road, made them its especial mark. The town was soon made untenable, and an effort made by the rebel battery planted above the village to return our fire was driven off with one gun disabled. The enemy again retired before our fire, and the skirmishers, following up as rapidly as the nature of the ground would admit, threatened the capture of his guns, which he fired rapidly, and which we could not return, as he had cut down a bridge, obliging us to search a crossing more than one-half a mile down the creek. When our battery again appeared, the enemy had drawn off, but we threw several shots in the direction of his retreat. We were not again in action until the evening of December 30, when the 2d brigade was ordered to support the right of General Davis's division, threatened by rebel cavalry. They showed themselves in force, but, having secured a good position, a few shells threw their ranks into confusion and made them retire. The right of General Davis was at this time suffering from the shells of the enemy's battery, to which we turned our attention, and had the satisfaction of silencing the battery after a few rounds. Knowing our danger on the right, we planted two (2) pieces on the road by which it was supposed the enemy would come, kept the horses harnessed all night, and took every precaution we thought necessary to guard against surprise. At daylight on the morning of the 31st instant the pickets gave the alarm, and skirmishers were firing, but as yet could see no enemy. The horses were quickly hitched, except a few, perhaps one-half of which were on their return from water, and were brought up at once. Failing to distinguish the enemy, two shells were thrown in the direction of their fire, and, when they appeared, canister. Six rounds were poured into the moving mass with great effect, but, attacked in front and flank, we soon saw our horses shot down, the work evidently of sharpshooters, who moved in the advance and on the right and left until the whole column being now upon us we had not horses enough to save our guns. The number of deaths amongst our men, and particularly the fact that two of them were bayonetted at their guns, will show conclusively the courage and tenacity which influenced them on the occasion. Completely overpowered, it became necessary to retire with a few horses, perhaps thirty.

In conclusion, allow me to express my heartfelt regret at the loss of Captain Edgarton, whose manly voice rung out above the din of musketry, encouraging his men and giving orders coolly and judiciously. He preferred to go a prisoner with his battery to leaving his much cherished pieces. In mentioning the other officers and men, the name of Lieutenant Burwick comes foremost, who, an adopted citizen, rushed to arms at the first call, and, in acts as well as words, proved his unchangeable love of the freedom which enticed him from his bonnie hills. The sergeants and men behaved with noble devotion, as the death of three of the former will fully testify, whilst the alacrity shown by all to enter the service anywhere, so they could fight for their country, proves patriotism and courage.

Accompanying this report I append the names of those known to have been killed and wounded.

Respectfully, your obedient servant,

A. G. RANSOM,
First Lieutenant Commanding.

Captain D. C. WAGNER,
Acting Assistant Adjutant General, Second Brigade.

HEADQUARTERS BATTERY F,
1ST REGIMENT OHIO VOLUNTEER ARTILLERY.

SIR: I have the honor to submit the following report of the part taken by battery F, 1st regiment Ohio volunteer artillery, in the march from Nashville and the recent engagements near Murfreesboro', Tennessee.

Our battery numbered, on the morning of the 26th December, 1862, one hundred and twenty-five enlisted men and three commissioned officers, Captain Daniel Y. Cockerill commanding. We left our camp near Nashville about 9 a.m., 26th December, 1862, receiving orders from you to march with the 19th brigade, commanded by Colonel W. B. Hazen. Went into camp late in the evening near Lavergne, having taken no part in any of the skirmishing during the day.

December 27.—Received orders to move with the 19th brigade on the Smyrna pike. We came upon the enemy's cavalry at the crossing of the railroad. Colonel Hazen ordered a section of our battery to the front. Our cavalry made a brilliant charge and drove the enemy beyond the Stewart Creek bridge, when the enemy rallied under cover of a wood and formed. We threw a few well-directed shell into their lines, which dispersed them, killing some two or three as we afterwards ascertained. Bivouacked near the bridge for the night.

December 28.—Sunday.—Remained on the same ground during the day.

December 29.—We moved with the 19th brigade to the Murfreesboro' and Nashville turnpike, joined our division, and encamped for the night on the right of the turnpike, about three miles from Murfreesboro'.

December 30.—Heavy cannonading and brisk skirmishing during the day, but we being held in reserve did not take any part.

December 31.—We were ordered forward with the 19th brigade early in the morning to take a position near a burnt brick house on the right of the turnpike, but before we gained the position designated we discovered the right wing giving way so rapidly before the enemy that it was deemed imprudent to advance further. We received orders from Colonel Hazen to fall back; we then took up position between the railroad and turnpike; the enemy opened a destructive fire of shot and shell from two batteries before we got into position. Captain Cockerill, deeming it prudent, ordered the caissons to the rear under cover, but the drivers, misunderstanding the order, did not go where ordered, excepting one. Five of them got entirely separated from the battery and could not be found until 12 o'clock m. We opened upon the enemy and maintained our position, with the support of the gallant 19th brigade, which suffered terribly from an enfilading fire of the enemy's artillery, until our ammunition was exhausted. In the mean time we had one man killed and six wounded; we had sixteen horses killed and disabled, Captain Cockerill having one horse shot under him. One limber was blown up by a shell from the enemy's artillery, killing and disabling the team so as to render it impossible for us to bring the piece off the field, but was saved from falling into the enemy's hands by the unflinching courage of our supporting infantry. Two of our other pieces upon examination were found to be unfit for service, the axles being badly shivered. After finding our caissons, replenishing our limbers, and repairing one of the disabled pieces, we discovered the enemy's cavalry attacking our train on the opposite side of the river, and we brought our guns to bear upon them, fired a few rounds, when a field officer ordered us to cease firing, that we were firing upon our own men; but we afterwards found that he was mistaken. We were then ordered by Captain Mendenhall to take a position in a cornfield to the left of the railroad, supported by the 19th brigade on our left, and the 10th brigade, Colonel Grose commanding, on our right. No sooner had we taken our position than the enemy opened upon us with two batteries, one in front, the other on our left. Our fire for a short time was directed at the enemy's advancing columns of infantry with marked effect. But our attention was soon drawn to the enemy's artillery, which was doing us much damage; our fire was now directed at their batteries. We soon succeeded in silencing the battery on our left, but the one in our front kept up a destructive fire. Our ammunition again becoming exhausted, we drew off the field with the loss of one man killed. Our gallant and much-esteemed captain was severely wounded in the foot by a twelve-pound solid shot, and had to be borne from the field, to the great mortification of his whole command. Eight enlisted men wounded, also eight horses killed and disabled, we retired to the rear to replenish our ammunition chests and prepare some refreshments, also to seek some rest, which was so much needed. The command of the battery now devolved upon me.

January 1, 1863.—We were held in reserve with the 19th brigade.

January 2.—We took position early in the morning to the left of the railroad, by order of Captain Mendenhall, supported by the 21st brigade, Colonel Waggoner commanding, the 7th Pennsylvania battery on our right. Our skirmishers advanced across the field in our front, when, nearing the wood on the opposite side of the field, about one thousand yards distant, the enemy opened upon them with artillery, to which we promptly replied, silencing the enemy's guns in a very few moments. We remained silent until 3 o'clock p. m., when the enemy made an advance on our left on the opposite side of the river. We opened fire on a battery in our immediate front, which was operating against our infantry, which was on the opposite side of the stream. We then received orders from Captain Mendenhall to change front, to fire to the left on the advancing columns which were pressing our left wing back. We here fired several shot, when we received orders from one of General Rosecrans's aids to take position in an open field to our left, on the right of the Chicago battery. We here kept up a continuous fire until ordered to cease. We then bivouacked for the night upon the field.

January 3.—We were ordered to take the same position that we occupied the morning of the 2d instant. We were ordered inside the fortifications in the evening, where we remained during the night.

Not expecting to be called upon at the beginning of the recent engagements to make a report of the part taken by us, I am not prepared to give it as minutely as I desire, but I sum up our casualties as follows: Two enlisted men killed; one commissioned officer and thirteen enlisted men wounded; two enlisted men missing; twenty-four horses killed and disabled; lost two sets wheel harness, six sets lead harness, six sergeant's saddles and bridles, seven navy revolvers, and twelve paulins; two gun-carriages disabled, and one limber blown up.

I cannot speak too highly of the non-commissioned officers and men of the battery, who, with a very few exceptions, displayed great coolness throughout the entire contest, being the first time they were ever under fire of any consequence.

N. OSBURN,
Lieutenant, Commanding Battery F, 1st Ohio Volunteer Artillery.

Captain W. E. STANDART,
Chief of Artillery, 4th Division, Army of the Cumberland.

CAMP NEAR STONE RIVER, TENNESSEE,
January 5, 1862.

CAPTAIN: Agreeably to instructions of yesterday, I have the honor to report the part taken by batteries H and M, 4th United States artillery, under my command, in the recent operations against the enemy at this point.

These batteries opened fire for the first time on the morning of December 29, from their position, commanding Stewart's creek. After a few rounds of shell the enemy's pickets were dislodged from their shelter, in the opposite heights, when, upon receiving information from General Palmer that our own infantry had forded the creek, I returned to the pike, crossed the bridge, and moved forward with our first line of reserves. About one mile from the creek I observed indications that the enemy had taken position, with his artillery, awaiting our approach. With General Palmer's permission we opened fire with our rifles, and again dislodged him, after which the advance was continued. We fired no more during the day, and at night moved into park, in rear of the line of battle, three miles from Murfreesboro'.

On the morning of the 30th the enemy's artillery opened upon Cox's battery, to our left and front; during a spirited cannonading one of his shells struck in battery H, killing one private, one horse, and wounding one sergeant. We moved at once into the position assigned us by General Palmer, and formed the batteries in echelon, supported on the left by the 16th and on the right by the 22d brigade. I found no oc[illegible]ion, however, to open fire until about 4 p. m., when, upon receiving informat[illegible] an artillery demonstration from the left wing to support our right, then hotly pressed, was necessary, we commenced shelling the enemy's rifle-pits beyond the brick house; at the same time elavating the range of the rifle pieces, in order, if possible, to awaken the enemy's batteries. The latter effort was successful; but after exchanging a few shots, during which but one of my men was wounded, the enemy's fire was silenced. Satisfied that my position was an unfit one for artillery at night, I retired from the cedars after dark, and went into park in the open field behind them.

On the morning of the 31st I thought it most in accordance with my instructions from General Palmer to remain in the position where I then was, in order to check the advance of the enemy, should he turn our right. At about 8 a. m. our infantry came falling back from the pine wood in this direction, when our batteries were swung around and brought at once into action. The approach of the enemy was parallel, instead of perpendicular, to our front, and when he had arrived within about three hundred yards we opened upon his first line and column of reserves an enfilade fire of canister. The attempt to advance was continued for a few moments; then an effort to change front was followed by a feeble charge upon the batteries, when, upon being repulsed, the enemy fell back beyond our view. He reappeared shortly afterwards to our left, but again, upon receiving our fire, fell back, and a portion of our infantry. I then took position upon the slight elevation, nearer the pike, in season to assist in checking the enemy's advance upon General Rousseau's position; after which both batteries changed front and opened fire, by order of General Palmer, upon the brick house, to co-operate with Colonel Hazen's brigade. So soon as I believed the enemy dislodged from this position our pieces were moved to the front and directed upon his infantry, advancing into the cedar wood formerly held by the 22d brigade. The enemy, meanwhile, directed one of his batteries upon us, but I did not think it proper to reply so long as our ammunition could be used with better effect upon his infantry. At about 12 m., just as I had nearly given out of ammunition, I received orders from Captain Mendenhall to retire. At about 4 o'clock I moved to the front, by order of General Palmer, and from the elevation on either side of the railroad opened upon the enemy's infantry. His advance was effectually checked, and at sunset I was ordered to retire and refit.

At daylight, of January 1, we moved to a position on General Rousseau's front, where I was ordered by General Rosecrans; except for the fire of the enemy's sharpshooters, whom we dispersed at intervals by firing spherical case, we were not actively engaged during the day, and at night retired to a position near the pike, where our horses were fed and watered. During the night, and on the next morning, I was ordered by different officers to resume my previous position. I was obliged to decline obeying these orders, owing to those I had received from Captain Mendenhall, directing me to await his own. The position in which I was placed by this conflict of orders was exceedingly painful, but I found myself justified by subsequent events.

At about 4 p. m. of the 2d instant, after I had been placed in position by Captain Mendenhall on an elevation near Negley's division, two of the enemy's batteries opened upon us from our front, while a third gave signal for his last attack upon our left. I advanced the four rifles, holding my howitzers in reserve for the shortest range. The batteries around me were silenced far too soon, and when my rifled ammunition was exhausted, I found that some scoundrel had led off my cassions, and I was left only with the howitzers to reply to the enemy's concentrated artillery fire. Fortunately, Captain Swallow's battery came up beside us, and the crest of the hill was held until our re-enforcements came up, when, with the assistance of Captain Stokes's battery, the enemy's guns were silenced. We ceased firing, with our last round exhausted. We have not again been engaged, or under fire. I have to remark, in this connexion, that if through the five consecutive days, during which we were thus more or less severely engaged, we expended an unusual amount of ammunition, it must be recognized that we have been longer, and, in general, more closely engaged than perhaps any other batteries of the army, and that nearly all our ammunition has been expended at short range.

The following are our casualties, &c.: Number of men killed, 2; number of men wounded, 14; number of men missing, 6; horses killed, 20; pieces disabled, 1; rounds of ammunition fired, 2,299.

In place of the piece disabled, the 19th Illinois gave me one captured by them from the enemy.

I do myself honor, sir, in asking your attention to the efficient and meritorious services of Lieutenant Harvey C. Cushing and Lieutenant Henry A. Huntington, both of the 4th United States artillery. Disregarding all personal exposure under all circumstances, and especially during the hottest fires of December 31 and 2d instant, these gallant officers discharged their duty with such coolness and fidelity that they deserve my most grateful mention.

My brave men look for their reward to the generous appreciation which has been freely offered them by the troops with whom they fought, and the general commanding the division in which they serve.

I am, captain, very respectfully, your obedient servant,

CHARLES C. PARSONS,
First Lieutenant 4th U. S. Artillery, Commanding Battalion.

Captain D. W. NORTON,
Assistant Adjutant General.

A list of the killed and wounded of the (2d) second division, left wing, fourteenth army corps, in the battle before Murfreesboro', as far as reported by the regimental surgeons up to this date, January 6, 1863, by A. J. Phelps, surgeon medical division left wing.

THIRTY-FIRST INDIANA VOLUNTEERS.

Killed.—Company A: Private Alexander Ficklin. Company B: Corporal James Reynolds. Company F: Corporal Henry D. Lehman. Company G: Corporal Jacob Meadows. Company I: Sergeant William F. Davis.

Wounded.—Company A: First Sergeant John Cook, hand; Privates McLagha Cliff, side; John T. Derrel, face; Adam T. Dowry, Filmon S. Gidroson, arm; William Hobert, side; John Lyons, arm; Washington Miller, hand, and David Wells, hand. Company B: First Lieutenant James W. Pickens, chest and side; Sergeant Joseph Combs, hand; Corporals Jacob Williams, cheek, and Lorenzo D. Garo, wrist; Privates J. H. Grane, right hip; Jos. Renger, arm, amputated; and Michael Frock, hip, slightly. Company C: Corporal John Mallery, right temple, and Private Sylvinis Taly, left leg. Company D: Privates William Strain, face; Nat. Henderson, slightly, and Ezra Pitzen, neck, slightly. Company E: Sergeants Eli Sums, hip, slightly, and Jos. Jeresher, slightly; Corporal Henry Appnan, slightly; Privates Jackson Messer, hand, slightly; David Stuard, head, severe; Samuel France, slightly, and Robert Campbell, cheek and shoulder. Company F: Corporal A. V. Peters, leg, slightly; Privates Adam J. Alison, leg, severely; William O'Donald, neck, slighty, and J. B. Lazenger, leg, slightly. Company G: Sergeant Frank Fee, slightly. Company H: Second Lieutenant F. M. Hatfield, slightly cut from shell; Sergeant F. Hatfield, slightly, and Private John D. Sanders, hand. Company I: Sergeants E. D. Letzer, mouth, severely, and I. B. Konkey, foot, slightly; Corporals W. N. Enzey, arm, severely; Morris N. Lambert, knee, severely, and Thomas B. Fench, back, severely; Privates J. H. Adams, shoulder, slightly; Henry B. Cord, shoulder, severely, and H. Williams, left leg, severely. Company K: Sergeant John W. Johnson, thigh, severely, and Private W. E. Gaston, leg, slightly.

Summary.—Killed, 5; wounded, 46—total, 51.

SECOND KENTUCKY VOLUNTEERS.

Killed.—Company E: Sergeant H. Jasen. Company F: Corporal Robert Hosten. Company G: Private —— Vinegar. Company H: Corporal Fred. Hemple; Privates Henry Evans, and Pat. Galliger. Company I: Private Aug. Belt. Company K: Private C. Looker.

Wounded.—Company A: Sergeants S. Quiby, slight, and John Sodlefield, slight; Corporal S. Harth, face, severe; Privates P. McLaughlin, shoulder, severe; and J. McGinniss, hip, slight. Company B: Sergeant J. H. Henrie. Company C: Privates F. Bowers, side, serious; S. Blackburn, side, serious; and Fred. Swartz, serious. Company D: Sergeant Major John Poe, forearm fractured; Privates S. B. Gibner, abdomen, slight; W. V. Smith, both hips; and Denis Fox, both legs, serious. Company E: Sergeant Ben. Long, slight. Company G: Sergeant George Perkins, slight. Company H: Privates Samuel White, right leg fractured, tibia; William Smith, forefinger, amputated; Alfred Flisher, arm; and —— Dilerhurst, serious. Company I: Sergeant L. Wise, arm and shoulder; Privates W. H. Carnaway, slight; and J. Simmer, shoulder, slight. Company K: Privates George Falkner, shoulder; George Darling, shoulder, slight; A. Lindennan, leg, slight; C. Coppersmith, forearm, slight; Z. Sahner, foot, serious; and K. Oagker, forearm, serious.

Summary.—Killed, 8; wounded, 28—total, 36.

STANDART'S BATTERY.

Killed.—First Sergeant Thomas J. Thompson; Sergeant George Wolf; Privates John Elliott, C. Lyons, and S. B. Ruple.

Wounded.—Privates William Bro, severely; John Blanchard, severely; N. Laughlin, severely; A. French, severely; J. W. Shankland, severely; and B. F. Sarles, slight.

Summary.—Killed, 5; wounded, 6—total, 11.

SIXTH KENTUCKY VOLUNTEERS.

Killed.—Lieutenant Colonel George T. Colton. Company A: Private James Mulberry. Company B: Private H. C. Cardwell. Company C: Captain Charles Todd. Company D: Private J. A. Porter. Company E: Private Frank Bossell. Company G: Privates Joseph Moss, B. Schuller, John Matley, Joseph Kram. Company K: Private Charles Hitner.

Wounded.—Company A: Privates William Losey, left leg, slightly; Albert Yeager, right shoulder, severe; William Murphy, knee, severe; A. McGlassen, foot, severe; and James Cooper, arm, severe. Company B: Lieutenant Joseph Dawkins, left thigh, slight; Corporal Abe Souther, left hand, slight; Privates Henry Johnson, right hand, slight; E. Wordan, thigh, slight; James Bennett, hip, slight; Frank Porks, left groin, slight; A. Ladd, wrist, seriously; W. A. Ford, right elbow, seriously; J. Riley, left thigh, slight; R. Nichols, right hand, slight; and H. C. Cardwell, slight; Corporal B. McGruder, head, slight. Company C: Privates Haner Eagle, left thigh, slight; George Riling, forehead, severe; George Munk, left foot, slight; Conrad Cockler, wrist, slight; Sergeant N. Reider, slight. Company D: Captain Elisha Hedder, hip and back, slight; Sergeants J. J. Bennett, left leg fractured, and J. P. Easeby, right leg, severe; Privates George Richey, right groin, slight; William Ramsay, right leg, fractured tibia; Thomas White, shoulder, slight; Isaiah Porks, elbow, slight; Samuel Watters, left leg, slight; and William Hill, left hand, slight. Company E: Lieutenant Robert Armstrong, left leg, slight; Sergeant Vol Metcher, forehead, slight; Privates John Deible, right foot, slight; George Goetz, forehead, slight; John Laux, right shoulder, slight; and Thomas Shannon, right shoulder, slight. Company F: Sergeant William Robbitt, right thigh, slight; Corporal J. Watson, forehead, serious; Privates Denis Vaugh, knee, slight; Aaron Findall, right hand, slight; Samuel Findall, left leg, slight; John Taffe, scrotum, slight; Patrick Murphy, slightly; Charles Clark, side and back, serious; Charles Booker, left hip and arm, serious; J. Waldron, left leg, serious; Stephen Maddox, chest and arm, serious; Michael Keefe, left chest, serious; and J. P. Starks, chin, slight. Company G: Sergeants D. Wessendor, left leg, serious, and Charles Woods, thigh and scrotum, serious; Privates Martin King, left temple, slight; Philip Osum, left leg, slight; Gus. Laws, right thigh, slight; and Andrew Wagner, seriously. Company H: Privates Robert Hytcher, slightly; Samuel Kelly, slightly; William Smith, right thigh, slight; John Sherron, left breast, slight; Noble Bryant, thigh, slight; John McRae, left side, slight; and Jacob Shaljohn, left arm, serious. Company I: Lieutenant William Frank, heel contusion, slight; Private H. Alfutis, slightly. Company K: M. Neff, right thigh, slight; Charles Sarrod, hips, serious; William Adams, face, slight; James Graham, right thigh, slight; H. Williecher, left arm, slight; W. Hart, left arm.

Summary.—Killed, 11; wounded, 71—total, 82.

FIRST KENTUCKY REGIMENT.

Killed.—Company A: Privates J. J. Wadud, Patrick Rice, Samuel Weal, Henry Riley, Edward Williams, and C. Williamson. Company C: Color Corporal Cyrus, Block. Company F: Corporal Adam Warfield; Privates Louis Daws, J. B. Inezdes, and Michael Connelly. Company H: Sergeant Aug. Willhelms. Company K: Privates William Roppinhill and William Boctkger.

Wounded.—Company A: Sergeant James R. Macky, left breast, slight; Privates Thomas Brown, arm, compound fracture, severe; and Charles Rice, right thigh. Company B: Privates Robert McLure, back, slight; Henry Armstead; Joseph Woodwin, arm, slight; and Robert Loyd, left thigh, slight. Company C: Corporals Frank Hodkins, head, slight, and J. W. Cronse, both thighs, severe; Privates Joseph Crook, hips; Arnold Pfister, temple, slight; A. Bishop, right thigh, fracture severe; P. Foreman, leg, compound fracture; P. Flanigan, breast, slight; John Manyor, left leg, slight, and Wesley Quigley, shoulder fracture of scapula; Company D: John C. Hatch, left foot, severe; George Fry, left leg, slight; Jno. Gilmaster, right thigh, slight; Jno. Hitch, left foot; Augustus Ruff, right foot, severe; Christopher Smith, right hand, slight; and John Weaver, right thigh, severe. Company F: Privates James Hendly, left shoulder, severe, and Walter Eversele, right hand, severe. Company G: Privates H. Schneider, left hand, and Francis Bake, wrist fracture, severe. Company H: Corporal Eli Anderson, left arm, slight; Privates J. W. Colcher, right hip, slight; Donald Buck; thigh, severe; Jno. Coltseen, right hip, severe, and Michael Larkin, right arm, severe. Company I: Lieutenant James Fawand, right leg fracture; Privates Mathias Gibb, left hand, slight, and Arthur Fleetwood, slight; Corporal Thomas Fannan, left side, slight; Privates G. Gill, left hand, slight; Edward Baker, right hand, severe; W. H. Meyers, wrist fracture; Edward Parsells, right thigh, severe; Charles Wibber, left leg, slight. Company K: Sergeant John Hess, left foot, slight; Corporal Martin Ruffie, right ankle, slight; Privates J. Wolf, arm fracture; R. Miller, C. Inttigan, side and hand, severe; Peter Heinback, left leg, slight; Frederick Wreser, left side, slight; Frederick Bannan, right arm; Frederick Simmons, right leg; Daniel Karr, left leg, severe; Aug. Wudkind, left leg, severe, and Clen Vanderham, left leg, severe.

Summary.—Killed, 14; wounded, 53—total, 67.

TWENTY-THIRD KENTUCKY VOLUNTEERS.

Killed.—Company A: Sergeants Jasper Hutchison and Jas. E. Botts; Private John Noll. Company B: Privates Wm. Smith and Nicholas Korrell. Company E: Corporal Wm. H. Link. Company F: Corporal Jno. Jones.

Wounded.—Company A: Sergeants W. B. Sherrell, left leg, severely; and G. M. Greene, right breast, slightly; Corporal J. E. Calvert, left breast, slightly; Privates J. H. Lome, left hand, slightly; G. W. Collins, left thigh, severely; W. H. Williamson, left thigh, severely; and Pat. Moncey, left foot, slightly. Company B: Sergeant Lambert Scott, head; Privates Joseph Rock, left foot, slightly; and J. R. J Pasten, both legs, slightly. Company C: Captain W. G. Holden, left leg, slightly; Private John Hobbs, head, severely. Company D: Sergeant Reuben Hammer, scrotum, slightly; Corporals Jno. Bell, head, slightly; and J. F. Foyer, left knee, slightly; Privates John Wilson, head, slightly; Julius Hay, right arm; Lewis Shemshag, ankle, severely; and James Wilson, ankle, slightly. Company E: Sergeant L. C. Miller, left breast, slightly; Corporal F. Brockman, head, slightly; Privates W. H. Hook, abdomen, mortally; Henry Beaty, right leg, severely; and A. Millische, shoulder, slightly. Company F: Sergeant Henry Hemyhan, abdomen, severely; Corporal W. Christian, left cheek, slightly; Privates N. Gregory, head, slightly; Patrick Ryan, left arm, severely; and John Loux, arm, slightly. Company G: Privates F. Cullum, left knee, slightly; and M. Harrison, lung, slightly. Company H: Privates S. S. Smith, both legs, severely; and F. Hollingshead, right thigh, severely. Company I: Lieutenant F. A. Black, left arm, slightly; Privates George Miller, right shoulder, slightly; James Cooper, left leg, slightly; J. Weidright, left thigh, severely; Joseph Peak, right thigh, severely; F. Harrington, head, slightly; F. L. Briggs, left ankle, slightly; F. Howell, left leg, slightly; J. W. Glover, left arm, slightly; James Hage, slightly. Company K: Sergeant W. H. Spencer, arm, severely; Corporal W. A. Plumber, left leg, severely; Privates W. A. Crawford, right shoulder, severely; Solomon Purows, left hand, slightly; James McKee, right hand, slightly; Ruben Jones, leg, slightly; and D. M. Evans, left ankle, slightly.

Summary.—Killed, 7; wounded, 50; missing, 20—total, 77.

NINETIETH OHIO VOLUNTEERS.

Killed.—Company A: Sergeant Markly and Private G. W. Wood. Company B: Privates F. S. Miller and F. W. Roach. Company C: Privates J. Creamer and Daniel Smith. Company E: Privates Isaac Carpenter and W. Bryan. Company F: W. Arknim, Frederick Reynolds, and S. Frederick. Company I: Corporal Wm. Mason. Company K: Corporal A. Porter; Privates D. Shrevely, James Carris, and J. R. Cose.

Wounded.—Company A: Privates S. Bowling, both hips, severely; and J. Morris, right side, severely. Company B: Privates —— Gasten, left arm, severely; W. Edson, ankle; W. Hepelder, right shoulder, severely; J. Jaker, left shoulder, severely; J. Walter, knee, slightly; J. Burns, slightly; J. McQuade, right hip, slightly; J. Wycroft, head, slightly; and A. Jolley, hand, slightly. Company C: Privates J. Doiston, left leg, amputated; Paris Robinson, breast, slightly; D. C. Conor, hand, shoulder, and leg; Oliver Homey, left ankle; and H. McIntire, slightly. Company D: Captain A. Perry, missing; Lieut. —— Welch, right arm, severely; Privates A. Smith, severely; John Berger, right arm, severely; and John Andregg, both legs, severely. Company E: Privates J. Wood, left arm, severely; S. S. Rogers, left hand; J. Armstrong, left arm, severely; Lewis Jamen, right arm, severely; W. Buckingham, leg, severely; William Mock, head, slightly; A. Bowers, hip, slightly; H. Guest, hip, slightly; and Joseph Berry, right hand, slightly. Company F: Lieut. Thomas Rains, right foot, severely; Privates S. B. Haddennan, left hand wrist, severely; F. Kector, mortal; J. McAlister, neck, severely; Solomon Bets, left arm, severely; and J. Delong, neck, slightly. Company G: Privates J. Wood, hand; B. W. Cofland, lung, severely; R. Chulcoat, left side, slightly; Allen Oldfield, side; slightly; W. Switser, leg, slightly; James Dobins, foot, slightly; A. D. Eoland, slightly; J. Westenhaner, shoulder and leg, severely; J. S. Maxwell, hip, slightly; J. Phillips, hand, slightly; J. Switzer, right side, slightly; Robert Matton, left hip, slightly; J. Hoffman, right thigh, severely; and J. Pattett, arm, slightly. Company H: Privates J. W. Graves, right hip, severely; and J. N. Selly, left leg, slightly. Company I: Lieutenant Thomas Baker, foot, severely; Sergeants D. Hupford, left shoulder; and J. W. Strent, right shoulder, slightly; Privates J. W. Powell, shoulder, severely; E. Silus, left thigh, severely; H. Conrad, leg, severely; and S. Shaffer, right hand, severely. Company K: Captain M. Rowe, wrist, severely; Lieutenants F. Read, foot, slightly; J. Cook, missing; Privates J. Smithly, unknown; W. Straib, left hand, severely; J. R. Core, severely; H. McChristy, foot, slightly; J. Gibson, left thigh, severely; Henry Harper, left thigh, severely; Howard Schreiver, left shoulder, slightly; and Patrick Murphy, right thigh, severely.

Summary.—Killed, 16; wounded, 70; missing, 2—total, 88.

EIGHTY-FOURTH ILLINOIS REGIMENT.

Killed.—Company A: Private Aaron McKinner. Company B: Privates J. A. Murphy, John A. Sellers, John Minor. Company C: Sergeant G. F. Yocum; Corporals Charles Shainer and Ben. Price; Privates R. W. Pennington, George Gordon, R. Parrott. Company D: Sergeant —— Perry; Privates Samuel Leeper, William Franklin, J. M. Winecup. Company F: Corporal Eli Elval. Company H: Lieutenant L. T. Ball; Sergeants A. E. Abercrombie, A. J. Wellings, John M. Weidner, Bigelow Kyle, H. Willner, George W. Femer, W. M. Tipton, John J. Kidwell. Company I: Privates Crawford Scott, Dick Miller, F. J. Galloway, A. Crook. Company K: Sergeant S. G. Plummer, Corporal Samuel Wilkins, Private John Yocker.

Wounded.—Company A: Lieutenant S. G. Wisdom, both legs, severely; Sergeants L. N. Michell, scalp, severely; Willis Edson, shoulder, severely, and E. A Rall, hand, severely; Corporals James K. Wirtman, shoulder, severely; Privates S. R. Spears, left arm, amputated; Milford Mitchell, hand fractured; D. J. Yuggle, hand, slightly; P. Slighter, fractured thumb; George Porks, left hand; C. C. Roberts, hand; L. Patrick, left lung, severely; J. J. Shepherd, shoulder, severely; John A. Crane, neck, slightly; James Deerdoff, back, slightly; James Waters, foot, slightly. Company B: Lieutenant L. Scott, left knee and thigh; Corporals J. R. Minor, slightly; D. Hanlan, knee, amputated; Privates Abner Weldman; Robert Chaslock, back and head, died since; Isaac Druell, left hip and testicle; E Walker, back; C. Mitchell; L. Moore, groin; J. A. Walters, left thigh; D. Hughes, elbow joint, slightly; Levi Bodhamer; Levi Fancher, arm and chest, slightly; James Belford, scalp, contusion by cannon ball. Company C: Privates G. W. McDaniel, right shoulder, severely; Albert Marken, scalp, severely; A. Pendam, severely; Daniel Aben, leg, slightly; W. T. Harris, both cheeks; Nelson Butcher, thighs, slightly; W. McGleeson, leg, slightly; T. J. Martin, back, slightly; W. A. Chapman, slightly; G. W. White, thigh. Company D: Captain —— Davis, neck and arm, severely; Sergeants —— Miller, severely; Thomas Sprigg, right side and arm; Privates John Logan, slightly; S. Leeper, severely; James Furlong, both hips, severely; A. Mallard, right thigh, severely; A. Stinson, left leg, severely; Barlow McCoy, slightly; James Jones, knee, slightly; R. Oldfield, right arm. Company E: Lieutenant —— Roberts, leg and side, severely; Sergeants —— Slater, left shoulder and hip; —— Will, arm, severely; Privates D. A. Davis, severely; A. Sherman, lungs, died January 7; E. Lightle, hand, severely; Jacob Worth, J. A. Malone, right hip, contusion; David Hoffman, thigh, slightly; Thomas Abbott, thigh, slightly; Thomas Bugbee, wrist, slightly; John Connar, face, slightly. Company F: Lieutenant Samuel Frost, left foot, slightly; Corporal D. W. Litchfield, died January 10; Corporals John Pryce, neck, slightly; R. M. Miller, neck, slightly; Privates W. Walker, back, died January 5; F. B. Turner, right shoulder, fracture; W. Foster, shoulder, fracture; W. Thomas, shoulder, slightly; M. F. Weamigen, thigh and side, severely; V. B. Clark, right arm, severely; W. A. Kurch, left thigh, severely. Company G: Corporal Charles Green, head, severely; Privates W. R. Pinkerton, right shoulder, severely; G. W. Thompkins, left knee, amputated; R. W. Kelly, hand, slightly; J. Crandall, slightly; R. Sanott, slightly; Alexander Beck, right shoulder, severely. Company H: Captain John C. Pepper, left hip, slightly; Corporals W. W. McCandless, knee, amputated; H. C. White, leg, severely; J. W. White, back, slightly; Eli Detwiler, slightly; Privates J. Baldwin, leg and arm, severely; W. Fuller, right leg, severely; John Gilvain, leg, severely; M. Sullivan, leg, severely; E. L. Spicer, face, slightly; Thomas Miller, slightly; J. Brown, neck and shoulder; P. McClain, thigh, slightly; John Dean, slightly; W. H. Burgess, arm, severely; Thomas Cody, severely; L. McMann, left arm, severely; Grant Deharen, thigh, severely. Company I: Corporals Samuel King, left hand, severely; D. A. Alexander, scalp, severely; A. J. Hony, right arm and foot; Privates W. Nye, slightly; S. Johnson, right foot, slightly; Nelson Cain, both shoulders, severely; W. D. Crawford, left lung, died; Hall Higley, neck, severely; A. Turner, severely; George Stevens, right thigh, severely; David Malone, shoulder, severely; Dudley Dunahoe, severely; John Boyles, severely; Crawford Scott, severely; Dick Miller, severely; S. J. Galloway, severely; A. Crook, severely; Corporal David Slagle, left hand. Company K: Lieutenant —— Millis, scalp, slightly; Corporal George Bell, thigh and penis; Privates S. A. Snyder, left thigh, slightly; George Craft, slightly; W. Stanley, left lung, died January 9; Amos Rea; Niles Pearson, severely; George Tucker, severely.

Summary.—Killed, 31; wounded, 125—total, 156.

SIXTH OHIO REGIMENT.

Killed.—Company A: Lieutenant C. Foster and Adjutant Alfred Williams. Company B: Corporal David Madeny and Private ——— Burst. Company E: Privates M. Schwab, C. Davis, and ——— Shattock. Company F: Private H. Willis. Company G: First Sergeant G. Kidnom and Corporal Oliver Rockenfield. Company I: ——— Springereyser. Company K: First Sergeant G. B. Nicholson, Sergeant Thomas Drake, Private S. Huber, and F. Wesselman.

Wounded.—Colonel L. T. Anderson. Company A: Sergeant H. Hennan, left shoulder, severely; and Sergeant J. F. Howard, left shoulder, severely; Privates F. H. Holiday; J. Freel, hand, severely; A. Stetman, severely; William Klomer, back, severely; Charles Thompson, arm, severely; and John Ranny, back, severely. Company B: Captain ——— McAlpin, shoulder, severely; Corporal G. Nearing and Corporal E. Hanford, shoulder, severely; Privates J. Halfenberger, severely; Jos. Mitchell, shoulder; J. Kleine; ——— Hochslatter, abdomen, severely; H. Stocklin, severely; J. Stocklin, severely; A. Shatenhelm, back, severely; A. Gettle, slightly; and T. F. Miller, leg, slightly. Company C: Color Sergeant J. Critty, arm, slightly; Corporal E. G. Hem; Privates F. Tieman, slightly; A. Schuler, thigh; Jno. Leek, unknown; H. Stockhelm, hand, severely; William Lidel, contusion, slightly; J. Lyken, unknown; and

J. Heffernan, gluteal region, slightly. Company D: Sergeant A. Willowby, thigh, slightly; Sergeant W. Bowers, leg, severely; Corporal J. H. Jenks, left arm, slightly; Privates R. Hoffman, hip; A. Hugh, knee, severely; J. L. Williams, finger, amputated; M. Werleck, slightly; S. Weeker, severely; F. Doller, thigh, slightly; F. Lozen; J. W. Peters, ball entered gluten nax; A. C. Drips, shoulder, severely; H. Wake, lumbar region; W. Stephenson, left shoulder, severely; F. Mannus, flesh wound, slightly; M. Weidesecht, flesh wound, slightly; W. W. Williams, left forearm, severely; and A. Huger, knee, severely. Company E: Corporal E. West, abdomen, slightly; Privates J. L. Fordan, left lung, severely; C. H. Baldwin, back, severely; F. Greenward, head and thigh, severely; J. Scheader, unknown; M. Smith, back, severely; J. O'Neil, left hand, slightly; E. Eckhardt, unknown; W. Leak, unknown; C. Davis, leg, mortally; J. L. Ferdan, left lung; and E. M. Hall, right hand, slightly. Company F: Lieutenant T. Shafer, flesh, severely; Sergeant W. E. Jackson, thigh, severely; Corporal Siegel, leg, slightly; Privates W. R. Wood, arm and back, severely; J. Neippier, thigh, slightly; A. Strafer, slightly; G. Hillman, right arm, severely; J. Lawrence, thigh, severely; A. Keseman, hand, slightly; J. Lawrence, leg, slightly; ——— Aumer, face, slightly; J. Linceman, leg and knee, severely; and ——— Witle, shoulder, severely. Company G: Corporal H. Simons, left heel, slightly; J. Schenck, hand, severely; A. Schenck, hand, severely; J. T. Stallcup, leg, severely; J. A. Calwell, leg, severely; H. Bradbury, leg, severely; F. Burnett, unknown; and W. A. Clark, unknown. Company H: Sergeant G. W. Comany, scalp, slightly; Private W. E. Dangerty, scalp, slightly; A. Clapper, leg, severely; and J. Melfinber, head. Company I: Privates John Stacker, arm, severely; G. Haller, shoulder, slightly; F. Linkcome, face, severely; and A. Roy, foot, severely. Company K: Captain E. H. Finker, head, severely; Sergeant W. Paperbrook, left leg, severely; Corporal D. Krayhanzen, abdomen, mortally; Corporal Charles Dowby, arm, severely; Corporal J. Martin, arm, severely; Privates G. Kelch; W. Gaines, left leg, severely; James Hadock, thigh, severely; H. Beekman, back and thigh, severely; H. Elsing, leg, slightly; D. Kleme, shoulder, severely; C. Alberts, left hand, severely; and J. Nichols, left shoulder.

Summary.—Killed, 15; wounded, 104—total, 119.

TWENTY-FOURTH OHIO VOLUNTEERS.

Killed—Colonel Frederick C. Jones; Major Henry Teny; Captain Enoch Weller; First Lieutenant Charles R. Harmon, company E; Sergeant Alfred Morrison, company C; Daniel S. Porter and Jas. R. Puntry, company D; Corporal E. Newman and Privates William Keller and Joseph Bowland, company H; Private J. H. Barker, company I; Corporal Francis Riggins, company K.

Wounded.—Company B: Sergeant W. L. Dural, right leg, slightly; Corporal J. Haley, cheek, severe; Privates J. Bottenbrook, breast; William Erbenen, breast; Thomas Kelly, breast; Theston Reed, left foot, compound fracture; Denis Sulivan, left hand, severe; Hiram Doisler, left hand, fracture; George Shocks, right thigh; B. Willis, hand, slightly; M. Gittings, mortally. Company C: Corporals James Orton, left thigh, severely; Henry Roberts, leg, severely; Privates Lewis Ruble, right hand; Richard Tullis, right thigh; Jacob Warner, right arm and left hand; William Roller, right thigh; J. M. Waldrof, right thigh; George Dark, right thigh; Simeon Bausten, right thigh; D. Stagle, thigh, slight. Company D: Corporals John McManus, neck, severely; G. Collins, scalp, slightly; Privates John Shirly, lumbar region; Jeff. Bradley, lumbar region; John Grooms, left arm and thigh; James Potter, thigh; Jabes Rothwell, left thigh, slightly; R. S. Parish, thigh, severely; Clark Compton, thigh; John River, left leg; D. Hoover, left leg; John Fibbs, left leg; Alexander Thompson, left leg; John Parrish, left leg; Allen Parks, left leg; Allen

Murry, left leg; Allen Guthridge, left leg; Sewall Pointer, left leg; William Dragon, left leg; John Dragon, right hip; John Cameron, right hip; Jas. Armstrong, slightly. Company E: Sergeant Henry Shery, scalp, slightly; Privates John Galloway, left leg, fractured; Hugh McGainlan, left leg, amputated; George Smith, scalp; Charles Hand, left arm, severely; G. W. Dowdy, right hand; Abram Menis, breast, slightly. Company G: First Lieutenant John Ocker, bruised. Company H; First Lieutenant Jacob Diehl, slightly; Second Lieutenant August Dryer, severely. Company K: Privates Armstrong Kiggins, severely; John Miller, left leg; William A. White, thigh, severely; Michael Adams, scalp; J. Babcock, right leg; Levi Johnston, slightly; Bernard Short, mortally.

Summary.—Killed, 12; wounded, 61—total, 73.

ONE HUNDRED AND TENTH ILLINOIS REGIMENT.

Killed.—Company A: Privates James Rice, A. Wilson, and W. G. Stricklin. Company F: Second Lieutenant Jesse Payne and Privates Moses Ward and John Underwood.

Wounded.—Company A: Lieutenant —— Denning, right knee, severely; Privates J. Ice, right hand, slightly; S. Tonny, right eye; W. Therbitt, scalp; W. Essay, left hip. Company B: Privates Z. Casey, arm, fracture; John Whittenberg, scalp; R. D. Osborn, thorax. Company C: Captain J. Darks, head, severely; Lieutenant Hossea Ferrill, scalp, severely; Sergeants F. M. Parks, arm and ankle, severely; C. L. Parks, left thigh, slightly; Corporal Francis Parks, right thigh; Privates H. Sutherland, left shoulder; Henry Cooper, arm, fracture; D. Payne, left leg; A. Stricklone, slightly. Company D: Privates George Howard, left leg, slightly; Jas. Barnett, left knee joint, slightly; S. Fairchild, left leg, slightly; S. Palmer, right shoulder; A. H. Camp, left hip. Company F: W. Dungny, left shoulder. Company G: Privates Jas. Scott, left eye; F. M. Treeble, right leg, contusion; Willis Jones, scalp. Company H: Private A. T. Thompson, right shoulder. Company K: Private W. S. Butler, scalp and leg.

Summary.—Killed, 7; wounded, 27—total, 34.

THIRTY-SIXTH INDIANA REGIMENT.

Killed.—Company A: Privates Harry Manor and Jesse Shackel. Company B: Corporals A. Fisher, R. D. Tape, and B. F. Warrington. Company D: Private A. W. James. Company E: Captain W. H. Kichler and Private T. E. Kent. Company F: Private John Gantz. Company G: Captain James S. King. Company H: Privates Henry Williams and Jacob Eckhart. Company I: Captain William Davidson, Privates Joseph Haynes, and Samuel Thornton. Company K: Privates J. D. Hall and John W. Johnston.

Wounded.—Major Isaac Kinley, severely. Company A: Corporals George Warrick, leg, severely; F. Elliott, thigh, slightly; Privates Samuel Bell, arm, slightly; W. McKinney, groin. Company B: Captain A. D. Shutts, side, mortally; Corporal E. H. Laughlin, thigh, slightly; Privates Peter Bassenger, leg; R. Johnson, face; Jacob Rislig, scalp; John H. Conell, leg; W. H. H. Kitchey, thigh, mortally. Company C: Privates Absalom Julian, thigh, mortally; Geo. Haggard, thigh, severely; William Weaver, leg, slightly; F. H. Gum, leg, severely; H. Reichart, shoulder, severely; J. Vores, shoulder, severely; F. D. Shepherd, leg, severely; H. H. Henderson, knee, severely. Company D: Sergeants F. S. Swain, leg, severely; G. M. Cantly, leg shot off; D. S. Boyers, foot, severely; Corporal Anson Bird, breast, severely; Privates John Leckridge, both legs; F. Pike, three fingers shot off; Henry Gresees, three fingers shot off; E. Lamb, leg shot off; A. D. Lacy, hand shot off. Company E: Sergeants Thomas Beubau, hand shot off; E. H. Parkman, arm shot off; Privates Jerry

Hays, thigh and leg shot off; C. Canaway, leg shot off; A. H. Grave, jaw slightly; E. A. Taylor, thigh, slightly; S. H. Henry, hand, slightly; L. B Morris, leg, slightly; B. F. Weaver, hand. Company F: Privates David Fany' slightly; James Potter, ankle; F. G. Diggs, thigh; Joshua Stephole, ankle; A. Hays, both arms; William Robinson, both arms; Isaac Fargner, groin. Company G: Lieutenants W. J. Smith, hand, slightly; John C. Byron, leg, severely; Sergeant William Dimolen, scalp, severely; Corporals J. H. Harthaway, foot, severely; D. E. Ball, thigh, severely; Joseph Asboath, thigh, severely; John Surider, left leg; Albert Peoris, back, slightly; H. Maloney, leg, slightly; J. Penticost, thigh, slightly. Company H: Sergeants G. Mulligan, slightly; R. Carr, slightly; George Velott, slightly; Corporals S. Simpson, slightly; George Nathaway, slightly; William Gordon, slightly; Privates Lewis Loughton, slightly; R. Sutten, slightly; John Woods, slightly; Henry Velot, slightly; Lyman Funk, slightly; John McGlin, mortally; M. Conner, slightly. Company I: Sergeant Isaac Duthyan, head, slightly; Corporal Newton Parmer, leg; Privates Meredith Berry, head, slightly; Jacob Thornton, leg and shoulder. Company K: Captain M. Penden, right thigh, severely; Lieutenant John Ross, shoulder and leg, severely; Sergeants James A. Steel, mortally; M. Thorberg, leg, slightly; Corporal William Flinn, leg, slightly; Privates Isaac Hawker, mortally; George W. Bates, leg, severely; William Sherry, leg, slightly; Calvin Cross, thigh, slightly; W. M. L. Wood, leg.

Summary.—Killed, 17; wounded, 82—total, 99.

FORTY-FIRST OHIO REGIMENT.

Killed.—Company A: Captain J. McCarry, First Lieutenant C. C. Hart' and Private A. McFarland. Company B: Private W. Beck. Company E: Sergeant R. Sénnonels, Privates S. Winchester and J. Quicks. Company F: Sergeant ——— Kidwell and Private ——— Parrich. Company G: Privates J. Stung and D. Hughes. Company I: Sergeant ——— Kirk and Private R. Snyder. Total, 13.

Wounded.—Company A: Captain O. A. McClary, leg; Sergeants S. Brooks, slightly; J. J. Mattocks, right shoulder; Corporal P. A. Bowers, slightly; Privates J. Wagoner, mortally, (since died;) J. Cutler, face; C. R. Smith, severely; A. Flint, left hand; C. A. Bennett, thigh; H. C. Kepler, right hip and left arm; A. Hessett, left hip; E. Plonts, slightly; W. Slures, contusion; —— Richin, wound unknown. Company B: First Lieutenant E. F. Ford, chest; Sergeant C. F. Judd, right arm; Corporal H. Belon, eye; Privates J. A. Burk, left thigh; C. Dawfoot, leg; George Patterson and J. Johnson, slightly; G. Wilder, right thigh; D. A. Bartlett, contusion; F. Scott, slightly; F. Harley, contusion; —— Latham, hand. Company C: First Lieutenant ——— Patcher, foot; Sergeant C. Huston, arm; Color Sergeant C. F. Titus, right thigh; Corporals James Carlun, F. W. Eahirman, and J. Dunham, slightly; Privates R. Hinkle, right thigh; F. McConigle, lungs; J. Wright, leg; H. Morris, slightly; J. Huester, neck; T. Bonham, hand. Company D: Second Lieutenant L. Fisher, right foot; Corporals William Dunke, right thigh; A. Emerson, contusion; Privates O. Matthews, contusion; J. Hist, forearm; ——— Sawyer, locality of wound unknown; W. Smith, thigh; J. Davidson, slightly; W. Narley, abdomen; C. Wassoon, leg; H. Conaway, leg; P. Conoway, leg; P. Farrell, leg. Company E: Corporal D. Neville, contusion; Privates William Neville, contusion; D. Cockran, contusion; J. Canfield, left leg; J. Coldwell, left leg; N. Stibbins, left thigh; J. Ryan, right thigh; R. Davidson, head. Company F: Sergeant R. A. Gaalt, neck; Privates S. J. Ewing, head; D. Aikins, contusion; M. Fredericks, severely; J. Hunt, thigh; William Fry, right leg; D. Lawrence, left shoulder and arm; H. Olden, right shoulder; G. Webb, leg; J. Goff, contusion; C. Edney, contusion. Company G: Sergeant H. Young, contusion; Corporals D. Young, left hand; J. Bridgomar, contusion; Privates D. H. Worthington, severely; O. Stephenson, left temple and ear; H. B. Hunt, F. G. Gray, W. Searles, C. Moss, J. Picket, M. Watts, contusion. Company H: Sergeant H. Disland, right arm and hip; Corporal H. Cose, both legs; Privates ——— Sewbart, mortally; G. Rositer, right arm and hip; H. Moore, leg; S. Fishall, right thigh; G. E. Tift, left hip and leg; W. H. Prince, shoulder; G. Clark, shoulder. Company I: Privates A. Conchain, both thighs; D. Hays, hand; J. Hall, contusion. Company K: First Lieutenant ——— Beebe, hand; Second Lieutenant H. Wulcott, severely; Sergeants J. Orr, mortally; J. O. Smith, left leg; Privates W. M. Elherin, leg; A. Winters, shoulder; J. Ryan; J. Thompson, left side; D. Regan, forearm; C. Griffin, slightly. Total, 103.

NINTH INDIANA REGIMENT.

Killed.—Company A: Second Lieutenant H. Kessler, Sergeant S. Soyer, and Private —— Links. Company C: Sergeant C. Yelens and Private G. W. Hughgler. Company D: Corporal G. D. Shon. Company E: Private G. S. Weathes. Company F: Private J. Hanald. Company K: Sergeant M. Chowan, Corporal D. Willis, and Private D. O. Hall. Total, 11.

Wounded.—Lieutenant Colonel J. B. C. Suman, slightly. Hospital Steward T. J. McMullin, severely. Company A: Corporal G. Thompson, right arm, slightly; Privates —— English, right arm, slightly; J. Fox, right arm, severely; G. Guth-erig, right arm, severely; G. McComac, left leg, slightly; H. Hamlin, right hand; H. Mercer, left leg. Company B: Privates W. Weberton, right elbow fractured; H. Pallard, right shoulder; C. O. Beetle, cheek; L. Williams, left shoulder; R. Disbron, knee; A. Jackson, left leg. Company C: First Lieutenant D. Braden, severely; Corporals J. Knapp, right hand; N. Vonatchin, right hand; Privates S. Morris, right leg; H. A. Olmstead, right leg; W. D. Sayer, right leg; W. F. Shaver, left side; John Wolf, left knee; A. B. Chapman, neck. Company D: Sergeants T. D. Robinson, left knee; Peter Knoch, right shoulder; Corporal Alfred Allen, side and chest; Privates J. Bunnell, left ankle; J. W. Berger, left ankle; G. Ferganden, left groin; M. E. Richards, left thigh; A. Sward, left hand, severely; E. J. Williams, left foot, slightly. Company E: Sergeant T. Prichert, right knee; Corporal Thomas Powers, right knee; Privates W. Sink, severely; P. Rasher, right arm; J. W. Dutcher, left thigh, slightly; R. Maror, left thigh, slightly; G. Robbett, little finger, severely; J. Peterson, left shoulder, severely; S. Mackey, abdomen, slightly; D. McKnight, left foot, slightly; J. Simon, right side, slightly; A. Ketchum, right side, severely. Company F: Sergeant L. C. Shepherd, right hip, severely; Corporal J. Kopplin, right foot, slightly; Privates B. Heelson, left knee, slightly; T. A. Doremus, right arm, slightly; J. Dockly, right arm, slightly; J. Ellinger, knee, slightly; F. McNabb, left hip, slightly; E. Milroy, slightly; C. Kinger, both legs; J. C. Roberts, left elbow, severely; J. Stahler, left breast, slightly; G. Vantukin, right cheek, slightly; J. C. Culp, left foot, slightly. Company G: Sergeant B. R. Farris, right groin, slightly; Corporal J. F. Farris, left knee, slightly; Privates J. Byris, left knee, slightly; J. Brenton, right groin, slightly; P. Bartholomew, left leg, slightly. Company H: Privates F. H. Davidson, right knee; A. Naire, hips, severely; D. Bryant, left arm, slightly; M. Slate, left arm, slightly; H. Kerwig, left arm, slightly; A. Glover, left thigh, severely; J. Bullis, left hand, slightly; J. Edson, left hand, slightly. Company I: Captain J. M. Pettit, severely; Second Lieutenant W. H. Criswell, slightly; Privates B. Anderson, left hand, severely; C. E. Hard, left knee, slightly; J. C. Drislin, right arm, severely; P. E. Janney, right arm, severely; O. O. Knowlton, compound fracture, severely; W. A. Markell, left hip, severely; W. S. Morris, breast, slightly; C. O. Newman, foot, slightly; G. H. Nodwright, left wrist, severely; H. Perry, right cheek, slightly; W. W. Rossin, left thigh, severely; H. Shafer, left breast; A Steward, right forefinger. Company K: Sergeant S. H. James, left foot; Corporal A. Prittell, left foot, seriously: Privates J. Chandler, right shoulder; —— Hilton, left breast; Y. Miller, right shoulder; W. Coran, left groin, slightly; W. G. Jewell, left knee, slightly. Total, 93.

COCKERELL'S BATTERY.

Killed.—Privates A. Jones and A. Nichols. Total, 2.

Wounded.—Severely: Captain D. T. Cockerell, and Privates Harrison Frazier, William Lear, A. W. Carlisle, and Harry Glenn. Slightly: Privates Thomas Gilrugh, Henry Bright, Asher Wycoff, Alexander Highland, F. C. Lidam, Owen Doty, William Barney, and John Hartzell. Total, 13.

HEADQUARTERS 1ST BRIGADE, 2D DIVISION, LEFT WING,
Army of the Cumberland, in field before Murfreesboro', Tennessee, January 4, 1863.

CAPTAIN: In conformity to orders received from division headquarters the following rough approximate statement is made of the operations of the brigade before Murfreesboro', Tennessee. An extended and correct report will be submitted in a few days giving the proper details of all matters.

The brigade left camp near Nashville on the morning of the 26th ultimo. The effective strength of the brigade on leaving camp at that time was twelve hundred and seven, (1,207,) all told. It consisted of the 1st Kentucky volunteers, (Colonel Enyart,) 2d Kentucky volunteers, (Colonel Sedgwick,) 31st Indiana volunteers, (Colonel Osborn,) 10th Ohio volunteers, (Colonel Ross;) Standart's Ohio battery (company B) was assigned to the command for temporary service. After leaving the picket line near Nashville this brigade had the advance, preceded by a portion of Colonel Kennett's cavalry command. After various trifling skirmishes and some artillery firing, the enemy's skirmishers were forced to the village of Lavergne. Here quite a force of cavalry, artillery, and infantry, (or dismounted cavalry,) of the enemy disputed our occupancy of the place. I was ordered by General Palmer, commanding division, to drive the enemy from the woods on the left and take possession of the village from this quarter if daylight would permit. The 31st Indiana and 1st Kentucky (under command of Colonel Enyart) were sent by me to accomplish this. These regiments advanced under cover of the cedars on the left, and finding the enemy in force near the frame church on the west of Stony creek, attacked him, and after a sharp discharge of musketry, ran in on a bayonet charge and routed him, forcing him across the creek and occupying the bank. The conduct of both regiments and all their officers was excellent. In this action the casualties were three killed and eight wounded.

On the 27th the brigade reached Stewart's creek. On the 29th half the brigade was on picket at Stewart's creek. On the 30th position was taken in the front line of battle, on the right of the turnpike, in the cedars, near Cowan's burnt house. An effective line of skirmishers was thrown forward, and the enemy's line during the evening was driven from the crest near the burnt house. His temporary shelters were occupied by my troops and held by them till near daylight the following morning. If re-enforced this point would doubtless have been held. One-half of my effective strength was kept out all night on picket trying to hold this advanced line. The attempt was partially successful.

On the 31st ultimo an order was received about 8 o'clock a. m. to advance in line, with the brigade supporting me on the right and left. My brigade promptly did so, formed in two lines as follows: 2d Kentucky and 31st Indiana, (under general charge of Colonel Sedgwick,) constituting the first line; 1st Kentucky and 90th Ohio, (under general charge of Colonel Enyart,) constituting the second line. The artillery was formed in half battery on each flank of front line. The brigade by this formation exhibited a front of, say, six hundred men, *or less than an ordinary regiment.* Colonel Hazen's 3d brigade was formed to my left and rear, and a brigade of General Negley's division on the right. Upon the order being given to advance, my skirmishers ran rapidly forward and engaged those of the enemy. They drove them back. The front line advanced promptly up to the fence in the margin of the wood. The enemy rushed forward rapidly and in great force, and the fight became very severe and obstinate about 9 o'clock a. m. My troops fought with heroism. Each officer and man acted handsomely, and seemed to me to accomplish more than could be expected of him. We drove the enemy back, although in superior numbers. His line of formation appeared to be in four ranks with double lines. The first line, I thought, carried the United States flag; my attention was called to this by some of my officers, and seemed to be confirmed by my glass. After first repulsing the enemy, and before I could advance, he attacked our lines again. The engagement was very severe. My troops fought in a sturdy manner, and after some thirty minutes' firing drove him back a short distance. A respite of perhaps ten minutes in active firing enabled me to execute a passage of lines to the front and relieve the first line, the ammunition of which was wholly exhausted. The manœuvre was well executed, considering that the fire of the enemy's skirmishers was still brisk and that my line was wholly flanked. The rear line (now front) was soon actively engaged. The brigade on the left was not pressed up to my front. General Negley's brigade, yielding on the right to the desperate charge of the enemy, broke and drifted to my rear, and we were thus left completely flanked and exposed to an enfilading fire of artillery and musketry. It was impossible to get re-enforcements from the rear. It was impossible to get ammunition up or to communicate with the general commanding the division. In this condition I held the ground for some *forty minutes* longer than my conscience justified. Seeing my little brigade falling rapidly, and my best men carried wounded to the rear, without hope of support or fresh ammunition, I withdrew it to the wood. Here the enemy pressed me closely. We covered the retreat of General Negley's men as well as could be done. The 2d Kentucky brought off three pieces of artillery by hand. We saved my own battery completely and got across to the edge of the wood on the west side. Here finding fresh troops advancing I reported to General Thomas, and with his permission fell back to the turnpike with my shattered forces, then numbering about five hundred. We were then sent over to the railway by a member of General Rosecrans's staff to guard a battery, and held this position during the afternoon.

On January 1 the brigade was placed in line on the right of the division, in rear of the interval between the 1st and 3d divisions. After remaining here till noon it was advanced to the support of Swallow's battery on the hill to the right of the railway, and exposed to occasional shelling from the enemy's guns. On the 2d the brigade lay supporting the artillery, having constructed rough breastworks in rear of it. It held this position during the severe fight on the left across the creek exposed to a heavy cross fire of the enemy's artillery, but three men were killed by shells, however. When the enemy were driven on the left the brigade was advanced by General Palmer, he taking personally two regiments, 90th Ohio and 31st Indiana, to the point of woods half a mile to the front and left of our artillery and in line with our advance across the creek. I followed with the residue of the brigade across the open field to his right, on line, knowing the position of a masked battery of the enemy back of a crest in the field. I had the men to cheer loudly as we approached it, it having now become dark. The enemy immediately opened fire of shrapnell from four small guns; my line laid down under the shelter of the crest for some thirty minutes, during which the enemy continued to play at our position. But one man was killed here, by shell, and but four in the woods. A strong picket was posted for the night, and the line brought back to the hill in support of the artillery, where it has since remained.

The casualties of the brigade since leaving Nashville may be roughly stated as follows:

	Killed.	Wounded.	Prisoners.	Total.
1st Kentucky	9	52	42	103
2d Kentucky	6	56	23	85
31st Indiana	7	45	38	90
90th Ohio	5	75	79	159
Standart's battery	4	10	10	24
	31	238	192	461

I have been able to get no returns from the surgeons. This statement of casualties is only approximate. The list of killed includes only those known to be dead on the field, and will be doubtless largely swelled from those now rated as missing. The stragglers have been nearly all gathered up, and the report of this morning shows some eight hundred present. A full and complete report will be furnished as soon as reports of my commanding officers can be had and any conveniences be obtained for making it.

You may assure the general commanding that the men of all my regiment and battery, and every officer of them, behaved well in battle, and have endured the privations of the field cheerfully. Of all this, and of the results and details of our fights, I will report on a future occasion. My brigade sent in about one hundred prisoners.

I am, in great haste, captain, yours truly,

CHARLES CRUFT.
Brigadier General 22d Brigade.

Captain D. W. NORTON,
Acting Adjutant General, 2d Division, Left Wing.

HEADQUARTERS 1ST BRIGADE, 2D DIVISION, LEFT WING,
In field before Murfreesboro', Tennessee,
January 8, 1863.

CAPTAIN: I herewith submit, for the consideration of the general commanding division, the following report of the operations of this brigade in the recent action before Murfreesboro', Tennessee.

The brigade broke camp near Nashville on the morning of the 26th ultimo. The effective infantry strength of the command, on leaving camp, was twelve hundred and seven, (1,207.) It consisted of the 1st Kentucky volunteers, Colonel B. A. Enyart; 2d Kentucky volunteers, Colonel T. D. Sedgwick; 31st Indiana volunteers, Colonel John Osborn; and 90th Ohio volunteers, Colonel J. N. Ross. Captain Standart's Ohio battery, company B, 1st regiment, was attached to the command for temporary service.

After passing the picket lines near Nashville this brigade had the advance, preceded by a portion of Colonel Kennett's cavalry command. After various trifling skirmishes and some artillery firing, the enemy's skirmishers were forced into the village of Lavergne. Here quite a force of cavalry, artillery, and infantry, (or dismounted cavalry,) of the enemy disputed the occupancy of the place. General Palmer ordered me to drive the enemy from the woods on the left and take possession of the village from that quarter if daylight would permit. The 31st Indiana and 1st Kentucky volunteers were placed under command of Colonel Enyart, and sent by me to accomplish this. Colonel Murray, of 3d Kentucky cavalry, having been ordered to report to me for temporary duty, was placed upon the left flank of these regiments, and with his command acted very handsomely in protecting it and scouring the woods beyond. The regiments above named advanced, towards nightfall, under cover of the cedars on the left, and finding the enemy in force near the frame church, on the west of Stony creek, attacked him, and after a sharp discharge of musketry, ran in on a bayonet charge and routed him, forcing him across the creek and occupying the west bank; our line of skirmishers was then placed in the field beyond the creek and along the outskirts of the village; the conduct of both regiments and all their officers in this skirmish was excellent. The casualties in my command were eight wounded. The 31st Indiana was withdrawn to the rear to encamp, and Colonel Enyart, with his regiment, (1st Kentucky,) and a section of artillery under Lieutenant Newall, was left to occupy the position until morning.

On the 27th ultimo the brigade reached Stewart's creek, and went into camp at night.

On the 28th (Sunday) the command lay at Stewart's creek—one-half of the brigade on picket duty.

On the 29th the brigade advanced from Stewart's creek in line of battle across the field, and at night took position in the front, on the right of the Nashville turnpike, in the cedars, near Cowan's burnt house, about three and a half miles west from Murfreesboro'; an effective line of skirmishers was thrown forward and the open ground to our front firmly held.

On the 30th the brigade rested in position, holding the point of woods where it was bivouacked, and the line of pickets to the front during the fierce engagement which occurred on the right of our line during the night; the 2d Kentucky volunteers (Colonel Sedgwick) was on picket duty.

This regiment succeeded in driving the enemy's picket from the crest in the field near the burnt house. His temporary shelters along the row of peach trees on the lane, some sixty yards east of the burnt house, were occupied by my troops after a sharp night skirmish, and held by them against two charges of cavalry until daylight the following morning. No pains were spared to explain my position during the night. Support was promised on my left, but did not come. If re-enforced on the flank, this position could probably have been held. One-half the effective force of my brigade was kept out *all night* on picket, trying to hold this advanced line. The attempt was partially successful. It was suspected that the enemy had rifle-pits and a large force beyond the crest; but the best reconnoissance I could make by night could not furnish the facts. Subsequent knowledge evinced the correctness of the supposition, and also demonstrated the fact that *five thousand troops* could not have taken and held the crest which my brigade of *twelve hundred* attempted to reach and hold.

On the 31st ultimo an order was received from the general commanding division, about 8 o'clock a. m., to advance in line, with the brigade supporting me on the right and left. The brigade was promptly put in motion, formed in two lines as follows: 2d Kentucky and 31st Indiana volunteers (under general charge of Colonel Sedgwick as ranking officer,) constituting the front line; and 1st Kentucky and 90th Ohio, (under general charge of Colonel Enyart as ranking officer,) forming the second line; Captain Standart's artillery was formed in half battery on each flank of the front line. The brigade, by this formation, exhibited a front of, say, *six hundred men*, (600,) *or less than a full regiment.* Colonel Hazen's (3d) brigade was in position on my left and rear, and brigades of General Negley's division on the right; upon giving the orders to advance, my skirmishers ran rapidly forward from the wood and engaged those of the enemy in the open field. They drove them, and my front line advanced promptly up to the rail fence in the margin of the woods.

The enemy pushed towards us rapidly, and charged my line in great force and in solid rank. The fight became very severe and obstinate about 9 o'clock a. m.

My troops fought with heroism. Every officer and soldier *acted well*, and seemed to me to accomplish more than could be expected of him for sturdy endurance, stalwart bravery, and manly courage; it does not seem to me that the conduct of these two regiments here could be surpassed. The enemy were driven back, although superior in numbers. His charge was made in two lines, with the appearance of a four-rank formation, and in most admirable order and discipline. After the first repulse, and before my line could be advanced, the enemy made a second charge, (reserving fire until a close approach was had,) which was more furious than before. The 2d Kentucky and 31st Indiana nobly held their ground, and, after some thirty minute's well-directed fire, drove him back again for a short distance. A respite of a few minutes in active firing enabled me to execute a passage of lines to the front, to relieve the first line, the ammunition of which was nearly exhausted. This manœuvre was well executed, considering that it was done under a brisk fire of the enemy's skirmishers, the cross fire of flanking parties that had already passed to the right and left of the line, and in face of two of the enemy's batteries.

The rear line (now front) was soon actively engaged; I attempted, with it, to assail the enemy, and ordered an advance. The 1st Kentucky, Colonel Enyart, on the right of the line, made a gallant charge, and drove the enemy before it—rushing forward to the crest of the hill—clear beyond and to the right of the burnt house. The fire was so severe from the enemy's force at the burnt house, on the left, that the order to move up the 90th Ohio was countermanded, not, however, until many of the officers and men of this gallant regiment had pressed forward over the fence in line with the "Old" *First Kentucky*. The sad list of the killed and wounded of the 90th and 1st regiments speaks loudly of the courage and manhood they evinced in this charge. Standart, with his gallant gunners, was throwing in grape and canister from the flanks, as my men ran forward to the charge, and thinning the enemy's ranks. He was too strong for us, however, and soon my gallant advance was beaten back to the point of woods. This point was still held. The brigade on the left was never pressed up to my front, and left me exposed from this quarter. General Negley's brigade, on the right, first advanced with me, but yielding to the impulsive charge of the enemy, broke up, and a portion of it drifted in disorder immediately to my rear, and left me exposed to the cross fire of the enemy from the woods on the right. We were now completely flanked. Our own troops impeded my retreat. Cannon, caissons, artillery wagons, and bodies of men in wild retreat, filled the road and woods to my rear, precluding everything like a proper and orderly retreat. Captain Standart's artillery ammunition was failing rapidly; he was shifting front constantly to keep off the enemy. The cartridges of my men were becoming short; messages were sent to the rear for re-enforcements and for the reserve brigade of the division. The enemy's fire was upon three sides of my position, and apparently exactly to the rear, in the woods. It was impossible to get ammunition up, to communicate with the general commanding the division, or to obtain re-enforcements. In this condition the ground was still held for some forty (40) minutes longer than seemed right or proper. My command had some cover in the edge of the woods from the enemy's bullets, and still kept up a fire sufficiently strong to keep them from rushing into the woods. Seeing my little brigade failing rapidly, and many of its best men carried wounded to the rear, without hope of support, or further ability to hold on, I withdrew it in as good order as practicable. The enemy pressed closely, firing constantly into the retreating mass. We faced to rear and covered the retreat of General Negley's men as well as could be done. The 2d Kentucky regiment brought off three pieces and the 90th Ohio volunteers one piece of abandoned artillery *by hand*, which the enemy were rushing upon and about to capture.

Standart's battery was saved with a loss of three men and seven horses. It had but *sixteen* rounds of ammunition when the order to retire was given. Upon falling back to the edge of the wood, on the west side, I met Major General Thomas, and reported to him, and with his consent continued to fall back across the open ground to the turnpike with my shattered forces, now numbering about *five hundred*. After forming in line along the turnpike, (about 12 o'clock m.,) the brigade was ordered, by a member of General Rosecrans's staff, to the left, to support a battery on the railroad; it took this position and held it during the remainder of the day and the night following.

On the 1st instant the brigade was placed in line on the right of the division, in rear of the interval between the 1st and 3d divisions. After remaining thus until noon it was advanced to the front to support Swallow's (Indiana) battery, posted on a commanding elevation to the left of the railway, and near the ford across Stone river. During the day it was exposed to occasional shelling from the enemy's batteries.

On the 2d instant rude breastworks were constructed back of the batteries, and the brigade held the same position behind them. It lay here during the severe fight across the creek on our left, supporting the batteries, and exposed to a heavy cross fire from the enemy's guns. A higher scene of cool moral courage, perhaps, has not been evinced during the war than that exhibited by my brigade on this memorable day. The line lay still and quiet behind the frail works we had been able to construct, with the shot and shell of the enemy coming from three directions and bursting above, in front of it, and all around it, while our own masked batteries were belching out their contents in front of and over it. The roar of artillery was terrific. The smoke from our own pieces and the bursting shell of the enemy at times obscured the line from view. By some wonderful Providence but three men of the brigade were killed here by the enemy's shells.

About dark, and when the enemy were driven upon our left, the brigade was advanced by General Palmer, he gallantly leading two regiments, the 31st Indiana and 90th Ohio, to the point of woods, a half mile to the front and left of our artillery position, and in line with our advance on the left, across the creek. I followed rapidly with the residue of the brigade across the open field to the General's right, and on line with him, knowing nearly the position of a masked battery of the enemy hid by a crest in the field. I ordered the men to cheer loudly as we approached the latter. It had now become dark. As the noise of the last cheer died away, the enemy opened a fire of shrapnell from four small guns. The line immediately laid down under shelter of the crest, and for some thirty minutes the enemy continued to play at us. His shot passed just over our heads and struck the ground not to exceed one hundred feet to the rear of the line.

Only a single casualty occurred here—the death of one man struck by a shell. He was a straggler, not connected with my command, who was attempting to get to the rear. A strong picket from my brigade was posted in the wood and across the field, and the residue brought back to camp near the artillery. The latter position was maintained by the brigade until the evacuation of the enemy.

The following statement, condensed from the report of the medical officer of my staff, and the returns of the regimental commanders, exhibits the casualties of the brigade and the battery, to wit:

Regiments.	Killed.		Wounded.			Missing.			Aggregate.
	Non-com. officers and privates.	Total.	Officers.	Non com. officers and privates.	Total.	Officers.	Non-com. officers and privates.	Total.	
31st Indiana	5	5	1	44	45	3	34	37	87
1st Kentucky	13	13	1	51	52	1	30	31	96
90th Ohio	17	17	5	67	72	2	46	48	137
2d Kentucky	9	9	2	56	58	......	10	10	77
Standart's battery	5	5	......	12	12	......	3	3	20
	49	49	9	230	239	6	123	129	417

It may be observed that the above statement includes as wounded only those disabled from duty; slight hurts and trivial injuries are not included. Of those rated as missing, about one-half the number are stated by their officers to have been captured by the enemy in the battle of the 31st ultimo. The number of casualties, it will be noted, reaches nearly one-third of my effective strength. Herewith are enclosed the reports of Colonels Enyart, Sedgwick, Osborn, and Ross, commanding the various regiments of the brigade, and the report of Surgeon J. B. Armstrong, medical officer of my staff. These reports will convey to the general commanding the division a better knowledge of many of the details of the recent actions than can be embraced in this general statement. They make honorable mention of many line and subaltern officers, which is deserving and to which I crave special attention.

Before concluding, I beg to say to the general commanding the division that the officers and men of all the regiments under my command behaved uniformly well. Three of the regiments are veteran ones, and have left their impress upon former battle-fields. The 90th Ohio, though for the first time thrown into a severe engagement, behaved admirably, and achieved for itself a right to rank with its associates in the old "twenty-second," or any brigade where high-toned valor is displayed.

Colonels Sedgwick, Enyart, Ross, and Osborn displayed marked gallantry on the field during the engagement, and handled their commands with courage, skill, and prudence. Their associates, field and staff officers, nobly seconded them. It is not in my power to make distinctions among these, where all performed their duty so bravely and cheerfully.

To Captain Standart and his gallant battery I am under peculiar obligations. This brave officer and his command have long been associated with this brigade. Although chief of artillery to the division, he preferred to fight his own battery, and was with it constantly. It rendered most effective service whenever put in action. His associate officers, Lieutenants N. A. Baldwin and E. P. Sturgis, acted nobly throughout, and, with the gunners, drivers, and artillerymen of all grades, stood bravely to their work in the fight on the 31st ultimo, almost against hope, and safely brought away their battery. The battery was chiefly instrumental in saving the brigade in this position.

Of my personal staff, it affords me pleasure to say that Captain W. H. Fairbanks, of the 31st Indiana volunteers, acting assistant adjutant general, was at his post constantly, and, as on former occasions, behaved gallantly. Lieutenant John Wright, of the 1st Kentucky, acting aide-de-camp, displayed high courage on the field and most soldierly bearing throughout. I recommend his promotion for gallantry in the action of the 31st ultimo. Lieutenant J. C. Beeler, of the 31st Indiana volunteers, acting quartermaster to the brigade, discharged his duties properly and fearlessly, stayed with his transportation while under fire, took care of it, and lost no government property.

Surgeon J. B. Armstrong made very ample and efficient arrangements for the wounded of the brigade, and by his care and attention, in conjunction with the regimental surgeons, got them speedily from the field, and had them as well cared for as those of any other command. He reports to me good conduct on the part of all regimental surgeons.

The department of Captain Robinson, commissary of subsistence, was well managed. Though absent himself, it was left in good hands, and my troops were at all times during the days of the battles furnished with proper rations, regardless of the danger of conveying them.

Two orderlies from my escort—Corporal James T. Slater and Private William Hayman, both of the 2d Indiana cavalry—deserve notice for their good conduct on the field, and are worthy of promotion.

With assurances of esteem to the brigadier general commanding the division, I am, captain, very truly, yours, &c.,

CHARLES CRUFT,
Brigadier General, Commanding 1st Brigade.

Captain NORTON, *Acting Assistant Adjutant General,*
2d Division, Left Wing, 14th Army Corps.

HEADQUARTERS FIRST BRIGADE,
Hospital 2d Division, January 9, 1863.

DEAR SIR: I have the honor to forward to you the following report of casualties of the 1st brigade in the late battle near Murfreesboro', Tennessee:

	Killed.	Wounded.
31st regiment Indiana volunteers	5	46
1st regiment Kentucky volunteers	13	52
2d regiment Kentucky volunteers	1	31
90th regiment Ohio volunteers	17	72
Total	36	201

I cannot close this report without mentioning the names of Surgeon R. H. Tipton, of the 90th Ohio, Assistant Surgeons James E. Cox, of the 2d Kentucky, and John Dixon, of the 1st Kentucky, who were regularly detailed as assistant operative surgeons in the hospital of the 2d division, and who most cheerfully performed their entire duty, aiding and assisting the wounded in all cases of emergency, and assisting in all the grave operations necessary to the relief of the wounded. Their untiring exertion, as well as great care and judgment in their duty, require an honorable mention to be made of them.

Perhaps it is inappropriate, yet I do not feel willing to close this brief report without mentioning the name of our superior surgeon in charge of this hospital—Surgeon M. G. Sherman, acting medical director 2d division—whom I cannot make too high mention of for his high medical knowledge as a skilful surgeon and careful operator, ever ready and willing at all times, day and night, to render any service in his power to aid and comfort the wounded and dying.

Indeed, it is not saying too much when I say, never have I seen a physician and surgeon more attentive to his duty, and, without exception, has rendered entire satisfaction to all. He has endeared himself by the most tender ties to both patients and surgeons, and we shall ever feel grateful that he was in charge of this hospital during this most trying time.

Excuse the great brevity of this report, as time is precious, and we are yet very, very busy in the performance of our many duties to the afflicted.

With the most profound respect, I am, respectfully, your obedient servant, &c.,

J. B. ARMSTRONG, *Acting Brigade Surgeon,*
1st Brigade, 2d Division, Army of the Cumberland.

Brigadier General CHARLES CRUFT, *1st Brigade.*

List of casualties of the thirty-first Indiana volunteers.

Company A.—Killed: Private Alexander Ficklin. Wounded: Sergeant John Cook, slightly in hand, (missing;) Privates Adam J. Dounine, severely, (missing;) John T. Duval, slightly in face; McCafa Clift, hip; Tilghman H. Gilkison, arm; William Hobart, side; John Lyons, arm; Washington Miller, hand; David Wells, hand. Missing: Captain Richard M. Waleman, Privates Robert Dix, William J. Dounine, William Hilon, Edward Pfeiffer, Samuel Prevo, Gustus Yollin, Harvie Taylor.

Company B.—Killed: Corporal James Reynolds. Wounded: First Sergeant James W. Pickens, severely, and since died; James Corus, slightly in right hand; Corporals Lorenzo D. Gard, wrist; Jacob B. Williams, cheek; Privates Michael Frock, hip; Joseph Renyer, arm; John H. Green, hip.

Company C.—Wounded: Corporal John G. Malory, slightly on right temple, and missing; Private Syvanius Loby, slightly in left leg. Missing: Privates Thomas F. Roberts, Thomas J. Beauchamp, Joseph B. Fouts.

Company D.—Wounded: Privates William Strain, slightly in face; Ezra Pitzer, neck. Missing: Second Lieutenant John N. Clark, First Sergeant Charles A. Powers, Sergeant Jackson R. Eaton, Privates Lewis S. Burnett, Henry H. Chase, Joel James, William R. Knotts, William Posey, Samuel Thomas, William Wilkins, Adam M. Wilson.

Company E.—Wounded: First Sergeant Eliphalet M. Surns, slightly in hip; Sergeant James G. Swisher, seriously in hip; Corporals Henry Uppman, arm; Jackson Mercer, hand; Privates David Stewart, hand; Robert Campbell, cheek; James Burns, face. Missing: John Runney, William A. Lewis, William St. Clair.

Company F.—Killed: Corporal Henry Leahman. Wounded: Corporal Andrew W. Peaters, slightly in leg; Privates Adam S. Ellison, leg; William Oelonal, neck; James B. Setzinger, leg. Missing: Sergeant William J. Bonvell, color-bearer.

Company G.—Killed: Corporal Jacob Meadows. Missing: Corporal B. F. Riley.

Company H.—Wounded Second Lieutenant F. M. Hatfield, stunned by a shell; Privates John D. Sanders and Jeremiah Hatfield, slightly in hand. Missing: Corporals James W. Ault and Solomon Tucker; Privates Isham King, George Johnson, and James E. Wilson.

Company I.—Killed: Sergeant William S. Davis. Wounded: Sergeants E. D. Litsey, severely in mouth and neck; and Jesse B. Connelly, slightly in foot; Corporal William N. Ense, arm; Privates Henry B. Cord, shoulder; Morris L. Lambert, knee; Thomas B. Fouts, back; James H. Adams, back; Harrison Williams, thigh; Thomas Ratcliffe, shoulder.

Company K.—Wounded: Sergeant John W. Johnson, slightly in the thigh; Private William H. Gaston leg. Missing: Corporal Andrew Gosnell, Privates John Leeds and John Day.

Missing of staff and non-commissioned staff.—Second Assistant Surgeon James W. Morgan, Hospital Steward Asa W. McKinney.

RECAPITULATION.

	Killed.	Wounded.	Missing.
Company A	1	9	8
B	1	7	0
C	0	2	3
D	0	2	11
E	0	7	3
F	1	4	1
G	1	0	1
H	0	3	5
I	1	9	0
K	0	2	3
Commissioned and non-commissioned staff	0	0	2
	5	45	37

HEADQUARTERS 31ST REGIMENT INDIANA VOLUNTEERS,
Camp near Murfreesboro', Tenn., January 9, 1863.
JAMES R. HALLOWELL, *Aid and Adjutant.*

List of killed, wounded, and missing, 1st regiment Kentucky infantry, 2d division, 1st brigade.

Company A.—Killed: Corporal Joseph Nandand, Privates Clark Williamson, Edward Williams, Henry Peleg, Patrick Rice, and Samuel Nuby. Wounded: Private Charles Rice, slight in groin; Sergeant James R. Markey, slight, and captured. Missing: Privates John Beardmore, Joseph Reed, P. Jory Voges, William Duyer, John E. Walters, and Thomas Brown.

Company B.—Wounded: Privates Robert Loyd, slight, and captured; Robert McLure, flesh wound, back. Missing: Privates August Andrews, Richard Corcoran, McMaher, Edward Wimz, Thomas Ranagan, and William Morris.

Company C.—Killed: Corporal Cyrus Black and Private Charles Rice. Wounded: Corporal James Crouse, severely in thigh; Sergeant Pfister, slight in head, and captured; Privates Joseph Crock, severely in both thighs and testicle; Phillip Foreman, flesh wound, right leg; Patrick Flannagan, severely in body, and captured; John Mangon, slight in leg; and Wesley Quegley, slight in body, and captured. Missing: Private Absalom Bishop.

Company D.—Wounded: Corporal Gustavus Ruff, severely, and captured; Privates John Gillmartin, slight, and captured; George Fry, slight in left foot; Jacob Weaver, severely, and captured; Christopher Smith, severely in right hand; and John Hetch, severely in right foot. Missing: Private Edward Butler.

Company F.—Killed: Corporal Adam Warful, Privates John B. Snyder and Michael Connelly. Wounded: Privates Walter Ebersole, severely, and missing; Louis Danz, mortally and missing; and James Hendry, severely in body, and missing. Missing: Sergeants N. C. Noe and Q. W. English, Corporals Alexander Noe and James F. Shade, and Private Alonzo Hay.

Company G.—Wounded: Privates Henry Schnyder, slight in hand, and

Francis Rourke, slight in hand and arm. Missing: Privates Michael Maher, Pat Lonard, and Corporal William M. Cole.

Company H.—Killed: Sergeant August Wilhelm. Wounded: Corporal Eli Henderson, flesh wound, thigh; Privates Michael Larkin, shot through the hand; Donald Brick, severely in left thigh; Joseph Diginan, back, flesh wound; John M. Coltsier, slight in neck. Missing: Privates John Bayliss, William Tracey, and Daniel J. Anderson.

Company I.—Wounded: Corporal George F. Gill, severely in right shoulder; Thomas B. Furman, slight in breast; Edward Burks, slight in hand; John Freelinger, slight in leg; Edward A. Jones, slight in shoulder; Mathew Gill, slight in hand; William H. Myers, slight in hand; Edward Parsell, slight in left leg; Charles Weber, slight in right leg; and Lieutenant James Farran, severely in right leg. Missing: Privates Fred. Artz, George Hagan, and James Sheridan.

Company K.—Wounded: Sergeant John Hess, slight in foot; Corporal Martin Ruffel, severely in foot and ankle; Privates Christian Letty, slight in hand and side; Will. Koppenhill, severely in knee-joint; Frederick Weiser, severely in left side; William Bettger, slight in foot; Peter Himbuk, slight in ankle; Stacy Wedkind, flesh wound in leg; Frederick Simon, right leg severely; Daniel Kaw, severely in both legs; Clemens Onderhave, severely in left arm; Jacob Wolf, and Frederick Bauman, wounded and captured. Missing: Captain John Baker, Corporal August Poppe, Private H. Burien, and Sergeant Major William McKee.

Killed, 12; wounded, 51; missing, 31—total, 94.

Report of killed and wounded in the ninetieth regiment Ohio volunteer infantry in battle near Murfreesboro', Tennessee, from December 31, 1862, *until January* 3, 1863.

Company A.—Killed: Private George W. Wood. Wounded: Sergeant Henry R. Markley, severely in hip. Privates Fred. Owens, right thigh, severely; Seymour Bolin, severely through hips; Joe Morris, right hip, severely.

Company B.—Killed: Privates Thomas W. Roach and Thomas S. Miller. Wounded: William Edson, severely in right ankle; William Heselden, severely in right shoulder; J. Eichon, severely in left shoulder; Leroy Gaston, severely in right arm; J. Walters, slightly in right hand; J. Burns, missing; D. McQuade, slightly in right hip; S. Wycroft, slightly on head; and Allen Jolly, slightly in left wrist.

Company C.—Killed: Private J. Creamer. Wounded: Privates J. Doyster, right leg, severely, (amputated;) D. Connor, severely in left hand and shoulder; H. McIntire, severely and missing; Paris Robinson, slightly in breast; and Oliver Horney, ankle.

Company D.—Wounded: Lieutenant S. W. Welch, severely in right arm. Privates A. Smith, severely in left arm; S. Holdiman, severely in left arm and wrist; John Berger, severely in right forearm; and John Andregg, severely in both legs.

Company E.—Killed: Privates J. Carpenter and W. Bryan. Wounded: Privates James Wood, severely in left arm; J. Armstrong, severely in left arm; Lewis Samon, severely in right arm: W. Buckingham, severely, and missing; S. Rodgers, slightly in left hand; W. Mock, slightly on forehead; A. Bowers, slightly in hip; S. Guest, slightly in hip; J. Shore, slightly on left leg; and Jos. C. Berry, slightly on right hand.

Company F.—Killed: Privates Almer Porter and Francis Rector. Wounded: Lieutenant Thomas Pavis, wind shock. Privates S. B. Betts, left arm, severely; John McAllister, neck, severely; and J. A. DeLong, neck, slightly.

Company G.—Killed: Privates W. Ankrum, Geo. Harkless, and S. Tedrick. Wounded: Lieutenant T. E. Baker, severely in right foot; Sergeant James Dobbins, slightly in left shoulder. Privates Fred. Reynolds, mortally in forehead; B. Cofland, left lung, severely; A. D. Eveland, and missing; J. Wiestenberger, in shoulder and left leg; James Wood, severely in hand; J. L. Maxwell, slightly in left hip; A. Oldfield, left side, severely; Jos. Phillips, slightly in right hand; W. Switzer, slightly in right leg and foot; John Switzer, side, slightly, (left;) Robert Maddox, right hip, slightly; Jos. Pellet, slightly in right arm; and S. Hoffman, severely in right thigh.

Company H.—Wounded: Lieutenant J. N. Selby, slightly in left leg. Privates J. W. Smithly, and missing; W. H. Walker, and missing; W. Strait, severely in hand; and J. W. Graves, severely in left hip.

Company I.—Killed: Corporal Wm. Mason. Wounded: Sergeant D. Hufford, severely in shoulder. Privates E. Sites, in right thigh, severely; H. Coonrod, severely in left knee; J. W. Powell, severely in left shoulder; S. Shafer, severely in right hand; and J. W. Strentz, severely in right shoulder.

Company K.—Killed: Privates James Paris, D. Sively, and J. R. Core. Wounded: Captain M. B. Rowe, slightly in right wrist; Lieutenant L. W. Reihard, slightly in ankle; Sergeant J. M. Christie, slightly in right foot. Privates J. McKeever, and missing; James Gibson, severely in left thigh; H. Harper, severely in left knee; B. F. Elliott, and missing; H. Weimer, in left shoulder; Pat. Murphy, and missing.

I hereby certify that this report is true to the best of my knowledge and belief.

R. H. TIPTON,
Surgeon 90th Regiment Ohio Volunteer Infantry.

JANUARY 6, 1863.

RECAPITULATION.

	Killed.	Wounded.
Company A	1	4
B	2	9
C	1	5
D		5
E	2	10
F	2	5
G	3	15
H		5
I	1	6
K	3	9
Total	15	72

Report of the casualties in the 90th regiment Ohio volunteer infantry in the battle at Murfreesboro'.

Company A.—Killed, 1; wounded, 4; Sergeant H. R. Markley, wounded and missing; Jas. Serable and John Huffman, missing.

Company B.—Killed, 2; wounded, 9; C. S. Turner and Jasper Pennell, prisoners; H. E. Redform, missing.

Company C.—Killed, 1; wounded, 5; John Hayne and John McIntyre, wounded and missing.

Company D.—Lieutenant G. W. Welch and two enlisted men, wounded; Captain Alva Perry and John Andregg, prisoners; Sergeant John D. Nicely, Mahlan Harps, P. H. Elnght, Amos Reed, Davis Williamson, John Cross, and Wilson Hickle, missing.

Company E.—Killed, 2; wounded, 8; Brazilea Wortman, Daniel Smith, William D. Buckingham, and William Brine, missing.

Company F.—Killed, 1; wounded, 4; A. J. Tunmons, Corporal William Hedricks, William Tarbell, and L. K. Davis, missing.

Company G.—Killed 4; Lieutenant Baker and 12 enlisted men wounded; Wesley Beard and John English, missing.

Company H.—Lieutenant J. N. Selby and four enlisted men, wounded; William H. Walker, Henry S. Adcock, Thomas Minor, J. Chenny, Erasmus Cooper, Thomas Spicer, Michael Kulp, Abraham Tracy, J. M. Bamcrots, John Kennon, and Samuel Hook, missing.

Company I.—Killed, 2; wounded, 5; Emanuel Siles and Henry Conrad, prisoners and wounded; Clay Leist, missing.

Company K.—Killed, 2; Captain M. B. Rowe, Second Lieutenant S. W. Rehards and eight enlisted men, wounded; Lieutenant James F. Cook, prisoner; J. D. Williams, James P. Mills, William Smith, George Hampton, B. F. Elliot, and Harry Culberson, missing.

The within report is as full as I can possibly get at present. I cannot get the names of the killed and wounded while the regiment is absent, the only report being in the hands of Colonel Rippey, which I cannot find.

Yours,

D. W. KINGERY,
Adjutant 90th Ohio.

Captain FAIRBANKS.

HEADQUARTERS HOSPITAL DEPARTMENT 2D KENTUCKY REGIMENT,
January 8, 1863.

SIR: I have the honor to report to you the following as the casualties of the 2d Kentucky regiment, Colonel T. D. Sedgwick commanding, during the late battle at Stone river, all of which is respectfuly submitted, &c.:

Killed.—Sergeant H. Jasen, company E; Corporal R. Horton and Private S. Blackburn, company F; —— Vinegar, company G; Corporal Fred. Hemple and Privates Henry Evans and Pat. Golliger, company H; Private A. Belt, company I.

Wounded.—Sergeant S. Griegly; Corporals G. Hurth, face; P. McGlauchlin, shoulder; Privates J. McGinnis, hip, slightly; John Soderfield; Frank Conley, company A; Sergeant John A. Hearny; Second Assistant Sergeant W. L. Reed, company B; Corporal —— Stankey, thigh; Privates F. Bowers, shoulder; F. Grok; C. Horning Fair, right side, company C; Sergeant Major Jas. Pae, fractured arm; Privates —— Fox, both legs; S. B. Gibner, company D; Sergeant B. Long, company E; Private G. Perkins, company G; Sergeant D. Mahunter, shoulder; Privates S. White, right leg; William Smith, shot his own finger off; A. Hesher, arm, slightly, company H; Sergeant L. Wise, arm and shoulder; Private W. H. Carnaghey, company I; Privates Cris. Looker, abdomen; G. Falkner, shoulder; G. Darling, shoulder, slightly; A. Sinderman, slightly; C. Coppersmith, arm; —— Sabagier, toe; H. Ogken.

Summary.—Killed, 8; wounded, 30.

This does not include the wounded in Murfreesboro'.

J. E. COX,
Surgeon in charge of 2d Kentucky.

Major J. B. ARMSTRONG,
Surgeon 22d Brigade.

HEADQUARTERS 1ST REGIMENT KENTUCKY VOLUNTEERS,
Camp near Murfreesboro', Tennessee, January 8, 1863.

GENERAL: I have the honor to make the following report of the operations of the 1st regiment Kentucky volunteer infantry during the late engagement:

Pursuant to orders, we left our camp, near Nashville, on the morning of the 26th ultimo, and proceeded towards Murfreesboro' on the direct road.

Arriving within one mile of Lavergne about 4 o'clock that evening, a considerable force of the enemy were discovered on the left of the road, and the 1st brigade, 2d divison, left wing, was ordered to operate against them. General Cruft ordered the 1st Kentucky to the front, and after considerable skirmishing with the enemy we charged and drove him across the creek into the woods near the town with a loss of two men wounded. The position thus gained was picketed and held during the night by the 1st Kentucky regiment. Soon after dark a force of the enemy's cavalry attacked the left of our picket line, but were repulsed by companies I and C, losing one man wounded. On the 27th ultimo the regiment marched with the division as far as Stewart's creek, where we bivouacked until the morning of the 29th; we then moved forward slowly and bivouacked about 2½ miles from Murfreesboro'. On the 30th the regiment was assigned its position in line of battle, being on the right of the second line of the brigade. The brigade (General Cruft) being on the right of the division, (General Palmer,) and of General Crittenden's command. The 90th Ohio was on our left, and the 31st Indiana in our front in the first line. We lay on our arms during the day. On the morning of the 31st ultimo, about 8 o'clock, General Negley's division took position on our right, and soon after the engagement commenced on our right wing. About 9 o'clock our front was hard pressed, and the brigade moved forward, the first line to the edge of the woods, and the 1st Kentucky to support Standart's battery. The right of our army was being driven back, and the engagement was getting warm in our front, when General Cruft ordered the 1st Kentucky to move forward, and march over the 31st Indiana into the cornfield, 300 yards in front of them, where we were exposed to the fire of two pieces of artillery supported by a regiment of infantry about 100 yards distant, and directly on our left flank. Our position here was in advance of that held by any other regiment in the army. Being in danger of being cut off by a heavy column of the enemy advancing on our right, we retired in good order to the woods, where we took a new position behind a fence. We remained here but a short time, when the brigade fell back through the woods slowly and reformed on the road. About 12 o'clock we were ordered forward to the support of a battery; remaining there but half an hour, the brigade was moved to the railroad, and in the evening formed a new line in rear of the division, where we lay during the night. On the morning of the 1st instant we were again moved to the left to a new postition, our left resting on the bank of Stone river. About noon we were ordered further to the left, to support Captain Swallow's battery, which was posted on an eminence. Here the regiment remained during the night. On the 2d instant we threw up a breastwork of rails and stones, behind which we remained during the attempt of the enemy to turn the left of our line. After the signal defeat of the enemy at this point, we were ordered forward by General Cruft, until coming in range of a battery of the enemy, we lay down until the fire had ceased. It being dark and nothing further to do, we retired to our former position, where we remained until the 4th instant. A fuller and more definite report of the operations of the regiment will be made hereafter.

Very respectfully, your obedient servant,

D. A. ENYART,
Colonel, Commanding 1st Regiment Kentucky Volunteer Infantry.

HEADQUARTERS 31ST REGIMENT INDIANA VOLUNTEERS,
Camp near Murfreesboro', Tennessee, January 7, 1863.

CAPTAIN : I have the honor of submitting to you the following report of the part this regiment participated in the late action with the rebel army before Murfreesboro', commencing on the 26th day of December, 1862, at the town of Lavergne, and ending before Murfreesboro' on the 3d day of January, 1863. On the morning of the 26th of December, when the United States forces were put in motion, our regiment was on picket duty some six miles southeast of Nashville. Before the pickets could be called in, and the regiment in line of march, the brigade to which they belonged was some four miles in advance. The regiment had a very fatiguing march through mud and rain; in passing the forces we had to take the fields, that made the march more arduous. At 3 o'clock p. m. we joined the brigade one mile west of Lavergne; we were ordered to the advance, the 1st Kentucky regiment on the right and our regiment on the left, the 2d Kentucky regiment and the 90th Ohio regiment our support; we were ordered across a field to a woods to the left of the Murfreesboro' road. Shortly after we had taken our position the enemy commenced throwing shells into the woods. We immediately sent out two companies (E and K) and deployed them as skirmishers in advance of our line, and moved on the enemy in line. After advancing about one mile, we came in reach of the enemy's rifles; they opened a heavy fire from their rifles and two pieces of artillery, which overreached our line. Our men rushed forward with a shout which caused the enemy to leave in great confusion. We remained in this position until dark; we then moved a short distance to the right and bivouacked for the night. Both officers and men conducted themselves with coolness and bravery, without receiving any injury whatever. The next day we moved forward in line of battle, which was continued from day to day until the evening of the 29th of December; we arrived at nightfall within a few miles of Murfreesboro', our brigade filing to the right of Murfreesboro' pike about one quarter of a mile, when we bivouacked for the night. Nothing occurred during the night, except heavy skirmishing in our front. Early on the morning of the 30th December, 1862, we were ordered forward to the front of the grove in which we were bivouacked, which order was promptly executed, our regiment on the right and the 2d Kentucky on our left, the 90th Ohio supporting the 2d Kentucky, and the 1st Kentucky supporting our regiment. Upon arriving at this position, I was ordered by you to report to Colonel Sedgwick, of the 2d Kentucky, whom you informed me would command the front line. I was ordered to deploy two companies in front of our line as skirmishers, connecting with a like corps from General Negley's division on the right, and the 2d Kentucky on the left, which was immediately done by sending out companies C and E. Before our lines were established, the enemy opened on us a brisk fire of shell and ball, which continued all day, the balls from the enemy's sharpshooters reaching our lines. About 4 o'clock in the evening we were ordered to advance our line to support a battery, which was done, and we remained in that position during the night, companies A, B, I, D, and H, relieving alternately C and E as skirmishers. Early in the morning of the 31st we were again ordered to move our lines forward, which was done. Shortly after our skirmishers were driven in by the enemy, our men reserving their fire until all their comrades had joined the line.

At this time a heavy force of the enemy appeared in our front in an open field on a piece of rising ground, when they opened a severe fire upon our line, which was returned with a steady nerve by our men, which soon made them fall back. In a few moments they again returned to the crest of the field and attempted to charge our line, but the steady nerve of our boys and their deadly aim caused them again to retire. Our men getting short of ammunition, the 1st Kentucky regiment came to our aid, and passing by our line, followed the enemy up into the field; but the heavy force of the enemy in front, and the regiment being exposed to a cross fire from the enemy's battery, they were compelled to fall back with considerable loss. Our regiment, remaining in its former position, held their fire until their Kentucky friends had passed to their rear; they again, with the coolness of veterans, poured another volley into the lines of the enemy, thinning their ranks, and making them the third time fall back to their former hiding-place. In a short time the enemy changed their point of attack, and appeared in great force on the left of our brigade, and on the right between our regiment and General Negley's forces. Both our right and left falling back, I was forced to order the regiment to fall back. The men obeying the order so reluctantly, and our left being so far turned before orders to fall back were received, caused our list of missing to be so large. We were also exposed to a cross fire of the enemy's artillery. Our regiment occupied the front line from the morning of the 30th until 11 o'clock a. m. on the 31st, with the exception of a few moments, when the 1st Kentucky occupied the front. The brigade falling back through a dense growth of cedar, became scattered somewhat, but were formed again in line ready for any emergency. Next morning, January 1, 1863, the regiment, with the brigade, took a position further to the left, as a reserve. January 2, the regiment again took a position, sending out company F as skirmishers, and during this day they laid in rifle-pits, exposed to a terrific fire from the enemy's artillery. Late in the evening Lieutenant Colonel Smith and Captain I. T. Smith, acting major, with General Palmer, led them into a splendid charge on the enemy, cleaning out a piece of woods occupied by them in force, both officers and men acting heroically to the entire satisfaction of the brave general. I herewith send you a list of casualties.

I cannot close this report without calling your attention to the gallant conduct of the officers under my command during the action. Lieutenant Colonel Smith was always on the alert, cheering the men, passing along the line of skirmishers and the regiment; wherever duty called him, there he was during the whole engagement. Captain Smith, acting major, was always at his post, calm and collected, cheering the men and directing them where to strike the hardest blow. Captain Hallowell, acting adjutant, was always on duty, visiting the outposts and cheering the men; and where the balls flew thickest he appeared the oftenest. Captain Waterman, of company A: I cannot speak too highly of his bravery. When one of his men fell, he picked up his gun and nobly kept it still in use. Captains Neff, of company D, and Grimes, of company G, were always at their posts, discharging their whole duty. Lieutenant Peeken, of company B; Lieutenant Ray, of company C; Lieutenant Scott, of company E; Lieutenant Leas, of company F; Lieutenant Brown, of company H; Lieutenant Pike, of company I; and Lieutenant Hagen, of company K, were in command of their respective companies during the whole action, and conducted like old veterans, cheering their men, and directing them to fire with deliberation. Lieutenant Ford, of company A, after the regiment fell back on the morning of the 31st, after Captain Waterman was missing, took command of his company, and nobly imitated the gallant conduct of his veteran captain. Lieutenants Cloak, of company D; Hatfield, of company H; Brown, of company F; Fielding, of company E; Rody and McPhelredge, of company G; and Havelin, of company B, were at their places throughout the whole action, vieing with each other in noble deeds of valor. Assistant Surgeon Morgan was ever attentive to his profession, close in the rear of the regiment, close thereby he established his hospital, and refused to leave the wounded soldiers, but nobly remained with them, suffering himself to be taken prisoner, rather than leave them to suffer. The same is also true in regard to Dr. McKinney, hospital steward, who was also taken prisoner. I cannot speak in too high terms of the conduct of Sergeant Major Noble, who gallantly buckled on the cartridge-box nd took a rifle, and was in the front rank of the line dealing out lead pills for the secesh; Sergeant Douglass, of company K, who was discharging the duties of a lieutenant, was active in leading his brave men to the post of honor. And indeed it is not necessary for me to speak of *individuals;* every commissioned officer and non-commissioned officer and private of my command did their whole duty, without an exception, as did all the officers and men that came under my notice of the entire brigade. Brigadier General Cruft was at his post, ever watchful of his command, fearing no danger where duty called him; frequently riding along the line waving his hat and cheering his command in the hottest of the contest. Of the few killed on the field, three were of the color guard.

JOHN OSBORN,
Colonel, Commanding 31st Regiment Indiana Volunteers.

Captain W. H. FAIRBANKS,
Captain and Acting Assistant Adjutant General.

CAMP NEAR MURFREESBORO',
January 8, 1863.

SIR: I herewith furnish a report of the part taken by the 90th regiment Ohio volunteer infantry, first brigade, second division, left wing of the army of the Cumberland, in the series of movements beginning with the crossing of Stewart's creek on Monday, the 29th of December, 1862, and closing with the final repulse of the enemy on Saturday, the 3d of January, 1863. Monday forenoon the regiment moved across Stewart's creek, on the Murfreesboro' pike, deployed to the right of the pike and formed in double columns, closed at half distance in the rear of the 2d Kentucky regiment, and on the left of the 1st Kentucky regiment. It then moved parallel with the pike, and met no resistance during the day. Monday night it bivouacked within three miles of Murfreesboro', still at the right of the pike, and nothing worthy of notice occurred during the night.

Tuesday morning the regiment moved by the right flank into a cedar forest, still further to the right of the pike, and took position. The 31st Indiana and 2d Kentucky regiments forming the first line; whilst it, with the 1st Kentucky on the right, formed the second line, about one hundred and fifty paces in the rear. The regiment maintained this position during the day, and was frequently under the fire of shells. Tuesday night it bivouacked in the same position and in line of battle. Wednesday morning, about eight o'clock, the battle opened all along the right wing, with both cannonading and musketry, with indications that our forces were being pressed back. About ten o'clock the brigade moved forward in the order previously named; the 90th Ohio being ordered to support the 2d Kentucky, in case it needed assistance, and immediately the first line was engaged with the enemy.

Firing continued to increase in rapidity and fierceness until the 2d Kentucky sent back word that they needed support, when the 90th Ohio was ordered forwarded on double-quick. It moved to the front and was immediately engaged with the enemy, who appeared in great force with two batteries planted within one hundred and fifty yards of our position, which raked us with grape and canister. In noticing the movements of the enemy, I observed him massing a heavy force behind a large house in our front and left, and preparing to plant a battery in the same position, and I also observed that our support on the left had given way. After consulting with Lieutenant Colonel Rippey, I determined to report the situation of affairs to Brigadier General Cruft, commanding the brigade, who was on the field, and ask support. Receiving no support, I immediately returned to the regiment and ordered it to fall back, we having maintained our position until the enemy in overwhelming masses were within at least twenty-five yards of us. The regiment now fell back with considerable disorder, through the cedar forest in which it held position in the morning, to the railroad, where it rallied and formed on the left of the brigade supporting a battery; this position it maintained until dark, when the engagement closed. It then moved with the brigade to the right, towards the pike, and bivouacked for the night. Thursday it moved to the left of the railroad and lay in line ot battle all day, during which time it was exposed to the enemy's artillery, which frequently sent shell and shot into our ranks. The same day the brigade was moved forward to a small eminence, where it formed the advance line of battle and supported the batteries which had taken position here. The regiment was on the right of the brigade. About nine o'clock that evening it was moved back into a skirt of woods where it bivouacked for the night. Friday morning, at seven o'clock, we moved to the same position, and in the same order of the day previous. Here we threw up a hasty breastwork, the enemy firing a scattering shell into our ranks, until about eleven o'clock a. m., when he opened a fierce cannonade which lasted about an hour. About four o'clock that evening the enemy attacked our position in great fury with both musketry and artillery, manifestly endeavoring to turn our left. The regiment held its position on the right of the brigade, behind the breastworks, which formed a protection from the enemy's shot and shell, which fell now in abundance all around us and once drove our artillery to the rear. Many of the shells struck our works, but none of the regiment were wounded. Just before dark the brigade was ordered to fix bayonets and charge across the plain and clear a wood in our front of the enemy. This charge was made in gallant style, and for its behavior during this movement the 90th received the thanks of the division commander. After dark the regiment returned to the position it had occupied during the day, and there remained all night. The charge just mentioned was the closing operation of the day's work.

All day Saturday the regiment was held in the same position until late at night, when it moved into a skirt of woods just in the rear of its former position. It was not again brought into action, but held the position in the wood all day Sunday, when information came that the enemy had evacuated Murfreesboro'.

Where there was a general effort to perform duty, it would be difficult to designate individual acts of bravery. Yet I would say of the field officers, that Lieutenant Colonel C. H. Rippey was at his post during the series of engagements doing his whole duty, and doing it well; Major S. N. Yeoman was also at his post, cheering on the men and discharging his duty fully.

With one or two exceptions, the line officers performed their duty in a praiseworthy manner. Some of them exposed themselves to great danger in their efforts to save our artillery. Under the direction of Lieutenants Rains and Crow, a piece of artillery that had been abandoned was brought off of the field in the very face of the enemy and delivered to Captain Standart. Lieutenant Welch was wounded early in the engagement of Wednesday; Lieutenant Rains was injured by the concussion of a ball, but kept the field during that day; Captain Rowe and Lieutenants Baker and Selby were also wounded in the same action; whilst Captain Perry and Lieutenant Cook were taken prisoners.

In all the movements of the regiment the general commanding the brigade was present on the field, and, better than myself, can judge of its efficiency and the manner of its behavior during the entire series of engagements.

The following is a list of the killed and wounded in the 90th regiment in the recent battles of December 31, 1862, and January 2, 1863:

Killed.—Company A: George W. Wood. Company B: Thomas W. Roach and Thomas S. Miller. Company C: John Creamer. Company E: Isaac Carpenter and William Bryan. Company F: Almer Porter and Frank Rector, (died of wounds since engagement.) Company G: William Ankrum, George Harkness, S. Tedrick, and Fred. Reynolds, (died of wounds since engagement.) Company I: William Mason. Company K: James Paris, D. Sireby, J. R. Cue, and Pat. Murphy. Total, 17.

Wounded.—Company A: Sergeant H. R. Markley, Fred. Owen, James Morris, and S. Bolin. Company B: William Edson, W. Hesselden, J. Eicher, L. Gaston, J. Walters, J. Burns, D. McQuade, S. Wycroft, and A. Jolly. Company C: J. Doyster, D. Conner, H. McIntire, Paris Robinson, and Oliver Horney. Company D: Lieutenant G. W. Welch, E. Smith, S. Holderman, John Berger, and J. Andregg. Company E: James Wood, J. Armstrong, Lewis Lamen, W. Buckingham, S. Rodgers, J. Mock, A. Bowers, S. Gust, John Shere, and Joseph C. Berry. Company F: Lieutenant Thomas Rains, S. B. Betz, John McAllister, and J. A. Lelong. Company G: Lieutenant T. E. Baker, Sergeant James Dobbins, B. Cofland, A. D. Eveland, J. Westernhaver, James Wood, J. L. Maxwell, A. Oldfield, Joseph Phillips, William Switzer, John Switzer, R. Madduz, Joseph Pittit, and S. Hoffman. Company H: J. W. Smittly, William H. Walker, William Strait, and J. W. Graves. Company I: Sergeants D. Hufford and J. W. Strantz, Emanuel Sites, H. Conrod, J. W. Powell, and J. Shafer. Company K: Captain M. B. Rowe, Lieutenant L. W. Reabards, Sergeant J. M. Christie, J. McKeener, James Gibson, Henry Harper, B. F. Elliott, H. Weimer, and Daniel Smith. Total, 70.

Unaccounted for.—Company A: John Burten, James Crabill, and John Huffman. Company B: John Burns and Harrison E. Redfern. Company C: Harma McIntire and John C. Hoge. Company D: Orderly John Nicely, Corporal ——— Elright, John Cross, Amos Reid, Wilson Hickle, Mallen Harps, and David Williamson. Company E: William Bryan and Brazill Worthman. Company F: Corporal William Kendrick, A. J. Timmons, L. K. Davis, and William Tarbell. Company G: Wesley Beard and John English. Company H: William Strait, Henry Adcock, John Smithly, Jared Chana, Thomas Spicer, Erasmus M. Carper, and Jno. Kinnan. Company I: Clay List and Andrew Westenberger. Company K: Henry Culversen, George Hampton, William Smith, John Godden, John Williams, and James Mills. Total, 37.

Total killed, wounded, and missing, 124.

The regiment went into this engagement with about three hundred men, and came out with one hundred and seventy-six.

The foregoing report is respectfully submitted.

I. N. ROSS,
Colonel, Commanding 90th Regiment Ohio Volunteers.

Captain W. H. FAIRBANKS, *A. A. G.*

HEADQUARTERS 2d KENTUCKY VOLUNTEERS,
Camp near Murfreesboro', Tennessee, January 18, 1863.

DEAR SIR: In compliance with orders, I have the honor herewith to submit a report of the part taken by the 2d Kentucky regiment in the operations before Murfreesboro', from the 26th December, 1862, to January 4, 1863, and also my report as commander of the front line of the 1st brigade, composed of the 2d Kentucky regiment and 31st Indiana, forming the extreme advance of the 2d division in the action of the 31st December, 1862.

Leaving our camps beyond Nashville on the morning of the 26th December, 1862, the brigade being the advance of the division, the division forming the advance of the left wing, and my regiment being the advance of the brigade, was deployed as skirmishers on each side of the road. This position was observed until we arrived within one mile of Lavergne, when meeting with an obstinate resistance from the enemy's artillery and infantry, our cavalry and several regiments of infantry were sent forward, who drove the enemy from his ground; here we bivouacked for the night.

On the morning of the 27th we took our position in the line of march, and in the evening bivouacked on Stewart's creek, remaining in said position until the morning of the 29th, when I was placed in command of the 2d Kentucky and 31st Indiana volunteers, acting as reserve to the 3d brigade, in the general advance, in line towards Murfreesboro'. Arriving within three miles of Murfreesboro', we halted for the night, and on the morning of the 30th, the brigade being moved to a position about half a mile to the right of the pike, the two regiments under my command were thrown forward in the extreme advance of the division, in a cedar wood, and fronting an extensive open field, in which the enemy had thrown up upon commanding crests two rows of rifle-pits, and placed in position and embrasures two batteries.

Upon our right my front line skirmishers were supported by General Negley's division, and upon the left by Colonel Grose, commanding 3d brigade of our division.

Upon the crest of the first hill, immediately in front of and about two hundred yards distant from my front line, the enemy had posted a number of sharpshooters, who annoyed us considerably during the day.

This position I determined to take, and with General Cruft's consent I strengthened my skirmishers and advanced towards that point, driving the enemy from it. The skirmishers of General Negley kept up the alignment and support on the right, but, through some misunderstanding or otherwise, *we had no support on the left,* and during the night the enemy, being re-enforced, advanced and drove my outposts, holding this commanding and important position, back some twenty-five yards. This position, which would have been of immense advantage to us on the succeeding day, could not have been held or regained by the 1st brigade, (without the support on the left,) without bringing on a sharp and unwished-for engagement.

On the morning of the 31st the entire line of General Negley's, immediately upon our right, became seriously engaged, and at 8 a. m. I received the command from you to move forward. I pushed forward the skirmishers until they had driven the enemy from and gained the crest of the second hill in our front; the front line of the brigade moved forward to a fence at the edge of the woods and at the foot of the first hill. At this juncture, I found that the skirmishers and front line of General Negley's division had fallen back to a point in our rear, and that those on the left had come to a halt, and were engaged two hundred yards in my rear.

By this time the enemy commenced emerging in heavy force from the woods in our front and on the right, and advanced in column, driving my skirmishers back to the front lines.

They moved forward in splendid style until they reached the crest of the first hill in our front, there halted and delivered a well-directed volley full upon us. Captain Standart's battery immediately on my right, and my two regiments in front, simultaneously opened upon them, and with such effect that their front line gave way and fled to the rear; another line was forced up to the same position only to share the same fate; again fresh troops were advanced to the same point in the most perfect order. They planted their colors in the ground, and then extended their line by deploying to the right and left. The entire line threw themselves upon the ground and at once opened upon us and kept up a murderous fire. Here I reported the position of affairs in the front to General Cruft, and, in obedience to his order, hastened to the left, where I found that our support on the left had fallen back to a point near half a mile in the rear, and further to the left. In returning to report to the general, I discovered that General Negley's entire lines had apparently given way, and his troops, artillery and infantry, were then hurrying through the woods in our rear to some point on the left; thus leaving our entire right flank open and unprotected. Our position at this moment was one of great peril and danger. The enemy having driven back the brigade on our left, and gained possession of the high grounds around the "burnt house," had there posted a battery, one section of which was turned on our position, hurling with fearful accuracy perfect showers of grape and shell. On the right they had pressed closely upon the retiring forces of General Negley, and had gained a point within one hundred and fifty yards of our position, when Captain Standart, wheeling one section of his battery to the right, opened upon them with such effect that they were checked, but immediately opened upon our position a terrible fire of musketry. Meanwhile their batteries and infantry in our front kept up an incessant firing. Thus we were completely exposed to an enfilading fire of artillery and musketry, rendering our position untenable, and our capture or annihilation almost certain if we remained. The men, however, stood up nobly, preventing several different attempts to gain our position from the front. At this moment I was informed that the 2d Kentucky and 31st Indiana, who had for over two hours held their position at the fence, fighting against superior numbers, had nearly exhausted their ammunition. I immediately informed General Cruft of the fact, and also of our situation in the front and on the flanks, and asked permission to withdraw; he refused, saying that it was necessary for us to hold our position, in order to protect the retreat of General Negley's artillery. I immediately went forward and relieved the 2d Kentucky at the fence by the 90th Ohio, the 31st Indiana being relieved by the 1st Kentucky. The passage of lines by the advancing and retreating regiments was executed in the most perfect manner and in good order.

By the time the line had again been formed at the fence, the enemy, re-enforced, were pressing steadily forward on our flanks, and a force, eight columns deep, was advancing directly to our front. The 1st Kentucky sprang over the fence and advanced to meet them, but after delivering several volleys was forced to fall back to the fence. Here this regiment and the 90th Ohio kept them in check. I returned to the rear line, and found that all efforts to obtain a fresh supply of ammunition for the 2d Kentucky and 31st Indiana had proved fruitless. I informed the general of the fact, and also that it was impossible for the two regiments, then hotly engaged in the front, to hold their position against such odds. He again sent me to see the situation on our left and in the rear. I found the 2d brigade still holding their ground far in our rear, and one brigade of Negley's division formed in line, facing immediately to our rear, and firing at the enemy, who appeared to be advancing in that direction. Of these facts and our isolated position I informed General Cruft, when he reluctantly gave me the order to have the brigade fall slowly back. After returning through the woods about two hundred yards, I took command of my regiment, which was then reformed and faced to the front, and again advanced; but having little support, and seeing the enemy advancing in strong bodies, I determined to withdraw and rejoin the brigade. Just here I was informed that three pieces of artillery belonging to Negley's division had been abandoned in the woods some four hundred yards to my right, and were about falling into the hands of the enemy. I immediately moved my regiment by the flank double-quick to the spot, and, having cut the traces, I brought them off in safety, and placing them out of danger, I rejoined the brigade, which was formed on the railroad in rear of former position. The brigade remained near this place until 4 a. m. next morning, when we were advanced further to the front, where we remained but a short time, when we returned to our former position. After daylight my regiment moved with the brigade to a position further to the left, where we remained until afternoon, when we were moved still further to the left, near Stone river, to the support of Swallow's battery. Here we built small breastworks in our front and around the guns of the battery, and remained in our exposed condition amid the rain until the evening of January 3, 1863.

During the severe battle of that day, on the left my regiment was exposed to a terrible fire from the enemy's batteries, which had engaged those of Swallow and Parsons, which the brigade was supporting. Here I had one man mortally wounded by the explosion of a shell. From that time to date we have participated with the brigade in all its movements. From the time our forces left Nashville up to this date my regiment has been in the advance, never in reserve; and on all occasions, and under all circumstances, both men and officers have performed nobly and heroically the task allotted them. In the action on the 31st, and during the fight on the 2d January, 1863, soldiers never displayed more undaunted courage than those of the 2d Kentucky. Those that live are heroes, every one; those that died are martyrs to their country's cause.

Lieutenant Colonel Warner Spencer, Major J. R. Hurd, and Captain A. J. M. Brown deserve special mention and commendation for their gallantry and daring. In fact, every officer of the regiment is deserving of the greatest praise. Colonel Osborne, Lieutenant Colonel Smith, and Captain Hallowell, of the 31st Indiana volunteers, merit great praise for the manner in which they discharged their various duties during the action of the 31st.

Below I give you a list of the casualties in my regiment:

Killed.—Corporal James R. Jones, company A; Sergeant Henry Tessin, company E; Corporal Robert Hurton, company F; Private Frederick Weineger, company G; Corporal Fred. Hemple and Private Henry Evans, company H; and Privates August Belso and W. H. Carnagey, company I.

Wounded.—Assistant Surgeon W. Lyman Reed, slightly; Sergeant Major J. A. Poe, seriously. Company A: Lieutenant Thomas N. Davis, slightly; Sergeant Sylvester Quigly, slightly; Corporals William C. Pitts, slightly, and Gilbert Hurst, seriously; Privates E. Welty, Josiah Anderson, John McGinnis, Benjamin F. Stevenson, and John Garrell, slightly; John McPherson, mortally; Frank McLaughlin, Frank Connelly, and Daniel Mays, seriously; and John Godelfeld, mortally. Company B: Sergeants John A. Herne and Thomas Langdon, severely; and Private Michael Kelley, prisoner. Company C: Corporals Frank Bauer, seriously, and Barnard Stinkle, slightly; Private Fred. Groh, seriously and prisoner; William Winkleman and John Haigin, slightly. Company D: Privates Wm. O. Smith and Samuel D. Gibner, seriously, and prisoners; Daniel Fox, seriously; and James T. Hays, slightly. Company E: Sergeant B. F. Long, seriously, and prisoner; and Private George Long, slightly. Company F: Sergeant Samuel Crawford, slightly, and prisoner; Corporal A. Crawford, seriously; Privates C. Burn, Solomon Blackburn, Lafayette Vancyoe, and Thompson Hodges, seriously. Company G: Privates Christian Horning, seriously, and George Perkins, seriously, and prisoner. Company H: Sergeant John Delehuntie, seriously; Privates Joseph Redman, slightly; Samuel White and Patrick Gallagher, seriously; John Rome, F. Shriver, F. W. Bringman, and C. Smith, slightly. Company I: Orderly Sergeants L. Wise and Andrew Ereck, seriously; Corporals Frank McKinnen, seriously, and John Flynn, slightly; Privates Joseph Zimmer, and C. Ritchie, seriously; and John Zimmerman, slightly. Company K: Corporals Cristian Luckett, seriously, and Henry Sebexen, slightly; Privates George Fackler and Caspar Kupperschmit, seriously; George Lunleen and August Lenderman, slightly; and Herman Ogre, slightly, and prisoner.

Missing.—Privates Fred. Meyer and Fred Tuman, company C; Corporal E. S. Owens and James W. Patterson, company F; First Sergeant T. L. Hamilton, Sergeants M. O'Brien and Charles O'Brien, Corporal John V. Hunt, and Private Patrick Fitzgerald, company H; Private Joseph McKimm, company I.

Recapitulation.

Killed	8
Mortally wounded	2
Seriously wounded	30
Slightly wounded	27
Missing	10
Total	77

Nine wounded were taken prisoners.

I have the honor to be, with much respect, your obedient servant,

T. D. SEDGWICK,
Colonel 2d Kentucky Volunteers.

Captain W. H. FAIRBANKS, *A. A. A. G.*

HEADQUARTERS 19TH BRIGADE, ARMY OF THE CUMBERLAND,
2D BRIGADE, 2D DIVISION, LEFT WING,
Camp near Murfreesboro', Tennessee, January 5, 1863.

SIR: I have the honor to submit the following report of the operations of troops under my command since leaving Nashville, December 26:

The 19th brigade, which I have commanded since its organization in January, 1862, is now composed as follows: The 6th Kentucky volunteers, Colonel Walter C. Whitaker; the 9th Indiana volunteers, Colonel William H. Blake; the 110th Illinois volunteers, Colonel Thomas S. Casey, and the 41st Ohio volunteers, Lieutenant Colonel Aquila Wiley and upon leaving Nashville; numbered an effective aggregate of one thousand three hundred and ninety-one officers and men.

Being summoned before the commission then sitting for the investigation of the official course of Major General Buell, I did not, until evening, join the brigade, which had marched to within two miles of Lavergne. Just before my arrival, two regiments of the brigade had been thrown forward to the right of the road into a dense cedar brake; and as its temporary commander did not think it necessary to throw forward skirmishers, the flank was marched upon a force of the enemy, who, firing from under cover upon the head of the column, killed one of the 9th Indiana, wounded another, and wounded two of the 6th Kentucky. At 12 m. of December 27 I was ordered to proceed, *via* the Jefferson pike, to Stewart's creek, and save, if possible, the bridge crossing it. Ninety cavalry of the 4th Michigan, under Captain Maxey, were sent to me. I placed these under charge of my assistant inspector general, Captain James McCleery, 41st Ohio volunteers, with directions to keep me thoroughly informed of all that transpired, and as soon as the advance of the enemy was started, to put spurs to his troop, and not slack rein until the bridge was crossed. The distance did not exceed five miles, and by disposing flankers for perfect security, and urging the artillery and infantry to its fullest speed, I was enabled to keep within supporting distance all the time. The enemy was not three miles from the bridge, and, by closely following my directions, a steeple chase was made of the whole affair; the rebel force amounting to full five to our one. By the time the bridge was reached, they had formed upon the opposite side of the creek, but were soon dispersed by a few discharges from our artillery. In this affair we lost one cavalryman killed and two captured by the enemy. We took ten prisoners, one of whom an officer, and killed one commissioned officer and several men.

Too much credit cannot be given to Captain McCleery, of my staff, and Captain Maxey, of the 4th Michigan cavalry, for spirit and daring in this affair. On reaching the bridge my little party were upon the heels of the fugitives, and had they been armed with sabres in place of rifles, by slashing upon their rear the rout would have been pushed to a panic.

On the 29th I was ordered across to the Nashville and Murfreesboro' pike, and joining the division, proceeded to within three miles of Murfreesboro'. On the night of the 30th the brigade was ordered to the front line to relieve the 10th brigade. This position we held at the commencement of the general action of the 31st, and it deserves special notice. It was in a cotton-field, two and a half miles from Murfreesboro', on the place of Mr. Cowan; the line being at right angles with the Nashville and Murfreesboro' pike, the left resting on the pike at a point about five hundred yards towards Nashville from the intersection of the pike with the Nashville and Chattanooga railroad. The railroad and pike, at this point, crossed at a sharp angle; the position was utterly untenable, it being commanded by ground in all directions with covers of wood embankment, and palisading at good musket range in front, right, and left. My brigade was formed in two lines, the right resting against a skirt of woods, which, widening and extending to the right, gave concealment to the 22d brigade, which was adjacent to mine, and, further on, the entire division of Negley. On the left of the pike was Wagner's brigade, of Wood's division; the 6th Kentucky and 41st Ohio were in the front line, the 6th being on the right, and the 41st on the left. The 9th Indiana and 110th Illinois were in the second line, the 9th being on the right and the 110th on the left. A fierce battle had commenced at daylight on our right, and progressed with ominous changes of position until about 8.30 a. m., when it could no longer be doubted that our entire right was being driven around in rear to a position nearly at right angles to its proper line. At this moment authority was given to move forward to seize the commanding positions in front, and the burnt house of Mr. Cowan. The line advanced about twenty yards, when orders were given to face to the rear, the necessity of which was apparent, the enemy having by this time pushed forward quite to our rear. He at the same moment broke cover over the crest in front, at double-quick, in two lines. I faced my two right regiments to the rear, and moving them into the skirt of woods, commenced to engage in that direction. My two left regiments were retired some fifty yards and moved to the left of the pike to take cover of a slight crest, and engaged to the front; the regiment of Wagner's brigade occupying that ground (the 40th Indiana, Colonel Blake) having fallen much to the rear of it. The enemy had by this time taken position about the burnthouse, and the action became at my position terrific. The efforts of the enemy to force back my front and cross the cotton-field, out of which my troops had moved, were persistent, and were prevented only by the most unflinching determination upon the part of the 41st Ohio volunteers to hold their ground to the last. All the troops of General Wood, posted on our left, except two regiments guarding a ford some distance to our left and rear, were withdrawn to repel the assault upon the right, so that the 19th brigade was the extreme left of the army. Upon this point, as a pivot, the entire army oscillated from front to rear the entire day. The ammunition of the 41st Ohio volunteers was by this time nearly exhausted, and my efforts to replenish were up to this time fruitless. I despatched word to the rear that assistance must be given, or we must be sacrificed, as the position I held could not be given up, and gave orders to Lieutenant Colonel Wiley to fix his bayonets, and to Colonel Casey (without bayonets) to club his guns and hold the ground at all hazards as it was the key of the whole left. The responses satisfied me that my orders would be obeyed so long as any of those regiments were left to obey them. I now brought over the 9th Indiana from the right, and immediately posted it to relieve the 41st Ohio volunteers. It is pro per to state here that, in advancing to this position under a galling fire, a cannon shot passed through the ranks of the 9th Indiana, carrying death with it, and the ranks were closed without checking a step. The 41st Ohio volunteers retired with its thinned ranks in as perfect order as on parade, cheering for the cause and crying for ammunition.

A few discharges from the fresh regiments sufficed to check the foe, who drew out of our range, and at 9.30 lull and rest came, acceptably to our troops upon the left; their advance upon the right having also been checked. At about 10 a. m. another assault was made by the enemy, in several lines, furiously upon our front, succeeding in pushing a strong column past the burnt house, covered by the palisading, to the wood occupied by the 22d brigade and the 6th Kentucky. All of our troops occupying these woods now fell back, exposing my right flank, and threatening an assault from this point that would sweep away our entire left. General Palmer seeing this danger, and knowing the importance of this position, sent the 24th Ohio volunteers, Colonel Jones, and a fragment of the 36th Indiana, under Captain Woodruff, to my support. I posted these with the 41st Ohio volunteers, with the left of the line resting upon the 9th Indiana, and extending to the right and rear so as to face the advancing column. It was a place of great danger, and our losses were here heavy, including the gallant Colonel Jones, of the 24th Ohio volunteers; but with the timely assistance of Parsons's battery the enemy was checked, and the left again preserved from what appeared certain annihilation.

The enemy now took cover in the wood, keeping up so destructive a fire as to make it necessary to retire behind the embankments of the railroad, which only necessitated the swinging to rear of my right, the left having been posted on it when the action commenced in the morning. A sharp fight was kept up from this position till about 2 p. m., when another assault in regular lines, supported by artillery, was made upon this position in force. This assault was resisted much more easily than the previous ones, there being now a large force of our artillery bearing upon this point. The enemy also extended his lines much further to the left, causing something of a diversion of our troops in that direction. The 100th Illinois, Colonel Bartleson, was sent to me by the general commanding the army, which was posted with the 110th Illinois and 9th Indiana, in line to the front, with the right resting on the railroad. Here, with a German regiment, (I think the 2d Missouri,) these regiments fought the remainder of the day, the troops previously occupying this position retiring on the last approach of the enemy. A period of about one hour now ensued with but little infantry firing, but a murderous shower of shot and shell was rained from several directions upon this position which was covered by a thick growth of timber. A portion of Wood's division, now commanded by General Hascall, was also posted in these woods, in rear of my troops.

At about 4 p. m. the enemy again advanced upon my front in two lines. The battle had hushed, and the dreadful splendor of this advance can only be conceived, as all description must fall vastly short. His right was even with my left, and his left was lost in the distance. He advanced steadily, and, as it seemed, certainly to victory. I sent back all of my remaining staff successively to ask for support, and braced up my own lines as perfectly as possible. The 6th Kentucky had joined me from the other side some time previously, and was posted just over the embankment of the railroad. They were strengthened by such fragments of troops as I could pitch up until a good line was formed along the track. A portion of Sheridan's division was also but a few hundred yards in rear, replenishing their boxes. A portion of General Hascall's troops was also on the right of the railroad.

The fire of the troops was held until the enemy's right flank came in close range, when a single fire from my men was sufficient to disperse this portion of his lines, his left passing far around to our right. This virtually ended the fight of the day. My brigade rested where it had fought, not a stone's throw from where it was posted in the morning, till withdrawn at dawn next day.

The 6th Kentucky was not under my immediate observation from the first assault till late in the day, but the portion of time it was with me (and I have reason to believe at all other times) it fought unflinchingly, and is deserving of all praise. It repelled three assaults of a rebel brigade from the burnt house, endeavoring to reach the wood, and only retired when its ammunition was exhausted. Among its killed are Lieutenant Colonel Cotton and Captain Todd, men possessing in the highest degree the esteem and confidence of their brothers in arms, and who will be deeply lamented by a large circle of friends.

The 110th Illinois, a new regiment never before under fire, displayed that fearless courage one admires in veterans. Its losses from artillery were heavy. The 9th Indiana and 41st Ohio maintained fully their well-known reputation of perfect discipline, dauntless courage, and general fighting qualities. Their steadiness under fire was incredible. The latter regiment was taken by its commander, while resting, without orders, to repel an assault of the enemy's cavalry upon our train, which object it effected and returned to its position.

The casualties of this day were as follows:

Regiments.	Killed.		Wounded.		Missing.	Total.
	Officers	Men.	Officers.	Men.		
Forty-first Ohio volunteeers	1	12	4	98	17	132
One hundred and tenth Illinois	1	6	3	43	12	65
Ninth Indiana	1	9	5	89	13	117
Sixth Kentucky	2	11	5	85	10	113
Making a total of						427

A large list also occurred among the other troops under my immediate control on the field, but they will be reported by their proper brigade commanders. I am under many obligations to the commanders of these troops (many of their names I do not know) for their implicit obedience to my orders, but particularly to Colonel Bartleson, of the 100th Illinois, for valuable services.

To the officers commanding regiments of this brigade too much consideration cannot be given, both by their commanding generals and their country. Besides the actual service rendered their country this day, such heroic and daring valor justly entitles these men to the profound respect of the people of the country. To them the commander of the brigade feels that he owes everything this day, as there were times when faltering upon their part would have been destruction to the left of the army. He owes the success of this day, not only to proper conduct on the field, but more to strict obedience to orders, and a manly co-operation in bringing this brigade to its present high state of efficiency and discipline, through constant care, labor, and study, for a period of over twelve months. This alone has insured this proud result. To Lieutenant Colonel Suman, also, of the 9th Indiana, twice wounded, great credit is due for gallantry.

Captain Cockerill, battery F, 1st Ohio volunteer artillery, showed, as he always has, great proficiency as an artillery officer. He was also severely wounded. Lieutenant Osborne, of the same battery, being at the rear to fill his caissons when the train was menaced, turned his pieces upon the enemy, and greatly assisted in dispersing them.

Lieutenant Parsons, of the 4th United States artillery, who was in the thickest of the fight near my position all day, is also deserving of the warmest consideration of the government for the efficient manner in which his battery was manœuvred.

To my staff, also, everything can be said in their praise. To Major R. L. Kimberly, 41st Ohio volunteers, acting assistant adjutant general; to Lieutenants Wm. M. Beebe and E. B. Atwood, of the same regiment, aides-de-camp to Captan L. A. Cole, 9th Indiana topographical officer, for intelligently carrying orders and assisting to post troops, under a galling fire, the whole day; to Captain James McCluny, 41st Ohio volunteers, acting inspector general, for assisting to bring forward ammunition even after being wounded; to Harry Morton, 6th Kentucky volunteers, aide-de-camp, for similar service; to Lieutenant F. D. Cobb, 41st Ohio volunteers, acting commissary of subsistence, for keeping me intelligibly informed of what was transpiring beyond my immediate vision—all, for unqualified bravery, are deserving, as they have my warmest thanks, the consideration of the government.

Dr. M. G. Sherman, 9th Indiana, surgeon of the brigade, was acting medical director of the division, and removed from my immediate notice, yet I have reason to call favorable notice to this officer.

Lieutenant Q. L. Chilton, 6th Kentucky, acting brigade quartermaster, in the absence of Captain Johnson, exercised great capacity in caring for, and keeping from the enemy, the train of the brigade.

I am under many obligations to the general commanding the division for the confidence reposed in me in vesting with me the management of so important a portion of the field. By seizing the little crest occupied by my troops early in the morning, not exceeding two feet in height, and later, the railroad embankment, hundreds of lives were saved, the strength of my brigade doubled, and the position successfully held. This will account for the smaller list of casualties than that of some brigades which did less fighting.

I am happy to report, with some twenty miserable exceptions, no straggling in this brigade.

The casualties of my *personnel* were as follows: The colonel commanding the brigade was bruised by a ball upon the shoulder, and his horse was killed; Captain James McCluny, 41st Ohio volunteers, acting inspector general, shot through the leg; First Lieutenant Wm. M. Beebe, 41st Ohio volunteers, aide-de-camp, wounded in the head, and horse shot; Captain L. A. Cole, 9th Indiana, topographical officer, slightly wounded in the foot; Orderly Deaderick, sergeant 4th Kentucky cavalry, mortally wounded, and horse shot; and Bugler Leaman, 6th Kentucky, horse shot.

Close observation of the conduct and character of our troops for the past few days has confirmed me in a long-settled belief that our army is borne down by a lamentable weight of official incapacity in regimental organizations. The reasonable expectations of the country can, in my opinion, never be realized until this incubus is summarily ejected, and young men of known military ability and faculty to command men, without regard to previous seniority, are put in their places. I saw upon the field company officers of over a year's standing, who neither had the power to, or knowledge how, to form their men in two ranks.

On the 2d instant my brigade was ordered across the river to support Colonel Grose, commanding the 10th brigade, then in reserve to General Van Cleve, whose division (the only one on that side of the river) had been vigorously attacked by the enemy. I reached the field about 4 p. m., finding his entire division put to rout. The enemy had been checked by Colonel Grose and a portion of Negley's division, and the several batteries from the point occupied by General Cruft's brigade. It was difficult to say which was running away the most rapidly, the division of Van Cleve to the rear, or the enemy in the opposite direction. I found myself in command of all the troops on that side of the river. Leaving three of my regiments in position as a reserve, I pushed forward with the portion of Colonel Grose's brigade already moving, and the 41st Ohio volunteers, pursuing the enemy beyond all the ground occupied by our forces before the fight. I here formed the best line circumstances would admit of, the 41st Ohio volunteers being the only regiment wholly in hand. The others were badly broken; the only idea of their officers seeming to be to push on pell-mell, which, if carried beyond the point occupied, might have resulted disastrously. I succeeded in checking the straggling to the front, with the aid of Colonel Grider, of the —— Kentucky, who came forward and performed this valuable service after his regiment had gone to the rear.

I was relieved by the fresh division of General Jefferson C. Davis, who arrived just at dark. When far advanced in the pursuit, a portion of General Negley's batteries, far in the rear, were firing on my line, and continued to (without damage) till an aide-de-camp was sent to ask that it be discontinued.

After forming my advance line, a battery of the enemy, about four hundred yards in front, continued to fire upon us with great rapidity. I ordered the 41st Ohio volunteers to fire one volley upon it. No more firing took place on either side, and the weakness of my line prevented my going further. The next day three caissons and several dead men and horses were found at this point.

It was in this fight that the famous rebel General Roger B. Hanson was killed and General Adams was wounded, whether in their advance or retreat I never knew.

First Lieutenant F. D. Cobb, 41st Ohio volunteers, acting aide-de-camp, comported himself with great gallantry on the field. Seizing the colors of the 36th Indiana, that had been shot down, he galloped forward, rallying many stragglers, who, though going in the right direction, were doing so inefficiently, and on their own account.

My casualties in this action were slight, and in all, since leaving Nashville, are:

Commissioned officers: Killed	5	
Wounded	17	
Total commissioned		22
Enlisted men: Killed	41	
Wounded	318	
Total enlisted		359
Missing		52
Aggregate		433

I would respectfully call the attention of the general commanding the division to accompanying reports of regimental commanders, and of Lieutenant Chilton, in charge of train; also to explanatory sketch.

I am, very respectfully, your obedient servant,

W. B. HAZEN,

Colonel Commanding 19th Brigade, 2d Brig., 2d Div., Left Wing.

ASSISTANT ADJUTANT GENERAL, 4TH DIVISION,

Army of the Cumberland, 2d Division, Left Wing.

HOSPITAL OF 2D DIVISION,

Left Wing, near Murfreesboro'.

SIR: As brigade surgeon of your brigade, I have the honor to submit the following report of the casualties in the brigade during the several days' fight before Murfreesboro'.

110th Illinois.—Killed, 7; wounded ,28—total, 35.
9th Indiana volunteers.—Killed, 14; wounded, 93—total, 107.
6th Kentucky.—Killed, 12; wounded, 71—total, 83.
41st Ohio volunteers.—Killed, 17; wounded, 100—total, 117.
The whole number killed in the brigade, 50; wounded, 292—total, 342.

In consequence of our hospital being nearer the battle-field than any other during the time of the engagement, our hospital was necessarily crowded with hundreds of the wounded from other divisions, making our duties very responsible and laborious.

And I cannot in justice submit this report without making honorable mention of all the medical officers in your brigade. They have been untiring in their exertions, night and day, to relieve the sufferings of all who came under their notice. After looking after the wounded in their respective regiments, they devoted their skill and attention cheerfully to others, relaxing no effort to make them comfortable. Their unwearied attention to duty during this engagement merits the esteem and confidence of all who know them.

Very respectfully,

M. G. SHERMAN,
Brigade Surgeon, 2d Brigade, 2d Division, Left Wing.

Colonel W. B. HAZEN,
Commanding 2d Brigade of Left Wing.

CAMP NEAR MURFREESBORO', TENNESSEE,
January 8, 1863.

DEAR SIR: In compliance with an order from you of this morning, I herein submit to you a report of what transpired with the train of your brigade during the engagement near Murfreesboro', Tennessee, on Wednesday, January 1, 1863.

Having arrived on the field, Monday, December 30, 1862, at a late hour in the night, I parked the train near to and on the left of where the brigade was then lying. On Tuesday, December 31, 1862, early in the morning, believing that the train was too near to what I supposed to be our line of battle, I moved the train to the left and rear of where the brigade had rested the night previous, a distance of about one-fourth of a mile, where it remained until the fight began on Wednesday, January 1, 1863. Soon after the fight began I received an order from a lieutenant (whom I supposed to be an aid to General Rosecrans) to form the train into a hollow square. I had not more than completed the work before I received another order to move the train toward Stone river, and to the rear of the left of our army; the several trains of the army were ordered to the same place. Arriving at the crossing over the railroad at the same time, there seemed to be a disposition among the teamsters to crowd through and break the trains. I halted my train until others crossed. During this time of waiting I put several men, who seemed to have nothing to do, to work carrying rails to make another crossing, which by the time it was completed the way was clear. I moved my train over and near the river, and had it drawn up in park, when a shell from a gun of the rebels fell among the wagons, wounding a mule of the train, so much so that it had to be cut loose and left; then I moved nearer to the river, when an order came for us to cross the river and to halt, which was not more than accomplished before an order came to recross the river, which was done. I recrossed, held the train in moving order, and in a few minutes a squad of rebel cavalry came in view, causing a panic among the teamsters and stragglers who had by this time gathered along the train. I cautioned the teamsters of my train to be composed while I moved up and assisted in clearing the road, which was soon done. I then moved my train off in good order into the woods to the rear of the centre of our army, where I held it until late in the evening, when I moved it to the side of the pike. When night came on, Lieutenant Blythe, quartermaster 41st Ohio volunteers, and myself rode along to the right of our army to see if we could not pick upon some place to park the train that it might be safe during the next day, and thought best to move near the hospital of our division, which we did; but at 10 o'clock at night I received an order from General Palmer to issue all rations on hand and return to Nashville with the train, which was done, leaving the field at 8 o'clock a. m., January 2, arriving at Nashville at 5 o'clock p. m. of the same day without any loss or disturbance save the threatening of an attack from rebel cavalry; the casualties in all amounting to the loss of one mule belonging to the 110th Illinois volunteers, and one single set lead harness belonging to same.

Yours, respectfully,

Q. L. CHILTON,

First Lieut. and Assistant Quartermaster, 6th Kentucky Volunteers.

Colonel W. B. HAZEN,

Commanding 2d Brigade.

HEADQUARTERS 6TH KENTUCKY INFANTRY,
Battle-field of Stone river, January 5, 1863.

The undersigned, Walter C. Whitaker, colonel commanding 6th Kentucky infantry, of the 2d brigade, late the 19th, commanded by Colonel W. B. Hazen, of the 2d division, late the 4th, commanded by General Palmer, makes the following report of the part taken by the 6th Kentucky infantry in the battle of Stone river.

On the night of the 30th December the 6th Kentucky and 41st Ohio volunteers were drawn up in line of battle, fronting east and towards Murfreesboro', in advance of the army, on a cotton-field lying south of the Nashville and Murfreesboro' turnpike road, and near where the same crosses the Nashville and Chattanooga railroad, and also near where both roads strike the bank of Stone river. On the east, some two hundred and fifty yards in front of the 6th Kentucky, on a high piece of ground, in a curtilage surrounded with a strong palisade of cedar timbers some seven or eight feet high, firmly set in the ground, stands the burned brick dwelling-house of Mr. Cowan; in the rear of this house the enemy had their rifle-pits. Beyond the house the ground gently rose higher for some three hundred yards to the crest of the ridge, on the top of which, in a southeast direction, the enemy had a battery. Beyond the crest of the hill, and towards the river from the house, the ground gently sloped until it reached the river and a grove of timber in the rear. On this slope, concealed from our view, the enemy had an earthen breastwork for infantry and artillery. On the right, and south of the position of the 6th, was a dense wood of oak and tall cedar. In the same direction, his left resting on the right of the 6th, with an interval of two hundred and fifty yards between them, General Cruft had his brigade drawn up in line of battle. Immediately in rear of and west of the 6th was an open field, with a few old houses, some scattered trees, and large surface rocks, through which the turnpike and railroad ran. Directly north of this line of battle was an embankment of the railroad some seven or eight feet in height. On the edge of this field the gallant 9th Indiana and 110th Illinois were drawn up as reserve. Company D, Captain Proctor, and company I, Lieutenant Patchen, from the 41st Ohio volunteers, and company C, Captain Todd, and company I, Captain Stein, of the 6th Kentucky, were acting as pickets; companies C and I occupying the curtilage of the brick-house, with a small interval between them and the enemy's pickets. Shortly after sunrise on the morning of the 31st the pickets were attacked by the enemy, but maintained their position. Heavy firing was soon heard on the right of our army, and gave indications of the rapid advance of the enemy. The enemy soon made a most furious attack upon our left; the pickets of the 6th were driven in by a large force, who, protected by the palisade and out-buildings of Mr. Cowan's house and the high ground, opened a galling fire on the 6th, who were in the open ground. They gradually advanced under cover, with the intention of flanking the 6th on the right. Changing position by the right flank the regiment was formed in line of battle in the skirt of timber south of the cotton-field—an advantageous position—under cover of the timber. Here we were assaulted by a large body of the enemy; from their numbers I estimated them as a brigade. Three times they advanced, and as often were they driven back with great slaughter. From this position the 6th was enabled to protect the left flank of the 22d brigade, General Cruft, who was gallantly maintaining his position. Some of the enemy's skirmishers having, after two hours' hard fighting, gained position in the edge of the wood, the 6th was thrown forward to drive them from their cover. While in the act of advancing, the enemy, who had driven in General Negley's force on the right, opened a fire on the right flank of the 6th, by which my lieutenant colonel (Colton) was killed. After some hard fighting the enemy were driven from their cover. Then changing front, the right wing defending one flank and the left wing the other, the 6th fought the advancing foe until their ammunition was exhausted. Changing position in good order, they took another position in rear of the railroad, where, having replenished their ammunition, they formed in line of battle on the north side of and under cover of the embankment of the railroad, the 9th Indiana being on their left, and the 41st Ohio and 110th Illinois being in reserve in the rear. The battle had been furiously raging from eight in the morning until noon. About two o'clock p. m., the right of the army having been driven back, the enemy appeared in heavy force on the crest of the ridge east of Mr. Cowan's burned dwelling. Massing their forces, they intended, if possible, to crush the 19th brigade, which had maintained its position during the day against overwhelming numbers. Onward they came; the colors of five or six regiments advancing abreast in line of battle were visible on the crest of the ridge. A further view of this line was intercepted by intervening inequalities of ground and woods. Firmly they advanced until within good range of the guns of the 6th and 9th. A most destructive fire was opened upon them by these regiments, by Captain Cockerill's and Captain Parsons's batteries, and by the 40th Indiana regiment, commanded by Colonel Blake. They broke in confusion, but rallying, advanced again. Three or four times they rallied and advanced to the attack; each time they were driven back with great loss, the last time in such confusion that it became a rout. The day was *ours*. We camped that night on the position that had been so ably and successfully defended. The 6th has to regret the loss of two of her bravest and most gallant officers: Lieutenant Colonel George T. Colton was killed, nobly encouraging the men on the right; Captain Charles S. Todd, commander of company C, the color company, fell pressing his men on to victory—scion of illustrious patriots, a braver spirit has not been offered up on the altar of his country. The total loss in killed is two officers and eleven enlisted men. Six commissioned officers were wounded: Lieutenant Bates, company A; Lieutenant Dawkins, company B; Lieutenant Armstrong, company F; Lieutenant Frank, of company I; and others. Eighty-eight enlisted men were wounded. Total killed and wounded, one hundred and four. Lieutenant Dawkins, acting as adjutant, rendered me very great assistance, until he was so severely wounded as to be carried from the field. Lieutenant Rockingham, of company A, deserves the highest commendation for courage, coolness, and efficiency as an officer. Sergeant William A. Jones, of company A; Captain Dawkins, of company B; Lieutenant McCampbell, of company D; Lieutenant Armstrong, of company F; Captain Marker, of company G; Captain Johnston and Lieutenant Whitaker, of company H; Captain Stein and Lieutenant Frank, of company I; Lieutenant Campbell and Sergeant Furr, of company K, are specially noticed for gallant conduct and efficient services. I can speak in the most approving manner of the soldierly bearing and courage of the men of the 6th Kentucky. Three or four times regiments retreating in confusion would break through their lines, yet they never faltered in their duty, but obeyed implicitly the orders of the officer commanding. I was personally cognizant of very gallant conduct on the part of Lieutenant Meeker, of the signal corps, under very heavy fire, in endeavoring to rally some of the fugitive regiments that were breaking through my lines; I was attracted by his bearing, inquired of him his name, and gave him merited commendation. On Friday, in the evening, the 2d January, 1863, the enemy made a most violent and determined attack upon the left of our forces, which had been advanced beyond Stone river. The 6th Kentucky was ordered with the brigade, by Colonel Hazen, to cross the river and aid the forces engaged. This order was immediately obeyed. In double-quick time the 6th advanced through a heavy shower of solid shot, shell, grape, and Minie balls, cheering as they went. The timely aid brought inspired the forces engaged with the enemy, who, pressing forward, drove the enemy with great slaughter from the field. While they were advancing, great numbers of one of the divisions attacked (said to be General Van Cleve's) ran in great affright. Throwing down their arms, they broke through the ranks of the 6th, saying "all was lost." This did not throw the 6th into confusion. Steadily they advanced, every man and officer doing his duty. In the advance two men of company G were killed by a rifled cannon shot, and two from company H were wounded. The regiment remained encamped on the opposite side of the river till the 4th January, whence it moved to its present quarters, where it learned of the flight of the enemy. A detail was made, and all its noble dead entombed with their soldier's honors in a soldier's grave, on the ground where the 19th brigade made its memorable stand against such overwhelming numbers. Great credit is due to the talented and indefatigable surgeons of the 6th Kentucky, Dr. Joseph T. Drane and Dr. E. T. Long, for their faithful and indefatigable attention to the wounded; they not only cared for and attended the wounded of their regiment, but many others beside. They were on the field in discharge of their duty amidst the thickest of the fight.

Respectfully submitted.

WALTER C. WHITAKER,
Colonel Commanding 6th Kentucky Infantry.

Major KIMBERLY,
Assistant Adjutant General, 2d Brigade, 2d Division.

HEADQUARTERS 110TH ILLINOIS VOLUNTEERS,
Camp near Murfreesboro', Tennessee, January 8, 1863.

As commander of the 110th regiment Illinois volunteers, I have the honor to submit the following report of its operations and casualties in the recent engagements before Murfreesboro'.

On the morning of the 31st December the regiment which was in double column in reserve, was advanced to take position in the second line of battle, its left resting on the right of and near the Murfreesboro' and Nashville pike. About 8 o'clock a. m. the regiment began its advance on Murfreesboro', just then the firing, which had been heard at an early hour on our right, appeared to be rapidly nearing our right and rear; and the regiment had advanced scarce its front, when the "right about" was ordered, and it was moved to its former position, faced to the front, and almost immediately after moved by the left flank to a slight elevation on the right of the railroad, the highest point of which joins the railroad embankment, and there faced to the front, its left extending across the railroad, its entire right wing about twenty paces in rear of, and parallel to, the left wing of the 41st Ohio volunteers, which was then engaged with the enemy, who had advanced upon the front of our brigade. This position was maintained for a considerable time. I advanced the left wing of the regiment to the crest of the hill, where they became immediately engaged with the enemy, who had broken cover at the burnt brick. Twice the enemy came forward as if intending to charge, when Colonel Hazen directed me to have my command "fix bayonets;" I replied that we had no bayonets, and received the answer that we should "club muskets" if attacked. But the enemy did not charge our position. The whole right of the army having apparently given way, I was ordered to cross the railroad. Having crossed the road, we took a position perpendicular to it, and in front of the wood facing the enemy, the 100th Illinois volunteers being on our right. This position had scarcely been taken before the enemy appeared in force beyond the fence, and across the cotton-field, directly in our front. The firing began at once. Here the fire of small arms was incessant and terrific. My command suffered mostly from the rebel batteries to the left and rear of the burnt brick house. Here the enemy appeared twice on our front in column, but failed to cross the fence. Night ended the conflict. My command slept on the ground we fought on, in the extreme advance, until the early dawn of the 1st instant, when we, with the rest of the brigade, took a position on the bank of Stone river.

My command was not again engaged with the enemy. On Friday, the 2d instant, with the rest of the brigade, my command crossed the river to repel the attack of the enemy, but did not become engaged, the enemy having retired from before the assaults of the 3d brigade, commanded by Colonel Grose.

I subjoin the following list of casualties:

Company A, (Captain M. D. Hoge, commanding.)—Killed: Privates Willis J. Strickland, James L. Rice, and Aquilla Wilson. Wounded: Captain M. D. Hoge, slightly; Second Lieutenant W. B. Denning, slightly; Corporal Franklin S. Minor, slightly; Privates George M. D. Parish, slightly; William Threewit, slightly; James J. Ice, slightly; William Essery, seriously; Samuel Young, seriously; and Derald Wiltington, seriously.

Company B, (First Lieutenant Samuel T. Maxay, commanding.)—Wounded: First Sergeant Hiram R. Allen, slightly; Corporal C. C. Estes, slightly; Privates H. H. Wilson, slightly; R. B. Osborne, slightly; Zadoc Casey, seriously; and J. H. Wittenberg, slightly.

Company C, (Second Lieutenant J. L. Parks, commanding.)—Wounded: Second Lieutenant J. L. Parks, slightly; Privates F. M. Parks, slightly; C. L. Parks, slightly; Nath. Mondrell, slightly; Alexander Sutherland, slightly; Henry Copher, slightly; Daniel Payne, slightly; and H. V. Frell, slightly. Missing: Private James Edwards.

Company D, (Captain E. H. Topping, commanding.)—Killed: Private Charles Holt. Wounded: Privates James Barnett, seriously; Samuel Fairchild, seriously; James Ewbank, seriously; Samuel Palmer, slightly; George Howard, slightly; and Charles Benjamin, seriously.

Company E, (First Lieutenant W. A. Spiller, commanding.)—Wounded: Corporal James H. Scott, slightly, and Private M. P. Tribble, slightly.

Company F, (Captain Drapon Dewitt, commanding.)—Killed: Second Lieutenant Jesse G. Payne, and Privates John Underwood and Moses Ward. Wounded: Sergeant A. J. Sweaton, slightly; Corporal Miron Wells, slightly; Privates A. H. Coombs, slightly; Willis Jones, slightly; William Lance, slightly; and William Dungee, slightly. Missing: Private Ellis Gulley.

Company G, (Captain John F. Day, commanding.)—Wounded: Captain J. F. Day, slightly; Privates Harvey Cass, slightly; T. H. Ballinger, slightly; and J. M. Brookins, slightly.

Company H, (Captain William K. Murphy, commanding.)—Wounded: Corporal W. H. Mulligan, slightly; and Privates John F. Lynch and Andrew Thompson, slightly.

Company I, (Captain William L. Britton, commanding.)—Wounded: Privates Archibald Smith, and Isaac Bolton, slightly.

Company K, (First Lieutenant James S. Wycough, commanding.)—Wounded: First Lieutenant J. S. Wycough, slightly; Privates W. A. Redferrin and W. Butler, slightly.

Summary.—Killed, 7; wounded, 49; missing, 2—total, 58.

Respectfully submitted.

THOS. S. CASEY,
Colonel 110th Illinois Volunteers.

Major R. S. KIMBERLY,
Acting Assistant Adjutant General.

HEADQUARTERS 9TH INDIANA INFANTRY,
In Camp near Murfreesboro', Tennessee, January 6, 1863.

CAPTAIN: I have the honor to submit the following report of the part taken by the 9th Indiana infantry in the battle of Stone river, December 31, 1862.

Bivouacking in the dense cedars on the right of the Nashville pike the night preceding the engagement, I moved at dawn in double column to the front, relieving the 36th Indiana infantry of the 3d brigade. As there was no indication of an immediate advance I stacked arms, and permitted my men to build fires. At half past 6 a. m. heavy cannonading and continued discharges of musketry were heard on our extreme right, which gradually approached our position and was borne rapidly to our rear, until the sound of conflict was immediately in our rear on the Nashville pike.

At 7 a. m. I received an order to advance in line of battle, supporting the 6th Kentucky infantry; moving forward but a short distance, received orders to face by the rear rank and march to the rear. At this time the enemy's artillery in our rear had opened fire on our columns; was halted, and moved by the left flank in the direction of the pike and railroad. I here received orders to move rapidly to the support of Colonel Grose's brigade, then hotly engaged with the enemy's infantry, but a few paces to my right and rear. While forming on the left of the 3d brigade I lost two men killed and several wounded by an enfilading fire from the enemy's artillery on my former front. The 3d brigade was closely engaged firing obliquely to their right. The enemy did not appear in my front, and by orders I changed front to the rear in 1st company, and ordered my men to lie down. The enemy had advanced in our front, occupying the burned house and grounds with a force of infantry and a battery of artillery. Remaining in this position but a short time, I was ordered to relieve the 41st Ohio infantry, whose ammunition was said to have been exhausted at this early hour in the action. I marched by the left flank at double-quick time, passing under the enemy's fire; five men of company H were knocked down by a single shell, two of whom were mortally wounded. Forming on the left of the pike with my right resting near it, my left on the railroad, I moved forward in line of battle to the low crest and relieved the 41st Ohio volunteers.

The rebels then occupied the burned house with one battery, and their infantry partially covered by the out-houses and a stockade fence extending to the pike, I at once opened fire on them, and but a short time intervened until their artillery limbered up and retired in confusion to the rifle-pits on the ridge where they went to battery and opened fire. After three-quarters of an hour the fire from the infantry in our front slackened, and many of them ran to the rear in disorder. At this time a brigade of the enemy's infantry advanced from their rifle-pits and marched obliquely in the direction of my position; although at long range, I at once opened fire on them which thinned their ranks as they continued to approach. As they drew nearer one of the regiments moved to the front and advanced at the charge step upon my position. My men poured upon them a galling and deliberate fire that halted them within seventy-five yards of our line, where they lay down, covered somewhat by the cotton-furrows, and opened fire on us, from which we suffered. Their colors had been struck down three times during their advance, and every field officer of the regiment was killed. (The regiment was the 16th Louisiana, Colonel Fish, of General Chalmer's brigade, composed of the 9th and 10th Mississippi and 16th Louisiana. These facts were obtained from prisoners and burial parties that evening, and I presume are reliable.) I received orders to fix bayonets and hold the position until details could be sent to the rear for cartridges; my sixty rounds were almost entirely exhausted. At this period of the engagement Lieutenant Colonel Suman received a wound in the arm and side; Lieutenant Kesler was mortally wounded; Captain Pettit was severely wounded in the thigh, and borne from the field; Lieutenant Brinton and Lieutenant Creswell were both severely wounded; also Sergeant Major Armstrong severely wounded in the leg; and many enlisted men killed and wounded.

The 110th Illinois infantry, Colonel Casey, were in reserve directly in my rear, quietly awaiting an opportunity to render me support, which was not needed.

Captain Cockerill advanced one section of his battery to my support, and opened on the enemy with marked effect, and continued his fire until his ammunition was exhausted; he had his horse shot under him while directing the fire of his guns, and displayed the utmost coolness and courage.

At 11 o'clock a. m. our forces were being driven from the cedar grove on the right of the field. The enemy began to cross troops from the burnt house to the timber. Being well within range, I opened fire on them as they marched by the flank. The whole line was subjected to a severe fire as it passed successively the open space. At half past 11 a. m. the enemy's fire in my front had grown feeble; many had retired in disorder; many were killed or wounded, (as the ground where they fought clearly attested at the close of the day. I picketed the ground near their line that night.)

The enemy occupying the heavy timber on my right, and the whole line on my right having retired, I received orders to withdraw my right and open fire on the forces in the timber, who were then opening fire on us. In performing this movement, my brave color-bearer, Charles Zellers, was killed. My left and centre still engaged the enemy in front. I was compelled again to withdraw my right from the severe flanking fire from the timber which brought me to the railroad, where I received orders to cross and open fire upon the enemy moving upon my left and rear. Facing by the rear rank, I opened fire upon the enemy obliquely to my left, (then my right,) detaching at the same time company's "K," "G," and "B," in charge of Major Laselle, to occupy the elevation on the right of the railroad, that had just been held by my left. At this time Lieutenant Braden fell severely, if not mortally, wounded; he was an officer, brave, and without reproach. The 110th Illinois infantry were ordered up to my support and formed on my right. At half past 1 p. m. General Rosecrans appeared in person on this part of the field, and ordered the 2d Missouri and 73d Illinois infantry to assist in holding the position. The 2d Missouri came into action gallantly, both forming on the railroad; the colonel of the 2d Missouri was killed at this point. At half past 2 p. m. these regiments were withdrawn, and the 6th Kentucky infantry forming on my right, I was ordered to open fire over the railroad track upon heavy bodies of the enemy then occupying the timber opposite—then directly in our front. Maintained this fire until the enemy, re-enforced, again appeared on my left and rear; I again faced by the rear rank and opened obliquely to my left.

During the time my regiment occupied the position on the left of the railroad we were subjected to a cross fire from two of the enemy's batteries on their right and centre; but owing to the nature of the position did not suffer severely. At 4 p. m. the fire of the enemy's musketry ceased, while that of their batteries continued until the close of the day. Before twilight I sent details to collect and bury my dead upon the ground where they fell; a mutual truce was granted, in which the soldiers of both sides, without arms, gathered their fallen comrades without interruption. The fierce acerbity of the deadly strife had given place to the mutual expressions of kindness and regard. While thus engaged, one gun of Captain Cockerill's battery, having been abandoned well to the front by the explosion of a caisson, I had it removed well to the rear; the movement drew a fire from one of the enemy's batteries, but without effect.

For the brave men who stood by their colors from 7 a. m. until 4 p. m., continually under fire, no word of mine could do justice to their unfaltering courage. The officers of the 9th Indiana infantry I regard as amongst the *bravest* of the *brave.* Many of the captains and commandants of companies exhibited the highest courage and capacity under a severe and long-continued fire; but where, perhaps, none failed in doing their duty, it would be an invidious distinction to name any one for marked honor. Lieutenant Colonel Suman stood gallantly at the post of duty until wounded, and retired from the field. Major Laselle exhibited great courage, coolness, and efficiency throughout the day; Adjutant Willard repeated his heroism of Shiloh; Sergeant Major Armstrong was wounded severely while executing an order. A sergeant, ten enlisted men, and one corporal, deserted their colors during the action; I will take prompt measures to publish the infamy of their conduct and bring them to punishment.

I regret to say that when the action opened with such violence the arrangements made with the surgeons and musicians for carrying the wounded to the rear utterly failed; they were borne with the tide of terrified stragglers so far to the left that many of them were captured by the enemy's cavalry, who penetrated their hiding-places. Doctor Gilmore, assistant surgeon, with some hospital attendants and one ambulance, fell into the hands of the enemy The surgeons were subsequently released, and I am told rendered efficient service in their attention to the wounded after the engagement. By reason of this most criminal neglect, many of my wounded had to crawl with shattered limbs to the rear, while others, unable to be removed, lay under the enemy's fire. I am glad to report two bright exceptions to the base conduct of the hospital corps. Mr. Hurlburt, from the beginning to the close of the action, continually entered our line of fire and bore back the wounded; he exhibited a heroism worthy of all praise, because it was voluntary and out of the line of his duty. And William Morgan, chief bugler, displayed courage and efficiency in the discharge of his duty. The regiment, in addition to the sixty rounds to the man, fired during the day 16,000 rounds of cartridges. The regiment entered the action with 345 enlisted men and 27 commanding officers.

Loss.—Killed: officers, 1; enlisted men, 10—total, 11. Wounded: officers, 5; enlisted men, 82—total, 87. Missing: enlisted men, 11—total, 11. In aggregate, loss of 109.

I remain, with great respect, your obedient servant,

W. H. B. LAKE,
Colonel Commanding.

Captain R. S. KIMBERLY,
Acting Assistant Adjutant General, 2d Brigade.

HEADQUARTERS 41ST REGIMENT OHIO VOLUNTEERS,
Camp near Murfreesboro,' Tennessee, January 6, 1863.

As commander of the 41st regiment Ohio volunteers, I have the honor to submit the following report of its operations and casualties in the recent engagements before Murfreesboro.' On the evening of the 30th of December the regiment, which was then in double column in reserve, was ordered to take position in the first line of battle, its left resting on the right of and near the Murfreesboro' and Nashville turnpike, with two companies deployed as skirmishers, about one hundred and fifty yards in advance, covering its front. A little before daylight, on the morning of the 31st, companies D and I were deployed as skirmishers, and relieved companies A and F, which were then assembled and took their position in line. About 8 o'clock the signal "forward" was sounded, and the regiment commenced to advance toward Murfreesboro.' At this time the firing, which had commenced at an early hour on our right, appeared to be nearing the pike to our right and rear, and the regiment had not advanced more than about one hundred paces when the command "right-about" was given, and it returned to its former position and again faced to the front. At this time the enemy appeared advancing in line across the open country direct in our front. The regiment was then moved by the left flank across the turnpike, its left resting on a slight elevation to the right of and near the railroad. The enemy, then moving by his left flank to gain cover of a wood on our right, made an oblique change of front to rear on the left company. The skirmishers, who during this time under the command of Captain J. H. Williston, acting major, had been engaged with the enemy with slight loss, were now rallied and put in position on the right of the regiment. In this position the regiment opened fire, and continued firing until its ammunition was about exhausted, when it was relieved by the 9th Indiana, and retired a short distance and replenished its boxes. It then took up position on the right of the brigade, extending obliquely across the turnpike, and again opened fire. It here continued firing until a battery of the enemy's opened upon our right flank, when it retired across the railroad, and took up position on the left of the brigade, the right resting near and perpendicular to the railroad, the rest of the brigade having taken position behind, and parallel with the railroad. After remaining in this position for some time, the enemy not being within effective range of infantry, and suffering considerably from his artillery, one shell from which, exploding in the ranks, killed and wounded eight men, it retired about fifty yards behind a ridge which afforded some protection. Shortly after, hearing that the enemy's cavalry was attempting to cross the creek to our left and rear, and seeing a section of artillery unsupported opening in that direction, without waiting for orders I placed the regiment in position on the right of the artillery; a few discharges from the artillery, however, repulsed them. I was here met by a number of the staff of the colonel commanding the brigade, and directed to remain there until further orders. Shortly after, by direction of General Rosecrans, the regiment took its former position in the field behind the crest of the hill, which it occupied during the remainder of the day, sustaining some loss from the enemy's artillery, but without opportunity of returning its fire. During the following day the regiment was not engaged, remaining in double column in reserve on the left of the railroad and near the creek, as it did also during Friday, until in the afternoon, when the enemy made his attack on our left. The column was then moved by the left flank across the creek, to our extreme left, where it was deployed. The enemy was at this time repulsed and retiring in confusion. I was ordered to advance the regiment in line, and did so without firing, until ordered to halt at the skirt of a wood. The enemy having retreated across an open field and disappeared in a wood beyond, a single battery of the enemy's posted in the skirt of the wood was continuing its fire. The regiment was directed to fire one volley in the direction of the battery, and did so, immediately after which the firing on both sides ceased. It being now dark, the regiment remained in this position until relieved by the 21st Illinois, when it was ordered into position to the rear, which terminated its part in the engagement. The following is a list of casualties:

Company A, (Lieutenant C. C. Hart commanding.) Number engaged: Commanding officers, 2; enlisted men, 45.

Killed.—First Lieutenant C. C. Hart, Privates Albert McFarland and John M. Waggoner. Total, 3.

Wounded.—Sergeants James J. Mattocks, severely, and Shelden Crooks, slightly; Corporal Phillip A. Bower, severely; Privates Julius A. Cutler, severely; C. A. Bennett, severely; Hiram C. Kesler, severely; George A. Clark, severely; Edward Pfouts, severely, and missing; Charles R. Smith, severely; Alfred Frost, slightly; Mile Ritchie, slightly; Wm. Shivey, slightly; Adolphus Flint, slightly; and Asbury Hewitt, slightly. Total, 14.

Missing.—John Little and Addison Lincoln. Total, 2.

Company B, (Lieutenant E. A. Ford, commanding.) Number engaged: Commanding officers, 1; enlisted men, 52.

Killed.—Private William Buck. Total, 1.

Wounded.—First Lieutenant E. A. Ford, severely; Sergeant C. F. Judd, slightly; Corporal H. Belden, slightly; Privates D. R. Bartlett, slightly; C. Danforth, slightly; J. Burke, severely; J. B. Johnson, severely; G. B. Patterson, severely. Total, 8.

Company C, (First Lieutenant S. B. Hodil, commanding.) Number engaged: Commanding officers, 1; enlisted men, 39.

Wounded.—Sergeants Cunningham Huston, severely, and Cornelius F. Titus, severely; Corporals Frank Eckerman, slightly, and James Carlin, slightly. Privates Richard Hinkle, severely; Samuel Omiveg, severely; Thomas McGunigal, mortally; Thomas Benham, slightly; Joseph Dunham, slightly; James Huston, slightly; John Wright, slightly; Clement Vallandigham, slightly. Total, 12.

Company D, (Captain H. E. Proctor, commanding.) Number engaged: Commanding officers, 2; enlisted men, 32.

Wounded.—First Sergeant and Acting Lieutenant Lloyd Fisher, severely; Corporals William Dunker, slightly, and Arthur Emerson, slightly; Privates Joseph Hist, severely; W. E. Smith, severely; Joseph Davidson, severely; Spencer Sawyer, slightly; and Orlo. C. Matthews, slightly. Total, 9.

Missing.—Private Edward Kelly. Total, 1.

Company E, (First Sergeant F. A. McKay, commanding.) Number engaged: Enlisted men, 42.

Killed.—Sergeant Henry Scinous, Fifer S. M. Winchester, and Private Jesse Quick. Total, 3.

Wounded.—Corporal Richard Neville, slightly; Privates David Cochran, severely; William Nally, severely; John Ryan, severely; Nelson Stebbins, Clyde Wason, severely; Henry Conway, slightly; Thomas Conway, slightly; John Caldwell, slightly; John Canfield, slightly; Robert Davidson, slightly; and Patrick Farrell, slightly. Total, 12.

Missing.—Drummer Warren K. Scott. Total, 1.

Company F, (Captain E. S. Holloway, commanding.) Number engaged: Commanding officers, 2; enlisted men, 50.

Killed.—Privates Joseph Parrish and Sody B. Kidwell. Total, 2.

Wounded.—Sergeant R. A. Gault, slightly; Privates Samuel J. Ewing, severely; Henry Olden, severely; Julius Goff, severely; Charles Edney, severely; M. Fredericks, severely; Jackson Hewitt, severely; David Akins, slightly; Peter Lawrence, slightly; William Joy, slightly; and George A. Webb, slightly. Total, 11.

Missing.—Private James Davis. Total, 1.

Company G, (Captain W. W. Munn, commanding.) Number engaged: Commissioned officers, 2; enlisted men, 53.

Killed.—Privates H. T. Hurs and Joel Strong. Total 2.

Wounded.—Corporals John Bridgeman, William Garrett, D. W. Young, and Private Daniel Worthington, severely; Sergeant H. S. Young, Corporal H. B. Hunt, Privates T. J. Gray, L. Housworth, Charles Moss, O. Stephenson, Martin Searle, M. Watts, and G. Pickett, slightly. Total 13.

Missing.—Horton Smith. Total, 1.

Company H, (Captain William J. Morgan, commanding.) Number engaged: Commissioned officers, 2; enlisted men, 21.

Killed.—Private John C. Lenhart. Total, 1.

Wounded.—Sergeant Henry S. Divlan, Corporals Wm. H. Rossitur, Chester J. Case, Privates Samuel Fishel, Harrison Moore, Wm. H. Prince, and George H. Tifft, severely; Corporal Josiah Staples, Privates George Clark, Joseph Cross, Aquilla Maims, slightly; Emmer E. Rossiter, mortally, since dead. Total 12.

Company I, (First Lieut. L. T. Patchen, commanding,) Number engaged: Commissioned officers, 2; enlisted men, 36.

Killed.—Corporal J. K. Snyder, Private E. Troutman. Total, 2.

Wounded.—Lieutenant L. T. Patchin, severely; Privates Andrew Coucharm and Charles Dougherty, slightly. Total 3.

Company K, (Captain James Horner, commanding.) Number engaged: Commissioned officer, 1; enlisted men, 23.

Wounded.—First Sergeant and Acting Lieutenant H. P. Wollcott, severely; Sergeant John Orr, mortally, since dead; Sergeant L. O. Smith, severely; Privates A. J. Winters and John Thompson, severely, and Daniel Ryan, William McEchran, and J. P. Butter, slightly. Total, 8.

Total commissioned: Killed, 1; wounded 2.

Total enlisted: Killed, 13; wounded, 102; missing, 6.

Total engaged: Commissioned officers, 19; enlisted men, 394.

Of the above list five (5) were wounded in the engagement on Friday evening. Sergeants Titus and Huston were carrying the colors at the time they were wounded. Lieutenant Blythe, quartermaster, was with the regiment during the engagement on Wednesday, and rendered efficient service. Both officers and men displayed great coolness and steady bravery throughout the entire engagement, performing all manœuvres with accuracy and precision; and even when not engaged, and suffering severely from the enemy's artillery, not attempting to move until ordered to do so.

Sergeant McKay, of company E, commanding the company from the commencement of the engagement, and Sergeant McMahon, temporarily in command of company H, displayed great coolness and courage, and are eminently deserving of promotion. Corporal J. P. Patterson, of the color guard, seized the colors when Sergeant Huston fell, and bore them gallantly during the remainder of the engagement.

I have the honor to be your most obedient servant,

AQUILA WILEY,

Lieut. Colonel 41st Ohio Vols., Commanding Regiment.

Major R. L. KIMBERLY,

Acting Assistant Adjutant General.

HEADQUARTERS 3D BRIGADE, 2D DIVISION,
LEFT WING, ARMY OF THE CUMBERLAND,
Near Murfreesboro', Tennessee, January 8, 1863.

SIR: In accordance with duty, I have the honor to submit the report of the part this brigade, under my command, took in the recent battles before Murfreesboro'.

The five regiments—36th Indiana, Major Kinley; 24th Ohio, Colonel Jones; 6th Ohio, Colonel Anderson; 84th Illinois, Colonel Waters; 23d Kentucky, Major Hamrick; aggregate officers and men, 1,788—left our camp near Nashville, December 26, 1862, with the division, bivouacked that night in front of Lavergne, twelve miles distant. Next day, 27th, we moved to the west bank of Stewart's creek, five miles, and my brigade was put in position in front to the right of the pike. The pickets of the enemy were separated from ours by the creek. With light skirmishing, we rested here until Monday morning, the 29th, when we received orders and moved forward in double lines of battle on the right of the pike. The 36th Indiana and 84th Illinois in the front line, wading Stewart's creek, waist-deep to most of the men, to within two and a half miles of Murfreesboro', where we arrived near sunset, with skirmishing all the way, which was only ended by the close of the day. We there rested for the night. At early morn skirmishing again commenced and continued during the day with more severity than before, the artillery taking a heavy part. This ended again with the day. Up to this time the loss in my brigade was ten wounded. During the night it was relieved from the front by the brigade of Colonel Hazen, and retired to the rear to rest, and to be held in reserve.

Thus, on the bright Wednesday morning, December 31, the division, under command of its brave general, at early day was in battle-line. The brigade of General Cruft on the right, that of Colonel Hazen on the left, both in double lines, with my brigade in reserve in rear of the centre, in supporting distance, with the batteries of Cockerill and Parsons in position to support the lines. Whilst we were perfecting our lines in the morning, the divisions of Generals Negley and Rousseau filed by my rear, through a heavy cedar grove which lay in rear of General Cruft's brigade, and immediately up to the right of my brigade, the brigade of Colonel Hazen in an open cotton-field, the pike dividing his left from the division of General Wood, the lines of these two divisions resting nearly perpendicular to the pike. The engagement had been raging fiercely some distance to our right during the early morning, and at near 8 o'clock the clash of arms to our right had so far changed position that I saw the rear of my brigade would soon be endangered. Hence I set to work changing my front to rear, which was done in quick time, with the left, when changed, a little retired, to support the right of Colonel Hazen's brigade, then closely engaged with the enemy, our two brigades forming a V. My brigade was not more than thus formed to the rear before the enemy appeared in heavy lines, pressing the forces of ours that had been engaged to the right of our division on our front in fearful confusion. In this new formation the 6th Ohio and the 36th Indiana were in the front lines, the latter on the right, supported in the second line by the 84th Illinois and 23d Kentucky, with the 24th Ohio in an oblique form, a little to the right of the rear line. In this shape the 36th Indiana and 6th Ohio advanced into the woodland about two hundred and fifty yards, and there met the enemy in overwhelming numbers. Here Major Kinley and Captain Shultz, of the 36th Indiana fell, the former-named badly wounded, the latter killed; Colonel Anderson, of the 6th Ohio, was here wounded, and his adjutant, A. G. Williams, and Lieutenant Forster fell dead, with several others of their comrades. These two regiments were forced from the woodland, and retired to the right, in direction of the pike, while the other three regiments, aided by the eight-gun battery, commanded by Lieutenant Parsons, with the efficient aid of Lieutenant Huntington and Cushing, poured a galling fire into the ranks of the pursuing enemy, causing them to break in confusion and retire back to the woods out of our reach, leaving the field covered with their dead and dying, with the heavy loss of the 36th Indiana and 6th Ohio lying with them on the bloody field. After some half an hour or three-quarters the enemy renewed his attempts to advance, but was again repulsed with heavy loss on both sides. After this, then, between 11 and 12 o'clock, the enemy not appearing in our immediate front, and the lines of our forces that had retired or been driven from the right, by this time were reformed parallel with the pike, so that the front of the brigade was again changed, so as to assist the brigade of Colonel Hazen in the direction as formed in the morning. The 24th Ohio and 36th Indiana were soon thrown forward near the pike and had a terible conflict with the enemy. Here Colonel Jones and Major Terry both fell and were carried off the field in a dying condition. Each regiment of the brigade from this, until night closed the awful scene, alternately took its part in holding the position that we occupied in the morning. The enemy having gained the heavy cedar woods to the right, where we first took position in the morning, it became necessary to so change our position as to not be in reach of small arms from that woodland; hence at nightfall the centre of the front line of the brigade laid on the pike and diagonally across the same, fronting to the southeast, our left resting at the right of the lines of General Wood's division; we were then a little retired, and the centre of the brigade, about 250 yards to the left where we commenced in the morning. We ceased fighting for the night, with the front lines on the pike. During the day each of the regiments, having exhausted, had to replenish their ammunition, many of them having fired over 100 rounds.

When Major Kinley, of the 36th Indiana, fell, nearly at the commencement in the morning, the command devolved upon Captain Woodward; and upon the fall of Colonel Jones and Major Terry, of the 24th Ohio, Captain Weller was left in command. Although I was at Shiloh, and commanded in that battle, at the head of General Buell's army, and fought throughout that battle with that army, yet this battle, the last day of the old year, was by far the most terrible and bloody in my command that I have ever witnessed. During the latter part of the night, or rather in the early morning, of the 1st day of January, 1863, our whole line was retired, for a more eligible position, six or seven hundred yards, and my brigade was relieved from the front, and retired for rest.

During Thursday, January 1, we were ordered across the north bank of Stone river to support a division on the extreme left of our line, an attack being anticipated in that direction, but returned to our resting place before night, no attack being made that day. On the next day, January 2, in the forenoon, we were again ordered across the river to support the division there in position, with its right resting on the river bank, and its lines (double lines) formed at right angles to the river, extending therefrom about one-half a mile. The river below the right of the division line, about 800 yards, changes direction, running about one-half mile in the rear, and nearly parallel to the lines of the division formed as above. When my brigade arrived on the ground, I was requested to put it in position so as to protect the left flank of the division referred to, and repel any attack that might be made in that direction. The 23d Kentucky was posted to the left of the division spoken of, about two hundred yards retired; the 24th Ohio, three hundred yards to its rear, fronting same way; the 36th Indiana to the rear of the 24th Ohio, fronting diagonally to the flank of the other two, the right of the 36th Indiana distant from the left of the 24th Ohio about 150 yards, and with directions specially given to each of these regiments to change front as the exigencies of the case might require in case of an attack. The 84th Illinois and 6th Ohio were placed 150 yards from the left of the 36th Indiana in one line, fronting the same direction of the 24th and 23d, as well as in the same direction of the division so posted as above, to our right and front, the right of the 84th Illinois resting on the bluff at the river with the 3d Wisconsin battery, near the left and front of the 84th; the 6th Ohio on the left of the 84th Illinois. Thus in position, I took the precaution to have each regiment hurriedly throw before them barricades of such materials, "fences, buildings," &c., as were at command. About 3½ p. m. the enemy came in against the division in front and right (as above shown in position) in strong force, perhaps in three lines, and with three batteries distributed along the front, and a heavy contest ensued, which lasted from one-half to three-fourths of an hour, when the lines of the division gave way in considerable confusion, retiring toward the river, and many of them breaking through the lines of my brigade. I went to my front regiments and superintended the changing of their fronts respectively, so as to meet the enemy the best we could, coming from an unexpected direction, which, to some extent, threw the 23d Kentucky and 24th Ohio, my advanced front regiments, into confusion, and caused them to retire toward the left of the main line of the brigade, but they kept up a strong fire on the advancing enemy as they retired. The 36th Indiana changed its front, and, as the enemy's lines came near, opened on them a deadly fire; but on they came, until in reach of the 84th Illinois and 6th Ohio, behind their barricades, when both these regiments saluted them with a terrible fire; and by this time all my regiments were engaged, and the masses of the enemy began to falter and soon broke in disorder and commenced their flight back over the farm they had so fiercely advanced upon, pursued by the 36th Indiana, 23d Kentucky, and 24th Ohio to the line occupied by the out-picket posts of the division before the battle commenced. Here night overtook us, the battle was over, and the enemy was gone beyond the reach of our guns. Colonel Hazen's brigade crossed the river to our rear to support us about the time of the enemy's retreat, and moved closely after my pursuing regiments to give assistance if needed. Some other forces collected or crossed the river to my right, and moved up the river bank in pursuit of the enemy as my regiments advanced; what forces these were I have not learned. The battery posted near the brigade at the commencement of this day's fight fired a few rounds and took a hasty leave from the field, and I have not made its acquaintance since.

Artillery from the opposite side of the river rendered valuable aid by playing upon the enemy in his advance and retreat. Our loss this day was not large compared with that of the 31st. That of the enemy was very heavy.

I cannot too favorably notice the coolness and promptness of each and every field officer of the brigade. They seemed to vie with each other which should most promptly execute every command, without regard to danger. And the line officers and men of the respective regiments appeared not to fear or know danger. New and old regiments alike acted the heroic part and braved every peril.

Captain Weller, in command of the 24th Ohio, fell at his post on the last battle-field and left Captain Cockerill in command, who bravely and skilfully performed his whole duty. And as much may be said of Captain Woodward, who succeeded to the command of the 36th Indiana upon the fall of Major Kinley at a critical and perilous moment in the first day's engagement.

I am under lasting obligations to my staff and orderlies for their efficent assistance during these several days' fighting. Captain Peden, 36th Indiana, is entitled to great credit for his aid rendered me up to the time he fell wounded on the 31st.

Lieutenant J. P. Duke, of the 23d Kentucky, also on my staff, deserves a high meed of praise for promptness and aid rendered me at all times during the whole of these engagements. Dr. Silas H. Kersey, acting brigade surgeon, with unsurpassed industry and skill, has rendered invaluable assistance to the wounded.

My mounted orderlies, Frank Brough, Frank Webb, Albert Woods, William

D. Smith, Martin Mann, and Lewis Miller, of the 2d Indiana cavalry, George Shirk and Isaac Biglow, of the 36th Indiana infantry, rendered me valuable service. But I am left to remember and lament with friends the fall, in this mighty struggle for human prowess, of such brave spirits as Colonel Jones, Major Terry, Captain Weller, Captain Shultz, Captain King, Adjutant Williams, Lieutenant Foster, Lieutenant Ball, Lieutenant Abercrombie, and others whose earthly conflicts have closed with these battles. I may truthfully add that I mourn with those who mourn over these irreparable losses. To the brave wounded whose fate may or may not be uncertain, you have my earnest prayers for a speedy restoration to health and usefulness.

The casualties of the brigade, as near as can be ascertained, are as follows:

Regiments.	Officers killed.	Officers wounded.	Men killed.	Men wounded.	Men missing.	Total.
24th Ohio	4	4	10	68	12	98
23d Kentucky	......	3	8	50	22	83
84th Illinois	2	5	33	119	8	167
36th Indiana	2	6	23	85	18	134
6th Ohio	2	4	23	134	14	177
Total	10	22	97	456	74	659

Lists of which, with the reports of the regimental commanders for further details, are herewith respectfully forwarded.

I have the honor to remain your obedient servant,

W. GROSE,

Colonel Commanding 3*d Brigade,* (*Old* 10*th.*)

Captain D. W. NORTON,

Acting Assistant Adjutant General, 2d Division.

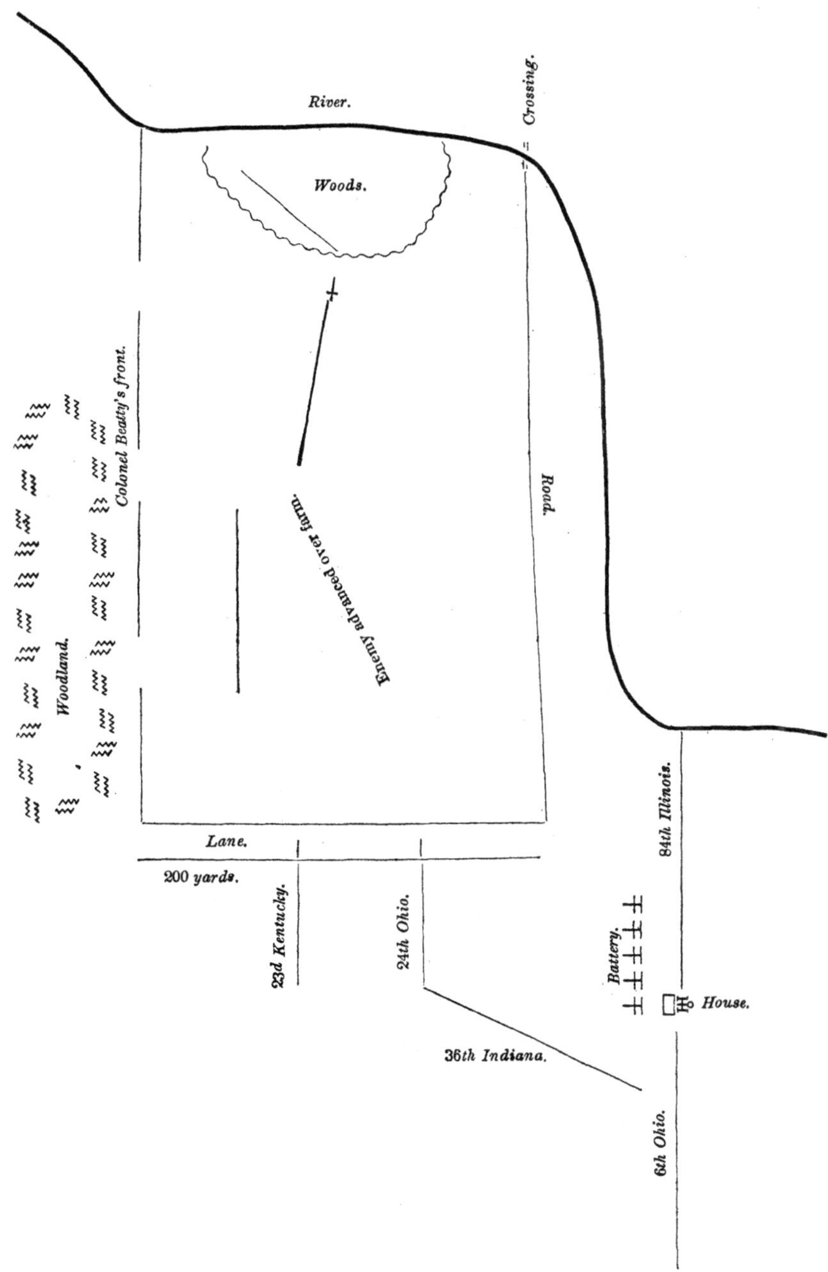

The above shows the position on the 2d of January, before the battle over the river, of Colonel Beatty's division and Colonel Grose's brigade. Barricades before regiments of brigade.

HEADQUARTERS MEDICAL DEPARTMENT 3D BRIGADE,
January 9, 1863.

DEAR SIR: I have the honor to transmit the following list of casualties suffered by your command in the recent series of engagements with the enemy before Murfreesboro', to wit:

6th regiment Ohio volunteers.

Killed	25
Wounded	124

24th regiment Ohio volunteers.

Killed	12
Wounded	97

36th regiment Indiana volunteers.

Killed	20
Wounded	95

23d regiment Kentucky volunteers.

Killed	7
Wounded	50

84th regiment Illinois volunteers.

Killed	35
Wounded	119
Total	584

Before closing this report, permit me respectfully to call attention to the faithful manner in which the regimental medical officers of the several regiments composing the 3d brigade have discharged the arduous duties incumbent on them under circumstances the most trying, viz: T. S. Badge, assistant surgeon 36th regiment Indiana volunteer infantry, was assigned the duty of administering anæsthetics, which he has so far accomplished in every operation without producing any untoward symptoms in a single case, and at the same time attended to the dressing of all the slighter wounds of his own regiment, thus performing double duty by day and night since the commencement of the battle.

I would also make honorable mention of A. M. Morrison, assistant surgeon 23d regiment Kentucky volunteers, who was appointed to keep the register, which necessarily occupied a large portion of his time, notwithstanding which, by constant industry and energy, his wounded have been well cared for.

Assistant Surgeon McDill, of the 84th Illinois, had so large a list of wounded that his time has been almost wholly occupied with them; they, too, have been as well attended as circumstances would permit.

We have, up to this date, a smaller proportional list of deaths from wounds after entering hospital than any other division hospital in the left wing of this army corps. Two cases of erysipelas have appeared in stumps—one of the arm, near the shoulder; the other the leg. They were immediately separated from the other inmates and cared for in a tent to themselves. The utmost care and vigilance is constantly evercised over the wounded that the limited room and means will permit.

I have, sir, the honor to be, respectfully, your obedient servant,

L. H. KERSEY,
Acting Surgeon 3d Brigade.

W. GROSE,
Colonel Commanding 3d Brigade.

HEADQUARTERS 84TH ILLINOIS VOLUNTEERS,
Near Murfreesboro', January 6, 1863.

SIR: Early in the morning of December 31, by direction of Colonel Grose, commanding 3d brigade, my command took position on the left of the brigade, front perpendicular to the pike, with the 23d Kentucky on my right and the 24th Ohio in my rear. In a short time it became evident that the division on our right was being rapidly driven in, whereupon I changed front to the right and got my command under the protection of a ledge of rocks. The enemy soon appeared in the cedar woods in our front, and we opened fire upon him. We here had five men severely wounded. Lieutenant Parsons's battery having changed position from our left to the pike in its rear, I retired my left to support the battery, moving my right to the position before occupied by my left. About 12 o'clock, the battery having moved forward on the pike nearly to the cotton-field in front, by direction of Colonel Grose, we moved forward to support the battery on the right, and immediately commenced firing upon the enemy lying across the cotton-field and meadow in our front. During this time there were two regiments of some other division upon my right, engaging the enemy somewhat to their right, and Stevens's Pennsylvania battery was in rear of my centre. Both these regiments gave way and left the field in considerable confusion, leaving Stevens's battery without any support. I immediately retired the right of my regiment so as to protect this battery as far as possible, until it could be taken from the field. It had done excellent service, and was not to be lost without a struggle. As soon as it was started from the field I again retired my right so as to have the protection of a ledge some sixty paces to the rear. From this ledge we kept up a steady fire upon the enemy, now occupying the skirt of the cedar woods in our front, until Lieutenant Parsons's battery, for want of ammunition or support on his left, was compelled to retire beyond the pike. While occupying this position we suffered terribly from the fire of stragglers who had sought cover behind some cabins in our rear, and were firing wildly at the enemy over our line. Captain Higgins and others of my command called to me that their men were being wounded by the firing from the cabins. I reluctantly withdrew my command to the railroad, some three hundred and fifty yards distant, and from thence, by Colonel Grose's direction, to some woods to the left, where we rested for the night. At the ledge where we made our last stand we left 24 of our dead. In the fight on the 2d instant we were posted by Colonel Grose on the left of his brigade line, and I cannot report anything that did not occur under the observation of Colonel Grose, who on this occasion, as on the 31st, was wherever duty called him, regardless of danger. After the enemy commenced retreating I advanced my command to the cornfield in our front, and there learned to my surprise that our ammunition was exhausted. We had fired fifty rounds. My command, on the morning of the 31st ultimo, consisted of three field and staff and 21 company officers and 336 enlisted men. Lieutenants Ball and Abercrombie, two as gallant gentlemen as ever fought beneath the "stars and stripes," fell at their posts in the first engagement. On the 31st we lost in killed thirty-five officers and men, and had wounded one hundred and twenty-one. On the 2d we had five wounded. On both occasions my command, as well as the other regiments of Colonel Grose's brigade, was nearly crushed by the herd of officers and men of other divisions, as they fled, panic-stricken, before the enemy; yet it stood like a "human wood," and officers and men vied with each other in beating back the fugitives.

To the coolness and fearlessness of Lieutenant Colonel Hamer, Major Morton, and my company officers, and the bravery of our men, are we indebted for whatever of credit the regiment may deserve. In this connexion I cannot omit the opportunity of bearing testimony to the gallantry of Lieutenant Parsons and the efficiency of his battery.

I herewith enclose a list of my killed and wounded, which is as nearly correct as I can now make. Many slightly wounded are not included in the list.

Very respectfully, your obedient servant,

L. H. WATERS,
Colonel, Commanding 84th Illinois Volunteers.

Captain R. SOUTHGATE,
Assistant Adjutant General, 3d Brigade.

List of the killed, wounded, and missing, of the 84th. regiment Illinois volunteers, in the battle of Stone river, near Murfreesboro'.

Lieutenant Colonel Hamer, wounded in breast; Major Morton, wounded in left knee, both slightly.

Company A.—Killed: Private A. Macumber. Wounded: Lieutenant T. G. Wisdom, in both legs; First Sergeant L. N. Mitchell, ankle; Third Sergeant B .E. Ball, right thumb; Fifth Sergeant, Willis Edson, shoulder; Corporal J. B. Wortman, shoulder; Privates Thomas J. Shepherd, shoulder; C. C. Roberts, finger; Wilford Mitchell, left hand; George Parks, left hand; D. J. Tuggle, left hand; Philo Slyter, right thumb; Samuel R. Spears, right arm, amputated; John Crain, neck, slight; J. G. Waters, left ankle; Samuel Patrick, lung, severely; J. C. Pelsor, right hand; Joseph Deerdoff, back, slightly. Total: 1 killed, 17 wounded.

Company F.—Killed: Corporal Eli Ewell; Privates Christopher Enders and Vachall Benson. Wounded: Lieutenant Frost, left foot; Corporals D. W. Litchfield, head and neck; William Walker, back; Joseph Price, neck, slight; Privates T. B. Turner, right shoulder; M. Swearingen, thigh and side; R. M. Miller, right shoulder; William A. Knock, left thigh; William A. Thomas, shoulder; V. B. Clark, right arm; William T. Foster, in foot. Missing: William Shaw. Total: 3 killed, 11 wounded, 1 missing.

Company D.—Killed: Second Sergeant Luke A. Perry; Privates Samuel Luper, J. Van Wisecup and William Franklin. Wounded: Captain M. N. Davis, neck and arm; First Sergeant Miller, slightly; Fifth Sergeant Thomas Sprigg, right side and arm; Privates James Furlong, hip and back; B. A. McCoy, left leg; Aaron Stinson, left leg; Alexander Mallard, right thigh; E. D. Oldfield, right arm; G. B. Clayton, right thigh; James Jones, knee; William Briscow, shoulder; John Stinson, back, slight; John Logston, head, slight. Total: 4 killed, 13 wounded.

Company I.—Killed: Privates Crawford Scott, Thomas J. Galloway, Archibald B. Clark, and Dirk Miller. Wounded: Corporals D. E. Alexander, head; A. S. Horner, arm and feet; Samuel Cane, left hand; David Slagel, severely; Privates George M. Stevens, left leg; W. H. Myers, breast; H. Higley, neck and hip; D. Manlove, right shoulder; W. D. Crawford, right leg and left lung, severely; Cyrus Johnson, severely; Nelson Cane, slightly; Dudley Shahoney, slightly; John Bogles, slightly. Total: 4 killed, 13 wounded.

Company C.—Killed: Color Sergeant George F. Yocumb; Private Richard W. Pennington. Wounded: Privates Abram Purdam, left thigh; A. Markham, head; G. W. White, thigh; William T. Harris, face; G. W. McDaniel, shoulder; Daniel Avery, leg, slightly; Thomas J. Martin, back, slightly; W. M. Gleason, leg; Nelson Butcher, thigh; William A. Chapman, slightly. Total: 2 killed, 10 wounded.

Company H—Killed: First Lieutenant Luther T. Ball, Second Lieutenant Henry E. Abercrombie, First Sergeant A. J. Hellings, Second Sergeant J. M.

Widner, and Privates Bigelow Kyle, William Lipton, George McFarren, Henderson Wooliver, and James Kidwell. Wounded: Captain J. C. Pepper, ankle, slightly; Fourth Sergeant W. M. McCandless; Corporals H. C. White, right leg; J. N. White, slightly; Privates E. L. Spicer, face; Joseph Ballien, thigh; Garret Dehaven, thigh and arm; Eli Ditwilier, slightly; William Fuller, leg; John Gilrain, leg; W. H. Boggness, arm; Joshua Brown, neck and shoulder; Lawrence McMauris, left arm; Martin Sullivan, leg; Peter McLane, thigh; Thomas Miller, slightly; John Desch, severely; W. H. Boggs, slightly; Thomas C. Oden, side. Missing: Avery Kyle. Total: 9 killed, 19 wounded, 1 missing.

Company E.—Killed: Privates David Davis and Jacob Worth. Wounded: First Lieutenant H. P. Roberts, leg and side; First Sergeant S. S. Slater, hip, lungs, and foot; Third Sergeant J. M. Will, left arm; Privates Alfred Shannon, lungs; Enoch Lightle, fingers; S. A. Malone, hip; David Huffman, thigh; Thomas Abbott, thigh; Thomas Bagby, wrist; John Conoway, face. Total: 2 killed, 10 wounded.

Company K.—Killed: First Sergeant S. G. Plumer, Corporal Samuel Wilkins, and Private John Tucker. Wounded: Lieutenant M. H. Mills, head; Corporal George Bell, groin and thigh; Privates Nels. Pearson, hand; William Stanley, breast; William J. Allaman, shoulder and leg; Amos Ray, arm; George Graff, knee and leg; S. A. Snyder, hip; William Abramson, hand. Total: 3 killed, 9 wounded.

Company G.—Killed: Corporals Charles Spanier and Benjamin C. Pierce, and Privates George Gordon and Richard Parrott. Wounded: Corporal Charles W. Green, head, severely; Privates A. Beck, shoulder; W. R. Pinkerton, body; George W. Tompkins, thigh, (amputated;) John G. Curtis, hip; Lafayette Crandall, neck; Albert Hoskinson, leg; R. W. Kelley, hand, Total: 4 killed, 8 wounded.

Company B.—Killed: Privates John Sellers, George Murphy, and John W. Miner. Wounded: First Lieutenant L. L. Scott, left knee; Corporals P. R. Miner, hip, slightly; David Harland, left leg; Privates Thomas A. Walters, thigh; David Hughes, elbow; Isaac Grewell, groin; Robert Chaddock, head; Seymour Moore, side; Levi Bartholomew, hand; Coleman Mitchell, shoulder; Abner Wileman, lung; Eleazer Walker, back; Levi Fancher, arm, slightly; James Belford, head, slightly. Missing: Joseph Parks and Henry Johnson. Total: 3 killed, 14 wounded, 2 missing.

RECAPITULATION.

	Officers engaged.	Men engaged.	Killed.	Wounded.	Missing.	Total engaged.	Total loss.
Company A	2	37	1	17	----	-----	-----
F	2	37	3	11	1	-----	-----
D	2	34	4	13	----	-----	-----
I	2	33	4	13	----	-----	-----
C	1	29	2	10	----	-----	-----
H	3	51	9	19	1	-----	-----
E	2	27	2	10	----	-----	-----
K	2	28	3	9	----	-----	-----
G	3	27	4	8	4	-----	-----
B	2	33	3	14	2	-----	-----
	21	336	35	124	8	357	167

Number of killed, wounded, and missing of the 84th regiment Illinois volunteers, in the battle of Stone river, near Murfreesboro'.

Lieutenant Colonel Hamer, wounded in left breast, slightly; Major Morton, wounded in left leg, slightly.

Company A.—Killed: Private A. Newcomer. Wounded: Lieutenant F. G. Wisdom, both legs, severely; First Sergeant L. N. Mitchell, left ankle, slightly; Third Sergeant E. B. Rall, right thumb, slightly; Fifth Sergeant Willis Edson, right shoulder, severely; Corporal J. B. Wortman, shoulder, severely; Privates Thomas J. Shepard, right shoulder, slightly; C. C. Roberts, fingers, slightly; Wilferd Mitchell, left hand, severely; George Parks, left hand, slightly; D. J. Tuggel, left hand, slightly; Philo Slighter, slightly; Samuel R. Spears, right arm amputated; John Crane, neck, slightly; J. G. Walters, left ankle, Samuel Patrick, left lung, severely; J. C. Pelsor, right hand, slightly; Joseph Deardorff, back, slightly. Total: 1 killed, 17 wounded.

Company F.—Killed: Corporal Eli Elwell, and Privates Christopher Adams and Vachal Benson. Wounded: Lieutenant Frost, left foot, slightly; Corporals D. W. Litchfield, head and neck, severely; William Walker, back, severely; Privates T. B. Turner, right arm, severely; M. Swearingen, thigh and side, slightly; R. M. Miller, right shoulder, severely; William Knock, left thigh, severely; William A. Thomas, shoulder, severely; V. B. Clark, right arm, severely; Joseph Price, neck, slightly; William F. Foster. Total: 3 killed, 11 wounded, and 1 missing.

Company D.—Killed: Second Sergeant Luke A. Perry, and Privates Samuel Leeper, J. Vanwisecup, and William Franklin. Wounded: Captain M. W. Davis, neck and arm, severely; First Sergeant Miller, slightly; Fifth Sergeant Thomas Sprigg, right arm, slightly; Privates James Furlong, hips and back, severely; B. A. McCoy, left leg; Aaron Stinson, left leg, slightly; Alexander Mallard, right thigh, slightly; E. D. Oldfield, right arm, slightly; J. B. Claton, right thigh, severely; James Jones, knee, severely; William Briscow, shoulder; John Stinson, back, slightly; John Lugston, head, slightly. Total: 4 killed, 13 wounded.

Company I.—Killed: Privates Thomas J. Galloway, Archibald B. Clark, and Dirk Miller. Wounded: Corporals D. A. Alexander, slightly; A. S. Horney, arm and feet, slightly; Samuel Cane, left hand; D. N. Slagel, left arm, severely; Privates George M. Stevens, slightly; Private W. H. Myers, breast, slightly; H. Higly, neck and hip, slightly; D. Manlove, right shoulder, severely; W. D. Crawford, left lung and right leg, severely; Cyrus Johnson, right foot, slightly; Dudley Shahoney, hip, slightly. Total: 4 killed, 11 wounded.

Company C.—Killed: Color Sergeant George Yocum and Private Richard W. Pennington. Wounded: Privates Abram Purdan, left thigh, severely; A. Markton, slightly; G. W. White, slightly; Wm. T. Harris, face, severely; G. W. McDaniel, left shoulder, slightly; Daniel Avery, leg, slightly; Thomas J. Martin, back, slightly; W. M. Gleason, left leg, slightly; Nelson Butcher, thigh, severely. Total: 2 killed, 9 wounded.

Company H.—Killed: First Lieutenant L. T. Ball, Second Lieutenant H. E. Abercrombie, First Sergeant A. I. Hellings, Second Sergeant J. M. Widner, and Privates Biglow Kyle, William Lipton, George McFarren, Henderson Wooliver, and James Kidwell. Wounded: Captain J. C. Pepper, left heel, slightly; Fourth Sergeant W. W. McCandless, right knee, amputated; Corporals H. C. White, right leg, slightly; and J. N. White, slightly; Privates E. L. Spear, face, slightly; Joseph Ballein, hip, slightly; Garrot Dehaven, right leg; Wm. Fuller, right leg, slightly; John Gilrain, leg, slightly; W. M. Boggness, arm, slightly; Joshua Brown, neck and shoulder, severely; Lawrence

McMannis, left arm, slightly; Martin Sullivan, leg, slightly; John Desh, severely; W. H. Boggs, slightly; Thomas C. Odea, side. Missing: Avery Kyle. Total: 9 killed, 15 wounded, 1 missing.

Company E.—Killed: Privates David Davis and Jacob Worth. Wounded: First Lieutenant Hiram P. Roberts, right side and right leg, severely; First Sergeant S. Slater, right lung, left hip, and left foot, severely; Third Sergeant J. M. Will, left arm, severely; Privates Alfred Sherman, left lung, severely; Enoch Lightle, fingers, slightly; S. A. Malone, spent cannon ball, slightly; David Hofman, thigh, slightly; Thomas Abbott, thigh, severely; Thomas Bagby, wrist, slightly; John Conaway, face, severely. Total: 2 killed, 10 wounded.

Company K.—Killed: First Sergeant S. G. Plummer, Corporal Samuel Wilkins, and Private John Tucker. Wounded: Second Lieutenant M. H. Mills, head, slightly; Corporal George Bell, through privates, severely; Privates Nelson Pierson, right hand, slightly; Wm. Stanley, left lung, severely; W. J. Almon, right leg, mortally; Amos Ray, arm, slightly; George Graft, right thigh, slightly; S. A. Snider, left hip, slightly; Wm. Abrehampson, right hand, slightly. Total: 3 killed, 9 wounded.

Company G.—Killed: Corporals Charles Spanier and Benjamin Pierce, and Privates George Gordon and Richard Parrott. Wounded: Corporal Charles Green, right eye, severely; Privates A. Beck, left side, slightly; W. R. Pinkerton, right shoulder, severely; George Tompkins, left leg, amputated; John Curtis, right thigh and leg, slightly; A. Hoskinson, left leg, amputated; R. W. Kelly, left hand, slightly. Missing: Lafayette Crandal, John Hensley, and Perry Wycoff. Total: 4 killed, 7 wounded, 3 missing.

Company B.—Killed: Privates John Sellier, George Murphy, and John W. Miner. Wounded: First Lieutenant W. W. Scott, left knee, slightly; Corporals P. R. Miner, hip, slightly; and David Harlin, left leg, slightly; Privates Thomas Walters, left thigh, slightly; David Hews, left arm, severely; Coleman Mitchell, left arm and shoulder, slightly; Isaac W. Grewell, in privates, severely; Robert Chaddock, in head, severely; Seymore More, side, slightly; Levi Bartholomew, hand, slightly; Abner Wildman, lungs, severely; Ebenezer Walker, back, severely; Levi Fancher, arm, slightly; James Belferd, head, slightly. Missing: Joseph Parks and Henry Johnson. Total: 3 killed, 14 wounded, 2 missing.

Recapitulation.

	Killed.	Wounded.	Missing.
Company A	1	17	..
Company F	3	11	1
Company D	4	13	..
Company I	4	12	..
Company C	2	9	..
Company H	9	15	1
Company E	2	10	..
Company K	3	9	..
Company G	4	7	3
Company B	3	14	2
	35	117	7

Total loss, 159.

HEADQUARTERS 23D KENTUCKY INFANTRY,
Camp in front of Murfreesboro', Tennessee, January 5, 1863.

SIR: I hereby beg leave to make my report of the part taken by the 23d Kentucky infantry in the two battles before Murfreesboro', 31st December, 1862, and 2d January, 1863. On the 26th of December, 1862, we left our camp near Nashville, with 282 men, and took up our line of march, with the brigade, under the command of Colonel Wm. Grose, in the rear of the 6th Ohio; halted near Lavergne at dusk, where we bivouacked during the night. On the morning of the 27th my regiment was detailed as guard to General Palmer's division train; at night we took our position with the brigade. On the 28th (Sunday) we moved to the front with our brigade, and were placed as reserve to the 84th Illinois. On the 29th we moved forward, crossed Stewart's creek, waist deep, and followed the 84th Illinois, in line of battle; remained in front all night with the brigade. On the 30th I was ordered forward some four hundred yards, to support Parsons's regular battery on the right, where we remained until dusk, when we were relieved, and ordered some four hundred yards to the rear, and into the timber for rest.

On the 31st (Wednesday) I was ordered to form line on the left of the 6th Ohio, fronting the enemy's battery in front, when the fire becoming heavy upon our right and rear, Colonel Grose ordered me to change my front, which I immediately did, facing the direction of the enemy's fire, when I was ordered to unsling knapsacks. I was then ordered to move forward and support the 6th Ohio, which I did, moving as far as the skirt of the wood on my left, when General Palmer rode up, and ordered me to retire to the support of Parsons's battery. At this time the stampede from the right became general, from the woods in our front. I had some fear of being carried away with it, but found no difficulty in moving my men to the support of the battery, forming my right on the battery, and my left resting on the wood. The enemy appeared on our front, and poured in a galling fire upon us, with the intention, it seemed, to charge the battery. Some regiment formed upon my left, resting in the woods. The battery opened a cross fire upon the enemy, as did also my regiment and the one upon my left, driving him back in great confusion and with heavy loss. The battery retired, when I was ordered to change my front and form behind a ledge of rock, and cause my men to lie down and await the approach of the enemy. The enemy's fire becoming very heavy, I was ordered to fall back with my command to the railroad, in rear of the 24th Ohio, which I did slowly and in good order.

After remaining there for some thirty minutes, I was ordered to move forward, and relieve the 24th Ohio, whose ammunition was exhausted. This I did under a heavy fire from the enemy. That position I held for fifty-five minutes, driving the enemy back with my superior guns, under cover of the woods, when we were relieved and ordered to the rear for ammunition. At 5½ o'clock p. m. I was again ordered to the front, when I took the position in the wood, in front of the railroad, occupied by me before I was ordered to the rear, which point I occupied until I was relieved at 1 o'clock a. m., when I was again ordered to the rear for refreshments and rest. On the 1st January, 1863, I was ordered to the rear and centre of Van Cleve's and Wood's divisions, where I remained until 12 o'clock m., when I was ordered to cross the river to our left, where I remained until 2½ o'clock p. m., when I was ordered to recross the river and go into camp for a night's rest.

On January 2, 1863, I was again ordered with the brigade to cross the river, when Colonel Grose ordered me to take a position behind a fence, on the extreme front and left. I threw out three companies as skirmishers. I remained in position until 3½ o'clock p. m., when the enemy appeared, driving back the forces upon my right. The 59th Ohio broke and ran across my front, and some of them over my men, who were lying behind the fence in line. I saw that the enemy were driving back the forces upon my right, so I changed my front and opened upon him. I had no sooner done so than a battery opened upon my left with grape, and at the same time a fire of small arms was opened upon my left and rear, placing me within a cross fire. I then attempted to move my men back to the brigade, when some stragglers raised the cry, "*We are surrounded*," and I found it was impossible to keep my men in order; they there fell back in confusion. I succeeded in rallying most of them in the woods on the left of the brigade; the balance, with a few exceptions, rallied and returned.

The enemy were then driven back with heavy loss. I then moved forward beyond my original position, keeping open a heavy fire upon him. When we halted we were five hundred yards in advance and to the right of our original position, and occupying the ground of our former picket line, which position, we held until dark, when, being relieved, we returned to our position occupied before the engagement, having lost in the two days' engagements 8 killed, 51 wounded, and 22 missing; the names of them you will find attached. Chaplain Wm. H. Black deserves especial praise for the manner in which he acted, being always at his post, and rendering aid and comfort to the wounded. both while the fight was going on and during the two succeeding nights, Doctor A. M. Morrison also deserves great praise for his kindness and attention to the wounded at all hours, day and night. My officers, line and staff, acted with great coolness and bravery, with a few exceptions, which I cannot particularize in this report.

I have the honor to remain your most obedient servant,

THOMAS H. HAMSICK,
Major, Commanding Regiment.

Captain R. SOUTHGATE,
Acting Assistant Adjutant General, 3*d Brigade,* 2*d Divison.*

List of killed and wounded.

Officers wounded.—Captain W. G. J. Holden, slightly in the leg; Lieutenant T. B. Black, severely in the arm; and Lieutenant Hennessey, slightly in the head.

Killed.—Corporals Henry Link, Company E, and John Jones, Company F; Sergeants Jasper Hutchinson and Jasper E. Botts, and Private John Noll, Company A; Private Rudolph Kerides, Company C; Privates William Smith and Nicholas Korrell, Company B.

Wounded.—Company A: First Sergeant William B. Sherrill, leg, severely; Sergeant George M. Green, side, severely; Corporal John E. Calvert, breast, slightly: Privates Patrick Marcey, foot, slightly; W. H. Williamson, leg, severely, Jarrett H. Lowe, hand, severely; and George W. Collins, leg, slightly. Company B: Sergeant Lambert Scott, neck, severely; Privates Joseph Rock, severely in breast; and Jonathan R. F. Poston, in leg, severely. Company C: Privates John Dobbs, in neck, seriously; and Michael Ryan, in head, slightly. Company D: First Sergeant Reuben Hamer, severely in abdomen; Corporals John T. Bell, slightly in head; and James J. Fryer, leg, slightly; Privates John Wilson, head, slightly; Simon Wilson, hand, slightly; Julius Hay, arm, slightly; Lewis Sheanshang, foot, severely; and Christian Steger, breast, slightly. Company E: Sergeant L. G. Miller, two ribs broken; Corporal Frank Brockman, slightly in the head; Privates Antony Millisch, severely in shoulder and arm; Henry Beatty, flesh wound in leg; A. G. McKay, slightly in hand; and W. H. Hook, mortally in head, by shell. Company F: Sergeant John Henryhan, left side, severely;

Privates John Lux, left thigh, severely; John Stickrod, left side, severely; Patrick Ryan, left arm, severely; and Nicholas Gregory, head, slightly. Company G: Corporal John Cullamer, leg, slightly; and Private Moses Harrison, jr., abdomen, dangerously. Company H: Privates Thomas Smith, both legs, severely; and Thomas Hollinshead, leg, severely. Company I: Privates John Weedwright, leg, severely; Joseph Peak, leg, severely; Joseph Howell, leg, slightly: Joshua Glover, arm; John Harrington, head, mortally; Felix Briggs, ankle, very severely; James Cooper, leg, severely; and George Miller, hand, slightly. Company K: First Sergeant William Spencer, arm, severely; Corporal William A. Plummer, leg, severely; Privates Samuel J. Crawford, shoulder, severely; David M. Evans, foot, severely; Reuben Jones, hip, severely; Soloman Purvis, finger shot off; and James H. McKee, finger shot off.

A list of the killed and wounded of the 23d regiment Kentucky volunteers, United States army, in the four days' battle near Murfreesboro', Tennessee.

Killed.—Company A: Sergeants Jasper Hutchison, Jasper E. Botts, and Private John Noll. Company B: Privates William Smith and Nicholas Corell. Company E: Corporal W. H. Link. Company F: Corporal John Jones.

Wounded.—Company A: First Sergeant W. B Sherrell, severely; Sergeant George M. Green, slightly; Corporal J. E. Calvert, slightly; Privates J. H. Lowe, slightly; George W. Collins, severely; W. H. Williamson, severely; and Patrick Marcey. Company B: Sergeant Lambert Scott, severely; Privates Joseph Rock, severely; and J. R. J. Poston, severely. Company C: Captain W. G. Holden, slightly; and Private John Hobbs, slightly. Company D: First Sergeant Reuben Hamer, slightly; Corporals John Bell, slightly; and James J. Fryer, slightly; Privates John Wilson, slightly; Julius Hay, severely; Lewis Shingshang, slightly; and Simon Wilson, slightly. Company E: Sergeant L. G. Miller, slightly; Corporal F. Brockman, slightly; Privates W. H. Hook, mortally; Henry Beatty, severely; and Antony Millische, severely. Company F: Sergeant J. Henryhan, severely; Corporal William Christian, slightly; Privates Nicholas Gregory, slightly; Patrick Ryan, severely; and John Lux, slightly. Company G: Privates M. Harrison, mortally; and John Cullum, slightly. Company H: Privates S. J. Smith, severely; and J. Hollingshead, severely. Company I: Second Lieutenant F. A. Black, slightly; Privates George Miller, slightly; James Cooper, slightly; John Wiedright, severely; Joseph Peak, slightly; F. L. Briggs, severely; J. Harrington, severely; Joseph Howell, slightly; J. W. Glover, slightly; and James Hugo, slightly Company K: First Sergeant William H. Spencer, slightly; Corporal W. A. Plumber, severely; Privates D. J. Crawford, severely; S. Purvis, slightly; James McKee, slightly; Reuben Jones, severely; and David Evans, severely.

Summary.

Killed	7
Mortally wounded	2
Severely wounded	20
Slightly wounded	28
Missing	20
Total	77

HEADQUARTERS 36th REGIMENT INDIANA VOLUNTEERS,
January 6, 1863.

SIR: It devolves upon me, as the temporary commander of the 36th regiment, to report the part taken by it in the recent engagements before Murfreesboro', and on the march thither.

On the 28th ultimo we were bivouacked on the west bank of Stewart's creek, ten miles from Murfreesboro', in sight of the enemy's cavalry pickets. At an early hour the next morning, 29th ultimo, we moved forward in line of battle, and arrived within sight of the enemy's rifle-pits, two and a half miles from Murfreesboro', at 4 o'clock, p. m. There we retained our position in front, the regiment doing picket duty the night of the 29th, and losing one man of company "D" wounded.

We retained our position in front during the day and night of the 30th ultimo, losing one man wounded in company "I." We were relieved on the morning of the 31st ultimo by the 9th Indiana regiment, and, at daylight of the same day, our regiment was called out under arms, expecting to participate in a general attack on the enemy's positions at Murfreesboro'. Just as we had formed our line, and were preparing to advance, a terrific fire, on the right of our position disclosed the fact that the battle had opened. In compliance with orders from you, my regiment countermarched, changed front, and advanced to the edge of a cedar thicket, to the right and rear of our first position, forming the right flank of the brigade, where it was evident our services would soon be needed. Hardly had we taken our position, when the enemy was upon us. Concealed from the view of my men by the thick undergrowth of cedar, the first indication they had of his presence was a volley from his muskets, which riddled our ranks. It was my impression that the 15th United States infantry was in my front, as we had been informed that such was the fact, on entering the thicket; hence the precaution of throwing out skirmishers had not been taken.

Up to this time Major Isaac Kinley retained command of the regiment, but at this point was seriously, perhaps fatally, wounded, being struck in the thigh by a musket ball. Here, too, Captain A. D. Shultz, of company B, fell mortally wounded, while bravely encouraging his men; and every mounted officer of the regiment, except the adjutant, had his horse shot under him.

After delivering a few well-aimed volleys at the enemy it became apparent that our position could not be held, the line having been already confused by the 15th regulars passing out between my left and the right of the 6th Ohio, and our right and left flanks, as well as our front, being exposed to the enemy's fire.

He quickly discovered his advantage, and charging upon my regiment with four times its number, compelled it to retire, cutting it off from the brigade and separating two of my companies, A and C, from the regiment. The strongest efforts were made by all the officers of my regiment to rally the men, and though their bravery was unquestioned, and they exhibited a strong disposition to maintain their ground, the fire of the enemy was too hot to admit of it, and they were retired to a point a short distance from the scene of our first conflict. Here, with the valuable assistance of Captain Gilbert Trusler and Adjutant J. H. McClung and other officers of the regiment, I succeeded in forming our line and again advanced, under a heavy fire, to the front. Not a man of my command flinched, and for eight long hours we assisted in maintaining our position against the furious assaults of the enemy.

First Lieutenant J. W. J. Smith and Second Lieutenant J. C. Byram, both of company G, were wounded in the early part of the day and compelled to retire from the field.

At 4 o'clock p. m., the fire having slackened, we noted our condition and strength, and found that out of four hundred and thirty commissioned officers and men, with whom we had entered the battle in the morning, two hundred and thirteen remained. This number was increased by the arrival of those who had become separated from the regiment during the day to two hundred and eighty-three.

On the 1st of January, 1863, we rested, and although my men were exposed to a heavy fire from the enemy's artillery during several hours of the day, none of them were killed or wounded. On the morning of the 2d, by your order, we moved across the river, taking a position on its northeast bank behind a barricade constructed by my men. We had remained here but a few hours, when the enemy made a strong and sudden attack on our position from the direction of our right flank, while his batteries to our right gave my line a raking fire. Then, by your order, I changed position, moving by the left flank a distance of two hundred yards. It was a terrible struggle, but the terrific fire to which the enemy was exposed for an hour compelled his lines to break and retire in disorder. At this juncture my men were ordered to charge the enemy, which they did with alacrity, halting not till darkness put an end to the pursuit. Captain J. H. King, of company G, was killed in this last engagement while gallantly encouraging his men at the barricade. He died nobly, bravely.

Our loss, colonel, in this series of engagements, is as follows:

Killed.—Company A: Privates Henry Maner, shot in head; and Jesse Shackle, killed by a cannon ball taking off his left leg. Company B: Captain A. D. Shultz, shot through both hips; Privates Andrew Fisher, Benjamin F. Warrington, and Robert D. Lake. Company C: Private Absalom Julian. Company D: Private Austin W. James. Company E: Corporal William Richter; Privates James E. Wood, Thomas E. Kent, musket shot through shoulder and bayonetted; and John H. Leavell, the latter burned to death, a house on the field in which he was lying wounded taking fire and burning to the ground before he could be rescued. Company F: Corporal David Furry and Private John Gautz. Company G: Captain J. H. King, shot through the head, ball entering above the left eye. Company H: Privates Henry Williams, Jacob Eckhart, and John McGlinn. Company I: Sergeant William Davidson, shot through the head; Privates Samuel Thornton and Joseph Haines, the latter by a cannon ball. Company K: Sergeant James A. Steel; Privates John Hall, John N. Johnson, and Isaiah Hawhee. Total killed, 25.

Wounded.—Major Isaac Kinley, in thigh, dangerously. Company A: Corporals George Warrick, flesh wound in leg; Franklin Elliott, flesh wound in thigh; Privates Samuel Bell, flesh wound in arm; and Wilson McKinney, slightly in groin. Company B: Corporal Ephraim McLauglin, leg shattered, seriously; Privates Robert Johnson, in face, badly; Jacob Kisling, slightly on head; John H. Power, in leg, slightly; William H. H. Ritchie, in thigh, badly; Peter Baisinger, in leg, badly; and John M. Favusett, in shoulder, badly. Company C: Privates George Hazzard, in hip, severely; William Weber, in leg, severely; Lorenzo D. Sheppard, in leg, slightly; Henry Reichart, in shoulder, slightly; Fabor W. Ginn, in shoulder, slightly; Abraham Miller, Robert Burns, James Vores, and William Horton, all in hand, slightly; and Henry Henderson, in knee, slightly. Company D: Sergeants George Cantley, in leg, slightly; David Byers, in foot, slightly; and Thomas M. Swain, in leg; Corporal Anson Bird, in breast, slightly; Privates A. D. Lacey, in hand; John Lockridge, in both legs, seriously; Samuel F. Pike, three fingers shot off; Henry Groves, in hand, slightly; and Erie Lamb, in leg. Company E: Sergeants E. W. Parkinson, in arm, slightly; and Thomas Benton, in hand, slightly; Privates Isaac D. Keeney, in hand, slightly; Jeremiah Hayes, badly in thigh and leg; Charles Conoway, arm broken; Edward Taylor, in thigh, badly; A. H. Grove, badly in jaw; B. F. Weaver, in hand, slightly; and L. B. Mannis, in leg, slightly. Company F: Sergeant James Porter, slightly in ankle; Corporals Isaac J.

Farquhar, slightly in groin; and William Low, slightly on head; Privates Aaron Hughes, seriously in both arms; William F. Robertson, in arm and leg; Francis C. Diggs, slightly in thigh; Joshua W. Stevenson, severely in ankle; Reuben W. Ray, slightly on head; Joseph Wills, slightly on hand. Company G: First Lieutenant J. W. J. Smith, right thumb shot away; Second Lieutenant John C. Bryan, flesh wound in leg; Sergeant William H. Duvall, slightly on head; Corporal Albert Parvis, small of back, slightly; Privates John F. Hattamay, in foot, slightly; Levi J. Pentecost, slightly in thigh; Douglas E. Ball, in breast, supposed mortally; John Snyder, in leg, slightly: Henry E. Mallory, in leg, slightly; Joseph Gossett, in leg, slightly; Abraham M. Miller, in foot, slightly; James Ashworth, in hip, supposed mortally. Company H: Sergeants George Mullikin, slightly; Rhoderick B. Carr, George and S. Vilott, slightly; Corporals Stanhope Limpus, George M. Hathaway, and William Jordan, slightly; Privates John A. Woods, seriously; Lewis Langston, Harrison Vilott, James H. Sutton, Michael O'Conner, Lyman A. Frink, Charles Webb, Milton L. Stephens, Albert Cully, and John Schæffer, all slightly. Company I: Sergeant Isaac Dulhagen, in head and hand, slightly; Corporal Newton Johns, slightly in leg; Privates Jacob Thornton, in shoulder and thigh, seriously; Meredith Berry, in hand, slightly; Isaac Luster, in breast, slightly. Company K: Captain Milton Pider, topographical engineer, third brigade, flesh wound in leg; First Lieutenant Charles M. Davis, slightly in leg; Second Lieutenant John Ross, in leg, and collar bone broken; Sergeant Milton Thornburg, slightly in leg; Corporal William Flynn, slightly; Privates George W. Bates, slightly in thigh; William Sherry, slightly in calf of leg; Calvin Cross, slightly in thigh; W. H. S. Woods, slightly in calf of leg. Total wounded, 91.

Missing.—Corporal John Little; Privates Joseph Barnie, and James C. Thorn, Company B; Private Noah W. Coon, company D; Sergeant John R. Erwin; Privates B. C. Hornaday, George Gephart, Joseph Jenkins, and D. S. Erwin, company E; Privates Isaiah L. Smith, John Zimmer, and Thomas Lawless, company F; Privates Charles C. Wilson, James M. Talbert, Sanford Limpus, company G; Privates Emery Mullen and Charles L. Scott, company I; Private Franklin Threewits, Company K. Total, 18.

Total loss in killed, wounded, and missing, 134.

In concluding my report to you, colonel, I wish again to call your attention to the bravery and gallant conduct of both the officers and men of my regiment, and to thank them for their noble conduct and bearing throughout all the trying scenes from the 28th of December to the 3d of January. They are worthy of immortal honor.

Too much cannot be said in praise of the glorious dead. Captains Shultz and King still live with us, though their bodies moulder in the earth. The enemy encountered no braver or truer spirits in those trying battles.

> "How sleep the dead who sink to rest,
> By all their country's wishes blest."

I am, colonel, with great respect, your most obedient servant,

PYRRHUS WOODWARD,

Captain, Commanding 36*th Regiment Indiana Volunteers.*

J. H. McClung, *Adjutant.*

A list of the killed and wounded of the 36th regiment Indiana volunteers in the battles before Murfreesboro', Tennessee.

Major Isaac Kinley, wounded in the left thigh, bone broken, seriously.

Company A.—Killed: Privates Henry Manor, shot in head; Jesse Sheckle, cannon shot, taking off his left leg. Wounded: Corporals George Warrick, leg; Franklin Elliot, thigh; Privates Samuel Bell, arm; Wilson McKinny, groin, slightly.

Company B.—Killed: Captain Abram D. Shultz, Privates Andrew Fisher, Benjamin F. Warrington, Robert D. Lake. Wounded: Corporal Ephraim McLaughlin, by musket ball, seriously; Privates Robert Johnson, face, seriously; Jacob Kisling, head, slightly; John H. Power, leg, slightly; William H. H. Richey, thigh, seriously; Peter Basinger, leg, seriously; John M. Tampsitt, shoulder, seriously. Missing: Corporal John Little, Privates Joseph Boinée, and James C. Thorn.

Company C.—Wounded: Privates Absalom Julian, abdomen, mortally; George Hazard, hip, seriously; William Weber, leg, seriously; Leander Shephard, leg, slightly; Henry Richart, shoulder, slightly; Tabor W. Ginn, shoulder; Abraham Miller, hand, slightly; Robert Burns, hand, slightly; James Veres, hand, slightly; Henry Henderson, knee, slightly; William Horton, hand, slightly.

Company D.—Killed: Private Austin W. James. Wounded: Sergeants George M. Cantly, leg, slightly; D. S. Byers, foot, slightly; T. S. Swain, leg, slightly; Corporal Anson Bird, breast, slightly; Privates A. D. Lacy, hand, severely; John Lockridge, both legs, slightly; S. F. Pike, fingers; Henry Grove, hand, slightly; Eri Lamb, leg, slightly. Missing: N. W. Coon, supposed to be wounded.

Company E.—Killed: Corporal William Richter, shot through the neck; Privates Thomas E. Kent, musket ball through right shoulder and bayonet through breast; James E. Wood, shot through the breast. Wounded: Sergeants E. W. Parkinson, arm; Thomas Benbow, hand, slightly; Corporal John H. Leavell, mortally; Privates Ike D. Keeney, hand, slightly; Jerry Hays, thigh, and leg, seriously; Charles Conoway, arm broken, seriously; Ed. Taylor, thigh, seriously; A. H. Greve, jaw, seriously; B. F. Weaver, hand, slightly; L. B. Morris, leg, slightly. Missing: Privates B. C. Homaday, George Giphart, James Jenkins, and D. S. Irwin. Taken prisoner: Sergeant John R. Irwin.

Company F.—Killed: Corporal David Furry, and Private John Gantz. Wounded: Sergeant James Porter, ankle, slightly; Corporals T. J. Farquhar, groin, slightly; William Levy, head, slightly; Privates Aaron Hughes, both arms, seriously; William Robinson, leg; Francis C. Diggs, thigh, slightly; Joshua H. Stephens, ankle, seriously; Reuben H. Ray, hand, slightly; Joseph Mills, right hand, slightly. Missing: Privates Isaiah L. Smith, John Zimmer, and Thomas Lawles.

Company G.—Killed: Captain James H. King. Wounded: First Lieutenant Jesse W. J. Smith, right thumb, slightly; Second Lieutenant John C. Byrom, right leg, seriously; Sergeant William H. Duvalle, head, slightly; Corporal Albert Parvis, small of the back, slightly; Privates John M. Ratteway, left foot, slightly; Levi L. Pentecoste, right thigh, slightly; Douglas Ball, right breast, mortally; John Snider, left leg, slightly; Henry C. Mallery, left leg, slightly; Joseph Garrett, right leg, slightly; Abraham M. Miller, foot; and James Ashworth, right hip, mortally. Missing: Privates William Hill, Charles C. Wilson, James M. Talbert, and Sanford Limpers.

Company H.—Killed: Privates Henry Williams and Jacob Eckhart. Wounded: First Sergeant George Mullikin, slightly; Sergeants Roderick R. Carr, slightly, and George S. Velott, slightly; Corporals Stanhope Limpers, seriously; George M. Hathaway, seriously; and William Jordan, slightly; Privates John McGlinn, mortally; John A. Woods, seriously; Lewis Langston, slightly; Harrison Velott, slightly; James H. Sutton, slightly; Michael O'Connor, slightly; Lyman A. Frink, slightly; Charles Webb, slightly; Milton L. Stephen, slightly; Albert Cally, slightly, and John Shaffer.

Company I.—Killed: Sergeant William Davidson, Privates Samuel Thornton and Joseph Haynes. Wounded: Sergeant Isaac Dulhage, head and hand, slightly; Corporal Newton Palmer, calf of leg, slightly; Privates Jacob Thornton, shoulder and thigh, seriously; Meredith Berry, hand, slightly; and Isaac Leester, breast, slightly. Missing: Private Emery Mullen and Fife Major Charles L. Scott.

Company K.—Killed: Privates John N. Johnson and John Hall. Wounded: Captain Milton Peden, thigh, seriously; Second Lieutenant Jonathan Ross, shoulder and leg, seriously; Sergeants Milton Thornbury, leg, slightly, and James A. Steel, mortally; Corporal William Flinn, by a splinter, slightly; Privates George R. Bates, leg, seriously; William Sherry, calf of leg; Calvin Cross, thigh, seriously; William H. S. Wood, calf of leg, slightly; Isaiah Hawkee, mortally. Missing: Franklin Threewits.

The sum total foots up in killed, 20; wounded, 95; missing, 18; prisoners, 1.

This report is necessarily imperfect from the fact that a great many were sent to other hospitals, and from there to Nashville, and I could not find out the nature and locality of their wounds.

Respectfully,

T. S. BASYE,

Assistant Surgeon 36th Regiment Indiana Volunteers.

JANUARY 8, 1863.

NASHVILLE, *January* 7, 1863.

COLONEL: In accordance with orders from headquarters, I have the honor to make the following report of the part taken by the 6th regiment Ohio volunteers in the late series of battles, beginning on the morning of December 31. At about 8 o'clock a. m. on that day we were drawn up in line of battle in the open field to the north of the "burnt brick," and to the west of the cedars, while Rousseau's division filed by us to get position. Scarcely had the rear of that column passed, when heavy firing was heard to our right, coming from the cedars, and approaching rapidly. I was ordered with my regiment into the woods. I immediately changed front and advanced some two hundred yards, when I saw our troops flying in wild disorder, and hotly pursued by the enemy. I formed my line and awaited the escape of our men and the nearer advance of the enemy. In a few moments a terrible fire was opened on us, scarce a hundred yards distance from a rebel line apparently four deep; this fire we returned, and a dreadful carnage ensued on both sides. Finding myself hotly pressed, I had determined on a charge, and the order was already given to fix bayonets, when I saw my regiment flanked almost completely on both sides by two rebel regiments. I gave the order to fall back firing; as soon as we reached the edge of the woods, Lieutenant Parsons, of the 4th regular artillery, opened on the enemy with terrible effect, and I reformed my line behind his guns, having held my position against tremendous odds, but with great sacrifice, for forty minutes. I then replenished my ammunition, and was soon after ordered to throw my regiment diagonally across the Murfreesboro' pike, and hold that position; this I did under a destructive fire, and with much loss during the rest of the day and until midnight, when I was relieved by the 24th Ohio, and took my regiment a short distance to the rear. During the first day of January my regiment was moved from one place to another as the plan of the battle required, but did not get into any general action. On Friday, the second, my regiment was ordered with the brigade across the river, and placed in position on a slight eminence to the rear of and as a support to Van Cleve's division. All was quiet until about half past 3 o'clock p. m., when a tremendous fire was heard along our front, and whole masses of the enemy were hurled against Van Cleve's division, which soon gave way. The enemy came down boldly, when I brought my regiment into action, simultaneous with the 84th Illinois, and we opened a severe cross fire on the enemy. For more than an hour we held the hill; and under our heavy fire, and that of a battery from the other side of the river, the enemy gave way, and when re-enforcements poured in for us they were already in full retreat. We held our position without further molestation till Sunday morning, when we were ordered across the river into camp, the enemy having retreated. My regiment, both officers and men, behaved throughout with energy, courage, and discipline. The loss was 177 killed, wounded, and missing. Among the former was Adjutant Williams, who fell cheering the men on, regardless of all personal danger. Accompanying is a correct list of the casualties.

Respectfully,

N. L. ANDERSON,
Colonel, Commanding 6th Ohio Volunteers.

Colonel GROSE,
Commanding 10th Brigade.

Report of surgeon of sixth regiment Ohio Volunteer Infantry.

Killed.—Adjutant A. G. Williams. Company A: Second Lieutenant Charles Foster. Company B: Corporal D. Medary, Privates Hardy and Burst. Company C: Corporal A. Kadin and Private W. Boyd. Company E: Privates C. Davis, (died in hospital of gunshot wound of the left leg, dividing artery and nerve, and fracturing femor, twenty-four hours after injury,) M. Schwab, Simon Shaddock, Charles Dickmeyer, and Andrew Davis. Company F: Privates H. Willis, C. Ark, L. Evers, and T. Brown. Company G: Orderly Sergeant G. Ridenour and Corporal Oliver Rochenfield. Company H: Privates Ed. Ulm and Charles Wattermet. Company I: Privates S. C. Springmeyer, S. Pulver, and J. Rappeler. Company K: Sergeant T. G. Drake and Private T. Wesselman.

Wounded.—Colonel N. L. Anderson, thigh; Sergeant Major A. F. Graham, shoulder. Company A: Privates J. Freel, abdomen; F. H. Halliday, shoulder; H. Hermann, hip. Company B: Captain W. McAlpine, shoulder; Orderly Sergeant G. W. Cormany, head; Sergeant A. Willoughby, thigh; Corporal E. Hannaford, neck and shoulder; Privates Theophilus Davis, breast; F. J. Miller, leg; Hugo Hochstetter, abdomen; Guy Nearing, neck; W. E. Doherty, leg; John Cline, arm; Anson Clapper, legs; J. Cline, hip; A. Goettle; James Mitchell, shoulder; A. Schutenhelm, back; J. Heffenbine, both thighs and head. Company C: Color Sergeant John Crotly, arm; Sergeant G. W. Peters, hip; Corporal F. Theman, shoulder; Privates E. G. Hone, arm; W. Baldwin, leg; Ed. Eyers, arm; H. Stocklein, leg; Jacob Stocklein, contused; J. Learch, thigh; G. Stokle, knee; W. L. Leidel, contused; F. Tieman, shoulder; J. C. Heffeman, hip. Company D: Second Lieutenant J. L. Antram, hip; Sergeant W. Bowers, leg; Corporal L. H. Jenks, arm; Privates A. C. Dripp, breast; S. H. Weeks, side; S. W. Stephenson, shoulder; F. Manus, arm; R. Hoffman, hip; Frank Dreler, thigh; Fred. Sogen, hand; J. L. Williams, hand; A. Hugel, knee; M. Wiedericht, arm; W. W. Williams, arm. Company E: Corporal E. West, hand; J. O. Niel, hand; E. Eckhardt, hand; W. Leake, hand; F. Greenwood, head; S. Schroder; A. Otto, shoulder; M. Smith, neck; C. H. Baldwin, neck; J. L. Ferdon, lungs. Company F: Second Lieutenant F. Schaeffer, leg; Sergeant W. E. Jackson, thigh; Corporal —— Sigel, leg; Privates N. Kisemier, hand; J. Laurens, leg; J. O. Root, thigh; W. R. Wood, breast; —— Witte, shoulder; —— Anner, face; Francis Linceman, leg; Andrew Schaeffer, leg; W. R. Wood, arm and back; G. Heilaman, arm; J. Lawrence, thigh. Company G: Corporal W. A. Clark, arm; Privates T. Burnett, leg; H. Bradley, thigh; J. A. Colwell, leg; Robert Faulman, both legs; S. P. Stallcup, legs in three places; J. Fenhoff, arm; J. Schenck, hand; A. Schenck, head. Company H: Captain E. H. Tinker, head, Second Lieutenant J. F. Meline, leg; Corporals Charles Ashman, hand; Albert Speece, face; Privates Owen Murphy, hand; J. A. Bonner, leg; H. Ruscher, leg; S. Lawrence, both feet; M. Leibaur, leg; Del. Brown, arm; L. Geis, shoulder; Thomas Kennedy, breast. Company I: Sergeant G. T. Lewis, arm; Privates W. L. Wolverton, leg; —— Rodrigo, shoulder; F. Larkcom, face; G. Heller, shoulder; J. Stoker, arm; Andrew Ray, foot. Company K: Orderly Sergeant G. B. Nicholson, back; Sergeant W. Papenbrook, leg; Corporals A. Kimble, leg; J. Martin, arm; H. Kreyenhagen, through pelvis and contents; Corporal C. Donnelly, arm; Privates L. Frantz, breast; C. Warner, leg; F. Meyer, hand; P. Moutaldo, foot; D. Henrie, face; H. Sheldon, hand; J. Nickel, shoulder; George Kelch, both legs; L. Huber, leg; W. Gaines, leg; Jos. Haddock, thigh; H. Beckman, hip; H. Esling, leg; D. Cline, shoulder; C. Albord, hand; C. Albord, hand.

Recapitulation.

Killed	25
Wounded	124
Missing	18
Total	167

H. Y. SMITH,
Assistant Surgeon 24th Ohio Volunteer Infantry,
In charge of 6th Regiment O. V. I.

Report of the killed, wounded, and missing in the battle of before Murfreesboro', Tennessee, of the Sixth Ohio regiment.

Company A.—Killed: Second Lieutenant Charles H. Foster and Private W. S. Shaw. Wounded: Sergeant James F. Canady, Corporal Joseph Rey, Privates William Krohmer, H. Hermann, C. M. Thompson, and Frank H. Halliday. Missing: Corporal Joseph Newman and Private Fred. Dressel, (supposed to be prisoners.)

Company B.—Killed: Corporal David H. Medary, Privates Albert Hardel and John Burit. Wounded: Captain Henry McAlpin, First Sergeant George W. Cormany, Corporal Eben Hannaford, Privates Guy Nearin, T. Davis, Anson Clapper, J. Hahnemann, Andrew Schultenhelm, John Helfeubein, James Mitchell, Fred. J. Miller, Hugo Hochstetter, John Cline, Albert O. Grettle, and William E. Doherty.

Company C.—Killed: Corporal A. Karlin and Private Wm. Boyd. Wounded: First Sergeant William Brown, Sergeant John Crotty, Color Sergeant A. W. Peters, Corporals E. P. Horn, Francis Thiemann, James Jordan, J. C. Hefferman, John Sykes, Privates A. Shuba, John Lauch, John Stochlin, William Lydell, William Baldwin, Ed. Eyers, B. C. Myers, and H. Stocklin.

Company D.—Wounded: Lieutenant J. L. Antrain, Sergeants William

Bowers and Amos Willoughby, Corporal Liberty H. Jenks, Privates A. C. Dripps, Frank Deller, Adam Hugo R. Hoffman, S. H. Weeks, W. W. Williams, Simon Weeke, S. W. Stephenson, Fred. Soghan, John Wakeman, Frank Manns, and Martin Wirdesech. Missing: L. Carpenter, William Saxon, and J. H. Maham. Prisoner: William A. Cormany, drummer.

Company E.—Killed: Privates S. Shattock, Michael Schwab, Charles Dickmeyer, Robert Davis, and Charles Davis. Wounded: Corporal William Leeke, Privates J. L. Ferdon, A. Otto, P. Krepes, (taken prisoner,) Thomas Greenwood, E. M. Hall, E. West, Matthew Smith, Charles H. Baldwin, John O'Neal, G. W. Bowen, Samuel Schroeder, and Charles Eckhart.

Company F.—Killed: Privates Christian Ark, Lewis Eves, Henry Willis, and Thomas Brown. Wounded: First Lieutenant Frank Schaefer, Sergeant W. E. Jackson, Corporal Sigel, Privates Joseph Knepper, W. R. Wood, G. Hielman, W. Kesemier, John Lawrens, J. L. Root, A. Schaefer, ——— Witte, ——— Annear, ——— Linceman, and ——— Young. Missing: Corporal J. B. Miller, and Private Lerwilliger.

Company G.—Killed: First Sergeant G. B. Ridenour, and Corporal O. P. Rockinfield. Wounded: Corporals J. C. Schenck, W. A. Clark, and Harry Simmons, Privates T. Burnett, H. Bradbury, J. A. Caldwell, J. Penhoff, S. Stalleap, A. Schenck, R. A. Paulman, and Silas Dunn. Missing: Corporal C. S. Dunn and Private A. M. Dunn, (supposed to be prisoner.)

Company H.—Killed: Private Charles Waltermet. Wounded: Captain H. H. Tinker, Second Lieutenant James F. Maline, Corporals J. Kennedy, Charles Ashmann, Albert Spiess, and Privates Ed. Ulm, Henry Rusher, Sam'l Lawronce, Owen Murphy, John A. Bonner, Martin Srebaur, Del. Brown, and Lawrence Geiss. Missing: Corporal Joseph Gang.

Company I.—Killed: Jacob Raplee, F. W. Springmeyer, Samuel Pulver. Wounded: Sergeants George P. Lewis, William L. Wolverton, Corporal Roderigo, and Privates John M'Glone, Andrew Ray, Gotleib Heller, John Stoker, Frederick Larkum, Joseph Seiter, Samuel Parker, and Christian Coley.

Company K.—Killed: Sergeant Thomas G. Drake, and Privates Theodore Wessolmann, Henry G. Kreysuhajen, (mortally wounded.) Wounded: First Sergeant George B. Nicholson, Sergeants William Pappenbrook, Jethro P. Hill, Corporals Joseph Martin, Charles Donnelly, Albert Kimball, and Privates H. Buckmann, William Gaines, L. Huber, L. Frantz, H. Esling, J. Nickol, G. Kalch, D. Kline, P. Montaldo, C. Albert, Charles Warner, F. Mirer, D. Henry H. Shelton. Missing: Corporal A. Kimball, and Privates G. Burnwald, C. Cunningham.

Field and staff.—Colonel W. L. Anderson, slight wound in leg; Adjutant Albert G. Williams, killed; Sergeant Major Frank. Graham, severely wounded in shoulder.

Recapitulation.

Killed, 25; severely wounded, 62; slightly wounded, 76; missing, 11; prisoners, 3. Total, 177.

HEADQUARTERS 24TH OHIO REGIMENT, *January* 6, 1863.

SIR: I have the honor to submit the following report of the part taken by the 24th Ohio regiment in the recent battles before Murfreesboro', Tennessee, of December 31, 1862, and January 2, 1863.

Our regiment being one of the five regiments composing the 10th brigade, commanded by Colonel William Grose, of the 36th Indiana regiment, numbered on the morning of the 31st of December, 1862, three hundred and fourteen enlisted men and fourteen commissioned officers, (company "A" being detached and was not with the regiment;) Colonel Frederick C. Jones commanding, Major Henry Terry acting lieutenant colonel, Captain Enoch Weller acting major, Adjutant H. Y. Graham, Captain A. T. M. Cockerill commanding company "D," Captain George M. Bacon commanding company "E," Lieutenant Charles Harman commanding company "F," Lieutenant Benjamin F. Horton commanding company "I," Lieutenant D. W. C. Wadsworth commanding company "C," Lieutenant William C. Beck commanding company "C," Lieutenant Jacob Diehl commanding company "H," Lieutenant August Drager commanding company "H," Lieutenant John Acker commanding company "G," and Lieutenant Isaac N. Dryden commanding company "B."

Early in the morning of the 31st ultimo heavy artillery and musketry firing was distinctly heard on our right, and as the sound neared our position it was evident that our forces were falling back, and our position in danger of being flanked, when our front was immediately changed to the left and rear, immediately in rear of the 6th Ohio, which had now become earnestly engaged with the enemy, who were under cover of thick woods. We immediately moved forward to support the 6th, and were ordered to lie down in the open space about fifty paces in their rear, being much exposed to a galling fire of rebel infantry.

The deadly fire of the enemy in superior numbers was mowing down the ranks of the gallant 6th, and they were compelled to fall back. Colonel Jones now ordered the regiment to fall back, which was done in good order. We halted at about one hundred and fifty paces and lay down to await the enemy's approach from the cover of the woods into the open space that separated us. On they came like a tornado that would destroy every thing in its path. Encouraged by their success in driving the forces upon our right, they charged upon a battery lying upon our right, belonging to General Rousseau's command, when almost simultaneously our forces lying in their front opened upon them a tremendous fire from our infantry and artillery, mowing them down almost by ranks, causing dismay and confusion, when they broke and fled in disorder to the cover of woods from which they had but just emerged. We had rested but a few minutes after this terrible encounter, when an orderly of the gallant General Palmer delivered orders for us to move double-quick to the support of the 19th brigade, (Colonel Hazen's,) which was at this time gallantly resisting a furious charge of the rebel hordes in an open cotton-field on our left. We almost instantly formed on their right in the field, with Lieutenant Parsons's 4th regular battery on our right. We remained in this position about one hour and a half, amidst the most terrible shower of ball and shell, encouraged by the cool and daring courage of our brigade commander, who was apparently omnipresent, watching the movements of the enemy and issuing his orders in person, when we were ordered to fall back to the turnpike, where another stand was made. We had remained in this position but a few minutes, exposed to a severe cross fire of the enemy, when Colonel Jones was mortally wounded and carried from the field. The command now devolved upon Major Henry Terry, who displayed great coolness and bravery during the brief period he was permitted to command. Our position at this time was very much exposed, and it was here that the regiment suffered most. Major Terry was struck in the head and mortally wounded by a fragment of shell; Lieutenant Charles Harman was almost instantly killed, and Lieutenant Benjamin F. Horton had his leg fractured so severely that amputation was necessary. Captain Enoch Weller now assumed command, assisted by me, when our ammunition being exhausted, the regiment was relieved, and retired to the rear to replenish our cartridge-boxes, and again moved forward under cover of a cluster of timber, where we remained until dark, under a terrible and dangerous fire of the enemy's artillery, directed at some batteries upon our right and left, which wounded several of our men. Night closed the terrible carnage, and we retired to the rear to prepare some refreshments and receive some rest, which was so much needed after the fatigues of the day. After resting January 1, 1863, on the morning of January 2 our regiment, with the brigade, moved across the river to support the division of General Van Cleve, which was alone on that side of the river. We prepared a small protection by removing the rails from an adjoining fence and constructing a slight breastwork, where we remained until about 3 p. m., when the enemy made a desperate charge upon the division of General Van Cleve, and being in such force they were compelled to give way; our position being in the rear and on the left of Van Cleve, immediately behind the 23d Kentucky regiment, which formed the advance of our brigade, the 36th Indiana, 6th Ohio, and 84th Illinois being immediately in our rear. The forces of Van Cleve were retreating in confusion, running directly over our artificial covering, drawing the fire of the enemy directly toward us. Captain Weller, commanding the regiment, displayed great coolness and bravery, ordering us to hold our position. The enemy were now rushing wildly and madly on, and were near flanking our position, when Captain Weller was instantly killed; the regiment now retired in confusion under cover of some buildings and timber, when the 36th Indiana, 6th Ohio, and 84th Illinois regiments poured in such deadly volleys of musketry, causing a check in the enemy's advance, when the regiment rallied and again went gallantly into the fight with her colors in the front. The command now devolving upon me, the regiment was brought back and bivouacked with the brigade upon the spot that but a few moments before had been the scene of havoc and death. At 3 a. m. the 3d instant I moved the regiment to the front on picket duty, and remained until 12 m., when we were relieved and retired across the river, which was waist-deep to the men. Too much praise cannot be bestowed upon the heroic and gallant officers who sacrificed their lives in the late bloody encounters; they were true and brave men. What more can be said? Great praise is due personally to Captain George M. Bacon, Lieutenants Dryden, Horton, Deihl, Dorager, Wadsworth, Beck, and Adjutant Graham, for gallant and efficient services rendered during the entire engagement, displaying that coolness and bravery so necessary under such emergencies. The non-commissioned officers of the regiment performed well their part of the drama, several of the companies being commanded by 1st sergeants, who bravely and ably performed the tasks assigned them. Our killed and wounded were promptly cared for by the corps of musicians under directions of Dr. Ord, of the 36th Indiana regiment, who manifested great zeal and energy in having them comfortably provided for and dressing their wounds.

I cannot omit to notice that the gallant behavior of the regiment is attributable to the brave example of our gallant brigade commander, whose brave and heroic daring on the field of Shiloh was still fresh in their memories. Also Brigadier General Palmer, whose simplicity of manners and kind words of encouragement to the men, coupled with the cool and daring courage upon the field, cannot fail to inspire the men with confidence in their commanders. The command devolving upon me when the last engagement was nearly closed, I am unable to make a minute report in detail of the part taken by the regiment in the recent desperate and bloody engagements of December 31 and January 2. Our loss in killed, wounded, and missing is as follows: Commissioned officers killed, 4; wounded, 4. Enlisted men killed, 10; mortally wounded, 6; severely wounded, 62; missing, 12. Total killed, wounded, and missing, 98. Besides the foregoing, there are twenty (20) slightly wounded, but not disabled for duty.

I have the honor to be, respectfully, sir, your obedient servant,

A. T. M. COCKERILL,

Captain, Commanding 24th Ohio Regiment.

Captain R. SOUTHGATE, *Acting Assistant Adjutant General,*
Tenth Brigade, Fourth Division, Army of the Cumberland.

List of killed, wounded, and missing in the twenty-fourth Ohio regiment.

Killed.—Colonel Fred. C. Jones; Major Henry Terry; Captain Enoch Weller, (in command of regiment;) First Lieutenant Charles Harman, company F; Sergeants David S. Potter and James R. Puntenney, company D; Private Joseph Barker, company I; Sergeant A. Marson, company C; Corporal Emanuel Newman, and Privates Joseph Bortine and Wm. Keller, company H; Corporal F. Higgins and Private B. Schort, company K; Private Dennis O'Brien, company G.

Mortally wounded.—Sergeant Egbert Andrews and Corporal Robert Ewing, company F; Privates Robert S. Parrish, company D; Wm. B. Jones, company I; David Wilvalsky, company H; Thomas Kelly, company B.

Severely wounded.—Corporals Daniel Oswalt and Aaron Robbins, and Privates Wm. Adams, John Bock, James Chissholm, Edward Cox, Hugh Donnelly, Wm. Fuller, Patrick Hickey, and Charles Hayward, company F; Sergeant George Colling, Corporal John McManis, and Privates Thomas J. Bradley, John Grooms, James H. L. Potter, John W. River, Jabez C. Rothwell, John C. Dragoo, John Cameron, and John Phibbs, company D; First Lieutenant Benjamin F. Horton, and Privates Stephen E. Lemons and Daniel Rose, company I; Corporals J. R. Orton and J. H. Roberts, and Privates George Dart, L. Ruble, David Stigle, J. Warner, J. Taylor, W. A. Roller, R. B. Tullis, and J. M. Waldorf, company C; First Lieutenant Jacob Deihl, Second Lieutenant August Drager, and Privates Jacob Severs and John Suter, company H; Sergeant Henry Shaser, and Privates George W. Dowdney, Charles Hand, Hugh McGarhan, Abraham Morris, and John Galloway, company E; Sergeant A. M. Kitchen, and Privates M. Adams, J. Babcock, J. Miller, W. A. White, and L. Johnston, company K; First Lieutenant John Acker, Sergeants Wm. Bennett and James G. Breckinridge, and Privates Wm. H. Hughes, Berkhart Marts, Casper Seabold, and Benjamin T. Taylor, company G; Sergeant Wm. H. Durable, Corporal J. Healey, and Privates John Cottenbrook, Hiram Doyer, Wm. H. Ehrman, Wm. Gittings, Thurston Reed, G. B. Sparks, Dennis Sullivan, and Benoni Willis.

Missing.—Private Cornelius Holmes, company I; Private J. Dildine, company C; Corporal Max Federlie, and Privates Wm. Amberg and Gurst Federlie, company H; Corporals J. G. Butler and David Hagans, company K; Corporal Victor R. Monroe, and Privates Fred. Myers, Joseph Ryder, Paul Hager, and Alexander Grant, company G.

A. T. M. COCKERILL,
Captain, Commanding 24th Ohio Regiment.

JANUARY 8, 1863.

SIR: Being detailed by Brigade Surgeon Kersey to attend the brigade on the field, and acting there until the fighting ceased, I had poor opportunities for seeing the wounded of the twenty-fourth Ohio volunteer infantry, many of whom were sent to Nashville, before I knew their whereabouts among our local hospitals. The report is as complete as possible under the circumstances.

Very respectfully,

JAMES P. ORR, *Assistant Surgeon*
36th Indiana Volunteers, in charge 24th Ohio Volunteer Infantry.

Surgeon's report of the killed, wounded, and missing of the 24th Ohio volunteer infantry, 2d division, 3d brigade..

Killed.—Colonel Frederick C. Jones, Major Henry Terry, Captain Enoch Weller, (in command of regiment.) Company C: Sergeant A. Marson. Company D: Sergeants David S. Potter and James R. Punteney. Company F: First Lieutenant Charles Harman. Company H: Corporal Emanuel Newman; Privates Joseph Bortine and William Keller. Company K: Corporal F. Kiggings.

Mortally wounded.—Company B: Private Thomas Kelley. Company C: Private John E. Taylor, head. Company D: Private Robert S. Parrish, bowels. Company F: Sergeant Egbert Andrews, bowels; Corporal Robert Ewing, dorsal vertebra. Company H: Private John Suter, bowels. Company I: Private M. B. Jones, lumbar vertebra. Company K: Bernhart Scahrt, bowels.

Severely wounded.—Company B: Sergeant W. H. Durable; Corporal J. Healey; Privates Jno. Cottonbrook, Hiram Dozier, William H. Ehrman, flesh, right leg; William Gittings, flesh, right thigh; Thurston Reed, G. B. Sparks, Dennis Sullivan, Benoni Willis. Company C: Corporals J. R. Orton, flesh, left thigh; J. H. Roberts; Privates George Dart, L. Ruble, David Stigle, J. Warner, W. A. Roller, R. B. Tullis, flesh, left thigh; J. M. Waldorf, flesh, right thigh. Company D: Sergeant George Collings, scalp of occiput; Corporal John McMannis; Privates Thomas J. Bradley, lumbar region, (rifle-ball;) John Grooms, flesh, right arm and thigh; James H. L. Botler, flesh, right thigh; John W. River, flesh, left thigh; Jabez E. Rothwell, flesh, left thigh and right leg; John C. Dragoo, John Cameron, John Phebbs. Company E: Sergeant Henry Sherer; Privates George W. Dowdney, Charles Hand, Hugh McGarhen, Abrâm Morris, John Galloway. Company F: Corporals Daniel Oswalt, Aaron Robbins, flesh, right thigh; Privates William Adams, John Bock, flesh, left thigh; James Chisholm, flesh, right thigh; Edward Cox, Hugh Donnelley, William Fuller, flesh, left thigh; Patrick Hickey, flesh, left leg; Charles Hayward. Company G: First Lieutenant John Acker, dorsal region; Sergeants William Bennett, flesh, right leg, (double;) James G. Breckinridge; Privates W. H. Hughes, flesh, right shoulder; Bernhart Martz, ball in lumbar region; Caspar Sebold, flesh, right knee and near umbilicus; Benjamin T. Taylor, Joseph Rider, flesh, left arm; Frederick Myers, flesh, left leg; Company H: First Lieutenant Jacob Diehl, flesh, right arm; Second Lieutenant Augustus Dreger, flesh, right leg; Privates Jacob Severs, and David Wiebrashi, bruised by concussion in back. Company I: First Lieutenant Benjamin F. Horton, compound fracture, right leg; Privates Stephen E. Lemons, flesh, both thighs; Daniel Rose, flesh, left thigh. Company K: Sergeant A. M. Kitchen, head; Privates M. Adams, occiput, (no fracture;) J. Babcock, flesh, right leg; J. Miller, W. A. White, flesh, upper third thigh; L. Johnson.

Missing, January 8, 1863.—Company C: Private J. Dildine. Company G: Corporal Victor R. Monroe; Privates Paul Hagar and Alexander Grant. Company H: Corporal Max Federlie; Privates William Amberg and Gustavus Federlie. Company I: Private Cornelius Holmes. Company K: Corporals J. G. Butler and David Hagans.

HEADQUARTERS 3D DIVISION, LEFT WING,
ARMY OF THE CUMBERLAND.

MAJOR: I have the honor to submit the following report of the operations of my division on the 31st December, 1862. At 7 o'clock in the morning of that day I received an order to cross Stone river, on which my left rested, and march toward Murfreesboro'. The 1st brigade, Colonel Beatty, 3d brigade, Colonel Price, and the batteries, Captain Swallow commanding, were promptly moved over and formed in line. The 2d brigade, Colonel Fyffe, being retained on the south side by a subsequent order, my lines being formed and about to advance, by your order I recrossed the river, leaving the 3d brigade to guard the ford. With the 1st brigade I marched rapidly to the support of General Rousseau, whose division was hard pressed by the enemy. We formed in a wood on the south side of the Murfreesboro' and Nashville turnpike. Our lines were no sooner formed than the enemy was seen advancing, driving before him our scattered troops. Our ranks were opened to suffer these to pass, when they closed and opened on the enemy a withering fire, which soon brought him to a halt. A murderous fire was kept up on both sides about twenty minutes, when the enemy began to recoil. Our 2d line now relieving the 1st with hearty cheers, the rebels broke and retreated. The 2d brigade, coming up at this moment, formed on the right and joined in the pursuit. We pressed the enemy through this wood, then across an open field to another wood, where they appeared to have met with re-enforcements, and reformed.

The 1st Indiana battery, Captain Swallow, joined us in this open field and rendered efficient aid.

Here I received information from General Rosecrans that General Rousseau was driving the enemy, accompanied with an order for me to press them hard. At the same moment I was notified by a messenger from Colonel Harker, whose brigade was to my right and rear, that the enemy were in force on my right, in a wood, and were planting a battery there. I immediately sent a message to Colonel Harker to press the enemy hard, as I had no reserve to protect my right; to Captain Swallow, who was doing good service with his battery, not to suffer it to be captured; to Colonel Beatty to send two regiments, if they could possibly be spared, to the support of Colonel Fyffe, and a fourth to General Crittenden, to inform him of my critical situation. The enemy now poured a galling fire of musketry, accompanied with grape and shell, on our right. Colonel Fyffe's brigade, supported by Captain Swallow's battery, gallantly returned the fire, but, being overpowered by numbers on front and flank, were soon compelled to retire, followed but a short distance by the enemy. Captain Swallow, to whom too much praise cannot be awarded, brought off his battery safely. Colonel Beatty, who had been pressing the enemy on the left, as soon as he learned the condition of affairs, retired in good order. With two of his regiments he was ordered by General Rosecrans to protect a battery on the Murfreesboro' road. The remaining two regiments of his brigade and Colonel Fyffe's brigade were reformed and took a position on the left of General McCook's corps, and to the right of the pioneer; which position we occupied without further adventure till after dark. I cannot close this report without inviting your attention to the gallantry displayed by those under my command during this engagement. To both officers and men too much praise cannot be awarded. I would particularly notice the coolness, intrepidity, and skill of my brigade commanders, Colonels Beatty and Fyffe, and of Captain Swallow, chief of artillery. To the members of my staff, Captain E. A. Otis, assistant adjutant general; Captain C. H. Wood, inspector general; Captain William Starling, topographical engineer; Lieutenants T. F. Murdock and H. M. Williams, aides-de-camp, I owe much for the promptness, faithfulness, and gallantry with which they executed my orders and conveyed intelligence on the field. Sergeant R. B. Rhodes, of the 1st Ohio cavalry, in command of my escort, conducted himself like a true soldier, and deserves honorable mention.

Individual acts of bravery in the different brigades will be brought to your notice in the reports of their respective commanders.

A slight wound received early this day becoming exceeding painful, on the following morning I was compelled to turn over the command of the division to Colonel Beatty, and retire from the field.

Very respectfully, your most obedient servant,

H. P. VAN CLEVE,
Brigadier General.

Major LYNE STARLING,
Assistant Adjutant General, Left Wing.

HEADQUARTERS 3D DIVISION, LEFT WING,
Camp near Murfreesboro', January —, 1863.

MAJOR: I have the honor to submit the following report of the operations of this division for the time embraced between the first and third days of January, 1863, inclusive.

I was called to the command of the division on the morning of January 1, by General Van Cleve's disability from the wound received in the battle of the preceding day. At 3 a. m. on that day I received orders to cross Stone river, with my command, at the "Upper ford," and hold the hill overlooking the river, near the ford. Accordingly, at daybreak, the third brigade, Colonel Price commanding, crossed the river at the place indicated, throwing out skirmishers and flankers. Colonel Price was quickly followed by Colonel Fyffe's brigade, (2d;) the force being formed in two lines, the right resting on the high ground near the river and east of the ford, and the left thrown forward so that the direction of the line should be nearly perpendicular to the river.

In the mean time, the 1st brigade, Colonel Grider commanding, had been disposed as follows: Two regiments were formed in the hollow, near the hospital, as a reserve, the other two remaining on the other side of the river to support a battery.

The enemy's skirmishers were now discovered in a wood, distant half a mile or so from our first line, and occasional firing took place on both sides. Information of all these movements was sent to General Crittenden, who sent me word that if I needed artillery to order up a battery; the 3d Wisconsin battery, Lieutenant Livingston commanding, was accordingly, at about 10 o'clock a. m., ordered to cross the river and remain in the hollow near the ford.

Small parties of the enemy's cavalry and infantry were occasionally seen, and at length a strong line was distinctly visible through the openings in the wood. Lieutenant Livingston was now ordered to bring up his battery. It was accordingly placed in position on the rising ground in front of Colonel Fyffe's brigade. Several shells were thrown at the enemy's line, which caused its disappearance; it was supposed they had laid down. One section, Lieutenant Hubbard commanding, was now moved to the hill on the right, whence also one or two shells were thrown at detached parties. Colonel Fyffe's brigade was moved to the left of the battery, where it was covered by a skirt of woods. Our whole force had been constantly concealed by making the men lie down.

About one o'clock the remaining two regiments of Colonel Grider's brigade, the 19th Ohio and 9th Kentucky, were ordered to cross the river, which they did, forming near the hospital on the left of the other two regiments of the same brigade, to protect our left flank. The enemy's forces were occasionally seen moving to our left, and Generals Crittenden and Palmer were advised of that fact; Colonel Grose was, consequently, ordered to support me. His brigade formed so as to protect our left, relieving the 19th Ohio and 9th Kentucky. These two regiments then formed in rear of the right of the second line as a reserve, being posted in the hollow near the ford.

No other disturbance occurred during the day, except the occasional firing of the skirmishers, so Colonel Grose's brigade and Livingston's battery recrossed the river.

About midnight we were alarmed by sharp firing from the skirmishers. They reported that it was caused by the enemy's skirmishers advancing and firing upon us. One of our men was killed and one wounded. Nothing else occurred during the night.

On the morning of Friday, January 2, Livingston's battery came across the river again and was posted as before. There was light skirmishing during the earlier part of the day. The 79th Indiana regiment, Colonel Knefler, was ordered to take place in the first line, to close the gap between Colonel Fyffe's brigade and the others. Nothing of note occurred until about 11 o'clock, when the firing of the enemy's skirmishers became very constant and heavy, as they slowly crept up towards us. The skirmishers now reported a battery being planted in our front, and shortly afterwards that fifteen regiments of infantry and three pieces of artillery were moving to our left. Notice of all these movements was given to General Crittenden and General Palmer, and Colonel Grose's brigade again came over to our support. About noon the enemy's battery opened with occasional shell, directed at Lieutenant Hubbard's section of artillery on the hill. The enemy's artillery was now seen moving to our left, and soon another battery opened fire upon Lieutenant Hubbard's section. As the enemy's skirmishers were so near that their fire was annoying and dangerous to the artillery, I ordered Lieutenant Livingston to retire and take a position on the hill near the hospital. A few shells were still thrown by the enemy's battery on our left, and occasional ones from an apparently heavy battery across the river.

As the enemy's skirmishers pressed ours very closely, our line was strengthened by throwing out two more companies. The firing was very sharp, and many of our men, as well as theirs, were wounded.

At about half past two o'clock it was reported that four more of the enemy's guns were moving towards our left. Word was sent in this, as in cases of all other movements, to General Crittenden.

At about three p. m. our skirmishers reported that the enemy's skirmishers were throwing down the fence in front of our line. Orders were sent to Colonel Price to let his first line fall back behind the crest of the hill, but before he could receive them the enemy were advancing across the field to the charge. They were formed in column, with a front of apparently two regiments. The first column was three regiments, or six ranks deep; this was succeeded by a second of the same depth, and a third of apparently greater. At the same moment their artillery opened from three or four different points, throwing shot, shell, and canister directly into us. As the enemy's column approached to within a hundred yards or so, the first line rose up and delivered a heavy fire upon their column, which checked it for a moment; they soon pressed on, however. The regiments of the first line, (the 51st Ohio, 8th Kentucky, and 35th and 79th Indiana,) fought gallantly until the enemy were within a few yards of them, when, overpowered by numbers, they were compelled to retire. This movement confused and disorganized the second line, which also was ordered to fall back. The reserve, consisting of the 19th Ohio, 9th Kentucky, and 11th Kentucky, was now ordered up. They advanced most gallantly toward the crest of the hill and poured a destructive fire upon the enemy, whose first column was by this time almost annihilated. Their supporting columns soon came up, however, and at the same time a force advanced along the river bank upon our right flank. Our men fought with the most desperate courage, as will appear from their severe loss, until forced back by the actual pressure of the enemy. Even then they broke back from the right, file by file, stubbornly contesting the ground; at last, however, the right being forced back, the left was ordered to retire, which it slowly did, until the bank of the river was reached.

Attempts were made to rally the men at several points, but it was imposible, from the heavy fire and the close proximity of the enemy. Most of them were therefore forced across the river, where many of them rallied and returned with the first supporting troops; and I am proud to say that the colors of the 19th Ohio, 9th Kentucky, and 51st Ohio were the first to recross the stream after the enemy's check. The tremendous fire of our artillery on the south side of the river, with Livingston's battery on the other, with the determined resistance they had met, had stopped the enemy at the river; and now, as our troops pressed forward, they fled in confusion, leaving four of their guns

Several brave officers had rallied a great number of our men, and were the foremost in the advance. Night now came on and closed the pursuit. The regiments were rapidly reorganized, and in a few hours were in a state of efficiency, and turned out promptly and cheerfully at an alarm.

The second brigade, Colonel Fyffe's, was not attacked, the front of the enemy's column not extending to them; seeing the right driven back, they also retired in good order.

Lieutenant Livingston's battery fired constantly, and well, from the first appearance of the enemy, until the very last moment he could remain safely. He then crossed the river without losing a piece.

I cannot too much commend the gallant manner in which my men fought and the promptness with which, when forced to give way, they rallied and reorganized. Numerous instances of individual courage and devotion appear in the regimental and brigade reports.

To the commanders of the different brigades—Colonels Grider, Price, and Fyffe—my thanks are due for the gallantry and coolness of their behavior under very trying circumstances. Lieutenant Livingston, of the 3d Wisconsin battery, did efficient service, and performed his duty ably and handsomely.

Lieutenant Smock, 3d Kentucky cavalry, who commanded a detachment of couriers, remained constantly near me, and was of great use.

To the following officers, members of my staff, I tender my thanks for their assistance, and the manner in which it was rendered: Captain E. A. Otis, assistant adjutant general; Captain C. H. Wood, acting assistant inspector general; Captain William Starling, topographical engineers; Lieutenant T. F. Murdock, aide-de-camp; Lieutenant H. N. Williams, aide-de-camp.

For particulars of the action of the different brigades and detached regiments, I have the honor to refer you to their respective reports, herewith transmitted.

Most respectfully, your obedient servant,

SAMUEL BEATTY.

Colonel, Commanding 3d Division, Left Wing, 14th Army Corps.

Major LYNE STARLING,

Assistant Adjutant General.

HEADQUARTERS 3D DIVISION, LEFT WING,
January 16, 1863.

In my official report of the part the 3d division took in the engagement before Murfreesboro' I omitted to mention the valuable services rendered by the acting medical director of the division, Major M. C. Woodworth, surgeon of the 51st Ohio volunteers, and now take advantage of this opportunity to give credit and due praise to him as an able and efficient officer, and thank him for his valuable services rendered to the wounded of this division by his able and energetic efforts in their behalf.

Very respectfully, your obedient servant,

SAM'L BEATTY,

Colonel, Commanding 3d Division, Left Wing, 14th Army Corps.

Major LYNE STARLING,

Assistant Adjutant General.

Report of the number killed, wounded, and missing, from the 3d division, left wing, in the engagement before Murfreesboro', Tennessee.

Command.	KILLED.			WOUNDED.			MISSING.			Total—killed, wounded, and missing.
	Commissioned officers.	Enlisted men.	Total.	Commissioned officers.	Enlisted men.	Total.	Commissioned officers.	Enlisted men.	Total.	
Brig. Gen. H. P. Van Cleve	......	......	......	1	......	1	......	......	......	1
First brigade	7	59	66	16	303	319	......	81	81	466
Second brigade	4	76	80	14	225	239	2	160	162	481
Third brigade	6	75	81	21	307	328	2	146	148	557
Artillery corps	......	6	6	......	19	19	......	......	......	25
Total	17	216	233	52	854	906	4	387	391	1,530

Respectfully submitted.

SAMUEL BEATTY,
Colonel, Commanding 3d Division, Left Wing, 14th Army Corps,
Department of the Cumberland.

HEADQUARTERS 3D DIVISION, LEFT WING,
January 16, 1863.

In my official report of the part the 3d division took in the engagement before Murfreesboro' I omitted to mention the valuable services rendered by the acting medical director of the division, Major M. C. Woodworth, surgeon of the 51st Ohio volunteers, and now take advantage of this opportunity to give credit and due praise to him as an able and efficient officer, and thank him for his valuable services rendered to the wounded of this division by his able and energetic efforts in their behalf.

Very respectfully, your obedient servant,

SAM'L BEATTY,
Colonel, Commanding 3d Division, Left Wing, 14th Army Corps.

Major LYNE STARLING,
Assistant Adjutant General.

HEADQUARTERS LIGHT ARTILLERY BATTERY,
2RD DIVISION, LEFT WING,
January 5, 1863,

CAPTAIN: In accordance with your request, I have the honor to submit herewith, the reports of the several batteries of this division.

CAMP OF THE 3D WISCONSIN BATTERY,
Near Murfreesboro', January 5, 1863.

SIR: I would report, as follows, the part taken in the actions of the 31st of December, and the 1st, 2d, and 3d of January, 1863, by the 3d Wisconsin battery. At daybreak on the morning of the 31st December we moved from camp with our division, and crossed the ford of Stone river to the east and Murfreesboro, side. We took a commanding position in battery. In a short time we were ordered to recross to the west side and take up a position commanding the ford, (all the troops that had crossed were ordered to recross.) The 3d brigade, under Colonel Price, supported our flanks. Very early in the action the enemy gained on our right wing, and many wagons and ambulances moved across this ford. A hospital was established in some buildings there. I inquired of an officer, and was informed that we had infantry pickets and a small force of cavalry on the other side. About 12 m. I saw a great stampede among the ambulances, wagons, and stragglers opposite, and was told some rebel cavalry were charging on them. I was fearful of making a mistake and firing on our own cavalry. We could not see the enemy until he got among the wagons and was taking them off. We then opened upon them and disabled two wagons, which blocked the lane and obliged them to leave without their booty. I think they got off with only five wagons. They left one man killed, and carried off their wounded. We shelled the woods in the direction they had taken. We expended 50 rounds of ammunition that day. The only casualty was one man, Henry S. Netley, wounded in the thigh slightly. Thursday, January 1, the battery was advanced across the river with the 3d division, under command of Colonel Beatty, with orders to protect the left from any flank movement, but not to bring on a general engagement. After moving forward about half a mile we discovered two regiments of infantry on a hill-side; we threw a few shells among them, and they withdrew to the woods on their left. We fired very little that day, only when we saw evidences of their massing troops; we had one man, A. J. Uleric, slightly wounded by the sharpshooters.

January 2.—This morning we discovered the enemy had erected a fortification on the brow of the hill a mile and a half to our front. Soon they opened on us with their 24-pound brass pieces; we did not reply and they did us no injury. Soon they moved these guns nearer to us and more to their right; this gave them a flank fire, and we found it very dangerous to remain there. We were ordered to withdraw and take up a position a half mile to our rear and left, near the hospital; about a half hour after we had done so, we saw the enemy had drawn up in line and were advancing in great force. Just then General Rosecrans ordered me to change my position, so that I was a little late in opening my fire. The enemy advanced steadily, driving in our pickets. Our fire was very effective, but their ranks closed up immediately. Soon I saw our right had given way that rested on the river. A heavy column had advanced under cover of the bank of the river and its skirty woods, and had flanked the troops stationed there. I then sent my caisson across to the west side, and seeing everything giving way, I sent one section at a time across, still working those that remained, until the others were over. When the last section reached the ford, one regiment of the enemy was within 100 yards of it, and poured a galling fire into us. Many of our horses were shot dead in the river, but our brave boys cleared them from the teams, and everything was got across. We opened fire on them as soon as we had crossed, though many of our caissons had not yet come up. We opened fire at three different positions after we crossed, and soon after the enemy gave back. We recrossed to the east side to sustain General Davis, and took a position in advance of the one taken the day previous.

January 1.—We expended this day 300 rounds of ammunition. Our fire was very good, disabling two of the enemy's limbers and killing their horses, but our fire was directed mostly at their advancing lines. We lost 9 horses, 2 sets lead harness, and had two men, Sergeants Holenback and Daniel Robin, wounded, not seriously.

January 3.—We had remained in our position, assigned us by General Davis, all night and until noon this day, before we were relieved. Our horses had had nothing to eat for 48 hours, and our men were wet with wading the river and without shelter from the cold pelting rain; but when I told them it was the imperative order of General Davis, and of vital necessity that we should hold out a little longer, they cheerfully obeyed. General Davis kindly divided what little he had to eat with our men, as did also Colonel Beatty the day before. We had no rations issued since the 30th, and our provision and forage wagon had been sent back by order of some one. At 11 o'clock a. m we were relieved by the 26th Pennsylvania battery, and fell back a little to feed; at 11 o'clock p. m. we recrossed the river by order of Captain Mendenhall, and took up our old position on the west side commanding the ford.

January 4.—Remained at the ford until 5 p. m., when we were ordered to this camp. We have expended in all 358 rounds of ammunition, lost 9 horses, 2 sets harness, and have 4 men wounded. Present for duty, 3 commissioned officers and 107 men.

Yours, &c.,

CORTLAND LIVINGSTON,
Lieutenant, Commanding 3d Wisconsin Battery.

Captain SWALLOW,
Chief of Artillery Brigade,
3d Division, Left Wing, Army of the Cumberland.

HEADQUARTERS PENNSYLVANIA LIGHT ARTILLERY,
January 5, 1863.

SIR: I have the honor to make the following report of the part taken in the recent action by the Pennsylvania battery.

On the morning of the 31st December we were ordered to cross the river with the 1st brigade to take position, which we had barely time to do, when we were ordered back again; we then followed the 1st brigade towards the right wing, where the battle was raging fiercely. We found everything there in confusion, and it impossible to follow our brigade and the battery nearly in the lines of the enemy. You then gave me the permission to fight on my own hook, and do the best in my power. I then countermarched the battery and took position on the rising ground on the left of the old block-house, along the line of the railroad, and opened fire on the enemy, who were advancing through the woods on the right of the pike and in our front. We fired as rapidly as possible with spherical case from our smooth-bores and Schenkel shells from our rifles. When finding the enemy checked and our infantry advancing, we limbered to the front, advanced a short distance across the pike, where we came in position and fired a few rounds, when the Board of Trade battery advanced and took position on our left, covering all the intermediate ground in our front. We changed position by moving by the left flank and occupied the rising ground in the corn field to the right of the pike and covering the woods, out of which

Generals Rousseau's and Negley's troops were retiring. We reserved our fire until our own troops were clear of the woods, and the enemy's lines with banners flying came in sight on the verge of the timber within 500 yards of our battery. We opened upon them with spherical case, shell and canister, and fired briskly for about fifteen minutes, when seeing no more of the enemy, we ceased firing; some of the enemy's advance fell within fifteen or twenty yards of our guns. By General Rousseau's advice we then fell back on the rising ground between that and the railroad, firing a few shots at the enemy. By Captain Mendenhall's order we again advanced to our former position in the cornfield on the right of the pike, and met with a warm reception from the enemy's musketry from the woods in our front, and the right flank being at the same time under cross fire from one of the enemy's batteries on our left. We opened fire on the woods in our front and right, soon silencing the enemy's fire, when, finding that we had no support on either flanks or rear, we again withdrew to the rising ground between the pike and railroad. We then were ordered by Captain Mendenhall to take position across the pike near the old log-house in our extreme front, having to guard against the enemy's advance up the pike and from the woods on our right, from which a continued fire of musketry annoyed us. At the same time a battery opened upon us from the brick house near the pike, injuring one of our trails and limber, to which we replied until our long-range ammunition, the supply of which was small, was exhausted, when I had the smooth-bores withdrawn and take a position to rake the pike with canister, in case the enemy advanced, and kept the two rifles in the advance until night, when the whole battery was withdrawn about 500 yards to the rear, and supplied with ammunition. On the morning of the 1st of January, by your order, we took position on the left of the railroad, and at a right angle with it, the 6th Ohio battery on our left. We did no firing that day, with the exception of a few shots in the morning thrown at the woods in our front and kept in position ready for action in that vicinity nearly the whole day; at night went into park in rear of the log-house near the railroad.

At sunrise on the morning of the 2d of January, we were saluted with a shower of solid balls from the enemy's batteries falling in too close a vicinity to be agreeable. We mounted quickly and took position on the left of the railroad on a small rise commanding the approach of the enemy in our front. Captain Mendenhall then ordered us to the front to take a position commanding the open field to the left of the railroad. During the forenoon we were several times saluted with shots from the battery of the enemy planted in the woods beyond the opening in our front, to which we remained silent till near noon, when skirmishers of the 51st Indiana, which supported us on the right, advanced across the opening and drove the enemy's pickets, when the enemy opened upon them with canister at the same time upon us with solid shot. Our skirmishers falling back, we opened with solid shot, when their battery became silent and remained so until three o'clock p. m., when it again opened, and shortly after heavy musketry was heard upon our left; we opened at the battery in our front, when it became silent. When we saw the enemy advancing upon our left wing across the river, and our men falling back, we changed front, firing to the left; and opened a cross fire on them, and continued it till our forces in their front compelled them to fall back beyong our range. We remained in position until nine o'clock p. m., when we ascertained that our supports on our flanks had been withdrawn without we being notified of the fact, and no pickets in front between us and the enemy's lines, I withdrew the battery to the rear of the infantry and parked. On the morning of the 3d of January we returned to our position of the previous day, support having returned, where we remained till three o'clock p. m., when we were ordered across and take the place occupied by the 3d Wisconsin battery, where we remained till near midnight; when we were ordered to recross the river, which we did, and parked on the ground we now occupy. We expended about 1,650 rounds of ammunition, lost seven horses, two men killed, and seven wounded, a few small arms, and a large quantity of clothing, camp, and garrison equipage.

Yours, respectfully,

A. J. STEVENS,
First Lieutenant, Commanding Battery.

Captain G. R. SWALLOW,
Chief of Artillery, 3d Division, Left Wing, 14th Army Corps.

CAMP OF THE 7TH INDIANA BATTERY, 3D DIVISION,
January 5, 1863.

On the morning of the 31st of December I ordered Lieutenant Buckman to move the battery in rear of the 2d brigade of the 3d division. This brigade was not moved across the river at the time the 1st and 3d crossed and recrossed, but was ordered up the pike in the vicinity of our hospital, where the enemy's cavalry were trying to capture prisoners from our broken and retreating columns. The battery opened upon them with shell, our cavalry at the same time charging upon them, which caused them to retreat in disorder. The brigade then advanced to the right and front, through a cedar thicket into an open field, the battery following immediately in rear. While in the field, and nearly across it, our advance commenced skirmishing with the enemy. I immediately ordered the battery into position, and the firing to commence with shell to our right and front, where the enemy's infantry were rapidly advancing upon us. They soon entered the field, when I ordered the battery to open upon them with canister, at the same time ordering the caissons to the rear. I soon saw part of the brigade falling back in disorder and the enemy advancing across the field toward the battery with a yell. I then ordered the battery to limber to the rear and retire as rapidly as possible, which was done in not the best order. We reached the pike and took position near the old block-house, with a loss of First Lieutenant F. W. Buckman, seriously wounded, one man killed, and two wounded. During the day the battery occupied several different positions, engaging the enemy's artillery and infantry, but with what effect is not known. At night went into park a short distance from the old block-house, having had one lieutenant and four men wounded, and three killed.

On the morning of the 1st instant, by Captain Mendenhall's order, I took position near the ford, supported by General Cruft's brigade. Nothing worthy of note transpired during the day, and the morning of the 2d instant found us occupying the same position. During the day General Negley's command took position in my rear and near the ford. Six guns of the artillery under his command took position on my left, and Captain Mendenhall's battery of eight guns, under command of Lieutenant Parsons, came into position on my right and front. About 4 o'clock p. m. I received word that the enemy were advancing in force to attack the left of our wing. Their lines of infantry soon came in full view, and the batteries on my right and left, together with my own, opened a rapid and vigorous fire upon their advancing columns. They soon opened a galling artillery fire upon us from three different points. The battery on my left retired a short distance, and the one on my right commenced to fire, retiring. Seeing this, I ordered the battery to fix prolonge, to fire retiring. About this time the vent of my left piece became filled with friction primers, and was ordered to the rear for repair without my knowledge. The drivers of the other pieces seeing this piece moving to the rear supposed the order had been given to retire, and drove some forty yards to the rear before they could be halted. The order was then given to advance, and one piece was moved by hand to its first position; the rest were limbered and moved to the position first occupied, except the gun that had been ordered to the rear, when all the ammunition was expended, except a few rounds of canister. In this engagement we had one man killed and two wounded. January 3 found the battery in the same position. General Negley ordered the battery to open fire upon a line of the enemy's infantry, which did no good and wounded one of my own men by the premature discharge of one of the guns. During the whole engagement I expended 406 rounds of ammunition; had one lieutenant and seven men wounded; four men killed; four horses wounded, one killed, and four missing. I should have done more firing, but General Rosecrans told me he wanted some ammunition reserved for an emergency.

Respectfully,

G. R. SWALLOW,
Captain 7th Indiana Battery.

HEADQUARTERS LIGHT ARTILLERY BATTERY,
3D DIVISION, LEFT WING, *January* 5, 1863.

CAPTAIN: In accordance with your request, I have the honor to submit herewith the reports of the several batteries of this division.

CAMP OF THE 3D WISCONSIN BATTERY,
Near Murfreesboro', January 5, 1863.

SIR: I would report, as follows, the part taken in the actions of the 31st of December, and the 1st, 2d, and 3d of January, 1863, by the 3d Wisconsin battery.

At daybreak on the morning of the 31st of December we moved from camp with our division, and crossed the —— ford of Stone river to the east and Murfreesboro' side. We took a commanding position in battery. In a short time we were ordered to recross to the west side and take up a position commanding the ford, (all the troops that had crossed were ordered to recross.) The 3d brigade, under Colonel Price, supported our flank. Very early in the action the enemy gained on our right wing, and many wagons and ambulances moved across this ford. A hospital was established in some buildings there. I inquired of an officer, and was informed that we had infantry pickets and a small force of cavalry on the other side. About 12 m. I saw a great stampede among the ambulances, wagons, and stragglers opposite, and was told some rebel cavalry were charging on them. I was fearful of making a mistake and firing on our own cavalry. We could not see the enemy until he got among the wagons and was taking them off. We then opened upon them and disabled two wagons, which blocked the lane and obliged them to leave without their booty. I think they got off with only five wagons. They left one man killed, and carried off their wounded. We shelled the woods in the direction they had taken. We expended fifty rounds of ammunition that day. The only casualty was one man, Henry S. Nettey, wounded in the thigh, slightly.

Thursday, January 1.—The battery was advanced across the river with the 3d division, under command of Colonel Beatty, with orders to protect the left from any flank movement, but not to bring on a general engagement. After moving forward about half a mile we discovered two regiments of infantry on a hillside. We threw a few shells among them, and they withdrew to the woods on their left. We fired very little that day, only when we saw evidences of their massing troops. We had one man, A. J. Uline, slightly wounded by the sharpshooters.

January 2.—This morning we discovered the enemy had erected a fortification on the brow of the hill a mile and a half to our front. Soon they opened on us with their 24-pounder brass pieces. We did not reply, and they did us no injury. Soon they moved their guns nearer to us and more to their right. This gave them a flank fire, and we found it very dangerous to remain there. We were ordered to withdraw and take up a position a half mile to our rear and left, near the hospital. About a half hour after we had done so we saw the enemy had drawn up in line and were advancing in great force. Just then General Rosecrans ordered me to change my position, so that I was a little late in opening my fire. The enemy advanced steadily, driving in our pickets. Our fire was very effective, but their ranks closed up immediately. Soon I saw our right giving way that rested on the river. A heavy column had advanced under cover of the bank of the river and its skirty wood, and had flanked the troops stationed there. I then sent my caissons across to the west side, and seeing everything giving way I sent one section at a time across, still working those that remained until the others were over. When the last section reached the ford, one regiment of the enemy was within 100 yards of it, and poured a galling fire into us. Many of our horses were shot dead in the river, but our brave boys cleared them from the teams, and everything was got across. We opened fire on them as soon as we had crossed, though many of our caisson had not yet come up. We opened fire at three different positions after we crossed, and soon after the enemy gave back. We recrossed to the east side to sustain General Davis, and took a position in advance of the one taken the day previous.

January 2.—We expended this day 300 rounds of ammunition. Our fire was very good, disabling two of the enemy's limbers and killing their horses; but our fire was directed mostly at their advancing line. We lost nine horses, 2 sets lead harness, and had two men, Sergeant Holenback and Daniel Robin, wounded, not seriously.

January 3.—We had remained in our position, assigned us by General Davis, all night and until noon this day, before we were relieved. Our horses had had nothing to eat for forty-eight hours, and our men were wet with wading the river, and without shelter from the cold pelting rain; but when I told them it was the imperative order of General Davis, and of vital necessity, that we should hold out a little longer, they cheerfully obeyed. General Davis kindly divided what little he had to eat with our men, as did also Colonel Beatty the day before. We had no rations issued since the 30th, and our provision and forge wagon had been sent back by order of some one. At 11 o'clock a. m. we were relieved by the 26th Pennsylvania battery, and fell back a little to feed. At 11 o'clock p. m. we recrossed the river by order of Captain Mendenhall, and took up our old position on the west side commanding the ford.

January 4.—Remained at the ford until 5 p. m., when we were ordered to this camp.

We have expended, in all, 358 rounds of ammunition, lost nine horses, 2 sets harness, and have four men wounded. Present for duty, three commissioned officers and 107 men.

Yours, &c.,

CORTLAND LIVINGSTON,
Lieutenant, Commanding 3d Wisconsin Battery.

Captain SWALLOW,
Chief of Artillery Brigade, 3d Division,
Left Wing, Army of the Cumberland.

SIR: I have the honor to make the following report of the part taken in the recent action by the Pennsylvania battery.

On the morning of the 31st of December we were ordered to cross the river with the first brigade to take position, which we had barely time to do, when we were ordered back again. We then followed the first brigade towards the right wing, where the battle was raging fiercely. We found everything there in confusion, and it impossible to follow our brigade, and the battery nearly in the lines of the enemy. You then gave me permission to fight on my own hook, and do the best in my power. I then countermarched the battery, and took position on the rising ground on the left of the old block-house, along the line of the railroad, and opened fire on the enemy, who were advancing through the woods on the right of the pike and in our front. We fired as rapidly as possible with spherical case from our smooth-bores and Schenkel shells from our rifles, when finding the enemy checked, and our infantry advancing, we limbered to the front, advanced a short distance across the pike, where we came in position, and fired a few rounds, when the Board of Trade battery advanced and took position on our left, covering all the immediate ground in our front. We changed position by moving by the left flank, and occupied the rising ground in the cornfield to the right of the pike, and covering the woods out of which Generals Rousseau's and Negley's troops were retiring. We reserved our fire until our own troops were clear of the woods, and the enemy's lines, with banners flying, came in sight on the verge of the timber, within five hundred yards of our battery. We opened upon them with spherical case, shell, and canister, and fired briskly for about fifteen minutes, when, seeing no more of the enemy, we ceased firing. Some of the enemy's advance fell within fifteen to twenty yards of our guns. By General Rousseau's advice we then fell back on the rising ground between that and the railroad, firing a few shots at the enemy. By Captain Mendenhall's order we again advanced to our former position in the cornfield, on the right of the pike, and met with a warm reception from the enemy's musketry from the woods in our front, and the right flank being at the same time under cross fire from one of the enemy's batteries on our left. We opened fire on the woods in our front, and right soon silenced the enemy's fire, when, finding that we had no support on either flanks or rear, we again withdrew to the rising ground between the pike and the railroad. We then were ordered by Captain Mendenhall to take position across the pike, near the old log-house in our extreme front, having to guard against the enemy's advance up the pike and from the woods on our right, from which a continual fire of musketry annoyed us. At the same time a battery opened on us from the brick house near the pike, injuring one of our trails and limber, to which we replied until our long-range ammunition, the supply of which was small, was exhausted, when I had the smooth-bores withdrawn, and took a position to rake the pike with canister in case the enemy advanced, and kept the two rifles in the advance until night, when the whole battery was withdrawn about five hundred yards to the rear and supplied with ammunition.

On the morning of the 1st of January, by your order, we took position on the left of the railroad, and at a right angle with it, the sixth Ohio battery on our left. We did no firing that day with the exception of a few shots in the morning thrown at the woods in our front, and kept in position ready for action in that vicinity nearly the whole day. At night went into park in rear of the log-house near the railroad.

At sunrise on the morning of the 2d of January we were saluted with a shower of solid balls from the enemy's batteries falling in too close a vicinity to be agreeable. We mounted quickly and took position on the left of the railroad, on a small rise commanding the approach of the enemy in our front.

Captain Mendenhall then ordered us to the front to take a position commanding the open field to the left of the railroad. During the forenoon we were several times saluted with shots from the battery of the enemy planted in the woods beyond the opening in our front, to which we remained silent till near noon, when skirmishers of the fifty-first Indiana, which supported us on the right, advanced across the opening and drove in the enemy's pickets, when the enemy opened upon them with canister, and at the same time upon us with solid shot. Our skirmishers falling back, we opened with solid shot, when their battery became silent, and remained so until 3 o'clock p. m., when it again opened, and shortly after heavy musketry was heard upon our left. We opened at the battery in our front, when it became silent. When we saw the enemy advancing upon our left wing across the river, and our men falling back, we changed front, firing to the left, and opened a cross fire on them, and continued it till our forces in their front compelled them to fall back beyond our range. We remained in position until 9 o'clock p. m., when we ascertained that our supports on our flanks had been withdrawn without we being notified of the fact, and no pickets in front between us and the enemy's lines, I withdrew the battery to the rear of the infantry and parked. On the morning of the 3d of January we returned to our position of the previous day, support having returned, where we remained till 3 o'clock p m., when we were ordered across to take the place occupied by the third Wisconsin battery, where we remained till near midnight, when we were ordered to recross the river, which we did, and parked on the ground we now occupy. We expended about 1,650 rounds of ammunition, lost 7 horses, 2 men killed, and 7 wounded, a few small arms, and a large quantity of clothing, camp and garrison equipage.

Yours, respectfully,

A. J. STEVENS,
First Lieutenant, Commanding Battery.

Captain G. R. SWALLOW,
Chief of Artillery, Third Division, Left Wing, 14th Army Corps.

CAMP OF THE 7TH INDIANA BATTERY, 3D DIVISION,
January 5, 1863.

On the morning of the 31st December I ordered Lieutenant Buckman to move the battery in rear of the 2d brigade of the 3d division. This brigade was not moved across the river at the time the 1st and 3d crossed and recrossed, but was ordered up the pike in the vicinity of our hospital, where the enemy's cavalry were trying to capture prisoners from our broken and retreating columns. The battery opened upon them with shell, our cavalry at the same time charging upon them, which caused them to retreat in disorder. The brigade then advanced to the right and front through a cedar thicket into an open field, the battery following immediately in rear. While in the field, and nearly across it, our advance commenced skirmishing with the enemy, and immediately ordered the battery into position and the firing to commence with shell to our right and front, where the enemy's infantry were rapidly advancing upon us. They soon entered the field, when I ordered the battery to open upon them with canister, at the same time ordering the caissons to the rear. I soon saw part of the brigade falling back in disorder, and the enemy advancing across the field towards the battery with a yell. I then ordered the battery to limber to the rear and retire as rapidly as possible, which was done in not the best order. We reached the pike and took position near the old block-house, with a loss of First Lieutenant F. W. Buckman, seriously wounded; one man killed and two wounded. During the day the battery occupied several different positions engaging the enemy's artillery and infantry, but with what effect is not known. At night went into park a short distance from the old block-house, having had one lieutenant and four men wounded, and three killed.

On the morning of the 1st instant, by Captain Mendenhall's order, I took position near the ford, supported by General Cruft's brigade. Nothing worthy of note transpired during the day, and the morning of the 2d instant found us occupying the same position.

During the day General Negley's command took position in my rear and near the ford. Six guns of the artillery under his command took position on my left, and Captain Mendenhall's battery, of eight guns, under command of Lieutenant Parsons, came into position on my right and front. About 4 o'clock p. m. I received word that the enemy were advancing in force to attack the left of our wing. Their lines of infantry soon came in full view, and the batteries on my right and left, together with my own, opened a rapid and vigorous fire upon their advancing columns; they soon opened a galling artillery fire upon us from three different points. The battery on my left retired a short distance, and the one on my right commenced to fire retiring. Seeing this, I ordered the battery to fix prolonge, to fire retiring. About this time the vent of my left piece became filled with friction primers, and was ordered to the rear for repairs without my knowledge. The drivers of the other pieces, seeing this piece moving to the rear, supposed the order had been given to retire, and drove some forty yards to the rear before they could be halted. The order was then given to advance, and one piece was moved by hand to its first position; the rest were limbered and moved to the position first occupied, except the gun that had been ordered to the rear, when all the ammunition was expended except a few rounds of canister. In this engagement we had one man killed and two wounded.

January 3 found the battery in the same position. General Negley ordered the battery to open fire upon a line of the enemy's infantry, which did no good, and wounded one of my own men by the premature discharge of one of my guns. During the whole engagement I expended 406 rounds of ammunition, had one lieutenant and seven men wounded, four men killed, four horses wounded, one killed, and four missing. I should have done more firing, but General Rosecrans told me he wanted some ammunition reserved for an emergency.

Respectfully,

G. R. SWALLOW,
Captain 7th Indiana Battery.

CAMP OF THE THIRD WISCONSIN BATTERY,
Near Murfreesboro', January 5, 1863.

CAPTAIN: Our part taken in the actions of 31st of December, 1st, 2d, and 3d of January, 1863, I would report as follows:

At daybreak on the morning of the 31st December we moved from camp with our division, and crossed the ford of Stone river to the east and Murfreesboro' side. We took a commanding position in battery. In a short time we were ordered to recross the ford, (all had crossed,) and take a position commanding the ford; the 3d brigade, under Colonel Price, supported us. Very early in the action the enemy gained ground on our left wing, and many wagons and ambulances moved back and across the ford in the confusion. A hospital was established on the other side in some buildings. I inquired of Colonel Price, and was informed that he had pickets stationed there. Another told me there was a force of cavalry there—about twelve men. I saw a great stampede among the ambulances, wagons, and stragglers opposite, and was told some rebel cavalry was charging on them; I could not see or learn from what direction, and was fearful of firing into our own cavalry. I did not see the enemy until he had got among the wagons When they commenced moving them off, we fired upon them, disabling the wagons so that they blocked the lane, and the enemy were obliged to leave all but five. They carried off their wounded. One horse and rider were left dead. We shelled the woods and road in the direction they had taken. We expended that day fifty rounds of ammunition. Had one man wounded.

January 1.—We crossed the river with the division. After advancing half a mile we saw a line of infantry concealed a mile and a half to our front. We shelled them, and they withdrew from our sight. We fired very little that day; only when we saw evidences of their moving towards us. We had one man slightly wounded by their sharpshooters.

January 2.—The enemy, who had erected a fortification on the hill, opened upon us with their 24-pounder guns, but did us no injury. Soon they moved the guns nearer to us and to their right, which gave them a flanking fire, and obliged us to withdraw. We were not allowed to reply to the battery. Our second position was on the hill, near the hospital. When the army advanced we were a little slow in opening our fire, as General Rosecrans ordered us just then to change our position. Our fire was slow and very effective. Their battery opened upon us, but we replied to it with only one gun, directing our fire upon the advancing lines. When I saw that our right had been turned and flanked by a column moving under cover of the bank of the river, I ordered the caissons across, and then the left section, the other remaining guns keeping up their fire until the others had crossed. When the last section crossed, the enemy were within one hundred yards of the ford, and poured a steady fire into us. One horse was shot dead in the river, but the brave boys cleared him, and everything was got·across. We opened fire at three different points after we had crossed. When the enemy began to fall back, we recrossed the river to support General Davis, and remained in position all night and until 11 o'clock next day.

Our loss was nine horses shot, and two sets lead harness. We had four men wounded. Our men behaved bravely under the most discouraging circumstances. Lieutenant Hubbard, commanding the left section, was out, and fought his section well. Lieutenant Currier also showed fine points of a good officer. He had his horse shot in two places. Lieutenant Colburn was not with us. Too much praise cannot be bestowed upon my command for their good conduct.

N. B.—We fired in all 358 rounds.

C. LIVINGSTON,
Lieutenant, Commanding Third Wisconsin Battery.

Captain E. A. OTIS, *Assistant Adjutant General,*
3d Division, 14th Army Corps, Department of the Cumberland.

A list of the killed and wounded of the 3d division, left wing, 14th army corps, in the battle before Murfreesboro', as far as reported by the regimental surgeon, up to this date, January 6, 1863.

Brigadier General Van Cleve, wounded.

THIRTY-FIFTH INDIANA.

Killed.—Company A: Sergeant George A. Kirkland. Company D: Private James McClean. Company E: Sergeant Michael Rafferty; Corporals Austin E. Sanders, Thomas Woods, and Patrick Connel; Privates John James

Charles Meeks, George Miller, Cornelius Donavan, Hugh Green, John Lyons, Amasa Perkinson, Michael Kenary, John Stanton, and George Butler. Company F: Sergeant Edward Bolen; Corporal E. F. Hurlbut; Privates John Y. Flora and William Martin. Company G: Orderly Sergeant Isaac M. Cassidy; Private George Kessler. Company H: Private John Bridenbaugh. Company I: Corporal Samuel Lockland; Private Lerick Moore. Company K: Orderly Sergeant John Kinsella; Private Thomas Willey. Total 27.

Wounded.—Colonel B. J. Muller. Company A: Corporal Charles Murray, thigh, severe; Privates Jacob Shearer, arm, severe, and side; Michael Henley, side, serious, (died;) John McMahon, chest, mortal, (since died;) Michael Murphy, hand, severe; Michael Barrett, hand, severe; William H. Mock, left arm, slight. Company B: Captain John P. Duffieg, (acting major,) prisoner; Privates Zacariah Upp, neck, severe; Jeremiah Sullivan, thigh, slight; Peter Quinn, arm, severe; Lawrence Sheridan, arm, slightly; Anthony Malcolm, arm, serious; Frederick Whitenbrook, arm, serious. Company C: Sergeants Daniel Kelley, thigh, slightly; Patrick Morrison, severe, right wrist; Privates Thomas Mitchell, hand, slightly; William Cramer, severe; George Peterson, head, slight. Company D: First Lieutenant William H. Kilboy, fatal, side; Privates Bernard Smith, foot, shattered; Henry C. Hargis, left side and right thigh; William H. Farmer, left shoulder and thigh; Milton D. Cotton, thigh and testicles; Thomas Alvey, abdomen, serious; John Elder, shoulder; John Avis, foot. Company E: Captain Henry Proper, neck, severe, died. Lieutenant James A. Cavisk, thigh, slightly; Sergeant Mathew McGuire, side, severe; Corporal Patrick Connel, mortal; Privates John O'Brien, fracture of thigh, serious; John Murphy, fracture, slight; John McCrillion, fracture, serious; Michael Clark, thigh, slight; Dennis Bowers, leg, severe; Michael O'Brien, thigh fractured; Company F: Sergeant John Lowe, side, severe, shell; Privates Rowland Carpenter, left lung, serious; John Goldsmith, fracture of leg, slight; Drummer Karley Barker, fracture of leg, severe. Company G: Sergeant James Conway, chest, mortal; Corporals Bernard McCabe, neck; Joseph Donigan, mortal; Rowland Fagan, leg, slight; Alfred Phelps, left arm; Privates Thomas Carroll, arm, slight; Thomas Ryan, left thigh, severe; Samuel Mounts, wrist fractured by ball. Company H: Captain John Crowe, thigh, slightly; Sergeant Charles M. Ware, right thigh, severe; Privates Jacob Richinan, neck; George Stokes, fracture of thigh; George W. Reever, left hip, serious; Thomas Hughes, right lung, severe; James Bradford, slight. Company I: Sergeant Porter Lyman, chest, severe; Private Andrew Seylong, right shoulder. Company K: Captain Frank Bagot, spine, fatal; Private William Regan, serious. Total, 60.

NINETY-NINTH OHIO VOLUNTEER INFANTRY.

Killed.—Company A: Privates R. Hamilton and J. Sparks. Company B: Privates E. S. Jolly and E. Touquet. Company C: Private J. L. Lucky. Company F: Sergeant E. W. Heyline, Privates Henry Hult, G. W. Mapes, and P. Duet. Company H: Corporal J. W. Murphy.

Wounded.—Colonel P. T. Swayne, slightly. Company A: Captain W. C. Scott, severely, since died; Corporal W. A. Hill, head, mortal; Privates G. W. Little, leg; J. Kampf, leg and thigh; W. A. Roberts, groin; M. Booth, shoulder, slightly; S. Snepp, hip; G. S. Shaffer, shoulder; D. Diesbold, wounded; and S. B. Moneysmith, abdomen, slightly. Company B: Privates P. Charpin, face; and W. Mumaugh, leg. Company D: Sergeant W. B. Richards, neck, severely; Corporal J. S. Selby, breast, severely; Privates M. Vance, side; J. Lonk, side, slightly; J. Miller, finger shot off; M. Haunch, arms, slightly; F. Rumbaugh, arms, slightly; A. Snyder, arms, slightly; M. Hammel, arms, slightly; and N. W. Jenkins, thigh, slightly. Company F: Corporals J. Rice, hand; B.

T. Burrows, hand; Privates W. Hattel, foot, slightly; C. Smith, foot, slightly; J. Kempler, arm; J. Neiville, arm; and H. Fried, arm, slightly. Company G: Captain O. P. Capell, thigh, mortal. Company H: Privates W. C. Peirod, arm, slightly; S. Dumberger, neck and shoulders; D. W. Kleine, hip and knee; J. W. Swader, wrist; and G. W. Kiger, head, slightly. Company I: Corporal J. Beurent, breast, since died; Privates J. Ashfeller, arm, slightly; J. Fry, shoulder, slightly; and D. Sideres, head, slightly. Company K: First Lieutenant R. S. Kishler, hip, slightly; Sergeant F. E. Stephenson, side; Corporal A. J. Mony, head, mortal; Privates N. Sprague, arm, slightly; J. Allspaugh, arm, head, foot, and leg; P. Shuf, arm, slightly; G. Hackerman, arm and hand; and D. McKercher, head, mortal.

Summary.

Killed	10
Wounded	48
Total	58

EIGHTY-SIXTH INDIANA VOLUNTEER INFANTRY.

Killed.—Company A: First Lieutenant G. W. Smith, Sergeant Robert Myers; Privates Richard Storves and James O. Solan. Company B: Privates George E. Ames, Richard C. Crowell, and A. M. Saxon. Company C: Privates Ed. Blanchfield, William J. Board, W. H. H. Martin, Derrick Lanbaugh, Benjamin Frullinger, and J. Williams. Company D: Privates Nathan Pringle and William Lamb. Company E: Sergeant Abram Fiske, Privates W. B. Fleming and James H. Clinton. Company F: Sergeants J. W. Wilson, James A. Howard; Privates William Stockdale, E. P. Stephenson, Henry Door, and Floyd N. Worrell.

Wounded. Company A: Captain A. Frazer, slightly; Sergeants William Dinmore, slightly; Eli Elder, thigh, severely; Perry Gorham, leg, severely; Privates Charles H. Campbell, ankle, slightly; Samuel L. Ross, slightly; John H. Mount, face and wrist; Ephraim Wings, side; George E. Lindsey, both arms; Bangor Wells, hip and leg; John W. Franch, hands; Thomas Hester, leg, severely; and James F. Dinsmore, hand. Company B: Privates Albert Rekafoot, slightly; Benjamin Ashley, John F. Whiche, and Daniel W. Oliver. Company C: Sergeants C. C. Sylvester, hips; William Coffin, thigh; Privates J. Schoolcroft, Nathaniel Ellis, Charles Patten, A. B. O'Dill, Nathan Craffuberg, neck and foot, severely; Eli Swartz, both legs; H. Morehouse, arms, slightly; C. W. Gilger, thigh, severely; David Stevens, thigh, severely. Company D: First Lieutenant Jackson Hickman; Corporal Lewis Stevens; Privates James Guest, Winter Crabb, Robert Newhexter, Erwin J. Greaves, and Joseph W. Stephens. Company E: Privates Peter Grimes and William Duncan. Company F: Corporal William Stevens; Privates John B. Smith, G. Baldwin, and John C. Beard. Company G: Privates Israel Wells, hip; Alonzo More, arm; Jacob A. Nesser; Silas F. Collins, shoulder; and James Cambridge, abdomen. Company H: Privates John Wilson; William M. Barnes; Luke Barker; and W. J. Moss, wrist. Company I: First Lieutenant John Gullion, thigh; Privates John O. Heaton, side; H. B. Gant, hand; Joseph Sheets, wrist; Daniel Startle; John J. Creeks; and John Starks. Company K: Privates Bast. Green, breast; William Flythe, side; Henry Oxly, leg; Joseph Bown; Patten English; James Picknell; Morris Wild; and James Williams.

Summary.

Commissioned officers—Killed	1
Wounded	4
Non-commissioned officers and privates—Killed	23
Wounded	62
Total	90

SEVENTY-NINTH INDIANA VOLUNTEERS.

Killed.—Company B: Privates John Calter and Jacob Clouard. Company D: Privates Thomas Eller and Martin Van Stanley. Company E: Privates Benjamin Fose. Company F: Lieutenant Thomas Poynter.

Wounded.—Company A: Corporals S. B. Gaylord, thigh; and William Kinsley, hip; Privates Thomas S. Lawson, left arm; George Steinman, left arm and right foot; William P. Moore, right leg; Aaron P. Lawson, left hip and right thigh; John Nelson, thigh; Timothy Halsey, heel; G. W. Williams, leg; William Carr, arm; and J. M. Paddock, arm. Company B: Second Lieutenant Arthur Vance, leg; Privates William Hatton, right leg; Samuel S. Hook, left thigh; John W. Hopper, lung; James Bellis, side; and J. Winkle, thigh. Company C: Second Lieutenant Benjamin Vallequette, right leg; Privates Andrew Eakes, thumb; Benjamin Lester, head; and J. McMannis, head. Company D: Privates Darius A. King, right thigh and wrist; W. Hines, arm; and George Harris, arm. Company E: Captain John L. Scott, left arm; Second Lieutenant Jones Luman, right arm; Privates Richard M. Clarke, right knee; William C. Rogers, side; John E. Dill, hand; Henry Slusher, arm; and G. M. Hadde, breast. Company F: Second Lieutenant Zantes Catterdon, foot; Private N. Brooks, foot. Company G: Privates Cyrus C. Hyzer, shoulder; Joshua Halton, hand; and A. S. Hardin, right arm, amputated. Company H: Second Lieutenant Edgar Foster, left thigh; Privates James M. Mashiet, left shoulder; J. M. Petitt, right leg; John S. McClane, left thigh, amputated; Milton Henwese, left leg, amputated; —— Halsizer, right leg; James Garrold, leg; Chas. Hattin, arm; and Charles Tyler, arm. Company I: Privates J. Edmond Clark, left arm; John S. Mitchell, breast; Ealing Wheaton, breast; John Sereal, breast; and William McCano, left side, mortally. Company K: Private James Dolson, right thigh.

Summary.

Killed	6
Wounded	51
Total	90

NINTH KENTUCKY VOLUNTEERS.

Killed.—Company A: Captain D. B. Coyle; Privates Andrew Bray and Iroam Fooley. Company B: Captain William Bryan. Company C: Sergeants R. D. Napier and J. S. Mayhew; Private J. J. Raglan. Company D: Lieut. A. S. Leggett; Privates Claiborne Borden, Obediah Leonard, and Ralston Jenkins. Company E: Private Henry Bacon. Company F: Lieutenant F. F. Carpenter; Sergeant G. W. McReynolds; Privates J. W. Richards and John W. England. Company K: Privates Ephraim Thomas, Philip Murphy, and John Gammon.

Wounded.—Company B: Lieutenants Silas Clarke, slightly; and B. M

Johnson, slightly; Privates Andrew Moss, hand, slightly; W. Gass, neck, slightly; George Marsh, left knee; J. A. Johnson, chest, slightly; and Gilbert Wakefield, left leg. Company C: Lieutenant F. Heter, slightly; Sergeant Roly Howell, slightly; Corporal L. W. Meadows, arm, amputated; Privates B. H. Y. Alexander, mortally, since died; G. L. Andrews, hand, slightly; W. Spear, thigh fractured; J. R. Stewart, thigh; J. M. Huntsman, thigh fractured; L. Garman, thigh, slightly; Bradford Howell, fracture, seriously; James Stewart, fracture, seriously; W. R. Clark, foot, slightly; J. W. Huntsman, hand, slightly; J. W. Mathews, hand, slightly; G. W. Spear, arm, seriously; Rit. Stewart, thigh, seriously; and G. W. Bradley, thigh, slightly. Company D: Privates J. C. Whitley, leg fractured, seriously; John Austin, arm, slightly; J. H. Glover, arm, severely; H. P. Jenkins, abdomen, doing well; J. M. Bean, right leg, slightly; and J. H. Bell, left arm. Company E: Privates W. J. Norvall, neck; S. Ratrain, right leg; W. L. Adams, right arm; J. H. Barbee, head; R. W. Barbee, arm; John H. Donohue, contusion; and Henry Bokan, both kidneys. Company F: Captain R. A. Reed, seriously; Sergeant E. Reeds, right hand, slightly; Corporal M. Patten, right hand, slightly; Privates J. R. McElroy, abdomen and leg, mortally; Calvin Bracken, right thigh and testicles; M. J. Miles, left leg fractured, severely; Joseph Taylor, severely; M. S. Yoke, right hand, slightly; R. Harris, both feet, severely; R. J. Clarkston, right hand, slightly; W. Chandler, right hand, slightly; and Riley A. Read, chest. Company G: Corporal J. Proffit, right hand, slightly; Privates J. A. Passley, left thigh fractured, severely; W. D. Boyle, arm, slightly; J. S. Creek, right leg, slightly; Joseph Finner, fracture, severely; and Payton Jenkins, right leg fractured. Company H: Lieutenant J. W. Crain, seriously; Corporal J. E. Ayers, side, slightly; Privates A. F. Register, leg fractured; J. M. Vaughn, side, slightly; J. M. Vaugh, side, slightly; John Waxham, right forearm fractured, severely; R. D. Frazer, hand, slightly; Isaam Fooley, hand, slightly; F. J. Meadow, hand, slightly; F. J. Cooley, hand, slightly; R. Frazer, hand, slightly; and W. J. Croon, lower jaw, badly. Company I: Corporal J. M. Gray, chest, severely; Privates A. Blankenship, left hand; J. T. Brooks, leg, slightly; J. F. Mayhew, leg, slightly; Asa Tracy, left shoulder, slightly; L. P. Cox, hand, slightly; and Joel Barker, right arm, slightly. Company K: Privates R. Goad, left arm fractured, severely; John Shivers, right arm, slightly; William Simmons, left leg, slightly; J. Lemons, right arm, slightly; W. J. Dorsey, right chest, slightly; Jasper Hayes, right chest, severely; Joshua Lancaster, leg fractured; D. D. Kirby, left hand, slightly; and Hagan A. Bishop, chest, mortally.

Summary.

Killed	19
Wounded	83
Total	102

THIRTEENTH OHIO INFANTRY.

Killed.—Colonel J. G. Hawkins. Company A: Lieutenant James A. Whitaker; Orderly Sergeant Samuel D. Huber; Privates M. Miller, Robert Roan, Jacob A. Lawrence, Henry McKnight, and C. D. Oyler. Company C: Sergeants Aden A. Wood and James Q. Holland; Private Thomas Keiser. Company D: Privates Nelson Bennett, William Brooks, John Griffith, and Grafton Downer. Company F: Sergeant Joseph Dunlop. Company H: Private Joseph G. Moody. Company I: Privates Jacob Oberdef and James R. Kirk. Company K: Privates Henry Calback and John Campbell.

Wounded.—Company A: Lieutenant John Murphy, mortally; Sergeant John Reiger, mortally; Sergeant Francis Reiger, severely; Privates Wm. G.

Weaver, slightly; S. B. Hawkins, severely; Alexander M. Duck, severely; Wm. H. Mateson, slightly; E. D. Cline, mortally; Peter Leonard, severely; Wm. Wilson, severely; Wm. J. Messenger, severely; Wm. Herron, slightly; Lewis Walters, severely; John Westbaugher, severely; Samuel Boney, severely; Edward Seely, slightly; John Ritter, severely; Robert Allen, severely; James C. Reed, severely; George McLaughlin, severely; Joseph Allen, severely; and Wm. S. Kelley, severely. Company B: Corporal Samuel Lindsey, slightly; Corporal Samuel Williams, slightly; Privates Joseph Briggs, severely; John Cooper, severely; Lewis Harkleroad, slightly; James Pucket, slightly; and Williard Easterly, slightly. Company C: Captain E. M. Mast, slightly; Lieutenant Samuel C. Gould, severely; Orderly Sergeant James D. Caskey, severely; Corporal Thomas Moore, severely; Bugler Fred. Rupple, severely; Privates Adam Shade, severely; John A. Grubber, severely; H. H. Etzeller, slightly; Isaiah Cline, slightly; and Levi Beeson, severely. Company D: Orderly Sergeant J. W. G. Simmons, severely; Privates Andrew Reed, severely; Adam Weaver, slightly; James Heony, slightly; Asel J. Clark, slightly; George Ballou, severely; John Platner, slightly; William Culimber, slightly; and Solomon Gay, severely. Company E: Private August Keisel, severely. Company F: Lieutenant John E. Ray, severely; Orderly Sergeant S. W. Ripley, severely; Sergeant Pierce Hobble, slightly; Corporal Jasper McDonald, severely; Privates H. Wilkins, severely; John Derwester, severely; Eminet Derflinger, severely; Pat. H. Mahon, severely; Jacob Levis, severely; and Lewis Dunser, severely. Company G: Lieutenant John Fox, mortally; Sergeant Reuben Framen, severely; Privates John F. Rosenbum and Fred. Hose, severely. Company H: Private Ed. Harner, severely. Company I: Sergeant F. M. Hutcheson, slightly; Corporal Enos Jones, slightly; and Private C. H. Burge, slightly. Company K: Lieutenant Thomas Stone, slightly.

Summary.

Commanding officers—Killed	2
Wounded	4
Non-commissioned officers and privates—Killed	20
Wounded	64
Total	90

TWENTY-FIRST KENTUCKY VOLUNTEER INFANTRY.

Killed.—Company A: Private James Vanpelt. Company B: Privates Carlin Ferguson, Isaac Peirce, J. B. Wells. Company F: Sergeant William Lacey. Company G: Lieutenant B. Stone.

Wounded.—Major W. W. Dowden, right thigh, severely. Company A: Sergeants Newton Scarce, right leg, slightly; Henry Stahel, arm, severely; Privates E. W. McMinaway, finger, slightly; John Robertson, leg, slightly; Ed. Kennedy, leg, severely. Company B: Sergeant John F. Duff, both knees, mortally; Privates G. W. Nance, left leg, slightly; J. W. London, arm, severely; W. Jewell, arm, cheek, and jaw; Joel F. Jewel, left arm, slightly. Company C: Captain S. R. Sherrard, left side, slightly; Privates Pat. Welch, left side, severely; Charles Townsen, right foot, severely; Charles Redford, right foot, severely; Joseph Owens, chest, slightly. Company D: Private Joseph Wainscott, left leg, severely. Company E: Privates A. Elliot, right arm, slightly; Joseph Shaw, right arm, slightly; John Kidd, abdomen, by shell; F. Hieroumyes, both thighs. Company F: Lieutenant John H. Bevil, abdomen, mortally; Corporal William Reivil, neck, severely; Privates J. M. Tolls, left thigh, severely; James Fultz, chest, slightly. Company G: Corporal Al Campbell, head, slightly; Privates Jeremiah Crane, head, slightly; John Dodd, thigh, severely; William Burchald, leg, slightly. Company H: Lieutenant Fletcher Hardee, left thigh, severely; Privates Elijah Bell, abdomen, severely; Silas Hardee, right arm, severely; William Bates, head, slightly; David Sidebottom, right side, severely; J. H. Rhynes, chest, severely. Company K: Privates R. H. Swinney, right leg, slightly; W. H. Poynter, left side, mortally; George Thompson, right hand, slightly; John L. Scott, back, slightly.

Summary.

Commissioned officers killed	1
Commissioned officers wounded	4
Non-commissioned officers and privates killed	5
Non-commissioned officers and privates wounded	35
Total	45

FIFTY-NINTH REGIMENT OHIO VOLUNTEER INFANTRY.

Killed.—Company A: Corporal William Owens, Private William English. Company C: Privates Aaron Leach, Augustus Penn, (band.)

Wounded.—Company A: Orderly Sergeant J. Harbinton, back, slightly; Privates Henry Howe, left arm, slightly; William Hutchinson, back, severely. Company B: Private Aaron Moore, hand, slightly. Company C: Lieutenant W. B. Klins, right arm, severely; Corporal John Brockman, arm, severely; Privates Benjamin West, knees, severely; Silas English, left thigh and hand, severely; John English, hip, severely; William Beeker, hip, severely; Henry Reynolds, face, slightly; B. F. Ely, hip, since died; Thomas Purdy, foot, slightly; John Stephenson, slightly; Charles Hayle, slightly. Company D: Lieutenant John O'Connor, left hand, slightly; Corporal Alexander Crumm, left side, severely; Privates Ed. Ryan, right arm, severely; James Fryman, severely; Robert Feltieu, finger, slightly; William Nicols, severely; Andrew Pennery, severely; William Rounds, left thigh, severely; Alexander Conway, slightly. Company E: Corporal John Ferrie, right arm, slightly; Privates M. South, left knee, severely; Alfred Storey, hand, slightly. Company F: Private Willis Levis, right arm, slightly. Company H: Captain J. W. Hill, face, severely; Private Alfred Edan, right foot, slightly. Company I: Privates John Carr, arm, slightly; George Lewis, slightly. Company K: Orderly Sergeant Henry Miller, face, severely; Corporal John White, arm, severely; Privates William Clark, arm, severely; John Howe, neck, severely; John Hicks, arm, severely. B. B. Dougherty, (band,) shoulder, slightly.

Summary.

Commissioned officers wounded	3
Non-commissioned officers and privates killed	4
Non-commissioned officers and privates wounded	35
Total	42

ELEVENTH KENTUCKY INFANTRY.

Killed.—Company B: Private E. Parsons. Company C: Private Issac W. Emby. Company D: Private James Russ. Company E: Private S. B. Forbes. Company F: Sergeant Andrew B. Dabbs, and Private J. Wiley Winton. Company H: Private O. J. Norman.

Wounded.—Adjutant J. F. Kenmaid, severely. Company A: Sergeant George Chandle, severely; Corporal H. G. White, severely; Privates H. W. Scott, slightly; M. Young, severely; James Mulligan, slightly; A. Sanders, slightly; and Archy White, slightly. Company B: Lieutenant W. F. Ward, severely; Sergeants George White, severely; F. P. Martin, mortally; Corporals Jesse Smith, severely; Elijah Dobbs, slightly; Privates John Suddith, severely; A. King, slightly; A. Johnson, slightly; O. G. Gwynn, slightly; and W. Greenwood, slightly. Company C: Captain John Tyler, severely; Sergeant W. Furlow, severely; Corporals James Ebny, slightly; D. Keysinger, slightly; Privates Virgil Emby, slightly; D. R. Keysinger, severely; David Snodgrass, severely; Lewis Felty, severely; J. McKenney, slightly; L. Greathouse, slightly; S. Baugh, severely; Joseph Austin, severely; A. Graves, severely; Lewis Phelps, severely; R. Lee, slightly; L. Pea, slightly; and Wm. McKinney, severely. Company D: Sergeants William Jenkins, severely; J. Powell, slightly; W. Sheren, slightly; Privates Russel Jones, severely; W. Gaines, slightly; W. Goodman, slightly; J. W. Grubb, severely; J. B. Gaines, severely; and James Rassee, (missing.) Company E: Corporal S. B. Goulds, slightly; and Private G. W. Blair, slightly. Company F: Sergeant C. A. Dunn, slightly; Corporal D. Grubb, slightly; Privates B. Bringham, slightly; R. H. Peirsons, severely; S. P. Baughn, severely; C. C. Moore, severely; Stephen Bringham, severely; W. R. Erving, mortally; S. P. Vaughn, severely; and W. Manney, slightly. Company G: Sergeant J. M. Conway, slightly; Corporal P. Devoise, slightly; Privates James A. Phelps, severely; Thomas Hampton, slightly; J. P. Johnson, slightly; and W. P. Herrald, slightly. Company H: Lieutenant Columbus Neel, slightly; Sergeants G. B. Humpurg, slightly; —— Bertrand, slightly; Privates B. F. Cartsibin, slightly; David Holland, slightly; A. Stotcaugh, slightly; J. F. Duvall, slightly; M. S. Ham, slightly; Shauh Solomon, severely; J. L. Carnees, slightly; J. Beasley, severely; and C. P. Donahoo, slightly. Company I: Privates F. Mage, slightly; J. S. Campfield, slightly; J. N. Simmons, slightly; and W. Whitney, severely. Company K: Corporal Augustus Lewis, slightly; Privates J. B. Blackwell, slightly; Jesse Shanks, severely; John Allen, severely; W. P. Hill, severely; P. K. Harper, severely; and G. B. Steward, slightly.

Summary.

Non-commissioned officers and privates killed	7
Commissioned officers wounded	4
Non-commissioned officers and privates wounded	81
Total	92

FORTY-FOURTH INDIANA REGIMENT.

Killed.—Company B: Private Thomas Helsper. Company F: Privates John Webster, Jacob Parker, and George W. Wallace. Company G: Private Jefferson Shanon. Company I: Second Lieutenant Frank Baldwin, and Private Childs Drake. Company K: Private Harrison Harwood.

Wounded.—Company A: Corporal George W. Perris, leg, severely; Privates Frederick Swambaugh, back, severely; and Joseph Millens, leg, slightly. Company B: Sergeants Albert Ritz, foot, severely; and William Cartwright, leg, slightly; Privates John Cogan, head, severely; William Clark, finger, amputated; Scott Eddy, hip, severely; George Scott, finger, slightly; Gable Scott, thigh, severely; and Samuel Widner, thigh, severely. Company C: Second Lieutenant Sidney Livingston, slightly; Privates Jacob Smith, thigh severely; Samuel Sweet, finger, slightly; Owen Show, arm, slightly; and Jackson Hyser, nose, slightly. Company D: Privates John Holden, chest, mortally; William Apir, arm, slightly; Amos Britton, leg, severely; and William Routson, hand, severely. Company E: Second Lieutenant And. Read, slightly; Privates Hiram Biddle, back, severely; F. A. Gable, shoulder, severely; Frederick Banta, shoulder, slightly; and John Spurgeon, leg, severely. Company G: Private Lucius McGowan, thigh, severely. Company H: First Lieutenant J. H. Dancer, severely; Privates Peter Allspaugh, thigh, severely; Victor Ketchum, thigh and scrotum, severely; Van Buren Fisher, leg, severely; and John J. Crist, leg, severely. Company I: Privates David Robison, wound unknown; P. Robbins, arms, severely; David Greenwoult, leg, severely; Jacob Hicks, wrist, slightly; Francis Johnson, back and elbow, severely; Jacob Hicks, wrist, slightly; Francis Johnson, back and elbow, severely; George Castor, finger, slightly; Bennet Robe, arm, slightly; Lewis Tiffany, hip, severely; Asa Harwood, arm, severely; Chester Gwinnemyse, foot, severely; Robin E. Food, thigh, slightly; Frederick Javener, side and arm, severely; Frederick Strouss, arm, slightly; John Robison, wrist, slightly; Martin Danner, shoulder, severely; James A. Smith, arm fractured, severely; Martin G. Hurd, face, severely; and John Lesher, face, severely. Company K: Sergeant Frank Willis, foot, slightly; Privates Samuel Squires, hand, severely; and Orlando Wright, knee, severely.

Summary.—Missing and supposed to be wounded, 25; total killed and wounded, 60.

NINETEENTH OHIO VOLUNTEER INFANTRY.

Killed.—Company A: Privates Nicholas Taylor and John Clark. Company B: First Lieutenant Daniel Donavan; Corporals —— Marks and Daniel Cooper; Privates George Courtney, James Sewell, and Henry Ague. Company C: First Lieutenant Job D. Bell; Corporal —— Shafer; Private Lucius S. Scott. Company D: Second Lieutenant R. D. Wilson; Sergeant Major Lyman Tylee; Private Gustavus Boyson. Company E: Captain Urwin Bean; Private George Herald. Company F: Private William Gable. Company G: Private Charles Castimore. Company H: Corporal John Blythe. Company I: Corporal J. W. Warer. Company K: Private Valentine Murril.

Wounded.—Company A: Corporals Frank Shilty, shoulder and lung, severely; George Leipstag, right thigh, severely; Privates John Saylor, head, severely; M. L. Hower, right arm, severely; T. Jackson, left leg, severely; John Lovett, right arm, severely; John Cross, right arm, severely; Nicholas Kline, right arm, severely; Thomas Griffin, left arm, slightly; W. H. Betchel, slightly; James Holoday, slightly; —— Flinn, hand, slightly; George Nave, shoulder, severely. Company B: Privates James Balmore, shoulder, severely; James K. Bailey, left hand, severely; Henry Crum, left arm, severely; Samuel Clark, left arm, severely; William H. Dubes, left hand, severely; Isaac Davis, left foot, severely; David Hogg, right leg, severely; John C. Johnston, left thigh, severely; Charles Jacob, left hand, severely; George King, left hand, severely; William Lewis, right leg, severely; Hiram Lyons, left leg, severely; James Mathews, left thigh, severely; Harman McFall, head, slightly; Wm. McCurdy, head, slightly; Henry Patterson, left arm, severely; Ami Stilson, left shoulder, severely; Samuel Shafer, scalp, slightly. Company C: Captain H. G. Stratton, severely; Sergeant James Baly, hand, slightly; Corporals Areal Adams, ankle, slightly; Charles Talbertsen, left arm, severely; Ira Haight, left leg, severely; Privates Henry King, left leg, severely; W. P. Gartman, left leg, severely; Noah Dally, right leg, severely; Milo Wilson, left hand, severely; James Boyd, left leg, severely; J. B. Lewis, left leg, slightly; G. W. Allen, hand, slightly; H. W. Allen, arm, slightly; W. J. Miller, right leg, severely; Daniel Powell, right leg, severely; Joseph Scott, left leg, severely; Miller Wilson, both legs, severely; Hiram Rader, right lung, severely. Company D: Sergeants Jesse Ross, right arm, slightly; J. W. Meek, hand, severely; Corporal William Keefer, right lung, severely; Privates Washington Bryant, left leg, severely; James Bennett, nose, severely; G. S. Bradshaw, left foot, amputated; W. M. Best, left foot, amputated; James Craig, left hand; James Barber, leg, severely; Sylvester Craig, arm, severely. Company E: Sergeant G. I. Swank, face, severely; Corporals Thomas Gilson, hand, severely; Frederick Painer, face severely; William Clank, right leg, severely; George W. Little, left thigh, severely; Privates James Franks, hand, severely; Anthony Bollinger, left foot, severely; George Cobhouse, right leg, severely; William Cooper, left arm, severely; John T. Green, hand, slightly; Israel Granger, foot, severely; Thos. Harbaugh, arm, severely; J. H. Lamb, shell, severely; Jennings Northrop, breast, slightly; William Zeigle, right arm, severely. Company F: First Lieutenant Aurora C. Keel, severely; Sergeants Frederick G. Feller, knee, severely; Alonzo Himes, leg, severely; Privates Michael Koblity, left foot, slightly; Michael Graffee, leg, severely; Henry Rose, thigh, severely; Andrew English, foot, slightly; W. N. Fugate, both knees, severely; Daniel Stamer, slightly. Company G: Sergeant William Hunt, hand, slightly; Corporal Peter Shafer, leg, slightly; Privates George Lawson, chest, severely; Lyman Dunn, right hand, severely; J. C. Wilmarth, left arm, severely; Frank Hicock, brain, contusion, severely; Henry Townsend, hand, severely; Jacob Keefe, right thigh, severely; William Caley, left thigh, severely; Fisher McKee, arm, slightly. Company H: Corporals S. L. Parmour, hand, slightly; Wesly Desselin, hip, slightly; Charles Moore, left side, slightly; Privates Elias Culbertson, right leg, slightly; James Cox, left hand, slightly; Frank Dupon, thigh, slightly; Leander Knowles, foot, slightly; Joseph Polin, foot, slightly; Adolphus Patterson, left hand, slightly; John Reiter, right arm, slightly. Company I: Sergeants A. R. Raff, left hand, slightly; J. M. Dunlop, right leg, severely; Corporals William Bennett, left arm, slightly; Jeff. Dunbar, leg, by shell, slightly; E. Robinson, arm, severely; Peter Fisher, right side, severely; John Yellens, right leg, slightly; Private Hiram Doll, left hand, slightly. Company K: Privates Ed. Damp, left hand, slightly; Simon Cook, left hand, slightly; J. Carter, leg, severely; G. L. Bishop, right hand, slightly; Thomas King, right side, slightly; Joseph Martin, left hand, slightly.

Summary.

Officers killed	4
Enlisted men killed	17
Officers wounded	2
Enlisted men wounded	116
Total	139

Additional Names.

Wounded.—Company A: Privates Albert Rovutz, slightly: W. A. Sutherland, hip, by shell; Peter Moverer, slightly. Company B: Private Reynolds J. Cowder, slightly. Company C: Privates H. G. Stratton, severely; Robert Reed, slightly. Company D: James Craig, left hand, slightly; Company I: Private John White, severely. Company K: Corporal Ed. R. Houks, severely; Privates Charles Breede, severely; Isaac Preist, left hand, slightly; James Malone, severely.

Grand total, 151.

FIFTY-FIRST OHIO VOLUNTEER INFANTRY.

Killed.—Company A: William A. McKee. Company B: Sergeant B. F. Fry, Privates George Cunningham and Robert Flynn. Company C: Privates Henry Cosgrove, Clark Steward and N. Scott. Company D: Corporal S. M. Brown, and Private William Blackford. Company E: Corporal John A. Taggort, Privates John W. Dutton, F. H. Miller, and George W. Fetters. Company F: Corporal —— Murphy, Privates C. S. Meek, Wallie E. Davis, and Thomas Keslip. Company H: Privates John Davidson and George Morrow. Company I: Corporal Joseph Critchfield, Privates Francis M. Landes, Lyman D. Dyal, and Alma Richardson. Company K: Private Joel Davis.

Wounded.—Lieutenant Colonel R. H. McClain, abdomen, severely; Adjutant William Nicolay, chest; Company A: Corporal Simon Hale, ear, slightly; Privates John W. Kahn, left arm, slightly; Fred. Yucher, left arm, severely; Alex. Redden, left shoulder, severely; John Showacre, shoulder, slightly; Andrew Ald, neck, mortal; John Plotts, abdomen, severely; George Patterson, thigh and hand, severely; William R. Jennings, head, severely; William Moore, leg, severely; Helligan Kuhn, thigh and head, severely; John Park, leg and chest, severely; George Dunn, shoulder, slightly; —— Williams, leg, slightly; Napoleon Williams, leg, slightly; J. Cordery, back, slightly; John C. Herring, arm, slightly; George Wilson, head, slightly; Frederick Messley, thigh, slightly. Company B: First Sergeant A. G. Wood, chest, severely; Sergeant David Fisk, shoulder, slightly; Corporal M. F. Ault, chest, severely; Privates Wm. Rendee, left foot, severely; Theodore Everest, thigh, severely; Wesly Poland, arm and chest, severely; L. Coy, left leg and right arm, severely; Nathaniel Guthree, left leg, severely; Robert Thompson, thigh, severely; Gotleib Frost, foot, slightly; William Thome, back, slightly; John Aling, foot, slightly; and John Hatmaker, leg, slightly. Company C: Captain B. F. Heskett, wounded, since dead; Lieutenant D. M. Jones, abdomen, slightly; Lieutenant Philip Everbort, right arm; First Sergeant John Q. Winklepleck, left thigh, severely; Sergeant John Hock, ankle, slightly; Privates John Gunther, right hip, slightly; W. J. Jones, left arm and head, severely; Peter Dickey, head, severely; Jacob Miller, arm, slightly. Company D: First Sergeant Ed. Coun, head, severely; Sergeants Thomas A. Reed, shoulder, slightly; William Griffen, abdomen, severely; Corporals Jos. Stanford, thigh, severely; James Esline, hip and shoulder; John Paris, abdomen and head, severely; Musician Joshua Dickenson, perineum, slightly; Privates Thomas Titus, left arm, severely; William Jones, right side, severely; A. Pasmore, shoulder, slightly; Jacob Ginther, right arm and thigh, severely. Company E: Corporals Emanuel Yengling, arm, severely; Thomas E. Exby, leg, slightly; Privates Jacob Gross, leg, slightly; John Richman, both thighs, severely; Robert Jenkins, chest, mortal; Gideon Cogshell, chest, slightly; Jacob Shannon, thigh, severely; R. F. Thompson, arm, slightly; William Lenhark, leg, slightly; Samuel Cornelius, abdomen, severely; H. C. Barger, leg, slightly; J. S. Maxwell, abdomen, slightly; E. L. Beckwith, head, mortal, died January 3. Company F: First Sergeant William L. Reltely, left thigh, severely; Sergeant J. W. Sayers, head, slightly; Corporal S. Harper, leg, slightly; Privates James Davis, right leg, severely; Fred. Baret, right arm, slightly; W. F. Batty, leg, slightly; John D. Fox, right thigh and left leg, severely; William Welch, thorax, severely; John Killiker, leg, severely; John Weir, leg, slightly. Company G: Lieutenant —— Yoder, leg and shoulder, severely; Corporals Peter Rice, ankle, slightly; Samuel Hoag, left arm; D. B. Roming, leg, slight; Privates James Lamister, left arm, severely; George Mese, hand, slightly; Charles Gardner, back, severe; Daniel Madden, head, slightly; L. Wumer, slightly; John D. Corpman, head and left shoulder, severely; Luther Hixpon, right shoulder and thigh, severely; Joseph Hall, leg and foot, severely.

Company H: Corporal Nathan Shannon, thigh, severely; Privates C. B. Crawford, hip, slightly; John Cox, back, slightly; Israel Vanscoder, head severely; David Nicodemus, left shoulder, severely; B. F. Buck, mortal, since died; William Davidson, arm, severely; Lawrence Durban, hand, slightly; J. Walker, right leg and head, severely; William Wicker, right leg and head, severely; R. B. Whitaker, hand, severely; John Daker, arm, severely; —— Livinger, foot, slightly; Nat. Jones, leg and arm. Company I: Sergeant James McFarland, leg, slightly; Privates Daniel Trump, hand, severely; William Evans, shoulder; Thomas Elliot, left thigh; Isaac Herdock, chest, foot and leg; N. D. Carpenter, left leg, severely; Albert Ullman, left leg, slightly; W. Lapp, left leg, slightly; Samuel Muller, leg, severely; Harrison Bibb, arm and hand, severely; —— Ligman, arm, slightly. Company K: Corporals S. H. Elson, abdomen, severely; Fred. Weisenreid, left shoulder, slightly; Privates Samuel Bubb, left arm; Martin Huff, testicles; Jacob Evans, right side, severely; F. S. Nevitt, abdomen, mortal, died January 8; Martin Haltor, leg, slightly; Howard Kenedy, hips, slightly; J. C. Reaff, leg, severely.

Summary.

Commissioned officers wounded	5
Commissioned officers killed	0
Non-commissioned officers and privates killed	19
Non-commissioned officers and privates wounded	132
Total	156

EIGHTH REGIMENT KENTUCKY VOLUNTEER INFANTRY.

Killed.—Company B: Private James Collins; Company D: Privates Moses Dunaney, Benjamin F. Maguire, and Jno. Durbin; Company E: George W. Keeton; Company F: Captain Jno. Banton; Company I: Sergeant Wiley Baker; Company K: Private Henry Shepperd.

Wounded.—Company A: First Lieutenant W. B. Catching, hip, slight; Corporal John Tye, leg, slight; Private Lawson Burrfre, hand, slight. Company B: First Lieutenant Thomas Henderson, head, slight; Sergeant A. Akers, thigh, severe; Corporals George English, thigh, slight, and Will Hewson, ankle severe; Privates Nelson Neal, side, slight; William English, hip, slight; Henry Sheaver, side, slight; John Jordan, leg, slight; Silas Marford, leg, slight; Singleton Abner, hand and arm; James Eastis, leg, and Jno. Riley, arm, severe. Company C: First Lieutenant William Park, back, slight; Corporal Dillard Gunn, ankle, severe; Privates William Lynch, chin, severe; Martin Thomas, chest, mortal; William Barker, side, slight; Daniel Tudor, arm, severe; William Mansfield, arm, slight; Calvin Lynch, face, slight. Company D: Private Abel Gabbert, arm, slight. Company E: Lieutenant Colonel Reuben May, contusion; Captain R. B. Hickman, bowels, mortal; Second Lieutenant P. A. Nichols, hip, slight; Sergeant Jos. Jewell, hand, slight; Privates James Lacy, leg, severe; Simpson Battershell, hand, slight; Samuel Epperman, arm, slight; James Burrows, arm, severe; Harris Morgan, leg, slight, and Catlett Keaton, back, slight. Company F: Sergeant Henry Moore, thigh, mortal; Corporals Jno. Kneed, shoulder, slight, and Israel Moore, arm and lung, severe; Privates Jno. Cain, arm, slight, and R. Spridley, arm, slight. Company G: Captain Laudon C. Winter, both thighs, severe; Second Lieutenant Charles W. Burleigh, leg, severely; Sergeant Wheeler Wright, arm and leg, mortal; Privates Fletcher Bowman, arm and lung, severely, and Isaac Slatterly, back, slight. Company H: First Lieutenant Wade B. Cox, shoulder, hand, thigh, and leg, mortal; First Sergeant Clinton Wilbour, arm, severe;

Privates Jno. Wise, Jos. McLaughlin, neck and shoulder, slight; Michael Fritz, hand, slight; James Barnett, legs, slight; John H. Alkorn, legs, slight, and James Wouldon, knee, slight. Company I: Sergeant Marshall Webb, arm, slight; Corporal George Reconor, back, slight; Privates Daniel Lewis, legs, severe, and John Cooper, legs, severe. Company K: Captain Henry Thomas, left arm and head; Privates Jesse Reed, neck, slight; O. N. Ballugh, elbow, severe; Peasant Hendley, arm, severe; Elisha Richardson, arm, severe; Allen J. Jones, abdomen, mortal; Hardin Ingraham, side, slight, and Robert Rawlings, arm, slight.

Summary.—Killed, 9; wounded, 65; total, 74.

BATTERIES OF THE THIRD DIVISION, THIRD WISCONSIN BATTERY.

Wounded.—L. J. Uline, hip; H. Sutley, thigh; Daniel Robbins, arm, and R. D. Hollinbeck, thigh.—Total wounded, 4.

SEVENTH INDIANA BATTERY.

Killed.—Privates E. Dixon, M. McGregor, S. S. Bath, and Ches. Musverin.

Wounded.—Lieutenant F. W. Brecker, shoulder, mortal; Sergeant B. F. Roberts, back; Privates Geo. Vancleef, foot; J. Reno, leg; R. A. Craig, side; H. Smallwood, hip, and Thomas Bolus, hand.—Total 11.

TWENTY-SIXTH PENNSYLVANIA BATTERY.

Killed.—Privates E. Cuddy and C. Reins.

Wounded.—Sergeant Charles Lutja, hip; Privates L. Bittner, hand and thigh; William Miller, hand and thigh; William Buchanan, abdomen contused, George Schoffer, hip; Dos Forris, ankle dislocated, and Daniel Stoner, shoulder.—Total, 9.

HEADQUARTERS 1ST BRIGADE, 3D DIVISION,
LEFT WING, 14TH ARMY CORPS,
In Camp near Murfreesboro', January 9, 1863.

CAPTAIN: I have the honor to submit the following report of the 1st brigade, 3d division, left wing, of the 14th army corps, in the action of the 31st day of December, 1862.

At 8 o'clock a. m., on the 31st day of December, 1862, the 3d division having crossed Stone river, on the extreme left of the army, formed line of battle, with the right of the 1st brigade resting on the bank of the river. The line was scarcely established when an order was received to recross the stream and march to the right, across the Nashville and Chattanooga railroad track, and west of the Nashville and Murfreesboro' pike. Here the brigade, marching in advance of the division, was met by retreating columns bearing unmistakable signs of disaster, who reported themselves belonging to the command of Major General Rousseau. They broke through the lines of the brigade—infantry, cavalry, artillery, ambulances, baggage train, &c.—in the greatest confusion, frequently separating the regiments of the brigade, threatening serious trouble. Line of battle was finally formed upon a point indicated by Major General Rosecrans in person, consisting of the 19th regiment Ohio volunteers, Major Charles F. Manderson commanding, on the right; the 9th regiment Kentucky volunteers, Colonel Ben. C. Grider commanding, on the left; in front, the 19th Ohio volunteers, supported by the 79th regiment Indiana volunteers, Colonel Fred. Knefler commanding, and the 9th Kentucky, supported by the 11th regiment Kentucky volunteers, Major E. L. Motley commanding. It was with the utmost difficulty that the line established was maintained. It was impossible to prevent the retreating columns from breaking through and almost destroying it; but the brigade stood fast, and never wavered. The enemy was rapidly approaching in three heavy columns, to reach and capture the train of the army immediately in rear and across the pike. Fire had to be reserved on account of our own troops, who were in front of the line. The front at last having been cleared by our own men, and the enemy's column appearing at a short distance, a heavy fire was opened by the front line of the brigade, which was kept up with very destructive effect, and completely checked the enemy's advance, who for some time maintained the position, inflicting severe loss upon us. At this juncture, the 11th Kentucky and 79th Indiana regiments were ordered to relieve the 19th Ohio and 9th Kentucky regiments in front, who by this time expended many rounds of their ammunition, wheeled into column, and the two supporting regiments passed through the intervals. The whole movement was accomplished in fine order, under the very heavy fire of the enemy. The new line immediately opened fire upon the enemy, who commenced falling back; bayonets were ordered to be fixed, and the 79th Indiana and the 11th Kentucky were ordered to advance, supported by the other two regiments. They advanced rapidly, the enemy retreating. An uninterupted fire was kept up, and the enemy compelled, after a pursuit of nearly a mile from the position first occupied by the brigade, to take refuge behind his works, which could not be assailed for the want of artillery, which could not advance in that direction, owing to the very rough and uneven nature of the ground.

While in this position the 2d brigade of the 3d division, which had in the mean time advanced on the right of the first brigade, and was now in a line parallel with it, was forced back by strongly re-enforced columns of the enemy again appearing in front. The 1st brigade was ordered to fall back, to prevent a flank movement, which was accomplished in good order, to a distance of about three hundred yards, and took position in a cedar thicket, where skirmishers thrown to the front kept up a continual fire.

At this point I was ordered by Major General Rosecrans to move to the support of Mendenhall's and the Chicago Board of Trade battery, on the left of the brigade. The 9th and 11th Kentucky regiments were ordered to that point, and the 19th Ohio and the 79th Indiana regiments were ordered to fall back and to join the 2d brigade on the right.

In this position the brigade remained until midnight, when the brigade was ordered to recross the pike, and there bivouacked till morning. The brigade was hotly engaged for three hours. Regimental reports, which I have the honor herewith to transmit, have accurate lists of casualties, and I refer you to them for particulars.

Commanders of regiments, officers and soldiers, did their duty gallantly, and their splendid conduct, repulsing the enemy when victoriously pursuing our disordered troops, contributed, in no small measure, to the successful result of the day.

My thanks are due to Lieutenants Sheets and Percival, of my staff, and the soldiers of my escort, for their efficient services in the action.

I have the honor to be, captain, very respectfully, your obedient servant,

SAMUEL BEATTY,

Colonel, Commanding 3*d Division, Left Wing,* 14*th Army Corps.*

Captain E. A. OTIS,

A. A. G. 3*d Division, Left Wing,* 14*th Army Corps.*

HEADQUARTERS 1ST BRIGADE, 3d DIVISION,
Camp in front of Murfreesboro', Saturday, January 3, 1863.

COLONEL: I had the honor to be placed in command of the first brigade, third division, (formerly the 11th brigade,) on the morning of the 1st January, 1863; and being ordered by you as commander of the division, I at once marched with my command to the south side of Stone river, and bivouacked in the woods and fields belonging, as I learned, to a man named Hoover. Some skirmishing and picket firing was soon heard and some rebel cavalry seen, but nothing worthy of notice occurred during the day. That night the enemy attempted to drive in our pickets, but failed. Next morning opened with brisk cannonading on the part of the enemy, to which our artillery made no reply. Our skirmishers in front were actively engaged all day. It was then ascertained that the enemy had planted a battery in our front, and a section or more on our left, and that a portion of their guns across the river, which came down in a course parallel with our right, could reach us with a raking fire, and interfere with our crossing at the first ford, if compelled to recross. It was also suggested by myself and other officers, Major Manderson, commanding the 19th Ohio, particularly, that our right resting on the river was exposed, and might be attacked and turned, and that neither the depth of the stream nor character of the banks was a sufficient protection; that troops and artillery were needed on the opposite side to sustain our right. You and we all were assured that this was attended to, and we rested on that assurance. Thus matters stood until about an hour before sundown, when artillery firing on the part of the enemy, and heavy skirmishing on both sides commenced. We now supposed that the attack which we had all day expected would be postponed until daylight the next day, but were mistaken. The enemy was seen advancing in three lines, the front composed of a battalion of sharpshooters, and the other lines composed of the whole division of General John C. Breckinridge and Cheatham; Colonels Roger W. Hanson and Joseph H. Reins, of Kentucky, as I learn, were present in Breckinridge's command. The regiments of my brigade, the 19th Ohio, Major Manderson, on the right, the 9th Kentucky, Lieutenant Colonel Cram, in the centre, and the 11th Kentucky, Major Motley, on the left, were by your orders held in reserve. The 79th Indiana had been about noon ordered to form on and sustain the front line, composed of the 3d brigade, Colonel W. Price commanding, and were not again seen by me during the day. I doubt not they will receive justice at the hands of the colonel under whose command they were placed.

The onset of the enemy, sustained as they were by their artillery, succeeded in breaking and driving back our first and second line. You now sent me an order to bring up the reserve, which I instantly did, though it was almost manifest, from the character of the fire in front, that the force we had on the ground, unassisted as we at that moment were by artillery, could not check the enemy's advance. Yet our men, the 19th Ohio, 9th Kentucky, and 11th Kentucky, undaunted by the terrible and desperate state of affairs, with bravery that cannot be described, and led on by their officers, the most cool and daring, moved forward, some through a thick undergrowth of wild briers, which to some extent broke their lines, fearlessly meeting the enemy and breaking his first line. Seeing this from my position between and slightly in front of the 19th Ohio and 9th Kentucky, and noticing you just in my rear, I said to you, "Colonel, we have them checked; give us artillery and we will whip them." You replied, "You shall have it." I rode back and soon saw the right regiment, the 19th Ohio, falling back; calling to Major Manderson, who halted and came back, I said to him, "Major, the 9th is still standing; let us rally the 19th and sustain her." The major replied: "We are flanked on our right; we had better fall back and rally at the foot of the hill, if we can." I told him to do so, and I would order the 9th and 11th Kentucky to do the same. I rode forward for this purpose, but just as I was about to give the order to Lieutenant Colonel Cram, he gave it to his regiment, which was then receiving most of the fire hitherto directed against the 19th; the 11th Kentucky moved back about the same time, and both of these regiments almost in line with some of the enemy's troops, and were the last regiments to quit the field—the 19th Ohio leaving first, because first exposed to the flanking fire. We fell back fighting, though in some disorder, crossed the river, rallied under a very heavy fire, checked the enemy, and held him in check until we were re-enforced, when I, with the flags of the 19th Ohio and 9th Kentucky, recrossed the river, followed closely by Lieutenant Colonel Cram, Majors Motley and Manderson, men and officers from 19th Ohio, 9th Kentucky, and 11th Kentucky—Lieutenant Philip Reefry holding the colors of the 19th, and Private Moses Rourke those of the 9th Kentucky. The 21st Ohio, led by Captain ——, acting major, promptly followed. Our troops now crossed rapidly and opened fire on the south side of the river. Observing that the men would follow and stand by their colors, I here took the flag of my own regiment, the 9th Kentucky, and riding forward called on the troops to advance, to which they gallantly responded, and rushing upon the enemy drove them with great slaughter from and past the ground which they had occupied before the attack, the 11th Kentucky taking a stand of colors, and the three regiments capturing four of the enemy's guns, the "Washington artillery;" the colors of the 19th Ohio and the 9th Kentucky volunteers being the first to reach them. Lieutenant Colonel Cram, of the 9th, and Major Motley, of the 11th Kentucky, with myself, were the first mounted officers at these guns. All three of the above regiments were represented there, and at all times in the most advanced and exposed position. Lieutenant Colonel Cram and Major Motley ordered off a gun each, and I ordered off two. In short, each and every officer and man in these three regiments was all that could be asked, and far above the reach of encomiums. Of Lieutenant Colonel Cram, 9th Kentucky; Major Manderson, 19th Ohio, and Major Motley, 11th Kentucky, I make special mention as the commanders on that day of their respective regiments. I refer to their reports accompanying this for more special notice than I can here take of the officers and men under their commands.

The result of the day was, the enemy retreated in haste and disorder, acknowledging a defeat, and evacuated Murfreesboro' the next day; we bivouacked that night on the battle-field. The loss of the three regiments under my command, as nearly as can be ascertained, is two hundred and fifty officers and men killed, wounded, and missing—about one-third of the effective force which they had engaged. I refer for particulars to the enclosed regimental reports.

Most respectfully submitted.

B. C. GRIDER,
Colonel, Commanding 1st Brigade, 3d Division.

Colonel SAMUEL BEATTY,
Commanding 3d Division, Left Wing, 14th Army Corps

IN CAMP NEAR MURFREESBORO',
January 1, 1863.

LIEUTENANT: My regiment, the 9th Kentucky volunteer infantry, was early yesterday morning ordered on the south side of Stone river, and formed in line of battle in the front line, and on the left of the 19th Ohio volunteers, (Major Manderson.) We had advanced a short distance down the river when we were ordered to recross to support our forces in the centre and on the right, understanding that the enemy were driving them, and had turned our right and probably gained our rear. We moved by the flank, and at a double-quick, to the Murfreesboro' pike, and thence along that pike about half a mile to our rear, to a skirt of woods, through which we saw our men retreating, and heard that they had been before forced back through them. We formed on the pike, the 19th Ohio on the right, and the 9th Kentucky on the left, the two composing the front line, supported by the 11th Kentucky, Major Motley, and the 79th Indiana, Colonel Knefler, in the rear or second line. As soon as our retreating troops cleared the woods, our front, the 19th and 9th, opened upon the enemy a cool, well-aimed, and deadly fire, which brought them to a stand; after a few such rounds we were ordered to advance, which the men promptly did with the alacrity and steadiness of veterans, gallantly led on by *all* their officers, driving the enemy with great slaughter for half a mile or more; here the ammunition of the front line beginning to fail, and the enemy's fire having almost ceased, we were ordered to open our lines for the reserve, the 11th Kentucky and the 79th Indiana, to pass through, which they did in gallant style, seeing and hearing but little of the enemy for some hundreds of yards, when they found him rallied; but again he was forced to yield to the well-directed fire and gallantry of the 11th Kentucky and 79th Indiana, and thus, for a time, the advance was continued for some distance, when we found a body of our troops broken and retreating from our right in a direction which passed them diagonally through our lines; our men kept firm, and we tried to rally them, but with no effect. Thus our right was exposed and turned, and you gave the order to fall back, which we did in most excellent order under the heaviest shower of balls and missiles that we had encountered during the day. Our loss here was great, and the courage and coolness of men and officers was here put to a severer test than during the advance, and *well* did they meet the trying emergency. We came back a short distance and promptly formed in line to again meet the enemy. Here General Rosecrans, in person, ordered me to advance my regiment to close range of the enemy, and, after giving him a few fires, to charge. I ordered the advance, but had gone only a short distance when the general ordered us to halt and cause the men to lie down, while a battery in our rear opened over us upon the enemy. After remaining here for a short time, my regiment and the 11th Kentucky were ordered to take position to sustain the Chicago Board of Trade battery and another, the name of which I do not know, then threatened by the enemy. This we continued to do until late in the night, after the battle was all over for the day. We were, during this time, under fire from the enemy's artillery, and lost two men killed and several wounded. Our loss during the day was two commissioned officers, First Lieutenant Silas Clark and First Lieutenant W. J. Cram, wounded; two sergeants, one of whom was the color-bearer, killed; one private killed and nineteen wounded. A full list will be handed in as soon as practicable.

I have no terms of praise that can do justice to the noble bearing and unflinching bravery of all the officers and men. I mention the names of them all: Lieutenant Colonel George H. Cram, Major John H. Grider, Adjutant C. D. Bailey, Captains R. A. Reed, Rufus K. Somerby, D. B. Coyle, William F. Bryan; First Lieutenants A. Sidney Liggett, T. Freely Heeter, W. J. Cram, commanding companies; First Lieutenants Thomas Potter, Boyle O. Rodes, Henry Myers, Silas Clark; Second Lieutenants Fred. Carpenter, B. C. Downing, John F. Grinstead, James M. Simmons, Benjamin Johnston.

Company A, Captain Henry F. Liggett, was on detached duty, and, I regret, could not be in the battle, as their services, brave men and well officered as they are, would have been valuable. First Lieutenant John H. Wheat was not with the regiment, being detached on duty with the pioneer corps.

Respectfully submitted,

B. C. GRIDER,
Colonel Ninth Kentucky Volunteers.

Lieutenant H. H. SHEETS,
Acting Assistant Adjutant General, 1st Brigade

List of killed and wounded of the 9th regiment Kentucky (foot) volunteers before Murfreesboro', Tennessee.

Major John Grider and Adjutant C. D. Bailey, wounded.

Company B.—Killed: Captain W. T. Bryant, and Privates Anay Bray and Isom Judy. Wounded: First Lieutenant Silas Clark, Second Lieutenant Benjamin Johnson; Corporal J. W. Hinson, and Privates William Moss, Gilbert Wakefield, J. J. Johnson, G. W. Marshall, and W. C. Gass.

Company C.—Killed: Color Sergeant J. J. Raglin, Fifth Sergeant R. D. Napier, Corporal J. W. Mahew, and Private B. H. Y. Alexander. Wounded: Corporals G. S. Anderson, W. Spears, and Privates L. W. Meadow, G. R. Steward, H. W. Huntsman, John Garmen, Rolley Howell, Brad Howel, James Steuart, W. R. Clark, J. W. Huntsman, G. W. Mathis, D. W. Spear, R. N. Steward, and J. D. Bradley.

Company D.—Killed: First Lieutenant A. S. Liggett, and Privates Clayborn Borden, Obadiah F. Leonard, and R. Jenkins. Wounded: Sergeant Samuel Jones, and Privates J. C. Whittey, John Austin, J. H. Glover, B. P. Jenkins, J. M. Bein, J. H. Bell, Jaspar Hayze, and J. A. Lancaster.

Company E.—Killed: Private Henry Bacon. Wounded: Sergeants W. L. Norvell, J. N. Birtram, and Privates Shelly Birtram, G. W. Smith, W. L. Adams, J. H. Barbour, B. W. Barbour, and J. H. Donahu.

Company F.—Killed: Second Lieutenant F. F. Carpenter, Sergeant J. W. McReynolds, and Privates J. W. Ritchard, W. England, and G. B. McElroy. Wounded: Captain R. A. Reed, and Privates J. B. Buchanan, Calvin Bracken, W. J. Mills, Joseph Taylor, M. S. York, R. Harris, R. J. Clarkston, and W. Chandler.

Company G.—Killed: Captain D. B. Coyle. Wounded: Corporal J. W. Proffett, and Privates James Pausley, W. B. Bowls, J. S. Creek, J. F. Turner, A. F. Register, J. G. Agers, and J. M. Vaughn.

Company H.—Wounded: First Lieutenant W. J. Cram, and Privates John Washan, R. D. Frazier, and T. J. Meadon.

Company I.—Wounded: Corporal J. W. Gray, and Privates Allen Blankenship, Joel Barbe, J. Y. Broox, J. F. Mayhew, Aseay Tracy, and S. P. Cox.

Company K.—Killed: Privates Ephraim Thomas, Philip Murphy, and John C. H. Gamon. Wounded: Privates Flagon A. Bishop, Richard Good, John Shries, William Simmons, John Simmons, Leonidas Kirby, and William Dorsey.

I respectfully submit the following as my report of the part my regiment took in the engagement of 2d January, 1863, on the left wing of our army in front of Murfreesboro'.

Early in the forenoon Colonel Grider ordered me to hold my regiment in reserve, with another regiment of his brigade, (the nineteenth Ohio,) under cover of a hill about two hundred yards from the upper ford of Stone river, and told me that the enemy would probably attack us some time during the day, and ordered me to hold my regiment in readiness to re-enforce our line if the enemy should attack us in too great force. Nothing but heavy skirmishing and artillery firing, on the part of the enemy, occurred during the day, until about four o'clock in the evening, when our whole line was attacked by a heavy rebel force. My men were under arms, and I knew by the firing that our men were giving way. I was ordered forward, and moved up the hill at a double-quick, through briers and undergrowth, (tearing our line badly.) Arriving at the crest of the hill, we met our troops retreating in great confusion. Nothing could be more discouraging to my men than the aspect of affairs at that time, but they never faltered. I allowed the retreating mass to pass through my lines, the enemy all the time pouring into us a destructive fire, both infantry and artillery. Our lines closed up, and I ordered my men to commence firing.

The enemy gave way after the fourth or fifth round, the colors of the regiment in front of us having fallen no less than three times, and had we had but the enemy in front to contend with, our chances of success would have been tolerably certain; but just when the battle was being decided in our favor, we were flanked by a heavy force on our right, causing our support on that flank to give way, leaving us exposed to a raking fire, which was fast decimating my regiment. We had already suffered. Major Grider was wounded, Adjutant Bailey wounded, Captain Bryan killed, Captain Coyle killed, Captain Read badly wounded, Lieutenant Liggett killed, Lieutenant Carpenter killed, Lieutenant Huter wounded, and Lieutenant Johnson wounded. I do not hesitate to say that no regiment could have withstood this fresh attack. I ordered the regiment to fall back under the hill. Colonel Grider ordered me in person to rally my men at the foot of the hill. I found the ground almost in possession of a rebel regiment. We continued the retreat across the river, and I there rallied my men. We were here re-enforced by three or four regiments, and the enemy brought to a stand. The firing here was the most terrible I ever heard. The foe fought us bravely, but could not withstand such a terrible fire. He gave way slowly, and we not only retook the lost ground, but drove him over a mile, cutting him up badly, and capturing his artillery—changing the result of the battle from a defeat to a splendid victory. The colors of the ninth Kentucky recrossed the river by the side of those of the nineteenth Ohio, and under your leadership. The regiments of your brigade, shattered as they were, were the first to wave their flags over the captured guns of the enemy.

My officers and men fought splendidly under the most discouraging circumstances. Every man in the regiment knew what he had to encounter when we were ordered forward, but not one faltered. They knew that the gallant reserve, the nineteenth Ohio and ninth Kentucky, were insufficient to check the victorious enemy.

Major Grider was wounded while gallantly cheering on his men early in the engagement, and Adjutant Bailey soon afterwards. I felt the loss of these officers greatly. Captain Bryan was mortally wounded, doing his duty nobly. Captain Coyle was killed while cheering on his men. Lieutenants Liggett and Carpenter were killed at the head of their companies. Captain Read, Lieutenant Huter, and Lieutenant Johnson were wounded while fighting gallantly. I take pleasure in mentioning the following officers, whose gallant conduct deserves great praise: Captain Somerby, Lieutenants Patton, Downing, Grimstead, Rhodes, and Mayes. Private Moses Roaok, of company C, deserves special mention. When the colors were shot down, in the engagement of the 31st, he grasped them and brought them safely through the fight, and in the battle of the 2d January he carried them into the thickest of the fight, and was at times left almost alone. He is but eighteen years of age, and is one of the bravest soldiers in the army.

GEORGE H. CRAM,
Lieutenant Colonel, Commanding Ninth Kentucky Volunteers.

Our loss was as follows: Commissioned officers killed, 4; wounded, 7. Enlisted men killed, 18; wounded, 80; prisoners, 3, (wounded.) Of the above three were killed and twenty-one wounded on the 31st. (See Colonel Grider's regimental report.)

I have the honor to be your most obedient servant,

GEORGE H. CRAM,
Lieutenant Colonel, Commanding Ninth Kentucky Volunteers.

H. H. SHEETS, *Acting Assistant Adjutant General,*
First Brigade, Third Division, Left Wing, Fourteenth Army Corps.

HEADQUARTERS 11TH KENTUCKY VOLUNTEER MILITIA,
January 6, 1863.

SIR: I have the honor to report the part my regiment (11th Kentucky volunteers) took in the action of December 31, 1862. The night previous we bivouacked in an open field adjacent to the Murfreesboro' pike. Next morning, about 8 o'clock, we were ordered to follow the 9th Kentucky regiment and cross the river, where we were placed in line of battle, supporting them. We remained in that position about half an hour, when we recrossed the river, still moving in our position as first placed, having marched about half a mile parallel with the pike. Was then ordered to halt and front, still occupying my position in the rear of the 9th Kentucky volunteers. The firing then began by the regiments in front of me and continued about half an hour, when I was ordered to move forward and relieve the 9th Kentucky, which was about one hundred yards in advance. We did so, moving in line of battle about five hundred yards. We then halted, as our further advance was interrupted by about four regiments of scattered troops rushing through my line. After they had passed we opened a heavy and destructive fire on the enemy, who were advancing against me, and remained in that position, firing till the right of our division was nearly flanked, when we received an order from you to fall back, which I did (bringing several prisoners with me) in line of battle, till I reached a dense thicket, when I moved by the left flank. We then formed line in an open field, and was ordered by General Rosecrans in person to occupy the thicket through which we had just passed, and hold it at all hazards. We did so. Just at this moment the enemy were advancing in strong force on our left, when the left wing of the regiment opened an oblique galling fire upon them, making them fall back. We were then ordered back by you to the large open field on our left, to support two pieces of Tyrell's regular and the Chicago Board of Trade batteries, where we remained the remainder of the day, my entire regiment, both officers and men, doing their whole duty. Enclosed find list of casualties.

Very respectfully,

E. L. MONTLEY,
Major, Commanding 11th Kentucky Volunteers.

Colonel SAMUEL BEATTY,
Commanding 1st Brigade, 3d Division.

LIST OF CASUALTIES IN THE ELEVENTH KENTUCKY VOLUNTEER INFANTRY.

Company A, (commanded by Lieutenant James M. Elms.)—Wounded: Corporal James Miligan, slightly; Private Joseph B. Hildebrand, slightly.

Company B, (commanded by Lieutenant W. F. Ward.)—Killed: Private Irvine Parsons. Wounded: Captain John B. Tyler, acting major, severely.

Company C, (commanded by Lieutenant John B. Graves.)—Wounded: Orderly Sergeant W. B. Neel, slightly; Privates G. Phelps, severely; J. W. McKinney, severely; L. Greathouse, severely; Simeon Baugh, severely.

Company D, (commanded by Captain C. W. Hannay.)—Wounded: Privates James W. Grubb, severely; John N. Gaines, severely.

Company E, (commanded by Lieutenant N. Nash.)—Wounded: Privates F. M. Age, slightly; G. W. Blair, slightly.

Company F, (commanded by Captain I. S. Willis.)—Killed: Orderly Sergeants Andrew B. Dobbs. Wounded: Corporal C. C. Moore, severely; Privates S. A. Bingham, severely; N. R. Ewing, mortally; Sergeant C. A. Deem, slightly.

Company G, (commanded by Captain O. P. Johnson.)—Wounded: Sergeant John M. Conway, slightly; Corporal John A. Phelps; Private William Dervese. Missing: Private William G. Dervese.

Company H, (commanded by Lieutenant J. Yontes.)—Wounded: Privates J. D. Casebue, slightly; A. Stobauch, slightly; John Duvall.

Company I, (commanded by Lieutenant C. Niel.)—Wounded: Sergeant John N. Simmonds, slightly.

Company K, (commanded by Lieutenant C. H. Martin.)—Wounded: Corporal G. W. Lewis, severely.

Total killed, wounded, and missing, 27.

HEADQUARTERS 11TH REGIMENT KENTUCKY VOLUNTEER INFANTRY,
January 6, 1863.

SIR: I have the honor to report the part my regiment (eleventh Kentucky volunteers) took in the engagement, 2d January, 1863. Having crossed the river the morning of the 1st January, 1863, and bivouacked one hundred and fifty yards behind the main advance of our lines about half past three, 2d January, the enemy showed himself in strong force, sixteen regiments deep, advancing in column against us; also, a brigade on our left. The firing now became general all along the lines. Seeing the regiments on the left giving way, I ordered my regiment to take arms—the arms had previously been stacked. Just then the front was falling back, and I ordered my regiment forward under the most terrific storm of shot, shell, and musketry, it has ever been my lot to witness. I advanced about one hundred yards when I ordered a halt and commenced firing. I broke their [ranks] more than once, their colors shot down several times, but their broken ranks were speedily filled with fresh troops. Casting my eyes to the right, and seeing I had no support in that direction, and being nearly outflanked, I gave the order to fall back to the wood in our rear, the men being pressed so closely some of them crossed the river. After crossing the river, I, in conjunction with yourself and other officers, rallied parts of the different regiments of the brigade, and succeeded in putting the enemy to flight before us, and captured four pieces of the celebrated Washington artillery.

I must say, in conclusion, that my regiment was one of the very last to leave the grounds. For the gallantry of my entire regiment, they behaved as officers and soldiers should in such a cause.

The casualties of my regiment are as follows:

	Killed.	Wounded.	Missing.	Total.
Commissioned officers	..	3	..	3
Company A	..	5	4	9
Company B	..	9	1	10
Company C	1	10	..	11
Company D	1	7	1	9
Company E	1	1	2	4
Company F	1	4	..	5
Company G	..	5	..	5
Company H	1	8	..	9
Company I	..	3	1	4
Company K	..	6	..	6
Total killed, wounded, and missing				75

Very respectfully,

E. L. MATLEY,
Major, Commanding 11*th Kentucky Volunteers.*

Colonel BENJ. C. GRIDER,
Commanding 1*st Brigade,* 3*d Division.*

HEADQUARTERS 19TH REGIMENT OHIO VOLUNTEER INFANTRY,
Field near Murfreesboro', Tennessee, January 6, 1863.

LIEUTENANT: I transmit you the following report of the participation of the 19th regiment Ohio volunteers, United States army, (Charles F. Manderson, major commanding,) in the action in front of Murfreesboro', on Wednesday, December 31, 1862:

On the morning of that date the regiment was under arms in double column, between the Murfreesboro' turnpike and Chattanooga and Nashville railroad, being the right of the front line of the 3d division, left wing. By order of Colonel Samuel Beatty, commanding 1st brigade, after deploying column and loading, we moved by the right flank to the left, crossing Stone river at the ford, and forming line, (after throwing companies A and K as skirmishers,) with the right resting about one hundred yards from the river, the 9th Kentucky volunteers, which were first formed on our right, being moved to the left of the regiment. About 10 o'clock we were ordered to recall our skirmishers and recross the river, which being done we moved by the right flank across the open space between the railroad and pike, amidst the greatest confusion of retreating batteries, men, teams, and ambulances. At this point General Rousseau ordered the regiment to move across the turnpike, and form line in the woods, skirting the west of the pike. From this position we were immediately ordered by Colonel Beatty to march by the left flank back to the railroad, and then by the right flank back to our former position in the last-named woods, under a fire by which we lost several men. This scene was one of disorder and panic: regiment after regiment swept through our lines in the greatest confusion; but through it all our men preserved an unbroken front, and, when the pursuing enemy came within seventy-five or one hundred yards, and our front was clear of the retreating and broken columns, at the order to fire by file, poured most destructive volleys into the foe, breaking his lines into disorder. Major General Rosecrans, who was in the rear of the right of the regiment, cheering our men with his presence and words, then ordered a charge, and our regiment, with fixed bayonets, supported by the 9th Kentucky volunteers on our left, and the 79th Indiana volunteers in our rear, drove the foe in splendid style for about one-fourth of a mile, when our ammunition running low, the front line wheeled into column, and the 79th Indiana volunteers passed through to the front. The regiment, then forming the second line, (in the rear of the 79th Indiana volunteers,) advanced for about three-fourths of a mile to an open field, where we were separated from our front line by a cedar thicket. We were here but a few minutes when our right support gave way, and left our regiment greatly exposed to a flanking fire. I sent word twice to Colonel Beatty that the enemy had flanked our position in great force, but received no order. The regiment was suffering most terribly from the fire; and seeing the enemy within fifty yards of our right, and in position to destroy us, I ordered a change of front to the right and rear. Our men, while executing the movement, were thrown into temporary disorder by the scattered regiments on our right pouring through the line, but gathered on the instant, formed an excellent line in good position, and fired with such precision that, with the aid of a battery of artillery in our rear and left, we held the ground and drove the foe from the open field in our front. Being now entirely out of ammunition, and suffering loss from the fire of our own artillery, we moved by the right flank into the woods and formed line on the left of the 2d brigade, Colonel Fyffe, commanding the second battalion of the pioneer corps, supporting us on the left. We were supplied with ammunition by Captain Wood, assistant inspector general, 3d division, and threw out skirmishers, who met no enemy. About 4 o'clock we were relieved by the 1st brigade, 1st division, Colonel Walker commanding; bivouacked where we were until midnight, when we were ordered by Colonel Beatty to report to him on the left of the railroad. Our loss in this action is as follows, viz: Killed: One officer and eleven enlisted men; total, twelve. Wounded: One officer and sixty-six enlisted men; total, sixty-seven. Missing: Three enlisted men. Total loss, eighty-two men.

I subjoin as accurate a list as it is possible at this time to gather. My men behaved with the utmost bravery and coolness. Senior Captain Henry C. Stratton, of company C, assisted as field officer. He was severely wounded about noon. First Lieutenant Daniel Donavan, commanding company B, fell dead in front of his company while gallantly leading a charge. Orderly Sergeant Robert D. Wilson, commanding company D, was killed about the same time. The cool, manly daring of these gallant officers cannot be spoken of too highly. But the action of all of the 19th Ohio was under the directing eye of the colonel commanding the brigade, and the generals commanding, and to them I leave further comments.

Respectfully, yours,

CHARLES F. MANDERSON,
Major, Commanding 19th Regiment Ohio Volunteer Infantry.

Lieutenant HENRY H. SHEETS,
A. A. A. G. 1st Brigade, 3d Division, Left Wing,
14th Army Corps, Department of the Cumberland.

List of killed, wounded, and missing of the 19th Ohio volunteers in the action of December 31, 1862.

Company A.—Killed: Privates John Clark and Nicholas Sayler. Wounded: Privates John Layler, George Leptag, Tisch Jackson, and John Lovett, all severely; James Flinn and Thomas Griffith, slightly; Moses L. Horver, dangerously; John Cross, severely, (prisoner;) Nicholas Kline, severely, (prisoner.) Killed, 2; wounded, 9.

Company B.—Killed: First Lieutenant Daniel Donavan, Corporal John Marks, Private Matthew G. Courtney. Wounded: Privates James R. Bailey, dangerously; John A. Johnson, William Lewis, Ami Stilson, Henry Crum, William H. Dubes, George King, Samuel Clark, Isaac Davis, David Hoggands, and Hiram Lyons, all severely. Missing: Sergeant James Beatty, (probably wounded.) Killed, 3; wounded, 11; missing, 1.

Company C.—Wounded: Captain Henry G. Stratton, severely; Corporal Asail Adams, severely; Privates Henry King, Noah N. Dally, James Boyd, William R. Gartman, Milo Wilson, and N. S. Baldwin, all severely. Total, 8.

Company D.—Killed: First Sergeant Robert D. Wilson, Corporal William Keifer, Private William M. Best. Wounded: Privates James Bennett, Washington Bryan, and George S. Bradshaw, all severely; James Craig, slightly. Missing: Private John Keifer. Killed, 3; wounded, 4; missing, 1.

Company E.—Killed: Private Thomas Gilson. Wounded: Corporal William Clunk, Privates Anthony Bollinger, William H. Cooper, John F. Green, Isaac Granger, Thomas Harbaugh, George W. Little, and John H. Lamb, all severely; Corporal John Deavers, slightly. Killed, 1; wounded, 9.

Company F.—Killed: Private William Gables. Wounded: Sergeant Alonzo Himes, severely; Corporal Frederick Gfeller, seriously; Privates William N. Frigate, Michael Gabletz, and Henry Bose, all severely; Daniel Stramer, slightly. Killed, 1; wounded, 6.

Company G.—Wounded: Privates Gilbert Merwin, dangerously; George M. Lawson, Judson Wilmarth, Lyman Dunn, and Frank Hickok, all seriously. Total, 5.

Company H.—Wounded: Corporal S. L. Paramour, Privates Frank Dupoine, John H. Reitter, Elias Culbertson, James Cox, and Albert Koons, all severely. Total, 6.

Company I.—Killed: Private Levi McGregor. Wounded: Sergeant Almon K. Raff, slightly; Corporals E. M. Robinson and Peter Fisher, severely; Privates John H. Zellers, severely, and John White, slightly. Killed, 1; wounded, 5.

Company K.—Killed: Valentine Mummel. Wounded: Privates E. D. Damp, slightly, and Simon Cook, severely. Missing: Private Hiram Hilliard. Killed, 1; wounded, 4; missing, 1.

HEADQUARTERS 19TH REGIMENT OHIO VOLUNTEER INFANTRY,
Field near Murfreesboro', Tennessee, January 6, 1863.

LIEUTENANT: On Friday, January 2, 1863, the 19th Ohio volunteers, United States army, under my command, was formed, with the right resting near the high bank on Stone river, being held by the 9th regiment Kentucky volunteers, which joined us on the left, in reserve of the 2d and 3d brigades, 3d division, which position we had assumed on Thursday, January 1, about noon. Soon after 4 o'clock p. m. heavy firing on our front caused us to take arms and stand in line. The firing had continued about fifteen minutes, when Lieutenant Murdock, aide-de-camp to Colonel Beatty, commanding 3d division, rode up to the front and left of the regiment and ordered me to advance. Although the order, coming from that source, was contrary to rule and custom, presuming the occasion to be an emergency requiring such a deviation, I ordered the regiment forward in double-quick time. We advanced up a gradual slope for about two hundred yards, the lines in front of us pouring through our ranks in confusion, but the men preserved an excellent front, and rushed upon the enemy. In some parts of the line our pieces crossed those of the foe. His front line received a check of some few minutes, and was thrown into disorder; but a strong flanking party poured over the bank of the river, and broke our right flank to the rear, file after file. Seeing this, and that brave officers and many men of our right wing had fallen, I ordered the left to fall back. Colonel B. C. Grider, commanding 1st brigade, here rode up to me from the left and front, and w shed me to rally the men. I told him they were falling back by order; that the enemy had flanked me in force; and that I would form line at the foot of the hill. He said, "Do so;" and stated he would give the same order to the 9th Kentucky volunteers, on our left. The regiment rallied, and, forming line twice before the overwhelming force of the enemy, drove them across Stone river. The storm of missiles was terrific, and, for a few moments, no men could have stood under it. The bank of the river presented a scene of indescribable confusion. The colors of our regiment were seized by Second Lieutenant Philip Reefy, of company F, who gallantly dashed forward across the stream, followed by daring spirits of different regiments. At the same time Colonel Grider, bearing the colors of the 9th Kentucky volunteers, crossed with another party, and these flags, with two belonging to other regiments, rallied under their folds an indiscriminate mass of men and officers of the 3d division, which, supported by fresh troops that had been ordered to the conflict, drove back, in terrible confusion, the columns of the enemy, victorious but a moment before. The colors of the 19th Ohio and 9th Kentucky were placed on three pieces of the enemy's artillery, which were captured and brought into our lines by squads composed of the different regiments and brigades of the division. After this magnificent scene of individual heroism, the different detachments of the regiment formed on the same ground we occupied in the morning, and bivouacked that night. Again we have to regret the loss of brave officers and men. Captain Urwin Bean, of company E; First Lieutenant Job D. Bell, commandng company C; and Sergeant Major Lyman Tylee, were killed while gallantly performing their duties. First Lieutenant Aurora C. Reel, of company F, was severely wounded; Second Lieutenant William A. Sutherland, of company H, slightly. Captain William H. Allen, of company F, rendered most valuable and efficient aid as a field officer. All the line officers vied with each other in deeds of courage. I wish particularly to note the gallant bearing of First Lieutenant Charles Brewer, adjutant; Second Lieutenant Albert Upson, commanding company K; and Sergeant Jason Hurd, commanding company G. But all have done their duty, and the unpleasant task is not mine to record any acts of cowardice in the 19th Ohio regiment.

I annex a list of killed, wounded, and missing.

In this action we had killed two officers and thirteen enlisted men; total killed, fifteen, (15.) Wounded, two officers and fifty-six enlisted men; total wounded, fifty-eight, (58.) Missing, (supposed prisoners,) thirty-one enlisted men.

Respectfully, your obedient servant,

CHAS. F. MANDERSON,
Major, Commanding 19th Regiment Ohio Volunteers.

Lieutenant HENRY H. SHEETS,
A. A. A. G., 1st Brigade, 3d Division, Left Wing,
14th Army Corps, Department of the Cumberland.

List of killed, wounded, and missing of the 19th regiment Ohio volunteers in the action of January 2, 1863.

Company A.—Wounded: Corporal Frank Schiltz, dangerously; Privates Thomas Griffith and George Lane, slightly. Missing: Privates William H. Bachtel, since paroled; William H. Dierdorff, David Shortless, John Bowman, and James Flinn, all prisoners.

Company B.—Killed: Corporal Daniel Cooper, Privates James Jewell, Henry Ague, and James Balmer. Wounded: Sergeant Reynolds J. Cowden and Private Charles Jacobs, slightly; Privates James Mathews, Harmon McFall, William McCurdy, Henry Patterson, Samuel Shaffer, and John Burnett, all severely. Missing: Washington Sexton, William Myers, and James H. Smith, prisoners.

Company C.—Killed: First Lieutenant Job D. Bell, Corporal Henry Shaffer, and Private Lucius J. Scott. Wounded: Sergeant James G. Bailey, slightly; Corporals John B. Lewis, severely; Charles Talbitzer, severely; Privates Hiram Rader, mortally; George W. Allen, slightly; Henry W. Allen, slightly; Ira A. Haight, William J. Miller, Daniel Powell, Joseph Scott, Miller Wilson, all severely; Robert Reed, slightly. Missing: Thomas Jenkins, William Mahoney, and John Dunn, prisoners.

Company D.—Killed: Gustavus Boyson. Wounded: Sergeants Jesse E. Rose, severely; John W. Meek, slightly; Privates James A. Barber, severely; and Sylvester Craig, slightly. Missing: Corporals James Foster, Jonas Tulles, Christian Legrain, (since paroled,) and Private Alexander Templin, prisoners.

Company E.—Killed: Captain Urwin Bean, Privates George Herald and James Franks. Wounded: Sergeant George J. Swank, Corporal Frederick Panier, and Private William Zigler, all severely; Privates George Colehouse and Jennings F. Northop, both slightly. Missing: George W. Armstrong and Henry Ellis.

Company F.—Wounded: First Lieutenant Aurora C. Reel, dangerously; Privates Andrew J. English and Michael Grafe, severely. Missing: Corporal

David F. Weimer, Privates Edward Cotton, Absalom Gonser, James A. Maragon, and Robert Slater, prisoners.

Company G.—Killed: Private Charles Castimore. Wounded: Sergeant William F. Hurst, Privates William Caley, Jacob Reep, Henry Tounend, Peter Shaffer, and Fisher McKee, all severely. Missing: Privates Sanford Lawton and Charles Benedict, prisoners.

Company H.—Killed: Corporal James C. Blythe. Wounded: Second Lieutenant William A. Sutherland, slightly; Corporals Westly Dessellam, Charles Moore, and Private Joseph Polus, all severely; Privates Alexander S. Patterson, Peter Maner, and Leander Knowles, all slightly. Missing: Corporal H. C. Ellson, Privates John Hetzel and Benjamin Rigdon.

Company I.—Killed: Corporal Joseph W. Werner. Wounded: Sergeant J. M. Dunlap, severely; Corporals William Bennett, Jeff. Dunbar, and Private Hiram Doll, all slightly. Missing: Corporal J. W. Frederick, Privates Stanton Thomas, and John Whett, prisoners.

Company K.—Wounded: Corporal Edwin R. Hanks, Privates Joseph Martin, Joseph Carter, Thomas King, George S. Bishop, and James Malone, severely. Missing: Private Lyle Saunders, prisoner.

Field and staff.—Killed: Sergeant Major Lyman Tylee.

Summary.—Killed: 2 officers and 13 enlisted men. Wounded: 2 officers and 56 enlisted men. Missing: 31 enlisted men.

Total killed, wounded, and missing, 104.

HEADQUARTERS 79TH REGIMENT INDIANA VOLUNTEERS,
Near Murfreesboro', January 8, 1863.

LIEUTENANT: The undersigned has the honor to report that on the 31st day of December, 1862, after having recrossed Stone river, the regiment was ordered into position west of the Murfreesboro' pike, in rear of the 19th regiment Ohio volunteers, to check the columns of the enemy then pursuing our forces across the pike. After very heavy firing by the 19th Ohio, and the repulse of the enemy, the regiment was ordered forward to relieve it, by command of the colonel commanding the brigade. Bayonets were fixed, and the enemy rapidly pursued with very severe fire for about three-quarters of a mile, driving them to their position, behind works. At this point an order was received to fall back, as the support on the right had given way before the enemy. Having fallen back in good order a distance of about 300 yards, halted, and faced to the front, the regiment was ordered by Major General Rosecrans, in person, to move by the right flank to an open field, to check the advance of the approaching enemy, and to cover the retreating right; which being accomplished, the regiment was ordered to fall back to the original line, the supports of the right and left having given way, and there joined the 19th Ohio, the only regiment of the brigade remaining; the others having moved to the support of a battery on the left. The regiment remained in that position until ordered to recross the pike at midnight.

The regiment was engaged for three hours, and the loss severe. A report of the casualties is herewith submitted.

It may not be improper to remark that the behavior of the regiment—only a short time in the field, on a long march, constant and arduous service when in camp, with but few opportunities to drill—may be attributed, in a great measure, to the splendid conduct of the 19th regiment Ohio volunteers, Major Manderson commanding, the effect of whose example was not lost upon the officers and soldiers of this regiment.

Very respectfully, your obedient servant,

FRED. KNEFLER,
Colonel 79th Regiment Indiana Volunteers.

Lieutenant W. H. H. SHEETS,
Acting Assistant Adjutant General,
1st Brigade, 3d Division, 14th Army Corps.

List of wounded and missing of the 79th regiment of Indiana volunteers on Wednesday, December 31, 1862.

Wounded.—Company A: Corporal William Curr, right arm: Privates William Wigner, hip; Andrew Lawson, leg; Timothy Haley, foot; John Pettix, leg, severely; William T. Moore, leg; and George Steinman, foot and arm. Company B: Privates John T. Anderson, knee; James Hastings, neck; William Hutton, leg; and Samuel C. Hook, thigh, dangerously. Company C: Corporal Theodore Bryant, thigh; Privates Benjamin Lester, head; and George Dressler, hip. Company D: Privates William Shever, thigh, dangerously; and William Hines, hand. Company E: Sergeant P. S. Burtch, head, Private William C. Rodgers, side, severely. Company F: Privates James Chapman, ankle; and James Ward, shoulder. Company G: Privates C. C. Higer, shoulder, dangerously; John Allen, breast; C. W. Loucks, side; and M. S. Hardin, arm broken, and amputated. Company I: Corporals John T. Mitchell, leg and ankle, severely; and John Israel, breast; Privates Fielding Wheaton, breast; and James Cotton, left thigh. Company K: Sergeant William H. Lout, head, slightly; Privates J. A. C. Dobson, right thigh; J. S. McLain, left thigh, amputated; and D. F. Ray, left thigh broken.

Missing.—Company B: Privates James Boyce, Jacob Leonard, and Sylvester Crail. Company C: Corporal Sylvester Crail and Private William Vallentine. Company D: Privates Amos Deshong, William Herron, and William C Wright. Company F: Privates Thomas J. Pressel, John Lanner, and Robert Dunham. Company G: Privates Edward Ball and William Pennington. Company H: Privates Harrison Payton and William Dunegan. Company K: Privates B. S. McLain, A. R. Crafton, and S. Worrell.

HEADQUARTERS 79TH REGIMENT INDIANA VOLUNTEERS,
Near Murfreesboro', Tennessee, January 8, 1863.

CAPTAIN: The undersigned has the honor to submit the following report of the 79th regiment Indiana volunteers in the action of January 2, 1863:

Having marched on the 1st day of January, 1863, from the position east of the pike, across Stone river, the regiment was formed in line, on the left of the 11th regiment Kentucky volunteers, supporting the brigade in front, and remained in that position until the morning of the 2d, when it was detached from the 1st brigade, and, by order of Colonel S. Beatty, commanding the 3d division, took up a position in front, with the 35th regiment Indiana volunteers on the right, and the 44th regiment Indiana volunteers on the left; a company of skirmishers was deployed in an open wood to cover the front of the regiment. During the day several pieces of artillery were placed in position by the enemy, on a rise of ground some five hundred yards distant, throwing shell into our lines, severely wounding some of the men. The regiment was sheltered, as far as the nature of the ground would permit, by lying down.

About 4 o'clock p. m. the fire of the skirmishers increased, and a column of the enemy, four or five regiments deep, approached rapidly, supported by artillery, which was kept concealed (as it was dragged by men instead of horses,) until it opened fire within one hundred yards of our lines. The forces on the right soon became engaged, but the regiment was kept lying on the ground, until the enemy had approached within fifty yards, when it was ordered to rise up, and commenced firing with very destructive effect upon the enemy, volley after volley, until the line having given way on the right and left, the regiment being left alone, almost surrounded, the enemy in front, and on both flanks, it was forced to fall back across Stone river, where it rallied at the rendezvous of the 3d division.

The regiment went into action on the 3d of December with 341 rank and file, and lost during both engagements fully one-third of its available force, including more than half the commissioned officers, in killed and wounded; but very few men are missing or taken prisoners.

Officers and soldiers conducted themselves well, doing their duty, and there was no shirking or skulking from the field before or during action. It would be injustice to many to mention a few when all behaved well.

Lieutenant Eli F. Ritter, adjutant of the regiment, rendered me very valuable services, acting as a field officer in the absence of the lieutenant colonel.

A report of casualties is submitted herewith.

I have the honor to be, captain, very respectfully, your obedient servant,

FRED. KNEFLER,
Colonel 79th Regiment Indiana Volunteers.

Captain E. A. OTIS,
Assistant Adjutant General, 3d Division, 14th Army Corps.

List of killed, wounded, and missing of the 79th regiment Indiana volunteers in an action in which the regiment was engaged on Friday, January 2, 1863.

Killed.—Company A: Corporal Samuel B. Gaylord, and Privates Benjamin Krigler and Thomas Arnold. Company B: Private John W. Culte. Company D: Privates Noah D. Hevson, Martin V. Stanley, and Thomas Eller. Company F: Second Lieutenant Benjamin T. Poynter, Corporal James Bailey, and Privates Robert Potter and Herman Stout. Total, 11.

Wounded.—Major Perry M. Blankenship, in hip. Company A: Corporal William Hinesley, in both hips, dangerously; Privates John Nelson, in leg, severely; Thomas Lawson, in arm and side; George Williams, in nasal organ; Patrick Brennan, in cheek; Samuel Delzell, in leg. Company B: Second Lieutenant Arthur St. Clair Vance, in knee-joint; Privates John Hopper, in breast, dangerously; John Bellis, in side. Company C: First Lieutenant Benjamin Vallequette, in leg, dangerously; Privates A. D. Eakes, in hand, severely; John McManus, in hand. Company D: Sergeant George Harris, arm and leg; Private Dunas A. King, thigh and arm, dangerously. Company E: Captain John N. Scott, left arm, dangerously; First Lieutenant Luman Jones, right arm, dangerously; Corporal P. W. Martin, in left side; Privates Richard Clark, in knee; George W. Hadden, in neck; Henry Flusher, in hand; John Kendall, in side. Company F: First Lieutenant James P. Catterson, in left foot; Private N. Brooks, in foot and left side. Company G: First Sergeant George W. Clark, on head, slightly; Sergeant Benjamin F. Conner, in right shoulder; Private J. S. Hetton, two fingers shot off. Company H: Privates William Seachrist, arm broken; John Pettit, in leg, badly; James B. Mosier, in shoulder, severely; Wm. McKane, in back, dangerously. Company I: Privates James E. Clark, in arm, severely; William Sherer, in thigh; William Hines, in hand. Company K: First Lieutenant Ed. J. Foster, in left thigh, dangerously; Privates M. Hendricks, leg amputated; C. W. Tyler, in left arm; James Gorrell, in left leg, dangerously; —— Hulsiger, in left thigh, dangerously; H. C. Ratcliff, (prisoner,) on head; H. V. Kaywood, in left hand; William C. Amick, in right shoulder. Total, 42.

Missing.—Company A: Private John B. Ducker. Company B: Sergeant W. H. H. Phillips, and Private James Miller. Company C: Sergeant Charles Anderson, and Private Sidney Moore. Company D: Private Christian Spilker. Company E: Corporal P. W. Martin, and Privates Joshua E. Diee and Daniel Fox. Company G: Privates Benjamin F. Marshall, John Shuman, and Andrew J. Bolin. Company H: Sergeant Joseph Hodges, and Privates Henry Crane and Henry Sutherland. Company I: Privates Silas Martin and Milton Gillespie. Company K: Sergeant William H. Tout. Total, 18.

HEADQUARTERS 2D BRIGADE, 3D DIVISION, LEFT WING,
Army of the Cumberland, January 5, 1863.

CAPTAIN: I herewith transmit my report of the operations of the 2d brigade in front of Murfreesboro', where it arrived with the balance of the left wing December 29, 1862, up to 3d January, 1863.

December 30.—The brigade was under arms in close column of divisions all day; considerable firing in the afternoon, in the direction of the right wing.

December 31.—The brigade was ordered across Stone river; prior to reaching the same, an order was received from General Crittenden to countermarch the brigade, together with Swallow's battery, in double-quick to the rear, as the train was attacked. Passing quickly through the woods, as the wagons had blocked up the road, we came out into the open field beyond, and formed a line of battle, perpendicular to the road, on the left, in a cornfield, through which the rebels were seen leading off the train slowly, as the ground was soft. Beyond the train, in the same field, was about a squadron of cavalry, guarded by rebels. On our appearance the cavalry began capturing their guard; one escaped, one was killed. The rebel cavalry were drawn up in line across the field, in the edge of the woods. Captain Swallow, who had managed to get his battery through the obstructions expeditiously, soon had his pieces in position, and opened fire on the rebel lines, who began dispersing, and were charged by a force of our cavalry, which had passed down the road to the right of the train, doing excellent service. The effect of the charge I could not see from where we were. Captain Swallow now moved his pieces to a more elevated position, which commanded the country for a great distance, from whence he opened on their scattered forces, driving them out of view.

At this point an order was received from General Van Cleve to return to the 3d division, and form on the right of the 1st brigade in two lines, to support it; that Colonel Harker would support my right. The order was immediately complied with; the division began advancing down the slope of the cedar ridge, south of the road, passing Colonel Harker's on my right, beyond the foot of the slope. After passing his brigade, which did not move, my right flank became exposed, with strong indications of a heavy force approaching in front, extending beyond my right flank. As we continued advancing I sent three different messengers, by my aids, calling Colonel Harker's attention to my exposed flank; and at length reported in person to General Van Cleve. While doing this the 65th Ohio, which, it appeared, had been lying down at the edge of the field, rose to their feet in the place where a force was needed. Supposing it would remain there, I passed back again to my position, to see the 65th march by the right flank back to Colonel Harker's left. The firing in front of my first line, composed of the 59th Ohio and 44th Indiana, was getting to be heavy, and the skirmishers running in reported a heavy force advancing through the woods, outflanking my right. Lieutenant Temple, of my staff, was sent at once to Lieutenant Colonel Dick with orders to wheel his regiment to the right, and place it in the woods to secure my flank. Before the order reached him the enemy appeared coming through the woods. Seeing the force would have to fall back, I galloped to the battery and ordered it to open fire to the right of my flank into the woods, for the purpose of checking and confusing the outflanking force, to save my brigade from the effects of the cross fire, while falling back, as much as possible.

The order to fire was complied with instantly, the whole battery opening several volleys in quick succession and with decided effect into the woods, while the column fell back rapidly, the front line having sustained itself gallantly until outflanked. The artillery came safely out of the field under fire, Lieutenant Buckner, a gallant officer, being shot from his horse and badly wounded, just as he was passing out of the field. After falling back from the field the 13th Ohio, under Major Jarvis, and part of the 86th Indiana, Lieutenant Colonel Dick, was formed near the road, the 44th being placed on duty elsewhere, and ordered to move up the road to meet the force that had followed from the field, who were represented advancing. Going in advance of the force, I found the 59th Ohio, under Lieutenant Colonel Howard and Major Frambus, hotly contesting the cedar ridge, and hard pressed, their left flank being exposed, encouraging the men to hold on and that they should have help immediately; the force following me was hurried up; the remnant of the 13th Ohio, though sadly repressed by the death of the gallant and loved Colonel Hawkins, shot dead on the field, answered the command to go forward with a cheer, and got into line on the left, opening fire just as a regiment on the right of the 59th marched to the rear, leaving my right flank again exposed, which the enemy were not slow to perceive, and began taking advantage of. Sorely annoyed, I crossed the road and asked the officer in command, whom I do not know, what it meant; he said he had been ordered back, but on my representations he immediately marched his regiment up again, delivering a heavy fire as he reached the crest of the ridge. I then ordered the whole line to charge, which was gallantly done with a cheer, the enemy being driven from the crest of the ridge down the southern slope, and back across the field.

One of the skirmishers, William Brown, of company B, 59th Ohio, met me on the edge of the ridge marching back through the line at the head of twenty-eight prisoners, besides two officers (lieutenants) he had captured in a sink-hole; many other prisoners were captured by the 2d brigade, amounting to sixty, as near as can be ascertained. After the enemy were repulsed, as stated, there was no more fighting on this day by the left wing, General Van Cleve turning over the command of the division to me, he having been wounded, Colonel Beatty being on duty elsewhere.

January 1, 1863.—Crossed with the brigade over the river, where the 2d brigade was placed on the left of the 1st, in an open field in rear of a belt of timber on a ridge, the 44th Indiana and 13th Ohio in the front line, with the 35th and 79th Indiana on their right, the 59th Ohio and 86th Indiana in reserve. This arrangement left an open space on the left; on the front line, between it and a road running through a lane beyond the road, was an open field unoccupied by troops, except a line of skirmishers from Colonel Grose's command; in the rear, towards Stone river, was a cornfield, and behind the fence was a Kentucky regiment, with their right resting on the lane. This left a gap between my left and their right of about five hundred yards, thus the forces rested during the day, with sharp skirmishing in our front.

January 2.—The skirmishing commenced early and was brisk throughout the day, until about 3 o'clock, when the indications of an attack in front became so threatening, a battery having been planted in the woods on my left flank, that I ordered my reserve into the front line, deflecting the 86th Indiana back, and placing them behind the fence across the lane to sweep the open field in front of the Kentucky regiment. Company A, of the 59th regiment, under Sergeant Carr, was placed on the left of the 86th, connecting the two forces, which gave them a cross fire over the open field in front.

About 4 o'clock p. m. Colonel Beatty, commanding the division, came over and was shown the disposition of the brigade, which he approved, suggesting, in case we were compelled to fall back, we should do so through the low ground. We then went to the point near the ford, where the artillery was stationed, and while examining that, Major General Rosecrans arrived at the same point In a few moments a messenger from the front arrived and reported a large force was being massed in front of our lines. Colonel Beatty and myself immediately started to our respective positions. I was shortly met by Adjutant Holten, of the 59th Ohio, with a report that the enemy were in motion, advancing on our front. Sixteen regimental flags had been counted in one column. Acting Assistant Adjutant General C. F. King was ordered to make report of the facts to General Rosecrans immediately. Passing on to the 86th regiment, it and company A were ordered to strengthen their position with rails. Only a short time elapsed when a tremendous fire indicated that the attack had fallen on Colonel Beatty's right. Another column, it appeared, had crossed Stone river and participated in the attack, while still another was coming on my left, but for some cause its advance was somewhat delayed. The main column of attack moved diagonally across the front of the wood, striking toward a wooded height on the bank of the river, where Captain Drury's battery of artillery had been posted in the morning, under the command of Lieutenant Livingston. The weight of the column of attack fell first on the 8th Kentucky and 51st Ohio in the front line. They stood gallantly for a few moments, but were swept away. The enemy, still pushing on, received a heavy flank and oblique fire from the 35th, 44th, and 86th Indiana, and 13th Ohio. The column next encountered the 99th Ohio, 21st Kentucky, and 19th Ohio, which were successively borne backward, as were the 9th and 11th Kentucky. In the mean time, after the giving way of our second line, and as soon as our infantry had got out of the way, Lieutenant Livingston opened upon them with his battery with good effect. The enemy's artillery, following their column, took position on the high ground to the right of the wood, which commanded the field of battle, and, as their infantry passed on driving our right across the river, opened with grape and canister. The second brigade, not being exactly in line of their charge, held their ground until the column of attack had passed our second line.

The brigade then fell back through the low ground, as directed, (being myself disabled, my horse having thrown and dragged me for a short distance,) and took position behind the buildings on the hill. The artillery, after the giving way of our last line of infantry, recrossed Stone river. The column of attack, pushing on towards the ford, was exposed to a severe flank fire from Colonel Grose's force, together with those of my brigade, who had collected about the buildings upon the hill, and also to our artillery and the infantry that had taken position on the opposite bank of the river; thus extending the fire around their front to their left flank, encircling them on three sides. A cross fire of artillery and small arms, delivered for a short time with terrible effect, was too much for them, and their broken and discomfited columns turned back upon their path, closely pursued by the troops which had rallied, together with the fresh troops which General Rosecrans had ordered up, taking a portion of the celebrated Washington battery. This repulse closed the operations in front of Murfreesboro', the second brigade going into camp on the field for the night.

I cannot close this report without favorably noticing many of the officers and men of my command throughout the trying ordeal of so many days' fighting. My acting assistant adjutant general, C. F. King, J. B. Temple, aide-de-camp, Captain Charles A. Sheaf, provost marshal, Lieutenant Joseph Dancer, inspector, who was severely wounded in the last day's fight, and Orderlies H. J. Higgins, E. D. Thomas, members of my staff, are entitled to much credit for their conduct on the field. Colonel Williams, Lieutenant Colonel Aldrich, and Joseph C. Hodges, adjutant of the 44th Indiana; Colonel J. G. Hawkins, (killed in the first day's fight while gallantly doing his duty;) Major Jarvis, upon whom the command devolved after the fall of Colonel Hawkins, and Adjutant L. B. George; Lieutenant Colonel Howard, Major Frambus, Adjutant Holter, of the 59th Ohio; Colonel Dick, Major Dresser, of the 86th Indiana, (severely wounded in the engagement of the first day,) are deserving of particular notice. Colonel Hamilton, although unacquainted with military matters, was present, assisting all in his power. Also Surgeons Martin Hays and Gordon, with the assistance of the brigade band, in getting and attending to the wounded, in which Gus. Penn was shot dead, and Dougherty, both of the band, badly wounded, for their good conduct are especially noticed. Lieutenants Kibler and Woods attracted my attention by their gallantry while in command of the skirmishers on the cedar ridge. I will also notice the gallantry and death of color-bearer Sergeant Wood, shot dead with the flag in his hand on the first day's fight; also of Nelson Shields, who seized the colors and bore them aloft, upon the fall of the color sergeant, until wounded himself, when he delivered them to Private Lord, all of the 13th Ohio. I also notice Color-bearers Benjamin Snellinger and Nathan Coffenberry, of the 86th Indiana, who were both shot down, the first killed instantly, the latter mortally wounded, in the fight of the first day. Both of these flags were lost. I also notice the good conduct of Sergeant Ely and Thomas Hayden, of the 59th Ohio, who, on the last day's fight, were raised in the air by a cannon ball ploughing the earth beneath their feet, and thrown violently to the earth. I recommend that William Brown, of company B, 59th Ohio, who captured the prisoners above referred to, and Nelson Shields, of the 13th Ohio, who saved his regimental flag, as proper persons to receive, each, one of the medals ordered to be prepared by Congress for those who particularly distinguish themselves in battle.

In closing this report, I wish also to render my thanks to Major Lyne Starling, adjutant general on General Crittenden's staff, for words of encouragement and cheer to a portion of my command when hard pressed on the cedar ridge in the first day's fight; and also to express my gratitude to our commander-in-chief, General Rosecrans, for the same favor at the place and about the same time. All of which is respectfully submitted, together with the reports of the different regimental commanders, appropriately marked, with a corrected account of the killed, wounded, and missing, which foot up: Officers killed, 4; wounded, 15; enlisted men killed, 75; enlisted men wounded, 251; missing, officers, 2; enlisted men, 166—total, 513, distributed, as will more fully appear by abstract herewith enclosed, marked A.

JAMES P. FYFFE,
Colonel, Commanding 2d Brigade, 3d Division,
Left Wing, 14th Army Corps.

Captain E. A. OTIS,
Acting Assistant Adjutant General.

HEADQUARTERS FORTY-FOURTH INDIANA VOLUNTEERS,
Camp near Murfreesboro', Tennessee, January 5, 1863.

DEAR SIR: It becomes my duty to make a brief report of engagements before Murfreesboro'. We went into the field on the 31st December with 316 men, officers included. We took our position, by your order, in brigade on the right, and marched in line of battle through an open field south of the pike. In passing through this field, we discovered the enemy making a flank movement on our right, in a wood bordering upon the field. Intelligence was conveyed to you, and, as I understand, by you to our division commander. We made a stand at the edge of the wood in our front, but were soon ordered to advance, which we did. After entering the wood, our skirmishers were ordered in, as the line of the enemy was in sight. We still advanced to within, as near as I could judge, one hundred yards of their line, and opened fire. They replied, and advanced their line; at the same time the flanking force opened a galling cross fire upon us. We held the position as long as we could do so without sacrificing our whole regiment; we then fell back to our battery, and formed line of battle. We were ordered, by General Van Cleve, to remain here till further orders. We soon had orders from you to join the brigade at the right, which we did. Here we formed a new line, and remained till some time in the night, when we were ordered to march to the left again, where we remained through the night.

Permit me to pass over occurrences not important, for want of room, to the 2d day of January, when we were in line of battle on the left. About 4 o'clock p. m. the enemy was discovered to be advancing. I received orders from you to fall back to low ground, if it was found we could not hold our position. The enemy attacked on our right, 79th and 35th Indiana engaged, and held their position firm for some time; in the mean time I directed my fire at right oblique. The enemy pressed on, and the 35th and 79th gave way. I still held my men and kept up the fire till the enemy had passed by us on the right, and then gave orders to fall back, which we did, to a rail fence. Then we rallied again, and gave them a cross fire; but they still advancing made it necessary to fall back to the ground you designated. I gave the command, and we fell back to the building on the hill. Here Adjutant Hodges and myself, together with other officers, succeeded in rallying a large force together with our regiment, and opened a destructive cross fire on the enemy, which soon had its effect upon their extreme left, and assisted very much in their final repulse. We followed them till ordered to fall back. I must here mention that at the first rally at the rail fence was last seen Colonel Williams. I suppose him to be taken prisoner. Our loss as it stands now is 56 wounded, 10 killed, 47 missing.

I must make mention of some officers and men that acted with great bravery: First is our colonel, William C. Williams. Adjutant Joseph Hodges was among the most efficient and brave; Acting Lieutenant Joseph Burch, company A; Lieutenants Gundinghouser and Thomas, company F; Lieutenants Getty and Murray, company B; Lieutenant Wilson, company K; Lieutenant Hilderbrand, company E; Acting Lieutenants, company G; Lieutenant Story, company C; Lieutenant King, company H; Lieutenant Shell, company D; Acting Lieutenant Belnap, company I. Color-bearer Owen Shaw, company C, acted with distinguished bravery; and, with few exceptions, our men and officers acted finely.

Many things I am obliged to omit for want of room and poor health. I must, however, not close without giving our brigade commander high praise and credit for his coolness, bravery, and judgment upon those eventful days.

I remain, sir, your obedient servant,

S. C. ALDRICH,

Lieutenant Colonel, Commanding 44th Indiana Volunteers.

Colonel FYFFE,

Commanding 2d Brigade, 3d Division.

P. S.—I would state that on the 31st December I had my horse shot.

S. C. A.

HEADQUARTERS 86TH REGIMENT INDIANA VOLUNTEERS,
Camp near Murfreesboro', Tennessee, January 5, 1863.

SIR: I have the honor to report as follows: My command arrived in front of Murfreesboro' at 8 o'clock p. m., December 30, 1852. On the following morning the regiment numbered 368, rank and file. About noon of the 31st December, with the brigade, we were marched in line of battle across the Nashville turnpike road, about one-half mile south, across an open field to the skirt of a heavy wood, in which the enemy lay concealed in heavy force. My regiment was on the extreme right of the brigade; we were halted behind a fence at the edge of the wood, to await the arrival of troops to come up to support us on the right, who failed to come. Our right was totally exposed to the enemy, who immediately attacked us in overwhelming numbers in front, our right flank extending round partially to the rear of our right wing.

Our regiment fought bravely until their ranks were being rapidly cut down and thinned, when we fell back to the turnpike road, where a portion of them again rallied, with portions of other regiments of the brigade, and drove the enemy back.

Our loss in the engagement was as follows:

Commissioned officers killed, 1; wounded, 5; missing, 2; enlisted men killed, 33; wounded, 54; missing, 99—total officers killed, wounded, and missing, 8; enlisted men killed, wounded, and missing, 186—aggregate, 194. Both the color-bearers were shot down and the colors left on the field.

On the following morning we were marched some mile and a half across Stone river to the front, and placed in line of battle early in the day, where we skirmished with the enemy all day, lying on our arms that night. The next day we occupied the same ground, skirmishing with the enemy till 3 o'clock p. m., when the enemy in vast numbers attacked the right of our line, composed of the 1st and 3d brigades of our division, who maintained the ground, fighting obstinately for some time, when they were forced to yield to superior numbers, and fell back; when our regiment fell back to a high piece of ground, near a house on the hill, some one hundred rods to the rear, where we again made a stand, again rallied with other troops, and drove the enemy from the field, retaking and holding our former position. Our loss here was one private wounded.

Captain Frazer, of company A, Captain Dick, of company C, Lieutenant Hixon, of company D, and Lieutenant Gillilan, of company I, were wounded in the fight of the first day and compelled to remain at the hospital. I take pleasure in saying that Captain Philip Gamen was present with his command during the whole of the different actions, rendering efficient service and aid. Lieutenant Colonel George F. Dick was present at all times during the different engagements, behaved in the most gallant manner, giving direction to and encouraging the troops to maintain their ground, and has my warmest thanks for the efficient aid rendered me during the whole affair.

Respectfully, your obedient servant,

A. S. HAMILTON,
Colonel 86*th Regiment Indiana Volunteers.*

Colonel JAMES P. FYFFE,
Commanding 2d Brigade, 3d Division, Army of the Cumberland.

Official report of the 13*th regiment Ohio volunteer infantry of the battles before Murfreesboro', Tennessee.*

SIR: I have the honor to report the following as the part taken by the 13th regiment Ohio volunteer infantry in the series of battles before Murfreesboro, Tennessee, commencing December 30, 1862, and terminating January 3, 1863.

On Wednesday, at 8 o'clock a. m., our regiment, under command of Colonel Joseph G. Hawkins, was ordered in from outpost duty, and took our place in line. Soon after we started for the south side of Stone river, but got but a short distance when, by your orders, we countermarched at double-quick a distance of about one mile, to a cornfield on the right of the Murfreesboro' road, to repel an attack of cavalry upon our train. Our lines were here formed, my regiment occupying the right of the 2d brigade. The enemy being driven from the field by our cavalry and artillery, my regiment was not engaged, and about 10 o'clock, under your directions, took a position in the woods south of the cornfield. My regiment was now ordered to cover the 59th Ohio, which, with the 44th Indiana, formed the first line of attack; my regiment, with the 86th Indiana on its right, forming the second line. In consequence of the unevenness of the ground and the density of the thicket, it was difficult to keep our lines properly, but on emerging from the woods into the open field beyond we advanced regularly to the edge of the next woods. The first line having advanced some twenty yards into the woods, my regiment was ordered to lie down. Now it became evident that the enemy was attempting to outflank us upon the right; and this was reported to you, but just at that moment our first line was attacked, and it was compelled to fall back in some disorder, and over my men, who were lying down close to the fence. At this moment our gallant colonel fell, mortally wounded, whilst encouraging the men to keep cool and to fire low; and the command devolved upon myself. I held the position until the enemy completely outflanked us, and was then compelled to fall back in disorder to the line of reserves, where I rallied my command, and this time drove the enemy back, they now being in the open field, whilst we had the advantage of the cover of the woods. We inflicted considerable loss upon them in killed and wounded, besides capturing some thirty prisoners. My loss in this engagement was quite severe, Colonel J. G. Hawkins and Second Lieutenant J. C. Whitaker being killed, together with twenty-seven enlisted men. Captain E. M. Most, Lieutenants John Murphy, John E. Ray, S. C. Gold, John Fox, (since dead,) and Thomas J. Stone were wounded, and sixty-eight enlisted men, besides thirty-nine missing.

No other movement of importance in which my regiment participated occurred until Friday, January 2, 1863, when we occupied the extreme left of our lines on the south side of Stone river, having taken our position the day previous under your immediate supervision. On the morning of the 2d my skirmishers were thrown forward, and by their vigilance I was enabled to report to you the movements of the enemy and the probability of an attack, as the enemy were massing troops on our right, and artillery had moved to my front. At 3 o'clock p. m. the firing of the skirmishers on the right plainly indicated the enemy's advance, and in half an hour after their infantry engaged the brigade on our right, their lines being formed diagonal to our front. My regiment was not exposed to the infantry; but a battery opened upon our front with grape and canister, so that I was compelled to order a retrograde movemfnt, which was executed in as good order as was possible. At about 300 yards I made a stand again, but by this time their battery occupied our former position in line, and we were ordered to fall back to the other side of the river, which was done in good order. Our loss in this engagement was ten enlisted men wounded and thirty missing.

The following exhibits a detailed account of my casualties in both engagements, viz:

Killed.—Colonel J. G. Hawkins, Second Lieutenant J. C. Whitaker; enlisted men, 29.

Wounded.—Captain E. M. Most; First Lieutenants John Murphy, John C. Ray, and Samuel C. Gold; Second Lieutenant John Fox, (since died,) and Second Lieutenant Thomas J Stone; enlisted men, 79.

Missing.—69.

Aggregate loss in killed, wounded, and missing, 185.

Respectfully submitted.

D. JARVIS, JR.,
Major, Commanding 13th Regiment Ohio Volunteer Infantry.

Colonel JAMES P. FYFFE,
Commanding 2d Brigade, 3d Division, Left Wing,
14th Army Corps, Department of the Cumberland.

HEADQUARTERS 59TH REGIMENT OHIO VOLUNTEER INFANTRY,
Camp near Murfreesboro', Tennessee, January 5, 1863.

SIR: I have the honor to transmit to you the report of the 59th regiment Ohio volunteer infantry, of your command, of the battles from the 31st December, 1862, to the 3d January, 1863.

On the morning of that day my command was formed at 4 o'clock, in accordance with previous orders, and, with the balance of the brigade, started at 8 o'clock to take position on the left, when we received orders to march immediately to defend the wagon train against the attack of the enemy, which was done with promptness, and they were driven back with loss, and the whole train was saved. We then received orders to march back and take position on the right of Colonel Beatty's command, in front, as our forces were hard pressed at that point, in line of battle, and moved forward to attack the enemy; and after moving across the woods we came into an open field, which we moved rapidly across until we reached the woods, and my skirmishers soon discovered the enemy in heavy force and in strong position in front, and fired upon him and fell back to the line, which I immediately ordered forward and made the attack; and after firing upon them several rounds, and holding them in check for some time, we were forced back by superior numbers about twenty paces, when, by the prompt assistance of my officers, we succeeded in rallying the regiment and took position behind a fence, and then poured volley after volley into the advancing ranks of the enemy, and held them in check until Major Frambus, upon the right, informed me that we were being flanked upon that wing and that the balance of the brigade was falling back, when I gave the order to fall back, inclining to the right in a skirt of woods, and thereby protecting, to a great extent, my command against a most galling fire in rear, and, to some extent, a flanking fire also. My officers again coming promptly to my assistance, we succeeded in rallying the regiment again, and moved to the right, through the woods in front of the enemy, and by a well-directed fire checked his onward movement, and held him at that position until the balance of the brigade was put in position, when we moved forward and drove the enemy from the field with great slaughter and in complete disorder. We then, by your orders, took a strong position in the woods, and I threw forward my skirmishers; but the enemy, although making several demonstrations on the right, did not dare again to approach. We held our position until darkness closed the controversy for the day. We then, during the night, moved to the left, and went into camp, but were soon ordered to get in line of battle, and there remained until daylight, when we moved across Stone river and took position upon the extreme left, and during that day had heavy skirmishing, until night ended the fight.

On the next morning we were ordered to form in column of divisions, and take position near the woods and throw out our skirmishers, who soon came in collision with the enemy's, and each in turn advanced and fell back until about 11 o'clock, when the enemy got a battery in position and commenced to throw an occasional shell in the direction of our line, evidently feeling our position, when, by your orders, Major Frambus moved my command back and took position upon some low ground, and gave the orders to lay close to protect themselves against the enemy's shells, and there remained until about 2 o'clock, when the skirmishers were driven in, when I gave the orders to Major Frambus to deploy into line and move forward near the woods. About that time the enemy succeeded in planting a second battery directly in our front, and commenced to throw shells, when we again laid close to the ground. The enemy then planted another battery still further upon his right and our left. About 3 o'clock our skirmishers were driven in, and it was very soon apparent that the enemy was approaching in force to attack, and at that time he opened with musketry and artillery along his whole line, and moved forward upon our forces in five heavy columns of brigades; but in his movement all in front of us was entirely clear of our army, and his right had passed our right, and we were about wheeling to give him a flank fire, when we discovered emerging from the woods the same number of his columns, moving with his right upon our left and passing us, when Major Frambus was ordered to fall back with the command, which order was executed in excellent style until the enemy, by his terrible discharges of musketry and artillery, and the weight of his columns, bore down and threw into disorder our whole lines, when we were thrown back in confusion, but succeeded in again rallying our line at a fence in our rear; but all in vain, for no human power of our strength could withstand such a force. But about that time the scene was destined to change. Our artillery and musketry opened upon their advancing ranks and columns with fearful destruction, but still he moved steadily forward. At that time every officer in my command seemed aroused to a sudden sense of duty, and dashed in to rally what he could for a grand stand, without reference to a general rallying of the regiment, and went into this terrible battle, Major Frambus taking command of one wing, Adjutant Holten of another, and each officer with all he could gather; and at that time the fight became terribly fearful, and the enemy was turned and thrown into complete confusion, and was driven, with awful slaughter, from the field. And I am proud to say that every officer and soldier in my command did his whole duty, and we gained on that day a magnificent victory.

We lost during the several battles from the 31st December to the 3d January: in killed, three; in wounded, thirty-seven; and we had forty-five missing, very few of whom were captured by the enemy, many of them being ordered to guard the train to Nashville. My command, in the several battles, captured fifty-six prisoners, among whom were one captain and one lieutenant. We commenced these battles with two hundred and ninety-one officers and soldiers, and we have now for duty two hundred and six officers and men. I had two officers wounded and there are two missing. It is due to my command to state that one part of them assisted in taking the battery which was captured.

I cannot close this report without awarding due praise to my officers, and in doing this I must name them here, so that the world may know who have actually played a prominent part in these splendid victories before Murfreesboro', that must electrify the world, and cause every true Union man's heart to thrill for joy. I can, under all circumstances, rely upon Major Frambus, who was everywhere present in the very hottest of the battle, fearless of his own safety. He deserves his country's praise. Adjutant Holten, amidst showers of bullets, carried my every order to any part of the field, regardless of his own safety. Let his country do him justice. Lieutenants Wood and Kibler deserve to be remembered by those who may live after them. Captain Vanosdol and Lieutenants Stevens and Smith can be relied upon in any emergency; and it was truly a source of pleasure to me to see Captain L. I. Egbert move steadily forward in battle. He deserves his country's honor. Lieutenant John O'Connor, after being severely wounded in the hand, bound it up himself, and he continued in command until night, at which time he had his finger amputated, and was compelled to leave the field. The name of such a patriot will live after him.

Captain Hill was severely wounded in the face, and was compelled to retire. A better officer I do not want. My surgeons, Doctors Hays and Gordon, have my sincerest thanks for their prompt attention to the wounded. Companies F, G, and H were commanded by Sergeants Jesse Ellis, Cohen, Hawkins, and Riley, each of whom deserve a commission, because they have fairly earned them. My color-bearers did not allow their flags to trail in the dust, but brought them safely from the field. In a word, I am perfectly satisfied with my whole command, and believe the 59th Ohio volunteer infantry has, in those four terrible days, faithfully discharged her duty, and deserves her country's admiration and esteem.

I am, very respectfully, your obedient servant,

WILLIAM HOWARD,
Lieutenant Colonel, Commanding 59th Regiment O. V. I.

JAMES P. FYFFE,
Colonel, Commanding 2d Brigade.

HEADQUARTERS 3D BRIGADE, 3D DIVISION,
LEFT WING, 14TH ARMY CORPS,
January 6, 1863.

SIR: I have the honor to submit the following report of the part the 3d brigade, which I command, (composed of the 51st Ohio, 8th and 21st Kentucky, 35th Indiana, and the 99th Ohio, infantry regiments,) took in the action near Murfreesboro' since the 31st ultimo:

On the morning of the 31st day of December last my brigade was ordered from the position it held on the north of the Nashville and Murfreesboro' railroad, across and on the east side of Stone river, crossing the river at a ford about one mile below where the railroad bridge crosses it. At the top of the hill, and about half a mile distant from the river, on the east side, I formed my brigade, on the left of the 1st brigade, then commanded by Colonel Samuel Beatty. No sooner had I thus formed the brigade than an order came from Brigadier General Van Cleve, then commanding the 3d division, for my brigade to cross the river at the same ford, and for me to arrange it so as to overlook and command the ford. I accordingly recrossed, and stationed the brigade on the crest of the hill, the 8th Kentucky regiment on the right of the front line, 2d Wisconsin battery (commanded by Lieutenant Livingston) on the left of the 8th Kentucky, 51st Ohio on the left of the artillery, and 35th Indiana regiment on the left of the 51st Ohio. The second or rear line was formed by the 21st Kentucky and 99th Ohio regiments—21st Kentucky on the right, and the 99th Ohio on the left.

During the entire day severe fighting was going on with the right wing and the centre. The battle-field was perfectly visible from the position I held, and although frequently in range of the enemy's cannon, and exposed at times to their bursting shells and solid shot, the men and officers of my command were perfectly cool and composed, and remained in ranks and conducted themselves as become soldiers and officers.

About 2 o'clock p. m. three or four hundred rebel cavalry appeared on the east and opposite side of the river, and made a dash at a number of government wagons containing camp equipage. Before they reached the wagons, Lieutenant Livingston, ever vigilant and prompt in the performance of his duties, opened a sharp fire of artillery on them, killing three of them and somewhat confusing the remainder. Notwithstanding, they succeeded in starting off a number of the wagons; but during their hasty retreat the artillery disabled one of the wagons, thereby blockading the road and saving the wagons in rear.

Expecting that an attempt would be made afterwards by the enemy to cross the river, I detached the 8th Kentucky, as sharpshooters, to command (under cover of the bank) the ford and prevent their success in such an attempt. Afterwards nothing unusual occurred on that day, and my brigade remained in *statu quo.*

On the next morning, January 1, 1863, I was ordered by Colonel Beatty, (who, by reason of General Van Cleve having been disabled by a shell in the action of the day previous, assumed command of the division,) to station the brigade again on the east side of the river; which I accordingly did, placing it half a mile up and perpendicular to the river, in two lines—51st Ohio on the right of the front line, 8th Kentucky in the centre, and 35th Indiana on the left—also, the 3d Wisconsin battery was in the front line, between the 8th Kentucky and 35th Indiana regiments, the 21st Kentucky and 99th Ohio forming the rear line, the 21st Kentucky on the right and 99th Ohio on the left. During the day there was heavy skirmishing in our front, and occasionally bodies of cavalry appeared in the distance in front of my command. Our artillery opened on them at different times and dispersed them; but after the firing ceased they reappeared. At sundown our artillery was ordered back to the rear to the west side of the river.

The night was passed without any interruption from the enemy, except about 12 o'clock there was very sharp firing on the skirmish line, when one of the skirmishers, a private of the 35th Indiana regiment, was killed. On the morning of the 2d of January the 3d Wisconsin battery was ordered up and occupied its former position. Through the day our skirmishers reported at different times the appearance of rebel artillery in our front, and also of fifteen rebel infantry regiments that seemed to pass toward our left, which was promptly reported to the commander of the 3d division, Colonel Beatty. The rebel artillery frequently shelled the woods we occupied, and killed a private of the 8th Kentucky, at the same time tearing the colors of that regiment in pieces. In the skirmishing of the day a private of the 51st Ohio was killed, and one or two of the 8th Kentucky and 35th Indiana regiments wounded. At 3.15 o'clock the rebels advanced in force through a cornfield in our front, supposed to be a division. As they advanced to our skirmish line, Captain Banton, of the 8th Kentucky, who was in command of the skirmishers of the 8th Kentucky regiment, was shot and instantly killed. When they had advanced to within gunshot of our line, the 51st Ohio regiment, commanded by Lieutenant Colonel R. W. R. McClain; the 8th Kentucky regiment, commanded by Lieutenant Colonel R. May, and the 35th Indiana regiment, commanded by Colonel B. F. Mullen, poured into their ranks a deadly and effective fire, which seemed for a while to stop their advancing column; but again they advanced slowly, and here the battle raged desperately. The gallantry and coolness there evinced by the officers and soldiers of the 51st Ohio, 8th Kentucky, and 35th Indiana regiments, deserve the highest praise, and heartily do I attribute it to them.

After these three regiment had contended with the enemy, far superior in numbers to my command, for ten or twelve minutes, and under a severe fire of three batteries of the enemy, (none on our side to respond to them,) and seeing that to oppose them further would only end in the slaughter of my men, I ordered the front line to fall back in order, which it did as far as possible, and for the second or rear line, composed of the 21st regiment, commanded by Lieutenant Colonel J. C. Evans, and 99th Ohio regiment, commanded by Colonel P. T. Swaine, to fire on the enemy as they advanced. Their lines being broken and confused by the front line retiring, also was compelled, after a few volleys, to fall back. The officers and men of these two regiments also deserve especial praise for their gallantry.

After crossing to the west side of the river, by the perseverance of the officers a great number of the men were rallied, and again returned to the scene of action, and aided in the ultimate defeat of the enemy. All the line officers behaved with the greatest coolness and courage during the entire engagement.

I cannot omit to make honorable mention of a circumstance of the scenes of the last day's engagement, which reflects great credit for the daring bravery and coolness of the parties concerned.

Corporal E. C. Hockensmith, of the color guard of the 21st Kentucky regiment, and who carried the colors that day, was confronted by a rebel in the retreat, and was ordered, while on the bank of the river, to surrender, to which he replied, "Myself I will surrender, but my colors never," at the same moment throwing them into the water. Sergeant J. T. Gunn, company E, of the same regiment, seized them and carried them safely through the battle. Corporal Hockensmith escaped and is safe.

I am indebted in the highest degree to the members of my staff, Lieutenant John Clark, acting assistant adjutant general; Lieutenant Carter B. Harrison, assistant adjutant inspector general, and Lieutenant Edward Noble, aide-de-camp, for their assistance, who, at all times, performed their duties with intelligence and zeal, and deserve especially the highest praise for valor and efficiency during the action of the 2d instant.

The loss on both sides has been very heavy. My loss in killed is small in proportion to the number of wounded. The enemy's loss, compared with ours, was at least four to one.

I am, with great respect, your obedient servant.

S. W. PRICE,
Colonel, Comm'g 3d Brigade, 3d Division, Left Wing, 14th Army Corps.

Captain E. A. OTIS,
Assistant Adjutant General, 3d Division of Left Wing.

HEADQUARTERS 8TH KENTUCKY VOLUNTEERS,
January 26, 1863.

SIR: I have the honor to make the following report of the part taken by the 8th regiment Kentucky volunteers in the battle of January 2, near Murfreesboro':

On the 1st January we took position near the crest of a hill, the 51st Ohio being on our right, and the 35th Indiana on our left. Nothing of special interest occurred until the morning of the 2d, when brisk skirmishing began along the whole line, and continued until about 2 o'clock, when the enemy advanced with infantry and artillery. The battle soon became general, and the enemy pressing hard upon the 51st Ohio forced them to retire, giving the enemy an opportunity to gain our right flank and rear, which they lost no time in accomplishing. Both men and officers of my regiment fought with becoming bravery, coolness and determination, until flanked on the right and left, and seeing no chance to stay the onward course of the enemy, we retired to the opposite side of the river just in time to save our capture.

Captain John B. Banton, of company F, was killed early in the action, while gallantly commanding a line of skirmishers. We lost seven men killed on the field, seven officers wounded, two of whom have since died; sixty-nine men wounded, twelve of which have since died, and twenty-seven missing.

Very respectfully,

G. B. BRODDUS,
Major, Commanding 8th Regiment Kentucky Volunteers.

Colonel STANLY MATTHEWS,
Commanding 3d Brigade.

HEADQUARTERS 1ST IRISH, 35TH REGIMENT INDIANA VOLUNTEERS,
In the field near Murfreesboro,' Tennessee, January 5, 1863.

COLONEL: In obedience to orders, I have the honor to report officially to brigade headquarters the part my regiment took in the battles since the 31st December, 1862. On the morning of the 31st day of December last my regiment moved with our brigade, the 3d, across Stone river, and took position on the extreme left of the brigade, fronting east. We remained but a short time, when orders came to recross the river and establish my line, the right resting upon the 51st Ohio; when the line was thus established my left rested upon the bank of the river. When in this position the action commenced on our right, and in an incredible short space of time I found hundreds of fugitives and numerous wagons and ambulances flying in confusion and attempting to cross the river. Orders came from you to arrest the flight of these fugitives, and to this end I directed my men to fix bayonets and halt the panic-stricken soldiers. To Captain John P. Dufficy, acting major, and Adjutant Scully, I am much indebted, as well as to the company officers, for energetic efforts to form the recusants into line. Two small battalions were formed, and under an officer sent back to the right of the line. The confusion was very great, and I feel as if it was due to my officers and men to mention particularly the cool and determined manner they brought order out of confusion. A short time after the subsidence of the panic on the west side of the river, I discovered a stampede arising among the teamsters who had crossed on the east side. An officer rode up and informed me that a battalion of the enemy's cavalry was about to charge upon and capture the wagons. Among them were two wagons belonging to the general-in-chief, and requesting me, if possible, to save them. I instantly put the regiment in march to the ford, in order to meet the cavalry force; on my road to the ford I was ordered by Acting Assistant Adjutant General Clark to form line again on the 51st Ohio; I did so, and saw the cavalry coming in full charge on the train. At this juncture I threw the left wing of the regiment back, and opened a severe fire on the enemy, the battery on our right shelling him handsomely at the same time. The result was, the enemy remained but a little while, and managed to get but a few of the rear wagons away with him. On the morning of January 1 our division (3d) recrossed to the east side of the river. The lines were formed in the following order: First line of our brigade consisted of the 51st Ohio, 8th Kentucky, and 35th Indiana; the latter regiment being posted on the extreme left of the brigade, and just behind a curtain of woodland. In the rear of my regiment was the 99th Ohio, on my left was the 79th Indiana. In the course of the day I furnished three companies of skirmishers, G, I, and E, under Captains Prosser and McKim. Skirmishing was kept up all day. In the evening I relieved companies E, I, and G, by sending out the other seven companies under command of Captain Dufficy. At midnight the enemy undertook to drive in my skirmishers by a vigorous assault. I am proud to report that in this they signally failed. The line of skirmishers never gave an inch. On the contrary, in the gallant ardor of the moment they drove the enemy beyond his own line and established the 35th upon it. In this affair I lost one man killed and two wounded. Captain Dufficy on the right, and Captain Crowe upon the left of skirmishers, behaved with distinguished gallantry. At daylight I found it necessary to relieve the line of skirmishers, as they had been all night and part of the preceding day without rest or nourishment. An order came from brigade headquarters for every regiment to throw out in front of their own line two companies of skirmishers. The skirmishers from my regiment were under command of Captain James McKim, a cool and daring officer. All day of the 2d instant skirmishing kept up heavy in the entire front. About 2 o'clock p. m. a rebel battery opened upon us and threw solid shot and shell until 4 o'clock p. m. when the enemy in force advanced upon us. I had directed my men to lie down and fix bayonets, and in no case to fire until I gave the word. The skirmishing became very brisk, and my skirmishers came in, fell into line with the regiment, reporting to me the approach of an immense force. The enemy advanced steadily in column by regiment in echelon. When within a short distance of the line of the 51st Ohio and 8th Kentucky, the first brigade of the enemy came into line, and both parties opened a crashing fire of musketry. The enemy's second brigade came up to the work yelling—they were immediately in my front. I considered it best to let them advance to within thirty or forty paces of my line, as I believed they had no knowledge of my position before I opened my fire; when their right flank was immediately opposite my line I gave the order to rise and fire. With a deafening cheer the order was gallantly obeyed. A plunging volley staggered the advancing columns, and before the enemy could recover his surprise my regiment had reloaded and commenced a well-aimed and telling file fire. The flash and rattle of my musketry gave information to the battery in my front, which opened furiously upon me. The close proximity of the belligerent lines obliged the gunners to throw their shells to my rear, on solid shot to my extreme left. This accounts for the left wing suffering so much more than the right. After twenty minutes of a murderous fire from the enemy, and seeing that he was steadily advancing upon the regiments on my right and left, I called for the 99th Ohio to come forward and support me. I intended to have tried the virtue of the bayonet, according to the instructions of our much-respected general-in-chief. I regret very much to say, after two appeals to the 99th Ohio, that regiment failed to come forward. The right wing of the 79th Indiana was now engaged, and the whole of our brigade line on our right. Through all this terrible fire of musketry and shell I am proud to say not a single officer or man flinched.

The enemy soon pressed forward. In my rear the 99th Ohio had gone from the field. The 79th Indiana then gave way under this terrific pressure. The regiments on my right the 51st Ohio, and 8th Kentucky, were slowly retiring, and fighting heroically. At the end of forty-three minutes of a desperate and unequal contest I found the enemy completely around my flanks. To prevent a useless destruction of life or entire capture of my regiment I gave the order to retire; I was obliged to repeat it, and even then the brave fellows complied reluctantly—many refused, and they were either killed or captured. On reaching the river in our rear, some four hundred yards, I rallied the torn ranks of my regiment. Here were the remaining fragments of the 51st Ohio, 8th and 21st Kentucky, with some other regiments that I cannot now designate. A bold and determined fire was opened by this new-formed line. The enemy paused, fought, and then at last broke and fled, our men pursuing them with cheers and a heavy straggling fire. So deafening was the musketry, I did not hear or know a single piece of artillery was giving us any aid until I reached the crest of the hill in the wood upon our right. The enemy made one stand more on this hill; it was but momentary, for our brave lads were upon them, and they fled, never again to rally. In my efforts, agreeable to your orders, to ascertain what officer or man particularly distinguished himself for gallantry, or disgraced himself by cowardice, I asked a special report from officers commanding companies; I received but one report: they commanded a body of heroes. My own observation goes to indorse the truthfulness of these officers' reports. In the rush for the advance, portions of the 35th Indiana, 51st Ohio, 8th and 21st Kentucky reached the enemy's battery. The boys of the 51st claim one piece, their comrades of the 35th another. To do justice, I think your entire brigade was freely represented in the capture of these pieces. Where two hundred and seventy-two men stand unflinchingly for forty-three minutes a combined fire of musketry and artillery at close range, it is certainly hard to give to any one a pre-eminence for gallantry. I had but few officers with me; each and every one had some peculiar tact of excellence—some one splendid soldierly virtue.

In conclusion, I feel obliged to call attention to the splendid conduct of my adjutant, John Scully; his escape was a miracle, freely exposing himself, and cheering the men throughout the action to deeds of valor. Sergeant Major Robert Stockdale fought desperately, but coolly; he deserves particular mention, not only for his conduct on this field, but for the faithful and cheerful manner he has ever performed his duties. To Doctor Averdick, my surgeon, I must acknowledge valuable services; brave and defiant on the field, he is kind and attentive in the hospital wards. Quartermaster Igoe was on the field attentive to the wounded, using every effort to have them carefully transported to the rear; by 10 o'clock that night not a wounded man of the 35th could be found on the field. To Father Cooney, our chaplain, too much praise cannot be given; indifferent as to himself, he was deeply solicitous for the temporal comfort and spiritual welfare of us all. On the field he was cool and indifferent to danger; and in the name of the regiment I thank him for his kindness and laborious attention to the dead and dying.

B. F. MULLEN,
Colonel 35th Indiana.

Colonel S. W. PRICE,
Commanding 3d Brigade.

HEADQUARTERS 99TH REGIMENT OHIO VOLUNTEER INFANTRY,
Near Murfreesboro', January 24, 1863.

SIR: The following is a copy of my remarks accompanying my report of killed, wounded, and missing of this regiment in the battle of Stone river, which report was made on the 4th day of January, A. D. 1363:

"SIR: I have the honor to make the following report:

"The 99th regiment went into action on the 2d of January, 1863, with 369 men, rank and file. The regiment lost, as the foregoing shows, one commissioned officer and eleven enlisted men killed; three commissioned officers and forty-one enlisted men wounded; one commissioned officer and thirty-five enlisted men are missing. Of this number some are known to have been wounded on the field, and some to be prisoners in the hands of the enemy.

"After the regiment was compelled to fall back, I found that, with but few exceptions, the men rallied and went back into the action. The conduct of the officers and men of the regiment was all that could be asked, and I might do injustice to some to mention particular instances of good conduct. Colonel Swaine, who was in command, and is wounded and absent from the regiment, sends back word that he was well satisfied with the conduct of all the officers and men of his command, and that they obeyed every order which he gave with promptness.

"J. E. CUMMINS,
"*Lieutenant Colonel, Commanding 99th Reg't Ohio Volunteer Infantry.*

"Colonel PRICE,
"*Commanding 3d Brigade, 3d Division, Left Wing.*"

There are several inaccuracies in the report made at that time. It should have reported one commissioned officer and twelve enlisted men killed, and one commissioned officer and twenty-nine enlisted men missing.

J. E. CUMMINS,
Lieutenant Colonel 99th Ohio.

Colonel STANLEY MATTHEWS,
Commanding 3d Brigade, 3d Division.

HEADQUARTERS 21ST KENTUCKY VOLUNTEERS,
Near Murfreesboro', Tennessee, January 3, 1863.

SIR: In obedience to your orders, I took my position, with the rest of the brigade, on Thursday morning, (1st,) on the Murfreesboro' side of Stone river, the 51st Ohio, 8th Kentucky, and 35th Indiana in the first line, running nearly north and south and fronting east, and my regiment and the 99th Ohio in the second line; my regiment in rear of the 51st, the 99th in rear of the 35th. During that day nothing of importance occurred, save the continual firing of the skirmishers. On Friday, (2d,) companies F and D of my regiment were ordered out on the extreme left of the division as skirmishers, and company B on the right, next to the river. During the fight of that day companies F and D did not come under my observation, but I am assured by Captain Evans, who commanded the two companies, that the men behaved like true soldiers. Special mention was made of the coolness and bravery of Lieutenant Frederick Temple, commanding company D. All the morning the skirmishing continued. About 1 o'clock p. m. the rebel artillery commenced throwing shells amongst us, greatly to our annoyance. At this time our artillery was withdrawn to the opposite side of the river, to the astonishment of all. It seems that our little brigade had been forgotten, or was left there all alone to be sacrificed, in order to draw the enemy on, which latter turned out to be the case. Near 3 o'clock the rebel column advanced. I could see company B, as they slowly fell back, fighting with the coolness and courage of veterans On they came, and when within thirty or forty yards of our line the 51st and 8th arose and poured into them a destructive fire. These two regiments fought like tigers—longer, too, than could have been expected under the circumstances. I being interested in the fight in front, failed to notice the rebels advancing around our right, until they completely flanked us. By this time the 8th and 51st were driven back, and I at once ordered my men to rise and fall back, but to fight as they went, which they did. We were driven back some two hundred yards to the bed of the river, where I rallied my men, but was ordered by Colonel Beatty, who commanded the division, to cross the river, and rally the men behind the batteries. We crossed, but owing to the firing of our artillery, and the fresh troops coming into line, my men were so scattered that it was impossible to rally all of them together; but I am glad to state that they all rallied upon one regiment or another, and again went in, and remained during the fight. I have no censure for a single man of my command, but the highest praise for them all. I did not see the 35th and 99th during the engagement.

My loss, in killed, wounded, and missing, was fifty-five.

With the greatest respect, I remain your obedient servant,

J. C. EVANS,
Lieutenant Colonel 21st Kentucky Volunteers, Commanding Regiment.

Colonel S. W. PRICE,
Commanding 3d Brigade.

HEADQUARTERS 51ST REGIMENT OHIO VOLUNTEER INFANTRY,
Camp near Murfreesboro', Tennessee, January, 1863.

COLONEL: I have the honor to make the following report of the operations of the 51st regiment Ohio volunteer infantry in front of Murfreesboro' during the late engagement.

On our arrival at Stone river, on Monday evening, December 29, 1862, my regiment was ordered on picket duty, to take post to the left of the pickets of General Wood's division, where we remained until Wednesday morning, December 31, when we received orders to rejoin our brigade, which was then *en route* for the purpose of crossing Stone river. After we had crossed over, the 51st was assigned its position in the centre of the first line of battle—the 8th Kentucky on our right, and the 35th Indiana infantry on our left. We had not been in line of battle over half an hour, when I received orders to recross the river, and take position opposite the ford, where we remained until 1 o'clock p. m., when the enemy's cavalry, with two pieces of artillery, made a dash at our hospital wagons, which had not yet recrossed. Thereupon the 51st was ordered to change position some forty paces to the rear, in order to open the way for one of our batteries to open fire upon the enemy. We remained in that position until 3 o'clock p. m. The enemy's shot commenced falling among us, and we were again ordered to change our position about one hundred yards to the rear, and out of range of the enemy's battery, where we remained during the night.

On Thursday morning, January 1, at 5.30 o'clock, I received orders from Colonel Samuel Beatty, then commanding the 3d division, "to take the 51st Ohio and throw it across Stone river immediately; then to deploy four companies as skirmishers, holding the remaining six companies as a 'reserve;'" adding, at the same time, "move your regiment forward," and he would throw additional forces to support me, and if possible to accomplish this before it was clearly light, which was done. Our line of skirmishers had not advanced far before a spirited fire was opened between them and the enemy's line of skirmishers. In a few minutes I received orders to "halt the line of skirmishers, and not bring on an engagement," which I did.

The six companies of reserve were then ordered to take position on the eminence on the right of the first line of battle, my right resting near Stone river, while the 8th Kentucky and 35th Indiana formed on our left. We immediately discovered a battery of the enemy's about twelve hundred yards in our front, which I reported to Colonel Beatty, who sent a battery to the front, posting two pieces to my right and four pieces to the left of the first line. Our battery then opened fire on the enemy, consisting of artillery, cavalry, and infantry, who were posted in the edge of the woods in front of us, the enemy feebly replying with their artillery, their sharpshooters at the same time keeping up a brisk fire on our line of skirmishers all day. Thus passed Thursday. In the evening the four companies that were skirmishing were relieved, and formed with the regiment, where we lay that night on our arms. On Friday morning, at daybreak, the enemy's sharpshooters opened on us with increased vigor. Two companies of the 51st were then sent to relieve the front line of skirmishers. At about 12 o'clock m. the enemy changed the position of their battery to the left of our front, and opened a heavy fire on us at this elevated point, and having got range of the two pieces of artillery posted where we were stationed, our pieces had to be withdrawn a short distance to the rear. The enemy's line of skirmishers was then strengthened, and drove our skirmishers back a short distance, and gained possession of some buildings which our skirmishers were unable to hold. Our line then rallied, drove the enemy from the buildings, who set them on fire before leaving them.

Between the hours of 1 and 2 o'clock p. m. we could distinctly see in the distance large bodies of infantry forming in our front and moving to our left, accompanied by artillery and cavalry. I immediately notified the proper officers of the movements of the enemy. Soon thereafter we saw large bodies of infantry forming in our front in line of battle, and moving toward us. They advanced to within between six and eight hundred yards of our front and halted, and commenced throwing down a line of fence running parallel to our line. I immediately directed Adjutant Nicholas to report the fact, and he informed Major Starling of the enemy's movements, as well as the brigade and division commanders that the enemy were in the act of attacking us. The enemy's artillery was playing on us up to this time, when it ceased, and their line of battle immediately advanced, their centre moving steadily, while their left was thrown around to Stone river. After advaning in this manner to within two hundred yards of our front, they set up a most hideous yell, and charged upon us in two lines of battle closed in mass, while their skirmishers rallied to their left. At this period the eight companies of the 51st were lying down, with bayonets fixed, being partially protected by a depression of the ground, the two companies of skirmishers still disputing the advance of the enemy's left, which was in advance of their centre, and moving more rapidly, in order to get between us and the river, to outflank us. When their line arrived within sixty yards of our front, so that we could plainly see their breasts, I gave the command to rise and fire, which was done, the enemy at the same time opening a terrific fire upon us, their front line, using revolving rifles, kept up a continuous fire, and advancing. Being pressed heavily, and our right forced back and outflanked, the artillery having been withdrawn previous to the charge, we were compelled to fall back and cross the river, where I rallied portions of the regiment under cover of our artillery, then recrossed the river, and advanced with our colors, and assisted in driving the enemy beyond our first position, capturing one piece of artillery belonging to the "Washington battery," our colors being the first to wave over the gun. It being dark, and the enemy driven from the field, we were ordered to seek quarters for the night.

The following is a list of the killed, wounded, and missing in the regiment during the engagement:

Killed, 24; wounded, 122; missing, 44—total, 190.

The following is a list of those especially noted for gallantry and ungallantry:

For gallant conduct: Sergeants Thomas Rodgers, (color-bearer,) and William Barnes, company H; Privates Jesse T. Beachler, company A; M. Morgan, John G. Fox, and John Hilliker, company F; N. Jones and Theophilus Phillips, company H; and Nathan A. Carpenter, company I.

For ungallantry: First Sergeant William A. Himes, company A. Privates Jacob Lenhart and Martin Hart, company F.

Great praise is due both officers and soldiers for the manner with which they sustained the first charge of the enemy; and although compelled to fall back, being pressed by superior numbers, still greater praise is due them for rallying with the advance, and assisting to drive the enemy from the field.

I am, colonel, your obedient servant,

R. W. McCLAIN,

Lieutenant Colonel, Com'g 51st Regiment O. V. I.

Colonel Stanley Matthews,

Com'g 3d Brigade, 3d Division, Left Wing.

14.—REPORT OF BRIGADIER GENERAL D. S. STANLEY, WITH THE REPORTS OF THE SUBORDINATE COMMANDERS OF CAVALRY.

Headquarters Cavalry Fourteenth Army Corps,
Department of the Cumberland, near Murfreesboro', January 9, 1863.

Major: I have the honor to submit, for the information of the general commanding the army, the following statement of the part taken by the cavalry under my command in the advance upon, and battle of, Murfreesboro'.

On the 26th of December I divided the cavalry into three columns, putting the 1st brigade, commanded by Colonel Minty, 4th Michigan cavalry, upon the Murfreesboro' pike, in advance of General Crittenden's corps. The 2d brigade, commanded by Colonel Zahn, 3d Ohio cavalry, was ordered to move on Franklin, dislodge the enemy's cavalry, and move parallel to General McCook's protecting his right flank. The reserve cavalry, consisting of the new regiments, viz: Anderson troop, 1st Middle Tennessee, 2d East Tennessee cavalry, and four companies of the 3d Indiana, I commanded in person, and preceded General McCook's corps on the Nolensville pike. Colonel John Kennett, commanding cavalry division, commanded the cavalry on the Murfreesboro' pike. For the operations of this column, and also the movements of Colonel Zahn up to the 31st of December, I would refer you to the enclosed reports of Colonel Kennett and Colonels Zahn and Minty.

On the morning of the 27th our cavalry first encountered the enemy on the Nolensville pike, one mile in advance of Bole Jack Pass. Their cavalry was in large force, and accompanied by a battery of artillery. Fighting continued from 10 o'clock until evening, during which time we had driven the enemy two miles beyond Lavergne.

The 3d Indiana and Anderson troop behaved very gallantly, charging the enemy twice, and bringing them to hand-to-hand encounters. The conduct of Majors Rosengarten and Ward, the former now deceased, was most heroic.

On the 28th we made a reconnoissance to College Grove, and found that Hardee's rebel corps had marched to Murfreesboro'. On the 29th Colonel Zahn's brigade, having joined, was directed to march upon Murfreesboro' by the Franklin road, the reserve cavalry moving on the Bole Jack road, the columns communicating at the crossing of Stewart's creek.

We encountered the enemy's cavalry, and found them in strong force at Wilkinson's Crossroads. Our cavalry drove them rapidly across Overall's creek, and within one-half mile of the enemy's line of battle. The Anderson cavalry behaved most gallantly this day, pushing at full charge upon the enemy for six miles. Unfortunately their advance proved too reckless. Having dispersed their cavalry, the "troop" fell upon two regiments of rebel infantry in ambush, and after a gallant struggle were compelled to retire with the loss of Major Rosengarten and six men killed, and the brave Major Ward and five men desperately wounded. With the loss of these two most gallant officers the spirit of the "Anderson troop," which gave such fine promise, seems to have died out, and I have not been able to get any duty out of them since. On the 30th the entire cavalry force was engaged in guarding the flanks of the army in position. Some small cavalry skirmishing occurred, but nothing of importance. At 11 o'clock p. m., the 30th, I marched for Lavergne with the 1st Tennessee and the Anderson cavalry. Near that place I was joined by detachments of the 4th Michigan and 7th Pennsylvania cavalry. At half past 9 o'clock, on the 31st, I received an order from the general commanding directing me to hasten to the right. I made all possible speed, leaving a strong detachment to protect the trains crowding the road at Stewartsboro', and to pick up stragglers. Upon arriving upon the right flank of the army I found order restored, and took position on General McCook's right, my right extending towards Wilkinson's Crossroads, occupying the woods about the meeting-house on Overall's creek. In this position we were attacked about 4 o'clock p. m. by a long line of foot skirmishers. My first impression was that these covered infantry, but I learned soon that they were only dismounted cavalry. We successfully held them at bay for one-half an hour with the 4th Michigan and 7th Pennsylvania, dismounted, when, being outflanked, I ordered our line to mount and fall back to the open field. The enemy followed here, and being re-enforced by detachments of the Anderson and 3d Kentucky cavalry, and by the 1st Tennessee, we charged the enemy and put him to rout. The cavalry held the same position this night they had taken upon my arrival upon the field. About 9 o'clock New Year's morning the enemy showed a line of skirmishers in the woods to our front, and soon after brought a six-gun battery to bear upon my cavalry. As we could not reach the enemy's skirmishers, nor reply to his artillery, I ordered my cavalry to fall back. A part of Zahn's brigade marched this day to Nashville to protect our trains. Colonel Zahn's report is enclosed.

The 2d and 3d of January the cavalry was engaged in watching the flanks of our position. Upon the 4th it became evident that the enemy had fled. The cavalry was collected and moved to the fords of Stone river. Upon the 5th we entered Murfreesboro'. Zahn's brigade marched in pursuit of the enemy on the Shelbyville pike—marched six miles, finding no opposition. With the remainder of the cavalry I marched on the Manchester pike and encountered the enemy in heavy force at Lyttle's creek, three and a half miles from town. We fought with this force till near sundown, pushing them from one cedar brake to another. When being re-enforced by General Spear's brigade of East Tennesseeans, we drove the enemy out of his last stand in disorder. We returned after dark and encamped on Lyttle's creek. Our troops all behaved well. The skirmishing was of a very severe character. The 4th United States cavalry, which was this day first under my control, behaved very handsomely.

Enclosed please find reports of division, brigade, and regimental commanders. Captain Otis's command acted independently until the 5th instant, when they came under my orders.

Enclosed find list of killed, wounded, and missing, excepting from Anderson cavalry; the report of this regiment I have not received. A special report of officers and soldiers deserving mention will be submitted. The duty of the cavalry was very arduous. From the 26th December till the 4th of January the saddles were only taken off to groom, and were immediately replaced.

A consolidated list of casualties, including those of 1st Tennessee, Anderson Troop, and 3d Indiana, as nearly as ascertained, will be submitted in the morning.

Respectfully submitted.

D. S. STANLEY.

Brigadier General, and Chief of Cavalry.

HEADQUARTERS CAVALRY,

Camp on Bradyville Pike, January 29, 1863.

COLONEL: In accordance with paragraph 743 Army Regulations, I have the honor to submit the names of the following officers deserving, in my opinion, of special notice:

1st. Major Kline, 3d Indiana, on the 27th, first engaged the enemy on the Nolensville pike, and soon put them to full flight.

Majors Ward and Rosengarten, (Anderson Troop,) both deceased, behaved with great bravery in the two affairs with the enemy. In the last one, on the 29th, both these gallant young officers received their death-wounds.

Colonel Minty, 4th Michigan, commanding 1st brigade, deserves credit for his management of his command on the march and in several actions.

Captain Otis, 4th United States cavalry, and Colonel Murray, 3d Kentucky cavalry, with their respective regiments, rendered important and distinguished service, gallantly charging and dispersing the enemy's cavalry in their attack upon our train, Wednesday, the 31st. Major John E. Wynkoop was, as always, a model to faithful soldiers.

Colonel Kennett was only a part of the time under my command; he rendered good service. Colonel Zahn, 3d Ohio cavalry, 2d brigade, though unfortunate with a portion of his command, on Wednesday morning contributed greatly, by his personal example, to the restoration of order and confidence in that portion of the 2d brigade stampeded by the enemy's attack. Enclosed please find subordinate reports. Colonel Zahn, having received an injury, has submitted no report.

Respectfully submitted.

D. S. STANLEY,
Brigadier General, Chief of Cavalry.

Colonel C. GODDARD,
Assistant Adjutant General and Chief of Staff.

Report of casualties in cavalry command, 14th army corps, from the advance from Nashville on the 26th December, and including the battles before Murfreesboro'.

Regiment.	KILLED.		WOUNDED.		MISSING.		TOTAL.		HORSES.	
	Officers.	Enlisted men.	Officers.	Enlisted men.	Officers.	Enlisted men.	Officers.	Enlisted men.	Killed.	Wounded.
2d Indiana cavalry	----	1	----	----	1	13	1	14	----	----
7th Pennsylvania cavalry	----	2	----	9	----	50	----	61	----	----
3d Kentucky cavalry	----	1	1	7	----	1	1	9	7	15
4th Michigan cavalry	----	1	1	6	----	12	1	19	11	17
1st Middle Tennessee cavalry	----	----	1	5	1	8	2	13	19	8
2d East Tennessee cavalry	1	2	----	10	----	5	1	17	----	----
4th United States cavalry	----	3	1	9	----	12	1	24	----	----
15th Pennsylvania cavalry	1	----	1	5	----	----	2	5	----	----
1st Ohio cavalry	3	2	1	10	*1	14	5	26	----	----
3d Ohio cavalry	----	6	----	15	----	13	----	34	----	----
4th Ohio cavalry	----	7	----	18	----	31	----	56	----	----
	5	25	6	94	3	159	14	278	37	40

*Surgeon.

List of officers killed and wounded in cavalry command, 14th army corps, department of the Cumberland, in operations before Murfreesboro', Tennessee.

Killed.—Colonel Minor Milliken, 1st Ohio cavalry; Major D. A. B. Moore, 1st Ohio cavalry; Lieutenant T. L. Condit, company L, 1st Ohio cavalry.

Wounded.—Captain Warsham, company C, 1st Tennessee cavalry; Captain Eli Long, company K, 4th United States cavalry; Adjutant William H. Scott, 1st Ohio; Lieutenant Thomas V. Mitchell, company H, 4th Michigan cavalry.

HEADQUARTERS CAVALRY,
Near Murfreesboro', January 12, 1863.

SIR: Enclosed please find consolidated report with list of commissioned officers killed, wounded, and missing, in the operations before Murfreesboro'. I send it unsigned, as the general is away.

I am your obedient servant,

WILLIAM. H. SINCLAIR,
Assistant Adjutant General.

C. GODDARD,
Assistant Adjutant General and Chief of Staff.

HEADQUARTERS 1ST MIDDLE TENNESSEE CAVALRY,
Camp near Murfreesboro', January 11, 1863.

SIR: In pursuance of General Orders No. 11, I have the honor to compliment the gallant conduct and prompt obedience to all my orders in the late battles before Murfreesboro' of the following officers:

Major Galbraith, Adjutant Murphy, Captain Waters, and Lieutenant Chastin, of company B; Lieutenants Sheppard and Martin, of company C; Lieutenant Snelling, of company D; Captain Smith, of company E; Lieutenant Couch, of company F; Captain Cane, of company G; Captain Julien and Lieutenant Van Juren, of company H; and Lieutenant Exune, of company I. The courageous conduct of Major Galbraith and Adjutant Murphy, in the charge on the evening of December 31, deserves special mention by their colonel; also Captain Julien, of company H, who assumed command of the 2d battalion, it having been surrendered to him by Major Cliff, who, in company with other commissioned officers, left the battle-field.

In conclusion, it is due to state that company A had been detached the day previous (30th) on courier duty. I regret to state that the brave Captain Wortham, of company C, was wounded while leading his men in a charge on the morning of the 30th, and was unable to appear again on the field.

Respectfully, your obedient servant,

W. B. STOKES,
Colonel, Commanding 1st Middle Tennessee Cavalry.

Captain T. H. CROSBY,
Aide-de-Camp, 1st Brigade of Cavalry.

Addenda to special report of distinguished officers.

CAMP SOUTH OF MURFREESBORO',
January 16, 1863.

DEAR SIR: I find, on examining my report made you with regard to meritorious conduct of my officers, that the name of Henry C. McQuiddy, my sergeant major, was omitted. I regret it exceedingly, as he proved himself a soldier in every sense of the word, showing by his bravery and gallantry that the confidence I put in him was not misplaced, and that I cannot bestow too much praise on him.

Respectfully, your obedient servant,

W. B. STOKES,
Colonel, Commanding 1st Middle Tennessee Cavalry.

T. H. CROSBY, *Captain and Aide-de-Camp.*

HEADQUARTERS BATTERY D, 1ST OHIO ARTILLERY,
Camp near Murfreesboro', Tennessee, January 12, 1863.

LIEUTENANT: On the 26th of December, 1862, Colonel Kennett ordered me to move with the 1st brigade, Colonel Minty, from camp near Nashville, on Murfreesboro pike, towards Lavergne. Two miles from Lavergne we came upon a body of confederate cavalry and went into action, dispersing them after firing four rounds. We then moved forward a mile; we there took position on the pike and opened fire on a section of rebel artillery, distanced about a mile. I fired sixty rounds, losing during the action one man killed—Private F. T. Coffin—and one horse disabled. I then moved into a field on the right of the pike, and opened fire. The enemy retired from their position to the left and rear. I then moved to the left of the pike, and took position near a small church, from which position we fired until dark, silencing the enemy after a few rounds.

That night I camped with the brigade on the right of the pike, and one mile back.

From the night of the 26th December to the morning of the 1st January I occupied different positions in and around Lavergne and Stewart's creek. On 1st January moved from Stewart's creek to Lavergne with Colonel Dickson, of the 4th Michigan cavalry, to re-enforce Colonel Innis, of the 1st Michigan engineers and mechanics, stationed near Lavergne. About one mile from that place I found Wheeler's rebel cavalry on the left of the pike. I went into action and drove them from the field, and then joined Colonel Innis's command, with whom I remained until the 9th instant. On the 9th instant received orders to report to General Stanley, chief of cavalry, and by him was ordered to report to Colonel Kennett, and am now in camp on Manchester pike, near 1st cavalry brigade.

Very respectfully,

N. W. NEWELL,

Lieutenant, Commanding Battery D, 1st Ohio Artillery.

Lieutenant M. B. CHAMBERLIN,

Acting Assistant Adjutant General, 1st Cavalry Division.

HEADQUARTERS 1ST CAVALRY DIVISION,

Camp Stanley, January 8, 1863.

SIR: I have the honor of submitting to you the reports of the part taken in the fighting of the two brigades composing the 1st cavalry division, from the 26th December, 1862, up to the night of the 5th January, 1863, from Nashville to Murfreesboro', and six miles beyond Murfreesboro', on the Manchester and Shelbyville pikes. On leaving Nashville the 2d brigade, under Colonel Zahn, took the road to Franklin; Brigadier General D. S. Stanley, with the 1st and 2d Tennessee cavalry and Anderson Troop, took the Nolensville pike; the 1st brigade, Colonel Minty commanding, under my charge, took the Murfreesboro' pike. I reported my command to General Palmer, who placed us in the advance. Our skirmishers drove the enemy some five miles. The afternoon was well spent when General Palmer relieved us with infantry skirmishers, the cavalry forming the reserve on the right and left flanks. The 1st brigade marched daily as a reserve to the advance skirmishers of the army composing the left wing on their flanks, up to the 30th December, 1862.

On the 31st December, 1862, we were posted as reserves on the flanks, throwing out our skirmishers and videttes, watching the movements of the enemy. We performed a variety of duty—as scouts on the different avenues leading to our camp and connecting with the roads centring upon Nashville, Tennessee, flankers, videttes, couriers—engaging the enemy daily on the right flank. For the details of each engagement I beg leave to refer you to the reports marked A and B. Some few incidents which could not well have fallen under the eye of the brigade commanders, having occurred under my immediate notice, I beg leave to append.

When the enemy charged upon our right wing, scattering a few regiments, who stampeded to the rear, I received orders from Major General Rosecrans in person to collect all the cavalry at my command, and proceed to rally the right wing and drive the enemy away. I found Colonel Murray, of the 3d Kentucky, in command of about a squadron of men. With that we made our way to the right. We found a complete stampede—infantry, cavalry, and artillery rushing to the rear, and the rebel cavalry charging upon our retiring forces on the Murfreesboro' pike.

Colonel Murray, with great intrepidity, engaged the enemy towards the skirts of the woods, and drove them in three charges. His men behaved like old veterans. Between his command and the field was filled with rushing rebel cavalry, charging upon our retreating cavalry and infantry, holding many of our soldiers as prisoners. I rallied the 3d Ohio, some two companies, who were falling back, and formed them in the rear of a fence, where volley after volley had the effect of driving back the rebels upon the run, they(the 3d Ohio) charging upon them effectually, thereby relieving the pike of their presence, saving the train, one piece of artillery, and rescuing from their grasp many of our men taken as prisoners. One of my staff, Lieutenant Rilley, being a prisoner in their hands, was released.

Lieutenant Colonel Murray, of the 3d Ohio, displayed energy, coolness, and courage upon this occasion in executing my orders. I also take great pride in mentioning the prompt manner with which my staff conveyed my orders in all these engagements.

Two of my orderlies displayed high order of chivalry. Jaggers charged upon two rebel cavalry, rescuing two men of the 4th Ohio volunteer cavalry, who were being taken off as prisoners. The other, Farrish, shot two of the rebels and came to my rescue in a personal encounter with a rebel, who was in the act of levelling his pistol at my head; but he found a carbine levelled into his own face, and at my order to surrender, he delivered his pistols, carbine, and horse to me. They both deserve promotion, and would make good officers.

The able, undaunted spirit and ability which Colonel Minty has displayed whenever coming under my eye I take great satisfaction in noticing. The officers and men all displayed great self-sacrifice. Major Wynkoop, of the 7th Pennsylvania, commanding, and Lieutenant Woolley, assistant adjutant general of the 1st brigade, carried out every order with unhesitating energy and will, displaying the highest order of gallantry.

Captain Otis, of the 4th regiment cavalry, although he does not belong to my division, but being posted on the left wing of our skirmishers on the march on the Manchester road, I feel it my duty, as well as take great pleasure, in stating he is an able and efficient officer.

Brigadier General D. S. Stanley being in command of the forces pursuing the retiring rebels on this march, it fell to my lot to convey and see his orders executed. Before closing this report, it is my duty to make honorable mention of the meritorious conduct of Lieutenant Newell, commanding a section of artillery attached to my division. During the first day's engagement near Lavergne, he placed his two pieces in well-selected grounds and did great execution, killing three horses, dismounting seven, and scattering the rebel cavalry by his well and timely aimed shots. He has on several occasions displayed talents of the first order as an artillerist. It would not be amiss to state at this time that my entire command were short of rations, performing duty night and day in the wet fields, without shelter, exposed to the wet, cold, and hunger, without a murmur.

Major Paramour, of the 3d Ohio, displayed great presence of mind and determination in maintaining his position on the right flank with his battalion to cover an ammunition train long after the cavalry on his right had been driven away by the enemy's shells. I annex his report, all of which I respectfully submit for your review.

Your obedient servant,

JNO. KENNETT,
Colonel, Commanding 1st Cavalry Division.

Captain W. H. SINCAIR.

HEADQUARTERS 1ST CAVALRY BRIGADE,
Camp near Murfreesboro', Tennessee, January 7, 1863.

SIR: I have the honor to hand you the following report of the part taken by the 1st brigade, 1st division of the cavalry reserve, in the operations from the advance from Nashville to and including the battles before Murfreesboro':

I marched from Camp Rosecrans, near Nashville, on the morning of the 26th ultimo, with the 3d Kentucky, 4th Michigan, 7th Pennsylvania, and one company of the 2d Indiana, and reported to General Palmer on the Murfreesboro' road. In accordance with orders received from him through the colonel commanding the division, I placed the 3d Kentucky on the left, and the 7th Pennsylvania on the right of the road, keeping the 4th Michigan on the pike with a strong advanced guard out. Ten miles from Nashville I met the enemy's pickets, who, as they fell back before us, were continually re-enforced; until arriving at Lavergne, they disputed our progress with a force of two thousand five hundred cavalry and mounted infantry, supported by four pieces of artillery, under the command of General Wheeler. As the enemy had us most perfectly in range, after some sharp skirmishing, I moved under cover of a slight eminence, on which Lieutenant Newell, of battery D, 1st Ohio, had his section planted, leaving two companies of the 4th Michigan dismounted and in ambush, behind the fence to support the battery.

I must here mention that Lieutenant Newell did splendid service with his two three-inch Rodman's. Every shot was well planted, and he nobly fought the four guns of the enemy for over half an hour, when a battery from General Palmer's division moved up to his assistance. One of the gunners was killed by a shell from the enemy while serving his gun.

Saturday, December 27.—The 7th Pennsylvania, under Major Wynkoop, made a reconnoissance in front of General Palmer's division, which occupied a position on the left of the line. One battalion of the 4th Michigan, under command of Captain Mix, was sent out on the Jefferson pike, and did not rejoin the brigade until the following day. I beg to refer you to Captain Mix's report for particulars. The army advanced at about 11 o'clock a. m., the 3d Kentucky and one company of the 2d Indiana, under command of Colonel Murray, covering the left flank, and the 4th Michigan, under my immediate direction, covering the right flank. Camped near Stewart's creek this night.

Sunday, December 28.—Sent one battalion of the 7th Pennsylvania, to relieve the battalion of the 4th Michigan on Jefferson pike.

Monday, December 29.—Army again advanced; 7th Pennsylvania, under Major Wynkoop, on the left flank; 3d Kentucky on the right flank, under Colonel Murray; 4th Michigan in reserve, 2d Indiana on courier duty. Light skirmishing with the enemy all day. Found the enemy in position in front of Murfreesboro' at about 3 o'clock p. m. Bivouacked for the night immediately in rear of our line of battle.

Tuesday, December 30.—One battalion of the 7th Pennsylvania and one of the 3d Kentucky formed a chain of videttes in rear of the line of battle, with orders to drive up all stragglers. Under orders from the colonel commanding the division, I took the 4th Michigan and one battalion of the 7th Pennsylvania back on the Nashville pike, to operate against Wheeler's cavalry, who a few hours before had destroyed the train of the 28th brigade on the Jefferson pike. Between Stewart's creek and Lavergne I met the enemy about one hundred strong, and dressed in our uniforms. The 7th Pennsylvania drove them until after dark. I reported to Colonel Walker, 31st Ohio, commanding a brigade, and camped with him that night two and a half miles south of Lavergne.

Wednesday, December 31.—Under orders from Major General Rosecrans, I reported to Brigadier General Stanley, chief of cavalry, who came up the same morning with the 1st Middle Tennessee and part of the 15th Pennsylvania.

Under orders from General Stanley we moved rapidly across the country towards the right of General McCook's position, (leaving Lieutenant Colonel Dickinson, 4th Michigan cavalry, with one hundred and twenty men, to support Lieutenant Newell's section of artillery, at the crossroads northwest of Stewart's creek,) the enemy's cavalry falling back rapidly before us. When close to Overall's creek, our own artillery, in position to our left, opened on us with shell, and severely wounded one man of the 15th Pennsylvania.

Crossing Overall's creek, I took up position parallel to and three-fourths of a mile distant from the Nashville and Murfreesboro' road. The 4th Michigan dismounted, forming a line of skirmishers on the edge of the woods immediately in our front, out of which they had driven a large force of the rebel cavalry; they were supported by a part of the 1st Tennessee, also dismounted. Captain Jennings's battalion, 7th Pennsylvania, and two companies 3d Kentucky, under Captain Davis, were posted in the woods to the right, and in rear of the 4th Michigan, with the 15th Pennsylvania in their rear.

Our entire force at this time was nine hundred and fifty (950) men.

The enemy advanced rapidly with 2,500 cavalry, mounted and dismounted, with three pieces of artillery, all under the command of General Wheeler. They drove back the 4th Michigan to the line of the 1st Tennessee skirmishers, and then attacked the 7th Pennsylvania with great fury, but met with a determined resistance. I went forward to the dismounted skirmishers and endeavored to move them to the right to strengthen the 7th Pennsylvania; but the moment the right of the line showed itself from behind the fence where they were posted, the whole of the enemy's fire was directed on it, turning it completely round. At this moment the 15th Pennsylvania gave way, and retreated rapidly, leaving the battalion of the 7th Pennsylvania and the dismounted men almost entirely unsupported, and leaving them no alternative but retreat.

We fell back a couple of fields, and reformed in rear of a rising ground, which protected us from the enemy's artillery.

The rebel cavalry had followed us up sharply into the open ground, and now menaced us with three strong lines: two directly in front of my position, and one opposite our left flank, with its right thrown well forward, and a strong body of skirmishers in the woods to our right, and threatening that flank.

General Stanley gave the order to charge, and he himself led two companies (K and H) of the 4th Michigan cavalry and about fifty men of the 15th Pennsylvania against the line in front of our left, routed the enemy and captured one stand of colors, which was brought in by a sergeant of the 15th Pennsylvania. Captain Jennings's 7th Pennsylvania with his battalion supported this movement.

At the same time I charged the first line in our front with the 4th Michigan and 1st Tennessee, supported on the right by a fire from the 15th Pennsylvania, and drove them from the field. The second line was formed on the far side of a lane, with a partially destroyed fence on each side of it, and still stood their ground. I reformed my men, and again charged; the enemy was again broken and driven from the field.

Colonel Kennett, commanding 1st cavalry division, now arrived on the field with re-enforcements. I held the ground that night with the 1st Tennessee, 15th Pennsylvania, and 4th Michigan, picketing the whole of my first position.

A sergeant of the 7th Pennsylvania, who was taken prisoner by the enemy, states that before we charged we had killed twenty-seven, including many officers.

January 1, 2, *and* 3.—Had the brigade under arms all day, with two regiments on picket, and skirmishing with the enemy's pickets.

Sunday, January 4.—Moved the brigade to Wilkinson's Crossroads, and bivouacked there for the night, with the 4th cavalry.

Monday, January 5.—Marched through Murfreesboro' and took the Manchester pike; one mile out met the enemy's pickets, reported to General Stanley, who ordered an advance, and took the lead himself with the 4th cavalry. After crossing a small creek, about two miles from Murfreesboro', the bridge over which had been destroyed, the enemy commenced shelling us. I sent the 3d Kentucky well to the right and front, and the 7th Pennsylvania to the left, keeping the 1st and 2d Tennessee and the 4th Michigan in reserve. After some little delay, the general again ordered an advance; I placed the five companies, 4th Michigan on the right of the road, with one company advanced as skirmishers, the 3d Kentucky on the right of the 4th Michigan, and the 1st Tennessee on the right of the 3d Kentucky, with the 2d Tennessee in reserve; in this formation we advanced through a cedar wood with a dense undergrowth, rendering it almost impossible to force our way through. We had occasional skirmishing with the enemy, who continued to shell us as we advanced.

About six miles out we met the enemy in force; a sharp skirmish ensued. The 4th cavalry, 1st Tennessee infantry, and 7th Pennsylvania cavalry were chiefly engaged on our side. The enemy were driven from the field, and we returned within a mile and a half of Murfreesboro', and went into camp.

I beg to refer you to the reports of regimental commanders for particulars of operations of detached portions of the brigade.

Enclosed herewith I hand you a report of such officers and men as deserve special mention, also the report of casualties.

In explanation of the large number of "missing" reported by the 7th Pennsylvania, I would call your attention to the fact that the entire of one battalion was deployed as a chain of videttes in rear of our line of battle, where the right wing was driven back, and many of the men must have been captured by the enemy while endeavoring to drive up the straggling infantry. I have to call your particular attention to the reports of Colonel Murray, Captain Mix, and Lieutenant Eldridgé.

Colonel Murray, with a handful of men, performed services that would do honor to a full regiment.

Captain Mix, with about fifty men, not only drove two hundred of the enemy for over two miles, but he there held his position against an entire regiment of rebel cavalry.

Lieutenant Eldridge, with eighteen men, dismounted, attacked the enemy, routed them, and recaptured a wagon full of ammunition.

In the engagement of Wednesday, while leading his company in a charge, Captain Mix's horse was shot under him, and in the same charge Lieutenant Woolley, my acting assistant adjutant general, was thrown from his horse, severely hurting his leg; notwithstanding which, he immediately remounted and continued to perform all his duties.

The brigade has captured and turned over one hundred and ninety-two (192) prisoners.

I am, respectfully, your obedient servant,

ROBERT H. G. MINTY,
Colonel, Commanding 1st Cavalry Brigade.

Lieutenant CHAMBERLIN,
Acting Assistant Adjutant General 1st Cavalry Division.

HEADQUARTERS 1ST CAVALRY BRIGADE,
Camp near Murfreesboro', January 7, 1863.

SIR: In handing in a report of such officers and men as are deserving of special mention for gallantry in the field, I must confine myself to those who came under my personal observation, as the regimental commanders decline mentioning any one in particular where, undoubtedly, all did their duty well.

First Sergeant Bedtelyon, company K, 4th Michigan cavalry, rode by my side during both charges against the enemy in the engagement of Wednesday evening, December 31, and displayed great gallantry and coolness. I have recommended him to his excellency the governor of Michigan for promotion.

Quartermaster Sergeant Ed. Owen, 4th Michigan cavalry, and Bugler Ben. Depenbroch, 2d Indiana cavalry, when we were driven back in the early part of the evening of December 31, I was on foot and in rear of the dismounted skirmishers who were running for their horses, when these two gallant soldiers galloped to the front bringing up my horse.

Lieutenant John Woolly, 2d Indiana cavalry, acting assistant adjutant general 1st cavalry brigade, was thrown from his horse and so severely hurt that he could not walk without great difficulty. He continued to press to the front, secured another horse, and remained on the field until long after the engagement was over.

Captain Frank W. Wix, 4th Michigan cavalry, had his horse shot under him during the first charge. He pressed forward on foot, caught a stray horse, and led his company in the second charge.

Many others, undoubtedly, did as well as those I have mentioned, but the above are the special cases that came under my immediate notice.

I am, respectfully, your obedient servant,

ROBERT H. G. MINTY,
Colonel, Commanding 1st Cavaly Brigade.

Lieutenant CHAMBERLIN,
Acting Assistant Adjutant General 1st Cavalry Division.

HEADQUARTERS 3D KENTUCKY CAVALRY,
Camp Stanley, near Murfreesboro', Tennessee, January 7, 1863.

SIR: I have the honor herewith to transmit a report of the part taken by my command from the 26th December, 1862, the day of our advance from Nashville, the engagement before Murfreesboro', and pursuit of the enemy in their retreat.

On passing our outpost before Nashville, on the Murfreesboro' road, my command formed the left wing of the advance. We had proceeded but a short distance when we encountered the enemy, and, pressing them closely, soon engaged in quite a brisk skirmish. Driving them in a lively chase, we succeeded in capturing five of the enemy. Skirmishing all day long through dense cedar thickets, we found quite a force a Lavergne, with quite an engagement, exposed to the fire of their artillery, which resulted only in the loss of two horses. Changing my position, my command formed the left, joined to General Cruft's brigade, capturing one other of the enemy. We moved from there to Stewart's creek the following day, forming still the left, and capturing seven of the enemy. Advancing from thence, my command formed the right. Night found us on the ground afterwards occupied by General Negley in the beginning of the general engagement. Captain Wolfley, commanding 2d battalion, opened communication with Major General McCook during the day.

Major Shacklett, with his battalion, on the 30th, formed a line of couriers (in rear of line of battle) with Major General McCook. Captain Davis, with squadron, companies B and D, ordered to report to General Stanley at Wilkinson's Crossroads. This squadron was afterwards with Colonel Minty, and engaged, with his command, the enemy while detached from me. Fifteen men, under Lieutenant Smock, reported to General Van Cleve. At 8 o'clock on the 31st December,

1862, Colonel Kennett, commanding division, gave me orders to move to Wilkinson's Crossroads. Having moved but a short distance, and in direction of the crossroads, I found the greatest confusion, caused by the right wing of the army falling back. Going but little further, I found our whole train of baggage and ammunition in possession of the enemy. Captain Wolfley, with part of his battalion, and Captain Breathill, commanding 1st battalion, with a squad of his command, in all about eighty men, in a moment were engaged charging down the train. We came upon the enemy in all directions. Here were engagements hand to hand, but dashing onward my men were doing in earnest the work before them. The open field gave us the place for charging. The enemy were marching about 250 of our men to their rear as prisoners; these we recaptured. We also recaptured a portion of the 5th Wisconsin battery, also a section supposed to be the 1st Ohio. The hospital of General Palmer's division was still held by them. Bringing about forty men to dash upon them, their whole command fled. At one time it seemed as if my whole command were taking prisoners to the rear. There being no support near, I ordered the prisoners to be given to the nearest infantry, in order that I might bring all my force against them and hold the train. Major Shacklett here rejoined me, and having taken position near the hospital, our cavalry coming to the field took position on my left; again the enemy made a dash, but was again repulsed. Near two hours afterwards the enemy moved to the right. By order of Colonel Kennett we moved in that direction at the trot, again to find them about to attack the train; but after exchanging shots, and under fire from our artillery, again baffled in their design, withdrew. We took between fifty and sixty prisoners, killing and wounding about twenty-five. In the engagement the eighty men of my command drove from the field Wharton's brigade of rebel cavalry, saved the baggage and ammunition of a great part of our army, recaptured a portion of the 5th Wisconsin battery, and a section of, I think, the 1st Ohio battery, and, at least calculation, 800 of our men. From that time up to their retreat from Murfreesboro' we held our position with the 1st cavalry brigade, under the direct orders of Colonel Minty, commanding.

In the pursuit on Manchester road, moving with the brigade about one mile from Murfreesboro', Captain Cummins, with a squad, was sent out and discovered the enemy just before us. As the brigade moved he was in advance and engaged the enemy all along. My command carried the right of the pike and had several engagements, exposed several times to the fire of the artillery, capturing four prisoners. The casualties during the whole engagement were—

Killed.—Private John Weissel, company E.

Wounded.—Bugler John Decker, badly, and Private Robert Moses, mortally, company M; Private Charles Spitznagle, slightly, company C; Sergeant John Costello, and Private Phillip Peters, seriously, company H; Captain John M. Thomas, slightly, company I.

Missing.—Captain John Weatherholt, company I.

Seven horses killed and fifteen wounded.

I will make no mention of one officer above another. All did their duty, and led their men nobly to the action; and the men, their actions on the battle-field, are beyond what I could speak of them here. Not one of my command ran to rear; all acted bravely. In all, we captured eighty-seven prisoners.

Respectfully, your obedient servant,

E. H. MURRAY,
Colonel 3d Kentucky Cavalry.

JOHN WOOLEY,
Acting Assistant Adjutant General 1st Cavalry Brigade.

HEADQUARTERS 3D KENTUCKY CAVALRY,
Camp Stanley, Murfreesboro', Tennessee, January, 28, 1863.

SIR: In compliance with an order from brigade headquarters, that I would forward a special report of officers and men deserving special mention, I would report that throughout the whole engagement before Murfreesboro', every officer and man performed his duty nobly, and wherever my attention would be called it was to see that portion of my command engaged, acting with promptness and decision. I could not, where all acted bravely, make discriminations.

The officers and men all have my entire confidence, and thanks for the part borne by them. My wagons were near the town of Lavergne when the attack was made upon the train. Here I must mention the courageous conduct and presence of mind displayed by Private R. J. Tindle, company L, (wagoner;) gathering from the crowd of wagoners and stragglers twenty-seven men, armed with pistols, guns, and anything found in the confusion, he marched his men, met the enemy, and being driven back three times by their cavalry, now dashing upon them, at last succeeded in finally repulsing them and saving the train in his rear. In this fight Adjuant J. A. Minnis, 4th Tennessee rebel cavalry, was killed. In this affair Private Tindle has shown himself a brave man, worthy of the name of soldier.

Respectfully,

E. H. MURRAY,
Colonel 3d Kentucky Cavalry.

ROBERT BURNS,
Acting Assistant Adjutant General 1st Cavalry Brigade.

HEADQUARTERS 4TH MICHIGAN CAVALRY,
Camp near Murfreesboro', January 8, 1862.

SIR: In compliance with an order of Colonel Minty, commanding 1st cavalry brigade, I submit the following report of the troops under my command since my separation from the main body of my regiment at the crossroads near Stewart's creek, on the Murfreesboro' pike, December 31.

I remained there, by Colonel Minty's order, with two pieces of artillery and four companies of the 4th Michigan cavalry, viz: companies A, D, G, and L, until the morning of the 1st of January, when I was ordered by Colonel Burk, of the 10th Ohio infantry, to move with my command in the direction of Lavergne to engage the enemy who had attacked our baggage train. On arriving within three-fourths of a mile of that place we found the enemy attacking and burning our train. I immediately ordered a part of my men to dismount and protect the two pieces of artillery under my command, and the other to attack the enemy from the left. After a brisk fire of about half an hour the enemy retired, leaving fifteen killed and carrying off fifteen wounded. I was then ordered by Colonel Innis to patrol the pike between Stewart's creek and Lavergne, both day and night, until January 4, when, by General Stanley's command, I escorted O. M. Dudley's train to Nashville and back here, where I arrived on the evening of the 7th instant. On January 2 two prisoners were brought in by our pickets, whom I turned over to Captain Ward, of the 10th Ohio, commanding detachment at Stewart's creek. Enclosed you will find a report made by Lieutenant Eldridge, who was for a few days in command of a separate detachment.

Yours,

W. H. DICKINSON,
Lieutenant Colonel, Commanding 4th Michigan Cavalry.

Lieutenant J. WOOLEY,
Acting Assistant Adjutant General.

JANUARY 7, 1863.

SIR: The adjutant of the 4th Michigan cavalry was with the advance. On the 1st day of January instant I was ordered by Captain Henion to take twenty men of company K, 4th Michigan cavalry, and proceed towards Nashville as an advance guard of the train. At Lavergne the train was attacked, and the 2d Tennessee cavalry formed in line of battle, and I prepared to join them; but at the discharge of the enemy's second gun the Tennessee cavalry fled, and I, with my men, remained alone to protect the train. I left the pike and went to the right and passed around on to the pike again, and proceeded with the advance of the train to Nashville, while the enemy burned a portion of the rear of the train.

On the 3d I left Nashville to join my regiment, and at the asylum the train was attacked and I was ordered up, and proceeded at a double-quick and found that fighting was going on on both sides of the road; and seeing we were the weakest on the left, I formed on that side where a portion of the 2d Tennessee cavalry was engaging the enemy; but as we entered the field they broke and fled, and I dismounted my men and advanced as skirmishers, leaving our horses under cover of a hill. I followed the enemy nearly half a mile and retook one of our wagons loaded with ammunition, and then proceeded to join my regiment under Colonel Dickinson.

L. B. ELDRIDGE,
First Lieutenant Company K.

HEADQUARTERS 4TH MICHIGAN CAVALRY,
Camp near Murfreesboro', Tennessee, January 8, 1863.

COLONEL: In compliance with your order, on the 27th of December, 1862, I reported to General Palmer with four companies of the 4th Michigan cavalry, companies H, E, L, and B. I was ordered to take the advance of a brigade of infantry and one battery of artillery, and move off on the Jefferson pike to take and hold the bridge over Stewart's creek, about four miles east of Murfreesboro' pike. I sent company E into the woods to the left of the road as skirmishers, and company H to the right. When about one and a half mile out on the road our advance came upon their pickets. I immediately started with companies L and B after them. We were then two and a half miles from the bridge. At every rod their number increased; so that, when we came to the bridge, we were chasing about two hundred of them. Captain Prichard, with company L, had the advance, and was so close to them when we crossed the bridge that some of them were pushed off the side of the bridge and taken prisoners. As soon as we got possession of the bridge I sent couriers back to hurry up the infantry. While we were waiting they attacked us in strong force, but our boys nobly stood their ground and repulsed them. We heard no report from the infantry. I sent another courier back, and he soon came back to me saying there was about one hundred of them in our rear, between the infantry and my command. I then attempted to draw part of my command (company L) back of the bridge, but I no sooner started them back than they came down on us like bees, yelling as if they had us sure. I had company B, under Lieutenant Carter, posted on each side of the road where they had a good sight of them. Company L came back to the bridge on double-quick, with the enemy close to their heels. I ordered them to right about which they did handsomely, not a man flinching or wavering in the least. They immediately opened a fire upon the enemy, which soon made them leave for the woods. I soon heard firing in my rear, and sent Captain Prichard, with his company, back to find out the cause, as I instantly expected an attack from that quarter. I called company B in and placed them on the bridge. They again attempted to drive us from the bridge, but our boys were too much for them, and again drove them back under cover of the woods. Lieutenant Leach now came in with company H; he had run on to the party in our rear, and with twenty men drove them to the woods and joined my command. The artillery soon came up, and my trouble was over. The officers and men of these four companies are deserving great praise. With fifty men we charged and drove for two and a half miles two hundred of the 1st Alabama cavalry, and held the bridge for one-half hour against the whole regiment. The prisoners we took admit that their regiment was all there, and another regiment in Wheeler's brigade was two miles in their rear, on Stone river. I lost three men taken prisoners, between the infantry and my command, and had one slightly wounded. We took from them nine prisoners, wounded one lieutenant and three privates, and killed one lieutenant and one private. We also took four horses, two of them the infantry took possession of. We remained on the ground over night, and were relieved by the 7th Pennsylvania cavalry, when I immediately rejoined my regiment, all right, and perfectly satisfied with my trip.

I am, colonel, your most obedient servant,

FRANK W. MIX,

Captain, Commanding Detachment 4th Michigan Cavalry.

Lieutenant Colonel W. H. DICKENSON,

Commanding 4th Michigan Cavalry.

HEADQUARTERS 7TH PENNSYLVANIA CAVALRY,

Camp near Murfreesboro', Tennessee, January 6, 1863.

SIR: I have the honor to report that, on the morning of December 26, 1862, I was ordered with my regiment to move on the Murfreesboro' road in rear of the 1st cavalry brigade; the 1st cavalry brigade being the advance of that position of the army of the Cumberland. After proceeding on the road about six miles I was ordered with my entire command to the front, with instructions to use one-half in the advance and upon the right as a line of skirmishers, keeping the other half as a support. In this order we proceeded about three miles, when we commenced engaging the enemy, they falling back gradually one mile to a belt of woods where they made a stubborn stand; here there was considerable heavy firing, in which three of my men were wounded, and two horses killed. I ordered one company to charge, which was done with promptness, and which caused the enemy to retire, we pressing and skirmishing with him until night came on.

The 27th was occupied in skirmishing on the left; no casualties in my regiment this day.

Sunday, December 28.—But little skirmishing; my command chiefly in camp.

Monday, December 29.—Was ordered on the left of General Wood's division; throwing out a line of skirmishers to the left, moved with the line of battle; no casualties.

Tuesday, December 30.—Ordered to form a line of couriers from the extreme left, connecting with those on the right, keeping a reserve in the centre—one upon the right centre, and one upon the left centre. These duties were performed by the 2d and 3d battalions commanded by myself, the 1st battalion being with Colonel Minty upon a reconnoissance to Lavergne; the 1st battalion commanded by Captain Jennings.

Wednesday, December 31.—The 1st battalion absent with Colonel Minty; the 2d and 3d continuing as videttes and couriers until 9 o'clock a. m., when our right fell back, creating much consternation and disorder. My videttes and line of couriers were compelled to retire, which was done in good order, the men rallying upon their chiefs.

My command being collected together, I used my utmost exertions to press the troops to the front, who were coming back in much confusion. Finding my endeavors almost useless, the greatest confusion prevailing, I despatched a courier to General Rosecrans to know what position the cavalry should be assigned to. He directed me to take my command to the rear, which I accordingly did, and remained in the rear until about 2 o'clock p. m., when I received an order from Colonel Kennett (commanding cavalry division) to bring my command upon the Murfreesboro' pike, where a portion of the cavalry were engaging the rebel cavalry. We were thrown upon the front, and were for some time under a heavy fire from the enemy under cover. The officers and men here behaved with great coolness, and deserve much credit.

The 1st battalion, under command of Captain Jennings, returned from Lavergne with General Stanley and Captain Minty. Moving rapidly to the right and front, it took up position on the extreme right of our line. Dismounting, it met the advance of the rebels, and finally fell back. Mounting and reforming, the 1st battalion took up a new position on the left of the rest of the cavalry. After a half hour's more fighting darkness brought a cessation of the fighting. The loss this day was two killed, four wounded, and four taken prisoners.

Thursday, January 1.—I was ordered with my entire command upon the right to watch the movements of the enemy, who was continually moving upon the flank; considerable firing between the skirmishers, several of my horses being killed and wounded. This day my regimental train was burned by the enemy whilst en route for Nashville, having upon it all regimental books, papers, company property, camp equipage, officers' baggage, &c.

Friday, January 2.—Was placed on the right to watch that flank. Much skirmishing all day. No casualties to-day. This evening went on picket in right and rear.

Saturday, December 3.—On picket all day.

Sunday, December 4.—Relieved from picket; 2 p. m. was ordered to move with the brigade to Wilkinson's Crossroads.

Monday, December 5.—Ordered to move in rear of brigade towards Murfreesboro'; passed through Murfreesboro', three miles on Manchester road, when my command was ordered to the front. The position assigned me was on the left, when we immediately commenced engaging the enemy, which lasted with considerable severity for about one hour, we driving them from the ground they occupied to a belt of woods where they were under cover. I had one sergeant wounded severely.

The loss in my regiment since leaving Nashville to the present time was as follows: Two (2) killed; nine (9) wounded; fifty (50) prisoners and missing; total, sixty-one (61.)

I am, very respectfully, your obedient servant,

JNO. E. WYNKOOP,
Major, Commanding 7th Pennsylvania Cavalry.

Lieutenant JNO. WOOLLY,
Acting Assistant Adjutant General.

HEADQUARTERS 3D BATTALION 3D INDIANA CAVALRY,
Near Murfreesboro', January 7, 1863.

SIR: I have the honor to submit the following report of the part taken by this battalion in the field since leaving camp near Nashville, on the 26th ultimo, up to the 3d instant.

The four companies under my command left camp on the 26th, as ordered, and bringing up the rear of the 2d division, encamped beyond Nolensville. On the following morning, 27th, having orders, I reported to General Stanley, chief of cavalry, who, remarking he "had understood the 3d knew how to take these rebels," ordered me to move forward and take the advance of the column of cavalry then moving towards Triune. I succeeded in gaining the advance at about the point where the enemy's outposts were expected to be. I then threw out portions of company H, Lieutenant Young commanding, on either side of the pike, and putting out an advance guard, moved smartly down the pike. Our advance soon encountered the enemy in considerable force drawn up in line of battle. The column now moved on to them at a gallop, receiving the whole of their fire into one company, (company G, Captain Herriott,) the skirmishers on the flanks not being able to come up for some time on account of the soft nature of the ground and the fences intervening. Company G held their ground until company I, Captain Vanosdal, on the right, and company K, Lieutenant Lurke, on the left, advanced gallantly to the rescue, and, despite superior force, drove them across the narrow valley to a position beyond where their artillery covered them. Here we advanced with the remainder of our cavalry force and drove them from this hill, from which they fell back to Triune. Here we were ordered by General Stanley, with one company of the 15th Pennsylvania cavalry, to attack the enemy on the right side of the pike. They were posted behind a stone wall, heads only visible, one or more regiments strong; we advanced across the open fields and were pouring in a steady fire at easy range, when two pieces of artillery on our left, about five hundred yards, and two in front, opened on us, obliging us to retire to the cover of the woods from where we advanced. This movement was done *promptly*, but in good order. On the following morning my battalion was in advance of the reconnoisance under General Willich; did no fighting, but captured some sixteen of the enemy's stragglers on the Nolensville pike. We lost three killed: Sergeant Newell, company I; Private Moore, company H; and Private Dunn, company G; and three wounded: Privates Merritt and Russey, company G; and Henry Tunph, company I. We lost also a few horses wounded and disabled, and one killed by cannon shot. On the 29th and 30th nothing worthy of note occurred.

On the morning of the 31st ultimo my battalion was posted with our cavalry force beyond Wilson's Crossroad's pike, on the right and rear of the 2d division. When our forces first gave way before the overwhelming numbers of the enemy, the efficiency of my battalion was destroyed in being divided by one of our own cavalry regiments running through our ranks and scattering the men. This movement, had it been in the opposite direction, would have been a most gallant charge, and doubtless from its determination an efficient one. We kept falling back, forming and charging at intervals, until forced across to the Murfreesboro' pike, where one of my companies was first to form to drive the enemy from our train. We captured during the retreat eleven of the enemy. One of company G, Corporal Justice, recaptured our ambulance containing our surgeon, by shooting down one of its captors and frightening the others away. I regret to say that Corporal Justice was afterwards captured. We were formed near the centre of our cavalry, when the enemy in the afternoon again attempted to take our train. We participated in the fight and the charge that followed. We lost one man on that morning, Private Daniel Gibbons, on General Willich's escort, and two others wounded. On the following days of the fight my battalion was on provost duty.

Our loss sums up: Killed, 4; wounded, 6; missing, 10; captured, 5. Of the missing, doubtless nearly all were captured. Our total loss is 25; horses, 30; and one ambulance.

Respectfully, your obedient servant,

R. KLEIN,
Major, Commanding Battalion.

Captain BARTLETT,
Captain and Assistant Adjutant General.

NASHVILLE, *Tennessee, January* 2, 1863.

SIR: I have the honor to report that, in accordance with your order, I reported to Captain Otis, chief of couriers, on the 29th ultimo; and that on the same date, by his direction, my men were posted on the Nashville and Murfreesboro' road as couriers, commencing nine miles from Nashville and extending to the headquarters of Major General Crittenden.

On the 31st ultimo, at 3 p. m., the enemy made a raid upon Lavergne, at which point I had made my headquarters, capturing from my command one lieutenant and thirteen men, and making it necessary for two other courier posts to abandon their stations to prevent capture, all which I immediately reported to Major General Rosecrans the same evening. The places of my men were supplied from another command, and I proceeded to this place to collect the few men who still remained of my company. Those who were at General Crittenden's headquarters having been sent here as an escort with his headquarters train, I collected seventeen men for duty, and reported to Brigadier General Mitchell, commanding the post, and, by his command, I had placed them as couriers between Nashville and Lavergne.

I have to report, besides the loss already mentioned, fifteen government horses, ten mules, two wagons, all the equipage, tents, &c., of the company; fifteen Colt's revolving pistols and holsters, eleven Colt's revolving rifles, fourteen saddles, bridles, and halters, besides all of my own private baggage and personal effects.

Since occupying the present line I have to report one man killed whilst bearing a despatch.

I am, most truly, your obedient servant,

J. A. S. MITCHELL,
Captain, Commanding Company.

Colonel R. G. K. MINTY,
Commanding 1st Cavalry Brigade.

HEADQUARTERS 2D CAVALRY BRIGADE,
In camp, on Wilson's pike, near Nolensville crossing,
December 27, 1862.

GENERAL: In compliance with orders received, I moved from our old camp at Nashville yesterday morning, at eight o'clock, with the 1st, 3d, and 4th cavalry regiments, 950 strong in all. I crossed over on the Franklin pike, south of General Thomas's headquarters, as I afterwards learned. I passed the immense trains and troops on the Franklin pike, beyond Brentwood. I halted my command, as I had not seen General Thomas yet. I supposed he was on the move with the troops in front. I kept inquiring along the column, and was told that he was in the advance; I proceeded myself on the Wilson creek pike some two miles, almost to the head of the column, but then learning from General Rousseau that General Thomas was in the rear, I immediately started back some six miles; there ascertaining that General Thomas had cut across the country on to the Nolensville pike, I thought further pursuit would be useless. I started back to join my command, and to carry out the remainder of my instructions. I proceeded to Franklin, encountered the enemy's pickets 2½ miles out, drove them in; skirmishing continued until within half a mile of Franklin, when a sharp skirmish ensued, driving the rebels. They then made another halt in town. I dismounted some six companies to act as skirmishers on foot; came round on both flanks with mounted skirmishers, and their reserves finally charged through the river into town, where some considerable firing ensued; drove the rebels out; drove them some two miles beyond town; the lateness of the day prevented further pursuit, for by this time it began to be dark. The enemy was taken by surprise, could not get their forces together before we were upon them, therefore made it rather an easy task to drive them, as they were in several directions, formed several lines, but as we advanced and fired they invariably fled. We took 10 prisoners, one of them a lieutenant of General Bragg's escort, who was then on business with 16 men. We captured a private of the same escort; we captured that number of horses, several mules, some shot-guns and carbines, broke up their camps, and burned several tents for them. From the best information received, I made out the force to have been about 900, consisting of Colonel Smith's regiment, and an independent battalion. I shall send the prisoners to Nashville this morning.

I learned that quite a force of infantry and artillery were 9 miles out of Franklin, on the road leading to Murfreesboro'. I arrived in camp here at nearly 9 o'clock last evening; reported to General Rousseau, in the absence of General Thomas. We learned that the enemy had quite a force at Triune, some ten miles south of this. General Rousseau and myself came to the conclusion to use my brigade to day in reconnoitring the front and right, until further orders could be received from you. I shall therefore send some five hundred men towards Petersburg and Triune to reconnoitre; shall likewise send a smaller force over towards Franklin to ascertain whether the enemy has come back again or not. My force will be back in camp towards evening; will remain here and picket Wilson's creek pike, as instructed, until your further orders are received.

I forgot to mention that we killed three of the enemy; could not ascertain the number of wounded; must have wounded some in proportion to the killed. My men behaved nobly, both officers and men. The 3d cavalry had the advance, and did the principal part of the fighting; there was no flinch to them; they moved steadily onward, and finally made the charge through town.

I am, general, your obedient servant,

LEWIS ZAHN,
Colonel, Commanding 2d Cavalry Brigade.

General STANLEY,
Commanding Cavalry.

HEADQUARTERS 2D CAVALRY BRIGADE,
Nashville, Tennessee, 11 *o'clock, January* 2, 1863.

GENERAL: I have the honor to report that at 9 o'clock a. m. (yesterday) I proceeded with the 3d cavalry and the Anderson Troop, as directed, forward to guard the trains in motion on the road to Nashville. I took up every train in front of me which was in motion. At Stewart's creek I found the 3d division train just putting out. It detained me about one hour; at the same time I learned that a heavy cavalry force was to the left of me. I ordered the train to proceed at a brisk walk. We moved on until we arrived at Lavergne; the train had passed the flats at Lavergne; myself with command resting on the flat when my flanks discovered the enemy to our left and engaged him. I immediately turned into the field, formed line of battle, despatched orderlies to the front to move the train on a trot. The enemy formed, then ensued skirmishing with the skirmishers; the enemy formed a new line which I counteracted, kept him at bay ready to receive their charge; they, however, declined to charge—wheeled in column of fours, moved to the left of our train, and forward around a hill in front and to the left of the road with the intention of heading off the train. By this time the rear of the train was a half mile ahead of us. I immediately followed the train, sent flankers at a rapid pace towards the front to watch and engage the enemy if approaching. The enemy did not succeed in heading the train. After proceeding about two miles further, discovered the enemy charging up the pike on our rear. I met them and repulsed them. They charged again. I repulsed them again—charged them back for two miles, scattered them, killed nine, wounded eleven, and took two prisoners. I had a few men slightly wounded. After this they troubled my train no more. Not a wagon fell into their hands ahead of the escort. Some four or five wagons broke down, which we left and destroyed. The enemy's forces were Wheeler's brigade with two pieces of artillery, which they played upon us pretty lively. A short time before we were attacked, a large number of the 2d Tennessee came running by my column, running away from the front, stating that our forces were in full retreat. I placed a company in the road, halted every one of them, but, at the breaking out of the skirmish, they ran again like sheep. I am sorry to say that the Anderson Troop, with very few exceptions, as the enemy charged us in the rear, scampered off in most every direction; did not stand up to the work at all. The contrary caused, together with the negroes, (2d Tennessee,) all running, somewhat of a stampede among the wagons, which caused the few breakdowns above mentioned.

I arrived here at 9 o'clock p. m.; found no forage for horses; sent out a train after forage this morning, so it will be 5 o'clock this p. m. before our horses will get a mouthful to eat since 3 o'clock yesterday morning, and labored very hard; consequently not fit for any service to-day. Both horses and men are very much used up.

I am awaiting further orders. I have ordered the Anderson Troop to report to me early this morning, but they have not done so up to this time; they are very much demoralized. In any work for me to do, I ask you please not to count them as being any help to me. I would sooner do without them.

I am, very respectfully, your obedient servant,

LEWIS ZAHN.

General STANLEY,
Commanding Cavalry.

HEADQUARTERS 2D CAVALRY BRIGADE,
In camp, near Murfreesboro', January 6, 1863.

LIEUTENANT: I herewith have the honor to report the part taken and the work performed by my brigade since our departure from Nashville until the close of the battle before Murfreesboro'. I left Nashville on the morning of the 26th with three regiments of my brigade, viz: the 1st, 3d, and 4th Ohio cavalry; the 5th Kentucky remaining at Nashville. My force numbered 950 men. We marched out on the Franklin pike, the 3d Ohio having the advance. When within two miles of Franklin drove in the rebel pickets; skirmished all the way down to Franklin; drove the enemy out, and pursued him some two miles. From the best information received, the enemy were 900 strong, all cavalry, part of Wharton's brigade. We killed four, wounded several, and took ten prisoners, amongst them a lieutenant of General Bragg's escort, several horses and mules, and destroyed their camps, with some tents standing thereon. We retired from Franklin, moved over to the Wilson Creek pike, and picketed said pike.

On the 27th, sent the 1st Ohio, and most of the 4th Ohio, under command of Colonel Milliken, on the Wilson Creek pike, towards Triune, to reconnoitre. They proceeded within two miles of Triune, captured six of the rebel pickets, when the enemy opened on them with shells; threw some fifty, without damaging us any, then my force retired to camp. I likewise had sent a battalion of the 3d to Franklin to reconnoitre, which drove in the rebel pickets, who had returned in force, after my command had left the evening previous. Quite a skirmish ensued, in which three of the rebels were killed and several wounded. After skirmishing some two hours, and the enemy being too strong to drive, the battalion returned to camp in good order without any loss.

On the 28th, moved with the command to Triune without anything occurring worth mentioning. On the 29th, proceeded towards Murfreesboro', moving between the Franklin road and the road called Boley Jack road, which General McCook's corps moved on. I divided my brigade into three columns, marching parallel with one and the other, and with the main force, the right (the 4th Ohio) moving on the Franklin road, the 3d in the centre, and the 1st on the left, the columns being from one to one and a half mile apart, throwing out skirmishers connecting one column with the other, and connecting on the left with the main column. We thus proceeded for five miles, when the centre column encountered the enemy's pickets, which they drove in, the different columns steadily advancing.

Shortly after, both the right and the left encountered pickets, driving them in before them. After proceeding about a mile further, we came upon the enemy's cavalry, (Wharton's brigade;) engaged them for three hours, some time the right wing, then the left, then the centre, receiving several charges, which were repulsed, driving the enemy some two miles, when the brigade concentrated, repelling a heavy charge from the enemy, driving him back under his guns, which were only a short distance from us. We then retired some two miles and went into camp. Some few casualties occurred this day. The officers and men behaved admirably during the whole day. The 4th had proceeded until the enemy threw shells into them pretty rapidly, when they retired. We were within four miles of Murfreesboro'.

On the morning of the 30th were ordered to proceed on the Franklin road towards Murfreesboro', to push the enemy hard. We had encamped that night near the brick church, on the road leading from General McCook's headquarters to the Franklin road. I proceeded that morning with my command and the 2d East Tennessee, which reported to me that morning, *via* that road to the Franklin road, at which crossing we encountered the enemy's pickets, and drove them in; sent a party of the 4th to reconnoitre on the road leading south to Salem, where they soon came upon a stronger force, and a brisk skirmish ensued. I increased the number of skirmishers, especially to the left, skirmished with the enemy for an hour or more, when a courier arrived, saying that the enemy was approaching with a heavy cavalry force and some artillery. In the mean time I had ascertained, likewise, that a heavy force of the enemy were encamped some little distance south of the Franklin road, and east of where my column halted. I did not think it prudent to advance, and owing to the bad grounds (being all timber) where my force halted, I retired to my camping ground, near which were large open fields, well adapted for cavalry movements. I soon formed a line of battle. The enemy made his appearance. Skirmishers engaged him pretty briskly. The enemy manœuvred with the design to outflank us, but did not succeed. I forestalled him every time. With the exception of severe skirmishing, nothing transpired. The enemy retired, when I concluded to join the main body of our army. After marching about a mile, met General Stanley with a brigade of infantry and a battery of artillery to re-enforce me. The general marched the whole command towards the enemy's camp. On reaching its vicinity, the enemy drew up in line of battle; skirmishing ensued; remained there about half an hour, when the general withdrew, with the remark that we were not ready yet to fight the whole of Hardee's army corps. That night we encamped one and a half mile from the enemy's camp, and laid on our arms all night.

At daybreak on the morning of the 31st I had my command drawn up in line of battle in the rear of my camp; sent out two squadrons to the front and to the right to reconnoitre. Had been in line about half an hour, when I heard heavy firing, cannon and musketry, to my left and a little to the front. Soon after, I beheld our infantry scattered all over the fields, running towards my line, when I learned that General Johnson's division was repulsed. At about the same time, my skirmishers engaged the enemy, when they were driven in, reporting that the enemy were approaching in heavy force. Sure enough, I soon discovered heavy lines of infantry coming towards my front, and on the left, where General Johnson's division had been posted; also to my right the enemy's cavalry were coming round in long columns, with the evident design to outflank us. I concluded to retire slowly towards the main body of our army, the enemy pressing hard on me; kept him at bay with my skirmishers. I retired in this wise for a mile, when I formed a line of battle with the 1st and 3d, when the enemy charged on them with their cavalry, but were repulsed by my men. About this time the enemy began to throw shells into my lines pretty lively. The first shell that landed mortally wounded Major Moore, of the 1st Ohio. I now fell back, formed a new line, received the enemy's charge, repulsed them, and made many of the rebels bite the dust. Shells coming pretty thick again, I retired further, when I made another stand, supported by Willich's regiment of infantry; received the enemy's charge, and repulsed him again. I then withdrew my whole command through a large strip of woods to another open lot—shells of the enemy helping us along—passing by a line of rebel infantry marching parallel with my column, not over 200 yards from us, so that we were nearly surrounded, as the enemy's cavalry were working round our right all the time, and the infantry and artillery following us closely in our rear and to our left. They had cavalry enough to spare to strike, or to take position, whenever required. When arrived on the open ground, General McCook's aid told me that the whole of General McCook's ammunition train was close by, on a dirt road running by that point, and that I must try to save it. I soon formed my command in line, when the enemy made his appearance in a position occupying two-thirds of a circle. They prepared to charge upon us; likewise commenced throwing shells, at which the 2d East Tennessee broke and ran like sheep. The 4th, after receiving several shells, which killed some of their men and horses, likewise retired from their line, as it became untenable. The 1st had been ordered to proceed further on into another lot, to form and to receive a charge from another line of the enemy's cavalry. The 3d moved to the left, in the vicinity of a white house. About the time the 1st was formed, the enemy charged upon the 4th, which, being on the retreat, owing to the shells coming pretty freely, moved off at a pretty lively gait. The 3d moved further to the left, and, somewhat sheltered by the house and barns, the 1st charged upon the enemy; did not succeed in driving them back. On returning from said charge the gallant Colonel Milliken and a lieutenant were killed, another lieutenant severely wounded. At this juncture the 1st and 4th retired pretty fast, the enemy in close pursuit after them, the 2d East Tennessee having the lead of them all. Matters looked pretty blue now: the ammunition train supposed to be gone up, when the 3d charged upon the enemy, driving him back, capturing several prisoners, and recapturing a good many of our men, and saved the train. I was with the three regiments that skedaddled, and among the last to leave the field; tried hard to rally them, but the panic was so great that I could not do it. I could not get the command together again until I arrived at the north side of the creek; then I found that only about one-third of the 1st and 4th regiments were there, and nearly all of the 2d East Tennessee. These I marched back across the creek, when, joined by the 3d, we had several skirmishes with the enemy's cavalry all day long; received several charges, and repulsed them. All the officers and men behaved well through all the fighting, up to the stampede, which was not very creditable. All of them that I brought back into action again behaved well during the rest of the day. I must say the 3d deserves great credit for this day's fighting—for the coolness and bravery of its officers and men, and for its determination to save the train, which they accomplished. I don't wish to take any credit away from the other regiments, as they all fought nobly, and did first rate, with the exception of the stampede. On the 1st day of January, after being in line of battle since 3 o'clock a. m., I was ordered to take the 3d Ohio and the Anderson Troop, proceed to Nashville, and escort the army wagon train through to Nashville. I left about 9 o'clock. A little below Lavergne, was attacked by General Wheeler's cavalry brigade; repulsed him twice; killed nine and wounded several, took two prisoners; saved all the train but two or three wagons, which broke down in the excitement; saved several cannon belonging to a Wisconsin battery, going along with the train, which were abandoned by the drivers, horses still hitched to the cannon. Some of my men mounted the horses and took the cannon into Nashville. The enemy threw shells at us, but did not succeed in hurting any of the men. The Anderson Troop, I am sorry to say, were of very little benefit to me, as the majority of them ran as soon as we were attacked. Arrived in Nashville at 9 o'clock p. m.; found no forage for my horses. Next day, the 2d of January, had to send out a foraging party; they returned at 5 o'clock p. m., when my horses were fed for the first time since leaving the front the day previous, at 3 o'clock a. m. At 1 o'clock on the 3d were ordered to leave at 3 o'clock to escort a hospital store train and an ammunition train through to the front. When two miles out had to wait for Colonel McCook to come up with two and a half regiments of infantry, and some 150 of the 3d Tennessee cavalry. Two companies of the 4th Ohio, under command of Lieutenant White, were with me likewise. It was 11 o'clock before we got started. All of this force combined formed the escort to the train. We proceeded about eight miles, when we were attacked by Wheeler's brigade. We repulsed them, taking twelve prisoners, amongst them two lieutenants; killed fifteen, and wounded many. They did but little damage to the train, which was done through the cowardice of the teamsters. I had one man killed and one wounded. The enemy tried to attack us the second time, but retired before our forces met. We brought the train through safe, and arrived with it at 1 o'clock the next morning. During my three days' absence, the 1st and 4th were busily employed reconnoitring, and doing picket duty, and skirmishing with the enemy's cavalry. On the 4th, marched my command to the front, near Murfreesboro', to reconnoitre, the enemy having withdrawn their forces.

On the 5th, marched to the front some four and a half miles beyond Murfreesboro', on the Shelbyville road, on a reconnoissance, capturing quite a number of rebel stragglers; pushed a squadron of the 4th some three miles further, to a point where they could overlook the pike for five miles ahead, when they discovered that the enemy had entirely disappeared. The skirmishers of the 4th had some skirmishing with some of the rebel cavalry. By 7 o'clock was back to camp again. You will observe that my command had fought nearly every day from the time we left Nashville up to this time. They worked very hard, and deserve a great deal of credit for what they have done, as both officers and men fought bravely.

Herewith find list of casualties, which are not large, considering the number of engagements we were in. All respectfully submitted.

I am, very respectfully, your obedient servant,

LEWIS ZAHN,

Colonel, Commanding 2d Ohio Volunteer Cavalry.

Lieutenant M. B. CHAMBERLIN,

Acting Assistant Adjutant General,

1st Cavalry Division, Army of the Cumberland.

Official report of casualties, &c., of 1st Ohio volunteer cavalry, from December 26 to December 31, 1862.

HEADQUARTERS 1ST OHIO VOLUNTEER CAVALRY,
January 6, 1863.

December 26.—Left Nashville for Franklin. Arrived at Franklin at 3 o'clock p. m. Found the enemy occupying the town; drove them from it, and proceeded to Wilson Creek pike, and encamped for the night.

December 27.—Left camp at 8 o'clock; proceeded towards Triune. Struck the enemy's pickets within five miles of Triune. Drove in their pickets, captured six, and returned to the camp occupied the previous night.

December 28.—Left camp at 8 o'clock for Triune, where we encamped.

December 29.—Left camp at 9 o'clock on a reconnoissance towards Murfreesboro'. Struck the enemy's scouts when within one mile of Stewart's creek, when active skirmishing commenced, and continued until sundown, having driven the enemy's cavalry at least three and a half miles. One man missing while crossing Stewart's creek. At sundown we retired back across Stewart's creek, and encamped.

December 30.—Skirmished with the enemy all day on the right of General Johnson's division, driving the enemy's cavalry whenever they made their appearance, and retired and encamped in the camp occupied by us the night before.

December 31.—At 7 o'clock a. m. I was ordered by you to take two companies and make a thorough reconnoissance up the creek in the woods on our right. After throwing out skirmishers into the woods, I received orders from you to withdraw my command as soon as possible, for the enemy were advancing in force on my left. I immediately withdrew at full speed, and passed the enemy's left (infantry) within 150 yards, under a heavy fire, slightly wounding only one man and two horses. After passing their flank half a mile, I discovered your brigade formed in line of battle in the cornfield on the opposite side of the creek. Being unable to join my regiment at this point, I proceeded down the creek half a mile and crossed, joining the brigade on the right—my regiment was on the left—retiring slowly in column of fours. After retiring half a mile we were again formed in line of battle, and remained until we were under a heavy fire from the enemy's artillery, when we were compelled to retire. Here the brave and heroic Major D. A. B. Moore fell mortally wounded. We then retired across a cornfield, the enemy in full and fast pursuit, with at least three times our number, when we again formed, receiving three heavy charges from the enemy's cavalry, but repulsed them every time with a fire from our carbines. Their artillery was still open on us. We then retired through the woods towards the Nashville pike, when we formed in a cornfield. The enemy (cavalry and infantry) immediately appearing, our noble commander, Colonel Minor Milliken, ordered our regiment, five companies, to charge them. Being unable to hold his position after the charge, he ordered the regiment to retire, when he received the fatal shot that killed him instantly. About this time Second Lieutenant Condit was killed, and our adjutant, First Lieutenant William Scott, fell seriously wounded. The companies then retired to the pike, and crossed Stewart's creek on the pike, and found myself in command, and repulsed the enemy, who had pursued to the creek, and took possession of our wagon train, killing two and wounding four. At this time the brigade came across the creek and organized.

January 1.—Nine o'clock a. m. Major Laughlin reported for duty, and took command of the regiment.

Recapitulation of casualties.

Commissioned officers killed	3
Privates killed	2
Commissioned officers wounded	1
Privates wounded	10
Commissioned officers missing, (surgeon)	1
Privates missing	14
Total	31

Respectfully submitted.

VALENTINE CUPP,
Captain, Commanding 1st Ohio Volunteer Cavalry.

Colonel LEWIS ZAHN,
Commanding 2d Cavalry Brigade, 1st Division, 14th Army Corps.

CAMP 1ST OHIO VOLUNTEER CAVALRY,
Near Murfreesboro', January 6, 1863.

SIR: I have the honor to submit the following report of the 1st Ohio volunteer cavalry:

On the morning of the 1st of January I was ordered to take command of the regiment, and was immediately ordered in the rear of Stewart's creek and on the right, on picket or outpost duty. In the evening I was ordered back in front of Stewart's creek and on the right, to stand on picket for the night. On the morning of the 2d I was ordered to advance my regiment forward on the right, which I did, and found the enemy in my front, and skirmished with them until dark. I was then ordered into camp for the night. The morning of the 3d I was ordered to march my regiment to the rear of Stewart's creek, which I did. In the evening I was ordered to join my command with the 4th Ohio volunteer cavalry, and make a reconnoissance on our left, which was done, and we returned to camp the same night. Remained in camp on the 4th until evening; was ordered to the front, and left to guard the railroad bridge for the night. On the morning of the 5th went on scout beyond Murfreesboro', on the Shelbyville pike, and returned, no casualties having happened during the time included.

Your most obedient,

JAMES LAUGHLIN,
Major, Commanding 1st Ohio Volunteer Cavalry

Colonel LEWIS ZAHN,
Commanding 2d Cavalry Brigade.

HEADQUARTERS THIRD OHIO CAVALRY,
In camp, near Murfreesboro', Tennessee, January 6, 1863.

COLONEL: In compliance with instructions received from your headquarters, I have the honor to report for your information the part taken by the 3d Ohio cavalry in the several engagements in which the regiment was engaged since leaving Nashville, Tennessee, on the 26th of December last, on which day we proceeded to Franklin, driving the enemy therefrom, and taking possession of the town; took some ten prisoners. Remaining in town some time, we recrossed the river, and marched across the country to Wilson Creek pike, about fourteen miles from Nashville, and encamped, arriving in camp at about 10 o'clock, p. m. On the 27th the 3d battalion of the regiment moved towards Franklin, and found that the enemy had in strong force again taken possession of the town; the battalion drove in their pickets under a heavy fire, killing three of them. Seeing that the enemy were in such force, the commander deemed it prudent to retire, and rejoined the regiment, which picketed the roads, &c., in the vicinity of its camp. On the 28th ultimo proceeded to Triune and encamped, leaving early next morning across the country towards Murfreesboro', proceeding about five miles in that direction, when attacked by the enemy's pickets in force, which we drove, skirmishing, they frequently making a stand, which we each time broke, and still drove them about five miles. The 30th ultimo, ordered to proceed to Stone river; proceeded but a short distance when attacked by the enemy's pickets; the enemy were in force in our front with artillery; we therefore retired, forming on the high ground in our rear to receive them, their pickets, or patrol, advancing, which we repulsed. In the evening our brigade was re-enforced by one battery of artillery and three regiments of infantry, and proceeded in reconnoissance to the left of the enemy's lines, where we found General Hardee's corps d'armé ready, in line of battle, to receive us. We retired and encamped in the woods, about two miles in front of the enemy's lines. On the morning of the 31st we formed; shortly after the enemy appeared in large force, both on our left, centre, and right, evidently endeavoring to cut us off. The brigade of infantry to our left gave way, retreating in confusion through our lines, letting the whole force of the enemy's artillery, cavalry, and infantry fall upon us, which compelled us gradually to retire towards the main body of our army. The regiment covering the entire rear of the brigade, supporting one infantry regiment on our right, drove back, with heavy loss, a large force of cavalry which charged upon us, under cover of a piece of artillery firing well-directed shells, which passed over us. The enemy being in such force, we had to retire about three-fourths of a mile, when an aide-de-camp of General McCook rode up, informing us that the train close by was General McCook's entire ammunition train, which must be saved at all hazards; on intimation of which, the regiment was immediately formed for its protection, holding the enemy in check until the entire train, with the exception of a few disabled wagons that could not be moved, were safely withdrawn. The regiment then moved between the enemy and train as far as the Murfreesboro' pike, where we found the enemy making a fierce attack upon General Thomas's train, where we again repulsed them at several points, taking many prisoners, and saving that entire portion of the train. The attack of the enemy was furious and desperate, which required the greatest firmness and bravery to resist. Colonel Kennett was an eye-witness to the determined bravery of a portion of the regiment rescuing the train from the enemy, which were in force at the hospital on the Murfreesboro' pike. The regiment then formed in the field, near the hospital, where the brigade soon assembled and reformed, and advanced towards the enemy's left. Soon came up to the enemy's cavalry, supported by artillery, when several other skirmishes ensued during the evening, the enemy's entire object seeming to be to take the train.

On the 1st instant received orders to proceed to Nashville in charge of train consisting of some two or three hundred wagons. When about two miles on the Nashville side of Lavergne we were attacked by General Wheeler's brigade of cavalry, which made several dashes on the train, and were repulsed. They then attacked our rear in force. After a well-contested fight, our regiment put them to flight in disorder, killing nine of them and wounding several, and arrived in Nashville at 9 o'clock p. m., and encamped. The 2d instant remained in Nashville, and procured forage for our horses, furnishing working party and escort to forage train. The 3d instant left Nashville for Murfreesboro', in charge of hospital and ammunition trains; attacked again in force by Wheeler's brigade of cavalry on the Nashville side of Lavergne, which were repulsed with the loss of fifteen on their side and some eight or nine prisoners taken; amongst the latter the adjutant of the 3d Alabama cavalry. Two of our non-commissioned officers, I regret to inform you, were severely and dangerously wounded, whom we had to leave in a house on the road-side. Arrived at camp, near Murfreesboro', at 1 o'clock a. m., 4th instant, with the train all safe, with the exception of one wagon of the regiment that was cut off by the enemy, and is now supposed to have returned to Nashville. On the evening of the 4th proceeded with brigade towards Murfreesboro' as far as Stone river, and returned to camp. On the 5th instant proceeded again with brigade to Murfreesboro', and beyond it about four and a half miles, where we halted, taking several prisoners, and returning to camp about 7 o'clock p. m.

I have much pleasure in informing you that the conduct and behaviour of both officers, non-commissioned officers, and privates of the regiment has been highly creditable, with not a single instance to the contrary in the regiment.

Enclosed please find list of casualties that have occurred since the 26th of December, 1862, to the 5th of January, 1863.

Very respectfully, I have the honor to be your obedient servant,

D. A. MURRAY,

Lieutenant Colonel 3d Ohio Cavalry, Commanding Regiment.

Colonel LEWIS ZAHN,

Commanding 2d Cavalry Brigade, 1st Cavalry Division.

HEADQUARTERS 3D OHIO CAVALRY,

January 8, 1863.

SIR: There are a few incidents in the recent series of battles in which we were engaged which, not having fallen immediately under your observation, or of the regimental commander, have escaped notice; and being under my immediate command, in justice to the brave officers and men engaged, I deem it my duty to make this special report.

In the severe fighting of Wednesday, the 31st ultimo, which fell so heavily upon your brigade, you will recollect, when we had been forced back as far as General McCook's ammunition train, and were drawn up in front of it for its protection, the furious charge of the enemy's cavalry, preceded by a shower of shells, caused a pretty general stampede of our cavalry, led off by the 2d Tennessee on our right, and followed by the 4th and 1st Ohio and the 1st battalion of the 3d Ohio cavalry. At that juncture an aid of General McCook came up to me, and informed me that "that was their entire ammunition train, and must be held at all hazards." I gave orders accordingly to the left wing of the 3d Ohio cavalry under my command, and I am happy to report that they held their position and did not break their lines nor join in that stampede, but received the galling fire of the enemy with the firmness of heroes, and maintained their ground till all of the wagons, except a few that were disabled or deserted by the teamsters, had safely reached the lines of our infantry. The enemy seeing our determination and bold resistance, turned and left us, and pursued the broken columns of our cavalry that had fled. We then wheeled, and charged upon their rear with terrible effect—scattering their columns in worse confusion, if possible, than they had just routed the balance of our brigade, killing a number of men and horses, and taking some ten or twelve prisoners, and releasing a large number of our brigade that they had captured. We pursued them over to the Murfreesboro' pike, Captain McClelland, commanding the squadron E and F, taking the right of the pike, and the balance of the command, with myself, taking the left. When within a short distance of the hospital we again encountered a large force of the enemy coming back to take possession of the train. We at once engaged them, although at least double our numbers, and after a severe struggle put them to flight with a loss of several killed, wounded, and prisoners. The bravery and daring of Captains Wood and Colver, and their respective commands, on this occasion, challenged my admiration. I also learned that Captain McClelland. with his squadron, engaged the enemy further up the pike, beyond the hospital, with Colonel Kennett and a portion of the 3d Kentucky cavalry, and, after a fierce contest, repulsed them. We then quietly formed in line and awaited the reassembling of the brigade. Then be it spoken to their praise, that the 2d and 3d battalions of the 3d Ohio cavalry did not run nor break their lines during that day's severe fighting. This result is greatly attributable to the coolness and bravery of Captains McClelland, Wood, and Colver, and their lieutenants. It was also this portion of the regiment that repulsed the attack of the enemy on the rear of our train the next day near Lavergne as we were proceeding to Nashville, and brought safely into Nashville two pieces of cannon, three caissons full of ammunition, and a wagon loaded with new carbines and ammunition, which had been abandoned by their cowardly teamsters. All of which is respectfully submitted.

MAJOR J. W. PARAMORE,
Commanding Left Wing 3d Ohio Cavalry.

Colonel L. ZAHN,
Commanding 2d Cavalry Brigade.

IN CAMP, *January* 6, 1862.

COLONEL: We left camp, near Nashville, December 26, with 2d brigade cavalry and marched to Franklin, and assisted in driving out a force of rebel cavalry; next day remained in camp, and on the 28th ultimo marched for Triune. On the 29th was ordered by you to march on the dirt road leading to Murfreesboro' and to throw out a line of skirmishers to the front and flank, connecting with skirmishers of the 3d Ohio, on our left. We had proceeded but five or six miles until we came on to the enemy's advance picket, driving them in, and occasionally had slight skirmishes with squads of the enemy's cavalry, who were evidently sent out for the purpose of ascertaining our number. When within three or four miles of Murfreesboro', came on a battery of two pieces of artillery and a support of infantry or dismounted men posted in a wood, who opened a fire of grape on our advance. In reconnoitring their position, we found a body of cavalry was passing on our flank, and soon discovered they were on our rear and flank. I faced the column about, and ordered Captain Johnson to attack a body of cavalry posted in the road, which he did, driving them into the woods; then we attacked their whole force posted at the edge of the wood, when a sharp skirmish ensued, resulting in a loss on our part of two killed, seven wounded, (one mortally, and has since died,) and nine prisoners. We captured seven prisoners from the enemy. The loss was principally sustained by companies K and M, Lieutenants White and Megrue commanding, who behaved themselves admirably, as did all the officers. On the day following we were, together with the 1st and 3d Ohio, engaged during the day reconnoitring and skirmishing with the enemy. 31st, were by your orders formed in the field on ——— creek; had been in our position but a short time, when the enemy were discovered advancing with infantry, cavalry, and artillery, in line of battle, capturing two batteries of our artillery and engaging our infantry, who were soon driven back. Our position now became untenable, and we fell back to another position, and had but just got my line formed when we discovered the enemy's cavalry were out flanking us. We then took a position in woods adjoining, and charged the enemy's cavalry with company A, Lieutenant Hamilton; company B, Captain Teeton; company C, Captain Matthews; company E, Captain Gotwald, who succeeded in checking their advance and driving them back a short distance; they were re-enforced, and, in turn, drove our men from the field. At this point an aid from General McCook rode up and asked me to form my command so as to protect the train, which I did, but soon was driven away from it by shells from the enemy's guns and cavalry. The panic now became so general that our regiment in leaving the field got scattered, but the majority of it were in skirmishes of the afternoon. On the days of January 1, 2, and 3, was in line of battle all day. On the 31st, whilst in line near the train, and on leaving the field, we lost in killed, wounded, missing and prisoners, some thirty-five or six men, also three horses killed and five wounded; the enemy had also captured some twenty more, who were afterwards released by our own men, having been previously disarmed and dismounted. On the 5th, crossed Stone river, and proceeded to a distance of three or four miles south of Murfreesboro'; lost two men prisoners, being captured by rebel pickets. Annexed please find a list of killed, wounded, missing, and prisoners.

Killed, 7; wounded, 18; missing, 16; prisoners, 15—total, 56.

I am, very respectfully, your obedient servant,

J. L. PUGH,
Major, Commanding 4th Ohio Volunteer Cavalry.

Colonel L. ZAHN,
Commanding 2d Brigade.

IN CAMP NEAR MURFREESBORO', TENNESSEE,
January 12, 1863.

DEAR SIR: In the action of Wednesday, December 31, 1862, I take pleasure in calling your especial attention to a brilliant little achievement accomplished by a portion of your command while temporarily and unavoidably detached from your immediate supervision. While there was apparently a general consternation among other cavalry regiments, you ordered the right of your command to rest at a point commanding a road; and while superintending the alignment, which was very difficult at that time, owing to said confusion, a portion of Tennessee cavalry came pursued hotly up the road upon which your right was resting. A regiment of Texas rangers were in full pursuit, and were endeavoring also to take two pieces of artillery, one ambulance, and six wagons, which were following the fleeing Tennessee cavalry. It was an emergency, and demanded coolness, bravery, and expedition to save the property, as well as change the wavering fortunes of that day. In fact, it was so immensely critical as, for the time being, at least, to waive the precedence of rank, or military etiquette of waiting for orders, and seize upon the golden chance of saving the honor of the regiment and, measurably, the fortunes of the day.

Captain Peter Mathews, being in command of the 1st squadron, consisting of companies A, B, and C, seeing the exigency, and, at the same time, being aware of your attention being preoccupied with the speedy alignment of the left of the regiment, took the authority ostensibly warranted by the emergency, and ordered his squadron to charge down the road and drive back the enemy, and save the property imperilled. I had the honor to be in the charge, and can testify with pride that I saw the enemy severely repulsed, driven back, the two pieces of cannon saved, and the ambulance and the six government wagons. In that charge I had one man killed, one wounded, and one taken prisoner, and the other two companies suffered proportionately.

I trust to be pardoned for the vanity I display in calling your particular attention to this glorious little episode of that day. I know well the pride you take in anything done meritorious by your command, and this, in addition to the reflection that there seems to be a design somewhere to detract from the old 4th's glory, induces me to make mention thus. I moreover say that "honor to whom honor is due" should apply in the case in which we are all so much interested; and if the old 4th did anything creditable, it is my duty, and your duty, and every man's duty, to see that she meets not with detraction. In your report of this conduct of the regiment, I deem this may justly take a conspicuous part. I was in all the fight, and I can proudly testify as to the conduct of our regiment, whatever else others may say to the contrary notwithstanding.

I am, sir, with much respect, your obedient servant,

H. B. TEETOR,
Captain A, B, 4th O. V. C.

Lieutenant Colonel J. L. PUGH,
Commanding 4th Ohio Volunteer Cavalry.

HEADQUARTERS 4TH UNITED STATES CAVALRY,
Camp near Murfreesboro', Tenn., January 8, 1863.

SIR: I have the honor to transmit herewith my report of the operations of the 4th United States cavalry during the recent fight near Murfreesboro', Tennessee. I send it directly to you, as my regiment was, until the battle was finished, detached. A report has also been furnished General Stanley.

I am, sir, very respectfully, your obedient servant,

ELMER OTIS,
Captain 4th Cavalry, Commanding Regiment.

Major C. GODDARD,
A. A. A. G., Headquarters 14th Army Corps,
Department of the Cumberland, Tennessee.

HEADQUARTERS 4TH UNITED STATES CAVALRY,
In camp, near Murfreesboro', January 7, 1863.

SIR: I have the honor to make the following report of the operations of the 4th United States cavalry in the late battle in front of Murfreesboro'. On the 30th December the 4th United States cavalry left camp at Stewart's creek, leaving the train and baggage under charge of a strong guard commanded by Lieutenant Rendelbrook. The regiment proceeded to join General Rosecrans on the field of battle, and was drawn up in line of battle in rear of the general's headquarters, but took no immediate part in the action. That day company L, commanded by Lieutenant Roys, was detached as General Rosecrans's immediate escort, (about 10 o'clock in the morning,) and so remains at the present time. Company M, strengthened by fifty men detailed from companies B, C, D, G, I, and K, commanded by Lieutenant L'Hommedieu, proceeded to establish a courier line from General Rosecrans's headquarters to Lavergne, and so remained doing good service until relieved, January 4, 1863. These details left me with only six small companies, numbering in the aggregate 260 men, rank and file.

On the morning of the 31st Colonel Garesché informed me that rebel cavalry were appearing on the right flank of the line of battle, and ordered me to proceed with the 4th United States cavalry to look after them. This must have been between 7 and 8 o'clock in the morning. I crossed the Murfreesboro' pike, and drew up the six companies in line of battle in the following way: Each company was in a column of fours, led by the company commanders; the companies on a line parallel to each other, company distance apart according to the following diagram, leading the centre myself:

This was done owing to the wooded country and fences that were obstructions to the ordinary line of battle. Proceeding to the right of the line, I found our entire right flank had given way. Learning from some men of General Davis's division the position of the enemy's cavalry, I made a turn to the right, moving about one-quarter of a mile, and discovered the enemy. I came out of a piece of timber I was in, and, getting over the fence rapidly, charged the enemy with my entire command, completely routing them, with the exception of two pieces of artillery, supported by about 125 cavalry, stationed between my right and the Murfreesboro' and Nashville pike, who were not at first discovered. I rallied my men again, and, whilst rallying, I saw about 300 of volunteer cavalry on my right. I rode over to them and asked them to charge the artillery with me and the few men I had rallied to take the pieces. The officer replied that he was placed there to protect a train, and would not charge with me. I have no doubt I could have taken the artillery. Before I could get my command rallied the artillery moved off. About the time I had got my men rallied I received an order from General Rosecrans to proceed to the Nashville and Murfreesboro' pike as soon as possible. I did so immediately. I have since thought the general did not know my position, or he would have allowed me to follow up the enemy. I was much nearer the pike than I thought I was. I saw no more of the enemy's cavalry on the pike that morning. In this charge I cannot speak in too high terms of the officers and men. Every man charged and kept in position, taking over a hundred prisoners of the enemy and releasing a large number of our own captured men. More redounds to their credit, considering that a large majority are recruits from volunteer infantry, and only some five days drilled and mounted. Two companies of infantry were released in body. The train on the pike, I have since learned, was in possession of the enemy with a large number of stragglers who were being disarmed at the time. These stragglers did nothing at all to protect the wagons, scarcely firing a shot. From prisoners taken I have learned that the 4th United States cavalry charged at this time an entire brigade of cavalry, and routed them to such an extent that they disappeared from the field at that point entirely. Later in the day I sent seventy-nine prisoners in one body to the 10th Ohio infantry, stationed in our rear at Stewart's creek. Another body of about forty men started, but, I regret to say, were recaptured. Of the seventy-nine sent to the rear, there was one captain and two lieutenants. I have no doubt there were other officers, but did not have an opportunity to examine them closely enough to find out.

Of the officers engaged it is almost impossible to particularize, they all did so well. Captain Eli Long led his company with the greatest gallantry, and was wounded by a ball through his left arm. Lieutenants Mouck, Kelly, Lee, and Healy could not have done better. It was a matter of surprise to me, considering the ground passed over, to find Dr. Comfort so soon on the field with his ambulance caring for the wounded. He was in time to capture a prisoner himself. First Sergeant Martin Murphy led company G, and commanded it with great gallantry. He reports having counted eleven dead of the enemy on the ground over which his company charged. Sergeant Major John G. Webster behaved gallantly, taking one lieutenant mounted on a fine mare. First Sergeant James McAlpin led company K, after Captain Long was wounded, and reports having killed two with two successive shots of his pistol. First Sergeant John Dolan, company B, captured a captain and received his sword. No one could have acted more bravely than First Sergeant Charles McMasters, of company I. First Sergeant Christian Haefling, in charge of courier line near headquarters, proceeded in the thickest of the fire and recovered the effects of Colonel Garesché, on his body, killed in this day's fight. Our loss in this charge was trifling. Captain Eli Long and six privates wounded.

Proceeding on the Nashville pike, I was ordered to escort a train to the rear. I afterwards got orders to return to report to General Rosecrans. I returned, and for two hours looked for the general with my command, but was unable to find him, although I found several of his staff. I then proceeded to the right flank and formed my regiment in front of some rebel cavalry who showed themselves in the distance, in order to protect our train. I returned to General Rosecrans's headquarters that night and bivouacked near him. The next morning, January 1, I was ordered to make a reconnoissance on the right flank, which I did, making my reports frequently to Major Goddard, acting assistant adjutant general; that night bivouacking near Overall's creek, where my command remained watching the movements of the enemy as far as possible, and making reports thereon, until the 4th of January, when my command was moved to Wilkinson's Crossroads. On the 5th my command proceeded, under command of General Stanley, to engage the enemy's rear guard, on the Manchester pike, driving them some two or three miles. Private Snow, of company L, orderly to General Rosecrans, was ordered, on the 2d of January, to pick up fifteen stragglers, which he did, and was then ordered to take them to the front and turn them over to some commissioned officer. Failing to find one, he put them into line and fought them himself, telling them the first one who attempted to run he would shoot. Private Snow reports they fought bravely.

Enclosed I give a list of killed and wounded during the entire engagement. Twelve men were taken prisoners while doing courier duty. Lieutenant Rendelbrook was exceedingly vigilant guarding the train, and of great service in sending forward supplies.

I am, sir, very respectfully, your obedient servant,

ELMER OTIS,
Captain, Commanding 4th United States Cavalry.

Major C. GODDARD,
Acting Assistant Adjutant General,
Headquarters Department of the Cumberland, in the Field.

Killed.—Private Daniel McDonald, company D; Sergeant Jos. P. Richmond, company K; Private C. P. Cole, company L.

Wounded.—Privates Patrick Hearn and Charles Smith, company B; Private William Dalton, company C; Private George Deiter, company D; Privates Joseph Kohler and Farrier Strickland, company G; Private Samuel Tate, company I; Captain Eli Long and Private William Ellis, company K; Private A. Jennet, company L.

HEADQUARTERS THIRD CAVALRY BRIGADE,
Fourteenth Army Corps, January 16, 1863.

SIR: I have the honor to make the following special report in reference to officers and non-commissioned officers who deserve special mention for the conspicuous manner in which they acted in the late battle of Stone river. The officers and men all behaved so well that it is difficult to discriminate among them.

Captain Eli Long led his company with the greatest gallantry, and was wounded in the left arm during the charge of the 31st. No officer could have behaved more handsomely. Lieutenants Mauck, Michael J. Kelly, John Lee, and Thomas Healy, each commanded companies, and led them with great gallantry into the thickest of the fight. First Sergeant Martin Murphy commanded company G, and handled it as well as any commissioned officer could have done. He reports having counted eleven of the enemy's dead upon the field over which his company had charged. Sergeant Major John G. Webster behaved gallantly, capturing a lieutenant mounted on a fine horse. First Sergeant James McAlpin led company K, after the wounding of Captain Long, and reports having killed two of the enemy with two successive shots of his pistol. No one could have acted more bravely than 1st Sergeant Charles McMaster, of company I. First Sergeant John Dolan, of company B, captured and received the sword of a rebel captain. Sergeant A. J. Williamson, of company G, behaved with great coolness and discretion. All of the above-named officers and non-commissioned officers deserve special mention for the handsome manner they conducted themselves in the charge of the 31st, charging, as they did, a force greatly outnumbering our own, and effecting an entire rout.

Lieutenant T. L'Hommedieu was detached in charge of a courier line, and did efficient service in keeping open communication to the rear. Lieutenant Joseph Rendlebrook was in charge of the camp guard and wagons left back at Stewart's creek, and there did efficient service, protecting the trains on the road and forwarding supplies to the regiment. He acted with great vigilance and activity. Lieutenant E. D. Baker, adjutant, rendered excellent service in carrying messages, and was, at the time of the charge, conveying one to General Rosecrans. First Sergeant Christian Haefling, in charge of the courier station near General Rosecrans's headquarters, was several times under heavy fire, and proceeded in the midst and took possession of the effects of Colonel Garesché after he fell, and delivered them up with fidelity.

The above-named officers and non-commissioned officers are fully deserving of the highest commendation for the manner in which they performed their duties.

I am, sir, very respectfully, your obedient servant.

ELMER OTIS,
Captain 4th United States Cavalry, Commanding 3d Brigade.

Captain W. H. SINCLAIR,
Acting Assistant Adjutant General,
Headquarters Cavalry Corps, in the Field.

CAMP NEAR MURFREESBORO', TENNESSEE,
January 9, 1863.

SIR: In compliance with your request, I have the honor to report the following operations of which the 2d East Tennessee cavalry took an active part in the late battle before Murfreesboro', viz:

On the 27th of December, 1862, while attached to the command of Colone Stokes, we engaged a strong party of the rebel cavalry, southeast of the Nolensville pike, and after a sharp engagement put the enemy to flight. On the following day, while under the same command, we encountered the enemy near Triune, and, after an obstinate engagement, drove the enemy in the direction of Shelbyville, Tennessee, in which engagement we sustained a loss of four horses killed, and captured a first lieutenant and five privates belonging to the 50th Alabama cavalry. The following day we rested near Triune. The next day, December 29, 1862, we started in pursuit in the direction of Murfreesboro, taking the mountain path, leaving all our wagons behind, with the exception of the ambulances. On the afternoon of said day, being in the advance, we discovered the enemy strongly posted about six miles in front of Murfreesboro', near the Murfreesboro' pike. We, in connexion with the 1st cavalry brigade, came up in line of battle. The enemy not showing a disposition to engage us, we waited the coming up of our infantry and artillery. We remained in that condition until Major General McCook came up. At dark, by the order of General Stanley, chief of cavalry, we were placed on the extreme right as a picket. The succeeding day we were skirmishing with the enemy during the entire day. Our loss was, in killed and wounded, Captain Morris, of company L, one private in company F, and five slightly wounded. Several horses shot from under the men.

During the remainder of the battle we were held in readiness, but not actively engaged, with the exception of Sunday. We were sent to the river to protect the railroad bridge, within about one mile of Murfreesboro', which was on fire. We had a slight engagement with the enemy's rear guard; no damage sustained.

I am, sir, respectfully,

WM. S. HALL,

Adjutant, Second East Tennessee Regiment of Cavalry.

Captain OTIS,.

United States Army, Brigadier Commander.

HEADQUARTERS ANDERSON CAVALRY,

Camp Gareschè, Murfreesboro', Tennessee, February 19, 1863.

I have the honor to report the following as the losses sustained by the Anderson cavalry during the battle of Stone river:

Killed.—Major Adolph G. Rosengarten. Company B: Private Robert Edys Company C: Sergeant William H. Kimber and Private Orlando Weikel. Company E: Private Richard W. Chase. Company H: Private Anthony R. Kentigh. Company K: Sergeant Alexander S. Drake and Private Wm. Brooks. Company L: Sergeant Silas F. Herring—total, 9.

Wounded.—Major Frank B. Ward, mortally, since dead. Company C: Sergeant William P. Rockhill, jr.; Privates Jacob R. Steinwetz and Edward C. Smith. Company H: Private Joseph Hilty. Company L: Privates C. Lewis Diehl, (since discharged,) Frank S. Eaton, (since dead,) William H. Powell, (since dead,) and Isadore Weiler, (since dead,)—total wounded, four of which have died of wounds, 9.

Prisoners.—Company B: Sergeant William Wagner; Corporal Charles L. Hayden; Privates Arthur H. Craig, (sick,) John C. Fleming, (sick,) William K. Rile, John C. Sinclair, George P. Socum, and Joseph D. Little, (wounded.) Company C: Privates Henry W. Arnold, M. Baldwin Colton, and William F. Jamison, (wounded.) Company D: Privates Frank F. Adams (sick) and Horatio D. Snyder (sick.) Company E: Sergeant William Conrad; Corporal Harry Paschall; Privates Andrew J. Buchanan, William B. Chase, Richard Pancoast, William Tarr, Mahlon H. Williamson, and James H. Cornwell.

Company F: Corporal Robert W. Brownlee; Privates Robert R. Taylor and Samuel Robinson. Company G: Privates Edward Patterson, jr., (sick,) Alexander Ramsey, jr., (sick,) and D. Eugene Bigler. Company H: Privates Geo. Fisher, John Pinkerton, William S. Moore, Samuel Trimble, and Josiah Warg. Company I: Sergeants Geoffrey P. Dennis and Francis P. Drinker; Privates William H. Baldwin, John W. Hall, Abraham Horn, Edward E. Lynch, John Richards, (wounded,) and Jacob B. Garber. Company K: Private Wilber F. Jamison. Company L: Corporal Charles E. Scheide; Privates Benjamin Baitman, Samuel S. Curtis, Harry B. Ecky; Johnson Hubbell, Harry H. Jacobs, John G. Marshall, Edward L. Mills, Alexander Robinson, Wilbur Watts, Chas. T. Wilson, and William T. Nieman, (wounded,)—total number of prisoners, of which four were wounded and taken, 53.

N. B.—A large number of these prisoners were captured with wagon train near Lavergne at the time of the raid of Wheeler's brigade of cavalry.

Recapitulation.

	Commissioned officers.	Enlisted men.
Killed and mortally wounded	2	11
Wounded and not captured	0	5
Prisoners, including four (4) wounded and captured	0	53
Total loss	2	69

Very respectfully,

WILLIAM J. PALMER,
Colonel, Commanding Anderson Cavalry.

ADJUTANT GENERAL OF THE UNITED STATES.

15.—REPORT OF CAPTAIN JAMES ST. CLAIR MORTON, COMMANDING PIONEER BRIGADE.

HEADQUARTERS PIONEER BRIGADE, 14TH ARMY CORPS,
Camp three miles north of Murfreesboro', Tennessee, January 5, 1863.

MAJOR: According to your order, I have the honor to submit the following report of the part taken in the late battle by my brigade, which is composed of three battalions of pioneers and Stokes's (Chicago Board of Trade) battery.

On the march hither from Nashville my brigade constructed two bridges over Stewart's creek between the hours of 4 p. m. and 4 a. m. December 29th and 30th, arriving here on the 30th.

On the morning of the 31st the brigade was engaged in improving the fords of Stone river, in which the right battalion sustained the fire of some rebel cavalry, when I was ordered to take position in the line of battle, and formed my brigade, by the orders of the commanding general in person, fronting towards the right, where the enemy appeared on a rise of ground in front of us, from which they had driven one of our batteries. I immediately opened fire with canister from Stokes's battery and drove them back. I then, by order of the commanding general in person, advanced to the said rise and held it under the fire of three rebel batteries. I supported the battery by the first battalion of pioneers on the left, posted in a thicket, and by the third battalion on the right; the second battalion was placed in a wood still further to the right.

Shortly after I had formed my line the enemy appeared across the field preparing to charge upon some of our troops who were retiring, but had been rallied by the commanding general. I opened fire upon these from Stokes's battery, which played over the head of the commanding general and our troops, and arrested their advance. My right battalion was soon after attacked, the object of the enemy being to penetrate through the line under cover of the woods; said battalion changed front so as to obtain a flanking fire, and by a single volley repulsed the enemy, composed of the 11th and 14th Texas regiments. In this the batallion was aided by the 79th Indiana, which had rallied on its right.

Towards sundown, the enemy appearing on my left, I brought two sections of Stokes's battery to the left of my first battalion, and repulsed a brigade of the enemy which attacked that battalion in the thicket. They left their dead within fifty paces of my line. In this affair both the batallion and battery behaved very creditably.

The brigade slept on their arms the night of the 31st. Early on the 1st instant the enemy appeared on my left, apparently to advance through the gap between it and the pike. I changed my front and occupied the gap, and sustained and returned their volleys of musketry, playing upon them from the battery, and preventing their advance beyond the edge of the woods. We held this position till after nightfall when the brigade was relieved and formed in reserve.

On the morning of the 2d part of the pioneers were engaged in making road crossings over the railroad when the enemy opened a cannonade which reached our camp. I brought out Stokes's battery and returned the fire; the battalions advanced, supporting it, under a fire of solid shot and shell. The cannonade having ceased, I received orders to fall back to my assigned position in reserve, and remained till late in the afternoon, when the commanding general, in person, ordered me to the left as re-enforcement. I then marched my command at a double-quick and arrived on the line, occupying a gap in it, under the fire of a rebel battery, which was, however, soon silenced by Stokes's battery, which was worked with exceeding vigor and skill.

General Negley now approached me and requested me to re-enforce his troops, who, after a violent contest, had gained ground on the opposite side of the river. I accordingly moved my command there at a double-quick and formed the third battalion in second line, behind General Davis's command, the first battalion extending beyond it and throwing out its own advance, occupying the space between it and the river. The battery was posted on a knoll between the first and third battalions, the second battalion being in second line on the extreme right. In this position we remained till after nightfall, when I received orders to recross the river and again assume a position in reserve, and to furnish the second battalion to construct rifle-pits in the front and near the pike, and also on the extreme right. Said battalion worked all night in the rain.

On the 3d the third battalion relieved the 1st on duty in the trenches, and on the 4th the 2d and 3d battalions began two lunettes on the north bank of the river, and the 1st battalion began a trestle bridge across it; on the 5th the said work was continued, and the 3d battalion with the advance of the army in pursuit of the enemy.

The loss of the brigade is as follows:

First battalion.—Killed, 4; wounded, 3 commissioned officers and 5 enlisted men.

Second battalion.—Killed, 4; wounded, 5 enlisted men.

Third battalion.—Killed, 4; wounded, 10 enlisted men.

Stokes's battery.—Killed 3; wounded, 1 commissioned officer and 9 enlisted men.

Total, killed and wounded, 48.

The force of the brigade actually engaged was sixteen hundred men, there being ten companies or one thousand pioneers employed on the fortifications between Gallatea and Nashville, and two hundred detached guarding the implement train; of the force above mentioned, ninety-five belong to Stokes's battery.

During the engagement the pioneers behaved as well as could be wished, and, when required, worked zealously by night and day, although insufficiently provided with rations, in spite of inclement weather and under fire. The artillerymen displayed the highest discipline, and worked their guns with extreme rapidity and accuracy. As the commanding general was everywhere present on the field with his staff, he cannot but have remarked the good service done by Captain Stokes, who manifested the greatest zeal, and managed his battery with the utmost precision and success.

I beg leave to mention to the favorable notice of the commanding general my adjutant, Lieutenant Lambesson, of the 19th Illinois volunteers; my inspectors, Lieutenants Clark, of the 16th United States infantry, and Murphy, of the 21st Wisconsin volunteers; and my aids, Lieutenant Reeve, of the 37th Indiana volunteers, and Assistant Engineer Pearsall; all of whom exhibited the utmost order and alacrity in the performance of their duty.

I beg leave, also, to mention Captain Hood, of the 11th Michigan volunteers, commanding 2d battalion; Captain Clements, of the 69th Ohio volunteers, commanding 3d battalion; and Captain Bridges, of the 19th Illinois volunteers, commanding 1st battalion, who, though wounded on the first day, retained the command of his battalion throughout.

I have the honor to enclose the sub-reports of the chiefs of battalions, of the commander of the battery, and of the surgeon of the brigade.

I have the honor to be, sir, very respectfully, your obedient servant,

JAS. ST. C. MORTON,
Captain of Engineers United States Army, Chief Engineer 14th Army Corps, Commanding Pioneer Brigade.

Major C. GODDARD,
Acting Assistant Adjutant General.

HEADQUARTERS 1ST BATTALION PIONEER BRIGADE,
DEPARTMENT OF THE CUMBERLAND,
Stone river, near Murfreesboro', Tennessee, January 5, 1863.

CAPTAIN: In compliance with your order, I herewith furnish a report of the part this battalion took in the recent battle at this place.

I have the honor to report that, on the morning of December 30, 1862, having completed the bridge at Stewart's creek at 4 a. m., I received orders to hold my command in readiness to march at a moment's notice. At 8 a. m., by your order, I moved seven companies, six hundred strong, forward upon the Murfreesboro' pike, throwing out an advance guard and flankers upon either side, three companies being upon special duty. At 10 a. m., in accordance with orders received from you, I moved to the front and halted, awaiting your order. At 2 p. m. I moved my command to the river, taking position upon the left of Captain Stokes's Chicago Board of Trade battery, and built an abatis from the river towards General Rosecrans's headquarters, as directed by you. At 4 a. m., December 31, I improved a ford across Stone river. At 7 a. m. our right wing having been overpowered, and the enemy's advance being within eighty rods of my camp, I fell in with my command and followed Stokes's battery, as previously ordered by you. The battery having been ordered into position on the ridge between the pike and railroad, I forwarded my command in line of battle upon the left of Stokes's battery, the enemy having possession of the parallel ridge upon the opposite side of the pike, about twenty rods distant.

At that crisis General Rosecrans rode along our line and ordered me to charge and take the knob upon the opposite side of the pike, he sending the same order to Captain Stokes's battery. I moved one wing upon either side of the battery to the hill in good order. Soon after reaching the hill General Rosecrans ordered me to occupy the skirt of woods upon my left. I moved my entire command upon the left of the battery, the 3d battalion of this brigade relieving my right wing, changing position to the left.

The enemy continued a heavy fire of grape, canister, and musketry upon us as we advanced, and they fell back after gaining our new position. General Rosecrans rode to our front and rallied the 21st Ohio, 1st Kentucky, and 78th Pennsylvania, which had fallen back upon our right. At 12 m. the enemy, General McClernus's division, came down upon the double-quick, with their standards flying in splendid order. They were allowed to come within three hundred yards, when the musketry of the entire brigade and the battery opened with grape and canister a most deadly fire, which he returned as earnestly. Their column reeled and fell back in disorder, their colors struck down and barely rescued. Lieutenant Ritchie, company A, of 3d Ohio detachment, was here wounded while encouraging his men. The number of killed and wounded left upon the field tell how severe was his loss. Many of his wounded reached our lines during the day and night, all declaring that the 12 o'clock charge was an expensive one for them. The enemy again rallied his forces at 5 p. m., advancing a brigade upon my left flank through a skirt of woods, attempting a surprise. My pickets being fired upon by the enemy, who took advantage of a train of ambulances being in the vicinity, firing upon ambulances and pickets indiscriminately, I ordered this battalion to change front and commence firing. Lieutenant Stephens, of Stokes's battery, opened fire upon him simultaneously with grape and canister. Our new line fortunately rested upon the crest of the hill. Each volley by us thinned his ranks. He advanced, perhaps, forty paces, discharging repeated volleys of musketry, but his repulse was complete, and they fell back to the woods, one thousand yards in the rear, cursing their fate. Dozens of their wounded men found within our lines of skirmishers all corroborated each other in stating that a brigade was repulsed in attemping to take our position. He left sixty of his men upon the field. Lieutenant Smith, of company B, in charge of my skirmishers, with his company, captured one major, one captain, and thirty men. I received a slight wound in my left leg above the ankle, not so severe as to require me to leave the field. My command laid upon their arms during the night, holding the grounds gained early in the morning. Lieutenant Frolick, 22d Illinois, at daybreak next morning, January 1, 1863, while in charge of the skirmishers of and in front of my command, reported a large force of the enemy assembling near to the left of the position to which he returned the previous evening. I rode to the front and left flank of my line of battle. The fog being very dense the enemy could not be seen, but I could distinctly hear his commands, being satisfied that he was advancing on my left; and there being no support between my left and the Murfreesboro' pike, I informed you of my information and position. Receiving orders from you I immediately changed front, my left resting upon the Murfreesboro' pike. Captain Stokes moved his battery promptly upon my right. The sun had just risen, but the fog had not yet cleared. We took our position without accident. The enemy advanced within five hundred yards and opened fire, as he supposed, upon our flank. A few moment's return fire convinced him that we were not unaware of his movements; in half an hour he fell back behind his intrenchment, remaining there during the day.

No demonstration was made upon our front during the day. At 10 p. m. Colonel Buel relieved my command, and I moved, by your orders, one mile to the left and rear, having held the one position upon the front thirty-six hours without relief.

At sunrise, January 2, the enemy charged upon our left centre, capturing a section of a battery one-half a mile in our immediate front, and were forcing our position. I moved my command, as ordered by you, to the left and front; my right resting on the 3d battalion of this brigade; my left upon an open field near the river; remained an hour in line of battle; was then ordered to take a position at the bend of the river, forty rods further down; remained in position until 3 p. m., when, by your orders, I moved forward in good order to the support of Stokes's battery in the charge upon the hill, above the bend of the river, recently held by our left wing.

Lieutenant E. S. Dodd, acting lieutenant colonel, was wounded in the leg with a six-pound ball while the battalion was taking their position. By your order I moved forward in double-quick, forded the river and charged up the hill; formed line of battle over the crest of the hill, my left wing occupying an oak ridge, as indicated by you. I remained in position an hour until the several regiments that had done such gallant service rallied and formed in line of battle again.

By your order I changed position, my right resting upon the river; my left occupying a front of woods and supported by Stokes's battery; remained in position until 12 p. m., when I was ordered to move across the river.

January 3.—By your order this battalion commenced building a military bridge at the lower end of Stone river, which I have the honor to inform you is now completed and in use.

It is with pleasure that I mention with the highest regard and praise the officers and men of this battalion, who all did their duty so promptly and nobly during the past terrible week. To Lieutenant George Turner, adjutant, I am under many obligations for repeated and timely assistance.

Annexed is a list of the killed and wounded of this battalion.

I have the honor to be, very respectfully, your obedient servant,

LYMAN BRIDGES,
Captain Commanding.

Captain J. St. C. Morton,
Chief Engineer, 14th Army Corps, Commanding Pioneer Brigade.

Headquarters Centre Battalion, Pioneer Brigade,
Near Murfreesboro', Tennessee, January 5, 1863.

Sir: On the morning of December 30, 1862, my battalion was ordered by Captain J. St. C. Morton to report to General Rosecrans. By 4 o'clock a. m. I reported my command to the front ready for duty, when I received orders from the commanding general to report to General Thomas, who ordered me to cut and clear several roads through the thick woods on the right of the pike and in front. We worked all day under the fire of the enemy's guns, and by 5 o'clock p. m. cleared several roads for the passage of artillery and infantry. At 6 o'clock p. m. I was relieved, and reported my battalion in camp some three-fourths of a mile to the rear, and on the left of the M. and N. pike.

December 31, 1862, company F, under charge of Acting Lieutenant Colonel Lingerman, reported to General Negley to finish the previous day's work. Acting Major Stewart, with companies A, D, I, and E, was ordered to the front of General Crittenden's corps to cut the east bank, a portion of it on Stone river, passable for troops. Reaching the river they found it in possession of the rebels. Leaving a reserve of two companies on this side in charge of Captain Ak. Robinson, Major Stewart crossed with the balance of his men and drove the enemy from the ground and commenced work. At 8 o'clock a. m. heavy firing was heard on our right and in front of General Negley's division. Immediately the left wing of our battalion was ordered to form line, and soon we were on the march towards the direction of the firing that was becoming more terrific as we advanced. In the mean time Major Stewart was relieved by a portion of the 11th brigade, General Van Cleve's division, and, with the exception of company F, our battalion moved forward under a fire from the enemy's cannon, and supported Captain Stokes's Chicago battery, that opened, from the top of a slight elevation on the left of the pike, a terrific shower of grape into the enemy's ranks, who were at that moment driving our front line from the woods, on the right of the road, by heavy volleys of musketry; soon the enemy were forced back, our troops advancing with the battery into an open field some three hundred yards. By this time the rebels had renewed their fire, and were driving our advanced line, that had moved forward into a thick wook, panic-stricken back upon my men, who were ordered by Captain Morton to fix bayonets and charge upon the first man attempting to pass the line. The order was promptly enforced, and soon hundreds of confused stragglers were formed into line on our right, and with the shower of shell and grape from our battery succeeded in driving the enemy from the field. During the day my battalion was kept on the front, and at night threw forward company H, as advanced pickets and skirmishers, some four hundred yards.

The night being very cold, and no fires allowed, the men suffered much from the want of blankets as well as from the scarcity of rations, many of them having had nothing to eat since the previous night. At 6 o'clock a. m., January 1, 1863, I was ordered to change my line and support our battery, expecting an attack from the southeast, as it could be seen the enemy were advancing from the woods in that direction. My line was formed, and opened fire, together with the battery, that checked the enemy's advance, and heavy skirmishing was kept up during the entire day. Benjamin L. Wagner, of company C, wounded, was the only injury sustained by my men. At 9 o'clock p. m. my battalion was relieved and encamped, after 36 hours' duty, on the front, one-half mile toward the rear and on the left of the pike. At 7 o'clock a. m., January 2, the enemy commenced shelling our camp, having the night previous planted a battery in direct range of our camp-fires. I soon deployed my men from column into line, and moved forward with the battery to a slight rise of ground, and ordered my battalion to lie down so as to protect my line from the shot and shell that flew over us without doing much damage. Before I could get my battalion deployed, however, Sergeant John F. Burke, 20th Kentucky regiment, Corporal Peter Wagoner, 100th Illinois, and William Trimble, 3d Kentucky volunteers, were killed; Samuel S. M. Blankenship, 9th Kentucky volunteers, John Desch, 84th Illinois volunteers, John C. Pelser and Sergeant William Mason, 6th Kentucky volunteers, were wounded.

The enemy's guns being silenced, I was ordered to move my men by columns doubled in centre toward the rear, and remained under cover of woods near the river till 2½ o'clock p. m., when a sudden attack by the enemy was made on General Van Cleve's front, we were marched forward to the support of our battery. Reaching the top of a small bluff, I was ordered to halt my battalion. Orders were soon given, however, to advance, and we moved forward on a double-quick to the support of our front, who were obliged to fall back upon this side of the river, under cover of our artillery that was soon brought into position and played with great execution upon the advancing columns of the enemy, who were repulsed by a heavy cross fire from our guns. I was then ordered by General Negley to cross the river, and formed line just at dark on ground occupied in the morning by the rebel skirmishers. In this position my men lay until 9 o'clock p. m., suffering much from wet feet and a rain, when we were ordered back and went into camp.

January 3, an order came detailing 200 men for duty; the men, under charge of Lieutenant Benjamin F. West, reported to the front and threw up rifle-pits, until 8 o'clock p. m., when relieved. January 4, after spending a cold and rainy night without tents and half rations, I moved my battalion to the east three hundred yards from camp, and on a bluff near Stone river, where I was ordered to throw up a heavy breastwork while clearing the rubbish from an old building. Amos Hoak, 13th Ohio volunteers, was killed by the falling of a heavy timber. At 4 o'clock p. m. I was relieved and ordered to report, January 5, to General Thomas, at Murfreesboro', the enemy having evacuated the town.

I need not add that notwithstanding the inclemency of the weather, to which my men were exposed during the whole engagement, having no tents, few blankets, and without half rations, they went forward to the prompt execution of every order and command with a cheerfulness and bravery commendable only to a prompt and efficient soldier.

Respectfully,

R. CLEMENTS,
Captain Commanding.

Captain J. St. C. Morton,
Commanding Pioneer Brigade.

Headquarters Right Battalion Pioneer Brigade,
Camp in the field, January 5, 1863.

Sir: I have the honor to submit the following report of the part taken in the late battle by my battalion:

On the morning of the 31st of December we were ordered to improve a ford of Stone river near camp. Soon after commencing work we were fired upon by the enemy's cavalry, and retired, as we were ordered not to remain under fire.

At 9 a. m. we marched, and formed line of battle with the brigade between the railroad and pike, near the cedar woods. In front of us was hard fighting, when the enemy finally gave way, and our troops advanced to the field beyond the cedars. We moved forward in line with the brigade, my battalion on the right, and took position about midway of the woods, and about one hundred rods from the field. The troops in front of us there gave way, and regiment after regiment came through our lines entirely broken up. We here received orders from Captain Morton to fix bayonets and allow no stragglers to pass our lines, and to hold fire and give the enemy the cold steel. The retreating troops passed on our right, except the 79th Indiana, whose commander rallied them on my right and rear. The 11th and 14th Texas came on at a charge, and tried to flank our right, when my battalion changed positions by the right flank and fronted towards them. General Van Cleve here rode up from my right and asked what troops we were, and said we must fall back. I here learned that a small part of his command was on my right and near the pike. I replied that I was ordered to hold this position at all hazards. I then ordered my men to lie down and wait until the enemy were well upon us. They then rose, gave them a volley, and charged with the 79th Indiana, and drove them from the woods.

Our loss here was four killed, including my orderly, Bennett Smith, 11th Michigan, who was shot from his horse beside me, and several wounded. Lieutenant Sherman, 25th Illinois, was wounded in the arm slightly, but did not leave the field. We remained under arms all night, with one company under Lieutenant Sands, 36th Illinois, as advance picket, and brought from the field in front some twenty-five wounded men of our own and the enemy's.

Early in the morning of January 1 we changed position with the brigade to the front and centre of our lines, and on the brow of the hill. Here we remained all day under fire of the enemy's sharpshooters, with continual fighting with their skirmishers, our skirmishers being under command of Lieutenant Sands. Late in the evening we were relieved by the 33d Ohio, and retired beyond the brow of the hill and bivouacked. I then gave the immediate command to

Lieutenant Hartsough, 49th Ohio, acting lieutenant colonel, as I had become so hoarse that I could not speak aloud. Early in the morning of the 2d, while a part of my command were at fatigue duty, the enemy commenced firing solid shot from the centre at the battery in front of us and on the hill, but shooting too high, their shot struck in front of us and ricochetted, and made bad work with us. Our men formed and marched forward to the support of the Chicago Board of Trade battery, with shot falling amongst them thick and fast, and, as near as can be ascertained, three were killed and several wounded. Lieutenant Hartsough here had his horse shot from under him, and the command fell upon Lieutenant Moore, 6th Indiana, acting major, who commanded them gallantly. Firing soon ceased, and we remained upon the ground until late in the afternoon, when, as the enemy charged across the river upon General Negley's division, we were ordered to his support, and my command charged across the river under Lieutenant Moore. My command were ordered back, and, under the direction of General Thomas, worked all night in the rain on the rifle pits in front, and without rations.

With few exceptions, officers and men behaved gallantly, and on the day of the 31st behaved like veterans; and, taking into consideration that they are formed of detachments from forty different regiments, and have never drilled together in either company or battalion drills, moved in the face of the enemy splendidly.

I would especially mention Lieutenant Moore, 6th Indiana, acting major; Lieutenant Baker, 39th Indiana, acting adjutant; and Lieutenant Sands, 36th Illinois, who rendered me valuable assistance throughout.

Your obedient servant,

CALVIN HOOD,
Captain, Commanding Right Battalion.

Captain JAMES ST. CLAIR MORTON,
Commanding Pioneer Brigade.

List of the killed and wounded in the Pioneer Brigade, under the command of Captain James St. C. Morton, in the engagement before Murfreesboro' of the 30th and 31st December, 1862, *and the* 1*st,* 2*d, and* 3*d January,* 1863.

First battalion, (commanded by Captain Bridges.)—Killed: Captain James Brown, company B, 69th Ohio; Private Horace A. Cooper, company B, 111th Ohio, and one unknown. Wounded: Acting Colonel Lyman Bridges; Acting Lieutenant Colonel E. S. Dodd; Lieutenant John Richer, company A, 3d Ohio; Privates Moses Lam, company B, 69th Ohio; Adam Rutzel, company K, 70th Indiana; Levi Barnes, company C, 17th Ohio; John Van Acre, company C, 17th Ohio; Henry Boch, company K, 1st Wisconsin; and B. Greenluf, company G, 42d Illinois.

Second battalion, (commanded by Captain Hood.)—Killed, 4, names unknown. Wounded, 5, names unknown.

Stokes's battery.—Killed, 3, names unknown. Wounded, 9, names unknown.

Third battalion, (commanded by Captain Clements.)—Killed: Sergeant John T. Burke, 20th Kentucky; Corporal Peter Wagner, 84th Illinois; Privates William Trumble, 3d Kentucky; and Amos Hoak, 13th Ohio. Wounded: Sergeant William Mason, 6th Kentucky; Privates John Desh, 100th Illinois; James Aulton, 2d Kentucky; Samuel Blankenship, 9th Kentucky; Charles Dreggs, 57th Indiana; Benjamin S. Wagner, 15th Indiana; John Pelser, 84th Illinois; Timothy Arbeck, 41st Ohio; Thomas A. Scarpel, 41st Ohio; and James Head, 6th Kentucky.

E. HARWOOD,
Assistant Surgeon, acting for brigade.

STOKES'S BATTERY, IN CAMP NEAR MURFREESBORO',
January 5, 1863.

SIR: I have the honor to report that the battery under my command was called into action Wednesday morning, 31st ultimo, about 8 a.m., and at a time when the left of our right army corps, completely demoralized, was under full retreat. The battery, by a terrific fire of canister, drove back the enemy, the infantry rallying under its fire. The battery then moved still further to the front, and took a position commanding the approaches where our right had been dispersed. Under a fire, it is said, of three rebel batteries, well served, it held this key to our front through the entire day. About 4 p. m. a rebel brigade formed under cover of the woods to the right of the battery, and was only known by a foolish discharge of musketry on one of our ambulances picking up their wounded as well as ours. The battery, being charged with canister, opened upon this brigade, and, it is said by one of the wounded, entirely annihilated it. The killed and wounded prove the accuracy of the fire. This position was held through the night, until next evening. About 10 p. m. it was ordered to the rear to rest, having been thirty-six hours to the front. In this engagement the battery, with a strength of ninety-eight, all told, lost three privates killed; one officer, three non-commissioned officers, and five privates wounded, being twelve killed and wounded, or about one-eighth.

On Friday, the 2d instant, the battery was again called into action, about 4 p. m., by the retreat and threatened destruction of our left. The battery, under the direction of the commanding general, moved to the front through the retreating infantry and artillery, and did not halt to go into battery until it had moved far beyond the front. The infantry again rallied under its fire. The battery opened a destructive fire of shell on the rebel battery, so destructive to our troops, completely silencing and destroying it, so that several of its pieces were captured by our advancing infantry. The battery that night occupied the ground of this rebel battery.

The commanding general, who witnessed the bearing of this gallant little band, will do justice to its discipline and bravery. All were brave; all nobly did their duty to their country.

I am, captain, very respectfully, your obedient servant,

JAMES H. STOKES,
Captain, Commanding Battery.

Captain MORTON,
Com'g Pioneer Corps, Army of the Cumberland.

16.—REPORT OF WM. P. INNES, COLONEL COMMANDING FIRST MICHIGAN ENGINEERS AND MECHANICS.

HEADQUARTERS 1ST REG'T MICHIGAN ENGINEERS AND MECHANICS,
In Camp, January, 1863.

MAJOR: I have the honor to report that, in accordance with your orders, I broke camp at Mill creek on December 31, at 7 a. m., and took up line of march for this point, sending my wagon train around by the pike, and went into camp at this point, about three-quarters of a mile south of the village of Lavergne, on the Murfreesboro' pike.

About 2 o'clock on the following day my command, numbering 391 effective men, was attacked by a rebel force of cavalry under command of Generals Wheeler and Whorton and Colonel Morgan, of Alabama, said to number between 3,000 and 4,000 strong, with two pieces of artillery. They first dispersed the wagon guard and teamsters of the train going north, and fired and plundered about thirty wagons.

The enemy attacked us with great fury, making seven distinct charges upon us, attacking us on every side, mounted and on foot, dashing forward in a gallant and determined manner, but were again and again severely repulsed by my gallant regiment. During the interval between their cavalry charges their artillery were throwing shot and shell, some of them causing considerable damage.

At about 5 o'clock the enemy sent in two flags of truce, demanding an immediate surrender of our position, which I peremptorily refused. They sent in another flag of truce, asking permission to bury their dead, which I refused, and returned for answer that I would bury their dead and take care of their wounded.

In the mean time I had despatched a messenger to Colonel Burke, of the 10th Ohio infantry, stationed at Stewart's creek, asking him for re-enforcements, which was promptly answered by that gallant officer, who immediately came to my rescue with a section of the 1st Ohio battery, in command of Lieutenant Newall, and four companies of the 10th Ohio; and although he did not arrive until the enemy had retreated, yet too much credit cannot be given to that gallant officer for his promptness in coming to my aid, which he did under the *double-quick*.

It is impossible for me to make personal mention of either officers or men, where *all* behaved so gallantly. Every officer was at his post, and every man did his duty; the coolness and bravery of the officers was only equalled by the promptness and efficiency of the men.

The following is a statement of the casualities, as near as I have been able to learn: Our loss—2 killed, 9 wounded, 5 missing. Enemy's loss—6 killed, buried by our men; 6 wounded, taken to our hospital; 7 prisoners.

From what I have been able to learn from prisoners, the enemy acknowledge their own loss of killed and wounded at between 40 and 50.

We lost 41 horses and mules, and had three wagons entirely destroyed and others damaged by the bursting of shell.

I have the honor to remain, major, your most obedient servant,

WM. P. INNES,

Colonel, Commanding 1st Regiment Michigan Engineers and Mechanics.

Major C. GODDARD,
Acting Assistant Adjutant General,
14th Army Corps, Department of the Cumberland.

18.—EFFECTIVE FORCE OF INFANTRY AND ARTILLERY, DECEMBER 31, 1862.

Divisions, &c.	Strength.	Killed and wounded.	Percentage.
RIGHT WING.			
FIRST DIVISION.			
Brigadier General Davis.			
1st brigade, Colonel S. Post	1,418	161	11.33
2d brigade, Colonel W. P. Carlin	1,781	619	34.75
3d brigade, Colonel W. E. Woodruff	1,445	226	15.64
Total division	4,644	1,006	21.66
SECOND DIVISION.			
Brigadier General Johnson.			
1st brigade, Colonel Gibson	1,650	472	28.60
2d brigade, Colonel Dodge	2,100	405	19.28
3d brigade, Colonel Parrott	2,500	291	11.64
Total division	6,250	1,168	18.68
THIRD DIVISION.			
Brigadier General Sheridan.			
1st brigade, Colonel Grensel	1,839	479	26.05
2d brigade, Colonel Seiboldt	1,680	206	12.25
3d brigade, Colonel Bradley	1,520	443	29.14
Total division	5,039	1,128	20.72
Total right wing	15,933	3,302	20.72
CENTRE.			
FIRST DIVISION.			
Major General Rousseau.			
1st brigade, Colonel Sribner	1,588	208	13.10
2d brigade, Colonel G. Beatty	1,534	281	18.33
3d brigade, Colonel Starkweather	1,548	28	1.80
4th brigade, Colonel Sheppard	1,566	561	35.82
Total division	6,236	1,078	17.28
SECOND DIVISION.			
Brigadier General Negley.			
1st brigade, Brigadier General Spear	812	16	2.00
2d brigade, Colonel Stanley	1,822	500	27.44
3d brigade, Colonel Miller	1,998	410	20.00
Total division	4,632	926	20.00
Total centre corps	10,868	2,004	18.44

EFFECTIVE FORCE OF INFANTRY AND ARTILLERY, &c.—Continued.

Divisions, &c.	Strength.	Killed and wounded.	Percentage.
LEFT WING.			
FIRST DIVISION.			
Brigadier General Wood.			
1st brigade, Brigadier General Hascall	1,701	343	20.17
2d brigade, Colonel Wagner	1,644	329	20.00
3d brigade, Colonel Harker	1,747	454	26.00
Total division	5,092	1,126	22.11
SECOND DIVISION.			
Brigadier General Palmer.			
1st brigade, Brigadier General Crufts	1,207	255	21.12
2d brigade, Colonel Hazen	1,385	336	24.25
3d brigade, Colonel Grose	1,768	516	29.18
Total division	4,360	1,107	25.40
THIRD DIVISION.			
Brigadier General Van Cleve.			
1st brigade, Colonel S. Beatty	1,216	411	33.80
2d brigade, Colonel S. Tiffe	798	288	36.09
3d brigade, Colonel Matthews	1,822	342	18.75
Total division	3,836	1,041	27.14
Total left wing	13,288	3,274	24.64
PIONEER BRIGADE.			
Captain Morton	1,700	30	1.75
Cavalry	3,200	84	2.60

RECAPITULATION.

Right wing	15,944
Centre corps	10,868
Left wing	13,288
Pioneer brigade	1,700
Total infantry and artillery	41,800
Cavalry division	3,200
Total	45,000
Deducting wagon guard	1,600
Total	43,400

Combined loss, killed and wounded, 8,778, or 20.22 per cent. of the forces engaged.

www.ingramcontent.com/pod-product-compliance
Lightning Source LLC
LaVergne TN
LVHW021229110826
845150LV00002B/284

* 9 7 8 1 4 2 5 5 6 3 2 0 2 *